Publishers message

Robert Nicholson Pd
this new street map.
new aims : ● Clear le   ick
street-finding system
crowded central Lon
● A street by street check just before publication
to bring it up to date ● In addition we have
compiled the index by computer to a consistent
alphabetical system.

This London Street Finder is the result of three
years of design, research and experiment by a
team of designers, architects and cartographers
so that this carefully considered and developed
book now represents a real breakthrough in
London cartography.

Just before printing, a team of 40 observers
visited every London street to bring the maps
up to date.

**We hope you will be astounded at the
ease and speed with which you can find
the street you want.**

Designed by Romek Marber
and Robert Nicholson

© Robert Nicholson Publications
Based upon the Ordnance Survey
map with the sanction of the Controller
of H.M. Stationery Office.
Crown copyright reserved.

Published and distributed by
Robert Nicholson Publications Ltd.
3 Goodwin's Court, St. Martin's Lane,
London WC2.

Index Computer typeset by
Computerprint, London.
Street check by
Joan Wilkins Associates.
Printed in England by
Richard Clay (The Chaucer Press), Ltd.
Bungay, Suffolk
Paper supplied by
Frank Grunfeld, London.

SBN: 90056813 5
First edition

Nicholson's
London Street Finder

How to use the street finder

1. Look up the street in the alphabetical index at the back of the book. This example shows how to pinpoint the street you are looking for.
2. Adjacent maps are given within arrows shown at the corners of the pages.
3. The general map which follows this page, apart from giving map numbers and general orientation has been designed to show major road routes leading in to and out of London and London districts.

70 B 2 West End rd Southall

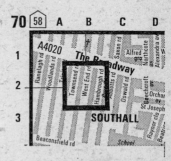

Symbols

†	Church	🚌	Coach station
⊕	Hospital	✦	Air terminal
🚗	Car park	⇌	British Rail terminal
🏛	Historic building	**PO**	Post Office
🏠	Small building	**Pol**	Police station
🏫	Schools	⋙	Lock
🏟	Sports stadium	⋮⋮⋮	Foot-path
⊖	London Underground station	◀ 200	Figure indicating the direction
🚆	British Rail station	300 ▶	of street numbering and the approximate position

Scale

Central area (coloured maps)		½ mile
		½ km
Outer area (black maps)		½ mile
		½ km

Nicholson &
THE OBSERVER

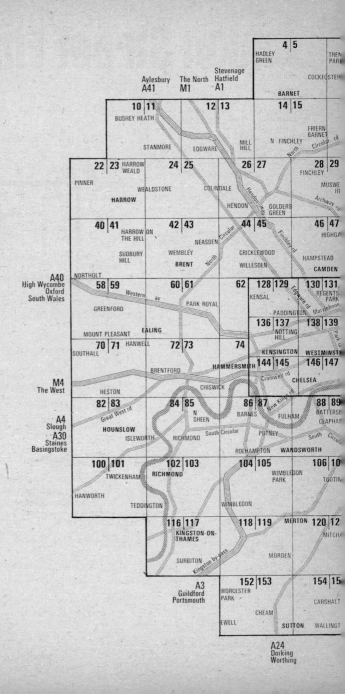

4 5
HADLEY
GREEN
TREN
PARK
COCKFOSTER

BARNET

Aylesbury
A41
The North
M1
Stevenage
Hatfield
A1

10 11
BUSHEY HEATH

12 13

14 15
N FINCHLEY
FRIERN
BARNET
North Circular rd

STANMORE
EDGWARE
MILL
HILL

22 23 HARROW
WEALD
24 25
26 27
28 29
FINCHLEY
PINNER
MUSWE
HI

WEALDSTONE
COLINDALE
Archway rd
HARROW
HENDON
GOLDERS
GREEN

40 41
HARROW ON
THE HILL
42 43
44 45
46 47
HIGHGA
Hendon way
NEASDEN
SUDBURY
HILL
WEMBLEY
CRICKLEWOOD
HAMPSTEAD
BRENT
WILLESDEN
CAMDEN

A40
High Wycombe
Oxford
South Wales
NORTHOLT

58 59
Western av
60 61
PARK ROYAL
62
128 129
KENSAL
Edgware rd
130 131
REGENTS
PARK
Marylebone

GREENFORD
PADDINGTON
136 137
NOTTING
HILL
138 139
Park la

MOUNT PLEASANT
EALING
70 71 HANWELL
SOUTHALL
72 73
74
KENSINGTON
WESTMINST
144 145
146 147

BRENTFORD
HAMMERSMITH
Cromwell rd
CHELSEA

M4
The West
HESTON
CHISWICK

A4
Slough
A30
Staines
Basingstoke

82 83
Great West rd
84 85
N
SHEEN
86 87
BARNES
New Kings rd
FULHAM
88 89
BATTERSE
CLAPHAM

HOUNSLOW
ISLEWORTH
RICHMOND
South Circular
PUTNEY
South Circula
ROEHAMPTON
WANDSWORTH

100 101
TWICKENHAM
102 103
RICHMOND
104 105
WIMBLEDON
PARK
106 10
TOOTIN

HANWORTH
TEDDINGTON
WIMBLEDON

116 117
KINGSTON-ON-
THAMES
118 119
MERTON
120 12
MITCHA

SURBITON
Kingston by pass
MORDEN

A3
Guildford
Portsmouth
152 153
WORCESTER
PARK
154 15
CARSHALT

EWELL
CHEAM
SUTTON
WALLINGT

A24
Dorking
Worthing

Maps and Routes

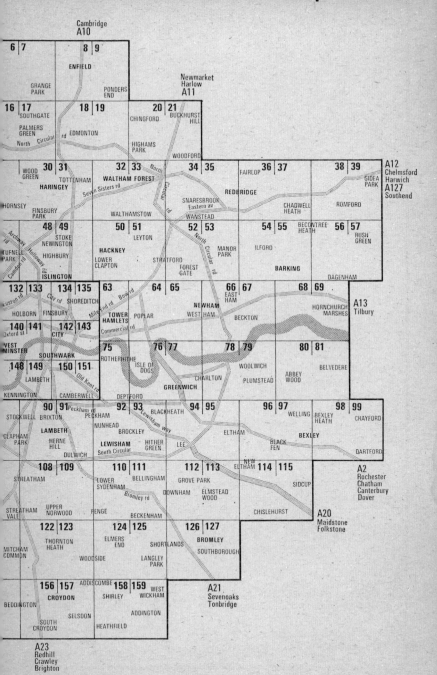

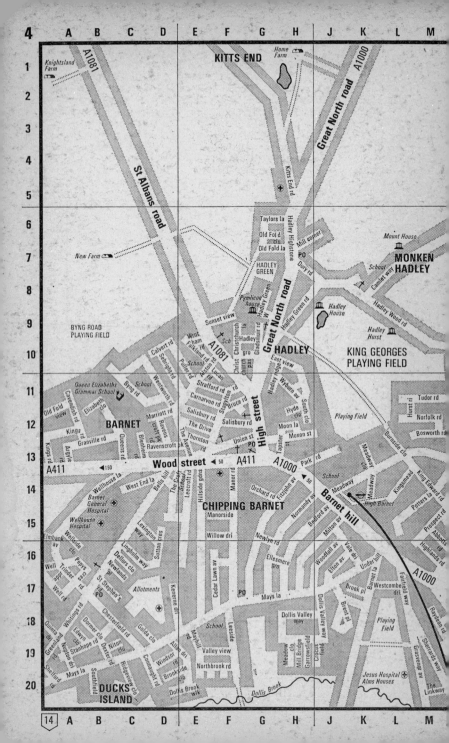

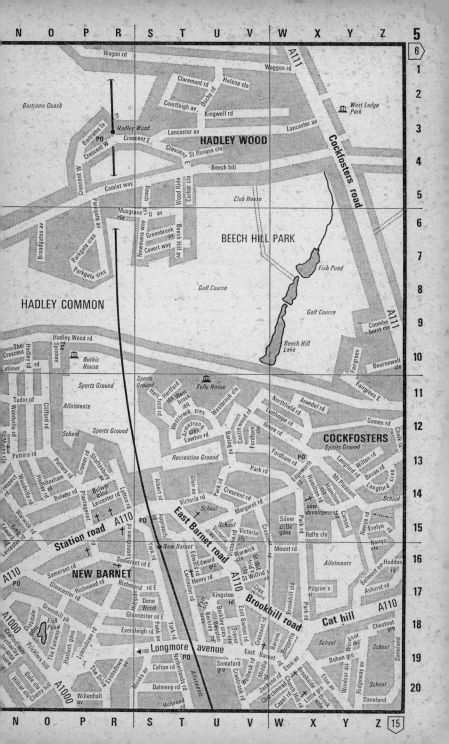

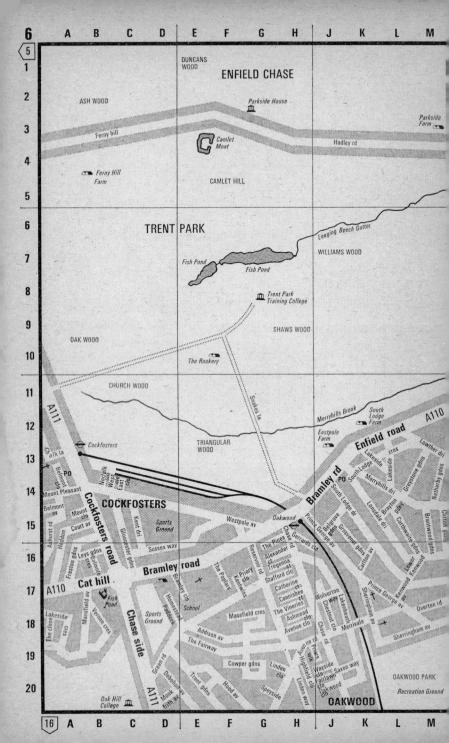

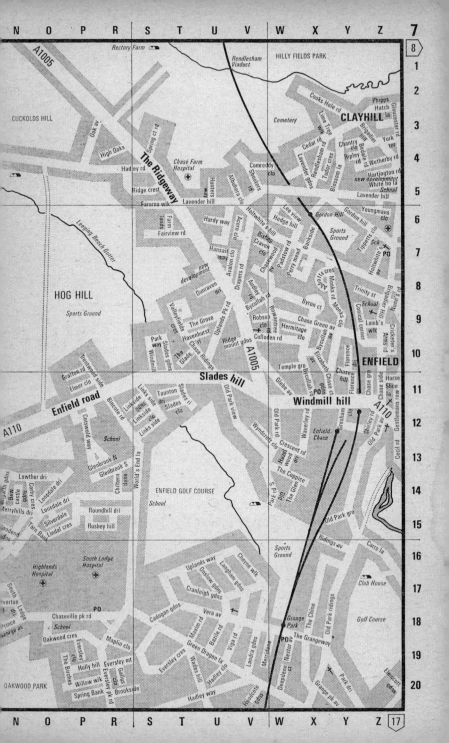

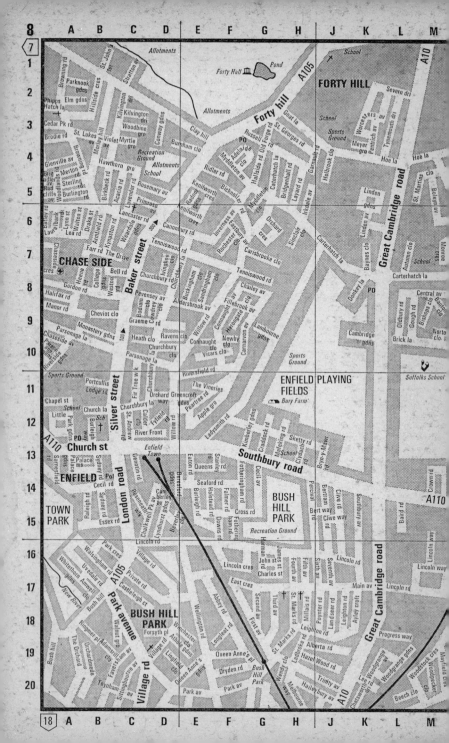

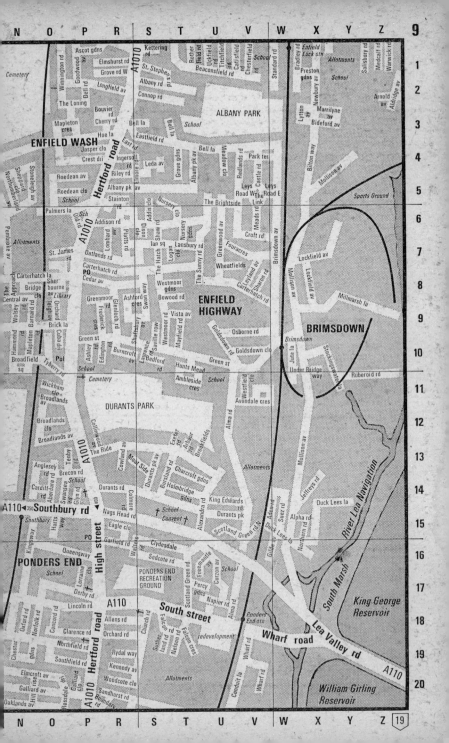

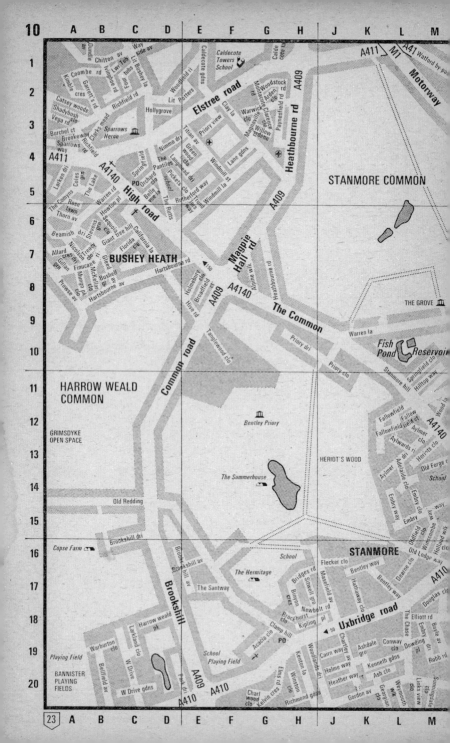

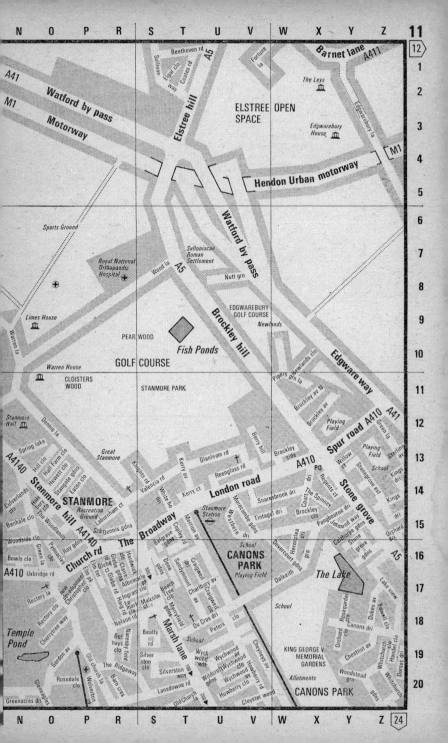

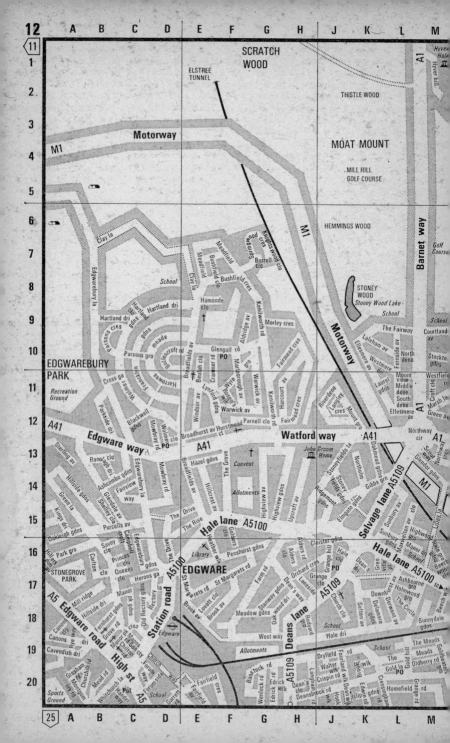

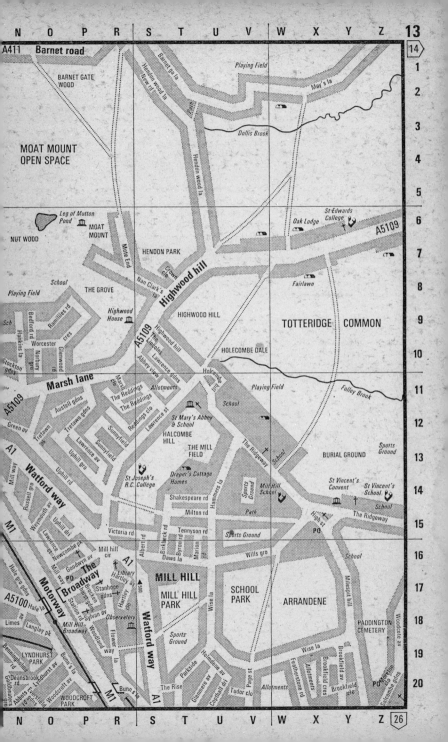

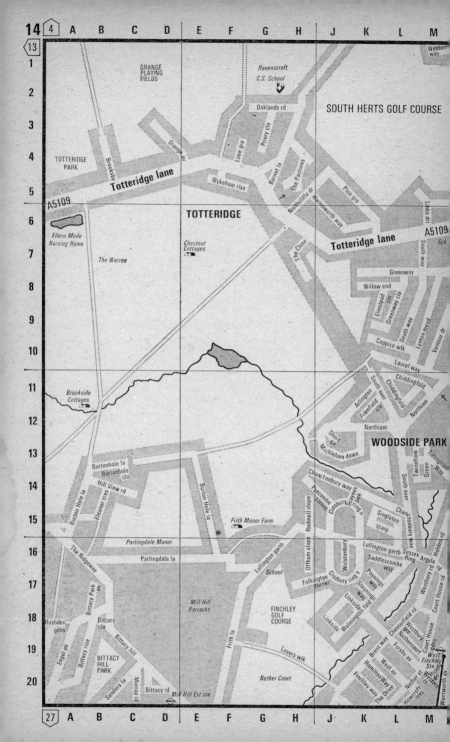

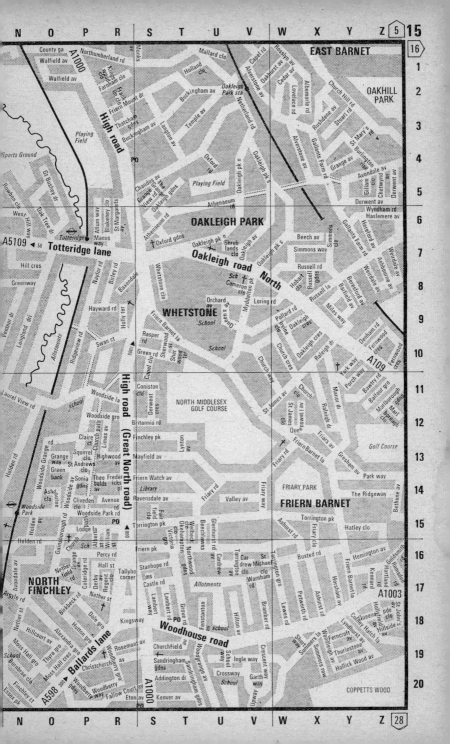

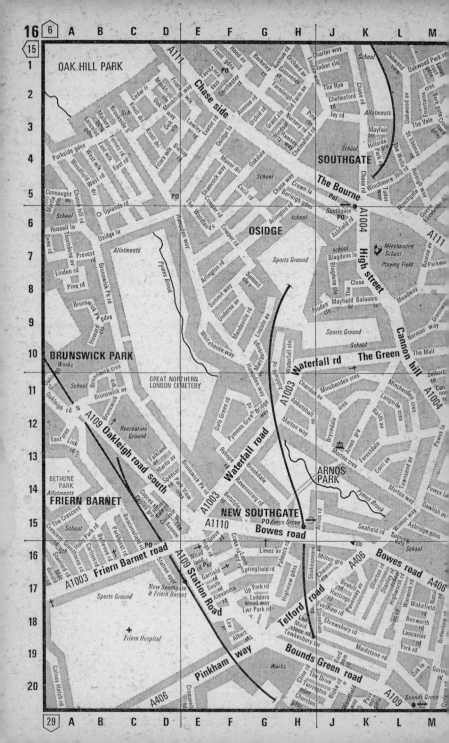

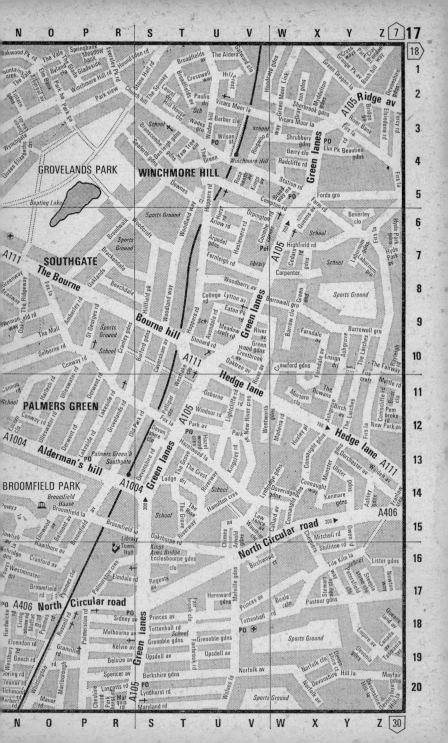

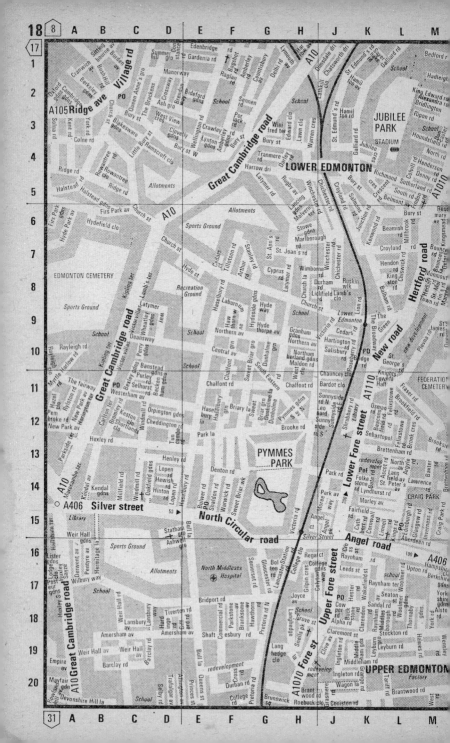

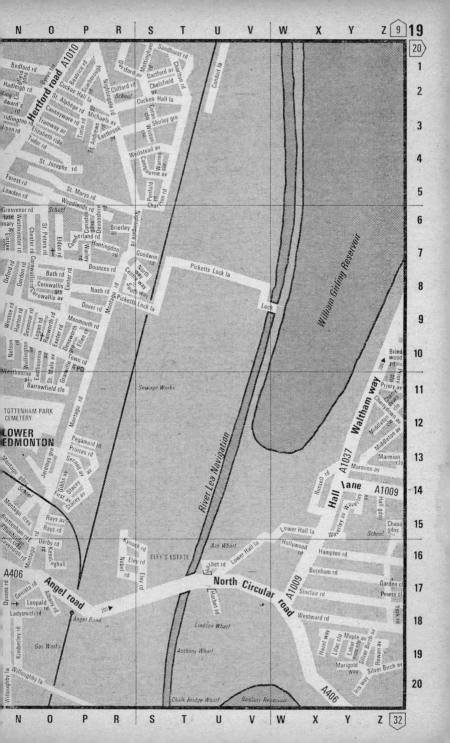

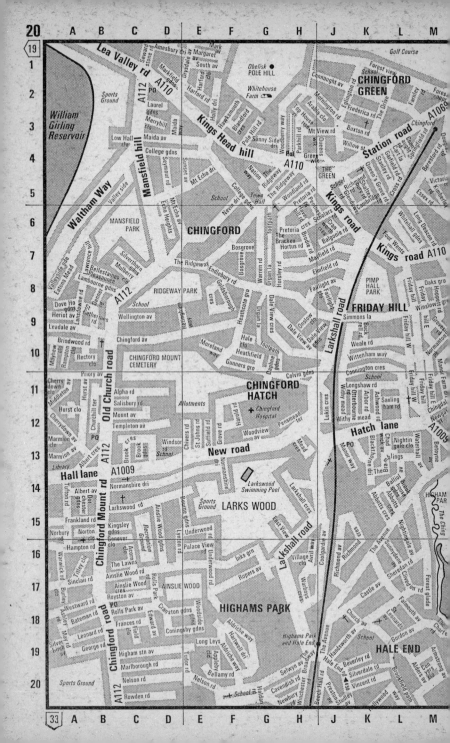

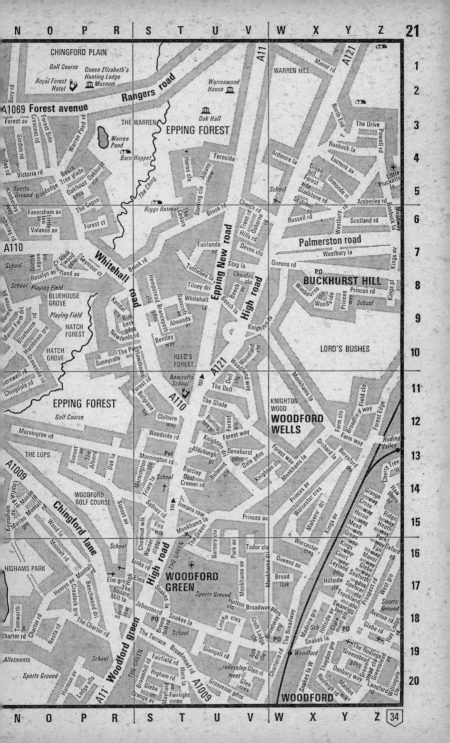

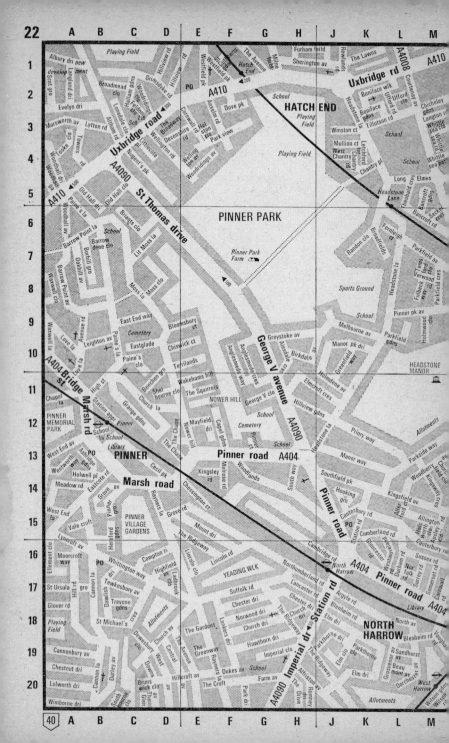

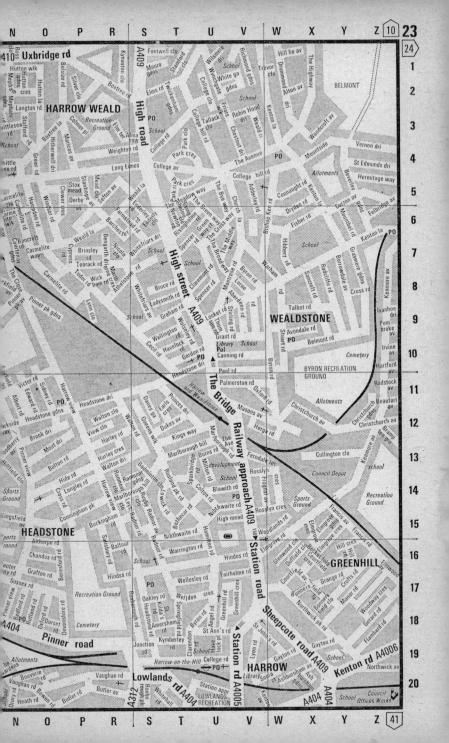

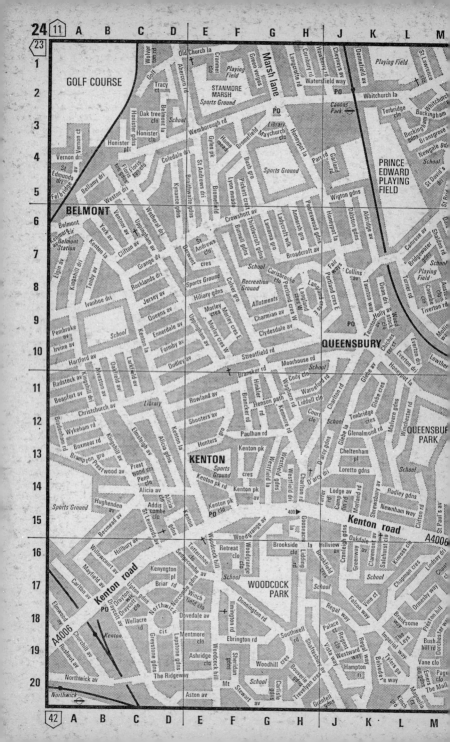

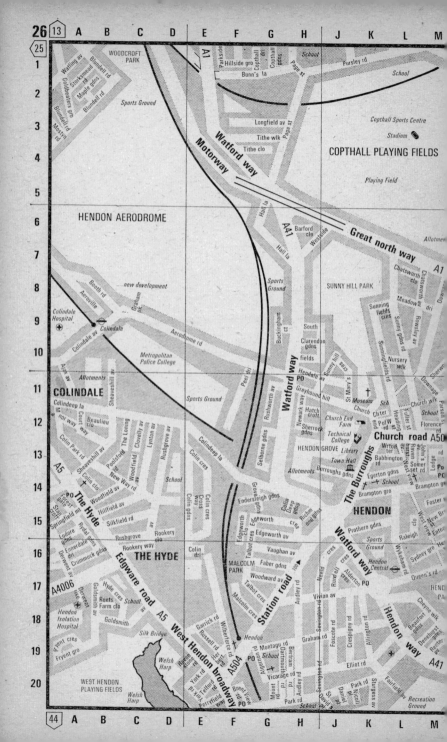

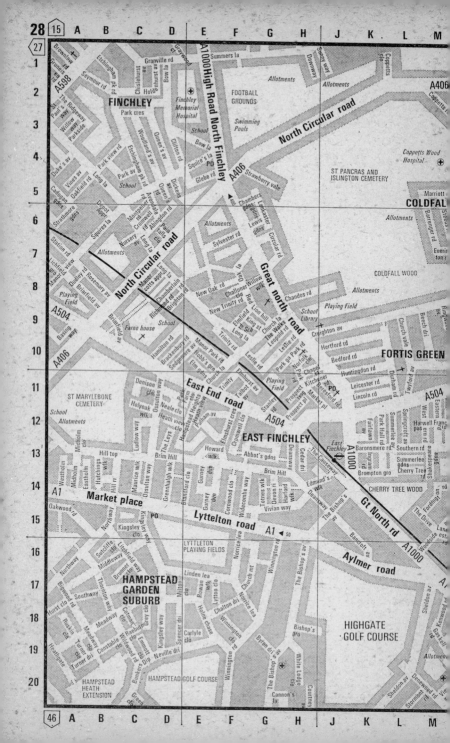

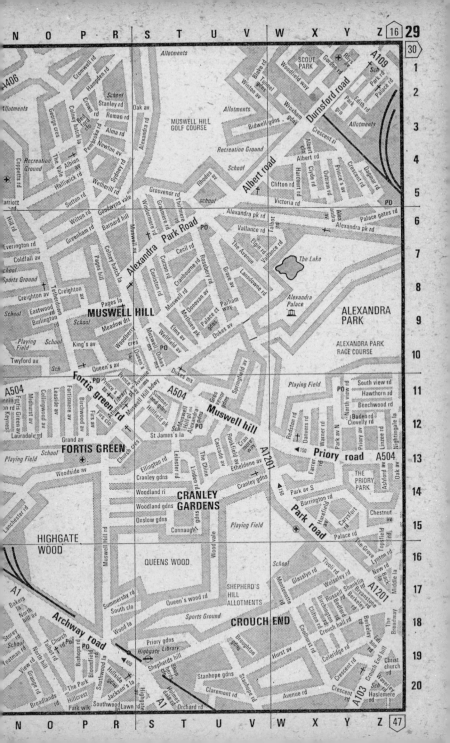

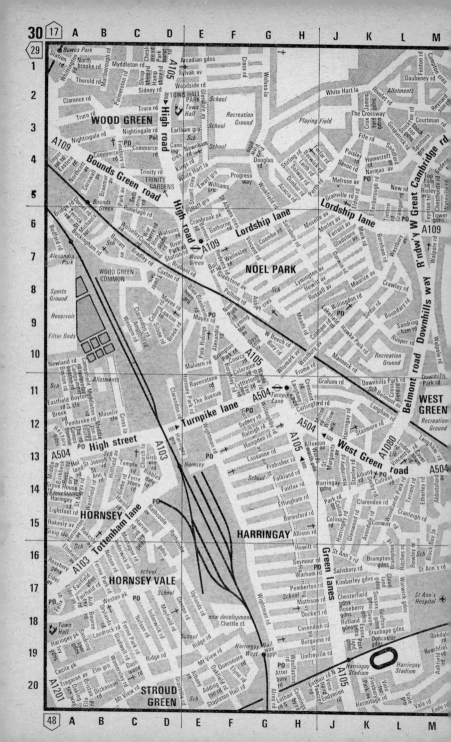

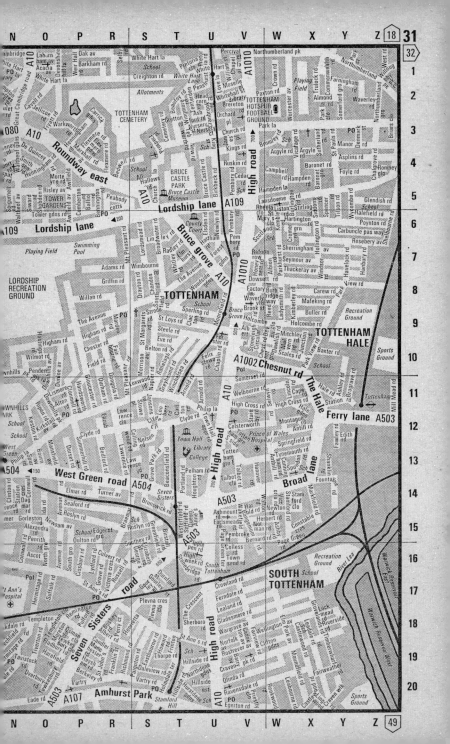

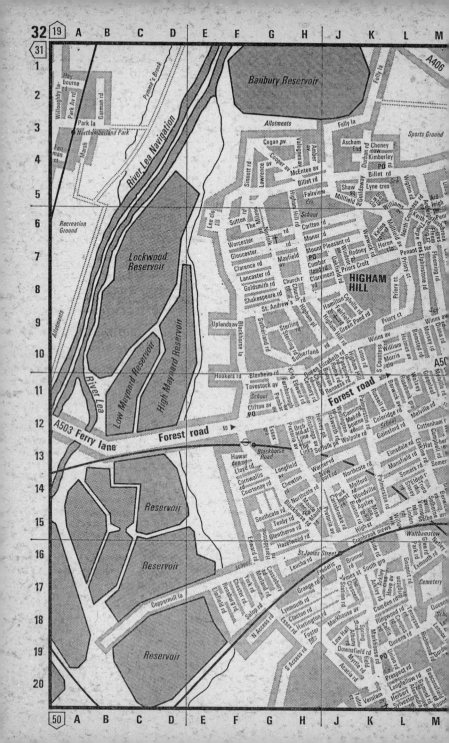

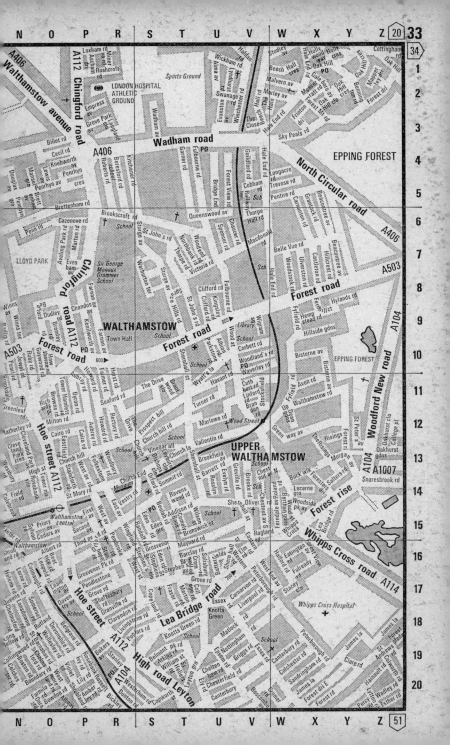

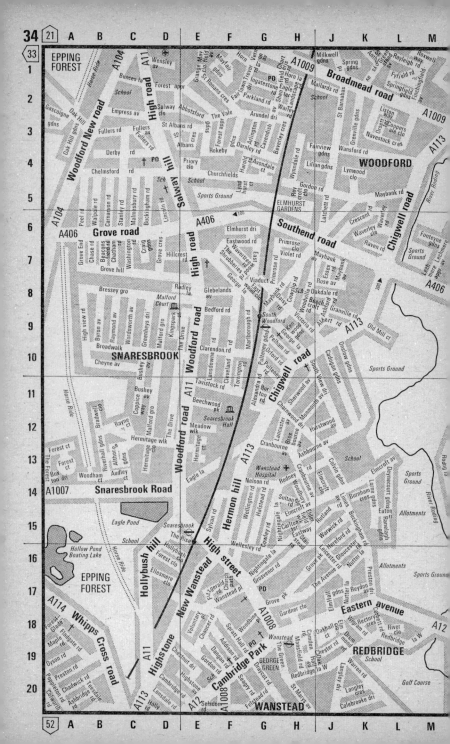

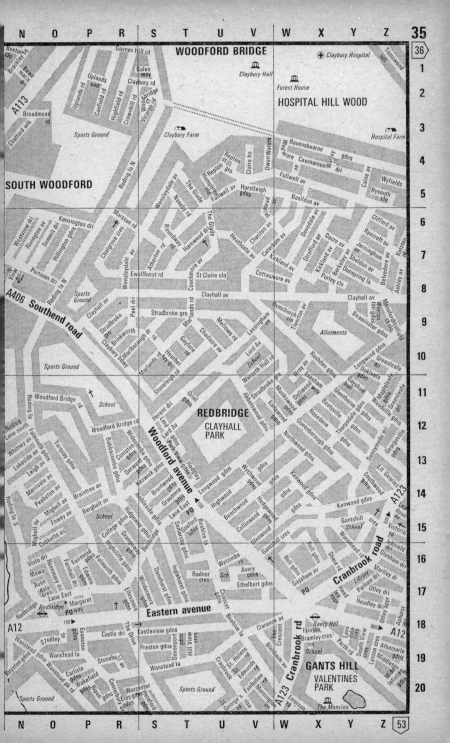

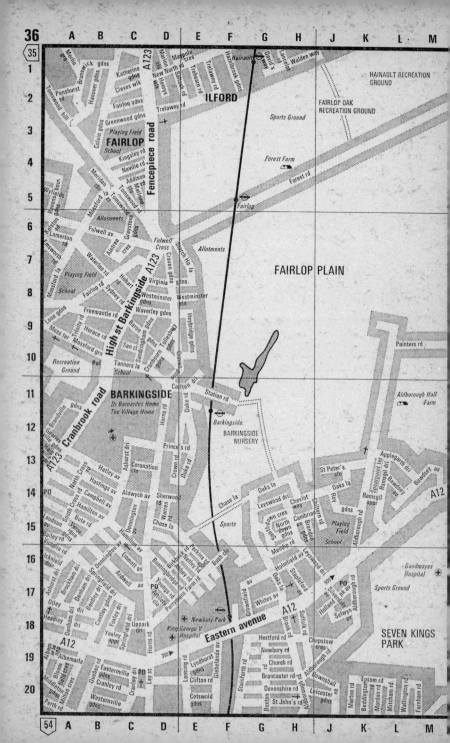

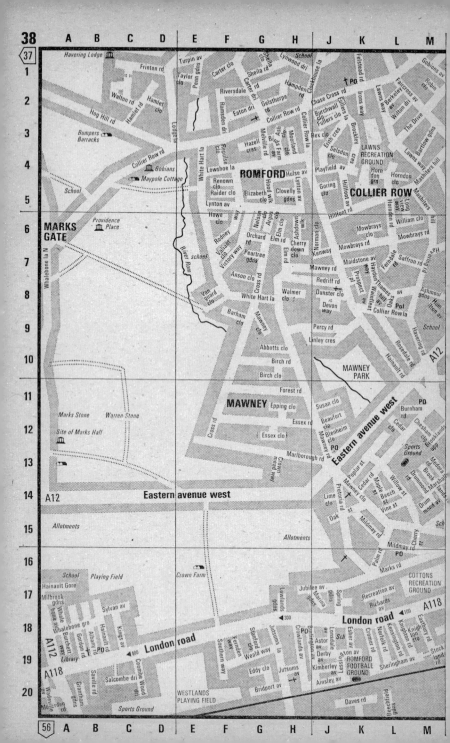

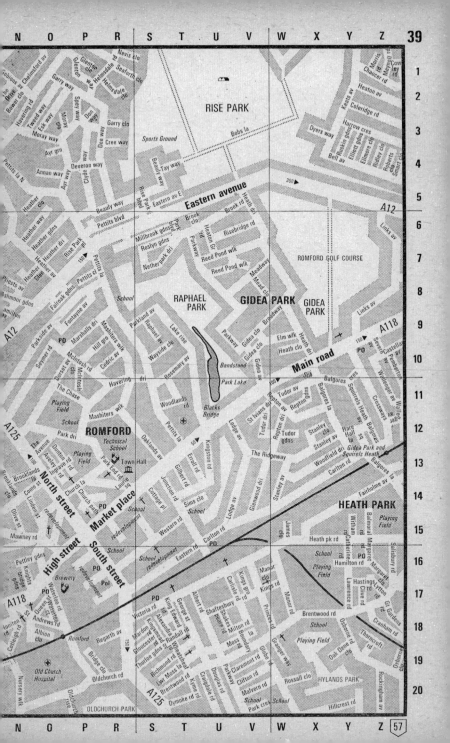

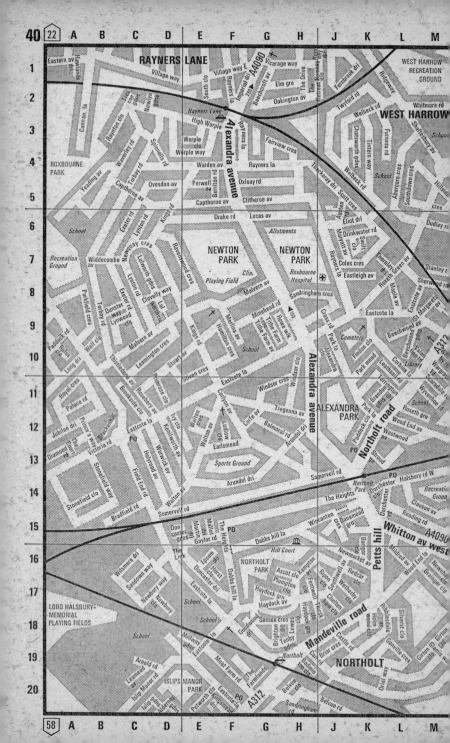

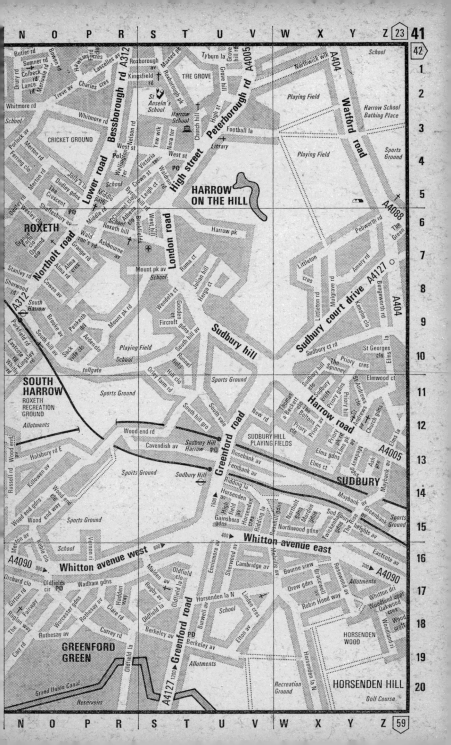

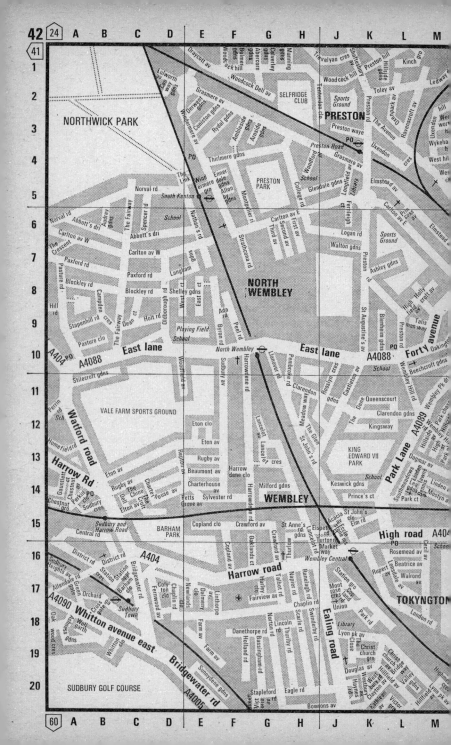

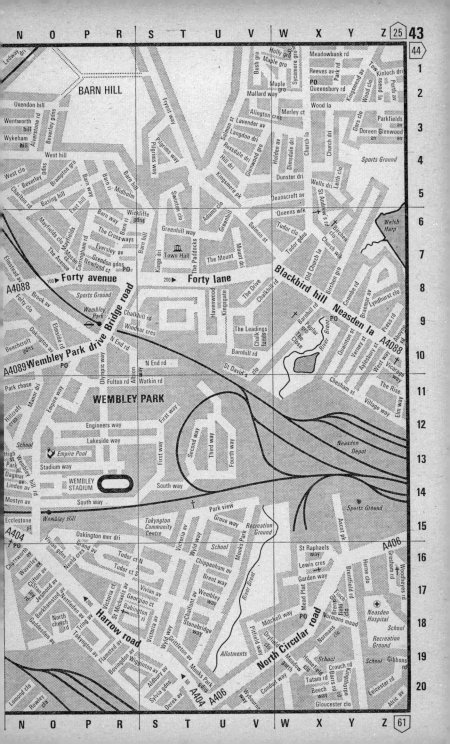

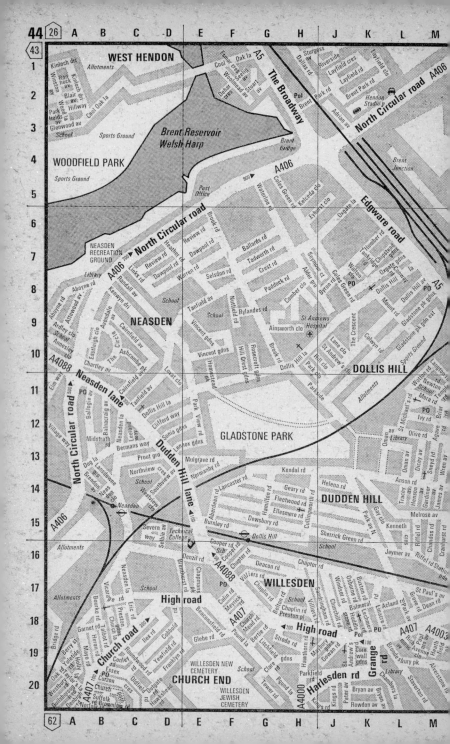

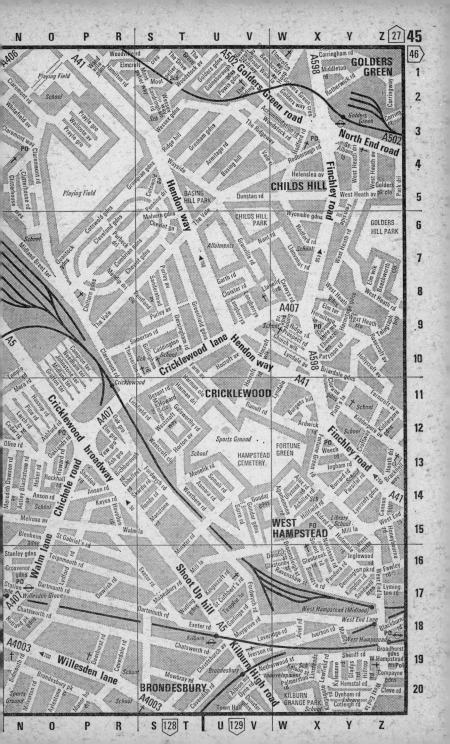

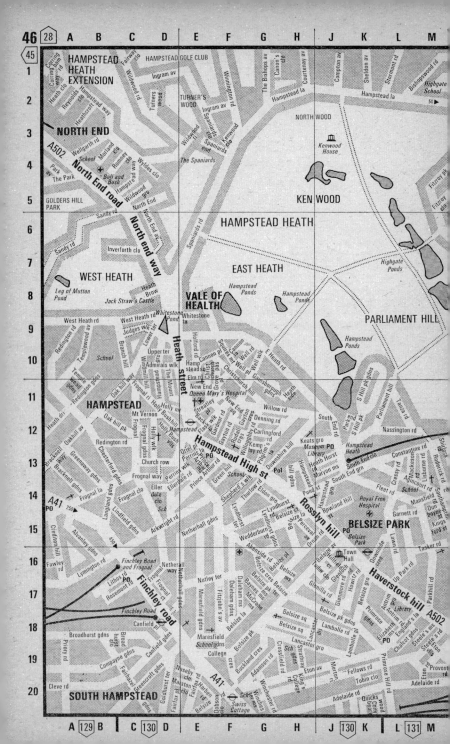

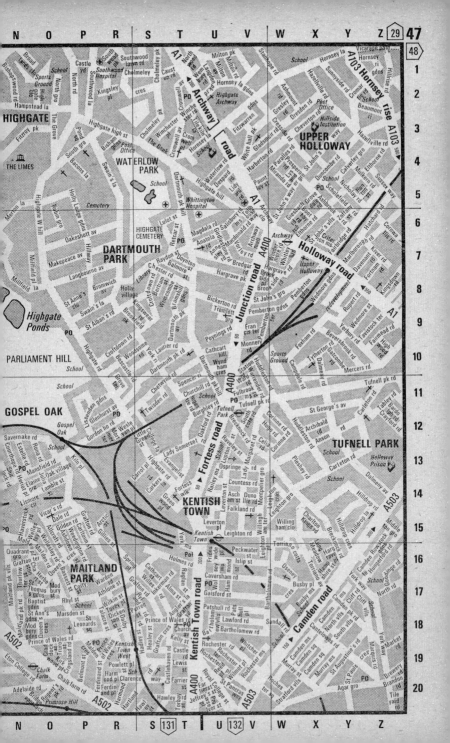

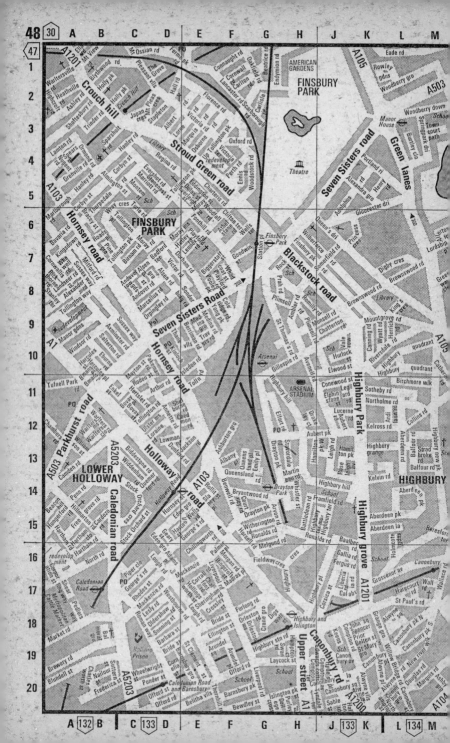

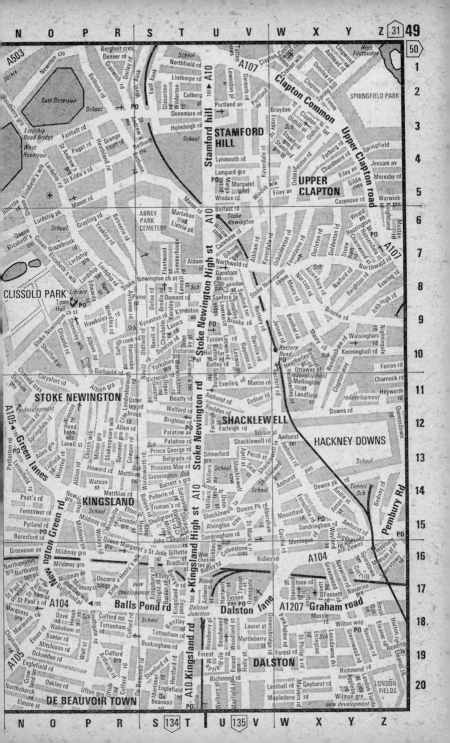

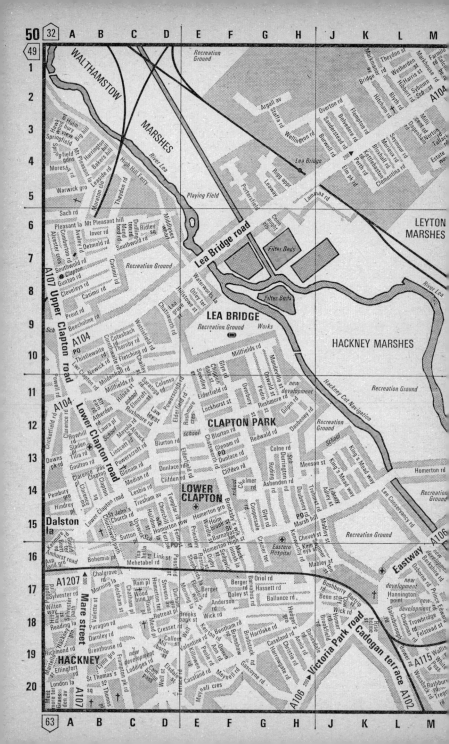

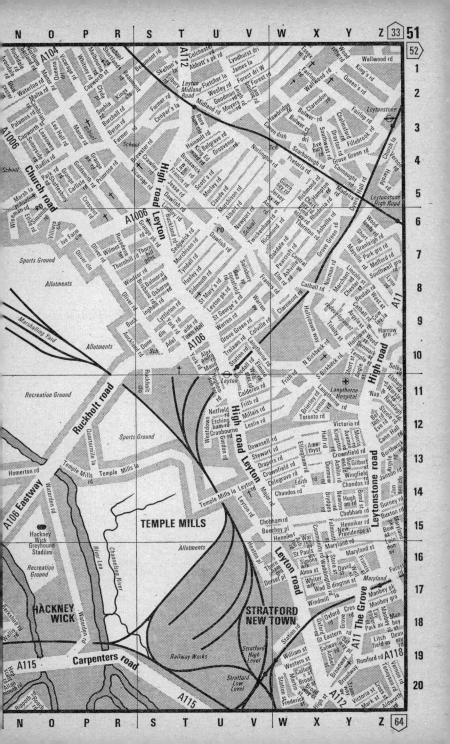

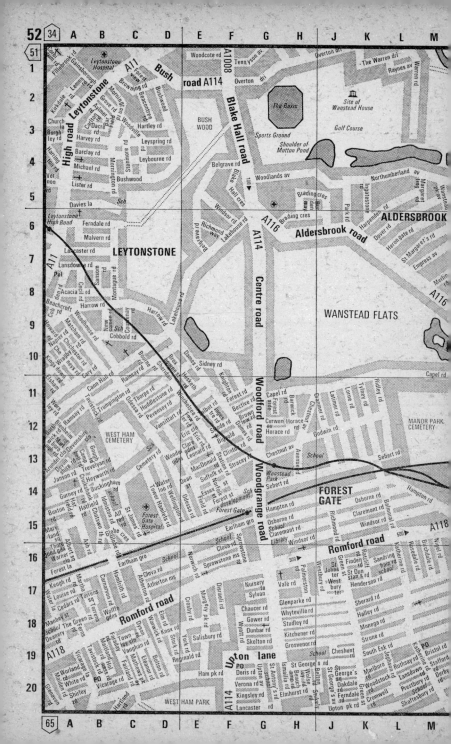

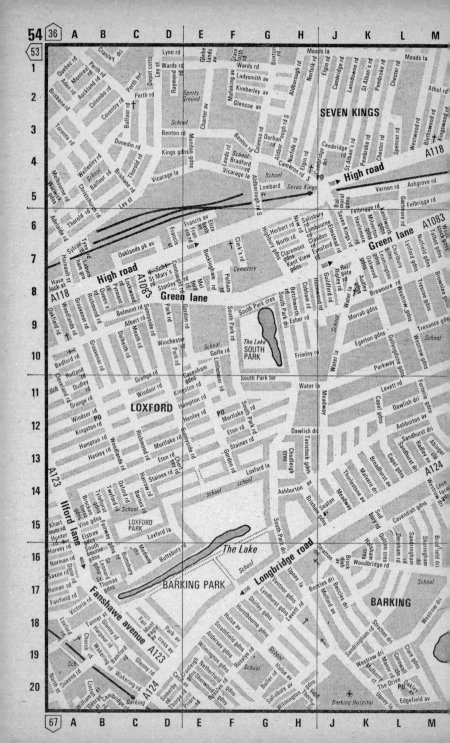

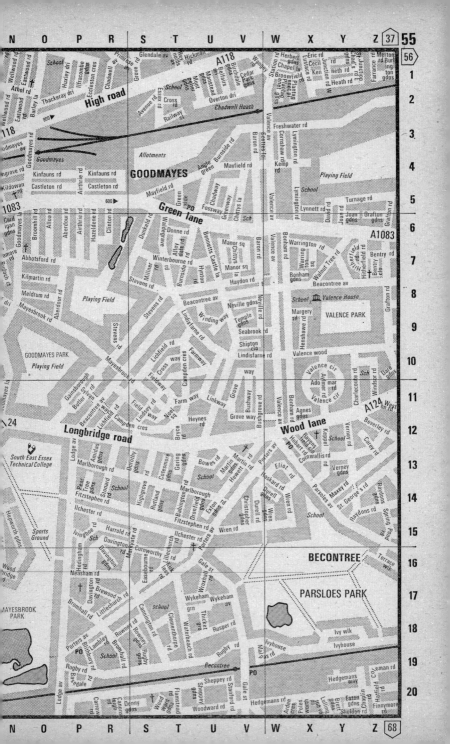

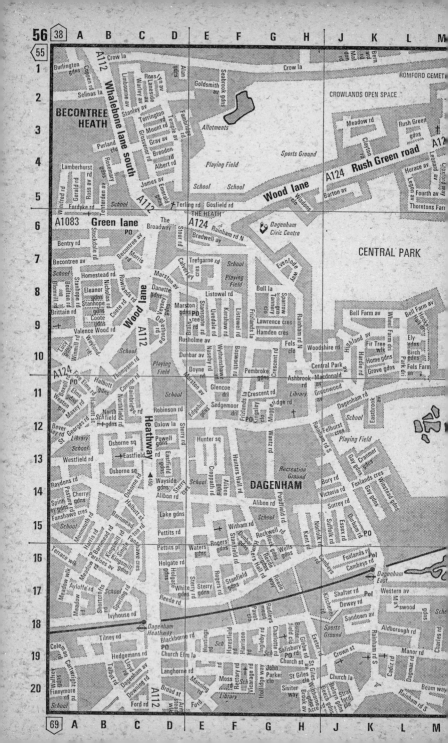

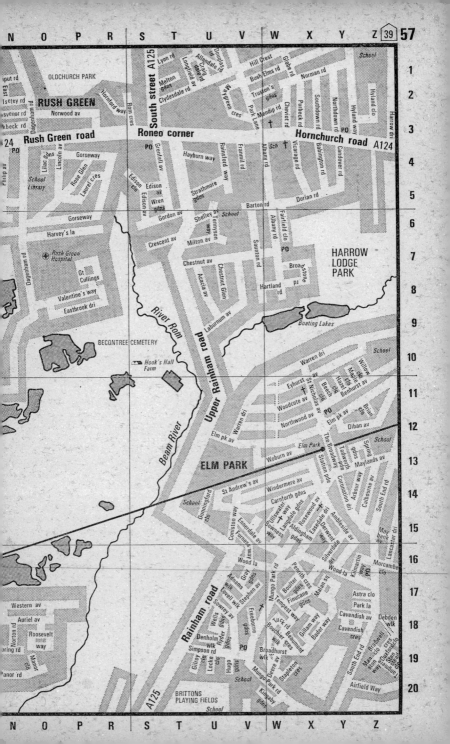

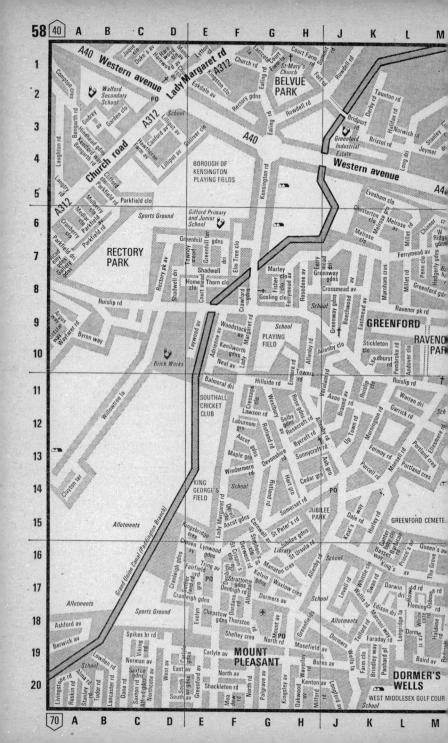

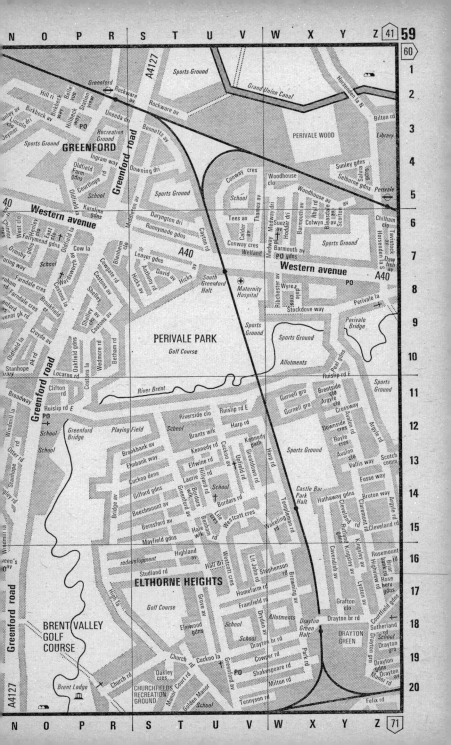

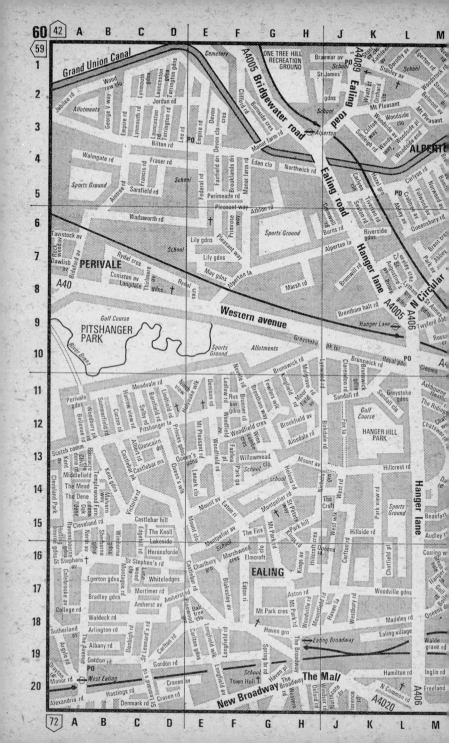

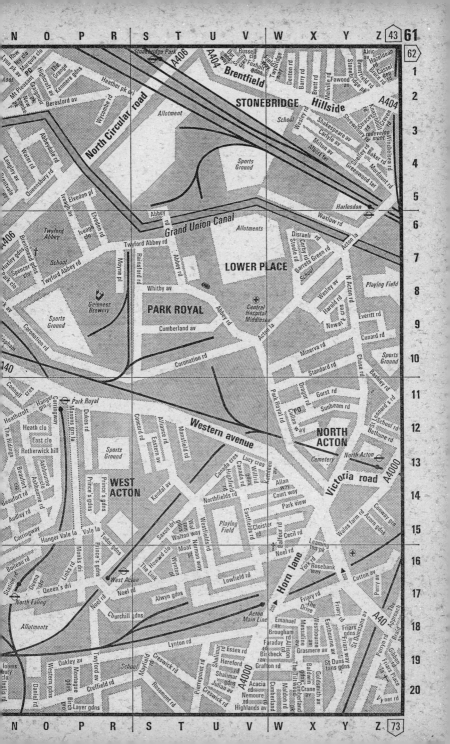

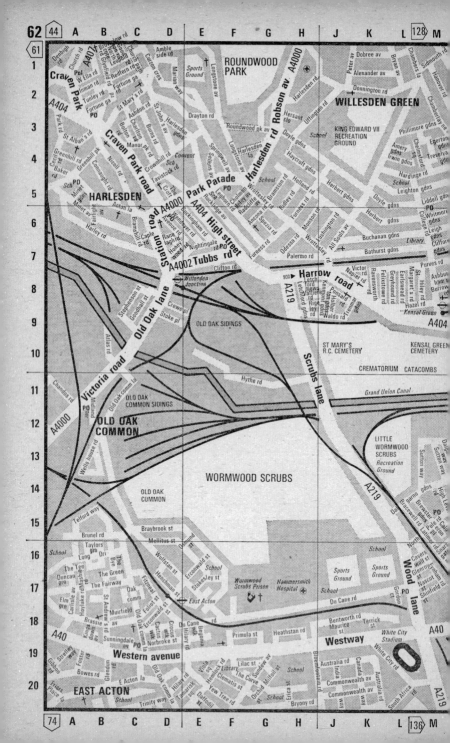

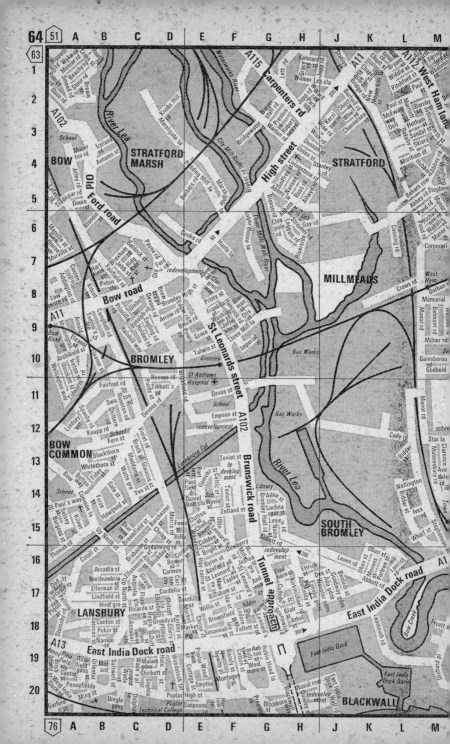

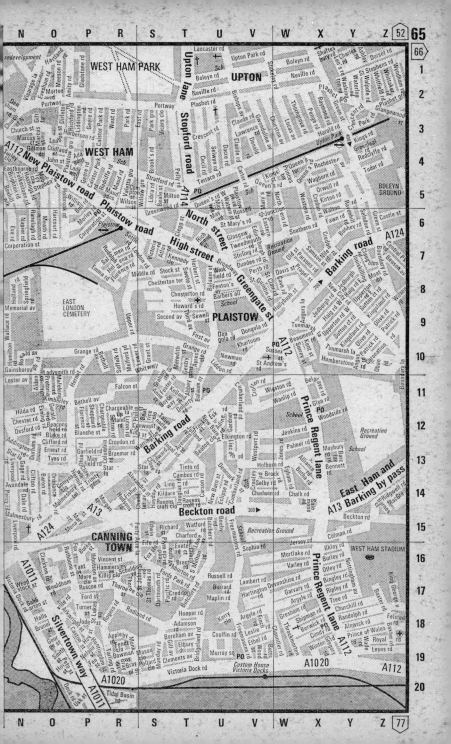

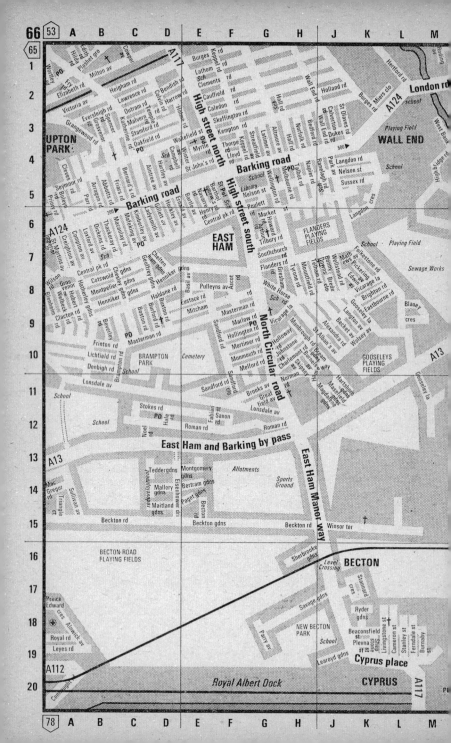

A B C D E F G H J K L M

1
2
3
4
5
6
7
8
9
10
11
12
13
14
15
16
17
18
19
20

A117

Edith rd
Plashet gro
Hilda rd
Cowper av
Milton av

Wortley
PO
Elizabeth rd
Victoria av
Grangewood rd
Eversleigh rd
Spencer rd
Katharine rd
Grosvenor rd

Heigham rd
Lawrence rd
Outram rd
Colvin rd
Malvern rd
Stamford rd
Oakfield rd

Bendish rd
Harrow rd
Temple rd
PO

High street north

Burges rd
Keppel rd
Lathom rd
Clements rd
Caulfield rd
Caledon rd
Skeffington rd
Kempton rd

Sch
Latimer av
Streatfield av
Thorpe rd
Keppel rd
Lloyd rd

Wall End rd
Holland rd
Norfolk rd
Bedford rd

St Olaves rd
Calverton rd
Wall End rd
Dukes rd

Burges rd. Miers clo
A124

Hertford rd
school
West Bank

London rd

Playing Field

WALL END

UPTON PARK

A124

Seymour rd
Bleyn
Priory rd
Parr rd
Cleves rd

Abbotts rd
Bernard s rd
Friars rd
Arragon rd

Barking road

Gillett av
Mafeking av
Hockley av
Erina av

High street south

St Martins av
Creighton av
Compton av
Lorkford av
Dickens rd

Macaulay rd
Thackeray rd
Kimberley av
Goldsmith av

Barnby
Navarre rd
Bartle av
Henry rd
Central pk rd

Barking road

School
Wellington rd
Melbourne rd
Talbot rd

Napier rd
Ranelagh rd
Park av
Langdon rd
Nelson st
Sussex rd
500

Langdon cres
School

Playing Field

Sewage Works

EAST HAM

Central pk gdns
Wilson
Grosvenor rd
Hubert rd
Hamberley gdns
Welbeck rd
Blenheim rd
Clacton rd

Cotswold gdns
Montpelier gdns
Henniker gdns

Chesley gdns
Geoffrey gdns
Henniker rd

Haldane rd
Burford rd
Boston rd

Pulleyns av

Thaxted rd

Henniker gdns

Southchurch
Tilbury rd
Flanders rd

FLANDERS PLAYING FIELDS

Howard rd
Market

Folkestone rd
Pickering
Wellsted rd
Felton rd
Brondy s
Bristol rd
Brede

Matthews
Pembroke
Gooseley la
Eastbourne rd
Brighton rd

School

Vicarage la

Blaney cres

Beverley rd
Frinton rd
Lichfield rd
Denbigh rd

Masterman rd
PO
Masterman rd

Haldane rd

Eustace rd
Mitcham

Masterman rd
Marlow rd
Hollington rd
Mortimer rd
Monmouth rd
Melford rd

White Horse
Sch

Vicarage rd

North Circular road

Holloway rd
Johnstone
rd
Manbrough av
Dream
rd
Charlemont rd
Barnes rd

St Alban s av

Alexandra rd
Becket rd
Langton av
Wolser av

GOOSELEYS PLAYING FIELDS

Gooseley la

A13

BRAMPTON PARK

Cemetery

School

Denbigh rd

Lonsdale av

School

School

Sandford rd

Sandford rd

Brooks rd
Great field av
Lonsdale av

Norman
rd

Skyner

way

Hartshorn
Masefield
gdns

Meadow
gdns

Stokes rd
PO
Noel
Hale rd

Fabian
rd

Saxon
rd

Roman rd

Roman rd

East Ham and Barking by pass

A13

Mac Gregor rd
Sullivan av
Triangle
ct

Tedder gdns
Mallory gdns
Maitland gdns

Montgomery gdns
Bertram gdns
Eisenhower dri
Paget gdns

Allotments

Sports Ground

East Ham Manor way

redevelopment

Becton
gdns

Beckton rd

Beckton gdns

Beckton rd

Winsor ter

BECTON ROAD PLAYING FIELDS

Sherbrooke gdns

Level Crossing

BECTON

Prince Edward cres
Alnwick av
Royal rd
Leyes rd

A112

Connaught

Savage gdns

Parry av

NEW BECTON PARK
School

Learoyd gdns

Stannard cres

Ryder gdns

Beaconsfield st
Plevna st
Stone st
23

Livingstone st
Cameron st
Stanley st
Ferndale st
Burnaby st

Cyprus place

CYPRUS

Royal Albert Dock

A117

A B C D E F G H J K L M

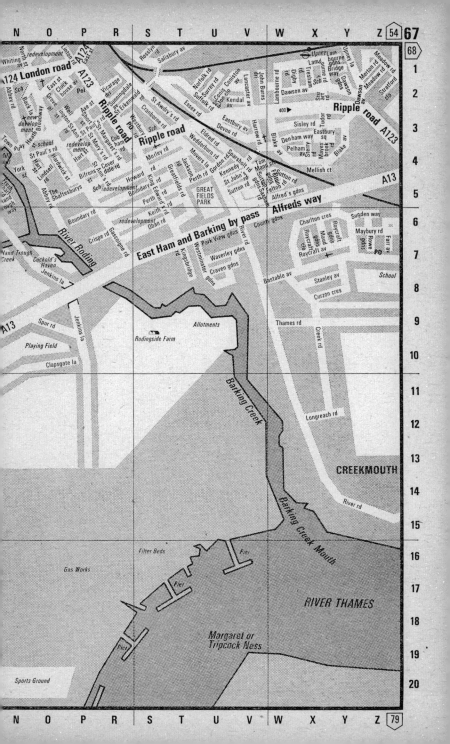

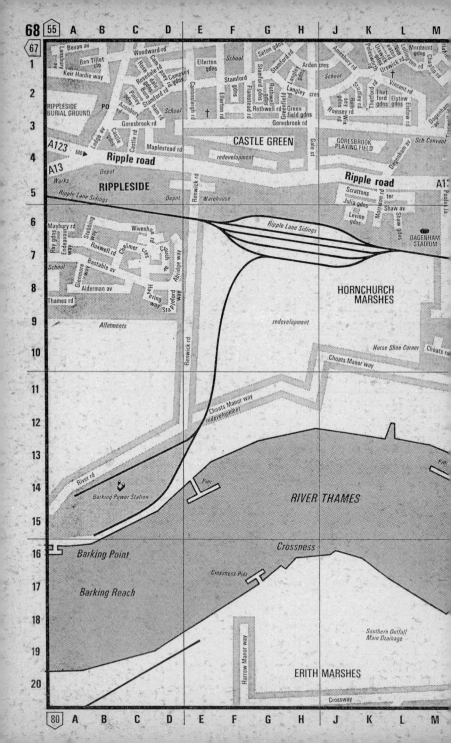

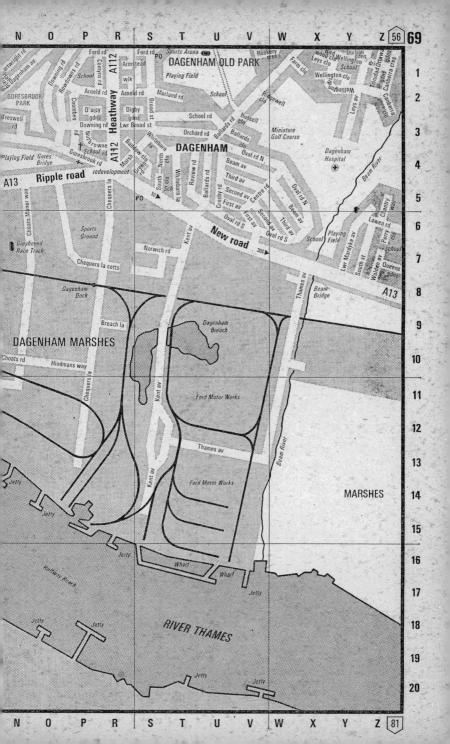

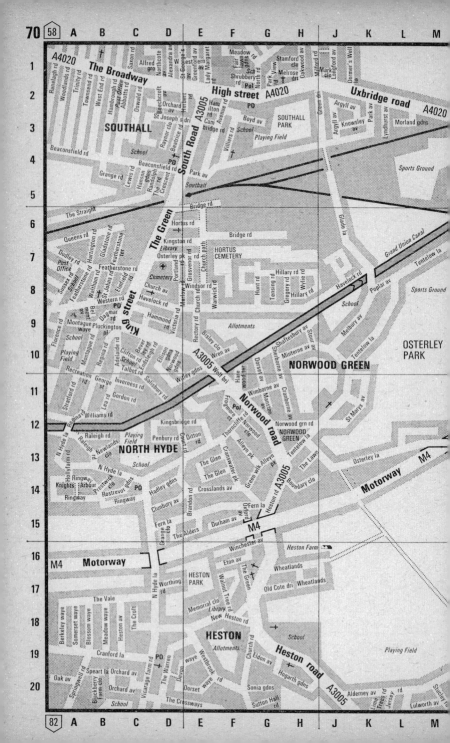

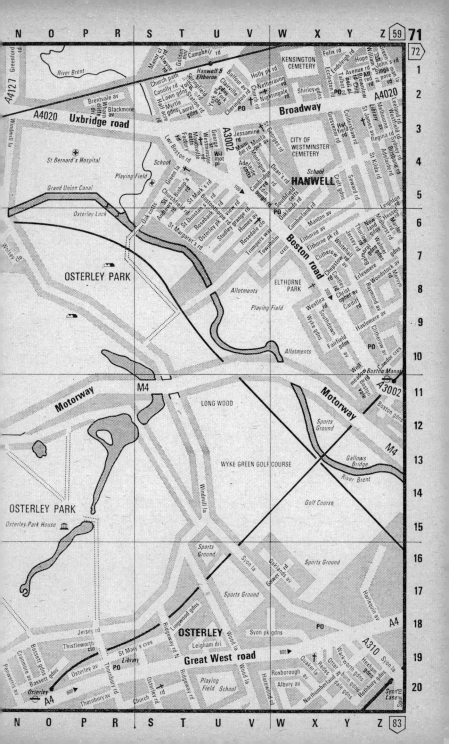

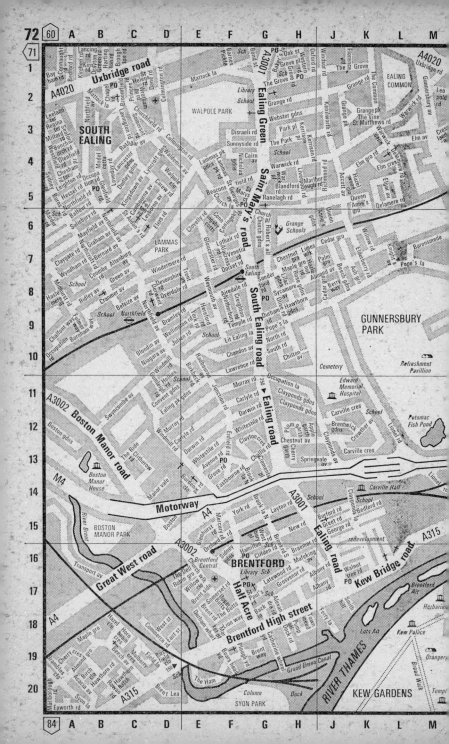

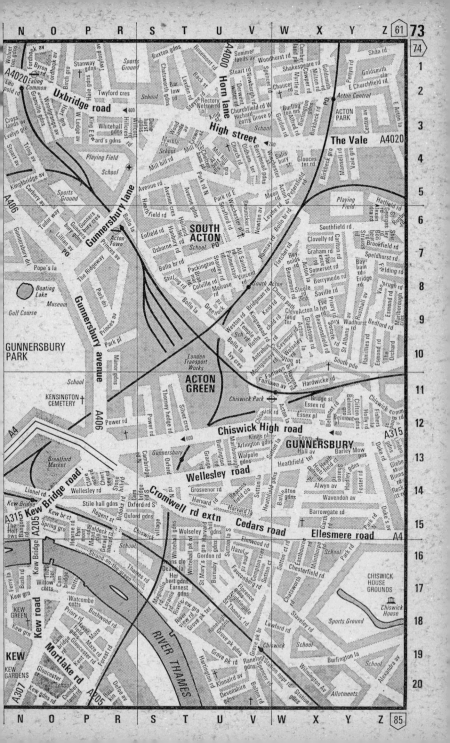

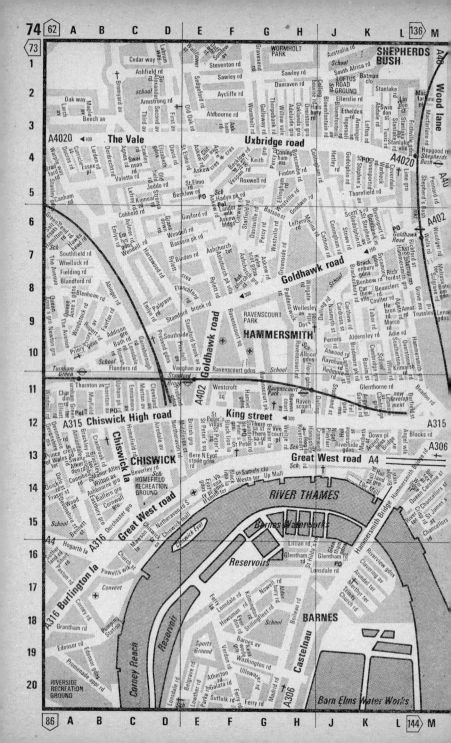

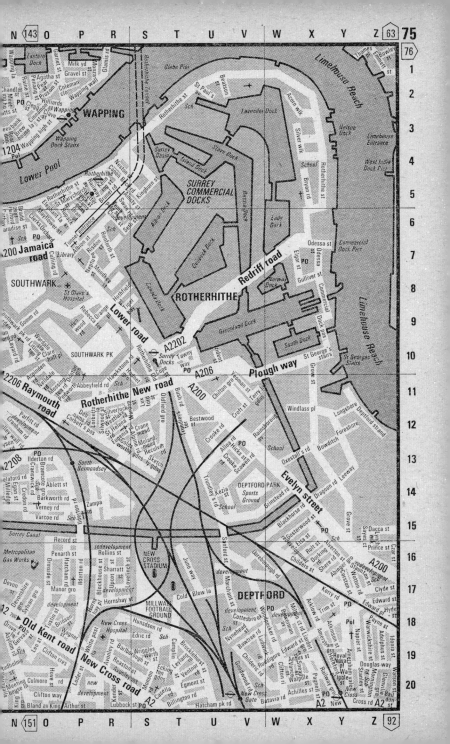

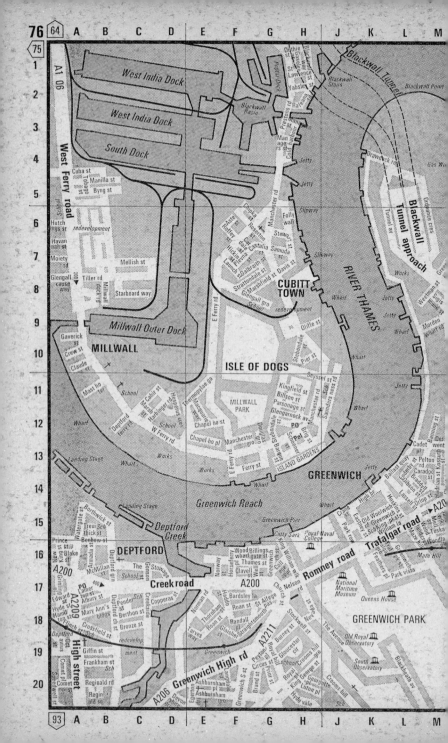

A B C D E F G H J K L M

A B C D E F G H J K L M

1
2
3
4
5
6
7
8
9
10
11
12
13
14
15
16
17
18
19
20

A1 06

West India Dock

West India Dock

South Dock

West Ferry road

Cuba st
Tobago st
Manilla st
Byng st

redevelopment

Hutch ings st
Havan nah st
Moiety rd
Glengall cause way

Mellish st

Tiller rd

Starboard way

Millwall Outer Dock

Gaverick st
Crew st
Claude st

MILLWALL

Mast ho ter
Marsh
Harbinger st

School

Cabit st

Deptford ferry rd

W Ferry rd

Landing Stage

Wharf

Wharf

Works

Hesperus av's
Macquarie
Thermopylae ga

School

Chapel ho st

Chapel ho pl
Manchester gro

E Ferry rd

E Ferry rd

Ferry st

Works

Wharf

Landing Stage

Borthwick st
Trevi Sch
thick st
Benbow st

Prince st
Blake st
McMillan st
Amelia st

Deptford gra

Grinling
Edward st
Lamb st
Albury st
Mary Ann's bldgs
Crossfield st

A200

A2209

PO

Hyde st
Hamil ton st
Finch st
Deptford lavis

High street

Giffin st
Frankham st Sch

Reginald rd
Regin ald sq

Comet st
Comet pl
Speedwell st

DEPTFORD

Creek road

Deptford Creek

The School

Gonson st
Stowage

Pender st
Berthon st
Bronze st

redevelopment

Greenwich High rd

A206

Ashburnham pl
Ashburnham
Egerton
Devon

Aste st
Rothey st
Hickin st
Castalia
Launch st
Strattondale st
Glengall gro

Chipka st
Rosetton st
Malabar st
Galbraith st
Marshfield st

St Davis st

Follywall
Stewet

Samuda st

E Ferry rd

Manchester rd

Blackwall Basin

Duthie
St Lawrence
Yabsley st

Preston's rd

Coldharbour

Managers
old rd

CUBITT TOWN

School

redevelopment

Oliffe st

ISLE OF DOGS

Stebondale st
Pier st

Seyssel st

Kingfield st
Billson st
Parsonage st
Glengarnock av

MILLWALL PARK

Manchester gro

Saunders ness rd

PO

Barque st

Schooner st

PO

Manchester rd

ISLAND GARDENS

GREENWICH

Greenwich Reach

Wharf

Greenwich Pier

Cutty Sark

Royal Naval College

King William st

Horseferry wharf gate st
Thames st
Clavell st
Wood st
Billings
Welland st

Norway st

Norman rd
Thornham
Bardsley la
Hadlo st
St Alfege pas

Tarves way

Randall
Straightsmouth
Glaisher st

Greenwich

A2211

Circus st
Brand st

Stockwell st

Greenwich S st

Gloucester cir

Peyton pl

Stockwell pas

Church st

Greenwich Church st

Nelson rd

Romney road

Trafalgar road

A200

National Maritime Museum

Queens House

GREENWICH PARK

The Avenue

Old Royal Observatory

South Observatory

Crooms hill

RIVER THAMES

Wharf

Jetty

Jetty

Wharf

Jetty

Blackwall Tunnel

Blackwall Point

Blackwall Stairs

Drawdock rd

Gas wks

Ordnance cres

Blackwall Tunnel approach

Tunnel av

Works

Westmab Sgs

Morden Wharf rd

Cadet

Derwent rd
Pelton rd

Caradoc st

Ballast quay

Old Woolwich rd

Trafalgar road

Maze Hill

Blackheath av

Wharf

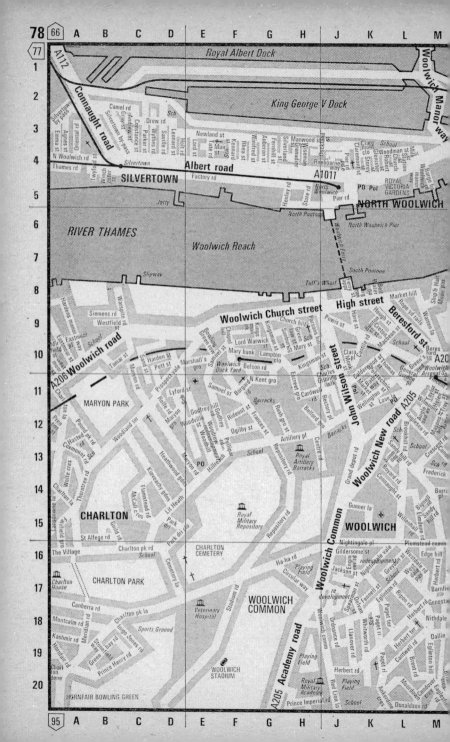

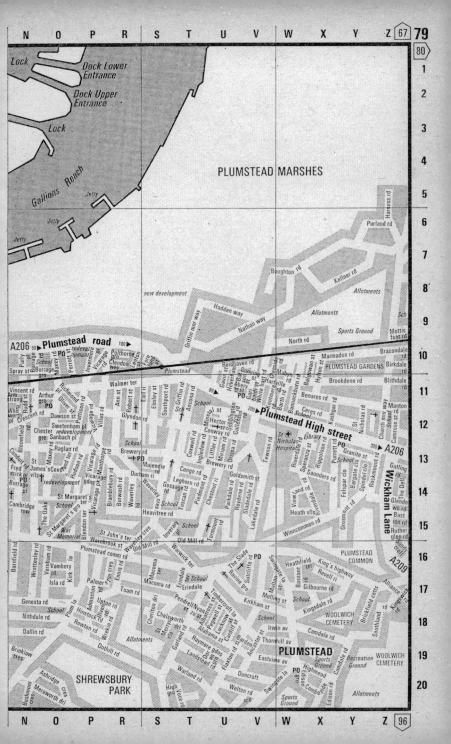

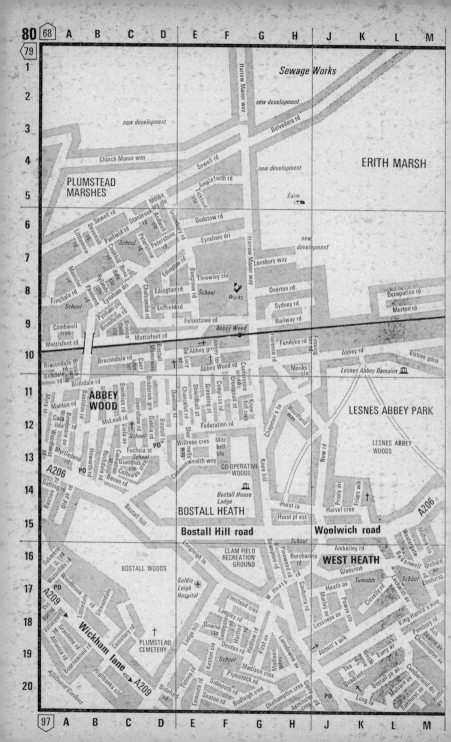

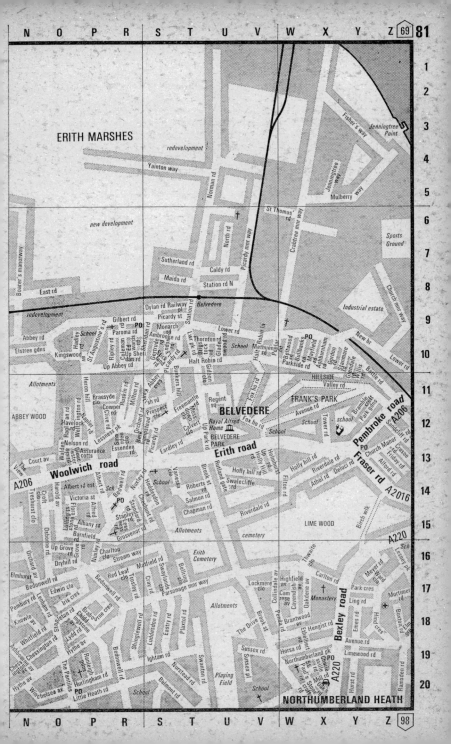

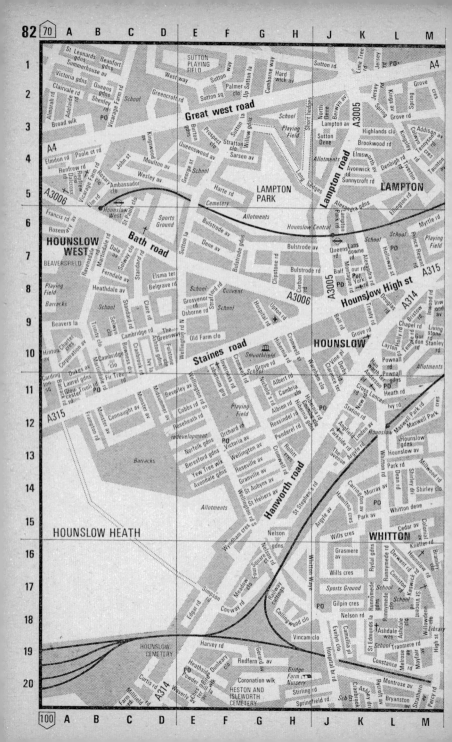

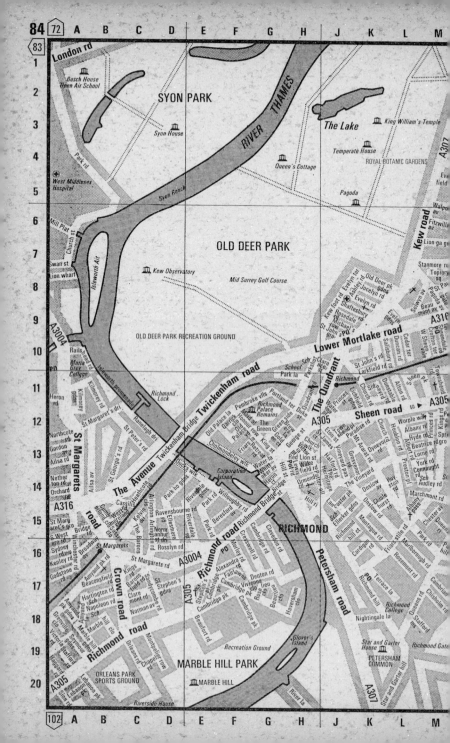

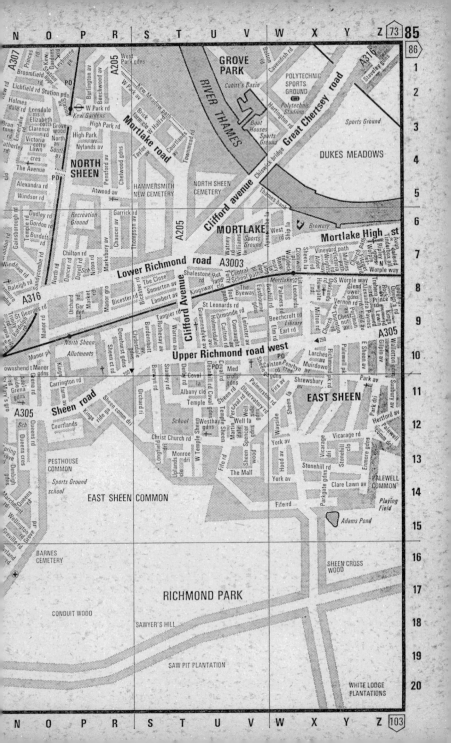

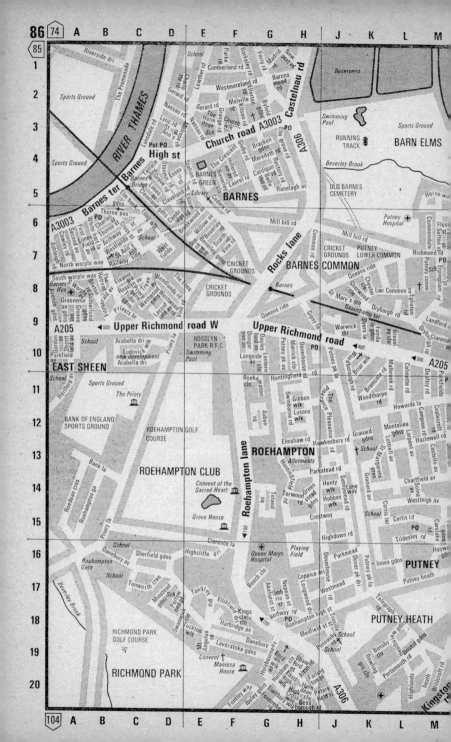

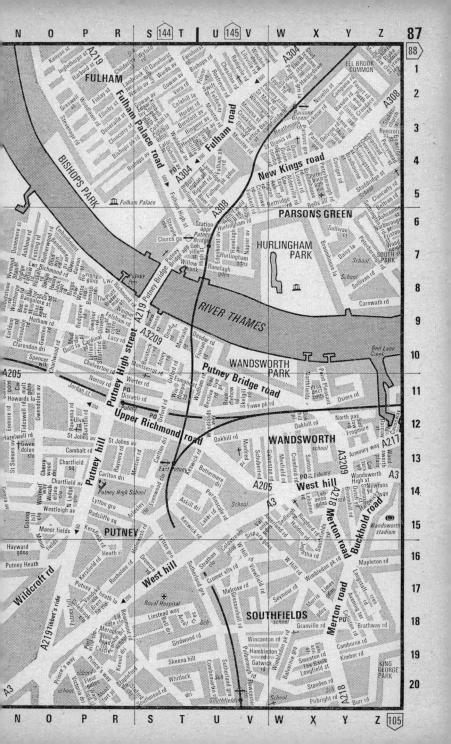

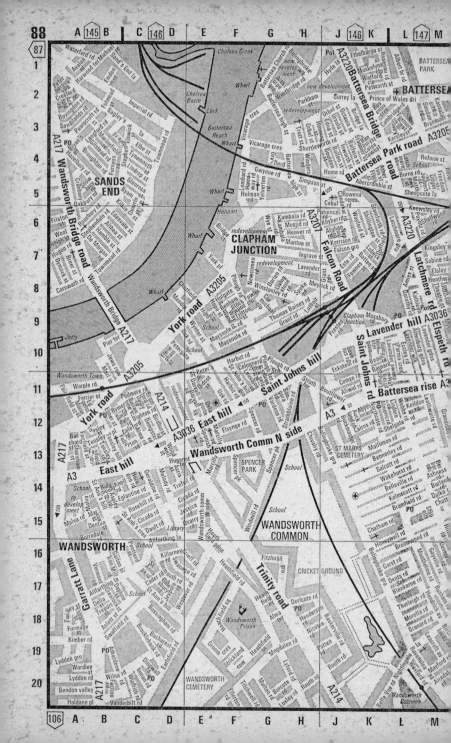

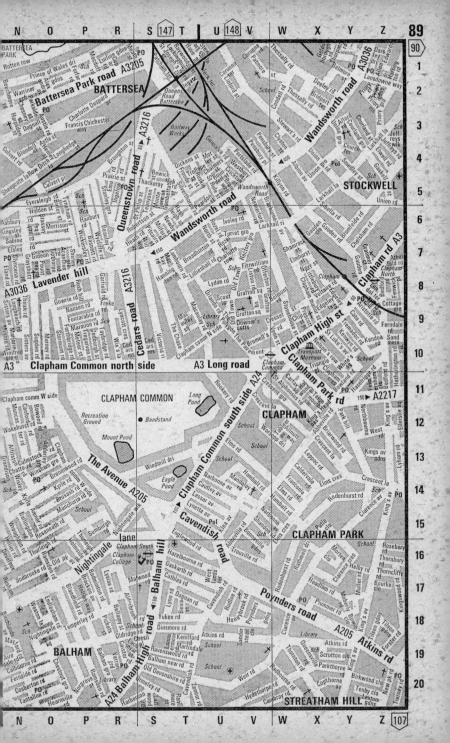

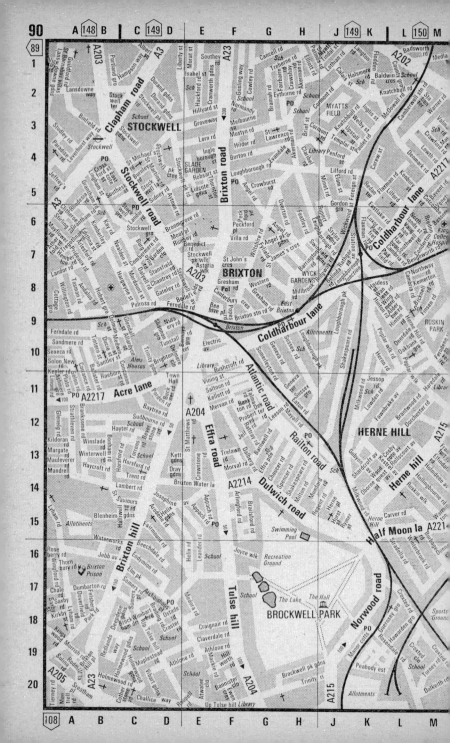

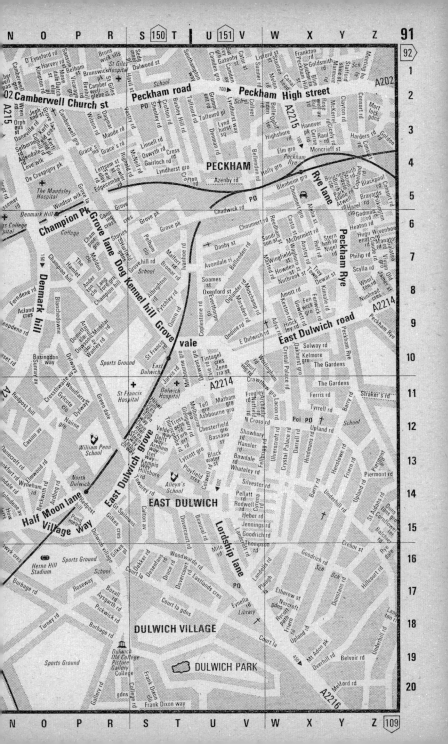

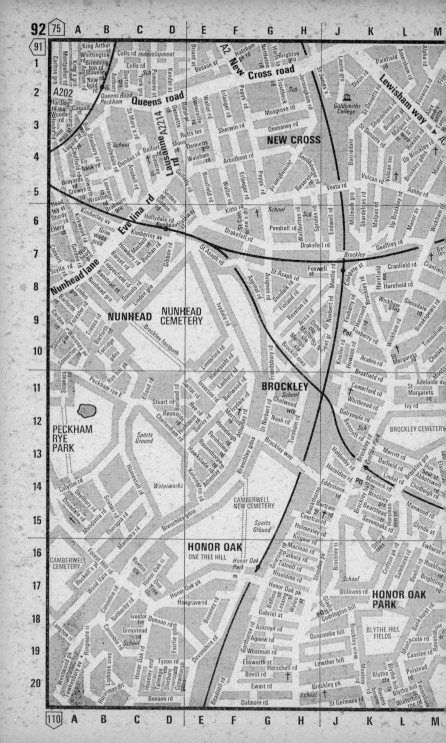

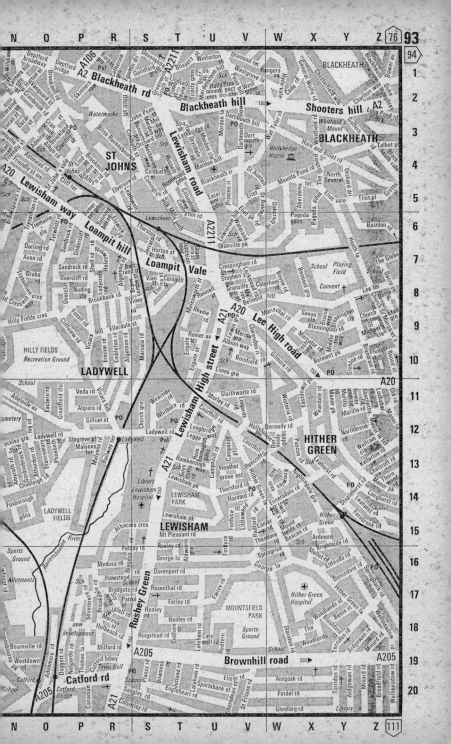

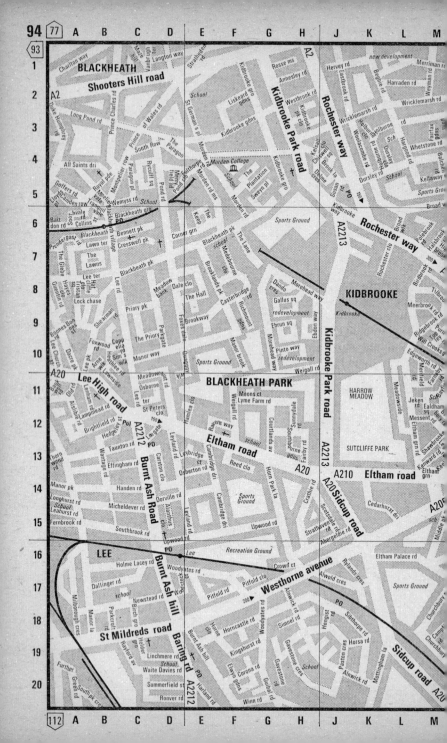

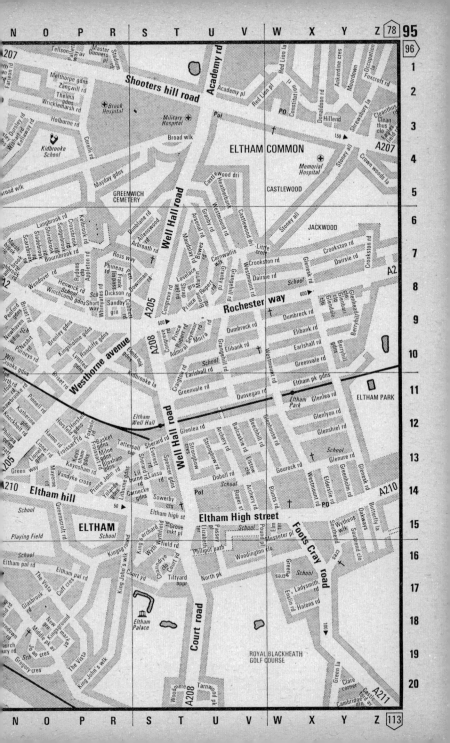

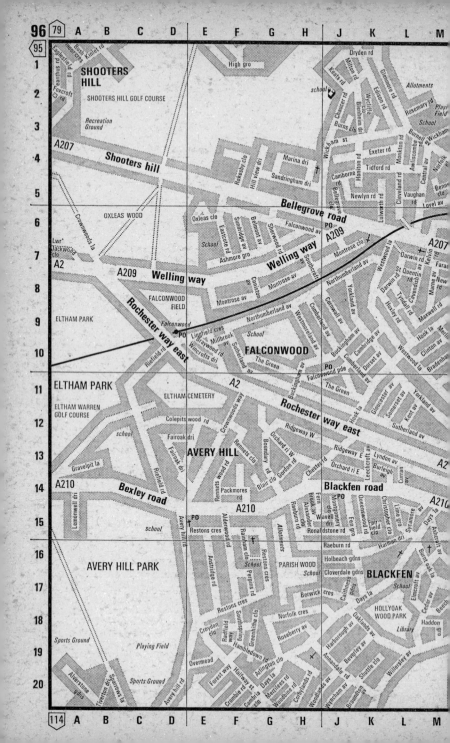

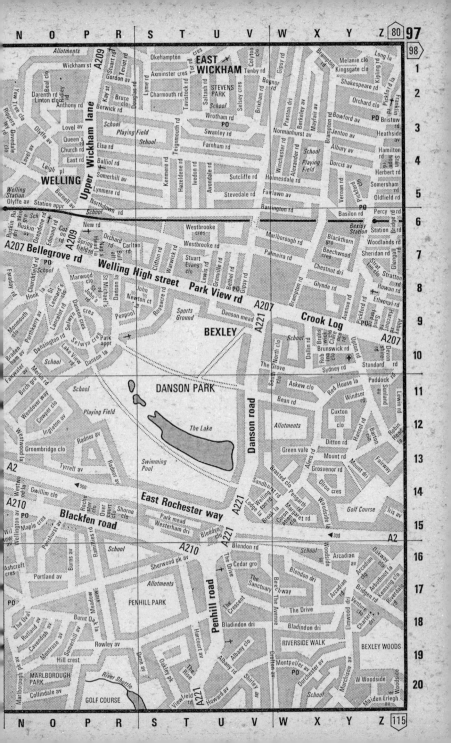

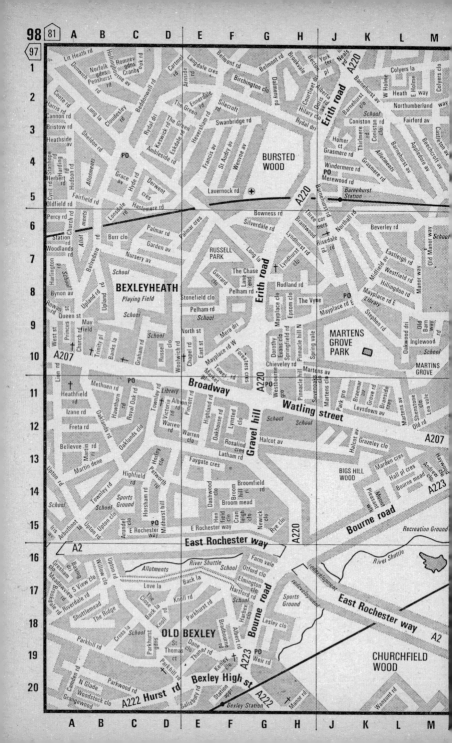

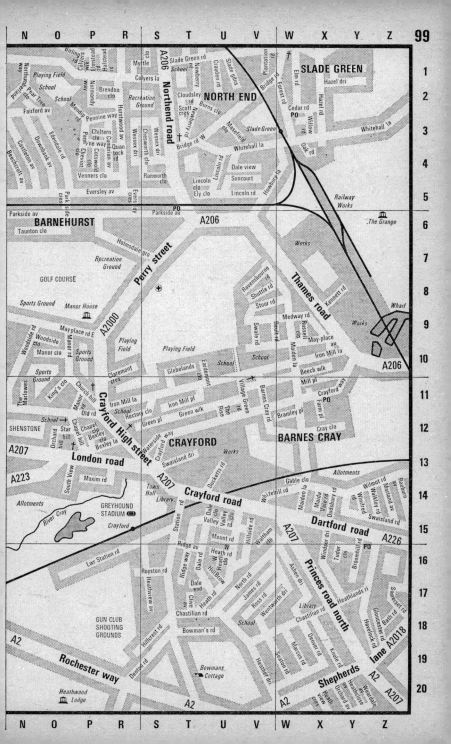

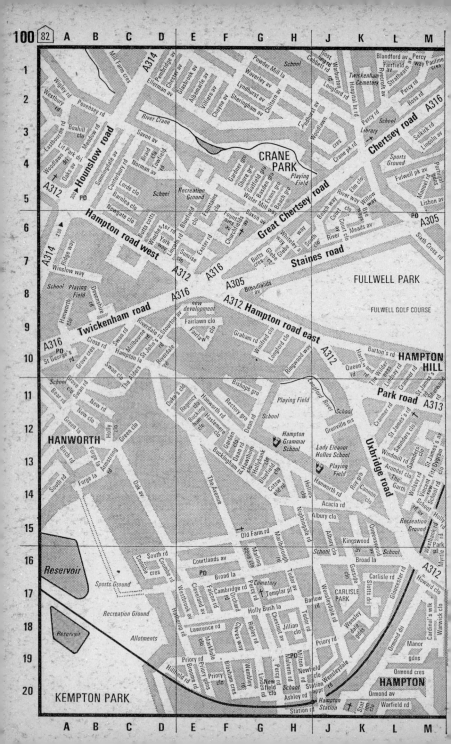

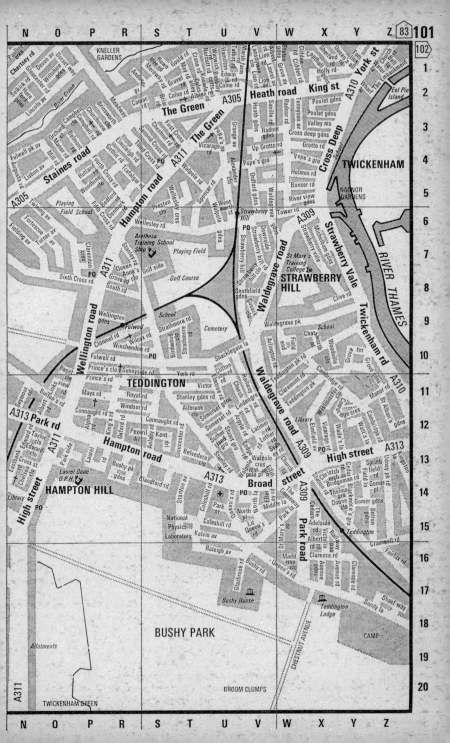

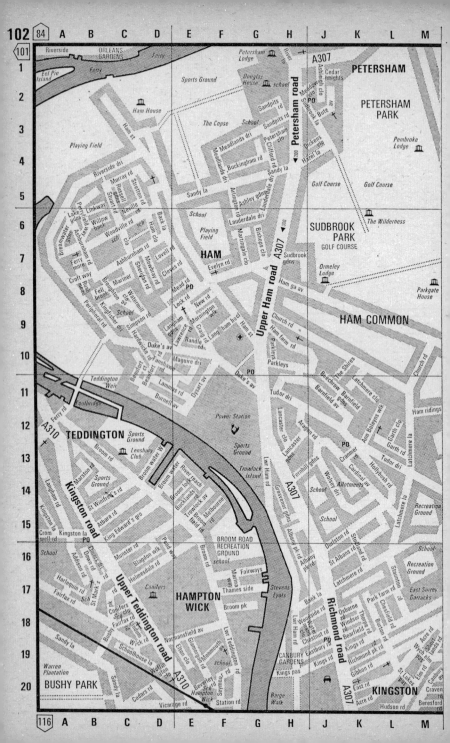

1

SIDMOUTH WOOD

Leg of Mutton Pond

2

White Lodge

3

Oak Lodge

RICHMOND PARK

Pen Ponds

SPANKERS HILL WOOD

4

White Ash Lodge

5

6

POND SLADE

7

PRINCE CHARLES'S SPINNEY

ISABELLA PLANTATION

8

BROOMFIELD HILL WOOD

Kingston Vale

A308

Derwent av

9

Ullswater cres

Grasmere av

HIGH WOOD

Kingstonhill Place

Ullswater clo

10

RICHMOND PARK

11

Kingston hill

Kenry House

12

Coombe pk

Coombe pk

Bowness cres

Coombe wood rd

13

Ladderstile ride

Coombe ridings

Coombe pk

Corscombe clo

14

Warboys rd

Warren rd

Park ga

COOMBE HILL GOLF COURSE

15

Warboys appr

Fairlawn clo

Warren House

Warren pk

Cotswold clo

16

KINGSTON UPON THAMES

Kings nympton pk

Ravenswood ct

COOMBE

Kelvedon clo

Up Park rd

School

COOMBE WOOD GOLF COURSE

Warren cutting

17

Park rd E
rd W

Park rd

Wilmer clo
Wilmer cres

Bockhampton rd

Bertram rd

Kingston gate

Winchester clo

Edgecombe clo

Coombe end

Golf club dri

Park Fields rds

Wyndham rd

Liverpool rd

Renfrew rd

Coombe neville

18

Wood cote clo

Park gdns

King's rd

New rd

Crescent rd

Morcoombe clo

Stoke rd

school

George rd school

school

Coombe

Tudor dri

Shortlands rd

Tudor rd

George rd

The Drive

Gatehouse clo

Coombe

19

Wing field rd

PO

Elm rd

Alexandra rd

Eaton dri

Dalziel of Wooler Home

Gatacre rd

Glen Eliam gdns

Ballard clo

Coombe Lane west

gdns
Cranleigh

Park rd

St George's rd

Princes rd

Arthur rd

Queen's rd

Kingston hill

Glenbuck rd

Lord Chanc
Southwood

Fitzgeorge av

Coombe ho
chase

Latchmere
Cross rd

York rd

Clifton rd

Borough

School

Brunswick rd

A308

Wolsey clo

Orchard rd

West rd

A238

Warren ri

The Neville av
The Fair

Crav en rd
Beres ford rd

Lowther rd

Dagmar rd

Glenville rd

Elton rd

Brook gdns

Coombe clo

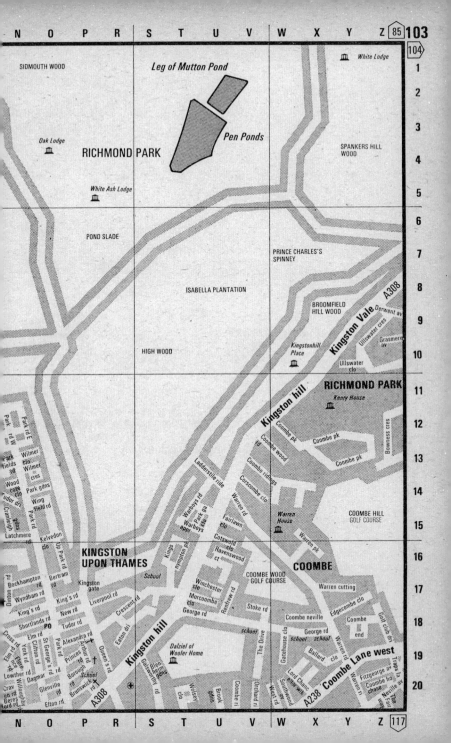

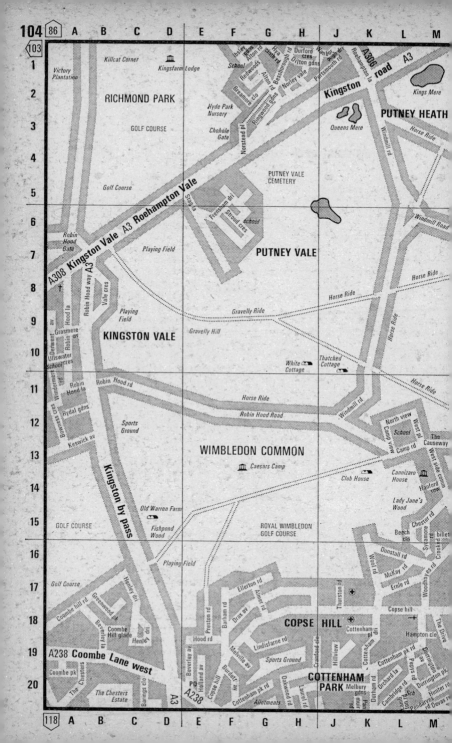

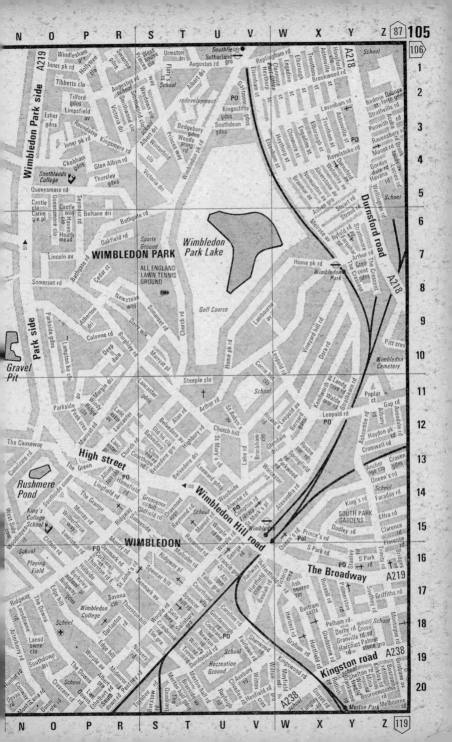

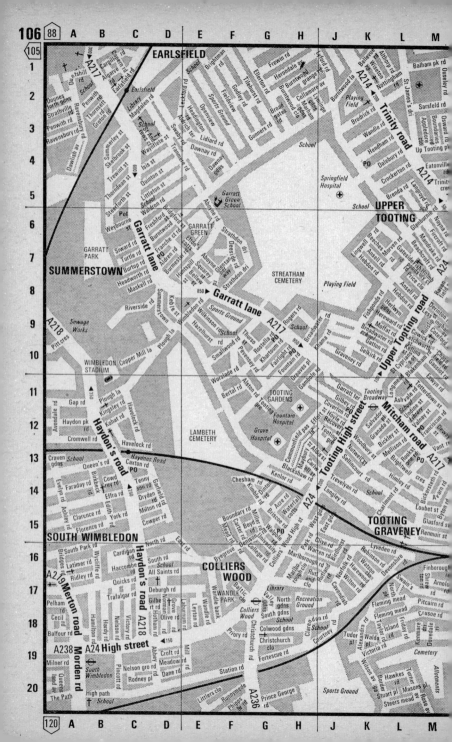

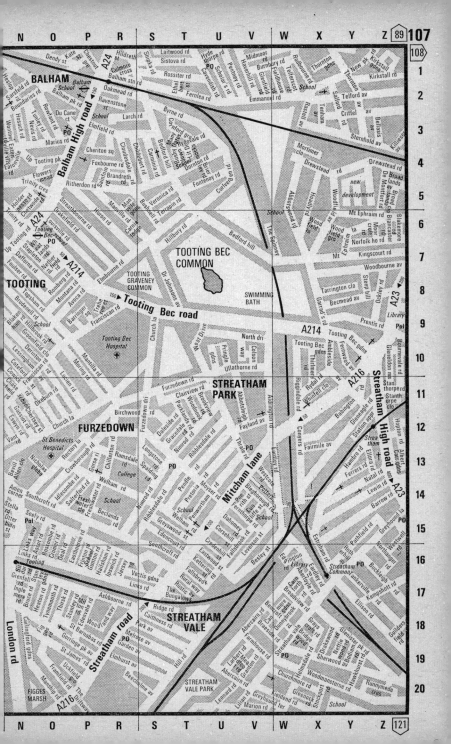

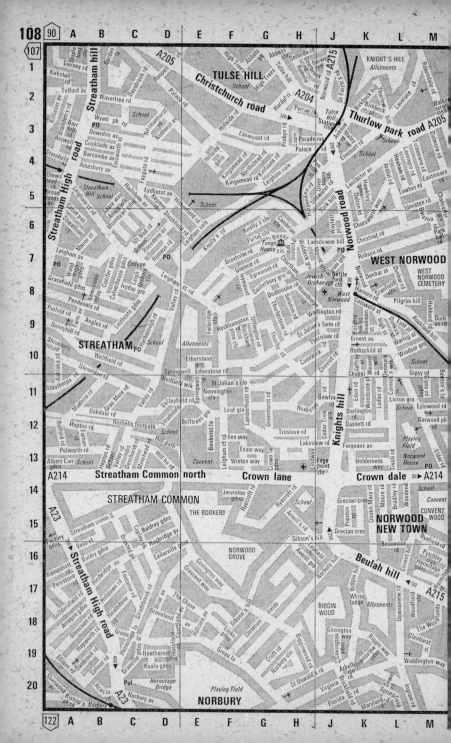

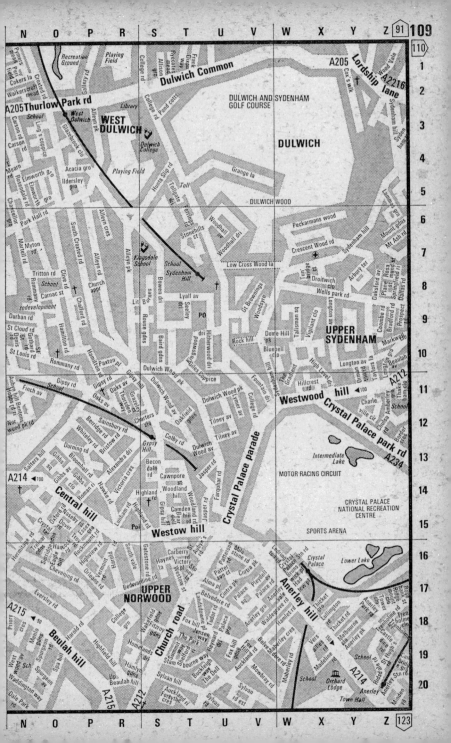

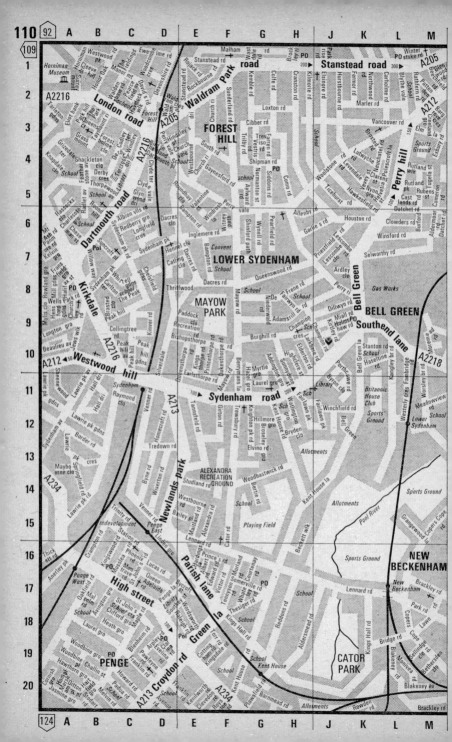

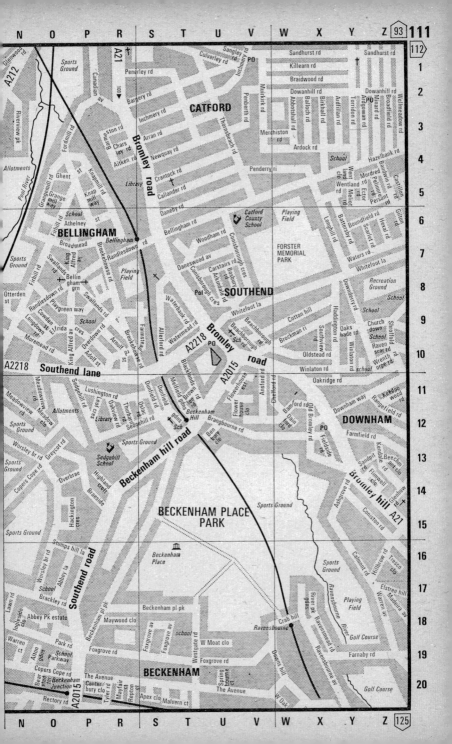

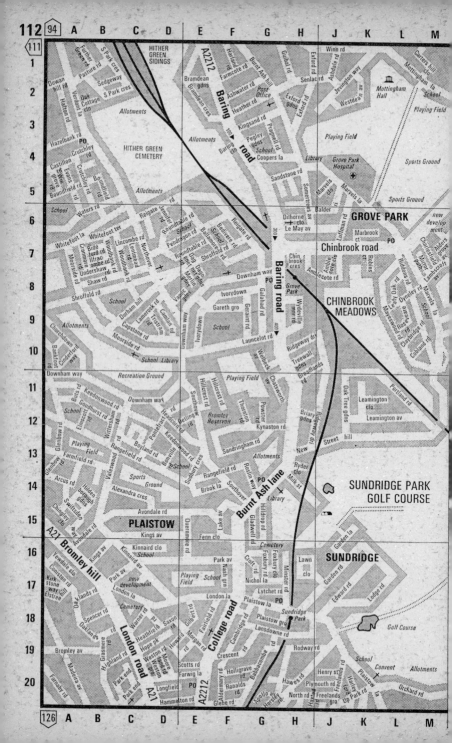

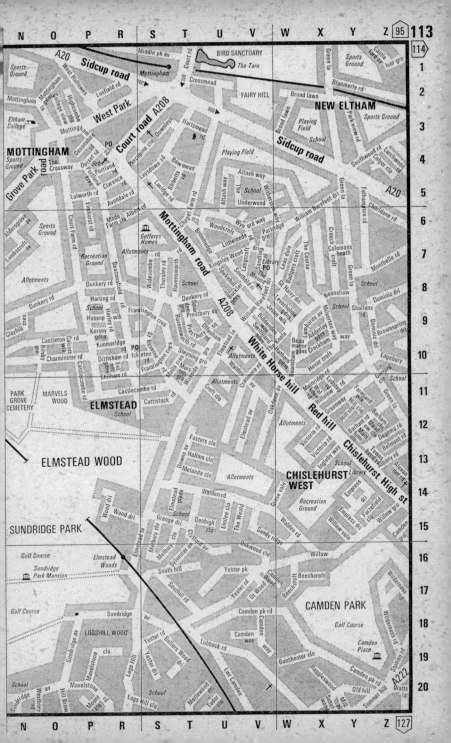

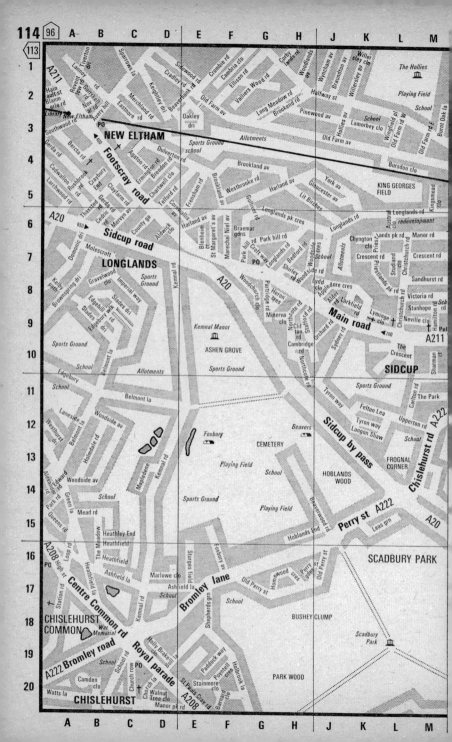

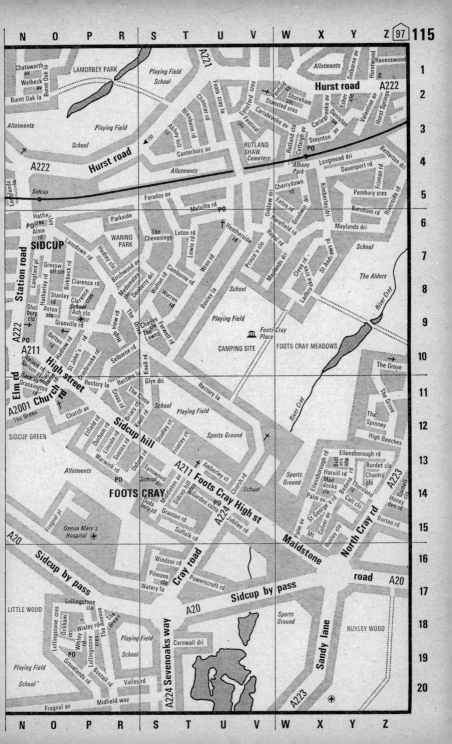

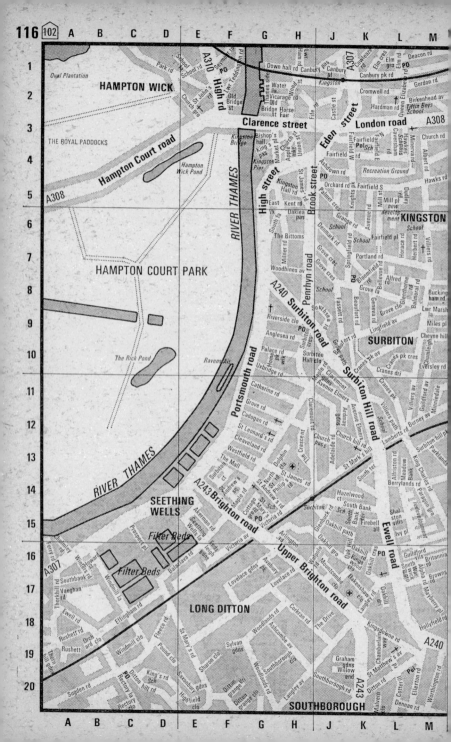

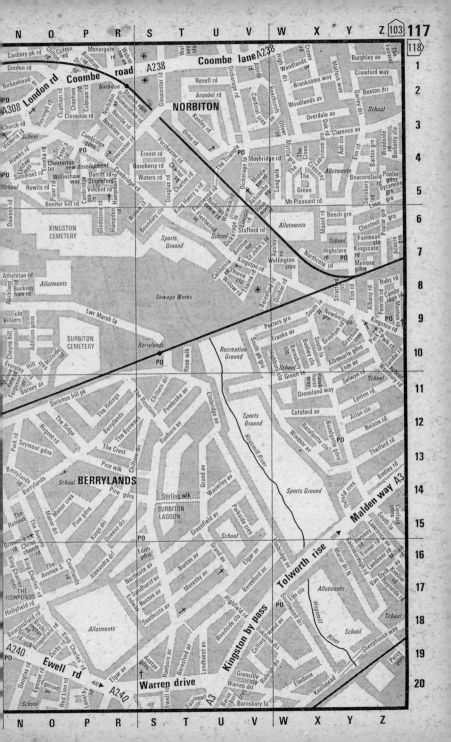

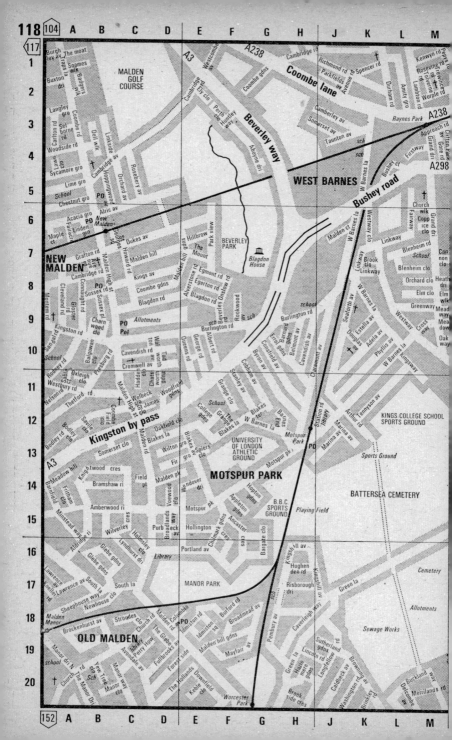

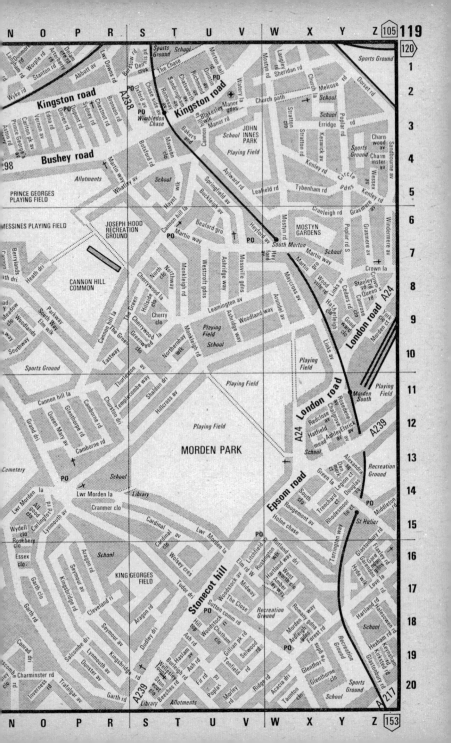

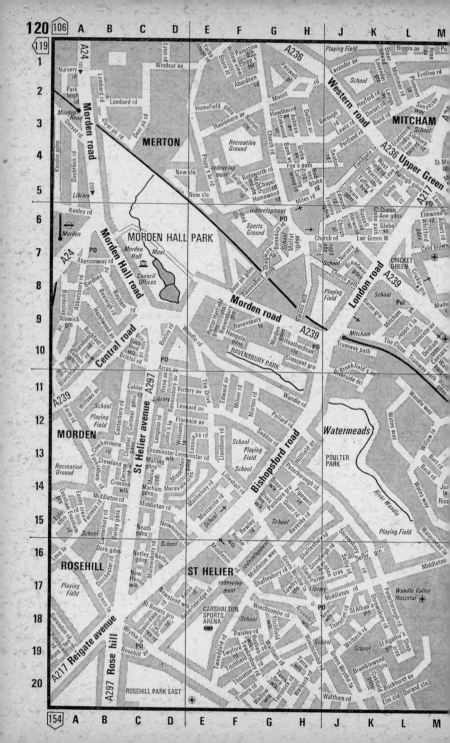

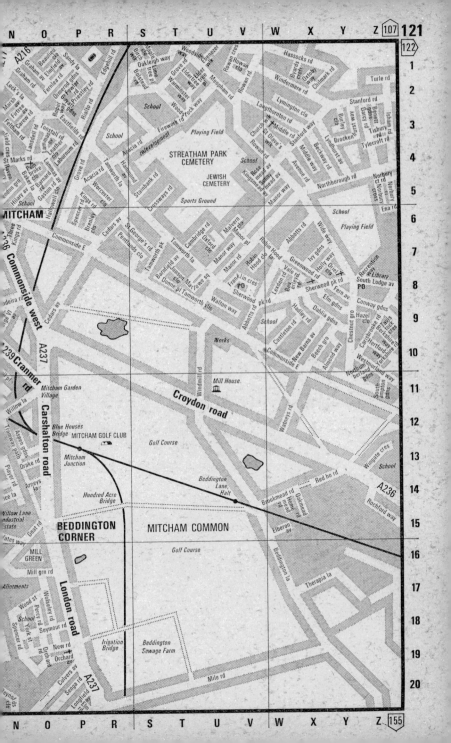

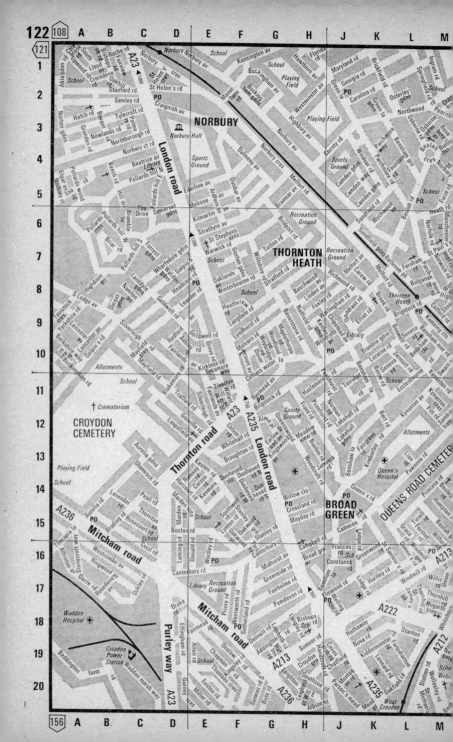

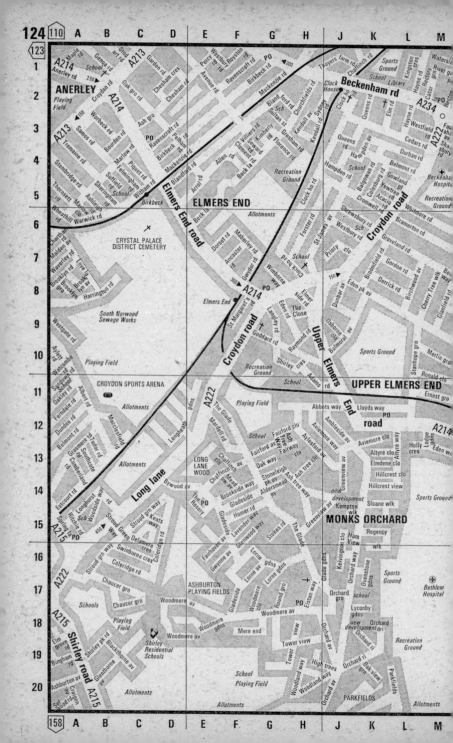

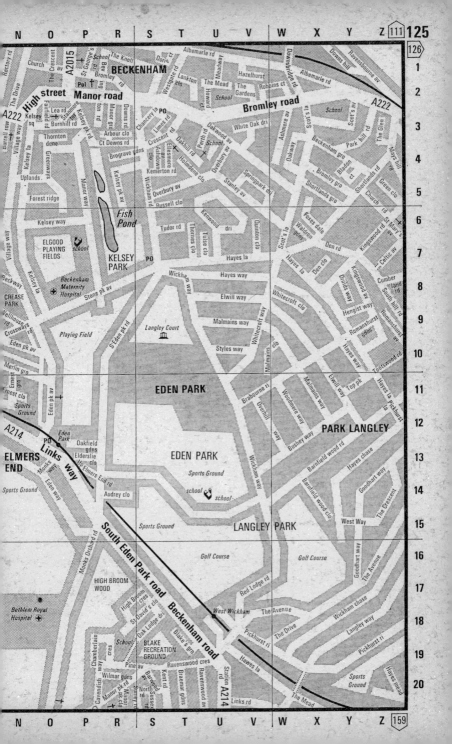

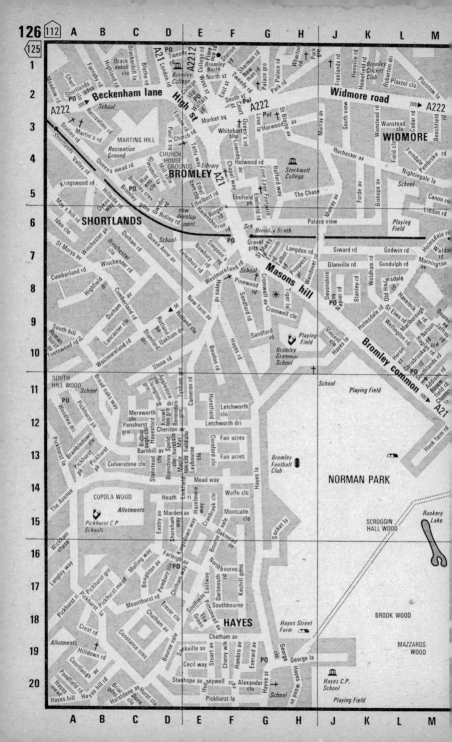

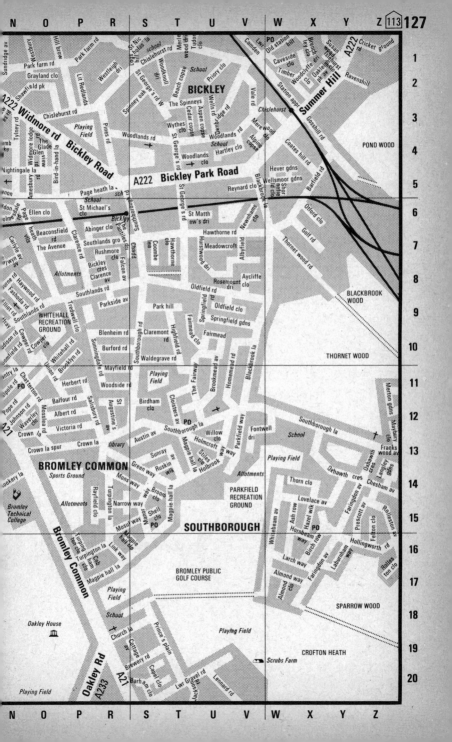

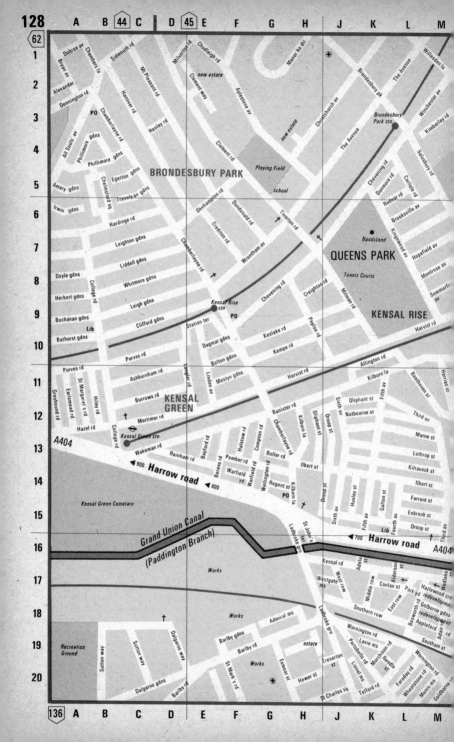

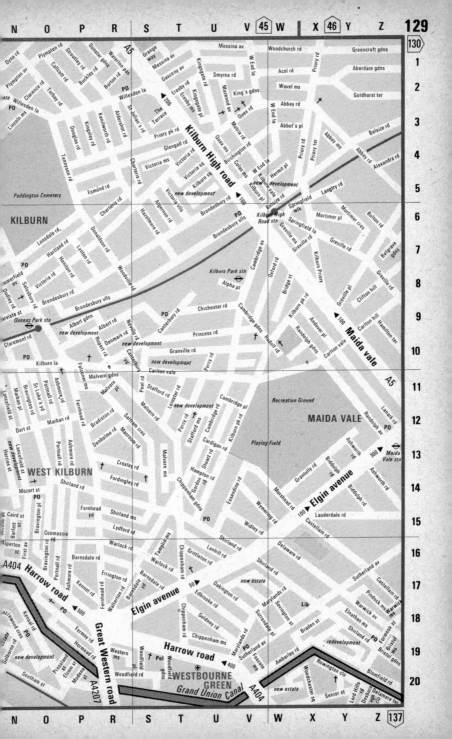

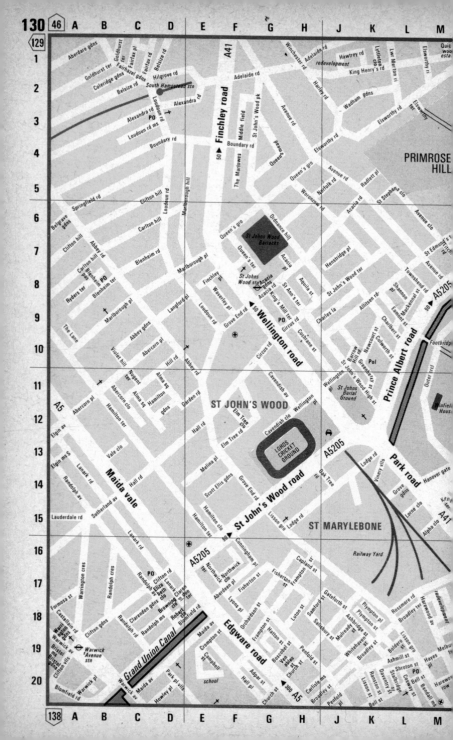

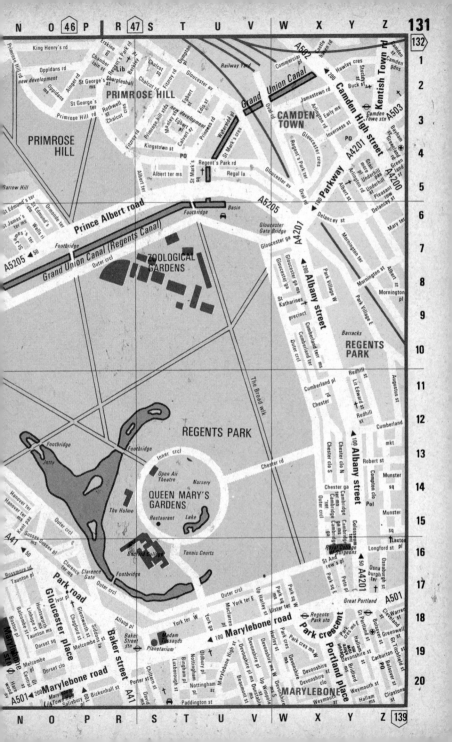

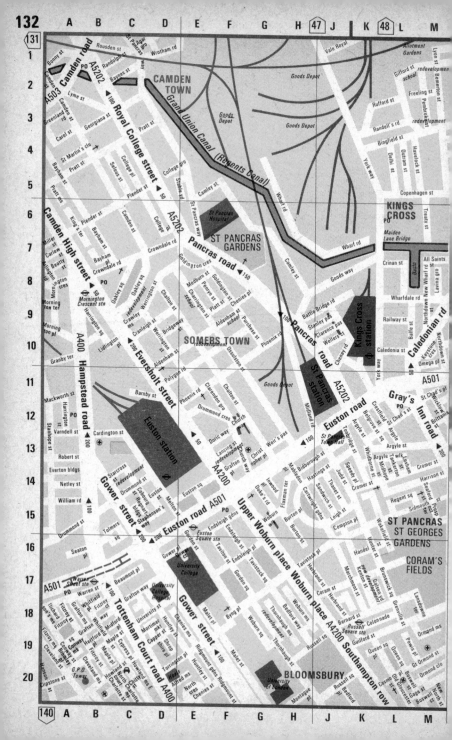

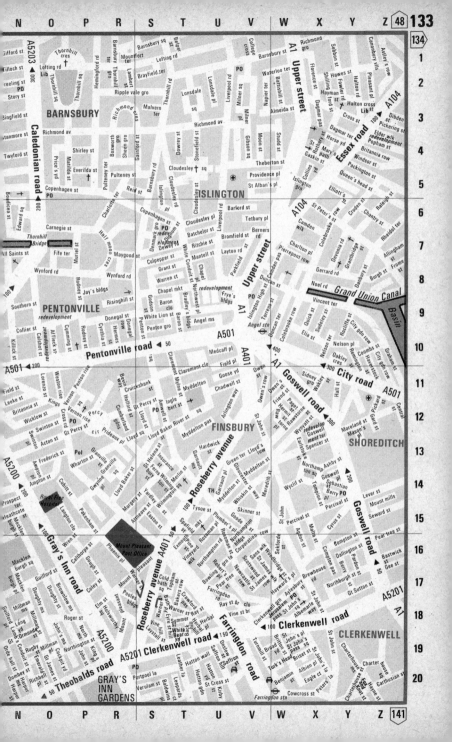

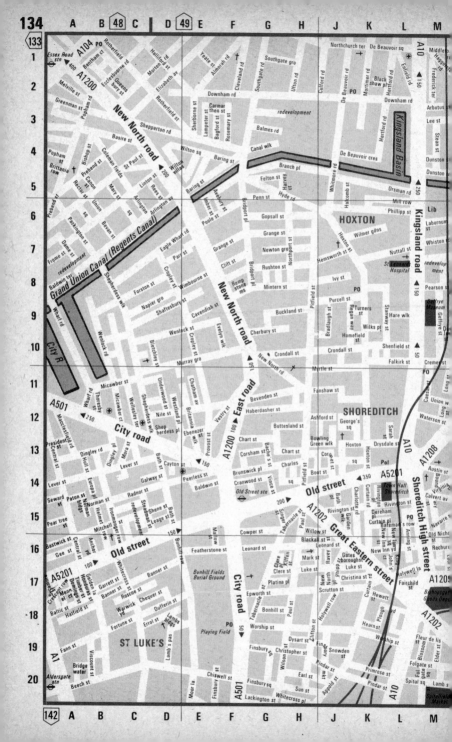

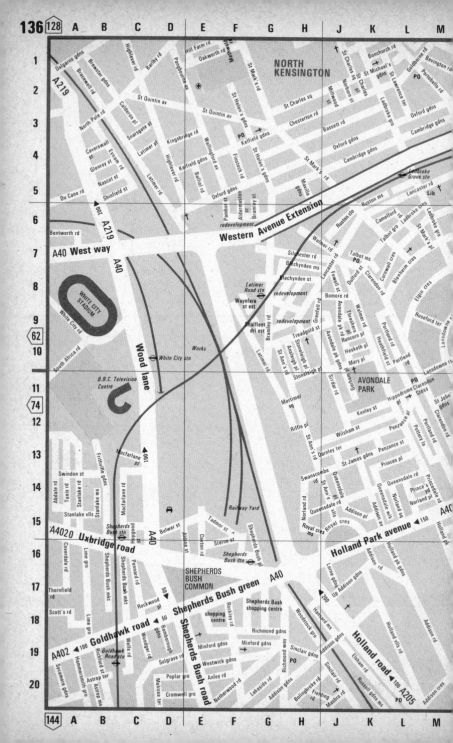

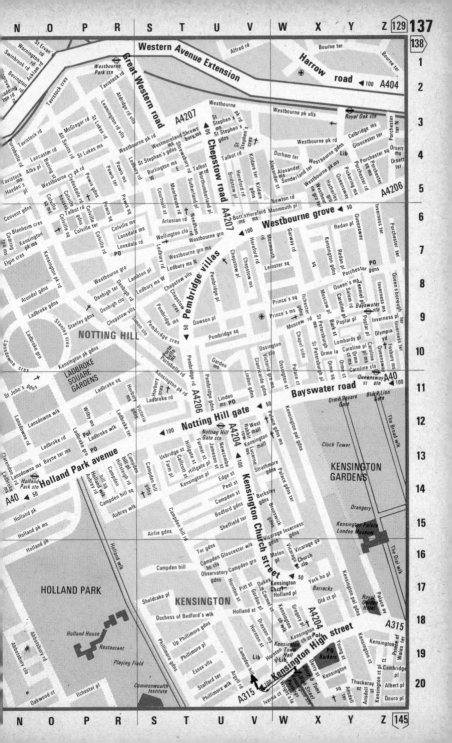

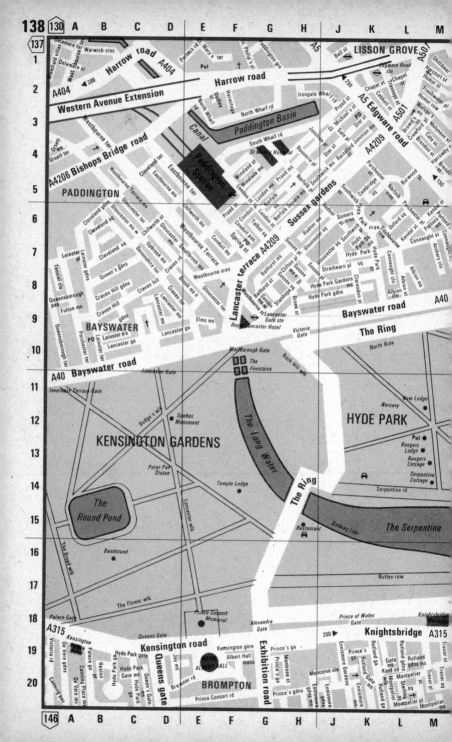

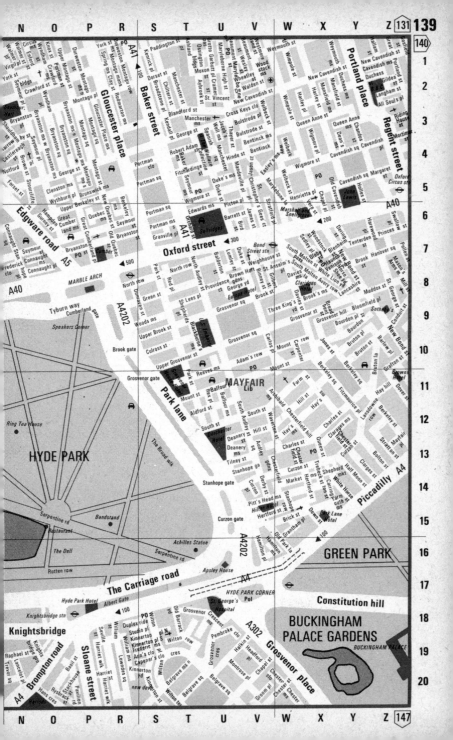

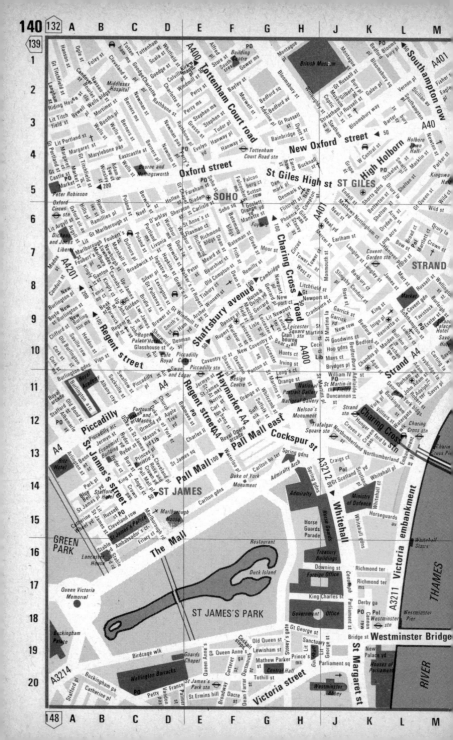

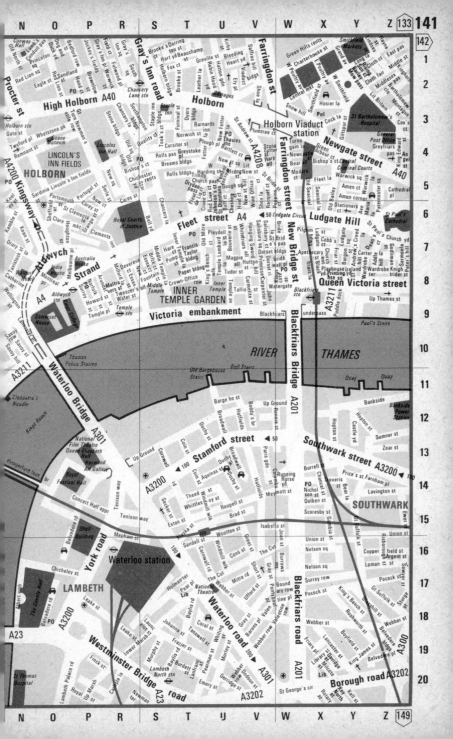

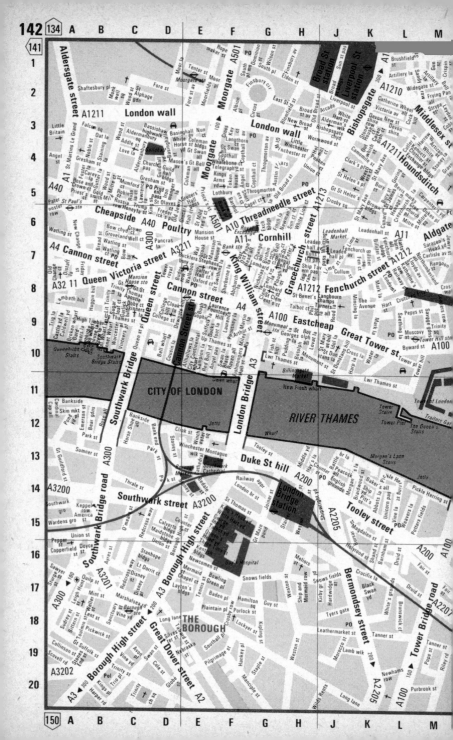

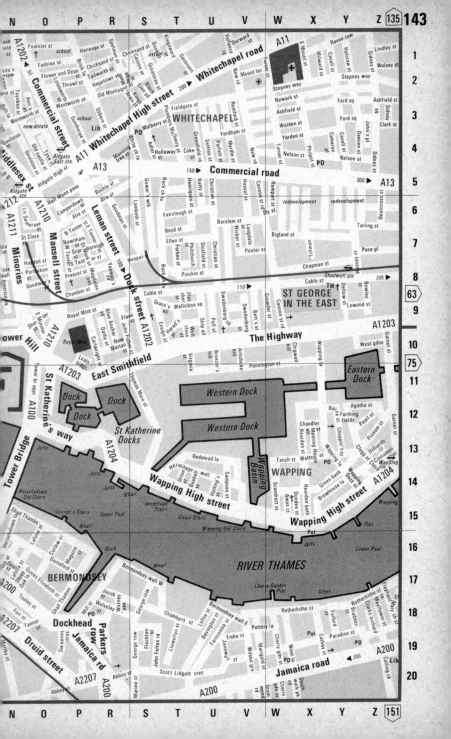

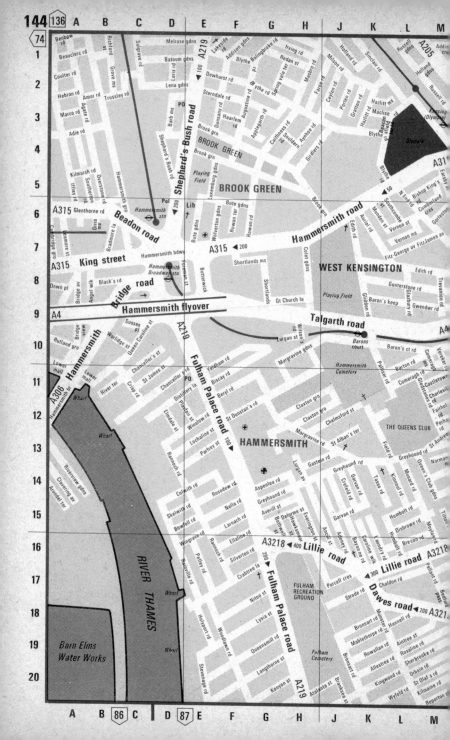

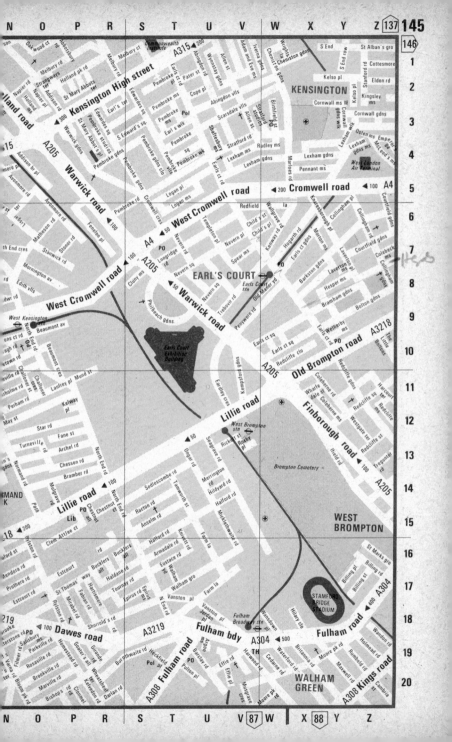

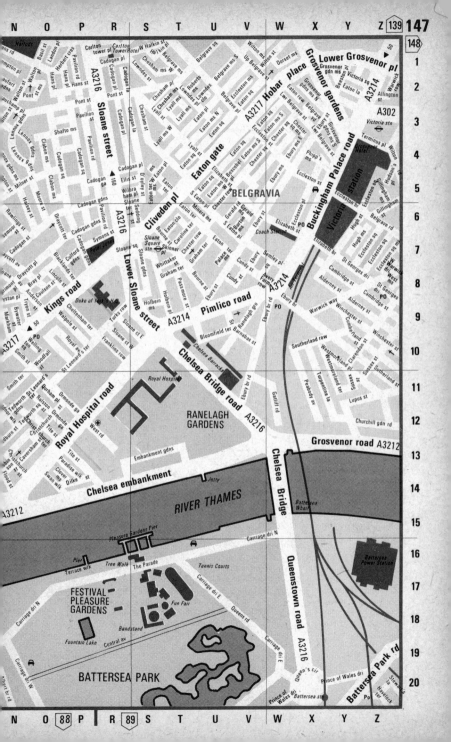

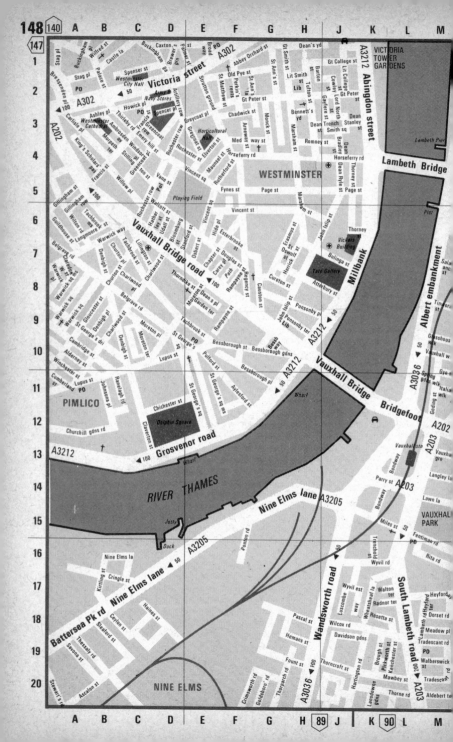

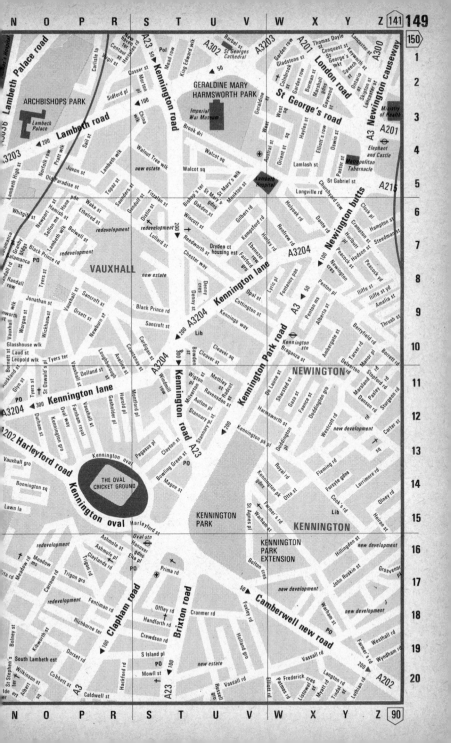

ARCHBISHOPS PARK

Lambeth Palace road

Lambeth Palace

Lambeth road

A3203

GERALDINE MARY HARMSWORTH PARK

Imperial War Museum

St Georges Cathedral

London road

St George's road

A201

Ministry of Health

A3 A201

Elephant and Castle

Metropolitan Tabernacle

A215

Newington butts

VAUXHALL

redevelopment

redevelopment

new estate

Kennington lane

A3204

A3204

Black Prince road

Kennington lane

A3204

Kennington road A23

NEWINGTON

Kennington stn

Kennington Park road

THE OVAL CRICKET GROUND

Kennington oval

Harleyford road

A202

KENNINGTON PARK

KENNINGTON

KENNINGTON PARK EXTENSION

new development

new development

Oval stn

Clapham road

Brixton road

Camberwell new road

A202

new development

new development

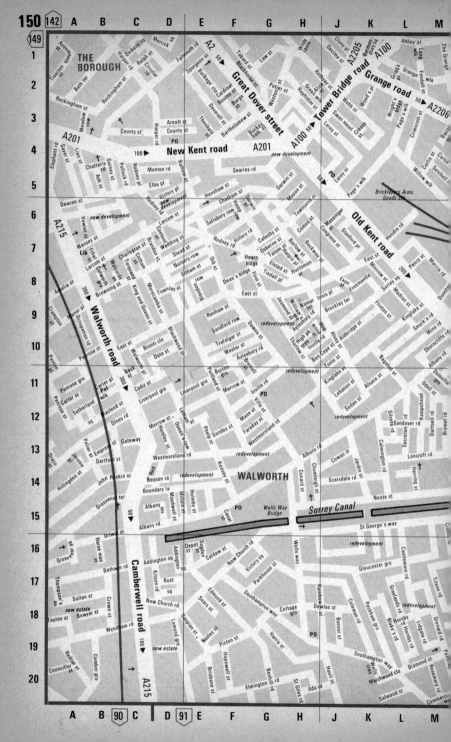

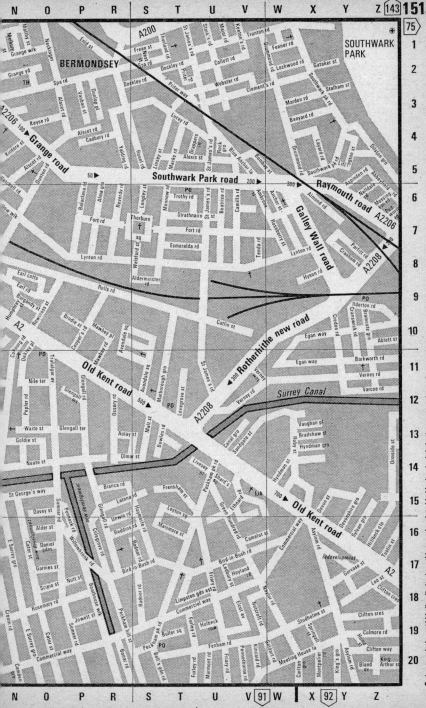

SOUTHWARK PARK

BERMONDSEY

A200

Enid st

Neckinger

Mallory st

Grange wlk

Melbourne st

Grange yd

TH

Spa rd

Dunlop pl

Vauban st

Alscot rd

Keyse rd

Kintere st

A2206 100

Grange road

Alscot rd

Omlton rd

50

Southwark Park road 200

PO

Rolls rd

A2 Old Kent road 500

A2208

Rotherhithe new road

Surrey Canal

Old Kent road 700

A2

SOUTHWARK PARK

Fenner rd

Gataker st

Stalham st

Marden rd

Banyard rd

Southwark pk rd (ctr)

Raymouth road A2206

Galley Wall road

A2208

Rotherhithe new road

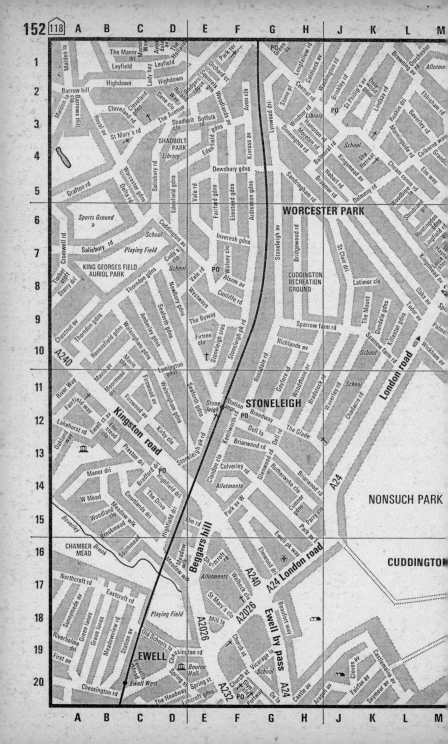

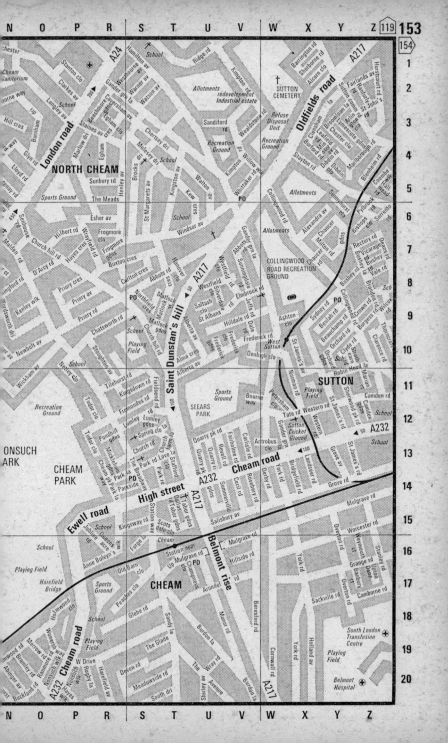

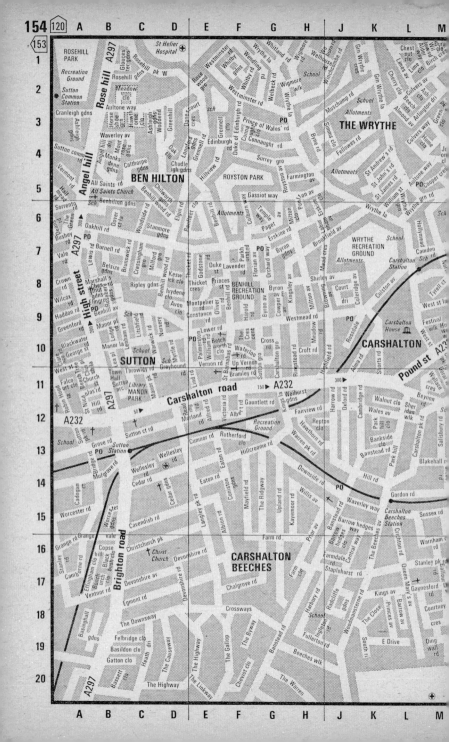

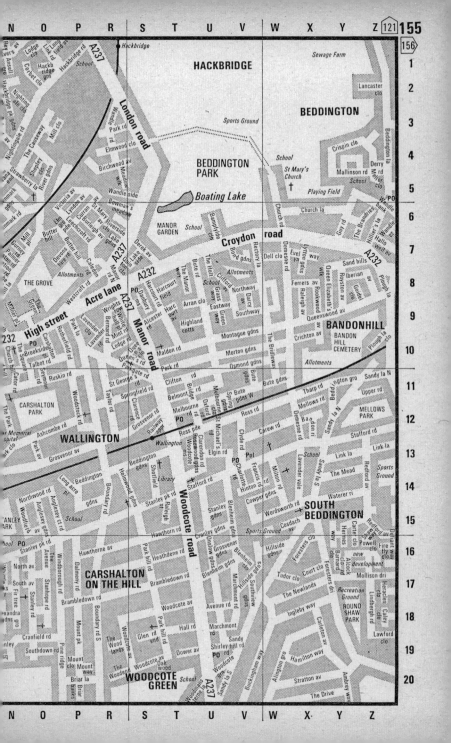

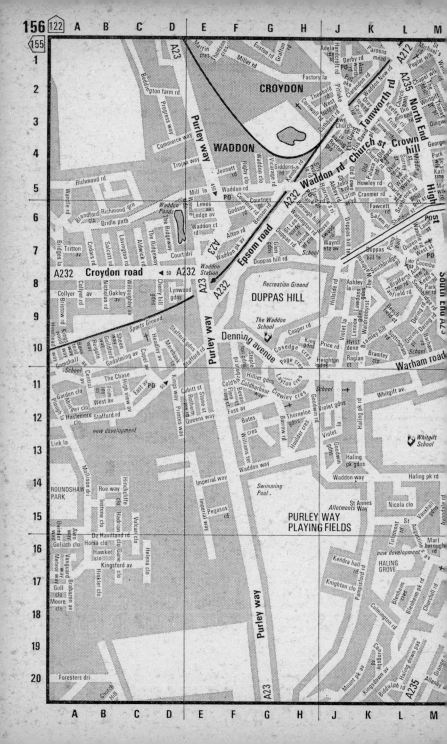

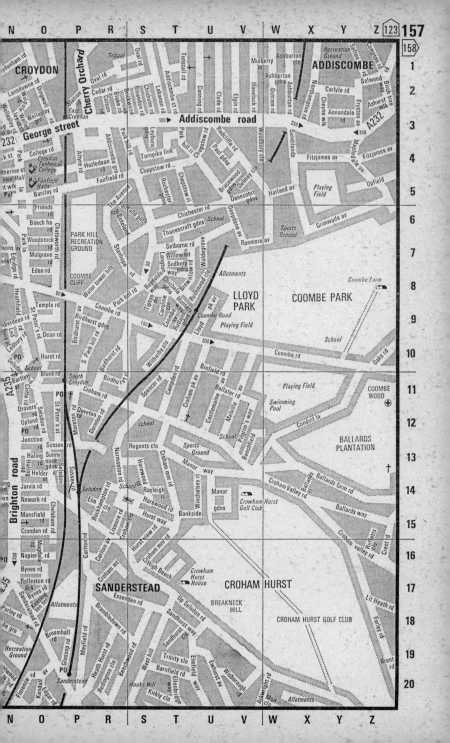

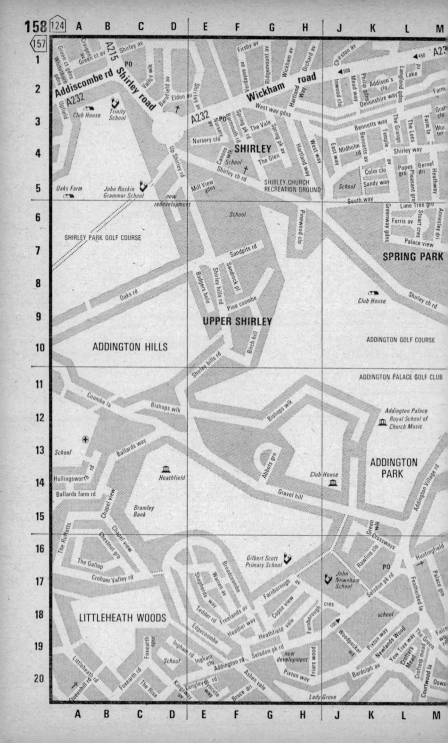

Alphabetical system

This has been programmed for computer typesetting and is consistent throughout the index in the following order.

Postal districts are in alphabetical order followed by numerical order
High av **NW1**
High av **WC1**
High av **WC2**

Outer districts follow postal districts in alphabetical order
High av **Dgnhm**
High av **Mitch**
High av **Wemb**

Strict alphabetical order is followed – disregarding any spacing between separate words
High**enden** st
High **Hill** st
High **st**

Abbreviations

Outer districts

Barking **Bark**
Barnet **Barnt**
Beckenham **Becknhm**
Belvedere **Blvdr**
Bexley **Bxly**
Bexley Heath **Bxly Hth**
Boreham Wood **Borhm wd**
Bromley **Brom**
Brentford **Brentf**
Buckhurst Hill **Buck HI**
Carshalton **Carsh**
Chislehurst **Chisl**
Croydon **Croy**
Dagenham **Dgnhm**
Dartford **Drtfrd**
East Molesey **E. Molesey**
Edgware **Edg**
Enfield **Enf**
Feltham **Felt**
Greenford **Grnfd**
Hampton **Hampt**
Hornchurch **Hornch**
Hounslow **Hounsl**
Ilford **Ilf**
Isleworth **Islwth**
Kingston **Kingst**
Mitcham **Mitch**
Morden **Mrdn**
New Malden **New Mald**
Orpington **Orp**
Pinner **Pinn**
Rainham **Rainhm**
Richmond **Rich**
Romford **Rom**
Ruislip **Ruis**
Southall **S'hall**
South Croydon **S. Croy**
Surbiton **Surb**
Teddington **Tedd**
Thornton Heath **Thntn Hth**
Twickenham **Twick**
Stanmore **Stanm**
Wallington **Wallgtn**
Wembley **Wemb**
West Wickham **W. Wckm**
Woodford Green **Wdfd Grn**
Worcester Park **Worc pk**

Streets etc.

Alley **all**
Approach **appr**
Arcade **arc**
Avenue **av**
Bank **bank**
Boulevard **blvd**
Bridge **br**
Broadway **bdwy**
Buildings **bldgs**
Church **ch**
Churchyard **chyd**
Circle **crcl**
Circus **cir**
Close **clo**
Common **comm**
Cottages **cotts**
Court **ct**
Crescent **cres**
Drive **dri**
East **east**
Embankment **emb**
Estate **est**
Gardens **gdns**
Gate **ga**
Great **gt**
Green **grn**
Grove **gro**
Hill **hill**
House **ho**
Junction **junc**
Lane **la**
Little **lit**
Lower **lwr**
Manor **mnr**
Mansions **mans**
Market **mkt**
Mews **ms**
Mount **mt**
North **north**
Palace **pal**
Parade **p'de**
Park **pk**
Passage **pas**
Path **pth**
Place **pl**
Rise **ri**
Road **rd**
Slope **slope**
South **south**
Square **sq**
Station **sta**
Street **st**
Terrace **ter**
Upper **up**
Villas **villas**
Walk **wlk**
Way **way**
West **west**
Yard **yd**

A

Ref	Entry
108 G 1	Abbess clo SW2
151 Z 19	Abbett st SE16
99 V 15	Abbeville rd SW4
60 L 5	Abbey av Wemb
8 S 11	Abbey cres Erith
130 C 9	Abbey Gdn ms NW8
8 E 10	Abbey gro SE2
115 T 3	Abbey Hill rd Sidcp
64 G 5	Abbey la E15
111 O 17	Abbey la Becknhm
129 X 3	Abbey ms NW6
148 F 1	Abbey Orchard st SW1
111 O 17	Abbey Pk estate Becknhm
64 L 5	Abbey rd E15
61 T 7	Abbey rd NW10
61 T 5	Abbey rd NW10
129 Y 4	Abbey rd NW6
130 B 7	Abbey rd NW8
106 D 19	Abbey rd SW19
67 N 2	Abbey rd Bark
81 N 9	Abbey rd Blvdr
80 K 10	Abbey rd Blvdr
97 Z 9	Abbey rd Bxly Hth
156 J 5	Abbey rd Croy
8 F 17	Abbey rd Enf
36 E 16	Abbey rd Ilf
5 T 11	Abbey st E13
143 O 20	Abbey st SE1
150 L 1	Abbey st SE1
80 F 10	Abbey ter Wemb
60 M 7	Abbey ter Wemb
13 S 10	Abbey view NW7
80 F 10	Abbey Wood rd SE2
61 O 3	Abbeydale rd Wemb
75 P 11	Abbeyfield rd SE16
151 Z 5	Abbeyfield rd SE16
49 T 17	Abbot st E8
28 G 13	Abbots gdns N2
158 G 13	Abbots grn Croy
142 K 14	Abbots la SE1
108 G 1	Abbots pk SW2
109 W 3	Abbots pl NW6
13 N 20	Abbots rd NW7
25 W 1	Abbots rd Edgw
124 H 11	Abbots way Becknhm
64 G 5	Abbotsbury clo E15
137 N 19	Abbotsbury clo W14
137 N 18	Abbotsbury rd W14
120 A 18	Abbotsbury rd Mrdn
30 M 14	Abbotsford av N15
34 E 2	Abbotsford gdns Wdfd Grn
55 O 7	Abbotsford rd Ilf
16 H 12	Abbotshall av N14
111 W 3	Abbotshall rd SE6
107 V 11	Abbotsleigh rd SW16
87 N 8	Abbotstone rd SW15
92 M 13	Abbotswell rd SE4
35 U 11	Abbotswood gdns Ilf
107 M 9	Abbotswood rd SW2
119 P 1	Abbotswood rd SW20
64 K 16	Abbott rd E14
38 G 10	Abbotts clo Rom
20 L 14	Abbotts cres E4
7 X 8	Abbotts cres Enf
42 A 6	Abbotts dri Wemb
51 U 1	Abbotts Pk rd E10
66 B 5	Abbotts rd E6
4 M 16	Abbotts rd Barnt
25 X 1	Abbotts rd Edg
121 X 6	Abbotts rd Mitch
70 C 2	Abbotts rd Sutton
153 V 7	Abbotts rd Sutton
80 J 19	Abbotts wlk Bxly Hth
61 Z 15	Abchurch la EC4
142 F 8	Abchurch la EC4
136 A 14	Abdale rd W12
74 K 3	Abdale rd W12
63 X 10	Aberavon rd E3
107 V 18	Abercairn rd SW16
120 A 7	Aberconway rd Mrdn
27 T 2	Abercorn clo NW7
130 C 11	Abercorn pl NW8
27 U 2	Abercorn rd NW7
24 D 2	Abercorn rd Stanm
40 L 4	Abercorn cres Harrow
42 G 1	Abercorn gdns Harrow
37 P 18	Abercorn gdns Rom
130 C 10	Abercorn pl NW8
88 K 5	Abercrombie st SW11
130 A 1	Aberdare gdns NW6
129 Z 1	Aberdare gdns NW6
27 O 2	Aberdare gdns NW7
9 O 14	Aberdare rd Enf
48 K 15	Aberdeen la N5
48 K 15	Aberdeen pk N5
130 F 17	Aberdeen pl NW8
44 E 14	Aberdeen rd NW10
18 L 15	Aberdeen rd N18
48 L 13	Aberdeen rd N5
120 F 2	Aberdeen rd SW19
157 N 9	Aberdeen rd Croy
23 V 9	Aberdeen rd Harrow
93 X 5	Aberdeen ter SE3
55 P 6	Aberdour rd Ilf
64 H 17	Aberfeldy st E14
107 X 17	Aberfoyle rd SW16
94 J 15	Abergeldie rd SE12
93 Z 11	Abernethy rd SE13
49 V 15	Abersham rd E8
79 U 11	Abery st SE18
28 D 6	Abingdon rd N3
122 A 1	Abingdon rd SW16
145 U 1	Abingdon rd W8
148 X 2	Abingdon st SW1
145 U 2	Abingdon vlls W8
153 N 20	Abinger clo Sutton
127 P 6	Abinger clo Brom
54 M 13	Abinger clo Ilf
156 A 12	Abinger clo Wallgtn
83 S 8	Abinger gdns Islwth
75 Y 16	Abinger gro SE8
74 B 8	Abinger rd W4
118 G 4	Aboyne dri SW20
44 B 8	Aboyne rd NW10
43 Z 9	Aboyne rd NW10
106 E 5	Aboyne rd SW17
68 D 7	Abridge way Bark
88 K 12	Abyssinia rd SW11
31 O 1	Acacia av N17
72 A 20	Acacia av Brentf
57 U 8	Acacia av Hornch
42 J 15	Acacia av Wemb
10 G 19	Acacia av Harrow
119 W 20	Acacia dri Sutton
130 G 8	Acacia gdns NW8
159 U 4	Acacia gdns W Wkhm
109 P 4	Acacia gro SE21
117 Z 7	Acacia gro New Mald
118 A 6	Acacia gro New Mald
130 G 8	Acacia pl NW8
52 A 8	Acacia rd E11
32 J 19	Acacia rd E17
130 G 8	Acacia rd NW8
30 G 5	Acacia rd N22
108 B 20	Acacia rd SW16
61 V 20	Acacia rd W3
8 C 5	Acacia rd Enf
100 J 14	Acacia rd Hampt
121 R 4	Acacia rd Mitch
123 V 20	Academy gdns Croy
58 A 7	Academy gdns Grnfd
95 U 2	Academy pl SE18
78 G 19	Academy rd SE18
95 U 1	Academy rd SE18
89 O 7	Acanthus rd SW11
45 W 3	Accommodation rd NW11
45 W 14	Achilles rd NW6
75 X 20	Achilles st SE14
88 A 2	Ackfold rd W4
137 O 1	Acklam rd W10
87 X 3	Ackmar rd SW6
92 G 18	Ackroyd rd SE23
91 N 8	Acland cres SE5
44 L 17	Acland rd NW2
129 N 1	Acol rd NW6
68 C 3	Aconbury rd Dgnhm
20 C 16	Acorn clo E4
7 V 6	Acorn clo Enf
123 T 1	Acorn gdns SE19
61 Z 15	Acorn gdns W3
75 W 2	Acorn wlk SE16
130 N 8	Acquila st NW8
90 C 11	Acre la SW2
155 R 8	Acre la Wallgtn
106 G 14	Acre rd SW19
56 H 20	Acre rd Dgnhm
102 K 20	Acre rd Kingst
88 D 14	Acris st SW18
61 Z 6	Acton la NW10
73 W 5	Acton la W4
73 W 12	Acton la W4
133 O 13	Acton st WC1
105 Z 3	Acuba rd SW18
150 H 3	Acworth st SE1
64 J 17	Ada gdns E14
65 P 4	Ada gdns E15
135 V 7	Ada pl E2
150 H 20	Ada rd SE5
42 F 9	Ada rd Wemb
135 V 5	Ada st E8
128 M 10	Adair rd W10
140 B 4	Adam & Eve ct W1
145 V 1	Adam & Eve ms W8
140 L 10	Adam st WC2
43 U 6	Adams clo NW9
75 P 5	Adams gdns SE16
48 D 16	Adams pl N7
31 R 7	Adams rd N17
24 H 11	Adams rd Becknhm
139 V 10	Adams row W1
65 T 18	Adamson rd E16
46 G 19	Adamson rd NW3
8 B 19	Adamsrill clo Enf
110 H 9	Adamsrill rd SE26
108 B 5	Adare way SW16
108 B 5	Adare wlk SW16
113 X 9	Adderley gdns SE9
89 O 13	Adderley gro SW11
23 V 5	Adderley rd Harrow
64 F 18	Adderley st E14
15 S 20	Addington dr N12
110 G 10	Addington gro SE26
65 K 12	Addington palace Croy
65 L 14	Addington park Croy
65 N 13	Addington rd E16
64 A 8	Addington rd E3
30 E 20	Addington rd N4
158 E 20	Addington rd S Croy
159 W 7	Addington rd W Wkhm
150 D 16	Addington sq SE5
158 M 14	Addington Village rd Croy
159 P 11	Addington Village rd Croy
9 S 6	Addis clo Enf
123 W 18	Addiscombe av Croy
24 D 15	Addiscombe clo Harrow
157 T 2	Addiscombe ct rd Croy
157 R 4	Addiscombe gro Croy
158 B 2	Addiscombe rd Croy
157 U 3	Addiscombe rd Croy
6 E 18	Addison av N14
136 K 15	Addison av W11
82 M 3	Addison av Hounsl
145 N 4	Addison Br pl W14
136 M 20	Addison cres W14
136 F 20	Addison gdns W14
144 F 1	Addison gdns W14
117 N 9	Addison gdns Surb
74 B 9	Addison gro W4
136 J 15	Addison pl W11
34 F 19	Addison rd E11
33 T 15	Addison rd E17
123 Y 9	Addison rd SE25
145 O 2	Addison rd W14
136 M 18	Addison rd W14
127 N 10	Addison rd Brom
126 M 10	Addison rd Brom
9 R 6	Addison rd Enf
36 C 5	Addison rd Ilf
102 A 16	Addison rd Tedd
27 X 13	Addison way NW11
158 K 2	Addisons clo Croy
141 Y 7	Addle hill EC4
142 C 3	Addle st EC2
118 K 10	Adela av New Mald
118 K 9	Adela st W10
128 K 17	Adela st W10
92 M 11	Adelaide av SE4
94 N 11	Adelaide av SE4
8 F 4	Adelaide clo Enf
10 K 13	Adelaide clo Stanm
71 V 4	Adelaide cotts W7
37 Y 15	Adelaide gdns Rom
74 H 3	Adelaide gro W12
51 T 9	Adelaide rd E10
47 N 20	Adelaide rd NW3
46 M 20	Adelaide rd NW3
71 Z 4	Adelaide rd W13
82 A 2	Adelaide rd Hounsl
54 A 6	Adelaide rd Ilf
85 N 11	Adelaide rd Rich
70 B 10	Adelaide rd S'hall
116 J 13	Adelaide rd Surb
101 X 15	Adelaide rd Tedd
140 J 11	Adelaide st WC2
156 J 1	Adelaide st Croy
135 Z 20	Adelina gro E1
63 O 14	Adelina gro E1
140 G 3	Adeline pl WC1
141 U 1	Adelphi ter WC2
49 O 13	Aden gro N16
9 V 15	Aden rd Enf
54 A 2	Aden rd Ilf
144 U 16	Adeney rd W6
93 O 19	Adenmore rd SE6
74 L 9	Adie rd W6
144 A 3	Adie rd W6
65 U 12	Adine rd E13
143 S 4	Adler st E1
50 J 14	Adley st E5
79 P 18	Admaston rd SE18
128 H 18	Admiral ms W10
95 T 9	Admiral Seymour rd SE9
93 O 3	Admirals st SE4
46 D 16	Admirals wlk NW3
57 V 17	Adnams wlk Rainhm
111 P 10	Adolf st SE6
48 J 5	Adolphus rd N4
75 Z 19	Adolphus st SE8
55 X 11	Adomar rd Dgnhm
130 G 20	Adpar st W2
44 J 3	Adrian av NW2
58 E 10	Adrienne av S'hall
91 W 9	Adys rd SE15
26 E 9	Aerodrome rd NW9
88 J 6	Afghan rd SW11
45 W 14	Agamemnon rd NW6
47 Y 20	Agar gro NW1
132 D 1	Agar gro NW1
140 K 10	Agar st WC2
74 L 8	Agate rd W6
144 A 3	Agate rd W6
143 Y 12	Agatha st E1
114 C 4	Agaton rd SE9
44 M 12	Agave rd NW2
133 W 15	Agdon st EC1
46 L 13	Agincourt rd NW3
53 X 11	Agnes av Ilf
55 X 11	Agnes gdns Dgnhm
74 C 4	Agnes rd W3
63 Y 16	Agnes st E14
78 A 3	Agnes st E16
92 G 18	Agnew rd SE23
83 Z 13	Ailsa av Twick
84 B 13	Ailsa av Twick
83 Z 13	Ailsa rd Twick
84 A 13	Ailsa rd Twick
64 G 14	Ailsa st E14
64 H 5	Ailwyn rd E15
131 P 2	Ainger rd NW8
22 H 10	Ainsdale cres Pinn
60 H 13	Ainsdale rd W5
38 J 19	Ainsley av Rom
63 N 8	Ainsley st E2
135 W 14	Ainsley st E2
20 C 17	Ainslie Wood cres E4
20 D 15	Ainslie Wood gdns E4
20 C 17	Ainslie Wood rd E4
75 R 5	Ainsty st SE16
44 H 9	Ainsworth clo NW2
63 P 1	Ainsworth rd E9
156 K 1	Ainsworth rd Croy
66 C 5	Aintree av E6
36 B 7	Aintree cres Ilf
60 B 5	Aintree rd Grnfd
144 L 18	Aintree st SW6
140 D 10	Air st W1
74 A 2	Airedale av W4
88 M 20	Airedale rd SW12
88 N 19	Airedale rd SW12
72 F 8	Airedale rd W5
57 Z 20	Airfield way Hornch
137 S 15	Airlie gdns W8
53 Z 5	Airlie gdns Ilf
55 P 5	Airthrie rd Ilf
94 A 12	Aislibie rd SE12
111 R 4	Aitken rd SE6
26 A 10	Ajax av NW9
45 W 14	Ajax rd NW6
86 G 17	Akehurst st SW15
46 G 16	Akenside rd NW3
90 H 4	Akerman rd SW9
116 E 15	Akerman rd Surb
79 T 18	Alabama st SE18
72 F 7	Alacross rd W5
56 D 1	Alan gdns Rom
105 T 12	Alan rd SW19
94 D 15	Alanthus clo SE12
141 T 16	Alaska st SE1
27 T 18	Alba gdns NW11
137 N 4	Alba pl W11
93 R 15	Albacore cres SE13
85 U 11	Albany clo SW14
97 U 19	Albany clo Bxly
25 R 2	Albany cres Edg
25 Z 4	Albany ct NW9
140 B 11	Albany Ct yd W1
150 O 15	Albany ms SE17
9 U 2	Albany park Enf
84 L 14	Albany pass Rich
9 R 5	Albany Pk av Enf
9 T 4	Albany Pk av Enf
9 T 4	Albany Pk rd Enf

102 H 16 Albany Pk rd Kingst
48 F 13 Albany pl N7
33 O 20 Albany rd E10
53 O 13 Albany rd E12
32 J 18 Albany rd E17
30 K 14 Albany rd N15
19 O 18 Albany rd N19
32 E 20 Albany rd N4
150 H 13 Albany rd SE5
105 Z 12 Albany rd SW19
60 B 19 Albany rd W13
81 P 15 Albany rd Blvdr
72 J 17 Albany rd Brentf
97 U 19 Albany rd Bxly
113 Z 13 Albany rd Chisl
9 S 2 Albany rd Enf
57 W 8 Albany rd Hornch
117 Y 8 Albany rd New Mald
84 L 12 Albany rd Rich
38 B 18 Albany rd Rom
131 X 8 Albany st NW1
21 P 13 Albany the Wdfd Grn
21 U 4 Albany view Buck Hl
79 T 18 Albatross st SE18
36 A 19 Albemarle appr Ilf
100 E 2 Albemarle av Twick
36 A 19 Albemarle gdns Ilf
35 Z 19 Albemarle gdns Ilf
11 R 17 Albemarle pk Stanm
15 X 2 Albemarle rd Barnt
125 X 1 Albemarle rd Becknhm
117 Y 10 Albemarle rd New Mald
140 A 12 Albemarle st W1
133 W 18 Albemarle way EC1
27 V 14 Alberon gdns NW11
20 B 14 Albert av E4
146 M 17 Albert br. SW11
88 L 1 Albert Br rd SW11
146 M 18 Albert Br rd SW11
147 N 20 Albert Br rd SW11
108 A 13 Albert Carr gdns SW16
107 Z 13 Albert Carr gdns SW16.
29 X 3 Albert clo N22
20 B 13 Albert cres E4
105 T 2 Albert dri SW19
141 N 17 Albert emb SE1
148 M 8 Albert emb SE1
63 S 18 Albert. gdns E1
129 P 9 Albert gdns NW6
105 P 20 Albert gro SW20
138 F 19 Albert Hall mans SW7
146 A 1 Albert ms W8
31 U 9 Albert pl N17
27 Y 4 Albert pl N3
137 Z 20 Albert pl W8
51 U 6 Albert rd E10
78 D 4 Albert rd E16
33 O 16 Albert rd E17
34 J 9 Albert rd E18
27 P 13 Albert rd NW4
129 R 9 Albert rd NW6
13 S 16 Albert rd NW7
31 R 18 Albert rd N15
29 V 5 Albert rd N4
48 D 3 Albert rd N4
110 E 16 Albert rd SE20
123 Z 4 Albert rd SE25
124 B 11 Albert rd SE25
113 R 6 Albert rd SE9
60 C 13 Albert rd W5
5 S 14 Albert rd Barnt
81 P 14 Albert rd Blvdr
127 P 12 Albert rd Brom
58 D 4 Albert rd Bxly
101 O 12 Albert rd Dgnhm
23 N 11 Albert rd Hampt
82 H 11 Albert rd Harrow
53 Z 10 Albert rd Ilf
54 C 9 Albert rd Ilf
120 M 6 Albert rd Mitch
8 E 10 Albert rd New Mald
84 L 13 Albert rd Rich
39 T 17 Albert rd Rom
154 F 12 Albert rd Sutton
101 X 15 Albert rd Tedd
101 V 1 Albert rd Twick
83 V 20 Albert rd Twick
81 P 14 Albert Rd est Blvdr
52 H 16 Albert sq E7
149 N 20 Albert sq SW8
90 C 1 Albert sq SW8
131 Z 8 Albert st NW1
16 F 19 Albert st N11
15 P 15 Albert st N12
131 S 4 Albert ter NW1
61 X 4 Albert ter NW10

131 S 4 Albert Ter ms NW1
73 U 4 Albert Vlls rd W3
153 U 10 Alberta av Sutton
8 J 19 Alberta rd Enf
98 J 2 Alberta rd Erith
149 X 9 Alberta st SE17
29 O 4 Albion av SW8
89 W 4 Albion av SW8
138 L 8 Albion clo W2
39 O 18 Albion clo Rom
135 O 2 Albion rd E8
74 H 10 Albion gdns W6
49 R 11 Albion gro N16
45 V 20 Albion mews NW6
138 L 7 Albion ms W2
133 W 19 Albion pl EC1
142 F 2 Albion pl EC2
33 U 9 Albion rd E17
49 P 10 Albion rd N16
31 W 7 Albion rd N17
98 D 11 Albion rd Bxly Hth
84 H 12 Albion rd Hounsl
117 V 1 Albion rd Kingst
154 E 15 Albion rd Sutton
101 T 2 Albion rd Twick
135 O 1 Albion sq E8
75 P 7 Albion st SE16
138 L 8 Albion st W2
122 H 20 Albion st W2
135 N 1 Albion ter E8
110 C 6 Albion Vlls rd SE26
93 V 3 Albion way SE13
43 R 10 Albion way Wemb
91 S 8 Albrighton rd SE22
7 U 5 Albuhera clo Enf
97 Y 4 Albury rd Bxly Hth
71 W 20 Albury av Islwth
100 J 15 Albury clo Hampt
22 A 1 Albury dri Pinn
76 B 17 Albury st SE8
127 V 7 Albyfield Brom
93 P 4 Albyn rd SE4
50 A 5 Alcester cres E5
155 S 9 Alcester rd Wallgtn
155 Y 16 Alcock clo Wallgtn
49 X 8 Alconbury rd E5
153 X 2 Alcorn clo Sutton
49 T 7 Aldam pl N16
56 K 18 Aldborough rd Dgnhm
54 H 1 Aldborough rd Ilf
54 F 5 Aldborough Rd south Ilf
36 K 15 Aldborough Rd south Ilf
74 F 3 Aldbourne rd W12
150 J 9 Aldbridge st SE17
43 S 19 Aldbury av Wemb
148 M 20 Aldebert ter SW8
149 N 20 Aldebert ter SW8
21 T 13 Aldeburgh pl Wdfd Grn
77 S 12 Aldeburgh st SE10
65 N 11 Alden av E15
132 D 10 Aldenham st NW1
74 K 9 Aldensley rd W6
44 H 8 Alder gro NW2
85 X 7 Alder rd SW14
114 J 8 Alder rd Sidcp
151 O 16 Alder st E15
154 L 1 Alder way Carsh
89 R 18 Alderbrook rd SW12
74 G 17 Alderbury rd SW13
68 B 8 Alderman av Bark
142 C 4 Aldermanbury EC2
142 C 3 Aldermanbury sq EC2
17 O 13 Aldermans hill N13
142 J 3 Aldermans wlk EC2
112 F 20 Aldermary rd Brom
136 F 6 Aldermaston st W10
151 S 9 Alderminster rd SE1
70 K 20 Aldermoor rd SE6
40 D 20 Alderney gdns Grnfd
63 T 11 Alderney rd E1
147 X 8 Alderney st SW1
148 A 10 Alderney st SW1
20 M 19 Alders av Wdfd Grn
12 H 16 Alders clo Edg
12 H 16 Alders rd Edg
17 U 1 Alders the N21
100 C 11 Alders the Felt
70 E 15 Alders the Hounsl
159 R 1 Alders the W Wkhm
8 E 1 Aldersbrook av Enf
53 V 10 Aldersbrook la E12
52 H 6 Aldersbrook rd E11
53 R 11 Aldersbrook rd E12
54 E 18 Aldersey gdns Bark
142 A 1 Aldersgate st EC1
112 M 7 Aldersgrove av SE9
113 N 6 Aldersgrove av SE9

129 R 3 Aldershot rd NW6
124 G 14 Aldersmead av Croy
110 H 18 Aldersmead rd Becknhm
128 L 16 Alderson st W10
26 J 17 Alderton cres NW4
90 L 9 Alderton rd SE24
123 V 16 Alderton rd Croy
87 W 5 Alderville rd SW6
83 P 7 Alderwick dri Hounsl
95 J 15 Alderwood rd SE9
93 T 11 Alford st N1
142 M 6 Aldgate EC3
143 N 4 Aldgate av EC3
143 O 5 Aldgate High st E1
136 E 16 Aldine st W12
57 X 15 Aldingham gdns Hornch
106 H 13 Aldis st SW17
45 X 15 Aldred rd NW6
106 D 7 Aldren rd SW17
159 V 19 Aldrich cres Croy
106 E 3 Aldrich ter SW18
20 F 19 Aldriche way E4
12 F 9 Aldridge av Edg
9 Z 2 Aldridge av Enf
24 K 6 Aldridge av Stanm
137 R 3 Aldridge Rd vlls W11
118 A 16 Aldridge ri New Mald
107 V 11 Aldrington rd SW16
114 D 6 Aldwick clo SE9
156 C 7 Aldwick rd Croy
93 T 16 Aldworth gro SE13
51 Z 20 Aldworth rd E15
64 M 1 Aldworth rd E15
64 L 1 Aldworth rd E15
141 O 7 Aldwych WC2
36 C 14 Aldwych av Ilf
97 X 13 Alers rd Bxly Hth
132 A 2 Alexander av NW10
62 K 1 Alexander av NW10
126 G 20 Alexander clo Brom
96 H 15 Alexander clo Sidcp
101 U 4 Alexander clo Twick
6 G 16 Alexander ct N14
137 W 4 Alexander ms SW7
146 J 4 Alexander pl SW7
48 A 8 Alexander rd N4
97 W 4 Alexander rd Bxly Hth
114 A 14 Alexander rd Chisl
113 Z 13 Alexander rd Chisl
146 J 4 Alexander sq SW7
137 N 5 Alexander st W2
29 Y 6 Alexandra av N22
89 O 2 Alexandra av SW11
73 Z 20 Alexandra av W4
40 F 4 Alexandra av Harrow
70 D 1 Alexandra av S'hall
153 X 6 Alexandra av Sutton
40 J 10 Alexandra clo Harrow
92 M 3 Alexandra cotts SE14
112 C 14 Alexandra cres Brom
109 R 13 Alexandra dri SE19
117 R 16 Alexandra dri Surb
29 T 12 Alexandra gdns N10
155 N 18 Alexandra gdns Carsh
82 K 5 Alexandra gdns Hounsl
15 O 18 Alexandra gro N12
48 K 5 Alexandra gro N12
29 W 9 Alexandra palace N22
29 Z 9 Alexandra park N22
40 J 11 Alexandra park Harrow
29 T 6 Alexandra Pk rd N22
123 P 11 Alexandra rd SE25
51 U 10 Alexandra rd E10
32 L 20 Alexandra rd E17
34 G 11 Alexandra rd E18
66 J 9 Alexandra rd E6
27 P 13 Alexandra rd N8
129 Z 4 Alexandra rd NW8
130 C 3 Alexandra rd NW8
29 S 3 Alexandra rd N10
31 O 15 Alexandra rd N15
30 F 9 Alexandra rd N8
110 E 15 Alexandra rd SE26
85 Z 8 Alexandra rd SW14
105 V 15 Alexandra rd SW19
73 Z 6 Alexandra rd W4
72 G 17 Alexandra rd Brentf
123 R 19 Alexandra rd Croy
9 T 15 Alexandra rd Enf
82 K 7 Alexandra rd Hounsl
116 P 18 Alexandra rd Kingst
106 K 19 Alexandra rd Mitch

18 M 2 Alexandra rd N .
85 N 5 Alexandra rd Rich
37 X 18 Alexandra rd Rom
39 S 18 Alexandra rd Rom
84 F 17 Alexandra rd Twick
119 Y 13 Alexandra sq Mrdn
65 R 14 Alexandra st E16
60 A 20 Alexandria rd W13
151 T 5 Alexis st SE16
50 B 11 Alfearn rd E5
159 W 15 Alford gdns Croy
89 Y 3 Alford rd SW8
81 Z 13 Alford rd Erith
30 H 13 Alfoxton av N15
58 C 20 Alfred gdns Shall
70 C 1 Alfred gro S'hall
132 E 20 Alfred ms W1
140 E 1 Alfred pl W1
52 C 15 Alfred rd E15
123 Y 10 Alfred rd SE25
71 Y 1 Alfred rd W13
137 U 1 Alfred rd W2
73 W 3 Alfred rd W2
81 P 14 Alfred rd Belvdr
116 L 7 Alfred rd Kingst
154 E 12 Alfred rd Sutton
63 Z 8 Alfred st E3
67 T 6 Alfreds way Bark
122 A 16 Alfriston av Croy
22 H 20 Alfriston av Harrow
89 N 13 Alfriston rd SW11
116 L 13 Alfriston rd Surb
83 Y 9 Algar clo Islwth
83 Y 8 Algar rd Islwth
106 B 2 Algarve rd SW18
26 G 19 Algernon rd NW4
129 S 5 Algernon rd NW6
93 R 7 Algernon rd SE13
93 P 11 Algiers rd SE13
56 F 14 Alibon gdns Dgnhm
150 H 2 Alice st SE1
24 C 14 Alicia av Harrow
24 D 14 Alicia clo Harrow
24 D 14 Alicia gdns Harrow
143 P 6 Alie st E1
43 V 3 Alington cres NW9
155 W 20 Alington gro Wallgtn
88 J 11 Aliwal rd SW11
74 B 13 Alkerden rd W4
49 V 7 Alkham rd N16
31 S 4 All Hallows rd N17
94 A 4 All Saints dri SE3
106 D 16 All Saints rd SW19
137 O 3 All Saints rd W11
73 V 7 All Saints rd W3
154 B 5 All Saints rd Sutton
132 M 7 All Saints st N1
133 N 7 All Saints st N1
62 J 6 All Souls av NW10
128 A 4 All Souls av NW10
139 Z 2 All Souls pl W1
117 Y 12 Allan clo New Mald
4 D 19 Allan dri Barnt
93 W 3 Allan way W3
27 T 10 Allandale av N3
57 U 1 Allandale rd Hornch
51 N 20 Allanmouth rd E9
50 A 7 Allard cres Bushey
90 C 10 Allardyce st SW4
63 R 9 Allas rd E2
101 T 11 Allbrook clo Tedd
47 O 15 Allcroft rd NW5
89 Z 1 Allen Edwards dri SW8
49 R 12 Allen rd N16
124 E 4 Allen rd Becknhm
122 E 19 Allen rd Croy
145 U 1 Allen st W8
58 J 10 Allenby clo Grnfd
110 H 6 Allenby rd SE23
58 H 10 Allenby rd S'hall
58 F 17 Allendale av S'hall
91 N 4 Allendale rd SE5
42 A 17 Allendale rd Grnfd
9 R 18 Allens rd Enf
95 S 6 Allenswood rd SE9
22 L 14 Allerford ct Harrow
111 S 10 Allerford rd SE6
48 N 6 Allerton rd N16
49 N 6 Allerton rd N16
144 K 19 Allestree rd SW6
55 T 7 Alleydale rd Dgnhm
109 P 6 Alleyn cres SE21
109 P 3 Alleyn pk SE21
70 F 13 Alleyn pk S'hall
109 P 7 Alleyn rd SE21
88 B 17 Allfarthing la SW18
119 O 15 Allgood clo Mrdn
142 E 10 Allhallows la EC4
65 X 13 Alliance rd E13
79 Z 17 Alliance rd SE18

80 A 19	Alliance rd	SE18
61 S 12	Alliance rd	W3
133 Z 7	Allingham st	N1
105 P 13	Allington clo	SW19
26 K 18	Allington rd	NW4
128 K 10	Allington rd	W10
22 M 15	Allington rd	Harrow
147 Z 2	Allington st	SW1
109 S 1	Allison gro	SE21
30 H 15	Allison rd	N8
61 W 19	Allison rd	W3
130 K 8	Allitsen rd	NW8
89 W 12	Alliutt way	SW4
75 U 13	Alloa rd	SE8
55 O 6	Alloa rd	Ilf
42 E 5	Allonby gdns	Wemb
63 W 9	Alloway rd	E3
131 R 18	Allsop pl	NW1
15 P 6	Allum way	N20
33 U 1	Alma av	E4
41 P 7	Alma cres	Harrow
153 T 10	Alma cres	Sutton
151 P 6	Alma gro	SE1
109 T 17	Alma pl	SE19
122 G 12	Alma pl	Thntn Hth
29 R 3	Alma rd	N10
88 C 11	Alma rd	N10
154 K 10	Alma rd	Carsh
9 U 12	Alma rd	Enf
41 O 7	Alma rd	Harrow
58 A 20	Alma rd	S'hall
115 O 6	Alma rd	Sidcp
23 R 3	Alma row	Har
130 D 11	Alma sq	NW8
51 X 16	Alma st	E15
47 T 17	Alma st	NW5
88 G 18	Alma ter	SW18
50 C 12	Almack rd	E5
133 W 3	Almeida st	N1
104 G 17	Almer rd	SW20
88 K 12	Almeric rd	SW11
84 A 8	Almington st	N4
72 J 8	Almond av	W5
154 L 3	Almond av	Carsh
91 Y 5	Almond clo	SE15
127 W 17	Almond clo	Brom
72 A 19	Almond gro	Brentf
31 X 2	Almond rd	N17
151 X 6	Almond rd	SE16
127 W 17	Almond way	Brom
121 Y 10	Almond way	Mitch
21 T 9	Almonds av	Buck Hl
82 A 2	Almorah rd	Hounsl
134 E 2	Almorah st	N1
66 A 18	Alnwick av	E16
124 A 9	Alnwick gro	Mrdn
65 Y 18	Alnwick rd	E16
94 H 17	Alnwick rd	SE12
60 G 7	Alperton la	Wemb
129 N 16	Alperton st	W10
130 L 15	Alpha clo	NW1
129 U 8	Alpha pl	NW6
146 M 13	Alpha pl	SW3
20 C 11	Alpha rd	E4
18 J 18	Alpha rd	N18
92 M 1	Alpha rd	SE14
123 R 20	Alpha rd	Croy
9 W 15	Alpha rd	Enf
116 M 16	Alpha rd	Surb
117 P 12	Alpha rd	Tedd
91 X 5	Alpha rd	SE15
127 W 3	Alpine copse	Brom
75 S 12	Alpine rd	SE16
10 G 8	Alpine wlk	Stanm
61 Z 1	Alric av	NW10
118 B 6	Alric av	New Mald
43 Z 20	Alrick av	NW10
30 G 20	Alroy rd	N4
150 K 11	Alsace st	SE17
151 O 5	Alscot rd	SE1
48 D 7	Alsen pl	N7
48 D 7	Alsen rd	N7
152 F 8	Alsom av	Worc Pk
18 M 18	Alston rd	N18
106 F 11	Alston rd	SW17
4 E 10	Alston rd	Barnt
105 U 17	Alt gro	SW19
113 U 5	Altash way	SE9
72 B 7	Altenburg av	W13
88 L 10	Altenburg gdns	SW11
22 B 3	Altham rd	Pinn
88 B 6	Althea st	SW6
117 N 7	Altheston rd	Kingst
34 B 13	Althorne gdns	E18
106 K 1	Althorp	SW17
88 G 2	Althorpe rd	SW11
23 O 16	Althorpe rd	Harrow
53 T 20	Altmore av	E6
66 G 4	Altmore av	E6
23 W 2	Alton av	Stanm
83 X 3	Alton clo	Islwth
11 N 19	Alton gdns	Becknhm
83 R 17	Alton gdns	Twick
31 O 11	Alton rd	N17
86 H 19	Alton rd	SW15
104 G 1	Alton rd	SW15
156 F 6	Alton rd	Croy
84 L 11	Alton rd	Rich
64 C 16	Alton st	E14
124 K 13	Altyre clo	Becknhm
157 P 4	Altyre rd	Croy
124 L 12	Altyre way	Becknhm
46 B 15	Alvanley gdns	NW6
123 S 11	Alverston gdns	SE25
105 X 5	Alverstone av	W6
15 V 2	Alverstone av	Barnt
96 A 20	Alverstone gdns	SE9
53 W 14	Alverstone rd	E12
44 M 20	Alverstone rd	NW2
118 E 8	Alverstone rd	New Mald
43 N 3	Alverstone rd	Wemb
75 X 16	Alverton st	SE8
24 B 11	Alveston av	Harrow
150 J 9	Alvey st	SE17
49 U 15	Alvington cres	E8
94 J 17	Alwald cres	SE12
73 X 14	Alwyn av	W4
159 S 17	Alwyn clo	Croy
61 T 17	Alwyn gdns	W3
48 K 19	Alwyne la	N1
48 K 19	Alwyne pl	N1
48 K 20	Alwyne rd	N1
105 V 14	Alwyne rd	SW19
71 S 1	Alwyne rd	W7
48 L 18	Alwyne sq	N1
48 K 20	Alwyne vlls	N1
27 X 18	Alyth gdns	NW11
82 C 5	Ambassador clo	Hounsl
140 C 15	Ambassadors ct	SW1
32 H 4	Amber av	E17
51 X 19	Amber st	E15
27 Z 10	Amberden av	N3
149 X 10	Ambergate st	SE17
115 U 13	Amberley ct	Sidcp
18 F 4	Amberley gdns	Enf
152 C 9	Amberley gdns	Epsom
109 Z 11	Amberley gro	SE26
123 U 18	Amberley gro	Croy
33 P 20	Amberley rd	E10
17 P 9	Amberley rd	N13
80 K 16	Amberley rd	SE2
129 W 19	Amberley rd	W9
21 Y 5	Amberley rd	Buck Hl
18 F 1	Amberley rd	Enf
119 W 17	Amberley way	Mrdn
118 B 15	Amberwood ri	New Mald
112 J 7	Amblecote clo	SE12
112 J 7	Amblecote rd	SE12
48 H 9	Ambler rd	N4
107 X 10	Ambleside av	SW16
124 J 12	Ambleside av	Becknhm
57 S 15	Ambleside av	Hornch
9 T 11	Ambleside cres	Enf
35 S 14	Ambleside gdns	Ilf
42 F 3	Ambleside gdns	Wemb
62 D 1	Ambleside rd	NW10
98 D 4	Ambleside rd	Bxly Hth
57 Y 20	Ambrey way	Wallgtn
81 S 9	Ambrooke rd	Belvdr
148 B 3	Ambrosden av	SW1
27 U 20	Ambrose av	NW11
151 V 6	Ambrose st	SE16
149 Z 8	Amelia st	SE17
48 A 8	Amelia st	SE17
141 Y 5	Amen corner	EC4
107 N 14	Amen corner	SW17
141 Y 5	Amen ct	EC4
143 N 8	America sq	EC3
142 A 15	America st	SE1
87 W 15	Amerland rd	SW18
75 X 18	Amersham gro	SE14
18 B 19	Amersham rd	N18
92 L 1	Amersham rd	SE14
123 N 13	Amersham rd	Croy
23 S 18	Amersham rd	Harrow
75 Y 19	Amersham vale	SE14
128 A 5	Amery gdns	NW10
62 L 3	Amery gdns	NW10
41 Y 7	Amery rd	Harrow
108 B 4	Amesbury av	SW2
20 D 1	Amesbury dri	E4
127 O 5	Amesbury rd	Brom
51 X 13	Amethyst rd	E15
60 C 17	Amherst av	W13
60 D 17	Amherst av	W13
83 Y 4	Amhurst gdns	Islwth
49 W 13	Amhurst pas	E8
31 R 20	Amhurst pk	N16
49 Z 15	Amhurst rd	E8
50 A 16	Amhurst rd	E8
49 W 12	Amhurst rd	E5
55 P 12	Amidas gdns	Dgnhm
63 P 1	Amiel st	E1
88 L 8	Amies st	SW11
118 L 2	Amity gro	SW20
65 O 2	Amity rd	E15
64 E 7	Ammiel ter	E3
89 O 15	Amner rd	SW11
74 L 8	Amor rd	W6
144 B 2	Amor rd	W6
143 W 15	Amos ct	E1
91 W 8	Amott rd	SE15
64 A 19	Amoy pl	E14
80 F 5	Ampleforth rd	SE2
133 N 13	Ampton pl	WC1
133 N 14	Ampton st	WC1
8 B 17	Amwell clo	Enf
83 U 5	Amwell rd	Islwth
133 S 12	Amwell st	EC1
84 A 18	Amyand la	Twick
84 A 18	Amyand Pk gdns	Twick
83 Z 19	Amyand Pk rd	Twick
84 B 17	Amyand Pk rd	Twick
93 N 13	Amyruth rd	SE4
47 U 6	Anatola rd	N19
118 F 15	Ancaster cres	New Mald
124 F 7	Ancaster rd	Becknhm
79 V 19	Ancaster st	SE18
77 X 11	Anchor And Hope la	SE7
151 W 6	Anchor st	SE16
134 E 18	Anchor yd	EC1
105 Z 13	Anchorage clo	SW19
144 J 15	Ancill st	W6
62 G 6	Ancona rd	NW10
79 T 12	Ancona st	SE18
90 A 8	Andalus rd	SW9
82 K 11	Anderson pl	Hounsl
50 F 17	Anderson rd	E9
147 O 9	Anderson st	SW3
91 P 8	Anderton clo	SE5
58 L 10	Andover clo	Grnfd
48 C 8	Andover gdns	N7
48 C 8	Andover gro	N7
129 X 9	Andover pl	NW6
48 C 8	Andover rd	N7
101 R 2	Andover rd	Twick
48 C 8	Andover row	N7
49 Y 14	Andre st	E8
98 M 14	Andrew clo	Bxly
89 X 1	Andrew pl	SW8
64 G 17	Andrew st	E14
78 C 3	Andrew st	E16
135 X 6	Andrews rd	E8
80 D 6	Andwell clo	SE2
109 V 18	Anerley gro	SE19
109 W 19	Anerley rd	SE19
109 Y 17	Anerley Park rd	SE20
110 A 17	Anerley pk	SE20
109 Y 18	Anerley rd	SE20
109 Y 20	Anerley rd	SE20
124 A 1	Anerley rd	SE20
109 Z 20	Anerley Station rd	SE20
109 W 17	Anerley vale	SE19
114 C 14	Angel ct	EC1
142 F 5	Angel ct	EC2
18 H 15	Angel ct	N18
91 M 8	Angel Hill	Sutton
154 B 4	Angel Hill dri	Sutton
51 X 18	Angel la	E15
133 T 9	Angel ms	N1
142 F 10	Angel pas	EC4
18 J 15	Angel pk	N18
90 G 7	Angel Pk gdns	SW19
19 O 17	Angel rd	N18
90 F 5	Angel rd	SW9
9 O 14	Angel rd	Enf
23 U 18	Angel rd	Harrow
142 A 4	Angel rd	EC1
141 Z 4	Angel rd	EC1
74 L 12	Angel wlk	W6
52 K 12	Angela st	E2
135 N 12	Angela st	E2
82 K 12	Anfield	Hounsl
55 U 4	Angle green	Dgnhm
51 Y 10	Angle st	E11
47 T 17	Anglers la	NW5
108 B 9	Angles rd	SW16
78 M 12	Anglesea av	SE18
78 L 12	Anglesea rd	SE18
116 Q 9	Anglesea rd	Kingst
155 O 15	Anglesey Ct rd	Carsh
155 O 15	Anglesey gdns	Carsh
30 J 3	Anglesey rd	Enf
22 G 10	Anglesmede cres	Pinn
22 F 10	Anglesmede way	Pinn
63 Y 6	Anglo rd	E3
25 Z 5	Angus gdns	NW9
65 Y 10	Angus rd	E13
75 X 19	Angus st	SE14
146 L 19	Anhalt rd	SW11
95 Y 1	Ankerdine cres	SE18
78 L 20	Ankerdine cres	SE18
101 S 12	Anlaby rd	Tedd
136 E 20	Anley rd	W14
24 H 6	Anmersh gro	Stanm
146 F 16	Ann la	SW10
79 R 11	Ann st	SE18
64 C 18	Annabel clo	E14
39 O 4	Annan way	Rom
77 P 14	Annandale rd	SE10
74 A 13	Annandale rd	W4
157 Y 3	Annandale rd	Croy
96 J 19	Annandale rd	Sidcp
102 K 12	Anne Boleyns la	Kingst
153 R 16	Anne Boleyns wlk	Sutton
65 S 11	Anne st	E13
25 Z 10	Annesley av	NW9
44 A 10	Annesley clo	NW10
158 M 6	Annesley dri	Croy
47 U 7	Annesley rd	N19
94 G 2	Annesley rd	SE3
48 D 12	Annette rd	N7
134 L 15	Anning st	EC2
29 N 11	Annington rd	N2
50 H 19	Annis rd	E9
139 S 19	Anns clo	SW1
143 O 2	Anns pl	E1
123 N 7	Annsworthy av	Thntn Hth
123 P 4	Annsworthy cres	Thntn Hth
92 C 5	Ansdell rd	SE15
137 Y 20	Ansdell st	W8
137 Y 20	Ansdell ter	W8
155 N 1	Ansell rd	Carsh
106 K 7	Ansell rd	SW17
145 S 15	Anselm rd	SW6
22 E 3	Anselm rd	Pinn
111 V 11	Ansford rd	Brom
136 H 10	Ansleigh pl	W11
38 F 7	Anson clo	Rom
44 L 14	Anson rd	NW2
45 P 14	Anson rd	NW2
47 X 12	Anson rd	N7
91 X 7	Anstey rd	SE15
96 E 16	Anstridge rd	SE9
63 W 8	Anthill rd	E3
123 X 15	Anthony rd	SE25
59 S 7	Anthony rd	Grnfd
97 O 2	Anthony rd	Welling
31 W 13	Antill rd	N15
63 S 17	Antill ter	E1
49 Y 14	Anton st	E8
46 L 17	Antrim gro	NW3
46 L 17	Antrim rd	NW3
153 W 13	Antrobus clo	Sutton
73 V 10	Antrobus rd	W4
111 S 20	Apex clo	Becknhm
112 G 20	Apollo av	Brom
146 F 17	Apollo pl	SW10
141 W 7	Apothecary st	EC4
90 E 14	Appach rd	SW2
72 H 12	Apple garth	Brentf
8 E 12	Apple gro	Enf
116 H 4	Apple mkt	Kingst
140 D 12	Apple Tree yd	SW1
20 E 19	Appleby clo	E4
65 R 18	Appleby rd	E16
49 X 20	Appleby rd	E8
135 N 8	Appleby st	E2
98 L 4	Appledore av	Bxly Hth
106 L 3	Appledore clo	SW17
126 D 11	Appledore clo	Brom
25 O 4	Appledore clo	Edg
114 J 8	Appledore cres	Sidcp
128 M 8	Appleford rd	W10
159 S 14	Applegarth	Croy
36 L 13	Applegarth dri	Ilf
144 G 3	Applegarth rd	W14

95 P 7	Appleton rd SE9	
134 J 20	Appold st EC2	
63 P 7	Approach rd E2	
118 M 3	Approach rd SW20	
5 S 15	Approach rd Barnt	
61 Z 17	Approach the W3	
9 N 8	Approach the Enf	
27 N 13	Aprey gdns NW4	
49 V 13	April st E8	
22 M 15	Apsley clo Harrow	
32 K 15	Apsley rd E17	
123 Z 9	Apsley rd SE25	
117 W 7	Apsley rd New Mald	
141 T 14	Aquinas st SE1	
66 C 10	Arabella dri SW15	
20 F 2	Arabia clo E4	
92 K 10	Arabin rd SE4	
152 H 20	Aragon av Epsom	
102 N 12	Aragon rd Kingst	
119 P 16	Aragon rd Mrdn	
37 O 19	Arandora cres Rom	
63 V 7	Arbery rd E3	
20 K 11	Arbor rd E4	
63 R 11	Arbor sq E1	
17 N 2	Arboreal av N14	
125 R 3	Arbour clo Beoknhm	
9 T 12	Arbour rd Enf	
57 Y 14	Arbour way Hornch	
95 S 7	Arbroath rd SE9	
109 Y 8	Arbury ter SE26	
97 Z 16	Arbuthnot la Bxly	
98 A 15	Arbuthnot la Bxly	
92 F 4	Arbuthnot rd SE14	
142 J 2	Arcade the EC2	
27 X 6	Arcadia av N3	
64 B 16	Arcadia st E14	
91 Y 16	Arcadian av Bxly	
97 Y 16	Arcadian clo Bxly	
30 E 1	Arcadian gdns N22	
97 Y 17	Arcadian rd Bxly	
90 D 17	Archbishops pl SW2	
91 V 11	Archdale rd SE22	
145 P 13	Archel rd W14	
123 Z 8	Archer st SE25	
140 E 9	Archer st W1	
138 M 7	Archery clo W2	
95 U 12	Archery rd SE9	
139 W 11	Archibald ms W1	
47 X 12	Archibald rd N7	
64 A 10	Archibald st E3	
47 V 6	Archway clo N19	
47 V 6	Archway mall N19	
29 O 18	Archway rd N6	
47 U 3	Archway rd N6	
86 B 7	Archway st SW13	
49 U 14	Arcola st E8	
47 R 15	Arctic st NW5	
112 A 14	Arcus rd Brom	
108 A 3	Arewell rd SW2	
91 O 14	Ardbeg rd SE24	
10 G 2	Arden clo Bushey Watf	
41 P 10	Arden clo Harrow	
55 W 20	Arden cres Dgnhm	
68 H 1	Arden cres Dgnhm	
27 V 9	Arden rd N3	
122 E 5	Ardfern av Becknhm	
111 Y 3	Ardfillan rd SE6	
111 Y 3	Ardgowan rd SE6	
93 Y 19	Ardgowan rd SE6	
48 L 12	Ardilaun rd N5	
119 X 19	Ardleigh gdns Sutton	
32 L 5	Ardleigh rd E17	
49 P 19	Ardleigh rd N1	
32 M 5	Ardleigh ter E17	
44 A 9	Ardley clo NW10	
110 J 7	Ardley clo SE6	
108 L 4	Ardlui rd SE27	
116 J 12	Ardmay gdns Surb	
93 X 15	Ardmere rd SE13	
21 W 4	Ardmore la Buck Hl	
111 W 4	Ardock rd SE6	
152 F 5	Ardrossan gdns Worc Pk	
36 C 17	Ardwell av Ilf	
45 X 12	Ardwick rd NW2	
50 G 2	Argall av E10	
141 Z 16	Argent st SE1	
145 U 19	Argon ms SW6	
66 G 6	Argus clo Rom	
58 A 9	Argus way Grnfd	
82 J 15	Argyle av Hounsl	
59 Y 11	Argyle clo W13	
74 K 11	Argyle pl W6	
63 S 11	Argyle rd E1	
51 Z 13	Argyle rd E15	
65 U 18	Argyle rd E16	
14 L 16	Argyle rd N12	
15 N 17	Argyle rd N12	
31 W 4	Argyle rd N17	
18 L 13	Argyle rd N18	
59 Z 12	Argyle rd W13	
60 A 19	Argyle rd W13	
4 A 13	Argyle rd Barnt	
22 J 17	Argyle rd Harrow	
82 K 13	Argyle rd Hounsl	
53 W 6	Argyle rd Ilf	
101 U 12	Argyle rd Tedd	
132 L 12	Argyle sq WC1	
51 Y 9	Argyle st E11	
132 L 13	Argyle st WC1	
132 L 13	Argyle wlk WC1	
70 J 2	Argyll av Shall	
25 T 7	Argyll gdns Edg	
137 U 20	Argyll rd W8	
140 A 6	Argyll st W1	
92 H 9	Arica rd SE4	
45 X 18	Ariel rd NW6	
89 Y 9	Aristotle la SW4	
108 K 19	Arkell clo SE19	
111 U 8	Arkindale rd SE6	
32 K 17	Arkley la E17	
32 K 17	Arkley rd E17	
75 X 17	Arklow rd SE14	
46 D 15	Arkwright rd NW3	
157 V 20	Arkwright rd S Croy	
65 P 18	Arkwright st E16	
90 A 7	Arlesford rd SW9	
87 S 14	Arlesley clo SW15	
90 F 15	Arlingford rd SW2	
14 K 12	Arlington N12	
134 D 6	Arlington av N1	
96 G 19	Arlington clo Sidcp	
153 Y 3	Arlington clo Sutton	
84 C 14	Arlington clo Twick	
154 L 3	Arlington dri Carsh	
73 V 13	Arlington gdns W4	
53 V 3	Arlington gdns Ilf	
131 Y 5	Arlington rd NW1	
132 A 8	Arlington rd NW1	
32 K 17	Arlington rd N14	
60 B 18	Arlington rd W13	
102 F 5	Arlington rd Rich	
116 H 15	Arlington rd Surb	
101 V 10	Arlington rd Tedd	
84 C 15	Arlington rd Twick	
34 G 3	Arlington rd Wdfd Grn	
134 C 6	Arlington sq N1	
140 A 13	Arlington st SW1	
133 U 12	Arlington way EC1	
17 U 6	Arlow rd N21	
76 B 16	Armada st SE8	
145 T 16	Armadale rd SW6	
63 Y 4	Armagh rd E3	
121 N 3	Armfield cres Mitch	
8 B 6	Armfield rd Enf	
74 K 3	Arminger rd W12	
45 U 4	Armitage rd NW11	
87 Y 13	Armoury way SW18	
69 R 1	Armstead wlk Dgnhm	
56 D 20	Armstead wlk Dgnhm	
20 M 19	Armstrong av Wdfd Grn	
5 T 12	Armstrong cres Barnt	
77 Y 12	Armstrong gdns SE7	
79 N 11	Armstrong pl SE18	
74 D 2	Armstrong rd W3	
100 C 13	Armstrong rd Felt	
78 M 12	Armstrong st SE18	
87 S 18	Arnal cres SW18	
140 L 6	Arne st WC2	
94 B 10	Arne wlk SE3	
148 F 3	Arneway st SW1	
37 W 11	Arneways av Rom	
121 N 13	Arneys la Mitch	
93 W 19	Arngask rd SE6	
91 S 13	Arnhem way SE22	
9 Z 2	Arnold av E	
135 N 14	Arnold av E	
25 N 20	Arnold clo Harrow	
83 R 13	Arnold cres Islwth	
17 U 15	Arnold gdns N13	
64 A 9	Arnold rd E3	
31 O 11	Arnold rd N15	
106 M 17	Arnold rd SW17	
69 P 2	Arnold rd Dgnhm	
69 R 1	Arnold rd Dgnhm	
40 C 19	Arnold rd Grnfd	
16 K 12	Arnos gro N14	
16 J 15	Arnos rd N11	
150 D 3	Arnott st SE1	
91 P 9	Arnould av SE5	
42 G 3	Arnside gdns Wemb	
98 E 2	Arnside rd Bxly Hth	
111 R 10	Arnulf st SE6	
108 H 15	Arnulls rd SW16	
90 D 15	Arodene rd SW2	
110 D 19	Arpley rd SE20	
108 A 18	Arragon gdns SW16	
66 B 4	Arragon rd E6	
83 Z 20	Arragon rd Twick	
155 T 8	Arran clo Wallgtn	
111 S 3	Arran rd SE6	
120 D 10	Arras av Wdfd	
124 E 5	Arrol rd Becknhm	
64 D 9	Arrow rd E3	
95 T 6	Arsenal rd SE9	
105 N 19	Arterberry rd SW20	
137 T 6	Artesian rd W2	
64 M 3	Arthingworth st E15	
79 O 11	Arthur gro SE18	
66 G 6	Arthur rd E6	
48 D 11	Arthur rd N7	
18 F 7	Arthur rd N9	
105 W 7	Arthur rd SW19	
103 P 9	Arthur rd Kingst	
118 K 12	Arthur rd New Mald	
37 U 19	Arthur rd Rom	
142 F 9	Arthur st EC4	
143 V 10	Artichoke hill E1	
36 D 17	Artillery clo Ilf	
142 L 1	Artillery la E1	
142 H 12	Artillery pl SE18	
148 D 2	Artillery row SW1	
142 M 4	Artizan st E1	
119 W 9	Arundel av Mrdn	
52 A 13	Arundel clo E15	
98 C 15	Arundel clo Bxly	
156 H 7	Arundel clo Croy	
100 L 13	Arundel clo Hampt	
40 F 14	Arundel dri Harrow	
34 G 2	Arundel dri Wdfd Grn	
117 U 8	Arundel gdns N21	
137 M 8	Arundel gdns W11	
25 Y 2	Arundel gdns Edg	
25 Y 2	Arundel gdns Edgw	
55 N 6	Arundel gdns Ilf	
49 R 15	Arundel gro N16	
48 F 19	Arundel pl N1	
5 X 12	Arundel rd Barnt	
123 O 15	Arundel rd Croy	
117 U 2	Arundel rd Kingst	
153 U 17	Arundel rd Sutton	
48 F 19	Arundel sq N1	
141 P 8	Arundel st WC2	
74 K 12	Arundel ter SW12	
144 A 14	Arundel ter SW12	
74 K 17	Arundel ter SW13	
48 G 15	Arvon rd N5	
148 B 20	Ascalon st SW8	
33 P 1	Ascham dri E4	
32 J 3	Ascham end E17	
47 V 14	Ascham st NW5	
40 G 16	Ascot clo Grnfd	
9 P 1	Ascot gdns Enf	
58 F 15	Ascot gdns S'hall	
43 Y 15	Ascot pk NW10	
66 F 8	Ascot rd E6	
31 O 16	Ascot rd N15	
18 K 13	Ascot rd N18	
107 N 19	Ascot rd SW17	
72 J 5	Ascott av W5	
154 L 2	Ash clo Carsh	
117 Y 3	Ash clo New Mald	
38 G 3	Ash clo Rom	
96 D 16	Ash clo Sidcp	
10 X 19	Ash clo Stanm	
135 X 5	Ash gro E8	
45 R 13	Ash gro NW2	
124 C 3	Ash gro SE20	
72 K 7	Ash gro W5	
18 D 2	Ash gro Enf	
58 J 13	Ash gro S'hall	
159 V 1	Ash gro W Wckm	
47 Y 13	Ash gro Wemb	
52 B 15	Ash rd E15	
159 O 2	Ash rd Croy	
119 T 19	Ash rd Sutton	
127 W 15	Ash row Brom	
150 B 5	Ash st SE17	
124 H 13	Ash Tree clo Croy	
25 X 15	Ash Tree dell NW9	
124 H 14	Ash Tree way Croy	
34 H 13	Ashbourne av E18	
27 V 14	Ashbourne av NW11	
15 Z 7	Ashbourne av N20	
81 N 19	Ashbourne av Bxly Hth	
41 R 7	Ashbourne av Harrow	
107 R 17	Ashbourne av Mitch	
15 O 14	Ashbourne clo N12	
61 O 13	Ashbourne clo W5	
12 L 17	Ashbourne gro NW7	
91 U 12	Ashbourne gro SE22	
74 B 14	Ashbourne gro W4	
60 M 11	Ashbourne rd W5	
61 O 13	Ashbourne rd W5	
105 W 17	Ashbourne ter SW19	
24 E 19	Ashbridge clo Harrow	
34 A 20	Ashbridge rd E11	
130 K 18	Ashbridge st NW8	
47 X 5	Ashbrook rd N19	
56 H 10	Ashbrook rd Dgnhm	
146 A 5	Ashburn gdns SW7	
146 B 5	Ashburn ms SW7	
146 A 5	Ashburn pl SW7	
23 W 20	Ashburnham av Harrow	
23 X 20	Ashburnham gdns Harrow	
76 E 20	Ashburnham gro SE10	
76 E 20	Ashburnham pl SE10	
62 M 8	Ashburnham rd NW10	
128 C 11	Ashburnham rd NW10	
146 D 19	Ashburnham rd SW10	
81 X 10	Ashburnham rd Erith	
102 C 7	Ashburnham rd Rich	
123 Z 20	Ashburton av Croy	
54 G 14	Ashburton av Ilf	
157 W 1	Ashburton clo Croy	
157 W 2	Ashburton gdns Croy	
48 F 13	Ashburton gro N7	
65 T 17	Ashburton rd E16	
123 W 20	Ashburton rd Croy	
157 W 2	Ashburton rd Croy	
37 V 16	Ashbury gdns Rom	
89 N 6	Ashbury rd SW11	
48 M 20	Ashby gro N1	
31 W 15	Ashby rd N15	
92 L 5	Ashby rd SE4	
93 N 5	Ashby rd SE4	
133 X 13	Ashby st EC1	
74 F 8	Ashchurch ct W12	
74 A 10	Ashchurch ct W4	
74 F 7	Ashchurch gro W12	
74 F 8	Ashchurch Pk vlls W12	
74 F 7	Ashchurch ter W12	
116 G 18	Ashcombe av Surb	
12 B 14	Ashcombe gdns Edg	
44 C 10	Ashcombe pk NW2	
105 Y 12	Ashcombe rd SW19	
155 O 12	Ashcombe rd Carsh	
117 V 5	Ashcombe sq New Mald	
87 Z 6	Ashcombe st SW6	
96 M 15	Ashcroft av Sidcp	
97 N 16	Ashcroft cres Sidcp	
53 V 9	Ashcroft rd E3	
82 L 18	Ashdale clo Twick	
10 K 19	Ashdale gro Stanm	
112 J 1	Ashdale rd SE12	
82 L 18	Ashdale way Twick	
21 V 19	Ashdon clo Wdfd Grn	
62 C 3	Ashdon rd NW10	
125 S 4	Ashdown clo Becknhm	
116 J 4	Ashdown rd Kingst	
47 O 15	Ashdown st NW5	
38 H 6	Ashdown wlk Rom	
99 W 16	Ashen dri Drtfrd	
105 X 5	Ashen gro SW19	
158 G 20	Ashen vale S Croy	
50 G 14	Ashenden rd E5	
102 J 1	Ashfield clo Rich	
114 C 17	Ashfield la Chisl	
63 O 16	Ashfield rd E1	
16 G 11	Ashfield rd N14	
30 M 19	Ashfield rd N4	
74 C 1	Ashfield rd W3	
143 W 3	Ashfield st E1	
29 Z 14	Ashford av N8	
9 R 8	Ashford cres Enf	
34 J 8	Ashford rd E18	
53 V 20	Ashford rd NW2	
45 O 12	Ashford rd NW2	
31 U 2	Ashford rd N17	
134 J 12	Ashford st N1	
111 Y 14	Ashgrove rd Brom	
54 L 5	Ashgrove rd Ilf	
55 N 4	Ashgrove rd Ilf	
87 W 5	Ashington rd SW6	
108 A 10	Ashlake rd SW16	
139 T 1	Ashland pl W1	
102 J 1	Ashleigh cl Rich	
102 J 2	Ashleigh clo Rich	
154 A 3	Ashleigh gdns Sutton	
154 C 3	Ashleigh gdns Sutton	
124 B 5	Ashleigh rd SE20	
86 A 7	Ashleigh rd SW14	

Ref	Entry
35 Z 8	Ashley av Ilf
119 Y 12	Ashley av Mrdn
27 N 7	Ashley clo NW4
30 G 8	Ashley cres N22
82 K 20	Ashley dri Twick
17 Y 14	Ashley gdns N13
102 G 5	Ashley gdns Rich
42 K 7	Ashley gdns Wemb
27 N 7	Ashley la NW7
156 J 8	Ashley la Croy
148 B 3	Ashley pl SW1
20 A 18	Ashley rd E4
65 Y 1	Ashley rd E7
31 Y 11	Ashley rd N17
48 A 2	Ashley rd N4
106 A 15	Ashley rd SW19
9 P 10	Ashley rd Enf
100 H 20	Ashley rd Hampt
84 K 8	Ashley rd Rich
122 D 10	Ashley rd Thntn Hth
27 N 2	Ashley wlk NW7
51 Y 13	Ashlin rd E15
123 X 20	Ashling rd Croy
87 N 6	Ashlone rd SW6
6 H 18	Ashmead clo N14
93 O 4	Ashmead rd SE4
125 W 3	Ashmere av Becknhm
90 A 11	Ashmere gro SW2
130 L 19	Ashmill st NW1
149 R 16	Ashmole pl SW8
149 R 16	Ashmole st SW8
96 F 7	Ashmore gro Welling
129 O 11	Ashmore rd W9
31 U 14	Ashmount rd N15
47 W 2	Ashmount rd N19
38 M 8	Ashmour gdns Rom
39 N 8	Ashmour gdns Rom
42 A 19	Ashness gdns Grnfd
88 M 13	Ashness rd SW11
24 E 19	Ashridge clo Harrow
79 O 20	Ashridge cres SE18
18 M 15	Ashridge gdns N13
17 N 16	Ashridge gdns N13
22 B 13	Ashridge gdns Pinn
119 U 8	Ashridge way Mrdn
49 X 1	Ashtead rd E5
153 W 9	Ashton clo Sutton
82 D 10	Ashton gdns Hounsl
37 Z 19	Ashton gdns Rom
51 X 16	Ashton rd E15
64 G 19	Ashton st E14
120 H 3	Ashtree av Mitch
35 Z 18	Ashurst dri Ilf
36 C 13	Ashurst dri Ilf
15 X 17	Ashurst rd N12
6 Z 17	Ashurst rd Barnt
6 A 15	Ashurst rd Barnt
157 Z 2	Ashurst wlk Croy
106 L 11	Ashvale rd SW17
51 W 8	Ashville rd E11
112 F 2	Ashwater rd SE12
18 D 16	Ashwell gro N18
63 U 7	Ashwell rd E3
49 T 17	Ashwin st E8
20 K 11	Ashwood rd E4
129 Y 13	Ashworth rd W9
74 F 6	Askew bldgs W12
97 X 11	Askew clo Bxly Hth
74 E 4	Askew cres W12
74 E 4	Askew rd W12
74 F 3	Askham rd W12
87 T 14	Askill dri SW15
88 B 18	Aslett st SW18
45 U 14	Asmara rd NW2
27 X 15	Asmuns hill NW11
27 W 15	Asmuns pl NW11
127 U 3	Aspen copse Brom
74 K 13	Aspen gdns W6
121 N 12	Aspen gdns Mitch
144 G 14	Aspenlea rd W6
92 F 8	Aspinal rd SE4
75 O 10	Aspinden rd SE16
151 Y 5	Aspinden rd SE16
60 A 16	Aspland gro E8
88 B 14	Aspley rd SW18
31 Y 4	Asplins rd N17
63 P 13	Assembly pas E1
120 H 18	Assembly wlk Carsh
81 P 13	Assurance cotts Blvdr
92 B 1	Aste st SE15
76 F 6	Aste st E14
146 K 9	Astell st SW3
89 O 3	Astle st SW11
45 N 14	Astley av NW2
133 Z 1	Astleys row N1
24 E 20	Aston av Harrow
115 O 9	Aston clo Sidcp
119 N 3	Aston rd SW20
60 H 17	Aston rd W5
63 V 16	Aston st E14
105 X 2	Astonville st SW18
38 J 18	Astor av Rom
90 E 7	Astoria wlk SW9
57 Y 17	Astra clo Hornch
136 B 20	Astrop ms W6
74 L 7	Astrop ms W6
74 L 7	Astrop ter W6
136 B 20	Astrop ter W6
136 B 20	Astropter W6
48 A 8	Astwood ms SW5
75 N 20	Asylum rd SE15
92 A 1	Asylum rd SE15
151 X 16	Asylum rd SE15
144 J 20	Atalanta st SW6
102 C 15	Atbara rd Tedd
83 O 10	Atcham rd Hounsl
88 B 20	Atheldene rd SW18
111 P 6	Athelney st SE6
117 N 8	Athelstan rd Kingst
63 X 7	Athelstane gro E3
48 F 6	Athelstane rd N4
23 R 8	Athelstone rd Harrow
41 R 5	Athena clo Harrow
59 Y 12	Athenaeum pl N10
15 S 6	Athenaeum rd N20
92 F 13	Athenlay rd SE15
50 B 12	Atherden rd E5
89 Z 7	Atherfold rd SW9
90 A 7	Atherfold rd SW9
146 C 4	Atherstone ms SW7
105 P 9	Atherton dri SW19
52 D 17	Atherton ms E7
52 C 17	Atherton rd E7
74 E 20	Atherton rd SW13
35 S 7	Atherton rd Ilf
85 X 5	Atherton st SW11
60 G 6	Athlon rd Wemb
69 W 8	Athlone rd SW2
47 R 17	Athlone st NW5
81 X 14	Athol rd Erith
54 N 2	Athol rd Ilf
54 N 1	Athol rd Ilf
64 H 18	Athol st E14
8 D 19	Athole gdns Enf
93 O 13	Athurdon rd SE4
33 S 19	Atkins rd E10
89 Z 19	Atkins rd SW12
75 Y 18	Atkinson st SE14
77 X 10	Atlantic rd SW19
77 X 10	Atlas gdns SE7
65 S 7	Atlas rd E13
62 B 10	Atlas rd NW10
64 A 4	Atley rd E3
87 S 10	Atney rd SW15
30 G 19	Atterbury rd N4
148 I 18	Atterbury st SW1
44 A 9	Attwood av NW10
133 R 15	Attneave st WC1
90 E 20	Atwater clo SW2
91 Y 5	Atwell rd SE15
85 R 5	Atwood av Rich
74 J 10	Atwood rd W6
78 G 3	Auberon st E16
48 H 12	Aubert pk N5
48 J 12	Aubert rd N5
33 P 11	Aubrey rd E17
30 B 18	Aubrey rd N8
137 R 15	Aubrey wlk W8
109 N 11	Aubyn hill SE27
86 G 12	Aubyn sq SW15
123 U 1	Auckland clo SE19
123 T 1	Auckland gdns SE19
108 M 9	Auckland hill SE27
51 R 9	Auckland rd E10
109 U 19	Auckland rd SE19
123 T 3	Auckland rd SE19
88 J 12	Auckland rd SW11
53 Z 3	Auckland rd Ilf
54 A 2	Auckland rd Ilf
117 N 8	Auckland rd Kingst
109 T 20	Auckland ri SE19
149 N 11	Auckland st SE11
34 C 14	Audley ct E18
54 K 8	Audley gdns Ilf
26 H 19	Audley rd NW4
60 M 15	Audley rd W5
61 N 14	Audley rd W5
7 V 8	Audley rd Enf
84 M 14	Audley rd Rich
139 V 13	Audley sq W1
125 R 14	Audrey clo Becknhm
42 B 6	Audrey gdns Wemb
53 Y 10	Audrey rd Ilf
135 T 8	Audrey st E2
65 X 9	Augurs la E13
101 N 5	Augusta rd Twick
64 C 17	Augusta st E14
144 F 3	Augustine rd W14
105 S 1	Augustus rd SW19
131 Z 11	Augustus st NW1
151 R 13	Aulay st SE1
149 U 12	Aulton pl SE11
154 L 4	Aultone way Carsh
154 B 2	Aultone way Sutton
C 13	Aurelia gdns Croy
122 B 14	Aurelia rd Croy
57 O 18	Auriel av Dgnhm
144 K 6	Auriol rd W14
13 O 11	Austell gdns NW7
40 J 6	Austen rd Harrow
127 S 13	Austin av Brom
142 G 5	Austin friars EC2
89 O 2	Austin st SW11
134 M 14	Austin st E2
114 L 6	Austral clo Sidcp
149 W 4	Austral st SE11
62 J 19	Australia rd W12
74 J 1	Australia rd W12
117 S 19	Austyn gdns Surb
8 L 7	Autumn clo Enf
64 B 4	Autumn st E3
59 Y 13	Avalon clo W13
7 U 7	Avalon clo Enf
88 A 1	Avalon rd SW6
59 Y 12	Avalon rd W13
106 M 14	Avarn rd SW17
141 Y 6	Ave Maria la EC4
116 G 16	Avebury pk Surb
51 X 3	Avebury rd E11
105 V 19	Avebury rd SW19
134 F 6	Avebury st N1
50 A 6	Aveley rd E5
39 O 13	Aveley rd Rom
149 R 10	Aveline st SE11
33 O 6	Aveling Park rd E17
48 H 10	Avenell rd N5
87 Y 18	Avening terr SW18
65 T 12	Avenons rd E13
144 L 19	Avenue clo NW2
130 L 6	Avenue clo NW8
73 S 5	Avenue cres W3
116 J 11	Avenue elmers Surb
123 W 5	Avenue gdns SE25
86 A 8	Avenue gdns SW14
73 T 5	Avenue gdns W3
101 X 16	Avenue gdns Tedd
29 S 11	Avenue ms N10
108 J 3	Avenue Pk rd SE27
51 Y 12	Avenue rd E11
52 H 13	Avenue rd E7
62 D 6	Avenue rd NW10
130 J 4	Avenue rd NW8
15 R 14	Avenue rd N12
6 G 20	Avenue rd N14
16 G 1	Avenue rd N14
31 O 16	Avenue rd N15
29 W 20	Avenue rd N6
110 D 20	Avenue rd SE20
124 E 2	Avenue rd SE20
123 V 4	Avenue rd SE25
121 X 4	Avenue rd SW16
118 K 2	Avenue rd SW20
71 Y 1	Avenue rd W13
73 S 5	Avenue rd W3
81 W 11	Avenue rd Blvdr
72 E 13	Avenue rd Brentf
97 Y 9	Avenue rd Bxly Hth
81 Y 19	Avenue rd Erith
83 U 3	Avenue rd Islwth
116 K 6	Avenue rd Kingst
118 B 7	Avenue rd New Mald
22 A 9	Avenue rd Pinn
55 S 2	Avenue rd Rom
70 F 2	Avenue rd S'hall
101 X 16	Avenue rd Tedd
155 U 18	Avenue rd Wallgtn
21 Z 18	Avenue rd Wdfd Grn
117 V 7	Avenue ter New Mald
142 M 3	Avenue the EC3
34 J 17	Avenue the E11
20 J 19	Avenue the E4
128 J 4	Avenue the NW6
29 U 7	Avenue the N10
31 P 9	Avenue the N17
7 Y 7	Avenue the N3
30 E 11	Avenue the N8
76 J 19	Avenue the SE10
77 X 18	Avenue the SE7
89 P 13	Avenue the SW4
60 A 19	Avenue the W13
74 A 9	Avenue the W4
4 E 13	Avenue the Barnt
111 U 20	Avenue the Becknhm
127 O 7	Avenue the Brom
97 W 18	Avenue the Bxly
155 O 16	Avenue the Carsh
157 R 5	Avenue the Croy
100 F 14	Avenue the Hampt
23 U 12	Avenue the Harrow
23 V 4	Avenue the Harrow
82 J 13	Avenue the Hounsl
115 R 18	Avenue the Orp
22 E 19	Avenue the Pinn
22 G 1	Avenue the Pinn
85 N 4	Avenue the Rich
39 O 13	Avenue the Rom
117 O 15	Avenue the Surb
153 U 20	Avenue the Sutton
84 D 14	Avenue the Twick
126 A 14	Avenue the W Wkhm
125 W 18	Avenue the W Wkhm
42 K 3	Avenue the Wemb
43 O 7	Avenue the Wemb
152 D 3	Avenue the Worc Pk
108 H 16	Averill gro SW16
144 G 15	Averill st W6
147 V 8	Avery Farm row SW1
35 V 16	Avery gdns Ilf
114 B 2	Avery hill Sidcp
96 B 16	Avery Hill park SE9
96 D 20	Avery Hill rd SE9
139 X 8	Avery row W1
124 K 12	Aviemore clo Becknhm
124 J 12	Aviemore way Becknhm
92 G 8	Avignon rd SE4
110 B 17	Avington gro SE20
63 T 17	Avis sq E1
107 P 8	Avoca rd SW17
154 D 8	Avon clo Sutton
152 F 2	Avon clo Worc Pk
157 N 14	Avon path S Croy
142 C 19	Avon pl SE1
33 X 11	Avon rd E17
93 O 7	Avon rd SE4
58 J 11	Avon rd Grnfd
44 B 9	Avondale av NW2
15 N 17	Avondale av N12
15 Y 4	Avondale av Barnt
118 C 19	Avondale av Worc Pk
9 V 11	Avondale cres Enf
35 O 17	Avondale cres Ilf
34 G 4	Avondale ct E18
82 E 14	Avondale gdns Hounsl
136 K 11	Avondale park W11
136 J 10	Avondale Pk gdns W11
136 J 9	Avondale Pk rd W11
62 M 13	Avondale rd E16
65 N 14	Avondale rd E16
51 N 1	Avondale rd E17
17 U 9	Avondale rd N13
30 K 15	Avondale rd N15
28 C 5	Avondale rd N3
113 R 5	Avondale rd SE9
85 Z 7	Avondale rd SW14
105 Z 12	Avondale rd SW19
106 A 12	Avondale rd SW19
112 C 15	Avondale rd Brom
23 X 9	Avondale rd Harrow
156 M 15	Avondale rd S Croy
97 U 5	Avondale rd Welling
91 U 7	Avondale ri SE15
151 S 11	Avondale sq SE1
75 R 19	Avonley rd SE14
75 R 19	Avonley ms SE14
145 N 4	Avonmore pl W14
145 N 5	Avonmore rd W14
150 A 1	Avonmouth st SE1
82 K 4	Avonwick rd Hounsl
20 H 16	Avril way E4
156 A 15	Avro way Wallgtn
31 P 5	Awlfield av N17
96 L 4	Awliscombe rd Welling
67 O 3	Axe st Bark
25 R 4	Axholme av Edg
80 H 20	Axminster cres Welling
97 S 1	Axminster cres Welling
48 B 9	Axminster rd N7
139 T 2	Aybrook st W1
127 V 8	Aycliffe clo Brom
74 F 2	Aycliffe rd W12
150 H 9	Aylesbury rd SE17
126 E 7	Aylesbury rd Brom
133 W 17	Aylesbury st EC1
43 Y 10	Aylesbury st NW10
124 H 13	Aylesford av Becknhm
148 F 11	Aylesford st SW1
45 O 20	Aylestone av NW6
128 F 2	Aylestone av NW6
123 Z 10	Aylett rd SE25
124 A 10	Aylett rd SE25
83 U 5	Aylett rd Islwth
8 K 18	Ayley croft Enf
10 L 12	Aylmer clo Stanm

10 K 13 Aylmer dri Stanm
52 B 2 Aylmer rd E11
28 K 16 Aylmer rd E1
74 C 6 Aylmer rd W12
55 X 11 Aylmer rd Dgnhm
56 A 17 Ayloffe dr Dgnhm
110 G 5 Aylward rd SE23
119 V 5 Aylward rd SW20
63 R 16 Aylward rd E1
10 L 13 Aylwards ri Stanm
144 H 3 Aynhoe rd W14
85 V 6 Aynscombe la SW14
39 O 4 Ayr grn Rom
39 Q 4 Ayr way Rom
65 T 10 Ayres clo E13
142 B 16 Ayres st SE1
49 R 8 Ayrsome rd N16
91 P 17 Aysgarth rd SE21
90 D 5 Aytoun rd SW19
91 U 4 Azenby rd SE15
77 N 12 Azof st SE10

B

48 J 15 Baalbec rd N5
35 P 12 Babbacombe gdns Ilf
112 G 19 Babbacombe rd Brom
26 K 13 Babbington rd NW4
107 Y 11 Babington rd SW16
55 T 14 Babington rd Dgnhm
57 X 4 Babington rd Hornch
43 R 18 Babington ri Wemb
140 E 12 Babmaes st SW1
134 G 13 Baches st N1
143 T 5 Back Ch la E1
133 T 18 Back hill EC1
46 E 12 Back la NW3
29 Z 17 Back la N8
67 N 2 Back la Bark
72 G 18 Back la Brentf
98 E 17 Back la Bxly
98 C 18 Back la Bxly
25 V 5 Back la Edg
102 D 6 Back la Rich
37 X 20 Back la Rom
115 N 10 Back rd Sidcp
73 T 2 Back st W3
150 M 3 Bacon gro SE1
25 T 13 Bacon la NW9
25 P 3 Bacon la Edg
135 R 16 Bacon st E2
47 P 4 Bacons la N6
63 R 8 Bacton st E2
69 S 4 Baddow clo Dgnhm
142 F 17 Baden pl SE1
29 Z 12 Baden rd N8
53 Y 14 Baden rd Ilf
57 X 18 Bader way Rainhm
152 E 2 Badgers copse Worc Pk
113 W 7 Badgers croft SE9
158 E 8 Badgers hole Croy
118 A 2 Badgers wlk New Mald
33 N 9 Badlis rd E17
40 H 19 Badminton clo Grnfd
23 S 14 Badminton clo Har
89 P 17 Badminton rd SW12
90 L 1 Badsworth rd SE5
134 E 3 Bagford st N1
63 Y 13 Baggallay st E3
88 C 3 Bagleys la SW6
37 Z 12 Bagleys spring Rom
18 F 1 Bagshot rd Enf
150 K 10 Bagshot st SE17
75 Z 20 Baildon st SE8
110 E 15 Bailey pl SE26
36 A 15 Bailey rd Ilf
56 C 11 Bainbridge rd Dgnhm
140 G 3 Bainbridge st WC1
58 M 19 Baird av S'hall
25 V 18 Baird clo NW9
109 S 10 Baird gdns SE21
8 K 14 Baird rd Enf
94 A 6 Baizdon rd SE3
93 Z 6 Baizdon rd SE3
121 N 4 Baker la Mitch
61 Z 4 Baker la NW10
62 A 4 Baker la NW10
131 R 19 Baker st NW1
139 S 2 Baker st W1
8 D 6 Baker st Enf
142 K 14 Bakers all SE1
33 R 19 Bakers av E17
119 T 3 Bakers end SW20
50 B 4 Bakers hill E5
29 N 17 Bakers la N6

72 G 1 Bakers la W5
139 T 4 Bakers ms W1
133 T 17 Bakers row EC1
64 L 5 Bakers row E15
65 U 11 Balaam st E13
16 K 8 Balaams la N14
151 P 6 Balaclava rd SE1
116 D 16 Balaclava rd Surb
95 V 12 Balcaskie rd SE9
94 M 4 Balchen rd SE3
91 Z 15 Balchier rd SE22
131 N 18 Balcombe st NW1
63 R 1 Balcorne st E9
112 J 6 Balder ri SE12
139 U 7 Balderton st W1
64 C 7 Baldock st E3
108 B 16 Baldry gdns SW16
90 K 2 Baldwin cres SE5
61 X 19 Baldwin gdns W3
134 E 14 Baldwin st EC1
134 A 8 Baldwin ter N1
141 S 1 Baldwin's gdns EC1
133 S 20 Baldwins pl EC1
132 L 9 Balfe st NW1
74 B 14 Balfern gro W4
88 J 4 Balfern st SW11
53 Z 7 Balfour appr Ilf
71 V 2 Balfour av W7
15 Z 11 Balfour gro N20
139 V 11 Balfour ms W1
139 U 11 Balfour pl W1
48 M 13 Balfour rd N5
123 X 10 Balfour rd SE25
106 A 18 Balfour rd SW19
72 A 6 Balfour rd W13
61 W 15 Balfour rd W3
127 P 11 Balfour rd Brom
154 M 17 Balfour rd Carsh
23 R 16 Balfour rd Harrow
82 K 7 Balfour rd Hounsl
53 Z 7 Balfour rd Ilf
54 C 3 Balfour rd Ilf
150 D 5 Balfour st SE17
20 J 6 Balgonie rd E4
39 Y 11 Balgores cres Rom
39 X 11 Balgores la Rom
39 Y 12 Balgores sq Rom
118 B 10 Balgowan clo New Mald
124 K 4 Balgowan rd Becknhm
79 X 11 Balgowan st SE18
89 R 19 Balham gro SW12
89 R 19 Balham High rd SW12
107 P 3 Balham High rd SW17
89 S 16 Balham hill SW12
89 S 19 Balham New rd SW12
106 M 1 Balham Pk rd SW12
107 O 2 Balham Pk rd SW12
18 L 8 Balham rd N9
107 R 1 Balham Stn rd SW12
142 G 7 Ball ct EC3
112 F 7 Ballamore rd Brom
50 G 17 Ballance rd E9
88 C 11 Ballantyne st SW18
103 X 19 Ballard clo Kingst
69 V 3 Ballards clo Dgnhm
157 Y 14 Ballards Farm rd Croy
158 A 14 Ballards Farm rd Croy
27 Z 3 Ballards la N3
44 G 7 Ballards rd NW2
69 V 2 Ballards rd Dgnhm
157 X 14 Ballards ri S Croy
158 C 13 Ballards way Croy
157 Y 15 Ballards way S Croy
76 L 13 Ballast quay SE10
90 B 11 Ballater rd SW2
157 U 11 Ballater rd S Croy
92 B 17 Ballina st SE23
89 N 15 Ballingdon rd SW11
20 K 4 Balliol av E4
31 P 5 Balliol rd N17
136 E 5 Balliol rd W10
97 R 4 Balliol rd Welling
111 X 3 Balloch rd SE6
44 B 11 Ballogie av NW10
49 O 17 Balls Pond pl N1
49 R 17 Balls Pond rd N1
63 Y 7 Balmer rd E3
134 G 3 Balmes rd N1
124 J 9 Balmoral av Becknhm
71 Y 7 Balmoral gdns SW13
54 J 5 Balmoral gdns Ilf
48 B 18 Balmoral gro N7
51 S 8 Balmoral rd E10
52 L 14 Balmoral rd E7

44 K 17 Balmoral rd NW2
40 G 12 Balmoral rd Harrow
116 L 8 Balmoral rd Kingst
39 Y 15 Balmoral rd Rom
152 J 4 Balmoral rd Worc Pk
6 B 16 Balmore cres Barnt
47 T 7 Balmore st N19
87 N 11 Balmuir gdns SW15
44 B 12 Balnacraig av NW10
106 F 17 Baltic clo SW19
134 A 18 Baltic st EC1
87 W 20 Balvernie gro SW18
136 D 18 Bamborough gdns W12
63 T 1 Bambury rd E9
60 M 5 Bamford av Wemb
54 B 19 Bamford rd Bark
111 W 11 Bamford rd Brom
155 U 6 Bamfylde clo Wallgtn
110 E 6 Bampton rd SE23
101 U 2 Banbury cotts Twick
140 K 8 Banbury ct WC2
153 Z 17 Banbury ct Sutton
88 K 4 Banbury st SW11
77 V 19 Banchory rd SE3
28 K 15 Bancroft av N2
21 T 9 Bancroft av Buck Hl
22 M 10 Bancroft gdns Harrow
63 T 11 Bancroft rd E1
23 N 6 Bancroft rd Har
22 M 11 Bancroft rd Harrow
155 X 12 Bandon ri Wallgtn
87 O 8 Bangalore st SW15
73 N 15 Bangor rd Brentf
74 K 10 Banim st W6
128 G 12 Banister rd NW10
144 G 4 Bank av Mitch
142 D 12 Bank end SE1
86 B 13 Bank la SW15
102 J 17 Bank la Kingst
47 S 3 Bank the N6
112 A 10 Bankfoot rd Brom
92 L 18 Bankhurst rd SE6
98 B 10 Banks la Bxly Hth
141 Y 11 Bankside SE1
142 A 11 Bankside SE1
7 X 7 Bankside SE1
157 T 15 Bankside S Croy
154 K 13 Bankside clo Carsh
90 F 12 Bankton rd SW2
94 A 11 Bankwell rd SE13
134 B 18 Banner st EC1
23 Z 7 Bannersfield la Harrow
76 M 12 Banning st SE10
90 F 20 Bannister clo SW2
79 W 11 Bannockburn rd SE18
18 F 10 Banstead gdns N9
154 K 13 Banstead rd Carsh
92 B 8 Banstead rd SE15
156 A 10 Banstead way Wallgtn
12 G 20 Banstock rd Edg
8 M 8 Banton cl Enf
8 M 9 Banton clo Enf
75 V 18 Bantree rd SE14
76 N 9 Banyard rd SE16
151 X 3 Banyard rd SE16
47 O 17 Baptist gdns NW5
52 B 3 Bar field E11
144 D 3 Barb ms W6
48 D 10 Barbara st N7
76 R 10 Barbauld rd N16
149 V 1 Barbel st SE1
65 U 8 Barbers all E13
64 E 5 Barbers rd E15
58 L 15 Barbican rd Grnfd
88 A 13 Barchard st SW18
23 R 6 Barchester rd Harrow
64 D 15 Barchester st E14
21 T 14 Barclay oval Wdfd Grn
52 B 4 Barclay rd E11
65 Y 13 Barclay rd E13
33 T 16 Barclay rd E17
32 B 19 Barclay rd N18
88 A 1 Barclay rd SW6
157 O 5 Barclay rd Croy
108 B 4 Barcombe av SW2
79 U 19 Barden st SE18
120 B 8 Bardney rd Mrdn
158 K 20 Bardolph av Croy
47 Z 12 Bardolph rd N7
85 N 9 Bardolph rd Rich
18 J 11 Bardot clo N9
63 O 13 Bardsey pl E1

76 F 17 Bardsley la SE10
129 N 15 Barfett st W10
15 Y 8 Barfield av N20
127 X 5 Barfield rd Brom
26 H 6 Barford clo NW4
133 U 6 Barford st N1
92 A 8 Barforth rd SE15
92 B 9 Barforth rd SE15
79 Y 13 Bargate clo SE18
118 G 16 Bargate clo New Mald
78 M 4 Barge Ho rd E16
141 U 11 Barge Ho st SE1
111 S 2 Bargery rd SE6
110 M 2 Bargrove cres SE6
127 G 20 Barham clo Brom
113 Z 12 Barham clo Chisl
42 E 9 Barham clo Rom
42 C 17 Barham clo Wemb
104 F 18 Barham clo SW20
113 Y 12 Barham rd Chisl
156 M 10 Barham rd S Croy
112 F 4 Baring clo SE12
112 F 2 Baring rd SE12
94 D 19 Baring rd SE12
94 E 18 Baring rd SE12
5 U 12 Baring rd Barnt
123 Y 19 Baring rd Croy
134 E 5 Baring st N1
104 C 20 Barings clo New Mald
137 X 9 Bark st W2
146 B 14 Barker st SW10
31 P 1 Barkham rd N17
65 Y 14 Barking By pass E16
67 T 6 Barking By pass Bark
54 E 17 Barking park Bark
65 S 12 Barking rd E16
66 F 4 Barking rd E6
145 X 7 Barkston gdns SW5
75 O 14 Barkworth rd SE16
151 Y 11 Barkworth rd SE16
75 R 19 Barlborough st SE14
128 F 19 Barlby gdns W10
128 F 9 Barlby rd W10
136 D 1 Barlby rd W10
55 O 2 Barley la Ilf
37 R 14 Barley la Rom
73 Y 13 Barley Mow pas W4
141 Y 1 Barley Mow pas EC1
63 Y 20 Barleycorn way E14
139 Z 10 Barlow pl W1
73 T 2 Barlow rd W3
100 J 17 Barlow rd Hampt
150 G 2 Barlow st SE17
111 R 3 Barmeston rd SE6
59 X 6 Barmouth av Grnfd
88 D 17 Barmouth rd SW18
158 F 3 Barmouth rd Croy
11 R 20 Barn cres Stanm
43 S 7 Barn hill Wemb
43 R 5 Barn ri Wemb
49 P 8 Barn st N16
55 R 5 Barn way Wemb
50 F 15 Barnabas ter E9
50 G 17 Barnabus rd E9
63 S 19 Barnado st E1
114 F 20 Barnard clo Chisl
155 Y 16 Barnard clo Wallgtn
118 G 9 Barnard gdns New Mald
29 R 6 Barnard hill N10
88 K 10 Barnard rd SW11
9 N 9 Barnard rd Enf
121 O 4 Barnard rd Mitch
141 T 3 Barnards inn EC4
64 L 2 Barnby sq E15
64 L 2 Barnby st E15
132 C 11 Barnby st NW1
98 L 4 Barnehurst av Bxly Hth
98 K 2 Barnehurst clo Erith
98 J 5 Barnehurst rd Bxly Hth
74 F 19 Barnes av SW13
99 V 11 Barnes Cray rd Drtfrd
65 Z 14 Barnes ct E16
118 H 12 Barnes end New Mald
86 C 4 Barnes High st SW13
72 F 1 Barnes pickle W5
54 C 14 Barnes ri Ilf
63 U 17 Barnes st E14
86 B 5 Barnes ter SW13
13 T 1 Barnet Ga la Barnt
135 S 13 Barnet gro E2
4 J 14 Barnet hill Barnt
14 G 5 Barnet la N20
4 K 16 Barnet la Barnt

11 X 1 Barnet la Brhm Wd
12 L 7 Barnet way NW7
A 14 Barnfield New Mald
158 D 2 Barnfield av Croy
122 J 11 Barnfield av Kingst
121 T 7 Barnfield av Mitch
102 K 11 Barnfield gdns Rich
78 M 17 Barnfield rd SE18
79 N 16 Barnfield rd SE18
60 C 11 Barnfield rd W5
81 P 15 Barnfield rd Blvdr
25 U 5 Barnfield rd Edg
157 T 20 Barnfield rd S Croy
125 X 14 Barnfield Wood clo W Wkhm
125 X 13 Barnfield Wood rd Beckhm
58 M 7 Barnham rd Grnfd
59 N 8 Barnham rd Grnfd
58 A 14 Barnham st SE1
126 C 13 Barnhill av Brom
43 W 9 Barnhill rd Wemb
100 C 5 Barnlea clo Felt
56 C 15 Barnmead gdns Dgnhm
110 G 20 Barnmead rd Beckhm
56 B 15 Barnmead rd Dgnhm
117 X 10 Barnsbury clo New Mald
117 U 20 Barnsbury cres Surb
48 E 19 Barnsbury gro N7
117 V 20 Barnsbury la Surb
48 F 20 Barnsbury pk N1
133 S 5 Barnsbury rd N1
133 T 1 Barnsbury sq N1
133 V 1 Barnsbury st N1
133 R 1 Barnsbury ter N1
129 P 16 Barnsdale av E14
9 S 17 Barnsdale yd W9
63 N 12 Barnsley st E1
135 X 17 Barnsley st E1
90 G 13 Barnwell rd SW2
77 T 2 Barnwood ct E16
133 S 9 Baron cl N1
36 C 9 Baron gdns Ilf
120 K 8 Baron gro Mitch
65 O 14 Baron rd E16
55 V 3 Baron rd Dgnhm
133 T 9 Baron st N1
55 N 11 Baroness rd E2
31 X 4 Baronet gro N17
31 X 4 Baronet rd N17
144 L 10 Barons Ct rd W14
145 N 10 Barons Ct rd W14
59 W 18 Barons ga Barnt
144 K 8 Barons keep W14
145 N 8 Barons pl SE1
54 C 15 Barons the Twick
120 H 9 Barons wlk Mitch
84 C 17 Baronsfield rd Twick
86 G 2 Baronsmead rd SW13
72 M 7 Baronsmede W5
28 K 13 Baronsmere rd N2
76 G 13 Barque st E14
82 A 11 Barrack rd Hounsl
30 B 6 Barratt av N22
28 M 6 Barrenger rd N10
33 U 13 Barrett rd E17
139 V 6 Barrett st W1
61 X 7 Barretts Green rd NW10
49 T 13 Barretts gro N16
92 J 4 Barriedale SE14
107 P 9 Barringer sq SW17
53 W 17 Barrington rd E12
29 W 14 Barrington rd N8
90 H 7 Barrington rd SW9
97 W 6 Barrington rd Bxly Hth
153 X 1 Barrington rd Sutton
154 L 18 Barrow av Carsh
17 W 10 Barrow clo N21
154 J 15 Barrow Hedges clo Carsh
154 J 15 Barrow Hedges way Carsh
152 A 2 Barrow hill Worc Pk
152 A 2 Barrow Hill clo Worc
130 J 10 Barrow Hill rd NW8
22 A 8 Barrow Point av Pinn
22 A 6 Barrow Point la Pinn
107 Z 14 Barrow rd SW16
156 G 12 Barrow rd Croy
22 B 7 Barrowdene clo Pinn
17 W 9 Barrowell grn N21
19 O 11 Barrowfield clo N9
73 X 15 Barrowgate rd W4
43 X 20 Barrs rd NW10
31 V 19 Barry av N15
80 L 19 Barry av Bxly Hth
43 X 20 Barry rd NW10

61 X 1 Barry rd NW10
91 X 14 Barry rd SE22
92 B 7 Barset rd SE15
108 M 6 Barston rd SE27
140 L 3 Barter st WC1
79 W 11 Barth rd SE18
141 Z 2 Bartholomew clo EC1
142 F 5 Bartholomew la EC2
47 W 17 Bartholomew rd NW5
150 F 3 Bartholomew st SE1
47 U 18 Bartholomew vlls NW5
66 E 5 Bartle av E6
141 V 4 Bartlett ct EC4
64 E 13 Bartlett st E14
157 N 11 Bartlett st Croy
38 M 3 Bartlow gdns Rom
56 J 5 Barton av Rom
97 Z 12 Barton clo Bxly Hth
117 Z 4 Barton grn New Mald
144 L 10 Barton rd W14
57 V 5 Barton rd Hornch
115 Z 15 Barton rd Sidcp
148 H 2 Barton st SW1
92 J 14 Bartram clo Sutton
5 F 3 Bartrams la Barnt
50 K 17 Bartrip st E9
52 H 11 Barwick rd E7
125 S 20 Barwood av W Wkhm
100 G 5 Basden gro Felt
55 P 20 Basedale rd Dgnhm
61 Z 11 Bashley rd NW10
66 E 8 Basil av E6
139 O 19 Basil st SW3
145 O 1 Basil st SW3
35 W 5 Basildon av Ilf
154 B 19 Basildon clo Sutton
80 B 11 Basildon rd SE2
92 J 6 Basildon rd Bxly Hth
98 A 16 Basing dri Bxly
45 U 4 Basing hill NW11
43 O 5 Basing hill Wemb
137 O 4 Basing st W11
27 Z 10 Basing way N3
28 A 9 Basing way N3
91 O 10 Basingdon way SE5
142 D 3 Basinghall av EC2
154 B 18 Basinghall gdns Sutton
142 D 4 Basinghall st EC2
134 B 3 Basire st N1
88 J 18 Baskerville rd SW18
95 P 13 Basket gdns SE9
89 P 7 Basnett rd SW11
91 U 12 Bassano st SE22
79 W 17 Bassant rd SE18
74 E 7 Bassein Pk rd W12
58 K 16 Basset way Grnfd
154 B 20 Bassett clo Sutton
71 O 19 Bassett gdns Islwth
136 J 3 Bassett rd W10
47 P 17 Bassett st NW5
88 D 18 Bassingham rd SW18
42 G 19 Bassingham rd Wemb
142 C 3 Bassishaw highwalk EC2
67 W 8 Bastable av Bark
68 B 7 Bastable av Bark
79 Z 15 Bastion rd SE2
80 A 14 Bastion rd SE2
133 Z 16 Bastwick st EC1
134 A 16 Bastwick st EC1
87 Y 2 Basuto rd SW6
75 W 20 Batavia rd SE14
133 T 6 Batchelor st N1
63 Y 19 Bate st E14
20 B 18 Bateman rd E4
140 F 6 Bateman st W1
140 F 6 Batemans bldgs W1
134 L 15 Batemans row EC2
128 F 12 Bates clo Croy
133 S 17 Bath ct EC1
53 N 19 Bath rd E12
19 O 8 Bath rd N9
74 B 10 Bath rd W4
99 Z 18 Bath rd Drtfrd
82 D 7 Bath rd Hounsl
37 Y 18 Bath rd Rom
30 D 14 Bath st EC1
150 A 2 Bath ter SE1
105 P 7 Bathgate rd SW19
62 K 7 Bathurst gdns NW10
128 A 10 Bathurst gdns NW10
138 G 8 Bathurst ms W2
53 Z 5 Bathurst rd Ilf

138 G 8 Bathurst st W2
78 K 11 Bathway SE18
49 U 10 Batley pl N16
49 U 10 Batley rd N16
8 A 6 Batley rd Enf
74 K 2 Batman clo W12
144 M 8 Batoum gdns W6
144 D 1 Batoum gdns W6
58 A 18 Batson st SE18
74 H 6 Batson st W12
120 F 5 Batsworth rd Mitch
88 K 9 Batten st SW11
111 Y 6 Battersby rd SE6
146 J 18 Battersea br SW11
88 K 2 Battersea Br rd SW11
146 J 19 Battersea Br rd SW11
88 G 1 Battersea Church rd SW11
146 J 20 Battersea Church rd SW11
88 G 2 Battersea High st SW11
88 M 1 Battersea park SW11
147 M 1 Battersea park SW11
147 Z 20 Battersea Pk rd SW11
89 O 2 Battersea Pk rd SW11
88 J 11 Battersea Pk rd SW11
148 A 18 Battersea Pk rd SW8
88 J 11 Battersea ri SW11
133 W 2 Battishill st N1
142 J 13 Battle Br la SE1
132 J 9 Battle Bridge rd NW1
81 Y 11 Battle rd Erith
48 H 15 Battledean rd N5
143 T 5 Batty st E1
111 Z 5 Baudwin rd SE6
87 X 19 Baulk the SW18
122 B 3 Bavant rd SW16
42 A 4 Bavaria rd N4
90 M 5 Bavent rd SE5
91 V 13 Bawdale rd SE5
36 L 14 Bawdsey av Ilf
15 Y 11 Bawtry rd N20
135 S 11 Baxendale E2
15 R 8 Baxendale N20
65 Z 17 Baxter rd E16
49 O 18 Baxter rd N1
31 X 10 Baxter rd N17
18 M 13 Baxter rd N18
53 Y 15 Baxter rd Ilf
94 M 11 Bayfield rd SE9
128 E 13 Bayford rd NW10
63 N 1 Bayford st E8
135 X 1 Bayford st E8
132 B 7 Bayham pl NW1
72 A 1 Bayham rd W13
73 Y 7 Bayham rd W4
120 B 8 Bayham rd Mrdn
131 Z 3 Bayham st NW1
132 A 4 Bayham st NW1
140 F 2 Bayley st WC1
141 S 19 Baylis rd SE1
8 K 7 Baynes clo Enf
46 G 17 Baynes ms NW3
132 C 2 Baynes st NW1
74 K 16 Bayonne rd W6
49 V 10 Bayston rd N16
137 W 11 Bayswater rd W2
138 K 9 Bayswater rd W2
63 Z 14 Baythorne st E3
90 D 12 Baytree rd SW2
117 X 13 Bazalgette clo New Mald
117 X 13 Bazalgette gdns New Mald
64 F 19 Bazely st E14
18 A 18 Bazile rd N21
100 H 5 Beach gro Felt
100 J 5 Beach way Twick
111 V 10 Beachborough rd Brom
52 A 8 Beachcroft rd E11
106 L 6 Beachcroft rd SW17
64 A 1 Beachy rd E3
48 A 15 Beacon hill N7
93 W 15 Beacon rd SE13
77 S 17 Beaconsfield clo SE3
73 U 14 Beaconsfield clo W4
51 U 8 Beaconsfield rd E10
65 O 12 Beaconsfield rd E16
32 M 20 Beaconsfield rd E17
34 B 7 Beaconsfield rd E18

16 C 15 Beaconsfield rd N11
31 T 14 Beaconsfield rd N15
18 J 12 Beaconsfield rd N9
77 R 17 Beaconsfield rd SE3
113 R 8 Beaconsfield rd SE9
73 X 9 Beaconsfield rd W4
72 F 5 Beaconsfield rd W5
127 O 6 Beaconsfield rd Brom
123 O 14 Beaconsfield rd Croy
9 U 1 Beaconsfield rd Enf
117 Z 5 Beaconsfield rd New Mald
70 D 4 Beaconsfield rd S'hall
117 N 18 Beaconsfield rd Surb
84 B 17 Beaconsfield rd Twick
66 K 18 Beaconsfield st E6
37 X 19 Beaconsfield ter Rom
144 K 3 Beaconsfield Ter rd W14
87 V 3 Beaconsfield wlk SW6
33 Y 7 Beacontree av E17
55 T 8 Beacontree av Dgnhm
52 C 2 Beacontree rd E11
108 K 9 Beadman st SE27
92 F 20 Beadnell rd SE23
74 M 11 Beadon rd W6
144 C 6 Beadon rd W6
126 E 10 Beadon rd Brom
119 V 6 Beaford gro SW20
140 B 8 Beak st W1
97 O 2 Beal clo Well
53 W 7 Beal rd Ilf
17 W 17 Beale clo N13
63 X 4 Beale rd E3
65 S 5 Beale st E13
69 V 4 Beam av Dgnhm
56 M 20 Beam way Dgnhm
35 Y 9 Beaminster gdns Ilf
10 A 6 Beamish dri Bushey
18 L 6 Beamish rd N9
97 W 11 Bean rd Bxly Hth
113 X 10 Beanshaw SE9
37 Z 9 Beansland gro Rom
141 W 4 Bear all EC4
142 B 12 Bear gdns SE1
141 Y 14 Bear la SE1
100 A 11 Bear rd Felt
140 G 10 Bear st WC2
109 T 15 Beardell st SE19
102 K 18 Berdfield rd Kingst
92 K 14 Bearstead ri SE4
111 O 20 Bearsted ter Becknhm
122 C 4 Beatrice av SW16
42 L 16 Beatrice av Wemb
33 O 16 Beatrice rd E17
48 G 1 Beatrice rd N4
19 P 2 Beatrice rd N9
151 U 6 Beatrice rd SE1
84 L 13 Beatrice rd Rich
70 D 3 Beatrice rd S'hall
65 S 12 Beatrice rd E13
75 U 1 Beatson st SE16
49 T 11 Beatty rd N16
11 S 18 Beatty st Stanm
132 A 7 Beatty st NW1
35 X 12 Beattyville gdns Ilf
146 M 2 Beauchamp pl SW3
147 N 3 Beauchamp pl SW3
52 H 20 Beauchamp rd E7
123 P 2 Beauchamp rd SE19
88 K 10 Beauchamp rd SW11
153 Y 9 Beauchamp rd Sutton
83 Z 19 Beauchamp rd Twick
141 T 1 Beauchamp st EC1
86 K 8 Beauchamp ter SW15
74 L 8 Beaufort av W6
144 A 1 Beauclerc rd W6
23 Z 11 Beaufort av Harrow
24 A 11 Beaufort av Harrow
61 N 13 Beaufort clo W5
38 J 12 Beaufort clo Rom
102 C 10 Beaufort ct Rich
27 Y 12 Beaufort dri NW11
26 L 19 Beaufort gdns NW4
147 N 2 Beaufort gdns SW3
146 M 1 Beaufort gdns SW3
Hounsl
53 W 4 Beaufort gdns Ilf
60 M 15 Beaufort rd W5
61 N 13 Beaufort rd W5
116 J 10 Beaufort rd Kingst
102 D 10 Beaufort rd Rich

84 E 18	Beaufort rd Twick	
146 H 15	Beaufort st SW3	
152 G 18	Beaufort way Epsom	
31 T 2	Beaufoy rd N17	
89 R 6	Beaufoy st SE11	
109 Z 10	Beaulah av SE26	
109 P 19	Beaulah hill SE19	
110 A 10	Beaulieu av SE26	
26 B 12	Beaulieu clo NW6	
121 O 1	Beaulieu clo Mitch	
84 G 17	Beaulieu clo Twick	
17 Y 4	Beaulieu gdns N21	
39 R 5	Beauly way Rom	
113W 10	Beaumanor gdns SE9	
35 N 2	Beaumaris dri Wdfd Grn	
132 C 17	Beaumont WC1	
145 O 9	Beaumont av W8	
22 L 19	Beaumont av Harrow	
84 M 9	Beaumont av Rich	
42 E 14	Beaumont av Wemb	
145 U 10	Beaumont cres W14	
57 X 18	Beaumont cres Rainhm	
63 S 13	Beaumont gro E1	
59 V 1	Beaumont ms W1	
51 R 2	Beaumont rd SE19	
65 W 9	Beaumont rd E13	
108 L 15	Beaumont rd SE19	
87 R 18	Beaumont rd SW19	
73 W 8	Beaumont rd W4	
47 Z 2	Beaumont ri N19	
63 T 13	Beaumont st W1	
131 V 20	Beaumont st W1	
139 V 1	Beaumont st W1	
91 U 15	Beauval rd SE22	
114 D 2	Beaverbank rd Sidcp	
82 A 9	Beavers la Hounsl	
114 J 14	Beaverwood rd Chisl	
74 G 12	Beavor la W6	
79 U 12	Bebbington rd SE18	
54 J 17	Beccles dri Bark	
63 Z 19	Beccles st E14	
124 E 6	Beck la Becknhm	
135 X 4	Beck rd E8	
120 M 13	Beck rd Mitch	
150 C 11	Beck st SE17	
18 C 11	Beckenham gdns N9	
125 X 4	Beckenham gro Brom	
111 S 13	Beckenham Hill rd Becknhm	
126 A 3	Beckenham la Brom	
111 P 18	Beckenham Pl pk Becknhm	
111 T 16	Beckenham place Becknhm	
111 T 15	Beckenham Place park Becknhm	
124 K 2	Beckenham rd Becknhm	
125 U 18	Beckenham rd W Wkhm	
66 J 9	Becket av E6	
123 X 14	Becket clo SE25	
23 X 16	Becket fold Har	
100 S 13	Beckett wlk SE28	
110 H 15	Beckett wlk Bcknhm	
123 V 15	Beckford rd Croy	
74 E 5	Beckford wlk W12	
66 E 15	Beckton gdns E6	
65 T 15	Beckton rd E16	
66 H 15	Beckton rd E6	
124 H 8	Beckway Becknhm	
125 N 7	Beckway Becknhm	
121 X 4	Beckway rd SW16	
150 H 7	Beckway st SE17	
91 O 14	Beckwith rd SE24	
107 R 14	Beclands rd SW17	
107 Y 8	Becmead av NW10	
24 B 15	Becmead av Harrow	
100 S 13	Becondale rd SE19	
56 A 7	Becontree av Dgnhm	
87 U 11	Bective pl SW15	
52 G 11	Bective rd E7	
87 U 11	Bective rd SW15	
66 E 15	Becton pl E6	
98 H 1	Becton pl Erith	
7 Y 4	Bedale rd Enf	
142 E 14	Bedale st SE1	
156 C 2	Beddington Farm rd Croy	
122 B 19	Beddington Farm rd Croy	
155 P 14	Beddington gdns Carsh	
155 Y 11	Beddington gro Wallgtn	
121W 16	Beddington la Croy	
155 Z 3	Beddington la Wallgtn	

36 K 20	Beddington rd Ilf	
98 C 2	Beddonwell rd Bxly Hth	
63 Y 14	Bede rd E3	
37 T 18	Bede rd Rom	
115 Y 14	Bedens rd Sidcp	
130 G 2	Bedford av WC1	
4 J 15	Bedford av Barnt	
29 P 3	Bedford clo N10	
140 K 10	Bedford ct WC2	
137 V 15	Bedford gdns W8	
107 V 6	Bedford hill SW16	
144 M 17	Bedford pass SW6	
122 M 20	Bedford pk Croy	
140 K 1	Bedford pl WC1	
132 K 20	Bedford pl WC1	
123 O 20	Bedford pl Croy	
33 O 8	Bedford rd E17	
34 E 9	Bedford rd E18	
66 H 3	Bedford rd E6	
13 N 9	Bedford rd NW7	
31 R 13	Bedford rd N15	
28 J 10	Bedford rd N2	
30 A 6	Bedford rd N22	
29 Y 17	Bedford rd N8	
18 M 1	Bedford rd N9	
19 N 2	Bedford rd N9	
89 Z 8	Bedford rd SW9	
72 A 1	Bedford rd W13	
73 Z 9	Bedford rd W4	
72 K 15	Bedford rd Brentf	
9 S 10	Bedford rd Enf	
23 N 17	Bedford rd Harrow	
53 Z 10	Bedford rd Ilf	
54 A 10	Bedford rd Ilf	
114 H 7	Bedford rd Sidcp	
141 O 1	Bedford rd Twick	
101 P 5	Bedford rd Twick	
153 N 14	Bedford rd Worc Pk	
141 O 1	Bedford row WC1	
140 G 2	Bedford sq WC1	
140 K 9	Bedford st WC2	
48 D 7	Bedford ter N7	
132 H 18	Bedford way WC1	
140 J 10	Bedfordbury WC2	
105 T 3	Bedgebury gdns SW19	
94 M 11	Bedgebury rd SE9	
112 F 6	Bedivere rd Brom	
96 M 20	Bedonwell rd SE2	
81 O 16	Bedonwell rd Blvdr	
81 R 17	Bedonwell rd Bxly Hth	
109 H 17	Bedwardine rd SE19	
31 R 4	Bedwell rd N17	
81 R 14	Bedwell rd Blvdr	
65 U 15	Beeby rd E16	
15 X 6	Beech av N20	
74 B 3	Beech av W3	
72 J 8	Beech av Brentf	
21 V 8	Beech av Buck Hl	
96 M 19	Beech av Sidcp	
86 G 17	Beech clo SW15	
104 L 15	Beech clo SW19	
154 L 2	Beech clo Carsh	
8 L 20	Beech clo Enf	
57 X 11	Beech clo Hornch	
127 T 2	Beech copse Brom	
28 L 9	Beech dri N2	
72 J 8	Beech gdns W5	
56 J 20	Beech gdns Dgnhm	
121 X 10	Beech gro Mitch	
117 Y 6	Beech gro New Mald	
33 W 1	Beech Hall cres E4	
33 V 2	Beech Hall rd E4	
20 J 20	Beech Hall rd E4	
5 U 4	Beech hill Barnt	
5 S 5	Beech Hill av Barnt	
5 V 7	Beech Hill park Barnt	
157 O 6	Beech Ho rd Croy	
21 U 9	Beech la Buck Hl	
15 U 19	Beech lawns N12	
17 N 19	Beech rd N11	
122 B 4	Beech rd SW16	
134 A 20	Beech st EC1	
38 L 14	Beech st Rom	
11 S 17	Beech Tree clo Stanm	
21 O 4	Beech Tree glade E4	
154 A 11	Beech Tree pl Sutton	
43 X 20	Beech way NW10	
12 M 18	Beech wlk NW7	
99 X 10	Beech wlk Dtford	
113W 17	Beechcroft Chisl	
45 V 1	Beechcroft av NW1	
40 G 2	Beechcroft av Harrow	
117W 2	Beechcroft av New Mald	
70 D 2	Beechcroft av S'hall	
43 N 10	Beechcroft gdns Wemb	

34 H 8	Beechcroft rd E18	
85 W 9	Beechcroft rd SW14	
17 R 8	Beechdale N21	
90 D 16	Beechdale rd SW2	
22 D 11	Beechen gro Pinn	
106 K 6	Beeches clo SW17	
119 T 20	Beeches rd Sutton	
154 H 19	Beeches wlk Carsh	
51 W 15	Beechey pl E15	
156 L 9	Beechfield ct S Croy	
38 L 20	Beechfield gdns Rom	
31 N 18	Beechfield rd N4	
110 M 1	Beechfield rd SE6	
126 M 3	Beechfield rd Brom	
95 V 12	Beechhill rd SE9	
89 N 2	Beechmere rd SW11	
111 Z 13	Beechmore clo Brom	
153 R 3	Beechmore gdns Sutton	
89 N 2	Beechmore rd SW8	
59 S 14	Beechmount av W7	
107 R 19	Beecholme av Mitch	
50 A 9	Beecholme rd E5	
98 M 4	Beechroft av Bxly Hth	
102 J 11	Beechrow Rich	
97W 17	Beechway Bxly	
27W 11	Beechwood av N3	
58 J 8	Beechwood av Grnfd	
40 L 9	Beechwood av Harrow	
85 P 2	Beechwood av Rich	
122 H 8	Beechwood av Thntn Hth	
12 M 16	Beechwood clo NW7	
97 Y 7	Beechwood cres Bxly Hth	
21 P 17	Beechwood dri Wdfd Grn	
40 L 9	Beechwood gdns Harrow	
35 U 14	Beechwood gdns Ilf	
34 E 11	Beechwood pk E18	
49 U 18	Beechwood rd E8	
29 Y 11	Beechwood rd N8	
157 R 19	Beechwood rd S Croy	
45 Z 8	Beechworth clo NW3	
92 J 12	Beecroft rd SE4	
35 T 15	Beehive la Ilf	
90 F 9	Beehive pl SW19	
120 B 8	Beeleigh rd Mrdn	
127 X 2	Been ct E4	
86 H 20	Beesborough rd SW16	
147 Y 2	Beeston pl SW1	
5 U 19	Beeston pl Barnt	
11 T 1	Beethoven rd Borhm Wd	
128 L 11	Beethoven st W10	
94 K 2	Begbie rd SE3	
152 E 15	Beggars Hill Epsom	
62 E 18	Begonia wlk W12	
89 T 17	Beira st SW12	
55 U 1	Belfairs dri Rom	
49 U 6	Belfast rd N16	
123 Z 10	Belfast rd SE25	
78 H 12	Belford gro SE18	
92 C 4	Belfort rd SE15	
49 T 13	Belfrade rd N16	
129 Z 7	Belgrave gdns NW8	
130 A 6	Belgrave gdns NW8	
6 J 15	Belgrave gdns N14	
11 S 15	Belgrave gdns Stanm	
147 V 1	Belgrave ms SW1	
147 T 1	Belgrave Ms w SW1	
147 U 3	Belgrave pl SW1	
51 U 3	Belgrave rd E10	
52 F 4	Belgrave rd E11	
65 X 11	Belgrave rd E13	
33 O 18	Belgrave rd E17	
123 V 8	Belgrave rd SE25	
148 C 8	Belgrave rd SW1	
74 E 20	Belgrave rd SW13	
53 T 4	Belgrave rd Ilf	
120 F 5	Belgrave rd Mitch	
147 U 1	Belgrave sq SW1	
63 U 17	Belgrave st E1	
21 S 11	Belgrave ter Wdfd Grn	
147 X 3	Belgrave yd SW1	
139 S 20	Belgrave Ms north SW1	
139 T 20	Belgrave sq SW1	
132 K 12	Belgrove st WC1	
91 P 1	Belham st SE5	
90 J 8	Belinda pl SW9	
48 E 20	Belitha vlls N1	

39 Y 4	Bell av Rom	
87 S 18	Bell drive SW18	
56 K 9	Bell Farm av Dgnhr	
110 J 12	Bell green SE26	
110 K 10	Bell Green la SE26	
142 H 7	Bell Inn yd EC3	
142 M 2	Bell la E1	
143 N 3	Bell la E1	
77 R 2	Bell la E16	
26 N 14	Bell la NW4	
9 U 4	Bell la Enf	
101 Z 1	Bell la Twick	
8 C 7	Bell rd Enf	
82 J 9	Bell rd Hounsl	
130 K 20	Bell st NW1	
138 J 1	Bell st NW1	
78 K 8	Bell Water ga SE18	
142 D 10	Bell Wharf la EC4	
141 S 6	Bell yd WC2	
141 S 7	Bell yd WC2	
24 B 5	Bellamy dri Stanm	
20 F 20	Bellamy rd E4	
89 R 18	Bellamy st SW12	
107 Z 3	Bellasis av SE2	
110 X 8	Belle grn SE26	
33 W 7	Belle Vue rd E17	
88 K 20	Belle Vue rd SW17	
90 E 8	Bellefields rd SW9	
96 J 5	Bellegrove clo Welling	
91 V 4	Bellenden rd SE15	
20 B 7	Bellestaines E4	
88 L 14	Belleville rd SW11	
59 P 2	Bellevue Grnfd	
10 C 5	Bellevue la Bushey	
122 L 7	Bellevue pk Thntn Hth	
16 B 16	Bellevue rd N11	
86 G 5	Bellevue rd SW13	
106 K 1	Bellevue rd SW17	
60 A 12	Bellevue rd W13	
98 A 13	Bellevue rd Bxly Hth	
116 K 8	Bellevue rd Kingst	
106 E 7	Bellew st SW17	
10 B 20	Bellfield av Harrow	
96 G 5	Bellgrove rd Welling	
97 O 7	Bellgrove rd Welling	
63 V 3	Bellhaven st E3	
111 P 8	Bellingham grn SE6	
111 S 6	Bellingham rd SE6	
77 N 12	Bellot st SE10	
87 X 5	Bells all SW6	
151 S 20	Bells Gdns rd SE15	
4 D 14	Bells hill Barnt	
108 E 12	Belltrees gro SE16	
92 F 11	Bellwood rd SE15	
17 O 15	Belmont av N13	
30 L 11	Belmont av N17	
18 L 5	Belmont av N9	
5 Z 17	Belmont av Barnt	
6 A 14	Belmont av Barnt	
118 H 10	Belmont av New Mald	
70 B 9	Belmont av S'hall	
96 G 6	Belmont av Welling	
60 M 2	Belmont av Wemb	
24 A 6	Belmont cir Harrow	
6 A 14	Belmont clo Barnt	
21 U 13	Belmont clo Wdfd Grn	
93 X 8	Belmont gro SE13	
73 X 11	Belmont gro W4	
93 Y 8	Belmont hill SE13	
114 B 10	Belmont la Chisl	
24 D 3	Belmont la Stanm	
93 X 10	Belmont pk SE13	
33 S 19	Belmont Pk rd E10	
73 Y 12	Belmont pl W4	
64 M 9	Belmont rd E15	
30 L 12	Belmont rd N17	
124 A 13	Belmont rd SE25	
89 W 8	Belmont rd SW8	
73 X 12	Belmont rd W4	
124 L 4	Belmont rd Becknhm	
113 Z 12	Belmont rd Chisl	
81 S 20	Belmont rd Erith	
98 F 1	Belmont rd Erith	
23 X 10	Belmont rd Harrow	
54 C 9	Belmont rd Ilf	
101 P 3	Belmont rd Twick	
155 T 11	Belmont rd Wallgtn	
153 V 18	Belmont ri Sutton	
47 P 19	Belmont st NW1	
89 Y 2	Belmore st SW8	
133 T 1	Belper st E1	
50 C 17	Belsham st E9	
46 J 16	Belsize av NW3	
17 R 19	Belsize av N13	
72 C 8	Belsize av W13	
46 G 16	Belsize cres NW3	
46 H 15	Belsize ct NW3 · ·	
154 B 7	Belsize gdns Sutton	

Ref	Name
46 K 17	Belsize gro NW3
46 F 18	Belsize la NW3
46 G 16	Belsize ms NW3
46 F 19	Belsize pk NW3
46 J 17	Belsize Pk gdns NW3
46 G 16	Belsize pl NW3
46 E 20	Belsize rd NW6
29 Z 3	Belsize rd NW6
30 D 1	Belsize rd NW6
23 P 1	Belsize rd Harrow
46 H 18	Belsize sq NW3
46 G 17	Belsize ter NW3
78 F 10	Belson rd SE18
05 P 6	Beltane dri SW19
51 Z 12	Belton rd E11
52 J 20	Belton rd E7
47 G 17	Belton rd NW2
31 S 10	Belton rd N17
15 O 9	Belton rd Sidcp
64 A 14	Belton way E3
87 Z 5	Beltran rd SW6
01 W 10	Beltwood rd Blvdr
05 T 12	Belvedere av SW19
35 Z 8	Belvedere av Ilf
41 Z 19	Belvedere bldgs SE1
01 T 13	Belvedere clo Tedd
01 T 13	Belvedere dri SW19
05 S 13	Belvedere gro SW19
41 Z 19	Belvedere pl SE1
50 J 3	Belvedere rd E10
41 O 18	Belvedere rd SE1
09 U 17	Belvedere rd SE19
80 H 3	Belvedere rd SE2
98 B 7	Belvedere rd Bxly Hth
05 S 12	Belvedere sq SW19
24 K 19	Belvedere way Harrow
91 Y 19	Belvoir rd SE22
40 H 20	Belvue clo Grnfd
58 H 2	Belvue park Grnfd
40 J 20	Belvue rd Grnfd
32 M 2	Bemerton st N1
87 P 8	Bemish rd SW15
32 L 9	Bemsted rd E17
150 H 10	Ben Cope st SE17
97 P 2	Ben Hill rd SE5
63 U 15	Ben Johnson rd E1
68 B 1	Ben Tillet clo Bark
79 X 11	Benares rd SE18
74 K 8	Benbow rd W6
44 A 1	Benbow rd W6
76 B 15	Benbow st SW8
111 U 12	Benbury clo Brom
57 V 13	Benchfield S Croy
10?W 17	Bencroft rd SW16
30 M 20	Bendall ms NW1
87 D 7	Bendemeer rd SW15
66 D 2	Bendish rd E6
80 A 12	Bendmore av SE2
88 A 20	Bendon valley SW18
90 E 7	Benedict clo SW9
120 G 7	Benedict rd Mitch
C 12	Benenden grn Brom
?21 Z 3	Benett gdns SW16
154 D 6	Benfleet clo Sutton
142 G 7	Bengal ct EC3
23 R 7	Bengal rd Ilf
23?R 7	Bengarth dri Harrow
58 A 3	Bengarth rd Grnfd
90 L 7	Bengeworth rd SE5
41 Z 8	Bengeworth rd Harrow
11 N 15	Benhale clo Stanm
59 U 15	Benham rd W7
88 F 9	Benham st SW11
154 B 9	Benhill av Sutton
150 G 20	Benhill rd SE5
154 C 5	Benhill rd Sutton
154 C 5	Benhill Wood rd Sutton
154 B 6	Benhilton gdns Sutton
57 Y 11	Benhurst av Hornch
108 E 12	Benhurst la SW16
93 Y 18	Benin st SE13
133 W 20	Benjamin st EC1
64 J 17	Benledi st E14
59 Y 17	Benn st E9
88 K 13	Bennerley rd SW11
44 A 13	Bennet st SW1
96 M 5	Bennett clo Welling
93 S 13	Bennett gro SE13
94 C 6	Bennett pk SE3
65 X 13	Bennett rd E13
37 Z 20	Bennett rd Rom
74 A 15	Bennett st W4
158 K 4	Bennetts av Croy
59 S 3	Bennetts av Grnfd
158 K 3	Bennetts way Croy
148 H 3	Bennetts yd SW1
13 N 19	Benningholme rd Edg
31 P 5	Bennington rd N17
33 Y 2	Bennington rd Wdfd Grn
86 K 19	Bensby clo SW15
122 L 10	Bensham clo Thntn
122 L 3	Bensham gro Thntn Hth
122 J 10	Bensham la Thntn Hth
122 M 9	Bensham Mnr rd Thntn Hth
123 N 10	Bensham Mnr rd Thntn Hth
65 Z 7	Benson av E6
92 D 20	Benson rd SE23
156 G 6	Benson rd Croy
49 X 10	Benthall rd N16
134 B 1	Bentham ct N1
50 F 18	Bentham rd E9
139 V 3	Bentinck ms W1
139 V 4	Bentinck st W1
36 B 17	Bentley dri Ilf
10 G 12	Bentley priory Stanm
49 S 18	Bentley rd N1
10 K 17	Bentley way Stanm
21 S 9	Bentley way Wdfd Grn
54 D 3	Benton rd Ilf
108 M 11	Bentons la SE27
109 N 11	Bentons ri SE27
55 Z 7	Bentry clo Dgnhm
55 Z 7	Bentry rd Dgnhm
56 A 7	Bentry rd Dgnhm
136 A 6	Bentworth rd W12
62 J 18	Bentworth rd W12
48 F 14	Benwell rd N7
63 Z 8	Benworth st E3
88 M 13	Berber rd SW11
114 A 4	Bercta rd SE9
63 T 19	Bere st E1
128 F 13	Berens rd NW10
15 Y 8	Beresford av N20
59 S 15	Beresford av W7
117 T 19	Beresford av Surb
84 F 15	Beresford av Wemb
61 P 2	Beresford av Wemb
21 Y 13	Beresford dri Buck Hl
8 D 14	Beresford gdns Enf
82 E 14	Beresford gdns Hounsl
37 Z 17	Beresford gdns Rom
33 R 4	Beresford rd E17
20 M 4	Beresford rd E4
28 J 11	Beresford rd N2
49 N 15	Beresford rd N5
30 H 15	Beresford rd N8
23 O 16	Beresford rd Harrow
102 M 20	Beresford rd Kingst
103 N 20	Beresford rd Kingst
117 V 8	Beresford rd New Mald
153 V 18	Beresford st Sutton
78 M 10	Beresford sq SE18
78 L 9	Beresford st SE18
48 M 15	Beresford ter N5
74 E 13	Berestede rd W6
50 F 17	Berger rd E9
50 E 17	Berger rd E9
35 P 14	Bergholt av Ilf
49 R 1	Bergholt cres N16
97 X 2	Berkeley av Bxly Hth
41 S 18	Berkeley av Grnfd
35 Y 7	Berkeley av Ilf
38 L 2	Berkeley av Rom
16 G 1	Berkeley ct N14
18 A 2	Berkeley gdns N21
17 V 14	Berkeley gdns W8
139 R 5	Berkeley ms W1
105 P 17	Berkeley pl SW19
53 R 16	Berkeley rd E12
25 P 14	Berkeley rd NW9
31 P 19	Berkeley rd N15
29 Y 17	Berkeley rd N8
86 F 1	Berkeley rd SW13
139 Y 11	Berkeley sq W1
139 Z 12	Berkeley st W1
70 A 18	Berkeley waye Hounsl
81 R 12	Berkhampstead rd Blvdr
81 S 12	Berkhamstead rd Belv
43 O 18	Berkhamsted av Wemb
5 U 18	Berkley cres Barnt
131 R 1	Berkley rd NW1
17 S 20	Berkshire gdns N13
18 M 17	Berkshire gdns N18
50 M 16	Berkshire rd E9
51 N 17	Berkshire rd E9
121 Z 10	Berkshire way Mitch
122 A 10	Berkshire way Mitch
44 C 13	Bermans way NW10
150 K 1	Bermondsey sq SE1
142 J 17	Bermondsey st SE1
143 U 18	Bermondsey Wall east SE16
143 S 18	Bermondsey Wall west SE16
72 B 7	Bernard av W13
105 W 12	Bernard gdns SW19
31 V 15	Bernard rd N15
56 K 1	Bernard rd Rom
155 R 9	Bernard rd Wallgtn
132 K 18	Bernard st WC1
11 R 19	Bernays clo Stanm
90 D 9	Bernays gro SW9
122 K 10	Berne rd Thntn Hth
158 M 4	Bernel dri Croy
140 C 2	Berners ms W1
140 C 4	Berners pl W1
133 V 6	Berners rd N1
30 E 6	Berners rd N22
140 C 3	Berners st W1
21 N 11	Bernwell rd E4
109 P 12	Berridge rd SE19
48 E 9	Berriman rd N7
40 E 5	Berriton rd Harrow
17 W 4	Berry clo N21
11 V 13	Berry hill Stanm
133 X 14	Berry pl EC1
133 X 16	Berry st EC1
44 A 19	Berry st NW10
72 J 8	Berry way W5
149 Y 10	Berryfield st SE17
95 Y 9	Berryhill SE9
95 Y 10	Berryhill gdns SE9
119 N 7	Berrylands SW20
117 R 12	Berrylands Surb
116 N 13	Berrylands rd Surb
117 N 13	Berrylands rd Surb
110 F 10	Berrymans la SE26
73 V 4	Berrymead gdns W3
73 X 8	Berrymede rd W4
122 K 12	Bert rd Thntn Hth
8 J 14	Bert way Enf
106 F 11	Bertal rd SW17
33 W 15	Berthan gdns E17
76 C 18	Berthon st SE8
44 G 18	Bertie rd NW10
110 G 14	Bertie rd SE26
105 X 18	Bertram cotts SW19
66 E 14	Bertram gdns E6
26 H 19	Bertram rd NW4
8 J 14	Bertram rd Enf
103 O 17	Bertram st Kingst
47 S 8	Bertram st N19
93 R 7	Bertrand st SE13
25 R 3	Bertridge grn Edg
96 H 17	Berwick cres Sidcp
65 X 18	Berwick rd E16
32 M 14	Berwick rd E17
30 H 4	Berwick rd N22
97 R 3	Berwick rd Welling
140 C 4	Berwick st W1
72 L 3	Berwyn av Hounsl
82 J 2	Berwyn av Hounsl
108 J 1	Berwyn rd SE21
85 S 10	Berwyn rd Rich
144 F 11	Beryl rd W6
45 S 11	Besant rd NW2
107 V 16	Besley st SW16
148 G 10	Bessborough gdns SW1
148 F 10	Bessborough pl SW1
104 G 1	Bessborough rd SW15
41 R 2	Bessborough rd Harrow
148 F 10	Bessborough st SW1
148 G 10	Bessborough way SW1
90 M 6	Bessemer rd SE5
91 N 5	Bessemer rd SE5
92 E 1	Besson st SE14
75 T 12	Bestwood st SE8
154 F 10	Betchworth clo Sutton
54 H 8	Betchworth rd Ilf
159 T 18	Betchworth way Croy
59 R 10	Betham rd Grnfd
23 T 14	Bethecar rd Harrow
97 U 8	Bethel rd Welling
65 P 11	Bethell av E16
53 W 1	Bethell av Ilf
110 M 19	Bethersden clo Becknhm
135 U 14	Bethnal Green rd E2
135 Z 11	Bethnal Green museum E2
15 Z 14	Bethume av N11
49 S 3	Bethune clo N16
61 Z 12	Bethune rd NW10
49 S 4	Bethune rd N16
150 C 17	Betwin rd SE15
20 M 13	Betoyne av E4
16 F 14	Betstyle rd N11
115 Z 4	Batterton dri Sidcp
140 K 5	Betterton st WC2
87 W 5	Bettridge rd SW6
65 V 19	Betts rd E16
143 V 9	Betts st E1
12 E 10	Beulah clo Edg
122 M 4	Beulah cres Thntn Hth
122 M 15	Beulah gro Croy
108 K 16	Beulah hill SE19
51 Y 8	Beulah rd E11
33 T 14	Beulah rd E17
105 V 17	Beulah rd SW19
153 Y 9	Beulah rd Sutton
122 L 5	Beulah rd Thntn Hth
99 W 9	Beult rd Drtford
68 A 1	Bevan av Bark
156 F 11	Bevan ct Croy
80 C 14	Bevan rd SE2
5 Z 13	Bevan rd Barnt
134 B 6	Bevan st N1
134 G 12	Bevenden st N1
104 E 19	Beverley av SW20
82 F 11	Beverley av Hounsl
96 J 19	Beverley av Sidcp
17 Y 6	Beverley clo N21
55 S 14	Beverley clo SW13
8 D 15	Beverley clo Enf
34 H 3	Beverley cres Wdfd Grn
92 M 7	Beverley ct SE4
25 R 9	Beverley dri Edg
27 T 20	Beverley gdns NW11
86 E 7	Beverley gdns SW13
23 Y 5	Beverley gdns Stanm
43 O 3	Beverley gdns Wemb
104 B 18	Beverley la Kingst
118 F 7	Beverley park New Mald
20 K 19	Beverley rd E4
66 B 9	Beverley rd E6
123 Z 3	Beverley rd SE20
86 E 6	Beverley rd SW13
74 C 14	Beverley rd W4
98 L 6	Beverley rd Bxly Hth
55 Z 12	Beverley rd Dgnhm
56 A 12	Beverley rd Dgnhm
102 E 20	Beverley rd Kingst
121?M 8	Beverley rd Mitch
118 F 9	Beverley rd New Mald
70 C 10	Beverley rd S'hall
152 L 3	Beverley rd Worc Pk
118 G 3	Beverley rd SW20
47 Y 10	Beverstock rd N19
90 C 12	Beverstone rd SW2
122 H 9	Beverstone rd Thntn Hth
107 N 13	Bevill allen SW17
107 N 13	Bevill Allen clo SW17
133 R 11	Bevin way WC1
136 M 1	Bevington rd W10
137 N 2	Bevington rd W10
125 P 3	Bevington rd Becknhm
143 U 18	Bevington st SE16
142 L 5	Bevis marks EC3
7 N 14	Bewcastle gdns Enf
48 F 20	Bewdley st N1
89 S 4	Bewick st SW8
143 Z 8	Bewley st E1
63 O 19	Bewley st E1
108 J 11	Bewlys rd SE27
100 A 3	Bexhill clo Felt
16 J 17	Bexhill rd N11
92 L 17	Bexhill rd SE4
85 W 8	Bexhill rd SW14
65 N 5	Bexhill wlk E15
99 P 12	Bexley clo Drtford
18 B 11	Bexley gdns N9
98 F 20	Bexley High st Bxly
99 P 12	Bexley la Drtford
115 U 18	Bexley la Sidcp
96 Z 14	Bexley rd SE9
154 L 11	Beynon rd Carsh
151 R 14	Bianca rd SE15
27 V 8	Bibsworth rd N3
85 S 8	Bicester rd Rich
131 P 20	Bickenhall st W1
106 M 14	Bickersteth rd SW17
47 U 8	Bickerton rd N19

127 U 5 Bickler Pk rd Brom
127 R 8 Bickley cres Brom
33 R 20 Bickley rd E10
127 P 4 Bickley rd Brom
106 L 13 Bickley st SW17
90 M 8 Bicknell rd SE5
8 F 5 Bicknoller rd Enf
126 C 12 Bidborough clo Brom
132 H 13 Bidborough st WC1
88 E 11 Bidcot st SW11
113 V 9 Biddenden way SE9
64 L 14 Bidder st E16
48 C 13 Biddestone rd N7
129 Y 14 Biddulph rd W9
156 L 20 Biddulph rd S Croy
9 X 3 Bideford av Enf
60 A 7 Bideford av Grnfd
25 O 5 Bideford clo Edg
18 E 2 Bideford gdns Enf
112 B 7 Bideford rd Brom
9 X 3 Bideford rd Enf
80 D 20 Bideford rd Welling
29 V 3 Bidwell gdns N11
92 A 3 Bidwell st E15
67 P 5 Bifrons st Bark
50 A 3 Big Hill E5
78 M 14 Big Nell rd SE18
64 G 2 Biggerstaff rd E15
48 E 7 Biggerstaff st N4
120 L 1 Biggin av Mitch
108 K 17 Biggin hill SE19
108 K 19 Biggin way SE19
108 H 19 Bigginwood rd SW16
87 O 8 Biggs row SW15
63 N 18 Bigland st E1
143 W 7 Bigland st E1
52 F 13 Bignold rd E7
28 A 17 Bigwood rd NW11
37 W 10 Billet clo Rom
32 J 5 Billet rd E17
33 O 3 Billet rd E17
37 V 10 Billet rd Rom
145 Y 17 Billing pl SW10
145 Z 16 Billing rd SW10
145 Y 17 Billing st SW6
76 G 16 Billingsgate st SE10
75 T 20 Billington rd SE14
142 K 7 Billiter sq EC3
142 K 7 Billiter st EC3
78 G 11 Billson st E14
113 O 10 Bilsby gro SE9
59 Z 3 Bilton rd Grnfd
60 D 3 Bilton rd Grnfd
9 X 4 Bilton way Enf
146 B 8 Bina gdns SW5
7 R 12 Bincote rd Enf
74 E 7 Binden rd W12
90 A 3 Binfield rd SW4
157 U 10 Binfield rd S Croy
132 L 4 Bingfield st N1
133 N 3 Bingfield st N1
131 T 19 Bingham pl W1
123 Y 20 Bingham rd Croy
49 O 17 Bingham st N1
65 X 17 Bingley rd E16
59 N 14 Bingley rd Grnfd
139 V 8 Binney st SW1
73 Z 13 Binns rd W4
10 H 17 Binyon cres Stanm
113 T 5 Birbetts rd SE9
17 Y 12 Birch av N13
91 Y 5 Birch clo SE15
72 B 19 Birch clo Brentf
38 G 10 Birch clo Rom
154 M 1 Birch cres Carsh
56 L 10 Birch gdns Dgnhm
94 C 18 Birch gro SE12
61 P 20 Birch gro W3
73 O 2 Birch gro W3
97 N 11 Birch gro Welling
158 G 10 Birch hill Croy
100 A 13 Birch rd Felt
38 G 10 Birch rd Rom
127 X 16 Birch row Brom
157 Z 2 Birch Tree way Croy
81 Y 15 Birch wlk Erith
121 S 1 Birch wlk Mitch
123 X 12 Birchanger rd SE25
55 V 1 Birchdale gdns Rom
52 M 15 Birchdale rd E7
43 X 6 Birchen clo NW9
7 F 19 Birches the N21
72 D 19 Birchfield clo Brentf
64 A 19 Birchfield st E14
142 G 1 Birchin la EC3
98 G 1 Birchington clo Bxly Hth
129 V 4 Birchington rd NW6
29 X 17 Birchington rd N8
117 O 10 Birchington rd Surb

88 M 18 Birchlands av SW12
89 N 18 Birchlands av SW12
48 L 11 Birchmore wlk N5
29 P 11 Birchwood av N10
124 L 8 Birchwood av Becknhm
115 R 7 Birchwood av Sidcp
155 R 4 Birchwood av Wallgtn
17 V 16 Birchwood ct N13
25 V 8 Birchwood ct Edg
107 R 11 Birchwood rd SW17
110 D 4 Bird In The hand SE23
139 V 6 Bird st W1
82 E 20 Bird wlk Twick
151 R 17 Bird-In-Bush rd SE15
127 O 4 Bird-In-Hand la Brom
94 M 8 Birdbrook rd SE3
140 C 19 Birdcage wlk SW1
127 S 12 Birdham clo Brom
157 P 9 Birdhurst av S Croy
157 P 9 Birdhurst gdns S Croy
88 C 12 Birdhurst rd SW18
106 J 16 Birdhurst rd SW19
157 R 10 Birdhurst rd S Croy
157 R 11 Birdhurst ri S Croy
98 G 3 Birds Farm av Rom
69 Y 2 Birdwood clo Dgnhm
61 W 19 Birkbeck av W3
59 O 3 Birkbeck av Grnfd
89 R 8 Birkbeck gdns Wdfd Grn
73 X 4 Birkbeck gro W3
108 K 2 Birkbeck hill SE21
108 K 2 Birkbeck pl SE21
49 U 16 Birkbeck rd E8
13 S 16 Birkbeck rd NW7
15 O 17 Birkbeck rd N12
31 U 5 Birkbeck rd N17
30 A 13 Birkbeck rd N8
106 B 14 Birkbeck rd SW19
73 X 3 Birkbeck rd W3
72 E 10 Birkbeck rd W5
124 D 4 Birkbeck rd Becknhm
8 B 5 Birkbeck rd Enf
36 D 16 Birkbeck rd Ilf
57 N 3 Birkbeck rd Rom
115 O 7 Birkbeck rd Sidcp
135 Y 14 Birkbeck st E2
63 O 10 Birkbeck st E2
59 O 2 Birkbeck way Grnfd
22 H 10 Birkdale av Pinn
79 Z 10 Birkdale rd SE2
80 A 11 Birkdale rd SE2
60 J 12 Birkdale rd W5
116 M 2 Birkenhead av Kingst
111 X 3 Birkhall rd SE6
89 Y 20 Birkwood clo SW12
15 R 8 Birley rd N20
89 O 6 Birley st SW11
99 R 1 Birling rd Erith
48 C 7 Birnam rd N4
31 T 15 Birstall rd N15
144 F 11 Biscay rd W6
93 X 9 Biscoe way SE13
157 S 2 Bisenden rd Croy
47 R 3 Bisham gdns N6
7 V 7 Bishop Craven clo Enf
234 L 6 Bishop Ken rd Harrow
144 L 5 Bishop Kings rd W14
16 D 4 Bishop rd N14
134 B 4 Bishop st N1
65 U 2 Bishops av E13
87 R 4 Bishops av SW6
126 K 5 Bishops av Brom
37 T 18 Bishops av Rom
28 H 16 Bishops Av the N2
46 G 2 Bishops Av the N2
138 B 4 Bishops Bridge rd W2
33 S 13 Bishops clo E17
8 M 9 Bishops clo Enf
102 G 6 Bishops clo Rich
153 Z 6 Bishops clo Sutton
141 X 4 Bishops ct EC4
141 R 4 Bishops ct WC2
28 H 18 Bishops gro N2
100 G 11 Bishops gro Hampt
116 Q 3 Bishops hall Kingst
87 O 4 Bishops pk SW6
108 A 20 Bishops Pk rd SW16
122 B 1 Bishops Pk rd SW16
87 R 4 Bishops Pk rd SW6
29 P 19 Bishops rd N6

87 U 1 Bishops rd SW6
145 O 20 Bishops rd SW6
71 T 5 Bishops rd W7
122 H 18 Bishops rd Croy
149 T 5 Bishops ter SE11
63 O 6 Bishops way E2
135 Y 8 Bishops way E2
158 G 12 Bishops wlk Croy
120 G 13 Bishopsford rd Mrdn
142 K 3 Bishopsgate EC2
142 J 3 Bishopsgate chyd EC2
110 E 9 Bishopsthorpe rd SE26
46 M 1 Bishopswood rd N6
46 N 2 Bishopswood rd N6
70 E 9 Bisley clo S'hall
119 N 20 Bisley clo Worc Pk
61 N 9 Bispham rd NW10
64 G 5 Bisson rd E15
33 X 10 Bisterne av E17
14 B 18 Bittacy hill NW7
14 C 19 Bittacy hill NW7
27 S 2 Bittacy hill NW7
14 B 19 Bittacy Hill park NW7
14 B 18 Bittacy Park av NW7
14 D 20 Bittacy rd NW7
14 A 19 Bittacy rise NW7
142 A 18 Bittern st SE1
116 H 6 Bittoms the Kingst
30 M 16 Black Boy la N15
135 N 20 Black Eagle st E1
150 F 2 Black Horse ct SE1
115 O 10 Black Horse rd Sidcp
74 F 12 Black Lion la W6
143 S 2 Black Lion yd E1
149 O 7 Black Prince rd SE11
142 F 10 Black Raven alley EC4
142 K 17 Black Swan yd SE1
134 H 16 Blackall st EC2
70 B 20 Blackberry Farm clo Hounsl
43 W 8 Blackbird hill NW9
56 D 19 Blackborne rd Dgnhm
127 V 5 Blackbrook la Brom
45 Z 18 Blackburn rd NW6
139 T 10 Blackburnes ms W1
37 V 10 Blackbush av Rom
154 B 16 Blackbush clo Sutton
87 O 8 Blackett st SW15
96 K 14 Blackfen rd Sidcp
97 P 15 Blackfen rd Sidcp
141 W 10 Blackfriars br EC4
141 X 7 Blackfriars la EC4
141 W 17 Blackfriars rd SE1
141 V 9 Blackfriars underpass EC4
93 Z 1 Blackheath SE10
94 C 6 Blackheath gro SE3
93 T 2 Blackheath hill SE10
94 F 7 Blackheath pk SE3
93 R 2 Blackheath rd SE10
93 U 14 Blackheath ri SE13
93 Z 4 Blackheath vale SE3
94 A 3 Blackheath vale SE3
94 B 6 Blackheath village SE3
32 F 9 Blackhorse la E17
123 Y 17 Blackhorse la Croy
32 G 14 Blackhorse rd E17
75 W 15 Blackhorse rd SE8
111 T 11 Blacklands rd SE6
147 O 8 Blacklands ter SW3
71 R 2 Blackmore av S'hall
101 Y 14 Blackmores gro Tedd
91 Z 5 Blackpool rd SE15
74 M 12 Blacks rd W6
144 B 8 Blacks rd W6
134 L 2 Blackshaw pl N1
106 H 13 Blackshaw rd SW17
48 H 7 Blackstock rd N4
45 N 14 Blackstone rd NW2
124 B 19 Blackthorn av Croy
97 Y 7 Blackthorn gro Bxly Hth
64 B 13 Blackthorn st E3
20 K 13 Blackthorne dri E4
64 H 20 Blackwall tunnel E14
77 P 11 Blackwall tunnel SE10
64 H 20 Blackwall way E14
76 H 1 Blackwall way E14
154 A 10 Blackwater st Sutton
91 U 13 Blackwater st SE22

12 C 12 Blackwell gdns Edg
150 D 10 Blackwood st SE17
97 V 18 Bladindon dri Bxly
125 Y 4 Bladon ct Brom
16 J 5 Blagdens clo N14
16 J 7 Blagdens la N14
118 F 7 Blagdon house New Mald
93 R 16 Blagdon rd SE13
118 C 9 Blagdon rd New Mald
102 D 16 Blagdon wlk Tedd
137 N 2 Blagrove rd W10
44 A 2 Blair av NW9
96 G 14 Blair clo Sidcp
64 H 18 Blair st E14
108 A 3 Blairderby rd SW2
67 W 4 Blake av Bark
87 Z 1 Blake gdns SW6
52 F 5 Blake Hall cres E11
52 F 1 Blake Hall rd E11
65 O 12 Blake rd E16
16 J 20 Blake rd N11
29 V 2 Blake rd N11
157 R 2 Blake rd Croy
120 H 5 Blake rd Mitch
76 A 16 Blake st E14
154 M 13 Blakehall rd Carsh
52 L 8 Blakeley cotts SE1
107 Z 6 Blakemore rd SW16
122 D 11 Blakemore rd Thnth Hth
110 M 20 Blakeney av Becknhm
15 P 6 Blakeney clo N20
110 M 19 Blakeney rd Becknhm
106 M 10 Blakenham rd SW1?
107 N 9 Blakenham rd SW1?
64 F 4 Blaker rd E15
118 E 13 Blakes av New Mal
125 T 19 Blakes grn W Wkh
118 D 13 Blakes la New Male
150 L 19 Blakes rd SE15
118 G 12 Blakes ter New Mal
119 V 2 Blakesley av W5
13 C 8 Blakesware gdns N?
118 U 3 Blanchard st E8
91 O 8 Blanche st E16
120 A 11 Blanchedowne SE5
75 O 20 Blanchland rd Mrdn
100 L 1 Bland av SE15
28 E 14 Blandford av Twick
156 A 6 Blandford clo Croy
20 F 3 Blandford cres E4
74 A 8 Blandford rd W4
72 H 5 Blandford rd W5
101 S 14 Blandford rd Tedd
139 T 3 Blandford st W1
66 L 9 Blaney cres E6
113 Y 2 Blanmerle rd SE9
114 A 2 Blanmerle rd SE9
146 T 19 Blantyre st SW10
93 Y 18 Blashford st SE13
23 U 14 Blawith rd Harrow
59 Y 6 Bleasdale av Grnfd
59 X 6 Bleasdale av Grnfd
136 H 7 Blechynden ms W11
136 H 8 Blechynden st W11
97 U 15 Bleddyn clo Bxly
59 N 6 Bledlow ri Grnfd
141 U 1 Bleeding Heart yd EC1
107 V 14 Blegborough rd SW16
97 W 17 Blendon dri Bxly
150 E 9 Blendon rd SE17
97 V 18 Blendon rd Bxly
35 V 19 Blendon ter SE18
118 L 1 Blenheim clo SW2?
59 R 7 Blenheim clo Grnfd
38 J 12 Blenheim clo Rom
155 V 16 Blenheim clo Wallgtn
136 L 7 Blenheim cres W11
137 W 6 Blenheim cres W11
156 L 17 Blenheim cres S Croy
114 E 6 Blenheim ct Sidcp
96 K 3 Blenheim dri Wellir?
45 N 15 Blenheim gdns NW?
90 B 15 Blenheim gdns SW?
103 S 19 Blenheim gdns Kingst
155 V 15 Blenheim gdns Wallgtn
42 K 9 Blenheim gdns Wemb
30 E 8 Blenheim gro N22

Ref	Name
91 W 5	Blenheim gro SE15
30 B 8	Blenheim pas NW8
56 L 17	Blenheim Pk rd S Croy
52 A 12	Blenheim rd E15
32 G 10	Blenheim rd E17
26 A 8	Blenheim rd E6
30 C 7	Blenheim rd NW8
30 E 8	Blenheim rd N22
10 C 18	Blenheim rd SE20
18 L 7	Blenheim rd SW20
74 B 8	Blenheim rd W4
22 K 18	Blenheim rd Barnt
27 R 9	Blenheim rd Brom
22 K 18	Blenheim rd Har
22 J 17	Blenheim rd Harrow
15 T 3	Blenheim rd Sidcp
53 Z 4	Blenheim rd Sutton
39 X 7	Blenheim st W1
88 L 17	Blenkarne rd SW11
25 V 4	Blessbury rd Edg
93 X 9	Blessington clo SE13
93 X 9	Blessington rd SE13
34 C 10	Bletchley st N1
93 R 3	Bliss ravensbourne
93 T 1	Bliss
55 P 18	Bisset st SE10
79 Z 11	Blitbury rd Dgnhm
80 B 11	Blithdale rd SE2
45 W 3	Blithdale st W8
75 R 17	Blithfield st W8
74 J 3	Blockhouse st SE15
62 H 19	Blockley rd Wemb
74 J 3	Bloemfontein av W12
72 Z 20	Bloemfontein rd W12
30 E 18	Blomfield rd W9
142 G 3	Blomfield rd W9
138 A 1	Blomfield st EC2
16 M 8	Blomfield vlls W2
58 N 4	Blomvill rd Dgnhm
20 C 10	Blondell st SW11
64 B 6	Blondin av W5
108 J 7	Blondin st E3
45 N 20	Bloom gro SE27
36 A 19	Bloom Pk rd SW6
79 Y 8	Bloomburg st SW1
29 P 19	Bloomfield pl W1
73 N 13	Bloomfield rd N6
130 A 20	Bloomfield rd SE18
26 M 11	Bloomfield rd W9
27 N 10	Bloomfield rd Brom
116 K 8	Bloomfield rd Brom
118 P 13	Bloomfield rd Kingst
109 P 13	Bloomfield ter SW1
10 N 19	Bloomhall rd SE19
140 L 3	Bloomsbury clo W5
22 E 9	Bloomsbury ct WC1
140 L 1	Bloomsbury ct Pinn
140 K 1	Bloomsbury pl WC1
140 H 2	Bloomsbury sq WC1
140 K 3	Bloomsbury st WC1
7 X 5	Bloomsbury way WC1
34 M 19	Blossom la Enf
70 B 18	Blossom st E1
63 N 16	Blossom wave Hounsl
50 K 4	Blount st E14
100 P 19	Bloxhall rd E10
95 P 13	Bloxham cres Hampt
150 C 20	Bloxham gdns SE9
91 X 1	Blucher rd SE5
51 V 5	Blue Anchor la SE16
43 R 9	Blue Anchor la SE16
40 B 14	Blue Anchor yd E1
89 S 5	Blue Bell yd SW1
00 E 6	Bluebell clo SE26
00 G 13	Bluefield clo Felt
21 N 9	Bluefield clo Felt
25 Z 4	Bluehouse rd E4
26 A 3	Blundell rd Edg
48 A 20	Blundell rd Edg
97 O 11	Blundell st N7
95 W 14	Blunt rd S Croy
50 D 13	Blunts st SE9
50 L 2	Blurton rd E5
92 L 20	Blyth rd E17
92 L 20	Blythe clo SE6
13 H 16	Blythe hill SE6
10 L 1	Blythe Hill la SE6
44 K 3	Blythe Hill la SE6
26 C 1	Blythe rd W14
35 V 13	Blythe rd Brom
10 L 2	Blythe st E2
54 M 4	Blythe vale SE6
	Blythswood rd Ilf
48 B 1	Blythwood rd N4
81 N 7	Boarers manorway Blvdr
72 F 19	Boars Head yd Brentf
151 P 18	Boathouse wlk SE15
39 U 3	Bobs la Rom
103 N 17	Bockhampton rd Kingst
135 X 4	Bocking st E8
141 V 12	Boddys br SE1
8 C 9	Bodiam clo Enf
107 Y 19	Bodiam rd SW16
118 A 13	Bodley clo New Mald
117 Z 13	Bodley rd New Mald
118 C 12	Bodley rd New Mald
120 A 10	Bodmin grn Mrdn
105 Z 2	Bodmin st SW18
49 Z 14	Bodney rd E5
97 V 2	Bognor rd Welling
50 B 16	Bohemia pl E8
5 Y 19	Bohun gro Barnt
74 H 18	Boileau rd SW13
60 M 17	Boileau rd W5
61 N 16	Boileau rd W5
93 P 4	Bolden st SE4
130 L 19	Boldero st NW8
159 R 3	Bolderwood way W Wkhm
8 M 5	Boleyn av Enf
56 J 20	Boleyn gdns Dgnhm
159 S 4	Boleyn gdns W Wkhm
66 A 5	Boleyn rd E6
65 V 1	Boleyn rd E7
49 S 14	Boleyn rd N16
88 K 16	Bolingbroke gro SW11
136 H 20	Bolingbroke rd W14
144 G 1	Bolingbroke rd W14
88 H 1	Bolingbroke wlk SW11
73 T 7	Bollo Br rd W3
73 R 6	Bollo la W3
73 V 10	Bollo la W4
149 N 18	Bolney st SW8
131 Z 19	Bolsover st W1
121 S 2	Bolstead rd Mitch
141 U 5	Bolt ct EC4
149 V 16	Bolton cres SE5
128 F 10	Bolton gdns NW10
146 A 8	Bolton gdns SW5
101 Y 15	Bolton gdns Tedd
52 D 19	Bolton rd E15
62 G 3	Bolton rd NW10
129 Z 6	Bolton rd NW8
18 G 17	Bolton rd N18
73 V 20	Bolton rd W4
85 W 1	Bolton rd W4
139 V 13	Bolton st W1
149 P 6	Bolwell st SE11
151 V 5	Bombay st SE16
136 J 8	Bomore rd W11
151 R 20	Bonar rd SE15
113 W 19	Bonchester clo Chisl
154 B 17	Bonchurch clo Sutton
136 K 1	Bonchurch rd W10
72 A 4	Bonchurch rd W13
155 V 7	Bond gdns Wallgtn
52 X 3	Bond rd Mitch
51 X 15	Bond st E15
73 Z 12	Bond st W4
72 G 1	Bond st W5
139 Z 10	Bond St See New Old Bond st W1
148 K 14	Bondway SW8
90 B 13	Bonham rd SW2
55 W 7	Bonham rd Dgnhm
73 Y 7	Bonheur rd W4
134 G 18	Bonhill st EC2
22 K 3	Boniface gdns Harrow
22 K 2	Boniface wlk Harrow
93 V 10	Bonfield rd SE13
117 O 5	Bonner Hill rd Kingst
63 P 6	Bonner rd E2
63 S 7	Bonner st E2
23 X 17	Bonnersfield clo Harrow
23 Z 17	Bonnersfield la Harrow
89 V 15	Bonneville gdns SW4
149 N 14	Bonnington sq SW8
66 J 7	Bonny Downs rd E6
132 A 1	Bonny st NW1
100 W 5	Bonser rd Twick
150 J 18	Bonsor st SE5
112 D 13	Bonville rd Brom
93 Z 10	Boone st SE13
94 A 9	Boone st SE13
134 H 14	Boot st N1
26 B 8	Booth rd NW9
25 Z 6	Booth rd NW9
47 X 6	Boothby rd N19
149 S 14	Booths pl W1
59 U 14	Bordars rd W7
59 T 14	Bordars wlk W7
18 B 1	Borden av Enf
86 G 19	Borden wlk SW15
29 Z 12	Border cres SE26
106 K 20	Border ga Mitch
159 P 7	Border gdns Croy
110 B 13	Border rd SE26
120 A 9	Bordesley rd Mrdn
16 J 19	Bordham rd N11
65 T 18	Boreham av E16
51 T 3	Boreham clo E10
30 K 6	Boreham rd N22
135 O 14	Boreham st E2
78 F 11	Borgard rd SE18
92 D 11	Borland rd SE15
87 N 8	Borneo st SW15
142 B 19	Borough High st SE1
156 H 6	Borough hill Croy
141 X 20	Borough rd SE1
83 T 1	Borough rd Islwth
103 P 19	Borough rd Kingst
120 J 3	Borough rd Mitch
149 Z 10	Borrett rd SE17
88 B 15	Borrodale rd SW18
23 Y 8	Borrowdale av Harrow
52 A 13	Borthwick rd E15
51 Z 13	Borthwick rd E15
76 B 15	Borthwick st SE8
32 K 11	Borwick av E17
111 U 8	Bosbury rd SE6
47 R 10	Boscastle rd NW5
147 V 4	Boscobel pl SW1
130 C 19	Boscobel st NW8
33 V 20	Boscombe av E10
107 N 15	Boscombe rd SW17
105 Z 19	Boscombe rd SW19
74 H 4	Boscombe rd W12
143 N 19	Boscombe rd Worc Pk
20 F 7	Bosgrove E4
143 N 16	Boss st SE1
80 E 14	Bostall heath SE2
80 C 15	Bostall Hill SE2
80 F 14	Bostall Hill rd SE2
80 F 14	Bostall House lodge SE2
80 D 12	Bostall la SE2
80 D 10	Bostall manorway SE2
80 L 20	Bostall Pk av Bxly Hth
115 P 19	Bostall rd Orp
71 Z 12	Boston gdns Brentf
72 A 12	Boston gdns Brentf
72 B 13	Boston Manor house Brentf
72 B 12	Boston Mnr rd Brentf
72 D 15	Boston Pk rd Brentf
131 N 18	Boston pl NW1
33 N 19	Boston rd E17
66 C 9	Boston rd E6
71 X 9	Boston rd W7
122 D 15	Boston rd Croy
25 V 2	Boston rd Edg
135 S 7	Boston st E2
71 Y 11	Boston vale W7
71 U 5	Bostonthorpe rd W7
132 M 20	Boswell ct WC1
122 L 9	Boswell rd Thntn Hth
132 M 20	Boswell st WC1
32 K 5	Bosworth clo E17
16 L 18	Bosworth rd N11
128 L 18	Bosworth rd W10
4 M 12	Bosworth rd Barnt
65 R 10	Bosworth rd Dgnhm
144 G 15	Bothwell st W6
142 H 9	Botolph all EC3
142 H 10	Botolph la EC3
64 C 9	Botolph rd E3
119 S 4	Botsford rd SW20
137 V 6	Botts ms W2
57 W 18	Bouchier wlk Rainhm
126 C 17	Boughton av Brom
79 W 7	Boughton rd SE18
63 U 18	Boulcott st E1
122 M 14	Boulogne rd Croy
123 N 14	Boulogne rd Croy
57 X 17	Boulter gdns Rainhm
56 A 8	Boulton rd Dgnhm
18 M 7	Bounces la N9
19 P 8	Bounces rd N9
106 M 3	Boundaries rd SW12
107 N 2	Boundaries rd SW12
117 S 6	Boundary clo Kingst
70 H 14	Boundary clo S'hall
65 Z 11	Boundary la E13
150 D 14	Boundary la SE17
65 Z 7	Boundary rd E13
33 O 20	Boundary rd E17
30 D 4	Boundary rd NW8
30 L 8	Boundary rd N22
19 R 1	Boundary rd N9
106 F 15	Boundary rd SW19
67 S 5	Boundary rd Bark
67 O 6	Boundary rd Enf
39 V 18	Boundary rd Rom
155 R 18	Boundary rd S Wallgtn
96 G 13	Boundary rd Sidcp
55 R 14	Boundary rd Wallgtn
141 W 17	Boundary row SE1
134 M 15	Boundary st E2
159 O 11	Boundary way Croy
111 Y 6	Boundfield rd SE6
112 A 5	Boundfield rd SE6
16 J 19	Bounds Green rd N11
30 R 4	Bounds Green rd N22
140 E 7	Bourchier st W1
139 X 9	Bourdon pl W1
124 B 3	Bourdon rd SE20
139 X 9	Bourdon st W1
89 Z 17	Bourke clo SW2
44 B 18	Bourke rd NW10
140 B 2	Bourlet clo W1
31 O 13	Bourn av N15
37 O 1	Bournbridge gdns Ilf
95 O 7	Bournbrook rd SE3
16 M 7	Bourne av N14
20 E 15	Bourne gdns E4
7 E 9	Bourne hill N13
98 L 14	Bourne mead Bxly
52 C 10	Bourne rd E7
30 B 18	Bourne rd N8
126 M 8	Bourne rd Brom
127 N 8	Bourne rd Brom
126 M 8	Bourne rd Brom
98 K 15	Bourne rd Bxly
99 N 13	Bourne rd Dtford
147 S 7	Bourne st SW1
156 J 3	Bourne st Croy
137 X 1	Bourne ter W2
17 O 8	Bourne the N14
16 J 5	Bourne the N14
126 D 19	Bourne vale Brom
41 W 16	Bourne view Grnfd
153 V 12	Bourne way Sutton
9 A 3	Bourne Way bushey Watf
91 X 4	Bournemouth rd SE15
105 Z 20	Bournemouth rd SW19
107 Z 10	Bournevale rd SW16
80 A 19	Bournewood rd SW2
93 N 18	Bournville rd SE6
5 Z 10	Bournwell clo Barnt
92 E 55	Bousfield rd SE4
88 J 11	Boutflower rd SW11
24 H 20	Bouverie gdns Harrow
138 H 4	Bouverie pl W2
49 R 6	Bouverie rd N16
23 O 20	Bouverie rd Harrow
141 U 7	Bouverie st EC4
9 R 3	Bouver rd Enf
48 C 11	Bovay pl N7
48 C 11	Bovay st N7
92 E 18	Boveney rd SE23
92 G 20	Bovill rd SE20
43 R 19	Bovingdon av Wemb
188 A 3	Bovingdon rd SW6
182 B 4	Bow chyd EC4
64 A 13	Bow Common la E3
142 C 7	Bow Common la E3
28 D 1	Bow la N12
63 Y 10	Bow rd E3
64 C 8	Bow rd E3
51 Z 15	Bow st E15
140 L 7	Bow st WC2
25 X 16	Bowater clo NW9
77 W 19	Bowater pl SE3
149 T 10	Bowden st SE11
75 X 12	Bowditch SE8
33 N 20	Bowdon rd E17
109 S 8	Bowen dri SE21
41 O 1	Bowen rd Harrow
23 O 20	Bowen rd Harrow
64 D 16	Bowen st E14
93 Z 1	Bower av SE10
39 N 2	Bower clo Rom
50 L 19	Bower rd E9

63 T 18	Bower st E1
87 Z 3	Bowerdean st SW6
75 W 18	Bowerman av SE14
16 G 15	Bowes rd N11
62 A 20	Bowes rd W3
55 U 13	Bowes rd Dgnhm
144 E 15	Bowfell rd W6
97 Y 3	Bowford av Bxly Hth
89 Y 18	Bowie clo SW4
89 X 11	Bowland rd SW4
151 S 13	Bowles rd SE1
75 Z 1	Bowley st E14
142 E 17	Bowling Green pl SE1
78 E 9	Bowling Green row SE18
149 T 13	Bowling Green st SE11
134 H 12	Bowling Green wlk N1
86 K 19	Bowling Grn clo SW15
133 V 17	Bowling Grn la EC1
11 N 16	Bowls clo Stanm
65 R 19	Bowman av E16
155 R 6	Bowmans meadow Wallgtn
48 I 18	Bowmans mews N7
48 I 18	Bowmans pl N7
99 T 18	Bowmans rd Drtford
113 T 4	Bowmead SE9
103 Z 12	Bowness cres SW15
104 A 12	Bowness cres SW15
82 C 10	Bowness dri Hounsl
93 S 19	Bowness rd SE6
98 G 6	Bowness rd Bxly Hth
57 W 15	Bowness way Hornch
89 O 12	Bowood rd SW11
9 T 8	Bowood rd Enf
42 H 20	Bowrons av Wemb
150 B 19	Bowyer st SE5
91 R 17	Boxall rd SE21
56 A 11	Boxall rd Dgnhm
80 E 8	Boxgrove rd SE2
120 D 10	Boxley rd Mrdn
77 V 3	Boxley st E16
24 A 13	Boxmoor rd Harrow
23 O 3	Boxtree la Harrow
133 R 4	Boxworth gr N1
78 L 13	Boyard rd SE18
65 T 12	Boyce way E13
25 W 18	Boycroft av NW9
70 G 3	Boyd av S'hall
106 F 15	Boyd rd SW19
143 T 7	Boyd st E1
141 Y 19	Boyfield st SE1
112 C 13	Boyland rd Brom
10 M 18	Boyle av Stanm
140 A 9	Boyle st W1
27 R 12	Boyne av NW4
93 W 8	Boyne rd SE13
56 E 10	Boyne rd SW9
137 O 13	Boyne Ter ms W11
150 D 14	Boyson rd SE17
30 A 11	Boyton clo N8
30 A 11	Boyton rd N8
30 D 7	Brabant rd N22
156 A 17	Brabazon av Wallgtn
64 C 16	Brabazon st E14
92 B 6	Brabourn gro SE15
81 P 18	Brabourne cres Bxly Hth
125 V 11	Brabourne ri Becknhm
41 X 17	Bracewell av Grnfd
62 L 14	Bracewell rd W10
136 B 2	Bracewell rd W3
157 V 5	Bracewood gdns Croy
48 B 6	Bracey st N4
89 P 7	Bracken av SW12
159 P 6	Bracken av Croy
86 G 4	Bracken gdns SW13
74 K 7	Brackenbury gdns W6
28 D 10	Brackenbury rd N2
74 K 8	Brackenbury rd W6
17 R 7	Brackendale N21
40 B 12	Brackenhill Ruis
126 C 1	Brackenhill clo Brom
126 C 1	Brackenhill la Brom
74 B 12	Brackenhill rd W4
110 M 20	Brackley rd Becknhm
111 O 17	Brackley rd Becknhm
35 N 1	Brackley sq Ilf
74 B 13	Brackley ter W4
45 Y 13	Bracknell cl NW3
46 A 13	Bracknell gdns NW3
45 Z 13	Bracknell way NW3
46 A 13	Bracknell way NW3
79 Z 10	Bracondale rd SE2
80 C 10	Bracondale rd SE2
141 U 15	Brad st SE1
98 F 18	Bradbourne rd Bxly
87 Y 4	Bradbourne st SW6
49 T 16	Bradbury st N16
50 N 6	Braddon rd Rich
75 N 6	Braddon st SE16
143 Y 18	Braddock st SE16
76 L 13	Braddyll st SE10
129 X 18	Braden st W9
96 M 10	Bradenham av Welling
97 N 10	Bradenham av Welling
24 A 12	Bradenham rd Harrow
54 T 16	Bradfield dri Bark
77 T 4	Bradfield rd E16
40 C 15	Bradfield rd Ruis
9 N 10	Bradfield sq Enf
152 C 14	Bradford dri Epsom
109 Z 9	Bradford rd SE26
74 A 4	Bradford rd W3
54 F 4	Bradford rd Ilf
52 H 19	Bradgate rd SE6
52 H 5	Brading cres E11
90 D 18	Brading rd SW2
122 B 15	Brading rd Croy
129 R 12	Bradiston rd W9
134 J 9	Bradlaugh st N1
60 B 17	Bradley gdns W13
30 C 7	Bradley rd N22
108 L 14	Bradley rd SE19
9 X 1	Bradley rd Enf
133 T 9	Bradleys bldgs N1
144 B 7	Bradmore la W6
74 K 10	Bradmore Pk rd W6
151 X 13	Bradshaw st SE15
50 G 19	Bradstock rd E9
152 H 11	Bradstock rd Epsom
56 E 6	Bradwell av Dgnhm
34 B 12	Bradwell clo E18
57 Z 19	Bradwell clo Hornch
63 T 9	Bradwell st E1
63 N 14	Brady st E1
135 X 20	Brady st E1
43 Y 8	Braemar av NW10
30 B 5	Braemar av N22
105 X 5	Braemar av SW19
98 X 11	Braemar av Bxly Hth
157 N 20	Braemar av S Croy
122 G 5	Braemar av Thntn Heath
60 J 1	Braemar av Wemb
25 Z 6	Braemar gdns NW9
114 F 6	Braemar gdns Sidcp
125 T 20	Braemar gdns W Wkhm
65 R 13	Braemar rd E13
31 R 15	Braemar rd N15
73 T 8	Braemar rd W3
72 H 16	Braemar rd Brentf
152 J 5	Braemar rd Worc Pk
54 K 8	Braemore rd Ilf
105 T 20	Braeside SW19
72 N 4	Braeside Becknhm
98 K 11	Braeside cres Bxly Hth
107 V 18	Braeside rd SW16
81 P 11	Braesyde clo Blvdr
156 L 8	Brafferton rd Croy
149 N 10	Braganza st SE17
61 Z 18	Braid av W3
100 C 4	Braid clo Felt
111 X 2	Braidwood rd SE6
142 K 14	Braidwood st SE1
90 G 15	Brailsford rd SW2
35 P 14	Braintree av Ilf
56 E 9	Braintree rd Dgnhm
63 P 10	Braintree st E2
24 E 5	Braithwaite gdns Stanm
90 G 2	Bramah rd SW9
15 V 18	Bramber rd N12
145 P 14	Bramber rd W14
159 P 8	Bramble clo Croy
122 C 6	Bramble la Croy
79 P 14	Bramblebury rd SE18
81 Y 13	Bramblecroft Erith
126 A 13	Brambles clo Brom
155 P 17	Brambledown rd Carsh
157 R 18	Brambledown rd S Croy
72 A 20	Brambles clo Brentf
72 A 20	Bramblewood clo Carsh
120 L 9	Bramcote av Mitch
151 Z 10	Bramcote gro SE16
75 O 13	Bramcote gro SE16
86 K 11	Bramcote rd SW15
112 E 2	Bramdean cres SE12
112 E 2	Bramdean gdns SE12
124 L 6	Bramerton rd Beck
146 J 13	Bramerton st SW3
88 L 14	Bramfield rd SW11
88 C 11	Bramford rd SW18
145 Y 8	Bramham gdns SW5
77 W 16	Bramhope la SE7
6 D 17	Bramley clo N14
82 M 16	Bramley clo Twick
156 K 10	Bramley clos S Croy
35 X 18	Bramley cres Ilf
156 K 9	Bramley hill S Croy
99 W 12	Bramley pl Drtfrd
6 D 17	Bramley pl N14
136 G 9	Bramley rd W11
72 D 9	Bramley rd W5
6 L 13	Bramley rd Enf
153 N 19	Bramley rd Sutton
154 F 11	Bramley rd Sutton
136 G 6	Bramley rd W10
159 S 3	Bramley way W Wkhm
30 K 16	Brampton gdns N15
26 K 14	Brampton gro NW4
23 Z 12	Brampton gro Harrow
24 A 13	Brampton gro Harrow
43 O 4	Brampton gro Wemb
30 F 10	Brampton Park rd N8
66 C 10	Brampton rd E6
25 R 15	Brampton rd NW9
30 L 16	Brampton rd N15
80 G 16	Brampton rd SE18
80 G 18	Brampton rd Bxly Hth
97 X 1	Brampton rd Bxly Hth
123 T 16	Brampton rd Croy
50 F 19	Bramshaw rd E9
118 B 14	Bramshaw ri New Mald
47 T 8	Bramshill gdns NW5
62 C 6	Bramshill rd NW10
77 U 16	Bramshot av SE7
62 G 5	Bramshot rd NW10
89 O 5	Bramwell pl SW8
53 U 13	Brancaster rd E12
107 Z 6	Brancaster rd SW16
36 G 19	Brancaster rd Ilf
21 S 9	Brancepeth Buck'Hl
46 C 10	Branch hill NW3
134 G 4	Branch pl N1
63 V 19	Branch rd E14
24 F 10	Brancker rd Harrow
76 G 20	Brand st SE10
87 V 11	Brandlehow rd SW15
33 V 12	Brandon rd E17
47 Z 20	Brandon rd N7
70 E 14	Brandon rd S'hall
153 Z 8	Brandon rd Sutton
150 C 7	Brandon st SE17
93 Y 10	Brandram rd SE13
107 R 4	Brandreth rd SW17
155 Z 6	Brandries the Wallgtn
36 A 12	Brandville gdns Ilf
111 U 12	Brangbourne rd Brom
144 J 20	Branksea st SW6
18 F 18	Branksome av N18
105 Y 20	Branksome rd SW19
90 A 12	Branksome rd SW2
24 L 18	Branksome way Harrow
117 X 2	Branksome way New Mald
17 S 3	Branscombe gdns N21
93 R 8	Branscombe st SE13
24 M 3	Bransgrove rd Edg
85 N 5	Branstone rd Rich
59 U 12	Brants wlk W7
83 Y 8	Brantwood av Erith
33 S 11	Brantwood clo E17
6 M 15	Brantwood gdns Enf
35 S 14	Brantwood gdns Ilf
18 L 20	Brantwood rd N17
90 L 12	Brantwood rd SE24
98 H 6	Brantwood rd Bxlyhth
157 N 20	Brantwood. rd S Croy
89 O 6	Brassey sq SW11
62 B 18	Brassie av W3
110 B 9	Brasted clo SE26
97 W 13	Brasted clo Bxly Hth
87 Z 18	Brathway rd SW18
58 J 11	Braund av Grnfd
114 J 1	Braundton av Sidcp
96 K 20	Braundton av Sidcu
129 O 15	Bravington av W9
128 K 16	Bravington rd W9
92 K 11	Braxfield rd SE4
108 C 15	Braxted pk SW16
65 R 19	Bray dri E16
65 R 19	Bray pl E16
147 N 8	Bray pl SW3
91 Z 5	Brayards rd SE15
92 A 5	Brayards rd SE15
62 D 15	Braybrook st W12
89 K 9	Brayburne av SW4
49 W 2	Braydon rd E5
133 S 2	Brayfield ter N1
6 L 14	Brayton gdns Enf
96 E 10	Braywood rd SE9
69 R 9	Breach la Dgnhm
142 B 7	Bread st EC4
93 N 6	Breakspears rd SE4
92 M 9	Breakspears rd SE4
66 J 10	Bream gdns E6
4 A 2	Bream st E3
104 G 2	Breamore clo SW15
55 N 7	Breamore rd Ilf
54 K 8	Breamore rd Ilf
141 S 4	Breams bldgs EC4
102 A 6	Breamwater gdns Rich
86 L 9	Breasley clo SW15
146 C 8	Brechin pl SW7
47 Y 15	Brecknock rd N7
144 L 15	Brecon rd W6
9 O 13	Brecon rd Enf
66 J 8	Brede clo E6
47 V 7	Bredgar rd N19
90 M 6	Bredon rd SE5
123 U 17	Bredon rd Croy
88 A 7	Breer st SW6
143 U 10	Breezers hill E1
138 D 20	Bremner rd SW7
126 D 13	Brenchley clo Brom
127 X 1	Brenchley clo Chisl
92 D 15	Brenchley gdns SE23
106 L 5	Brenda rd SW17
44 A 14	Brendon av NW10
99 P 2	Brendon clo Erith
40 K 11	Brendon gdns Harrow
86 H 16	Brendon gdns Ilf
114 D 4	Brendon rd SE9
50 D 6	Brendon rd Dgnhm
138 M 4	Brendon st W1
18 D 2	Brendon way Enf
121 P 6	Brenley clo Mitch
95 O 9	Brenley gdns SE9
60 M 7	Brent cres Wemb
27 O 16	Brent grn NW4
44 H 2	Brent Park rd NW4
4 J 18	Brent pl Barnt
65 T 18	Brent rd E16
78 L 19	Brent rd SE18
72 H 16	Brent rd Brentf
157 Z 19	Brent rd S Croy
72 E 17	Brent side Brentf
27 O 15	Brent st NW4
26 F 20	Brent View rd NW9
14 K 20	Brent way N3
72 G 19	Brent way Brentf
43 U 17	Brent way Wemb
61 V 1	Brentfield NW10
43 X 17	Brentfield clo NW10
27 P 20	Brentfield ct NW11
43 Y 17	Brentfield rd NW10
61 V 1	Brentfield rd NW10
72 G 18	Brentford high Brentf
60 K 9	Brentham Halt rd W5
60 F 11	Brentham way W5
50 B 19	Brenthouse rd E9
14 E 17	Brenthurst rd NW10
72 D 20	Brentlea Brentf
61 N 7	Brentmead gdns NW10
27 P 18	Brentmead pl NW11
63 W 17	Brenton st E14
59 Y 11	Brentside clo W13
71 P 2	Brentvale av S'hall
60 A 6	Brentvale av Wemb
61 N 6	Brentvale av Wemb
72 J 12	Brentwick gdns Brentf
39 X 18	Brentwood rd Rom
31 V 2	Brereton rd N17
148 A 3	Bressenden pl SW1
34 C 8	Bressey gro E18
55 Y 20	Brett gdns Dgnhm
87 P 7	Brett Ho clo SW15
50 A 16	Brett rd E8
61 X 1	Brett rd NW10

150 F 10	Brettell st SE17
33 O 5	Brettenham av E17
23 E 1	Brettenham rd E17
18 K 13	Brettenham rd N18
19 N 15	Brettenham Rd east N18
140 D 9	Brewer st W1
148 D 1	Brewers grn SW1
84 G 12	Brewers la Rich
47 Z 19	Brewery rd N1
48 A 19	Brewery rd N7
79 R 19	Brewery rd SE18
53 S 19	Brewery rd Bron
64 D 8	Brewery yd E3
143 Y 14	Brewhouse la E1
87 S 9	Brewhouse la SW15
133W 17	Brewhouse yd EC1
55 R 17	Brewood rd Dgnhm
136 B 2	Brewster gdns W10
62 M 14	Brewster gdns W10
51 S 4	Brewster rd E10
57 Y 11	Brian clo Hornch
37 U 14	Brian rd Rom
92 E 1	Briant st SE14
22 C 6	Briants clo Pinn
108 D 17	Briar av SW16
155 P 20	Briar banks Carsh
17 Z 11	Briar clo N13
83W 12	Briar clo Islwth
40 J 19	Briar cres Grnfd
153 N 8	Briar ct Sutton
126 B 20	Briar gdns Brom
155 P 20	Briar la Carsh
159 R 7	Briar la Croy
44 M 11	Briar rd NW2
122 B 7	Briar rd SW16
24 D 17	Briar rd Harrow
101 S 2	Briar rd Twick
86 K 10	Briar wlk SW15
25W 2	Briar wlk Edg
25W 18	Briar Wood clo NW9
59 Z 16	Briarbank rd W13
13 N 20	Briardale gdns NW3
28 B 8	Briarfield av N3
31 Z 3	Briars clo N17
89 X 12	Briarwood rd SW4
152 F 13	Briarwood rd Epsom
115 R 12	Briary ct Sidcp
112 H 12	Briary gdns Brom
12 B 12	Briary la N9
141 S 8	Brick ct WC2
85 S 3	Brick Farm clo Rich
135 P 19	Brick la E1
143 P 2	Brick la E1
8 L 9	Brick la Enf
9 O 9	Brick la Enf
139W 15	Brick st W1
79 Y 18	Brickfield cotts SE18
64 D 10	Brickfield rd E3
122 K 2	Brickfield rd Thntn Hth
41 R 6	Brickfields Harrow
52 Z 17	Brickwood rd Croy
141W 6	Bride la EC4
20 D 19	Bride st N7
141W 7	Bridewell pl EC4
131 Y 19	Bridford ms W1
47 N 20	Bridge appr NW3
74 K 12	Bridge av W6
144 A 8	Bridge av W6
59 R 14	Bridge av W7
9 N 8	Bridge clo Enf
39 P 19	Bridge clo Rom
88 F 6	Bridge ct SW11
33 U 4	Bridge ga N21
17 Y 3	Bridge ga N21
27 S 14	Bridge la NW11
88 K 3	Bridge la SW11
123 P 18	Bridge pl Croy
64 K 2	Bridge rd E15
50 K 2	Bridge rd E17
53 T 20	Bridge rd E6
44 A 18	Bridge rd NW10
30 A 6	Bridge rd N22
18 K 10	Bridge rd N9
110 L 18	Bridge rd Becknhm
97 Z 6	Bridge rd Bxly Hth
99 V 1	Bridge rd Erith
83 P 6	Bridge rd Hounsl
70 E 5	Bridge rd S'hall
84 B 14	Bridge rd Sutton
84 A 15	Bridge rd Twick
99 T 3	Bridge rd W Erith
155 T 11	Bridge rd Wallgtn
43 R 9	Bridge rd Wemb
129W 8	Bridge st NW6
140 K 18	Bridge st SW1
73 Y 11	Bridge st W4
22 A 10	Bridge st Pinn
84 G 14	Bridge st Rich
24 K 1	Bridge ter E15
23 U 11	Bridge the Harrow
144 A 9	Bridge view W6
27 V 16	Bridge way NW11
16 G 12	Bridge way N11
83 O 20	Bridge way Twick
153 X 14	Bridgefield rd Sutton
148 L 12	Bridgefoot SE1-
65 T 18	Bridgeland rd E16
101 X 14	Bridgeman st Tedd
130 J 9	Bridgeman st NW8
97 Y 17	Bridgen rd Bxly
8 H 5	Bridgenhall rd Enf
156 A 7	Bridges la Croy
87W 2	Bridges pl SW6
105 Z 16	Bridges rd SW19
106 A 16	Bridges rd SW19
10 H 17	Bridges rd Stanm
74 L 13	Bridgeview W6
24 M 7	Bridgewater gdns Edg
64 F 3	Bridgewater rd E15
42 C 17	Bridgewater rd Grnfd
42 C 17	Bridgewater rd Wemb
134 A 20	Bridgewater st EC1
67 X 1	Bridgeway Bark
42 L 19	Bridgeway Wemb
132 D 9	Bridgeway st NW1
107 X 18	Bridgewood rd SW16
152 H 7	Bridgewood rd Worc Pk
106 D 6	Bridgford st SW18
73 V 8	Bridgman rd W4
140 C 8	Bridle la W1
156 B 6	Bridle path Croy
159 O 1	Bridle rd Croy
159 P 9	Bridleway Croy
155W 10	Bridleway the Wallgtn
19 N 3	Bridlington rd N9
18 M 2	Bridlington rd N9
38 G 20	Bridport av Rom
134 F 6	Bridport pl N1
134 F 8	Bridport pl N1
18 E 18	Bridport rd N18
58 K 3	Bridport rd Grnfd
122 G 6	Bridport rd Thntn Hth
89 X 2	Bridport ter SW8
75 O 18	Bridson st SE15
137 U 5	Bridstow pl W2
90 H 3	Brief st SE5
159 R 15	Brierley Croy
19 R 6	Brierley av N9
51 X 12	Brierley rd E11
107 T 4	Brierley rd SW12
63 P 8	Brierly st E2
76 H 12	Brig st E14
8 A 5	Brigadier av Enf
7 Y 3	Brigadier hill Enf
64 E 16	Bright st E14
94 B 12	Brightfield rd SE12
92 M 17	Brightling rd SE4
63 X 20	Brightlingsea pl E14
106 E 1	Brightman rd SW18
32 L 17	Brighton av E17
40 G 18	Brighton dri Grnfd
92 H 1	Brighton gro SE14
65 N 5	Brighton rd E15
66 K 8	Brighton rd E6
49 T 12	Brighton rd N16
28 D 8	Brighton rd N2
157 N 13	Brighton rd S Croy
116 E 14	Brighton rd Surb
154 B 17	Brighton rd Sutton
90 D 10	Brighton ter SW9
93 X 15	Brightside rd SE13
9 U 5	Brightside the Enf
106 L 13	Brightwell cres SW17
81 T 10	Brigstock rd Blvdr
122 L 9	Brigstock rd Thntn Hth
28 D 13	Brim hill N2
92 A 1	Brimmington rd SE15
80 C 9	Brimpsfield clo SE2
9W 7	Brimsdown av Enf
92 L 3	Brindley st SE14
58 K 19	Brindley way S'hall
19 Z 10	Brindwood rd E4
20 A 10	Brindwood rd E4
80 B 10	Brinkburn clo SE2
25 S 9	Brinkburn clo Edg
25 R 9	Brinkburn gdns Edg
152 J 2	Brinkley rd Worc Pk
78 M 20	Brinklow cres SE18
79 N 19	Brinklow cres SE18
35 R 9	Brinkworth rd Ilf
27 O 11	Brinsdale rd NW4
9W 7	Brinsdown av Enf
23 P 7	Brinsley st Harrow
101 P 2	Brinsworth clo Twick
105 Z 19	Brisbane av SW19
51 S 8	Brisbane rd E10
71 Z 4	Brisbane rd W13
54 A 2	Brisbane rd Ilf
67 Z 20	Brisbane st SE5
106 G 15	Briscoe rd SW19
95 N 8	Briset st SE1
86 L 19	Briset st EC1
133W 19	Bristol gdns SW15
129 Z 19	Bristol gdns W9
130 A 19	Bristol gdns W9
129 Z 19	Bristol ms W9
130 A 19	Bristol ms W9
52 M 19	Bristol rd E12
53 N 18	Bristol rd E12
64 G 2	Bristol rd Grnfd
120 C 10	Bristol rd Mrdn
30 B 20	Bristol gro N8
109 R 12	Bristow rd SE19
97 Z 3	Bristow rd Bxly Hth
98 A 3	Bristow rd Bxly Hth
82 M 9	Bristow rd Hounsl
15 S 12	Britannia rd N12
145 X 19	Britannia rd SW6
53 Y 11	Britannia rd Ilf
116 M 16	Britannia rd Surb
117 N 16	Britannia rd Surb
133 Y 4	Britannia row N1
133 Z 10	Britannia st WC1
134 E 12	Britannia wlk N1
74 E 12	British gro W4
74 E 14	British Grove pass W6
21 O 7	British Legion rd E4
140 H 2	British museum WC1
63 Z 10	Britten st E3
56 A 9	Brittain rd Dgnhm
134 A 4	Brittania row N1
132 M 12	Brittania st WC1
146 J 10	Britten st SW3
133W 19	Britton st EC1
54 H 14	Brixham gdns Ilf
97 V 2	Brixham rd Welling
90 C 16	Brixton hill SW2
90 A 19	Brixton Hill pl SW2
149 T 18	Brixton rd SW9
90 F 5	Brixton rd SW9
90 F 9	Brixton Stn rd SW9
90 E 14	Brixton Water la SW2
140 L 6	Broad ct WC2
122 H 16	Broad Grn av Croy
31W 14	Broad la N15
100 F 16	Broad la Hampt
113W 2	Broad lawn SE9
126 B 11	Broad Oaks way Brom
51 X 20	Broad st E15
56 D 20	Broad st Dgnhm
69 S 2	Broad st Dgnhm
101 V 14	Broad st Tedd
142 H 2	Broad St av EC2
142 T 2	Broad St bldgs EC2
45 V 1	Broad Walk la NW1
23 U 7	Broad Way the Harrow
95 T 3	Broad wlk SE18
56 L 8	Broad wlk SE3
82 A 3	Broad wlk Hounsl
139 X 9	Broad yd EC1
159 X 9	Broadbent st W1
77 S 19	Broadbridge clo SE3
158 F 17	Broadcoombe S Croy
24 H 7	Broadcroft av Stanm
22 E 18	Broadfield ct Bushey Watf
93 Z 20	Broadfield rd SE6
111 Z 3	Broadfield rd SE6
21 Y 12	Broadfield way Buck Hl
22 K 6	Broadfields Harrow
17 T 1	Broadfields av N21
12 L 14	Broadfields av Edg
5 O 7	Broadgates av Barnt
106 G 3	Broadgates rd SW18
89 T 7	Broadhinton rd SW4
12 E 12	Broadhurst av Edg
54 K 13	Broadhurst av Ilf
26 B 18	Broadhurst clo NW6
45 Z 19	Broadhurst gdns NW6
46 B 18	Broadhurst gdns NW6
57W 19	Broadhurst walk Rainhm
107 Z 4	Broadlands av SW16
9 O 12	Broadlands av Felt
100 G 8	Broadlands av Felt
47 N 1	Broadlands Av clo N6
107 Z 5	Broadlands clo SW16
9 O 12	Broadlands clo Enf
29 N 20	Broadlands rd N6
112 H 10	Broadlands rd Brom
118 D 15	Broadlands way New Mald
30 H 20	Broadley st NW8
30 L 18	Broadley ter NW8
111 P 7	Broadmead SE6
118 F 18	Broadmead av Worc Pk
22 C 2	Broadmead clo Pinn
34 K 2	Broadmead rd Wdfd Gn
35 N 3	Broadmead rd Wdfd Gn
21 S 18	Broadmead rd Wdfd Gn
139 S 2	Broadstone pl W1
57W 7	Broadstone rd Hornch
25 P 19	Broadview NW9
107W 17	Broadview rd SW16
34 B 10	Broadwalk E18
17 R 6	Broadwalk N21
31 S 6	Broadwater rd N17
106 H 9	Broadwater rd SW17
65 U 7	Broadway E13
51 Y 20	Broadway E15
140 F 20	Broadway SW1
148 E 1	Broadway SW1
72 A 2	Broadway W13
71W 2	Broadway W7
67 O 3	Broadway Bark
98 E 11	Broadway Bxly Hth
152 G 12	Broadway Epsom
59 N 11	Broadway Grnfd
39W 9	Broadway Rom
123 O 12	Broadway av Croy
84 A 16	Broadway av Twick
21W 18	Broadway clo Wdfd Grn
51 X 20	Broadway ct E15
120 J 7	Broadway gdns Mitch
21W 18	Broadway gdns Wdfd Grn
135 U 5	Broadway mkt E8
17W 5	Broadway ms N21
20 H 19	Broadway the E4
13 P 17	Broadway the NW7
29 Z 18	Broadway the N8
18 K 9	Broadway the N9
105 X 16	Broadway the SW19
56 C 6	Broadway the Dgnhm
57 Y 13	Broadway the Hornch
22 D 3	Broadway the Pinn
70 C 1	Broadway the S'hall
11 S 15	Broadway the Stanm
153 S 14	Broadway the Sutton
21W 18	Broadway the Wdfd Grn
140 C 7	Broadwick st W1
64 C 15	Brock pl E3
65 C 14	Brock rd E13
54 J 16	Brockdish av Bark
123 Z 16	Brockenhurst Croy
118 B 18	Brockenhurst Worc Pk
13 P 17	Brockenhurst gdns NW7
54 B 14	Brockenhurst gdns Ilf
121 Y 3	Brockenhurst way SW16
105 V 13	Brockham clo SW19
90 C 18	Brockham dri SW2
36 A 17	Brockham dri Ilf
10 H 18	Brockhurst clo Stanm
92 H 10	Brockill cres SE4
88 C 19	Brocklebank rd SW18
75 T 19	Brocklehurst st SE14
123 Z 10	Brocklesby rd SE25
11 X 11	Brockley av Stanm
11 X 11	Brockley Av north Stanm
11 X 14	Brockley clo Stanm
38 K 3	Brockley cres Rom
92 C 9	Brockley footpath SE15
92 L 4	Brockley gdns SE4
93 N 12	Brockley gros SE4
92 K 14	Brockley gros SE4

92 K 14 Brockley Hall rd SE4
11 U 9 Brockley hill Edg
92 J 20 Brockley pk SE23
92 J 8 Brockley rd SE4
110 H 1 Brockley rd SE4
92 J 16 Brockley ri SE23
110 H 1 Brockley rd SE23
92 K 18 Brockley side Stanm
150 J 9 Brockley ter SE17
92 K 18 Brockley view SE23
92 G 13 Brockley way SE4
111 W 9 Brockman ri Brom
153 S 4 Brocks dri Sutton
142 B 9 Brocks wharf EC4
90 H 18 Brockwell park SE24
90 H 20 Brockwell Pk gdns SE24
80 D 11 Broderick gro SE2
49 T 8 Brodia rd N16
20 H 7 Brodie rd E4
8 A 4 Brodie rd Enf
161 P 10 Brodie st SE1
63 S 19 Brodlove la E1
106 K 3 Brodrick rd SW4
125 R 4 Brograve gdns Becknhm
31 Y 11 Brograve rd N17
135 R 4 Broke E8
142 A 9 Broken wharf EC4
63 Y 10 Brokesley st E3
95 U 8 Brome rd SE9
24 E 5 Bromefield Stanm
89 V 10 Bromells rd SW4
91 T 7 Bromer st SE5
89 Y 6 Bromfelde rd SW4
133 U 7 Bromfield st N1
55 P 18 Bromhall rd Dgnhm
113 U 7 Bromhedge SE9
80 B 9 Bromholm rd SE2
112 A 19 Bromley av Brom
126 L 11 Bromley comm Brom
127 P 16 Bromley comm Brom
126 C 5 Bromley cres Brom
126 C 5 Bromley cres Brom
125 X 5 Bromley gro Brom
64 G 14 Bromley Hall rd E14
64 D 8 Bromley High st E3
111 Z 15 Bromley hill Brom
112 A 16 Bromley hill Brom
114 E 18 Bromley la Chisl
132 A 19 Bromley pl W1
33 S 20 Bromley rd E10
33 O 9 Bromley rd E17
31 W 3 Bromley rd N18
38 B 12 Bromley rd N18
111 T 8 Bromley rd SE6
125 V 2 Bromley rd Becknhm
114 B 19 Bromley rd Chisl
63 O 17 Bromley st E1
28 K 13 Brompton gro N2
147 N 1 Brompton pl SW3
139 O 19 Brompton rd SW3
139 O 3 Brompton rd SW3
146 K 2 Brompton sq SW3
101 Z 15 Bromwell rd Tedd
102 A 15 Bromwell rd Tedd
47 R 8 Bromwich av N6
74 B 2 Bromyard av W3
44 L 19 Bromyard av NW2
45 O 20 Brondesbury pk NW6
128 K 2 Brondesbury pk NW6
129 U 7 Brondesbury rd NW6
129 T 7 Brondesbury vlls NW6
144 J 19 Bronsart rd SW6
119 R 3 Bronson rd SW20
150 C 10 Bronti pl SE17
76 C 18 Bronze st SE8
16 H 20 Brook av Dgnhm
12 F 18 Brook av Edg
43 O 8 Brook av Wemb
27 U 3 Brook clo NW7
118 K 7 Brook clo SW20
39 T 6 Brook clo Rom
20 C 13 Brook cres E4
18 L 13 Brook cres N9
149 T 3 Brook dri SE11
23 O 12 Brook dri Harrow
20 C 13 Brook gdns E4
86 E 7 Brook gdns SW13
103 U 20 Brook gdns Kingst
144 E 4 Brook grn W6
94 J 4 Brook la SE3
112 E 14 Brook la Brom
97 V 14 Brook la Bxly
72 G 14 Brook La north Brent
138 E 8 Brook Ms north W2
4 K 17 Brook pl Barnt

44 E 6 Brook rd NW2
30 D 9 Brook rd N22
42 B 10 Brook rd N8
21 U 6 Brook rd Buck Hl
36 H 18 Brook rd Ilf
39 U 5 Brook rd Rom
42 B 10 Brook rd Thntn Hth
83 Z 15 Brook rd Twick
72 G 15 Brook Rd south Brentf
31 V 9 Brook st N17
139 Y 7 Brook st N18
138 H 9 Brook st W2
81 U 16 Brook st W2
116 H 4 Brook st Kingst
12 K 20 Brook hill Edg
59 S 13 Brookbank av W7
93 P 8 Brookbank rd SE13
33 N 11 Brookdale rd E17
93 R 17 Brookdale rd SE6
98 A 17 Brookdale rd Bxly
79 Y 11 Brookdene rd SE18
41 O 9 Brooke av Harrow
33 V 14 Brooke rd E17
49 X 9 Brooke rd N16
18 E 12 Brooke rd N18
141 T 2 Brooke st EC1
10 A 3 Brooke way Bushey Watf
111 P 6 Brookehowse rd SE6
114 H 2 Brookend rd Sidcp
141 S 1 Brookes ct EC1
33 U 13 Brookfield av E17
60 H 12 Brookfield av W5
154 H 7 Brookfield av Sutton
13 Y 20 Brookfield clo NW7
13 X 20 Brookfield cres NW7
24 J 16 Brookfield cres Harrow
59 O 8 Brookfield ct. Grnfd
20 L 20 Brookfield path Wdfd Grn
47 R 9 Brookfield pk NW5
50 L 8 Brookfield rd E9
18 L 11 Brookfield rd N9
73 Z 7 Brookfield rd W4
9 T 13 Brookfields Enf
120 J 10 Brookfields av Mitch
159 X 16 Brookham cres Croy
5 W 17 Brookhill clo SE18
78 L 12 Brookhill rd SE18
5 W 18 Brookhill rd Barnt
20 L 14 Brookhouse gdns E4
114 G 4 Brookland av Sidcp
27 Z 13 Brookland clo NW11
27 Z 13 Brookland garth NW11
27 Z 13 Brookland hill NW11
27 Z 12 Brooklands app N2
38 M 12 Brooklands appr Rom
105 Z 4 Brooklands av SW19
39 N 14 Brooklands clo Rom
60 F 4 Brooklands dri Grnfd
39 N 13 Brooklands la Rom
94 E 7 Brooklands pk SE3
38 M 14 Brooklands rd Rom
124 E 8 Brooklyn av SE25
124 A 8 Brooklyn av SE25
127 P 10 Brooklyn rd Brom
152 B 15 Brookmead Epsom
127 U 11 Brookmead av Brom
121 W 14 Brookmead rd Croy
93 O 2 Brookmill rd SE4
66 F 11 Brooks av E6
10 D 18 Brooks hill Harrow
20 C 16 Brooks hill dri Bushey Watf
139 X 8 Brooks ms W1
65 S 4 Brooks rd E13
73 R 15 Brooks rd W4
14 B 4 Brooksby N20
50 F 15 Brooksbys wlk E9
33 R 6 Brookscroft rd E17
11 P 4 Brookshill av Harrow
7 R 20 Brookside N21
5 X 20 Brookside Barnt
155 O 10 Brookside Carsh
4 D 20 Brookside clo Barnt
24 H 16 Brookside clo Harrow
40 C 11 Brookside clo Harrow
118 H 20 Brookside cres Worc Pk
47 V 8 Brookside pl N19
27 U 18 Brookside rd NW11
47 W 8 Brookside rd N19
18 M 13 Brookside rd N9

124 F 14 Brookside way Croy
27 U 13 Brookside wlk NW11
14 J 19 Brookside wlk N3
128 L 6 Brooksville av NW6
98 H 1 Brookvale Erith
107 T 1 Brookview rd SW16
145 O 19 Brookville rd SW6
94 E 9 Brookway SE3
86 E 6 Brookwood av SW13
105 X 1 Brookwood rd SW18
82 K 4 Brookwood rd Hounsl
127 S 14 Broom clo Brom
159 P 6 Broom gdns Croy
98 F 14 Broom Hill ri Bxly Hth
102 E 14 Broom lock Tedd
98 F 14 Broom mead Bxly Hth
102 F 17 Broom pk Tedd
159 O 6 Broom rd Croy
102 B 13 Broom rd Tedd
102 D 14 Broom water Tedd
100 E 19 Broome rd Hampt
17 P 15 Broomfield av N13
17 O 14 Broomfield house N13
17 R 15 Broomfield la N13
17 N 13 Broomfield park N13
72 B 2 Broomfield pl W13
17 O 17 Broomfield rd N13
72 C 2 Broomfield rd W13
124 K 7 Broomfield rd Beck
98 F 14 Broomfield rd Bxly Hth
85 N 1 Broomfield rd Rich
55 W 1 Broomfield rd Rom
117 O 18 Broomfield rd Surb
102 E 15 Broomfield rd Tedd
64 C 15 Broomfield st E14
25 P 4 Broomgrove gdns Edg
90 D 6 Broomgrove rd SW4
157 O 18 Broomfield rd S Croy
87 V 14 Broomhill rd SW18
99 Y 16 Broomhill rd Drtfrd
55 O 6 Broomhill rd Ilf
21 S 20 Broomhill rd Wdfd Grn
21 S 18 Broomhill rd Wdfd Grn
87 X 7 Broomhouse la SW6
87 X 5 Broomhouse rd SW6
153 Y 3 Broomloan la Sutton
45 W 16 Broomsleigh st NW6
102 D 13 Broomwater west Tedd
88 L 16 Broomwood rd SW11
89 P 13 Broomwood rd SW4
110 G 12 Broseley gro SE26
148 K 19 Brough st SW8
135 T 3 Brougham rd E8
61 W 18 Brougham rd W3
27 R 10 Broughton av N3
102 C 8 Broughton av Rich
29 V 19 Broughton gdns N6
88 B 4 Broughton rd SW6
72 C 1 Broughton rd W13
122 F 13 Broughton rd Thntn Hth
89 R 4 Broughton st SW8
73 V 6 Brouncker rd W3
139 V 7 Brown Hart gdns W1
19 N 5 Brown st W1
64 E 18 Brownfield st E14
93 V 19 Brownhill rd SE6
59 W 17 Browning av W7
154 J 8 Browning av Sutton
118 K 19 Browning av Worc Pk
130 D 17 Browning clo. W9
52 C 2 Browning rd E11
52 C 12 Browning rd E12
8 A 2 Browning rd Enf
150 B 8 Browning st SE17
54 M 8 Brownlea gdns Ilf
111 T 11 Brownlow ms WC1
133 O 20 Brownlow ms WC1
52 G 12 Brownlow rd E7
135 R 3 Brownlow rd E8
62 B 1 Brownlow rd NW10
44 B 20 Brownlow rd NW10
16 M 18 Brownlow rd N11
28 A 1 Brownlow rd N3
71 Y 2 Brownlow rd W13
157 U 18 Brownlow rd Croy
141 P 2 Brownlow st WC1
142 K 5 Browns bldgs EC3

138 L 3 Browns ct W1
33 O 11 Browns rd E17
116 M 17 Browns rd Surb
113 Z 9 Brownspring dri SE
114 A 8. Brownspring dri SE
48 K 8 Brownswood rd N4
89 P 14 Broxash rd SW11
34 H 12 Broxbourne av E18
52 D 10 Broxbourne rd E7
108 F 7 Broxholm rd SE27
110 K 3 Broxted rd SE6
31 S 4 Bruce Castle museum N17
31 T 4 Bruce Castle park N17
31 U 5 Bruce Castle rd N1
99 K 7 Bruce clo Welling
158 F 20 Bruce dri S Croy
31 T 6 Bruce gro N17
64 E 9 Bruce rd E3
61 Z 1 Bruce rd NW10
123 O 8 Bruce rd SE25
4 F 12 Bruce rd Barnt
23 T 8 Bruce rd Harrow
107 N 17 Bruce rd Mitch
107 N 8 Brudenell rd SW17
34 N 2 Brune st E1
75 R 5 Brunel rd E16
62 B 15 Brunel rd W3
65 O 18 Brunel st E16
16 B 1 Brunner clo NW11
32 J 16 Brunner rd E17
60 F 11 Brunner rd W5
16 B 16 Brunswick av N11
97 X 9 Brunswick clo Bxly Hth
22 C 20 Brunswick clo Pinn
16 B 11 Brunswick cres N11
142 L 19 Brunswick ct SE1
92 J 10 Brunswick gdns W5
137 W 15 Brunswick gdns Ilf
36 B 1 Brunswick gdns Ilf
16 B 12 Brunswick gro N11
139 P 5 Brunswick ms W1
91 P 1 Brunswick pk SE5
16 B 9 Brunswick Pk gdns N11
134 F 14 Brunswick pl N1
109 W 16 Brunswick pl SE20
51 T 4 Brunswick rd E10
64 G 18 Brunswick rd E14
16 B 8 Brunswick rd N11
31 S 15 Brunswick rd N15
60 K 10 Brunswick rd W5
97 X 10 Brunswick rd Bxly Hth
103 P 20 Brunswick rd Kingst
154 C 7 Brunswick rd Sutton
8 G 20 Brunswick sq N17
132 L 17 Brunswick sq WC1
33 T 16 Brunswick st E17
91 R 1 Brunswick vlls SE5
63 W 18 Brunton pl E14
60 J 7 Brunwild rd W5
143 N 1 Brushfield st E1
142 L 1 Brushfield st E1
88 G 11 Brussels rd SW11
139 Y 9 Bruton la W1
139 Y 9 Bruton pl W1
139 C 10 Bruton rd Mrdn
139 Y 10 Bruton st W1
59 Z 14 Bruton way W13
44 K 20 Bryan av NW10
128 A 1 Bryan av NW10
62 L 1 Bryan av NW10
75 X 5 Bryan rd SE16
88 A 34 Bryans alley SW6
82 L 20 Bryanston av Twick
139 N 4 Bryanston ms W1
139 O 3 Bryanston Ms east W1
139 N 3 Bryanston Ms west W1
139 N 3 Bryanston pl W1
139 O 4 Bryanston sq W1
29 Y 17 Bryanstone rd N8
32 T 15 Bryant st E15
47 A 8 Bryantwood rd N7
55 T 12 Bryce rd Dgnhm
16 J 12 Brycedale cres N14
110 H 12 Bryden clo SE26
51 X 14 Brydges rd E15
150 M 12 Brymer rd SE5
8 J 13 Bryn-Y-Mawr rd Enf
88 M 3 Brynmaer rd SW11
62 H 20 Bryony rd W12
62 K 7 Buchan rd SE15
62 K 7 Buchanan gdns NW10

88 D 19 Bucharest rd SW18
25 X 16 Buck la NW9
131 Y 2 Buck st NW1
33W 14 Buck wlk E17
150 F 4 Buckenham st SE1
120 B 10 Buckfast rd Mrdn
135 T 14 Buckfast st E2
87 Y 16 Buckhold rd SW18
120 L 20 Buckhurst av Carsh
63 O 12 Buckhurst st E1
135 Y 17 Buckhurst st E1
140 L 12 Buckingham arcade WC2
15 R 3 Buckingham av N20
122 G 1 Buckingham av Thntn
96 H 11 Buckingham av Welling
8 E 8 Buckingham clo Enf
100 E 12 Buckingham clo Hampt
26 G 9 Buckingham ct NW4
140 B 20 Buckingham ga SW1
24 L 3 Buckingham gdns Edg
122 F 2 Buckingham gdns Thntn Hth
139 Z 19 Buckingham palace SW1
140 A 19 Buckingham palace SW1
139 X 18 Buckingham palace gdns SW1
147 X 6 Buckingham Palace rd SW1
148 A 1 Buckingham pl SW1
51 R 9 Buckingham rd E10
34 K 15 Buckingham rd E11
52 B 14 Buckingham rd E15
34 C 6 Buckingham rd E18
62 E 6 Buckingham rd NW10
49 S 19 Buckingham rd N1
30 B 7 Buckingham rd N22
24 M 2 Buckingham rd Edg
25 N 1 Buckingham rd Edg
100 F 13 Buckingham rd Hampt
23 R 15 Buckingham rd Harrow
54 E 7 Buckingham rd Ilf
116 M 8 Buckingham rd Kingst
117 N 8 Buckingham rd Kingst
122 A 10 Buckingham rd Mitch
102 G 4 Buckingham sa SW1
148 D 1 Buckingham sa SW1
140 L 11 Buckingham st WC2
155 V 20 Buckingham way Wallgtn
46 G 19 Buckland cres NW3
51 T 6 Buckland rd E10
153 N 20 Buckland rd Sutton
134 G 9 Buckland st N1
118 L 20 Buckland way Worc Pk
120 C 10 Buckland wlk Mrdn
102 E 14 Bucklands rd Tedd
143 R 5 Buckle st E1
119 V 5 Buckleigh av SW20
107 Z 16 Buckleigh rd SW16
109 T 19 Buckleigh way SE19
113 U 18 Buckler gdns SE9
145 R 16 Bucklers all SW6
142 E 7 Bucklersbury EC4
129 P 2 Buckley rd NW6
88 G 12 Buckmaster rd SW18
140 H 4 Bucknall st WC2
90 D 11 Buckner rd SW2
20 K 9 Buckrell rd E4
18 K 18 Buckstone rd N18
92 H 14 Buckthorne rd SE4
142 D 8 Budge row EC4
80 G 20 Budleigh cres Welling
55 N 7 Budoch ct Ilf
55 N 8 Budoch dri Ilf
87 U 5 Buer rd SW6
77 V 10 Bugsby rd SE7
122 L 7 Bulganak rd Thntn Hth
148 J 1 Bulinga st SW1
97 R 7 Bull av Welling
140 L 9 Bull Inn ct WC2
18 E 15 Bull la N18
114 O 19 Bull la Chisl
56 G 8 Bull la Dgnhm
65 P 5 Bull rd E15
142 B 9 Bull Wharf la EC4

91 X 2 Bull yd SE15
63 S 9 Bullards pl E1
81W 10 Bullbanks rd Blvdr
88 J 4 Bullen st SW11
128 G 13 Buller rd NW10
31 X 9 Buller rd N17
30 E 7 Buller rd N22
54 G 20 Buller rd Bark
123 O 6 Buller rd Thntn Hth
151 T 19 Buller sq SE15
115 X 13 Bullers clo Sidcp
113 T 19 Bullers Wood dri Chisl
12 D 10 Bullescroft rd Edg
64 G 19 Bullivant st E14
146 L 5 Bulls gdns SW3
142 H 7 Bulls Head pas EC3
42 F 1 Bulmer gdns Harrow
82 F 6 Bulstrode av Hounsl
82 F 7 Bulstrode gdns Hounsl
139 V 3 Bulstrode pl W1
82 H 7 Bulstrode rd Hounsl
139 V 3 Bulstrode st W1
51 X 3 Bulwer Ct rd E11
5 P 14 Bulwer gdns Barnt
51 X 3 Bulwer rd E11
18 E 15 Bulwer rd N18
5 P 14 Bulwer rd Barnt
136 D 15 Bulwer st W12
34 C 1 Bunces la Wdfd Grn
123 S 9 Bungalow rd SE25
107 S 17 Bungalows the SW16
134 D 16 Bunhill row EC1
81 S 11 Bunkers hill Blvdr
13 P 19 Bunns la NW7
26 F 1 Bunns la NW7
63 U 6 Bunsen st E3
36 D 16 Buntingbridge rd Ilf
78 K 9 Bunton st SE18
32 J 10 Bunyan rd E17
150 E 2 Burbage rd SE21
90 M 15 Burbage rd SE24
91 O 17 Burbage rd SE24
117 Z 4 Burberry clo New Mald
31W 8 Burbridge rd N17
64 F 17 Burcham st E14
80 H 16 Burcharbro rd SE2
10 A 3 Burchel ct Bushey Watf
51 R 3 Burchell rd E10
92 A 3 Burchell rd SE15
38 A 18 Burchett way Rom
38 J 2 Burchwall clo Rom
88 G 20 Burcote rd SW18
72 E 14 Burden clo Brentf
52 H 5 Burden way E11
85 S 9 Burdenshott av Rich
49 S 17 Burder rd N1
115 Z 13 Burdet clo Sidcp
104 F 20 Burdett av SW20
63 Y 15 Burdett st E14
123 P 15 Burdett rd Croy
85 O 6 Burdett rd Rich
141 T 20 Burdett st SE1
153 V 20 Burdon la Sutton
74 L 11 Burfield st W6
17 S 10 Burford gdns N13
64 J 2 Burford rd E15
68 L 9 Burford rd E6
110 M 6 Burford rd SE6
72 J 15 Burford rd Brentf
151 R 10 Burford rd Brom
153 X 4 Burford rd Sutton
118 F 18 Burford rd Worc Pk
159 V 15 Burford way Croy
151 N 9 Burgandy st SE1
150 F 3 Burge st SE1
53 V 20 Burges rd E6
66 E 1 Burges rd E6
66 K 2 Burges rd E6
25 Y 18 Burgess av NW9
45W 11 Burgess hill NW2
51 V 13 Burgess rd E15
153 Z 9 Burgess rd Sutton
64 A 15 Burgess st E14
133 Z 8 Burgh st N1
110 G 9 Burghill rd SE26
105 R 9 Burghley rd SW19
117 Y 1 Burghley av New Mald
118 A 1 Burghley av New Mald
52 A 3 Burghley rd E11
47 U 11 Burghley rd NW5
30 F 10 Burghley rd N8
141 Y 7 Burgon st EC4
93 R 1 Burgos gro SE10
30 H 19 Burgoyne rd N4
123 U 8 Burgoyne rd SE25
90 C 7 Burgoyne rd SW9

22 B 7 Burhill gro Pinn
65 P 16 Burke st E16
88 M 14 Burland rd SW11
96 K 13 Burleigh av Sidcp
155 P 6 Burleigh av Wallgtn
16 G 5 Burleigh gdns N14
8 E 14 Burleigh rd Enf
119 T 19 Burleigh rd Sutton
140 M 8 Burleigh st WC2
8 B 12 Burleigh way Enf
121 Y 3 Burley clo E4
107 Y 18 Burley clo SW16
65 X 6 Burley rd E16
21 U 12 Burlin pl Wdfd Grn
85 P 2 Burlington av Rich
38 H 18 Burlington av Rom
140 A 11 Burlington gdns W1
73 X 3 Burlington gdns W3
73W 14 Burlington gdns W4
65 Z 1 Burlington gdns Rom
58 A 1 Burlington gdns Rom
73 Y 19 Burlington la W4
74 A 17 Burlington la W4
73W 3 Burlington ms W3
137 T 4 Burlington Ms east W2
137 S 4 Burlington Ms west W2
87 T 5 Burlington pl SW6
21 U 12 Burlington pl Wdfd Grn
29 O 9 Burlington rd N10
31 X 5 Burlington rd N17
87 J 5 Burlington rd SW6
73 U 13 Burlington rd W4
8 A 5 Burlington rd Enf
83 P 2 Burlington rd Islwth
118 F 9 Burlington rd New Mald
122 M 4 Burlington rd Thntn Hth
123 N 3 Burlington rd Thntn Hth
15 Y 4 Burlington rise Barnt
49 O 12 Burma rd N16
149 X 2 Burman st SE1
106 D 7 Burmester rd SW17
73 U 16 Burnaby gdns W4
66 M 19 Burnaby st E6
146 D 19 Burnaby st SW10
15 N 19 Burnbrae clo N12
107 V 1 Burnbury rd SW12
102 D 11 Burncroft av Enf
96 L 3 Burnell av Well
97 O 5 Burnell av Welling
24 F 7 Burnell gdns Stanm
154 B 7 Burnell rd Sutton
66 H 10 Burnels av E6
149 N 10 Burnett rd SE11
116 L 12 Burney av Surb
117 N 11 Burney av Surb
76 G 19 Burney st SE10
87 T 3 Burnfoot av SW6
8 E 4 Burnham clo Enf
34 K 14 Burnham cres E11
119 P 1 Burnham dri Worc Pk
19 X 17 Burnham rd E4
68 C 2 Burnham rd Dgnhm
120 A 10 Burnham rd Mrdn
38 L 11 Burnham rd Rom
115 X 5 Burnham rd Sidcp
83 P 8 Burnham st E2
117 P 1 Burnham st Kingst
72 A 9 Burnham way W13
125 O 3 Burnhill rd Becknm
44 F 15 Burnley rd NW10
90 C 4 Burnley rd SW9
58 J 19 Burns av S'hall
97 O 16 Burns av Sidcp
99 U 2 Burns clo Erith
96 J 3 Burns clo Welling
62 C 3 Burns rd NW10
88 L 4 Burns rd SW11
72 A 5 Burns rd W13
23 U 13 Burns rd Harrow
60 J 6 Burns rd Wemb
146 L 10 Bunsall st SW3
4 L 13 Burnside clo Barnt
83 X 15 Burnside clo Twick
60 G 3 Burnside cres Wemb
55 U 3 Burnside rd Dgnhm
63 V 8 Burnside st E3
112 G 1 Burnt Ash hill SE12
94 F 20 Burnt Ash hill SE12
112 G 14 Burnt Ash la Brom
94 C 13 Burnt Ash rd SE12
25 T 4 Burnt Oak bdwy Edg
96 M 16 Burnt Oak la Sidcp
114 M 3 Burnt Oak la Sidcp

106 H 2 Burntwood Grange rd SW18
106 D 6 Burntwood la SW17
98 C 6 Burr clo Bxly Hth
87 Y 20 Burr rd SW18
79 O 10 Burrage gro SE18
78 M 14 Burrage pl SE18
79 N 14 Burrage rd SE18
79 O 10 Burrage rd SE18
65 U 17 Burrard rd E16
45 Y 13 Burrard rd NW6
12 G 7 Burrell clo Edg
125 N 3 Burrell row Becknhm
141 X 13 Burrell st SE1
117 R 4 Burritt rd Kingst
26 J 13 Burroughs gdns NW4
26 K 13 Burroughs the NW4
141W 16 Burrows ms SE1
62 M 8 Burrows rd NW10
128 D 11 Burrows rd NW10
142 J 15 Bursar st SE1
114 L 4 Bursdon clo Sidcp
9 S 13 Bursland rd Enf
143 U 6 Burslem st E1
37 P 1 Burstead gdns Ilf
87 S 10 Burstock rd SW15
87 P 12 Burston rd SW15
105 S 20 Burstow rd SW20
119 S 1 Burstow rd SW20
120 M 13 Burt rd Mitch
145 S 19 Burthwaite rd SW6
48 L 3 Burtley clo N4
82 E 3 Burton gdns Hounsl
150 F 11 Burton gdns SE17
147 U 6 Burton mews SW1
132 H 15 Burton pl WC1
34 G 11 Burton rd E18
129 R 2 Burton rd NW6
90 F 4 Burton rd SW9
102 L 18 Burton rd Kingst
132 H 15 Burton st WC1
14 B 14 Burtonhole clo NW7
14 B 13 Burtonhole la NW7
46 L 1 Burtons ct E15
100 K 10 Burtons rd Hampt
100 O 11 Burtons rd Hampt
106 C 7 Burtop rd SW17
79 R 14 Burwash rd SE18
41 T 18 Burwell av Grnfd
50 J 3 Burwell rd E10
138 L 5 Burwood pl W2
142 K 5 Bury EC3
120 A 10 Bury grn Mrdn
140 K 2 Bury pl WC1
21 N 2 Bury rd E4
30 G 10 Bury rd N22
56 J 14 Bury rd Dgnhm
142 K 5 Bury st EC3
140 C 13 Bury st SW1
18 H 4 Bury St west N9
146 J 8 Bury wlk SW3
47 X 17 Busby ms NW5
47 X 17 Busby pl NW5
135 R 16 Busby st E2
36 F 16 Bush clo Ilf
57W 1 Bush Elms rd Hornch
43 V 1 Bush gro NW9
25W 20 Bush gro Stanm
24 F 4 Bush gro Stanm
18 A 1 Bush hill N21
17 Y 2 Bush hill N21
8 B 18 Bush hill Enf
18 B 1 Bush Hill N21
24 M 19 Bush Hill rd Harrow
142 E 9 Bush la EC4
52 D 1 Bush rd E11
75 T 11 Bush rd SE8
73 N 17 Bush rd Rich
50 J 17 Bushberry rd E9
10 B 8 Bushell grn Bushey Watf
143 T 14 Bushell st E1
34 C 10 Bushey av E18
117 X 10 Bushey clo New Mald
118 L 4 Bushey ct SW20
91 T 2 Bushey Hill rd SE5
153 Z 6 Bushey la Sutton
101 S 18 Bushey park Tedd
65 Y 6 Bushey rd E13
18 R 18 Bushey rd N15
114 L 4 Bushey rd SW20
119 P 4 Bushey rd SW20
159 O 3 Bushey rd Croy
154 A 7 Bushey rd Sutton
153 Z 8 Bushey rd Sutton
125W 13 Bushey way Becknhm
12 E 8 Bushfield clo Edg
12 F 8 Bushfield cres Edg
55 V 11 Bushgrove rd Dgnhm
55 V 12 Bushgrove rd Dgnhm

96 A 1	Bushmoor cres SE18
79 N 20	Bushmoor cres SE18
107 S 5	Bushnell rd SW17
55 V 11	Bushway Dgnhm
52 D 2	Bushwood E11
73 P 18	Bushy Hill park Enf
8 G 15	Bushy Hill park Enf
101 R 13	Bushy Pk gdns Tedd
102 B 18	Bushy Pk rd Tedd
101 V 16	Bushy rd Tedd
107 T 3	Bushydown SW12
101 U 17	Bushyhouse Tedd
63 U 19	Butcher row E14
65 T 17	Butcher st E16
102 J 2	Bute av Rich
144 E 6	Bute gdns W6
55 V 11	Bute gdns Wallgtn
155 V 11	Bute Gdns west Wallgtn
122 G 20	Bute rd Croy
36 B 15	Bute rd Ilf
155 U 7	Bute rd Wallgtn
146 F 6	Bute st SW7
23 R 20	Butler av Harrow
55 P 11	Butler rd Dgnhm
23 P 20	Butler rd Harrow
41 N 1	Butler rd Harrow
63 R 8	Butler st E2
112 A 11	Butt rd Brom
155 O 6	Butter hill Carsh
56 H 18	Butterfield clo Dgnhm
33 U 16	Butterfields E17
95 Z 15	Butterfly la SE9
155 P 7	Butterhill Wallgtn
87 U 13	Buttermere dri
144 E 8	Butterwick W6
134 G 12	Buttesland st N1
100 C 6	Butts cotts Felt
100 G 7	Butts cres Felt
72 F 18	Butts the Brentf
54 C 16	Buttsbury rd Ilf
15 X 16	Buxted rd N12
92 C 16	Buxton clo SE23
35 N 1	Buxton clo Wdfd Grn
153 R 7	Buxton cres Sutton
34 A 14	Buxton dri E11
117 Z 2	Buxton dri New Mald
118 A 2	Buxton dri New Mald
73 S 1	Buxton gdns W3
51 Z 15	Buxton rd E15
52 A 15	Buxton rd E15
32 K 15	Buxton rd E17
20 K 3	Buxton rd E4
66 D 9	Buxton rd E6
44 K 17	Buxton rd NW2
86 B 8	Buxton rd SW13
81 Z 18	Buxton rd Erith
36 G 20	Buxton rd Ilf
54 G 1	Buxton rd Ilf
122 H 13	Buxton rd Thntn Hth
135 R 18	Buxton st E1
88 C 5	Byam st SW6
121 X 1	Byards croft SW16
58 H 13	Bycroft rd S'hall
110 H 17	Bycroft st SE20
7 X 9	Bycullah rd Enf
7 V 9	Bycullah rd Enf
62 B 16	Bye the W3
23 U 5	Bye Way the Harrow
100 K 5	Bye ways Twick
106 G 16	Byegrove rd SW19
85 V 8	Byeway the SW14
117 R 12	Byeways the Surb
86 G 3	Byfeld gdns SW13
83 Y 8	Byfield rd Islwth
159 R 15	Bygrove Croy
64 C 18	Bygrove st E14
17 O 1	Byland clo N21
110 D 14	Byne rd SE26
154 H 3	Byne rd Carsh
157 O 17	Byne rd S Croy
132 F 18	Byng pl WC1
4 C 11	Byng rd Barnt
76 B 5	Byng st E14
98 A 8	Bynon av Bxly Hth
107 T 2	Byrne rd SW12
53 P 19	Byron av E12
34 B 9	Byron av E18
25 T 11	Byron av NW9
118 G 10	Byron av New Mald
154 G 9	Byron av Sutton
154 G 9	Byron Av east Sutton
110 J 11	Byron clo SE26
7 X 9	Byron ct Enf
154 G 7	Byron dri N2
41 R 5	Byron Hill rd Harrow
51 R 3	Byron rd E10
33 P 11	Byron rd E17
44 J 8	Byron rd NW2
13 T 16	Byron rd NW7
73 O 1	Byron rd W5
23 T 18	Byron rd Harrow
23 W 10	Byron rd Harrow
42 E 9	Byron rd Wemb
16 E 8	Byron st E14
19 O 1	Byron terr N9
58 B 9	Byron way Grnfd
35 Z 5	Bysouth clo Ilf
106 M 14	Byton rd SW17
142 L 10	Byward st EC3
147 N 9	Bywater st SW3
152 E 9	Byway the Epsom
154 F 18	Byway the Sutton
140 A 3	Bywell pl W1
124 D 14	Bywood av Croy

C

138 K 2	Cabbell st NW1
63 N 19	Cable st E1
143 X 8	Cable st E1
88 J 5	Cabul rd SW11
62 D 18	Cactus wlk W12
151 P 4	Cadbury rd SE16
45 S 10	Caddington rd NW2
93 W 2	Cade rd SE10
76 L 12	Cadeb pl SE10
88 C 17	Cader rd SW18
56 L 19	Cadiz rd Dgnhm
56 L 17	Cadiz st SE17
110 C 3	Cadley ter SE23
89 Y 9	Cadmus clo SW4
154 A 14	Cadogan ct Sutton
147 P 5	Cadogan ga SW3
34 J 10	Cadogan gdns E18
7 S 18	Cadogan gdns N21
28 A 5	Cadogan gdns N3
147 P 5	Cadogan gdns SW3
147 S 3	Cadogan la SW1
147 R 2	Cadogan la SW1
147 R 1	Cadogan pl SW1
116 G 12	Cadogan rd Surb
147 O 4	Cadogan sq SW1
147 N 7	Cadogan st SW3
50 L 18	Cadogan ter E9
31 V 18	Cadoxton av N15
114 A 4	Cadwallon rd SE9
48 E 12	Caedmon rd N7
80 C 10	Caerleon ter SE2
35 W 4	Caernarvon dri Ilf
134 M 11	Caesar st E2
104 F 13	Caesars camp SW19
120 M 10	Caesars wlk Mitch
121 N 10	Caesars wlk Mitch
76 C 11	Cahir st E14
72 G 4	Cairn av W5
129 N 15	Cairn st W10
10 J 19	Cairn way Stanm
44 C 11	Cairnfield av NW2
88 K 12	Cairns rd SW11
33 O 12	Cairo rd E17
65 P 3	Cairo st Croy
65 P 3	Caistor Park rd E15
65 P 4	Caistor pk E15
89 R 19	Caistor rd SW12
96 J 17	Caithness gdns Sidcp
144 G 3	Caithness rd W14
107 S 18	Caithness rd Mitch
48 K 17	Calabria rd N5
90 J 1	Calais st SE5
57 Z 14	Calbourne av Hornch
89 N 19	Calbourne rd SW12
113 O 10	Calcott wlk SE9
118 J 19	Caldbeck av Worc Pk
91 N 4	Caldecot rd SE5
10 K 1	Caldecote gdns Bushey Watf
10 G 1	Caldecote la Bushey Watf
59 V 6	Calder av Grnfd
8 C 12	Calder clo Enf
25 O 9	Calder gdns Edg
120 C 11	Calder rd Mrdn
62 M 15	Calderon pl W10
136 C 3	Calderon rd E11
51 V 11	Calderon rd E11
89 X 13	Caldervale rd SW4
78 K 10	Calderwood st SE18
150 E 16	Caldew st SE5
149 P 20	Caldwell st SW9
142 A 9	Caldwell yd EC4
81 U 7	Caldy rd Blvdr
146 L 8	Cale st SW3
66 F 2	Caledon rd E6
155 P 7	Caledon rd Wallgtn
132 L 10	Caledonia st N1
132 M 9	Caledonian rd N1
128 A 1	Caledonian rd N1
48 C 15	Caledonian rd N7
77 O 13	Caletock st SE10
155 Z 18	Caley clo Wallgtn
10 C 7	California la Bushey Watf
117 U 7	California rd New Mald
111 S 5	Callander rd SE6
17 W 15	Callard av N13
129 C 1	Callcott rd NW6
137 T 13	Callcott st W8
32 L 18	Callis rd E17
146 E 13	Callow st SW3
150 K 13	Calmington rd SE5
111 Y 16	Calmont rd Brom
35 Y 4	Calne av Ilf
105 P 9	Calonne rd SW19
133 O 10	Calshot st N1
115 Y 14	Calt clo Sidcp
11 Y 16	Calthorpe gdns Edg
154 C 4	Calthorpe gdns Sutton
133 P 16	Calthorpe st WC1
91 S 14	Calton av SE21
5 S 19	Calton st Barnt
56 D 7	Calverley cres Dgnhm
42 G 1	Calverley gdns Harrow
47 Y 4	Calverley gro N19
152 F 14	Calverley rd Epsom
134 M 14	Calvert av E2
81 T 12	Calvert clo Blvdr
77 U 18	Calvert rd SE3
4 D 10	Calvert rd Barnt
131 T 3	Calvert st NW1
66 J 3	Calverton rd E6
142 D 15	Calverts bldgs SE1
135 N 18	Calvin st E1
77 W 14	Calydon rd SE7
101 R 2	Camac rd Twick
87 P 13	Cambalt rd SW15
32 M 12	Cambell rd E17
118 J 3	Camberley av SW20
8 D 14	Camberley av Enf
91 O 2	Camberwell Church st SE5
91 P 2	Camberwell glebe SE5
91 N 1	Camberwell grn SE5
91 O 2	Camberwell gro SE5
149 W 18	Camberwell New rd SE5
91 N 2	Camberwell pas SE5
150 C 17	Camberwell rd SE5
90 L 2	Camberwell Stn rd SE5
56 K 16	Cambeys rd Dgnhm
87 Y 19	Camborne rd SW18
123 W 18	Camborne rd Croy
119 P 12	Camborne rd Mrdn
115 T 8	Camborne rd Sidcp
153 Z 17	Camborne rd Sutton
154 A 16	Camborne rd Sutton
96 J 4	Camborne rd Welling
82 G 1	Camborne way Hounsl
19 S 4	Cambourne av N9
72 C 5	Cambourne av W13
89 W 20	Cambray rd SW12
82 H 11	Cambria clo Hounsl
96 F 20	Cambria clo Sidcp
114 F 1	Cambria clo Sidcp
90 L 7	Cambria rd SE5
145 Z 20	Cambria st SW6
36 H 15	Cambrian av Ilf
108 H 6	Cambrian clo SE27
51 N 2	Cambrian rd E10
84 M 17	Cambrian rd Rich
129 V 7	Cambridge av NW6
41 V 16	Cambridge av Grnfd
118 B 4	Cambridge av New Mald
96 K 10	Cambridge av Welling
140 G 7	Cambridge cir WC2
104 J 20	Cambridge cl SW20
104 J 20	Cambridge clo SW20
82 C 10	Cambridge clo Hounsl
73 O 17	Cambridge cotts Rich
63 N 7	Cambridge cres E2
135 W 9	Cambridge cres E2
101 X 11	Cambridge cres Tedd
94 E 13	Cambridge dri SE12
54 J 4	Cambridge dri Ilf
131 X 15	Cambridge ga NW1
131 Y 15	Cambridge Ga ms NW1
129 V 9	Cambridge gdns NW6
31 N 1	Cambridge gdns N17
18 A 2	Cambridge gdns N21
136 K 4	Cambridge gdns W10
8 K 9	Cambridge gdns Enf
117 P 3	Cambridge gdns Kingst
95 Y 20	Cambridge grn SE9
109 Z 19	Cambridge gro SE20
144 A 7	Cambridge gro W6
74 K 10	Cambridge Gro rd Kingst
117 P 5	Cambridge Gro rd Kingst
63 O 9	Cambridge Heath rd E2
135 Y 5	Cambridge Heath rd E8
63 N 3	Cambridge Ldge vlls E9
50 D 19	Cambridge pass E11
34 F 19	Cambridge pk E11
84 E 17	Cambridge pk Twick
129 U 11	Cambridge pl NW6
137 Z 19	Cambridge pl W8
34 D 20	Cambridge rd E11
20 K 5	Cambridge rd E4
129 U 12	Cambridge rd NW6
123 Z 5	Cambridge rd SE20
88 L 3	Cambridge rd SW11
86 D 6	Cambridge rd SW13
118 H 1	Cambridge rd SW20
104 L 20	Cambridge rd SW20
71 V 5	Cambridge rd W7
54 B 20	Cambridge rd Bark
112 F 18	Cambridge rd Brom
154 K 11	Cambridge rd Carsh
100 F 17	Cambridge rd Hampt
22 J 16	Cambridge rd Harrow
82 C 9	Cambridge rd Hounsl
54 J 2	Cambridge rd Ilf
117 R 5	Cambridge rd Kingst
121 U 6	Cambridge rd Mitch
117 Z 8	Cambridge rd New Mald
118 B 8	Cambridge rd New Mald
73 O 19	Cambridge rd Rich
70 E 3	Cambridge rd S'hall
114 H 10	Cambridge rd Sidcp
101 X 11	Cambridge rd Tedd
84 G 15	Cambridge rd Twick
73 S 13	Cambridge Rd north W4
73 S 14	Cambridge Rd south W4
79 N 14	Cambridge row SE18
138 K 5	Cambridge sq W2
147 Y 8	Cambridge st SW1
148 A 10	Cambridge st SW1
131 X 14	Cambridge ter NW1
131 Y 14	Cambridge Ter ms NW1
65 T 13	Cambus rd E16
79 X 19	Camdale rd SE18
91 V 1	Camden av SE15
114 B 20	Camden clo Chisl
131 Z 1	Camden gdns NW1
153 Z 12	Camden gdns Sutton
122 J 4	Camden gdns Thntn Hth
91 W 1	Camden gro SE15
151 N 20	Camden gro SE15
113 Z 15	Camden gro Chisl
131 Y 2	Camden High st NW1
132 A 6	Camden High st NW1
109 T 15	Camden Hill rd SE19
47 Z 16	Camden Hurst st E14
47 Z 16	Camden la N7
47 V 13	Camden ms NW1
113 X 17	Camden park Chisl
133 V 8	Camden pas N1
47 V 18	Camden Pk rd NW1
113 Y 20	Camden Pk rd Chisl
113 Y 19	Camden place Chisl
34 H 18	Camden rd E11
32 K 18	Camden rd E17
132 A 2	Camden rd NW1
47 X 18	Camden rd N7
48 A 14	Camden rd N7
98 A 20	Camden rd Bxly

154 L7	Camden rd Carsh
153 Z11	Camden rd Sutton
94 A5	Camden row SE3
47 X19	Camden sq NW1
131 Z1	Camden st NW1
132 A2	Camden st NW1
113 V19	Camden way Chisl
122 J5	Camden way Thntn Hth
133 W6	Camden wlk N1
113 V17	Camden wood Chisl
78 B2	Camel rd E16
136 K6	Camelford rd W11
82 J18	Camellia pl Twick
151 V16	Camelot SE15
146 E14	Camera pl SW10
15 U8	Cameron clo N12
15 V8	Cameron clo N20
143 Y4	Cameron pl E1
110 M5	Cameron rd Brom
126 E11	Cameron rd Brom
122 J15	Cameron rd Croy
54 H4	Cameron Rd south Ilf
66 L19	Cameron st E6
151 V6	Camilla rd SE16
112 D9	Camlan rd Brom
135 N16	Camlet st E2
4 L8	Camlet way Barnt
5 R5	Camlet way Barnt
132 E5	Camley st NW1
142 K4	Camomile st EC3
104 L13	Camp rd SW19
104 L12	Camp view SW19
87 Y2	Campana rd SW6
36 B14	Campbell av Ilf
101 O3	Campbell clo Twick
12 C15	Campbell croft Edg
52 A13	Campbell rd E15
64 B9	Campbell rd E3
66 D4	Campbell rd E6
31 W4	Campbell rd N17
71 T1	Campbell rd W7
122 H15	Campbell rd Croy
101 P3	Campbell rd Twick
130 E19	Campbell st W2
47 W10	Campdale rd N7
55 T10	Campden cres Dgnhm
42 B8	Campden cres Wemb
137 V16	Campden gro W8
137 S16	Campden hill W8
137 S14	Campden Hill gdns W8
137 R13	Campden Hill.pl W8
137 T15	Campden Hill rd W8
137 R15	Campden Hill sq W8
137 V16	Campden Ho clo W8
157 T11	Campden rd S Croy
137 U14	Campden st W8
143 O6	Camperdown st E1
94 M18	Campfield rd SE9
95 N18	Campfield rd SE9
142 E10	Campion clo E4
86 L12	Campion rd SW15
83 W11	Campion rd Islwth
45 P10	Campion ter NW2
24 J14	Camplin rd Harrow
75 T19	Camplin st SE14
30 B12	Campsbourne rd N8
30 A11	Campsbourne rd N8
30 A12	Campsbourne the N8
68 D2	Campsey gdns Dgnhm
68 D1	Campsey rd Dgnhm
93 U13	Campshill pl SE13
93 U13	Campshill rd SE13
32 L18	Campus rd E17
24 L6	Camrose av Edg
25 R2	Camrose av Edg
81 W17	Camrose av Enf
119 Y9	Camrose clo SW19
79 Z12	Camrose st SE2
17 Z18	Canada av N18
61 U13	Canada cres W3
61 U13	Canada rd W3
62 K20	Canada way W12
93 P20	Canadian av SE6
111 P2	Canadian av SE6
151 U13	Canal gro SE15
91 W1	Canal head SE15
93 W12	Canal rd E3
150 E15	Canal st SE5
134 G3	Canal walk N1
69 Z2	Canberra clo Dgnhm
69 Z1	Canberra cres Dgnhm
78 A17	Canberra rd SE18
77 Y18	Canberra rd SE7
80 H17	Canberra rd Bxly Hth
102 M19	Canbury av Kingst
116 H1	Canbury pas Kingst
116 K1	Canbury Pk rd Kingst
117 N1	Canbury Pk rd Kingst
116 J1	Canbury pl Kingst
90 G1	Cancell rd SW9
88 J5	Candahar rd SW11
31 P18	Candler st N15
57 Y4	Candover rd Hornch
140 B2	Candover st W1
140 A1	Candover st W1
63 Z3	Candy st E3
86 D19	Canfield gdns NW6
46 C18	Canfield pl NW6
35 P2	Canfield rd Wdfd Grn
58 D3	Canford av Grnfd
117 Z15	Canford gdns New Mald
89 N12	Canford rd SW11
123 S6	Canham rd SE25
74 A5	Canham rd W3
107 W18	Canmore gdns SW16
2 J12	Cann Hall rd E11
30 D4	Canning cres N22
91 R6	Canning cross SE5
138 A20	Canning pas W8
146 A1	Canning pl W8
138 B20	Canning Place ms W8
64 L6	Canning rd E15
32 K12	Canning rd E17
48 K9	Canning rd N5
157 U2	Canning rd Croy
23 U10	Canning rd Harrow
55 S18	Cannington rd Dgnhm
104 M13	Cannizard house SW19
105 N13	Cannizard rd SW19
118 M7	Cannon clo SW20
119 N7	Cannon clo SW20
100 K14	Cannon clo Hampt
45 Z14	Cannon hill N14
16 L9	Cannon hill N14
119 R8	Cannon Hill la SW10
46 F9	Cannon la NW3
22 B20	Cannon la Pinn
40 A3	Cannon la Pinn
46 F10	Cannon pl NW3
16 M11	Cannon rd N14
17 N11	Cannon rd N14
98 A3	Cannon rd Bxly Hth
140 K18	Cannon row SW1
142 A7	Cannon st EC4
143 W9	Cannon St rd E1
142 D10	Cannon St station EC4
22 A19	Cannonbury av Pinn
28 G20	Cannons la N2
11 X20	Cannons park Stanmore
37 V17	Canon av Rom
75 R4	Canon Beck rd SE16
126 M5	Canon rd Brom
127 N5	Canon rd Brom
134 B5	Canon st N1
92 B17	Canonbie rd SE23
48 J19	Canonbury av N1
48 J20	Canonbury gro N1
48 L18	Canonbury Pk north N1
48 L19	Canonbury Pk south N1
48 K19	Canonbury pl N1
48 J19	Canonbury rd N1
8 D6	Canonbury rd Enf
48 J20	Canonbury sq N1
48 L20	Canonbury st N1
133 Y1	Canonbury vlls N1
46 G1	Canons clo N2
12 A18	Canons clo Edg
11 Y18	Canons dri Edg
12 A19	Canons dri Edg
158 F4	Canons wlk Croy
55 R20	Canonsleigh rd Dgnhm
68 E2	Canonsleigh rd Dgnhm
135 W13	Canrobert st E2
47 X18	Cantelowes rd NW1
35 R20	Canterbury av Ilf
53 S2	Canterbury av Ilf
115 T3	Canterbury av Sidcp
111 P20	Canterbury clo Becknhm
58 K15	Canterbury clo Grnfd
108 G8	Canterbury gro SE27
33 U20	Canterbury rd E10
129 T9	Canterbury rd NW6
122 G16	Canterbury rd Croy
100 C4	Canterbury rd Felt
22 M16	Canterbury rd Harrow
23 N16	Canterbury rd Harrow
120 B12	Canterbury rd Mrdn
129 S10	Canterbury yd NW6
123 V1	Cantley gdns SE19
36 B18	Cantley gdns Ilf
71 X8	Cantley rd W7
64 B18	Canton st E14
63 Z12	Cantrell rd E3
78 L19	Cantwell rd SE18
31 X1	Cape rd N17
156 C10	Cape av Wallgtn
15 S10	Capel clo N20
127 S20	Capel clo Brom
142 G5	Capel ct EC2
54 K12	Capel gdns Ilf
22 F12	Capel gdns Pinn
53 O11	Capel rd E12
52 M10	Capel rd E7
15 V1	Capel rd Barnt
5 W20	Capel rd Barnt
139 S19	Capeners clo SW1
106 B1	Capern rd SW18
130 H16	Capland st NW8
62 C6	Caple rd NW10
132 D19	Capper st WC1
123 V18	Capri rd Croy
112 C9	Capstone rd Brom
40 E5	Capthorne av Harrow
33 S20	Capworth st E10
51 R1	Capworth st E10
76 M13	Caradoc st SE10
109 T16	Carberry rd SE19
73 O5	Carbery av W3
63 Y17	Carbis rd E14
31 Y6	Carbuncle Pas way N17
131 Z19	Carburton st W1
76 F7	Cardale st E14
92 A9	Carden rd SE15
71 Y8	Cardiff rd W7
9 O14	Cardiff rd Enf
79 U18	Cardiff st SE18
55 N6	Cardigan gdns Ilf
63 Z6	Cardigan rd E3
129 U13	Cardigan rd NW6
86 G4	Cardigan rd SW13
106 C16	Cardigan rd SW19
84 K16	Cardigan rd Rich
145 S10	Cardigan st SE11
119 S15	Cardigan st SE11
102 K14	Cardinal av Mrdn
150 F3	Cardinal Bourne st SE1
142 A11	Cardinal Cap all SE1
119 S15	Cardinal clo Mrdn
117 V3	Cardinal cres New Mald
87 P9	Cardinal pl SW15
100 M18	Cardinals wlk Hampt
82 A17	Cardington sq Hounsl
132 B13	Cardington st NW1
48 B15	Cardozo rd N7
15 U16	Cardrew av N12
15 V16	Cardrew clo N12
74 J9	Cardross st W6
78 H11	Cardwell rd SE18
31 X8	Carew rd N17
72 D5	Carew rd W13
121 N3	Carew rd Mitch
72 J17	Carew rd Thntn Hth
155 W12	Carew rd Wallgtn
90 K4	Carew st SE5
142 B4	Carey la EC2
148 F7	Carey pl SW1
55 Z12	Carey rd Dgnhm
141 R5	Carey st WC2
89 W11	Carfax sq SW4
106 B1	Cargill rd SW18
123 V10	Cargreen rd SE25
110 L2	Carholme rd SE23
121 Z9	Carisbrooke Mitch
115 V2	Carisbrooke av Bxly
8 G7	Carisbrooke av Enf
24 G7	Carisbrooke clo Stanm
32 J15	Carisbrooke rd E17
110 J16	Carisbrooke rd Brom
47 S14	Carkers la NW5
155 X18	Carleton av Wallgtn
47 Z11	Carleton rd N1
63 Z7	Carlile clo E3
46 G12	Carlingford rd NW3
30 H12	Carlingford rd N15
119 O15	Carlingford rd Mrdn
142 M7	Carlisle av EC3
62 A18	Carlisle av W3
24 G20	Carlisle gdns Harrow
35 P19	Carlisle gdns Ilf
141 R20	Carlisle la SE1
149 P1	Carlisle la SW1
130 H20	Carlisle mews NW8
148 A3	Carlisle pl SW1
51 P5	Carlisle rd E10
128 L5	Carlisle rd NW6
25 W9	Carlisle rd NW9
48 G2	Carlisle rd N4
100 K17	Carlisle rd Hampt
39 U17	Carlisle rd Rom
153 V13	Carlisle rd Sutton
140 E5	Carlisle st W1
139 V9	Carlos pl W1
132 Z7	Carlow st NW1
6 K16	Carlton av N14
24 A17	Carlton av Harrow
157 R16	Carlton av S Croy
42 G6	Carlton Av east Wemb
42 C7	Carlton Av west Wemb
12 B16	Carlton clo Edg
153 S8	Carlton cres Sutton
87 R14	Carlton dri SW15
36 D11	Carlton dri Ilf
140 E14	Carlton gdns SW1
60 E19	Carlton gdns W5
92 A1	Carlton gro SE15
151 X20	Carlton gro SE15
129 Z9	Carlton hill NW8
130 C6	Carlton hill NW8
140 G13	Carlton House ter SW1
119 O3	Carlton Park av SW20
52 B3	Carlton rd E11
53 O13	Carlton rd E12
32 H6	Carlton rd E17
16 B16	Carlton rd N11
31 T12	Carlton rd N15
48 F2	Carlton rd N4
85 U9	Carlton rd SW14
73 Y7	Carlton rd W4
60 D19	Carlton rd W5
81 X17	Carlton rd Erith
118 A3	Carlton rd New Mald
39 Y13	Carlton rd Rom
157 P16	Carlton rd S Croy
114 M11	Carlton rd Sidcp
97 R7	Carlton rd Welling
63 T11	Carlton rd sq E1
140 E12	Carlton st SW1
34 H15	Carlton ter E11
110 B8	Carlton ter SE26
18 B12	Carlton ter N18
147 R1	Carlton Tower pl SW1
129 S10	Carlton vale NW6
47 P15	Carltoun st NW5
106 H13	Carlwell st SW17
61 X3	Carlyle av NW10
127 N7	Carlyle av Brom
58 F19	Carlyle av S'hall
28 E19	Carlyle clo N2
58 D19	Carlyle gdns S'hall
53 R12	Carlyle rd E12
72 F11	Carlyle rd W5
157 U6	Carlyle rd Croy
146 H12	Carlyle sq SW3
40 G13	Carlyon av Harrow
60 J4	Carlyon clo Wemb
60 L4	Carlyon rd Wemb
87 N11	Carmalt gdns SW15
134 E3	Carmarthen st N1
137 V17	Carmel ct W8
23 N5	Carmelite clo Harrow
23 O8	Carmelite rd Harrow
141 V8	Carmelite st EC4
23 O7	Carmelite way Harrow
23 N6	Carmelite wlk Harrow
64 D11	Carmen st E14
88 G9	Carmichael clo SW11
123 W10	Carmichael rd SE25
107 S4	Carminia rd SW17
138 U4	Carnaby st W1
109 O8	Carnac st SE27
33 X5	Carnanton rd E17
8 F10	Carnarvon av Enf
33 U17	Carnarvon rd E10
52 B17	Carnarvon rd E15
34 B6	Carnarvon rd E18
4 E11	Carnarvon rd Barnt

80 C 13	Carnation st SE2
95 S 14	Carnecke gdns SE9
105 N 6	Carnegie pl SW19
133 O 6	Carnegie st N1
57 W 14	Carnforth gdns Hornch
107 W 17	Carnforth rd SW16
107 R 6	Carnie lodge SW17
87 Y 8	Carnwath rd SW6
88 A 8	Carnwath rd SW6
132 A 4	Carol st NW1
122 K 2	Carolina rd Thntn Hth
137 Y 10	Caroline clo W2
137 S 9	Caroline clo Croy
137 Y 10	Caroline pl W2
137 Y 9	Caroline pl W2
137 Y 10	Caroline Pl ms W2
105 U 18	Caroline rd SW19
63 T 18	Caroline st E1
147 T 6	Caroline ter SW1
44 K 18	Caroline wlk SW6
17 W 8	Carpenter gdns N21
139 W 10	Carpenter st W1
64 G 2	Carpenters rd E15
51 O 19	Carpenters rd E15
142 M 5	Carpenters yd EC3
32 M 7	Carr rd E17
40 H 19	Carr rd Grnfd
41 U 18	Carr rd Grnfd
63 W 15	Carr st E14
147 W 19	Carriage Dri east SW11
147 W 16	Carriage Dri north SW11
147 N 19	Carriage Dri west SW11
31 P 3	Carrick gdns N17
82 K 14	Carrington av Hounsl
85 P 11	Carrington rd Rich
139 X 14	Carrington st W1
47 S 13	Carrol pl NW5
64 D 17	Carron clo E14
149 O 17	Carroun rd SW8
55 R 20	Carrow rd Dgnhm
7 Z 16	Carrs la N21
154 G 10	Carshalton gro Sutton
154 L 9	Carshalton house Carsh
154 M 10	Carshalton Pk rd Carsh
155 O 10	Carshalton pl Carsh
121 O 12	Carshalton rd Mitch
154 E 11	Carshalton rd Sutton
86 M 15	Carslake rd SW15
65 T 14	Carson rd E16
109 N 3	Carson rd SE21
5 Y 15	Carson rd Barnt
111 U 7	Carstairs rd SE6
94 D 13	Carston clo SE12
93 U 18	Carswell rd SE6
20 L 4	Cart la E4
38 F 1	Carter clo Rom
15 Y 15	Carter clo Wallgtn
38 G 2	Carter dri Rom
141 Y 7	Carter la EC4
150 B 11	Carter pl SE17
65 U 4	Carter rd E13
106 F 15	Carter rd SW19
127 Z 12	Carter st SE17
150 A 12	Carter st SE17
140 F 19	Carteret st SW1
9 N 8	Carterhatch la Enf
8 L 7	Carterhatch la Enf
9 P 8	Carterhatch rd Enf
112 M 1	Carters Hill clo SE9
87 Y 13	Carters yd SW18
74 J 8	Carthew rd W6
74 K 8	Carthew vlls W6
133 Z 20	Carthusian st EC1
140 M 10	Carting la WC2
120 C 12	Cartmel gdns Mrdn
98 D 1	Cartmel rd Bxly Hth
139 R 4	Carton st W1
118 H 14	Cartwright gdns WC1
56 A 19	Cartwright rd Dgnhm
69 N 1	Cartwright rd Dgnhm
9 P 10	Cartwright st E1
90 L 15	Carver rd SE24
72 J 12	Carville cres Brentf
49 O 11	Carysfort rd N16
29 Y 15	Carysfort rd N8
91 O 12	Cascade av N10
75 T 20	Casella rd SE14
92 A 15	Casewick rd SE27
50 B 7	Casimir rd E5
91 O 12	Casino av SE24
135 N 13	Casket st E2
137 Y 17	Caslon pl E1
150 E 18	Caspian st SE5
61 Z 1	Casselden rd NW10
80 A 12	Cassilda rd SE2
84 C 14	Cassilis rd Twick
32 G 17	Cassiobury rd E17
50 H 19	Cassland rd E9
123 N 9	Cassland rd Thntn Hth
92 L 19	Cassles rd SE14
143 S 1	Casson st E1
76 G 7	Castalia st E14
39 Z 10	Castella av Rom
129 X 15	Castellain rd W9
130 A 18	Castellain rd W9
39 Z 10	Castellan av Rom
86 M 13	Castello. av SW15
74 H 18	Castelnau SW13
86 H 2	Castelnau SW13
94 F 8	Casterbridge rd SE3
78 J 10	Castle bri SE18
111 Z 5	Castillon rd SE6
112 A 4	Castillon rd SE6
110 L 5	Castlands rd SE6
20 K 1	Castle av E4
152 H 20	Castle av Epsom
15 S 17	Castle clo N12
105 O 5	Castle clo SW19
142 G 7	Castle ct EC3
35 R 18	Castle dri Ilf
68 B 3	Castle gdns Dgnhm
159 U 18	Castle Hill av Croy
148 B 1	Castle la SW1
47 T 19	Castle rd NW1
15 S 17	Castle rd N12
68 C 4	Castle rd Dgnhm
9 V 4	Castle rd Enf
40 J 19	Castle rd Grnfd
83 V 4	Castle rd Islwth
66 A 6	Castle st E6
65 Z 6	Castle st E6
116 J 2	Castle st Kingst
105 O 5	Castle way SW19
47 P 1	Castle yd N6
141 Y 12	Castle yd SE1.
142 A 9	Castle Yd la EC4
60 C 15	Castlebar hill W5
60 C 13	Castlebar ms W5
60 B 13	Castlebar pk W5
60 E 16	Castlebar rd W5
87 R 19	Castlecombe dri SW19
113 P 11	Castlecombe rd SE9
109 Z 19	Castledine rd SE20
95 Z 20	Castleford av SE9
113 Z 1	Castleford av SE9
84 M 9	Castlegate Rich
47 S 19	Castlehaven rd NW1
131 X 1	Castlehaven rd NW1
8 C 17	Castleleigh ct Enf
150 L 16	Castlemain rd SE15
157 U 11	Castlemaine S Croy
152 K 19	Castlemaine av Epsom
139 N 3	Castlereagh st W1
98 M 3	Castleton av Bxly
99 N 4	Castleton av Bxly Hth
42 J 12	Castleton av Wemb
33 X 7	Castleton rd E17
113 O 10	Castleton rd SE9
55 O 4	Castleton rd Ilf
121 W 9	Castleton rd Mitch
144 M 11	Castletown rd W14
145 N 10	Castletown rd W14
35 S 18	Castleview gdns Ilf
95 V 4	Castlewood dri SE9
49 V 1	Castlewood rd E5
31 X 20	Castlewood rd N16
5 V 20	Castlewood rd Barnt
64 A 19	Castor st E14
135 V 5	Cat & Mutton bndge E8
5 X 18	Cat hill Barnt
6 A 18	Cat hill Barnt
35 V 7	Caterham av Ilf
93 V 8	Caterham rd SE13
150 G 7	Catesby st SE17
93 P 19	Catford bdwy SE6
93 P 19	Catford rd SE6
51 X 8	Cathall rd E11
143 X 18	Cathay st SE16
75 N 16	Cathay st SE16
17 N 19	Cathcart hill N19
146 A 13	Cathcart rd SW10
47 S 16	Cathcart st NW5
141 Z 5	Cathedral pl EC4
142 E 13	Cathedral st SE1
48 M 10	Catherall rd N5
6 H 17	Catherine ct N14
83 P 11	Catherine gdns Hounsl
93 R 1	Catherine gro SE10
140 B 20	Catherine pl SW1
39 Y 16	Catherine rd Rom
116 G 11	Catherine rd Surb
141 N 8	Catherine st WC2
140 B 15	Catherine wheel SW1
142 K 2	Catherine Wheel all E1
72 G 19	Catherine Wheel yd Brentf
89 T 17	Cathles rd SW12
74 J 7	Cathnor rd W12
9 V 1	Catisfield rd Enf
151 U 10	Catlin st SE16
110 D 7	Catling clo SE23
89 Y 9	Cato rd SW4
138 M 3	Cato st W1
108 A 6	Caton pas SW16
110 D 4	Cator la Becknhm
110 J 19	Cator park Becknhm
110 F 15	Cator rd SE26
155 N 11	Cator rd Carsh
151 O 17	Cator st SE15
150 M 17	Cator st SE15
151 O 17	Cator st SE15
10 A 5	Catsey woods Bushey Watf
95 S 4	Cattistock rd SE9
66 E 2	Caulfield rd E6
92 A 4	Caulfield rd SE15
28 H 13	Causeway the N2
87 Z 12	Causeway the SW18
104 M 12	Causeway the SW19
105 N 12	Causeway the SW19
155 O 4	Causeway the Carsh
154 B 19	Causeway the Sutton
101 W 14	Causeway the Tedd
19 O 3	Causewayre rd N9
47 T 1	Causton rd N6
148 G 8	Causton st SW1
88 H 1	Cautley av SW4
146 O 12	Cavaye pl SW10
65 M 8	Cave rd E13
31 O 2	Cavell rd N17
63 N 16	Cavell st E1
143 Y 4	Cavell st E1
130 G 11	Cavendish av NW8
27 X 8	Cavendish av N3
59 Y 18	Cavendish av W13
81 W 17	Cavendish av Erith
41 T 13	Cavendish av Harrow
118 H 10	Cavendish av New Mald
97 N 18	Cavendish av Sidcp
34 G 3	Cavendish av Wdfd Grn
96 M 8	Cavendish av Welling
130 G 12	Cavendish clo NW8
57 Y 18	Cavendish cres Hornchurch
142 K 3	Cavendish ct EC2
51 V 3	Cavendish dri E11
12 A 19	Cavendish dri Edg
54 L 15	Cavendish gdns Bark
53 W 3	Cavendish gdns Ilf
37 Z 17	Cavendish gdns Ilf
139 Y 1	Cavendish ms W1
139 Y 3	Cavendish pl W1
20 H 20	Cavendish rd E4
45 U 19	Cavendish rd NW6
19 N 16	Cavendish rd N18
30 H 18	Cavendish rd N4
89 T 16	Cavendish rd SW12
106 J 17	Cavendish rd SW19
107 T 1	Cavendish rd SW4
85 W 1	Cavendish rd W4
4 A 12	Cavendish rd Barnt
122 J 19	Cavendish rd Croy
118 C 10	Cavendish rd New Mald
154 C 15	Cavendish rd Sutton
139 Y 4	Cavendish sq W1
134 E 9	Cavendish st N1
125 P 20	Cavendish way W Wkhm
54 C 10	Cavenham gdns Ilf
118 H 14	Caverleigh way Worc Pk
17 T 10	Caversham av N13
153 R 2	Caversham av Sutton
47 U 17	Caversham rd NW5
30 L 13	Caversham rd N15
147 N 13	Caversham st SW3
136 B 4	Caverswall rd W10
62 L 16	Caverswall rd W12
127 V 1	Caveside clo Chisl
71 Z 10	Cawdor cres W7
63 U 2	Cawley rd E9
109 T 14	Cawnpore st SE19
64 A 7	Caxton gro E3
30 D 7	Caxton rd N22
106 C 13	Caxton rd SW19
136 E 16	Caxton rd W12
65 P 19	Caxton st E16
148 D 1	Caxton st SW1
77 R 1	Caxton St south E16
59 U 7	Cayton rd Grnfd
134 D 14	Cayton st EC1
33 O 6	Cazenove rd E17
49 Y 5	Cazenove rd N16
54 D 20	Cecil av Bark
8 G 14	Cecil av Enf
42 M 16	Cecil av Wemb
140 H 10	Cecil ct WC2
22 D 13	Cecil pk Pinn
121 N 11	Cecil pl Mitch
65 T 4	Cecil rd E11
33 O 3	Cecil rd E17
62 A 4	Cecil rd NW10
25 Z 11	Cecil rd NW9
29 T 7	Cecil rd N10
16 F 5	Cecil rd N14
106 A 18	Cecil rd SW19
61 W 15	Cecil rd W3
122 C 16	Cecil rd Croy
7 Z 13	Cecil rd Enf
8 B 14	Cecil rd Enf
23 S 10	Cecil rd Harrow
83 N 6	Cecil rd Hounsl
53 Y 12	Cecil rd Ilf
55 X 1	Cecil rd Rom
153 R 2	Cecil rd Sutton
126 E 19	Cecil way Brom
30 A 19	Cecile pk N8
49 W 15	Cecilia rd E8
15 W 1	Cedar av Barnt
9 P 8	Cedar av Enf
37 Y 15	Cedar av Rom
96 M 17	Cedar av Sidcp
82 M 15	Cedar av Twick
38 L 12	Cedar clo Rom
127 T 3	Cedar copse Brom
105 P 8	Cedar ct SW19
28 H 13	Cedar dri N2
154 D 14	Cedar gdns Sutton
72 J 7	Cedar gro W5
97 V 16	Cedar gro Sidcp
58 H 14	Cedar gro S'hall
102 J 1	Cedar heights Rich
14 F 7	Cedar Lawn av Barnt
55 V 1	Cedar Park gdns Rom
8 A 3	Cedar Park rd Enf
45 N 12	Cedar rd NW2
31 V 4	Cedar rd N17
126 L 3	Cedar rd Brom
157 R 2	Cedar rd Croy
7 X 4	Cedar rd Enf
99 V 2	Cedar rd Erith
38 K 14	Cedar rd Rom
154 C 14	Cedar rd Sutton
13 Y 13	Cedar rd Tedd
16 C 2	Cedar rd N14
84 L 10	Cedar ter Rich
108 J 12	Cedar Tree gro SE27
74 C 1	Cedar way W3
94 K 14	Cedarhurst dri SE9
145 W 19	Cedarne rd SW6
33 O 15	Cedars av E17
121 P 8	Cedars av Mitch
27 O 10	Cedars clo NW4
18 E 7	Cedars ct N9
89 R 10	Cedars ms SW4
52 A 18	Cedars rd E15
17 W 7	Cedars rd N21
18 J 9	Cedars rd N9
86 F 5	Cedars rd SW13
89 S 10	Cedars rd SW4
73 V 15	Cedars rd W4
124 L 3	Cedars rd Becknhm
156 B 7	Cedars rd Croy
102 D 20	Cedars rd Kingst
119 Y 8	Cedars rd Mrdn
21 T 6	Cedars the Buck HI
101 X 5	Cedars the Tedd
108 D 16	Cedarville gdns SW16
39 R 10	Cedric av Rom
114 B 6	Cedric rd SE9
137 Y 3	Celbridge ms W2
47 V 12	Celia rd N19
125 Z 7	Celtic av Brom
126 A 7	Celtic av Brom
64 F 13	Celtic st E14
78 D 17	Cemetery la SE7
52 D 13	Cemetery rd E7
31 T 3	Cemetery rd N17
80 C 19	Cemetery rd SE2
149 R 1	Centaur st SE1
51 X 7	Central av E11
28 F 8	Central av N2

18 F 10	Central av N9
8 M 8	Central av Enf
9 N 8	Central av Enf
83 O 12	Central av Hounsl
22 D 19	Central av Pinn
156 B 11	Central av Wallgtn
96 M 4	Central av Welling
109 P 14	Central hill SE19
141 W 2	Central mkt EC1
56 L 7	Central park Rom
56 H 10	Central Park av Dgnhm
59 Y 8	Central pde Grnfd
66 F 6	Central Pk rd E6
65 Z 7	Central Pk rd E6
120 B 10	Central rd Mrdn
42 B 15	Central rd Wemb
152 H 2	Central rd Worc Pk
85 V 7	Central School path SW14
27 Z 17	Central sq NW11
133 Z 12	Central st EC1
134 A 16	Central st EC1
154 J 16	Central way Carsh
73 Y 3	Centre av W3
114 B 17	Centre Common rd Chisl
52 F 6	Centre rd E11
78 H 13	Centre rd E7
69 V 5	Centre rd Dgnhm
63 N 7	Centre st E2
38 W 9	Centre st E2
19 S 8	Centre way N9
32 H 11	Century rd E17
63 R 12	Cephas av E1
63 O 12	Cephas st E1
135 Z 17	Cephas st E1
79 X 12	Ceres rd SE18
91 X 3	Cerise rd SE15
120 C 14	Cerne rd Mrdn
144 J 2	Ceylon rd W14
148 B 18	Ceylon st SW8
63 X 5	Chad st E3
35 U 9	Chadacre av Ilf
152 J 12	Chadacre rd Epsom
64 E 15	Chadbourn st E14
127 S 7	Chadd dri Brom
37 V 16	Chadville gdns Rom
55 U 5	Chadway Dgnhm
55 R 1	Chadwell av Rom
37 S 17	Chadwell Heath la Rom
133 U 11	Chadwell st EC1
20 L 12	Chadwick av E4
34 A 20	Chadwick rd E11
91 U 5	Chadwick rd SE15
148 F 3	Chadwick st SW1
65 V 14	Chadwin rd E13
124 F 13	Chaffinch av Croy
124 F 13	Chaffinch clo Croy
124 K 1	Chaffinch rd Becknhm
37 S 14	Chaford way Rom
131 P 18	Chagford st NW1
8 F 8	Chailey av Enf
50 C 10	Chailey st E5
80 D 8	Chalcombe rd SE2
131 R 3	Chalcot cres NW1
131 S 2	Chalcot rd NW1
131 T 1	Chalcot sq NW1
46 L 18	Chalcote gdns NW3
93 Z 13	Chalcroft rd SE13
144 L 17	Chaldon rd SW6
90 A 17	Chale rd SW2
43 T 18	Chalfont av Wemb
18 F 10	Chalfont grn N9
48 E 17	Chalfont rd N7
18 F 11	Chalfont rd N9
123 V 6	Chalfont rd SE25
72 A 9	Chalfont way W13
109 P 8	Chalford rd SE21
35 N 3	Chalford wlk Wdfd Grn
119 Y 12	Chalgrove av Mrdn
35 P 7	Chalgrove cres Ilf
27 T 10	Chalgrove gdns N3
50 B 17	Chalgrove rd E9
31 Z 4	Chalgrove rd N17
154 F 17	Chalgrove rd Sutton
47 O 20	Chalk Farm rd NW1
5 Z 12	Chalk la Barnt
6 A 13	Chalk la Barnt
65 W 14	Chalk rd E13
43 R 9	Chalkhill rd Wemb
43 V 9	Chalklands Wemb
8 C 15	Chalkwell Pk av Enf
90 D 20	Challice way SW2
110 B 19	Challin st SE20
72 G 13	Challis rd Brentf
28 F 8	Challoner clo N2
145 O 11	Challoner cres W14
145 O 11	Challoner st W14
89 U 4	Chalmers rd SW8

49 T 10	Chalmers ter N16
92 M 10	Chalsey rd SE4
28 F 18	Chalton dri N2
132 D 8	Chalton st NW1
143 P 8	Chamber st E1
125 P 19	Chamberlain cres W Wkhm
28 D 8	Chamberlain rd N2
131 P 1	Chamberlain st NW1
116 K 19	Chamberlain way Surb
62 M 2	Chamberlayne rd NW10
128 D 7	Chamberlayne rd NW10
28 F 5	Chambers gdns N2
44 L 20	Chambers la NW10
128 B 1	Chambers la NW10
62 L 1	Chambers la NW10
48 A 11	Chambers rd N7
143 T 18	Chambers st SE16
135 O 13	Chambord st E2
110 H 9	Champion cres SE26
91 P 6	Champion gro SE5
91 O 7	Champion hill SE5
91 R 8	Champion hill SE5
110 J 9	Champion sq SE26
153 T 17	Champneys clo Sutton
141 X 14	Chancel st SE1
109 N 6	Chancellor gro SE21
108 M 5	Chancellor gro SE24
74 M 15	Chancellors rd W6
144 D 11	Chancellors rd W6
74 M 14	Chancellors st W6
144 C 10	Chancellors st W6
80 E 11	Chancellot rd SE2
141 R 3	Chancery la WC2
125 S 3	Chancery la Becknhm
14 J 14	Chanctonbury way N12
65 S 14	Chandler av E16
75 N 2	Chandler st E1
143 X 12	Chandler st E1
33 P 8	Chandos av E17
16 H 11	Chandos av N14
15 S 5	Chandos av N20
72 F 10	Chandos av W5
21 V 8	Chandos clo Buck Hl
25 N 2	Chandos cres Edg
140 K 10	Chandos pl WC2
51 W 14	Chandos rd E15
62 A 11	Chandos rd NW10
44 M 15	Chandos rd NW2
31 S 8	Chandos rd N17
28 H 8	Chandos rd N2
23 O 16	Chandos rd Harrow
139 Y 3	Change all EC3
142 G 7	Change all EC3
64 J 3	Channelsea rd E15
64 K 1	Chant rd E15
90 D 8	Chantrey rd SW9
7 Y 3	Chantry clo Enf
24 M 16	Chantry clo Harrow
115 Z 14	Chantry clo Sidcp
126 M 11	Chantry la Brom
127 N 11	Chantry la Brom
22 K 4	Chantry pl Harrow
22 K 4	Chantry rd Harrow
133 Y 6	Chantry st N1
69 Z 5	Chantry way Rainhm
99 P 12	Chapel clo Drtfrd
28 H 10	Chapel ct N2
142 E 17	Chapel ct SE1
113 T 6	Chapel Farm rd SE9
78 F 9	Chapel hill SE18
99 P 12	Chapel hill Drtfrd
76 E 12	Chapel Ho pl E14
76 E 12	Chapel Ho st E14
22 A 11	Chapel la Pinn
55 W 1	Chapel la Rom
133 S 8	Chapel mkt N1
133 T 8	Chapel pl EC1
31 V 1	Chapel pl N17
139 X 5	Chapel pl W1
108 K 10	Chapel rd SE27
72 B 2	Chapel rd W13
98 E 10	Chapel rd Bxly Hth
82 M 9	Chapel rd Hounsl
120 F 5	Chapel rd Mitch
84 C 19	Chapel rd Twick
72 M 5	Chapel side W2
64 K 1	Chapel st E15
138 K 2	Chapel st NW1
139 V 19	Chapel st SW1
8 A 11	Chapel st Enf
158 B 15	Chapel view S Croy
126 F 4	Chapel way Brom
44 H 18	Chapel wlk Croy
31 U 10	Chaplin rd N17
55 Z 20	Chaplin rd Dgnhm

68 M 1	Chaplin rd Dgnhm
42 H 18	Chaplin rd Wemb
24 L 17	Chapman cres Harrow
50 L 18	Chapman rd E9
81 T 14	Chapman rd Blvdr
122 E 19	Chapman rd Croy
63 N 19	Chapman st E1
143 X 8	Chapman st E1
80 G 12	Chapmans la SE2
44 E 17	Chapmans pk NW10
44 F 16	Chapter rd NW2
149 Y 12	Chapter rd SE17
12 T 5	Chapter st E7
148 E 7	Chapter st SW1
149 X 13	Charc-field ter SE17
9 T 13	Charcroft gdns Enf
74 A 11	Chardin rd W4
49 X 4	Chardmore rd N16
65 T 15	Charford st E16
65 R 11	Chargeable la E13
65 R 11	Chargeable st E16
140 G 7	Charing Cross rd WC2
130 K 9	Charlbert st NW8
11 T 17	Charlbury av Stanm
54 L 7	Charlbury gdns Ilf
60 E 16	Charlbury gro W5
110 A 6	Charldane rd SE9
55 Y 11	Charlecote gro SE26
	Charlecote rd Dgnhm
68 E 6	Charlemont rd E6
115 S 9	Charles clo Sidcp
41 P 2	Charles cres Harrow
78 J 10	Charles Grinling wlk SE18
140 E 12	Charles Ii st SW1
130 J 9	Charles la NW8
65 Y 1	Charles rd E7
56 M 19	Charles rd Rom
37 V 19	Charles rd Rom
134 H 14	Charles.sq N1
77 Z 3	Charles st E16
86 B 6	Charles st SW13
139 V 12	Charles st W1
156 L 5	Charles st Croy
8 G 17	Charles st Enf
112 M 7	Charlesfield SE9
150 C 7	Charleston st SE17
81 X 19	Charlesville rd Erith
48 B 20	Charlesworth st N1
109 V 12	Charleville cir SE26
144 M 11	Charleville rd W14
145 N 10	Charleville rd W14
106 L 14	Charlmont rd SW17
89 P 2	Charlotte Despard av SW8
132 C 20	Charlotte ms W1
134 K 14	Charlotte rd EC2
86 D 2	Charlotte rd SW13
56 G 18	Charlotte rd Dgnhm
155 V 14	Charlotte rd Wallgtn
89 U 7	Charlotte row SW4
132 C 20	Charlotte st W1
140 D 2	Charlotte st W1
133 R 6	Charlotte ter N1
81 R 16	Charlton clo Blvdr
67 X 6	Charlton cres Bark
78 A 20	Charlton dene SE18
77 Z 19	Charlton dene SE7
78 A 17	Charlton house SE18
47 X 15	Charlton Kings rd NW5
78 B 17	Charlton park SE18
78 C 18	Charlton Pk la SE7
78 B 16	Charlton Pk rd SE7
133 W 7	Charlton pl N1
62 C 3	Charlton rd NW10
19 T 1	Charlton rd N9
77 O 14	Charlton rd SE10
77 W 17	Charlton rd SE7
24 J 11	Charlton rd Harrow
43 N 5	Charlton rd Wemb
93 Y 2	Charlton way SE10
77 P 20	Charlton way SE3
94 A 1	Charlton way SE3
10 G 20	Charlwood clo Harrow
148 C 8	Charlwood pl SW1
87 O 10	Charlwood rd SW15
148 B 9	Charlwood st SW1
97 S 2	Charmaith rd Welling
24 G 9	Charmian av Stanm
119 Z 4	Charminster av SW19
113 O 10	Charminster rd SE9
143 O 12	Charminster rd Worc Pk
49 Z 11	Charnock rd E5

118 B 9	Charnwood clo New Mald
34 G 12	Charnwood dri E18
123 P 10	Charnwood rd SE25
49 Y 7	Charnwood st E5
132 E 8	Charrington st NW1
111 R 4	Charsley rd SE6
126 A 2	Chart clo Brom
134 G 13	Chart st N1
54 E 3	Charter av Ilf
82 A 10	Charter cres Hounsl
97 Y 18	Charter dri Bxly
117 T 5	Charter rd Kingst
20 M 18	Charter Rd the Wdfd Grn
21 P 18	Charter Rd the Wdfd Grn
117 T 4	Charter sq Kingst
16 J 1	Charter way N14
27 V 11	Charter way N3
42 C 14	Charterhouse av Wemb
133 Y 19	Charterhouse ms EC1
133 Y 19	Charterhouse sq EC1
133 Y 20	Charterhouse st EC1
141 W 1	Charterhouse st EC1
129 R 5	Charteris rd NW6
48 E 5	Charteris rd N4
34 G 3	Charteris rd Wdfd Grn
21 W 19	Charteris rd Wdfd Grn
109 S 12	Charters clo SE19
87 N 14	Chartfield av SW15
87 P 13	Chartfield sq SW15
108 H 7	Chartham gro SE27
123 Z 7	Chartham rd SE25
44 B 10	Chartley av NW2
10 J 19	Chartley av Stanm
77 Y 14	Charton Ch la SE7
114 D 5	Chartwell clo SE9
7 X 9	Chase Creen av Enf
38 J 2	Chase Cross rd Rom
7 X 11	Chase Ct gdns Enf
19 Z 16	Chase gdns E4
83 S 17	Chase gdns Twick
7 Z 11	Chase grn Enf
7 Y 10	Chase hill Enf
36 D 15	Chase la Ilf
34 B 7	Chase rd E18
61 Y 10	Chase rd NW10
6 H 15	Chase rd N14
16 K 2	Chase rd N14
7 T 10	Chase ridings Enf
7 Z 11	Chase side Enf
119 S 2	Chase Side av SW20
53 N 12	Chase the E12
108 E 19	Chase the SW16
119 T 1	Chase the SW20
89 T 9	Chase the SW4
126 H 5	Chase the Brom
98 G 7	Chase the Bxly Hth
25 S 5	Chase the Edg
57 T 9	Chase the Pinn
22 D 12	Chase the Pinn
39 O 11	Chase the Rom
37 Y 18	Chase the Rom
10 L 18	Chase the Stanm
158 B 11	Chase the Wallgtn
16 G 5	Chase way N14
106 M 10	Chasefield rd SW17
107 N 11	Chasefield rd SW17
63 V 17	Chaseley st E14
8 A 9	Chaseside av Enf
8 A 7	Chaseside cres Enf
7 O 18	Chaseville Pk rd N21
7 V 7	Chasewood av Enf
99 X 17	Chastilian rd Dart
47 N 16	Chaston st NW5
60 K 16	Chatfield pl W5
88 E 8	Chatfield rd SW11
122 J 19	Chatfield rd Croy
26 D 18	Chatham av N11
134 E 11	Chatham av N1
27 Z 16	Chatham clo NW11
119 V 18	Chatham clo Sutton
50 C 17	Chatham pl E9
32 H 11	Chatham rd E17
34 C 7	Chatham rd E18
88 L 15	Chatham rd SW11
117 O 2	Chatham rd Kingst
150 F 5	Chatham st SE17
26 L 8	Chatsworth av NW4
119 T 2	Chatsworth av SW20
112 G 11	Chatsworth av Brom
115 O 1	Chatsworth av Sidcp
43 N 16	Chatsworth av Wemb
26 L 8	Chatsworth clo NW4

83 P 9 Chatsworth cres Hounsl
18 J 1 Chatsworth dri Enf
8 K 20 Chatsworth dri Enf
73 S 2 Chatsworth gdns W3
40 K 4 Chatsworth gdns Harrow
118 D 11 Chatsworth gdns New Mald
101 X 9 Chatsworth pl Tedd
52 B 15 Chatsworth rd E15
50 S 8 Chatsworth rd E5
45 M 18 Chatsworth rd NW2
73 W 17 Chatsworth rd W4
60 M 12 Chatsworth rd W4
157 O 7 Chatsworth rd Croy
153 R 9 Chatsworth rd Sutton
150 B 4 Chatsworth ri W5
108 K 6 Chatsworth way SE27
150 B 4 Chatteris rd SE17
48 J 9 Chatterton rd N4
127 N 11 Chatterton rd Brom
85 R 6 Chatto rd SW11
89 N 13 Chatto rd SW11
16 J 16 Chaucer av Rich
35 U 17 Chaucer clo N11
124 C 17 Chaucer gdns Sutton
34 F 18 Chaucer rd E11
35 U 6 Chaucer rd E17
52 G 18 Chaucer rd E7
90 G 14 Chaucer rd SE24
73 W 2 Chaucer rd W3
39 Z 1 Chaucer rd Rom
115 U 3 Chaucer rd Sidcp
153 X 7 Chaucer rd Sutton
96 J 2 Chaucer rd Welling
18 J 10 Chauncey av
95 T 16 Chaundrye clo SE9
65 W 19 Chauntler rd E16
152 L 4 Cheam Comm rd Worc Pk
153 P 14 Cheam park Sutton
153 R 13 Cheam Pk way Sutton
153 P 20 Cheam rd Sutton
142 B 6 Cheapside EC2
12 C 12 Cheddington rd N18
111 W 11 Chelford rd Brom
68 C 7 Chelmer cres Bark
50 F 14 Chelmer rd E9
39 O 1 Chelmsford av Rom
33 O 1 Chelmsford gdns Ilf
97 S 17 Chelmsford rd E11
33 N 18 Chelmsford rd E17
34 B 4 Chelmsford rd E18
16 H 4 Chelmsford rd N14
62 L 4 Chelmsford sq NW10
128 B 5 Chelmsford sq NW10
144 J 12 Chelmsford st W6
147 W 13 Chelsea br SW1
147 U 11 Chelsea Br rd SW1
25 O 7 Chelsea clo Edg
101 N 13 Chelsea clo Hampt
147 T 13 Chelsea embankment SW3
146 H 16 Chelsea embankment SW3
146 L 12 Chelsea Manor st SW3
146 K 12 Chelsea Mnr gdns SW3
146 F 14 Chelsea Pk gdns SW3
146 H 10 Chelsea sq SW3
19 S 2 Chelsfield av N9
110 D 8 Chelsfield gdns SE26
89 Y 7 Chelsham rd SW4
157 O 15 Chelsham rd S Croy
79 S 18 Chelsworth dri SE18
83 Y 19 Cheltenham av Twick
40 J 17 Cheltenham clo Grnfd
66 D 7 Cheltenham gdns E6
73 T 4 Cheltenham pl W3
24 J 13 Cheltenham pl Harrow
33 U 19 Cheltenham rd E10
92 D 12 Cheltenham rd SE15
147 P 9 Cheltenham ter SW3
87 P 10 Chelverton rd SW15
85 R 4 Chelwood gdns Rich
92 G 11 Chelwood wlk SE4
116 M 10 Chemleigh wlk Surb
132 J 10 Cheney rd NW1
32 K 4 Cheney row E17

52 A 10 Cheneys rd E11
132 E 18 Chenies ms WC1
132 F 8 Chenies pl NW1
132 E 20 Chenies st WC1
145 W 1 Cheniston gdns W8
145 X 1 Cheniston gdns W8
137 T 8 Chepstow cres W11
58 F 18 Chepstow gdns S'hall
137 V 7 Chepstow ms W2
137 U 7 Chepstow pl W2
137 U 4 Chepstow pl W2
71 X 7 Chepstow rd W7
157 S 4 Chepstow rd Croy
157 T 5 Chepstow ri Croy
137 R 9 Chepstow vlls W11
38 J 19 Chepstow way Ilf
134 D 18 Chequer st EC1
69 R 5 Chequers la Dgnhm
69 R 7 Chequers La cotts Dgnhm
17 X 15 Chequers way N13
134 G 9 Cherbury st N1
71 V 2 Cherington rd W7
126 D 12 Cheriton av Brom
35 V 6 Cheriton av Ilf
79 S 18 Cheriton dri SE18
107 P 4 Cheriton sq SW17
154 L 2 Cherry clo Carsh
119 S 9 Cherry clo Mrdn
72 A 19 Cherry cres Brentf
72 H 13 Cherry garth Brentf
143 W 19 Cherry Gdn st SE6
56 A 14 Cherry gdns Dgnhm
5 O 20 Cherry hill Barnt
156 D 8 Cherry Hill gdns Croy
77 X 17 Cherry orchard SE7
157 P 1 Cherry orchard Croy
123 R 20 Cherry Orchard rd Croy
9 R 3 Cherry rd Enf
38 M 15 Cherry st Rom
28 L 13 Cherry Tree rd N2
21 Z 13 Cherry Tree ri Buck Hl
124 M 8 Cherry Tree wlk Becknhm
28 L 14 Cherry Tree woods N2
126 F 19 Cherry wlk Brom
19 Z 11 Cherrydown av E4
20 A 12 Cherrydown av E4
19 Z 11 Cherrydown clo E4
20 A 11 Cherrydown clo E4
38 H 7 Cherrydown clo Rom
115 W 5 Cherrydown rd Sidcp
11 O 18 Cherrytree way Stanm
87 O 13 Cherrywood dri SW15
119 S 8 Cherrywood la Mrdn
153 T 4 Chertsey dri Sutton
51 X 5 Chertsey rd E11
73 P 14 Chertsey rd W4
54 D 13 Chertsey rd Ilf
100 L 3 Chertsey rd Twick
83 W 17 Chertsey rd Twick
101 N 1 Chertsey rd Twick
107 N 12 Chertsey st SW17
110 A 6 Cheseman st SE26
102 L 18 Chesfield rd Kingst
127 Z 14 Chesham av Brom
38 M 12 Chesham clo Rom
124 D 1 Chesham cres SE20
147 E 1 Chesham ms SW1
147 S 2 Chesham ms SW1
147 S 1 Chesham pl SW1
124 D 2 Chesham pl SE20
106 F 13 Chesham rd SW19
117 P 2 Chesham rd Kingst
43 Y 11 Chesham st NW10
147 S 3 Chesham st SW1
72 A 4 Chesham ter W13
141 U 6 Cheshire ct EC4
17 P 20 Cheshire rd N22
30 C 1 Cheshire rd N22
135 S 16 Cheshire st E2
49 S 9 Chesholm rd N16
52 J 19 Cheshunt rd E7
81 R 14 Cheshunt rd Blvdr
89 R 19 Chesil pl SW12
87 U 1 Chesilton rd SW6
66 C 8 Chesley gdns E6
159 U 15 Chesney cres Croy
89 N 2 Chesney st SW11
31 W 10 Chesnut rd N17
27 V 11 Chessington av N3
80 M 19 Chessington av Bxly Hth

22 E 14 Chessington ct Pinn
81 O 19 Chessington rd Bxly Hth
152 B 20 Chessington rd Epsom
159 S 3 Chessington way W Wkhm
145 P 13 Chesson rd W14
82 E 20 Chester av Hounsl
84 M 15 Chester av Rich
100 D 1 Chester av Twick
139 W 20 Chester clo SW1
86 K 8 Chester clo SW15
53 Y 3 Chester clo Sutton
131 X 13 Chester Clo north NW1
131 X 13 Chester Clo south NW1
22 H 17 Chester dri Harrow
131 X 14 Chester ga NW1
9 N 19 Chester gdns Enf
120 C 13 Chester gdns Mrdn
79 O 12 Chester gro SE18
139 W 20 Chester ms SW1
131 X 11 Chester pl NW1
34 J 19 Chester rd E11
53 N 20 Chester rd E12
65 N 12 Chester rd E16
32 F 17 Chester rd E17
131 V 13 Chester rd NW1
31 P 9 Chester rd N17
47 S 7 Chester rd N19
19 N 7 Chester rd N9
104 M 15 Chester rd SW19
54 L 2 Chester rd Ilf
96 H 13 Chester rd Sidcp
147 T 7 Chester row SW1
147 U 6 Chester row SW1
147 V 4 Chester Sq SW1
147 W 3 Chester Sq ms SW1
51 Y 8 Chester st E11
139 W 20 Chester st SW1
147 T 7 Chester way SE11
30 K 17 Chesterfield gdns N4
139 W 13 Chesterfield gdns W1
91 U 12 Chesterfield gro SE22
139 W 12 Chesterfield hill W1
33 U 20 Chesterfield rd E10
14 L 18 Chesterfield rd N3
73 W 17 Chesterfield rd W4
4 B 18 Chesterfield rd Enf
9 V 1 Chesterfield rd Enf
139 W 13 Chesterfield st W1
139 W 13 Chesterfield wlk SE10
46 B 13 Chesterfield gdns NW3
53 U 17 Chesterford rd E12
104 A 20 Chesters the New Mald
58 K 6 Chesterton clo Grnfd
68 E 13 Chesterton rd E13
136 H 3 Chesterton rd W10
65 S 8 Chesterton ter E13
117 P 4 Chesterton ter Kingst
30 M 5 Chesthunte rd N17
145 R 15 Chestnut all SW6
52 K 13 Chestnut av E7
29 Z 15 Chestnut av N8
33 V 14 Chestnut av SE17
85 Y 9 Chestnut av SW14
72 H 12 Chestnut av Brentf
11 Y 19 Chestnut av Edg
152 A 9 Chestnut av Epsom
100 G 18 Chestnut av Hampt
57 U 7 Chestnut av Hornch
42 A 14 Chestnut av Wemb
33 V 13 Chestnut Av north E17
6 J 18 Chestnut clo N14
154 L 1 Chestnut clo Carsh
145 R 15 Chestnut ct SW6
34 E 19 Chestnut dri E11
97 X 8 Chestnut dri Bxly Hth
23 V 3 Chestnut dri Harrow
22 A 19 Chestnut dri Pinn
154 B 8 Chestnut gdns Sutton
57 U 8 Chestnut glen Hornch
89 O 19 Chestnut gro N17
107 P 1 Chestnut gro W12
72 G 7 Chestnut gro W12
5 Z 18 Chestnut gro Barnt
83 Y 10 Chestnut gro Islwth
121 Y 9 Chestnut gro Mitch

118 A 5 Chestnut gro New Mald
158 B 16 Chestnut gro S Croy
42 A 14 Chestnut gro Wemb
108 K 6 Chestnut rd SE27
119 R 3 Chestnut rd SW20
102 J 18 Chestnut rd Twick
101 S 3 Chestnut rd Twick
79 U 14 Chestnut rd SE18
21 S 16 Chestnut wlk Wdfd Grn
158 J 1 Cheston av Croy
99 S 3 Chesworth clo Erith
30 E 18 Chettle ct N8
107 N 5 Chetwode rd SW17
15 Z 5 Chetwynd av Barnt
47 S 11 Chetwynd rd NW5
146 L 1 Cheval pl SW7
128 G 9 Chevening rd NW6
77 R 14 Chevening rd SE10
109 O 16 Chevening rd SE19
115 S 6 Chevenings the Sidcp
47 X 3 Cheverton rd N19
50 H 15 Chevet st E9
99 P 4 Cheviot clo Bxly Hth
8 B 9 Cheviot clo Enf
154 F 20 Cheviot clo Sutton
45 S 8 Cheviot ga NW2
45 R 7 Cheviot gdns NW2
108 J 10 Cheviot rd SE27
57 W 2 Cheviot way Hornch
36 H 14 Cheviot way Ilf
32 H 14 Chewton rd E17
34 B 10 Cheyne av E18
100 F 2 Cheyne av Twick
146 M 14 Cheyne gdns SW3
116 M 9 Cheyne hill Surb
117 N 10 Cheyne hill Surb
146 K 15 Cheyne row SW3
146 K 16 Cheyne walk SW3
26 M 18 Cheyne wlk NW4
7 V 16 Cheyne wlk N21
146 F 17 Cheyne wlk SW10
146 L 15 Cheyne wlk SW3
157 X 3 Cheyne wlk Croy
11 V 19 Cheyneys av Edg
24 J 1 Cheyneys av Edg
157 T 8 Chichele gdns Croy
45 P 13 Chichele rd NW2
22 M 2 Chicheley gdns Harrow
23 N 3 Chicheley rd Harrow
141 O 16 Chicheley st SE1
24 L 10 Chichester ct Stanm
53 S 2 Chichester gdns Ilf
52 A 10 Chichester rd E11
129 U 9 Chichester rd NW6
18 J 5 Chichester rd N9
157 U 6 Chichester rd Croy
141 R 5 Chichester rents WC2
148 D 11 Chichester st SW1
143 R 1 Chichester st E1
14 L 11 Chiddingfold N12
87 Y 4 Chiddingstone SW6
81 P 18 Chiddingstone av Bxly Hth
98 G 10 Chieveley rd Bxly Hth
71 Y 2 Chignell pl W13
143 X 10 Chigwell hill E1
34 H 10 Chigwell rd E18
64 D 18 Chilcot clo E14
107 S 4 Childebert rd SW17
75 V 19 Childeric rd SE14
87 R 1 Childerley st SW6
75 X 16 Childers st SE8
145 V 6 Childs st SW5
145 V 6 Childs pl SW5
27 W 15 Childs way NW11
59 Z 6 Chilham clo Grnfd
113 R 10 Chilham rd SE9
126 D 17 Chilham way Brom
150 D 17 Chilham way Brom
107 P 13 Chillerton rd SW17
48 E 16 Chillingworth rd N7
118 F 15 Chilmark gdns New Mald
121 X 2 Chilmark rd SW16
100 G 2 Chiltern av Twick
99 P 3 Chiltern clo Bxly Hth
7 R 14 Chiltern dene Enf
117 S 13 Chiltern dri Surb
45 P 8 Chiltern gdns NW2
64 B 12 Chiltern rd E3
36 J 14 Chiltern rd Ilf
139 S 2 Chiltern st W1
131 S 19 Chiltern st W1
77 T 12 Chiltern way Wdfd Grn
72 G 10 Chilton av W5

75 U 11 Chilton gro SE8
12 C 19 Chilton rd Edg
85 P 7 Chilton rd Rich
135 R 15 Chilton st E2
154 D 5 Chilworth gdns Sutton
138 E 6 Chilworth ms W2
138 D 6 Chilworth st W2
17 U 15 Chimes av N13
149 S 3 China wlk SE11
112 H 7 Chinbrook cres SE12
112 H 7 Chinbrook rd SE12
29 U 13 Chine the N10
7 X 18 Chine the N21
42 C 14 Chine the Wemb
20 M 11 Chingdale rd E4
21 N 11 Chingdale rd E4
20 C 9 Chingford av E4
21 O 14 Chingford la Wdfd Grn
20 B 16 Chingford Mount rd E4
20 B 19 Chingford rd E4
33 P 2 Chingford rd E4
112 A 15 Chingley clo Brom
58 M 6 Chinnor cres Grnfd
59 N 6 Chinnor cres Grnfd
89 W 9 Chip st SW4
76 F 6 Chipka st E14
50 F 10 Chippendale st E5
43 U 16 Chippenham av Wemb
129 T 14 Chippenham gdns NW6
129 U 19 Chippenham ms W9
129 T 18 Chippenham rd W9
122 J 9 Chipstead av Thntn Hth
44 L 7 Chipstead gdns NW2
87 Y 3 Chipstead st SW6
63 V 5 Chisenhalle rd E3
157 S 2 Chisholm rd Croy
84 M 17 Chisholm rd Rich
28 C 2 Chislehurst av N3
113 Z 14 Chislehurst High st Chisl
127 S 1 Chislehurst rd Chisl
84 K 14 Chislehurst rd Rich
114 M 13 Chislehurst rd Sidcp
94 H 4 Chiswell sq SE3
134 E 20 Chiswell st EC2
74 C 13 Chiswick la NW4
74 D 15 Chiswick la SW4
85 V 4 Chiswick br W4
73 Z 11 Chiswick Comm rd W4
73 U 12 Chiswick High rd W4
74 B 12 Chiswick High rd W4
74 D 15 Chiswick mall W4
18 L 8 Chiswick rd N9
73 V 12 Chiswick rd W4
22 E 10 Chiswick st Pinn
73 S 15 Chiswick village W4
132 C 20 Chitty st W1
55 V 5 Chittys la Dgnhm
88 N 13 Chivalry rd SW11
20 E 13 Chivers rd E4
68 E 12 Choats Manor way Bark
69 N 5 Choats Manor way Dgnhm
68 M 10 Choats rd Dgnhm
69 N 10 Choats rd Dgnhm
105 O 4 Chobham gdns SW19
51 W 15 Chobham rd E15
47 S 1 Cholmeley cres N6
47 S 1 Cholmeley pk N6
116 A 16 Cholmley rd Th Dith
62 F 5 Cholmondeley av NW10
84 F 13 Cholmondeley wlk Rich
143 Y 13 Choppins ct E1
91 X 5 Choumert gro SE15
91 V 6 Choumert rd SE15
91 X 5 Choumert sq SE15
64 E 18 Chrisp st E14
64 C 15 Chrisp st E14
64 D 15 Chrisp st E14
85 S 12 Christ Church rd SW14
45 U 19 Christchurch av NW6
128 J 3 Christchurch av NW6
15 P 19 Christchurch av N12

24 B 12 Christchurch av Harrow
101 X 13 Christchurch av Tedd
42 L 19 Christchurch av Wemb
106 G 19 Christchurch clo SW19
23 Z 12 Christchurch gdns Harrow
42 K 19 Christchurch grn Wemb
46 F 10 Christchurch hill NW3
4 F 10 Christchurch la Barnt
46 F 10 Christchurch pas NW3
4 F 10 Christchurch pas Barnt
154 C 16 Christchurch pk Sutton
29 Z 19 Christchurch rd N8
106 G 19 Christchurch rd SW19
108 E 2 Christchurch rd SW2
54 A 5 Christchurch rd Ilf
114 L 8 Christchurch rd Sidcp
117 N 16 Christchurch rd Surb
147 O 12 Christchurch rd SW3
147 O 13 Christchurch ter SW3
76 M 14 Christchurch way SE10
108 G 18 Christian fields SW16
143 U 7 Christian st E1
37 R 20 Christie gdns Rom
50 H 19 Christie rd E9
134 J 17 Christina st EC2
71 Y 8 Christopher av W7
96 K 15 Christopher clo Stanm
11 P 17 Christopher clo Stanm
55 V 14 Christopher gdns Dgnhm
132 G 13 Christopher pl NW1
132 G 19 Christopher st EC2
139 V 5 Christophers pl W1
54 H 13 Chudleigh cres Ilf
63 T 17 Chudleigh st E1
109 Z 12 Chulsa rd SE26
150 H 14 Chumleigh st SE5
109 P 8 Church appr SE21
20 K 18 Church av E4
47 T 18 Church av NW1
85 Y 9 Church av SW14
125 O 1 Church av Becknhm
58 D 1 Church av Grnfd
22 D 19 Church av Pinn
70 D 8 Church av S'hall
115 P 17 Church av Sidcp
16 X 11 Church clo N20
137 W 16 Church clo W18
137 W 16 Church clo W8
12 J 18 Church clo Edg
63 S 1 Church cres E9
29 R 13 Church cres N10
15 W 10 Church cres N20
27 V 5 Church cres N3
43 X 3 Church dri NW9
22 G 18 Church dri Harrow
159 Z 6 Church dri W Wkhm
18 E 16 Church end E17
26 K 11 Church end NW4
141 X 7 Church entry EC4
153 T 13 Church Farm la Sutton
87 S 6 Church ga SW6
72 G 6 Church gdns W5
41 Y 12 Church gdns Wemb
93 S 12 Church gro SE13
116 E 2 Church gro Kingst
33 P 13 Church hill E17
17 R 2 Church hill N21
78 H 9 Church hill SE18
105 W 12 Church hill SW19
155 N 10 Church hill Carsh
156 B 20 Church hill Harr
99 P 11 Church hill Drtfrd
41 T 3 Church hill Harr
33 S 12 Church Hill rd E17
5 W 20 Church Hill rd Barnt
15 X 1 Church Hill rd Barnt
16 A 5 Church Hill rd Barnt

116 J 12 Church Hill rd Surb
153 S 10 Church Hill rd Sutton
51 Z 4 Church la E11
52 A 3 Church la E11
33 T 13 Church la E17
44 B 18 Church la NW10
31 S 5 Church la N17
25 X 18 Church la N17
31 S 4 Church la N17
28 G 9 Church la N2
30 C 13 Church la N8
18 H 8 Church la N9
107 O 12 Church la SW17
119 X 2 Church la SW19
72 F 5 Church la W5
127 R 18 Church la Brom
114 D 20 Church la Chisl
56 J 20 Church la Dgnhm
8 B 12 Church la Enf
23 V 6 Church la Harrow
22 C 11 Church la Pinn
39 P 14 Church la Rom
154 B 11 Church la Sutton
101 W 13 Church la Tedd
155 X 6 Church la Wallgtn
81 Y 13 Church Manor rd SE18
80 C 4 Church Manor way SE18
44 G 18 Church Mead rd NW10
79 Z 12 Church Mnr way SE2
81 Z 8 Church Mnr way Erith
28 F 17 Church mt N2
142 C 4 Church pas EC2
116 J 12 Church pas Surb
44 B 20 Church path NW10
62 C 1 Church path NW10
15 P 13 Church path N12
85 Y 7 Church path SW14
119 W 2 Church path SW19
73 W 8 Church path W4
71 S 2 Church path W7
156 L 2 Church path Croy
120 J 8 Church path Mitch
39 P 14 Church path Rom
70 E 7 Church path S'hall
140 D 11 Church pl SW1
72 G 6 Church pl W5
120 J 6 Church pl Mitch
51 N 3 Church rd E10
53 W 14 Church rd E12
32 G 8 Church rd E12
44 C 19 Church rd NW10
26 M 12 Church rd NW4
31 T 3 Church rd N17
29 O 18 Church rd N6
109 S 20 Church rd SE19
86 F 3 Church rd SW13
105 R 13 Church rd SW19
73 V 4 Church rd W3
59 T 19 Church rd W7
71 V 2 Church rd W7
125 Y 5 Church rd Brom
126 E 3 Church rd Brom
21 V 5 Church rd Buck Hl
98 A 9 Church rd Bxly Hth
156 K 4 Church rd Croy
159 N 10 Church rd Croy
9 S 18 Church rd Enf
58 B 4 Church rd Grnfd
70 F 19 Church rd Hounsl
36 G 19 Church rd Ilf
71 S 20 Church rd Islwth
83 R 1 Church rd Islwth
116 M 3 Church rd Kingst
117 N 3 Church rd Kingst
120 G 4 Church rd Mitch
84 K 12 Church rd Rich
102 M 10 Church rd Rich
70 E 8 Church rd S'hall
115 O 11 Church rd Sidcp
115 W 13 Church rd Sidcp
11 P 16 Church rd Stanm
153 S 13 Church rd Sutton
101 U 11 Church rd Tedd
97 P 4 Church rd Welling
118 C 18 Church rd Worc Pk
110 F 2 Church ri SE23
46 C 13 Church row NW3
114 C 20 Church row Chisl
65 N 3 Church st E15
78 L 4 Church st E16
18 D 6 Church st N9
76 G 17 Church st SE10
130 G 20 Church st W2
74 C 16 Church st W4
156 K 4 Church st Croy
56 H 19 Church st Dgnhm

152 F 19 Church st Epsom
84 A 7 Church st Islwth
116 H 3 Church st Kingst
154 B 11 Church st Sutton
101 Z 1 Church st Twick
65 N 3 Church St north E1
89 O 11 Church Stretton clo Hounsl
26 L 11 Church ter SE13
93 Y 9 Church ter SE13
89 Y 4 Church ter SW8
28 L 9 Church vale N2
110 L 4 Church vale SE23
132 F 12 Church way NW1
15 V 10 Church way N20
12 D 19 Church way Edg
45 W 9 Church wlk NW2
26 M 11 Church wlk NW4
43 X 7 Church wlk NW9
49 P 13 Church wlk N16
86 F 3 Church wlk SW13
121 V 3 Church wlk SW16
118 M 5 Church wlk SW20
72 E 16 Church wlk Brentf
84 H 12 Church wlk Rich
8 D 10 Churchbury clo Enf
8 C 12 Churchbury la Enf
95 N 19 Churchbury rd SE9
94 M 17 Churchbury rd SE9
8 D 8 Churchbury rd Enf
111 Z 9 Churchdown Brom
112 A 9 Churchdown Brom
22 M 13 Churchfield clo Harrow
72 C 3 Churchfield rd W13
71 S 5 Churchfield rd W7
97 N 8 Churchfield rd Welling
73 V 2 Churchfield Rd west W3
34 F 4 Churchfields E18
100 F 6 Churchfields av Felt
124 H 2 Churchfields rd Becknhm
24 A 19 Churchill av Harrow
148 A 12 Churchill gdns SW1
147 Z 12 Churchill gdns SW1
61 R 18 Churchill gdns W3
65 Y 17 Churchill rd E16
44 J 18 Churchill rd NW2
47 T 11 Churchill rd NW5
12 A 20 Churchill rd Edg
156 M 17 Churchill rd S Croy
20 B 12 Churchill ter E4
50 D 15 Churchill wlk E9
110 A 9 Churchley rd SE26
5 W 20 Churchmead clo Barnt
107 W 20 Churchmore rd Brom
101 P 3 Churchview rd Twic
50 B 15 Churchwell path E9
149 X 5 Churchyard row SE17
65 V 3 Churston av E13
119 R 12 Churston dri Mrdn
16 H 20 Churston gdns N11
148 B 7 Churton pl SW1
148 B 8 Churton st SW1
114 K 6 Chyngton clo Sidcp
110 G 3 Cibber rd SE23
88 D 15 Cicada rd SW18
91 X 3 Cicely rd SE15
112 A 10 Cinderford way Brom
60 M 10 Cinema pde W5
75 O 3 Cinnamon st E1
143 Z 13 Cinnamon st E1
109 V 16 Cintra pk SE19
119 Y 5 Circle gdns SW19
44 C 10 Circle the NW2
12 L 19 Circle the NW7
31 V 9 Circular rd N17
28 G 7 Circular rd N2
150 C 2 Circular rd SE1
78 H 16 Circular way SE18
139 N 1 Circus ms W1
142 G 3 Circus pl EC2
130 G 10 Circus rd NW8
76 G 19 Circus st SE10
31 P 16 Cissbury rd N15
14 K 15 Cissbury Ring north N12
14 K 16 Cissbury Ring south N12
142 E 10 City And Continenta wharf EC4
133 Y 10 City Gdn row N1
133 Y 11 City rd EC1
134 C 12 City rd EC1
147 O 4 Clabon ms SW1
75 R 6 Clack st SE16
32 H 18 Clacton rd E17

66 A9 Clacton rd E6
31 U9 Clacton rd N17
27 Z5 Claigmar gdns N3
15 P12 Claire ct N12
11 R17 Claire gdns Stanm
35 V4 Claire ho Ilf
82 A2 Clairvale rd Hounsl
07 T11 Clairview rd SW16
32 A2 Clairville gdns W7
10 G18 Clamp hill Stanm
87 Z5 Clancarty rd SW6
52 E14 Clandon clo Epsom
27 Y11 Clandon gdns N3
54 H7 Clandon rd Ilf
93 O3 Clandon st SE4
37 Y10 Clanricarde gdns W2
89 P10 Clapham Comm North side SW4
89 U12 Clapham Comm South side SW4
89 N11 Clapham Comm West side SW4
89 R11 Clapham common SW4
89 X11 Clapham cres SW4
89 X9 Clapham High st SW4
89 X8 Clapham Manor st SW4
89 R18 Clapham Pk rd SW4
89 Y8 Clapham rd SW8
90 C2 Clapham rd SW9
69 O10 Clapsgate la Bark
47 W2 Clapton comm E5
50 B14 Clapton pas E5
50 B14 Clapton sq E5
49 X3 Clapton ter N16
49 X11 Clapton way E5
78 J10 Clara pl SE18
95 Y20 Clare corner SE9
52 E13 Clare gdns E7
54 L19 Clare gdns Bark
54 K7 Clare Lawn av SW14
41 O6 Clare mkt WC2
33 V17 Clare rd E11
44 G19 Clare rd NW10
81 R18 Clare rd Grnfd
82 C9 Clare rd Hounsl
36 X9 Clare st E2
35 X9 Clare st E2
48 A7 Claredale st E2
75 O10 Clarehall pl SE16
24 K16 Claremont av Harrow
18 H10 Claremont av New Mald
78 K3 Claremont clo E16
33 T11 Claremont clo N1
99 R10 Claremont cres Drtfrd
54 G7 Claremont gdns Ilf
16 J10 Claremont gdns Surb
21 Y18 Claremont gro Wdfd Grn
27 T5 Claremont pk N3
51 W9 Claremont rd E11
32 J8 Claremont rd E17
52 K15 Claremont rd E7
45 N2 Claremont rd NW2
29 U20 Claremont rd N6
59 Y14 Claremont rd W13
29 N10 Claremont rd W9
5 T2 Claremont rd Barnt
27 S10 Claremont rd Brom
23 Y19 Claremont rd Croy
23 U8 Claremont rd Harrow
39 V19 Claremont rd Hornch
19 V19 Claremont rd Hornch
16 H11 Claremont rd Surb
01 W11 Claremont rd Tedd
34 C17 Claremont rd Twick
33 S10 Claremont sq N1
78 K4 Claremont st E16
18 J18 Claremont st N18
52 E18 Claremont st SE10
45 N13 Claremont way NW2
59 Y14 Clarence av SW4
27 R8 Clarence av Brom
35 V18 Clarence av Ilf
17 Y3 Clarence av New Mald
10 G3 Clarence clo Bushey Watf
92 H19 Clarence cres SW4
15 P8 Clarence cres Sidcp
31 P16 Clarence gate NW1
86 E15 Clarence la SW15
50 A14 Clarence ms E5

132 J9 Clarence pas NW1
50 A14 Clarence pl E5
53 N14 Clarence rd E12
64 M13 Clarence rd E16
32 F7 Clarence rd E17
50 A12 Clarence rd E5
129 C2 Clarence rd NW6
31 N14 Clarence rd N15
30 A2 Clarence rd N22
113 R5 Clarence rd SE9
106 A15 Clarence rd SW19
105 Z15 Clarence rd SW19
73 P14 Clarence rd W4
127 P7 Clarence rd Brom
97 X9 Clarence rd Bxly Hth
123 O16 Clarence rd Croy
9 P18 Clarence rd Rich
85 O3 Clarence rd Rich
115 P8 Clarence rd Sidcp
153 Z10 Clarence rd Sutton
154 A10 Clarence rd Sutton
101 X16 Clarence rd Tedd
S15 S12 Clarence rd Wallgtn
116 H3 Clarence st Kingst
84 J10 Clarence st Rich
82 J10 Clarence ter Hounsl
131 O16 Clarence Ter ms NW1
47 R20 Clarence way NW1
101 P7 Clarendon cres Twick
136 L11 Clarendon cross W11
86 M9 Clarendon dri SW15
87 N10 Clarendon dri SW15
26 H19 Clarendon gdns NW4
130 C18 Clarendon gdns W9
53 V2 Clarendon gdns Ilf
42 H11 Clarendon gdns Wemb
132 E11 Clarendon gro NW1
121 N5 Clarendon gro Mitch
138 K8 Clarendon pl W2
51 X2 Clarendon rd E11
33 R18 Clarendon rd E17
34 E10 Clarendon rd E18
30 K14 Clarendon rd N15
18 K13 Clarendon rd N18
30 C9 Clarendon rd N22
30 D11 Clarendon rd N8
106 H18 Clarendon rd SW19
136 K8 Clarendon rd W11
137 N13 Clarendon rd W11
60 J10 Clarendon rd W5
156 K2 Clarendon rd Croy
23 T19 Clarendon rd Harrow
155 U13 Clarendon rd Wallgtn
93 V9 Clarendon ri SE13
147 Y10 Clarendon st SW1
130 D17 Clarendon ter W9
17 Z1 Clarendon way N21
110 K4 Clarens st SE6
146 C7 Clareville gro SW7
146 D7 Clareville st SW7
139 X12 Clarges ms W1
139 Y13 Clarges st W1
90 H4 Claribel rd SW19
27 Y11 Clarindon gdns N3
110 D19 Claris rd SE20
37 U20 Clarissa rd Rom
135 N4 Clarissa st E8
143 Z3 Clark rd E1
63 O16 Clark st E1
153 P2 Clarkes av Worc Pk
10 B3 Clarks mead Bushey Watf
143 Z18 Clarks orchard SE16
142 J4 Clarks pl EC3
54 F7 Clarks rd Ilf
65 O16 Clarkson rd E16
135 W12 Clarkson st E2
51 U5 Claude rd E10
65 U4 Claude rd E13
91 Z7 Claude rd SE15
76 A10 Claude st E14
65 Y7 Claughton rd E13
40 L14 Clauson av Grnfd
75 O3 Clave st E1
143 Z13 Clave st E1
76 F18 Clavell st SE10
90 F19 Claverdale rd SW2
74 K16 Clavering av SW13
144 A14 Clavering rd E12
53 N6 Clavering rd E12
27 Z4 Claverley gro N3
148 C12 Claverton st SW1
144 H11 Claxton gro W6
8 C2 Clay hill Enf
10 F3 Clay la Bushey Watford
12 B7 Clay la Edg

139 R2 Clay st W1
112 M9 Claybridge rd SE12
35 R10 Claybury bdwy Ilf
35 V1 Claybury hall Wdfd Grn
35 R2 Claybury rd Wdfd Grn
114 B5 Clayfarm rd SE9
159 W15 Claygate cres Croy
72 A7 Claygate rd W13
35 U5 Clayhall av Ilf
8 E3 Clayhall av Ilf
113 N9 Clayhill cres SE9
149 R16 Claylands rd SW8
64 G6 Claypole rd E16
72 J13 Clayponds av Brentf
72 H11 Clayponds gdns W5
72 K14 Clayponds la Brentf
42 K20 Clayton av Wemb
72 G13 Clayton cres Brentf
91 Y2 Clayton rd SE15
72 H11 Clayton rd Islwth
56 K4 Clayton rd Rom
149 T13 Clayton st SE11
58 A14 Clayton ter Hayes
95 Z3 Cleanthus clo SE18
95 Z2 Cleanthus rd SE18
96 A2 Cleanthus rd SE18
110 B1 Cleave hill SE23
116 G12 Cleaveland rd Surb
149 U10 Cleaver sq SE11
149 U10 Cleaver st SE11
123 Z14 Cleaverholme clo SE25
75 O3 Clegg st E1
143 Y13 Clegg st E1
75 P6 Clegg st E13
145 O15 Clem Attlec ct SW6
62 F20 Clematis st W12
63 Y16 Clemence st E14
50 K5 Clementina rd E10
65 T19 Clements av E16
141 P6 Clements inn WC2
142 G8 Clements la EC3
53 Z9 Clements la Ilf
72 G13 Clements pl Brentf
52 E6 Clements rd E6
151 V3 Clements rd SE16
53 Z9 Clements rd Ilf
79 H10 Clendon way SE18
153 X3 Clensham la Sutton
139 O5 Clenston ms W1
49 N19 Clephane rd N1
134 G16 Clere pl EC2
134 G17 Clere st EC2
64 E8 Clergion way E3
133 V17 Clerkenwell clo EC1
133 V17 Clerkenwell grn EC1
133 W18 Clerkenwell rd EC1
75 O6 Clerks orchard SE16
75 P6 Clerks orchard SE16
63 P2 Clermont rd E9
45 Z20 Cleve rd NW6
46 A20 Cleve rd NW6
115 W7 Cleve rd Sidcp
49 U8 Clevedon pas N16
62 C20 Clevedon rd SE20
117 P3 Clevedon rd Kingst
84 G18 Clevedon rd Twick
49 U8 Clevedon st N16
90 A4 Cleveland av W4
100 E17 Cleveland av Hampt
45 P6 Cleveland gdns NW2
30 L1 Cleveland gdns N4
86 C5 Cleveland gdns SW13
138 B6 Cleveland gdns W2
152 C2 Cleveland gdns Worc
63 P12 Cleveland gro E1
152 B20 Cleveland ms W1
60 A14 Cleveland park W13
33 N13 Cleveland Park av E17
33 N13 Cleveland Park cres E17
140 D13 Cleveland pl SW1
34 F10 Cleveland rd E18
134 F2 Cleveland rd N1
86 D5 Cleveland rd SW13
59 Y15 Cleveland rd W13
60 B15 Cleveland rd W13
53 Z9 Cleveland rd Ilf
54 A11 Cleveland rd Ilf
83 Y10 Cleveland rd Islwth

96 L5 Cleveland rd Welling
152 C3 Cleveland rd Worc Pk
119 R17 Cleveland ri Mrdn
140 B15 Cleveland row SW1
138 B7 Cleveland sq W2
132 A19 Cleveland st W1
131 Z18 Cleveland st W1
140 R1 Cleveland st W1
138 C4 Cleveland ter W2
73 W9 Cleveland ter W4
63 P12 Cleveland way E1
60 A8 Cleveley cres W5
152 J19 Cleves av Epsom
66 A4 Cleves rd E6
102 D7 Cleves rd Rich
100 F18 Cleves way Hampt
36 C2 Cleves wlk Ilf
23 P5 Clewer cres Harrow
50 D14 Clifden rd E5
72 F16 Clifden rd Brentf
101 W1 Clifden rd Twick
83 X20 Clifden rd Twick
47 Y17 Cliff rd NW1
93 P4 Cliff ter SE4
47 Y17 Cliff vlls NW1
65 P13 Cliff wlk E16
157 O11 Cliff rd S Croy
95 U6 Clifford av SW14
113 T15 Clifford av Chisl
35 Z6 Clifford av Ilf
155 U8 Clifford av Wallgtn
58 B5 Clifford clo Grnfd
62 M7 Clifford gdns NW10
128 C9 Clifford gdns NW10
110 C18 Clifford gro SE20
65 O13 Clifford rd E13
33 U8 Clifford rd E17
133 W9 Clifford rd E25
19 R2 Clifford rd E25
5 O12 Clifford rd Barnt
102 H4 Clifford rd Rich
60 F3 Clifford rd Wemb
84 A9 Clifford st W1
44 D12 Clifford way NW1
93 O9 Cliffview rd SE13
134 F8 Clift st N1
32 G12 Clifton av E17
27 V4 Clifton av N3
74 E4 Clifton av W12
24 C7 Clifton av Stanm
43 N17 Clifton av Wemb
75 O19 Clifton cres SE15
151 Z18 Clifton cres SE15
27 X18 Clifton gdns NW11
31 W18 Clifton gdns N15
30 B18 Clifton gdns W9
6 M15 Clifton gdns Enf
49 X17 Clifton gro E8
129 Y8 Clifton hill NW6
130 C5 Clifton hill NW8
110 M3 Clifton Park av SW20
119 N3 Clifton Park av SW20
138 H7 Clifton pl W2
53 O18 Clifton rd E12
65 N13 Clifton rd E16
62 F7 Clifton rd NW10
29 W5 Clifton rd N22
28 D4 Clifton rd N3
29 X18 Clifton rd N8
123 S10 Clifton rd SE25
105 O15 Clifton rd SW19
130 D17 Clifton rd W9
59 O11 Clifton rd Grnfd
24 L15 Clifton rd Harrow
39 V19 Clifton rd Hornch
36 E20 Clifton rd Ilf
83 S4 Clifton rd Islwth
03 O19 Clifton rd Kingst
117 O1 Clifton rd Kingst
70 C10 Clifton rd S'hall
114 H9 Clifton rd Sidcp
11 U10 Clifton rd Tedd
155 T11 Clifton rd Wallgtn
97 S7 Clifton rd Welling
75 W19 Clifton rd SE14
134 H19 Clifton st EC2
48 F6 Clifton ter N4
130 A20 Clifton vlls W9
75 O20 Clifton way SE15
151 Z20 Clifton way SE15
60 K3 Clifton way Wemb
65 T16 Clinch ct E16
16 H19 Cline rd N11
142 D12 Clink st SE1
96 M9 Clinton av Welling
63 V9 Clinton rd E3
52 F13 Clinton rd E7
31 N14 Clinton rd N14

82 G8 Clipstone rd Hounsl
131 Z20 Clipstone st W1
132 A20 Clipstone st N1
49 N11 Cissold cres N16
49 N8 Cissold park N16
49 O9 Cissold rd N16
40 G5 Clitheroe av Harrow
90 A6 Clitheroe rd N16
71 X7 Clitherow av W7
72 C13 Clitherow rd Brentf
45 N5 Clitterhouse cres NW2
45 N5 Clitterhouse rd NW2
18 J19 Clive av N18
99 T17 Clive av Drtfrd
109 O8 Clive rd SE21
106 J15 Clive rd SW19
81 P12 Clive rd Blvdr
8 J14 Clive rd Enf
39 Y17 Clive rd Rom
101 X8 Clive rd Twick
8 J15 Clive way Enf
15 P14 Cliveden clo N17
147 S6 Cliveden pl SW1
105 U20 Cliveden rd SW19
60 A13 Clivedene rd W13
20 L17 Cliveden rd E4
142 D8 Cloak la EC4
124 H5 Clock Ho rd Bechnhm
149 Y6 Clock pl SE17
67 O2 Clockhouse av Bark
38 H2 Clockhouse la Rom
123 Z14 Cloister gdns SE25
12 J16 Cloister gdns Edg
48 U8 Cloister rd NW2
61 V15 Cloister rd W3
127 T12 Cloisters av Brom
49 R12 Clonbrock rd N16
87 R3 Cloncurry st SW6
41 R5 Clonmel clo Harrow
87 W1 Clonmel rd SW6
145 P20 Clonmel rd SW6
101 P10 Clonmel rd Tedd
31 P11 Clonmell rd N17
105 W2 Clonmore st SW18
45 X11 Clorane gdns NW3
33 V3 Close the E4
16 K8 Close the N14
14 H7 Close the N20
6 A18 Close the Barnt
124 H9 Close the Becknhm
98 C17 Close the Bxly
154 K18 Close the Carsh
23 N8 Close the Harrow
83 P3 Close the Islwth
120 K10 Close the Mitch
117 X4 Close the New Mald
85 S7 Close the Rich
37 X19 Close the Rom
115 R11 Close the Sidcp
119 V17 Close the Sutton
42 J18 Close the Wemb
43 W10 Close the Wemb
141 Y1 Cloth ct EC1
141 Y2 Cloth fair EC1
142 L4 Clothier st E1
107 R4 Cloudesdale rd SW17
133 T6 Cloudesley pl N1
133 T5 Cloudesley rd N1
98 C12 Cloudesley rd Bxly Hth
133 T4 Cloudesley sq N1
133 T5 Cloudesley st N1
99 T2 Cloudsley rd Erith
52 F16 Clove rd E7
65 S13 Clove st E13
26 C12 Clovelly av NW9
18 D3 Clovelly gdns Enf
38 H5 Clovelly gdns Rom
29 Y12 Clovelly rd N8
73 X7 Clovelly rd W4
72 E6 Clovelly rd Bxly Hth
80 K17 Clovelly rd Bxly Hth
40 D8 Clovelly way Harrow
147 O13 Clover ms SW3
96 J16 Cloverdale gdns Sidcp
110 L6 Clowders rd SE6
1 V20 Cloyster wood Edg
135 N16 Club row E2
70 D14 Clunbury av S'hall
145 S8 Cluny ms SW5
150 J1 Cluny pl SE1
64 E15 Clutton st E14
8 H13 Clydach rd Enf
31 S12 Clyde cir N15
51 P2 Clyde pl E10
77 T2 Clyde rd N22
31 T12 Clyde rd N15
29 X4 Clyde rd N22
123 U20 Clyde rd Croy

157 L12 Clyde rd Croy
153 Y10 Clyde rd Sutton
155 V13 Clyde rd Wallgtn
75 Z17 Clyde st SE8
110 D4 Clyde ter SE23
110 D5 Clyde vale SE23
39 P4 Clyde way Rom
9 S16 Clydesdale av W11
24 G9 Clydesdale av Stanm
85 S10 Clydesdale gdns Rich
137 P5 Clydesdale rd W11
57 T2 Clydesdale rd Hornch
89 W3 Clyston st SW8
86 M12 Coalecroft rd SW15
135 U8 Coate st E2
127 X4 Coates Hill rd Brom
11 T2 Coates rd Borehm Wd
142 M3 Cobb st E1
95 R8 Cobbett st SE9
100 J1 Cobbett rd Twick
149 O20 Cobbett st SW8
52 C9 Cobbold rd E11
44 D18 Cobbold rd NW10
74 C6 Cobbold rd W12
141 X7 Cobbs ct EC4
82 E12 Cobbs rd Hounsl
150 L16 Cobden pl SE15
52 A8 Cobden rd E11
123 Y12 Cobden rd SE25
64 E15 Cobden st E15
118 G10 Cobham av New Mald
127 P16 Cobham clo Brom
33 J5 Cobham rd E17
30 J9 Cobham rd N22
67 R4 Cobham rd Bark
54 H8 Cobham rd Ilf
117 P2 Cobham rd Kingst
112 M10 Cobland rd SE12
63 Y9 Coborn rd E3
63 Y9 Coborn st E3
151 N1 Cobourg rd SE5
132 C14 Cobourg st NW1
30 D9 Coburg rd N22
105 U18 Cochrane rd SW19
132 B14 Cochrane st NW8
142 L3 Cock hill E1
141 X3 Cock la EC1
6 A13 Cockfosters rd Barnt
5 X4 Cockfosters rd Barnt
140 F19 Cockpit steps SW1
133 O19 Cockpit yd WC1
140 G13 Cockspur ct SW1
135 P18 Code st E1
92 J18 Codrington hill SE23
137 N7 Codrington ms W11
24 H11 Cody clo Harrow
64 L12 Cody rd E16
32 G3 Cogan av E17
63 Y17 Cogenhagen pl E14
141 T13 Coin st SE1
47 P17 Coity rd NW5
143 U4 Coke st E1
109 N2 Cokers la SE21
129 V4 Colas mews NW6
146 A7 Colbeck ms SW7
41 N1 Colbeck rd Harrow
49 T2 Colberg pl N16
153 N2 Colborne way Worc Pk
152 M3 Colborne way Worc Pk
154 F6 Colburn way Sutton
109 T13 Colby rd SE19
53 U10 Colchester av E12
33 V20 Colchester rd E10
33 N20 Colchester rd E17
25 W2 Colchester rd Edg
75 T17 Cold Blow la SE14
120 M7 Cold blows Mitch
76 H4 Cold harbour E14
133 S17 Coldbath sq EC1
93 S4 Coldbath st SE13
71 Y3 Coldershaw rd W13
29 N7 Coldfall av N10
90 H9 Coldharbour la SW9
156 G11 Coldharbour rd Croy
156 K11 Coldharbour way Croy
87 V16 Coldstream gdns SW18
83 Y14 Cole Pk gdns Twick
83 Y18 Cole Pk rd Twick
83 Y15 Cole Pk rd Twick
83 Y17 Cole rd Twick
142 D19 Cole st SE1
145 Z7 Colebeck ms SW5
83 R11 Colebert av E1
87 P17 Colebrook clo SW15

33 N14 Colebrook rd E17
122 A1 Colebrook rd SW16
60 A17 Colebrooke av W13
34 K20 Colebrooke dri E11
133 X7 Colebrooke row N1
24 D4 Coledale dri Stanm
88 C12 Coleford rd SW18
51 V13 Colegrave rd E15
151 R16 Colegrove rd SE15
145 Y12 Coleherne ms SW10
145 X11 Coleherne rd SW10
87 S3 Colehill gdns SW6
87 S3 Colehill la SW6
75 P2 Coleman clo E1
134 B4 Coleman fields N1
150 K18 Coleman rd SE5
81 R10 Coleman rd Blvdr
55 Z19 Coleman rd Dgnhm
56 A19 Coleman rd Dgnhm
142 E5 Coleman st EC2
142 E3 Coleman St bldgs EC2
113 X7 Colemans heath SE9
50 D11 Colenso rd E5
54 G4 Colenso rd Ilf
96 D12 Colepits Wood rd SE9
30 F10 Coleraine rd N8
77 R16 Coleraine rd SE3
53 R17 Coleridge av E12
154 K8 Coleridge av Sutton
130 B2 Coleridge gdns NW6
32 L12 Coleridge rd E17
15 P17 Coleridge rd N12
48 F8 Coleridge rd N4
29 X19 Coleridge rd N8
124 C16 Coleridge rd Croy
39 V3 Coleridge rd Rom
27 X14 Coleridge wlk NW11
40 K7 Coles cres Harrow
44 H5 Coles Green rd NW2
10 B6 Coles grn Bushey Watf
124 K5 Colesburg rd Becknhm
101 U15 Coleshill rd Tedd
88 K4 Colestown st SW11
144 H7 Colet gdns W14
133 P17 Coley st WC1
110 G1 Colfe rd SE23
26 B14 Colin clo NW9
158 K4 Colin clo Croy
26 E15 Colin cres NW9
26 H14 Colin Deep gdns NW4
26 F13 Colin Deep la NW9
26 E15 Colin dri NW9
26 E16 Colin gdns NW9
26 A13 Colin Park rd NW9
44 F17 Colin rd NW10
30 J14 Colina ms N15
30 J15 Colina rd N15
25 Z11 Colindale av NW9
26 B10 Colindale av NW9
86 L10 Colinette rd SW15
55 R6 Colinton rd Ilf
87 Y18 Coliston rd SW18
106 H3 Collamore av SW18
76 G16 College appr SE10
23 T4 College av Harrow
23 U2 College av Harrow
46 F19 College cres NW3
133 V1 College cross N1
20 D4 College gdns E4
18 H16 College gdns N18
91 R20 College gdns SE21
8 B8 College gdns Enf
35 R15 College gdns Ilf
118 E12 College gdns New Mald
109 R18 College grn SE19
132 D5 College gro NW1
142 D9 College hill EC4
23 U3 College Hill rd Harrow
23 V4 College Hill rd Harrow
47 S12 College la NW5
18 F20 College Pk rd N17
33 Z12 College pl E17
132 C4 College pl NW1
33 T17 College pl E17
62 M6 College rd NW10
128 B8 College rd NW10
18 F20 College rd N17
17 U8 College rd N21
91 R19 College rd SE21
109 S1 College rd SE21
106 G19 College rd SW19
111 P6 College rd W13
112 F18 College rd Brom
126 E1 College rd Brom
157 O4 College rd Croy

23 T3 College rd Harrow
23 U19 College rd Harrow
83 V3 College rd Islwth
42 H5 College rd Wemb
126 E2 College slip Brom
142 D9 College st EC4
63 X8 College ter E3
27 W6 College ter N3
113 O3 College view SE9
50 D18 Collent st E9
63 X16 Colless rd N15
151 U2 Collett rd SE16
25 P7 Collier dri Edg
38 H3 Collier Row la Rom
38 C4 Collier Row rd Rom
133 N9 Collier st N1
122 A19 Colliers Water la Thntn Hth
106 G16 Colliers Wood High st SW19
81 V17 Collindale av Erith
97 O20 Collindale av Sidcp W12
74 J2 Collingbourne rd W12
145 Z7 Collingham gdns SW5
145 Y6 Collingham pl SW5
145 Z26 Collingham rd SW5
29 O11 Collingwood av N10
117 V18 Collingwood av Surb
82 H18 Collingwood clo Twick
33 N18 Collingwood rd E17
31 S12 Collingwood rd N15
120 G5 Collingwood rd Mitch
153 W5 Collingwood rd Sutton
26 N12 Collingwood st E1
135 X17 Collingwood st E1
24 K7 Collins av Stanm
48 C12 Collins rd N5
94 B6 Collins st SE3
133 X5 Collins yd N1
142 A19 Collinson st SE1
9 P12 Collinwood av Enf
35 V5 Collinwood gdns Ilf
92 C1 Colls rd SE15
91 V2 Collyer av Croy
91 V2 Collyer pl SE15
156 A8 Collyer rd Croy
65 Y15 Colman rd E16
63 T11 Colmar st E1
23 P3 Colmer Pl Harrow
108 B19 Colmer rd SW16
9 R14 Colmore rd Enf
149 W2 Colmworth st SE1
50 H13 Colne rd E5
18 A3 Colne rd N21
101 U2 Colne rd Twick
29 P2 Colney Hatch la N1
15 Y18 Colney Hatch la N1
16 A20 Colney Hatch rd N11
88 G10 Cologne rd SW11
77 N14 Colomb st SE10
54 B2 Colombo rd Ilf
141 W15 Colombo st SE1
82 M15 Colonial av Twick
83 N15 Colonial av Twick
132 K15 Colonnade WC1
131 Y15 Colosseum ter NW1
157 R2 Colson rd Croy
107 V10 Colson way SW16
31 V2 Colsterworth rd N15
154 K8 Colston av Carsh
53 N18 Colston rd E12
85 W10 Colston rd SW14
80 C13 Coltness cres SE2
23 U14 Colton rd Har
25 X4 Columbia av Edg
118 E18 Columbia av Worc Pk
65 R13 Columbia rd E13
135 S10 Columbia rd E2
93 T5 Columbine way SE13
101 T2 Colus all Twick
49 U16 Colvestone cres E8
18 L4 Colvill rd N9
137 P6 Colville gdns W11
137 N6 Colville houses W11
137 R6 Colville ms W11
140 D2 Colville pl W1
51 V9 Colville rd E11
32 J8 Colville rd E17
137 R7 Colville rd W11
73 U8 Colville rd W3
137 O6 Colville sq W11
137 O5 Colville Sq ms W11
137 P6 Colville ter W11
34 J13 Colvin gdns E11

20 H 11 Colvin gdns E4
46 B 3 Colvin gdns Ilf
56 D 2 Colvin rd E6
22 F 12 Colvin rd Thntn Hth
74 K 11 Colvin st W6
91 U 14 Colwell rd SE22
64 K 9 Colwith rd W6
06 G 18 Colwood gdns SW19
43 Z 19 Colworth rd E11
34 A 20 Colworth rd E11
23 X 20 Colworth rd Croy
92 M 3 Colwyn av Grnfd
59 X 6 Colwyn cres Hounsl
92 M 3 Colwyn rd NW2
13 Z 4 Colyer clo SE9
98 M 1 Colyers clo Erith
38 L 1 Colyers la Erith
39 S 1 Colyers la Erith
97 V 1 Colyers wlk Erith
37 V 1 Colyton clo Welling
52 A 14 Colyton clo Wemb
32 A 14 Colyton rd SE22
18 H 17 Colyton rd N18
77 P 19 Combe av SE3
77 Y 16 Combe lodge SE1
77 P 19 Combe ms SE3
03 Y 14 Combe Wood Golf course Kingst
97 S 14 Combedale rd SE10
87 T 20 Combemartin rd SW18
94 K 2 Comber clo NW2
50 B 20 Comber gro SE5
90 C 7 Combermere rd SW9
50 A 6 Comberton rd E5
28 B 13 Comberton rd Mrdn
79 X 20 Combesides SE18
80 A 9 Combwell cres SE2
33 T 15 Comely Bank rd E17
44 M 10 Comeragh ms W14
44 L 11 Comeragh rd W14
45 X 14 Comeragh rd W14
92 K 11 Comerford rd SE4
76 A 19 Comet pl SE8
76 A 20 Comet st SE8
30 B 4 Commerce rd N22
72 C 18 Commerce rd Brentf
56 D 4 Commerce way Croy
75 X 8 Commercial Dock pas SE16
31 W 1 Commercial pl NW1
63 O 17 Commercial rd E1
43 U 5 Commercial rd E1
18 F 19 Commercial rd N18
43 O 2 Commercial st E1
51 T 18 Commercial way SE15
50 M 20 Commercial way SE15
77 N 13 Commerell st SE10
63 V 13 Commodore st E1
86 H 7 Common rd SW13
10 D 11 Common rd Stanm
72 K 2 Common the W5
10 H 9 Common the Stanm
86 M 6 Commondale SW15
06 M 16 Commonfield la SW17
06 H 13 Commonfield pas SW17
21 P 7 Commonside east Mitch
21 N 8 Commonside west Mitch
62 K 20 Commonwealth av W12
37 S 20 Commonwealth institute W8
31 X 1 Commonwealth rd N17
80 E 13 Commonwealth way SE2
51 X 16 Community rd E15
10 H 5 Como rd SE23
51 N 14 Como st Rom
45 Z 19 Compayne gdns NW6
46 B 19 Compayne gdns NW6
46 A 6 Compton av E6
48 J 19 Compton av N1
44 J 1 Compton av N6
31 Z 14 Compton clo NW1
31 N 2 Compton cres N17
73 V 17 Compton cres W4
54 A 1 Compton cres Grnfd
33 X 16 Compton pas EC1
32 J 15 Compton pl WC1
28 G 13 Compton rd NW10
6 K 19 Compton rd N1
17 V 5 Compton rd N21
05 V 14 Compton rd SW19

123 Z 20 Compton rd Croy
157 Z 1 Compton rd Croy
22 D 16 Compton ri Pinn
133 X 16 Compton st EC1
65 R 5 Compton st E13
48 H 19 Compton ter N1
7 V 4 Comreddy clo Enf
150 H 6 Comus st SE17
88 J 11 Comyn rd SW11
65 O 14 Comyns clo E16
69 P 1 Comyns rd Dgnhm
10 A 6 Comyns the Bushey Watf
90 B 10 Concanon rd SW2
141 P 14 Concert Hall appr SE1
61 S 12 Concord rd W3
9 O 18 Concord rd Enf
89 W 2 Condell rd SW8
63 V 17 Conder st E14
90 L 7 Conderton rd SE5
158 C 18 Condover cres SE18
140 K 8 Conduit ct WC2
19 U 2 Conduit la N9
157 X 12 Conduit la S Croy
138 F 7 Conduit ms W2
138 G 6 Conduit pl W2
78 M 13 Conduit rd SE18
79 N 13 Conduit rd SE18
139 Z 8 Conduit st W1
140 A 8 Conduit st W1
43 V 20 Conduit way NW10
48 J 11 Conewood st N5
80 G 10 Conference rd SE2
79 T 13 Congo st SE18
80 F 11 Congress rd SE2
95 S 8 Congreve rd SE9
150 J 7 Congreve st SE17
7 Y 9 Conical corner Enf
108 B 8 Conifer gdns SW16
102 C 18 Conifers clo Tedd
87 X 4 Coniger rd SW6
156 K 19 Coningby rd S Croy
74 H 4 Coningham ms W12
74 J 4 Coningham rd W12
20 D 18 Coningsby gdns E4
72 F 6 Coningsby rd W5
93 T 5 Conington rd SE13
111 U 7 Conisborough cres SE6
17 Z 12 Coniscliffe rd N13
67 U 2 Coniston av Bark
60 B 8 Coniston av Grnfd
96 G 8 Coniston av Welling
55 S 11 Coniston clo N20
67 U 2 Coniston clo Bark
98 K 3 Coniston clo Bxly Hth
25 Y 16 Coniston gdn N9
19 P 6 Coniston gdns N9
35 R 13 Coniston gdns Ilf
154 F 14 Coniston gdns Sutton
42 E 3 Coniston gdns Wemb
29 S 7 Coniston rd N10
J 20 Coniston rd N17
111 Y 15 Coniston rd Brom
112 A 17 Coniston rd Brom
98 K 3 Coniston rd Bxly Hth
123 X 17 Coniston rd Croy
82 L 17 Coniston rd Twick
57 V 15 Coniston way Hornch
128 L 17 Conistone st W10
44 C 19 Conley rd NW10
20 J 2 Connaught av E4
85 V 9 Connaught av SW14
16 A 5 Connaught av Barnt
8 F 9 Connaught av Enf
82 C 12 Connaught av Hounsl
50 G 6 Connaught clo E10
138 L 20 Connaught clo W2
8 F 10 Connaught clo Enf
154 F 3 Connaught clo Sutton
27 Z 13 Connaught dri NW11
29 T 15 Connaught gdns N10
17 W 15 Connaught gdns N13
54 D 8 Connaught la Ilf
139 N 7 Connaught ms W2
139 N 7 Connaught pl W2
51 Y 4 Connaught rd E11
78 B 3 Connaught rd E16
66 A 20 Connaught rd E16
33 N 16 Connaught rd E17
20 L 4 Connaught rd E4
62 B 5 Connaught rd NW10

48 F 1 Connaught rd N4
72 A 1 Connaught rd W13
4 D 20 Connaught rd Barnt
23 W 5 Connaught rd Harrow
54 D 8 Connaught rd Ilf
118 B 8 Connaught rd New Mald
84 L 13 Connaught rd Rich
154 G 4 Connaught rd Sutton
101 S 12 Connaught rd Tedd
139 N 6 Connaught sq W2
138 M 7 Connaught sq W2
17 S 12 Connaught st SE18
138 M 6 Connaught st W2
17 X 14 Connaught way N13
60 M 10 Connell cres W5
61 N 11 Connell cres W5
72 F 6 Conningsby cotts W5
30 H 20 Conningsby rd N4
20 K 10 Connington cres E4
6 H 17 Connisbee ct N14
9 S 2 Connop rd Enf
56 C 11 Connor rd Dgnhm
63 S 3 Connor st E9
71 S 2 Conolly rd W7
149 X 1 Conquest st SE1
119 N 19 Conrad dr Worc Pk
141 U 16 Cons st SE1
91 Z 5 Consort rd SE15
92 A 7 Consort rd SE15
118 G 18 Consfield av New Mald
83 S 14 Consort ms Islwth
91 Z 2 Consort rd SE15
28 B 19 Constable clo NW11
31 X 15 Constable cres N15
25 O 6 Constable gdns Edg
83 O 13 Constable gdns Hounsl
126 C 19 Constance cres Brom
122 J 16 Constance rd Croy
18 D 1 Constance rd Enf
154 E 9 Constance rd Sutton
82 L 19 Constance rd Twick
78 C 3 Constance st E16
46 L 13 Constantine rd NW3
139 Y 17 Constitution hill SW1
95 W 2 Constitution ri SE18
150 C 7 Content st SE17
137 N 6 Convent gdns W11
72 D 11 Convent gdns W5
10 L 19 Conway clo Stanm
59 V 4 Conway cres Grnfd
37 S 19 Conway cres Rom
8 D 3 Conway gdns Enf
121 Z 9 Conway gdns Mitch
42 D 2 Conway gdns Wemb
61 Z 14 Conway gro W3
132 B 19 Conway ms W1
44 L 8 Conway rd NW2
17 O 10 Conway rd N14
30 K 15 Conway rd N15
79 U 12 Conway rd SE18
105 N 20 Conway rd SW20
82 F 18 Conway rd Hounsl
65 S 12 Conway st E13
132 A 19 Conway st W1
46 K 20 Conybeare NW3
20 M 19 Conyers clo Wdfd Grn
107 W 12 Conyers rd SW16
80 C 7 Cookhill rd SE2
7 X 2 Cooks Hole rd Enf
66 C 8 Cooks rd E3
149 X 13 Cooks rd SE17
44 B 3 Cool Oak la NW9
65 U 19 Coolfin rd E16
20 J 16 Coolgardie av E4
29 X 18 Coolhurst rd N8
129 O 15 Coomassie rd W9
157 T 9 Coombe av Croy
24 M 9 Coombe clo Edg
82 H 12 Coombe clo Hounsl
17 V 6 Coombe corner N21
100 D 16 Coombe cres Hampt
103 Y 18 Coombe end Kingst
118 B 12 Coombe Field clo New Mald
118 G 2 Coombe gdns SW20
118 C 8 Coombe gdns New Mald
103 Y 14 Coombe hill Kingst
104 C 18 Coombe Hill glade SW20
104 A 18 Coombe Hill rd Kingst
103 Z 20 Coombe Ho chase Kingst
118 H 1 Coombe la SW20

158 B 12 Coombe la Croy
117 U 1 Coombe la Kingst
103 Y 19 Coombe La west Kingst
104 C 19 Coombe La west Kingst
127 S 7 Coombe lea Brom
103 X 18 Coombe neville Kingst
157 X 8 Coombe park Croy
103 X 13 Coombe pk Kingst
104 A 20 Coombe pk Kingst
43 Y 8 Coombe rd E8
30 G 7 Coombe rd N22
109 Z 9 Coombe rd SE26
72 B 8 Coombe rd W13
74 B 14 Coombe rd W4
10 B 1 Coombe rd Bushey Watford
157 W 10 Coombe rd Croy
100 D 16 Coombe rd Hampt
117 P 1 Coombe rd Kingst
118 A 3 Coombe rd New Mald
103 V 20 Coombe ri Kingst
103 V 13 Coombe ridings Kingst
153 Z 5 Coombe wlk Sutton
38 C 20 Coombe Wood dri Rom
103 W 13 Coombe Wood rd Kingst
5 Z 9 Coombehurst clo Barnt
69 P 3 Coombes rd Dgnhm
133 Y 19 Coombs st N1
154 M 5 Cooper cres Carsh
62 H 16 Cooper rd NW10
156 H 9 Cooper rd Croy
51 S 3 Coopers la E10
112 G 4 Coopers la E10
50 P 1 Coopers rd SE1
142 M 8 Coopers row EC3
34 L 3 Coopersale clo Wdfd Grn
50 G 15 Coopersale rd E9
98 A 2 Coote gdns Dgnhm
98 B 6 Coote rd Bxly Hth
145 U 2 Cope pl W8
75 T 10 Cope st SE16
33 S 17 Copeland rd E17
91 Y 5 Copeland rd SE15
63 Y 13 Copenhagen pl E14
32 S 6 Copenhagen st N1
132 L 5 Copenhagen st WC1
111 O 20 Copers Cope rd Beckhnm
16 D 14 Copies gro N11
42 F 16 Copland av Wemb
42 E 15 Copland clo Wemb
42 J 17 Copland rd Wemb
91 U 9 Coplestone rd SE15
108 C 15 Copley pk SW16
11 T 15 Copley rd Stanm
63 T 5 Copley st E1
94 C 10 Coppelia rd SE3
56 A 1 Coppen rd Dgnhm
106 C 10 Copper Mill la SW17
76 D 17 Copperas st SE8
63 W 13 Copperfield rd E3
141 Z 16 Copperfield st SE1
142 A 16 Copperfield st SE1
32 D 18 Coppermill la E17
28 K 1 Coppetts clo N12
28 M 2 Coppetts rd N10
29 N 4 Coppetts rd N10
118 M 6 Coppice clo SW20
86 H 17 Coppice dri SW15
7 W 13 Coppice the Enf
34 C 11 Coppice way E18
14 L 10 Coppice wlk N20
9 S 15 Coppins the Croy
52 A 9 Copse av W Wkhm
104 E 20 Copse clo SE12
154 B 16 Copse hill Sutton
118 K 2 Copse hill SW20
21 P 6 Copse the E4
158 G 18 Copse view S Croy
142 F 4 Copthall av EC2
142 F 4 Copthall clo EC2
142 G 5 Copthall ct EC2
13 U 20 Copthall dri NW7
26 G 1 Copthall dri NW7
26 G 1 Copthall gdns NW7
101 X 1 Copthall gdns Twick
89 X 1 Copthorne av SW12
140 J 2 Coptic st WC1
141 T 18 Coral st SE1
132 J 17 Coram st WC1

19 S2	Coran clo N9	
82 H8	Corban rd Hounsl	
5 T5	Corbar clo Barnt	
155 O2	Corbet clo Wallgtn	
34 K18	Corbett rd E1	
33 V10	Corbett rd E17	
75 P12	Corbetts pas SE16	
52 A1	Corbicum rd E11	
105 P16	Corbiere clo SW19	
40 L10	Corbins la Harrow	
7 O14	Corby cres Enf	
61 X7	Corby rd NW10	
96 H20	Corbylands la Sidcp	
114 H1	Corbylands rd Sidcp	
48 A5	Corbyn st N4	
64 E14	Cordelia st E14	
64 D16	Cording st E14	
63 I8	Cordova rd E3	
95 P3	Corelli rd SE3	
40 F12	Corfe av Harrow	
63 N10	Corfield st E2	
135 X15	Corfield st E2	
60 J16	Corfton rd W5	
47 W12	Corinne rd N19	
140 A10	Cork st W1	
140 A10	Cork St ms W1	
116 H17	Corkran rd Surb	
159 X5	Corkscrew hill W Wkhm	
90 H3	Cormont rd SE5	
24 H1	Cornbury rd Edg	
48 D19	Cornelia st N7	
115 Z14	Cornell clo Sidcp	
94 D7	Corner grn SE3	
74 B18	Corney rd W4	
91 Z15	Cornflower ter SE22	
126 E13	Cornford clo Brom	
107 T3	Cornford gro SW12	
142 G6	Cornhill EC3	
110 A20	Cornish gro SE20	
93 T8	Cornmill la SE13	
55 W3	Cornshaw dri Dgnhm	
50 B10	Cornthwaite rd E5	
63 O9	Cornwall av E9	
30 B5	Cornwall av N22	
27 Z2	Cornwall av N3	
58 G15	Cornwall av S'hall	
54 L19	Cornwall clo Bark	
136 L7	Cornwall cres W11	
115 T18	Cornwall dri Orp	
44 K19	Cornwall gdns NW10	
145 Z3	Cornwall gdns SW7	
146 A3	Cornwall gdns SW7	
145 Y3	Cornwall Gdns wlk SW7	
74 B15	Cornwall gro W4	
146 A3	Cornwall Ms south SW7	
145 X2	Cornwall Ms west W8	
31 O5	Cornwall rd N15	
18 K15	Cornwall rd N18	
48 F2	Cornwall rd N4	
141 T14	Cornwall rd SE1	
156 H3	Cornwall rd Croy	
22 M17	Cornwall rd Harrow	
22 E3	Cornwall rd Pinn	
153 W19	Cornwall rd Sutton	
83 Z20	Cornwall rd Twick	
63 N19	Cornwall st E1	
19 O8	Cornwallis av N9	
19 N8	Cornwallis av N9	
114 D5	Cornwallis av SE9	
19 O9	Cornwallis gro N9	
32 G14	Cornwallis rd E17	
47 Z6	Cornwallis rd N19	
48 A7	Cornwallis rd N4	
55 X13	Cornwallis rd N9	
95 U7	Cornwallis wlk SE9	
28 F14	Cornwood clo N2	
55 S16	Cornworthy rd Dgnhm	
94 F19	Corona rd SE12	
97 W15	Coronation clo Bxly	
36 C13	Coronation clo Ilf	
57 Y14	Coronation dri Hornch	
65 Z10	Coronation rd E13	
61 O9	Coronation rd NW10	
82 G20	Coronation wlk Twick	
134 J13	Coronet st N1	
82 A10	Corporation av Hounsl	
133 U16	Corporation row EC1	
65 P6	Corporation st E15	
64 M7	Corporation st E15	
47 Z20	Corporation st N7	
48 E11	Corrall rd N7	
90 A11	Corrance rd SW2	
16 L13	Corri av N14	
45 Z2	Corrina ct NW11	
45 X1	Corringham rd NW11	
46 A1	Corringham rd NW11	
43 P7	Corringham rd Wemb	
45 Z2	Corringway NW11	
45 Z2	Corringway NW11	
60 M16	Corringway W5	
61 O11	Corringway W5	
103 V14	Corscombe clo Kingst	
107 U15	Corsehill st SW16	
134 G13	Corsham st N1	
48 J17	Corsica st N5	
75 Y17	Corston st SE8	
87 W5	Cortayne rd SW6	
86 L15	Cortis rd SW15	
86 L15	Cortis ter SW15	
89 V1	Corunna rd SW8	
89 U1	Corunna ter SW8	
89 N20	Cosberton rd SW12	
90 L13	Cosbycote av SE24	
155 X15	Cosdach av Wallgtn	
156 H10	Cosedge cres Croy	
132 L20	Cosmo pl WC1	
92 A2	Cossall st SE15	
149 S2	Cosser st SE1	
91 W6	Costa st SE15	
59 R8	Costons av Grnfd	
59 O8	Costons la Grnfd	
130 L20	Cosway st NW1	
64 B16	Cotall st E14	
106 M9	Coteford st SW17	
107 N10	Coteford st SW17	
157 S6	Cotelands Croy	
50 C9	Cotesbach rd E5	
55 T13	Cotesmore gdns Dgnhm	
122 M8	Cotford rd Thntn Hth	
150 C7	Cotham st SE17	
90 C20	Cotherstone rd SW2	
87 O15	Cotinghill clo SW15	
115 W3	Cotleigh av Bxly	
45 Y20	Cotleigh rd NW6	
39 N18	Cotleigh rd NW6	
28 C18	Cotman clo NW11	
25 O7	Cotman gdns Edg	
97 O6	Cotman rd Welling	
117 X12	Cotsford av New Mald	
99 P4	Cotswold clo Bxly Hth	
103 U15	Cotswold clo Kingst	
45 S5	Cotswold ga NW2	
66 B8	Cotswold gdns E6	
45 P6	Cotswold gdns Ilf	
36 E20	Cotswold gdns Hampt	
100 G14	Cotswold rd Hampt	
7 F12	Cotswold way Enf	
127 S19	Cottage av SW9	
150 H18	Cottage grn SE5	
90 A8	Cottage gro SW9	
89 Z8	Cottage gro Surb	
116 G15	Cottage gro Surb	
133 Y12	Cottage la EC1	
146 J2	Cottage pl SW3	
39 S14	Cottage pl Rom	
64 E19	Cottage st E14	
104 K18	Cottenham dri SW20	
104 G20	Cottenham Pk rd SW20	
104 K18	Cottenham pl SW20	
32 M12	Cottenham rd E17	
116 L20	Cotterill rd Surb	
75 U18	Cottesbrook st SE14	
35 V7	Cottesmore av Ilf	
145 Z1	Cottesmore gdns W8	
146 A1	Cottesmore gdns W8	
33 N1	Cottingham rd E17	
110 E19	Cottingham rd SE20	
59 V9	Cottington st SE11	
63 Y12	Cottisford rd E3	
61 Y16	Cotton av W3	
111 W9	Cotton hill Brom	
64 F19	Cotton st E14	
49 Y17	Cottrill rd E8	
29 X18	Couch Hall rd N8	
43 X19	Couch rd NW11	
35 T7	Couchmore av Ilf	
92 J8	Coulgate st SE4	
147 O8	Coulson st SW3	
74 K8	Coulter rd W6	
144 A2	Coulter rd W6	
150 A20	Councillor st SE5	
149 S10	Countenay st SE11	
142 E15	Counter ct SE1	
142 J13	Counter st SE1	
47 V14	Countess rd NW5	
18 G1	Countisbury av Enf	
114 C6	County ga SE9	
15 O1	County ga Barnt	
67 V6	County gdns Bark	
90 L1	County gro SE5	
141 N18	County hall SE1	
146 J4	County rd Thntn Hth	
150 C3	County st SE1	
30 F10	Courcy rd N8	
89 Y3	Courland gro SW9	
89 Y3	Courland st SW8	
113 X7	Course the SE9	
81 N13	Court av SE2	
24 H12	Court clo Harrow	
155 X17	Court clo Wallgtn	
100 J6	Court Clo av Twick	
125 R3	Court Downs rd Becknhm	
156 D7	Court dri Croy	
11 X14	Court dri Stanm	
153 X7	Court dri Sutton	
58 G1	Court Farm la Grnfd	
113 O6	Court Farm rd SE9	
58 H1	Court Farm rd Grnfd	
14 M19	Court House gdns N3	
14 M18	Court House rd N12	
91 V18	Court la SE21	
91 T17	Court la gdns SE21	
91 T17	Court Lane gdns SE21	
58 E8	Court mead Grnfd	
123 V5	Court rd SE25	
113 S3	Court rd SE9	
95 U7	Court rd SE9	
116 B5	Court rd Kingst	
70 E13	Court rd S'hall	
126 F2	Court st Brom	
40 A15	Court the Ruislip	
26 B12	Court way NW9	
61 W14	Court way W3	
83 W18	Court way Twick	
21 Y16	Court way Wdfd Grn	
95 S17	Court yd SE9	
95 T16	Court yd SE9	
46 H1	Courtenay av N6	
22 L2	Courtenay av Harrow	
23 N6	Courtenay av Harrow	
23 N6	Courtenay rd Har	
23 N7	Courtenay gdns Harrow	
52 C9	Courtenay rd E11	
32 G14	Courtenay rd E17	
110 G16	Courtenay rd SE20	
153 N5	Courtenay rd Worc Pk	
23 W17	Courtfield av Harrow	
23 X16	Courtfield cres Harrow	
145 Z6	Courtfield gdns SW5	
57 Y3	Courtfield gdns W13	
146 A6	Courtfield rd SW7	
159 Y5	Courtfield ri W Wkhm	
93 W13	Courthill rd SE13	
47 N13	Courthope rd NW3	
105 R13	Courthope rd SW19	
59 P5	Courthope rd Grnfd	
105 T5	Courthope vlls SW19	
21 P8	Courtland av E4	
12 M9	Courtland av NW7	
108 D18	Courtland av SW16	
126 A20	Courtland av Brom	
53 T6	Courtland av Ilf	
94 G12	Courtlands Rich	
100 E16	Courtlands av SE12	
85 T3	Courtlands av Rich	
152 C14	Courtlands dri Epsom	
117 P17	Courtlands rd Surb	
117 P16	Courtlands rd Surb	
98 H2	Courtleet dri Erith	
5 T3	Courtleigh av Barnt	
27 T14	Courtleigh gdns NW11	
30 M2	Courtman rd N17	
31 N3	Courtman rd N17	
137 S5	Courtnell st W2	
28 H20	Courtney av N6	
48 G14	Courtney av N7	
106 J18	Courtney rd SW19	
156 F5	Courtney rd Croy	
92 H15	Courtrai rd SE23	
158 M20	Courtswood la Croy	
142 D10	Cousin la EC4	
77 W18	Couthurst rd SE3	
63 X13	Coutts rd E3	
85 U11	Coval gdns SW14	
85 T10	Coval la SW14	
85 U10	Coval rd SW14	
140 L8	Covent gdn WC2	
108 L16	Covent hill SE19	
63 N12	Coventry rd E1	
135 Y17	Coventry rd E1	
123 X8	Coventry rd SE25	
53 X5	Coventry st Ilf	
54 B3	Coventry st Ilf	
140 E10	Coventry st W1	
45 R19	Coverdale rd W12	
74 L4	Coverdale rd W12	
136 A16	Coverdale rd NW2	
67 R4	Coverdale rd Bark	
5 S7	Covert way Barnt	
106 J11	Coverton rd SW17	
108 J19	Covington gdns SW16	
108 J18	Covington way SW16	
108 E16	Covington way SW16	
59 P7	Cow la Grnfd	
150 J13	Cowan st SE5	
25 N13	Cowbridge rd Harrow	
133 X20	Cowcross st EC1	
111 O9	Cowden st SE6	
8 D9	Cowdrey clo Enf	
50 J17	Cowdry st E9	
41 O8	Cowen av Harrow	
59 R7	Cowgate rd Grnfd	
106 M9	Cowick rd SW17	
107 N10	Cowick rd SW17	
9 R13	Cowland av Enf	
116 K1	Cowleaze rd Kingst	
63 P18	Cowley gdns E1	
51 Z9	Cowley la E11	
34 G16	Cowley rd E11	
86 A7	Cowley rd SW14	
90 F2	Cowley rd SW9	
149 Y20	Cowley rd SW9	
74 C4	Cowley rd W3	
53 U2	Cowley rd Ilf	
39 Z1	Cowley rd Rom	
148 J2	Cowley st SW1	
54 E9	Cowper av E6	
64 G9	Cowper av Sutton	
127 O10	Cowper clo Brom	
97 O12	Cowper clo Welling	
6 F19	Cowper gdns N14	
155 V14	Cowper gdns Wallgtn	
16 E5	Cowper rd N14	
49 R13	Cowper rd N16	
18 J12	Cowper rd N18	
106 D15	Cowper rd SW19	
73 X2	Cowper rd W3	
59 V19	Cowper rd W7	
81 P11	Cowper rd Blvdr	
127 N10	Cowper rd Brom	
134 G15	Cowper st EC2	
89 X1	Cowthorpe rd SW8	
78 A13	Coxmount rd SE7	
141 Z3	Coxs ct EC1	
109 Y2	Coxs wlk SE21	
79 T13	Coxwell rd SE18	
111 W18	Crab hill Becknhm	
37 W12	Crabtree av Rom	
60 K5	Crabtree av Wemb	
144 F17	Crabtree la SW6	
81 W7	Crabtree Mnr way Belvdr	
8 G13	Craddock rd Enf	
47 O19	Craddock st NW5	
114 C2	Cradley rd SE9	
24 C7	Craig gdns E18	
18 M15	Craig Park rd N18	
102 E9	Craig rd Rich	
39 U20	Craigdale rd Hornch	
57 U1	Craigdale rd Hornch	
124 A20	Craigen av Croy	
158 A1	Craigen av Croy	
77 U19	Craigerne rd SE3	
61 O2	Craigmuir pk Wemb	
90 E18	Craignair rd SW2	
122 D2	Craignish av SW16	
140 J13	Craigs ct SW1	
95 T11	Craigton rd SE9	
11 U17	Craigweil clo Stanm	
11 U17	Craigweil clo Stanm	
110 B16	Crampton rd SE20	
149 Y6	Crampton st SE17	
150 A9	Crampton st SE17	
58 A6	Cranberry clo Grnf	
70 H11	Cranborne av S'hall	
67 S3	Cranborne rd Bark	
36 D10	Cranbourn gdns Ilf	
140 H9	Cranbourn st WC2	
140 H9	Cranbourne all W	
34 H13	Cranbourne av E11	

Ref	Name
27 U 16	Cranbourne gdns NW11
51 U 12	Cranbourne rd E15
29 T 8	Cranbourne rd N10
26 E 15	Cranbrook clo Brom
32 K 20	Cranbrook dri Twick
63 S 7	Cranbrook estate E2
32 K 15	Cranbrook mews E17
30 E 6	Cranbrook pk N22
04 J 12	Cranbrook rd N17
95 N 7	Cranbrook rd SE3
33 O 2	Cranbrook rd SE4
05 S 18	Cranbrook rd SW19
44 B 13	Cranbrook rd W4
5 V 20	Cranbrook rd Barnt
98 C 1	Cranbrook rd Bxly Hth
32 C 10	Cranbrook rd Hounsl
5W 19	Cranbrook rd Ilf
36 A 12	Cranbrook rd Ilf
53 N 2	Cranbrook rd Ilf
22 M 2	Cranbrook rd Thntn Hth
35 U 19	Cranbrook rise Ilf
38 A 5	Cranbury rd SW6
31 X 20	Crane av W3
33 Y 13	Crane av Islwth
11 U 5	Crane ct EC4
08 G 18	Crane gro N7
75 S 12	Crane mead SE16
00 G 4	Crane park Twick
00 J 4	Crane Pk rd Twick
01 T 1	Crane rd Twick
33 O 17	Crane st SE10
33 O 17	Crane way Twick
83 U 19	Craneford clo Twick
83 U 19	Craneford way Twick
16 K 10	Cranes dri Surb
16 K 11	Cranes la Surb
16 K 10	Cranes Pk av Surb
16 L 10	Cranes Pk cres Surb
92 L 7	Cranfield rd SE4
55 O 19	Cranfield rd Carsh
48 C 18	Cranfield vlls SE27
17 O 16	Cranford av N13
04 H 19	Cranford clo SW20
70 B 19	Cranford la Hounsl
63 T 1	Cranford st E1
75 N 12	Cranham rd SE16
5 Y 8	Cranham rd Hornch
39 Z 18	Cranham rd Hornch
24 M 2	Cranhurst rd NW2
23 Z 2	Cranleigh clo SE20
98 F 15	Cranleigh clo Bxly
7 T 17	Cranleigh gdns N21
23 S 5	Cranleigh gdns SE25
54 E 19	Cranleigh gdns Bark
24 J 16	Cranleigh gdns Harrow
03 N 15	Cranleigh gdns Kingst
58 D 17	Cranleigh gdns S'hall
54 A 3	Cranleigh gdns Sutton
30 L 14	Cranleigh rd N15
19 X 6	Cranleigh rd SW19
32 C 9	Cranleigh st NW1
36 C 20	Cranley dri Ilf
54 C 1	Cranley dri Ilf
29 S 14	Cranley gdns N10
29 V 14	Cranley gdns N10
17 R 10	Cranley gdns SW7
55 U 15	Cranley gdns Wallgtn
46 D 9	Cranley ms SW7
46 F 7	Cranley pl SW7
54 V 14	Cranley rd E13
36 B 20	Cranley rd Ilf
29 R 14	Cranmer av W13
24 E 2	Cranmer clo Mrdn
24 E 2	Cranmer clo Stanm
57 Y 7	Cranmer ct SW4
56 K 13	Cranmer gdns Dgnhm
52 J 11	Cranmer rd E7
52 U 18	Cranmer rd SW9
56 K 5	Cranmer rd Croy
12 E 10	Cranmer rd Edg
00 L 11	Cranmer rd Hampt
42 K 13	Cranmer rd Kingst
21 N 10	Cranmer rd Mitch
39 U 2	Cranmer st W1
12 B 7	Cranmore rd Brom
13 V 11	Cranmore rd Chisl
29 V 12	Cranmore way N10
20 D 18	Cranston gdns E4
10 H 2	Cranston rd SE23
F 13	Cranswater pk S'hall
75 O 13	Cranswick rd SE16
151 Y 10	Cranswick rd SE16
111 S 4	Crantock rd SE6
18 A 1	Cranwich av N21
49 R 1	Cranwich rd N16
134 F 14	Cranwood st EC1
20 J 6	Cranworth cres E4
90 E 2	Cranworth gdns SW9
90 D 18	Craster rd SW2
94 H 14	Crathie rd SE12
93 T 7	Crathorn st SE13
60 D 20	Craven av W5
20 A 9	Craven av S'hall
105 Z 13	Craven gdns SW19
106 A 13	Craven gdns SW19
67 U 7	Craven gdns Bark
36 D 7	Craven gdns Ilf
138 D 8	Craven hill W2
138 C 8	Craven Hill gdns W2
138 C 9	Craven Hill gdns W2
140 K 12	Craven pas WC2
62 C 4	Craven Pk rd NW10
31 V 19	Craven Pk rd N15
61 Z 3	Craven rd NW10
138 D 7	Craven rd W2
60 D 20	Craven rd W5
123 Z 20	Craven rd Croy
102 M 20	Craven rd Kingst
103 N 20	Craven rd Kingst
140 K 12	Craven st WC2
138 D 8	Craven ter W2
49 W 1	Craven wlk E5
31 Y 20	Craven wlk N16
42 G 15	Crawford av Wemb
83 T 4	Crawford clo Islwth
17 W 10	Crawford gdns N13
58 F 8	Crawford gdns Grnfd
139 O 2	Crawford ms W1
139 O 1	Crawford ms W1
133 T 17	Crawford pas EC1
138 L 3	Crawford pl W1
90 M 3	Crawford rd SE5
139 D 2	Crawford st W1
132 C 9	Crawley ms NW1
51 S 4	Crawley rd E10
30 L 7	Crawley rd N22
18 E 3	Crawley rd Enf
90 H 2	Crawshay rd SW9
91 V 11	Crawthew gro SE22
9 X 12	Cray clo Drtfrd
81 S 17	Cray rd Blvdr
115 T 16	Cray rd Sidcp
115 P 10	Craybrooke rd Sidcp
114 B 5	Craybury end SE9
99 U 1	Crayden rd Erith
99 R 12	Crayford High st Drtfrd
47 Z 12	Crayford rd N7
99 S 12	Crayford way Drtfrd
21 P 17	Crealock gro Wdfd Grn
88 B 17	Crealock st SW18
150 K 3	Creasy st SE1
91 Y 16	Crebor st SE22
107 U 16	Credenhill st SW16
46 A 15	Crediton hill NW6
65 T 17	Crediton rd E16
128 E 6	Crediton rd NW10
65 X 7	Credon rd E13
151 Y 10	Credon rd SE16
39 R 3	Cree way Rom
142 L 6	Creechurch la EC3
142 L 6	Creechurch pl EC3
141 Y 6	Creed la EC4
67 S 8	Creek rd SE8
67 X 9	Creek rd Bark
76 C 17	Creekside SE8
110 M 3	Creeland gros SE6
144 J 14	Crefeld rd W6
61 R 20	Creffield rd W3
66 A 7	Creighton av E6
29 N 10	Creighton av N10
28 J 9	Creighton av N2
128 H 8	Creighton rd NW6
31 S 1	Creighton rd N17
72 F 9	Creighton rd W5
134 M 10	Cremer st E2
146 F 16	Cremorne est SW10
146 E 17	Cremorne rd SW10
57 T 7	Crescent av Hornch
	Crescent east Barnt
105 Y 7	Crescent gdns SW19
89 V 11	Crescent gro SW4
120 H 10	Crescent gro Mitch
89 X 13	Crescent la SW4
146 L 5	Crescent pl SW3
51 P 5	Crescent rd E10
65 T 3	Crescent rd E13
34 K 6	Crescent rd E18
21 N 3	Crescent rd E4
65 Y 3	Crescent rd E6
16 A 15	Crescent rd N11
30 H 11	Crescent rd N15
29 Y 4	Crescent rd N22
27 V 4	Crescent rd N3
29 Y 19	Crescent rd N8
18 K 5	Crescent rd N9
78 M 13	Crescent rd SE18
79 N 12	Crescent rd SW20
125 S 3	Crescent rd Becknhm
112 F 19	Crescent rd Brom
56 G 10	Crescent rd Dgnhm
7W 13	Crescent rd Enf
103 R 17	Crescent rd Kingst
114 M 7	Crescent rd Sidcp
29 X 3	Crescent ri N22
5 V 17	Crescent ri Barnt
136 A 17	Crescent row EC1
32 J 17	Crescent the E17
44 K 9	Crescent the NW2
16 A 15	Crescent the N11
31 T 17	Crescent the N15
86 F 4	Crescent the SW13
105 Y 8	Crescent the SW19
5 N 10	Crescent the Barnt
125 O 1	Crescent the Becknhm
97 U 18	Crescent the Bxly
123 O 13	Crescent the Croy
41 P 5	Crescent the Harrow
35W 18	Crescent the Ilf
117 X 4	Crescent the New Mald
70 D 5	Crescent the S'hall
114 L 10	Crescent the Sidcp
116 H 13	Crescent the Surb
154 F 9	Crescent the Sutton
125 Z 14	Crescent the W Wickhm
42 A 7	Crescent the Wemb
15 V 19	Crescent way N20
93 N 8	Crescent way SE4
108 E 17	Crescent way SW16
5 P 5	Crescent west Barnt
109W 7	Crescent Wood rd SE26
88 A 2	Cresford rd SW6
26 J 18	Crespigny rd NW4
58 F 11	Cressage clo S'hall
50 D 18	Cresset rd E9
89W 9	Cresset st SW4
63 R 13	Cressey ct E1
47W 3	Cressida rd N19
154 C 7	Cressingham gro Sutton
93 U 7	Cressingham rd SE13
12 L 20	Cressingham rd Edg
25 Y 2	Cressingham rd Edg
49 S 13	Cressington rd N16
94 C 7	Cresswell pk SE3
123 Y 9	Cresswell rd SE25
84 F 16	Cresswell rd Twick
17 T 2	Cresswell way N21
63 R 14	Cressy clo E1
63 R 14	Cressy pl E1
46 L 13	Cressy rd NW3
9 P 4	Crest dri Enf
44 G 7	Crest rd NW2
126 B 18	Crest rd Brom
157 Z 16	Crest rd S Croy
29 O 14	Crest the NW4
17 T 13	Crest the N13
117 R 13	Crest the Surb
17 V 10	Crestbrook av N13
132 K 12	Crestfield st WC1
86 H 15	Crestway SW15
146 A 9	Creswell gdns SW10
146 B 11	Creswell pl SW10
61 S 19	Creswick rd W3
27W 13	Creswick wlk NW11
78 K 9	Creton st SE18
76 A 10	Crew st E14
149 S 19	Crewdson rd SW9
62 D 8	Crewe pl NW10
45W 8	Crewys rd NW2
92 A 5	Crewys rd SE15
155 X 9	Crichton av Wallgtn
154 L 16	Crichton rd Carsh
120 L 8	Cricket grn Mitch
127 Z 1	Cricket Ground rd Chisl
7 Z 9	Cricketers Arms rd Enf
108 B 4	Cricklade av SW2
40 O 12	Cricklewood bdwy NW2
45 T 10	Cricklewood la NW2
65 O 4	Cridland st E15
88 E 16	Criffel av SW2
107 Y 2	Criffel av SW2
150 L 3	Crimscott st SE1
148 F 20	Crimsworth rd SW8
132 L 7	Crinan st N1
148 C 17	Cringle st SW8
74 M 15	Crisp rd W6
144 C 11	Crisp rd W6
67 P 6	Crispe rd Bark
155 Z 4	Crispin clo Wallgtn
12 J 20	Crispin rd Edg
142 M 1	Crispin st E1
87 V 5	Cristowe rd SW6
47 X 7	Criterion ms N19
106 L 5	Crockerton rd SW17
113 X 10	Crockham way SE9
4 J 19	Crocus field Barnt
62 D 18	Crocus wlk W12
159 V 1	Croft av W Wkhm
12 M 11	Croft clo NW7
81 O 14	Croft clo Blvdr
113 V 11	Croft clo Chisl
71 X 5	Croft gdns W7
21 V 18	Croft Lodge clo Wdfd Grn
108 G 19	Croft rd SW16
106 D 19	Croft rd SW16
112 G 16	Croft rd Brom
9 V 7	Croft rd Enf
154 H 10	Croft rd Sutton
75 V 12	Croft st SE8
62 D 5	Croft the NW10
60 J 14	Croft the W5
4 D 14	Croft the Barnt
70 C 18	Croft the Hounsl
22 F 20	Croft the Pinn
42 C 14	Croft the Wemb
102 B 8	Croft way Rich
114 G 7	Croft way Sidcp
47 S 8	Croftdown rd NW5
158 L 19	Crofters mead Croy
158 M 20	Crofters mead Croy
92 K 16	Crofton Pk rd SE4
65 V 10	Crofton rd E13
91 T 2	Crofton rd SE5
84 M 10	Crofton ter Rich
5 N 19	Crofton way Barnt
23 Y 14	Crofts rd Harrow
45 Y 12	Croftway NW3
47 P 19	Crogsland rd NW1
57 R 15	Croham clo S Croy
157 T 13	Croham Manor rd S Croy
157 R 16	Croham mt S Croy
157 T 11	Croham Park av S Croy
157 V 10	Croham Valley rd S Croy
157W 14	Croham Valley rd S Croy
158 C 17	Croham Valley rd S Croy
122 B 2	Croindene rd SW16
47 Y 2	Cromartie rd N19
114 F 1	Crombie rd Sidcp
126 F 20	Crombie rd Sidcup
33W 20	Cromer rd E10
31W 6	Cromer rd N17
123 Z 6	Cromer rd SE25
107 O 15	Cromer rd SW19
5 P 13	Cromer rd Barnt
37 Z 18	Cromer rd Rom
38 K 18	Cromer rd Rom
21 T 14	Cromer rd Wdfd Grn
132 K 14	Cromer rd WC1
87 U 19	Cromer Vlls rd SW18
87 X 13	Cromford rd SW18
117 Z 1	Cromford way New Mald
19 W 2	Crompton st W2
47 T 2	Cromwell av N6
74 J 12	Cromwell av W6
126 G 8	Cromwell av Brom
118 C 10	Cromwell av New Mald
28 F 13	Cromwell clo N2
126 H 9	Cromwell clo Brom
145 S 5	Cromwell cres W8
146 H 4	Cromwell gdns SW7
136 D 20	Cromwell gro W6
54 F 5	Cromwell ms SW7
47 T 3	Cromwell pl N6
85W 7	Cromwell pl SW14
146 G 5	Cromwell pl SW7
33 T 16	Cromwell rd E17
52 K 20	Cromwell rd E7
29 P 1	Cromwell rd N10
16 E 20	Cromwell rd N3
28 C 6	Cromwell rd N3
105 Z 12	Cromwell rd SW19
106 A 12	Cromwell rd SW19
145 X 5	Cromwell rd SW5
146 C 5	Cromwell rd SW7

123 N 17 Cromwell rd Croy
82 H 13 Cromwell rd Hounsl
116 K 2 Cromwell rd Kingst
60 J 6 Cromwell rd Worc Pk
152 A 6 Cromwell rd Worc Pk
73 T 15 Cromwell Rd ext NW4
82 H 10 Cromwell st Hounsl
87 Y 2 Crondace rd SW6
134 J 10 Crondall st N1
150 M 15 Cronin rd SE15
151 N 18 Cronin rd SE15
97 X 9 Crook log Bxly Hth
75 U 12 Crooke rd SE8
104 M 15 Crooked billet SW19
27 S 10 Crooked usage N3
87 V 3 Crookham rd SW6
95 Y 7 Crookston rd SE9
76 J 20 Crooms hill SE10
76 H 19 Crooms Hill gro SE10
134 E 10 Cropley st N1
56 E 14 Croppath rd Dgnhm
52 E 17 Crosby rd E7
69 U 5 Crosby rd SE7
142 F 18 Crosby row SE1
142 J 5 Crosby sq EC3
101 X 4 Cross deep Rich
101 W 3 Cross Deep gdns Rich
101 W 3 Cross Deep gdns Twick
12 B 11 Cross ga Edg
142 F 3 Cross Key ct EC2
139 U 2 Cross Keys clo W1
142 J 10 Cross la EC3
30 B 12 Cross la N8
98 C 18 Cross la Bxly
82 K 11 Cross Lances rd Hounsl
20 L 5 Cross rd E4
16 F 15 Cross rd N11
18 F 20 Cross rd N17
30 F 1 Cross rd N22
91 T 4 Cross rd SE5
105 Y 18 Cross rd SW19
123 P 20 Cross rd Croy
8 F 15 Cross rd Enf
100 B 10 Cross rd Felt
23 P 14 Cross rd Harrow
23 Y 8 Cross rd Harrow
40 J 9 Cross rd Harrow
103 N 18 Cross rd Kingst
38 F 12 Cross rd Rom
55 T 2 Cross rd Rom
115 R 11 Cross rd Sidcp
154 G 10 Cross rd Sutton
51 Z 20 Cross st E15
64 A 1 Cross st E3
133 Y 3 Cross st N1
18 J 16 Cross st N18
86 C 6 Cross st SW13
101 N 13 Cross st Hampt
15 U 19 Cross way N12
10 Y 10 Cross way Dgnhm
21 Y 14 Cross way Wdfd Grn
23 U 6 Cross Way the Harrow
95 P 6 Crossbrook rd SE3
46 C 19 Crossfield rd NW3
30 L 11 Crossfield st N17
76 B 18 Crossfield st SE8
90 B 4 Crossford st SW9
42 B 18 Crossgate Grnfd
122 H 14 Crossland rd Thntn Hth
72 M 3 Crosslands av W5
73 N 3 Crosslands av W5
70 E 14 Crosslands av S'hall
48 F 18 Crossley st N7
113 U 2 Crossmead SE9
58 J 8 Crossmead av Grnfd
91 O 11 Crossthwaite av SE5
135 U 3 Crosston st E8
142 M 8 Crosswall EC3
143 N 7 Crosswall EC3
26 E 14 Crossway NW9
49 T 15 Crossway N16
68 J 20 Crossway SE2
118 M 9 Crossway SW20
59 Y 11 Crossway W13
18 D 2 Crossway Enf
30 K 3 Crossway the N22
113 O 4 Crossway the SE9
23 U 6 Crossway the Harrow
17 Y 1 Crossways N21
39 Z 11 Crossways Rom
158 K 16 Crossways S Croy
154 F 18 Crossways Sutton

145 S 5 Crossways rd Mitch
70 E 20 Crossways the Hounsl
43 R 7 Crossways the Wemb
68 D 7 Crouch av Bark
113 X 7 Crouch croft SE9
29 Z 19 Crouch End hill N8
48 A 1 Crouch hill N4
56 H 1 Crow la Rom
107 P 13 Crowborough rd SW17
143 W 9 Crowder st E1
90 G 5 Crowhurst rd SW9
16 M 3 Crowland gdns N14
31 V 16 Crowland rd N15
123 N 9 Crowland rd Thntn Hth
49 N 20 Crowland ter N1
120 B 13 Crowland wlk Mrdn
38 H 18 Crowlands av Rom
156 H 11 Crowley cres Croy
92 D 20 Crowmarsh gdns SE23
13 T 7 Crown clo NW7
13 S 7 Crown clo NW7
142 C 6 Crown ct EC4
94 G 16 Crown st SE12
140 M 7 Crown ct WC2
108 L 14 Crown dale SE19
16 H 5 Crown la N14
108 G 14 Crown la SW16
127 O 13 Crown la Brom
119 Z 7 Crown la Brom
127 O 13 Crown la Spur Brom
108 G 13 Crown la gdns SW16
140 C 14 Crown pas SW1
29 P 2 Crown rd N10
31 W 1 Crown rd N17
8 M 14 Crown rd Enf
36 D 13 Crown rd Ilf
119 Z 8 Crown rd Mrdn
117 X 1 Crown rd New Mald
153 Z 9 Crown rd Sutton
154 A 8 Crown rd Sutton
84 C 17 Crown rd Twick
150 B 18 Crown st SE5
73 T 3 Crown st W3
56 J 19 Crown st Dgnhm
41 S 4 Crown st Harrow
84 M 9 Crown ter Rich
95 Z 4 Crown Woods la SE18
141 T 8 Crown-Office row EC4
132 B 8 Crowndale rd NW1
36 F 17 Crownfield av Ilf
51 W 13 Crownfield rd E15
62 D 4 Crownhill rd NW10
35 R 3 Crownhill rd Wdfd Grn
38 H 13 Crownmead way Rom
96 A 7 Crownwoods la SE9
96 F 12 Crownwoods way SE9
64 L 8 Crows rd E15
24 F 6 Crowshott av Stanm
90 E 13 Crowstone rd SW2
72 K 12 Crowther av Brentf
123 X 10 Crowther rd SE25
120 C 14 Croxden wlk Mrdn
30 K 3 Croxford gdns N22
56 L 4 Croxford way Rom
129 R 13 Croxley rd W9
90 L 19 Croxted clo SE21
109 N 2 Croxted rd SE21
90 L 18 Croxted rd SE24
59 O 9 Croyde av Grnfd
96 E 18 Croydon clo Sidcp
122 H 19 Croydon gro Croy
65 R 12 Croydon rd E13
110 D 20 Croydon rd SE20
123 Z 4 Croydon rd SE20
124 L 6 Croydon rd Becknhm
156 B 8 Croydon rd Croy
121 T 11 Croydon rd Mitch
155 V 7 Croydon rd Wallgtn
18 J 5 Croyland N9
50 G 16 Crozier ter E9
142 K 17 Crucifix la SE1
133 Y 6 Cruden st N1
133 R 11 Cruickbank st WC1
52 B 14 Cruikshank rd E15
26 B 16 Crummock gdns NW9
80 F 11 Crumpsall st SE2
25 R 17 Crundale av NW9
157 O 15 Crunden rd S Croy
106 M 18 Crusoe rd Mitch
142 L 8 Crutched friars EC3

112 A 4 Crutchley rd SE6
109 Y 12 Crystal Palace park SE26
109 V 13 Crystal Palace pde SE19
91 W 10 Crystal Palace rd SE22
109 W 16 Crystal Palace Stn rd SE19
109 O 15 Crystal ter SE19
9 O 9 Cuba dri Enf
76 A 4 Cuba st E14
133 O 14 Cubitt st WC1
156 E 11 Cubitt st Croy
59 U 13 Cuckoo av W7
59 S 13 Cuckoo dene W7
19 P 2 Cuckoo Hall la N9
59 U 19 Cuckoo la W7
152 D 7 Cudas clo Epsom
152 D 6 Cuddington av Worc Pk
93 T 18 Cudham st SE6
135 X 16 Cudworth st E1
63 N 11 Cudworth st E1
95 P 17 Cuff cres SE9
147 O 7 Culford gdns SW3
49 R 19 Culford ms N1
49 R 18 Culford ms N1
134 J 2 Culford rd N1
49 R 18 Culford rd N1
7 N 13 Culgarth gdns Enf
61 W 12 Cullen way NW10
75 O 7 Culling rd SE16
143 Z 20 Culling rd SE16
23 X 13 Cullington clo Harrow
44 H 15 Cullingworth rd NW10
7 V 9 Culloden rd Enf
64 G 17 Culloden st E14
142 J 7 Cullum st EC3
51 X 20 Cullum st E15
72 D 3 Culmington rd W13
156 K 18 Culmington rd S Croy
107 R 1 Culmore cross SW4
75 O 20 Culmore rd SE14
151 Z 19 Culmore rd SE15
89 O 13 Culmstock rd SW11
133 S 7 Culpepper st N1
30 K 14 Culross rd N15
139 S 9 Culross st W1
24 F 3 Culver gro Stanm
108 C 8 Culverhouse gdns SW16
11 N 14 Culverlands clo Stanm
93 R 20 Culverley rd SE6
111 U 1 Culverley rd SE6
154 L 2 Culvers av Carsh
155 N 1 Culvers av Carsh
121 O 19 Culvers av Mitch
155 N 2 Culvers retreat Carsh
154 L 3 Culvers way Carsh
126 C 13 Culverstorte clo Brom
89 O 6 Culvert pl SW8
31 R 16 Culvert rd N15
89 N 4 Culvert rd SW8
150 B 8 Culworth gro SE17
130 K 10 Culworth st NW8
123 W 7 Cumbedow rd SE25
61 T 9 Cumberland av NW10
96 K 10 Cumberland av Welling
84 B 15 Cumberland clo Twick
144 M 5 Cumberland cres W14
80 M 20 Cumberland dri Bxly Hth
98 A 1 Cumberland dri Bxly Hth
27 R 6 Cumberland gdns NW4
133 R 12 Cumberland gdns WC1
131 Z 12 Cumberland mkt NW1
61 X 20 Cumberland pk W3
73 W 1 Cumberland pk W3
131 X 12 Cumberland pl NW1
53 N 14 Cumberland rd E12
65 V 11 Cumberland rd E13
32 H 7 Cumberland rd E17
30 D 6 Cumberland rd N22
19 P 7 Cumberland rd N9
86 E 1 Cumberland rd SW13
61 W 20 Cumberland rd W3
71 W 6 Cumberland rd W7
125 Z 8 Cumberland rd Brom

126 C 8 Cumberland rd Bro
22 K 15 Cumberland rd Harrow
73 O 20 Cumberland rd Rich
25 N 11 Cumberland rd Stanm
147 N 9 Cumberland st SW
148 A 11 Cumberland st SW
131 X 10 Cumberland Terr m NW1
124 A 13 Cumberland va SE1
31 P 5 Cumberton rd N17
99 R 4 Cumberton rd Bxly Hth
45 R 7 Cumbrian gdns NV
133 O 9 Cumming st N1
72 H 15 Cumnor gdns Epso
154 E 13 Cumnor rd Sutton
142 K 6 Cunard pl EC3
61 Z 9 Cunard rd NW10
150 H 14 Cunard st SE5
65 X 18 Cundy rd E16
147 V 7 Cundy st SW1
152 F 8 Cunliffe rd Worc P
107 V 18 Cunliffe st SW16
159 S 3 Cunningham clo W Wknm
23 P 15 Cunningham pk Harrow
17 F 16 Cunningham pl NV
31 W 13 Cunningham rd N1
73 W 10 Cunnington st W4
89 R 1 Cupar rd SW11
148 G 6 Cupar st SW1
143 O 16 Curate st SE1
107 U 5 Curlverden rd SW1
108 L 11 Curnicks la SE27
155 P 6 Curran av Wallgtn
96 L 14 Curran av Sidcp
47 P 18 Currey rd Grnfd
74 A 4 Currick st W3
105 V 10 Currie Hill clo SW
141 S 4 Cursitor st EC4
134 K 15 Curtain pl EC2
134 K 14 Curtain rd EC2
6 L 15 Curthwaite gdns Er
82 D 20 Curtis rd Hounsl
150 M 4 Curtis st SE1
62 F 20 Curve the W12
52 G 12 Curwen av E7
74 F 6 Curwen rd W12
9 U 17 Curzon av Enf
23 Y 5 Curzon av Stanm
44 B 20 Curzon cres NW10
62 C 1 Curzon cres NW10
67 X 8 Curzon cres Bark
139 V 14 Curzon pl W1
29 S 7 Curzon rd N10
60 B 12 Curzon rd W5
122 E 14 Curzon rd Thntn Ht
139 V 13 Curzon st W1
101 V 8 Cusack clo Twick
81 Z 13 Cusoe rd Erith
141 U 17 Cut the SE1
90 M 5 Cutcombe rd SE5
33 V 11 Cuthbert rd E17
18 K 15 Cuthbert rd N18
156 J 3 Cuthbert rd Croy
91 O 3 Cuthill rd SE5
142 L 1 Cutler st E1
97 X 12 Cuxton clo Bxly Hth
135 O 16 Cygnet st E2
133 P 9 Cynthia st N1
83 N 18 Cypress av Twick
132 C 19 Cypress pl W1
123 T 3 Cypress rd SE25
23 P 7 Cypress rd Harrow
27 U 7 Cyprus av N3
27 T 6 Cyprus gdns N3
63 P 7 Cyprus pl E2
63 R 7 Cyprus pl E2
66 K 19 Cyprus place E6
27 V 8 Cyprus pl N3
18 G 7 Cyprus rd N9
63 R 7 Cyprus st E2
91 V 14 Cyrena rd SE22
98 A 5 Cyril rd Bxly Hth
133 X 15 Cyrus st EC1

D

40 J 14 Dabbs Hill la Grnrd
93 T 2 Dabia cres SE10
75 Z 15 Dacca st SE8
64 A 2 Dace rd E3
35 X 7 Dacre av Ilf
93 Z 7 Dacre pk SE13
94 A 10 Dacre pk SE13
93 Z 8 Dacre pl SE13
52 B 3 Dacre rd E11

85 U 4 Dacre rd E13
22 A 17 Dacre rd Croy
4 F 20 Dacre st SW1
10 D 6 Dacres clo SE23
16 F 20 Dacres rd SE23
74 E 1 Daffodil rd W12
62 E 20 Daffodil st W12
07 N 7 Dafforne rd SW1
58 M 3 Dagenham av Dgnhm
26 C 20 Dagenham av Dgnhm
89 N 1 Dagenham av Dgnhm
69 U 1 Dagenham Old park Dgnhm
50 M 3 Dagenham rd E10
6 J 11 Dagenham rd Dgnhm
37 N 4 Dagenham rd Rom
42 L 13 Dagmar av Wemb
43 N 13 Dagmar av Wemb
28 E 10 Dagmar gdns NW10
43 X 3 Dagmar pas N1
31 O 14 Dagmar rd N15
19 Y 4 Dagmar rd N22
23 R 10 Dagmar rd SE25
41 R 3 Dagmar rd SE5
66 L 19 Dagmar rd Dgnhm
23 O 19 Dagmar rd Kingst
70 C 9 Dagmar rd S'hall
33 X 3 Dagmar ter N1
23 P 13 Dagnall pk SE25
23 R 11 Dagnall rd SE25
39 N 3 Dagnall st SW11
39 T 17 Dagnan rd SW12
12 E 8 Dagonet gdns Brom
21 X 9 Dagonet rd Brom
30 U 12 Dahlia rd SE2
07 U 15 Dahomey rd SW16
56 A 15 Daimler way Wallgtn
53 V 10 Daines clo E12
11 W 12 Dainford clo Brom
85 Y 7 Dairsie rd SE9
68 R 9 Dairy wlk SW19
87 Y 7 Daisy la SW6
18 M 8 Daisy rd E18
90 F 13 Dalberg rd SW2
01 Cl Dalby rd SW18
17 R 18 Dalby st NW5
32 A 5 Dalcross rd Hounsl
26 M 7 Dale av Edg
24 M 6 Dale av Edg
92 C 7 Dale av Hounsl
94 D 8 Dale clo SE3
5 N 20 Dale clo Barnt
99 U 14 Dale clo Drtfrd
99 U 17 Dale end Drtfrd
21 V 13 Dale gdns Wdfd Grn
16 F 12 Dale Green rd N11
51 P 18 Dale gro N12
55 N 3 Dale Park av Carsh
54 M 3 Dale Park av Carsh
09 N 20 Dale Park rd SE19
17 O 15 Dale rd NW5
99 U 16 Dale rd Drtfrd
58 K 15 Dale rd Grnfd
53 V 9 Dale rd Sutton
74 A 14 Dale st W4
99 V 4 Dale view Erith
20 H 9 Dale View av E4
20 G 9 Dale View cres E4
20 H 9 Dale View gdns E4
06 K 4 Dalebury rd SW17
16 F 17 Daleham gdns NW3
46 F 17 Daleham ms NW3
07 S 12 Daleside rd SW16
31 S 19 Daleview rd N15
52 L 2 Dalewood gdns Worc Pk
50 F 17 Daley st E9
58 C 20 Dalgarno gdns W10
36 A 1 Dalgarno gdns W10
62 L 1 Dalgarno gdns W10
62 M 12 Dalgarno way W10
62 D 19 Dalgarno way W10
63 X 17 Dalgleish st E14
17 M 17 Dalkeith gro Stanm
90 M 20 Dalkeith rd SE21
04 C 10 Dalkeith rd Ilf
44 H 1 Dallas rd NW4
82 R 3 Dallas rd SE26
50 M 14 Dallas rd W5
53 T 14 Dallas rd Sutton
58 N 18 Dallin rd SE18
79 N 18 Dallin rd SE18
70 K 10 Dallin rd Bxly Hth
74 J 9 Dalling rd W6
81 B 17 Dallinger rd SE12
33 X 16 Dallington st EC1
92 F 20 Dalmain rd SE23
23 W 17 Dalmally rd Croy

47 Z 14 Dalmeny av N7
122 F 4 Dalmeny av SW16
18 G 4 Dalmeny clo Wemb
47 X 10 Dalmeny rd N1
5 S 20 Dalmeny rd Barnt
98 G 2 Dalmeny rd Bxly Hth
155 P 17 Dalmeny rd Carsh
152 K 5 Dalmeny rd Worc Pk
108 M 3 Dalmore rd SE21
92 J 12 Dalrymple rd SE4
24 J 6 Dalston gdns Stanm
50 A 15 Dalston la E5
49 V 18 Dalston la E8
33 P 13 Dalston av Mitch
108 K 5 Dalton st SE27
91 S 1 Dalton st SE5
90 C 8 Dalyell rd SW9
103 T 19 Dalziel Of Wooler home Kingst
134 A 7 Dame st N1
146 C 19 Damer ter SW10
52 F 12 Dames rd E7
63 N 17 Damien st E1
143 Y 4 Damien st E1
108 B 19 Danbrook rd SW16
37 V 10 Danbury clo Rom
155 S 8 Danbury ms Wallgtn
133 Y 8 Danbury st N1
21 Y 20 Danbury way Wdfd Grn
91 U 7 Danby st SE15
85 P 7 Dancer rd SW6
94 G 8 Dancer rd Rich
94 E 3 Dando cres SE3
159 T 9 Dane clo Bxly
157 V 5 Dane Court gdns Croy
63 X 6 Dane pl E3
106 D 20 Dane rd SW19
72 D 2 Dane rd W13
54 A 16 Dane rd Ilf
58 C 20 Dane rd S'hall
86 B 16 Danebury av SW15
111 S 5 Daneby rd SE6
91 N 13 Danecroft rd SE24
35 S 17 Danehurst gdns Ilf
87 S 1 Danehurst st SW6
5 Z 20 Daneland Barnt
40 K 15 Danemead gro Grnfd
87 N 7 Danemere st SW15
23 S 11 Danes ga Harrow
38 K 20 Danes rd E7
159 U 14 Danesbury Croy
154 D 3 Danescourt cres Sutton
27 R 16 Danescroft av NW4
27 R 16 Danescroft gdns NW4
50 H 18 Danesdale rd E9
111 T 7 Daneswood av SE6
42 F 18 Danethorpe rd Wemb
56 D 8 Danette gdns Dgnhm
91 N 3 Daneville rd SE5
34 E 19 Dangan rd E11
64 E 14 Daniel Bolt clo E14
151 O 17 Daniel gdns SE15
26 J 20 Daniel pl NW4
61 O 20 Daniel rd W6
135 R 13 Daniel st E2
92 C 8 Daniels rd SE15
140 F 9 Dansey pl W1
97 O 9 Dansington rd Welling
97 O 9 Danson cres Welling
97 P 10 Danson la Welling
97 V 9 Danson mead Welling
149 Y 12 Danson rd SE17
52 L 2 Danson rd Bxly Hth
149 X 6 Dante rd SE17
148 L 9 Danube st SW3
29 W 12 Danvers rd N8
146 H 15 Danvers st SW3
20 G 10 Daphne gdns E4
88 B 17 Daphne st SW18
140 D 6 Darblay st W1
143 R 19 Darby st E1
155 V 8 Darcy av Wallgtn
24 H 14 Darcy dri Harrow
69 P 2 Darcy gdns Dgnhm
24 J 13 Darcy gdns Harrow
121 Z 3 Darcy rd SW16
153 O 8 Darcy rd Sutton
55 Z 10 Dare gdns Dgnhm
85 P 7 Darell rd Rich
49 V 2 Darenth rd N16
97 O 2 Darenth rd Welling
92 K 13 Darfield rd SE4
87 O 8 Darfur st SW15
88 G 8 Darien rd SW11
142 B 9 Darkhouse la EC4
145 R 20 Darlan rd SW6

105 R 18 Darlaston rd SW19
117 Y 3 Darley dri New Mald
18 G 4 Darley rd N9
93 O 7 Darling clo SE4
63 N 13 Darling row E1
135 Y 19 Darling row E1
108 K 12 Darlington rd SE27
50 B 19 Darnley rd E9
34 G 4 Darnley rd Wdfd Grn
136 J 13 Darnley ter W11
91 X 13 Darrell rd SE22
89 Z 1 Darley dri SW8
129 N 12 Dart st W10
19 R 1 Dartford av N9
99 Y 15 Dartford rd Drtfrd
150 B 13 Dartford st SE17
93 V 3 Dartmouth gro SE10
93 V 3 Dartmouth hill SE10
47 T 9 Dartmouth Pk av NW5
47 T 5 Dartmouth Pk hill NW5
47 S 10 Dartmouth Pk rd NW5
110 D 4 Dartmouth pl SE23
65 S 19 Dartmouth rd E16
45 O 17 Dartmouth rd NW2
26 G 19 Dartmouth rd NW4
110 C 5 Dartmouth rd SE26
126 F 17 Dartmouth rd Brom
93 V 3 Dartmouth row SE10
140 F 19 Dartmouth st SW1
150 M 12 Dartnell rd SE5
123 U 17 Dartnell rd Croy
146 E 18 Dartrey rd SW10
88 E 11 Darvall sq SW18
88 E 11 Darvall st SW18
49 V 10 Darville rd N16
58 L 17 Darwin dri S'hall
150 F 6 Darwin pl SE17
30 J 7 Darwin rd N22
72 F 12 Darwin rd W5
96 L 8 Darwin rd Welling
58 N 17 Darwin st SE17
98 E 14 Dashwood clo Bxly Hth
30 C 19 Dashwood rd N8
108 K 12 Dassett rd SE27
91 P 2 Datchelor pl SE5
110 L 6 Datchet rd SE6
150 D 10 Date st SE17
30 H 12 Daubeney rd E5
30 L 2 Daubeney rd N17
88 C 15 Daulte rd SW18
47 Z 7 Davenant rd N19
143 T 2 Davenant st E1
93 T 16 Davenport rd SE6
115 Y 4 Davenport rd Sidcp
33 O 17 Daventry av E17
130 X 20 Daventry st NW1
77 O 13 Davern st SE10
151 O 15 Davey st SE15
59 T 8 David av Grnfd
131 S 20 David ms W1
55 X 6 David rd Dgnhm
141 X 19 Davidge st SE1
12 H 20 Davids clo Edg
110 C 2 Davids rd SE23
36 G 1 Davids way Ilf
148 J 18 Davidson dris SW1
123 U 15 Davidson rd Croy
52 A 5 Davies la E11
139 W 8 Davies ms W1
139 W 8 Davies st W1
55 R 16 Davington gdns Dgnhm
135 R 18 Davis av E1
74 D 4 Davis rd W3
65 W 7 Davis st E13
76 G 8 Davis st E14
74 G 6 Davisville rd W12
83 X 11 Dawes av Islwth
144 K 17 Dawes rd SW6
145 P 18 Dawes rd SW6
150 G 9 Dawes st SE17
16 M 14 Dawlish av N13
17 N 15 Dawlish av N13
106 A 4 Dawlish av SW18
59 Z 7 Dawlish av Grnfd
60 A 7 Dawlish av Grnfd
54 H 12 Dawlish dri Ilf
22 B 17 Dawlish dri Pinn
51 T 5 Dawlish rd E10
45 P 17 Dawlish rd NW2
31 W 9 Dawlish rd N17
106 E 3 Dawnay gdns SW18
106 E 3 Dawnay rd SW18
44 E 7 Dawpool rd NW2
13 T 16 Daws la NW7
67 W 2 Dawson av Bark
67 Y 2 Dawson av Bark

67 Y 2 Dawson gdns Bark
137 U 9 Dawson pl W2
45 N 13 Dawson rd NW2
117 N 6 Dawson rd Surb
30 S 9 Dawson st E2
120 A 4 Daybrook rd SW19
86 G 9 Daylesford av SW15
96 G 20 Days la Sidcp
108 C 2 Daysbrook rd SW2
92 C 1 Dayton gro SE15
49 R 20 De Beauvoir rd N1
134 J 2 De Beauvoir sq N1
49 S 20 De Beauvoir sq N1
134 K 1 De Beauvoir sq N1
6 D 20 De Behun av N14
91 O 4 De Crespigny pk SE5
110 H 8 De Frene rd SE26
156 B 16 De Havilland rd Croy
25 S 8 De Havilland rd Edg
156 B 16 De Havilland rd Croy
149 W 11 De Laune st SE17
80 E 10 De Lucy st SE2
107 Z 5 De Montford rd SW16
88 B 7 De Morgan rd SW6
31 O 4 De Quiney rd N17
138 A 19 De Vere gdns W8
53 T 5 De Vere gdns Ilf
138 A 20 De Vere ms W8
139 V 2 De Walden st W1
44 G 16 Deacon rd NW2
116 M 1 Deacon rd Kingst
150 A 6 Deacon st SE17
107 O 15 Deal rd SW17
135 S 19 Deal st E1
86 L 10 Dealtry rd SW15
148 J 4 Dean Bradley st SW1
42 C 9 Dean st Wemb
24 K 8 Dean dri Stanm
140 F 20 Dean Farrar st SW1
33 W 12 Dean gdns E17
44 M 17 Dean pl NW2
157 O 9 Dean rd Croy
100 F 13 Dean rd Hampt
82 L 14 Dean rd Hounsl
148 J 4 Dean Ryle st SW1
52 E 14 Dean st E7
140 F 7 Dean st W1
148 J 3 Dean Stanley st SW1
148 J 3 Dean Trench st SW1
12 K 20 Dean wlk Edg
143 Z 6 Deancross st E1
63 O 17 Deancross st E1
139 U 13 Deanery ms W1
51 Z 18 Deanery rd E15
52 A 19 Deanery rd E15
139 W 1 Deanery st W1
85 U 10 Deanhill rd SW14
150 F 8 Deans bldgs SE17
73 T 16 Deans clo W4
12 H 20 Deans clo Edg
141 Y 7 Deans ct EC4
12 K 16 Deans clo Edg
73 T 16 Deans la W4
12 H 18 Deans la Edg
139 X 4 Deans ms W1
148 E 8 Deans pl SW1
71 W 4 Deans rd W7
153 Z 7 Deans rd Sutton
154 A 6 Deans rd Sutton
12 G 17 Deans way Edg
148 H 1 Deans yd SW1
25 U 1 Deansbrook clo Edg
25 U 1 Deansbrook clo Edgw
13 N 20 Deansbrook rd NW7
43 V 5 Deanscroft av NW9
28 G 13 Deansway N2
18 E 10 Deansway N9
120 J 5 Dearn gdns Mitch
10 L 17 Dearne clo Stanm
64 H 3 Deason st E15
57 Z 18 Debden wlk Nornch
75 P 12 Debnams rd SE16
106 D 17 Deburgh rd SW19
150 J 1 Decima st SE1
27 U 14 Decoy av NW11
85 W 9 Dee rd Rich
64 J 16 Dee st E14
39 P 3 Dee way Rom
89 X 2 Deeley rd SW8
61 O 17 Deena clo W3
105 N 10 Deepdale SW19
157 V 5 Deepdene av Croy
7 W 20 Deepdene ct N21
90 C 18 Deepdene gdns SW2
91 N 9 Deepdene rd SE5

97 O 6 Deepdene rd Welling
120 C 3 Deer Pk rd SW19
108 H 1 Deerbrook rd SE24
90 L 9 Deerdale rd SE24
57 W 19 Deere av Rainhm
26 F 17 Deerfield cotts NW9
45 P 19 Deerhurst rd NW2
108 C 13 Deerhurst rd SW16
106 F 7 Deeside rd SW16
155 Z 16 Defiant way Wallgtn
73 R 20 Defoe av Rich
49 S 8 Defoe rd N16
113 Y 13 Degema rd Chisl
44 F 2 Dehar cres NW9
91 S 16 Dekker rd SE21
77 V 20 Delacourt rd SE3
77 X 13 Delafield rd SE7
75 N 14 Delaford rd SE16
145 N 16 Delaford st SW6
124 C 15 Delamere cres Croy
12 K 18 Delamere gdns NW7
119 P 1 Delamere rd SW20
72 L 4 Delamere rd W5
138 A 1 Delamere st W2
138 A 1 Delamere ter W2
131 Z 6 Delancey pas NW1
131 X 6 Delancey st NW1
88 L 12 Delaporte sq SW18
129 W 16 Delaware rd W9
91 N 16 Delawyk cres SE24
118 L 20 Delcombe av Worc Pk
91 S 12 Delft way SE22
18 G 1 Delhi rd Enf
132 L 4 Delhi st N1
88 B 18 Delia st SW18
64 L 3 Dell clo E15
155 W 7 Dell clo Wallgtn
12 N 11 Dell clo Wdfd Grn
152 F 12 Dell la Epsom
9 P 2 Dell rd Enf
152 G 12 Dell rd Epsom
109 U 19 Dell the SE19
79 Z 14 Dell the SE2
21 U 11 Dell the Wdfd Grn
42 C 14 Dell the Wemb
118 B 4 Dell wlk New Mald
4 C 16 Dellors clo Barnt
63 N 20 Dellow st E1
143 Y 8 Dellow st E1
35 X 11 Dellwood gdns Ilf
83 P 9 Delmany cres Hounsl
94 J 4 Delme cres SE3
90 D 10 Delmere clo SW19
157 V 5 Delmey clo Croy
93 N 2 Deloraine st SE4
4 B 19 Delorme st W6
152 C 5 Delta rd Worc Pk
135 R 12 Delta st E2
81 Y 13 Deluci rd Erith
78 K 17 Delvan st SE18
149 Y 10 Delverton rd SE17
87 X 3 Delvino rd SW6
155 W 7 Demesne rd Wallgtn
88 C 12 Dempster rd SW18
125 X 7 Den clo Becknhm
125 X 7 Den rd Brom
115 S 8 Denberry dri Sidcp
137 R 8 Denbigh clo W11
113 T 15 Denbigh clo Chisl
58 F 17 Denbigh clo S'hall
153 V 10 Denbigh clo Sutton
85 N 14 Denbigh gdns Rich
148 B 9 Denbigh pl SW1
66 B 10 Denbigh rd E6
44 A 20 Denbigh rd NW10
62 A 1 Denbigh rd NW10
137 R 8 Denbigh rd W11
60 C 19 Denbigh rd W13
82 L 4 Denbigh rd Hounsl
58 F 17 Denbigh rd S'hall
148 C 10 Denbigh rd SW1
137 R 8 Denbigh ter W11
127 V 2 Denbridge rd Brom
107 O 1 Dendy st SW12
82 E 7 Dene av Hounsl
97 S 19 Dene av Sidcp
92 H 9 Dene clo SE4
126 C 20 Dene clo Brom
152 D 2 Dene clo Worc Pk
11 S 16 Dene gdns Stanm
16 A 7 Dene rd N11
60 A 14 Dene the W13
42 J 12 Dene the Wemb
5 S 17 Dene wood Barnt
26 M 19 Denehurst gdns NW4
73 S 3 Denehurst gdns W3
85 R 10 Denehurst gdns Rich
83 R 19 Denehurst gdns Twick

28 M 20 Denewood rd N6
120 M 10 Denham cres Mitch
36 A 18 Denham dri Ilf
15 Y 10 Denham rd N20
67 W 3 Denham way Bark
57 U 18 Denholm wlk Rainhm
129 R 12 Denholme rd W9
28 C 11 Denison clo N2
106 F 16 Denison rd SW19
60 E 11 Denison rd W5
115 Y 3 Deniston av Bxly
17 S 4 Denleigh gdns N21
27 Z 15 Denman dri NW11
27 Z 14 Denman Dri north NW11
27 Z 15 Denman Dri south NW11
91 U 3 Denman rd SE15
140 E 9 Denman st W1
105 S 17 Denmark av SW19
119 Y 13 Denmark ct Mrdn
155 N 5 Denmark gdns Carsh
133 S 7 Denmark gro N1
91 O 10 Denmark hill SE5
140 G 5 Denmark pl WC2
129 R 9 Denmark rd NW6
123 Y 11 Denmark rd SE25
90 L 4 Denmark rd SE5
105 R 16 Denmark rd SW19
155 N 6 Denmark rd Carsh
60 C 20 Denmark rd Grnfd
116 J 6 Denmark rd Kingst
101 R 6 Denmark rd Twick
51 Y 10 Denmark st E11
65 U 13 Denmark st E13
31 Y 3 Denmark st N17
140 H 5 Denmark st WC2
118 L 10 Denmark wlk SE27
116 L 20 Denmark rd Surb
135 P 5 Denne ter E8
20 B 8 Denner rd E4
122 C 18 Dennett rd Croy
92 E 4 Dennetts gro SE14
92 D 3 Dennetts rd SE14
156 G 10 Denning av Croy
46 G 12 Denning rd NW3
45 Y 16 Dennington Pk rd NW6
42 L 14 Dennis av Wemb
11 R 15 Dennis gdns Stanm
11 O 12 Dennis la Stanm
119 S 1 Dennis Pk cres SW2
149 V 8 Denny cres SE11
55 S 20 Denny gdns Dgnhm
18 M 5 Denny st N9
149 T 8 Denny st SE11
64 M 2 Densham rd E15
65 N 3 Densham rd E15
19 P 10 Densworth gro N9
61 W 1 Denton rd NW10
18 F 14 Denton rd N18
30 E 17 Denton rd N8
99 S 19 Denton rd Drtfrd
84 G 17 Denton rd Twick
80 F 19 Denton rd Welling
88 B 15 Denton st SW18
88 L 17 Dents rd SW11
49 R 1 Denver rd N16
99 X 19 Denver rd Drtfrd
146 M 6 Denyer st SW3
44 E 16 Denzil rd NW10
85 O 20 Deodar rd SW15
28 B 6 Depot appr N3
54 C 1 Depot cotts Ilf
83 P 7 Depot rd Hounsl
150 E 16 Depot st SE5
93 O 1 Deptford bdwy SE4
93 O 1 Deptford br SE4
76 B 17 Deptford Ch st SE8
76 B 12 Deptford Ferry rd E14
76 B 16 Deptford grn SE8
75 Y 12 Deptford strand SE8
15 P 17 Derby av N12
23 P 5 Derby av Harrow
38 J 19 Derby av Rom
140 K 17 Derby ga SW1
110 C 4 Derby hill SE23
110 B 4 Derby Hill cres SE23
53 N 19 Derby rd E12
52 M 20 Derby rd E18
34 B 4 Derby rd E18
63 S 3 Derby rd E9
30 K 13 Derby rd N15
19 O 16 Derby rd N18
85 T 10 Derby rd SW14
105 Y 18 Derby rd SW19
156 J 1 Derby rd Croy
9 P 7 Derby rd Enf
58 K 2 Derby rd Grnfd
82 K 10 Derby rd Hounsl
117 O 18 Derby rd Surb
153 W 14 Derby rd Sutton

139 V 14 Derby st W1
135 U 14 Derbyshire st E2
135 K 15 Dereham pl EC2
54 L 16 Dereham rd Bark
155 S 7 Derek av Wallgtn
43 S 20 Derek av Wemb
135 V 4 Dericote st E8
156 L 9 Dering pl Croy
156 M 9 Dering rd Croy
139 X 6 Dering st W1
106 M 8 Derinton rd SW17
107 N 10 Derinton rd SW17
93 W 12 Dermody gdns SE13
93 W 12 Dermody rd SE13
108 H 1 Deronda rd SE24
124 L 8 Derrick gdns SE7
155 Z 4 Derry rd Wallgtn
137 X 19 Derry st W8
53 V 14 Dersingham av E12
53 V 12 Dersingham av E12
53 V 16 Dersingham av E12
45 T 9 Dersingham rd NW2
12 L 18 Derwent av NW7
26 A 16 Derwent av NW9
18 A 17 Derwent av N18
103 Z 9 Derwent av SW15
104 A 10 Derwent av SW15
15 Y 5 Derwent av Barnt
15 S 11 Derwent cres N20
98 D 5 Derwent av Bxly Hth
24 E 7 Derwent cres Stanm
35 R 13 Derwent gdns Ilf
42 E 2 Derwent gdns Wemb
91 T 10 Derwent gro SE20
17 P 11 Derwent rd N13
123 Y 3 Derwent rd SE20
72 C 8 Derwent rd W5
58 F 16 Derwent rd S'hall
82 L 16 Derwent rd Twick
26 A 17 Derwent rise NW9
76 M 12 Derwent st SE10
57 Y 15 Derwent way Hornch
73 V 2 Derwentwater rd W3
91 S 16 Desenfans rd SE21
65 N 12 Desford rd E16
47 U 4 Despard rd N19
112 E 12 Detling rd Brom
50 B 7 Detmold rd E5
155 N 5 Devana end Carsh
104 M 20 Devas rd SW20
15 N 20 Devas rd SW20
77 N 1 Devas st E3
86 B 6 Devenish rd SE2
91 S 12 Deventer cres SE22
150 E 3 Deverell st SE1
141 R 7 Devereux ct WC2
88 M 16 Devereux rd SW11
39 P 4 Deveron way Rom
101 O 1 Devon av Twick
31 W 9 Devon clo N17
21 V 7 Devon clo Buck Hl
60 E 3 Devon clo Grnfd
60 E 3 Devon cres Grnfd
30 K 18 Devon gdns N4
67 U 3 Devon rd Bark
153 S 19 Devon rd Sutton
28 G 14 Devon ri N2
151 X 15 Devon st SE15
75 N 17 Devon st SE15
38 J 8 Devon way Rom
70 E 19 Devon way Hounsl
83 Z 19 Devoncroft gdns Twick
17 Y 19 Devonia gdns N18
133 X 7 Devonia rd N1
35 T 19 Devonport gdns Ilf
74 K 4 Devonport rd W12
63 R 18 Devonport st E1
154 C 17 Devons rd E3
154 C 17 Devonshire av Sutton
52 A 13 Devonshire clo E15
17 S 12 Devonshire clo N13
131 X 20 Devonshire clo W1
27 P 1 Devonshire cres NW7
17 Y 19 Devonshire ct N18
76 D 20 Devonshire dri SE10
93 S 1 Devonshire dri SE10
17 Z 20 Devonshire gdns N18
17 Z 2 Devonshire gdns N21
73 U 20 Devonshire gdns W4
75 N 17 Devonshire gro SE15
151 Y 16 Devonshire gro SE15
31 O 1 Devonshire Hill la N17
18 A 20 Devonshire Hill la N17

45 X 9 Devonshire ms NW
74 A 13 Devonshire ms W4
131 X 20 Devonshire Ms nor W1
131 W 20 Devonshire Ms sou W1
131 V 19 Devonshire Ms we W1
131 V 19 Devonshire pl W1
131 V 19 Devonshire Pl ms W1
52 A 13 Devonshire rd E15
65 W 17 Devonshire rd E16
33 O 18 Devonshire rd E17
21 N 1 Devonshire rd NW
17 Z 20 Devonshire rd N13
19 P 6 Devonshire rd N9
92 E 19 Devonshire rd SE2
110 D 2 Devonshire rd SE2
113 P 4 Devonshire rd SW
106 L 16 Devonshire rd SW
74 A 13 Devonshire rd W4
72 D 8 Devonshire rd W5
97 Z 10 Devonshire rd Bxly Hth
123 N 16 Devonshire rd Cro
100 B 8 Devonshire rd Felt
23 O 18 Devonshire rd Harrow
36 G 20 Devonshire rd Ilf
22 D 3 Devonshire rd Pinn
58 G 13 Devonshire rd S'hal
154 D 16 Devonshire rd Sutt
155 O 7 Devonshire rd Wallgtn
142 K 3 Devonshire row E1
131 Y 19 Devonshire Row m W1
142 L 3 Devonshire sq E1
126 J 8 Devonshire sq Bro
151 X 15 Devonshire st SE1
74 A 15 Devonshire st W1
138 C 7 Devonshire st W4
158 K 2 Devonshire way C
159 N 1 Devonshire way Cr
91 X 8 Dewar st E14
64 F 15 Dewberry st E14
22 C 19 Dewsbury clo Pin
133 S 7 Dewey rd N1
56 J 18 Dewey rd Dgnhm
106 M 12 Dewey st SW17
144 F 2 Dewhurst rd W14
152 F 4 Dewsbury gdns Worc Pk

44 G 15 Dexter rd NW1
90 G 12 Dexter rd SE24
4 B 19 Dexter rd Barnt
31 N 4 Deyncourt rd N17
34 L 14 Deynecourt gdns E11
91 O 1 Deynsford rd SE5
140 E 5 Diadem ct W1
40 A 13 Diamond st Pinn
150 L 19 Diamond st SE15
93 V 1 Diamond ter SE10
32 M 9 Diana rd E17
80 C 13 Dianthus clo SE2
57 Y 12 Diban av Hornch
153 Y 4 Dibdin clo Sutton
153 Y 4 Dibdin rd Sutton
44 L 13 Dicey av NW2
28 D 5 Dickens av N3
102 J 3 Dickens clo Rich
66 B 6 Dickens rd E6
150 C 1 Dickens sq SE1
89 T 4 Dickens st SW8
30 B 20 Dickenson rd N8
47 R 18 Dickenson st NW5
123 X 14 Dickensons la SE2
123 X 15 Dickensons pl SE2
117 V 4 Dickerage la New Mald
117 V 2 Dickerage rd King
95 R 8 Dickson rd SE9
88 E 11 Dickson st SW11
48 K 7 Digby cres N4
82 D 2 Digby gdns Dgnhm
50 F 16 Digby rd E9
67 W 1 Digby rd Bark
63 R 9 Digby st E2
63 S 15 Diggon st E1
88 C 12 Dighton rd SW18
133 S 6 Dignum st N1
48 G 18 Digswell st N7
112 H 6 Dilhorne clo SE12
147 P 13 Dilke st SW3
110 J 8 Dillwyn rd SE26
75 P 11 Dilston gro SE16
151 Z 4 Dilston gro SE16
104 H 1 Dilton gdns SW15
74 K 11 Dimes pl W6
43 W 4 Dimsdale dri NW9

18 J 1 Dimsdale dri Enf
64 B 20 Dingle gdns E14
134 B 13 Dingley pl EC1
134 B 13 Dingley rd EC1
5 N 3 Dingwall av Croy
157 N 3 Dingwall av Croy
27 X 19 Dingwall gdns NW11
28 C 19 Dingwall rd SW18
154 M 19 Dingwall rd Carsh
157 O 2 Dingwall rd Croy
35 V 9 Dinmont st E2
5 O 18 Dinsdale gdns Barnt
77 O 15 Dinsdale rd SE3
89 S 18 Dinsmore rd SW12
106 G 14 Dinton rd SW19
103 N 17 Dinton rd Kingst
63 E 15 Dirleton rd E15
144 L 15 Disbrowe rd W6
142 C 17 Disney pl SE1
142 C 17 Disney st SE1
9 S 6 Dison clo Enf
52 F 17 Disraeli rd E7
61 X 6 Disraeli rd NW10
87 R 11 Disraeli rd SW15
72 F 3 Disraeli rd W5
135 O 11 Diss st E2
142 A 7 Distaff la EC4
144 E 11 Distillery la W6
82 B 16 District rd Wemb
93 R 2 Ditch all SE10
64 G 20 Ditchborn st E14
113 N 10 Dittisham rd SE9
116 F 20 Ditton Grange dri Surb
116 F 20 Ditton Grange dri Surb
116 C 20 Ditton Hill rd Surb
110 A 20 Ditton pl SE20
97 Y 13 Ditton rd Bxly Hth
70 T 13 Ditton rd S'hall
116 K 20 Ditton rd Surb
159 R 1 Dixon pl W Wkhm
92 K 1 Dixon rd SE14
123 T 6 Dixon rd SE25
95 U 13 Dobell rd SE9
62 A 1 Dobree av NW10
128 A 1 Dobree av NW10
46 F 20 Dobson clo NW6
142 C 9 Doby ct EC4
65 P 20 Dock rd E16
77 P 1 Dock rd E16
72 H 18 Dock rd Brentf
143 P 18 Dockhead SE1
33 J 3 Dockland st E16
151 S 2 Dockley rd SE16
49 R 17 Docwras bldgs N1
63 Z 17 Dod st E14
64 A 17 Dod st E14
108 H 8 Dodbrooke rd SE27
149 X 12 Doddington gro SE17
149 W 13 Doddington pl SE17
141 V 20 Dodson st SE1
141 O 1 Dog And Duck yd WC1
91 S 8 Dog Kennel hill SE5
62 A 1 Dog la NW10
93 O 19 Doggett rd SE6
5 W 18 Doggetts ct Barnt
65 T 11 Doherty rd E13
141 X 14 Dolben st SE1
87 V 6 Dolby rd SW6
149 P 11 Dolland st SE11
27 V 4 Dollis av N3
4 D 20 Dollis Brook wlk Barnt
44 L 8 Dollis Hill av NW2
14 H 10 Dollis Hill la NW2
27 V 3 Dollis pk N3
27 T 3 Dollis rd NW7
4 H 18 Dollis Valley way Barnt
90 B 9 Dolman st SW4
16 G 13 Dolphin clo Surb
64 C 20 Dolphin la E14
148 D 12 Dolphin sq SW1
133 N 20 Dolphin sq WC1
109 V 9 Dome Hill pk SE26
91 P 9 Domett clo SE5
134 A 17 Domingo st EC1
123 U 16 Dominion rd Croy
142 G 1 Dominion st EC2
138 A 7 Domonic dri SE9
114 A 7 Domonic dri SE9
150 M 11 Domville gro SE5
39 P 3 Don way Rom
37 T 16 Donald dri Rom
65 V 4 Donald rd E13
62 E 16 Donald rd E13
129 P 6 Donaldson rd NW6
78 L 20 Donaldson rd SE18

95 X 2 Donaldson rd SE18
40 E 17 Doncaster dri Grnfd
30 L 19 Doncaster gdns N4
40 D 15 Doncaster gdns Grnfd
18 M 3 Donegal row N1
133 R 9 Donegal row N1
133 R 9 Donegal st N1
87 P 3 Doneraile st SW6
65 V 9 Dongola rd E13
65 U 9 Dongola rd E13
31 R 11 Dongola rd N17
8 K 8 Donkey la Enf
51 X 13 Donmow rd E15
90 M 16 Donne clo SE24
146 L 5 Donne pl SW3
121 T 8 Donne pl Mitch
55 T 6 Donne rd Dgnhm
24 K 1 Donnefield av Edg
36 C 15 Donnington av Ilf
62 K 2 Donnington rd NW10
128 A 3 Donnington rd NW10
24 G 18 Donnington rd Harrow
152 H 3 Donnington rd Worc Pk
107 W 18 Donnybrook rd SW16
29 T 8 Donovan av N10
101 X 14 Doone clo Tedd
105 X 10 Dora st E14
63 Y 16 Dora st E14
154 M 11 Doral way Carsh
79 U 19 Doran grn SE18
17 Y 13 Dorchester av Bxly
97 X 19 Dorchester av Bxly
22 L 20 Dorchester av Harrow
40 L 14 Dorchester clo Grnfd
16 F 2 Dorchester ct N14
20 B 14 Dorchester gdns E4
27 Y 12 Dorchester gdns NW11
74 B 15 Dorchester gro W4
90 L 12 Dorchester rd SE24
40 L 14 Dorchester rd Grnfd
120 B 17 Dorchester rd Mrdn
152 L 1 Dorchester rd Worc Pk
153 N 1 Dorchester rd Worc Pk
24 M 18 Dorchester way Harrow
25 N 17 Dorchester way Harrow
97 Y 4 Dorcis av Bxly Hth
74 B 4 Dordrecht rd W3
53 W 15 Dore av E12
120 B 16 Dore gdns Mrdn
43 Y 3 Doreen av NW9
58 F 15 Dorell clo S'hall
87 W 4 Dorest rd SW6
57 X 5 Doria rd Hornch
125 S 1 Doric ct Becknhm
132 E 13 Doric way NW1
132 F 13 Doric way NW1
119 P 3 Dorien rd SW20
98 J 2 Doris av Erith
52 F 20 Doris rd E7
75 X 16 Dorking rd SE8
88 H 17 Dorlcote rd SW18
87 Z 12 Dormay st SW18
4 B 18 Dormer clo Barnt
58 G 17 Dormers av S'hall
58 L 18 Dormers ri S'hall
58 J 19 Dormers Wells la S'hall
70 K 1 Dormers Wells la S'hall
77 U 19 Dornberg rd SE3
87 T 4 Dorncliffe rd SW6
45 W 16 Dornfell st NW6
107 T 4 Dornton rd SW12
157 P 12 Dornton rd S Croy
60 L 1 Dorothy av Wemb
98 G 10 Dorothy Evans clo Bxly Hth
55 S 13 Dorothy gdns Dgnhm
88 L 8 Dorothy rd SW11
141 T 1 Dorrington st EC1
43 Y 3 Dors clo NW9
39 O 10 Dorset av Rom
70 G 10 Dorset av S'hall
96 K 10 Dorset av Welling
141 V 7 Dorset bldgs EC4
131 O 19 Dorset clo NW1
11 Z 20 Dorset dri Edg
122 B 8 Dorset gdns Mitch
147 W 1 Dorset ms SW1
51 W 17 Dorset pl E15

65 Z 1 Dorset rd E7
31 P 13 Dorset rd N15
30 A 6 Dorset rd N22
113 P 4 Dorset rd SE9
119 Z 2 Dorset rd SW19
120 A 3 Dorset rd SW19
105 X 20 Dorset rd SW19
148 M 18 Dorset rd SW8
149 P 19 Dorset rd SW8
72 F 7 Dorset rd W5
124 E 6 Dorset rd Becknhm
23 O 18 Dorset rd Harrow
120 K 3 Dorset rd Mitch
141 V 7 Dorset ri EC4
131 O 18 Dorset sq NW1
139 S 1 Dorset st W1
101 O 7 Dorset way Twick
70 E 20 Dorset waye Hounsl
74 H 9 Dorville cres W6
94 D 14 Dorville rd SE12
79 P 19 Dothill rd SE18
133 N 17 Doughty ms WC1
133 O 17 Doughty st WC1
33 N 4 Douglas av E17
32 M 5 Douglas av E17
118 K 9 Douglas av New Mald
42 K 19 Douglas av Wemb
10 M 17 Douglas clo Stanm
159 N 5 Douglas dri Croy
76 G 12 Douglas gro E14
102 G 1 Douglas house Rich
65 T 14 Douglas rd E16
20 M 4 Douglas rd E4
21 N 4 Douglas rd E4
129 P 3 Douglas rd NW6
48 L 19 Douglas rd N1
30 G 4 Douglas rd N22
39 U 19 Douglas rd Hornch
57 U 1 Douglas rd Hornch
82 L 8 Douglas rd Hounsl
37 N 19 Douglas rd Ilf
117 T 5 Douglas rd Kingst
117 N 19 Douglas rd Surb
97 R 2 Douglas rd Welling
119 Y 14 Douglas sq Mrdn
148 F 7 Douglas st SW1
52 Z 19 Douglas way SE8
105 Z 2 Dounceforth gdns SW18
106 A 2 Dounesforth gdns SW18
137 Z 20 Douro pl W8
64 A 5 Douro st E3
20 A 8 Dove House gdns E4
146 B 8 Dove ms SW5
22 F 2 Dove pk Pinn
49 O 18 Dove rd N1
135 T 7 Dove row E2
30 G 10 Dovecote av N22
24 E 18 Dovedale av Harrow
35 X 6 Dovedale av Ilf
97 N 3 Dovedale clo Welling
92 A 15 Dovedale rd SE22
106 M 19 Dovedale ri Mitch
146 J 11 Dovehouse st SW3
154 B 6 Dover Ct la Sutton
86 K 16 Dover Pk dri SW15
52 K 6 Dover rd E12
19 P 9 Dover rd N9
109 O 15 Dover rd SE19
37 Z 19 Dover rd Rom
139 Z 11 Dover st W1
122 G 10 Dovercourt av Thntn Hth
11 W 16 Dovercourt gdns Stanm
91 T 15 Dovercourt rd SE22
90 B 18 Doverfield rd SW2
86 H 10 Doverhouse rd SW15
17 W 14 Doveridge gdns N13
63 P 12 Doveton st E1
111 X 2 Dowanhill rd SE6
14 A 2 Dowanhill rd SE6
10 L 18 Dowding pl Stanm
155 T 19 Dower av Wallgtn
142 D 9 Dowgate hill EC4
150 J 18 Dowlas st SE5
116 G 1 Down Hall la Kingst
74 K 12 Down pl W6
144 A 8 Down rd W6
102 B 16 Down rd Tedd
139 W 15 Down st W1
26 M 8 Downage NW4
99 O 4 Downbank av Bxly Hth
111 Y 8 Downderry rd Brom
80 F 18 Downe clo Welling
89 U 9 Downers cotts SW4
17 T 5 Downes ct N21

118 E 20 Downfield Worc Pk
134 E 2 Downham rd N1
111 Y 11 Downham way Brom
112 A 11 Downham way Brom
31 O 10 Downhills av N17
31 O 11 Downhills av N17
30 L 11 Downhills Pk rd N17
30 M 9 Downhills way N17
12 L 17 Downhurst av NW7
59 S 4 Downing dri Grnfd
56 C 20 Downing rd Dgnhm
69 O 1 Downing rd Dgnhm
140 J 16 Downing st SW1
113 T 3 Downleys SE9
95 S 8 Downman rd SE9
113 T 13 Downs av Chisl
22 D 20 Downs av Pinn
125 W 1 Downs Br rd Becknhm
125 X 1 Downs hill Becknhm
111 W 20 Downs hill Becknhm
50 A 13 Downs Pk rd E8
49 X 14 Downs Pk rd E8
49 Y 12 Downs rd E5
125 R 2 Downs rd Becknhm
9 N 2 Downs rd Enf
108 L 20 Downs the Thntn Hth
105 O 18 Downs the SW20
83 X 1 Downs view Islwth
51 V 12 Downsell rd E15
32 J 19 Downsfield rd E17
36 J 19 Downshall av Ilf
46 G 13 Downshire hill NW3
101 V 6 Downside Twick
46 K 16 Downside cres NW3
59 Y 12 Downside cres W13
154 H 14 Downside rd Sutton
108 K 19 Downsview gdns SE19
108 L 17 Downsview rd SE19
154 C 18 Downsway the Sutton
108 B 3 Downton av SW2
28 H 1 Downway N12
133 T 4 Dowrey st N1
31 V 8 Dowsett rd N17
91 P 10 Dowson clo SE5
142 B 16 Doyce st SE1
62 H 3 Doyle gdns NW10
128 A 8 Doyle gdns NW10
123 X 9 Doyle rd SE25
147 S 5 Doyley st SW1
47 T 7 Doynton st N19
107 S 7 Dr Johnson av SW17
150 A 13 Draco st SE17
120 G 7 Dragonia la Mitch
75 X 14 Dragoon rd SE8
61 X 11 Dragor rd NW10
93 O 8 Drake st SE4
121 N 13 Drake rd Croy
122 D 17 Drake rd Croy
40 F 6 Drake rd Harrow
8 B 6 Drake st Enf
92 F 6 Drakefell rd SE14
107 O 6 Drakefield rd SW17
48 H 12 Drakeley ct N5
107 X 18 Drakewood rd SW16
51 V 13 Drapers rd E15
7 V 8 Drapers rd Enf
151 T 4 Drapers rd SE16
76 K 4 Drawdock rd SE10
104 F 18 Drax av SW20
105 T 14 Draxmont appr SW19
90 D 13 Dray gdns SW2
34 G 19 Draycot rd E11
146 K 6 Draycott av SW3
147 N 7 Draycott av SW3
224 B 18 Draycott av Harrow
42 D 1 Draycott av Harrow
24 C 18 Draycott clo Harrow
147 N 7 Draycott pl SW3
147 O 6 Draycott ter SW3
137 V 18 Drayson ms W8
59 Z 20 Drayton av W13
59 Y 19 Drayton Br rd W7
17 W 2 Drayton gdns N21
146 B 9 Drayton gdns SW10
59 Z 19 Drayton gdns W13
72 B 1 Drayton Gr rd W13
72 B 1 Drayton Green rd W13
59 Z 19 Drayton grn W13
59 Z 19 Drayton grn W13
48 G 15 Drayton pk N5
51 X 3 Drayton rd E11
62 E 3 Drayton rd NW10
31 S 8 Drayton rd N17
60 A 19 Drayton rd W13
166 K 2 Drayton rd Croy
24 C 17 Drayton wlk Harrow
47 X 2 Dresden rd N19

41 W 17 Drew gdns Grnfd
78 D 3 Drew rd E16
107 X 4 Drewstead rd SW16
108 A 5 Drewstead rd SW16
63 R 18 Drewton st E1
63 W 5 Driffield rd E3
107 P 20 Driftway the Mitch
40 K 6 Drinkwater rd Harrow
33 S 11 Drive the E17
34 E 9 Drive the E18
20 K 3 Drive the E4
27 S 20 Drive the NW11
45 T 1 Drive the NW11
16 H 20 Drive the N11
28 L 15 Drive the N2
14 L 20 Drive the N3
122 C 6 Drive the SW16
104 M 18 Drive the SW20
61 X 17 Drive the W3
54 L 20 Drive the Bark
5 P 20 Drive the Barnt
4 E 12 Drive the Barnt
125 N 2 Drive the Becknhm
21 Y 3 Drive the Buck Hl
97 W 18 Drive the Bxly
12 E 15 Drive the Edg
8 C 7 Drive the Enf
152 C 14 Drive the Epsom
81 V 18 Drive the Erith
22 H 20 Drive the Harrow
40 H 2 Drive the Harrow
35 R 18 Drive the Ilf
53 T 2 Drive the Ilf
83 P 4 Drive the Islwth
103 V 19 Drive the Kingst
120 E 11 Drive the Mrdn
38 L 3 Drive the Rom
39 N 2 Drive the Rom
115 R 9 Drive the Sidcp
18 J 18 Drive the Surb
123 N 8 Drive the Thntn Hth
125 W 18 Drive the W Wckhm
155 X 20 Drive the Wallgtn
43 V 18 Drive the Wemb
109 X 8 Droitwich clo SE26
87 S 16 Dromore rd SW15
55 T 14 Dronfield gdns Dgnhm
128 J 14 Droop st W10
75 N 18 Drovers la SE15
157 N 12 Drovers rd S Croy
91 T 16 Druce rd SE21
142 L 16 Druid st SE1
143 O 19 Druid st SE1
125 Y 8 Druids way Brom
38 M 14 Drummond av Rom
132 E 12 Drummond cres NW1
23 W 2 Drummond dri Stanm
34 K 18 Drummond rd E11
143 W 20 Drummond rd SE16
151 W 1 Drummond rd SE16
156 L 2 Drummond rd Croy
38 L 13 Drummond rd Rom
140 L 5 Drury la WC2
41 N 2 Drury rd Harrow
23 N 20 Drury rd Harrow
87 O 8 Dryad st SW15
25 R 10 Dryburgh gdns NW9
86 M 9 Dryburgh rd SW15
59 V 19 Dryden av W7
149 U 7 Dryden Ct Housing est SE11
141 U 5 Dryden pass EC4
106 C 14 Dryden rd SW19
8 F 19 Dryden rd Enf
23 W 6 Dryden rd Harrow
96 K 1 Dryden rd Welling
140 L 6 Dryden st WC2
43 V 18 Dryfield clo NW10
12 J 19 Dryfield rd Edg
81 O 16 Dryhill rd Blvdr
30 B 18 Drylands rd N8
20 E 1 Drysdale av E4
93 T 3 Drysdale rd SE13
134 L 13 Drysdale st N1
107 O 2 Du Cane ct SW17
62 E 18 Du Cane rd W12
136 A 5 Du Cane rd W12
11 U 18 Du Cros st Stanm
139 X 2 Duchess ms W1
137 T 18 Duchess Of Bedfords wlk W8
139 Y 2 Duchess st W1
5 U 2 Duchy rd Barnt
141 T 12 Duchy st SE1
90 B 10 Duck la SW4
140 D 7 Duck la W1
9 V 15 Duck Lees la Enf
30 H 18 Duckett rd N4
63 U 13 Duckett st E1

99 T 13 Ducketts rd Drtfrd
84 D 13 Ducks wlk Twick
142 E 9 Ducksfoot la EC4
74 A 4 Ducros rd W3
44 E 14 Dudden Hill la NW10
24 D 10 Dudley av Harrow
119 S 18 Dudley dri Mrdn
72 C 5 Dudley gdns W13
41 O 5 Dudley gdns Harrow
33 O 9 Dudley rd E17
129 N 8 Dudley rd NW6
28 A 8 Dudley rd N3
105 Y 15 Dudley rd SW19
40 N 6 Dudley rd Harrow
41 N 5 Dudley rd Harrow
53 Z 11 Dudley rd Ilf
54 A 11 Dudley rd Ilf
116 L 5 Dudley rd Kingst
85 O 6 Dudley rd Rich
70 A 7 Dudley rd S'hall
138 E 2 Dudley st W2
50 C 6 Dudlington rd E5
146 H 9 Dudmason ms SW3
99 X 14 Dudsbury rd Drtfrd
115 S 14 Dudsbury rd Sidcp
64 C 18 Duff st E14
134 D 18 Dufferin st EC1
23 W 16 Duffield clo Harrow
88 K 7 Duffield st SW11
140 C 7 Dufours pl W1
93 Z 2 Duke Humphrey rd SE3
94 A 2 Duke Humphrey rd SE3
83 R 16 Duke Of Cambridge clo Twick
154 F 4 Duke Of Edinburgh rd Sutton
140 D 12 Duke Of York st SW1
73 Z 13 Duke rd W4
36 E 13 Duke rd Ilf
140 C 12 Duke st SW1
139 U 7 Duke st W1
84 H 12 Duke st Rich
154 E 8 Duke st Sutton
142 G 13 Duke St hill SE1
102 F 11 Duke's av Kingst
29 U 9 Dukes av N10
27 Z 4 Dukes av N3
28 A 4 Dukes av N3
73 Z 15 Dukes av W4
11 Z 18 Dukes av Edg
40 D 20 Dukes av Grnfd
58 C 1 Dukes av Grnfd
22 F 20 Dukes av Harrow
23 T 12 Dukes av Harrow
82 A 10 Dukes av Hounsl
102 G 11 Dukes av Kingst
118 C 7 Dukes av New Mald
100 D 11 Dukes clo Hampt
137 V 17 Dukes la W8
29 T 10 Dukes ms N10
139 U 4 Dukes ms W1
142 M 6 Dukes pl EC3
66 J 3 Dukes rd E6
132 G 14 Dukes rd WC1
61 P 12 Dukes rd W3
110 F 10 Dukesthorpe rd SE26
48 E 5 Dulas st N4
136 J 8 Dulford st W11
88 M 14 Dulka rd SW11
114 D 4 Dulverton rd SE9
109 T 1 Dulwich comm SE21
91 U 19 Dulwich park SE21
91 P 15 Dulwich village SE21
109 S 11 Dulwich Wood av SE19
111 T 1 Dulwich Wood pk SE19
90 B 17 Dumbarton rd SW2
95 V 9 Dumbreck rd SE9
49 T 9 Dumont rd N16
131 T 1 Dumpton pl NW1
122 F 5 Dunbar av SW16
124 J 8 Dunbar av Becknhm
56 E 10 Dunbar av Dgnhm
56 F 15 Dunbar gdns Dgnhm
52 G 18 Dunbar rd E7
30 H 5 Dunbar rd N22
108 L 7 Dunbar rd SE27
117 W 8 Dunbar rd New Mald
108 K 7 Dunbar rd SE27
95 S 6 Dunblane rd SE9
46 M 14 Dunboyne st NW5
135 V 16 Dunbridge st E2
62 A 17 Duncan gro W3
135 V 4 Duncan rd E8
84 L 10 Duncan rd Rich
133 V 8 Duncan st N1

133 W 9 Duncan ter N1
140 J 11 Duncannon st WC2
92 J 18 Duncombe hill SE23
47 X 4 Duncombe rd N19
93 Y 16 Duncrievie rd SE13
79 U 20 Duncroft SE18
92 G 8 Dundalk rd SE4
92 C 4 Dundas rd SE15
65 V 7 Dundee rd E13
124 A 12 Dundee rd SE25
143 X 15 Dundee st E1
152 K 9 Dundela gdns Worc Pk
128 F 6 Dundonald rd NW10
105 U 19 Dundonald rd SW19
51 S 9 Dunedin rd E10
54 C 3 Dunedin rd Ilf
63 S 17 Dunelm st E1
111 S 11 Dunfield gdns SE6
111 S 11 Dunfield rd SE6
48 D 13 Dunford rd N7
86 F 9 Dungarvan av SW15
122 F 13 Dunheved clo Thntn Hth
122 G 14 Dunheved Rd south Thntn Hth
122 F 14 Dunheved Rd west Thntn Hth
18 G 10 Dunholme grn N9
18 G 12 Dunholme la N9
18 G 12 Dunholme rd N9
143 S 1 Dunk st E1
123 O 8 Dunkeld rd SE25
55 S 6 Dunkeld rd Dgnhm
113 O 8 Dunkery rd SE9
108 L 9 Dunkirk st SE27
50 D 13 Dunlace rd E5
82 F 19 Dunleary clo Hounsl
159 N 14 Dunley dri Croy
31 O 10 Dunlop av N17
135 P 9 Dunloe st E2
151 P 3 Dunloe st E2
135 N 8 Dunlop pl SE16
128 K 5 Dunmore rd NW6
105 O 20 Dunmore rd SW20
119 N 1 Dunmore rd SE15
37 S 15 Dunmow clo Rom
49 U 14 Dunn st E8
57 U 14 Dunningford clo Hornch
47 V 14 Dunollie rd NW5
92 D 18 Dunoon rd SE23
7 U 8 Dunraven dri Enf
74 H 2 Dunraven rd W12
139 S 8 Dunraven st W1
144 E 3 Dunsany rd W14
123 T 10 Dunsdale rd SE25
159 T 11 Dunsfold way Croy
49 T 3 Dunsmure rd N16
35 Y 8 Dunspring la Ilf
131 V 20 Dunstable ms W1
84 K 11 Dunstable rd Rich
104 L 16 Dunstall rd SW20
45 X 5 Dunstall rd NW11
91 Z 15 Dunstans gro SE22
91 Y 17 Dunstans rd SE22
119 P 19 Dunster av Mrdn
38 J 8 Dunster clo Rom
43 V 4 Dunster dri NW9
45 V 20 Dunster gdns NW6
129 P 1 Dunster gdns NW6
40 B 9 Dunster way Harrow
135 N 5 Dunston rd E8
150 M 8 Dunston rd SE1
134 M 4 Dunston st E8
33 R 20 Dunton rd E10
151 O 5 Dunton rd SE1
39 O 13 Dunton rd Rom
106 A 1 Duntshill rd SW18
95 V 11 Dunvegan rd SE9
98 B 2 Dunwich rd Bxly Hth
139 R 18 Duplex ride SW1
119 P 3 Dupont rd SW20
63 X 16 Dupont st E14
156 K 7 Duppas Hill la Croy
156 G 7 Duppas Hill rd Croy
156 J 7 Duppas Hill ter Croy
156 J 7 Duppas rd Croy
77 U 13 Dupree rd SE7
120 L 20 Durand clo Carsh
154 M 1 Durand clo Carsh
90 D 2 Durand gdns SW9
61 U 1 Durand way NW10
135 T 10 Durant st E2
9 R 11 Durants park Enf
9 U 15 Durants pk av Enf
9 S 13 Durants Pk av Enf
9 R 14 Durants rd Enf
69 Y 1 Durban gdns Dgnhm
69 Y 2 Durban gdns Dgnhm
64 M 8 Durban rd E15
32 K 4 Durban rd E17
18 F 20 Durban rd N17

108 M 9 Durban rd SE27
109 N 9 Durban rd SE27
124 L 4 Durban rd Becknhm
54 G 3 Durban rd Ilf
58 F 17 Durdans rd S'hall
55 W 14 Durell gdns Dgnhm
55 V 14 Durell rd Dgnhm
104 H 1 Durford cres SW15
126 C 9 Durham av Brom
70 F 15 Durham av Hounsl
50 D 17 Durham gro E9
140 L 11 Durham Ho st WC2
147 O 11 Durham pl SW3
53 N 13 Durham rd E12
65 O 12 Durham rd E16
31 R 11 Durham rd N7
28 L 11 Durham rd N2
48 D 7 Durham rd N7
18 J 8 Durham rd N9
104 K 20 Durham rd SW20
118 L 2 Durham rd SW20
72 G 9 Durham rd W5
126 C 6 Durham rd Brom
56 J 15 Durham rd Dgnhm
22 L 16 Durham rd Harrow
115 P 12 Durham rd Sidcp
79 R 14 Durham ri SE18
63 U 15 Durham row E1
149 O 12 Durham st SE11
137 W 4 Durham ter W2
72 E 18 Durham wharf Bren
122 F 13 Dunheved Rd north Thntn Hth
22 B 19 Durley av Pinn
49 R 1 Durley rd N16
49 X 7 Durlston rd E5
102 J 15 Durlston rd Kingst
31 T 17 Durnford st N15
109 P 13 Durning rd SE19
105 Y 4 Durnsford av SW19
29 Y 1 Durnsford rd N11
87 U 3 Durrell rd SW6
104 M 19 Durrington av SW20
104 M 20 Durrington pk SW20
50 G 13 Durrington rd E5
94 K 4 Dursley clo SE3
95 N 2 Dursley gdns SE3
94 K 4 Dursley rd SE3
95 N 2 Dursley rd SE3
135 W 20 Durward st E1
143 V 1 Durward st E1
139 R 1 Durweston ms W1
139 P 1 Durweston st W1
4 H 7 Dury rd Barnt
87 Y 14 Dutch yd SW18
76 H 1 Duthie st E14
93 U 1 Dutton st SE10
57 Z 19 Duxford clo Hornch
141 T 3 Dyers bldgs EC1
51 Y 5 Dyers Hall rd E11
86 K 9 Dyers la SW15
39 X 3 Dyers way Rom
126 B 5 Dykes way Brom
81 S 8 Dylan rd Blvdr
91 P 10 Dylways SE5
35 W 9 Dymchurch clo Ilf
88 A 7 Dymock st SW6
39 T 20 Dymoke rd Hornch
145 V 20 Dyne rd NW6
129 N 1 Dyne rd NW6
112 L 8 Dyneley rd SE12
49 S 10 Dynevor rd N16
84 K 13 Dynevor rd Rich
45 Y 20 Dynham rd NW6
140 H 3 Dyott st WC1
102 E 11 Dysart av Kingst
134 H 19 Dysart st EC2
34 A 19 Dyson rd E11
52 C 18 Dyson rd E15
19 N 17 Dysons rd N18

E

30 M 20 Eade rd N4
31 O 20 Eade rd N4
48 L 1 Eade rd N4
9 R 15 Eagle clo Enf
133 W 20 Eagle ct EC1
109 O 16 Eagle hill SE19
34 E 14 Eagle la E11
140 D 11 Eagle pl SW1
140 M 2 Eagle pl WC1
42 H 20 Eagle st Wemb
141 O 2 Eagle st WC1
34 H 2 Eagle ter Wdfd Grn
134 D 7 Eagle Wharf rd N1
95 Z 3 Eaglesfield rd SE18
96 A 1 Eaglesfield rd SE18
78 M 20 Eaglesfield rd SE18
63 P 12 Eaglet pl E1

64 C 9 Eagling rd E3
94 M 11 Ealdham sq SE9
72 G 2 Ealing grn W5
72 D 11 Ealing Pk gdns W5
72 J 16 Ealing rd Brentf
58 G 7 Ealing rd Grnfd
42 J 17 Ealing rd Wemb
60 J 6 Ealing rd Wemb
60 L 18 Ealing village W5
130 L 9 Eamont st NW8
99 T 10 Eardemont clo Drtfrd
145 U 11 Eardley cres SW5
107 X 17 Eardley rd SW16
81 S 13 Eardley st Blvdr
151 N 9 Earl cotts SE1
151 N 9 Earl rd SE1
85 W 9 Earl rd SW14
79 S 12 Earl rd E18
134 H 20 Earl st EC2
87 N 9 Earldom rd SW15
F 16 Earlham gro E7
30 D 3 Earlham av N22
140 J 6 Earlham st WC2
23 T 12 Earls cres Harrow
145 T 10 Earls Ct Exhibition building SW5
145 X 7 Earls Ct gdns SW5
145 T 2 Earls Ct rd W8
145 W 10 Earls Ct sq SW5
145 R 3 Earls ter W8
145 T 3 Earls wlk W8
106 C 1 Earlsfield rd SW18
88 D 19 Earlsfield rd SW18
95 V 10 Earlshall rd SE9
40 F 13 Earlsmead Harrow
128 A 11 Earlsmead rd NW10
62 L 8 Earlsmead rd NW10
31 U 15 Earlsmead rd N15
110 E 11 Earlsthorpe rd SE26
133 W 13 Earlstoke st EC1
63 N 3 Earlston gro E9
122 G 12 Earlswood av Thntn Hth
35 W 12 Earlswood gdns Ilf
77 N 14 Earlswood st SE10
131 X 3 Early ms NW1
73 T 17 Earnest gdns W4
140 H 4 Earnshaw st WC2
145 N 6 Earsby st W14
144 M 5 Earsby st W14
120 A 15 Easby cres Mrdn
55 S 16 Easebourne rd Dgnhm
57 X 15 Easedale dri Hornch
139 V 4 Easleys ms W1
63 S 17 East Abour st E1
62 B 20 East Acton la W3
73 Z 3 East Acton la W3
53 R 20 East av E12
33 R 14 East av E17
58 D 20 East av S'hall
156 C 11 East av Wallgtn
5 V 18 East Barnet rd Barnt
73 Y 2 East Churchfield rd W3
61 O 12 East clo W5
6 C 14 East clo Barnt
59 O 6 East clo Grnfd
16 A 12 East cres N11
8 G 17 East cres Enf
42 E 8 East ct Wemb
154 K 19 East drive Carsh
91 R 14 East Dulwich gro SE22
91 V 10 East Dulwich rd SE22
28 C 10 East End rd N2
27 Y 8 East End rd N3
22 C 9 East End way Pinn
76 E 9 East Ferry rd E14
106 J 15 East gdns SW17
65 Y 14 East Ham And Barking By pass E16
66 F 13 East Ham And Barking By pass E6
67 S 7 East Ham By pass Bark
66 H 14 East Ham Manor way E6
131 V 5 East Harding st EC4
46 G 10 East Heath rd NW3
43 P 5 East hill Wemb
98 L 1 East holme Erith
64 J 20 East India dock E14
64 K 18 East India Dock rd E14
116 G 5 East la Kingst
42 D 10 East la Wemb
30 J 9 East minster E1
143 X 1 East Mount st E1
37 X 16 East Park clo Rom

141 Z 1 East pas EC1
108 L 9 East pl SE27
141 X 1 East Poultry av EC1
65 R 3 East rd E15
134 F 12 East rd N1
106 E 15 East rd SW19
16 B 4 East rd Barnt
81 O 8 East rd Blvdr
25 U 4 East rd Edgw
9 R 3 East rd Enf
102 K 20 East rd Kingst
37 X 14 East rd Rom
57 N 2 East rd Rom
97 P 4 East rd Welling
98 F 15 East Rochester way Bxly Hth
98 K 18 East Rochester way Bxly Hth
97 T 15 East Rochester way Sidcup
128 L 17 East row W10
85 V 10 East Sheen av SW14
143 R 11 East smithfield E1
142 G 2 East st EC2
67 P 1 East st Bark
67 O 2 East st Bark
72 D 19 East st Brentf
126 F 2 East st Brom
98 E 10 East st Bxly Hth
151 N 17 East Surrey gro SE15
143 P 6 East Tenter st E1
20 G 15 East view E4
4 H 10 East view Barnt
158 J 4 East way Croy
16 B 4 East wlk Barnt
97 Z 20 East woodside Bxly
101 N 13 Eastbank rd Hampt
61 Y 19 Eastbourne av W3
85 V 8 Eastbourne gdns SW14
138 D 5 Eastbourne ms W2
66 K 8 Eastbourne rd E15
31 S 19 Eastbourne rd N15
107 P 16 Eastbourne rd SW17
73 X 16 Eastbourne rd W4
72 F 14 Eastbourne rd Brentf
100 A 3 Eastbourne rd Felt
138 D 5 Eastbourne ter W2
19 O 10 Eastbournia av N9
19 P 3 Eastbrook av N9
56 K 12 Eastbrook av Dgnhm
57 P 8 Eastbrook dri Rom
94 J 1 Eastbrook rd SE3
67 V 3 Eastbury av Bark
8 F 6 Eastbury av Enf
74 B 14 Eastbury gro W4
102 J 19 Eastbury gro Kingst
38 M 18 Eastbury rd Rom
67 X 3 Eastbury sq Bark
140 C 4 Eastcastle st W1
142 H 9 Eastcheap EC3
77 N 15 Eastcombe av SE7
41 Z 16 Eastcote av Grnfd
40 L 8 Eastcote av Harrow
58 G 1 Eastcote la Grnfd
40 E 17 Eastcote la Grnfd
40 E 11 Eastcote la Harrow
41 N 10 Eastcote rd Harrow
22 B 14 Eastcote rd Pinn
96 F 6 Eastcote rd Welling
90 B 5 Eastcote st SW9
152 B 17 Eastcroft rd Epsom
33 X 11 Eastdown pk SE13
34 K 17 Eastern av E11
61 T 12 Eastern av W3
36 F 18 Eastern av Ilf
35 T 18 Eastern av Ilf
40 A 1 Eastern av Pinn
39 V 5 Eastern av Rom
37 T 13 Eastern av Rom
39 S 5 Eastern Av east Rom
38 M 10 Eastern Av west Rom
65 V 6 Eastern rd E13
33 V 15 Eastern rd E17
28 M 12 Eastern rd N22
30 A 4 Eastern rd N22
93 O 11 Eastern rd SE4
39 T 16 Eastern rd Rom
36 B 19 Easternville gdns Ilf
56 D 13 Eastfield gdns Dgnhm
33 O 12 Eastfield rd E17
30 A 11 Eastfield rd N8
61 V 14 Eastfield rd W3
56 C 13 Eastfield rd Dgnhm
9 S 3 Eastfield rd Enf
121 P 3 Eastfields rd Mitch
22 C 10 Eastgate Pinn
28 B 14 Eastholm NW11
90 K 6 Eastlake rd SE5

91 U 17 Eastlands cres SE21
40 K 8 Eastleigh av Harrow
44 B 10 Eastleigh clo NW2
98 L 7 Eastleigh rd Bxly Hth
86 G 19 Eastleigh wlk SW15
58 K 9 Eastmead av Grnfd
108 M 4 Eastmearn rd SE21
109 N 4 Eastmearn rd SE21
78 A 10 Eastmoor pl SE7
78 A 10 Eastmoor st SE7
76 K 15 Eastney st SE10
114 C 2 Eastnore rd SE9
133 S 15 Easton st WC1
126 D 15 Eastry av Brom
81 S 18 Eastry rd Erith
27 U 14 Eastside rd NW11
79 V 19 Eastview av SE18
27 U 17 Eastville av NW11
34 H 15 Eastway E11
51 N 14 Eastway E9
50 L 16 Eastway E9
126 E 17 Eastway Brom
119 H 10 Eastway Mrdn
155 U 9 Eastway Wallgtn
34 G 8 Eastwood clo E18
34 F 6 Eastwood rd E18
29 O 8 Eastwood rd N10
55 N 2 Eastwood rd Ilf
37 N 20 Eastwood rd Ilf
107 U 16 Eastwood st SW16
33 W 16 Eatington rd E10
147 T 6 Eaton clo Stanm
11 P 14 Eaton clo Stanm
103 S 18 Eaton dri Kingst
38 F 3 Eaton dri Rom
147 U 4 Eaton gate SW1
55 Y 20 Eaton gdns Dgnhm
25 R 12 Eaton gro NW9
147 T 2 Eaton la SW1
147 U 3 Eaton Ms north SW1
147 V 4 Eaton Ms south SW1
147 U 5 Eaton Ms west SW1
17 U 9 Eaton Pk rd N21
147 U 2 Eaton pl SW1
26 M 15 Eaton rd NW4
90 H 12 Eaton rd SW9
8 E 13 Eaton rd Enf
83 R 11 Eaton rd Hounsl
115 W 5 Eaton rd Sidcup
154 E 14 Eaton rd Sutton
34 L 14 Eaton ri E11
60 F 17 Eaton ri W5
147 W 2 Eaton row SW1
147 U 3 Eaton sq SW1
147 T 6 Eaton ter SW1
147 S 5 Eaton Ter ms SW1
20 A 8 Eatons mead E4
106 M 4 Eatonville rd SW17
107 N 4 Eatonville rd SW17
107 N 4 Eatonville vlls SW17
152 M 2 Ebbisham rd Worc Pk
94 H 9 Ebdon way SE3
45 X 9 Ebenezer ms NW2
149 V 7 Ebenezer row SE11
134 E 13 Ebenezer st N1
121 U 1 Ebenezer wlk Mitch
88 B 12 Ebner st SW18
134 M 16 Ebor st E2
24 F 19 Ebrington rd Harrow
94 G 9 Ebrun sq SE3
45 R 13 Ebsfleet rd NW2
92 G 19 Ebsworth st SE23
48 B 10 Eburne rd N7
147 W 9 Ebury br SW1
147 W 4 Ebury Br rd SW1
147 W 4 Ebury ms SW1
147 W 4 Ebury Ms east SW1
147 V 7 Ebury sq SW1
147 W 6 Ebury st SW1
88 L 9 Eccles rd SW11
17 S 16 Ecclesbourne clo N13
17 S 16 Ecclesbourne gdns N13
134 B 2 Ecclesbourne rd N1
122 L 11 Ecclesbourne rd Thntn Hth
147 Y 5 Eccleston br SW1
37 O 20 Eccleston clo SE27
55 P 1 Eccleston cres Rom
147 V 2 Eccleston ms SW1
147 W 2 Eccleston pl SW1
71 X 2 Eccleston rd W13
147 Y 6 Eccleston sq SW1
147 Z 7 Eccleston sq SW1
147 Z 7 Eccleston Sq ms SW1
147 X 5 Eccleston st SW1
42 K 15 Eccleston ct Wemb

42 J 15 Ecclestone ms Wemb
43 N 15 Ecclestone pl Wemb
20 D 6 Echo heights E4
135 R 18 Eckersley st E1
75 S 19 Eckington gdns SE14
88 J 10 Eckstein rd SW11
65 U 14 Eclipse rd E13
111 Y 5 Ector rd SE6
129 U 18 Edbrooke rd W9
48 E 5 Eddington st N4
87 W 4 Eddiscombe rd SW6
38 G 19 Eddy clo Rom
92 J 14 Eddystone rd SE4
60 F 4 Eden clo Wemb
33 S 15 Eden gro E17
48 D 15 Eden gro N7
125 T 13 Eden park Becknhm
124 K 8 Eden Pk av Becknhm
125 P 10 Eden Pk av Becknhm
33 S 15 Eden rd E17
108 K 11 Eden rd SE27
124 G 8 Eden rd Becknhm
157 O 8 Eden rd Croy
116 J 9 Eden st Kingst
124 M 12 Eden way Becknhm
125 O 14 Eden way Becknhm
63 T 1 Edenbridge rd E9
18 E 1 Edenbridge rd Enf
107 T 15 Edencourt rd SW16
99 O 4 Edendale rd Bxly Hth
152 E 4 Edenfield gdns Worc Pk
87 U 7 Edenhurst av SW6
74 B 19 Edensor gdns W4
74 A 19 Edensor rd W4
107 P 18 Edenvale rd Mitch
88 C 6 Edenvale st SW6
122 E 5 Ederline av SW16
64 D 9 Edgar rd E3
82 E 18 Edgar rd Hounsl
37 V 20 Edgar rd Rom
157 O 20 Edgar rd S Croy
87 S 2 Edgarley ter SW6
78 M 16 Edge hill SE18
105 O 17 Edge hill SW19
27 X 11 Edge Hill av N3
137 V 14 Edge st W8
114 A 10 Edgbury Chisl
113 Z 10 Edgbury Chisl
114 B 9 Edgbury wlk Chisl
103 X 18 Edgcombe clo Kingst
91 R 5 Edgecombe rd SE5
158 E 18 Edgecombe S Croy
31 R 15 Edgecot gro N15
54 L 20 Edgefield av Bark
56 E 12 Edgehill gdns Dgnhm
60 C 15 Edgehill rd W13
114 B 9 Edgehill rd Chisl
121 R 1 Edgehill rd Mitch
88 A 11 Edgel st SW18
89 X 8 Edgeley la SW4
89 X 8 Edgeley rd SW4
108 J 13 Edgepoint clo SE27
26 C 15 Edgeworth av NW4
26 B 15 Edgeworth clo NW4
26 C 15 Edgeworth cres NW4
95 N 11 Edgeworth rd SE9
94 L 10 Edgeworth rd SE9
5 X 13 Edgeworth rd Barnt
107 W 16 Edgington rd SW16
12 C 20 Edgware High st Edg
44 L 6 Edgware rd NW2
25 W 9 Edgware rd NW9
26 D 18 Edgware rd NW9
130 F 19 Edgware rd W2
138 K 3 Edgware rd W2
139 N 6 Edgware rd W2
12 A 18 Edgware way Edg
12 B 17 Edgware way Edg
11 Y 11 Edgware way Edg
12 C 16 Edgwarebury gdns Edg
11 X 3 Edgwarebury house Borhm Wd
11 Y 3 Edgwarebury la Borhm Wd
12 B 8 Edgwarebury la Edg
12 C 14 Edgwarebury la Edg
12 A 10 Edgwarebury park Edg
65 V 7 Edinburgh rd E13
32 M 16 Edinburgh rd E17
18 L 15 Edinburgh rd N18
71 V 5 Edinburgh rd W7
154 E 4 Edinburgh rd Sutton
80 D 7 Edington st SE2
9 P 10 Edington rd Enf
131 U 2 Edis st NW1

an evening out

at

Dinner

three course

Dancing

to Ian Harper and his music
and the Gentle People

Stage Show

A Jack Fallon production

Map Reference
140 J 12

STRAND CORNER HOUSE
Trafalgar Square W.C.2

Reservations **930 2781**

57 T 4 Edison av Hornch
57 S 4 Edison clo Hornch
56 K 17 Edison dri S'hall
79 X 20 Edison gro SE18
29 Z 19 Edison rd N8
79 Y 20 Edison rd SE18
79 Y 20 Edison rd S18
126 D 3 Edison rd Brom
96 K 2 Edison rd Welling
117 S 16 Edith gdns Surb
146 B 15 Edith gro SW10
51 X 14 Edith rd E15
66 A 1 Edith rd E6
29 Y 2 Edith rd N11
31 Y 12 Edith rd N13
123 P 12 Edith rd SE25
106 B 15 Edith rd SW19
144 J 6 Edith rd W14
145 N 8 Edith rd W14
37 V 20 Edith rd Rom
146 C 17 Edith ter SW10
145 O 8 Edith vlls W14
90 B 7 Edithna st SW9
120 J 5 Edmund rd Mitch
97 O 6 Edmund rd Welling
150 F 18 Edmund st SE5
28 H 14 Edmunds wlk N2
119 O 3 Edna rd SW20
88 J 3 Edna st SW11
75 S 18 Edric rd SE14
12 G 20 Edrick rd Edg
12 G 20 Edrick wlk Edg
157 N 7 Edridge rd Croy
20 C 18 Edward av E4
120 F 11 Edward av Mrdn
18 H 3 Edward clo N9
101 N 13 Edward clo Hampt
5 T 16 Edward gro Barnt
75 Z 17 Edward pl SE8
32 G 16 Edward rd E17
110 F 16 Edward rd SE20
5 T 16 Edward rd Barnt
112 J 17 Edward rd Brom
114 A 13 Edward rd Chisl
123 T 16 Edward rd Croy
101 N 12 Edward rd Hampt
23 N 11 Edward rd Harrow
37 X 18 Edward rd Rom
133 N 6 Edward sq N1
65 S 13 Edward st E8
75 Z 17 Edward st SE8
76 A 17 Edward st SE8
115 R 3 Edwardes sq W8
48 H 19 Edwards cotts N1
49 P 8 Edwards la N16
139 T 5 Edwards mans W1
81 R 9 Edwards rd Blvdr
66 K 8 Edwin av E6
81 O 17 Edwin clo Bxly Hth
12 K 20 Edwin rd Edg
101 U 1 Edwin st E1
63 R 12 Edwin st E1
65 S 15 Edwin st E16
35 P 16 Edwina gdns Ilf
4 A 18 Edwyn clo Barnt
145 U 19 Effie rd SW6
145 U 19 Effie rd SW6
154 B 17 Effingham clo Sutton
30 H 14 Effingham rd N8
94 C 13 Effingham rd SE12
122 D 18 Effingham rd Croy
116 C 18 Effingham rd Surb
106 J 12 Effort st SW17
52 A 16 Effra pde SW2
106 B 14 Effra rd SW19
105 Z 14 Effra rd SW19
90 E 13 Effra rd SW2
75 N 14 Egan st SE16
151 X 10 Egan way SE16
131 T 3 Egbert pl NW1
146 L 4 Egerton cres SW3
76 E 20 Egerton dri SE10
93 S 1 Egerton dri SE10
62 M 3 Egerton gdns NW10
128 C 5 Egerton gdns NW10
26 K 13 Egerton gdns NW4
146 K 4 Egerton gdns SW3
60 B 17 Egerton gdns Ilf
54 K 10 Egerton gdns Ilf
146 L 3 Egerton Gdns ms SW3
31 U 20 Egerton rd N16
123 R 7 Egerton rd SE25
118 E 8 Egerton rd New Mald
83 U 17 Egerton rd Twick
60 L 1 Egerton rd Wemb
146 K 3 Egerton ter SW3
153 R 3 Egham clo Sutton
153 R 4 Egham cres Sutton
65 W 14 Egham rd E13
88 C 14 Eglantine rd SW18
120 A 15 Egleston rd Mrdn

20 K 2 Eglington rd E4
78 M 19 Eglinton hills SE18
78 K 17 Eglinton rd SE18
86 L 8 Egliston rd SW15
117 O 20 Egmont av Surb
118 E 7 Egmont rd New Mald
117 O 20 Egmont rd Surb
154 C 18 Egmont rd Sutton
75 T 20 Egmont st SE14
108 G 7 Egremont rd SE27
53 U 11 Eighth av E12
123 P 12 Eileen rd SE25
66 D 14 Eisenhower dri E6
47 N 14 Elaine gro NW5
90 J 5 Elam st SE25
156 H 5 Eland pl Croy
89 N 7 Eland rd SW11
156 H 5 Eland rd Croy
150 C 5 Elba pl SE17
88 C 4 Elbe st SW6
121 W 15 Elberon av Croy
123 W 11 Elborough rd SE25
105 X 2 Elborough st SW18
65 T 19 Elbury dri E16
146 L 19 Elcho st SW11
129 P 19 Elcom st W10
151 V 18 Elcot av SW15
30 A 17 Elder av N8
108 M 13 Elder rd SE27
134 M 19 Elder st E1
72 K 7 Elderberry rd W5
50 D 12 Elderfield rd E5
34 H 15 Elderfield wlk E11
125 P 13 Elderslie clo Becknhm
95 X 14 Elderslie rd SE9
110 H 10 Elderton rd SE26
121 U 1 Eldertree pl Mitch
121 T 2 Eldertree way Mitch
158 D 2 Eldon av Croy
70 G 19 Eldon av Hounsl
46 G 14 Eldon gro NW3
123 Z 8 Eldon pk SE25
32 L 14 Eldon rd E17
30 K 5 Eldon rd N22
19 O 7 Eldon rd N9
145 Z 2 Eldon rd W8
142 A 2 Eldon rd W8
142 G 1 Eldon st EC2
67 U 3 Eldred rd Bark
14 B 15 Eleanor cres NW7
56 A 8 Eleanor gdns Dgnhm
86 C 8 Eleanor gro SW13
52 D 19 Eleanor rd E15
49 Z 18 Eleanor rd E8
17 N 20 Eleanor rd N11
64 A 9 Eleanor st E3
64 B 10 Eleanor st E3
90 E 10 Electric av SW9
149 Z 4 Elephant And castle SE1
143 Z 17 Elephant la SE16
75 O 5 Elephant la SE16
150 A 4 Elephant rd SE17
72 D 6 Elers rd W13
35 R 20 Eley gdns Ilf
19 R 16 Eley rd N18
63 R 19 Elf row E1
101 V 13 Elfin gro Tedd
90 M 13 Elfindale rd SE24
91 N 14 Elfindale rd SE24
48 G 12 Elfort rd N5
111 O 9 Elfrida cres SE6
59 U 13 Elfwine rd W7
122 A 5 Elgar av SW16
72 K 5 Elgar av Surb
117 R 19 Elgar av Surb
11 S 2 Elgar clo Borehm Wd

75 W 7 Elgar st SE16
130 A 14 Elgin av W9
129 T 17 Elgin av W9
24 A 7 Elgin av Harrow
136 M 8 Elgin cres W11
137 N 7 Elgin cres W11
139 A 13 Elgin Ms south W9
130 A 13 Elgin Ms south W9
29 V 7 Elgin rd N22
157 V 2 Elgin rd Croy
123 U 20 Elgin rd Croy
54 J 1 Elgin rd Ilf
154 D 6 Elgin rd Sutton
155 U 13 Elgin rd Wallgtn
149 S 16 Elia st SE11
133 W 9 Elia st N1
95 V 10 Elibank rd SE9
110 A 3 Eliot bank SE23
40 J 16 Eliot dri Harrow
93 V 5 Eliot hill SE13
93 V 5 Eliot pk SE13
93 Y 5 Eliot pl SE13
55 W 13 Eliot rd Dgnhm
93 X 5 Eliot vale SE13
156 J 4 Elis David pl Croy
156 J 4 Elis David rd Croy
22 D 2 Elizabeth av N1
7 X 10 Elizabeth av Enf
54 E 6 Elizabeth av Ilf
147 X 7 Elizabeth Bridge SW1
64 D 17 Elizabeth clo E14
130 D 17 Elizabeth clo W9
4 B 12 Elizabeth clo Barnt
52 K 6 Elizabeth clo Rom
85 O 2 Elizabeth cotts Rich
74 D 4 Elizabeth gdns W3
46 L 18 Elizabeth ms NW3
66 A 2 Elizabeth rd E6
31 S 15 Elizabeth rd N15
19 O 3 Elizabeth rd N9
147 W 6 Elizabeth st SW1
95 U 15 Elizabeth ter SE9
31 P 12 Elizabethan pl N15
65 U 12 Elkington rd E13
30 B 20 Ella rd N8
144 F 15 Ellaline rd W6
19 N 16 Ellambridge cress N18
92 C 11 Elland rd SE15
22 A 16 Element clo Pinn
127 O 6 Ellen clo Brom
19 P 10 Ellen ct N9
143 T 7 Ellen st E1
30 K 5 Ellenborough rd N20
115 Y 13 Ellenborough rd Sidcp
157 T 20 Ellenbridge way S Croy
101 V 14 Ellerby rd Tedd
87 P 2 Ellerby st SW6
46 D 14 Ellerdale clo NW3
46 D 13 Ellerdale rd NW3
93 R 9 Ellerdale st SE13
83 O 11 Ellerdine rd Hounsl
84 J 15 Ellerker gdns Rich
74 J 2 Ellerman st E14
92 Z 12 Ellerslie rd W12
68 E 1 Ellerslie sq SW4
86 F 2 Ellerton rd SW13
88 F 20 Ellerton rd SW18
106 G 1 Ellerton rd SW18
106 G 17 Ellerton rd SW20
68 F 2 Ellerton rd Dgnhm
26 M 20 Ellerton rd Surb
92 A 6 Ellery st SE15
125 S 4 Ellesmere av Becknhm
34 D 16 Ellesmere clo E11
35 R 17 Ellesmere gdns Ilf
4 G 17 Ellesmere gro Barnt
77 T 2 Ellesmere rd E16
63 V 5 Ellesmere rd E3
44 H 15 Ellesmere rd NW10
73 X 15 Ellesmere rd W4
58 M 12 Ellesmere rd Grnfd
84 D 15 Ellesmere rd Twick
64 C 17 Ellesmere st E14
50 A 19 Ellingfort rd E8
51 X 13 Ellingham rd E15
74 G 5 Ellingham rd W12
29 S 13 Ellington rd N10
82 L 5 Ellington rd Hounsl
48 F 18 Ellington st N7
26 K 19 Elliot rd NW4
126 M 9 Elliot rd Brom
127 N 9 Elliot rd Brom
122 K 9 Elliot rd Thntn Hth
39 Y 4 Elliott gdns Rom
149 V 20 Elliott rd SW9
90 H 1 Elliott rd W4
74 A 11 Elliott rd W4
10 M 18 Elliott rd Stanm
149 X 4 Elliotts row SE11
77 X 16 Ellis ms SE7
147 R 4 Ellis st SW1
77 Y 15 Elliscombe rd SE7
87 U 19 Ellisfield dri SW15
70 D 10 Ellison gdns S'hall
86 E 5 Ellison rd SW13
105 A 19 Ellison rd SW16
107 Y 18 Ellison rd SW16
114 F 2 Ellison rd Sidcp
39 Y 4 Ellmore clo Rom
93 R 9 Ellora rd SW16
63 N 9 Ellsworth st E2
135 X 12 Ellsworth st E2
72 L 4 Elm av W5
17 O 2 Elm ms N14
86 C 5 Elm Bank gdns SW13
34 J 18 Elm clo E11
27 O 17 Elm clo NW4
113 M 8 Elm clo SW20
120 L 20 Elm clo Carsh

22 J 19 Elm clo Harrow
38 G 6 Elm clo Rom
157 P 14 Elm clo S Croy
117 W 17 Elm clo Surb
100 K 5 Elm clo Twick
72 K 4 Elm clo W5
116 K 1 Elm cres Kingst
22 J 18 Elm dri Harrow
28 E 10 Elm gdns N2
8 A 2 Elm gdns Enf
121 X 6 Elm gdns Mitch
62 A 17 Elm grn W3
45 R 12 Elm gro NW2
30 B 19 Elm gro N8
91 W 4 Elm gro SE15
105 S 18 Elm gro SW19
81 Z 18 Elm gro Erith
40 G 2 Elm gro Harrow
116 L 1 Elm gro Kingst
154 B 9 Elm gro Sutton
21 R 19 Elm Gro pde Wallgtn
155 P 6 Elm Gro pde Wallgtn
124 A 18 Elm Grove rd Croy
34 J 18 Elm Hall gdns E11
110 M 3 Elm la SE6
31 W 18 Elm Park av N15
90 C 17 Elm pk SW2
11 P 17 Elm pk Stanm
57 U 12 Elm Pk av Hornch
27 O 17 Elm Pk av Harrow
146 F 11 Elm Pk gdns NW4
146 E 12 Elm Pk la SW3
50 J 4 Elm Pk rd E10
17 X 4 Elm Pk rd N21
27 W 2 Elm Pk rd N3
123 T 6 Elm Pk rd SE25
146 E 13 Elm Pk rd SW3
146 F 10 Elm pl SW7
33 V 16 Elm rd E10
51 V 7 Elm rd E11
33 V 16 Elm rd E17
52 D 18 Elm rd E7
46 E 10 Elm rd NW3
85 W 9 Elm rd SW14
124 L 2 Elm rd Becknhm
152 E 15 Elm rd Epsom
99 W 1 Elm rd Erith
82 B 5 Elm rd Hounsl
102 M 19 Elm rd Kingst
103 O 18 Elm rd Kingst
116 L 1 Elm rd Kingst
117 Y 4 Elm rd New Mald
38 G 7 Elm rd Rom
114 M 12 Elm rd Sidcp
123 N 10 Elm rd Thntn Hth
121 P 20 Elm rd Wallgtn
42 K 15 Elm rd Wemb
119 V 16 Elm Rd west Sutton
133 P 17 Elm st WC1
45 X 9 Elm ter NW2
95 W 15 Elm ter Harrow
23 R 3 Elm ter Harrow
11 P 17 Elm ter Stanm
130 T 12 Elm Tree clo NW8
58 F 7 Elm Tree rd Grnfd
130 F 13 Elm Tree rd NW8
43 Z 11 Elm way NW10
44 A 11 Elm way NW10
152 M 4 Elm way Worc Pk
45 Z 8 Elm wlk NW3
118 M 8 Elm wlk SW20
119 O 9 Elm wlk Rom
39 W 9 Elm wlk Rom
31 P 14 Elmar rd N15
4 A 18 Elmbank av Barnt
59 S 13 Elmbank way W7
107 R 7 Elmbourne rd SW17
117 W 16 Elmbridge av Surb
95 S 10 Elmbrook gdns SE9
153 V 8 Elmbrook rd Sutton
108 K 3 Elmcourt rd SE27
34 H 14 Elmcroft av E11
45 W 1 Elmcroft av NW11
9 N 20 Elmcroft av Enf
96 L 17 Elmcroft av Sidcp
34 J 13 Elmcroft clo E11
60 G 16 Elmcroft clo Grnfd
45 R 1 Elmcroft cres NW11
22 J 11 Elmcroft cres Harrow
25 P 14 Elmcroft gdns NW9
50 C 11 Elmcroft st E5
17 R 17 Elmdale rd N13
144 D 12 Elmdene Surb
117 X 20 Elmdene Surb
124 K 13 Elmdene Becknhm
78 M 15 Elmdene rd SE18
82 A 4 Elmdon rd Hounsl
7 P 11 Elmer clo Enf
25 S 2 Elmer gdns Edg
83 R 8 Elmer gdns Islwth
93 U 19 Elmer rd SE6

LONDON STEAK HOUSES

Restaurants of intimate character and size serving excellent grills, veal and fish dishes and a wide range of sweets, cheeses and wines. Open seven days a week, lunchtime and evenings. (Weekdays until 11.00 pm Sundays 10.30 pm)

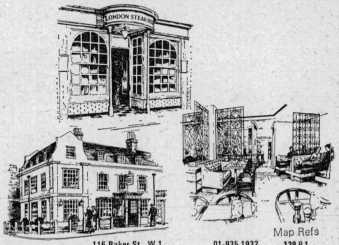

		Map Refs
116 Baker St., W.1	01-935 1932	139 R 1
8 Clifford St., W.1	01-734 5893	140 A 9
15-27 Davies St., W.1	01-493 6950	139 X 9
17-20 Kendal St., W.2	01-723 8891	138 M 6
130 Kensington High St., W.8	01-937 7500	137 V 20
10a Broadway, S.W.1	01-799 4420	140 F 20
11 Whitehall, S.W.1.	01-930 1656	140 J 14
29 Ebury St., S.W.1	01-730 5456	147 X 4
31 Basil St., S.W.3	01-589 2191	139 O 19
94 King's Road, S.W.3	01-589 2329	147 O 8
18 High St., Wimbledon, S.W.19	01-946 8377	105 R 13
73 Old Brompton Rd., S.W.7	01-584 6195	146 F 7
49a Lincolns Inn Fields, W.C.2	01-242 3956	141 O 5
7 South Grove, Highgate, N.6	01-348 0302	47 P 3
16-18 Montpelier Vale, Blackheath, S.E.3	01-852 6462	94 B 5
15-17 Streatham High Rd., S.W.16	01-769 6555	108 A 6
96-98 Dulwich Village, S.E.21	01-693 6880	91 R 17

BUSINESS & LEISURE

There's a London Steak House near you—consult your local telephone directory

102 B 16 Elmers dri Tedd
124 D 6 Elmers End rd Becknhm
123 Y 16 Elmers rd SE25
30 A 16 Elmfield av N8
121 O 1 Elmfield av Mitch
101 X 12 Elmfield av Tedd
126 F 5 Elmfield pk Brom
32 E 17 Elmfield rd E17
20 J 7 Elmfield rd E4
28 F 9 Elmfield rd N2
27 F 9 Elmfield rd N2
107 P 3 Elmfield rd SW17
126 G 5 Elmfield rd Brom
70 C 8 Elmfield rd S'hall
157 U 19 Elmfield way S Croy
12 K 15 Elmgate gdns Edg
23 X 15 Elmgrove cres Harrow
23 Y 15 Elmgrove gdns Harrow
86 G 4 Elmgrove rd SW13
72 K 4 Elmgrove rd W5
80 M 17 Elmhurst Blvdr
81 N 16 Elmhurst Blvdr
28 F 11 Elmhurst av N2
107 R 19 Elmhurst av Mitch
34 F 6 Elmhurst dri E18
52 H 20 Elmhurst rd E7
31 T 7 Elmhurst rd N17
113 P 6 Elmhurst rd SE9
89 X 7 Elmhurst st SW4
98 F 17 Elmington clo Bxly
150 G 20 Elmington rd SE5
93 S 8 Elmira st SE13
113 U 15 Elmlee clo Chisl
79 S 12 Elmley st SE18
51 V 10 Elmore rd E11
9 S 4 Elmore rd Enf
49 N 20 Elmore st N1
27 O 17 Elms av NW4
29 T 9 Elms av N10
89 X 14 Elms cres SW4
41 X 13 Elms ct Wemb
56 A 11 Elms gdns Dgnhm
41 X 13 Elms gdns Wemb
41 Z 9 Elms la Harrow
41 Z 12 Elms la Harrow
138 E 9 Elms ms W2
41 Y 12 Elms Pk av Wemb
89 U 13 Elms rd SW4
23 S 2 Elms rd Harrow
10 G 20 Elms rd Harrow
86 D 8 Elms the SW13
7 Z 20 Elmscott gdns N21
18 A 1 Elmscott gdns N21
112 A 12 Elmscott rd Brom
32 L 12 Elmsdale rd E17
86 H 13 Elmshaw rd SW15
28 F 12 Elmshurst cres N2
228 F 12 Elmshurst cres N2
9 R 1 Elmshurst rd Enf
159 S 14 Elmside Croy
43 O 9 Elmside rd Wemb
24 C 13 Elmsleigh av Harrow
101 R 4 Elmsleigh rd Twick
113 V 12 Elmstead av Chisl
43 N 7 Elmstead av Wemb
42 K 5 Elmstead av Wemb
14 K 8 Elmstead clo N20
152 B 12 Elmstead clo Epsom
80 F 17 Elmstead cres Bxly Hth
152 F 5 Elmstead gdns Worc Pk
113 T 14 Elmstead glade Chisl
113 U 10 Elmstead la Chisl
99 P 1 Elmstead rd Erith
54 J 7 Elmstead rd Ilf
87 V 1 Elmstead rd SW6
82 K 4 Elmsworth av Hounsl
101 U 11 Elmtree rd Tedd
17 O 15 Elmwood av N13
24 A 18 Elmwood av Harrow
23 Z 16 Elmwood av Harrow
155 R 4 Elmwood clo Wallgtn
25W 13 Elmwood cres NW9
41 Z 11 Elmwood ct Wemb
97 Y 18 Elmwood dri Bxly
152 G 16 Elmwood dri Epsom
55 T 18 Elmwood gdns W7
91 O 14 Elmwood rd SE24
73 V 16 Elmwood rd W4
122 J 17 Elmwood rd Croy
120 M 6 Elmwood rd Mitch
109 N 4 Elmworth gro SE21
119 Y 18 Elnathan ms W9
32 L 7 Elphinstone rd E17
48 J 11 Elphinstone st N5
49 X 18 Elrington rd E8
97 R 4 Elsa rd Welling
63 S 1 Elsa st E1

50 D 18 Elsdale st E9
31 U 6 Elsden rd N17
53 V 16 Elsenham rd E12
105 V 3 Elsenham st SW18
52 A 11 Elsham rd E11
51 Z 11 Elsham rd E11
136 K 19 Elsham rd W14
91 U 10 Elsie rd SE22
17 Z 3 Elsiedene rd N21
92 M 13 Elsiemaud rd SE4
110 J 2 Elsinore rd SE23
89 N 7 Elsley rd SW11
88 M 7 Elsley rd SW11
82 D 8 Elsma ter Hounsl
88 M 9 Elspeth rd SW11
42 J 15 Elspeth rd Wemb
119 Y 12 Elsrick av Mrdn
124 H 17 Elstan way Croy
150 G 8 Elsted st SE17
95 V 13 Elstow clo SE9
68 L 2 Elstow gdns Dgnhm
68 L 3 Elstow rd Dgnhm
19 N 7 Elstree gdns N9
80 M 10 Elstree gdns Blvdr
81 N 10 Elstree gdns Blvdr
112 A 17 Elstree gdns Blvdr
54 B 15 Elstree gdns Ilf
11 T 3 Elstree hill Borhm Wd
111 Z 17 Elstree hill Brom
10 E 3 Elstree rd Bushey Watf
93 R 6 Elswick rd SE13
88 C 3 Elswick st SW6
130 J 4 Elsworthy ri NW8
130 L 1 Elsworthy rd NW3
130 L 3 Elsworthy ter NW3
88 F 12 Elsynge rd SW18
95 E 14 Eltham common SE18
94 N 13 Eltham grn SE9
94 L 12 Eltham grn rd SE9
95 T 14 Eltham High st SE9
95 N 14 Eltham hill SE9
95 N 16 Eltham Pal rd SE9
94 L 16 Eltham Pal rd SE9
95 S 18 Eltham palace SE9
96 A 11 Eltham park SE9
95 X 11 Eltham Pk gdns SE9
94 H 12 Eltham rd SE12
150 E 8 Eltham st SE17
87 Y 2 Elthiron rd SW6
71 X 6 Elthorne av W7
71 X 6 Elthorne Pk rd W7
25 Y 20 Elthorne rd NW9
47 Z 4 Elthorne rd N19
25 Y 19 Elthorne way NW9
93 Y 16 Elthruda rd SE13
53 Y 12 Eltisley rd Ilf
4 J 17 Elton av Barnt
41 V 18 Elton av Grnfd
42 C 14 Elton av Wemb
102 E 19 Elton clo Kingst
49 R 14 Elton pl N16
103 O 20 Elton rd Kingst
106 E 6 Eltons cotts SW17
88 D 10 Eltringham st SW18
44 C 2 Elvaston ms SW7
146 C 2 Elvaston pl SW7
6 P 5 Eleveden pl NW10
61 P 6 Elveden rd NW10
93 R 5 Elvendon rd N13
93 R 5 Elverson rd SE4
148 E 4 Elverton st SW1
126 C 11 Elvington grn Brom
110 G 13 Elvino rd SE26
89 Z 4 Elwell rd SW4
125 U 8 Elwill way Becknhm
135 R 12 Elwin st E2
48 J 10 Elwood st N5
99 T 5 Elwyn gdns SE12
118 E 2 Ely clo New Mald
56 L 9 Ely gdns Dgnhm
141 U 2 Ely pl EC1
33 U 20 Ely rd E10
123 O 11 Ely rd Croy
30 F 19 Elyne rd N4
146 M 8 Elystan pl SW3
147 N 8 Elystan pl SW3
146 L 8 Elystan st SW3
61W 18 Emanuel av W3
143 V 19 Emba st SE16
87 O 6 Embankment SW15
147 S 13 Embankment gdns SW3
140 L 13 Embankment pl WC2
101 Z 1 Embankment the Twick
93 R 10 Embleton rd SE13
20 L 14 Embry clo Stanm
10 M 18 Embry dri Stanm

10 L 15 Embry way Stanm
88 B 2 Emden st SW6
56 D 5 Emerald gdns Dgnhm
133 N 19 Emerald st WC1
24 M 20 Emerson gdns Harrow
53 X 1 Emerson rd Ilf
35W 20 Emerson rd Ilf
142 A 12 Emerson st SE1
148 C 5 Emery Hill st SW1
141 T 20 Emery st SE1
81 Y 18 Emes rd Erith
48 G 13 Emily pl N7
74 B 6 Emlyn gdns W12
74 B 6 Emlyn rd W12
65 P 8 Emma rd E13
78 A 3 Emma st E16
107 V 2 Emmanuel rd SW12
133 U 8 Emmens bldgs N1
75 Z 1 Emmett st E14
36 C 16 Emmott av Ilf
28 C 19 Emmott clo NW11
63 V 12 Emmott st E1
135 V 8 Emms st E2
145 Z 4 Emperors ga SW7
146 A 4 Emperors ga SW7
17 Y 18 Empire av N18
60 E 3 Empire rd Grnfd
18 A 19 Empire sq N18
43 O 11 Empire way Wemb
52 M 7 Empress av E12
53 N 7 Empress av E12
33 P 2 Empress av E4
53 Y 4 Empress av Ilf
34 C 2 Empress av Wdfd Grn
113 Y 14 Empress dri Chisl
150 B 13 Empress rd SE10
64 F 12 Empson st E3
36 A 7 Emsworth rd Ilf
44 C 4 Emsworth st SW2
89 R 5 Emu rd SW8
121 Z 6 Ena rd SW16
122 A 5 Ena rd SW16
128 L 15 Enbrook st W10
68 A 7 Endeavour way Bark
140 J 5 Endell st WC2
76 L 13 Enderby st SE10
23 S 6 Enderley clo Har
23 S 6 Enderly clo Har
26 L 4 Endersleigh gdns NW4
20 F 8 Endlebury rd E4
89 O 17 Endlesham rd SW12
132 F 15 Endsleigh gdns WC1
53 U 5 Endsleigh gdns Ilf
116 E 16 Endsleigh gdns Surb
132 F 16 Endsleigh pl WC1
71 Y 1 Endsleigh rd W13
70 D 10 Endsleigh rd S'hall
132 F 15 Endsleigh st WC1
46 E 7 Endway NW3
117 R 17 Endway Surb
92 G 6 Endwell rd SE4
48 G 2 Endymion rd N4
30 J 20 Endymion rd N4
90 C 16 Endymion rd SW2
76 A 7 Enfield cres Enf
36 A 7 Enfield rd N1
49 N 19 Enfield rd N1
72 F 13 Enfield rd Brentf
6 L 12 Enfield rd Enf
7 O 12 Enfield rd Enf
139 N 1 Enford st W1
105W 2 Engadine st SW18
93 S 18 Engate st SE13
14 A 19 Engel pk NW7
78 K 16 Engineer rd SE18
43 P 12 Engineers way Wemb
46 L 18 Englands la NW3
49 N 18 Englefield rd N1
93 T 20 Englefield rd N1
89 Y 15 Englewood rd SW12
142 J 14 English grounds SE1
63 Y 12 English st E3
151 P 1 Enid st SE16
48 B 11 Enkel st N7
123 Y 11 Enmore av SE25
85 Z 13 Enmore gdns SW14
123 Y 11 Enmore rd SE25
58 N 12 Enmore rd S'hall
57 V 15 Enmore rd S'hall
24 D 9 Ennerdale av Stanm
25 Z 16 Ennerdale av Stanm
26 B 16 Ennerdale dri NW9
26 A 16 Ennerdale dri NW9
42 E 4 Ennerdale gdns Wemb
98 E 2 Ennerdale rd Bxly Hth
85 N 3 Ennerdale rd Rich

93W 14 Ennersdale rd SE13
48 F 4 Ennis rd N4
79 R 16 Ennis rd SE18
74 C 11 Ennismore av W4
41 U 16 Ennismore av Grnfd
146 J 1 Ennismore gdns SW7
138 J 20 Ennismore gdns SW7
146 J 1 Ennismore Gdns ms SW7
138 H 20 Ennismore Gdns ms SW7
138 K 20 Ennismore ms SW7
146 J 1 Ennismore ms SW7
17 X 10 Ensign dri N13
143 T 9 Ensign st E1
95W 17 Enslin rd SE9
146 E 9 Ensor ms SW7
63 O 10 Entick st E2
145 S 17 Epirus ms SW6
145 S 17 Epirus rd SW6
38 H 11 Epping clo Rom
21 U 3 Epping forest Buck HI
21 U 8 Epping New rd Buck HI
87W 2 Epple rd SW6
98 H 9 Epsom clo Bxly Hth
40 E 16 Epsom clo Grnfd
33 U 19 Epsom rd E10
156 G 7 Epsom rd Croy
36 K 20 Epsom rd Ilf
119W 14 Epsom rd Mrdn
72 A 20 Epworth rd Brentf
134 G 17 Epworth st EC2
148 H 6 Erasmus st SW1
62 D 18 Erconwald st W12
129 T 2 Eresby ms NW6
129 T 2 Eresby rd NW6
52 E 12 Eric clo E7
52 E 13 Eric rd E7
24 C 18 Eric rd NW10
55 X 1 Eric rd Rom
63 X 11 Eric st E3
159 P 7 Erica gdns Croy
62 H 20 Erica st W12
73 Y 8 Eridge rd W4
79 T 17 Erindale SE18
79 T 17 Erindale ter SE18
38 J 3 Erith cres Rom
80 L 14 Erith marshes Blvdr
81 U 13 Erith rd Blvdr
98 G 8 Erith rd Bxly Hth
98 J 3 Erith rd Erith
92 F 2 Erlanger rd SE14
93 R 10 Erlesmere gdns W13
93 R 10 Ermine rd E13
114 C 4 Ermington rd SE9
66 E 6 Ernald av E6
83W 17 Erncroft way Twick
108 K 9 Ernest av SE27
125 N 11 Ernest clo Becknhm
124 M 11 Ernest gro Becknhm
125 N 11 Ernest gro Becknhm
65 O 13 Ernest rd E16
117 S 4 Ernest st Kingst
63 U 13 Ernest st E1
104 L 17 Ernle rd SW20
86 M 7 Erpingham rd SW15
119 Y 3 Erridge rd SW19
129 R 17 Errington rd W9
118 G 10 Errol gdns New Mald
134 D 18 Errol st EC1
39 T 13 Erroll rd Rom
154 H 6 Erskine clo Sutton
27 Y 15 Erskine hill NW11
131 R 1 Erskine ms NW1
32 L 12 Erskine rd E17
131 R 1 Erskine rd NW1
154 G 7 Erskine rd Sutton
108 G 13 Esam way SW16
116 N 10 Escott gdns SE9
118 G 18 Escreet gro SE18
38 K 18 Esher av Rom
153 R 6 Esher av Sutton
115 Y 2 Esher clo Bxly
105 O 3 Esher gdns SW19
54 H 9 Esher rd Ilf
65 U 12 Esk rd E13
39 O 3 Esk way Rom
58 E 2 Eskdale av Grnfd
98 D 4 Eskdale rd Bxly Hth
44 F 1 Esmar cres NW9
151 T 8 Esmeralda rd SE1
129 P 5 Esmond rd NW6
73 Z 10 Esmond rd W4
87 T 11 Esmond st SW15
88 A 18 Esparto st SW18
68 V 13 Essan st E1
81 R 13 Essenden rd Blvdr
157 R 17 Essenden rd S Croy

THE
BELVEDERE
RESTAURANT

Only two minutes from Kensington High Street, with no parking problem, and set amongst the trees of Holland Park, the Belvedere is actually the ballroom of old Holland House. It inherits the charm of another age and offers a superb continental menu in accord with the classic recipes. Excellent personal service and a splendid cellar match the inspired skills of haute cuisine.

Reservations 01-602 1238

Map Reference 137 R 19

ABBOTSBURY ROAD
HOLLAND PARK W8

129 U 15 Essendine rd W9
83 T 8 Essex av Islwth
119 N 16 Essex clo Mrdn
38 G 12 Essex clo Rom
86 D 4 Essex ct SW13
141 S 7 Essex ct WC2
30 K 18 Essex gdns N4
32 G 12 Essex gro E17
109 P 15 Essex gro SE19
15 N 20 Essex pk N12
74 B 4 Essex pl W3
73 X 12 Essex pl W4
33 V 19 Essex rd E10
53 S 16 Essex rd E12
32 H 18 Essex rd E17
34 J 7 Essex rd E18
20 M 5 Essex rd E4
44 C 19 Essex rd NW10
49 N 18 Essex rd N1
133 Y 4 Essex rd N1
51 X 1 Essex rd SE11
61 U 19 Essex rd W3
73 X 13 Essex rd W4
97 T 3 Essex rd Bark
56 J 15 Essex rd Dgnhm
8 B 15 Essex rd Enf
38 H 12 Essex rd Rom
55 S 2 Essex rd Rom
51 X 1 Essex Rd south E11
52 E 14 Essex st E7
141 R 8 Essex st WC2
137 U 19 Essex vlls W8
50 M 4 Estate way E10
124 A 14 Estcourt rd SE25
145 N 17 Estcourt rd SW6
88 J 7 Este rd SW11
118 K 9 Estella av New Mald
47 N 13 Estelle rd NW3
148 F 6 Esterbrooke st SW1
33 Z 20 Esther rd E11
107 X 16 Estreham rd SW16
106 M 10 Eswyn rd SW17
107 N 12 Eswyn rd SW17
28 B 1 Etchingham Pk rd N3
51 U 12 Etchingham rd E15
115 P 12 Etfield rd Sidcp
65 V 19 Ethel rd E16
150 B 7 Ethel st SE17
126 E 5 Ethelbert clo Brom
35 V 17 Ethelbert gdns Ilf
105 V 20 Ethelbert rd SW20
126 E 5 Ethelbert rd Brom
81 W 19 Ethelbert rd Erith
107 T 2 Ethelbert st SW4
146 L 20 Ethelburga st SW11
88 K 1 Ethelburga st SW11
74 J 3 Ethelden rd W12
29 U 13 Etheldene av N10
149 P 6 Ethelred st SE11
30 L 14 Etherley rd N15
91 W 17 Etherow st SE22
108 E 10 Etherstone grn SW16
108 E 10 Etherstone rd SW16
151 V 15 Ethnard rd SE15
97 Z 8 Ethronvi rd Bxly Hth
51 N 6 Etloe rd E10
46 H 19 Eton av NW3
15 R 20 Eton av N12
5 X 19 Eton av Barnt
70 F 16 Eton av Hounsl
117 Y 10 Eton av New Mald
42 E 13 Eton av Wemb
47 N 19 Eton College rd NW3
42 E 12 Eton ct Wemb
93 Z 8 Eton gro SE13
46 M 19 Eton rd NW3
54 D 13 Eton rd Ilf
46 M 19 Eton vlls NW3
50 H 11 Etropol rd E5
75 X 15 Etta st SE8
64 H 16 Ettrick st E14
75 R 12 Eugenia rd SE16
117 O 4 Eureka rd Kingst
134 B 14 Europa pl EC1
66 E 8 Eustace rd E6
145 T 16 Eustace st SW6
55 X 1 Eustace rd Rom
52 E 15 Euston rd NW1
122 E 20 Euston rd Croy
156 G 1 Euston rd Croy
132 D 14 Euston sq NW1
132 D 14 Euston st NW1
132 D 13 Euston station NW1
90 G 4 Evandale rd SW9
47 T 13 Evangelist rd NW5
100 G 5 Evans gro Felt
112 A 5 Evans rd SE6
33 U 2 Evanston av E4
35 P 18 Evanston gdns Ilf

51 Z 12 Eve rd E11
65 N 7 Eve rd E15
31 T 9 Eve rd E17
83 Z 11 Eve rd Islwth
37 U 20 Eve rd Rom
92 C 6 Evelina rd SE15
110 D 19 Evelina rd SE20
120 L 2 Eveline rd Mitch
25 X 12 Evelyn av NW9
82 J 18 Evelyn av Twick
22 A 2 Evelyn dri Pinn
146 E 10 Evelyn gdns SW7
84 L 9 Evelyn gdns Rich
73 N 3 Evelyn gro W5
58 E 17 Evelyn gro S'hall
77 U 2 Evelyn rd E16
33 U 14 Evelyn rd E17
106 A 14 Evelyn rd SW19
73 X 9 Evelyn rd W4
5 Z 15 Evelyn rd Barnt
102 F 7 Evelyn rd Rich
84 K 8 Evelyn rd Rich
75 W 13 Evelyn st SE8
84 J 8 Evelyn ter Rich
155 X 7 Evelyn way Wallgtn
134 E 10 Evelyn wlk N1
140 E 4 Evelyn yd W1
56 H 7 Evenlode way Dgnhm
87 S 14 Evenwood clo SW15
126 G 19 Everard av Brom
74 F 18 Everdon rd SW13
95 S 13 Everest rd SE9
133 P 5 Everilda st N1
49 U 11 Evering rd N16
29 N 6 Evering rd N10
144 H 15 Everington st W6
61 Z 9 Everitt rd NW10
48 E 5 Everleigh st N4
13 N 20 Eversfield gdns NW7
84 M 4 Eversfield rd Rich
85 N 4 Eversfield rd Rich
120 A 14 Eversham grn Mrdn
132 C 10 Eversholt st NW1
48 C 4 Evershot rd N4
68 B 3 Eversleigh rd E6
87 W 2 Eversleigh rd N3
89 O 5 Eversleigh rd SW8
5 S 18 Eversleigh rd Barnt
99 P 5 Eversley av Bxly Hth
43 P 7 Eversley av Wemb
17 T 19 Eversley clo N21
99 R 5 Eversley cres Bxly Hth
83 R 2 Eversley cres Islwth
7 R 19 Eversley mt N21
7 R 20 Eversley Pk rd N21
17 R 1 Eversley Pk rd N21
109 O 17 Eversley rd SE7
77 V 16 Eversley rd SE7
117 N 10 Eversley rd Surb
116 M 10 Eversley rd Surb
59 M 6 Eversley way Croy
91 U 8 Everthorpe rd SE15
132 A 14 Everton bldgs NW1
24 L 10 Everton dri Stanm
123 W 19 Everton rd Croy
33 P 7 Evesham av E17
68 K 5 Evesham clo Grnfd
65 O 2 Evesham rd E15
16 J 18 Evesham rd N11
120 A 15 Evesham rd Mrdn
35 X 11 Evesham way Ilf
87 V 6 Ewald rd SW6
21 X 18 Ewanrigg ter Wdfd Grn
30 E 5 Ewart gro N22
92 G 20 Ewart rd SE23
152 G 18 Ewell By-pass Epsom
152 B 12 Ewell Ct av Epsom
152 D 12 Ewell Pk way Epsom
116 A 18 Ewell rd Surb
117 P 20 Ewell rd Surb
153 R 15 Ewell rd Sutton
35 S 8 Ewellhurst rd Ilf
110 D 1 Ewelme rd SE23
90 F 20 Ewen cres SW2
141 Z 15 Ewer st SE1
157 U 20 Ewhurst av S Croy
153 N 20 Ewhurst clo Sutton
92 M 16 Ewhurst rd SE4
93 N 16 Ewhurst rd SE4
63 W 11 Ewing st E3
110 M 4 Exbury rd SE6
93 U 5 Excelsior gdns SE13
117 O 4 Excelsior rd Kingst
142 L 4 Exchange bldngs E1
140 L 10 Exchange ct WC2
53 S 2 Exeter gdns Ilf
65 T 16 Exeter rd E16
33 N 15 Exeter rd E17

45 S 17 Exeter rd NW2
16 E 3 Exeter rd N14
19 O 9 Exeter rd N9
123 T 17 Exeter rd Croy
56 H 19 Exeter rd Dgnhm
9 T 12 Exeter rd Enf
100 E 7 Exeter rd Felt
40 C 6 Exeter rd Harrow
96 K 4 Exeter rd Welling
140 M 9 Exeter st WC2
112 H 2 Exford gdns SE12
112 H 2 Exford st SE12
138 G 19 Exhibition rd SW7
146 G 2 Exhibition rd SW7
128 H 20 Exmoor st W10
133 T 16 Exmouth mkt EC1
32 L 16 Exmouth rd E17
126 G 7 Exmouth rd Brom
80 E 20 Exmouth rd Welling
65 O 12 Exning rd E16
150 J 8 Exon st SE17
55 U 14 Exton gdns Dgnhm
141 T 15 Exton st SE1
57 W 11 Eyhurst av Hornch
108 M 11 Eyhurst clo NW2
91 V 17 Eylewood rd SE27
91 V 17 Eynella rd SE22
136 B 4 Eynham rd W12
62 M 17 Eynham rd W12
115 V 2 Eynsford cres Bxly
54 J 7 Eynsford rd Ilf
80 F 6 Eynsham dri SE2
115 S 13 Eynswood dri Sidcp
74 E 14 Eyot gdns W6
133 S 18 Eyre St hill EC1
90 G 2 Eythorne rd SW9
135 P 11 Ezra st E2

F

26 G 16 Faber gdns NW4
145 P 17 Fabian rd SW6
66 F 12 Fabian st E6
108 A 16 Factory gdns SW16
31 V 9 Factory la N11
156 H 2 Factory la Croy
78 E 4 Factory rd E16
71 T 3 Factory yd W7
126 F 13 Fair acres Brom
142 M 16 Fair st SE1
143 N 16 Fair st SE1
118 A 6 Fairacre New Mald
90 G 2 Fairbairn grn SW9
17 N 16 Fairbourne rd N17
47 Y 7 Fairbridge rd N19
17 T 18 Fairbrook clo N13
17 T 18 Fairbrook rd N13
94 H 13 Fairby rd SE12
134 L 17 Fairchild st EC2
143 T 6 Fairclough st E1
54 C 18 Faircross av Bark
38 L 2 Faircross av Bark
86 K 9 Fairdale gdns SW15
152 J 20 Fairfax av Epsom
94 M 3 Fairfax gdns SE3
46 D 20 Fairfax pl NW6
130 C 1 Fairfax pl NW6
46 E 20 Fairfax rd NW6
130 C 1 Fairfax rd NW6
30 H 14 Fairfax rd N8
74 B 9 Fairfax rd W4
101 Z 16 Fairfax rd Tedd
102 C 18 Fairfax rd Tedd
26 L 20 Fairfield av NW4
12 E 20 Fairfield av Edg
100 L 1 Fairfield av Twick
15 S 14 Fairfield clo N12
57 W 6 Fairfield clo Hornch
96 K 15 Fairfield clo Sidcp
12 E 20 Fairfield cres Edg
88 B 13 Fairfield dri SW18
60 E 4 Fairfield dri Grnfd
23 N 11 Fairfield dri Harrow
116 K 3 Fairfield east Kingst
30 B 17 Fairfield gdns N8
71 Y 10 Fairfield gro SE7
78 A 15 Fairfield gro SE7
116 K 3 Fairfield north Kingst
157 S 6 Fairfield path Croy
116 K 6 Fairfield pl Kingst
32 J 8 Fairfield rd E17
64 B 7 Fairfield rd E3
18 K 15 Fairfield rd N18
30 B 17 Fairfield rd N8
125 O 2 Fairfield rd Beckhm
112 E 18 Fairfield rd Brom
98 B 5 Fairfield rd Bxly Hth
157 R 5 Fairfield rd Croy
54 A 17 Fairfield rd Ilf
116 J 4 Fairfield rd Kingst

58 E 16 Fairfield rd S'hall
21 S 19 Fairfield rd Wdfd Grn
116 K 5 Fairfield south Kingst
88 A 11 Fairfield st SW18
4 L 17 Fairfield way Barnt
152 A 12 Fairfield way Epsom
116 K 4 Fairfield west Kings
25 W 15 Fairfields clo NW9
25 W 15 Fairfields cres NW9
64 B 11 Fairfoot rd E3
98 M 2 Fairford av Bxly Hth
99 N 2 Fairford av Bxly Hth
124 G 13 Fairford av Croy
124 G 12 Fairford clo Beckhm
152 E 5 Fairford gdns Worc Pk
149 V 7 Fairford gro SE11
5 Y 10 Fairgreen Barnt
5 Y 11 Fairgreen east Barnt
124 E 16 Fairhaven av Croy
130 C 2 Fairhazel gdns NW6
46 C 20 Fairhazel gdns NW6
39 Y 14 Fairholme av Rom
27 T 12 Fairholme clo N3
27 U 12 Fairholme rd W14
145 N 11 Fairholme rd W14
122 G 17 Fairholme rd Croy
23 V 17 Fairholme rd Harrow
35 V 20 Fairholme rd Ilf
53 V 13 Fairholme rd Sutton
49 P 3 Fairholt rd N16
146 L 1 Fairholt st SW7
52 C 19 Fairland rd E15
31 Z 2 Fairlands av Buck H
153 Z 2 Fairlands av Sutton
122 D 10 Fairlands av Thntn Hth
70 F 1 Fairlands gdns Shal
77 X 18 Fairlawn SE7
28 K 12 Fairlawn av N2
73 W 11 Fairlawn av W4
97 V 5 Fairlawn av Bxly Hth
6 J 20 Fairlawn av N14
100 E 9 Fairlawn clo Feth
103 U 15 Fairlawn clo Kingst
34 F 2 Fairlawn dri Wdfd Grn
70 F 1 Fairlawn gdns S'hall
73 W 10 Fairlawn gro W4
110 J 12 Fairlawn pk SE26
105 V 19 Fairlawn rd SW19
84 F 17 Fairlawns Twick
62 F 13 Fairlea pl W5
92 D 19 Fairlie gdns SE23
20 J 8 Fairlight av E4
62 B 6 Fairlight av NW10
21 T 20 Fairlight av Wdgd Grn
20 J 8 Fairlight clo E4
101 E 16 Fairlight rd SW17
57 Z 19 Fairlop clo Hornchurch
36 C 2 Fairlop gdns Ilf
36 H 7 Fairlop plain Ilf
51 X 2 Fairlop rd E11
36 B 8 Fairlop rd Ilf
127 U 10 Fairmead Brom
117 T 20 Fairmead Surb
127 U 10 Fairmead clo Brom
117 Z 7 Fairmead clo New Mald
12 H 11 Fairmead cres Edg
35 P 16 Fairmead gdns Ilf
47 Z 9 Fairmead rd N19
122 E 18 Fairmead rd Croy
107 X 12 Fairmile av SW16
90 D 15 Fairmount rd SW2
96 D 13 Fairoak dri SE9
39 O 8 Fairoak gdns Rom
77 T 13 Fairthorn rd SE7
48 G 17 Fairview av Wemb
32 H 5 Fairview clo E17
43 J 4 Fairview cres Harrow
34 J 4 Fairview gdns Wdfd Grn
31 V 18 Fairview rd N15
122 B 1 Fairview rd Enf
7 T 6 Fairview rd Enf
154 H 12 Fairview rd Sutton
12 C 14 Fairview way Edg
97 N 10 Fairwater av Welling
118 L 6 Fairway SW20
97 Z 13 Fairway Bxly Hth
21 Z 16 Fairway Wdfd Grn
57 T 10 Fairway av NW9
46 C 1 Fairway clo NW11
124 H 13 Fairway clo Croy
54 B 15 Fairway gdns Ilf
12 L 9 Fairway the NW7

FISHERMAN'S WHARF
215 BROMPTON ROAD, S.W.3.
01-584 1505   Map Reference **146** L 2
18 HIGH STREET, WIMBLEDON
S.W.19.   Map Reference **103** R14
01-946 6773

and

HOOK, LINE & SINKER
73 BAKER STREET, W.1.
01-935 0471   Map Reference **139** R 2

Seafood restaurants of outstanding merit, offering fish cooked and served in accord with classic recipes. The wine list is well considered and extensive and the service is in admirable support of both menu and establishment.

Open lunchtimes and evenings including Sunday

17 Z 10 Fairway the N13
6 E 19 Fairway the N14
18 A 11 Fairway the N18
62 B 17 Fairway the W3
5 O 19 Fairway the Barnt
127 T 11 Fairway the Brom
41 N 17 Fairway the Grnfrd
103 Z 20 Fairway the Kingst
117 Z 1 Fairway the New Mald
42 C 5 Fairway the Wemb
24 J 7 Fairways Stanm
102 G 16 Fairways Tedd
31 X 19 Fairweather rd N16
120 G 2 Fairwell pl Mitch
110 H 8 Fairwyn rd SE26
127 R 7 Falcon av Brom
9 T 18 Falcon cres Enf
88 J 7 Falcon gro SW11
88 B 3 Falcon rd SW11
9 S 18 Falcon rd Enf
100 F 17 Falcon rd Hampt
142 B 3 Falcon sq EC1
65 S 11 Falcon st E13
24 K 18 Falcon way Harrow
140 G 5 Falconberg ct W1
140 F 5 Falconberg ms W1
129 P 11 Faconer ms W9
96 H 6 Falconwood av Welling
96 J 10 Falconwood pde Welling
158 M 18 Falconwood rd Croy
159 N 17 Falconwood rd Croy
154 A 11 Falcourt clo Sutton
134 L 10 Falkirk st N1
16 D 13 Falkland av N3
27 Y 3 Falkland av N3
123 S 4 Falkland Pk av SE25
47 V 14 Falkland rd NW5
30 H 14 Falkland rd N8
8 F 14 Falkland rd Barnt
27 Y 13 Falloden way NW11
15 R 20 Fallow Court av N12
10 K 12 Fallowfield Stanm
10 L 12 Fallowfield ct Stanm
107 T 17 Fallsbrook rd SW16
33 P 10 Falmer rd E17
31 N 15 Falmer rd N15
8 F 14 Falmer rd Enf
20 L 17 Falmouth av E4
35 P 16 Falmouth gdns Ilf
35 N 2 Falmouth gdns Wdfd Grn
150 E 1 Falmouth rd SE1
51 Y 15 Falmouth rd E15
110 L 10 Falmouth rd SE26
56 D 3 Fambridge rd Dgnhm
145 P 12 Fane st W14
134 A 19 Fann st EC1
134 J 11 Fanshaw st N1
54 C 18 Fanshawe av Bark
56 A 15 Fanshawe cres Dgnhm
102 D 10 Fanshawe rd Rich
86 M 7 Fanthorpe st SW15
115 S 5 Faraday av Sidcp
52 B 19 Faraday rd E15
105 Z 14 Faraday rd SW19
106 A 14 Faraday rd SW19
128 L 20 Faraday rd W10
61 W 18 Faraday rd W3
58 K 18 Faraday rd S'hall
96 M 7 Faraday rd Well
97 N 8 Faraday rd Welling
150 G 12 Faraday st SE17
140 E 5 Fareham st W1
127 X 16 Faringdon av Brom
64 M 1 Faringford rd E15
95 N 1 Farjeon rd SE3
126 D 16 Farleigh av Brom
49 U 12 Farleigh pl N16
49 V 12 Farleigh rd N16
93 T 17 Farley rd SE6
157 Z 18 Farley rd S Croy
86 H 19 Farlington pl SW15
87 N 8 Farlow rd SW15
88 B 10 Farlton rd SW18
45 T 10 Farm av NW2
108 A 9 Farm av SW16
22 G 20 Farm av Harrow
42 E 18 Farm av Wemb
21 Y 12 Farm clo Buck HI
69 W 1 Farm clo Dgnhm
58 W 19 Farm clo S'hall
154 H 16 Farm clo Sutton
158 M 2 Farm dri Croy
21 Y 1 Farm dri Croy
145 V 16 Farm la SW6
158 M 3 Farm la Croy
137 S 13 Farm pl W8
99 X 11 Farm pl Drtfrd

17 X 5 Farm rd N21
12 G 17 Farm rd Edg
82 C 20 Farm rd Hounsl
120 A 12 Farm rd Mrdn
138 W 11 Farm rd Sutton
139 W 11 Farm st W1
98 G 16 Farm vale Bxly
21 Y 13 Farm way Buck HI
153 N 4 Farm way Worc Pk
27 X 17 Farm wlk NW11
112 F 1 Farmcote rd SE12
154 J 16 Farmdale rd Carsh
51 R 3 Farmer rd E10
137 T 13 Farmer st W8
149 Y 19 Farmers rd SE5
111 Y 12 Farmfield rd Brom
112 A 13 Farmfield rd Brom
107 V 19 Farmhouse rd SW16
50 M 1 Farmilo rd E17
33 N 20 Farmilo rd E17
154 H 5 Farmington av Sutton
113 Y 11 Farmland wlk Chisl
7 T 6 Farmlands Enf
40 G 19 Farmlands the Grnfd
111 N 14 Farmleigh N14
111 S 9 Farmstead rd SE6
23 R 6 Farmstead rd Harrow
55 T 11 Farmway Dgnhm
94 M 11 Farnaby rd SE9
111 Y 19 Farnaby rd Brom
112 A 20 Farnaby rd Brom
126 B 1 Farnaby rd Brom
33 R 10 Farnan av E17
42 A 12 Farnan rd SW16
32 G 11 Farnborough av E17
158 H 17 Farnborough av S Croy
143 U 18 Farncombe st SE16
17 X 9 Farndale av N13
59 N 8 Farndale av Grnfd
83 R 8 Farnell rd Islwth
15 R 2 Farnham clo N20
141 Y 14 Farnham pl SE1
36 M 20 Farnham rd Ilf
97 U 4 Farnham rd Welling
149 P 12 Farnham royal SE11
31 Y 2 Farningham rd N17
20 L 2 Farnley rd E4
123 P 9 Farnley rd SE25
144 H 2 Faroe rd W14
7 S 5 Farorna wlk Enf
109 U 14 Farquhar rd SE19
105 Y 7 Farquhar rd SW19
122 L 19 Farquharson rd Croy
67 Z 6 Farr av Bark
8 B 7 Farr rd Enf
37 Z 20 Farrance rd Rom
52 A 14 Farrance rd Rom
64 A 17 Farrance st E14
30 J 6 Farrant av N22
128 L 14 Farrant rd W10
110 G 4 Farren rd SE23
63 Z 18 Farrence st E14
29 X 13 Farrer rd N8
24 J 14 Farrer rd Harrow
47 U 20 Farrier st NW1
133 U 18 Farringdon rd EC1
133 U 17 Farringdon rd EC1
141 W 5 Farringdon st EC4
143 Y 12 Farthing fields E1
115 S 9 Farwell rd Sidcp
112 E 20 Farwig la Brom
143 O 2 Fashion st E1
127 N 8 Fashoda rd Brom
49 X 17 Fassett rd E8
116 J 8 Fassett rd Kingst
49 X 17 Fassett sq E8
73 V 17 Fauconberg rd W4
37 S 20 Fauna clo Rom
149 X 11 Faunce st SE17
87 Y 2 Favart rd SW6
21 O 6 Faversham av E4
8 B 19 Faversham av Enf
92 M 21 Faversham rd SE6
124 M 3 Faversham rd Becknhm
120 B 14 Faversham rd Mrdn
156 K 6 Fawcett rd Croy
146 A 14 Fawcett rd Croy
87 V 11 Fawe Pk rd SW15
64 D 15 Fawe st E14
45 Z 16 Fawley rd NW6
46 A 16 Fawley rd NW6
31 Y 12 Fawley rd N17
65 X 6 Fawn rd E13
90 K 12 Fawnbrake av SE24
61 Y 1 Fawood av NW10

108 C 4 Faygate rd SW2
107 V 12 Fayland av SW16
91 R 4 Fearnley rd SE5
77 S 12 Fearon st SE10
158 L 11 Featherbed la Croy
159 N 20 Featherbed la Croy
76 K 16 Feathers st SE10
110 B 4 Featherstone av SE23
13 X 20 Featherstone rd NW7
70 A 8 Featherstone rd S'hall
134 E 16 Featherstone st EC1
70 C 7 Featherstone ter S'hall
90 H 6 Featley rd SW9
60 E 5 Federal rd Grnfd
80 F 12 Federation rd SE2
23 Z 5 Felbridge av Stanm
24 A 5 Felbridge av Stanm
108 F 9 Felbridge clo SW16
154 C 19 Felbridge clo Sutton
54 L 5 Felbrigge rd Ilf
93 R 16 Felday rd SE13
87 U 2 Felden st SW6
22 C 3 Feldon clo Pinn
74 J 11 Felgate ms W6
113 Y 5 Felhampton rd SE9
56 J 12 Felhurst cres Dgnhm
30 A 17 Felix av N8
59 Z 20 Felix rd W13
71 X 1 Felix rd W13
63 N 6 Felix st E2
62 K 8 Felixstowe rd NW10
31 U 10 Felixstowe rd N17
18 L 12 Felixstowe rd N9
80 E 9 Felixstowe rd SE2
156 M 5 Fell rd Croy
91 V 13 Fellbrigg rd SE22
135 Y 18 Fellbrigg st E1
102 B 8 Fellbrook Rich
154 J 4 Fellowes rd Carsh
46 K 19 Fellows rd NW3
77 T 12 Felltram way SE7
89 Z 11 Felmersham clo SW4
124 C 4 Felmingham rd SE20
56 G 10 Fels clo Dgnhm
90 B 17 Fels Farm av Dgnhm
86 M 7 Felsberg rd SW2
87 R 9 Felsham rd SW15
79 Y 14 Felsham rd SW15
35 V 6 Felspar clo SE11
34 G 20 Felstead av Ilf
65 Z 18 Felstead rd E11
38 K 1 Felstead rd E16
50 M 18 Felstead rd Rom
121 N 3 Felstead st E9
127 Z 15 Feltham rd Mitch
56 ... Felton clo Brom
114 K 11 Felton gdns Bark
114 K 12 Felton lea Sidcp
72 C 5 Felton lea Sidcp
67 V 5 Felton rd W13
134 G 5 Felton rd Bark
142 K 7 Felton st N1
96 J 14 Fen ct EC3
65 P 19 Fen gro Sidcp
36 D 3 Fen st E16
142 J 7 Fencepiece rd Ilf
142 L 7 Fenchurch av EC3
142 J 8 Fenchurch bldgs EC3
150 L 2 Fenchurch st EC3
65 R 18 Fendall st SE1
80 H 4 Fendt clo E16
145 R 6 Fendyke rd Blvdr
151 U 19 Fenelon pl W14
32 A 4 Fenham rd SE15
112 E 15 Fenman ct N17
50 D 15 Fenn clo Brom
78 K 17 Fenn st E9
152 C 20 Fennell st SE18
151 W 1 Fennells mead Epsom
15 T 18 Fenner rd SE16
148 L 15 Fenstanton av N12
149 R 18 Fentiman rd SW8
30 M 1 Fentiman rd SW8
65 X 20 Fenton N17
91 X 8 Fenton av E13
89 Z 8 Fenwick gdns SE15
91 X 8 Fenwick rd SW9
47 R 20 Fenwick rd SE15
47 P 20 Ferdinand pl NW1
48 J 16 Ferdinand st NW1
117 N 11 Fergus rd N5
48 D 1 Ferguson av Surb
30 B 16 Ferme Pk rd N4
110 K 2 Ferme Pk rd N8
129 P 18 Fermor rd SE23
           Fermoy rd W9

58 K 13 Fermoy rd Grnfd
121 Y 8 Fern av Mitch
60 B 14 Fern dene W13
70 D 15 Fern la Hounsl
64 B 12 Fern st E3
41 V 14 Fernbank av Wemb
96 H 14 Fernbank av Sidcp
40 J 2 Fernbrook dri Harrow
93 Y 15 Fernbrook rd SE13
94 A 15 Fernbrook rd SE13
49 W 14 Ferncliffe rd E8
45 Z 11 Ferncroft av NW3
15 Y 18 Ferncroft av N12
126 L 4 Ferndale Brom
33 W 15 Ferndale av E17
82 C 8 Ferndale av Hounsl
52 B 6 Ferndale rd E11
52 J 20 Ferndale rd E7
31 V 17 Ferndale rd N15
124 A 12 Ferndale rd SE25
89 Z 9 Ferndale rd SW4
90 D 9 Ferndale rd SW9
38 L 7 Ferndale rd Rom
66 L 19 Ferndale st E6
23 V 13 Ferndale ter Harrow
38 F 19 Ferndene way Rom
90 M 10 Ferndene rd SE24
91 N 8 Ferndene rd SE24
59 N 9 Ferndown rd SE9
16 B 4 Ferney rd Barnt
35 P 16 Fernhall dri Ilf
122 L 7 Fernham rd Thntn Hth
129 P 11 Fernhead rd W9
129 P 15 Fernhead rd W9
33 X 8 Fernhill ct E17
102 H 13 Fernhill gdns Kingst
78 G 3 Fernhill st E16
76 L 16 Fernholme rd SE15
12 B 18 Fernhurst gdns Edg
87 T 1 Fernhurst rd SW6
123 Z 19 Fernhurst rd Croy
107 T 2 Fernlea rd SW12
121 C 2 Fernlea rd Mitch
22 L 26 Fernleigh ct Harrow
42 J 6 Fernleigh ct Wemb
17 U 7 Fernleigh rd N21
53 B 18 Ferns rd E15
133 S 18 Fernsbury st WC1
146 B 16 Fernshaw rd SW10
21 U 4 Fernside NW3
42 L 16 Fernside Buck HI
12 N 18 Fernside av NW7
89 N 19 Fernside rd SW12
107 V 15 Fernthorpe rd SW16
49 O 14 Ferntower rd N5
41 V 10 Fernwood av SW16
42 C 17 Fernwood av Wemb
16 C 15 Fernwood cres N20
6 B 3 Ferny hill Barnt
155 X 8 Ferrers av Wallgtn
107 V 13 Ferrers rd SW16
30 C 14 Ferrestone rd N8
131 T 9 Ferrett pas NW1
88 B 11 Ferrier st SW18
14 N 4 Ferring clo Harrow
109 S 6 Ferrings rd SE21
158 L 6 Ferris av Croy
91 X 11 Ferris rd SE22
49 Z 10 Ferron rd E5
78 J 8 Ferry appr SE18
31 Y 12 Ferry la N17
74 E 17 Ferry la SW13
72 J 18 Ferry la Brentf
73 N 17 Ferry la Rich
74 F 20 Ferry rd SW13
86 G 1 Ferry rd SW13
116 A 16 Ferry rd Surb
102 A 12 Ferry rd Tedd
76 F 13 Ferry st E14
58 H 8 Ferrymead av Grnfd
59 O 6 Ferrymead gdns Grnfd
102 B 7 Ferrymore Rich
73 O 7 Festing rd SW15
154 M 9 Festival wlk Carsh
141 T 4 Fetter la EC4
37 V 3 Fews la Rom
20 C 19 Ffinch st SE8
126 L 4 Field clo E4
20 C 19 Field clo Brom
141 R 1 Field clo Buck HI
141 R 1 Field ct WC1
101 W 10 Field end Tedd
40 C 14 Field End rd Ruis
72 D 19 Field la Brentf
101 Y 13 Field la Tedd
133 U 10 Field pl EC1
118 C 14 Field pl New Mald
33 N 14 Field rd E17

52 E 14 Field rd E7
31 P 10 Field rd N17
44 L 13 Field rd W6
33 N 11 Field st WC1
61 W 1 Field way NW10
59 S 15 Field way Croy
59 T 13 Field way Croy
07 W 20 Fieldend rd SW16
20 K 4 Fieldgate la Mitch
43 T 3 Fieldgate st E1
07 W 2 Fieldhouse rd SW12
01 N 8 Fielding av Twick
74 A 7 Fielding rd W14
74 A 7 Fielding rd W3
73 Z 18 Fielding rd W4
10 C 1 Fieldings the SE23
37 V 15 Fields Park cres Rom
53 S 11 Fieldsend rd Sutton
11 X 13 Fieldside rd Brom
06 F 2 Fieldview SW18
55 S 11 Fieldway Dgnhm
48 G 16 Fieldway cres N5
55 S 15 Fife rd E16
30 K 3 Fife rd N22
85 V 14 Fife rd SW14
16 H 3 Fife rd Kingst
33 O 7 Fife ter N1
53 T 12 Fifth av E12
28 K 15 Fifth av W10
8 H 17 Fifth av Enf
01 P 6 Fifth Cross rd Twick
07 O 18 Figges rd Mitch
49 W 5 Filey av N16
6 F 8 Filebrook av Enf
52 A 1 Filebrook rd E11
51 Y 3 Filebrook rd E11
87 T 1 Filmer rd SW6
45 N 16 Filmer rd SW6
81 W 14 Filton rd Erith
45 X 12 Finborough rd
       SW10
06 M 16 Finborough rd
       SW7
09 N 11 Finch av SE27
43 N 10 Finch clo NW10
42 G 6 Finch la E3
42 E 16 Finch rd E16
80 A 8 Finchale rd SE2
34 M 1 Finchingfield av
       Wdfd Grn
15 N 20 Finchley ct N12
27 O 12 Finchley la NW4
55 S 12 Finchley pk N12
30 E 8 Finchley pl NW8
27 W 15 Finchley rd NW11
45 X 4 Finchley rd NW3
46 D 18 Finchley rd NW3
30 F 3 Finchley rd NW8
27 Y 1 Finchley way N3
14 K 20 Finchley way N3
14 T P 19 Finck st SE1
52 K 16 Findon rd E7
64 G 16 Findon st E14
40 K 10 Findon clo Harrow
18 L 5 Findon rd W12
74 G 4 Findon rd W12
92 G 8 Finland rd SE4
87 P 2 Finlay st SW6
74 J 1 Finnemore rd Ilf
35 X 15 Finnis st E2
61 N 1 Finnis st E2
55 Z 20 Finnymore rd Dgnhm
42 A 20 Finnymore rd Dgnhm
42 H 1 Finsbury av EC2
42 G 2 Finsbury cir EC2
24 J 19 Finsbury mkt EC2
48 J 3 Finsbury pk N4
30 K 20 Finsbury Pk av N4
48 H 7 Finsbury Pk rd N4
30 B 4 Finsbury rd N22
34 G 20 Finsbury sq EC2
34 E 20 Finsbury sq EC2
90 M 9 Finsen rd SE5
36 F 4 Finstock rd W10
57 W 17 Finucane gdns
       Rainhm
10 B 7 Finucane rd Bushey
       Watford
18 E 13 Fir gro New Mald
61 Z 4 Fir of Sutton
59 O 7 Fir Tree gdns Croy
55 N 18 Fir Tree gro Carsh
82 C 11 Fir Tree rd Hounsl
56 K 10 Fir Tree wlk Dgnhm
8 C 11 Fir Tree wlk Enf
92 B 4 Firbank rd SE15
52 Y 9 Fircroft gdns Harrow
06 M 6 Fircroft rd SW17
53 M 4 Firebell all Surb
55 Z 16 Firefly clo Wallgtn
72 M 7 Firework rd Mitch
11 N 9 Firhill rd SE6
29 P 12 Firs av N10

85 W 11 Firs av SW14
29 P 12 Firs clo N10
17 Y 3 Firs la N21
18 B 6 Firs Park av N21
18 A 6 Firs Park gdns N21
60 F 15 Firs the W5
21 S 15 Firs wlk Wdfd Grn
158 F 1 Firsby av Croy
49 V 3 Firsby rd N16
17 Y 10 Firscroft N13
53 R 13 First av E12
65 T 10 First av E13
33 P 14 First av E17
27 N 13 First av N4
19 P 15 First av N18
86 A 7 First av SW14
146 M 4 First av SW3
129 N 16 First av W10
74 D 3 First av W3
69 V 5 First av Dgnhm
8 G 18 First av Enf
152 A 19 First av Epsom
37 V 4 First av Rom
80 G 19 First av Welling
42 H 6 First av Wemb
101 S 3 First Cross rd Twick
43 T 12 First way Wemb
118 L 4 Firstway SW20
52 C 12 Firswood av Epsom
152 C 11 Firswood av Epsom
87 S 3 Firth gdns SW6
121 N 2 Firtree av Mitch
152 E 10 Firtree clo Epsom
142 G 10 Fish St hill EC3
58 G 8 Fisher clo Grnfd
23 X 6 Fisher rd Harrow
65 R 14 Fisher st E16
140 M 2 Fisher st WC1
81 Y 3 Fisher's way Blvdr
73 Z 12 Fishers la W4
130 F 17 Fisherton st NW8
142 F 10 Fishmongers Hall st
       EC4
106 L 7 Fishponds rd SW17
106 K 8 Fishponds rd SW17
100 M 13 Fitz Dygram clo
       Hampt
144 M 6 Fitz James av W14
144 L 7 Fitz-George av W14
27 V 10 Fitzalan rd SE11
149 S 5 Fitzalan st SE11
103 Z 19 Fitzgeorge av Kingst
86 B 9 Fitzgerald av SW14
34 F 17 Fitzgerald rd E11
85 Y 7 Fitzgerald rd SW4
139 T 4 Fitzhardinge st W1
88 H 16 Fitzhugh gro SW18
157 Z 4 Fitzjames av Croy
4 H 14 Fitzjohn av Barnt
46 F 17 Fitzjohn's av NW3
139 X 12 Fitzmaurice pl W1
62 D 17 Fitzneal st W12
46 M 5 Fitzroy clo N6
132 B 18 Fitzroy gdns W11
109 S 18 Fitzroy gdns SE19
132 A 19 Fitzroy ms W1
46 M 5 Fitzroy pk N6
47 N 3 Fitzroy rd N6
131 T 2 Fitzroy rd NW1
132 A 18 Fitzroy sq W1
132 B 19 Fitzroy st W1
55 T 15 Fitzstephen rd
       Dgnhm
47 V 3 Fitzwarren gdns N19
84 M 6 Fitzwilliam av Rich
85 N 6 Fitzwilliam av Rich
89 V 7 Fitzwilliam rd SW4
56 A 11 Five Elms rd Dgnhm
31 O 19 Fladbury rd N15
34 A 18 Fladgate rd E11
23 Z 18 Flambard la Harrow
63 V 17 Flamborough st E14
78 C 14 Flamstead rd SE7
68 F 2 Flamstead rd Dgnhm
55 T 20 Flamstead rd Dgnhm
43 P 19 Flamstead av Wemb
74 E 8 Flanchford rd W12
66 G 7 Flanders rd E6
74 C 10 Flanders rd W4
50 E 17 Flanders way E9
143 R 9 Flank st E1
46 E 12 Flask walk NW3
119 Z 16 Flaxley rd Mrdn
140 E 6 Flaxman st W1
90 L 5 Flaxman rd SE5
132 H 14 Flaxman ter WC1
79 H 19 Flaxton rd SE18
10 J 16 Flecker clo Stanm
116 D 19 Fleece rd Surb
32 L 6 Fleeming clo E17
32 M 7 Fleeming rd E17
141 X 5 Fleet la EC4
46 K 14 Fleet rd NW3

141 T 6 Fleet st EC4
44 H 15 Fleetwood rd NW10
117 W 5 Fleetwood rd New
       Mald
117 W 6 Fleetwood sq New
       Mald
49 S 7 Fleetwood st N16
156 F 11 Fleming ct Croy
106 L 18 Fleming mead Mitch
149 X 13 Fleming rd SE17
58 M 17 Fleming rd S'hall
50 K 3 Flempton rd E10
51 U 1 Fletcher la E10
73 W 7 Fletcher rd W4
143 T 8 Fletcher st E1
50 C 10 Fletching rd E5
141 T 5 Fleur De Lis ct WC2
134 M 19 Fleur De Lis st E1
87 P 20 Fleur gates SW19
31 P 3 Flexmere gdns N17
31 R 4 Flexmere rd N17
111 Z 13 Flimwell clo Brom
150 G 8 Flint st SE17
150 K 9 Flinton st SE17
140 H 5 Flitcroft st WC2
143 S 19 Flockton st SE16
60 L 16 Flodden rd SE5
146 L 11 Flood st SW3
146 K 12 Flood wlk SW3
64 C 17 Flora clo E14
74 H 10 Flora gdns W6
37 S 19 Flora gdns Rom
81 P 14 Flora st Blvdr
140 L 7 Floral st WC2
7 Y 11 Florence av Enf
120 D 12 Florence av Mrdn
64 M 5 Florence cotts SE4
7 Y 10 Florence dri Enf
73 V 17 Florence gdns W4
65 R 7 Florence rd E13
26 L 12 Florence rd NW4
48 E 2 Florence rd N4
92 M 2 Florence rd SE14
80 G 10 Florence rd SE2
106 A 15 Florence rd SW19
73 X 7 Florence rd W4
60 V 20 Florence rd W5
72 J 1 Florence rd W5
124 G 4 Florence rd
       Becknhm
126 F 1 Florence rd Brom
139 N 19 Florence rd Kingst
157 N 20 Florence rd S Croy
70 A 9 Florence rd S'hall
65 P 12 Florence st E16
133 X 2 Florence st N1
92 M 1 Florence ter SE14
154 F 7 Florian av Sutton
87 U 10 Florian rd SW15
10 C 7 Florida clo Bushey
       (watf)
108 J 20 Florida rd Thntn Hth
122 J 1 Florida rd Thntn Hth
135 T 13 Florida st E2
24 C 4 Floriston clo Stanm
24 C 4 Floriston gdns
       Stanm
105 S 1 Florys ct SW19
86 M 6 Floss st SW15
143 O 2 Flower And Dean st
       E1
13 R 18 Flower la NW7
111 V 12 Flowerhouse clo SE6
111 V 14 Flowerhouse est SE6
107 O 4 Flowersmead SW17
77 Y 13 Floyd rd SE7
93 Z 10 Fludyer st SE13
31 X 1 Foley st W1
134 M 20 Folgate sq E1
134 L 20 Folgate st EC2
62 C 18 Foliot st W12
65 N 5 Folkestone rd E6
33 R 13 Folkestone rd E17
66 K 7 Folkestone rd E6
18 K 14 Folkestone rd N18
14 H 17 Folkington corner
       N12
64 F 18 Follett st E14
5 T 11 Folly house Barnt
32 J 3 Folly la E17
76 H 6 Folly wall E14
108 C 17 Fontaine rd SW16
89 P 9 Fontarabia rd SW11
39 P 9 Fontayne av Rom
149 W 8 Fontenoy pas SE11
107 U 4 Fontenoy rd SW4
34 M 6 Fonteyne gdns Ilf
48 E 6 Fonthill rd N4
86 F 20 Fontley way SW15
40 H 17 Fontwell clo Grnfd
23 T 1 Fontwell clo Harrow
127 V 12 Fontwell dri Brom
41 V 3 Football la Harrow

115 V 15 Footscray High st
       Sidcp
115 U 3 Footscray la Sidcp
115 U 9 Footscray place
       Sidcp
114 B 4 Footscray rd SE9
95 X 15 Footscray rd SE9
143 T 8 Forbes st E1
49 X 4 Forburg rd N16
41 P 1 Force clo Harrow
63 W 5 Ford rd E3
69 F 1 Ford rd Dgnhm
65 C 20 Ford rd Dgnhm
69 F 1 Ford rd Dgnhm
68 N 16 Ford sq E1
143 Y 3 Ford sq E1
65 P 17 Ford st E16
63 W 5 Ford st E3
126 K 5 Forde av Brom
93 W 20 Fordel rd E6
5 V 12 Fordham clo Barnt
5 W 13 Fordham rd Barnt
143 V 3 Fordham st E1
73 O 1 Fordhook av W5
129 R 14 Fordingley rd W9
28 M 14 Fordington rd N6
111 O 3 Fordmill rd SE6
17 X 5 Fords gro N21
55 T 17 Fords Park rd E16
45 S 13 Fordwych rd NW2
93 U 14 Fordwych ce SE13
56 A 5 Fordyke rd Dgnhm
142 D 2 Fore st EC2
142 E 2 Fore st EC2
18 H 19 Fore st N18
90 K 5 Foreign st SE5
27 R 5 Foreland ct NW4
79 S 10 Foreland st SE18
144 D 7 Foreman ct W6
75 Y 12 Foreshore SE8
20 M 2 Forest appr E4
34 D 1 Forest appr Wdfd
       Grn
21 N 2 Forest av E4
34 D 16 Forest clo E11
21 U 12 Forest clo Wdfd Grn
34 A 13 Forest ct E11
21 R 6 Forest ct E4
53 O 10 Forest dri Wdfd Grn
33 Z 2 Forest dri Wdfd Grn
33 X 20 Forest dri east E11
51 V 1 Forest Dri west E10
21 Z 12 Forest edge Buck Hl
26 A 14 Forest gate NW9
31 U 7 Forest gdns N17
33 Z 18 Forest glade E11
34 A 18 Forest glade E11
20 M 17 Forest glade E4
49 U 19 Forest gro E8
92 B 16 Forest Hill rd SE22
35 W 1 Forest house Wdfd
       Grn
52 D 15 Forest la E15
33 X 2 Forest Mt rd Wdfd
       Grn
51 V 1 Forest rd E11
33 X 20 Forest rd E11
51 Z 16 Forest rd E15
32 C 13 Forest rd E17
33 O 10 Forest rd E17
52 F 11 Forest rd E7
49 T 19 Forest rd E8
19 N 5 Forest rd N9
99 W 2 Forest rd Erith
36 H 4 Forest rd Ilf
73 P 19 Forest rd Rich
38 H 11 Forest rd Rom
119 X 18 Forest rd Sutton
2 S 11 Forest rd Wdfd Grn
33 Y 12 Forest ri E17
33 X 14 Forest ri E17
125 O 5 Forest ridge
       Becknhm
2 O 3 Forest side E4
52 G 11 Forest side E7
21 X 5 Forest side Buck Hl
118 D 19 Forest side Worc Pk
52 F 15 Forest st E7
34 A 13 Forest the E11
52 C 1 Forest view E11
20 K 1 Forest view E4
33 X 16 Forest View av E10
53 P 12 Forest View rd E12
33 U 4 Forest View rd E17
26 E 20 Forest way Sidcp
21 W 13 Forest way Wdfd
       Grn
21 U 12 Forest way Wdfd
       Grn
16 K 13 Forestdale N14
92 A 9 Forester rd SE15
63 W 11 Forester st E3

98 F 10	Foresters cres Bxly Hth	
33 X 14	Foresters dri E17	
155 Y 17	Foresters dri Wallgtn	
156 A 20	Foresters dri Wallgtn	
110 B 4	Forestholme clo SE23	
30 H 4	Forfar rd N22	
89 P 1	Forfar rd N22	
100 B 13	Forge la Felt	
153 S 16	Forge la Sutton	
24 D 10	Formby av Stanm	
129 Z 18	Formosa st W9	
27 X 19	Forres gdns NW11	
122 C 7	Forrest gdns SW16	
139 N 5	Forset st W1	
111 W 7	Forster Memorial park SE6	
31 U 9	Forster rd N17	
89 Z 18	Forster rd SW2	
124 H 6	Forster rd Bcknhm	
122 L 15	Forster rd Croy	
134 C 8	Forston st N1	
149 X 14	Forsyte gdns SE17	
8 D 18	Forsyth pl Enf	
109 S 20	Forsythe cres SE19	
123 S 1	Forsythe cres SE19	
151 T 7	Fort rd SE1	
58 H 2	Fort rd Grnfd	
142 L 1	Fort st E1	
77 V 3	Fort st E16	
54 L 11	Forterie gdns Ilf	
135 X 1	Fortescue av E8	
63 N 1	Fortescue av E8	
101 N 6	Fortescue av Twick	
106 G 19	Fortescue rd SW19	
25 X 2	Fortescue rd SW19	
47 U 12	Fortess rd NW5	
47 T 14	Fortess wlk NW5	
89 O 9	Forthbridge rd SW11	
29 N 12	Fortis Green av N2	
29 P 11	Fortis Green rd N10	
29 P 11	Fortismere av N10	
47 Z 7	Fortnam rd N19	
62 B 2	Fortune Ga rd NW10	
45 Y 14	Fortune Green rd NW6	
11 V 1	Fortune la Borehmwd	
134 B 19	Fortune st EC1	
65 R 15	Forty Acre la E16	
43 O 8	Forty av Wemb	
42 M 9	Forty av Wemb	
43 N 3	Forty clo Wemb	
85 V 8	Forty footpath SW14	
8 H 2	Forty hill Enf	
43 T 8	Forty la Wemb	
12 C 20	Forum way Edg	
12 D 19	Forumside Edg	
137 Z 10	Fosbury ms W2	
26 J 19	Foscote rd NW4	
87 V 5	Foskett rd SW6	
156 F 12	Foss av Croy	
77 W 14	Fossdene rd SE7	
59 Z 14	Fosse way W13	
93 P 9	Fossil rd SE13	
80 J 10	Fossington rd Blvdr	
65 U 5	Fossway Dgnhm	
142 A 4	Foster la EC2	
26 M 14	Foster pl NW4	
65 S 11	Foster rd E13	
32 H 18	Foster rd E17	
62 A 19	Foster rd W3	
73 Y 14	Foster rd W4	
113 T 12	Fosters clo Chisl	
8 F 13	Fotheringham rd Enf	
140 B 7	Foubert's pl W1	
49 U 11	Foulden rd N16	
146 F 9	Foulis ter SW7	
107 N 8	Foulser rd SW17	
123 N 7	Foulsham rd Thntn Hth	
148 H 19	Fount st SW8	
141 S 8	Fountain ct WC2	
109 V 11	Fountain dri SE19	
106 H 10	Fountain rd SW17	
120 L 4	Fountain rd Mitch	
122 K 4	Fountain rd Thntn Hth	
100 F 6	Fountains av Felt	
100 F 5	Fountains clo Felt	
17 N 1	Fountains cres N14	
16 M 2	Fountains cres N14	
31 X 14	Fountayne rd N15	
49 W 7	Fountayne rd N16	
82 G 16	Four Square ct SE18	
10 C 2	Four tubs Bushey	
20 L 6	Four wents E4	
9 V 7	Fouracres Enf	
12 J 19	Fourland wlk Edg	
143 O 1	Fournier st E1	
53 S 12	Fourth av E12	
128 L 15	Fourth av W10	
81 H 14	Fourth av Enf	
56 M 5	Fourth av Rom	
101 P 4	Fourth Cross rd Twick	
43 J 13	Fourth way Wemb	
136 J 8	Fowell st W11	
35 O 15	Fowey av Ilf	
88 G 8	Fowler clo SW11	
52 E 12	Fowler rd E7	
133 Y 2	Fowler rd N1	
121 P 2	Fowler rd Mitch	
91 R 4	Fowler st SE5	
60 G 11	Fowlers wlk W5	
88 K 7	Fownes st SW11	
133 Y 2	Fox And Knot st EC1	
63 H 11	Fox clo E1	
65 S 16	Fox clo E16	
141 S 1	Fox ct EC1	
109 V 19	Fox hill SE19	
109 U 19	Fox hill gdns SE19	
81 V 12	Fox Ho rd Blvdr	
17 O 8	Fox la N13	
60 J 12	Fox lane W5	
65 O 16	Fox st E16	
120 H 4	Fox's path Mitch	
92 K 8	Foxberry rd SE4	
93 N 14	Foxborough gdns SE4	
107 R 4	Foxbourne rd SW17	
114 F 16	Foxbury av Chisl	
115 N 19	Foxbury av Sidcp	
112 G 16	Foxbury clo Brom	
112 G 16	Foxbury rd Brom	
159 T 14	Foxcombe Croy	
86 G 20	Foxcombe rd SW15	
95 Z 2	Foxcroft rd SE18	
158 C 20	Foxearth rd S Croy	
158 C 19	Foxearth spur S Croy	
94 D 8	Foxes dale SE3	
125 X 6	Foxes dale Brom	
111 S 18	Foxgrove av Becknhm	
111 U 19	Foxgrove rd Becknhm	
47 X 9	Foxham rd N19	
95 P 12	Foxhole rd SE9	
61 V 1	Foxholt gdns NW10	
56 K 14	Foxlands cres Dgnhm	
56 K 16	Foxlands rd Dgnhm	
149 V 18	Foxley clo SW9	
122 H 8	Foxley rd Thntn Hth	
88 L 3	Foxmore st SW11	
92 H 7	Foxwell st SE4	
94 B 10	Foxwood rd SE3	
31 Y 4	Foyle rd N17	
77 O 17	Foyle rd SE3	
14 K 12	Framfield clo N12	
48 J 14	Framfield rd N5	
59 V 17	Framfield rd W7	
109 O 9	Framfield rd Mitch	
113 S 9	Framlington cres SE9	
50 C 20	Frampton Pk rd E9	
82 B 12	Frampton rd Hounsl	
130 H 17	Frampton st NW8	
93 O 13	Francemary rd SE4	
20 C 18	Frances rd E4	
122 J 16	Frances rd Croy	
78 G 12	Frances st SE18	
106 D 7	Franche Ct rd SW17	
98 F 4	Francis av Bxly Hth	
23 Y 15	Francis av Harrow	
54 E 6	Francis av Ilf	
89 P 3	Francis Chichester way SW11	
105 U 16	Francis gro SW19	
51 T 4	Francis rd E10	
28 M 12	Francis rd N2	
60 C 4	Francis rd Grnfd	
23 Z 15	Francis rd Harrow	
82 A 6	Francis rd Hounsl	
54 E 6	Francis rd Ilf	
155 V 14	Francis rd Wallgtn	
51 Y 16	Francis st E15	
148 B 4	Francis st SW1	
54 D 6	Francis st Ilf	
141 T 7	Francis Taylor bldng EC4	
47 V 9	Francis ter N19	
106 M 12	Franciscan rd SW17	
107 O 10	Franciscan rd SW17	
12 C 10	Francklin gdns Edg	
12 C 10	Francklyn gdns Edg	
89 W 14	Franconia rd SW4	
91 S 20	Frank Dixon clo SE21	
109 T 1	Frank Dixon way SE21	
65 T 12	Frank st E13	
90 M 13	Frankfurt rd SE24	
91 N 13	Frankfurt rd SE24	
76 B 19	Frankham st SE8	
21 Y 17	Frankland clo Wdfd Grn	
20 A 15	Frankland rd E4	
15 R 2	Franklin clo N20	
121 V 8	Franklin cres Mitch	
95 R 8	Franklin pass SE9	
110 D 20	Franklin rd SE20	
97 Z 2	Franklin rd Bxly Hth	
117 P 5	Franklin rd Kingst	
64 E 9	Franklin st E3	
31 R 19	Franklin st N15	
147 R 10	Franklins row SW3	
44 D 19	Franklyn rd NW10	
117 W 9	Franks av New Mald	
127 Z 13	Frankswood av Brom	
91 X 1	Frankton rd SE15	
17 Z 14	Franlaw cres N13	
57 V 4	Frant rd Hornch	
110 A 7	Fransfield gro SE26	
122 H 11	Frant rd Thntn Hth	
33 T 17	Fraser rd E17	
18 L 11	Fraser rd N9	
60 D 4	Fraser rd Grnfd	
74 A 14	Fraser st W4	
81 Z 14	Frason rd Erith	
141 T 19	Frazier st SE1	
151 S 1	Frean st SE16	
139 S 18	Frederic ms NW1	
32 H 17	Frederic st E17	
20 K 2	Frederica rd E4	
48 B 20	Frederica st N7	
139 N 7	Frederick clo W2	
153 V 10	Frederick clo Sutton	
149 W 20	Frederick cres SW9	
9 P 9	Frederick cres Enf	
153 U 10	Frederick gdns Sutton	
78 M 13	Frederick pl SE18	
79 M 13	Frederick pl SE18	
149 Y 12	Frederick rd SE17	
153 V 10	Frederick rd Sutton	
51 W 20	Frederick st E15	
133 O 13	Frederick st WC1	
134 M 2	Frederick ter E8	
142 D 6	Frederick's pl EC2	
15 R 14	Fredericks pl N12	
57 V 18	Freeborne rd Rainham	
88 M 5	Freedom st SW11	
48 B 15	Freegrove rd N7	
27 R 7	Freeland pk NW4	
60 M 20	Freeland rd W5	
68 F 18	Freelands av S Croy	
112 J 20	Freelands gro Brom	
112 J 20	Freelands rd Brom	
26 J 1	Freeland rd NW4	
132 M 2	Freeling st N1	
133 N 2	Freeling st N1	
9 T 16	Freemantle av Enf	
81 T 11	Freemantle rd Blvdr	
36 B 8	Freemantle rd Ilf	
55 K 8	Freemantle st SE17	
65 U 15	Freemasons rd E16	
123 R 18	Freemasons rd Croy	
135 Z 4	Freemont st E9	
89 P 9	Freke rd SW11	
63 O 3	Fremont st E9	
92 G 10	Frendsbury rd SE4	
104 F 5	Frensham dri SW15	
159 U 17	Frensham dri Croy	
114 E 5	Frensham rd SE9	
151 T 15	Frensham st SE15	
88 K 5	Frere st SW11	
67 N 5	Fresh Wharf rd Bark	
106 D 6	Freshford st SW18	
107 P 14	Freshwater clo SW17	
138 M 2	Freshwater pl W1	
55 W 3	Freshwater rd Dgnhm	
37 S 14	Freshwell av Rom	
6 A 16	Freston gdns Barnt	
27 V 7	Freston pk N3	
98 A 12	Freta rd Bxly Hth	
51 W 18	Frewin rd SW18	
141 X 7	Friar st EC4	
15 X 12	Friars av N20	
61 Y 18	Friars gdns W3	
84 F 13	Friars la Rich	
61 Z 19	Friars Place la W3	
62 A 20	Friars Place la W3	
66 B 4	Friars rd E6	
84 K 16	Friars Stile rd Rich	
16 D 4	Friars walk N14	
61 Y 19	Friars way W3	
16 D 2	Friars wlk N14	
6 H 19	Friars wlk N14	
80 K 14	Friars wlk SE2	
23 U 3	Friars wlk Harrow	
158 H 19	Friarswood Croy	
15 X 15	Friary clo N12	
140 C 15	Friary ct SW1	
25 S 14	Friary la Wdfd Grn	
15 W 14	Friary park N12	
15 W 13	Friary rd N12	
131 U 18	Friary rd SE15	
61 X 17	Friary rd W3	
15 X 11	Friary way N12	
20 L 8	Friday hill E4	
20 M 11	Friday Hill east E4	
20 L 10	Friday Hill east E4	
20 L 9	Friday Hill west E4	
81 Z 13	Friday rd Erith	
106 L 19	Friday rd Mitch	
142 A 7	Friday st EC4	
47 U 16	Frideswide pl NW5	
133 W 12	Friend st EC1	
93 N 4	Friendly st SE4	
93 N 4	Friendly St ms SE4	
157 O 6	Friends rd Croy	
15 S 9	Friern Barnet la N20	
16 C 17	Friern Barnet rd N11	
15 R 3	Friern Mount dri N20	
15 S 15	Friern pk N12	
91 W 18	Friern rd SE22	
15 N 12	Friern Watch av N12	
156 B 11	Frimley av Wallgtn	
159 V 16	Frimley clo Croy	
159 V 17	Frimley cres Croy	
115 T 13	Frimley ct Sidcp	
120 J 6	Frimley gdns Mitch	
54 H 10	Frimley rd Ilf	
63 T 13	Frimley way E1	
33 X 2	Frinton dri Wdfd Grn	
35 W 18	Frinton mews Ilf	
31 T 19	Frinton rd N15	
107 P 16	Frinton rd SW17	
38 D 1	Frinton rd Rom	
115 Z 4	Frinton rd Sidcp	
87 Z 6	Friston st SW6	
88 A 6	Friston st SW6	
27 T 2	Frith ct NW7	
14 F 19	Frith la NW7	
27 T 1	Frith la NW7	
51 W 11	Frith rd E11	
156 L 3	Frith rd Croy	
140 F 7	Frith st W1	
118 A 14	Fritham clo New Mald	
136 B 13	Frithville gdns W12	
74 L 3	Frithville gdns W12	
56 G 9	Frizlands la Dgnhm	
30 G 13	Frobisher rd N8	
91 V 11	Frogley rd SE22	
87 Y 12	Frogmore SW18	
153 R 7	Frogmore clo Sutton	
70 F 7	Frogmore ct S'hall	
153 R 7	Frogmore gdns Sutton	
46 C 12	Frognal NW3	
23 V 14	Frognal av Harrow	
115 O 20	Frognal av Orp	
46 C 12	Frognal clo NW3	
46 D 7	Frognal ct NW3	
46 C 12	Frognal gdns NW3	
46 B 14	Frognal la NW3	
115 O 15	Frognal pl Sidcp	
46 C 11	Frognal ri NW3	
46 C 13	Frognal way NW3	
95 P 12	Froissart rd SE9	
30 H 10	Frome rd N15	
133 Z 7	Frome st N1	
34 C 1	Frome st N1	
153 S 11	Fromondes rd Sutton	
89 T 5	Froude st SW8	
66 A 2	Fry rd E6	
31 O 3	Fryatt rd N17	
64 M 18	Fryatt st E14	
133 U 8	Frye's bldgs N1	
25 P 18	Fryent clo NW9	
26 A 19	Fryent cres NW9	
26 A 19	Fryent gro NW9	
25 P 17	Fryent way NW9	
43 S 2	Fryent way NW9	
142 M 2	Frying Pan all E1	
157 Z 3	Fryston av Croy	
80 C 13	Fuchsia st SE2	
22 M 8	Fulbeck way Harrow	
33 T 4	Fulbourne rd E17	
47 V 11	Fulbrook ms N19	
47 V 11	Fulbrook rd N19	
75 N 6	Fulford st SE16	
143 Y 18	Fulford st SE16	
145 T 18	Fulham Broadway SW6	
87 T 5	Fulham High st SW6	
87 P 5	Fulham palace SW6	

87 U 5. Fulham Pk gdns SW6
87 U 4 Fulham Pk rd SW6
146 G 9 Fulham rd SW3
145 T 19 Fulham rd SW6
87 U 3 Fulham rd SW6
118 D 19 Fullbrooks av Worc Pk
135 R 15 Fuller st E2
26 L 12 Fuller st NW4
34 C 3 Fullers av Wdfd Grn
38 J 3 Fullers clo Rom
32 J 2 Fullers la Rom
34 B 3 Fullers rd E18
23 U 17 Fullerton rd SE25
88 C 13 Fullerton rd SW18
154 H 18 Fullerton rd Carsh
100 K 8 Fullwell park Twick
88 B 2 Fulmead st SW6
72 A 9 Fulmer way W13
33 W 16 Fulready rd E10
82 D 10 Fulstone clo Hounsl
94 E 5 Fulthorpe rd SE3
138 A 9 Fulton ms W2
43 R 11 Fulton rd Wemb
35 W 4 Fulwell av Ilf
36 B 6 Fulwell av Ilf
100 L 4 Fulwell Pk av Twick
101 N 4 Fulwell Pk av Twick
101 P 10 Fulwell rd Tedd
60 L 5 Fulwood av Wemb
83 X 16 Fulwood gdns Twick
141 R 2 Fulwood pl WC1
Furham feild Pinn
151 T 18 Furley pl SE15
151 T 19 Furley rd SE15
48 F 18 Furlong rd N7
88 A 18 Furmage st SW18
68 K 12 Furneaux av SE27
62 G 7 Furness rd NW10
86 B 4 Furness rd SW6
40 L 3 Furness rd Harrow
128 B 15 Furness rd Harrow
57 V 15 Furness way Hornch
141 T 3 Furnival st EC4
50 D 15 Furrow la E9
14 L 19 Fursby av N3
94 A 20 Further Green rd SE6
112 A 1 Further Green rd SE6
122 M 5 Furze rd Thntn Hth
64 B 14 Furze st E3
107 S 12 Furzedown dri SW17
107 T 11 Furzedown rd SW17
113 Z 14 Furzefield clo Chisl
77 V 18 Furzefield rd SE3
33 W 9 Fyfield rd E17
90 G 7 Fyfield rd SW9
8 D 12 Fyfield rd Enf
34 L 1 Fyfield rd Wdfd Grn
148 F 5 Fynes st SW1

G

99 W 13 Gable clo Dartford
92 G 18 Gabriel st SE23
43 O 18 Gaddesden av Wemb
65 N 13 Gage rd E16
132 M 20 Gage st WC1
133 R 4 Gainford st N1
41 T 17 Gainsboro gdns Grnfd
55 P 11 Gainsborough Dgnam
53 W 14 Gainsborough av E12
45 U 1 Gainsborough gdns NW11
46 G 11 Gainsborough gdns NW3
25 O 7 Gainsborough gdns Edgw
83 P 13 Gainsborough gdns Islwth
52 A 1 Gainsborough rd E11
65 N 10 Gainsborough rd E15
64 M 10 Gainsborough rd E15
15 O 16 Gainsborough rd N12
74 C 10 Gainsborough rd W4
117 Y 15 Gainsborough rd New Mald

50 L 18 Gainsborough sq E9
32 K 13 Gainsford rd E17
143 O 17 Gainsford st SE1
122 K 13 Gairgreen rd Thntn Hth
91 S 4 Gairloch rd SE5
47 U 17 Gaisford st NW5
114 B 2 Gaitskell rd SE9
112 G 8 Galahad rd Brom
74 F 20 Galata rd SW13
91 Z 7 Galatea rd SE15
95 F 7 Galbraith st E14
64 B 14 Gale st E3
55 V 20 Gale st Dgnhm
68 H 4 Gale st Dgnhm
33 X 2 Galeborough av Wdfd Grn
140 K 2 Galen pl WC1
74 K 11 Galena rd W6
63 N 10 Gales gdns E2
35 S 1 Gales way Wdfd Grn
88 D 17 Galesbury rd SW18
15 Y 6 Gallants Farm rd Barnt
58 A 7 Gallery gdns Grnfd
91 R 20 Gallery rd SE21
109 P 2 Gallery rd SE21
151 W 7 Galley Wall rd SE15
75 N 12 Galley Wall rd SE16
48 J 16 Gallia rd N5
9 N 20 Galliard av Enf
9 P 20 Galliard clo Enf
18 K 4 Galliard rd N9
19 O 1 Galliard rd N9
158 B 16 Gallop S Croy
154 F 19 Gallop Sutton
79 U 12 Gallosson rd SE18
74 G 2 Galloway rd W12
7 R 20 Gallus clo N21
94 G 8 Gallus sq SE3
122 B 10 Galpin's rd Thntn Hth
132 K 17 Galsen yd WC1
37 P 20 Galsworthy av Rom
45 T 12 Galsworthy rd NW2
103 S 19 Galsworthy rd Kingst
63 X 17 Galt st E14
128 K 15 Galton st W.10
87 W 13 Galveston rd SW15
134 C 14 Galway st EC1
89 T 5 Gambetta st SW8
141 X 15 Gambia st SE1
106 H 11 Gambole rd SW17
5 Z 12 Games rd Barnet
87 O 9 Gamlen rd SW15
153 W 13 Gander Grn la Sutton
156 B 16 Gant clo Croy
140 B 7 Ganton st W1
35 V 15 Gantshill cres Ilford
105 Z 11 Gap rd SW19
106 A 11 Gap rd SW19
139 U 1 Garbutt pl W1
133 Y 12 Gard st EC1
98 D 6 Garden av Bxlyhth
107 R 19 Garden av Mitch
12 C 19 Garden city Edg
19 Z 16 Garden clo E4
20 C 20 Garden clo SW9
58 B 3 Garden clo Grnfd
100 F 13 Garden clo Hampt
156 A 11 Garden clo Wallgtn
115 U 14 Garden cotts Sidcp
108 B 1 Garden la SW2
112 J 15 Garden la Brom
137 U 10 Garden ms W2
130 E 11 Garden rd NW8
124 C 1 Garden rd SE20
112 J 17 Garden rd Brom
85 P 9 Garden rd Rich
149 W 1 Garden row SE1
139 W 2 Garden row SE1
82 T 15 Garden st E1
148 E 8 Garden ter SW1
43 X 17 Garden way NW10
134 J 15 Garden wlk EC2
142 A 9 Gardeners la EC4
63 U 7 Gardeners rd E3
18 E 1 Gardenia rd Enf
91 X 10 Gardens SE22
125 V 2 Gardens Becknhm
22 M 18 Gardens Harrow
22 E 18 Gardens Pinn
44 M 14 Gardiner av NW2
34 H 18 Gardner clo E11
100 F 4 Gardnor gro Felt
65 U 12 Gardner rd E13
142 B 9 Gardners la EC4
46 F 12 Gardnor rd NW3
119 Z 16 Garendon gdns Mrdn
119 Z 16 Garendon rd Mrdn
120 A 18 Garendon rd Mrdn
121 F 9 Gareth gro Brom

65 P 13 Garfield rd E13
20 L 4 Garfield rd E4
16 F 17 Garfield rd N11
89 P 8 Garfield rd SW11
106 D 14 Garfield rd SW19
9 R 16 Garfield rd Enf
83 Z 20 Garfield rd Twick
64 A 20 Garford st E14
79 U 11 Garibaldi st SE18
79 T 19 Garland rd SE18
24 J 4 Garland st Stanm
142 C 9 Garlick hill EC4
110 J 6 Garlie's rd SE23
45 U 18 Garlinge rd NW2
32 B 2 Garman rd N17
133 T 13 Garnault ms EC1
133 U 14 Garnault pl EC1
33 T 4 Garnault rd E17
33 T 4 Garner rd E17
33 T 4 Garner st E2
44 B 18 Garnet rd NW10
123 N 9 Garnet rd Thntn Hth
75 O 1 Garnet st E1
143 Z 10 Garnet st E1
46 L 14 Garnett rd NW3
39 N 16 Garnham st N16
151 O 17 Garnies st SE15
107 X 8 Garrad's rd SW16
98 F 8 Garrard clo Bxly Hth
113 Z 10 Garrard clo Chisl
106 G 9 Garratt la SW18
88 A 14 Garratt la SW18
25 R 1 Garratt rd Edgw
106 J 11 Garratt ter SW17
12 D 20 Garrett rd Edg
144 B 17 Garrett st EC1
10 B 2 Garretts rd Bushey Watt
27 U 19 Garrick av NW11
84 F 12 Garrick cl Rich
27 N 9 Garrick dri NW4
26 E 18 Garrick rd NW9
58 L 12 Garrick rd Grnfd
85 R 6 Garrick rd Rich
140 J 9 Garrick st WC2
27 O 12 Garrick way NW4
140 J 9 Garrick yd WC2
4 H 19 Garrows field Barnt
39 R 3 Garry clo Rom
39 O 2 Garry way Rom
100 K 16 Garside clo Hampt
25 N 18 Garth SE15
100 L 14 Garth Hampt
102 L 12 Garth clo Kingst
119 O 17 Garth clo Mrdn
45 U 8 Garth rd NW2
73 X 15 Garth rd W4
102 L 13 Garth rd Kingstn
119 O 18 Garth rd Mrdn
25 N 18 Garth the Harrow
15 V 20 Garth way N12
92 F 18 Garthorne rd SE23
105 V 2 Gartmoor gdns SW19
54 L 5 Gartmore rd Ilf
88 B 16 Garton pl SW18
144 K 14 Garvan rd W6
65 W 17 Garvary rd E16
74 H 2 Garway rd W2
34 A 2 Gascoigne gdns Wdfd Grn
135 N 12 Gascoigne pl E2
67 R 6 Gascoigne rd Bark
159 W 20 Gascoigne rd Croy
119 T 1 Gascony av NW6
50 G 19 Gascoyne rd E9
76 H 1 Gaselee st E14
149 R 12 Gasholder pl SE11
89 T 17 Gaskarth rd SW12
89 S 4 Gaskarth rd Edg
28 M 18 Gaskell rd N6
89 Z 5 Gaskell st SW4
133 X 4 Gaskin st N1
107 N 11 Gassiot rd SW17
154 G 5 Gassiot way Sutton
144 H 13 Gastein rd W6
121 O 5 Gaston rd Mitch
151 X 2 Gataker st SE16
47 V 10 Gatcombe rd N19
138 L 19 Gate ms SW7
18 K 14 Gate rd N18
141 N 3 Gate st WC2
130 J 17 Gateforth st NW8
103 W 19 Gatehouse clo Kingst
90 D 8 Gateley rd SW9
134 J 16 Gatesborough st EC2
106 L 7 Gateside rd SW17
15 S 16 Gatestone rd SE19
150 C 13 Gateway SE17

100 G 5 Gatfield gro Felt
30 F 6 Gathorne rd N22
147 W 11 Gatliff rd SW1
79 Z 13 Gatling st SE2
80 A 14 Gatling st SE2
91 U 1 Gatonby st SE15
154 C 19 Gatton clo Sutton
106 K 9 Gatton rd SW17
17 V 1 Gatward clo N21
87 V 19 Gatwick rd SW18
89 X 6 Gauden clo SW4
89 X 7 Gauden rd SW4
41 Z 14 Gauntlett ct Wemb
42 A 14 Gauntlett ct Wemb
154 G 12 Gauntlett rd Sutton
92 C 4 Gautrey rd SE15
76 A 9 Gaverick st E14
94 H 19 Gavestone cres SE12
94 G 18 Gavestone rd SE12
79 U 11 Gavin st SE18
83 P 8 Gawber st E2
64 A 6 Gawthorne st E3
44 K 14 Gay clo NW2
56 J 13 Gay gdns Dgnhm
64 H 6 Gay rd E15
35 T 9 Gayfere rd Ilf
148 J 2 Gayfere st SW1
74 E 6 Gayford rd W12
49 X 20 Gayhurst rd E8
40 E 15 Gaylor rd Grnfd
35 R 1 Gaynes Hill rd Edfd Grn
110 F 4 Gaynesford rd SE23
154 M 17 Gaynesford rd Carsh
35 W 17 Gaysham av Ilf
35 Y 11 Gaysham hall Ilf
46 F 12 Gayton cres NW3
46 F 1 Gayton rd NW3
23 W 19 Gayton rd Harrow
88 M 16 Gayville rd SW11
33 O 10 Gaywood st SE17
139 X 2 Gaywood st SE1
149 W 11 Gaza st SE17
36 A 12 Geariesville gdns Ilf
44 H 14 Geary rd NW10
48 D 15 Geary st N7
30 M 4 Gedeney rd N17
31 N 3 Gedeney rd N17
133 Z 16 Gee st EC1
34 A 16 Gee st EC1
65 P 3 Geere rd E15
139 V 6 Gees st W1
113 S 16 Gefferys homes SE9
134 M 9 Geffrye museum E2
134 M 9 Geffrye st E2
151 W 19 Geldart rd SE15
49 Y 7 Geldestone rd E5
92 P 5 Gellatly rd SE14
38 G 2 Gelsthorpe rd Rom
18 L 10 General Gordon pl SE18
93 X 1 General Wolfe rd SE10
78 M 17 Genesta rd SE18
79 N 17 Genesta rd SE18
37 Y 16 Geneva gdns Rom
90 G 10 Geneva rd SW9
116 K 8 Geneva rd Kingst
122 L 10 Geneva rd Thntn Hth
90 H 11 Geneva ter SW9
20 C 15 Genever clo E4
19 N 18 Genista rd N18
86 M 13 Genoa av SW15
87 N 14 Genoa av SW15
124 B 1 Genoa rd SE20
8 C 13 Genotin rd Enf
7 Z 12 Gentlemans row Enf
65 T 10 Gentry gdns E13
92 K 7 Geoffrey rd SE4
150 H 19 Geogian clo Brom
146 G 3 Geological museum SW7
29 O 3 George cres N10
140 L 11 George ct WC2
142 F 15 George Inn yd SE1
34 G 8 George la E18
93 S 16 George la SE13
126 H 19 George la Brom
20 B 19 George rd E4
72 J 15 George rd Brentf
103 V 18 George rd Kingst
118 E 10 George rd New Mald
143 S 19 George row SE16
65 O 18 George st E6
139 T 3 George st W1
71 U 3 George st W7
54 B 20 George st Bark
156 M 4 George st Croy
157 O 3 George st Croy
82 E 4 George st Hounsl
84 H 12 George st Rich
39 T 17 George st Rom

70 B 11 George st S'hall
154 A 10 George st Sutton
22 F 10 George V av Pinn
22 G 11 George V clo Pinn
60 B 3 George V way Gnfd
139 V 8 George yd W1
48 E 15 George's rd N7
134 K 12 George's sq N1
76 H 20 Georgette pl SE10
35 Z 12 Georgeville gdns Ilf
122 J 2 Georgia rd Thntn Hth
10 K 20 Georgian clo Stanm
43 R 17 Georgian ct Wemb
132 B 3 Georgiana st NW1
135 O 12 Georgina gdns E2
112 G 9 Gerald ms SW1
147 V 6 Gerald ms SW1
65 O 12 Gerald rd E16
147 U 6 Gerald rd SW1
56 A 5 Gerald rd Dgnhm
88 C 14 Geraldine rd SW18
73 P 16 Geraldine rd W4
149 V 3 Geraldine st SE1
146 D 15 Gertrude rd Belv
25 X 5 Gervase rd Edg
25 X 5 Gervase rd Edgw
75 N 18 Gervase st SE14
151 Y 17 Gervase st SE14
111 O 4 Ghent st SE6
10 B 7 Giant Tree hill Bushey
92 D 5 Gibbon rd SE15
61 Z 19 Gibbon rd W3
62 A 19 Gibbon rd W3
102 K 19 Gibbon rd Kingst
86 H 12 Gibbon wlk SW15
43 Z 19 Gibbons rd NW10
19 P 14 Gibbs av N18
109 O 13 Gibbs av SE19
109 P 13 Gibbs clo SE19
12 K 14 Gibbs grn Edg
109 O 13 Gibbs sq SE19
145 P 14 Gibraltar wlk E2
63 R 11 Gibson clo E1
49 U 7 Gibson gdns N16
133 V 4 Gibson sq N1
76 L 14 Gibson st SE10
108 H 15 Gibson's hill SW16
39 V 9 Gidea clo Rom
39 V 8 Gidea park Rom
81 U 10 Gideon clo Blvdr
89 O 7 Gideon rd SW11
39 V 10 Gides av Rom
47 W 6 Giesbach rd N19
18 D 18 Giffard rd N18
78 F 19 Giffin st SE8
59 S 14 Gifford gdns W7
132 L 2 Gifford st N1
133 N 1 Gifford st N1
65 N 3 Gift la E15
25 W 4 Gilbert gro Edg
140 J 2 Gilbert pl WC1
149 V 6 Gilbert rd SE11
106 C 17 Gilbert rd SW19
81 R 9 Gilbert rd Belvdr
E 18 Gilbert rd Brom
39 T 13 Gilbert rd Rom
51 Y 13 Gilbert st E15
139 V 7 Gilbert st W1
106 J 11 Gilbey rd SW17
79 X 17 Gilbourne rd SE18
49 Y 5 Gilda av Enf
49 Y 5 Gilda cres N16
139 Z 2 Gilda st W1
47 O 15 Gilden rd NW5
78 K 16 Gildersome st SE18
109 T 10 Giles coppice SE19
91 R 15 Gilkes cres SE21
91 R 16 Gilkes pl SE21
65 S 19 Gill av E16
63 Z 19 Gill st E14
15 Y 5 Gillam clo Barnt
57 X 18 Gillam way Rainhm
10 A 7 Gillan grn Bushey Watf
48 G 10 Gillespie rd N5
66 D 6 Gillett av E6
123 N 9 Gillett rd Thntn Hth
49 S 16 Gillett st N16
143 V 19 Gillian Pk rd Sutton
93 P 12 Gillian st SE13
47 P 15 Gillies st NW5

147 Z 5 Gillingham ms SW1
45 S 10 Gillingham rd NW2
147 Z 6 Gillingham row NW7
147 Z 5 Gillingham st SW1
147 Z 5 Gillingham st SW1
148 A 5 Gillingham st SW7
65 O 3 Gillman dri E15
146 G 19 Gillray sq SW10
93 W 10 Gilmore rd SE13
85 Z 10 Gilpin av SW14
18 H 17 Gilpin cres N18
82 K 17 Gilpin cres Twick
50 H 12 Gilpin rd E5
57 T 19 Gilroy clo Rainham
123 O 9 Gilsland rd Thntn Hth
88 B 4 Gilstead rd SW6
146 C 12 Gilston rd SW10
111 Z 6 Gilton rd SE6
141 X 3 Giltspur st EC1
109 X 15 Gipsy hill SE19
86 H 9 Gipsy la SW15
108 M 10 Gipsy rd SE27
109 O 11 Gipsy rd SE27
80 H 20 Gipsy rd Welling
97 W 1 Gipsy rd Welling
108 M 11 Gipsy Rd gdns SE27
120 H 4 Girdlers rd W14
47 U 7 Girdlestone rd N19
87 T 18 Girdwood rd SW18
145 R 19 Gironde rd SW6
64 C 17 Girsud st E14
25 R 11 Girton av NW9
40 M 19 Girton clo Grnfd
159 N 4 Girton gdns Croy
110 F 12 Girton rd SE26
40 M 18 Girton rd Grnfd
41 N 17 Girton rd Grnfd
30 C 13 Gisburn rd N8
53 O 11 Gladding rd E12
124 H 16 Glade gdns Croy
70 J 6 Glade la S'hall
17 O 1 Glade the N21
77 X 19 Glade the SE7
127 O 4 Glade the Brom
124 H 15 Glade the Croy
7 T 10 Glade the Enf
152 H 12 Glade the Epsom
35 T 5 Glade the Ilf
153 T 19 Glade the Sutton
159 T 6 Glade the W Wkhm
12 U 8 Glade the Wdfd Grn
17 P 1 Gladeside N21
124 F 17 Gladeside Croy
31 V 17 Gladesmore rd N15
81 U 10 Gladeswood rd Belvdr
92 J 18 Gladiator st SE23
49 U 11 Glading ter N16
47 V 4 Gladsmuir rd N19
4 G 10 Gladsmuir rd Barnt
53 R 19 Gladstone av E12
30 J 6 Gladstone av N22
83 R 19 Gladstone av Twick
44 G 12 Gladstone park NW2
44 L 10 Gladstone Pk Gdn est NW2
44 L 9 Gladstone Pk gdns NW2
65 P 1 Gladstone rd E15
105 X 18 Gladstone rd SW19
73 X 9 Gladstone rd W4
21 X 5 Gladstone rd Buck Hl
123 P 17 Gladstone rd Croy
117 R 6 Gladstone rd Kingst
120 L 3 Gladstone rd Mitch
70 B 7 Gladstone rd S'hall
139 W 1 Gladstone st SE1
89 T 1 Gladstone ter SW8
30 C 19 Gladwell rd N8
112 G 15 Gladwell rd Brom
87 O 7 Gladwyn rd SW15
45 Y 19 Gladys rd NW6
76 F 18 Glaisher st SE10
63 R 20 Glamis pl E1
63 R 18 Glamis rd E1
40 M 19 Glamis way Grnfd
102 E 19 Glamorgan rd Kingst
148 U 3 Glanfield rd Beckenhm
11 U 13 Glanleam rd Stanm
126 J 7 Glanville rd Brom
100 F 2 Glasbrook av Twick
49 T 2 Glaserton rd N16
30 H 16 Glasford st SW17
65 U 6 Glasgow rd E13
12 J 15 Glasgow rd N18
63 S 19 Glass House fields E1
95 O 17 Glassbrook rd SE9
141 Y 18 Glasshill st SE1

140 C 10 Glasshouse st W1
148 M 9 Glasshouse wlk SE11
149 N 9 Glasshouse wlk SE11
29 W 17 Glasslyn rd N8
126 D 5 Glassmill la Brom
119 Z 16 Glastonbury la Mrdn
45 W 16 Glastonby st NW6
64 C 13 Glaucus st E3
101 U 17 Glazbrook rd Tedd
144 L 9 Glazbury rd W14
109 O 3 Glazebrook clo SE21
77 W 11 Glebe av Enf
24 J 10 Glebe av Harrow
144 H 4 Glebe av Mitch
21 S 20 Glebe av Wdfd Grn
27 N 12 Glebe cres NW4
24 K 11 Glebe cres Harrow
100 G 7 Glebe ct Felt
144 L 5 Glebe ct Mitch
11 P 16 Glebe ct Stanm
118 B 16 Glebe gdns New Mald
24 J 12 Glebe la Harrow
120 K 6 Glebe path Mitch
146 K 13 Glebe pl SW3
49 U 20 Glebe rd E8
44 E 18 Glebe rd NW10
28 E 5 Glebe rd N3
30 C 14 Glebe rd N8
86 F 4 Glebe rd SW13
112 F 20 Glebe rd Brom
154 M 13 Glebe rd Carsh
155 N 14 Glebe rd Carsh
56 H 19 Glebe rd Dgnhm
11 R 16 Glebe rd Stanm
11 R 17 Glebe rd Stanm
153 S 18 Glebe rd Sutton
83 W 16 Glebe side Twick
120 K 6 Glebe sq Mitch
73 Z 13 Glebe st W4
64 C 8 Glebe ter E3
94 A 7 Glebe the SE3
93 Z 7 Glebe the SE3
118 D 19 Glebe the Worc Pk
100 G 7 Glebe way Felt
159 Y 3 Glebe way W Wkhm
21 Y 17 Glebe way Wdfd Grn
99 T 10 Glebelands Drtfrd
34 E 8 Glebelands av E18
36 F 19 Glebelands av Ilf
54 E 1 Glebelands av Ilf
146 A 8 Gledhow gdns SW5
120 L 11 Gledstanes rd W14
10 B 7 Gleed Bushey Watf
10 B 7 Gleed av Bushey Watf
105 P 4 Glen Albyn rd SW19
21 V 20 Glen cres Wdfd Grn
156 G 7 Glen gdns Croy
65 X 11 Glen rd E13
21 V 19 Glen ri Wdfd Grn
155 S 18 Glen Road end Wallgtn
125 Z 3 Glen the Brom
158 G 4 Glen the Croy
7 W 1 Glen the Enf
22 C 20 Glen the Pinn
70 F 13 Glen the S'hall
42 H 12 Glen the Wemb
24 K 12 Glenalmond rd Harrow
50 C 13 Glenarm rd E5
52 A 20 Glenavon rd E15
95 Y 8 Glenbarr clo SE9
111 Z 14 Glenbow rd Brom
112 A 13 Glenbow rd Brom
7 P 13 Glenbrook North Enf
7 R 13 Glenbrook South Enf
45 X 16 Glenbrook rd NW6
116 J 15 Glenbuck rd Surb
106 M 6 Glenburnie rd SW17
60 C 13 Glencairn dri W5
108 B 18 Glencairn rd SW16
54 F 2 Glencoe av Ilf
56 E 11 Glencoe dri Dgnhm
30 E 2 Glenesk av N22
12 B 15 Glendale av Edg
55 S 1 Glendale av Rom
95 X 8 Glendale clo SE9
105 V 12 Glendale dri SW19
42 J 5 Glendale gdns Wemb
81 Y 10 Glendale rd Erith
90 C 9 Glendall st SW9
87 P 7 Glendarvon st SW15
31 Z 5 Glendish rd N17
12 M 14 Glendor gdns NW7
85 Y 8 Glendower gdns SW14
146 F 6 Glendower pl SW7
20 K 5 Glendower rd E4

79 Z 14 Glendown rd SE2
62 B 20 Glendun rd W3
107 V 19 Gleneagle rd SW16
11 O 20 Gleneagles Stanm
107 Z 10 Glenelon ms SW1
108 D 10 Glenelon rd SW16
90 A 12 Glenelg rd SW2
95 Y 13 Glenesk rd SE9
107 V 1 Glenfield rd SW4
42 A 14 Glenfield rd W13
72 B 5 Glenfield rd W13
76 A 8 Glengall causeway E14
76 F 8 Glengall gro E14
151 P 12 Glengall ms SE15
129 T 4 Glengall rd NW6
151 P 12 Glengall rd SE15
97 Z 7 Glengall rd Bxly Hth
12 F 10 Glengall rd Edg
21 U 19 Glengall rd Wdfd Grn
151 P 13 Glengall ter SE15
76 G 12 Glengarnock av E14
91 U 12 Glengarry rd SE22
35 Z 16 Glenham dri Ilf
95 Y 8 Glenhead clo SE9
27 Y 7 Glenhill clo N7
95 W 12 Glenhouse rd SE9
47 P 12 Glenhurst av NW5
15 U 15 Glenhurst rd N12
72 E 15 Glenhurst rd Brentf
108 M 18 Glenhurst ri SE19
46 J 17 Glenilla rd NW3
107 Y 19 Glenister Pk rd SW16
77 P 13 Glenister rd SE10
78 K 4 Glenister st E16
95 X 11 Glenlea rd SE9
46 J 16 Glenloch rd NW3
9 R 9 Glenloch rd Enf
77 T 18 Glenluce rd SE3
95 X 12 Glenlyon rd SE9
13 T 20 Glenmere av NW7
46 J 17 Glenmore rd NW3
96 K 2 Glenmore rd Welling
68 A 8 Glenmore way Bark
108 F 7 Glennie rd SE27
52 H 17 Glenny rd Bark
52 J 17 Glenparke rd E7
88 C 5 Glenrosa st SW6
136 B 4 Glenroy st W10
46 H 15 Glenroy st W12
92 L 8 Glensdale rd SE4
95 X 12 Glenshiel rd SE9
79 W 10 Glenside rd SE18
108 F 7 Glentanner way SW17
74 J 16 Glentham gdns SW13
74 J 16 Glentham rd SW13
124 B 19 Glenthorne av Croy
119 X 19 Glenthorne clo Sutton
35 Y 11 Glenthorne gdns Ilf
119 X 19 Glenthorne gdns Sutton
32 H 15 Glenthorne rd E17
16 B 16 Glenthorne rd N11
144 A 6 Glenthorne rd W6
74 K 11 Glenthorne rd W6
116 L 8 Glenthorne rd Kings
119 P 12 Glenthorpe rd Mrdn
39 P 1 Glenton clo Rom
93 Y 10 Glenton rd SE13
39 P 2 Glenton way Rom
131 P 18 Glentworth st NW1
95 X 13 Glenure rd SE9
80 B 16 Glenview SE2
127 O 4 Glenview rd Brom
8 A 4 Glenville av Enf
75 Z 20 Glenville gro SE8
103 O 20 Glenville rd Kingst
43 Z 3 Glenwood av NW9
44 A 3 Glenwood av NW9
23 W 16 Glenwood clo Harrow
39 V 14 Glenwood dri Rom
39 V 15 Glenwood gdns Ilf
43 V 4 Glenwood gro NW9
13 O 10 Glenwood rd N15
30 K 15 Glenwood rd N15
110 M 1 Glenwood rd SE6
111 N 1 Glenwood rd SE6
152 G 13 Glenwood rd Epsom
83 P 8 Glenwood rd Houns
124 F 15 Glenwood way Croy
39 Z 3 Glergion way E3
144 N 8 Gliddon rd W14
52 B 15 Globe cres E15
52 B 15 Globe rd E15
52 B 15 Globe rd E2
39 V 19 Globe rd Hornch
57 W 1 Globe rd Hornch

21 Z 18 Globe rd Wdfd Grn
142 D 20 Globe st SE1
139 X 7 Globe yd W1
157 P 19 Glossop rd S Croy
142 C 16 Gloster rd New Mald
131 T 2 Gloucester av NW1
114 J 3 Gloucester av Sidcup
96 K 11 Gloucester av Welling
76 G 19 Gloucester cir SE10
43 X 20 Gloucester clo NW10
131 X 4 Gloucester cres NW1
73 O 20 Gloucester ct Rich
27 Y 13 Gloucester dri NW11
48 K 6 Gloucester dri N4
131 W 7 Gloucester ga NW1
131 W 7 Gloucester Ga. ms NW1
27 U 20 Gloucester gdns NW11
6 C 15 Gloucester gdns Barnt
53 S 1 Gloucester gdns Ilf
154 B 1 Gloucester gdns Sutton
150 K 17 Gloucester gro SE15
25 X 5 Gloucester gro Edg
138 D 6 Gloucester ms W2
138 C 6 Gloucester ms W2
131 O 18 Gloucester pl NW1
139 R 2 Gloucester pl W1
139 P 2 Gloucester Pl ms W1
51 N 2 Gloucester rd E10
34 J 16 Gloucester rd E11
53 T 11 Gloucester rd E12
32 F 7 Gloucester rd E17
31 P 11 Gloucester rd N17
18 G 17 Gloucester rd N18
146 C 8 Gloucester rd SW7
73 X 4 Gloucester rd W3
72 E 7 Gloucester rd W5
5 O 17 Gloucester rd Barnt
81 O 13 Gloucester rd Blvdr
123 P 18 Gloucester rd Croy
99 Z 18 Gloucester rd Dartford
5 R 18 Gloucester rd East Barnt
7 Z 3 Gloucester rd Enf
100 L 17 Gloucester rd Hampt
22 K 16 Gloucester rd Harrow
82 A 11 Gloucester rd Hounsl
73 P 19 Gloucester rd Richm
39 S 18 Gloucester rd Rom
101 S 13 Gloucester rd Tedd
101 N 1 Gloucester rd Twick
138 H 7 Gloucester sq W2
148 B 8 Gloucester ter W2
138 C 6 Gloucester ter W2
133 U 14 Gloucester way EC1
137 U 16 Gloucester wlk W8
22 A 18 Glover rd Pinn
5 T 14 Glyn av Barnt
157 F 20 Glyn clo Epsom
115 S 11 Glyn dri Sidcup
50 F 11 Glyn rd E5
9 P 14 Glyn rd Enf
153 O 4 Glyn rd Worc Pk
149 N 11 Glyn st SE11
89 N 7 Glyncena rd SW11
146 M 3 Glynde ms SW3
97 X 8 Glynde rd Bxly Hth
92 M 15 Glynde st SE4
79 R 12 Glyndon rd SE18
112 D 11 Glynfield rd NW10
110 C 5 Glynwood dri SE23
8 H 3 Goat la Enf
121 N 15 Goat rd Mitch
143 N 16 Goat st SE1
145 P 19 Goaters av SW6
38 M 1 Gobions av Rom
39 N 2 Gobions av Rom
156 B 10 Godalming av Wallgtn
64 C 16 Godalming rd E14
64 M 10 Godbold rd E15
148 G 9 Goddard rd Becknhm
83 R 18 Godfrey av Twick
78 E 12 Godfrey hill SE18
78 F 12 Godfrey rd SE18
64 G 4 Godfrey st E15
146 L 9 Godfrey st SW3
148 M 11 Goding st SE11
106 F 2 Godley rd SW18
141 Z 7 Godliman st EC4
91 Z 6 Godman rd SE15
74 J 4 Godolphin rd W12

58 B 3 Godrey av Grnfd
159 X 20 Godric cres Croy
156 F 6 Godson rd Croy
133 S 9 Godson st N1
154 E 7 Godstone rd Sutton
84 A 17 Godstone rd Twick
80 E 6 Godstow rd SE2
52 J 12 Godwin rd E7
126 L 7 Godwin rd Brom
94 A 4 Goffers rd SE3
93 Y 3 Goffers rd SE3
155 Y 8 Goidel clo Wallgtn
128 M 18 Golborne gdns W10
119 N 19 Golborne rd W10
136 L 1 Golborne rd W10
12 L 19 Gold hill Edg
12 L 20 Gold la Edg
4 C 18 Golda clo Barnt
26 A 2 Goldbesters gro Edg
12 M 19 Goldbesters gro Edg
13 N 20 Goldbesters gro Edg
128 M 20 Goldborne rd W10
159 X 18 Goldcrest way Croy
84 G 13 Golden ct Rich
134 B 17 Golden la EC1
59 T 20 Golden manor W7
71 T 1 Golden manor W7
140 C 9 Golden sq W1
12 F 15 Golders clo Edg
45 U 1 Golders gdns NW11
45 W 2 Golders Green cres NW11
45 V 1 Golders Green rd NW11
27 T 18 Golders Green rd NW11
45 Z 6 Golders Hill park NW3
46 A 5 Golders Hill park NW3
45 Z 5 Golders Manor dri NW11
45 Z 5 Golders Pk clo NW11
27 O 15 Golders ri NW4
45 W 2 Golders way NW11
74 K 6 Goldhawk mews W12
74 K 6 Goldhawk ms W12
74 G 8 Goldhawk rd N12
136 B 19 Goldhawk rd N12
130 B 1 Goldhurst st Enf
46 D 20 Goldhurst ter NW6
129 Y 2 Goldhurst ter NW6
127 N 13 Goldie st SE5
143 U 7 Golding st E1
132 E 7 Goldington cres NW1
132 F 8 Goldington st NW1
129 T 18 Goldney rd W9
20 F 8 Goldsborough cres E4
89 Y 1 Goldsborough rd SW8
9 V 10 Goldsdown clo Enf
8 U 9 Goldsdown rd Enf
53 R 17 Goldsmith av E12
26 B 17 Goldsmith av NW9
41 X 20 Goldsmith av W3
56 E 2 Goldsmith av Rom
73 Z 1 Goldsmith clo W3
25 V 13 Goldsmith la NW9
51 P 4 Goldsmith rd E10
32 G 8 Goldsmith rd E17
15 Z 16 Goldsmith rd N11
91 X 1 Goldsmith rd SE15
73 X 1 Goldsmith rd W3
142 B 5 Goldsmith st EC2
79 V 14 Goldsmith st SE18
79 U 14 Goldsmith st S18
135 T 9 Goldsmith's row E2
135 U 7 Goldsmith's sq E2
75 R 12 Goldsworthy gdns SE16
146 D 8 Goldwell rd Thntn Hth
24 C 2 Golf clo Stanm
103 Z 14 Golf Club dri Kingst
60 M 17 Golf rd W5
127 X 7 Golf rd Brom
101 S 7 Golf side Twick
54 F 10 Golfe rd Ilf
156 A 16 Goliath clo Wallgt
101 Y 14 Gomer gdns Tedd
101 Y 14 Gomer pl Tedd
75 N 9 Gomm rd SE16
156 A 10 Gomshall av Wallgtn
45 V 14 Gondar gdns NW6
89 U 4 Gonsalva rd SW8
76 C 17 Gonson st SE8
40 L 19 Gonville cres Grnfd

87 T 7 Gonville st SW6
51 V 10 Goodall rd E11
53 S 6 Goode st EC1
41 T 9 Gooden ct Harrow
105 U 18 Goodenough rd SW19
140 C 1 Goodge pl W1
140 D 1 Goodge st W1
62 C 9 Goodhall st NW10
125 Y 14 Goodhart way W Wkhm
47 Z 16 Goodlinge rd N7
51 U 2 Goodman rd E10
143 R 6 Goodman st E1
143 O 8 Goodman's yd E1
55 N 3 Goodmayes av Ilf
55 N 6 Goodmayes la Ilf
55 N 6 Goodmayes rd Ilf
91 V 15 Goodrich rd SE22
132 J 8 Goods way NW1
62 B 1 Goodson rd NW10
119 Y 9 Goodward clo Mrdn
64 J 17 Goodway gdns E14
115 W 6 Goodwin dri Sidcp
156 J 13 Goodwin gdns Croy
19 S 7 Goodwin rd N9
74 H 5 Goodwin rd W12
156 H 12 Goodwin rd Croy
48 F 7 Goodwin st N4
140 J 9 Goodwins ct WC2
9 P 1 Goodwood av Enf
40 G 18 Goodwood dri Grnfd
75 V 20 Goodwood rd SE14
13 P 16 Goodyear av NW7
29 R 5 Goodwyns vale N10
27 O 16 Goodyers gdns NW4
133 U 11 Goose rd EC1
24 H 15 Gooseacre la Harrow
66 K 9 Gooselire la E6
142 E 9 Gophir la EC4
144 E 6 Gopsall st N1
20 L 18 Gordon av E4
86 A 10 Gordon av SW13
57 T 6 Gordon av Hrnch
11 O 19 Gordon av Stanm
10 K 20 Gordon av Stanm
83 Z 13 Gordon av Twick
97 R 2 Gordon av Welling
123 T 19 Gordon cres Croy
62 L 17 Gordon ct W12
90 J 5 Gordon gro SE5
7 Y 6 Gordon hill Enf
47 P 12 Gordon Ho rd NW5
137 V 17 Gordon pl W8
34 E 19 Gordon rd E4
53 W 10 Gordon rd E15
51 U 13 Gordon rd E15
32 M 19 Gordon rd E17
34 H 5 Gordon rd E18
21 N 4 Gordon rd E4
129 T 14 Gordon rd NW6
29 X 1 Gordon rd N11
27 V 2 Gordon rd N3
19 N 8 Gordon rd N9
91 Z 3 Gordon rd SE15
92 A 7 Gordon rd SE15
73 W 3 Gordon rd W3
73 U 16 Gordon rd W4
60 D 19 Gordon rd W5
67 U 4 Gordon rd Bark
124 L 7 Gordon rd Becknhm
81 X 10 Gordon rd Blvdr
154 L 14 Gordon rd Carsh
8 A 8 Gordon rd Enf
23 T 10 Gordon rd Harrow
82 M 9 Gordon rd Hounsl
55 O 3 Gordon rd Ilf
117 N 19 Gordon rd Kingst
117 N 1 Gordon rd Kingst
116 M 2 Gordon rd Kingst
85 O 6 Gordon rd Rich
38 A 19 Gordon rd Rom
70 C 11 Gordon rd S'hall
96 H 13 Gordon rd Sidcp
132 F 17 Gordon sq WC1
132 E 16 Gordon st E13
93 N 13 Gordonbrook rd SE4
105 Z 4 Gordondale rd SW19
25 P 16 Gore ct NW9
145 Z 5 Gore rd E9
63 O 4 Gore rd E9
128 M 3 Gore rd SW20
69 P 4 Goresbrook rd Dgnhm
136 J 11 Gorham pl W11
38 J 5 Goring clo Rom
55 T 13 Goring gdns Dgnhm
16 M 19 Goring rd N11
17 N 19 Goring rd N11

57 N 19 Goring rd Dgnhm
142 L 5 Goring st EC3
59 N 7 Goring way Grnfd
31 O 15 Gorleston rd N15
120 M 6 Gorleston st W14
107 P 19 Gorringe Pk av Mitch
159 P 6 Gorse rd Croy
107 P 13 Gorse ri SW17
57 P 4 Gorseway Rom
61 X 11 Gorst rd NW10
88 L 17 Gorst rd SW11
135 N 11 Gorsuch pl E2
56 E 5 Gosfield rd Dgnhm
139 Z 1 Gosfield st W1
35 T 15 Gosford gdns Ilf
140 G 5 Goslett yd W1
58 G 8 Gosling clo Grnfd
90 F 2 Gosling way SW9
30 L 3 Gospatrick rd N17
31 N 4 Gospatrick rd N17
32 L 16 Gosport rd E17
79 S 14 Gossage rd SE18
135 P 13 Gosset St E2
127 X 3 Gosshill rd Chisl
75 W 15 Gosterwood st SE8
100 J 1 Gostling rd Twick
122 F 7 Goston gdns Thntn Hth
133 X 14 Goswell pl EC1
133 Y 15 Goswell rd EC1
133 X 12 Goswell ter EC1
101 R 4 Gothic rd Twick
112 B 12 Goudhurst rd Brom
52 B 13 Gough rd E15
8 L 9 Gough rd Enf
141 U 5 Gough sq EC4
133 P 16 Gough st WC1
101 T 1 Gould rd Twick
50 A 16 Gould ter E9
88 H 4 Goulden st SW11
143 O 4 Goulston st E1
50 A 13 Goulton rd E5
31 S 17 Gourley pl N15
31 S 17 Gourley st N15
95 W 13 Gourock rd SE9
87 S 2 Gowan av SW6
44 J 19 Gowan rd NW10
62 L 16 Gower ct WC1
140 F 1 Gower ms W1
132 O 16 Gower pl WC1
52 G 18 Gower rd E7
71 W 17 Gower rd Isl
132 C 15 Gower st NW1
132 C 15 Gower st WC1
143 S 5 Gower's wlk E1
124 L 4 Gowland pl Becknhm
91 W 8 Gowlett rd SE15
89 O 8 Gowrie rd SW11
98 C 4 Grace av Bxly Hth
64 H 1 Grace rd E15
146 L 15 Grace rd Croy
64 E 9 Grace st E3
143 T 9 Grace's all E1
91 P 3 Grace's ms SE5
91 R 3 Grace's rd SE5
142 H 8 Gracechurch st EC3
107 T 12 Gracedale rd SW16
108 A 8 Gracefield gdns SW16
109 W 11 Gradient the SE26
8 C 9 Graeme rd Enf
85 T 9 Graemesdyke av SW14
59 Y 17 Grafton clo W13
47 S 18 Grafton cres NW1
30 K 18 Grafton gdns N4
55 Z 6 Grafton gdns Dgnam
132 B 18 Grafton ms W1
132 F 13 Grafton pl NW1
47 S 17 Grafton rd NW5
61 V 19 Grafton rd W3
146 G 20 Grafton rd Croy
156 G 1 Grafton rd Croy
55 Z 6 Grafton rd Dgnhm
7 P 11 Grafton rd Enf
23 O 17 Grafton rd Harrow
118 B 7 Grafton rd New Mald
152 A 5 Grafton rd Worc Pk
89 V 8 Grafton sq SW4
139 Z 10 Grafton st W1
47 N 19 Grafton ter NW5
132 B 18 Grafton way W1
47 T 18 Grafton way NW5
72 B 7 Graham av W13
121 O 1 Graham av Mitch
158 M 2 Graham clo Croy
159 N 3 Graham clo Croy
116 J 19 Graham gdns Surb
26 B 8 Graham park NW9
65 S 10 Graham rd E13
49 X 18 Graham rd E8

26 H 19	Graham rd NW4	
30 J 11	Graham rd N15	
105 V 19	Graham rd SW19	
73 X 7	Graham rd W4	
98 C 10	Graham rd Bxly Hth	
100 F 9	Graham rd Hampt	
23 T 9	Graham rd Harrow	
145 N 1	Graham rd Mitch	
133 Z 10	Graham st N1	
147 T 7	Graham ter SW1	
40 M 16	Grainger clo Grnfd	
30 L 5	Grainger rd N22	
83 W 5	Grainger rd Islwth	
45 S 4	Grampian gdns NW2	
106 L 12	Granada rd SW17	
86 K 14	Granard av SW15	
86 K 13	Granard gdns SW15	
88 M 18	Granard rd SW12	
139 N 7	Granby bldgs SW1	
95 U 6	Granby rd SE9	
135 P 15	Granby row E2	
135 P 16	Granby st E2	
132 A 10	Granby ter NW1	
141 X 1	Grand av EC1	
29 F 12	Grand av N10	
117 U 16	Grand av Surb	
43 P 16	Grand av Wemb	
78 J 13	Grand Depot rd SE18	
118 M 3	Grand dri SW20	
119 O 12	Grand dri SW20	
146 A 3	Granden rd SW16	
89 N 13	Grandison rd SW11	
88 M 12	Grandison rd SW4	
152 M 4	Grandison rd Worc Pk	
88 H 2	Granfield st SW11	
15 P 17	Grange av N12	
14 D 4	Grange av N20	
123 R 3	Grange av SE25	
15 Y 4	Grange av Barnt	
24 C 7	Grange av Stanm	
101 U 3	Grange av Twick	
21 S 20	Grange av Wdfd Grn	
34 E 1	Grange av Wdfd Grn	
123 R 3	Grange Cliffe gdns SE25	
12 J 17	Grange clo Edg	
70 D 15	Grange clo Hounsl	
118 F 11	Grange clo New Mald	
34 E 1	Grange clo Wdfd Grn	
141 P 6	Grange ct WC2	
113 S 15	Grange dri Chisl	
41 O 6	Grange Farm clo Harrow	
123 R 3	Grange gdns SE25	
22 C 12	Grange gdns Pinn	
48 K 18	Grange gro N1	
123 R 2	Grange hill SE25	
12 J 16	Grange hill Edg	
109 V 4	Grange la SE21	
72 K 3	Grange pk W5	
17 Y 1	Grange Pk av N21	
7 X 20	Grange Pk av N21	
51 P 4	Grange Pk rd E10	
147 N 7	Grange Pk rd Thntn Hth	
51 O 4	Grange rd E10	
65 R 10	Grange rd E13	
32 H 17	Grange rd E17	
18 K 20	Grange rd N17	
29 N 19	Grange rd N6	
150 L 2	Grange rd SE1	
123 P 5	Grange rd SE25	
86 F 3	Grange rd SW13	
73 T 13	Grange rd W4	
72 G 2	Grange rd W5	
12 M 20	Grange rd Edg	
41 P 7	Grange rd Harrow	
23 Y 17	Grange rd Harrow	
54 A 11	Grange rd Ilf	
116 J 6	Grange rd Kingst	
156 M 20	Grange rd S Croy	
70 B 4	Grange rd S'hall	
153 Z 16	Grange rd Sutton	
154 A 16	Grange rd Sutton	
134 G 7	Grange st N1	
15 S 5	Grange the N20	
150 M 1	Grange the SE1	
105 P 14	Grange the SW19	
158 L 3	Grange the Croy	
61 O 1	Grange the Wemb	
154 B 16	Grange vale Sutton	
15 S 5	Grange View rd N20	
15 O 13	Grange way N12	
21 Y 14	Grange way Wdfd Grn	
150 L 2	Grange wlk SE1	
151 N 1	Grange wlk SE1	
127 N 2	Grange sq SE1	
49 R 3	Grangecourt rd N16	
95 V 8	Grangehill rd SE9	
111 O 5	Grangemill rd SE6	
111 O 5	Grangemill way SE6	
39 W 19	Granger way Rom	
129 S 1	Grangeway NW6	
35 H 15	Grangeway gdns Ilf	
7 X 19	Grangeway the N21	
98 A 20	Grangewood Bxly	
110 M 15	Grangewood la Becknhm	
66 B 3	Grangewood rd E6	
65 Z 3	Grangewood st E6	
18 H 9	Granham gdns N9	
79 Y 13	Granite st SE18	
51 Z 7	Granleigh rd E11	
50 A 20	Granmore av Islwth	
74 D 6	Gransden rd W12	
16 G 3	Grant clo N14	
123 V 20	Grant pl Croy	
88 H 8	Grant rd SW11	
88 J 8	Grant rd SW11	
123 U 20	Grant rd Croy	
23 U 9	Grant rd Harrow	
65 S 10	Grant st E13	
133 S 7	Grant st N1	
133 Y 7	Grantbridge st N1	
38 A 20	Grantham gdns Rom	
139 W 15	Grantham pl W1	
53 W 11	Grantham rd E12	
90 A 5	Grantham rd SW9	
74 A 18	Grantham rd W4	
63 T 10	Grantley st E1	
33 X 5	Grantock rd E17	
107 V 19	Granton rd SW16	
55 N 5	Granton rd Sidcp	
115 T 15	Granton rd Sidcp	
27 N 1	Grants clo NW7	
128 W 14	Grantully rd W9	
19 P 11	Granville av N9	
82 G 14	Granville av Hounsl	
108 C 19	Granville gdns SW16	
73 O 2	Granville gdns W5	
93 W 8	Granville gro SE13	
93 U 6	Granville pk SE13	
139 S 6	Granville pl W1	
33 R 17	Granville rd E17	
34 J 8	Granville rd E18	
45 V 7	Granville rd NW2	
129 T 10	Granville rd NW6	
28 D 1	Granville rd N12	
17 O 18	Granville rd N22	
30 J 5	Granville rd N22	
30 D 20	Granville rd N4	
87 X 18	Granville rd SW18	
105 Y 18	Granville rd SW19	
4 B 13	Granville rd Barnt	
53 Y 5	Granville rd Ilf	
115 O 9	Granville rd Sidcp	
97 U 8	Granville rd Welling	
133 R 13	Granville sq WC1	
133 P 13	Granville st WC1	
140 J 4	Grape st WC1	
108 G 1	Gras Mere rd SW16	
80 A 18	Grasdene rd SE18	
103 Z 10	Grasmere av SW15	
104 A 9	Grasmere av SW15	
119 Y 6	Grasmere av SW19	
61 X 19	Grasmere av W3	
82 J 16	Grasmere av Hounsl	
42 J 4	Grasmere av Wemb	
23 Z 8	Grasmere gdns Harrow	
35 S 14	Grasmere gdns Ilf	
29 S 6	Grasmere rd N10	
18 J 20	Grasmere rd N17	
147 Z 13	Grasmere rd SE25	
148 A 13	Grasmere rd SE25	
112 B 19	Grasmere rd Brom	
98 K 4	Grasmere rd Bxly Hth	
27 V 5	Grass pk N3	
155 U 8	Grass way Wallgtn	
115 N 11	Grassington rd Sidcp	
110 B 3	Grassmount SE23	
4 M 19	Grasvenor av Barnt	
144 K 2	Gratton rd W14	
45 O 10	Gratton ter NW2	
27 W 7	Gravel hill N3	
98 G 13	Gravel hill Bxly Hth	
158 H 14	Gravel hill Croy	
142 M 4	Gravel la E1	
150 G 6	Gravel pits Brom	
101 S 2	Gravel rd Twick	
75 P 1	Gravel st E1	
114 B 8	Gravelwood clo Chisl	
106 J 10	Graveney rd SW17	
74 G 1	Gravesend rd W12	
54 C 4	Gray av Dgnhm	
57 V 16	Gray gdns Rainhm	
78 B 3	Gray st E16	
141 V 18	Gray st SE1	
141 P 1	Gray's Inn pl WC1	
133 O 16	Gray's Inn rd WC1	
141 R 1	Gray's Inn sq WC1	
117 Y 9	Grayham cres New Mald	
117 X 9	Grayham rd New Mald	
127 O 2	Grayland clo Brom	
150 L 17	Graylands rd SE15	
49 P 6	Grayling rd N16	
107 X 18	Grayscroft rd SW16	
89 N 7	Grayshot rd SW11	
20 D 1	Graywood ct N12	
49 O 7	Grazebrook rd N16	
98 K 12	Grazeley clo Bxly Hth	
109 R 11	Grazeley ct SE19	
28 G 8	Great North rd N2	
4 H 8	Great North rd Barnt	
74 J 14	Great West rd W6	
59 V 13	Greatdown rd W7	
66 G 11	Greatfield av E6	
93 O 11	Greatfield clo SE4	
67 T 4	Greatfields rd Bark	
143 S 2	Greatorex st E1	
106 H 10	Greaves pl SW17	
108 K 15	Grecian cres SE19	
140 G 7	Greek st W1	
141 X 4	Green Arbour ct EC1	
12 M 12	Green av NW7	
13 N 12	Green av NW7	
72 C 8	Green av W13	
75 N 3	Green bank E1	
143 Y 14	Green bank E1	
15 O 13	Green bank N12	
27 S 13	Green Bank cres NW4	
28 C 20	Green clo NW11	
25 W 17	Green clo NW9	
125 Z 5	Green clo Carsh	
154 M 3	Green clo Carsh	
100 C 12	Green clo Hampt	
158 A 1	Green Ct av Croy	
158 A 1	Green Ct gdns Croy	
91 R 11	Green dale SE5	
7 T 19	Green Dragon la N21	
17 X 1	Green Dragon la N21	
70 J 2	Green dri S'hall	
17 X 8	Green end N21	
46 T 14	Green hill NW3	
141 X 1	Green Hills rents EC1	
151 V 15	Green Hundred rd SE15	
27 P 16	Green la NW4	
110 E 18	Green la SE20	
113 X 4	Green la SE0	
95 Y 19	Green la SE9	
108 F 19	Green la SW16	
71 T 4	Green la W7	
14 A 14	Green la Chisl	
56 B 6	Green la Dgnhm	
11 Z 12	Green la Edg	
12 A 14	Green la Edg	
100 A 12	Green la Felt	
54 D 8	Green la Ilf	
55 O 5	Green la Ilf	
119 X 14	Green la Mrdn	
120 B 17	Green la Mrdn	
117 W 11	Green la New Mald	
11 O 16	Green la Stanm	
122 J 2	Green la Thntn Hth	
118 H 19	Green la Worc Pk	
122 K 2	Green La gdns Thntn Hth	
49 N 12	Green lanes N16	
17 X 4	Green lanes N21	
48 L 4	Green lanes N4	
30 H 16	Green lanes N8	
52 B 18	Green lanes Epsom	
72 A 1	Green Man la W13	
72 A 1	Green Man la W13	
17 W 2	Green Moor link N21	
139 X 16	Green park SW1	
99 S 12	Green pl Drtfrd	
32 J 9	Green Pond rd E17	
6 D 19	Green rd N14	
15 S 10	Green rd N20	
65 X 2	Green st E13	
52 K 20	Green st E7	
139 S 8	Green st N1	
9 P 9	Green st Enf	
133 U 13	Green ter EC1	
52 A 18	Green the E15	
16 K 10	Green the N14	
17 V 4	Green the N21	
18 K 9	Green the N9	
62 B 17	Green the W3	
126 E 18	Green the Brom	
98 D 3	Green the Bxly Hth	
155 O 9	Green the Carsh	
158 M 19	Green the Croy	
70 F 17	Green the Hounsl	
119 S 9	Green the Mrdn	
117 X 5	Green the N Mald	
115 R 18	Green the Orp	
84 G 12	Green the Rich	
70 C 8	Green the S'hall	
154 A 6	Green the Sutton	
101 T 2	Green the Twick	
21 T 16	Green the Wdfd Grn	
96 J 11	Green the Welling	
41 Z 6	Green the Wemb	
60 M 16	Green vale W5	
97 W 13	Green vale Bxly Hth	
24 F 1	Green verges Stanm	
95 N 13	Green way SE9	
151 S 14	Green way Brom	
21 Y 15	Green way Wdfd Grn	
20 H 4	Green wlk E4	
27 P 14	Green wlk NW4	
126 H 2	Green wlk SE1	
99 T 11	Green wlk Drtfrd	
158 K 15	Green wlk S Croy	
70 G 14	Green wlk S'hall	
154 K 1	Green Wrythe cres Carsh	
144 G 15	Green Wrythe gdns Carsh	
144 H 17	Green Wrythe la Carsh	
140 D 8	Green's ct W1	
78 L 10	Green's end SE18	
95 W 16	Greenacres SE9	
11 N 20	Greenacres dri Stanm	
46 B 13	Greenaway gdns NW3	
41 Y 15	Greenbank av Wemb	
78 B 19	Greenbay rd SE7	
130 K 10	Greenberry st NW8	
5 S 6	Greenbrook av Barnt	
148 C 4	Greencoat pl SW1	
148 D 3	Greencoat row SW1	
25 R 5	Greencourt av Edg	
46 D 19	Greencroft gdns NW6	
129 Y 1	Greencroft gdns NW6	
8 E 11	Greencroft gdns Enf	
82 D 2	Greencroft rd Hounsl	
74 A 6	Greenend rd W4	
76 M 7	Greenfell st SE10	
117 T 15	Greenfield av Surb	
45 T 9	Greenfield gdns NW2	
68 M 3	Greenfield gdns Dgnhm	
143 U 4	Greenfield rd E1	
31 S 15	Greenfield rd N15	
68 G 3	Greenfield rd Dgnhm	
22 J 10	Greenfield way Harrow	
58 H 18	Greenfields S'hall	
59 T 14	Greenford av W7	
70 E 1	Greenford av S'hall	
58 E 20	Greenford av S'hall	
58 M 8	Greenford gdns Grnfd	
59 N 8	Greenford gdns Grnfd	
59 O 10	Greenford rd Grnfd	
41 T 17	Greenford rd Grnfd	
71 N 1	Greenford rd Grnfd	
154 A 9	Greenford rd Sutton	
42 A 17	Greengate Grnfd	
65 V 8	Greengate st E13	
28 D 14	Greenhalgh wlk N2	
29 P 6	Greenham rd N10	
34 C 9	Greenheys dri E18	
21 X 4	Greenhill Buck Hl	
154 D 3	Greenhill Sutton	
43 U 6	Greenhill Wemb	
23 V 17	Greenhill cres Harrow	
58 E 6	Greenhill gdns Grnfd	
53 P 14	Greenhill gro E12	
62 A 4	Greenhill pk NW10	
5 O 18	Greenhill pk Barnt	
62 A 4	Greenhill rd NW10	
23 U 18	Greenhill rd Harrow	
58 E 7	Greenhill ter Grnfd	
43 T 6	Greenhill way Wemb	
96 F 18	Greenhithe clo Sidcp	
95 Y 14	Greenholm rd SE9	
95 Y 13	Greenholm rd SE9	
95 S 27	Greenhurst rd SE27	
80 F 11	Greening st SE2	
132 A 3	Greenland rd NW1	
131 Z 4	Greenland rd NW1	
4 A 19	Greenland rd Barnt	

131 Z4	Greenland st NW1
78 H9	Greenlaw st SE18
32 M11	Greenleaf rd E17
33 N11	Greenleaf rd E17
63 M6	Greenleaf rd E6
35 Z10	Greenleafe dri Ilf
134 A2	Greenman st N1
9 P8	Greenmoor rd Enf
107 X20	Greenock rd SW16
73 U9	Greenock rd W4
57 T5	Greenside Dgnhm
84 G12	Greenside Rich
74 G7	Greenside rd W12
74 A6	Greenside rd W4
122 G16	Greenside rd Croy
34 L1	Greenstead av Wdfd Grn
21 Z20	Greenstead av Wdfd Grn
34 K1	Greenstead av Wdfd Grn
21 Y19	Greenstead clo Wdfd Grn
86 H14	Greenstead gdns SW15
21 Y19	Greenstead gdns Wdfd Grn
95 U11	Greenvale rd SE9
124 J14	Greenview av Becknhm
124 H15	Greenview av Croy
17 N7	Greenway N14
16 M9	Greenway N14
14 L7	Greenway N20
15 N8	Greenway N20
118 M8	Greenway SW20
113 X11	Greenway Chisl
55 U5	Greenway Dgnhm
24 K16	Greenway Harrow
82 D9	Greenway Hounsl
33 V12	Greenway Wallgtn
25 X9	Greenway av E17
14 L9	Greenway clo NW9
155 U16	Greenway clo N20
48 M7	Greenway clo N4
23 U6	Greenway ct Harrow
25 X8	Greenway gdns NW9
158 K6	Greenway gdns Croy
58 J8	Greenway gdns Grnfd
25 Y8	Greenway the SE9
23 U6	Greenway the Harrow
22 E19	Greenway the Pinn
63 T8	Greenways E2
25 O4	Greenways Becknhm
131 Z18	Greenwell st W1
76 G16	Greenwich Ch st SE10
76 F19	Greenwich High rd SE10
76 L18	Greenwich park SE10
76 L18	Greenwich Pk st SE10
93 S2	Greenwich South st SE10
56 H11	Greenwood av Dgnhm
9 U7	Greenwood av Enf
10 E4	Greenwood clo Bushey Watf
119 S9	Greenwood clo Mrdn
17 V10	Greenwood gdns N13
36 C3	Greenwood gdns Ilf
104 B17	Greenwood pk Kingst
47 L14	Greenwood pl NW5
65 S5	Greenwood rd E13
49 X16	Greenwood rd E8
122 K16	Greenwood rd Croy
83 U7	Greenwood rd Islwth
121 X7	Greenwood rd Mitch
61 Y4	Greenwood ter NW10
23 O4	Greer rd Harrow
72 J15	Greet rd Brentf
141 V16	Greet st SE1
77 T20	Gregor ms SE3
95 O19	Gregory cres SE9
137 W18	Gregory pl W8
65 X19	Gregory rd E16
70 H8	Gregory rd S'hall
30 A15	Greig clo N8
85 N11	Grena gdns Rich
85 N11	Grena rd Rich
123 O18	Grenaby av Croy
123 O18	Grenaby rd Croy
123 Z20	Grenada rd SE7
63 Z20	Grenade st E14
78 H4	Grenadier st E16
150 M18	Grenard rd SE15
43 P7	Grendon gdns Wemb
57 T4	Grenfell av Hornch
24 J20	Grenfell gdns Harrow
136 H9	Grenfell rd W11
107 N17	Grenfell rd Mitch
154 E3	Grennell clo Sutton
154 E4	Grennell rd Sutton
117 V20	Grenville clo Surb
84 A18	Grenville clo Twick
34 K3	Grenville gdns Wdfd Grn
12 K16	Grenville pl NW7
146 A4	Grenville pl SW7
48 A4	Grenville rd N4
159 V20	Grenville rd Croy
132 L18	Grenville st WC1
15 Y13	Gresham av N20
98 A16	Gresham clo Bxly
7 Y12	Gresham clo Enf
37 R18	Gresham dri Rom
45 T3	Gresham gdns NW11
65 W18	Gresham rd E16
66 G7	Gresham rd E6
43 Z16	Gresham rd NW10
123 W10	Gresham rd SE25
90 G8	Gresham rd SW9
124 G3	Gresham rd Becknhm
12 A20	Gresham rd Edg
142 C5	Gresham rd Hounsl
47 W2	Gresham st EC2
140 E3	Gresley st N19
87 V17	Gresse st W1
87 V17	Gressenhall rd SW18
115 O7	Gresswell clo Sidcp
87 O2	Greswell st SW6
31 T3	Gretton rd N17
129 W6	Greville ms NW6
129 Y8	Greville pl NW6
33 U13	Greville rd E17
129 Z8	Greville rd NW6
85 N15	Greville rd Rich
141 T1	Greville st EC1
28 C19	Grey clo NW11
138 E3	Greycoat pl SW1
138 E3	Greycoat st SW1
111 O12	Greycot rd Becknhm
78 L16	Greydon st SE18
135 O19	Greyeagle st E1
141 Z4	Greyfriars pas EC4
26 H11	Greyhound hill NW4
107 Z15	Greyhound la SW16
31 T10	Greyhound rd N17
128 A12	Greyhound rd W10
144 J13	Greyhound rd W6
154 D10	Greyhound rd Sutton
107 V20	Greyhound ter SW16
92 C18	Greystead rd SE23
22 H10	Greystoke av Pinn
60 L12	Greystoke gdns W5
60 H9	Greystoke Pk ter W5
141 T4	Greystoke pl EC4
6 L14	Greystone gdns Enf
24 D19	Greystone gdns Harrow
36 C6	Greystone gdns Ilf
107 T15	Greyswood st SW16
92 G16	Grierson rd SE23
79 T9	Griffin Mnr way SE18
31 R8	Griffin rd N17
79 T11	Griffin rd SE18
105 Z17	Griffiths rd SW19
126 L2	Griggs pl SE1
33 V19	Griggs rd E10
135 P17	Grimsby st E2
22 D7	Grimsdyke rd Pinn
87 V6	Grimston rd SW6
157 Y6	Grimwade av Croy
92 B6	Grimwade cres SE15
83 X17	Grimwood rd Twick
75 Z17	Grinling pl SE8
76 A17	Grinling pl SE8
75 W14	Grinstead rd SE8
43 T19	Grittleton av Wemb
129 T16	Grittleton rd W9
110 A4	Grizedale ter SE23
154 K2	Grn Wrythe la Carsh
142 E6	Grocers' Hall ct EC2
142 E5	Grocers' Hall gdns EC2
100 J12	Gronville ms Hampt
88 F19	Groom cres SW18
139 V20	Groom pl SW1
63 T1	Groombridge rd E9
107 O9	Groomfield clo
79 Y14	Grosmont rd SE18
48 K17	Grosvenor av N5
49 N16	Grosvenor av N5
86 A8	Grosvenor av SW14
155 O13	Grosvenor av Carsh
22 L19	Grosvenor av Harrow
25 R13	Grosvenor cres NW9
139 T19	Grosvenor cres SW1
139 T18	Grosvenor Cres ms SW1
16 H1	Grosvenor ct N14
147 X2	Grosvenor Gdn ms SW1
66 A8	Grosvenor gdns E6
27 U17	Grosvenor gdns NW11
45 N16	Grosvenor gdns NW2
29 U11	Grosvenor gdns N10
6 K15	Grosvenor gdns N14
147 X2	Grosvenor gdns SW1
86 A9	Grosvenor gdns SW13
102 H14	Grosvenor gdns Kingst
155 U16	Grosvenor gdns Wallgtn
21 U20	Grosvenor gdns Wdfd Grn
147 X2	Grosvenor Gdns Ms north SW1
147 X3	Grosvenor Gdns Ms south SW1
105 S14	Grosvenor hill SW19
139 X9	Grosvenor hill W1
139 Z17	Grosvenor pk SE17
150 A16	Grosvenor pk SE5
33 P16	Grosvenor Pk rd E17
149 Z17	Grosvenor pl SE5
139 W19	Grosvenor pl SW1
51 U3	Grosvenor rd E10
34 G17	Grosvenor rd E11
66 B3	Grosvenor rd E6
52 H19	Grosvenor rd E7
29 S5	Grosvenor rd N10
27 W1	Grosvenor rd N3
19 N5	Grosvenor rd N9
123 W19	Grosvenor rd SE25
73 T14	Grosvenor rd SW1
71 X3	Grosvenor rd W7
81 R15	Grosvenor rd Belvdr
72 H17	Grosvenor rd Brentf
97 X13	Grosvenor rd Bxly Hth
56 C3	Grosvenor rd Dgnhm
82 E8	Grosvenor rd Hounsl
54 A9	Grosvenor rd Ilf
84 K13	Grosvenor rd Rich
57 N3	Grosvenor rd Rom
70 E7	Grosvenor rd S'hall
87 Y20	Grosvenor rd Twick
159 S1	Grosvenor rd W Wkhm
155 S12	Grosvenor rd Wallgtn
33 S16	Grosvenor ri E17
139 V9	Grosvenor sq SW1
139 W9	Grosvenor st W1
150 B15	Grosvenor ter SE5
93 Z5	Grotes pl SE3
106 L3	Groton rd SW18
139 U1	Grotto pas W1
101 W4	Grotto rd Twick
29 U8	Grove av N10
27 Y2	Grove av N3
59 U17	Grove av W7
22 B14	Grove av Pinn
153 T14	Grove av Sutton
101 W1	Grove av Twick
100 B11	Grove clo Felt
116 L9	Grove clo Kingst
146 L12	Grove cres SW3
34 D7	Grove cres E18
25 X13	Grove cres NW9
91 R5	Grove cres SE5
116 B10	Grove cres Felt
116 J7	Grove cres Kingst
51 Y18	Grove Crescent rd E15
34 A7	Grove end E18
130 F14	Grove End rd NW8
26 G14	Grove gdns NW4
130 K14	Grove gdns NW8
100 H6	Grove gdns Felt
9 T4	Grove gdns Enf
101 Z10	Grove gdns Tedd
51 V4	Grove Green rd E11
34 B7	Grove hill E18
41 U2	Grove hill Harrow
91 S7	Grove Hill rd SE5
41 U1	Grove hill rd Harrow
86 E15	Grove house SW15
80 A14	Grove House rd N8
91 N2	Grove la SE5
116 K8	Grove la Kingst
95 T15	Grove Market pl SE9
74 L8	Grove ms W6
85 V1	Grove park W4
33 P2	Grove Park av E4
73 V19	Grove Park dr W4
73 U19	Grove Park gdns W4
31 S13	Grove Park rd N15
113 N5	Grove Park rd SE9
112 M6	Grove Park rd SE9
73 T18	Grove Park rd W4
73 T18	Grove Park ter W4
135 K7	Grove pas E2
116 X7	Grove path SE5
63 N5	Grove pk E2
25 W12	Grove pk NW9
91 S6	Grove pk SE5
46 F11	Grove pl NW3
73 V3	Grove pl W3
72 H1	Grove pl W5
67 O2	Grove pl Bark
52 B2	Grove rd E17
33 P17	Grove rd E17
34 C6	Grove rd E3
63 V7	Grove rd E3
20 F13	Grove rd E4
44 L17	Grove rd NW2
16 F15	Grove rd N11
15 T18	Grove rd N12
31 P16	Grove rd N15
86 D4	Grove rd SW13
106 D18	Grove rd SW19
72 H1	Grove rd W5
5 V12	Grove rd Barnt
81 P16	Grove rd Blvdr
72 F14	Grove rd Brentf
98 K11	Grove rd Bxly Hth
12 B18	Grove rd Edg
82 G10	Grove rd Hounsl
83 U3	Grove rd Islwth
121 P4	Grove rd Mitch
22 D15	Grove rd Pinn
35 S19	Grove rd Rom
37 S19	Grove rd Rom
55 S1	Grove rd Rom
116 G11	Grove rd Surb
154 B13	Grove rd Sutton
153 Y14	Grove rd Sutton
122 E10	Grove rd Thntn Hth
101 R8	Grove rd Twick
91 R1	Grove rd West Enfield
18 H18	Grove st N18
75 X10	Grove st SE8
47 R11	Grove ter NW5
101 Y10	Grove ter Tedd
51 Y18	Grove the E15
45 T1	Grove the NW11
17 T13	Grove the N13
27 X3	Grove the N3
48 D1	Grove the N4
47 O3	Grove the N6
25 Y16	Grove the SE9
72 G2	Grove the W5
97 W10	Grove the Bxly Hth
12 F13	Grove the Edg
7 T9	Grove the Enf
58 M17	Grove the Grnfd
83 T3	Grove the Islwth
115 Z11	Grove the Sidcp
159 U1	Grove the W Wkhm
91 T9	Grove vale SE22
113 W14	Grove vale Chisl
55 V11	Grove way Dgnhm
43 U15	Grove way Wemb
80 D6	Grovebury rd SE2
47 X5	Grovedale rd N19
142 B6	Groveland EC4
108 D18	Groveland av SW16
124 L6	Groveland rd Becknhm
117 X11	Groveland way New Mald
17 P4	Grovelands park N21
17 R12	Grovelands rd N13
31 X18	Grovelands rd N15
115 P19	Grovelands rd Orp
92 D6	Groveside rd E4
21 O10	Groveside rd E4
90 E3	Groveway SW9
85 O3	Grovewood Rich
91 U2	Grummant rd SE15
64 D18	Grundy st E14
28 A1	Gruneisen rd N3
142 E4	Gt Bell all EC2

109 V 8 Gt brownings SE21
15 O 5 Gt Bushey dr N20
31 N 3 Gt Cambridge rd N17
18 B 11 Gt Cambridge rd N9
8 L 5 Gt Cambridge rd Enf
140 A 5 Gt Castle st W1
131 N 20 Gt Central st W1
140 E 5 Gt Chapel st W1
85 X 2 Gt Chertsey rd W7
100 H 6 Gt Chertsey rd Felt
144 G 8 Gt Church la W6
38 J 1 Gt College st SW1
57 P 7 Gt cullings Rom
139 O 6 Gt Cumberland ms W1
139 P 6 Gt Cumberland pl W1
150 F 2 Gt Dover st SE1
142 D 18 Gt Dover st SE1
51 X 18 Gt Eastern rd E15
134 J 15 Gt Eastern st EC2
126 L 8 Gt Elms rd Brom
39 Z 18 Gt Gardens rd Rom
140 H 18 Gt George st SW1
142 A 13 Gt Guildford st SE1
113 W 8 Gt Harry dri SE9
133 O 19 Gt James st WC1
140 B 6 Gt Marlborough st W1
142 G 15 Gt Maze pond SE1
140 H 8 Gt Newport st WC2
26 L 6 Gt North way NW4
27 P 9 Gt North way NW4
132 M 19 Gt Ormond st WC1
133 N 19 Gt Ormond st WC1
133 N 18 Gt Ormonde st WC1
133 P 12 Gt Percy st WC1
138 G 2 Gt Peter st SW1
139 Z 2 Gt Portland st W1
140 A 4 Gt Portland st W1
140 D 8 Gt Pulteney st W1
140 M 5 Gt Queen st WC2
140 J 2 Gt Russell st W1
140 J 14 Gt Scotland yd SW1
138 G 1 Gt Smith st SW1
91 R 14 Gt spilmans SE21
142 J 5 Gt St helen's EC2
141 Y 15 Gt Suffolk st SE1
142 A 19 Gt Suffolk st SE1
133 Y 17 Gt Sutton st EC1
142 E 4 Gt Swan all EC2
142 C 8 Gt Thomas apostle EC4
131 Z 19 Gt Titchfield st W1
140 A 2 Gt Titchfield st W1
142 J 9 Gt Tower st EC3
142 B 8 Gt Trinity la EC4
141 O 3 Gt turnstile WC1
72 B 17 Gt West rd Brentf
82 E 3 Gt West rd Hounsl
71 U 19 Gt West rd Islwrth
137 S 2 Gt Western rd W11
129 R 19 Gt Western rd W9
142 G 4 Gt Winchester st EC2
140 E 9 Gt Windmill st W1
113 V 17 Gt wood Chisl
90 K 13 Gubyon av SE24
68 Y 8 Guerim st E3
90 L 18 Guernsey gro SE24
51 W 5 Guernsey rd E11
112 G 1 Guibal rd SE12
94 G 20 Guibal rd SE12
142 C 4 Guild hall EC2
78 B 15 Guild rd SE18
107 G 17 Guildersfield rd SW16
108 A 17 Guildersfield rd SW16
116 M 11 Guildford av Surb
93 S 1 Guildford gro SE10
33 V 4 Guildford rd E17
90 A 1 Guildford rd SW8
123 O 14 Guildford rd Croy
54 J 8 Guildford rd Ilf
116 L 16 Guildford vls Surb
156 B 10 Guildford way Wallgtn
142 D 4 Guildhall bldgs EC2
142 D 4 Guildhall yd EC2
148 A 6 Guildhouse st SW1
32 X 5 Guildsway E17
133 N 18 Guilford rd WC1
132 K 19 Guilford st WC1
133 O 17 Guilford st WC1
44 A 20 Guilsborough rd NW10
87 W 4 Guion rd SW6
58 E 3 Gull clo Grnfd
156 A 17 Gull clo Wallgtn
114 G 5 Gulliver rd Sidcp
75 X 8 Gulliver st SE16

72 D 11 Gumleigh rd W5
83 X 7 Gumley gdns Islwth
142 M 1 Gun st E1
149 S 6 Gundulf st SE11
126 L 7 Gundulph rd Brom
63 X 3 Gunmakers la E3
78 K 14 Gunner la SE18
20 F 10 Gunners gro E4
106 G 3 Gunners rd SW18
73 P 9 Gunnersbury av W3
72 M 2 Gunnersbury av W5
73 P 6 Gunnersbury cres W3
73 N 7 Gunnersbury dri W5
73 P 5 Gunnersbury gdns W3
73 R 6 Gunnersbury la W3
72 K 9 Gunnersbury park W3
79 U 10 Gunning st SE18
49 S 11 Gunstor rd N16
18 N 17 Gunter gro SW10
25 X 4 Gunter gro Edgw
144 L 8 Gunterstone rd W14
107 P 16 Gunton rd SW17
77 U 14 Gurdon rd SE7
59 X 11 Gurnell gro W13
122 D 20 Gurney cres Croy
28 E 14 Gurney dri N2
52 A 14 Gurney rd E15
51 Z 14 Gurney rd E15
155 N 7 Gurney rd Carsh
150 B 4 Gurney st SE17
142 B 5 Gutter la EC2
142 G 17 Guy st SE1
121 P 2 Guy rd Wallgtn
93 T 13 Guyatt gdns Mitch
87 P 9 Guyscliffe rd SE13
87 O 11 Gwalior rd SW15
87 O 12 Gwendolen av SW15
87 O 12 Gwendolen clo SW15
65 V 3 Gwendoline av E13
144 M 9 Gwendwr rd W14
145 N 8 Gwendwr rd W14
97 O 14 Gwillim clo Sidcp
124 F 7 Gwydor rd Becknhm
126 D 5 Gwydyr rd Brom
124 E 16 Gwynne av Croy
133 P 14 Gwynne pl WC1
88 G 4 Gwynne rd SW11
138 M 10 Gye st SE11
91 P 11 Gylcote clo SE5
24 E 4 Gyles pk Stanm
54 L 10 Gyllyngdune gdns Ilf

H

78 H 16 Ha-Ha rd SE18
144 F 3 Haarlem rd W14
134 G 12 Haberdasher st N1
106 C 16 Haccombe rd SW19
155 O 2 Hackbridge grn Wallgtn
155 N 2 Hackbridge Pk gdns Carsh
155 P 1 Hackbridge rd Wallgtn
149 R 20 Hackford rd SW9
90 E 2 Hackford rd SW9
111 O 15 Hackington cres Becknhm
50 A 19 Hackney gro E8
135 T 9 Hackney rd E2
118 C 11 Hadden clo New Mald
79 U 9 Hadden way SE18
41 R 17 Hadden way Grnfd
111 X 9 Haddington rd Brom
76 F 17 Haddo st SE10
37 P 1 Haddon gdns W13
96 M 18 Haddon gro Sidcp
154 A 9 Haddon rd Sutton
63 P 11 Hadleigh clo E1
19 N 2 Hadleigh rd N9
18 M 2 Hadleigh rd N9
63 P 10 Hadleigh st E2
7 U 19 Hadley clo N21
5 N 9 Hadley common Barnt
73 Y 13 Hadley gdns W4
70 D 14 Hadley gdns S'hall
4 G 8 Hadley green West Barnt
4 H 9 Hadley Green rd Barnt
4 G 10 Hadley gro Barnt

4 J 8 Hadley house Barnt
6 G 3 Hadley rd Barnt
5 O 10 Hadley rd Barnt
81 O 9 Hadley rd Belvdr
7 R 4 Hadley rd Enf
145 X 9 Hadley rd Mitch
4 G 11 Hadley ridge Barnt
47 S 18 Hadley st NW1
7 T 20 Hadley way N21
4 K 9 Hadley Wood rd Barnt
5 O 9 Hadley Wood rd Barnt
109 W 17 Hadlow pl SE19
115 O 10 Hadlow rd Sidcp
80 G 19 Hadlow rd Belvdr
156 B 15 Hadrian clo Croy
76 M 14 Hadrian st SE10
74 F 5 Hadyn Pk rd W12
88 K 11 Hafer rd SW11
112 A 2 Hafton rd SE6
84 A 19 Haggard rd Twick
135 N 2 Haggerston rd E8
134 M 1 Haggerston rd E8
135 U 14 Hague st E2
11 R 17 Haig rd Stanm
65 Y 9 Haig Rd east E13
65 X 8 Haig Rd west E13
8 H 20 Haileybury av Enf
108 C 5 Hailsham av SW16
107 P 16 Hailsham rd SW17
18 A 15 Hailsham terr N18
95 O 12 Haimo rd SE9
38 A 17 Hainault gore Rom
37 S 11 Hainault house Rom
33 Z 20 Hainault rd E11
38 B 18 Hainault rd Rom
38 L 10 Hainault rd Rom
7 S 17 Hainault st Ilf
148 C 17 Haines st SW6
116 M 18 Hainthorpe rd SE27
56 B 11 Halbutt gdns Dgnhm
56 B 11 Halbutt st Dgnhm
134 J 6 Halcomb st N1
98 H 12 Halcot av Bxly Hth
63 O 16 Halcrow st E1
143 Y 1 Halcrow st E1
20 G 20 Haldan rd E4
33 V 1 Haldan rd E4
82 B 20 Haldane pl SW18
66 D 8 Haldane rd E6
145 R 17 Haldane rd SW16
58 M 18 Haldane rd Shall
87 W 15 Haldon rd SW18
20 G 10 Hale clo E4
12 J 16 Hale clo Edgw
12 K 19 Hale dri NW7
33 W 8 Hale End rd E17
20 J 19 Hale End rd E4
31 X 11 Hale gdns N17
73 P 2 Hale gdns W3
12 M 16 Hale Gro gdns NW7
13 N 17 Hale Gro gdns NW7
12 L 16 Hale la NW7
13 O 17 Hale la NW7
12 E 16 Hale la Edg
66 D 12 Hale rd E6
31 X 11 Hale rd N17
33 X 11 Hale the N17
59 U 15 Hale wlk W7
31 Z 6 Halefield rd N17
119 Z 18 Halesowen rd Mrdn
120 A 19 Halesowen rd Mrdn
93 P 7 Halesworth rd SE13
72 F 19 Half acre Brentf
71 S 2 Half Acre rd W7
135 R 7 Half Moon cres N1
90 L 15 Half Moon la SE24
91 N 15 Half Moon la SE24
139 Y 14 Half Moon st W1
143 O 5 Halfmoon pass E1
33 W 16 Halford rd E10
145 T 15 Halford rd SW6
84 J 13 Halford rd Rich
76 F 20 Halfway st Sidcp
114 J 2 Halfway st Sidcp
83 Z 12 Haliburton rd Twick
49 O 17 Haliday wlk N1
50 D 15 Halidon st E8
8 A 8 Halifax Enf
58 L 3 Halifax rd Grnfd
110 A 8 Halifax st SE26
157 N 14 Haling Pk rd S Croy
156 M 14 Haling Pk rd S Croy
157 O 13 Haling rd S Croy
147 S 1 Halkin pl SW1
156 C 16 Haling gro S Croy
156 K 13 Haling Pk gdns S Croy

139 U 19 Halkin st SW1
110 B 11 Hall dri SE26
59 U 16 Hall dri W7
11 O 13 Hall Farm clo Stanm
83 R 18 Hall Farm dri Twick
19 Z 14 Hall gdns E4
19 Y 14 Hall la E4
20 B 14 Hall la E4
26 G 7 Hall la NW4
132 G 20 Hall pl W2
98 L 14 Hall Pl cres Bxly
51 X 12 Hall rd E15
66 G 3 Hall rd E6
130 C 14 Hall rd W9
83 R 12 Hall rd Islwth
37 U 18 Hall rd Ro.
155 T 18 Hall rd Wallgtn
15 P 16 Hall st EC1
94 E 8 Hall the SE3
113 T 13 Hallam clo Chisl
22 C 2 Hallam gdns Pinn
131 Y 20 Hallam ms W1
129 Z 1 Hallam st W1
131 Y 19 Hallam st W1
52 K 18 Halley rd E7
53 P 15 Halley rd E7
63 V 15 Halley st E14
134 D 1 Halliford st N1
90 B 15 Halliwell rd SW2
29 O 4 Halliwick rd N10
153 Z 5 Hallmead rd Sutton
154 A 5 Hallmead rd Sutton
155 Z 7 Hallowell av Wallgtn
121 O 5 Hallowell clo Mitch
8 G 4 Hallside rd Enf
65 O 18 Hallsville rd E16
65 O 17 Hallsville rd E16
15 P 15 Hallswelle rd NW11
49 P 17 Hallway wik N1
95 X 17 Halons rd SE9
150 G 7 Halpin pl SE17
94 M 6 Halsbrook rd SE3
95 P 11 Halsbrook rd SE9
11 O 15 Halsbury clo Stanm
74 H 3 Halsbury rd W12
41 O 13 Halsbury Rd east Grnfd
40 L 14 Halsbury Rd west Grnfd
147 N 6 Halsey st SW3
54 K 16 Halsham cres Bark
90 K 2 Halsmere SE5
18 A 5 Halstead gdns N21
34 G 15 Halstead rd E11
18 A 5 Halstead rd N21
8 E 14 Halstead rd Enf
99 P 1 Halstead rd Erith
128 F 13 Halstow rd NW10
77 R 15 Halstow rd SE10
81 V 10 Halt Robin la Belvdr
81 T 10 Halt Robin rd Belvdr
133 Y 3 Halton Cross st N1
133 Y 2 Halton rd N1
48 J 20 Halton rd N1
102 D 6 Ham clo Rich
102 H 9 Ham Farm rd Rich
102 H 8 Ham Ga av Rich
102 C 2 Ham house Rich
52 E 20 Ham Pk rd E7
110 A 20 Ham pl SE20
102 M 11 Ham ridings Rich
102 C 3 Ham st Rich
72 C 20 Ham the Brentf
124 J 15 Ham view Croy
140 D 9 Ham yd W1
89 V 14 Hambalt rd SW4
88 B 7 Hamble st SW6
123 U 6 Hambledon gdns SE25
87 V 19 Hambledon rd SW18
96 F 19 Hambledown rd Sidcp
126 F 19 Hambro av Brom
107 Y 13 Hambro rd SW16
123 Z 6 Hambrook rd SE25
70 B 2 Hambrough rd S'hall
56 G 9 Hamden cres Dgnhm
64 G 18 Hamelin st E14
66 J 10 Hameway E6
52 C 17 Hamfrith rd E15
18 K 2 Hamilton av N9
36 B 14 Hamilton av Ilf
39 N 8 Hamilton av Rom
38 M 9 Hamilton av Rom
153 S 1 Hamilton av Sutton
130 E 15 Hamilton clo NW8
5 X 14 Hamilton clo Barnt
17 U 14 Hamilton cres N13
40 F 9 Hamilton cres Harrow

30 D 11 Hamilton gdns NW8
39 V 15 Hamilton mans W1
48 J 13 Hamilton pk N5
48 H 13 Hamilton Pk west N5
13 U 15 Hamilton pl W1
65 N 10 Hamilton rd E15
32 J 9 Hamilton rd E17
44 G 14 Hamilton rd NW10
45 R 1 Hamilton rd NW11
28 D 10 Hamilton rd N2
13 J 3 Hamilton rd N9
109 O 9 Hamilton rd SE27
106 B 18 Hamilton rd SW19
74 A 7 Hamilton rd W4
60 L 19 Hamilton rd W5
5 X 14 Hamilton rd Barnt
72 G 16 Hamilton rd Brentf
97 Z 4 Hamilton rd Bxly Hth
23 U 15 Hamilton rd Harrow
31 Y 16 Hamilton rd Ilf
39 Y 16 Hamilton rd Rom
70 E 2 Hamilton rd Shall
14 M 9 Hamilton rd Sidcp
123 N 5 Hamilton rd Thntn Hth
101 U 1 Hamilton rd Twick
76 A 18 Hamilton st SE8
130 B 12 Hamilton ter NW8
129 Z 9 Hamilton way N3
14 K 20 Hamilton way Wallgtn
155 X 19 Hamilton way Wallgtn
149 O 6 Hamish clo SE11
94 D 12 Hamlea clo SE12
39 D 2 Hamlet clo Rom
74 F 11 Hamlet gdns W6
109 W 18 Hamlet rd SE19
38 C 2 Hamlet rd Rom
91 P 7 Hamlet the SE5
63 Y 11 Hamlets way E3
109 R 19 Hamlyn gdns SE19
112 E 20 Hammelton rd Brom
13 U 15 Hammers la NW1
65 R 17 Hammersley av E16
144 D 7 Hammersmith bdwy W6
K 15 Hammersmith br W6
144 A 11 Hammersmith br W6
74 L 13 Hammersmith Br rd W6
144 B 10 Hammersmith Br rd W6
144 D 9 Hammersmith flyover W6
136 A 19 Hammersmith gro W6
144 C 5 Hammersmith gro W6
74 L 7 Hammersmith gro W6
144 H 6 Hammersmith rd W6
G 14 Hammersmith ter W6
121 R 4 Hammond av Mitch
9 N 10 Hammond rd Enf
70 D 9 Hammond rd S'hall
47 U 17 Hammond st NW5
12 E 9 Hamonde clo Edg
148 K 4 Hampden av Becknhm
139 O 6 Hampden Gurney st W1
31 W 5 Hampden la N17
29 P 1 Hampden rd N10
31 X 4 Hampden rd N17
30 G 13 Hampden rd N8
148 J 4 Hampden rd Becknhm
23 O 5 Hampden rd Harrow
117 R 5 Hampden rd Kingst
88 H 2 Hampden rd Rom
16 E 6 Hampden way Enf
18 M 17 Hampshire clo N18
74 H 12 Hampshire Hog la W6
30 D 1 Hampshire rd N22
47 X 16 Hampshire st NW5
90 C 1 Hampson way SW8
27 X 19 Hampstead gdns NW11
46 J 14 Hampstead grn NW3
46 D 11 Hampstead gro NW3
46 G 6 Hampstead heath NW3
28 E 11 Hampstead heights N2
46 F 13 Hampstead High st NW3
46 H 13 Hampstead Hill gdns NW3
47 N 2 Hampstead la N6
46 K 2 Hampstead la N6
132 B 11 Hampstead rd NW1

46 E 10 Hampstead sq NW3
46 C 4 Hampstead way NW1
27 X 16 Hampstead way NW1
104 L 18 Hampton clo SW20
116 C 8 Hampton Court park Kingst
48 H 18 Hampton ct N1
100 C 10 Hampton la Felt
51 X 5 Hampton rd E4
19 X 16 Hampton rd E4
19 X 16 Hampton rd E7
52 G 15 Hampton rd E7
129 U 14 Hampton rd NW6
146 M 14 Hampton rd Croy
147 N 15 Hampton rd Croy
54 B 13 Hampton rd Ilf
101 R 13 Hampton rd Tedd
101 R 6 Hampton rd Twick
152 H 3 Hampton rd Worc Pk
100 G 9 Hampton Rd east Felt
100 C 6 Hampton Rd west Felt
24 K 19 Hampton ri Harrow
129 Z 6 Hampton st E5
77 U 3 Hanmeel st E16
31 Y 7 Hanbury rd N17
89 P 6 Hanbury rd SW11
73 T 7 Hanbury rd W3
135 S 20 Hanbury st E1
64 F 9 Hancock rd E3
109 O 16 Hancock rd SE19
141 P 2 Hand ct WC2
122 H 19 Handcroft rd Croy
156 J 1 Handcroft rd Croy
11 Z 9 Handel clo Edg
132 K 16 Handel st WC1
12 C 20 Handel way Edg
25 O 1 Handen rd SE12
94 C 14 Handen rd SE12
149 S 18 Handforth rd SW9
139 S 18 Handforth rd SW9
63 R 2 Handley rd E9
20 J 19 Handsworth av E4
31 P 11 Handsworth rd N17
R7 N 5 Handtrough way Barking
104 M 14 Hanford row SW19
61 O 11 Hanger grn W5
60 K 12 Hanger Hill park W5
60 L 14 Hanger la W5
60 M 17 Hanger vale W5
61 O 15 Hanger Vale la W5
141 V 6 Hanging Sword all EC4
142 F 19 Hankey pl SE1
13 N 10 Hankins la NW7
48 A 5 Hanley rd N4
108 K 8 Hannen rd SE27
63 R 14 Hannibal rd E1
50 L 17 Hannington point E9
89 S 8 Hannington rd SW4
153 T 8 Hanover clo Sutton
130 M 13 Hanover gate NW1
139 S 16 Hanover gdns SE11
36 B 2 Hanover gdns Ilf
91 X 3 Hanover pk SE15
140 L 7 Hanover pl WC2
62 M 2 Hanover rd NW10
128 C 3 Hanover rd NW10
31 V 13 Hanover rd N15
139 Y 7 Hanover sq W1
131 N 14 Hanover ter NW1
131 N 15 Hanover Ter ms NW1
139 O 20 Hans cres SW3
147 O 2 Hans pl SW1
147 N 1 Hans rd SW3
147 P 2 Hans st SW1
7 U 7 Hansart way Enf
136 J 18 Hansard ms W14
105 Y 1 Hansford clo SW18
25 X 4 Hanshaw dri Edgw
91 V 13 Hansler rd SE22
97 Y 12 Hansol rd Bxly Hth
70 C 5 Hanson gdns S'hall
132 A 20 Hanson st W1
140 A 1 Hanson st W1
140 F 3 Hanway pl W1
140 F 4 Hanway st W1
100 A 9 Hanworth clo Felt
100 J 14 Hanworth rd Hampt
82 H 14 Hanworth rd Hounsl
82 K 10 Hanworth ter Hounsl
143 T 9 Harads pl E1
46 E 20 Harben rd NW6
65 P 3 Harberson rd E15
93 R 20 Harberson rd SW12
47 V 4 Harberton rd N19
19 U 17 Harbet rd E4
98 F 18 Harbex clo Bxly

76 D 12 Harbinger rd E14
87 X 1 Harbledown rd SW6
87 P 1 Harbord st SW6
96 J 18 Harborough av Sidcp
108 D 9 Harborough rd SW16
90 L 7 Harbour rd SE5
86 F 18 Harbridge av SW15
154 M 17 Harbury rd Carsh
88 F 11 Harbut rd SW11
49 R 10 Harcombe rd N16
53 T 14 Harcourt av E12
12 G 11 Harcourt av Edg
97 T 18 Harcourt av Sidcp
155 T 9 Harcourt av Wallgtn
155 T 8 Harcourt field Wallgtn
65 O 6 Harcourt rd E15
29 W 4 Harcourt rd N22
92 K 8 Harcourt rd SE4
105 Y 19 Harcourt rd SW19
97 Z 9 Harcourt rd Bxly Hth
122 D 14 Harcourt rd Thntn Hth
155 S 8 Harcourt rd Wallgtn
138 M 2 Harcourt st W1
145 Z 11 Harcourt ter SW10
146 A 12 Harcourt ter SW10
159 T 7 Hardcourts clo W Wkhm
108 G 2 Hardel ri SW2
90 G 1 Harden st SE18
78 A 9 Hardens manorway SE18
91 Z 2 Harders rd SE15
92 A 2 Harders Rd ms SE15
90 K 8 Hardess st SE24
56 K 10 Hardie rd Dgnhm
98 A 4 Harding rd Bxly Hth
62 L 4 Hardinge rd NW10
128 C 6 Hardinge rd NW10
18 D 18 Hardinge rd N18
63 R 19 Hardinge st E1
110 E 16 Hardings la SE20
77 U 13 Hardman rd SE7
116 K 2 Hardman rd Kingst
82 H 2 Hardwick av Hounsl
11 R 16 Hardwick clo Stanm
57 13 Hardwick st EC1
17 N 18 Hardwicke rd N13
73 X 11 Hardwicke rd W4
102 C 9 Hardwicke rd Rich
87 Z 1 Hardwicks way SW18
142 J 17 Hardwidge st SE1
77 R 17 Hardy rd SE3
88 B 19 Hardy rd SW19
7 U 6 Hardy way Enf
93 X 4 Hare And Billet rd SE13
94 A 4 Hare And Billet rd SE3
141 S 7 Hare ct EC4
39 Y 12 Hare Hall la Rom
54 S 18 Hare st SE18
134 L 9 Hare wlk N1
48 L 17 Harecastle ct N1
29 X 15 Haredale rd SE24
153 R 20 Harefield av N8
92 K 7 Harefield ms SE4
31 O 19 Harefield rd N15
92 L 8 Harefield rd SE4
93 N 8 Harefield rd SE4
108 D 18 Harefield rd SW16
115 W 6 Harefield rd Sidcp
56 F 19 Haresfield rd Dgnhm
131 N 20 Harewood av NW1
130 M 17 Harewood av NW1
58 T 1 Harewood clo Grnfd
60 P 1 Harewood dri Ilf
106 K 16 Harewood rd SW19
83 W 1 Harewood rd Islwth
71 V 20 Harewood rd Islwth
157 S 14 Harewood rd S Croy
130 M 20 Harewood row NW1
70 F 11 Harewood ter S'hall
91 R 7 Harfield gdns SE5
20 E 2 Harford clo E4
20 E 2 Harford rd E4
63 U 12 Harford st E1
28 G 14 Harford wlk N2
94 L 4 Hargood rd SE3
47 U 8 Hargrave pk N19
47 X 16 Hargrave rd N19
47 W 7 Hargrave rd N19
36 A 13 Hargville gdns Ilf
90 B 8 Hargwyne st SW9
30 D 13 Haringey gro N8
30 A 19 Haringey pk N8

30 A 14 Haringey rd N8
18 A 12 Harington ter N13
157 W 5 Harland av Croy
14 E 6 Harland rd Sidcp
94 E 20 Harland rd SE12
112 F 1 Harland rd SE12
17 O 11 Harlech rd N14
71 Z 17 Harlequin av Brentf
102 A 17 Harlequin rd Tedd
92 F 10 Harlescort st SE15
62 D 3 Harlesden gdns NW10
62 F 4 Harlesden la NW10
62 H 2 Harlesden rd NW10
44 J 20 Harlesden rd NW10
42 G 17 Harley clo Wemb
23 R 13 Harley cres Harrow
146 C 11 Harley gdns SW10
63 Z 9 Harley gro E3
139 W 2 Harley pl W1
62 B 6 Harley rd NW10
130 H 2 Harley rd NW3
23 R 12 Harley rd Harrow
139 X 2 Harley st W1
131 W 19 Harley st W1
12 K 20 Harleyford Brom
149 O 13 Harleyford rd SE11
149 S 15 Harleyford st SE11
126 G 14 Harling st SE17
98 A 7 Harlington rd Bxly Hth
18 A 10 Harlow rd N13
21 O 20 Harman av Wdfd Grn
45 T 11 Harman clo NW2
45 T 11 Harman dri NW2
96 L 15 Harman dri Sidcp
8 G 16 Harman rd Enf
30 A 15 Harmiston av N8
47 R 20 Harmood pl NW1
47 R 20 Harmood st NW1
149 W 12 Harmsworth st SE17
14 J 6 Harmsworth way N20
79 Z 6 Harness rd SE18
25 X 4 Harnshaw dri Edg
81 O 14 Harold av Belvdr
149 R 12 Harold pl SE11
51 Z 4 Harold rd E11
65 X 3 Harold rd E13
20 F 12 Harold rd E4
61 X 8 Harold rd NW10
31 V 14 Harold rd N15
30 C 14 Harold rd N8
109 R 16 Harold rd SE19
154 F 9 Harold rd Sutton
34 G 4 Harold rd Wdfd Grn
32 G 16 Haroldstone rd E17
141 V 4 Harp all EC4
142 J 10 Harp la EC3
59 V 12 Harp rd W7
52 K 6 Harpenden rd E12
108 H 5 Harpenden rd SE27
150 C 1 Harper rd SE1
142 B 20 Harper rd SE1
63 S 10 Harpley sq E1
54 B 19 Harpour rd Bark
89 O 3 Harpsden st SW11
133 N 20 Harpur ms WC1
133 N 20 Harpur st WC1
94 L 2 Harraden rd SE3
139 R 20 Harriet st SW1
139 R 19 Harriet wlk SW1
30 J 14 Harringay gdns N15
30 G 15 Harringay pass N8
30 J 14 Harringay rd N15
30 J 13 Harringay rd N15
146 A 7 Harrington gdns SW7
50 B 4 Harrington hill E5
52 A 4 Harrington rd E11
124 B 8 Harrington rd SE25
123 Y 9 Harrington rd SE25
146 E 6 Harrington rd SW7
132 N 3 Harrington sq NW1
132 A 12 Harrington sq NW1
98 A 2 Harris rd Bxly Hth
56 B 15 Harris rd Dgnhm
50 L 1 Harris st E17
150 G 19 Harris st SE5
56 F 19 Harrison rd Dgnhm
132 M 14 Harrison st WC1
156 J 5 Harrison's ri Croy
55 R 15 Harrold rd Dgnhm
28 H 1 Harrow av Enf
39 Z 3 Harrow cres Rom
18 G 4 Harrow dri N9
57 Z 3 Harrow dri Hornch
51 Z 9 Harrow grn E11
64 F 20 Harrow la E14
57 V 7 Harrow Lodge park Hornch

68 F 20 Harrow Manor way SE2
41 U 6 Harrow pk Harrow
142 M 3 Harrow pl E1
52 D 9 Harrow rd E11
66 D 2 Harrow rd E6
128 D 14 Harrow rd NW10
62 J 8 Harrow rd NW10
138 B 2 Harrow rd W2
129 O 17 Harrow rd W9
67 V 3 Harrow rd Bark
154 J 12 Harrow rd Carsh
54 C 14 Harrow rd Ilf
41 X 12 Harrow rd Wemb
43 P 17 Harrow rd Wemb
23 R 14 Harrow view Harrow
60 C 12 Harrow View rd W5.
10 D 18 Harrow Weald pk Harrow
88 F 5 Harrowway st W11
139 N 4 Harrowby st W1
138 M 4 Harrowby st W1
139 N 4 Harrowby st W1
42 F 14 Harrowdene clo Wemb
42 G 10 Harrowdene rd Wemb
12 D 10 Harrowes meade Edg
50 G 19 Harrowgate rd E9
73 O 2 Hart gro W5
58 G 14 Hart gro S'hall
142 L 8 Hart st EC3
67 O 4 Hart st Bark
141 S 1 Hart yd EC1
82 F 5 Harte rd Hounsl
105 V 17 Hartfield cres SW19
110 B 20 Hartfield gro SE20
105 W 18 Hartfield rd SW19
64 B 7 Hartfield ter E3
24 A 10 Hartford av Harrow
23 Z 10 Hartford av Harrow
98 F 17 Hartford rd Bxly
27 H 14 Hartford wlk N2
48 A 15 Hartham clo N7
83 X 1 Hartham clo Islwth
31 U 6 Hartham rd N17
48 A 15 Hartham rd N7
83 X 2 Hartham rd Islwth
113 P 8 Hartington rd SE9
7 Z 4 Hartingdon rd Enf
65 V 17 Hartington rd E16
32 H 19 Hartington rd E17
31 X 6 Hartington rd N17
J 10 Hartington rd N9
148 J 20 Hartington rd SW8
89 Z 1 Hartington rd SW8
72 B 1 Hartington rd W13
85 W 3 Hartington st W4
73 U 20 Hartington rd W4
70 B 7 Hartington rd S'hall
84 B 17 Hartington rd Twick
145 R 17 Hartismore rd SW6
50 G 18 Hartlake rd E9
12 C 9 Hartland clo Edg
12 B 9 Hartland dri Edg
52 B 20 Hartland rd E15
65 O 1 Hartland rd E15
147 R 20 Hartland rd NW1
129 O 7 Hartland rd NW6
15 Z 17 Hartland rd N11
100 K 10 Hartland rd Hampt
57 W 8 Hartland rd Hornch
83 Z 7 Hartland rd Islwth
119 Z 18 Hartland rd Mrdn
158 H 4 Hartland way Croy
158 H 2 Hartland way Croy
119 W 16 Hartland way Mrdn
66 D 4 Hartley av E6
13 R 17 Hartley av NW7
13 R 17 Hartley clo NW7
127 V 4 Hartley clo Brom
52 C 3 Hartley rd E11
122 K 16 Hartley rd Croy
80 F 18 Hartley rd Welling
63 R 8 Hartley st E2
48 D 15 Hartnoll st N7
19 N 9 Harton st SE4
93 N 1 Harton st SE4
120 L 17 Hartopp av SW4
92 G 1 Harts la SE14
53 Z 18 Harts la Bark
9 O 15 Harts way Enf
10 B 8 Hartsbourne av Bushey Watf
10 D 8 Hartsbourne rd Bushey Watf
142 L 7 Hartshorn all EC3
66 J 11 Hartshorn gdns E6
113 T 3 Hartsmead rd SE9
74 C 7 Hartswood rd W12
79 V 11 Hartville rd SE18.
20 F 19 Hartwell dri E4

49 U 17 Hartwell st E8
73 U 15 Harvard hill W4
73 V 15 Harvard la W4
93 V 14 Harvard rd SE13
73 T 14 Harvard rd W4
83 T 3 Harvard rd Islwth
80 J 14 Harvel cres SE2
134 G 5 Harvey ct N1
77 Z 13 Harvey gdns SE7
52 B 3 Harvey rd E11
30 C 15 Harvey rd N8
91 O 1 Harvey rd SE5
82 F 19 Harvey rd Hounsl
53 Z 16 Harvey rd Ilf
54 A 16 Harvey rd Ilf
57 P 6 Harvey's la Rom
115 X 13 Harvill rd Sidcp
128 H 11 Harvist rd NW6
129 O 9 Harviste st NW6
129 N 9 Harviste st NW6
28 L 12 Harwell pas N2
126 G 3 Harwood av Brom
120 J 6 Harwood av Mitch
145 V 19 Harwood rd SW6
88 A 1 Harwood ter SW6
18 F 12 Haselbury grn N9
18 E 12 Haselbury la N9
18 F 8 Haselbury rd N9
92 C 20 Haseley end SE23
89 Y 11 Haselrigge rd SW4
110 K 10 Haseltine rd SE26
55 W 13 Haskard rd Dgnhm
55 W 14 Haskard rd Dgnhm
146 M 4 Hasker st SW3
119 T 19 Haslam av Sutton
27 O 18 Haslemere av NW4
106 A 3 Haslemere av SW18
72 A 9 Haslemere av W13
15 Z 6 Haslemere av Barnt
144 F 3 Haslemere av Mitch
71 Z 9 Haslemere Av 1-84 W13
100 F 12 Haslemere clo Hampt
156 A 12 Haslemere clo Wallgtn
27 U 11 Haslemere gdns N3
17 V 7 Haslemere rd N21
29 Z 20 Haslemere rd N8
98 C 5 Haslemere rd Bxly Hth
54 K 6 Haslemere rd Ilf
122 H 11 Haslemere rd Thntn Hth
159 U 17 Hasley dri Croy
5 O 19 Hasluck gdns Barnt
135 P 12 Hassard st E2
77 V 18 Hassendean rd SE10
50 G 17 Hassett rd E9
145 X 1 Hassocks clo SE26
145 O 11 Hassocks rd SW16
113 P 9 Hassop wlk SE9
78 B 13 Hasted rd SE18
36 B 14 Hastings av Ilf
65 N 5 Hastings rd E15
16 J 17 Hastings rd N11
31 O 9 Hastings rd N17
60 B 20 Hastings rd W13
123 U 19 Hastings rd Croy
39 Y 17 Hastings rd Rom
132 J 14 Hastings st WC1
26 H 11 Hatch croft NW4
37 Z 13 Hatch gro Rom
20 K 12 Hatch la E4
146 A 3 Hatch rd SW16
9 S 7 Hatch the Enf
75 U 20 Hatcham Pk rd SE14
92 F 1 Hatcham Pk rd SE14
75 P 16 Hatcham rd SE15
47 Z 6 Hatchard rd N19
94 B 8 Hatcliffe clo SE3
35 Z 9 Hatfield clo Ilf
120 E 9 Hatfield clo Mitch
119 X 12 Hatfield mead Mrdn
52 A 14 Hatfield rd E15
71 Y 3 Hatfield rd W13
73 Z 5 Hatfield rd W4
55 Z 20 Hatfield rd Dgnhm
68 M 1 Hatfield rd Dgnhm
134 A 18 Hatfield st EC1
141 U 12 Hatfields SE1
10 K 17 Hathaway clo Stanm
53 U 17 Hathaway cres E12
59 Y 14 Hathaway gdns W13
37 V 15 Hathaway gdns Rom
122 K 18 Hathaway rd Croy
119 Y 9 Hatherleigh clo Mrdn
115 O 6 Hatherley cres Sidcp
66 B 8 Hatherley gdns E6
137 X 5 Hatherley gro W2
32 M 13 Hatherley rd E17

33 N 12 Hatherley rd E7
85 N 3 Hatherley rd Rich
115 O 8 Hatherley rd Sidcp
148 D 6 Hatherley st SW1
113 W 10 Hathern gdns SE9
100 D 18 Hathrop rd Hampt
92 D 6 Hathway st SE15
36 B 13 Hatley av Ilf
15 Y 15 Hatley clo N11
48 E 7 Hatley rd N4
75 P 5 Hatteraick st SE16
133 T 20 Hatton gdn EC1
141 U 1 Hatton gdn EC1
120 M 11 Hatton gdns Mitch
122 G 19 Hatton rd Croy
130 G 19 Hatton row W2
133 T 19 Hatton wall EC1
133 U 20 Hatton yd EC1
139 X 7 Haunch Of Venison rd W1
105 Z 4 Havana rd SW19
76 A 6 Havannah st E14
33 U 11 Havant rd E17
23 U 19 Havelock pl Harrow
31 Y 7 Havelock rd N17
106 C 12 Havelock rd SW19
81 O 12 Havelock rd Blvdr
150 L 8 Havelock rd Brom
126 L 8 Havelock rd Brom
157 V 2 Havelock rd Croy
99 Y 18 Havelock rd Drtfd
23 T 10 Havelock rd Harrow
70 D 8 Havelock rd S'hall
132 M 4 Havelock st N1
54 A 8 Havelock st N1
89 T 1 Havelock ter SW8
147 Z 20 Havelock ter SW8
110 C 2 Havelock wlk SE23
105 O 6 Haven clo SW19
60 G 18 Haven grn W5
60 J 17 Haven la W5
60 G 19 Haven pl W5
7 T 10 Havenhurst ri Enf
43 U 8 Havenwood Wemb
73 P 19 Haverfield gdns Rich
63 U 8 Haverfield rd E3
25 N 5 Haverford way Edg
20 H 6 Haverhill rd E4
107 V 2 Haverhill rd SW12
107 V 1 Haverhill rd SW4
39 P 11 Havering dri Rom
37 W 14 Havering gdns Rom
38 M 9 Havering rd Rom
39 N 3 Havering rd Rom
63 S 18 Havering st E1
68 D 8 Havering way Bark
84 H 17 Haversham clo Twick
46 K 17 Haverstock hill NW3
47 N 15 Haverstock hill NW5
133 Y 10 Haverstock st N1
126 J 20 Havil st SE5
91 S 1 Havil st SE5
90 L 18 Hawarden gro SE24
32 F 13 Hawarden rd E17
51 W 3 Hawbridge rd E11
125 V 19 Hawes la W Wkham
159 X 1 Hawes la W Wkham
18 L 19 Hawes rd N18
112 H 20 Hawes rd Brom
133 X 2 Hawes st N1
64 B 14 Hawgood st E3
30 K 9 Hawke Park rd N22
109 P 14 Hawke rd SE19
156 B 16 Hawker clo Croy
116 L 4 Hawkes pass Kingst
106 L 20 Hawkes rd Mitch
86 J 13 Hawkesbury rd SW15
110 K 5 Hawkesfield rd SE23
107 Y 19 Hawkeshead rd SW16
117 X 11 Hawkhurst way New Mald
159 S 2 Hawkhurst way W Wkham
41 P 1 Hawkins cres Harrow
108 K 5 Hawkley gdns SE27
57 T 19 Hawkridge clo Rom
71 N 4 Hawks ri Kingst
116 M 4 Hawks rd Kingst
44 D 20 Hawkshead rd NW10
74 A 7 Hawkshead rd W4
92 E 13 Hawkslade rd SE15
49 P 5 Hawksley ct N16
49 P 9 Hawksley rd N16
120 H 15 Hawksmoor st W6
20 F 3 Hawksmouth E4
75 R 10 Hawkstone rd SE16
50 A 3 Hawkwood mt E5
40 A 1 Hawlands dri Pinn
131 Y 1 Hawley cres NW1

47 S 20 Hawley rd NW1
47 S 20 Hawley st NW1
93 R 17 Hawstead rd SE6
10 E 6 Hawthorn av N13
122 H 1 Hawthorn av Thntn
98 F 13 Hawthorn clo Hamp
22 G 19 Hawthorn dri Harrow
72 H 8 Hawthorn gdns W5
110 A 19 Hawthorn gro SE20
8 C 4 Hawthorn gro Enf
72 C 20 Hawthorn hatch Brentf
27 S 5 Hawthorn ms NW7
44 H 19 Hawthorn rd NW10
18 F 18 Hawthorn rd N18
29 Y 11 Hawthorn rd N8
72 B 20 Hawthorn rd Brentf
21 Z 14 Hawthorn rd Buck H
98 B 12 Hawthorn rd Bxly Hth
154 H 12 Hawthorn rd Sutton
155 T 15 Hawthorn rd Wallgt
18 F 9 Hawthorn way N9
155 P 16 Hawthorne av Carsh
144 G 3 Hawthorne av Mitch
127 T 7 Hawthorne clo Brom
154 C 3 Hawthorne clo Brom
58 C 4 Hawthorne Farm av Grnfd
25 W 20 Hawthorne gro NW9
33 O 10 Hawthorne rd E17
127 U 6 Hawthorne rd Brom
21 S 10 Hawthorns Buck Hl
130 K 1 Hawtrey rd NW3
112 H 20 Haxted rd Brom
139 Z 11 Hay hill W1
25 X 13 Hay la NW9
149 H 13 Hay's la SE1
139 W 11 Hay's mans W1
57 U 4 Hayburn way Hornch
62 H 4 Haycroft gdns NW10
90 B 13 Haycroft rd SW2
64 E 16 Haycurrie st E14
25 S 14 Hayday rd E16
38 K 7 Hayden way Rom
137 N 5 Hayden's pl N11
40 G 17 Haydock av Grnfd
40 G 17 Haydock grn Grnfd
25 W 14 Haydon clo NW9
105 Z 12 Haydon Pk rd SW19
106 A 12 Haydon Pk rd SW19
55 V 7 Haydon rd Dgnhm
143 O 7 Haydon st EC3
85 B 3 Haydon's rd SW19
125 Y 13 Hayes chase W Wkham
94 A 8 Hayes clo SE13
15 S 12 Hayes cres NW11
153 P 7 Hayes cres Sutton
126 A 20 Hayes hill Brom
126 B 20 Hayes Hill rd Brom
125 U 7 Hayes la Brom
126 G 14 Hayes la Brom
126 A 20 Hayes mead Brom
125 Z 20 Hayes mead W Wkham
130 M 19 Hayes pl NW1
126 F 10 Hayes rd Brom
122 G 20 Hayes st Brom
153 P 20 Hayes walk Sutton
125 U 8 Hayes way Becknhm
126 H 20 Hayes Wood av Brom
150 D 12 Hayesford Pk dri Brom
63 S 14 Hayfield pass E1
25 X 14 Hayfield clo NW9
149 X 3 Hayles st SE11
49 T 15 Hayling rd N16
133 X 2 Hayman st N1
140 F 11 Haymarket SW1
124 L 2 Hayne rd Becknhm
133 Y 20 Hayne st EC1
141 Z 1 Hayne st EC1
109 S 16 Haynes la SE19
42 K 20 Haynes rd Wemb
119 T 5 Haynt wlk SW20
133 P 8 Hays bldgs N1
123 Y 4 Haysleigh gdns SE20
90 C 12 Hayter rd SW2
86 M 16 Hayward gdns SW15
87 N 16 Hayward gdns SW15
15 P 8 Hayward rd N20
133 W 17 Hayward's pl EC1
98 M 13 Haywood cl Bxly

27 N 8 Haywood rd Brom	101 V 2 Heath gdns Twick	87 W 3 Heathmans rd SW6	45 Y 20 Hemstal rd NW6
18 A 11 Hazel clo N13	110 B 18 Heath gro SE20	82 E 19 Heathside Hounsl	134 J 7 Hemsworth st N1
91 Y 5 Hazel clo SE15	46 J 13 Heath Hurst rd NW3	98 A 4 Heathside av Bxly Hth	146 K 11 Hemus pl SW3
72 B 18 Hazel clo Brentf	157 R 19 Heath Hurst rd S Croy	97 Z 3 Heathside av Bxly Hth	142 L 5 Henage la EC3
57 Y 11 Hazel clo Hornch	93 H 7 Heath la SE3	62 H 18 Heathstan rd W12	143 P 1 Hencage st E1
21 Z 9 Hazel clo Mitch	105 O 6 Heath mead SW19	99 S 17 Heathview av Drtfrd	62 D 17 Henchman st W12
33 O 18 Hazel clo Twick	39 X 15 Heath Pk rd Rom	99 X 20 Heathview cres Drtfrd	26 H 10 Hendale av NW4
39 X 2 Hazel dri Erith	89 R 7 Heath rd SW8	86 L 19 Heathview gdns SW15	52 K 17 Henderson rd E7
12 E 13 Hazel gdns Edg	99 T 17 Heath rd Drtfrd	122 F 8 Heathview rd Thntn Hth	18 M 4 Henderson rd N9
10 G 11 Hazel gro SE26	3 N 20 Heath rd Harrow	48 A 2 Heathville rd N4	88 H 18 Henderson rd SW18
37 X 9 Hazel gro Rom	83 P 10 Heath rd Hounsl	58 M 17 Heathwall st SW11	123 N 13 Henderson rd Croy
50 K 5 Hazel gro Wemb	82 L 11 Heath rd Hounsl	158 M 5 Heathway Croy	106 K 4 Henderson rd SW17
22 J 4 Hazel la Rich	55 Y 1 Heath rd Romford	56 C 12 Heathway Dgnhm	27 V 6 Hendon av N3
52 L 8 Hazel rd NW10	122 M 5 Heath rd Thntn Hth	69 R 2 Heathway Dgnhm	27 U 9 Hendon av N3
28 B 12 Hazel rd NW10	101 V 2 Heath rd Twick	78 D 13 Heathwood gdns SE18	13 S 7 Hendon park NW7
39 X 2 Hazel rd Erith	87 R 16 Heath ri SW13	99 O 20 Heathwood lodge Bxly	27 V 17 Hendon Pk row NW11
19 X 19 Hazel way E4	126 D 14 Heath ri Brom	39 Y 2 Heaton av Rom	18 K 7 Hendon rd N9
27 X 15 Hazel wlk Brom	46 H 11 Heath side NW3	39 U 6 Heaton Grange rd Rom	11 P 3 Hendon Urban motorway Edg
8 J 19 Hazel Wood rd Enf	67 N 3 Heath st Barking	91 Y 6 Heaton pl E15	45 T 6 Hendon way NW2
12 A 4 Hazelbank rd SE6	16 Z 16 Heath view N2	91 Y 6 Heaton rd SE15	26 L 18 Hendon way NW4
11 Z 4 Hazelbank rd SE6	28 D 12 Heath View clo N2	107 O 17 Heaton rd Mitch	13 T 4 Hendon Wood la NW7
9 T 16 Hazelbourne rd SW12	79 W 15 Heath vlls SE18	88 H 6 Heaver rd SW11	150 K 7 Hendre rd SE1
36 F 1 Hazelbrook gdns Ilf	77 S 20 Heath way SE3	79 S 14 Heavitree rd SE18	88 M 18 Hendrick av SW12
46 A 2 Hazelbury rd SW6	98 L 2 Heath way Erith	107 K 7 Hebdon rd SW17	98 E 15 Henfield clo Bxly
61 Z 1 Hazeldean NW10	21 Z 15 Heath way Wdfd Grn	45 O 14 Heber rd NW2	119 V 1 Henfield rd SW19
73 V 16 Hazeldene rd W4	83 V 19 Heatham pk Twick	91 V 15 Heber rd SE22	120 Y 20 Henfield rd SW19
55 P 6 Hazeldene rd W4	10 G 8 Heathbourne rd Stanm	144 A 2 Hebron rd W6	94 J 18 Hengist st SE12
95 T 5 Hazeldene rd Welling	99 V 20 Heathclose av Drtfrd	74 L 9 Hebron rd W6	81 X 18 Hengist rd Erith
92 J 13 Hazeldon rd SE4	35 U 7 Heathcote av Ilf	145 T 19 Heckfield pl SW6	125 Y 9 Hengist way Brom
25 V 1 Hazelhurst Becknhm	20 F 9 Heathcote gro E4	79 U 12 Heckford st E1	92 E 17 Hengrave rd SE23
06 E 9 Hazelhurst rd SW17	84 C 14 Heathcote rd Twick	83 Y 9 Heddon clo Islwth	46 E 12 Heniker ms SW3
38 G 3 Hazell cres Rom	133 N 15 Heathcote st WC1	6 A 15 Heddon Court av Bark	153 R 5 Henley av Sutton
47 X 2 Hazellville rd N19	61 Z 1 Heathcroft NW10	5 Z 16 Heddon rd Barnt	59 O 6 Henley clo Grnfd
29 S 6 Hazelmere rd NW6	46 B 3 Heathcroft NW11	140 B 10 Heddon st W1	83 V 3 Henley clo Islwth
26 E 14 Hazelmere way Brom	60 M 11 Heathcroft W5	7 W 6 Hedge hill Enf	60 C 18 Henley clo Kingst
87 N 12 Hazelwell rd SW15	61 N 12 Heathcroft W5	94 B 12 Hedgeley st SE12	37 Y 15 Henley gdns Rom
20 B 9 Hazelwood clo Mrdn	82 B 8 Heathdale av Hounsl	56 C 19 Hedgemans rd Dgnhm	78 H 5 Henley rd E16
72 K 5 Hazelwood clo W5	108 C 18 Heathdene rd SW16	55 W 20 Hedgemans rd Dgnhm	128 D 3 Henley rd N18
17 T 13 Hazelwood cres N13	155 T 16 Heathdene rd Wallgtn	55 Y 19 Hedgemans way Dgnhm	18 D 13 Henley rd N18
16 J 14 Hazelwood ct Surb	39 O 7 Heather av Rom	58 M 7 Hedgerly gdns Grnfd	54 B 13 Henley rd Ilf
7 W 13 Hazelwood dri Enf	39 N 5 Heather clo Rom	50 H 18 Hedgers gro E9	89 O 4 Henley st SW11
17 T 13 Hazelwood la N13	99 V 19 Heather dri Drtfd	35 V 14 Hedgewood gdns Ilf	110 E 7 Hennel clo SE23
32 H 16 Hazelwood rd E17	39 O 7 Heather dri Rom	35 T 13 Hedgley Ilf	66 D 7 Henniker gdns E6
57 R 4 Hazledean rd Croy	27 S 19 Heather gdns NW11	55 P 16 Hedingham rd Dgnhm	66 C 8 Henniker gdns E6
18 H 19 Hazlemere gdns Worc Park	39 O 6 Heather gdns Rom	115 R 7 Hedley clo Sidcp	51 Y 15 Henniker st SW11
72 H 8 Hazlenut rd W5	39 N 7 Heather glen Rom	8 A 8 Heene rd Enf	88 H 3 Henning st SW11
86 L 12 Hazlewell rd SW15	161 R 2 Heather Pk dri Wemb	66 C 2 Heigham rd E6	31 P 3 Henningham rd N17
28 M 17 Hazlewood cres W10	44 D 7 Heather rd NW2	156 J 10 Heighton gns Croy	129 W 5 Henrietta pl W1
29 N 18 Hazlewood cres W10	112 F 2 Heather rd SE12	77 Z 15 Heights the SE7	31 R 18 Henrietta rd N15
44 K 2 Hazlitt ms W14	39 N 6 Heather way Rom	40 F 15 Heights the Grnfd	140 K 9 Henrietta st WC2
44 K 3 Hazlitt rd W14	158 T 18 Heather way S Croy	139 Z 15 Heiron st SE17	143 T 6 Henriques st E1
63 S 16 Head st E1	10 J 20 Heather way Stanm	89 Y 16 Helby rd SW4	87 O 8 Henry Jackson rd SW15
31 U 2 Headcorn rd N17	12 E 16 Heather wlk Edg	56 C 19 Helder gro SE12	66 E 6 Henry rd E6
12 D 12 Headcorn rd Brom	95 V 5 Heatherbank SE9	157 O 13 Helder st S Croy	66 H 5 Henry rd N4
22 D 8 Headcorn rd Thntn Hth	144 H 10 Heatherdean clo Mitch	83 R 9 Heldman clo Islwth	5 T 17 Henry rd Barnt
39 V 19 Headford pl SW1	93 U 13 Heathergrove est SE13	78 M 11 Helen st SE18	112 J 20 Henry st Brom
26 K 12 Heading st NW4	35 S 9 Heatherley dri Ilf	156 C 16 Helena clo Croy	21 P 16 Henrys av Wdfd Grn
06 E 2 Headington rd SW18	49 W 10 Heatherley pl N16	60 G 14 Helena ct W5	36 D 2 Henrys wlk Ilf
89 X 17 Headlam rd SW4	49 W 11 Heatherley st N16	65 R 7 Helena rd E13	92 M 13 Henryson rd SE4
45 Y 18 Headlam st E1	108 D 19 Heatherset gdns SW16	33 N 17 Helena rd E17	93 N 13 Henryson rd SE4
63 N 12 Headlam st E1	115 V 6 Heatherside rd Sidcp	44 J 14 Helena rd NW10	110 A 9 Hensford gdns SE26
35 Y 17 Headley appr Ilf	20 G 10 Heathfield E4	60 H 14 Helena rd W5	49 P 18 Henshall st N1
56 D 10 Headley av Wallgtn	114 C 16 Heathfield Chisl	5 U 2 Helena clo Barnt	150 E 5 Henshaw st SE17
59 T 16 Headley dri Croy	158 D 14 Heathfield S Croy	45 X 4 Helenslea av NW11	55 X 9 Henshawe rd Dgnhm
35 Y 17 Headley dri Ilf	88 G 17 Heathfield ave SW18	90 D 15 Helix gdns SW2	91 Y 13 Henslowe rd SE22
36 A 18 Headley dri Ilf	73 X 13 Heathfield ct W4	90 E 16 Helix rd SW2	44 L 14 Henson av NW2
92 A 6 Headley st SE15	27 P 20 Heathfield gdns NW11	143 U 14 Hellings st E1	24 G 11 Henson path Harrow
23 P 11 Headstone dri Harrow	88 F 15 Heathfield gdns SW18	142 H 4 Helmet ct EC2	130 J 7 Henstridge pl NW8
23 O 12 Headstone gdns Harrow	73 V 14 Heathfield gdns W4	134 B 15 Helmet row EC1	86 J 14 Henty wlk SW15
22 L 8 Headstone la Harrow	114 B 17 Heathfield la Chisl	39 R 2 Helmsdale clo Rom	126 J 1 Henville rd Brom
22 M 11 Headstone manor Harrow	83 V 17 Heathfield north Twick	107 W 19 Helmsdale rd SW16	95 P 8 Henwick rd SE9
23 S 18 Headstone rd Harrow	44 M 19 Heathfield pk NW2	39 R 1 Helmsdale rd Rom	75 P 9 Henwood rd SE18
52 D 20 Headway the Epsom	88 F 16 Heathfield rd SW18	135 X 1 Helmsley st E8	51 N 19 Hepscott rd E9
06 C 8 Headworth rd SW17	73 S 6 Heathfield rd W3	22 E 3 Helston clo Pinn	55 N 15 Hepworth gdns Bark
93 N 2 Heald st SE4	112 D 18 Heathfield rd Brom	110 L 5 Helvetia st SE6	108 B 19 Hepworth rd SW16
47 S 18 Healey st NW1	98 A 11 Heathfield rd Bxly Hth	90 A 7 Hemberton rd SW9	155 Z 17 Heracles clo Wallgtn
50 G 8 Hearn bldgs SE17	157 N 9 Heathfield rd Croy	25 S 1 Heming rd Edg	137 Y 15 Herald st E2
34 K 18 Hearn st EC2	83 V 18 Heathfield south Twick	133 P 2 Hemingford rd N1	133 T 18 Herbal Hill EC1
73 P 15 Hearne rd W4	88 F 18 Heathfield sq SW18	153 N 8 Hemingford rd Sutton	133 T 18 Herbal pl EC1
90 J 20 Hearnville rd SW12	136 K 10 Heathfield st W11	15 Y 16 Hemington av N11	147 O 1 Herbert cres SW1
80 J 17 Heath av Bxly Hth	79 W 16 Heathfield ter SE18	62 E 20 Hemlock rd W12	62 J 5 Herbert gdns NW10
46 C 8 Heath brow NW3	73 W 13 Heathfield ter W4	135 U 17 Hemming st E1	128 A 8 Herbert gdns NW10
46 A 2 Heath clo NW11	158 G 18 Heathfield vale S Croy	126 F 6 Hemp row SE17	73 T 17 Herbert gdns W4
61 O 12 Heath clo W5	28 A 19 Heathgate NW11	21 S 8 Hempstead clo Buck Hl	55 W 1 Herbert gdns Rom
8 C 9 Heath clo Enf	27 A 19 Heathgate NW11	23 X 9 Hempstead rd E17	78 M 16 Herbert pl SE18
39 W 10 Heath dri NW3	49 P 3 Heathland rd N16	63 N 2 Hemsley st E8	53 R 14 Herbert rd E12
46 A 12 Heath dri NW3	99 Y 17 Heathlands ri Drtfrd		32 L 20 Herbert rd E17
45 Z 13 Heath dri NW3	94 B 10 Heathlee rd SE3		26 E 19 Herbert rd NW9
19 N 8 Heath dri SW20	114 C 15 Heathley end Chisl		17 N 20 Herbert rd N11
18 M 8 Heath dri SW20			31 W 15 Herbert rd N15
39 W 8 Heath dri Rom			18 M 8 Herbert rd N9
45 C 19 Heath dri Sutton			78 J 19 Herbert rd SE18
			105 W 18 Herbert rd SW19
			127 P 11 Herbert rd Brom
			98 A 5 Herbert rd Bxly Hth
			97 Z 4 Herbert rd Bxly Hth
			54 G 6 Herbert rd Ilf
			116 L 7 Herbert rd Kingst

70 E 2 Herbert rd S'hall
65 T 8 Herbert st E13
47 O 17 Herbert rd NW5
78 L 18 Herbert ter SE18
132 J 17 Herbrand st WC1
48 B 10 Hercules pl N7
149 R 1 Hercules rd SE1
48 A 10 Hercules st N7
15 Y 6 Hereford av Barnt
35 S 20 Hereford gdns Ilf
22 B 15 Hereford gdns Pinn
101 N 2 Hereford gdns Twick
137 V 6 Hereford ms W2
75 Y 19 Hereford pl SE14
34 J 15 Hereford rd E11
137 V 5 Hereford rd W2
61 U 19 Hereford rd W3
72 E 9 Hereford rd W5
146 C 7 Hereford sq SW7
135 T 15 Hereford st E2
35 S 12 Herent dri Ilf
17 U 17 Hereward gdns N13
106 K 8 Hereward st SW17
41 T 8 Herga ct Harrow
23 V 12 Herga rd Harrow
20 A 9 Heriot av E4
47 N 14 Heriot pl NW5
26 M 15 Heriot rd NW4
27 N 15 Heriot rd NW4
19 W 16 Heriot way E4
10 L 13 Heriots clo Dgnhm
108 K 8 Herlwyn gdns SW17
148 H 18 Hermans st SW8
133 R 9 Hermes st N1
155 Y 19 Hermes way Wallgtn
30 A 15 Hermiston av N8
129 W 4 Hermit pl NW6
65 P 13 Hermit rd E16
133 W 12 Hermit st EC1
34 C 13 Hermitage clo E18
7 W 9 Hermitage clo Enf
34 E 13 Hermitage ct E18
45 Y 9 Hermitage gdns NW2
108 M 16 Hermitage gdns SE19
45 X 9 Hermitage la NW2
18 B 17 Hermitage la N18
108 C 19 Hermitage la SW16
123 X 16 Hermitage la Croy
30 K 20 Hermitage rd N4
31 N 18 Hermitage rd N4
108 M 16 Hermitage rd SE19
109 D 14 Hermitage rd SE19
138 F 2 Hermitage st W2
86 E 3 Hermitage the SW13
84 J 14 Hermitage the Rich
143 T 14 Hermitage wall E1
23 Z 5 Hermitage way Stanm
34 C 12 Hermitage wlk E18
34 F 14 Hermon hill E11
88 C 14 Herndon rd SWU8
43 Y 16 Herne clo NW10
90 L 14 Herne hill SE24
90 L 9 Herne Hill rd SE24
90 J 14 Herne pl SE24
32 K 7 Heron clo E17
114 H 8 Heron cres Sidcp
126 L 10 Heron ct Brom
84 G 14 Heron ct Rich
81 P 12 Heron hill Belvdr
53 Y 2 Heron mews Ilf
44 B 19 Heron rd NW10
90 K 10 Heron rd SE24
83 Z 11 Heron rd Twick
84 A 11 Heron rd Twick
21 Y 15 Heron way Wdfd Grn
106 H 1 Herondale av SW15
8 F 9 Herongate clo Enf
52 L 7 Herongate rd E12
21 T 4 Herons clo Buck Hl
12 C 17 Herons ga Edg
60 D 16 Heronslade dri W13
11 W 16 Heronslea dri Stanm
48 L 9 Herrick rd N5
148 H 7 Herrick st SW1
129 N 13 Herries st W10
128 M 11 Herries st W10
150 L 14 Herron st SE17
77 Y 9 Herringham rd SE7
78 A 8 Herringham rd SE7
62 H 3 Hersant clo NW10
92 G 19 Herschell rd SE13
86 G 19 Hersham clo SW15
9 P 9 Hertfield rd Enf
85 Z 12 Hertford av SW13
86 A 11 Hertford av SW13
5 T 11 Hertford clo Barnt
132 B 19 Hertford pl W1
66 L 1 Hertford rd E6
144 L 2 Hertford rd N1

49 T 20 Hertford rd N1
28 J 10 Hertford rd N2
19 L 8 Hertford rd N9
53 X 20 Hertford rd Bark
5 S 11 Hertford rd Barnt
36 G 18 Hertford rd Ilf
139 V 14 Hertford rd W1
121 Z 10 Hertford way Mitch
48 C 11 Hertslet rd N7
27 V 4 Hervey clo N3
32 J 12 Hervey pk E17
94 G 2 Hervey rd SE3
27 Y 5 Hervey wlk N3
136 J 10 Hesketh pl W11
52 E 11 Hesketh rd E7
107 N 2 Heslop rd SW12
145 Y 8 Hesper ms SW5
76 D 11 Hesperus cres E14
71 Z 6 Hessel rd W13
72 A 5 Hessel rd W13
143 V 5 Hessel st E1
18 J 17 Hester rd N18
146 K 18 Hester st SW11
87 T 3 Hestercombe av SW6
70 C 18 Heston av Hounsl
70 G 15 Heston rd Hounsl
70 H 19 Heston rd Hounsl
92 M 2 Heston st SE4
93 N 2 Heston st SE4
89 Z 11 Hetherington rd SW4
74 J 4 Hetley rd W12
74 L 11 Hetton st W6
113 X 10 Hever croft SE9
127 W 4 Hever gdns Brom
79 U 11 Heversham rd SE18
98 E 3 Heversham rd Bxly Hth
128 H 20 Hewer st W10
11 O 13 Hewett clo Stanm
55 V 13 Hewett rd Dgnhm
134 K 18 Hewett st EC2
18 D 14 Hewish rd N18
30 H 8 Hewitt av N22
30 H 8 Hewitt rd N8
63 W 6 Hewlett rd E3
111 Z 6 Hexal rd SE6
71 Z 19 Hexham gdns Islwth
108 L 4 Hexham rd SE27
5 O 14 Hexham rd Barnt
119 Z 18 Hexham rd Mrdn
108 B 17 Heybourne rd N17
108 B 17 Heybridge av SW16
119 V 6 Heybridge gdns Ilf
148 M 17 Heyford av SW8
119 W 7 Heyford av Mrdn
62 H 2 Heyford rd Mitch
148 L 17 Heyford ter SW8
150 A 6 Heygate st SE17
55 T 12 Heynes rd Dgnhm
31 P 19 Heysham rd N15
105 W 3 Heythorp st SW18
52 B 14 Heyworth rd E15
49 Z 11 Heyworth rd E5
50 L 2 Hibbert rd E17
23 W 7 Hibbert st Harrow
88 E 9 Hibbert st SW11
82 H 12 Hibernia gdns Hounsl
82 H 12 Hibernia rd Hounsl
92 E 12 Hichisson rd SE15
76 F 7 Hickin st E14
53 Z 14 Hickling rd Ilf
55 T 1 Hickman rd Rom
59 S 8 Hicks av Grnfd
75 V 13 Hicks st SE8
148 E 6 Hide pl SW1
23 P 13 Hide rd Harrow
157 S 17 High beech S Croy
115 Z 12 High beeches Sidcp
125 R 17 High Broom cres W Wkhm
31 V 11 High Cross rd N17
86 H 20 High Cross way SW15
117 W 1 High dri New Mald
21 R 17 High elms Wdfd Grn
95 F 1 High gro SE18
79 S 20 High gro S18
79 S 20 High grove SE18
52 B 14 High Hill ferry E5
140 K 4 High holborn WC1
141 P 2 High holborn WC1
59 R 17 High la W7
109 X 10 High Level dri SE26
62 M 14 High Level rd W10
23 U 15 High mead Harrow
159 Y 3 High mead W Wkhm
25 X 16 High Meadow cres NW9
7 R 4 High oaks Enf

85 P 3 High Park av Rich
85 P 3 High Park rd Rich
106 B 20 High path SW19
150 H 20 High Pk cres SE17
34 E 7 High rd E7
44 J 18 High rd NW10
16 R 16 High rd N11
28 E 1 High rd N12
31 V 4 High rd N17
15 R 11 High rd N20/N12
30 D 6 High rd N20
10 C 5 High rd Bushey Watf
23 S 3 High rd Harrow
53 Y 9 High rd Ilf
54 B 8 High rd Ilf
116 F 4 High rd Kingst
37 X 20 High rd Rom
55 O 2 High rd Rom
21 S 18 High rd Wdfd Grn
42 L 16 High rd Wemb
28 G 7 High Rd e.finchley N12
33 R 19 High Rd leyton E10
51 S 5 High Rd leyton E10
51 U 13 High Rd leyton E15
51 Y 11 High Rd leytonstone E11
52 B 2 High Rd leytonstone E11
28 E 2 High Rd n.finchley N12
34 F 16 High st E11
65 T 7 High st E13
51 X 20 High st E15
64 G 4 High st E15
33 N 13 High st E17
62 F 6 High st NW10
13 X 15 High st NW7
16 K 7 High st N14
110 D 17 High.st SE20
147 W 8 High st SE25
105 R 13 High st SW19
87 U 7 High st SW6
73 U 3 High st W3
36 C 9 High st Barkingside Ilf
4 G 12 High st Barnt
125 N 2 High st Becknhm
126 F 5 High st Brom
155 O 9 High st Carsh
114 A 16 High st Chisl
156 M 5 High st Croy
9 P 17 High st Enf
101 N 15 High st Hampt
41 T 4 High st Harrow
23 T 7 High st Harrow
82 K 8 High st Hounsl
82 L 8 High st Hounsl
116 G 6 High st Kingst
118 C 9 High st New Mald
22 B 11 High st Pinn
39 O 16 High st Rom
70 G 2 High st S'hall
115 O 10 High st Sidcp
153 T 14 High st Sutton
154 B 9 High st Tedd
101 X 13 High st Tedd
123 O 8 High st Thntn Hth
122 M 8 High st Thntn Hth
82 M 18 High st Twick
183 M 18 High st Twick
43 N 13 High st Wemb
42 M 13 High st Wemb
116 E 3 High St hamptonwick Kingst
30 C 13 High St hornsey N8
53 P 14 High St north E6
66 F 4 High St north E6
66 F 4 High St south E6
57 T 5 High Timber st EC4
108 P 1 High trees SW2
124 J 19 High trees Croy
123 T 3 High View clo SE19
34 A 9 High View rd E18
115 R 9 High View rd Sidcp
40 E 3 High worple Harrow
32 J 10 Higham Hill rd E17
32 H 9 Higham pl E17
31 O 9 Higham rd N17
21 S 20 Higham rd Wdfd Grn
20 C 19 Higham Stn av E4
20 F 18 Highams park E4
21 N 16 Highams park E4
80 B 20 Highbanks clo Welling
147 N 19 Highbarrow rd Croy
76 K 14 Highbridge SE10
66 M 4 Highbridge rd Bark
94 M 7 Highbrook rd SE3
95 N 7 Highbrook rd SE3

117 W 10 Highbury clo New Mald
159 S 3 Highbury clo W Wkhm
48 H 17 Highbury cres N5
54 G 6 Highbury gdns Ilf
48 K 13 Highbury grange N
48 K 16 Highbury gro N5
48 G 11 Highbury hill N5
48 M 16 Highbury New pk N
48 K 11 Highbury pk N5
48 H 17 Highbury pl N5
48 K 10 Highbury quadrant N5
105 T 12 Highbury rd SW19
48 G 19 Highbury Stn rd N1
48 J 15 Highbury ter N5
48 H 15 Highbury Ter ms N
110 H 10 Highclare st SE25
117 Y 7 Highclere rd New Mald
86 E 16 Highcliffe dri SW15
35 R 16 Highcliffe gdns Ilf
77 W 16 Highcombe SE7
113 P 2 Highcombe clo SE9
25 Z 15 Highcroft NW9
61 O 1 Highcroft av Wemb
27 V 18 Highcroft gdns NW11
48 A 2 Highcroft rd N4
122 B 8 Highdaun dri Mitch
152 C 2 Highdown Worcr P
86 J 15 Highdown rd SW15
27 S 19 Highfield av NW11
25 W 15 Highfield av NW9
81 W 17 Highfield av Erith
41 U 15 Highfield av Grnfd
22 D 16 Highfield av Pinn
42 L 8 Highfield av Wemb
25 W 15 Highfield clo NW9
116 E 20 Highfield clo Surb
6 H 19 Highfield ct N14
126 A 8 Highfield dri Brom
152 D 14 Highfield dri Epsom
159 T 4 Highfield dri W Wkhm
27 S 19 Highfield gdns NW11
109 P 19 Highfield hill SE19
27 T 18 Highfield rd NW11
17 W 7 Highfield rd N21
61 U 13 Highfield rd W3
127 T 10 Highfield rd Brom
98 C 14 Highfield rd Bxly Hth
83 U 1 Highfield rd Islwth
117 U 17 Highfield rd Surb
154 J 10 Highfield rd Sutton
35 R 3 Highfield rd Wdfd Grn
29 S 20 Highgate av N6
47 O 4 Highgate clo N6
47 R 3 Highgate High st N6
47 S 13 Highgate hill N19
47 S 13 Highgate rd NW5
47 O 6 Highgate West hill N6
47 O 7 Highgate West hill N6
55 S 14 Highgrove rd Dgnhm
59 T 9 Highland av W7
56 K 9 Highland av Dgnhm
155 T 9 Highland cotts Wallgtn
111 R 13 Highland croft Becknhm
109 R 15 Highland rd SE19
126 B 1 Highland rd Brom
126 B 19 Highland rd Brom
98 E 12 Highland rd Bxly Hth
61 V 20 Highlands av W3
82 U 3 Highlands clo Hounsl
53 T 2 Highlands gdns Ilf
86 L 20 Highlands rd SW15
4 M 16 Highlands rd Barnt
25 T 6 Highlands the Edg
79 X 20 Highmead SE18
42 M 20 Highmead cres Wemb
77 N 18 Highmore rd SE3
91 W 3 Highshore rd SE15
12 M 11 Highstone av E11
12 M 11 Highview NW7
12 G 14 Highview av Edg
156 C 11 Highview av Wallgtn
16 H 17 Highview gdns N11
27 S 11 Highview gdns N3
12 G 14 Highview gdns Edg
109 P 16 Highview rd SE19
59 Z 16 Highview rd SE19
143 W 10 Highway the E1
63 S 20 Highway the E1

23 X 1 Highway the Stanm
54 D 20 Highway the Sutton
31 T 16 Highweek rd N15
15 R 13 Highwood av N12
35 U 14 Highwood gdns Ilf
42 M 15 Highwood gro NW7
73 S 10 Highwood hill NW7
13 R 9 Highwood house NW7
47 Z 10 Highwood rd N19
16 L 17 Highworth rd N11
21 N 5 Hilary av Mitch
45 X 18 Hilary clo SW6
08 H 2 Hilary clo Bxly Hth
52 D 20 Hilary rd W12
53 P 6 Hilbert rd Sutton
45 O 2 Hilborough rd E8
6 A 1 Hilda rd E6
120 H 13 Hilda rd E16
42 M 20 Hildenborough gdns Brom
90 F 4 Hilder rd SW9
07 R 1 Hildreth st SW12
45 U 14 Hildyard rd SW6
42 L 8 Hiley gdns NW10
28 B 11 Hiley rd NW10
90 D 2 Hilgrove rd NW6
43 O 20 Hill brow Brom
13 O 20 Hill brow Chisl
99 U 17 Hill brow Drtfrd
27 Z 18 Hill clo NW11
43 J 10 Hill clo NW2
13 Y 12 Hill clo Chisl
23 N 1 Hill clo Harrow
11 N 13 Hill clo Stanm
30 H 15 Hill court Grnfd
15 N 7 Hill cres N20
23 Y 16 Hill cres Harrow
77 O 10 Hill cres Surb
53 N 3 Hill cres Worc Pk
09 U 17 Hill crest Hornch
97 O 19 Hill crest Sidcp
44 F 10 Hill Crest gdns NW2
13 U 4 Hill dri NW9
46 C 5 Hill dri SW16
95 X 2 Hill end SE18
36 E 1 Hill Farm rd NW10
39 P 9 Hill gro Rom
23 W 1 Hill Ho av Stanm
08 D 13 Hill Ho rd SW16
17 T 2 Hill House clo N21
08 D 13 Hill path SW16
30 D 10 Hill rd NW8
29 N 6 Hill rd N10
54 K 14 Hill rd Carsh
23 Y 16 Hill rd Harrow
07 T 19 Hill rd Mitch
22 A 17 Hill rd Pinn
54 A 11 Hill rd Sutton
42 A 8 Hill rd Wemb
28 B 14 Hill ri NW11
23 U 1 Hill ri Grnfd
84 H 14 Hill ri Rich
19 N 1 Hill rise N9
39 V 12 Hill st W1
34 A 14 Hill st Rich
28 B 13 Hill top NW11
19 T 18 Hill top Sutton
36 G 4 Hill View dri Welling
79 Y 15 Hill View gdns NW9
44 B 14 Hill View rd NW7
70 H 8 Hillary rd S'hall
70 H 7 Hillary rd S'hall
27 Z 16 Hillbeck clo SE15
39 P 3 Hillbeck way Grnfd
08 O 9 Hillbrook rd SW17
28 E 7 Hillbrow New Mald
43 C 16 Hillbrow rd Brom
24 C 16 Hillbury av Harrow
07 T 6 Hillbury rd SW17
18 E 13 Hillcote av SW16
45 N 18 Hillcourt av N12
47 U 17 Hillcourt rd SE22
17 U 2 Hillcrest N21
29 P 20 Hillcrest N6
07 U 14 Hillcrest av NW11
24 L 16 Hillcrest av Edg
24 K 13 Hillcrest clo Becknhm
27 S 11 Hillcrest gdns N3
34 D 7 Hillcrest rd E17
29 X 11 Hillcrest rd E18
53 R 3 Hillcrest rd W3
50 L 13 Hillcrest rd W5
52 E 11 Hillcrest rd Brom
09 S 18 Hillcrest rd Drtfd
49 Y 20 Hillcrest rd Hornch
24 K 14 Hillcrest view Becknhm
22 E 20 Hillcroft av Pinn

60 H 16 Hillcroft cres W5
42 M 12 Hillcroft cres Wemb
43 N 12 Hillcroft cres Wemb
154 G 13 Hillcoome rd Sutton
119 S 11 Hillcross av Mrdn
153 V 9 Hilldale rd Sutton
108 B 17 Hilldown SW16
126 B 19 Hilldown rd Brom
47 Y 15 Hilldrop cres N1
13 S 1 Hilldrop la N1
47 Z 14 Hilldrop rd N1
112 G 15 Hilldrop rd Brom
95 Y 3 Hillend SE18
88 F 4 Hillersdon av SW13
12 A 16 Hillersdon av Edg
150 F 7 Hillery rd SE17
26 B 15 Hillfield av NW9
30 B 13 Hillfield av N8
120 H 13 Hillfield av Mrdn
42 M 20 Hillfield clo Harrow
23 N 13 Hillfield clo Harrow
46 J 16 Hillfield ct NW3
29 S 12 Hillfield pk N10
17 S 9 Hillfield pk N21
45 X 14 Hillfield rd NW6
100 D 19 Hillfield rd Hampt
38 K 5 Hillfoot av Rom
38 J 5 Hillfoot rd Rom
137 T 13 Hillgate pl W8
137 T 13 Hillgate st W8
75 O 2 Hilliards ct E1
143 Z 13 Hilliards ct E1
5 N 20 Hillier clo Barnt
156 G 11 Hillier gdns Croy
98 M 15 Hillier rd SW11
89 N 16 Hillier rd SW11
155 Z 6 Hilliers la Wallgtn
98 L 8 Hillingdon rd Bxly Hth
149 W 17 Hillingdon st SE5
35 O 7 Hillington gdns Wdfd Grn
50 A 18 Hillman st E8
48 A 14 Hillmarton rd N7
110 G 12 Hillmore gro SE26
78 E 13 Hillreach SE18
47 Z 1 Hillrise rd N19
140 B 6 Hills pl W1
21 V 6 Hills of Buck Hl
91 S 13 Hillsboro rd SE22
61 W 2 Hillside NW10
25 X 14 Hillside NW9
105 P 16 Hillside SW19
5 S 17 Hillside Barnt
15 Z 18 Hillside av N11
21 X 18 Hillside av Wdfd Grn
42 L 12 Hillside av Wemb
143 S 8 Hillside clo Mrdn
21 Y 17 Hillside clo Wdfd Grn
8 B 2 Hillside cres Enf
40 M 5 Hillside cres Harrow
12 B 18 Hillside dri Edg
31 U 20 Hillside est N15
33 X 9 Hillside gdns E17
29 R 19 Hillside gdns N6
108 F 4 Hillside gdns SW2
4 E 14 Hillside gdns Barnt
12 A 14 Hillside gdns Edg
42 K 1 Hillside gdns Harrow
155 V 17 Hillside gdns Wallgtn
26 F 1 Hillside gro NW7
16 K 3 Hillside gro N14
31 T 19 Hillside rd N15
108 F 3 Hillside rd SW2
60 J 15 Hillside rd W5
150 B 5 Hillside rd Brom
156 J 8 Hillside rd Croy
99 V 15 Hillside rd Drtfd
58 G 11 Hillside rd S'hall
117 O 10 Hillside rd Surb
153 V 16 Hillside rd Sutton
137 R 13 Hillsleigh rd W8
52 E 8 Hillstowe st E5
45 Y 19 Hilltop rd NW6
10 L 11 Hilltop way Stanm
104 J 19 Hillview SW20
24 J 16 Hillview av Harrow
27 R 13 Hillview gdns NW4
22 H 11 Hillview gdns Harrow
113 X 11 Hillview rd Chisl
22 B 17 Hillview rd Pinn
22 E 2 Hillview rd W
154 E 4 Hillview rd Sutton
83 Y 16 Hillview rd Twick
44 A 2 Hillway NW9
47 P 7 Hillway N6
97 W 18 Hillworth rd SW2
93 N 9 Hilly Fields cres SE4
7 X 1 Hilly Fields park Enf
59 U 14 Hillyard st SW9

90 E 3 Hillyard st SW9
50 C 11 Hilsea st E5
15 U 18 Hilton av N12
91 S 11 Hilversum cres SE22
106 K 14 Himley rd SW17
156 C 14 Hinchcliffe clo Croy
91 W 9 Hinckley rd SE15
81 Z 18 Hind cres Erith
141 U 5 Hind ct EC4
64 B 17 Hind gro E14
129 U 4 Hinde st W1
23 R 17 Hindes rd Harrow
58 B 3 Hindhead gdns Grnfd
156 A 10 Hindhead way Croy
91 X 13 Hindmans rd SE22
69 O 10 Hindmans way Dgnhm
50 A 15 Hindrey pl E5
110 D 3 Hindsleys pl SE23
156 B 17 Hinkler clo Croy
24 G 11 Hinkler rd Harrow
79 P 18 Hinstock rd SE18
82 A 10 Hinton av Hounsl
18 D 14 Hinton rd N18
90 K 9 Hinton rd SE24
155 V 14 Hinton rd Wallgtn
136 L 11 Hippodrome pl W11
50 K 3 Hitcham rd E17
93 V 14 Hither Green la SE13
108 E 5 Hitherfield rd SW16
55 Y 7 Hitherfield rd Dgnhm
23 O 4 Hitherwell dri Harrow
109 U 10 Hitherwood dri SE19
10 E 9 Hive rd Bushey Watf
107 X 5 Hoadly rd SW16
15 W 8 Hobart clo N20
123 N 6 Hobart gdns Thntn Hth
147 W 2 Hobart pl SW1
55 X 12 Hobart rd Dgnhm
36 C 8 Hobart rd Ilf
152 J 5 Hobart rd Worc Pk
86 J 14 Hobbes wlk SW15
109 N 11 Hobbs grn N2
109 N 11 Hobbs rd SE27
64 C 16 Hobday st E14
114 H 15 Hoblands end Chisl
135 R 20 Hobson pl E1
135 N 14 Hocker st E2
66 D 6 Hockley av E6
45 U 10 Hocroft av NW2
45 V 10 Hocroft wlk NW2
59 W 6 Hodder dri Grnfd
81 S 14 Hoddesdon rd Blvdr
45 W 3 Hodford rd NW11
75 R 10 Hodnet gro SE16
149 Y 7 Hodson st SE17
8 L 4 Hoe la Enf
9 P 3 Hoe la Enf
33 O 12 Hoe st E17
144 J 1 Hofland rd W14
38 B 2 Hog Hill rd Rom
122 M 17 Hogarth cres Croy
70 H 20 Hogarth ct Hounsl
27 W 13 Hogarth hill NW11
145 W 6 Hogarth rd SW5
25 O 6 Hogarth rd Edg
18 E 8 Hogarth rd N9
96 J 16 Holbeach gdns Sidcp
93 R 18 Holbeach rd SE6
151 U 9 Holbeach row SE15
147 S 8 Holbein ms SW1
147 S 9 Holbein ms SW1
147 S 9 Holbein pl SW1
62 J 8 Holberton gdns NW10
141 T 2 Holborn EC1
141 S 2 Holborn bldgs EC4
65 V 13 Holborn rd E13
141 W 3 Holborn viaduct EC1
114 Q 19 Holbrook la Chisl
65 O 5 Holbrook rd E15
127 U 13 Holbrook way Brom
94 K 3 Holburne clo SE3
94 M 3 Holburne gdns SE3
94 K 4 Holburne rd SE3
94 L 3 Holburne rd SE3
95 P 3 Holburne rd SE3
73 T 11 Holcombe hill NW7
31 W 9 Holcombe rd N17
53 W 2 Holcombe rd Ilf
74 K 12 Holcombe rd E11
63 R 1 Holcroft rd E9
43 W 4 Holden av NW9
15 N 15 Holden av N12
64 C 9 Holden rd E3
15 N 13 Holden rd N12

89 O 6 Holden st SW11
92 J 13 Holdenby rd SE4
28 C 2 Holdenhurst av N12
108 K 13 Holderness way SE27
107 N 5 Holdernesse rd SW17
27 P 9 Holders Hill av NW4
27 S 3 Holders Hill circus NW7
27 P 8 Holders Hill cres NW4
27 R 9 Holders Hill dri NW4
27 R 8 Holders Hill gdns NW4
27 S 4 Holders Hill rd NW7
46 E 9 Holford rd NW3
133 R 11 Holford st WC1
88 F 8 Holgate av SW11
56 D 17 Holgate gdns Dgnhm
56 D 16 Holgate rd Dgnhm
104 C 20 Holland av SW20
153 X 19 Holland av Sutton
15 T 1 Holland clo Barnt
144 L 1 Holland gdns W14
149 V 19 Holland gro SW9
145 O 2 Holland ms W14
137 P 17 Holland park W8
137 N 15 Holland pk W11
136 M 15 Holland pk W14
137 O 14 Holland Pk av W11
136 J 16 Holland Pk av W11
136 K 14 Holland Pk av W14
136 L 16 Holland Pk gdns W14
137 N 15 Holland Pk ms W11
145 P 2 Holland Pk rd W14
137 W 17 Holland pl W8
65 N 8 Holland rd E15
66 J 2 Holland rd E6
62 H 5 Holland rd NW10
30 A 14 Holland rd N8
147 Y 10 Holland rd SE25
136 K 19 Holland rd W14
145 N 2 Holland rd W14
42 F 19 Holland rd Wemb
137 U 18 Holland st W8
73 T 5 Holland ter W3
136 L 19 Holland Vlls rd W14
137 P 14 Holland wlk W8
137 R 16 Holland wlk W8
10 M 16 Holland wlk Stanm
118 E 20 Hollands the Worc Pk
152 D 1 Hollands the Worc Pk
49 U 9 Hollar rd N16
140 U 9 Hollen st W1
139 Y 5 Holles st W1
15 Y 5 Holles st W1
15 Y 19 Hollick Wood av N12
56 G 20 Holliday way Dgnhm
114 J 2 Hollies av Sidcp
100 M 14 Hollies clo Hampt
72 D 11 Hollies rd W5
114 L 1 Hollies the Sidcp
89 P 17 Hollies way SW12
112 F 20 Holligrave rd Brom
98 B 1 Hollingbourne av Bxly Hth
60 A 15 Hollingbourne gdns W13
90 L 14 Hollingbourne rd SE24
158 A 14 Hollingsworth rd Croy
48 E 17 Hollingsworth st N7
118 E 15 Hollington cres New Mald
66 F 9 Hollington rd E6
31 X 6 Hollington rd N17
127 Z 16 Hollingworth rd Brom
51 Y 9 Holloway rd E11
66 Y 9 Holloway rd E6
47 X 7 Holloway rd N19
48 B 13 Holloway rd N7
143 R 5 Holloway st E1
82 L 7 Hollows the Hounsl
73 N 15 Hollows the Brentf
24 K 8 Holly av Stanm
24 K 9 Holly av Stanm
14 D 19 Holly Brake clo Chisl
46 D 11 Holly Bush hill NW3
100 G 18 Holly Bush la Hampt
100 C 12 Holly clo Felt
148 L 13 Holly cres Becknhm
33 X 1 Holly cres Wdfd Grn
20 E 2 Holly dri E4
43 W 1 Holly gro NW9
91 W 4 Holly gro SE15
46 D 12 Holly hill NW3

7 P 19	Holly hill N21	27 P 15	Holmfield av NW4
81 X 13	Holly Hill rd Blvdr	36 H 16	Holmfield av Ilf
44 A 19	Holly la NW10	81 V 13	Holmhurst rd Belv
47 P 6	Holly Lodge gdns N6	49 T 3	Holmleigh rd N16
		99 R 7	Holmsdale gro Bxly Hth
46 D 11	Holly mt NW3		
16 B 15	Holly Park rd N11	16 D 14	Holmsdale rd N11
27 W 10	Holly pk N3	126 M 6	Holmsdale rd Brom
48 B 2	Holly pk N4	110 J 9	Holmshaw rd SE26
27 X 10	Holly Pk gdns N3	89 P 16	Holmside rd SW12
71 V 1	Holly Pk rd W7	118 C 16	Holmsley clo New Mald
34 D 20	Holly rd E11		
73 Y 12	Holly rd W4	25 V 8	Holmstall av Edg
100 M 14	Holly rd Hampt	90 C 19	Holmswood gdns SW2
82 L 9	Holly rd Hounsl		
101 X 1	Holly rd Twick	40 K 18	Holmwood clo Grnfd
49 V 19	Holly st E8	22 M 9	Holmwood clo Harrow
135 O 1	Holly st E8		
15 R 9	Holly ter N20	153 P 18	Holmwood clo Sutton
121 X 7	Holly way Mitch	27 Y 8	Holmwood gdns N3
46 D 12	Holly wlk NW3	155 R 14	Holmwood gdns Wallgtn
100 G 13	Hollybank clo Hampt		
34 D 16	Hollybush clo E11	12 L 17	Holmwood gro NW7
135 V 12	Hollybush gdns E2	54 H 8	Holmwood rd Ilf
63 N 8	Hollybush gdns E2	153 N 19	Holmwood rd Sutton
34 D 16	Hollybush hill E11	28 E 18	Holne chase N2
63 N 8	Hollybush pl E2	143 W 15	Holne chase Mrdn
102 L 13	Hollybush st Kingst	52 B 19	Holness rd E15
65 W 8	Hollybush st E13	86 M 12	Holroyd rd SW15
46 D 12	Hollybush vlls NW3	22 M 15	Holsworth clo Harrow
45 Y 10	Hollycroft av NW3		
42 M 8	Hollycroft av Wemb	133 R 19	Holsworthy sq WC1
92 B 4	Hollydale rd SE15	78 D 3	Holt rd E16
51 X 9	Hollydown way E11	42 C 9	Holt rd Wemb
70 A 13	Hollyfarm rd S'hall	155 U 7	Holt the Wallgtn
15 Z 18	Hollyfield av N11	63 S 11	Holton st E1
117 N 17	Hollyfield av N11	7 Z 7	Holtwhites av Enf
116 M 19	Hollyfield rd Surb	7 V 6	Holtwhites hill Enf
117 N 17	Hollyfield rd Surb	22 A 14	Holwell pl Pinn
10 D 3	Hollygrove Bushey Watf	89 X 11	Holwood pl SW4
		150 G 4	Holwood rd Brom
93 V 12	Hollyhouse ter SE13	86 G 19	Holybourne av SW15
154 L 7	Hollymead Carsh		
93 U 2	Hollymount cres SE10	149 W 6	Holyoak rd SE11
		28 C 12	Holyoak wlk N2
96 L 18	Hollyoak Wood park Sidcp	60 E 11	Holyoake wlk W5
		144 E 18	Holyport rd SW6
105 P 1	Hollytree clo SW19	40 C 13	Holyrood av Harrow
19 W 16	Hollywood rd E4	25 T 8	Holyrood gdns Edg
146 B 13	Hollywood rd SW10	5 T 20	Holyrood st Barnt
33 X 1	Hollywood way Wdfd Grn	142 J 16	Holyrood st SE1
		134 L 17	Holywell la EC2
88 F 5	Holman rd SW11	134 J 18	Holywell row EC2
9 T 14	Holmbridge gdns Enf	154 L 3	Home clo Carsh
27 R 14	Holmbrook dri NW4	58 E 8	Home clo Grnfd
50 F 15	Holmbrook st E9	56 K 10	Home gdns Dgnhm
106 L 7	Holmbury view E5	24 F 3	Home mead Stanm
87 S 16	Holmbush rd SW15	105 V 9	Home Pk rd SW19
150 E 15	Holmby st N17	116 G 10	Home Pk wlk Kingst
48 L 16	Holmcote gdns N5	88 J 4	Home rd SW11
127 U 13	Holmcroft way Brom	151 Y 19	Home st SE15
27 R 15	Holmdale gdns NW4	30 K 4	Homecourt rd N22
45 Y 15	Holmdale rd NW6	110 D 12	Homecroft rd SE26
114 B 13	Holmdale rd Chisl	59 V 17	Homefarm rd W7
31 T 19	Holmdale ter N15	43 X 19	Homefield clo NW10
13 U 19	Holmdene av NW7	120 E 2	Homefield gdns Mitch
90 M 13	Holmdene av SE24		
91 N 14	Holmdene av SE24	105 R 14	Homefield rd SW19
22 J 11	Holmdene av Harrow	74 C 12	Homefield rd W4
149 T 4	Holmdene clo Becknhm	126 K 1	Homefield rd Brom
		12 L 20	Homefield rd Edg
94 C 16	Holme Lacey rd SE12	42 A 12	Homefield rd Wemb
		134 K 10	Homefield st N1
66 E 3	Holme rd E6	109 R 19	Homelands dri SE19
10 J 19	Holme way Stanm	92 F 12	Homeleigh rd SE15
145 Z 19	Holmead rd SW6	127 U 11	Homemead rd Brom
10 E 8	Holmebury clo Bushey Watf	121 W 14	Homemead rd Croy
		98 J 3	Homer clo Bxly Hth
32 K 10	Holmes av E17	50 J 18	Homer rd E9
47 T 16	Holmes av E17	124 F 15	Homer rd Croy
101 W 4	Holmes rd Twick	138 M 2	Homer row W1
141 T 17	Holmes ter SE1	138 M 2	Homer st W1
10 E 8	Holmesbury clo Bushey Watf	117 R 3	Homersham rd Kingst
		50 E 15	Homerton gro E9
85 U 9	Holmesdale av SW14	50 F 16	Homerton High st E9
		50 M 14	Homerton rd E9
123 U 7	Holmesdale clo SE25	151 N 13	Homerton rd E9
		50 D 11	Homerton row E9
16 C 14	Holmesdale rd N11	50 D 15	Homerton ter E9
29 T 20	Holmesdale rd N6	92 C 14	Homestall rd SE22
123 U 7	Holmesdale rd SE25	6 D 17	Homestead paddock N14
127 N 6	Holmesdale rd Brom		
97 W 5	Holmesdale rd Bxly Hth	44 E 10	Homestead pk NW2
		145 P 19	Homestead rd SW6
85 N 2	Holmesdale rd Rich	56 A 8	Homestead rd Dgnhm
102 D 16	Holmesdale rd Tedd		
92 H 15	Holmesley rd SE23	114 H 16	Homewood cres Chisl
114 G 17	Holmewood cres Chisl		
		120 F 5	Homewood rd Mitch
123 S 7	Holmewood rd SE25	134 A 17	Honduras st EC1
90 B 20	Holmewood rd SW2	149 P 5	Hone pde SE11
27 V 14	Holmfield NW11		

142 C 6	Honey lane EC2	110 A 1	Horniman dri SE
45 Z 15	Honeybourne rd NW8	92 B 20	Horniman dri SE
		110 A 1	Horniman museu SE20
89 U 18	Honeybrook rd SW12		
		110 A 1	Horniman museu SE23
115 Z 14	Honeyden rd Sidcp		
25 N 13	Honeypot clo NW4	36 D 12	Horns rd Ilf
25 O 15	Honeypot rd Stanm	47 U 3	Hornsey la N6
24 J 6	Honeypot la Stanm	47 U 1	Hornsey La gdns
31 V 7	Honeysett rd N17	30 E 11	Hornsey Park rd
88 L 16	Honeywell rd SW11	48 B 7	Hornsey rd N4
62 D 7	Honeywood rd NW10	47 Z 2	Hornsey ri N19
		47 Z 1	Hornsey Ri gdns N19
83 Z 10	Honeywood rd Islwth		
		48 D 14	Hornsey st N7
154 M 9	Honeywood wlk Carsh	75 R 17	Hornshay pl SE1
		75 R 17	Hornshay st SE1
24 C 3	Honister clo Stanm	137 W 19	Hornton pl W8
24 C 3	Honister gdns Stanm	137 V 17	Hornton st W8
24 C 4	Honister pl Stanm	156 B 16	Horsa clo Croy
129 P 7	Honiton rd NW6	94 K 18	Horsa rd SE12
39 N 18	Honiton rd Rom	81 W 19	Horsa rd Erith
96 K 4	Honiton rd Welling	140 F 8	Horse & Dolphin W1
93 T 18	Honley rd SE6		
110 B 1	Honor Oak pk SE23	116 H 2	Horse fair Kings
92 C 19	Honor Oak rd SE23	104 M 3	Horse ride SW1
92 D 17	Honor Oak ri SE23	142 C 12	Horse Shoe all S
6 F 20	Hood av N14	154 B 3	Horse Shoe grn Sutton
16 F 1	Hood av N14		
85 W 13	Hood av SW14	7 Z 11	Horse Shoe la E
104 E 18	Hood rd SW20	139 X 7	Horse Shoe yd W
38 G 6	Hood wlk Rom	25 Y 2	Horsecroft rd Ed
25 O 15	Hoodcote gdns N21	76 F 16	Horseferry pl SE
17 V 2	Hoodcote gdns N21	148 F 4	Horseferry rd SV
126 M 12	Hook Farm rd Brom	140 K 15	Horseguards av W1
97 O 8	Hook la Welling		
96 J 12	Hook la Welling	140 J 15	Horseguards pde SW1
12 J 20	Hook wlk Edg		
32 F 11	Hookers rd E17	48 F 15	Horsell rd N5
22 J 14	Hooking grn Harrow	143 N 16	Horselydown la
56 L 9	Hooks Hall dri Dgnhm	150 B 16	Horseman st SE1
		41 U 14	Horsenden av Gr
92 A 3	Hooks dri SE22	41 V 15	Horsenden crs G
45 W 1	Hoop la NW11	41 U 17	Horsenden La no Grnfd
27 X 20	Hoop la NW11		
75 R 18	Hooper rd E16	59 Y 2	Horsenden La no Grnfd
143 S 7	Hooper st E1		
140 J 10	Hop gdns WC2	59 Z 7	Horsenden La so Grnfd
112 D 19	Hope pk Brom		
71 Y 1	Hope rd W13	95 P 12	Horsfeld gdns SE
88 E 9	Hope st SW11	95 P 12	Horsfeld rd SE9
77 V 17	Hopedale rd SE7	90 C 13	Horsford rd SW2
128 M 7	Hopefield av NW6	15 Y 17	Horsham av N12
143 R 2	Hopetown st E1	98 C 14	Horsham rd Bxly
150 F 19	Hopewell st SE5	159 V 17	Horsley dri Croy
74 M 4	Hopgood rd W12	159 V 17	Horsley dri Croy
126 C 15	Hopgood st W12	20 G 8	Horsley rd E4
140 D 7	Hopkins st W1	112 H 20	Horsley rd Brom
17 U 5	Hoppers rd N21	150 D 13	Horsley st SE17
20 M 8	Hoppett rd E4	92 L 15	Horsmonden rd
118 B 5	Hoppingwood av New Mald	146 A 17	Hortensia rd SW
		73 X 14	Horticultural pl V
118 G 14	Hopton gdns New Mald	45 T 12	Horton av NW2
		49 Z 18	Horton rd E8
108 A 12	Hopton rd SW16	93 S 7	Horton st SE13
107 Z 12	Hopton rd SW16	20 H 7	Hortus rd E4
141 X 12	Hopton st SE1	70 B 6	Hortus rd S'hall
		107 N 3	Hosack rd SW17
150 H 9	Hopwood st SE17	141 X 2	Hosier la EC1
56 L 4	Horace av Romford	100 K 2	Hosiotal Br rd T*
52 H 12	Horace rd E7	76 L 14	Hoskins st SE10
36 B 9	Horace rd Ilf	82 J 19	Hospital Br rd T*
116 L 7	Horace rd Kingst	83 V 13	Hospital la Islwt
135 P 10	Horatio st E2	82 G 9	Hospital rd Hour
137 S 11	Horbury cres W11	87 O 9	Hotham rd SW1
137 R 11	Horbury ms W11	106 D 18	Hotham rd SW1
106 D 15	Horbury st SW10	64 L 3	Hotham st E15
87 T 2	Horder rd SW6	159 S 8	Hothfield pl SE1
32 L 17	Hore av E17	149 S 8	Hotspur st SE11
98 D 13	Horley clo Bxly Hth	84 L 12	Houblon rd Rich
113 P 9	Horley rd SE9	78 K 9	Hough st SE18
129 P 9	Hormead rd W9	31 T 14	Houghton rd N1
77 S 11	Horn la SE10	141 O 6	Houghton st WC
61 V 18	Horn la W3	156 H 12	Houlder cres Cro
73 U 2	Horn la W3	17 R 1	Houndsden rd N
21 T 20	Horn la Wdfd Grn	142 L 4	Houndsditch EC
94 F 13	Horn Park la SE12	18 M 3	Houndsfield rd N
72 C 18	Hornbeam cres Brentf	100 B 4	Hounslow av Fel
		82 L 13	Hounslow av Hou
21 N 10	Hornbeam gro E4	82 L 13	Hounslow gdns Hounsl
127 X 16	Hornbeam rd Buckh		
150 L 18	Hornby rd SE15	82 B 5	Hounslow heath Hounsl
48 F 18	Horncastle rd SE12		
57 Y 3	Hornchurch rd Hrnch	82 K 9	Hounslow High s Hounsl
86 H 20	Horndean clo SW15		
38 L 4	Horndon clo Rom	82 M 16	Hounslow rd Tw
38 K 4	Horndon grn Rom	140 K 20	Hounslow rd Tw
38 L 5	Horndon rd Rom		House of parliam SW1
94 F 18	Horne clo SE12		
86 M 5	Horne way SW15	110 K 6	Houston rd SE23
77 Z 17	Hornfair rd SE7	32 L 17	Hove av E17
78 A 19	Hornfair rd SE7	75 O 20	Hove st SE15
57 R 2	Hornford way Romf	45 R 14	Hoveden rd NW2
		97 U 20	Howard av Bxly

45 S 11 Howard cl NW2
16 B 9 Howard clo N11
51 S 16 Howard clo W3
30 M 17 Howard clo Hampt
32 U 2 Howard ct Becknhm
52 A 9 Howard rd E11
3 P 10 Howard rd E17'
36 G 6 Howard rd E6
50 O 13 Howard rd NW2
31 S 18 Howard rd N15
9 R 13 Howard rd N16
10 C 20 Howard rd SE20
47 Y 12 Howard rd SE25
57 S 4 Howard rd Bark
12 E 19 Howard rd Brom
53 Z 12 Howard rd Ilf
45 V 8 Howard rd Islwth
28 C 7 Howard rd New Mald
68 L 17 Howard rd S'hall
41 P 8 Howard st WC2
46 A 17 Howard st Surb
28 E 13 Howard wlk N2
37 N 11 Howards la SW15
36 L 12 Howards la SW15
55 Y 9 Howards rd E13
30 B 13 Howarth rd SE2
1 U 20 Howberry clo Edgw
24 H 1 Howberry rd Edgw
1 V 19 Howberry rd Edgw
23 N 2 Howberry rd Thntn Hth
39 V 5 Howbury la Erith
32 C 7 Howbury rd SE15
14 L 20 Howcroft cres N3
27 Y 1 Howcroft cres N3
23 T 4 Howden rd SE25
91 W 7 Howden st SE15
37 V 16 Howe clo Rom
35 X 8 Howgate rd SW14
18 C 2 Howick pl SW1
10 K 19 Howie st SW11
46 K 17 Howitt rd NW3
32 C 20 Howland Ms east W1
32 B 20 Howland st W1
91 N 15 Howletts SE24
30 D 20 Howley pl W2
56 K 5 Howley rd Croy
55 N 7 Howley rd Croy
74 G 18 Howsman rd SW13
92 J 10 Howson rd SE4
10 B 6 Howton pl Bushey Watf
34 J 13 Hoxton sq N1
34 J 7 Hoxton st N1
65 P 18 Hoy st E16
62 A 18 Hoylake rd W3
51 V 17 Hoyland rd SE15
06 J 11 Hoyle rd SW17
08 M 8 Hubbard rd SE27
64 L 4 Hubbard st E15
90 B 8 Hubert gro SW9
46 A 8 Hubert rd E6
68 Z 14 Huddart st E3
47 V 10 Huddleston rd N1
52 C 12 Huddlestone rd E7
24 J 18 Huddlestone rd NW2
98 A 5 Hudson rd Bxly Hth
02 L 20 Hudson rd Kingstn
47 Z 5 Hudsons pl SW1
65 R 14 Hudsons rd E16
42 B 8 Huggin hill EC4
47 Y 7 Hugh ms SW1
47 Y 6 Hugh st SW1
51 Y 14 Hughan rd E15
24 B 14 Hughenden av Harrow
18 H 16 Hughenden rd Worc Park
51 U 11 Hughendon ter E15
52 U 19 Hugo gdns Rainhm
47 V 12 Hugo rd N19
47 A 7 Hugon rd SW6
48 Y 6 Huguenot rd SE15
34 D 14 Huguenot terr SW18
37 Y 18 Hull rd Rom
34 A 13 Hull st EC1
38 H 4 Hulse av Bark
38 H 4 Hulse av Rom
77 O 16 Humber rd NW3
77 O 16 Humber rd SE3
43 L 19 Humberstone rd E13
44 L 15 Humbolt rd W6
35 U 5 Humes av W7
31 U 8 Humphrey clo Ilf
51 N 11 Humphrey st SE1
41 N 13 Hungerford Foot br SE1
40 K 12 Hungerford la WC2
37 Z 16 Hungerford rd N1

48 A 15 Hungerford rd N7
75 S 18 Hunsdon rd SE14
63 R 8 Hunslett st E2
144 A 19 Hunston rd Mrdn
70 G 8 Hunt rd S'hall
104 M 20 Hunter clo SW20
105 N 20 Hunter clo SW20
53 Z 16 Hunter rd Bark
53 Z 16 Hunter rd Ilf
54 A 15 Hunter rd Ilf
123 N 6 Hunter rd Thntn Hth
56 E 13 Hunter sq Dgnhm
132 K 16 Hunter st WC1
24 E 13 Hunters gdns Harrow
56 F 14 Hunters Hall rd Dgnhm
157 T 9 Hunters way Croy
7 U 5 Hunters way Enf
152 M 6 Huntingdon gdns Worc Pk
8 K 10 Huntingdon rd N2
19 R 7 Huntingdon rd N9
65 P 19 Huntingdon st E16
158 M 16 Huntingfield Croy
86 H 13 Huntingfield rd SW15
56 E 19 Huntings rd Dgnhm
147 T 7 Huntley st WC1
132 D 18 Huntley st WC1
118 F 3 Huntley way SW20
14 M 19 Huntly dri N3
135 R 19 Hunton ct E1
135 R 19 Hunton st E1
140 N 10 Hunts ct WC2
64 F 7 Hunts la E15
9 T 10 Hunts mead Enf
63 P 20 Hunts ms E1
109 S 5 Hunts Slip rd SE21
150 H 8 Huntsman st SE17
88 D 12 Huntsmoor rd SW18
147 S 17 Huntspill st SW17
131 O 18 Huntsworth ms NW1
149 Y 7 Hurlbutt pl SE17
149 W 7 Hurley rd SE11
58 K 15 Hurley rd Grnfd
87 V 7 Hurlingham gdns SW6
87 X 8 Hurlingham house SW6
87 W 7 Hurlingham park SW6
87 U 6 Hurlingham rd SW6
81 P 20 Hurlingham rd Bxly
48 J 10 Hurlock st N5
123 R 10 Hurlstone rd SE25
107 F 6 Huron rd SW17
20 B 11 Hurn av E4
29 W 19 Hurst av N6
20 A 12 Hurst clo E4
28 A 18 Hurst clo NW11
126 C 20 Hurst clo Brom
40 E 16 Hurst clo Grnfd
80 H 14 Hurst la SE2
80 H 15 Hurst Pl est SE2
33 R 10 Hurst rd E17
17 U 6 Hurst rd N21
98 D 20 Hurst rd Bxly
115 Y 2 Hurst rd Bxly
157 O 10 Hurst rd Croy
81 Y 20 Hurst rd Erith
4 L 12 Hurst ri Barnt
115 Z 2 Hurst springs Bxly
90 J 15 Hurst st SE24
57 S 15 Hurst View rd S Croy
157 S 15 Hurst way S Croy
54 F 18 Hurstbourne gdns Bark
110 A 2 Hurstbourne rd SE23
153 Z 2 Hurstcourt rd Sutton
126 C 20 Hurstdene av Brom
31 T 20 Hurstdene av Brom
126 E 11 Hurstfield Brom
35 V 5 Hurstleigh gdns Ilf
34 J 12 Hurstmead ct Edg
32 J 12 Hurstwood av E18
115 Z 1 Hurstwood av Bxly
99 R 3 Hurstwood av Bxly
127 U 7 Hurstwood dri Brom
27 V 13 Hurstwood rd NW11
126 F 20 Husseywell cres Brom
76 A 6 Hutchings st E14
28 B 14 Hutchings wlk NW11
21 V 18 Hutton clo Wdfd Grn
23 N 2 Hutton gdns Harrow
15 P 18 Hutton rd N12
23 O 2 Hutton la Harrow
141 V 7 Hutton st EC4
23 N 1 Hutton wlk Harrow

92 M 13 Huxbear st SE4
55 P 1 Huxley dri Rom
61 N 7 Huxley gdns NW10
17 W 12 Huxley pl N13
51 U 7 Huxley rd E10
18 B 13 Huxley rd N18
96 L 9 Huxley rd Welling
18 A 16 Huxley sayze N18
18 A 18 Huxley st N18
128 K 14 Huxley st W10
104 G 1 Hyacinth rd SW13
4 H 12 Hyde clo Barnt
18 E 7 Hyde court N9
26 B 17 Hyde cres NW9
88 J 1 Hyde la SW11
138 K 12 Hyde park W2
139 O 14 Hyde park W2
17 Z 7 Hyde Park av N21
18 A 6 Hyde Park av N21
138 K 6 Hyde Park cres W2
138 C 20 Hyde Park ga SW7
138 C 20 Hyde Park Ga ms SW7
17 Z 6 Hyde Park gdns N21
138 J 9 Hyde Park gdns W2
138 J 8 Hyde Park Gdns ms W2
138 K 7 Hyde Park sq W2
138 K 7 Hyde Park Sq ms W2
138 K 7 Hyde rd N1
134 G 5 Hyde rd Bxly Hth
84 L 12 Hyde rd Rich
75 Z 17 Hyde st SE8
76 A 18 Hyde st SE8
26 B 15 Hyde the NW9
25 Y 11 Hyde the NW9
76 H 20 Hyde vale SE10
93 W 2 Hyde vale SE10
119 Z 17 Hyde wlk Mrdn
18 B 6 Hydefield clo N21
48 J 19 Hydes pl N1
18 F 9 Hydeside gdns N9
18 G 9 Hydethorpe av N9
89 V 20 Hydethorpe rd SW12
107 U 1 Hydethorpe rd SW12
18 G 9 Hydeway N9
57 Z 2 Hyland clo Hrnch
57 Y 3 Hyland way Hrnch
33 Y 8 Hylands rd E17
79 X 10 Hylton st SE18
151 X 13 Hyndman av SE16
151 W 14 Hyndman st SE15
156 K 17 Hynton rd Dgnhm
156 K 17 Hyrstdene S Croy
75 N 12 Hyson rd SE16
80 M 20 Hythe av Bxly Hth
81 O 19 Hythe av Bxly Hth
62 G 11 Hythe rd NW10
123 O 5 Hythe rd Thntn Hth
12 M 2 Hyver hill NW7

I

9 T 7 Ian sq Enf
65 P 16 Ibbotson av E16
63 R 10 Ibbott st E1
155 Y 8 Iberian av Wallgtn
104 F 1 Ibsley gdns SW15
86 F 20 Ibsley gdns SW15
64 B 4 Iceland rd E3
49 Z 9 Ickburgh rd E5
113 S 10 Ickleton rd SE9
36 A 16 Icknield dri Ilf
35 Z 16 Icknield dri Ilf
32 J 12 Ickworth rd E17
31 O 14 Ida rd N15
64 F 18 Ida st E14
126 A 6 Iden clo Brom
77 N 10 Idenden cotts SE10
107 O 13 Idlecombe rd SW17
52 B 14 Idmiston rd E15
108 M 5 Idmiston rd SE27
118 B 14 Idmiston rd Worc Park
118 E 18 Idmiston sq Worc Park
142 J 10 Idol la EC3
75 Z 19 Idonia st SE8
144 A 5 Iffley rd W6
14 Y 16 Iffley rd W6
145 Y 13 Ifield rd SW10
146 A 15 Ifield rd SW10
81 S 19 Ightam rd Erith
128 H 13 Ilbert st W10
137 X 9 Ilchester gdns W2
137 P 20 Ilchester pl W14

55 T 15 Ilchester rd Dgnhm
109 O 5 Ildersley gro SE21
75 P 17 Ilderton rd SE15
75 O 13 Ilderton rd SE16
44 C 18 Ilex rd W10
108 F 12 Ilex way SW16
53 Z 11 Ilford la Ilf
54 A 15 Ilford lane Ilf
55 P 1 Ilfracombe gdns Rom
112 B 7 Ilfracombe rd Brom
149 Y 8 Iliffe st SE17
149 Z 8 Iliffe St yd SE17
65 X 16 Ilkley rd E16
24 F 18 Ilmington rd Harrow
88 K 10 Ilminster gdns SW11
16 J 1 Imber clo N14
134 E 6 Imber st N1
42 G 9 Imperial clo Harrow
40 G 2 Imperial dri Harrow
22 H 19 Imperial dri Harrow
146 E 2 Imperial Institute rd SW7
66 A 7 Imperial mews E6
30 A 4 Imperial rd N22
88 C 2 Imperial rd SW6
64 F 10 Imperial st E3
149 U 3 Imperial War museum SE1
114 C 8 Imperial way Chisl
156 E 15 Imperial way Croy
24 L 19 Imperial way Harrow
111 S 3 Inchmery rd SE6
74 A 13 Incress rd W4
30 D 18 Inderwick rd N8
143 N 7 India st EC3
62 J 20 India way W12
77 Z 20 Indus rd SE7
65 T 13 Ingal rd E13
89 T 2 Ingate pl SW8
52 K 5 Ingatestone rd E12
123 Z 10 Ingatestone rd SE25
34 G 2 Ingatestone rd Wdfd Grn
89 R 5 Ingelow rd SW8
74 J 3 Ingersoll rd W12
9 R 4 Ingersoll rd Enf
140 D 7 Ingestre pl W1
52 F 12 Ingestre rd E7
47 T 11 Ingestre rd NW5
158 E 19 Ingham clo S Croy
158 E 19 Ingham rd NW6
158 D 19 Ingham rd S Croy
15 V 20 Ingle way N12
15 U 19 Ingle way N12
90 E 4 Ingleborough st SW9
56 G 19 Ingleby rd Dgnhm
53 Z 4 Ingleby rd Ilf
13 X 13 Ingleby way Chisl
155 X 18 Ingleby way Wallgtn
79 T 13 Ingledew st SE18
35 T 17 Inglehurst gdns Ilf
10 F 6 Inglemere rd SE23
107 N 17 Inglemere rd Mitch
133 S 12 Inglenert st EC1
111 N 17 Ingleside clo Becknhm
77 N 17 Ingleside gro SE10
87 O 1 Inglethorpe st SW6
97 O 12 Ingleton av Welling
18 J 19 Ingleton rd N18
154 H 18 Ingleton rd Carsh
45 Y 16 Inglewood rd NW6
98 M 9 Inglewood rd Bxly Hth
60 M 19 Inglis rd W5
61 N 20 Inglis rd W5
123 V 19 Inglis rd Croy
90 K 3 Inglis st SE5
46 D 1 Ingram av NW11
11 R 17 Ingram clo Stanm
142 H 8 Ingram ct EC3
28 K 13 Ingram rd N2
122 L 1 Ingram rd Thntn Hth
108 L 20 Ingram rd Thrtn Hth
59 R 4 Ingram way Grnfd
39 O 13 Ingrave rd Rom
88 H 7 Ingrave st SW11
78 C 18 Inigo Jones rd SE7
140 K 9 Inigo pl WC2
48 T 17 Inkerman rd NW5
20 H 15 Inks grn E4
62 A 2 Inman rd NW10
88 C 20 Inman rd SW18
21 T 15 Inmans row Wdfd Grn
131 S 13 Inner crcl NW1
105 P 1 Inner Pk rd SW19
49 S 19 Inner Temple la EC4
86 K 16 Innes gdns SW15
150 J 8 Innis pl SE17

65 Y7 Inniskilling rd E13
49 Z16 Institute pl E8
156 B15 Instone clo Croy
133 S13 Insurance st WC1
50 B6 Inver rd E5
79 S15 Inverary pl SE18
37 V14 Inverclyde gdns Rom
152 F6 Inveresk gdns Worc Pk
46 C7 Inverforth clo NW3
77 W14 Inverine rd SE7
8 F6 Inverness av SE7
137 W15 Inverness gdns W8
137 Z8 Inverness ms W2
137 Z9 Inverness pl W2
18 M15 Inverness rd N18
82 F10 Inverness rd Hounsl
70 C11 Inverness rd S'hall
119 O20 Inverness rd Worc Pk
131 X3 Inverness st NW1
137 Z9 Inverness ter W2
92 E11 Inverton rd SE15
77 T18 Invicta rd SE3
150 H10 Inville rd SE17
82 M8 Inwood av Hounsl
83 N8 Inwood av Hounsl
158 J2 Inwood clo Croy
132 G14 Inwood pl WC1
82 M8 Inwood rd Hounsl
88 J4 Inworth st SW11
31 T16 Ipplepen la N15
107 R16 Ipswich rd SW17
141 Y7 Ireland yd EC4
87 Y3 Irene rd SW6
64 A10 Ireton rd E3
97 Z15 Iris av Bxly
98 A15 Iris av Bxly
81 P17 Iris cres Bxly
19 Y20 Iris way E4
8 H5 Irkdale av Enf
99 X10 Iron Mill la Drtfd
99 T11 Iron Mill rd Drtfd
88 B16 Iron Mill rd SW14
138 H2 Irongate Wharf rd W2
142 D5 Ironmonger la EC2
144 C15 Ironmonger row EC1
144 C15 Ironmonger st EC1
38 K2 Irons way Rom
24 A10 Irvine av Harrow
23 Z10 Irvine av Harrow
15 W9 Irvine clo N20
120 H1 Irving rd W14
140 H10 Irving st WC2
79 V18 Irwin av SE18
62 L4 Irwin gdns NW10
128 A6 Irwin gdns NW10
90 E2 Isabel st SW9
50 C16 Isabella rd E9
141 V15 Isabella st SE1
91 S13 Isel way SE22
121 Z3 Isham rd SW16
106 C4 Isis st SW18
79 O17 Isla rd SE18
106 L19 Island rd Mitch
63 X19 Island row E14
48 E10 Isledon rd N7
127 Y1 Islehurst clo Chisl
84 B11 Isleworth promenade Twick
133 W5 Islington grn N1
133 V9 Islington High st N1
48 G20 Islington Pk st N1
133 S5 Islington pl N1
12 K20 Islip gdns Edg
40 C20 Islip gdns Grnfd
40 C20 Islip Manor rd Grnfd
47 V16 Islip st NW5
52 H20 Ismailia rd E7
148 M11 Italian wlk SE11
24 B8 Ivanhoe dri Harrow
22 A10 Ivanhoe dri Harrow
91 T7 Ivanhoe rd SE5
61 O6 Ive Farm clo E10
61 P5 Iveagh av NW10
61 P6 Iveagh clo NW10
97 T5 Ivedon rd Welling
89 U6 Iveley rd SW4
5 N19 Ivere dri Barnt
137 V20 Iverna ct W8
145 V1 Iverna gdns W8
159 S16 Ivers way Croy
45 V19 Iverson rd NW6
64 L14 Ives rd E16
146 L6 Ives st SW3
92 C18 Ivestor ter SE23
8 D7 Ivinghoe clo Enf
10 B2 Ivinghoe rd Bushey Watrd
55 P15 Ivinghoe rd Dgnhm
113 Z1 Ivor gro SE9
10 O17 Ivor pl NW1

47 U20 Ivor st NW1
112 F8 Ivorydown Brom
140 M10 Ivy Bridge la WC2
40 D12 Ivy clo Harrow
73 U10 Ivy cres W4
30 A19 Ivy gdns N8
145 X7 Ivy gdns Mitch
82 D10 Ivy la Hounsl
116 L15 Ivy pl Surb
33 P19 Ivy rd E17
44 M12 Ivy rd NW2
45 M12 Ivy rd NW2
16 J3 Ivy rd N14
93 O12 Ivy rd SE4
92 L11 Ivy rd SE4
82 L11 Ivy rd Hounsl
134 J8 Ivy st N1
55 Y18 Ivy wlk Dgnhm
92 F9 Ivydale rd SE15
155 N2 Ivydale rd Carsh
108 C8 Ivyday gro SW16
154 D8 Ivydene clo Sutton
135 U2 Ivydene rd E8
56 B18 Ivyhouse rd Dgnhm
55 W18 Ivyhouse rd Dgnhm
108 F8 Ivymount rd SE27
146 K7 Ixworth pl SW3
98 A12 Izane rd Bxly Hth

J

53 W13 Jack Cornwell st E12
135 V4 Jackman st E8
48 E13 Jackson rd N7
74 T4 Jackson rd Bark
5 V20 Jackson rd Barnt
127 T20 Jackson rd Brom
78 J16 Jackson st SE18
29 R20 Jackson la N6
143 R17 Jacob st SE1
139 V3 Jacobs Well ms W1
108 K10 Jaffray pl SE27
127 N9 Jaffray rd Brom
126 M9 Jaffray rd Brom
143 P19 Jamaica rd SE1
75 N7 Jamaica rd SE16
143 X20 Jamaica rd SE16
122 V13 Jamaica rd Thntn Hth
63 R16 Jamaica st E1
44 M14 James av NW2
56 C5 James av Dgnhm
39 W15 James clo Rom
30 K2 James gdns N22
33 X20 James la E11
31 U3 James pl N17
99 V17 James rd Drtfrd
140 M8 James rd WC2
139 V6 James st W1
8 H16 James st Enf
83 O8 James st Hounsl
137 T13 Jameson st W8
131 X2 Jamestown rd NW1
143 U19 Janeway st SE16
51 Z14 Janson clo E15
52 A14 Janson rd E15
51 Z13 Janson rd E15
31 S11 Jansons rd N15
58 C3 Japan cres N4
37 W20 Japan rd Rom
58 C1 Jaque clo Grnfd
150 K13 Jardin st SE5
37 U18 Jarrow rd Rom
91 T11 Jarvis rd SE22
157 O14 Jarvis rd S Croy
159 R6 Jasmine gdns Croy
159 P6 Jasmine gdns Croy
110 A20 Jasmine gro SE20
139 V4 Jason ct W1
113 W9 Jason wlk SE9
9 P4 Jasper clo Enf
109 U13 Jasper rd SE19
138 D19 Jay ms SW7
90 B16 Jebb av SW2
64 C2 Jebb st E3
65 X8 Jedburgh rd E13
89 P10 Jedburgh st SW8
74 D5 Jeddo rd W12
64 F9 Jefferson est E3
64 F9 Jefferson st E3
89 Z4 Jeffreys rd SW4
90 A5 Jeffreys rd SW4
9 X14 Jeffreys rd Enf
47 U20 Jeffreys st NW1
89 Z3 Jeffreys wlk SW4
153 V9 Jeffs rd Sutton
94 L11 Jeken rd SE9
90 F12 Jelf rd SW2
31 O3 Jellicoe rd N17

67 O8 Jenkins la Bark
65 W12 Jenkins rd E13
49 W9 Jenner rd N16
156 F4 Jennett rd Croy
112 D6 Jennifer rd Brom
91 V15 Jennings rd SE22
81 Y3 Jenningtree way Blvdr
97 Y3 Jenton av Bxly Hth
52 L19 Jephson rd E7
91 O3 Jephson st SE5
87 X16 Jeptha rd SW18
120 L9 Jeppos la Mitch
145 U18 Jerdan pl SW6
64 C18 Jeremiah st E14
19 P14 Jeremys grn N18
140 B12 Jermyn st SW1
35 Y7 Jerningham av Ilf
92 H2 Jerningham rd SE14
109 T18 Jernsen way SE19
150 A13 Jerome pl SE17
135 N19 Jerome st E1
93 S7 Jerrard st SE13
24 D8 Jersey av Stanm
51 W5 Jersey rd E11
65 X15 Jersey rd E16
107 R16 Jersey rd SW17
71 Y7 Jersey rd W7
82 L1 Jersey rd Hounsl
70 L20 Jersey rd Hounsl
53 Z13 Jersey rd Ilf
71 P18 Jersey rd Islwth
133 W18 Jerusalem pass EC1
108 F14 Jerviston gdns SW16
43 O17 Jesmond av Wemb
123 U17 Jesmond rd Croy
150 G9 Jesmond st SE17
11 Y15 Jesmond way Stanm
49 Z4 Jessam av E5
71 V3 Jessamine rd W7
51 T5 Jesse rd E10
81 E18 Jessica rd SW18
90 K11 Jessop rd SE24
58 A10 Jessop st SE15
112 J2 Jevington way SE12
33 N10 Jewel rd E17
142 M7 Jewry st EC3
88 D10 Jews row SW18
110 A9 Jews wlk SE26
44 L16 Jeymer av NW2
58 M4 Jeymer dri Grnfd
59 N3 Jeymer dri Grnfd
58 M4 Jeymer dri Grnfd
88 D17 Jeypore rd SW18
100 H18 Jillian clo Hampt
95 O19 Joan cres SE9
55 Y6 Joan gdns Dgnhm
55 Y6 Joan rd Dgnhm
141 V15 Joan st SE1
58 C3 Joave clo Grnfd
84 K8 Jocelyn rd Rich
141 P1 Jockeys fields WC1
63 Z2 Jodrell rd E3
141 S18 Johanna st SE1
140 L11 John Adam st WC2
147 N2 John Burns dri Bark
49 T15 John Campbell rd N16
141 V8 John Carpenter st EC4
143 S20 John Felton rd SE16
143 R10 John Fisher st E1
148 H8 John Islip st SW7
97 S8 John Newton ct Welling
56 G20 John Parker clo Dgnhm
93 S2 John Penn st SE13
149 Y17 John Ruskin st SE5
150 B15 John Ruskin st SE5
48 K18 John Spencer sq N1
65 O4 John st E15
123 Y9 John st EC1
133 P19 John st WC1
8 G16 John st Enf
82 C4 John st Hounsl
78 J10 John Wilson st SE18
10 N4 Johns av NW4
120 D12 Johns la Mrdn
133 O18 Johns ms WC1
143 Y4 Johns pl E1
127 M12 Johnson rd Brom
123 N17 Johnson rd Croy
63 P18 Johnson st E1
154 M4 Johnsons clo Carsh
141 U6 Johnsons ct EC4
148 B11 Johnsons pl SW1
21 S18 Johnston rd Wdfd Grn
66 H10 Johnstone rd E6
45 O10 Johnstone ter NW2
142 G14 Joiner st SE1

41 P4 Jollys la Harrow
149 O8 Jonathan st SE11
120 M14 Jones la Mitch
65 W13 Jones rd E13
139 X10 Jones st W1
121 T8 Jonson clo Mitch
87 P11 Jordan ct SW15
60 D2 Jordan rd Grnfd
83 U3 Jorden clo Islwth
63 Y13 Joseph st E3
90 D14 Josephine av SW2
64 F16 Joshua st E14
88 M5 Joubert st SW11
151 P19 Jowett st SE15
18 H17 Joyce av N18
90 G16 Joydon dri Rom
38 H17 Joydon dri Rom
90 G16 Joyce wlk SW2
18 H17 Joyce av N18
83 O20 Jubilee av Twick
25 Y18 Jubilee clo NW9
18 K4 Jubilee cres N9
40 A12 Jubilee dri Ruisl
58 H15 Jubilee gdns S'ha
18 L3 Jubilee park N9
146 M10 Jubilee pl SW3
60 A2 Jubilee rd Grnfd
115 U15 Jubilee rd Sidcp
153 P15 Jubilee rd Sutton
63 P17 Jubilee st E1
132 J14 Judd st WC1
65 P18 Jude st E16
46 C9 Judges wlk NW3
146 L19 Juer st SW11
68 J5 Julia gdns Bark
47 O14 Julia st NW5
61 U20 Julian av W3
41 T8 Julian hill Harrow
72 D9 Julien rd W5
93 T7 Junction appr SE13
128 K4 Junction ms W2
138 D1 Junction pl W2
65 V6 Junction rd E13
31 X9 Junction rd N17
47 V8 Junction rd N19
18 K6 Junction rd N9
72 F11 Junction rd W5
23 S19 Junction rd Harrow
55 Z1 Junction rd Rom
55 X1 Junction rd Rom
39 T14 Junction rd Rom
157 O12 Junction rd S Croy
63 P19 Junction st E1
75 T16 Juno way SE14
64 J1 Jupp rd E15
63 V10 Jupps rd E3
146 J15 Justice wlk SW3
9 W10 Jute la Enf
65 T12 Jutland rd E13
93 T19 Jutland rd SE6
38 H19 Jutsums av Rom
56 C9 Jutsums la Rom
149 P5 Juxon st SE11

K

88 G6 Kambala rd SW11
110 L10 Kangley Br rd SE26
59 R5 Karoline gdns Grn
79 X12 Kashgar rd SE18
78 A18 Kashmir rd SE7
88 M2 Kassala rd SW11
107 O1 Kate st SW12
156 M4 Katharine st Croy
157 N4 Katharine st Croy
95 N12 Katherine gdns SE
36 C1 Katherine gdns Ilf
66 C3 Katherine rd E6
52 L16 Katherine rd E7
83 Z20 Katherine rd Twick
61 W13 Kathleen av W3
60 K1 Kathleen av Wemb
42 K20 Kathleen av Wemb
88 L8 Kathleen rd SW11
90 B6 Kay rd SW9
64 K1 Kay st E15
135 T9 Kay st E2
97 R2 Kay st Welling
45 P14 Kayes rd Sutto
141 N6 Kean st WC2
108 X11 Keary house SW1
5 J15 Keat's way Grnfd
39 Y2 Keats av Rom
46 H12 Keats gro NW3
46 J1 Keats rd Welling
124 D15 Keats way Croy
41 O16 Keble clo Wor Pk
18 E20 Keble clo Worc Pk
106 D9 Keble st SW17

F 17 Kechill gdns Brom
B 11 Keedonwood rd Brom
Z 11 Keedonwood rd Brom
L 3 Keeley rd Croy
N 15 Keeley st W1
M 13 Keeling rd SE9
N 13 Keeling rd SE9
M 8 Keen's rd Croy
J 18 Keens yd N1
E 6 Keep the SE3
E 6 Keesey st SE17
V 1 Keetcn's rd SE16
R 19 Keevil dri SW19
D 2 Keightley dri SE9
L 11 Keildon rd SW11
A 1 Keir Hardie way Bark
G 4 Keith gro W12
L 6 Keith rd E17
S 6 Keith rd Bark
P 6 Kelbrook rd SE3
H 5 Kelby path SE9
A 5 Kelceda clo NW2
H 5 Kelfield gdns W10
Y 20 Kell st SE1
T 11 Kelland rd E13
M 5 Kellaway rd SE3
O 3 Kellaway rd SE3
Y 13 Kellerton rd SE13
F 11 Kellett rd SW2
L 9 Kellino st SW17
X 8 Kellner rd SE18
T 18 Kelly st NW1
Y 17 Kelly way Rom
X 10 Kelmore gro SE22
G 7 Kelmscot gdns W12
K 6 Kelmscott clo E17
L 14 Kelmscott rd SW11
K 12 Kelross rd N5
H 4 Kelsall clo SE3
N 7 Kelsey la Beckenhm
R 5 Kelsey Pk av Becknhm
P 3 Kelsey Pk rd Becknhm
O 3 Kelsey sq Becknhm
V 15 Kelsey st E2
O 6 Kelsey way Becknhm
Y 2 Kelso pl W8
E 17 Kelso rd Carsh
W 19 Kelson st NW6
A 6 Kelston rd Ilf
Z 7 Kelston rd Ilf
O 15 Kelvedon clo Kingst
P 20 Kelvedon rd SW6
R 18 Kelvin av N13
T 15 Kelvin av Tedd
G 20 Kelvin cres Harrow
C 15 Kelvin dri Twick
G 17 Kelvin gdns S'hall
A 7 Kelvin gro SE26
K 13 Kelvin rd N5
M 7 Kelvin rd Welling
J 16 Kelvington clo Croy
E 14 Kelvington rd SE9
P 12 Kelway pl W14
W 6 Kemble rd N17
G 2 Kemble rd SE23
B 14 Kemble rd Croy
N 8 Kemble st WC2
L 8 Kemerton rd SE5
U 17 Kemerton rd Becknhm
S 4 Kemerton rd Becknhm
H 16 Kemeys st E9
E 9 Kemnal manor Chisl
D 13 Kemnal rd Chisl
W 4 Kemp rd Dgnhm
G 10 Kempe rd NW6
S 13 Kempis way SE22
G 12 Kemplay rd NW3
V 11 Kempsford gdns SW5
V 6 Kempsford rd SE11
L 12 Kempshead rd SE5
Z 17 Kempshott rd SW16
A 17 Kempshott rd SW16
Z 1 Kempson rd SW6
H 16 Kempton av Grnfd
B 20 Kempton park Felt
F 3 Kempton rd E6
K 14 Kempton wlk Croy
Z 17 Kemsing clo Bxly
N 9 Kemsing clo Thntn Hth
S 14 Kemsing rd SE10
L 4 Kenbury st SE5
K 19 Kenchester st SW8
B 14 Kendal av N18
S 14 Kendal av W3

67 U 2 Kendal av Bark
21 R 9 Kendal clo Wdfd Grn
18 B 14 Kendal gdns N18
44 H 13 Kendal rd NW10
138 M 6 Kendal st W2
111 Z 13 Kendale rd Brom
124 H 3 Kendall av Becknhm
157 R 20 Kendall av S Croy
139 T 3 Kendall gdn W1
124 H 3 Kendall rd Becknhm
83 X 5 Kendall rd Islwth
75 R 20 Kender st SE14
89 Y 9 Kendoa rd SW4
120 A 4 Kendor gdns SW19
156 J 16 Kendra Hall rd S Croy
83 S 17 Kendrey gdns Twick
146 E 6 Kendrick ms SW7
146 E 6 Kendrick pl SW7
41 Y 9 Kenelm clo Harrow
4 D 17 Kenerne dri Barnt
4 D 18 Kenerne dri Barnt
89 T 18 Keniford rd SW12
33 P 9 Kenilworth av E17
105 X 11 Kenilworth av SW19
40 D 12 Kenilworth av Harrow
8 E 6 Kenilworth cres Enf
54 K 6 Kenilworth gdns Ilf
58 F 10 Kenilworth gdns S'hall
63 V 6 Kenilworth rd E3
129 R 3 Kenilworth rd NW6
110 E 20 Kenilworth rd SE20
72 J 3 Kenilworth rd W5
12 G 12 Kenilworth rd Edg
152 F 12 Kenilworth rd Epsom
98 F 19 Kenley clo Bxly
122 H 9 Kenley gdns Thntn Hth
120 A 5 Kenley rd SW19
119 X 4 Kenley rd SW19
117 U 3 Kenley rd Kingst
84 A 16 Kenley rd Twick
136 K 12 Kenley st W11
153 N 9 Kenley wlk Sutton
106 G 13 Kenlor rds SW17
106 M 19 Kenmare dri Mitch
17 Y 14 Kenmare gdns N13
122 E 14 Kenmare rd Thntn Hth
61 P 1 Kenmere gdns N Wemb
97 T 4 Kenmere rd Welling
62 J 8 Kenmont gdns NW10
23 Z 13 Kenmore av Har
22 A 7 Kenmore av Harrow
23 Z 8 Kenmore av Harrow
25 T 7 Kenmore gdns Edg
24 G 12 Kenmore rd Harrow
50 A 16 Kenmure rd E8
64 H 1 Kennard rd E15
15 Z 17 Kennard rd N11
78 F 3 Kennard st E16
9 K 19 Kennedy av Enf
65 T 7 Kennedy clo E13
59 V 12 Kennedy path W7
59 U 13 Kennedy rd W7
67 U 4 Kennedy rd Bark
129 P 17 Kennet rd W9
83 V 7 Kennet rd Islwth
142 B 9 Kennet Wharf la EC4
53 X 11 Kenneth av Ilf
44 L 15 Kenneth cres NW2
10 K 19 Kenneth gdns Stanm
55 X 1 Kenneth rd Rom
99 X 8 Kennett rd Drtfrd
75 R 5 Kenning st SE16
49 Y 10 Kenninghall rd E5
19 P 16 Kenninghall rd N18
149 V 9 Kennings way SE11
149 O 12 Kennington gro SE11
149 V 8 Kennington la SE11
149 P 15 Kennington oval SE11
149 P 14 Kennington park SE11
149W 14 Kennington Pk gdns SE11
149 V 13 Kennington Pk pl SE11
149 V 11 Kennington Pk rd SE11
149 T 11 Kennington rd SE11
37 N 1 Kennylands Ilf
139 S 1 Kenrick pl W1
129 N 18 Kensal rd W10
128 J 16 Kensal rd W10
53 R 18 Kensington av E12

137W 18 Kensington Ch ct W8
137 V 14 Kensington Ch st W8
137W 18 Kensington Ch wlk W8
137W 17 Kensington Church ct W18
137W 17 Kensington Church ct W8
137 Z 19 Kensington ct W8
137 Z 20 Kensington Ct pl W8
35 O 6 Kensington dri Wdfd Grn
138 B 20 Kensington ga W8
53 U 4 Kensington gdns SE11
137 X 7 Kensington Gdns sq W2
138 F 19 Kensington gore SW7
137W 19 Kensington High st W8
145 R 2 Kensington High st W8
137 V 13 Kensington mall W8
137W 12 Kensington Pal gdns W8
187 Z 15 Kensington Palace London museum W8
137 P 10 Kensington Pk gdns W11
137 N 6 Kensington Pk ms W11
137 O 7 Kensington Pk rd W11
137 T 14 Kensington pl W8
138 D 19 Kensington rd SW7
58 G 5 Kensington rd Grnfd
38 L 18 Kensington rd Rom
137 X 20 Kensington rd SW19
157 O 17 Kensington ter S Croy
60 A 15 Kent av W13
69 T 6 Kent av Dgnhm
96 L 11 Kent av Welling
6 C 15 Kent dri Barnt
101 S 13 Kent dri Tedd
60 B 14 Kent gdns W13
110 J 14 Kent House la Beckenhm
110 F 19 Kent House rd Beckenhm
131 N 15 Kent pas NW1
18 A 3 Kent rd N21
73 V 8 Kent rd W4
56 H 15 Kent rd Dgnhm
116 G 5 Kent rd Kingst
73 P 19 Kent rd Rich
125 S 20 Kent rd W Wkhm
65 X 10 Kent st E13
66 E 2 Kent st E2
130 M 14 Kent ter NW1
54 H 7 Kent View gdns Ilf
138 L 19 Kent yd SW7
58 B 4 Kentford way Grnfd
142 E 16 Kentish bldgs SE1
81 S 11 Kentish st Blvdr
131 Z 2 Kentish Town rd NW1
47 T 18 Kentish Town rd NW5
79 V 11 Kenton av SE18
58 H 20 Kenton av S'hall
24 D 15 Kenton gdns Harrow
10 H 19 Kenton la Harrow
24 C 10 Kenton la Harrow
23 X 5 Kenton la Harrow
24 F 14 Kenton Pk av Harrow
24 F 15 Kenton Pk clo Harrow
24 F 13 Kenton Pk cres Harrow
24 E 14 Kenton Pk rd Harrow
50 E 18 Kenton rd E9
24 C 17 Kenton rd Harrow
132 K 17 Kenton st WC1
15 S 20 Kenver av N12
94 L 13 Kenward rd SE9
38 J 7 Kenway Rom
94 W 5 Kenway rd SW5
92 D 1 Kenwood av SE14
6 L 17 Kenwood av Enf
46 F 3 Kenwood clo NW3
125 U 6 Kenwood dri Beckenhm
35W 14 Kenwood gdns Ilf

28 M 17 Kenwood rd N6
18 K 6 Kenwood rd N9
50 H 15 Kenworthy rd E9
44 C 8 Kenwyn dri NW2
118 M 1 Kenwyn rd SW20
89 Y 9 Kenwyn rd SW4
77 Z 20 Kenya rd SE7
24 D 17 Kenyngton pl Harrow
87 O 1 Kenyon st SW6
144 G 20 Kenyon st SW6
52 A 17 Keogh rd E15
90 A 10 Kepler rd SW4
66 E 1 Keppel rd E6
55 X 12 Keppel rd Dgnhm
142 A 15 Keppel row SE1
135 R 15 Kerbela st E2
64 D 18 Kerbey st E14
91 O 3 Kerfield cres SE5
91 O 3 Kerfield pl SE5
72 H 3 Kerrison pl W5
64 J 3 Kerrison rd E15
88 J 7 Kerrison rd SW11
72 H 4 Kerrison rd W5
11 T 13 Kerry av Stanm
65 U 18 Kerry clo E16
11 T 14 Kerry ct Stanm
75 X 17 Kerry st SE14
113 P 9 Kersey gdns SE9
87 P 15 Kersfield rd SW15
56 F 9 Kershaw rd Dgnhm
88 L 3 Kersley ms SW11
49 T 9 Kersley rd N16
88 L 3 Kersley st SW11
128 G 9 Keslake rd NW6
18 C 12 Keston clo N18
80 E 19 Keston clo Welling
31 O 12 Keston rd N17
91W 8 Keston rd SE15
122 E 13 Keston rd Thntn Hth
159 X 18 Kestral way Croy
90 L 13 Kestrel av SE24
104 A 12 Keswick av SW15
119 X 4 Keswick av SW19
154 D 8 Keswick clo Sutton
35 S 13 Keswick gdns Ilf
42 J 14 Keswick gdns Wemb
87 T 15 Keswick rd SW15
98 D 3 Keswick rd Bxly Hth
82 M 17 Keswick rd Twick
159 Z 1 Keswick rd W Wkhm
90 D 13 Kett gdns SW2
9 S 1 Kettering st Enf
107 U 16 Kettering st SW16
31 N 6 Kettlebaston rd E10
31 N 6 Kevelioc rd N17
73 O 15 Kew Br ct W4
73 O 16 Kew bridge Brentf
72 L 16 Kew Bridge rd Brentf
153 U 5 Kew cres Sutton
84 K 8 Kew Foot rd Rich
58 O 1 Kew gardens Brentf
85 O 1 Kew Gardens rd Rich
73 N 18 Kew grn Rich
85 S 3 Kew Meadow path Rich
84 C 7 Kew observatory Rich
72 L 18 Kew palace Brentf
73 N 17 Kew rd Rich
85 N 2 Kew rd Rich
141 Y 20 Key North st SE1
108 D 5 Keymer rd SW2
29 N 12 Keynes clo N2
21 N 14 Keynsham av Wdfd Grn
95 P 12 Keynsham gdns SE9
95 P 13 Keynsham rd SE9
119 Z 19 Keynsham rd Mrdn
151 O 4 Keyse rd SE1
132 M 10 Keystone cres N1
149 Y 1 Keyworth st SE1
75 U 14 Kezia st SE8
106 J 10 Khama rd SW17
65 V 10 Khartoum rd E13
106 G 10 Khartoum rd SW17
54 A 15 Khartoum rd Ilf
53 Z 15 Khartoum rd Ilf
88 J 6 Khyber rd SW11
149 O 19 Kibworth st SW8
94 F 3 Kidbrooke gdns SE3
94 F 2 Kidbrooke gro SE3
95 S 11 Kidbrooke la SE9
94 H 3 Kidbrooke Pk clo SE3
94 G 2 Kidbrooke Pk rd SE3
122 K 18 Kidderminster rd Croy
45 Y 12 Kidderpore av NW3
45 Z 12 Kidderpore gdns NW3
134 G 17 Kiffen st EC2

Ref	Name
129 T 3	Kilburn High rd NW6
45 V 20	Kilburn High rd NW6
128 K 11	Kilburn la W10
129 O 10	Kilburn la W9
129 V 12	Kilburn Pk rd NW6
129 V 5	Kilburn pl NW6
X 7	Kilburn priory NW6
129 T 5	Kilburn sq NW6
129 V 5	Kilburn vale NW6
137 V 5	Kildare gdns W2
65 T 14	Kildare rd E16
137 V 4	Kildare ter W2
90 A 15	Kildoran rd SW2
55 N 5	Kildowan rd Ilf
92 H 15	Kilgow rd SE23
88 C 5	Kilkie st SW6
88 D 16	Killarney rd SW18
111 X 1	Killearn rd SE6
152 L 9	Killester gdns Worc Pk
133 N 10	Killick st N1
108 A 2	Killieser av SW2
107 Z 3	Killieser av SW2
87 R 17	Killip clo E16
41 O 13	Killowen av Grnfd
50 E 19	Killowen rd E9
89 W 5	Killyon rd SW8
144 M 20	Kilmaine rd SW6
74 L 10	Kilmarsh rd W6
144 A 5	Kilmarsh rd W6
122 E 6	Kilmartin av SW6
55 O 7	Kilmartin rd Ilf
57 Y 16	Kilmartin way Hornch
74 F 17	Kilmington rd SW13
84 A 11	Kilmorey gdns Twick
84 B 11	Kilmorey rd Twick
110 H 2	Kilmorie rd SE23
47 P 13	Kiln pl NW5
64 A 15	Kilner st E14
128 L 13	Kilravock st W10
8 C 3	Kilvington dri Enf
87 S 2	Kimbell gdns SW6
88 A 19	Kimber rd SW18
66 L 6	Kimberley av E6
92 B 6	Kimberley av SE15
54 F 2	Kimberley av Ilf
38 J 19	Kimberley av Rom
115 X 5	Kimberley dri Sidcp
30 J 17	Kimberley gdns N4
8 G 13	Kimberley gdns Enf
51 X 6	Kimberley rd E11
65 O 12	Kimberley rd E16
32 K 4	Kimberley rd E17
20 M 5	Kimberley rd E4
21 N 6	Kimberley rd E4
128 M 3	Kimberley rd NW6
31 X 9	Kimberley rd N17
19 N 19	Kimberley rd N18
90 B 6	Kimberley rd SW9
122 K 13	Kimberley rd Croy
21 N 5	Kimberley way E4
124 G 3	Kimberly rd Becknhm
10 A 2	Kimble cres Bushey Watf
106 G 14	Kimble rd SW19
113 R 10	Kimmeridge rd SE9
153 V 2	Kimpton clo Sutton
91 O 1	Kimpton rd SE5
151 V 20	Kincaid rd SE15
24 L 20	Kinch gro Harrow
42 L 1	Kinch gro Harrow
55 O 4	Kinfauns rd Ilf
108 G 4	Kinfauns rd SW2
111 O 10	King Alfred av SE6
150 C 9	King And Queen st SE17
92 B 1	King Arthur st SE15
151 Z 20	King Arthur st SE15
140 J 17	King Charles st SW1
117 N 16	King Charles' cres Surb
116 M 13	King Charles' cres Surb
63 O 20	King David la E1
51 T 4	King Edward rd E10
32 G 11	King Edward rd E17
63 R 1	King Edward rd E9
18 M 2	King Edward rd N9
5 N 15	King Edward rd Barnt
4 M 14	King Edward rd Barnt
39 T 17	King Edward rd Rom
141 Z 4	King Edward st EC1
149 T 1	King Edward wlk SW1
73 R 3	King Edward's gdns W3
67 S 5	King Edward's rd Bark
9 U 14	King Edward's rd Enf
135 Y 3	King Edwards rd E9
19 N 3	King Edwards rd N9
156 H 10	King gdns Croy
65 Z 17	King George av E16
152 B 7	King George Field Auriol park Epsom
87 Z 20	King George park SW18
76 H 20	King George st SE10
121 N 8	King George vi Mitch
80 M 18	King Harold's way Bxly Hth
49 S 15	King Henry st N16
159 V 18	King Henry's dri Croy
131 O 1	King Henry's rd NW3
130 K 1	King Henry's rd NW3
117 T 5	King Henry's rd Kingst
49 R 17	King Henry's wlk N1
141 Y 19	King James st SE1
63 T 15	King John st E1
134 L 16	King John's ct EC2
95 P 19	King John's wlk SE9
142 C 6	King st EC2
65 S 12	King st E13
31 U 3	King st N17
28 G 9	King st N2
140 D 14	King st SW1
140 K 9	King st W2
73 U 3	King st W3
74 F 12	King st W6
144 B 7	King st W6
84 G 13	King st Rich
70 C 8	King st S'hall
101 X 2	King st Twick
76 K 15	King William la SE10
142 F 7	King William st EC4
76 H 16	King William wlk SE10
29 P 10	King's av N10
89 Z 14	King's av SW4
60 H 16	King's av W5
58 L 16	King's av Grnfd
141 Y 17	King's Bench st SE1
141 T 8	King's Bench wlk EC4
99 O 11	King's clo Drtfrd
46 H 20	King's College rd NW3
129 V 2	King's gdns NW6
75 N 20	King's gro SE15
151 Y 20	King's gro SE15
89 X 12	King's Head pass SW4
142 F 15	King's Head yd SE1
79 X 17	King's highway SE18
50 K 13	King's Mead way E2
130 G 9	King's Mill ter NW8
133 P 19	King's ms WC1
95 S 15	King's orchard SE9
51 Y 1	King's rd E11
147 T 4	King's rd SW1
85 Z 9	King's rd SW14
105 Y 14	King's rd SW19
145 Z 20	King's rd SW6
60 G 15	King's rd W5
116 D 20	King's rd Surb
101 P 12	King's rd Tedd
148 B 4	King's scholars' SW1
132 A 6	King's ter NW1
57 V 20	Kingaby gdns Rainham
75 S 5	Kingdom st SE16
85 U 8	Kingdon rd NW6
156 K 20	Kingdown av S Croy
60 H 10	Kingfield rd W5
76 G 11	Kingfield st E14
102 C 9	Kingfisher dri Rich
141 Z 2	Kinghorn st EC1
150 L 9	Kinglake st SE17
140 L 8	Kingly ct W1
140 B 7	Kingly st W1
143 S 2	Kings Arms ct E1
142 F 4	Kings Arms yd EC2
17 V 5	Kings av N21
112 B 16	Kings av Brom
21 Z 7	Kings av Buck Hl
154 K 18	Kings av Carsh
82 L 2	Kings av Hounsl
118 C 8	Kings av New Mald
38 C 18	Kings av Rom
89 Y 13	Kings Av gdns SW4
51 R 2	Kings clo E10
27 R 13	Kings clo NW4
133 O 12	Kings Cross rd WC1
132 K 9	Kings Cross station
65 W 4	Kings ct E13
11 Z 14	Kings dri Edg
12 A 14	Kings dri Edg
117 P 15	Kings dri Surb
43 S 7	Kings dri Wemb
85 O 11	Kings Farm av Rich
54 D 4	Kings gdns Ilf
39 V 17	Kings gro Rom
110 F 18	Kings Hall rd SE20
20 E 3	Kings Head hill E4
154 G 12	Kings la Sutton
34 D 9	Kings Park ct E18
102 H 19	Kings pas Kingst
116 G 4	Kings pas Kingst
142 B 20	Kings pl SE1
73 V 12	Kings pl W4
21 Z 8	Kings pl Buck Hl
20 J 5	Kings rd E4
65 Y 3	Kings rd E6
44 J 20	Kings rd NW10
31 V 3	Kings rd N17
18 L 15	Kings rd N17
30 E 4	Kings rd N22
123 Y 6	Kings rd SE25
146 J 12	Kings rd SW3
4 A 13	Kings rd Barnt
40 E 9	Kings rd Harrow
103 O 17	Kings rd Kingst
102 J 19	Kings rd Kingst
121 P 5	Kings rd Mitch
84 M 12	Kings rd Rich
39 V 17	Kings rd Rom
84 C 17	Kings rd Twick
85 P 12	Kings Ride ga Rich
156 D 11	Kings way Croy
23 T 12	Kings way Harrow
21 Y 16	Kings way Wdfd Grn
48 L 8	King's cres N4
112 G 3	Kingsbridge av W3
73 N 5	Kingsbridge av W3
58 E 15	Kingsbridge cres S'hall
136 E 3	Kingsbridge rd W10
67 T 7	Kingsbridge rd Bark
119 P 17	Kingsbridge rd Mrdn
70 D 12	Kingsbridge rd S'hall
25 U 15	Kingsbury rd NW9
49 S 17	Kingsbury rd N1
49 S 17	Kingsbury ter N1
86 F 17	Kingsclere clo SW15
105 V 3	Kingscliffe gdns SW19
73 X 10	Kingscote rd W4
123 Z 18	Kingscote rd Croy
117 Y 7	Kingscote rd New Mald
141 W 8	Kingscote st EC4
107 Z 7	Kingscourt rd SW16
45 U 17	Kingscroft rd NW2
79 X 17	Kingsdale rd SE18
110 F 19	Kingsdale rd SE20
72 C 5	Kingsdown av W13
62 B 18	Kingsdown av W3
52 A 10	Kingsdown rd E11
47 Z 8	Kingsdown rd N19
48 A 7	Kingsdown rd N19
153 S 11	Kingsdown rd Sutton
126 E 15	Kingsdown way Brom
116 M 19	Kingsdowne rd Surb
104 D 1	Kingsfarm lodge SW15
22 L 14	Kingsfield av Harrow
23 N 15	Kingsfield av Harrow
41 S 2	Kingsfield rd Harrow
156 B 17	Kingsford ac Croy
156 B 17	Kingsford av Croy
46 M 15	Kingsford st NW5
43 U 8	Kingsgate Wemb
27 V 10	Kingsgate av N3
97 Y 1	Kingsgate clo Bxly Hth
129 T 2	Kingsgate pl NW6
129 U 2	Kingsgate rd NW6
45 X 20	Kingsgate rd NW6
95 O 18	Kingsground SE9
24 B 13	Kingshill av Harrow
118 H 16	Kingshill av Worc Pk
24 B 11	Kingshill dri Harrow
63 P 1	Kingsholm rd SE9
95 P 9	Kingsholme gdns SE9
94 F 19	Kingshurst rd SE12
49 T 17	Kingsland High st E8
49 T 17	Kingsland pass N1
65 V 9	Kingsland rd E13
134 L 6	Kingsland rd E2
49 T 19	Kingsland rd E8
59 Y 16	Kingsley av W13
83 N 4	Kingsley av Hounsl
58 G 20	Kingsley av S'ha
154 G 8	Kingsley av Sutt
28 C 15	Kingsley clo N2
56 G 12	Kingsley clo Dg
20 B 15	Kingsley gdns E
145 Z 2	Kingsley ms W8
47 R 2	Kingsley pl N6
33 T 8	Kingsley rd E17
52 F 20	Kingsley rd E7
129 P 3	Kingsley rd NW
17 U 13	Kingsley rd SW
106 C 12	Kingsley rd SW
122 F 19	Kingsley rd Croy
41 N 10	Kingsley rd Hou
83 N 6	Kingsley rd Hou
82 L 4	Kingsley rd Hou
36 C 4	Kingsley rd Ilf
22 E 14	Kingsley rd Pinn
89 N 6	Kingsley st SW1
88 M 7	Kingsley st SW1
28 C 15	Kingsley way N2
113 U 7	Kingsley Wood SE9
123 R 1	Kingslyn cres S
78 G 9	Kingsman pk SE
78 G 9	Kingsman st SE
4 L 14	Kingsmead Barn
43 Y 1	Kingsmead av N
18 M 6	Kingsmead av N
121 V 5	Kingsmead av N
39 S 18	Kingsmead av F
152 J 4	Kingsmead av F Pk
114 M 5	Kingsmead clo S
40 E 20	Kingsmead rd S
108 F 5	Kingsmead rd S
43 U 5	Kingsmere pk N
105 R 4	Kingsmere rd S
56 B 16	Kingsmill gdns Dgnhm
56 B 16	Kingsmill rd Dgr
103 T 16	Kingsnympton p Kingst
116 T 10	Kingsthorpe rd S
153 T 5	Kingston av Sutt
104 B 15	Kingston By-pas SW20
118 B 12	Kingston By-pas New Mald
58 E 2	Kingston clo Grr
37 Y 9	Kingston clo Ro
124 L 1	Kingston cres Becknhm
116 F 3	Kingston dri King
103 P 17	Kingston gate K
116 H 5	Kingston Hall rd Kingst
103 S 18	Kingston hill Kin
37 Z 9	Kingston Hill av
103 W 10	Kingston Hill pla Rich
102 A 15	Kingston la Ted
101 Z 13	Kingston la Ted
51 V 12	Kingston rd E11
18 L 8	Kingston rd N9
86 M 20	Kingston rd SW
104 H 3	Kingston rd SW
105 Y 19	Kingston rd SW
119 P 2	Kingston rd SW
5 U 17	Kingston rd Bar
152 C 12	Kingston rd Eps
54 B 12	Kingston rd Ilf
117 V 7	Kingston rd New Mald
39 U 13	Kingston rd Rom
70 D 7	Kingston rd SW
102 D 15	Kingston rd Ted
104 A 8	Kingston vale S
103 Y 9	Kingston vale S
131 S 4	Kingstown st N
15 R 18	Kingsway N12
43 U 8	Kingsway SW1
141 N 5	Kingsway WC2
9 N 15	Kingsway Enf
118 L 10	Kingsway New
42 K 12	Kingsway Wem
158 D 20	Kingsway av S
22 M 14	Kingsway cres Harrow
140 M 4	Kingsway hall V
35 S 15	Kingsway rd Su
47 S 9	Kingswear rd N
79 Z 17	Kingswick rd SE
128 L 7	Kingswood av N
101 O 10	Kingswood av E
125 Y 8	Kingswood av E
100 K 15	Kingswood av N Hampt
2	Kingswood av V Hounsl
122 G 13	Kingswood av V Hth
15 R 1	Kingswood clo N

Grid	Street
K 16	Kingswood clo Surb
S 10	Kingswood dri SE19
V 5	Kingswood pk N3
Z 9	Kingswood pl SE13
B 16	Kingswood rd SE20
K 9	Kingswood rd SW2
A 18	Kingswood rd SW2
Z 17	Kingswood rd SW2
A 5	Kingswood rd Brom
Y 6	Kingswood rd Brom
M 3	Kingswood rd Ilf
N 2	Kingswood rd Ilf
A 10	Kingswood way Croy
Y 20	Kingthorpe rd NW10
T 1	Kingward st E1
U 3	Kingwell rd Barnt
L 20	Kingwood rd SW6
B 1	Kinlet rd SE18
Z 1	Kinloch dri NW9
A 1	Kinloch dri NW9
D 18	Kinloch st N7
D 18	Kinloss rd Carsh
U 11	Kinloss rd N3
U 20	Kinnaird av W4
C 16	Kinnaird av Brom
D 16	Kinnaird clo Brom
C 5	Kinnear rd W12
R 18	Kinnerton Pl north W1
R 19	Kinnerton Pl south W1
S 20	Kinnerton st SW1
S 19	Kinnerton yd SW1
L 14	Kinnowl rd W6
A 2	Kinross av Worc Pk
L 16	Kinross clo Harrow
X 8	Kinsale rd SE15
N 4	Kintore st SE1
C 13	Kinveachy gdns SE7
D 9	Kinver rd SE26
H 18	Kipling pl Stanm
Z 1	Kipling rd Bxly Hth
G 18	Kipling st SE1
C 9	Kipling terr N21/N9
D 12	Kirby clo Epsom
J 17	Kirby gro SE1
U 1	Kirby st EC1
U 20	Kirby st EC1
A 1	Kirchen rd W13
O 16	Kirk la SE18
O 13	Kirk st WC1
A 18	Kirkby st SW2
B 9	Kirkdale SE26
A 2	Kirkdale rd E11
V 18	Kirkham st SE18
SW 7	Kirkland av Ilf
M 9	Kirkland pl SE16
E 10	Kirklees rd Thntn Hth
S 16	Kirkless rd Dgnhm
Z 19	Kirkly rd SW19
S 20	Kirkly clo S Croy
	Kirkman pl W1
H 17	Kirkmichael rd E14
X 15	Kirks pl E3
X 17	Kirkside rd SE3
O 12	Kirkstall av N17
Z 1	Kirkstall gdns SW2
Z 1	Kirkstall rd SW2
A 1	Kirkstall rd SW2
Z 19	Kirksted rd Mrdn
A 17	Kirkstone way Brom
R 8	Kirkwall pl E2
O 19	Kirkwood pl NW1
A 1	Kirn rd W13
J 9	Kirtley rd SE26
B 17	Kirtling st SW8
X 5	Kirton rd E13
W 2	Kirton wlk Edg
B 8	Kitcat ter E3
R 4	Kitchener rd E17
H 18	Kitchener rd E7
H 11	Kitchener rd N2
J 17	Kitchener rd Dgnhm
N 5	Kitchener rd Thntn Hth
T 12	Kite pl E2
U 1	Kitley gdns SE19
D 17	Kitson rd SE5
F 3	Kitson rd SW13
F 6	Kitson rd SE14
H 5	Kitts End rd Barnt
Z 7	Kiver rd N19
A 5	Klea av SW4
Y 20	Knackers yd SW1
A 4	Knapdale clo SE23
P 5	Knapmill rd SE6
P 5	Knapmill way SE6
B 12	Knapp rd E3
X 6	Knaresborough pl SW5
Z 3	Knatchbull rd NW10
J 3	Knatchbull rd SE5
33 O 4	Knebworth av E17
80 G 13	Knee hill SE2
80 G 11	Knee Hill cres SE2
83 P 15	Kneller gdns Islwth
83 R 16	Kneller hall Twick
92 J 10	Kneller rd SE4
117 Z 17	Kneller rd New Mald
83 O 16	Kneller rd Twick
82 M 16	Kneller rd Twick
72 L 7	Knight's av W5
49 Z 6	Knightland rd E5
38 M 18	Knighton clo Rom
156 J 17	Knighton clo S Croy
21 V 13	Knighton clo Wdfd Grn
21 V 13	Knighton dri Wdfd Grn
21 V 9	Knighton la Buck Hl
110 G 12	Knighton Pk rd SE26
52 F 11	Knighton rd E7
38 L 18	Knighton rd Rom
141 Z 8	Knightrider st EC4
70 A 14	Knights arbour S'hall
108 J 12	Knights hill SE27
108 K 9	Knights hill SE27
18 K 10	Knights la N9
116 J 5	Knights pk Kingst
77 T 4	Knights rd E16
11 S 13	Knights rd Stanm
139 O 18	Knightsbridge SW7
138 L 19	Knightsbridge SW7
139 N 16	Knightsbridge gdns Rom
139 N 19	Knightsbridge grn SW7
12 G 8	Knightswood clo Edg
12 G 7	Knightswood clo Edg
118 B 14	Knightwood cres New Mald
93 W 6	Knivett rd SW6
64 D 2	Knobs Hill rd E15
95 N 12	Knockholt rd SE9
113 W 10	Knole SE9
99 X 19	Knole rd Drtfrd
60 C 15	Knoll W13
125 R 1	Knoll Becknhm
16 C 3	Knoll dri N14
98 D 17	Knoll rd Bxly
115 R 12	Knoll rd Sidcp
88 C 14	Knolle rd SW18
117 X 20	Knollmead Surb
108 G 6	Knolly's clo SW16
108 E 6	Knolly's rd SW16
63 S 8	Knottisford st E2
33 T 18	Knotts Green rd E10
81 N 18	Knowle av Bxly Hth
101 T 2	Knowle rd Twick
93 W 13	Knowles Hill cres SE13
88 M 6	Knowlesy rd SW11
12 D 10	Knowlton grn Brom
70 K 3	Knowsley av S'hall
52 D 18	Knox rd E7
139 O 1	Knox st W1
106 B 12	Kohat rd SW19
76 M 13	Kossuth st SE10
108 D 19	Kuala gdns SW16
45 Y 19	Kylemore rd NW6
87 X 19	Kymberley rd Harrow
39 T 20	Kyme rd Hornch
24 D 5	Kynance gdns Stanm
146 A 2	Kynance ms SW7
146 A 2	Kynance pl SW7
49 T 9	Kynaston av N16
122 L 11	Kynaston av Thntn Hth
23 R 1	Kynaston clo Harrow
122 M 14	Kynaston cres Thntn Hth
49 S 9	Kynaston rd N16
112 G 12	Kynaston rd Brom
18 B 7	Kynaston rd Enf
122 M 10	Kynaston rd Thntn Hth
19 R 16	Kynoch rd N18
89 O 14	Kyrle rd SW11
49 V 4	Kyverdale rd N16

L

Grid	Street
74 D 1	Labrum way W3
31 O 1	Laburnham av N17
154 H 6	Laburnham av Sutton
11 P 15	Laburnham ct Stanm
54 A 7	Laburnham gro Ilf
18 F 3	Laburnum av N9
57 U 9	Laburnum av Hornch
19 Y 19	Laburnum clo E4
121 P 4	Laburnum est Mitch
17 Y 7	Laburnum gdns N21
25 W 20	Laburnum gdns N21
17 Y 7	Laburnum gro N21
82 F 11	Laburnum gro Hounsl
117 X 4	Laburnum gro New Mald
58 F 12	Laburnum gro S'hall
106 E 18	Laburnum rd SW19
121 P 4	Laburnum rd Mitch
135 N 5	Laburnum st E2
134 M 6	Laburnum st E2
63 Z 6	Lacey st E3
134 G 20	Lackington st EC2
91 W 11	Lacon rd SE22
87 R 9	Lacy rd SW15
108 K 11	Ladas rd SE27
136 L 6	Ladbroke cres W11
137 O 9	Ladbroke gdns W11
128 H 16	Ladbroke gro W10
136 K 2	Ladbroke gro W10
137 P 13	Ladbroke gro W11
137 N 14	Ladbroke ms W11
137 O 13	Ladbroke rd W11
8 H 19	Ladbroke rd Enf
137 R 11	Ladbroke sq W11
137 O 10	Ladbroke Sq gdns W11
22 D 17	Ladbrook clo Pinn
123 P 8	Ladbrook rd SE25
115 X 8	Ladbrooke cres Sidcp
103 U 13	Ladderstile ride Kingst
16 G 17	Ladderswood way N11
158 J 20	Lady grove Croy
152 C 1	Lady hay Worc Pk
47 V 13	Lady Margaret rd NW5
58 D 2	Lady Margaret rd Grnfd
58 E 14	Lady Margaret rd S'hall
70 E 1	Lady Margaret rd S'hall
47 T 13	Lady Somerset rd NW5
93 P 8	Ladycroft rd SE13
24 G 6	Ladycroft wlk Stanm
66 C 6	Ladysmith av E6
54 F 2	Ladysmith av Ilf
65 O 10	Ladysmith rd E16
31 V 8	Ladysmith rd N17
19 N 19	Ladysmith rd N18
95 X 17	Ladysmith rd SE9
8 F 12	Ladysmith rd Enf
23 T 8	Ladysmith rd Harrow
93 S 12	Ladywell rd SE13
65 P 4	Ladywell st E15
143 N 17	Lafone st SE1
123 P 15	Lahore rd Croy
51 Z 16	Laindon av E15
120 K 2	Laings av Mitch
87 X 19	Lainson st SW18
89 S 20	Laitwood rd SW12
107 T 1	Laitwood rd SW12
112 F 15	Lake av Brom
56 D 15	Lake gdns Dgnhm
102 B 6	Lake gdns Rich
155 R 7	Lake gdns Wallgtn
105 U 13	Lake rd SW19
158 L 1	Lake rd Croy
39 T 9	Lake rise Rom
63 R 18	Lake st E1
10 B 5	Lake the Bushey Watf
11 Z 17	Lake view Edg
97 O 10	Lake View rd Welling
79 V 15	Lakedale rd SE18
30 J 8	Lakefield rd N22
122 J 12	Lakehall gdns Thntn Hth
122 J 12	Lakehall rd Thntn Hth
52 F 6	Lakehouse rd E11
152 A 12	Lakehurst rd Epsom
6 J 17	Lakenheath N14
87 U 15	Laker rd SW15
60 D 15	Lakeside W13
6 K 13	Lakeside Enf
155 S 7	Lakeside Wallgtn
35 N 13	Lakeside av Ilf
123 W 3	Lakeside clo SE25
6 A 18	Lakeside cres Barnt
48 K 6	Lakeside ct N4
17 P 12	Lakeside rd N13
136 G 20	Lakeside rd W14
144 E 1	Lakeside rd W14
43 P 13	Lakeside way Wemb
108 J 12	Lakeview rd SE27
11 Z 17	Lakeview view Edg
12 K 10	Laleham la NW7
93 T 18	Laleham rd SE6
87 S 3	Lalor st SW6
63 N 1	Lamb la E8
135 Y 1	Lamb la E8
134 M 20	Lamb st E1
135 N 20	Lamb st E1
142 J 19	Lamb wlk SE1
113 X 9	Lambarde av SE9
108 O 11	Lamberhurst rd SE27
56 A 4	Lamberhurst rd Dgnhm
85 S 8	Lambert av Rich
65 V 17	Lambert rd E16
15 S 17	Lambert rd N12
90 C 14	Lambert rd SW2
133 R 2	Lambert st N1
15 S 17	Lambert way N12
123 P 20	Lamberts pl Croy
116 L 12	Lamberts rd Surb
148 L 4	Lambeth br SW1
54 N 5	Lambeth High st SE1
142 A 8	Lambeth hill EC4
149 N 3	Lambeth palace SE1
149 N 2	Lambeth Palace rd SE1
141 O 20	Lambeth Palace rd SE1
149 P 3	Lambeth rd SE1
122 G 18	Lambeth rd Croy
143 S 6	Lambeth st E1
149 O 7	Lambeth wlk SE11
47 O 14	Lamble st NW5
55 R 18	Lamboley rd Dgnhm
46 K 18	Lambolle pl NW3
46 L 18	Lambolle rd NW3
89 T 7	Lambourn rd SW4
105 V 9	Lambourne av SW19
20 B 8	Lambourne gdns E4
67 X 1	Lambourne gdns Bark
8 G 9	Lambourne gdns Enf
51 V 2	Lambourne rd E11
67 W 2	Lambourne rd Bark
54 H 6	Lambourne rd Ilf
87 R 2	Lambrook ter SW6
134 D 18	Lambs bldgs EC1
18 J 8	Lambs clo N9
141 N 1	Lambs Conduit pas WC1
133 N 19	Lambs Conduit st WC1
134 D 19	Lambs pas EC1
18 C 8	Lambs terr N9
7 Z 9	Lambs wlk Enf
142 M 8	Lambscroft av SE9
113 N 7	Lambscroft av SE9
137 S 8	Lambton pl W11
118 L 2	Lambton rd SW20
104 L 20	Lambton rd SW20
112 D 9	Lamerock rd Brom
36 A 6	Lamerton rd Ilf
76 B 17	Lamerton st SE8
74 J 11	Lamington st W6
149 X 4	Lamlash st SW11
121 O 3	Lammas av Mitch
121 O 4	Lammas av Mitch
109 Z 5	Lammas grn SE26
72 E 4	Lammas Pk gdns W5
72 F 4	Lammas Pk rd W5
50 H 5	Lammas rd E10
63 U 1	Lammas rd E9
102 D 11	Lammas rd Rich
89 T 19	Lammermoor rd SW12
146 E 15	Lamont rd SW10
146 E 15	Lamont Rd pas SW10
114 K 3	Lamorbey clo Sidcp
115 P 1	Lamorbey park Bxly
24 G 6	Lamorna gro Stanm
49 U 4	Lampard gro N16
134 E 4	Lampeter st N1
94 B 12	Lampmead rd SE12
82 J 3	Lampton av Hounsl
78 G 19	Lampton clo SE18
105 O 10	Lampton Ho clo SW19
82 G 5	Lampton park Hounsl
82 J 6	Lampton Park rd Hounsl
48 A 3	Lamton rd N4
60 E 14	Lanark clo W5

49 T9	Lavers rd N16
86 F19	Laverstoke gdns SW15
45 Y8	Laverton mws SW5
45 Y7	Laverton pl SW5
13 S5	Lavidge rd SE9
28 K19	Lavie ms W10
32 M8	Lavina gro N1
72 C3	Lavington rd W13
52 C7	Lavington rd Croy
41 Z14	Lavington st SE1
50 G1	Law st SE1
56 K8	Lawdons gdns Croy
52 C9	Lawford clo Wallgtn
47 V18	Lawford rd NW5
73 W18	Lawford rd W4
16 E3	Lawley rd N14
50 D12	Lawley st E5
18 H3	Lawn clo N9
12 H16	Lawn clo Brom
18 A4	Lawn clo New Mald
65 N4	Lawn cres Rich
37 Y11	Lawn Farm gro Rom
71 T2	Lawn gdns W7
34 A18	Lawn la SW8
49 N15	Lawn la SW8
29 R20	Lawn rd N6
10 M18	Lawn rd Becknhm
11 N18	Lawn rd Becknhm
94 B7	Lawn ter SE3
70 H13	Lawn the S'hall
20 C17	Lawns the E4
23 O1	Lawns the SE19
94 B7	Lawns the SE3
22 K1	Lawns the Pinn
15 S9	Lawns the Sidcp
38 L2	Lawns way Rom
94 A12	Lawnside SE3
53 V11	Lawrence av E12
57 V14	Lawrence av E12
32 G4	Lawrence av E17
37 P13	Lawrence av NW7
17 V15	Lawrence av N13
17 Z15	Lawrence av New Mald
49 U9	Lawrence bldgs N16
31 R12	Lawrence clo N15
56 G9	Lawrence cres Dgnhm
25 P8	Lawrence cres Edg
13 O15	Lawrence ct NW7
13 S10	Lawrence gdns NW7
114 L15	Lawrence hill E4
42 C5	Lawrence la EC2
65 V3	Lawrence rd E13
64 A8	Lawrence rd E3
66 C2	Lawrence rd E6
31 R13	Lawrence rd N15
18 L14	Lawrence rd N18
23 V9	Lawrence rd SE25
72 F11	Lawrence rd W5
00 E18	Lawrence rd Hampt
02 E9	Lawrence rd Rich
39 Y17	Lawrence rd Rom
13 S12	Lawrence st NW7
46 J15	Lawrence st SW3
31 S13	Lawrence yd N15
10 B11	Lawrie Pk av SE26
10 A13	Lawrie Pk cres SE26
10 B12	Lawrie Pk gdns SE26
58 B14	Lawrie Pk rd SE26
58 G12	Lawson rd S'hall
51 T4	Lawton rd E10
63 W10	Lawton rd E3
30 D9	Lawton rd N22
5 T12	Lawton rd Barnt
31 Z16	Laxton pl NW1
75 N10	Layard rd SE16
51 X4	Layard rd SE16
8 H5	Layard rd Enf
23 O3	Layard rd Thntn Hth
57 N1	Laycock st N1
61 P20	Layer gdns W3
44 J1	Layfield clo NW4
44 J1	Layfield cres NW4
16 E18	Layfield pl E14
44 K2	Layfield rd NW4
44 J7	Layhams rd W Wkhm
33 S18	Laystall st EC1
56 H11	Layton cres Croy
72 G15	Layton rd Brentf
31 Z16	Layton rd Hounsl
42 D17	Laytons bldgs SE1
16 H6	Le May av SE12
33 T17	Lea Bridge rd E10
50 E6	Lea Bridge rd E10
33 X15	Lea Bridge rd E11
42 L14	Lea gdns Wemb
51 O3	Lea Hall rd E10

154 B10	Lea pl Sutton
125 O2	Lea rd Becknhm
8 A6	Lea rd Enf
70 B11	Lea rd S'hall
98 M11	Lea vale Bxly Hth
20 B1	Lea Valley rd E4
9 Y19	Lea Valley rd Enf
65 O3	Leabon st E15
31 W2	Leabourne rd N16
96 K13	Leachcroft av Sidcp
88 M18	Leacroft av SW12
20 A9	Leadale av E4
31 X18	Leadale rd N15
142 H7	Leadenhall av EC3
142 J6	Leadenhall market EC3
142 J7	Leadenhall pl EC3
53 X16	Leader av E12
43 V9	Leadings the Wemb
108 F11	Leaf gro SE27
108 H16	Leafield clo SW16
119 W5	Leafield rd SW20
153 Y4	Leafield rd Sutton
112 L8	Leafy Oak rd SE12
134 D15	Leage st EC1
50 D9	Leagrave st E5
93 X13	Leahurst rd SE13
94 A15	Leahurst rd SE13
141 R18	Leake st SE1
31 U17	Lealand rd N15
33 O17	Leamington av E17
112 K12	Leamington av Brom
119 U8	Leamington av Mrdn
112 K11	Leamington clo Brom
83 O12	Leamington clo Hounsl
40 C10	Leamington cres Harrow
54 K7	Leamington gdns Ilf
61 X16	Leamington pk W3
137 R3	Leamington Rd vlls W11
74 L11	Leamore st W6
144 A7	Leamore st W6
64 K18	Leamouth rd E14
90 E16	Leander rd SW2
122 E8	Leander rd Thntn Hth
63 X11	Lear st E3
66 J19	Learoyd gdns E6
113 W7	Leas dale SE9
114 L15	Leas grn Chisl
29 O11	Leaside av N10
50 B5	Leaside rd E5
51 O3	Leasowes rd E10
64 M4	Leather clo Mitch
141 T2	Leather gdns E15
133 T19	Leather la EC1
63 T10	Leatherdale st E1
142 J18	Leathermarket st SE1
40 L10	Leathsail rd Harrow
88 M11	Leathwaite rd SW11
93 R5	Leathwell rd SE4
59 S7	Leaver gdns Grnfd
50 G5	Leaway E10
87 X14	Lebanon gdns SW18
84 B20	Lebanon pk Twick
87 X14	Lebanon rd SW18
157 T2	Lebanon rd Croy
150 J11	Lebanon st SE17
34 M7	Lechmere appr Ilf
34 M7	Lechmere av Ilf
44 K18	Lechmere rd NW2
106 E2	Leckford rd SW18
80 L17	Leckwith av Bxly Hth
146 F10	Lecky st SW7
86 D9	Leconfield av SW13
49 N13	Leconfield rd N5
9 S4	Leda av Enf
137 T7	Ledbury Ms north NW11
137 S8	Ledbury Ms west W11
157 N9	Ledbury pl Croy
137 S7	Ledbury rd W11
137 S7	Ledbury rd Croy
151 U17	Ledbury st SE15
109 W16	Ledrington rd SE19
43 H1	Ledway dri Wemb
42 M1	Ledway dri Wemb
37 X19	Lee av Rom
94 A10	Lee Church st SE13
32 E6	Lee clo E17
50 L14	Lee Conservancy rd E9
93 V9	Lee High rd SE13
94 B10	Lee pk SE3
27 R2	Lee rd NW7
94 C11	Lee rd SE3

8 K20	Lee rd Enf
60 D3	Lee rd Grnfd
134 M3	Lee st E8
135 N3	Lee st E8
16 F18	Lee st N11
93 Z8	Lee ter SE3
94 A8	Lee terr SE3
7 W6	Lee view Enf
155 P6	Leechcroft rd Wallgtn
4 E14	Leecroft rd Barnt
54 F4	Leeds rd Ilf
18 J17	Leeds st N18
133 N12	Leeke st WC1
71 Z2	Leeland rd W13
72 A2	Leeland ter W13
44 C12	Leeland way NW10
139 T8	Lees pl W1
158 L3	Lees the Croy
4 F19	Leeside Barnt
27 U18	Leeside cres NW11
90 H12	Leeson rd SE24
105 U14	Leeward gdns SW19
75 Y13	Leeway SE8
64 A5	Lefevre rd E3
63 Z4	Lefevre wk E3
74 H6	Leffern rd W12
74 C5	Lefroy rd W12
48 J11	Legard rd N5
94 M13	Legatt rd SE9
95 N12	Legatt rd SE9
64 G6	Leggatt rd E15
93 T12	Legge st SE13
62 F5	Leghorn rd NW10
79 T14	Leghorn rd SE18
119 Y14	Legion ct Mitch
56 L5	Legon av Rom
122 A9	Leicester av Mitch
140 G9	Leicester pl WC2
152 M7	Leicester ct Worc Pk
36 J20	Leicester gdns Ilf
140 G9	Leicester pl W1
2 J16	Leicester rd E11
43 Z20	Leicester rd NW10
28 K11	Leicester rd N2
5 R14	Leicester rd Barnt
123 S18	Leicester rd Croy
140 G10	Leicester sq WC2
140 G9	Leicester st W1
35 O13	Leigh av Ilf
159 T16	Leigh clo New Mald
41 S5	Leigh ct Harrow
62 M6	Leigh gdns NW10
128 C9	Leigh gdns NW10
142 A17	Leigh Hunt st SE1
108 D7	Leigh Orchard clo SW6
97 O4	Leigh pl Welling
51 V2	Leigh rd E10
53 V19	Leigh rd E6
48 J13	Leigh rd N5
83 P10	Leigh rd Hounsl
132 J15	Leigh st WC1
108 A7	Leigham av SW16
108 B5	Leigham Ct rd SW16
71 U19	Leigham dri Islwth
108 E6	Leigham vale SW16
53 W16	Leighton av E12
22 D10	Leighton av Pinn
25 R7	Leighton clo Edg
47 W14	Leighton cres NW8
62 L5	Leighton gdns NW10
128 C7	Leighton gdns NW10
47 V14	Leighton gro NW5
47 V16	Leighton pl NW5
47 V15	Leighton rd NW5
72 A5	Leighton rd W13
71 Z5	Leighton rd W13
8 H18	Leighton rd Enf
122 H20	Leighton St east Croy
122 H20	Leighton St west Croy
85 V9	Leinster av SW14
138 B7	Leinster gdns W2
138 B10	Leinster ms W2
138 A7	Leinster pl W2
129 U11	Leinster rd NW6
27 T13	Leinster rd N10
137 W7	Leinster sq W2
138 B10	Leinster ter W2
43 Y4	Leith clo NW9
63 X14	Leith rd E3
30 H4	Leith rd N22
108 C9	Leithcote gdns SW16
143 R7	Leman st E1
11 R17	Lemark clo Stanm
52 A15	Lemna rd E11
96 A15	Lemonwell dri SE9

144 D2	Lena gdns W6
74 M9	Lena gdns W6
89 Y8	Lendal ter SW9
117 P20	Lenelby rd Surb
94 B11	Lenham SE12
81 O17	Lenham rd Bxly Hth
154 B9	Lenham rd Sutton
123 O4	Lenham rd Thntn Hth
110 K17	Lennard rd Becknhm
127 U20	Lennard rd Brom
122 K19	Lennard rd Croy
32 M18	Lennox av E17
44 E13	Lennox gdns NW10
147 N4	Lennox gdns SW1
156 K9	Lennox gdns Croy
53 S3	Lennox gdns Ilf
147 N4	Lennox Gdns ms SW1
32 M18	Lennox rd E17
48 E7	Lennox rd N4
65 X1	Lens rd E7
80 G7	Lensbury way SE18
80 G8	Lensbury way SE18
142 A18	Lent st SE1
146 B5	Lenthall pl SW7
49 W20	Lenthall rd E8
77 O12	Lenthorp st SE10
112 C7	Lentmead rd Brom
79 H10	Lenton st SE18
75 O19	Leo st SE14
151 Z17	Leo st SE15
111 P12	Leof cres SE6
120 D13	Leominster rd Mrdn
120 C13	Leominster wlk Mrdn
120 D12	Leonard av Mrdn
56 M4	Leonard av Rom
20 B19	Leonard rd E4
52 E13	Leonard rd E7
18 J12	Leonard rd N9
120 U20	Leonard rd SW16
134 G16	Leonard st EC2
78 D3	Leonard st E16
19 N18	Leonard rd N18
133 T20	Leopards ct EC1
105 V12	Leopold av SW19
33 O16	Leopold rd E17
62 B1	Leopold rd NW10
28 G9	Leopold rd N2
105 X11	Leopold rd SW19
73 N2	Leopold rd N5
72 M2	Leopold rd W5
63 Z14	Leopold st E3
149 N10	Leopold wlk SE11
89 X13	Leppoc rd SW4
150 J3	Leroy st SE1
50 C14	Lesbia rd E5
110 J7	Lescombe clo SE23
110 J7	Lescombe rd SE23
98 G18	Lesley clo Bxly
129 R20	Lesley gro Croy
123 S20	Leslie Pk rd Croy
51 V12	Leslie rd E11
65 V18	Leslie rd E16
28 G10	Leslie rd N2
63 O14	Leslie st E1
28 D18	Lesly rd N7
80 L12	Lesnes Abbey park SE2
80 L10	Lesnes Abbey remains Blvdr
81 Z16	Lesney pk Erith
63 U7	Lessada st E3
89 T14	Lessar av SW4
92 G17	Lessing st SE23
106 M8	Lessingham av SW17
107 N10	Lessingham av SW17
35 U9	Lessingham av Ilf
38 K19	Lessington av Rom
80 J18	Lessness av Bxly Hth
81 P12	Lessness pk Blvdr
81 R15	Lessness rd Mrdn
120 E13	Lessness rd Mrdn
65 N11	Lester av E15
49 U10	Leswin pl N16
49 U9	Leswin rd N16
62 H8	Letchford gdns NW10
62 H8	Letchford mews NW10
22 K4	Letchford terr Har
126 F11	Letchworth clo Brom
126 F11	Letchworth dri Brom
106 M9	Letchworth rd SW17
93 T4	Lethbridge rd SE10
64 G2	Lett rd E15
145 N19	Letterstone rd SW6
87 V3	Lettice st SW6
91 R4	Lettsom st SE5
32 H16	Leucha rd E17
64 J16	Leven rd E14

110 K 4 Levendale rd SE23
134 A 14 Lever st EC1
133 Y 14 Lever st EC1
113 W 9 Leverholme gdns SE9
90 A 4 Leverhurst way SW4
107 V 16 Leverson st SW16
47 U 15 Leverton pl NW5
47 U 14 Leverton st NW5
54 H 17 Levett rd Bark
54 H 18 Levett rd Bark
54 K 11 Levett rd Ilf
68 K 6 Levine gdns Bark
40 H 18 Lewes clo Grnfd
15 W 18 Lewes rd N12
151 N 3 Lewes rd Brom
127 N 3 Lewes rd Brom
49 U 2 Lewiston pl N16
59 W 18 Lewgars av NW9
85 Z 9 Lewin rd SW14
107 Z 13 Lewin rd SW16
97 Z 11 Lewin rd Bxly Hth
33 O 4 Lewis av E17
43 X 16 Lewis cres NW10
28 G 6 Lewis gdns N2
93 U 9 Lewis gro SE13
120 J 3 Lewis rd Mitch
84 H 13 Lewis rd Rich
70 C 5 Lewis rd S'hall
115 T 7 Lewis rd Sidcp
154 B 7 Lewis rd Sutton
97 U 8 Lewis rd Welling
47 T 19 Lewis st NW1
93 T 12 Lewisham High st SE13
93 U 6 Lewisham hill SE13
93 T 14 Lewisham pk SE13
93 T 3 Lewisham rd SE13
140 G 19 Lewisham st SW1
92 L 2 Lewisham way SE14
93 O 5 Lewisham way SE4
37 O 18 Lexden dri Rom
73 T 2 Lexden rd W3
121 W 8 Lexden rd Mitch
145 X 4 Lexham gdns W8
145 Y 4 Lexham Gdns ms SW7
145 V 4 Lexham ms W8
145 X 3 Lexham wlk W8
140 D 8 Lexington st W1
4 C 15 Lexington la Barnt
89 Z 20 Lexton gdns SW12
36 D 20 Ley st Ilf
53 Y 8 Ley st Ilf
54 C 5 Ley st Ilf
72 D 5 Leyborne av W13
85 O 1 Leyborne pk Rich
126 E 13 Leybourne clo Brom
52 C 4 Leybourne rd E11
25 O 15 Leybourne rd NW9
94 E 13 Leybridge ct SE12
33 T 13 Leyburn clo E17
157 S 3 Leyburn gdns Croy
18 L 19 Leyburn gro N18
18 L 19 Leyburn rd N18
142 M 2 Leyden st E1
143 N 3 Leyden st E1
66 A 19 Leyes rd E16
65 Z 19 Leyes rd E16
152 C 1 Leyfield Worc Pk
9 V 8 Leyland av Enf
21 Y 17 Leyland gdns Wdfd Grn
94 D 13 Leyland rd SE12
75 T 19 Leylang rd SE14
69 Y 2 Leys av Dgnham
69 X 1 Leys clo Dgnham
69 X 1 Leys clo Harrow
6 B 16 Leys gdns Barnt
9 V 5 Leys Rd east Enf
9 V 5 Leys Rd west Enf
28 D 13 Leys the N2
24 L 18 Leys the Harrow
98 K 11 Leysdown av Bxly Hth
113 S 4 Leysdown rd SE9
74 H 7 Leysfield rd W12
52 C 3 Leyspring rd E11
36 G 14 Leyswood dri Ilf
73 V 6 Leythe rd W3
33 T 20 Leyton Grn rd E10
51 V 14 Leyton Pk rd E10
51 V 14 Leyton rd E15
106 E 18 Leyton rd SW19
151 T 15 Leyton sq SE15
51 Y 13 Leytonstone rd E15
75 X 18 Liardet gro SE14
48 J 17 Liberia rd N5
90 D 1 Liberty st SW9
55 S 5 Libra rd E13
63 Y 4 Libra rd E3
141 X 19 Library st SE1
84 J 11 Lichfield gdns Rich

27 Y 5 Lichfield gro N3
28 A 7 Lichfield gro N3
66 B 10 Lichfield rd E6
45 S 11 Lichfield rd NW2
18 J 8 Lichfield rd N9
55 S 10 Lichfield rd Dgnham
85 N 2 Lichfield rd Rich
21 N 14 Lichfield rd Wdfd Grn
90 E 5 Lidcote gdns SW9
24 H 11 Liddell clo Harrow
62 M 5 Liddell gdns NW10
128 C 7 Liddell gdns NW10
126 M 6 Lidden rd Brom
24 H 16 Lidding rd Harrow
65 P 3 Liddington rd E15
65 U 10 Liddon rd E13
127 N 6 Liddon rd Brom
49 O 13 Lidfield rd N16
150 M 19 Lidgate rd SE15
106 E 3 Lidiard rd SW18
132 B 10 Lidlington pl NW1
47 V 5 Lidyard rd N19
79 T 13 Liffler rd SE18
87 P 10 Lifford st SW15
17 U 12 Lightcliffe rd N13
30 A 15 Lightfoot rd N8
19 Y 19 Lilac clo E4
72 G 8 Lilac gdns W5
159 O 5 Lilac gdns Croy
57 O 4 Lilac gdns Rom
62 F 19 Lilac st W12
95 R 13 Lilburne gdns SE9
95 S 13 Lilburne rd SE9
59 U 15 Lile cres W7
90 J 4 Liford rd SE5
34 J 4 Lilian gdns Wdfd Grn
107 U 20 Lilian rd SW16
55 T 15 Lillechurch rd Dgnham
120 F 14 Lilleshall rd Mrdn
12 M 15 Lilley la NW7
73 O 7 Lillian av W3
74 H 16 Lillian rd SW13
144 H 16 Lillie rd SW6
145 P 14 Lillie road SW6
89 T 7 Lillieshall rd SW4
148 C 7 Lillington st SW1
58 D 3 Lilliput av Grnfd
57 N 1 Lilliput rd Rom
60 E 7 Lilliput gdns Wemb
33 P 19 Lily rd E17
87 V 1 Lilyville rd SW6
56 B 2 Limbourne av Dgnham
88 K 11 Limburg rd SW11
154 L 1 Lime clo Carsh
38 J 14 Lime clo Rom
14 F 4 Lime gro N20
74 L 14 Lime gro W12
136 B 16 Lime gro W12
117 Z 6 Lime gro New Mald
96 L 15 Lime gro Sidcp
83 X 16 Lime gro Twick
142 J 7 Lime st EC3
32 H 13 Lime st E17
142 J 7 Lime St pas EC3
142 J 7 Lime St pas EC3
159 N 5 Lime Tree gro Croy
82 K 1 Lime Tree rd Hounsl
158 L 6 Lime Tree rd Hounsl
7 X 3 Lime Tree wlk Enf
70 K 20 Lime Trees rd Hounsl
63 Z 20 Limehouse causeway E14
146 E 15 Limerston st SW10
34 J 14 Limes av E11
27 T 20 Limes av NW11
13 N 18 Limes av NW7
16 G 16 Limes av N11
15 R 12 Limes av N12
86 C 5 Limes av SW13
154 A 1 Limes av Carsh
156 E 6 Limes av Croy
86 A 7 Limes Field rd SW14
87 Y 17 Limes gdns SW18
93 U 10 Limes gdns SE13
11 N 9 Limes house Stanm
125 S 3 Limes rd Becknhm
123 N 16 Limes rd Croy
72 H 7 Limes wlk W5
25 V 8 Limesdale gdns Edg
92 E 10 Limesford rd SE15
121 S 1 Limetree st EC1
60 C 16 Limewood clo W13
81 Y 19 Limewood rd Erith
105 P 3 Limpsfield av SW19
122 D 12 Limpsfield av Thntn Hth

44 K 18 Linacre rd NW2
94 D 19 Linchmere rd SE12
16 G 10 Lincoln av N14
105 O 7 Lincoln av SW19
57 O 4 Lincoln av Rom
101 O 2 Lincoln av Twick
100 M 3 Lincoln av Twick
99 T 5 Lincoln clo Erith
58 M 3 Lincoln clo Grnfd
59 N 3 Lincoln clo Grnfd
22 E 16 Lincoln clo Harrow
8 F 17 Lincoln cres Enf
53 S 1 Lincoln gdns Ilf
129 N 3 Lincoln ms NW6
53 N 19 Lincoln rd E12
65 U 13 Lincoln rd E13
34 D 6 Lincoln rd E18
31 W 11 Lincoln rd N17
28 K 11 Lincoln rd N2
123 Z 7 Lincoln rd SE25
9 P 18 Lincoln rd Enf
8 L 17 Lincoln rd Enf
99 U 4 Lincoln rd Erith
100 D 7 Lincoln rd Felt
22 F 16 Lincoln rd Harrow
117 V 6 Lincoln rd New Mald
115 R 12 Lincoln rd Sidcp
42 G 18 Lincoln rd Wemb
118 H 19 Lincoln rd Worc Pk
51 Y 7 Lincoln st E11
147 O 8 Lincoln st SW3
8 M 16 Lincoln way Enf
141 O 5 Lincolns Inn fields WC2
13 S 9 Lincolns the NW7
112 C 7 Lincombe rd Brom
45 Y 14 Lincroft gdns NW6
154 E 11 Lind rd Sutton
93 P 4 Lind st SE4
7 O 15 Lindal cres Enf
92 L 14 Lindal rd SE4
155 Z 18 Lindbergh rd Wallgtn
128 E 11 Linden av NW10
8 K 6 Linden av Enf
82 K 12 Linden av Hounsl
122 H 8 Linden av Thntn Hth
43 N 14 Linden av Wemb
42 M 14 Linden av Wemb
6 G 19 Linden clo N14
41 V 17 Linden cres Grnfd
117 N 4 Linden cres Kingst
21 U 18 Linden cres Wdfd Grn
74 L 2 Linden ct W12
137 V 4 Linden gdns W2
73 Z 13 Linden gdns W4
8 K 5 Linden gdns Enf
92 A 8 Linden gro SE15
110 D 16 Linden gro SE20
118 A 6 Linden gro New Mald
101 V 11 Linden gro Tedd
42 L 14 Linden lawns Wemb
28 E 17 Linden lea N2
159 X 2 Linden leas W Wkhm
137 U 11 Linden ms W11
32 L 15 Linden rd E17
29 T 13 Linden rd N10
16 A 8 Linden rd N11
30 L 13 Linden rd N15
100 G 20 Linden rd Hampt
39 O 14 Linden st Rom
6 H 20 Linden way N14
16 H 1 Linden way N14
159 H 13 Lindens Croy
46 B 14 Lindfield gdns NW3
60 D 11 Lindfield rd W5
123 V 15 Lindfield rd Croy
64 B 17 Lindfield st E14
104 G 19 Lindisfarne rd SW20
55 T 9 Lindisfarne rd Dgnham
51 T 6 Lindley st E1
63 O 14 Lindley st E1
143 Z 1 Lindley st E1
88 L 12 Lindore rd SW11
120 C 18 Lindores rd Carsh
88 C 4 Lindrop st SW6
24 M 16 Lindsay dri Harrow
100 L 19 Lindsay rd Hampt
152 K 2 Lindsay rd Worc Pk
67 O 4 Lindsell rd Bark
37 S 1 Lindsell st SE10
64 A 12 Lindsey est E3
55 S 11 Lindsey rd Dgnham
141 Y 1 Lindsey st EC1
102 C 18 Lindum rd Tedd
108 J 13 Lindway SE27
33 V 11 Linford rd E17
89 U 2 Linford st SW8
65 T 14 Ling rd E13

81 Y 17 Ling rd Erith
93 V 11 Lingards rd SE13
116 K 9 Lingfield av Kingst
8 D 19 Lingfield clo Enf
96 E 10 Lingfield cres SE9
19 N 2 Lingfield gdns N9
105 P 14 Lingfield rd SW19
152 M 6 Lingfield rd Worc
90 B 5 Lingham st SW9
4 C 16 Lingholm way Barn
109 O 3 Lings coppice SE2
106 K 6 Lingwell rd SW17
71 T 18 Lingwood gdns Islwth
49 Y 1 Lingwood rd E5
31 X 20 Lingwood rd N16
131 N 18 Linhope st NW1
155 Y 13 Link la Wallgtn
156 A 13 Link la Wallgtn
16 B 13 Link rd N11
155 O 1 Link rd Wallgtn
50 D 16 Link st E9
61 S 16 Link the W3
9 N 4 Link the Enf
40 D 16 Link the Grnfd
42 D 4 Link the Wemb
127 R 16 Link way Brom
126 E 14 Linkfield Brom
83 Y 5 Linkfield rd Islwth
119 Y 8 Links av Mrdn
39 Z 6 Links av Rom
14 M 6 Links dri N20
108 F 18 Links gdns SW16
44 C 8 Links rd NW2
107 N 17 Links rd SW17
61 P 16 Links rd W3
125 V 20 Links rd W Wkhm
21 S 16 Links rd Wdfd Grn
7 S 12 Links side Enf
10 L 20 Links View clo Wa
159 O 4 Links View rd Croy
101 O 11 Links View rd Ham
107 N 15 Links way SW17
125 O 13 Links way Becknhm
14 J 18 Linkside N12
118 B 4 Linkside New Mald
5 S 12 Linkside clo Enf
7 R 11 Linkside gdns Enf
27 O 8 Linkswood NW4
118 L 16 Linkway SW20
55 U 11 Linkway Dgnham
102 B 5 Linkway Rich
4 M 20 Linkway the Barnt
154 B 2 Linkway the Sutton
38 J 9 Linley cres Rom
31 S 7 Linley rd N17
27 Z 19 Linnell clo NW11
27 Z 20 Linnell clo NW11
18 K 15 Linnell rd N18
91 S 3 Linnell rd SE5
90 A 11 Linnom rd SW2
50 C 13 Linscott rd E5
151 S 5 Linsey st SE16
87 S 18 Linstead way SW
45 X 19 Linsteads NW6
42 F 17 Linthorpe av Wem
49 T 1 Linthorpe rd N16
5 W 12 Linthorpe rd Barnt
97 O 3 Linton clo Well
108 L 11 Linton clo SE27
54 B 20 Linton rd Bark
67 O 1 Linton rd Bark
67 P 1 Linton rd Bark
134 C 5 Linton st N1
87 W 5 Linver rd SW6
29 Z 13 Linzee rd N8
101 V 2 Lion av Twick
84 M 6 Lion Ga gdns Rich
85 N 5 Lion gdns Rich
18 J 9 Lion rd N9
98 A 10 Lion rd Bxly Hth
122 L 13 Lion rd Croy
101 V 1 Lion rd Twick
150 A 4 Lion st SE7
72 F 18 Lion way Brentf
84 A 8 Lion wharf Islwth
95 O 12 Lionel gdns SE9
95 O 12 Lionel ms W10
95 O 12 Lionel rd SE9
72 L 13 Lionel rd Brentf
73 O 14 Lionel rd Brentf
92 B 19 Liphook cres SE23
101 N 4 Lisbon av Twick
100 M 5 Lisbon av Twick
63 N 13 Lisbon st E1
46 M 13 Lisburne rd NW3
91 V 1 Lisford st SE15
98 E 15 Lisgar ter W14
94 F 2 Liskeard gdns SE3
140 G 9 Lisle st W1
47 N 14 Lismore circ NW5
83 Y 5 Lismore clo Islwth
31 O 11 Lismore rd N17

Lis–Loo

157 R 15 Lismore rd S Croy
47 P 12 Lissenden gdns NW5
130 G 15 Lisson gro NW8
130 K 20 Lisson st NW1
17 Z 16 Lister gdns N18
18 A 16 Lister gdns N18
17 Z 16 Lister gdns N18
52 A 5 Lister rd E11
31 W 5 Liston rd N17
89 V 8 Liston rd SW4
34 L 2 Liston way Wdfd Grn
56 E 8 Listowel rd Dgnhm
149 X 20 Listowel st SW9
49 T 6 Listria pk N16
51 Z 18 Litchfield av E15
119 V 16 Litchfield av Mrdn
44 G 19 Litchfield gdns NW10
63 W 9 Litchfield rd E3
154 B 9 Litchfield rd Sutton
140 H 8 Litchfield st WC2
28 C 16 Litchfield way NW11
46 C 17 Lithos rd NW3
25 O 10 Litlington st SE16
151 Y 5 Litlington st SE16
114 H 5 Little Argyll st W1
135 Z 10 Little birches Sidcp
146 A 11 Little Boltons the SW10
109 S 8 Little bornes SE21
142 A 3 Little britain EC1
141 Y 2 Little britain EC1
18 C 4 Little Bury st N9
10 C 1 Little Bushey la Bushey Watf
148 J 2 Little College st SW1
87 R 18 Little Cote clo SW19
159 Z 3 Little court W Wkhm
159 Z 3 Little ct W Wkhm
107 T 3 Little dimocks SW4
142 C 16 Little Dorrit ct SE1
72 F 9 Little Ealing la W5
131 Y 11 Little Edward st NW1
35 Z 13 Little gearies Ilf
140 J 19 Little George st SW1
47 S 12 Little Green st NW5
5 X 20 Little gro Barnt
78 D 14 Little heath SE7
37 P 14 Little heath Rom
81 P 20 Little Heath rd Bxly Hth
98 A 1 Little Heath rd Bxly Hth
157 Z 17 Little Heath rd S Croy
53 U 11 Little Ilford la E12
59 V 16 Little John rd W7
140 B 7 Little Marlborough st W1
22 C 7 Little Moss la Pinn
141 V 5 Little New st EC4
140 G 9 Little Newport st W2
100 A 4 Little Park dri Felt
8 A 12 Little Park gdns Enf
21 Z 5 Little Plucketts la Buck Hl
140 A 3 Little Portland st W1
10 D 2 Little potters Watf
101 V 15 Little Queens rd Tedd
127 P 2 Little redlands Brom
140 J 2 Little Russell st WC1
140 H 19 Little sanctuary SW1
148 H 1 Little Smith st SW7
143 N 6 Little Somerset st E1
8 B 15 Little St James st SW1
85 W 8 Little St leonards SW14
140 A 3 Little Titchfield st W1
142 B 8 Little Trinity la EC4
89 X 8 Littlebury rd SW4
77 W 16 Littlecombe SE7
22 C 3 Littlecote pl Pinn
95 V 7 Littlecroft SE9
80 A 17 Littledale SE2
25 U 1 Littlefield rd Edg
158 A 20 Littleheath rd S Croy
113 U 7 Littlemead SE9
54 E 10 Littlemoor rd Ilf
80 A 7 Littlemore rd SE2
106 F 20 Littlers clo SW19
21 O 6 Littleton av Ev
41 W 7 Littleton cres Harrow
41 X 8 Littleton rd Harrow

106 D 5 Littleton st SW18
93 V 15 Littlewood SE13
135 O 2 Livermere rd E8
150 D 11 Liverpool gro SE17
33 V 17 Liverpool rd E10
65 N 15 Liverpool rd E16
133 U 2 Liverpool rd N1
48 F 17 Liverpool rd N7
72 H 5 Liverpool rd W5
103 R 17 Liverpool rd Kingst
122 M 7 Liverpool rd Thntn
142 J 2 Liverpool st EC2
142 K 2 Liverpool St station EC2
151 T 14 Livesey pl SE15
64 H 4 Livingstone rd E15
33 R 18 Livingstone rd E17
17 N 18 Livingstone rd N13
88 G 8 Livingstone rd SW11
83 N 9 Livingstone rd Hounsl
82 M 9 Livingstone rd Hounsl
58 A 20 Livingstone rd S'hall
123 N 4 Livingstone rd Thntn Hth
66 L 18 Livingstone st SE6
140 D 7 Livonia st W1
77 V 19 Lizban st SE10
45 W 8 Llanelly rd NW2
78 K 18 Llanover rd SE18
42 G 10 Llanover rd Wemb
120 F 13 Llanthony rd Mrdn
45 W 7 Llanvanor rd NW2
143 T 18 Llewellyn st SE16
122 B 1 Lloyd av SW16
133 S 12 Lloyd Baker st WC1
33 N 7 Lloyd park E17
157 V 8 Lloyd park Croy
157 U 9 Lloyd Pk av Croy
32 F 13 Lloyd rd E17
66 F 4 Lloyd rd E6
56 C 19 Lloyd rd Dgnhm
153 N 4 Lloyd rd Worc Pk
133 R 13 Lloyd sq WC1
133 S 12 Lloyd st WC1
142 L 7 Lloyds ct EC3
94 A 5 Lloyds pl SE3
133 V 13 Lloyds row EC1
124 K 11 Lloyds way Becknhm
93 P 6 Loampit hills SE13
93 S 7 Loampit vale SE13
59 P 10 Loats bldgs E1
77 V 19 Locarno rd Grnfd
93 Z 11 Lochaber rd SE13
144 E 12 Lochaline st W6
89 R 19 Lochinvar st SW12
64 G 14 Lochnagar st E14
94 B 8 Lock chase SE3
102 E 8 Lock rd Rich
57 V 19 Locke clo Rainhm
23 U 9 Locket rd Harrow
9 X 8 Lockfield av Enf
63 Z 12 Lockhart st E3
50 F 12 Lockhurst st E5
89 T 1 Lockington rd SW8
31 Y 18 Lockmead rd N15
51 V 17 Lockmead rd SE13
81 V 17 Lockmere clo Erith
121 N 2 Locks la Mitch
63 Y 15 Locksley st E14
151 W 2 Lockwood SE16
54 C 8 Lockwood rd Ilf
142 F 18 Lockyer st SE1
50 C 20 Loddiges rd E9
75 P 20 Loder st SE15
85 Z 8 Lodge av SW14
156 E 6 Lodge av Croy
55 P 13 Lodge av Dgnhm
68 B 3 Lodge av Dgnhm
24 J 14 Lodge av Harrow
39 U 12 Lodge av Rom
18 A 17 Lodge clo N18
155 O 1 Lodge clo Wallgtn
6 K 13 Lodge cres Enf
17 T 14 Lodge dri N13
124 M 12 Lodge gdns Becknhm
80 E 18 Lodge hill Welling
15 P 15 Lodge la N12
97 V 14 Lodge la Bxly
159 P 15 Lodge la Croy
38 D 3 Lodge la Rom
26 M 12 Lodge rd NW4
130 H 15 Lodge rd NW8
12 K 17 Lodge rd Brom
122 K 15 Lodge rd Croy
122 L 17 Lodge rd Croy
154 B 9 Lodge rd Sutton
101 V 13 Lodge rd Tedd
155 R 10 Lodge rd Wallgtn

21 P 20 Lodge vlls Wdfd Grn
26 A 15 Lodore gdns NW9
64 F 13 Lodore st E14
133 U 18 Loftie st SE16
133 O 2 Lofting rd N1
74 K 3 Loftus rd W12
9 T 7 Logan clo Enf
95 N 19 Logan ms W8
145 T 5 Logan pl W8
145 T 5 Logan pl W8
29 V 9 Logan rd N9
42 J 6 Logan rd Wemb
113 R 19 Logs hill Chisl
127 S 1 Logs hill Chisl
113 R 20 Logs hill clo Chisl
143 O 2 Lolesworth st E1
141 Y 16 Lollard st SE11
9 R 7 Lombard av Enf
54 G 5 Lombard av Ilf
142 G 8 Lombard ct EC3
16 F 16 Lombard rd N11
88 F 5 Lombard rd SW11
120 B 2 Lombard rd SW19
142 G 7 Lombard st EC3
77 V 12 Lombard wall SE7
91 W 2 Lombardy pl W2
43 N 20 Lomond clo Wemb
150 D 19 Lomond gro SE5
150 L 13 Loncroft rd SE5
49 R 11 Londesborough rd N16
142 E 13 London br EC4
81 T 11 London Br st SE1
142 H 14 London Bridge station SE1
135 W 3 London fields E8
49 Y 20 London Fields W side E8
50 A 20 London la E8
112 F 17 London la Brom
138 G 5 London ms W2
137 Z 15 London museum W8
65 R 7 London rd E13
110 B 2 London rd SE23
14 X 2 London rd SW1
122 D 4 London rd SW16
66 M 2 London rd Bark
67 O 1 London rd Bark
112 C 19 London rd Brom
99 F 13 London rd Drtfd
8 C 14 London rd Enf
152 K 11 London rd Epsom
41 T 7 London rd Harrow
83 X 2 London rd Islwth
84 B 1 London rd Islwth
117 N 2 London rd Kingst
121 P 17 London rd Mitch
120 K 8 London rd Mitch
121 N 19 London rd Mitch
119 X 11 London rd Mrdn
38 F 18 London rd Rom
11 U 14 London rd Stanm
153 O 4 London rd Sutton
83 Y 17 London rd Twick
155 S 3 London rd Wallgtn
42 M 17 London rd Wemb
142 L 8 London st EC3
138 G 6 London st W2
142 G 3 London wall EC2
140 L 6 Long acre WC2
155 P 14 Long Acre rd Carsh
20 M 6 Long Deacon rd E4
62 B 16 Long dri W3
58 L 4 Long dri Grnfd
40 B 11 Long drive Pinn
23 R 4 Long elmes Harrow
22 M 5 Long elmes Harrow
82 H 3 Long hedges Hounsl
14 Y 1 Long la EC1
28 D 8 Long la N2
27 Z 3 Long la N3
142 D 18 Long la SE1
97 Z 1 Long la Bxly Hth
80 K 20 Long la Bxly Hth
124 B 14 Long la Croy
20 E 19 Long leys E4
47 X 16 Long meadow NW5
114 G 2 Long Meadow rd Sidcp
93 Z 3 Long Pond rd SE3
94 A 2 Long Pond rd SE3
89 U 10 Long rd SW4
51 U 8 Long st E8
150 L 1 Long wlk SE1
86 C 6 Long wlk SW13
117 W 5 Long wlk New Mald
133 N 18 Long yd WC1
33 W 4 Longacre rd E17
189 N 9 Longbeach rd SW11
45 V 8 Longberrys NW2
54 G 16 Longbridge rd Bark

93 T 12 Longbridge way SE13
113 V 7 Longcroft SE9
24 H 1 Longcrofte rd Edg
111 O 9 Longdown rd SE6
32 L 20 Longfellow rd E17
33 N 18 Longfellow rd E17
63 V 10 Longfellow rd E3
152 H 1 Longfellow rd Worc Pk
112 D 20 Longfield Brom
32 G 14 Longfield av E17
26 G 3 Longfield av NW7
60 E 20 Longfield av Enf
9 R 2 Longfield av Enf
57 T 1 Longfield av Hornch
121 P 20 Longfield av Wallgtn
155 P 1 Longfield av Wallgtn
42 J 5 Longfield av Wemb
110 C 6 Longfield cres SE26
85 S 13 Longfield dri SW14
60 F 18 Longfield rd W5
87 X 19 Longfield st SW18
60 E 18 Longfield wlk W5
70 J 1 Longford av S'hall
58 J 20 Longford av S'hall
100 G 10 Longford clo Hampt
154 D 4 Longford gdns Sutton
100 J 2 Longford rd Twick
131 Z 16 Longford st NW1
37 W 12 Longhayes av Rom
124 D 12 Longheath gdns Croy
89 P 3 Longhedge st SW11
111 X 6 Longhill rd SE6
93 Z 14 Longhurst rd SE13
94 A 14 Longhurst rd SE13
124 B 14 Longhurst rd Croy
124 A 14 Longhurst rd Croy
15 N 9 Longland dri N20
115 N 6 Longlands la Sidcp
114 H 6 Longlands Pk cres Sidcp
114 J 6 Longlands rd Sidcp
8 F 19 Longleat rd Enf
80 E 16 Longleigh la SE2
44 N 4 Longley av Wemb
106 J 14 Longley rd SW17
122 H 18 Longley rd Croy
23 P 14 Longley rd Harrow
151 S 6 Longley st SE1
115 X 4 Longmead dri Sidcp
106 L 11 Longmead rd SW17
148 B 6 Longmoore st SW1
5 R 19 Longmore av Barnt
63 U 10 Longnor rd E1
67 X 12 Longreach rd Bark
58 L 18 Longridge la S'hall
145 T 7 Longridge rd SW5
140 G 10 Longs ct WC2
20 K 11 Longshaw rd E4
75 Y 11 Longshore SE8
87 Z 17 Longstaff cres SW18
87 Z 17 Longstaff rd SW18
62 E 3 Longstone av NW10
107 S 13 Longstone rd SW17
121 W 3 Longthornton rd SW16
109 Y 10 Longton av SE26
110 A 9 Longton gro SE26
109 Z 10 Longton gro SE26
38 L 5 Longview way Rom
149 X 5 Longville rd SE11
86 H 17 Longwood dri SW15
58 B 12 Longwood gdns Ilf
26 B 12 Loning the NW9
96 G 11 Lonsdale av E6
38 J 18 Lonsdale av Rom
42 L 16 Lonsdale av Wemb
22 C 3 Lonsdale clo Pinn
35 Y 18 Lonsdale cres Ilf
21 O 4 Lonsdale dri Enf
6 K 14 Lonsdale dri Enf
122 C 8 Lonsdale gdns Thntn Hth
137 R 6 Lonsdale ms W11
85 O 2 Lonsdale ms Rich
133 U 2 Lonsdale pl N1
34 D 20 Lonsdale rd E11
129 O 6 Lonsdale rd NW6
124 Z 8 Lonsdale rd SE25
74 F 18 Lonsdale rd SW13
86 D 3 Lonsdale rd SW13
137 R 7 Lonsdale rd W11
74 C 10 Lonsdale rd W4
98 B 5 Lonsdale rd Bxly Hth
133 T 2 Lonsdale sq N1
31 T 11 Loobert rd N15
36 A 9 Looe gdns Ilf
114 A 16 Loop rd Chisl

18 D 13 Lopen rd N18
48 C 13 Loraine rd N7
23 S 17 Loraine rd W4
75 P 12 Lorbetts la SE16
35 U 10 Lord av Ilf
103 X 20 Lord Chancellor wlk Kingst
35 S 12 Lord gdns Ilf
129 Y 20 Lord Hills rd W9
148 J 2 Lord North st SW1
78 E 3 Lord st E16
78 F 9 Lord Warwick st SE18
100 C 5 Lords clo Felt
130 G 13 Lords Cricket grd NW8
49 P 7 Lordship gro N16
31 O 6 Lordship la N17
30 G 6 Lordship la N22
91 V 15 Lordship la SE22
48 M 7 Lordship pk N16
49 O 6 Lordship pk N16
146 K 15 Lordship pl SW3
49 O 4 Lordship rd N16
49 P 8 Lordship ter N16
31 S 6 Lordsmead rd N17
133 O 11 Lorenzo st WC1
24 J 13 Loretto gdns Harrow
15 V 8 Loring rd N20
83 V 4 Loring rd Islwth
144 D 2 Loris rd W6
90 E 4 Lorn rd SW9
42 F 16 Lorne av Croy
130 L 15 Lorne clo NW8
34 K 14 Lorne gdns E11
136 J 17 Lorne gdns W11
124 G 16 Lorne gdns Croy
33 N 17 Lorne rd E17
52 K 11 Lorne rd E7
48 E 3 Lorne rd N4
23 V 8 Lorne rd Harrow
84 L 13 Lorne rd Rich
9 P 17 Lorraine clo Enf
149 Y 14 Lorrimore rd SE17
149 Z 13 Lorrimore sq SE17
30 J 20 Lothair rd N4
72 F 7 Lothair rd N4
30 H 20 Lothair Rd south N4
88 H 8 Lothair st SW11
142 F 5 Lothbury EC2
90 J 1 Lothian rd SW9
90 J 1 Lothian rd SW9
128 L 13 Lothrop st W10
146 C 19 Lots rd SW10
106 M 14 Loudoun av Ilf
36 A 15 Loudoun av Ilf
35 Z 14 Loudoun av Ilf
130 D 5 Loudoun rd NW8
130 C 3 Loudoun Rd ms NW8
48 D 16 Lough rd N7
J 9 Loughborough pk SW9
90 J 7 Loughborough rd SW9
90 F 4 Loughborough rd SW9
149 R 10 Loughborough st SE11
63 S 13 Louisa st E1
52 A 17 Louise rd E15
107 O 6 Louisville rd SW17
88 G 11 Louvaine rd SW11
44 D 11 Lovat clo NW2
142 H 10 Lovat la EC3
12 E 18 Lovatt clo Edg
142 C 4 Love la EC2
31 U 2 Love la N17
78 L 11 Love la SE18
124 A 7 Love la SE25
98 D 17 Love la Bxly
120 K 4 Love la Mitch
119 Z 17 Love la Mrdn
120 A 16 Love la Mrdn
22 A 10 Love la Pinn
153 T 13 Love la Sutton
126 G 3 Love lane Brom
91 N 4 Love walk SE5
72 B 3 Lovedy rd W13
151 T 12 Lovegrove st SE1
96 M 5 Lovel av Well
97 N 4 Lovel av Welling
127 X 15 Lovelace av Brom
54 M 14 Lovelace gdns Bark
116 F 17 Lovelace gdns Surb
105 T 7 Lovelace grn SE9
108 L 2 Lovelace rd SE21
15 W 2 Lovelace rd Barnt
116 H 17 Lovelace rd Surb
75 R 17 Lovelinch st SE15
102 D 7 Lovell rd Rich
58 J 17 Lovell rd S'hall
57 V 17 Lovell wlk Rainhm

45 V 18 Loveridge rd NW6
14 H 19 Lovers wlk NW7
27 X 1 Lovers wlk N3
109 V 7 Low Cross Wood la SE21
20 L 9 Low Hall clo E4
32 J 19 Low Hall la E17
19 N 5 Lowden rd N9
90 K 11 Lowden rd SE24
58 B 19 Lowden rd S'hall
65 T 15 Lowe av E16
63 W 17 Lowells st E14
69 Z 6 Lowen rd Rainhm
123 W 20 Lower Addiscombe rd Croy
147 W 3 Lower Belgrave st SW1
71 T 4 Lower Boston rd W7
69 R 3 Lower Broad st Dgnhm
113 U 20 Lower camden Chisl
127 V 1 Lower camden Chisl
156 J 3 Lower Church st Croy
65 B 2 Lower Clapton rd E5
86 K 8 Lower Common south SW15
156 M 7 Lower Coombe st Croy
105 P 20 Lower Downs rd SW20
18 K 13 Lower Fore st N9
127 T 20 Lower Gravel rd Brom
120 K 7 Lower green W Mitch
147 Y 1 Lower Grosvenor pl SW1
19 W 15 Lower Hall la E4
102 G 13 Lower Ham rd Kingst
116 H 1 Lower Ham rd Kingst
96 A 7 Lower Jackwood clo SE9
140 C 9 Lower John st W1
6 M 16 Lower Kenwood av N14
16 H 18 Lower Maidstone rd N11
74 K 14 Lower mall W6
144 B 11 Lower mall W6
69 Y 7 Lower Mardyke av R'hm
141 R 19 Lower marsh SE1
117 R 9 Lower Marsh la Kingst
116 M 8 Lower Marsh la Kingst
119 P 14 Lower Morden la Mrdn
84 L 9 Lower Mortlake rd Rich
39 T 19 Lower Moss la Rom
16 G 18 Lower Pk rd N11
81 T 9 Lower Pk rd Blvdr
65 R 10 Lower rd E13
48 E 16 Lower rd N7
75 R 8 Lower rd SE16
81 U 9 Lower rd Blvdr
81 Z 10 Lower rd Blvdr
41 P 4 Lower rd Harrow
154 E 9 Lower rd Sutton
85 S 7 Lower Richmond rd SW14
87 O 7 Lower Richmond rd SW15
147 R 8 Lower Sloane st SW1
99 P 16 Lower Station rd Drtfd
102 F 18 Lower Teddington rd Kingst
116 F 2 Lower Teddington rd Kingst
46 D 9 Lower ter NW3
142 G 10 Lower Thames st EC3
10 B 1 Lower tub Watford
45 X 19 Lowfield rd NW6
61 V 17 Lowfield rd W3
23 T 15 Lowick rd Harrow
38 H 17 Lowlands gdns Rom
23 T 20 Lowlands rd Harrow
28 A 17 Lowman rd N7
147 U 2 Lowndes clo SW1
140 B 7 Lowndes ct W1
147 T 2 Lowndes pl SW1
139 M 19 Lowndes sq SW1
147 S 1 Lowndes st SW1
126 F 4 Lownds av Brom
63 O 20 Lowood st E1
143 Y 9 Lowood st E1

38 F 4 Lowshoe la Rom
90 M 4 Lowth rd SE5
6 M 13 Lowther dri Enf
7 N 14 Lowther dri Enf
92 J 19 Lowther hill SE23
86 E 2 Lowther st SW13
74 E 20 Lowther st SW13
103 N 19 Lowther rd Kingst
24 M 10 Lowther rd Stanm
66 B 7 Loxford av E6
72 A 18 Loxford av Ilf
54 A 18 Loxford rd Bark
33 P 1 Loxham av E4
132 L 13 Loxham st WC1
88 H 20 Loxley rd SW18
110 G 2 Loxton rd SE23
31 S 11 Loxwood rd N17
142 H 3 Lt winchester EC2
113 V 19 Lubbock rd Chisl
75 R 20 Lubbock st SE14
88 K 7 Lubeck st SW11
146 K 6 Lucan pl SW3
4 F 10 Lucan rd Barnt
65 W 3 Lucas av E13
40 G 6 Lucas av Harrow
110 D 16 Lucas rd SE20
93 N 3 Lucas st SE4
17 N 12 Lucerne clo N14
33 X 14 Lucerne gro E17
137 V 13 Lucerne ms W8
48 J 12 Lucerne rd N5
122 K 10 Lucerne rd Thntn Hth
151 T 4 Lucey rd SE16
107 O 10 Lucien rd SW17
105 Z 4 Lucien rd SW18
21 Y 4 Luctons av Buck Hl
61 V 13 Lucy cres W3
56 A 10 Lucy gdns Dgnhm
81 S 18 Luddesdon rd Erith
141 X 6 Ludgate broadway EC4
141 W 6 Ludgate cir EC4
141 X 6 Ludgate hill EC4
141 X 7 Ludgate sq EC4
40 F 12 Ludlow clo Harrow
60 E 11 Ludlow rd W5
55 W 2 Ludlow way N2
86 C 10 Ludovick wlk SW15
75 V 18 Ludwick rd SE14
80 D 8 Luffield rd SE2
112 J 6 Luffman rd SE12
92 A 4 Lugard rd SE15
134 H 17 Luke st EC2
20 J 12 Lukin cres E4
63 P 18 Lukin st E1
115 P 17 Lullingstone clo Orp
115 O 18 Lullingstone cres Orp
81 O 14 Lullingstone rd Blvdr
14 G 17 Lullington garth N12
109 X 18 Lullington rd SE20
68 L 1 Lullington rd Dgnhm
55 Y 20 Lullington rd Dgnhm
47 S 6 Lulot st N19
82 L 1 Lulworth av Hounsl
70 L 20 Lulworth av Hounsl
42 D 1 Lulworth av Wemb
40 C 9 Lulworth clo Harrow
22 A 20 Lulworth dri Pinn
40 C 8 Lulworth gdns Harrow
92 B 5 Lulworth rd SE15
113 P 5 Lulworth rd SE9
96 K 6 Lulworth rd Welling
140 L 9 Lulworth st W1
153 S 12 Lumley gdns Sutton
153 S 12 Lumley rd Sutton
139 U 7 Lumley st W1
123 N 5 Luna rd Thntn Hth
109 R 15 Lunham rd SE19
108 H 3 Lupin clo SW2
47 U 13 Lupton st NW5
147 Y 11 Lupus st SW1
148 A 11 Lupus st SW7
144 G 13 Lurgan av W6
144 H 9 Lurgan av W6
189 R 1 Lurline gdns SW11
148 J 17 Luscombe way SW8
62 J 6 Lushington rd NW10
111 P 11 Lushington rd SE6
101 V 12 Luther rd Tedd
76 H 20 Luton pl SE10
65 R 12 Luton rd E13
32 K 10 Luton rd E17
115 T 6 Luton rd Sidcp
130 H 18 Luton st NW8
86 K 13 Luttrell av SW15
110 K 4 Lutwyche rd SE6
141 T 19 Luxborough st W1
144 E 5 Luxemburg gdns W6
113 R 2 Luxfield rd SE9
75 S 11 Luxford st SE16

92 L 3 Luxmore st SE4
90 K 6 Luxor st SE5
119 R 1 Lwr Downs rd SW20
140 C 9 Lwr James st W1
130 K 1 Lwr Merton rd NW3
63 W 7 Lyal rd E3
147 S 3 Lyall Ms w SW1
147 S 3 Lyall st SW1
109 T 8 Lyalla av SE21
147 T 3 Lyalla ms SW1
124 K 18 Lyconby gdns Croy
114 J 8 Lyd clo Sidcp
81 O 18 Lydd rd Bxly Hth
45 W 18 Lydden gro SW18
88 A 20 Lydden rd SW18
53 T 20 Lydeard rd E6
77 Z 9 Lydenberg st SE7
45 O 17 Lydford rd NW2
31 P 16 Lydford rd N15
129 R 15 Lydford rd W9
108 D 5 Lyndhurst av SW2
89 U 8 Lydon rd SW4
113 X 11 Lydstep rd Chisl
88 H 20 Lyford st SW18
106 J 1 Lyford rd SW18
78 D 11 Lyford st SE18
90 A 15 Lyham rd SW2
89 Z 13 Lyham rd SW4
94 G 11 Lyme Farm rd SE12
50 B 19 Lyme gro E9
97 S 2 Lyme rd Welling
122 A 2 Lyme st NW1
132 A 2 Lyme st NW1
109 U 12 Lymer av SE19
153 Y 3 Lymescote gdns Sutton
114 L 9 Lyminge clo Sidcp
106 J 2 Lyminge gdns SW18
30 H 8 Lymington av N22
121 W 3 Lymington clo SW16
152 D 10 Lymington gdns Epsom
45 Z 17 Lymington rd NW6
8 B 16 Lymington rd NW6
55 W 3 Lymington rd Dgnhm
18 H 1 Lymouth av Enf
17 V 14 Lynbridge gdns N13
75 Z 15 Lynch wlk SE8
89 R 9 Lyncott cres SW4
22 A 16 Lyncroft av Pinn
72 D 4 Lyncroft gdns W13
152 E 20 Lyncroft gdns Epsom
83 N 12 Lyncroft gdns Hounsl
45 W 11 Lyndale NW2
45 W 10 Lyndale av NW2
77 P 17 Lyndale clo SE10
15 Y 18 Lyndhurst av N12
27 U 4 Lyndhurst av N3
54 G 17 Lyndhurst gdns Bark
8 D 15 Lyndhurst gdns Enf
36 E 19 Lyndhurst gdns Ilf
91 T 4 Lyndhurst gro SE15
33 U 1 Lyndhurst rd E4
46 G 14 Lyndhurst rd NW3
15 T 20 Lyndhurst rd N18
18 K 14 Lyndhurst rd N18
98 H 7 Lyndhurst rd Bxly Hth
58 K 10 Lyndhurst rd Grnfd
122 F 9 Lyndhurst rd Thntn Hth
91 U 3 Lyndhurst sq SE15
91 U 2 Lyndhurst ter SE15
96 K 13 Lyndon av Sidcp
155 P 6 Lyndon av Wallgtn
81 S 9 Lyndon rd Blvdr
108 J 13 Lyndway SE27
32 K 5 Lyne cres E17
89 T 15 Lynette av SW4
12 E 12 Lynford gdns Edg
54 L 7 Lynford gdns Ilf
97 R 5 Lynmere rd Welling
119 O 15 Lynmouth av Mrdn
60 C 2 Lynmouth gdns Grnfd
32 H 18 Lynmouth rd E17
49 U 4 Lynmouth rd N16

28 M 12 Lynmouth rd N2
27 M 12 Lynmouth rd N2
60 C 3 Lynmouth rd Grnfd
23 P 9 Lynn clo Harrow
51 Z 8 Lynn rd E11
89 T 17 Lynn rd SW12
54 D 1 Lynn rd Ilf
8 A 6 Lynn st Enf
55 X 5 Lynnett rd Dgnhm
98 F 12 Lynsted clo Bxly Hth
95 P 10 Lynsted gdns SE9
26 C 12 Lynton av NW9
51 T 13 Lynton av N12
59 Y 17 Lynton av W13
63 Z 17 Lynton av W13
38 F 5 Lynton av Rom
83 V 10 Lynton clo Islwth
25 Z 19 Lynton cres Ilf
18 E 4 Lynton gdns Enf
14 M 9 Lynton mead N20
51 X 12 Lynton rd E11
20 D 16 Lynton rd E4
29 P 7 Lynton rd NW6
72 Z 16 Lynton rd N8
51 X 8 Lynton rd SE1
61 T 18 Lynton rd W3
22 F 15 Lynton rd Croy
40 C 8 Lynton rd Harrow
17 Y 11 Lynton rd New Mald
34 K 4 Lynwood clo E18
64 B 9 Lynwood clo Harrow
38 H 1 Lynwood dri Rom
52 G 3 Lynwood dri Worc Pk
56 D 8 Lynwood gdns Croy
58 E 16 Lynwood gdns S'hall
06 M 8 Lynwood rd SW17
60 H 10 Lynwood rd W5
24 F 5 Lyon meade Stanm
61 N 1 Lyon Pk av Wemb
42 J 18 Lyon Pk av Wemb
20 D 1 Lyon rd SW19
23 V 19 Lyon rd Harrow
57 T 1 Lyon rd Hornch
32 M 1 Lyon st N1
30 F 17 Lyons pl NW8
5 R 19 Lyonsdown av Barnt
R'16 Lyonsdown rd Barnt
49W 8 Lyric pl SW11
83 D 3 Lyric rd SW13
47 W 4 Lysander gro N19
48 G 18 Lysia st SW6
89 R 17 Lysias rd SW12
16 K 15 Lysons wlk SW15
12 G 17 Lytchet rd Brom
91 T 13 Lytcott gro SE22
63 O 5 Lyte st E2
60 L 8 Lytham gro W5
50 E 12 Lytham st SE17
28 T 15 Lyttelton rd N2
30 F 11 Lyttelton rd N8
30 K 1 Lyttleton clo NW3
51 S 9 Lyttleton rd E10
17 V 8 Lytton av N13
9 X 3 Lytton av Enf
28 F 19 Lytton clo N2
51 E 1 Lytton clo Grnfd
55 X 7 Lytton gdns Wallgtn
37 S 16 Lytton gro SW15
33 Z 20 Lytton rd E11
5 R 14 Lytton rd Barnt
22 B 3 Lytton rd Pinn
37 Z 17 Lytton rd Rom
77 V 18 Lyveden rd SE10
06 L 16 Lyveden rd SW17

M

09W 18 Maberley cres SE19
09W 19 Maberley rd SE19
26 F 6 Maberley rd Becknhm
32 M 14 Mabledon pl WC1
44 K 18 Mablethorpe rd SW6
35 S 15 Mabley st E9
79 W 10 Macarthur ter SE7
78 B 16 Macarthur ter SE7
66 C 6 Macaulay rd E6
89 T 9 Macaulay rd SW4
97 T 9 Macaulay sq SW4
78 K 9 Macbean st SE18
74 K 12 Macbeth st W6
34 A 12 Macclesfield rd EC1
22 E 12 Macclesfield rd SE25
40 F 9 Macclesfield st W1
56 J 10 Macdonald av Dgnhm
33 V 7 Macdonald rd E17
52 E 13 Macdonald rd E7

16 A 17 Macdonald rd N11
47 V 6 Macdonald rd N19
89 P 1 Macduff rd SW11
136 C 14 Macfarlane rd W12
74 M 3 Macfarlane rd W12
136 C 13 Macfarlane pl W12
74 M 2 Macfarlane pl W12
113 U 18 Macfarren pl NW1
66 A 14 Macgregor rd E16
65 Z 14 Macgregor rd E16
92 C 7 Machell rd SE15
89 S 7 Mackay rd SW4
130 L 1 Mackennal st NW8
48 C 17 Mackenzie rd N7
124 D 4 Mackenzie rd Becknhm
46 L 13 Mackeson rd NW3
90 E 19 Mackie rd SW2
50 F 16 Mackintosh la E9
140 L 4 Macklin st WC2
151 T 5 Macks rd SE16
132 A 11 Mackworth st NW1
50 H 12 Maclaren st E5
92 H 16 Maclean rd SE23
150 B 12 Macleod st SE17
144 K 3 Maclise rd W14
79 S 17 Macoma rd SE18
79 S 16 Macoma ter SE18
76 E 11 Macquarie way E14
129 R 12 Macroom rd W9
131 S 19 Madame tussauds NW8
64 C 13 Maddams st E3
101 V 16 Maddison clo Tedd
115 X 14 Maddocks clo Sidcp
139 Z 8 Maddox st W1
140 A 7 Maddox st W1
117 Z 17 Madeira av Brom
112 A 20 Madeira av Brom
21 X 18 Madeira av Wdfd Grn
51 Y 5 Madeira rd E11
17W 12 Madeira rd N13
108 B 11 Madeira rd SW16
120 M 8 Madeira rd Mitch
121 N 8 Madeira rd Mitch
60 L 18 Madeley rd W5
109 X 19 Madeline rd SE20
80 G 19 Madison cres Welling
80 G 19 Madison gdns Welling
48 F 17 Madras pl N7
53 Z 12 Madras rd Ilf
74 G 20 Madrid rd SW13
86 G 1 Madrid rd SW13
150 L 8 Madron st SE17
66 C 6 Mafeking av E6
72 H 16 Mafeking av Brentf
54 F 2 Mafeking av Ilf
65 S 11 Mafeking rd E16
31 X 8 Mafeking rd N17
8 G 13 Mafeking rd Enf
47 U 6 Magdala rd N19
157 O 16 Magdala rd Croy
83 Z 8 Magdala rd Islwth
143 P 8 Magdalen pas E1
88 G 19 Magdalen rd SW18
106 C 3 Magdalen rd SW18
142 K 15 Magdalen st SE1
66 J 11 Magdalene gdns E6
149 T 14 Magee st SE11
10 G 3 Magnaville rd Bushey Watf
24 L 20 Magnolia at Harrow
73 S 17 Magnolia rd W4
141 V 7 Magpie all EC4
141 U 8 Magpie all EC4
127 S 16 Magpie Hall clo Brom
127 T 15 Magpie Hall la Brom
10 G 6 Magpie Hall rd Bushey Watf
102 E 10 Maguire dri Rich
143 P 16 Maguire st SE1
84 F 12 Maid Of Honour row Rich
20 D 3 Maida av E9
130 E 19 Maida av W2
81 S 8 Maida rd Blvdr
130 C 14 Maida Vale W9
99 X 14 Maida Vale dr Drtfrd
20 D 3 Maida way E4
97 Z 20 Maiden Erlegh av Bxly
140 L 9 Maiden la WC2
99W 10 Maiden la WC2
132 L 7 Maiden Lane bridge SE10
52 A 20 Maiden rd E15
93 U 2 Maidenstone hill SE10
63W 11 Maidman st E3

38 K 7 Maidstone av Rom
142 D 15 Maidstone bldgs SE1
16 K 18 Maidstone rd N11
115 Y 11 Maidstone rd Sidcp
135 T 7 Maidstone st E2
8 K 17 Main av Enf
39 X 10 Main rd Rom
114 J 8 Main rd Sidcp
113 X 11 Mainridge rd Chisl
151 T 16 Maismore st SE15
66 B 15 Maitland gdns E15
47 N 18 Maitland Pk rd NW3
47 N 17 Maitland Pk vlls NW5
52 B 19 Maitland rd E15
110 E 15 Maitland rd SE26
50 H 10 Maiwand rd E5
79 S 13 Majendie rd SE18
51 V 14 Major rd E15
151 U 1 Major rd SE16
47 O 7 Makepeace av N6
146 L 7 Makins st SW3
64 C 19 Malam gdns E14
57 X 17 Malan sq Rainhm
86 L 11 Malbrook rd SW15
26 F 17 Malcolm cres NW4
11 R 17 Malcolm ct Stanm
63 O 11 Malcolm pl E2
110 B 17 Malcolm rd SE20
123 X 15 Malcolm rd SE25
105 T 16 Malcolm rd SW19
123 Z 7 Malden av SE25
124 A 7 Malden av SE25
41 S 17 Malden av Grnfd
47 P 19 Malden cres NW1
118 J 6 Malden ct New Mald
118 F 19 Malden Green av Worc Pk
118 C 7 Malden hill New Mald
118 D 8 Malden Hill gdns New Mald
152 A 1 Malden la Worc Pk
118 D 14 Malden pk New Mald
47 N 15 Malden pl NW5
47 O 16 Malden rd NW5
118 C 13 Malden rd New Mald
153 N 7 Malden rd Sutton
117 Z 15 Malden way New Mald
91 R 7 Maldon clo SE5
18 H 10 Maldon rd N9
61 W 20 Maldon rd W3
56 J 1 Maldon rd Rom
155 T 10 Maldon rd Wallgtn
21 Y 20 Maldon wlk Wdfd Grn
132 E 18 Malet pl WC1
132 F 19 Malet st WC1
108 K 3 Maley av SE27
34 D 9 Malford gro E18
91 T 7 Malfort rd SE5
110 F 1 Malham rd SE23
74 K 13 Mall rd W6
16 L 10 Mall the N14
17 O 9 Mall the N14
140 D 15 Mall the SW1
85 V 13 Mall the SW1
62 H 19 Mall the W5
24 M 20 Mall the Harrow
116 F 13 Mall the Surb
15 U 1 Mallard clo Barnt
43 V 2 Mallard way NW9
34 J 2 Mallards rd Wdfd Grn
40 E 15 Mallet dri Grnfd
93 X 16 Mallet rd SE13
119 C 13 Malling gdns Mrdn
126 C 16 Malling way Brom
155 Z 4 Mallinson rd Wallgtn
88 K 12 Mallison rd SW11
146 G 13 Mallord st SW3
92 C 10 Mallory clo SE4
126 J 8 Mallory gdns E6
16 B 3 Mallory gdns Barnt
27 T 2 Mallow mead NW7
134 E 16 Mallow st EC1
125 V 10 Malmains clo Becknhm
125 V 9 Malmains way Becknhm
65 V 9 Malmesbury rd E16
64 M 13 Malmesbury rd E16
34 C 5 Malmesbury rd E3
63 Z 8 Malmesbury rd E3
120 C 16 Malmesbury rd Mrdn
65 O 14 Malmesbury ter E16
92 L 3 Malpas rd SE4
55 V 19 Malpas rd Dgnhm
151 S 13 Malt st SE1

51 N 2 Malta rd E10
133 X 15 Malta st EC1
151 N 1 Maltby st SE1
143 N 19 Maltby st SE1
79 V 17 Malton st SE18
141 P 8 Maltravers st WC2
33W 1 Malva av E4
80 L 20 Malvern av Bxly Hth
40 G 8 Malvern av Harrow
121 V 6 Malvern clo Mitch
116 K 20 Malvern clo Surb
111 T 20 Malvern ct Becknhm
54 K 13 Malvern dri Ilf
21 X 15 Malvern dri Wdfd
45 S 6 Malvern gdns NW2
129 P 11 Malvern gdns W9
24 L 12 Malvern gdns Harrow
129 S 13 Malvern ms W9
129 R 11 Malvern pl W9
52 B 6 Malvern rd E11
66 C 3 Malvern rd E6
135 S 1 Malvern rd E8
49W 20 Malvern rd E8
129 S 12 Malvern rd NW6
31W 9 Malvern rd N17
30 E 10 Malvern rd N8
100 H 19 Malvern rd Hampt
39 V 20 Malvern rd Hornch
122 F 10 Malvern rd Thntn Hth
133 S 3 Malvern ter N1
18 H 6 Malvern ter N9
60 B 14 Malvern way W13
89 R 17 Malwood rd SW12
93 P 13 Malyions rd SE13
93 P 13 Malyions ter SE13
76 G 3 Managers st E14
58 G 16 Manaton cres S'hall
91 Z 7 Manaton rd SE18
51 Z 17 Manbey gro E15
51 Z 17 Manbey Pk rd E15
51 Z 18 Manbey rd E15
51 Z 18 Manbey st E15
52 A 18 Manbey st E15
66 H 9 Manbrough rd E6
76 F 12 Manchester gro E14
139 T 3 Manchester ms W1
72 E 14 Manchester rd E14
31 P 19 Manchester rd N15
122 M 6 Manchester rd Thntn Hth
139 U 4 Manchester sq W1
139 T 2 Manchester st W1
89 P 14 Manchuria rd SW11
142 F 20 Manciple st SE1
89 U 14 Mandalay rd SW4
77 R 20 Mandeville clo SE10
139 V 5 Mandeville pl W1
16 F 9 Mandeville rd N14
40 H 19 Mandeville rd Grnfd
83 Y 4 Mandeville rd Islwth
50 G 10 Mandeville rd E5
106 M 6 Mandrake rd SW17
96 A 13 Mandrell rd SW2
140 G 6 Manette st W1
87 V 13 Manfred rd SW15
76 B 5 Manilla st E14
80 A 8 Manister rd SE2
131 T 3 Manley st NW1
150 F 12 Mann st SE17
37 P 20 Mannin rd Rom
42 H 1 Manning gdns Harrow
56 E 20 Manning rd Dgnhm
43 R 5 Manningtree st E1
30 J 10 Mannock rd N22
83W 12 Manns clo Islwth
12 C 19 Manns rd Edg
100 M 5 Manoel rd Twick
74 B 13 Manor alley W4
92 M 4 Manor av SE4
58 D 1 Manor av Grnfd
94 F 10 Manor brook SE3
25 R 14 Manor clo NW7
57 O 19 Manor clo Dgnhm
99 O 10 Manor clo Drtfrd
59 V 16 Manor clo Rom
118 C 20 Manor clo Worc Pk
28 C 9 Manor Cottages appr N2
90 K 19 Manor cotts SE24
28 D 8 Manor Cotts appr N2
59 T 20 Manor Court rd W7
20 M 10 Manor Court rd W7
117 O 14 Manor cres Surb
108 A 7 Manor ct SW16
71 S 1 Manor Ct rd W7

Ref	Name
118 B 20	Manor Dr the Worc Pk
12 L 16	Manor dri NW7
16 F 4	Manor dri N14
15 Y 11	Manor dri N20
152 B 14	Manor dri Epsom
117 Y 16	Manor dri North Surb
118 A 19	Manor dri North Worc Pk
117 O 15	Manor dri Surb
43 N 11	Manor dri Wemb
21 N 9	Manor Farm dri E4
122 F 2	Manor Farm rd SW16
60 F 5	Manor Farm rd Wemb
87 O 15	Manor fields SW15
48 A 9	Manor gdns N7
119 V 2	Manor gdns SW20
73 R 10	Manor gdns W3
100 L 18	Manor gdns Hampt
85 O 10	Manor gdns Rich
157 U 14	Manor gdns S Croy
75 O 17	Manor gro SE14
125 R 3	Manor gro Becknhm
85 R 9	Manor gro Rich
27 O 7	Manor Hall av NW4
27 O 8	Manor Hall dri NW4
45 P 20	Manor Ho dri NW6
128 H 1	Manor Ho dri NW6
99 O 9	Manor house Bxly Hth
94 B 18	Manor la SE12
93 Z 12	Manor la SE13
154 B 10	Manor la Sutton
93 Z 12	Manor la ter SE13
110 C 1	Manor mt SE23
53 R 10	Manor park E12
118 E 17	Manor park New Mald
93 Y 11	Manor pk SE13
94 A 14	Manor pk SE13
85 O 10	Manor pk Rich
125 R 20	Manor Pk clo W Wkhm
12 C 19	Manor Pk cres Edg
22 K 10	Manor Pk dri Harrow
12 C 18	Manor Pk gdns Edg
53 O 13	Manor Pk rd E12
62 C 4	Manor Pk rd NW10
28 E 10	Manor Pk rd N2
114 D 20	Manor Pk rd Chisl
154 C 11	Manor Pk rd Sutton
125 R 20	Manor Pk rd W Wkhm
149 Y 10	Manor pl SE17
150 A 10	Manor pl SE17
121 V 7	Manor pl Mitch
154 B 9	Manor pl Sutton
51 O 2	Manor rd E10
64 L 9	Manor rd E15
32 H 6	Manor rd E17
49 P 5	Manor rd N16
31 Y 3	Manor rd N17
17 O 20	Manor rd N22
119 V 3	Manor rd SE25
123 W 8	Manor rd SW20
60 A 20	Manor rd W13
59 Z 20	Manor rd W13
54 L 19	Manor rd Bark
4 F 14	Manor rd Barnt
125 R 2	Manor rd Becknhm
98 H 20	Manor rd Bxly
56 L 19	Manor rd Dgnhm
57 N 19	Manor rd Dgnhm
99 P 9	Manor rd Drtfrd
8 A 9	Manor rd Enf
23 Y 17	Manor rd Harrow
21 X 1	Manor rd Lghtn
121 V 7	Manor rd Mitch
155 R 8	Manor rd North Wallgtn
85 O 9	Manor rd Rich
37 U 19	Manor rd Rom
39 W 17	Manor rd Rom
114 M 6	Manor rd Sidcp
153 U 18	Manor rd Sutton
101 Z 11	Manor rd Tedd
101 O 4	Manor rd Twick
59 R 1	Manor rd W Wkhm
155 S 10	Manor rd Wallgtn
55 V 7	Manor sq Dgnhm
72 D 14	Manor vale Brentf
28 A 8	Manor view N3
27 Z 8	Manor view N3
78 M 2	Manor way E4
20 J 13	Manor way E4
24 A 12	Manor way NW9
94 D 10	Manor way SE3
125 P 5	Manor way Becknhm
127 S 15	Manor way Brom
98 L 8	Manor way Bxly Hth
157 U 14	Manor way Croy
18 D 1	Manor way Enf
22 K 13	Manor way Harrow
121 L 17	Manor way Mitch
21 Z 16	Manor way Wdfd Grn
118 C 20	Manor way Worc Pk
155 T 8	Manor Way the Wallgtn
117 R 1	Manorgate rd Kingst
4 F 15	Manorside Barnt
86 F 19	Manresa house SW15
146 J 11	Manresa rd SW3
49 V 11	Manse rd N16
33 N 4	Mansel gro E17
105 T 15	Mansel rd SW19
73 Y 4	Mansell rd W3
58 L 13	Mansell rd Grnfd
143 O 7	Mansell st E1
31 O 13	Mansfield av N15
6 B 18	Mansfield av Barnt
20 C 5	Mansfield hill E4
139 X 2	Mansfield ms W1
20 B 6	Mansfield park E4
34 H 19	Mansfield rd E11
32 L 13	Mansfield rd E17
84 M 14	Mansfield rd NW3
47 O 13	Mansfield rd NW3
61 T 12	Mansfield rd W3
53 X 6	Mansfield rd Ilf
157 O 15	Mansfield rd S Croy
139 X 2	Mansfield rd W1
135 U 10	Mansford st E2
107 O 20	Manship rd Mitch
142 E 7	Mansion House pl EC4
142 E 6	Mansion House st EC2
146 E 7	Mansion ms W8
146 E 7	Manson pl W8
55 U 1	Manstead gdns Rom
70 G 11	Manston av S'hall
57 Z 19	Manston way Hornch
45 S 14	Manstone rd NW2
133 T 7	Mantell st N1
79 P 13	Manthorpe rd SE18
92 J 8	Mantilla rd SW17
92 J 8	Mantle rd SE4
71 X 6	Manton av W7
79 Z 11	Manton rd SE2
80 A 11	Manton rd SE2
63 P 10	Mantus rd E1
88 H 7	Mantus rd SW11
15 P 6	Manus way N20
107 R 5	Manville gdns SW17
107 R 5	Manville rd SW17
92 M 15	Manwood rd SE4
78 L 4	Manwood st E16
107 T 3	Many gates SW12
135 V 16	Mape st E2
45 S 17	Mapesbury rd NW2
19 Y 19	Maple av E4
74 B 3	Maple av W3
40 L 8	Maple av Harrow
57 Y 10	Maple clo Hornch
121 S 1	Maple clo Mitch
97 N 15	Maple cres Sidcp
57 S 17	Maple ct New Mald
118 A 6	Maple ct New Mald
26 A 2	Maple gdns Edg
43 V 1	Maple gro NW9
72 H 7	Maple gro W5
72 B 18	Maple gro Brentf
58 F 13	Maple gro S'hall
63 N 15	Maple pl E1
132 B 19	Maple pl W1
34 A 19	Maple rd E11
110 C 18	Maple rd SE20
116 F 15	Maple rd W3
132 C 19	Maple st W1
38 K 14	Maple st Rom
157 Y 4	Mapledale av Croy
157 Y 4	Mapledale av W Wkhm
114 C 14	Mapledene Chisl
49 W 20	Mapledene rd E8
35 Z 11	Mapleleafe gdns Ilf
90 C 19	Maplestead rd SW2
68 D 4	Maplestead rd Dgnhm
122 G 9	Maplethorpe rd Thntn Hth
126 L 13	Mapleton clo Brom
9 O 3	Mapleton cres Enf
87 Z 16	Mapleton rd SW18
9 N 10	Mapleton rd Enf
78 B 19	Maplin clo N21
65 U 17	Maplin rd E16
63 X 10	Maplin st E3
129 N 11	Marban pl W9
129 O 12	Marban rd W9
73 S 3	Marble clo W3
84 B 18	Marble Hill clo Twick
84 A 18	Marble Hill gdns Twick
84 E 19	Marble Hill park Twick
112 K 6	Marbrook ct SE12
48 C 9	Marcellus rd N7
83 X 18	March rd Twick
51 Y 8	Marchant rd E11
75 O 17	Marchant st SE14
84 M 14	Marchmont rd Rich
85 N 14	Marchmont rd Rich
155 V 17	Marchmont rd Wallgtn
132 K 17	Marchmont st WC1
150 K 19	Marchwood clo SE5
60 F 16	Marchwood cres W5
150 M 7	Marcia rd SE1
88 E 19	Marcilly rd SW18
74 L 8	Marco rd W6
144 A 3	Marco rd W6
49 Z 16	Marcon pl E8
58 K 18	Marconi way S'hall
65 N 4	Marcus ct E15
99 W 19	Marcus rd Drtfrd
68 O 4	Marcus st E15
88 B 15	Marcus st SE18
25 Z 17	Mardale dri NW9
74 L 6	Mardale st W12
124 E 12	Mardell rd Croy
126 D 15	Marden av Brom
98 L 13	Marden cres Bxly
122 D 14	Marden cres Croy
31 R 9	Marden rd N17
151 X 3	Marden rd SE16
75 O 8	Marden rd SE16
122 D 15	Marden rd Croy
71 Z 6	Marder rd W13
72 A 6	Marder rd W13
39 S 18	Mardon rd Rom
135 Y 2	Mare st E8
50 A 19	Mare st E8
63 N 3	Mare st E8
114 F 6	Marechal Niel av Sidcp
46 E 18	Maresfield gdns NW3
67 M 1	Marg Bonfield av Bark
20 E 1	Margaret av E4
39 Y 16	Margaret clo Rom
140 A 4	Margaret st W1
49 U 5	Margaret gdns N16
49 U 5	Margaret rd N16
5 V 14	Margaret rd Barnt
97 W 15	Margaret rd Bxly
39 Y 16	Margaret rd Rom
139 Z 4	Margaret st W1
140 A 4	Margaret st W1
35 P 17	Margaret way Ilf
146 L 14	Margaretta ter SW3
52 L 5	Margaretting rd E12
90 A 13	Margate rd SW2
52 E 18	Margery Pk rd E7
55 X 8	Margery rd Dgnhm
133 R 15	Margery st WC1
105 P 11	Margin dri SW19
144 H 10	Margravine gdns W6
144 H 12	Margravine rd W6
106 H 3	Marham gdns SW18
62 C 14	Marham gdns SW18
83 S 13	Maria ter E1
153 Z 11	Marian ct Sutton
135 V 7	Marian pl E2
62 D 1	Marian way NW10
23 P 4	Maricas av Harrow
143 V 19	Marigold st SE16
19 Y 20	Marigold way E4
118 J 13	Marina av New Mald
96 H 4	Marina dri Welling
38 U 17	Marina gdns Rom
102 F 17	Marina way Tedd
143 S 20	Marine st SE16
88 B 4	Marinefield rd SW6
102 C 8	Mariner gdns Rich
36 D 1	Marion clo Ilf
21 O 14	Marion gro Wdfd Grn
13 T 16	Marion rd NW7
107 V 20	Marion rd SW16
123 N 11	Marion rd Thntn Hth
93 W 9	Marischal rd SE13
93 W 9	Marishal rd SE13
76 J 17	Maritime museum SE10
63 Y 12	Maritime st SE3
107 O 3	Marius rd SW17
89 N 10	Marjorie gro SW11
20 E 1	Mark av E4
70 J 2	Mark clo Shall
142 K 8	Mark la EC3
30 K 6	Mark rd N22
134 H 16	Mark st EC3
51 Z 20	Mark st E15
140 A 5	Market ct EC1
78 L 8	Market hill SE18
25 U 5	Market la Edg
25 V 5	Market la Edgw
139 X 14	Market ms W1
28 C 14	Market pl NW11
28 H 11	Market pl N2
140 A 5	Market pl W1
72 F 18	Market pl Brentf
98 E 10	Market pl Bxly Hth
116 G 4	Market pl Kingst
38 P 15	Market pl Rom
47 Z 19	Market rd N7
48 A 18	Market rd N7
85 P 9	Market rd Rich.
64 E 18	Market sq E14
64 C 18	Market sq E14
126 E 13	Market sq Brom
66 G 6	Market st E6
78 K 11	Market st SE18
64 E 18	Market way E14
42 J 16	Market way Wemb
20 D 1	Markfield gdns E4
31 X 14	Markfield rd N15
147 N 9	Markham sq SW3
146 M 9	Markham st SW3
100 E 19	Markhole clo Hamp
32 K 18	Markhouse av E17
32 K 18	Markhouse rd E17
50 M 1	Markhouse rd E17
50 K 1	Markmanor av E17
38 A 3	Marks hall Rom
38 L 16	Marks rd Rom
85 R 8	Marksbury av Rich
109 Z 9	Markwell clo SE26
55 R 16	Markyate rd Dgnhm
88 B 11	Marl st SW18
35 S 10	Marlanda av Ilf
35 T 8	Marlands rd Ilf
135 T 2	Marlborough av E8
16 G 10	Marlborough av N1
12 F 11	Marlborough av Edg
15 Z 12	Marlborough clo N20
106 H 16	Marlborough clo SW19
73 Z 8	Marlborough cres W4
140 B 7	Marlborough ct W1
35 R 10	Marlborough dri Ilf
15 Z 11	Marlborough gdns N20
151 T 12	Marlborough gro SE1
130 D 6	Marlborough hill NW8
23 T 13	Marlborough hill Harrow
140 D 15	Marlborough house SW1
77 Y 18	Marlborough la SE7
95 N 20	Marlborough Pk av Sidcp
130 B 9	Marlborough pl NW8
52 A 13	Marlborough rd E18
34 G 9	Marlborough rd E4
20 C 19	Marlborough rd E4
52 K 19	Marlborough rd E7
48 A 6	Marlborough rd N1
47 Y 7	Marlborough rd N1
17 O 20	Marlborough rd N2
30 H 20	Marlborough rd N2
18 H 7	Marlborough rd N9
140 D 15	Marlborough rd SW1
106 H 16	Marlborough rd SW19
73 U 13	Marlborough rd W4
72 H 5	Marlborough rd W5
72 A 20	Marlborough rd Brentf
126 M 9	Marlborough rd Brom
97 W 7	Marlborough rd Bxl Hth
55 T 14	Marlborough rd Dgnhm
100 H 15	Marlborough rd Hampt
23 U 13	Marlborough rd Harrow
84 L 16	Marlborough rd Rich
156 M 16	Marlborough rd S Croy

Call
01-589 7000

for a choice of

2500

beds in the heart of **LONDON**

Best locations — Budget to 'Luxe'

KENSINGTON PALACE, W.8 ● PRINCE OF WALES, W.8
ECCLESTON, S.W.1 ● SHAFTESBURY, W.C.2 ● PARKWAY, W.2
SOUTHWAY, S.W.1 ● QUEENSWAY, W.2 ● MONTAGUE, W.C.1

For London Airport ARLINGTON HOTEL
Out of town venue Grand Hotel, Folkestone

ASSOCIATED HOTELS LTD.

NO. 1 VICTORIA ROAD, KENSINGTON, W.8

146 K 8	Marlborough st SW3	
110 K 2	Marler rd SE23	
80 J 17	Marley av Bxly Hth	
58 G 7	Marley clo Grnfd	
100 G 16	Marlingdene clo Hampt	
145 W 4	Marloes rd W8	
124 A 5	Marlow clo SE20	
83 V 15	Marlow cres Twick	
153 P 4	Marlow dri Sutton	
66 F 9	Marlow rd E6	
124 B 4	Marlow rd SE20	
70 E 8	Marlow rd S'hall	
114 D 17	Marlow clo Chisl	
36 L 5	Marlowe clo Ilf	
33 U 12	Marlowe rd E17	
121 U 8	Marlowe sq Mitch	
130 F 4	Marlowes NW8	
79 X 10	Marmadon rd SE18	
20 A 13	Marmion av E4	
19 Y 13	Marmion av NW2	
20 A 13	Marmion clo E4	
89 P 9	Marmion rd SW11	
91 Y 1	Marmont rd SE15	
151 U 20	Marmont rd SE15	
92 C 15	Marmora rd SE22	
16 D 13	Marne av N11	
96 M 8	Marne av Welling	
90 M 3	Marne rd SE5	
128 L 12	Marne st W10	
89 O 10	Marney rd SW11	
45 S 11	Marnham av NW2	
58 K 8	Marnham cres Grnfd	
92 K 14	Marnock rd SE4	
63 V 15	Maroon st E14	
49 N 18	Marquess gro N1	
49 N 18	Marquess rd N1	
61 O 1	Marquis clo Wemb	
47 Z 19	Marquis rd NW1	
17 R 20	Marquis rd N22	
48 M 19	Marquis rd N4	
48 E 2	Marquis rd N4	
86 H 9	Marrick clo SW15	
9 X 3	Marrilyne av Enf	
64 L 2	Marriott rd E15	
28 M 5	Marriott rd N10	
29 N 5	Marriott rd N4	
48 C 5	Marriott rd N4	
4 D 12	Marriott rd Barnt	
105 S 10	Marryat pl SW19	
105 P 12	Marryat rd SW19	
93 S 10	Marsala rd SE13	
18 M 8	Marsden rd N9	
91 V 8	Marsden st SE15	
47 P 18	Marsden st NW5	
121 N 2	Marsh av Mitch	
13 R 11	Marsh clo NW7	
101 U 1	Marsh Farm rd Twick	
83 V 20	Marsh Farm rd Twick	
69 R 4	Marsh Green rd Dgnhm	
50 H 15	Marsh hill E9	
51 N 5	Marsh la E10	
12 M 12	Marsh la NW7	
11 S 18	Marsh la NW7	
13 O 11	Marsh la NW7	
32 H 3	Marsh la N17	
24 G 1	Marsh la Stanm	
60 H 8	Marsh rd W5	
22 C 14	Marsh rd Pinn	
76 C 11	Marsh st E14	
149 X 2	Marshall gdns SE1	
31 P 4	Marshall rd N17	
140 C 7	Marshall st W1	
39 P 9	Marshalls dri Rom	
78 E 10	Marshalls rd SE18	
38 M 14	Marshalls rd Rom	
154 B 8	Marshalls rd Sutton	
142 C 17	Marshalsea rd SE1	
113 Y 12	Marsham clo Chisl	
148 H 3	Marsham st SW1	
95 N 7	Marshbrook clo SE18	
76 G 8	Marshfield st E14	
64 D 3	Marshgate la E15	
149 Y 11	Marsland rd SE17	
56 D 8	Marston av Dgnhm	
46 E 20	Marston clo NW6	
56 D 8	Marston gdns Dgnhm	
35 R 6	Marston rd Ilf	
102 B 13	Marston rd Tedd	
22 A 3	Marsworth av Pinn	
140 L 8	Mart st E2	
140 L 8	Mart st WC2	
49 T 6	Martaban rd N16	
109 N 7	Martell rd SE21	
50 A 20	Martello st E8	
49 X 18	Martello st E8	
98 L 11	Marten rd E17	
98 J 10	Martens av Bxly Hth	
98 J 11	Martens clo Bxly Hth	
98 J 9	Martens Grove park Bxly Hth	
52 B 17	Martha rd E15	
63 O 19	Martha st E1	
23 R 8	Marthorne cres Harrow	
95 U 8	Martin Bowes rd SE9	
156 K 1	Martin cres Croy	
98 B 13	Martin dene Bxly	
40 E 15	Martin dri Grnfd	
55 U 13	Martin gdns Dgnhm	
119 X 7	Martin gro Mrdn	
142 F 9	Martin la EC4	
55 V 13	Martin rd Dgnhm	
98 B 19	Martin ri Bxly Hth	
51 W 20	Martin st E15	
119 R 4	Martin way SW20	
119 T 7	Martin way Mrdn	
89 V 12	Martindale SW14	
82 B 7	Martindale rd SW12	
89 T 19	Martindale rd SW12	
48 H 13	Martineau rd N5	
102 G 7	Martineau clo Rich	
126 A 3	Martins rd Brom	
140 L 7	Martlett ct WC2	
35 Z 16	Martley dri Ilf	
112 J 5	Marvels clo SE12	
112 K 5	Marvels la SE12	
122 M 11	Marvels la Thntn Hth	
135 O 20	Marville rd SW6	
97 P 8	Marwood clo Welling	
76 B 13	Mary Anns bldgs SE8	
78 F 10	Mary bank SE18	
136 K 10	Mary pl W11	
65 P 15	Mary st E16	
134 B 5	Mary st N1	
31 T 4	Mary ter NW1	
40 J 7	Maryatt av Harrow	
51 Z 15	Maryland pk E15	
51 Y 16	Maryland rd E15	
17 S 20	Maryland rd N22	
122 J 1	Maryland rd Thntn Hth	
108 K 20	Maryland rd Thntn Hth	
52 A 15	Maryland sq E15	
51 Y 16	Maryland st E15	
129 V 18	Marylands rd W9	
139 U 1	Marylebond High st W1	
131 V 19	Marylebond High st W1	
139 W 5	Marylebond la W1	
131 V 19	Marylebond rd NW1	
140 B 4	Marylebone pas W1	
139 U 2	Marylebone st W1	
131 N 19	Marylebone station NW1	
78 D 12	Maryon gro SE7	
46 J 13	Maryon ms NW3	
78 D 12	Maryon rd SE7	
83 Y 19	Marys ter Twick	
136 J 20	Masbro rd W14	
77 X 11	Mascalls rd SE7	
87 R 9	Mascotte rd SW15	
6 G 19	Masefield av N14	
58 H 19	Masefield av S'hall	
10 J 17	Masefield av Stanm	
99 U 3	Masefield clo Erith	
120 F 5	Masefield clo Mitch	
6 G 18	Masefield gdns E6	
62 A 17	Mashie rd W3	
39 R 9	Mashiters hill Rom	
39 M 9	Mashiters wlk Rom	
68 K 1	Maskell rd SW17	
88 K 1	Maskelyne clo SW11	
65 S 19	Mason clo E16	
43 O 7	Mason ct Wemb	
21 N 14	Mason la Wdfd Grn	
150 H 5	Mason st SE17	
133 Y 13	Mason's pl EC1	
139 Z 7	Masons Arm ms W1	
142 D 4	Masons av EC2	
157 N 7	Masons av Croy	
23 V 12	Masons av Harrow	
61 P 12	Masons Grn la W3	
38 M 2	Masons hill SE18	
126 G 7	Masons hill Brom	
133 Z 12	Masons pl EC1	
106 L 20	Masons pl Mitch	
140 C 12	Masons yd SW1	
35 Z 8	Massford ct Ilf	
150 J 6	Massie rd E8	
150 J 6	Massinger st SE17	
63 S 11	Massingham st E1	
76 B 11	Mast Ho ter E14	
95 R 1	Master Gunners pl SE18	
63 U 14	Masters st E6	
82 M 17	Maswell Park cres Hounslw	
82 L 17	Maswell Park rd Hounslw	
52 A 9	Matcham rd E11	
126 E 13	Matfield clo Brom	
81 S 16	Matfield rd Blvdr	
91 U 11	Matham gro SE22	
135 O 6	Matheson rd W14	
140 G 19	Mathew Parker st SW1	
66 K 7	Mathews av E6	
52 C 19	Mathews Pk av E15	
140 U 5	Mathews yd EC1	
133 O 4	Matilda st N1	
153 T 8	Matilda st N1	
153 T 9	Matlock cres Sutton	
153 T 8	Matlock gdns Sutton	
33 U 18	Matlock pl Sutton	
63 U 16	Matlock rd E10	
117 Y 1	Matlock st E1	
88 L 5	Matlock way New Mald	
49 R 14	Matthews st SW11	
49 R 14	Matthias rd N16	
30 H 17	Matthias sq N16	
72 E 2	Mattison rd N4	
67 X 6	Mattock la W13	
51 U 10	Maud gdns E13	
65 R 5	Maud gdns Bark	
32 H 15	Maud rd E10	
91 R 3	Maud rd E13	
32 H 15	Maude rd SE5	
95 U 7	Maude ter E17	
71 T 4	Maudslay rd SE9	
90 A 13	Maudsville cotts W7	
71 V 4	Mauleverer rd SW2	
148 E 4	Maunder rd W7	
30 K 8	Maunsel st SW1	
62 J 18	Maurice av N22	
28 C 14	Maurice st W12	
77 N 12	Maurice wlk NW11	
96 N 8	Mauritius rd SE10	
64 F 17	Maury rd N16	
113 P 19	Muve st E14	
113 P 20	Mavalstone clo Chisl	
64 A 4	Mavelstone rd Chisl	
152 B 10	Maverton rd E3	
151 P 10	Mavis av Epsom	
151 P 11	Mavis clo Epsom	
148 L 20	Mawbey pl SE1	
38 G 9	Mawbey rd SE1	
38 J 10	Mawbey st SW8	
42 J 7	Mawney rd Rom	
39 N 13	Mawney park Rom	
119 T 4	Mawney rd Rom	
74 C 15	Mawson clo SW20	
56 A 12	Mawson la W4	
55 Y 14	Maxey rd SE18	
136 H 5	Maxey rd Dgnhm	
7 T 18	Maxilla gdns W10	
99 P 14	Maxim rd N21	
41 T 1	Maxim rd Drtfrd	
91 W 7	Maxted pk Harrow	
145 Y 19	Maxted rd SE15	
96 M 9	Maxwell rd SW6	
12 L 15	Maxwell rd Welling	
12 L 15	Maxwelton av NW7	
60 E 7	Maxwelton clo NW7	
65 U 6	May gdns Wemb	
20 A 19	May rd E13	
101 T 1	May rd E4	
145 O 12	May rd Twick	
65 U 5	May st W14	
99 X 9	May wlk E13	
90 H 12	May-Place av Drtfrd	
34 J 7	Mayall rd SE24	
57 Z 15	Maybank av E18	
41 Y 14	Maybank av Hornch	
34 K 5	Maybank av Wemb	
116 M 17	Maybank rd E18	
110 A 13	Mayberry pl Surb	
127 Z 12	Maybourne clo SE26	
44 J 19	Maybury clo Brom	
65 X 13	Maybury gdns NW10	
67 Y 6	Maybury rd E13	
68 A 6	Maybury rd Bark	
106 H 13	Maybury rd Bark	
24 G 3	Maybury st SW17	
119 W 8	Maychurch clo Stanm	
94 S 4	Maycross av Mrdn	
95 H 4	Mayday gdns SE3	
122 H 15	Mayday rd Thntn Hth	
150 D 14	Maydwell st SE17	
95 O 13	Mayerne rd SE9	
30 E 9	Mayes rd N22	
30 C 7	Mayes rd N22	
55 N 17	Mayesbrook park	
67 X 4	Mayesbrook rd Ba	
55 O 9	Mayesbrook rd SE	
37 U 20	Mayesford rd Rom	
112 L 9	Mayeswood rd SE	
97 X 2	Mayfair av Bxly Hth	
53 U 7	Mayfair av Ilf	
37 X 19	Mayfair av Rom	
82 M 19	Mayfair av Twick	
118 F 19	Mayfair av Worc P	
111 R 20	Mayfair ct Becknh	
18 A 20	Mayfair gdn N17	
17 Z 20	Mayfair gdns N18	
34 F 1	Mayfair gdns Wdfc Grn	
139 Z 12	Mayfair pl W1	
16 K 3	Mayfair ter N14	
98 B 9	Mayfield Bxly Hth	
32 G 7	Mayfield av E17	
18 S 13	Mayfield av N12	
16 J 8	Mayfield av N14	
72 B 6	Mayfield av W13	
74 B 11	Mayfield av W4	
24 B 17	Mayfield av Harrow	
21 S 20	Mayfield av Wdfd Grn	
34 E 1	Mayfield av Wdfd Grn	
49 U 19	Mayfield clo Enf	
8 M 19	Mayfield clo Enf	
122 C 10	Mayfield cres Thnt Hth	
22 E 12	Mayfield dri Pinn	
27 P 18	Mayfield gdns NW	
59 S 15	Mayfield gdns W7	
65 P 13	Mayfield rd E13	
20 J 7	Mayfield rd E4	
135 N 1	Mayfield rd E8	
49 U 20	Mayfield rd E8	
30 D 18	Mayfield rd N8	
105 W 20	Mayfield rd SW19	
61 S 19	Mayfield rd W3	
81 X 10	Mayfield rd Blvdr	
127 R 11	Mayfield rd Brom	
157 P 19	Mayfield rd Croy	
55 S 5	Mayfield rd Dgnhm	
9 T 9	Mayfield rd Enf	
157 P 18	Mayfield rd S Croy	
154 F 15	Mayfield rd Sutton	
122 C 10	Mayfield rd Thntn Hth	
43 O 7	Mayfields Wemb	
90 A 6	Mayfields clo Wem	
43 Z 18	Mayflower rd SW9	
75 O 6	Mayflower st SE16	
89 N 18	Mayford rd SW12	
88 M 19	Mayford rd SW12	
133 R 7	Maygood st N1	
57 U 2	Maygreen cres Hornch	
45 V 18	Maygrove rd NW6	
20 A 10	Mayhew clo E4	
77 V 17	Mayhill rd SE7	
4 E 19	Mayhill rd Barnt	
115 W 7	Maylands av Hornch	
33 T 15	Maylands dri Sidcp	
44 B 19	Maynard rd E17	
12 N 12	Mayo rd NW10	
50 C 12	Mayo rd Croy	
110 E 9	Mayola rd E5	
110 F 11	Mayow park SE26	
98 G 9	Mayow rd SE26	
99 N 9	Mayplace clo Bxly Hth	
98 J 9	Mayplace av Bxly Hth	
98 F 10	Mayplace Rd east Bxly Hth	
36 D 1	Mayplace Rd west Bxly Hth	
140 J 10	Maypole cres Ilf	
125 Z 4	Mays bldgs WC2	
13 X 2	Mays Hill rd Brom	
4 G 18	Mays la Barnt	
101 P 11	Mays la Barnt	
88 F 9	Mays rd Tedd	
56 L 18	Maysoule rd SW11	
48 C 10	Mayswood gdns Dgnhm	
15 V 11	Mayton st N7	
53 Y 14	Mayville Ilf	
81 R 18	Mayville rd Ilf	
77 O 19	Maywood clo Becknhm	
54 C 1	Maze hill SE10	
94 C 1	Maze hill SE10	
73 P 19	Maze hill SE3	
129 U 2	Maze rd Rich	
	Mazenod av NW6	

78 C 14	Mccall cres SE7
46 G 17	Mccrone ms NW3
63 Y 4	Mccullum rd E3
91 W 6	Mcdermott rd SE15
90 L 2	Mcdowall rd SE5
32 H 4	Mcentee av E17
64 L 3	Mcewan way E15
137 P 3	Mcgregor rd W11
39 P 10	Mcintosh clo Rom
39 P 10	Mcintosh rd Rom
104 L 17	Mckay rd SW20
10 B 8	Mckellar clo Bushey Watf
91 Y 2	Mckerrel rd SE15
145 Z 4	Mcleads ms SW7
80 C 12	Mcleod rd SE2
146 A 4	Mcleods ms SW7
91 S 4	Mcmeil rd SE5
73 R 15	Mcmillan st SE8
7 S 15	Mead clo W4
23 R 5	Mead clo Harrow
39 V 8	Mead clo Rom
20 H 13	Mead cres E4
154 H 7	Mead cres Sutton
25 X 16	Mead ct NW9
37 X 9	Mead gro Rom
50 D 18	Mead pl E9
122 K 20	Mead pl Croy
43 X 17	Mead plat NW10
106 F 15	Mead rd SW19
114 B 15	Mead rd Chisl
12 B 20	Mead rd Edg
102 E 8	Mead rd Rich
149 T 1	Mead row SE1
60 A 14	Mead the W13
125 U 2	Mead the Becknhm
125 W 20	Mead the W Wkhm
155 Y 13	Mead the Wallgtn
126 E 14	Mead way Brom
158 J 2	Mead way Croy
21 Y 15	Mead way Wdfd Grn
12 E 7	Meadfield Edg
107 V 19	Meadfoot rd SW16
102 F 4	Meadlands dri Rich
148 F 14	Meadow av Croy
94 D 8	Meadow bank SE3
116 L 13	Meadow bank Surb
111 O 12	Meadow clo SE6
119 N 9	Meadow clo SW20
118 M 9	Meadow clo SW20
4 H 9	Meadow clo Barnt
113 Z 12	Meadow clo Chisl
9 U 4	Meadow clo Enf
82 G 17	Meadow clo Hounsl
102 J 2	Meadow clo Rich
154 B 4	Meadow clo Sutton
26 L 8	Meadow dri NW4
29 R 9	Meadow dri N10
43 W 19	Meadow garth NW10
12 G 18	Meadow gdns Edg
118 A 14	Meadow hill New Mald
149 O 16	Meadow ms SW8
148 M 18	Meadow pl SW8
106 D 19	Meadow rd SW19
149 N 16	Meadow rd SW8
67 Z 2	Meadow rd Bark
126 A 2	Meadow rd Brom
56 A 18	Meadow rd Dgnhm
100 B 3	Meadow rd Felt
22 A 14	Meadow rd Pinn
56 K 2	Meadow rd Rom
70 F 1	Meadow rd S'hall
58 F 20	Meadow rd S'hall
154 H 9	Meadow rd Sutton
150 A 3	Meadow row SE1
114 B 15	Meadow the Chisl
97 P 17	Meadow view Sidcp
122 H 12	Meadow View rd Thntn Hth
25 Z 15	Meadow way NW9
42 H 12	Meadow way Wemb
23 T 5	Meadow Way the Harrow
70 B 18	Meadow waye Hounsl
34 E 12	Meadow wlk E18
56 A 17	Meadow wlk Dgnhm
152 D 17	Meadow wlk Epsom
155 R 5	Meadow wlk Wallgtn
17 P 1	Meadowbank N21
43 X 1	Meadowbank rd NW9
94 D 11	Meadowcourt rd SE3
127 U 7	Meadowcroft Brom
17 U 9	Meadowcroft rd N13
94 L 11	Meadowside SE9
153 S 20	Meadowside rd Sutton
110 M 11	Meadowview rd SE6
111 N 11	Meadowview rd SE6
98 A 17	Meadowview rd Bxly
152 B 19	Meadowview rd Epsom
54 H 1	Meads la Ilf
36 J 20	Meads la Ilf
30 H 9	Meads rd N22
9 V 6	Meads rd Enf
12 M 19	Meads the Edg
153 R 5	Meads the Sutton
60 C 18	Meadvale rd W5
123 V 16	Meadvale rd Croy
27 Z 19	Meadway NW11
28 B 18	Meadway NW11
17 N 8	Meadway N14
16 L 8	Meadway N14
118 M 9	Meadway SW20
119 N 8	Meadway SW20
4 K 14	Meadway Barnt
125 U 1	Meadway Becknhm
21 Z 6	Meadway Buck Hl
54 J 11	Meadway Ilf
39 V 7	Meadway Rom
83 P 20	Meadway Twick
28 B 19	Meadway clo NW11
4 K 13	Meadway clo Barnt
27 Z 19	Meadway ga NW11
53 R 14	Meanley rd E12
140 E 7	Meard st W1
65 O 6	Meath rd E15
54 C 9	Meath rd Ilf
89 R 1	Meath st SW11
133 N 17	Mecklenburgh pl WC1
133 N 16	Mecklenburgh sq WC1
133 N 15	Mecklenburgh st WC1
132 E 8	Medburn st NW1
133 U 10	Medcalf pl N1
9 Z 1	Medcalf rd Enf
59 U 20	Medcroft gdns SW14
94 F 7	Medebourne clo SE3
88 H 18	Medfield st SW15
63 V 8	Medhurst rd E3
50 C 14	Median rd E5
48 E 9	Medina gro N7
58 A 6	Medina rd N7
90 M 1	Medlar st SE5
45 Y 18	Medley rd NW6
115 R 9	Medomsley clo Sidcp
50 C 16	Mehetabel rd E9
38 M 13	Medora rd SW2
93 R 16	Medora rd SE6
54 C 16	Medusa rd SE6
47 Y 13	Medway clo Ilf
59 W 6	Medway dri Grnfd
59 W 7	Medway gdns Wemb
63 W 7	Medway rd E3
99 W 9	Medway rd Drtfrd
148 F 3	Medwin st SW4
90 B 10	Medwin st SW4
146 B 19	Meek st SW10
94 L 8	Meerbrook rd SE3
65 O 1	Meeson rd E5
50 H 13	Meeson st E5
143 X 13	Meeting Ho all E1
75 N 2	Meeting Ho la E1
91 Z 1	Meeting Ho la SE15
151 M 20	Meeting Ho la SE15
75 N 20	Meeting House la SE15
13 S 11	Melanda clo Chisl
97 Y 1	Melanie clo Bxly Hth
93 S 3	Melba way SE13
17 R 18	Melbourne av N13
71 Z 2	Melbourne av W13
22 K 9	Melbourne av Pinn
119 N 18	Melbourne clo SE20
155 U 11	Melbourne clo Wallgtn
37 Y 14	Melbourne gdns Rom
91 T 10	Melbourne gro SE22
141 O 7	Melbourne pl WC2
51 P 1	Melbourne rd E10
32 J 12	Melbourne rd E17
66 G 5	Melbourne rd E6
105 Z 20	Melbourne rd SW19
54 A 4	Melbourne rd Ilf
53 Z 4	Melbourne rd Ilf
102 F 15	Melbourne rd Tedd
155 T 12	Melbourne rd Wallgtn
90 F 3	Melbourne sq SW9
8 H 20	Melbourne way Enf
70 K 9	Melbury av S'hall
113 S 15	Melbury clo Chisl
145 R 1	Melbury ct W14
145 R 1	Melbury ct W8
104 J 20	Melbury gdns SW20
145 O 1	Melbury rd W14
25 O 16	Melbury rd Harrow
151 N 1	Melbury st SE1
130 M 19	Melbury ter NW1
25 N 16	Melcombe gdns Harrow
131 N 19	Melcombe pl NW1
131 P 19	Melcombe st NW1
55 O 8	Meldrum rd Ilf
111 T 11	Melfield gdns SE6
54 J 17	Melford av Bark
51 Z 7	Melford rd E11
65 R 10	Melford rd E13
32 U 14	Melford rd E17
66 G 10	Melford rd E6
91 Y 20	Melford rd SE22
54 E 8	Melford rd Ilf
122 J 7	Melfort av Thntn Hth
122 K 7	Melfort rd Thntn Hth
48 G 16	Melgund rd N5
130 E 14	Melina pl NW8
74 H 6	Melina rd W12
142 H 16	Melior pl SE1
142 H 16	Meliors st SE1
111 Y 5	Meliot rd SE6
76 M 15	Mell st SE10
155 Z 4	Meller clo Wallgtn
79 V 17	Melling st SE18
49 X 11	Mellington rd E5
67 X 4	Mellish st E14
106 L 13	Mellison rd SW17
62 D 15	Mellitus st W12
35 U 9	Mellows rd Ilf
155 X 11	Mellows rd Wallgtn
113 T 10	Mells cres SE9
88 D 14	Melody rd SW18
137 W 16	Melon pl W8
91 W 1	Melon rd SE15
44 M 15	Melrose av NW2
45 N 14	Melrose av NW2
34 N 22	Melrose av N22
122 E 5	Melrose av SW16
105 X 6	Melrose av SW19
58 L 6	Melrose av Grnfd
107 R 18	Melrose av Mitch
82 L 19	Melrose av Twick
56 H 8	Melrose clo Grnfd
70 H 1	Melrose dri S'hall
144 D 1	Melrose gdns W6
25 T 9	Melrose gdns Edgw
117 Y 7	Melrose gdns New Mald
58 K 6	Melrose gro Grnfd
86 D 3	Melrose rd SW13
87 U 17	Melrose rd SW13
119 Y 2	Melrose rd SW19
73 U 8	Melrose rd W3
28 B 12	Melrose rd d'Pinn
136 E 20	Melrose ter W16
74 M 7	Melrose ter W6
120 C 14	Melsa rd Morden
95 P 2	Melthorpe gdns SE3
57 T 1	Melton gdns Rom
132 D 15	Melton st NW1
104 F 19	Melville av SW20
41 W 16	Melville av Grnfd
157 V 12	Melville av S Croy
17 U 17	Melville gdns N13
32 L 12	Melville rd E17
61 X 2	Melville rd NW10
86 F 2	Melville rd SW13
38 H 3	Melville rd Rom
115 T 5	Melville rd Sidcp
134 A 2	Melville st N1
110 B 20	Melvin rd SE20
65 N 9	Memorial av E15
64 M 8	Memorial av E15
70 E 17	Memorial clo Hounsl
45 R 8	Mendip dri NW2
88 D 8	Mendip rd SW11
99 P 3	Mendip rd Bxly Hth
57 W 2	Mendip rd Hornch
36 Y 16	Mendip rd Ilf
155 N 16	Mendora rd SW6
45 T 13	Menelik rd NW2
109 N 18	Menlo gdns SE19
134 A 17	Mennel st EC1
134 A 17	Mennel st EC1
24 E 17	Mentmore clo Harrow
50 A 20	Mentmore ter E8
135 X 1	Mentmore ter E8
73 W 5	Meon rd W3
121 U 2	Meopham rd Mitch
23 N 2	Mepham cres Harrow
23 N 2	Mepham gdns Harrow
141 R 15	Mepham st SE1
98 F 9	Mera dri Bxly Hth
93 X 9	Mercator rd SE13
140 H 6	Mercer st WC21
63 N 12	Merceron st E1
135 X 18	Merceron st E1
47 Y 10	Mercers rd N19
123 N 4	Mercham rd Thntn Hth
63 Z 10	Merchant st E3
111 W 3	Merchiston rd SE6
114 C 2	Merchland rd SE9
93 V 9	Mercia gro SE13
87 S 13	Mercier rd SW15
72 F 15	Mercury rd Brentf
87 R 18	Mere clo SW19
124 F 18	Mere end Croy
156 D 10	Merebank la Croy
45 N 14	Meredith av NW2
133 V 14	Meredith st EC1
65 T 10	Meredith st E13
86 G 4	Meredyth rd SW13
120 D 14	Merevale cres Mrdn
5 T 1	Mereway rd Twick
127 V 3	Merewood rd Brom
98 J 4	Merewood rd Bxly Hth
126 C 12	Mereworth clo Brom
79 O 20	Mereworth dri SE18
36 B 4	Meriden clo Ilf
78 A 18	Meridian rd SE7
94 C 10	Merifield rd SE9
87 T 10	Merivale rd SW15
41 O 2	Merivale rd Harrow
127 U 1	Merlewood dri Chisl
113 T 20	Merlewood dri Chisl
43 W 3	Merley ct NW9
25 N 4	Merlin cres Edgw
112 E 8	Merlin gdns Brom
124 M 10	Merlin gro Becknhm
125 N 10	Merlin gro Becknhm
36 A 1	Merlin gro Ilf
52 M 7	Merlin rd E12
96 M 9	Merlin rd Well
97 O 11	Merlin rd Welling
133 T 14	Merlin st WC1
40 F 9	Merlins av Harrow
142 E 16	Mermaid ct SE1
150 D 1	Merrick sq SE1
7 V 19	Merridene N21
118 M 20	Merrilands rd Worc Pk
96 G 20	Merrilees rd Sidcp
95 N 1	Merriman rd SE3
94 M 1	Merriman rd SE3
90 F 12	Merrington rd SW6
11 T 15	Merrion av Stanm
92 L 13	Merritt rd SE4
8 K 18	Merrivale N14
55 U 4	Merrivale Edg
55 U 4	Merrivale Edgw
35 O 13	Merrivale av Ilf
153 O 19	Merrow rd Sutton
150 F 11	Merrow st SE17
159 V 14	Merrow way Croy
11 T 18	Merryfield gdns Stanm
94 D 5	Merryfield rd SE3
20 D 3	Merryhill clo E4
7 N 15	Merryhills dri Enf
6 K 14	Merryhills dri Enf
32 L 9	Mersey rd E17
25 R 16	Mersham dri NW9
110 A 20	Mersham dri SE20
74 K 17	Merthyr ter SW13
74 C 11	Merton av W4
41 N 15	Merton av Grnfd
92 G 10	Merton clo SE4
127 Z 12	Merton gdns Brom
105 T 20	Merton Hall gdns SW20
105 T 20	Merton Hall rd SW19
119 U 1	Merton Hall rd SW19
106 D 19	Merton High st SW19
47 N 6	Merton la N6
33 T 17	Merton rd E17
123 W 17	Merton rd SE25
106 A 18	Merton rd SW19
67 Y 1	Merton rd Bark
8 A 4	Merton rd Enf
41 N 4	Merton rd Harrow
36 K 20	Merton rd Ilf
55 Z 1	Merton rd Rom
46 J 19	Merton ri NW3
92 F 13	Merttins st SE15
90 F 12	Mervan rd SW2
114 C 6	Mervyn av SE9
71 Z 8	Mervyn rd W13
61 X 18	Messaline av W3
54 M 12	Messent rd SE9
95 W 15	Messeter pl SE9
129 U 1	Messina av NW6
89 P 10	Meteor st SW11

156 A 16 Meteor wy Wallgtn
149 U 11 Methley st SE11
25 P 2 Methuen clo Edg
25 O 2 Methuen clo Edg
29 T 9 Methuen pk N10
81 V 10 Methuen rd Blvdr
98 B 11 Methuen rd Bxly Hth
25 O 3 Methuen rd Edg
136 F 1 Methwold rd W10
35 O 16 Mews the Ilf
87 W 15 Mexfield rd SW15
8 K 3 Meyer gro Enf
81 Y 16 Meyer rd Erith
141 W 14 Meymott st SE1
50 E 20 Meynell cres E9
50 F 20 Meynell rd E9
39 Z 1 Meynell rd Rom
44 F 17 Meyrick rd NW10
88 H 8 Meyrick rd SW11
110 K 9 Miall rd SE26
134 C 12 Micawber ct N1
134 C 11 Micawber st N1
52 A 4 Michael rd E11
123 R 7 Michael rd SE25
88 B 1 Michael rd SW6
84 J 9 Michaels row Rich
94 C 15 Micheldever rd SE12
101 X 6 Michelham gdns Twick
53 S 12 Michigan av E12
14 J 13 Michleham down N12
153 R 13 Mickleham gdns Sutton
159 X 15 Mickleham way Croy
135 U 15 Micklethwaite rd SW6
12 L 11 Middle dene NW7
130 F 3 Middle field NW8
29 Z 16 Middle la N8
101 V 14 Middle la Tedd
113 S 1 Middle Park av SE9
95 N 17 Middle Park av SE9
94 M 15 Middle Park av SE9
41 P 5 Middle path Harrow
65 S 8 Middle rd E13
121 W 3 Middle rd SW16
5 V 19 middle rd Barnt
41 R 5 Middle rd Harrow
118 K 17 Middle row W10
141 Z 1 Middle st EC1
156 L 4 Middle st Croy
141 S 7 Middle Temple la EC4
121 X 4 Middle way SW16
23 V 7 Middle Way the Harrow
142 H 13 Middle yd SE1
130 F 3 Middlefield NW8
60 A 14 Middlefield Ilf
36 A 19 Middlefield gdns Ilf
35 Z 20 Middlefield gdns Ilf
28 K 19 Middleham gdns N18
18 K 19 Middleham rd N18
8 K 18 Middlesborough rd N18
74 E 12 Middlesex ct W4
141 Z 1 Middlesex pas EC1
143 N 5 Middlesex st E1
142 M 3 Middlesex st E1
50 D 5 Middlesex wharf E5
20 A 11 Middleton av E4
19 Z 12 Middleton av E4
59 S 5 Middleton av Grnfd
115 S 14 Middleton av Sidcp
19 Y 12 Middleton clo E4
35 Z 19 Middleton gdns Ilf
36 A 20 Middleton gdns Ilf
47 Z 15 Middleton gro N7
134 M 1 Middleton rd E8
135 O 1 Middleton rd E8
45 X 1 Middleton rd NW11
120 C 14 Middleton rd Mrdn
120 J 17 Middleton rd Mrdn
119 Z 15 Middleton rd Mrdn
117 V 5 Middleton rd New Mald
135 W 11 Middleton st E2
63 N 8 Middleton st E2
93 X 9 Middleton way SE13
120 G 17 Middleton way Carsh
28 B 17 Middleway NW11
98 K 7 Midfield av Bxly Hth
115 R 20 Midfield way Orp
132 C 18 Midford pl W1
28 A 14 Midholm NW11
43 R 5 Midholm Wemb
28 A 13 Midholm clo NW11
158 J 4 Midholm rd Croy
132 K 13 Midhope st WC1
29 O 11 Midhurst av N10

122 G 16 Midhurst av Croy
98 D 15 Midhurst hill Bxly Hth
71 Z 6 Midhurst rd W13
72 A 8 Midhurst rd W13
44 M 3 Midland Brent ter NW2
51 U 3 Midland rd E10
132 H 12 Midland rd NW1
62 B 12 Midland ter NW1
45 O 10 Midland ter NW2
63 X 13 Midlothian rd E3
107 V 1 Midmoor rd SW12
105 R 19 Midmoor rd SW19
44 B 12 Midstrath rd NW10
82 D 11 Midsummer av Hounsl
119 V 17 Midway Sutton
66 K 2 Miers clo E6
35 O 14 Mighell av Ilf
146 C 12 Milborne gro SW10
50 D 19 Milborne st E9
94 A 17 Milborough cres SE12
141 X 19 Milcote st SE1
50 B 11 Mildenhall rd E5
49 O 16 Mildmay av N1
49 O 16 Mildmay gro N1
49 P 15 Mildmay pk N1
49 N 15 Mildmay rd N1
38 K 15 Mildmay rd Rom
49 P 17 Mildmay st N1
40 L 16 Mildred av Grnfd
63 T 12 Mile End pl E1
63 O 13 Mile End rd E1
91 U 16 Mile rd SE3
121 U 19 Mile rd Wallgtn
32 F 6 Milend the E17
142 F 10 Miles la EC4
116 M 9 Miles pl Surb
120 H 5 Miles rd Mitch
148 K 15 Miles st SW8
15 Y 9 Miles way N20
13 Y 17 Milespit hill NW7
109 U 18 Milestone rd SE19
62 G 20 Milfoil st W12
80 M 15 Milford clo SE2
25 P 3 Milford gdns Edg
42 G 14 Milford gdns Wemb
154 C 7 Milford gro Sutton
141 R 7 Milford la WC2
93 R 19 Milford rd SE6
72 A 3 Milford rd W13
58 H 20 Milford rd S'hall
70 H 1 Milford rd S'hall
89 S 6 Milford st SW8
142 B 5 Milk st EC2
78 L 4 Milk st E16
112 H 14 Milk st Brom
75 P 1 Milk yd E1
34 J 1 Milkwell gdns Wdfd Grn
90 K 11 Milkwood rd SE24
4 H 19 Mill bridge Barnt
155 O 3 Mill clo Carsh
4 H 7 Mill corner Barnt
100 C 1 Mill Farm cres Twick
110 A 8 Mill gdns SE26
121 Q 16 Mill Grn rd Mitch
13 H 16 Mill Hill cir NW7
14 D 20 Mill Hill East sta NW7
14 D 20 Mill Hill Estate sta NW7
73 U 4 Mill Hill gro W3
13 T 17 Mill Hill park NW7
86 G 6 Mill Hill rd SW13
73 S 4 Mill Hill rd W3
73 T 4 Mill Hill ter W3
121 U 11 Mill house Mitch
45 T 16 Mill la NW6
155 N 8 Mill la Carsh
156 E 5 Mill la Croy
152 E 18 Mill la Epsom
37 Y 19 Mill la Rom
21 R 17 Mill la Wdfd Grn
31 Z 11 Mill Mead rd N17
63 X 18 Mill pl E14
155 N 7 Mill pl Carsh
113 Y 20 Mill pl Chisl
99 X 11 Mill pl Drtfrd
116 K 5 Mill pl Kingst
83 Z 6 Mill plat Islwth
84 A 6 Mill plat Islwth
83 Y 5 Mill Plat av Islwth
77 W 3 Mill rd E16
106 E 17 Mill rd SW19
81 X 20 Mill rd Erith
53 W 9 Mill rd Ilf
101 O 4 Mill rd Twick
12 B 17 Mill ridge Edg
134 L 5 Mill row N1
143 P 18 Mill st SE1

139 Z 8 Mill st W1
116 K 6 Mill st Kingst
126 D 4 Mill vale Brom
158 E 5 Mill View gdns Croy
13 N 15 Mill way NW7
53 W 16 Millais av E12
25 P 7 Millais gdns Edg
51 V 12 Millais rd E11
8 H 18 Millais rd Enf
117 Z 16 Millais rd New Mald
150 D 14 Millais st SE17
49 S 15 Millard clo N16
148 K 7 Millbank SW1
100 C 9 Millbourne rd Felt
96 F 10 Millbrook av Welling
39 S 6 Millbrook gdns Rom
38 A 17 Millbrook gdns Rom
18 L 6 Millbrook rd N9
90 H 8 Millbrook rd SW9
75 N 14 Milledge st SE16
106 G 15 Miller rd SW19
122 E 20 Miller rd Croy
132 A 7 Miller st NW1
49 U 13 Millers av E8
49 U 14 Millers ter E8
58 L 8 Millet rd Grnfd
32 J 5 Millfield av N17
47 N 8 Millfield la N6
47 O 7 Millfield pl N6
18 C 14 Millfield rd N18
25 W 7 Millfield rd Edg
82 C 20 Millfield rd Hounsl
50 G 10 Millfields rd E5
25 Y 1 Milling rd Edg
133 N 18 Millman ms WC1
133 O 19 Millman pl WC1
128 J 8 Millman rd NW6
133 N 18 Millman st WC1
92 J 6 Millmark gro SE14
9 Y 8 Millmarsh la Enf
55 S 7 Millner rd Dgnhm
64 F 16 Mills gro E14
154 M 2 Millside Carsh
76 B 8 Millwall Dock rd E14
63 N 15 Millward st E1
40 E 19 Millway gdns Grnfd
82 M 13 Millwood rd Hounsl
83 N 13 Millwood rd Hounsl
136 J 2 Millwood st W10
146 G 16 Milman's rd SW10
95 P 13 Milne gdns SE9
22 G 1 Milnefield Pinn
83 P 18 Milner dri Twick
13 V 3 Milner pl N1
155 N 9 Milner pl Carsh
64 M 9 Milner st E15
106 A 19 Milner rd SW19
116 G 7 Milner rd Kingst
120 F 11 Milner rd Mrdn
123 N 5 Milner rd Thntn Hth
133 V 2 Milner sq N1
47 N 4 Milner st SW3
73 X 16 Milnthorpe rd W4
144 J 1 Milson rd W14
66 B 1 Milton av E6
61 X 4 Milton av NW10
25 U 11 Milton av NW9
47 V 1 Milton av N6
4 J 15 Milton av Barnt
123 P 18 Milton av Croy
57 U 6 Milton av Hornch
154 H 8 Milton av Sutton
28 C 17 Milton clo NW7
154 G 6 Milton clo Sutton
36 A 19 Milton cres Ilf
75 W 18 Milton Ct rd SE14
16 J 16 Milton gro N11
49 P 13 Milton gro N16
47 U 1 Milton pk N6
33 O 12 Milton rd E17
13 T 15 Milton rd NW7
30 J 12 Milton rd N15
47 V 1 Milton rd N6
90 H 14 Milton rd SE24
85 X 9 Milton rd SW14
106 C 15 Milton rd SW19
73 X 2 Milton rd W3
59 W 20 Milton rd W7
81 R 11 Milton rd Blvdr
147 P 18 Milton rd Croy
100 H 19 Milton rd Hampt
23 U 13 Milton rd Harrow
107 P 18 Milton rd Mitch
39 U 18 Milton rd Rom
153 Y 7 Milton rd Sutton
155 W 14 Milton rd Wallgtn
96 J 1 Milton rd Welling
65 T 5 Milton st E13
54 K 6 Milverton gdns Ilf
45 N 20 Milverton rd NW6
128 D 1 Milverton rd NW6
149 T 11 Milverton st SE11

113 X 9 Milverton way SE9
143 X 1 Milward st E1
87 V 2 Mimosa st SW6
150 M 9 Mina rd SE17
105 Z 20 Mina rd SW19
111 Z 3 Minard rd SE6
93 Y 19 Minard rd SE6
16 J 11 Minchenden cres N14
142 K 8 Mincing la EC3
109 Z 20 Minden rd SE20
108 C 13 Minehead rd SW16
40 G 9 Minehead rd Harrow
147 U 6 Minera ms SW1
79 T 12 Mineral st SE18
62 A 5 Minerva clo Sidcp
33 R 1 Minerva rd E4
61 X 10 Minerva rd NW10
116 L 3 Minerva rd Kingst
135 W 9 Minerva st E2
62 A 5 Minet av NW10
62 A 5 Minet gdns NW10
90 J 5 Minet rd SW9
136 E 19 Minford gdns W14
64 B 20 Ming st E14
116 M 11 Minniedale Surb
117 N 10 Minniedale rd Surb
150 K 8 Minnow st SE17
143 N 8 Minories EC3
89 X 3 Minshull st SW8
63 T 2 Minson rd E9
86 D 17 Minstead gdns SW15
118 A 15 Minstead way New Mald
153 Y 4 Minster av Sutton
45 T 15 Minster av NW2
112 H 17 Minster rd Brom
155 R 9 Mint rd Wallgtn
142 B 17 Mint st SE1
156 M 5 Mint wk Croy
157 N 5 Mint wk Croy
17 W 11 Mintern clo N13
25 O 17 Mintern rd N1
134 G 8 Mintern st N1
70 H 10 Minterne av S'hall
25 O 17 Minterne rd Harrow
135 P 17 Mirabel rd SW6
47 W 4 Miranda rd N19
78 A 10 Mirfield st SE7
79 U 13 Miriam rd SE18
112 M 7 Mirror path SE9
120 D 14 Missenden gdns Mrdn
32 J 15 Mission gro E17
121 T 15 Mitcham common Mitch
107 V 13 Mitcham la SW16
120 L 9 Mitcham pk Mitch
66 L 9 Mitcham rd E6
121 Z 14 Mitcham rd SW17
106 L 12 Mitcham rd SW17
122 C 16 Mitcham rd Croy
36 L 20 Mitcham rd Ilf
80 F 13 Mitchell clo SE2
17 X 15 Mitchell rd N13
134 B 15 Mitchell st EC1
43 W 18 Mitchell way NW10
49 O 19 Mitchison rd N1
31 W 9 Mitchley rd N17
48 A 7 Mitford rd N4
142 B 5 Mitre ct EC2
141 U 17 Mitre rd SE1
142 M 6 Mitre sq EC3
142 L 6 Mitre st EC3
27 Z 10 Moat cres N3
65 Y 8 Moat dri E13
23 O 13 Moat dri Harrow
40 F 19 Moat Farm rd Grnfd
90 D 7 Moat pl SW9
61 T 16 Moat pl W3
9 S 13 Moat side Enf
89 Y 17 Moberly rd SW4
47 N 18 Modbury gdns NW5
47 O 17 Modbury st NW5
87 P 9 Modder pl SW15
72 B 4 Model cotts W13
113 R 6 Model Farm clo SE9
129 P 20 Modena st W10
141 W 5 Modern ct EC4
120 G 7 Moffat gdns Mitch
17 N 18 Moffat rd N13
106 K 9 Moffat rd SW17
122 M 4 Moffat rd Thntn Hth
123 N 3 Moffat rd Thntn Hth
83 X 12 Mogden la Islwth
157 W 20 Moir clo S Croy
95 U 9 Moira rd SE9
75 S 12 Moland mead SE16
114 B 7 Molescroft SE9
153 S 4 Molesey dri Sutton
87 Y 3 Molesford rd SW6

93 T 8 Molesworth st SE13
9 W 8 Mollison av Enf
9 X 4 Mollison av Enf
156 B 14 Mollison dri Wallgtn
155 Z 17 Mollison dri Wallgtn
24 M 9 Mollison way Edg
25 O 8 Mollison way Edg
138 M 3 Molyneux st W1
92 D 4 Mona rd SE15
65 P 15 Mona st E16
81 S 9 Monarch rd Blvdr
8 B 9 Monastery gdns Enf
148 G 3 Monck st SW1
91 R 9 Monclar rd SE5
138 J 20 Moncorvo cl SW7
91 X 4 Moncrieff st SE5
53 P 17 Monega rd E12
52 K 18 Monega rd E7
64 K 16 Moness st E14
64 A 1 Monier rd E3
110 L 19 Monivea rd Becknhm
65 R 19 Monk dri E16
78 J 10 Monk st SE18
16 E 1 Monkfrith av N14
6 D 20 Monkfrith av N14
16 D 2 Monkfrith clo N14
16 D 2 Monkfrith way N14
21 V 17 Monkhams av Wdfd Grn
21 V 17 Monkhams dri Wdfd Grn
21 X 11 Monkhams la Buck Hl
21 T 15 Monkhams la Wdfd Grn
119 T 8 Monkleigh rd Mrdn
5 S 20 Monks av Barnt
15 S 1 Monks av Barnt
80 H 10 Monks clo SE2
7 X 9 Monks clo Enf
16 P 16 Monks dri W3
125 O 13 Monks Orchard rd Becknhm
43 U 16 Monks park Wemb
43 T 19 Monks Park gdns Wemb
7 X 8 Monks rd Enf
125 P 16 Monks way Becknhm
154 B 4 Monksdene gdns Sutton
35 W 11 Monkswood gdns Ilf
96 L 4 Monkton rd Welling
149 V 5 Monkton st SE11
27 V 13 Monkville av NW11
142 B 2 Monkwell sq EC2
34 H 11 Monmouth av E18
102 F 19 Monmouth av Kingst
97 N 9 Monmouth clo Welling
137 W 6 Monmouth pl W2
66 F 10 Monmouth rd E6
18 M 8 Monmouth rd N9
19 P 10 Monmouth rd N9
137 W 7 Monmouth rd W2
56 B 15 Monmouth rd Dgnhm
140 J 7 Monmouth st WC2
47 V 10 Monnery rd N19
11 T 6 Monnow rd SE1
23 S 1 Monro gdns Harrow
8 M 7 Monroe cres Enf
127 R 14 Mons way Brom
48 J 9 Monsell rd N4
33 X 2 Monserratt av Wdfd Grn
62 H 6 Monson rd NW10
75 S 20 Monson rd SE14
92 L 18 Montacute rd SE6
10 G 2 Montacute rd Bushey Watf
159 T 20 Montacute rd Mrdn
120 E 15 Montacute rd Mrdn
19 N 15 Montagu cres N18
19 N 14 Montagu gdns N18
139 R 2 Montagu mans W1
139 P 2 Montagu Ms north W1
139 P 4 Montagu Ms south W1
139 P 4 Montagu Ms west W1
139 P 2 Montagu pl W1
140 H 1 Montagu pl NW4
26 G 19 Montagu rd NW4
19 O 12 Montagu rd N18
139 R 2 Montagu row W1
139 P 3 Montagu sq W1
139 R 4 Montagu st W1
92 M 10 Montague av SE4
93 N 10 Montague av SE4
71 V 3 Montague av W7
142 F 13 Montague clo SE1

141 Z 3 Montague ct EC1
61 P 19 Montague gdns W3
155 V 9 Montague gdns Wallgtn
64 F 20 Montague pl E14
64 F 19 Montague pl E14
64 F 20 Montague pl E14
132 H 20 Montague pl WC1
52 B 8 Montague rd E11
49 W 15 Montague rd E8
31 W 12 Montague rd N15
30 C 16 Montague rd N8
105 Z 18 Montague rd SW19
60 B 17 Montague rd W13
71 V 4 Montague rd W7
122 J 19 Montague rd Croy
82 K 7 Montague rd Hounsl
84 K 15 Montague rd Rich
70 B 10 Montague rd S'hall
140 J 1 Montague st W1
70 B 9 Montague waye S'hall
21 O 16 Montalt rd Wdfd Grn
21 P 15 Montalt rd Wdfd Grn
107 O 3 Montana rd SW17
105 O 20 Montana rd SW20
113 Z 7 Montbelle rd SE9
126 F 15 Montcalm clo Brom
78 A 18 Montcalm rd SE7
135 O 15 Montclare st E2
54 C 18 Monteagle av Bark
89 S 5 Montefiore st SW8
63 Y 3 Monteith rd E3
92 K 19 Montem rd SE23
118 A 9 Montem rd New Mald
48 C 5 Montem st N4
117 Z 8 Monten rd New Mald
29 W 17 Montenotte rd N8
149 S 11 Montford pl SE11
87 R 20 Montford pl SW19
96 J 15 Montgomery clo Sidcp
66 E 13 Montgomery gdns E6
73 V 10 Montgomery rd W4
12 A 20 Montgomery rd Edg
88 M 16 Montholme rd SW11
82 R 2 Monthorpe st WC1
86 L 12 Montolieu gdns SW15
86 E 15 Montpelier av W5
97 W 19 Montpelier av Bxly
66 B 8 Montpelier gdns E6
55 T 1 Montpelier gdns Rom
47 V 14 Montpelier gro NW5
138 M 20 Montpelier ms SW7
138 L 20 Montpelier pl SW7
28 C 6 Montpelier rd N3
151 X 20 Montpelier rd SE15
92 A 1 Montpelier rd W5
60 G 15 Montpelier rd W5
154 E 8 Montpelier ri Sutton
45 S 1 Montpelier ri NW11
42 F 5 Montpelier ri Wemb
94 C 4 Montpelier row SE3
84 D 19 Montpelier row Twick
138 L 20 Montpelier sq SW7
138 M 20 Montpelier st SW7
94 B 5 Montpelier vale SE3
45 S 1 Montpelier way NW11
138 L 20 Montpelier wlk SW7
110 C 16 Montrave rd SE20
141 O 8 Montreal pl WC2
54 A 2 Montreal rd Ilf
90 A 20 Montrell rd SW2
128 M 7 Montrose av NW6
25 W 7 Montrose av Edg
97 O 18 Montrose av Sidcp
82 L 20 Montrose av Twick
96 G 8 Montrose av Welling
96 J 7 Montrose clo Welling
42 J 17 Montrose cres Wemb
138 G 20 Montrose ct SW7
120 M 5 Montrose gdns Mitch
154 B 4 Montrose gdns Sutton
139 U 20 Montrose pl SW1
23 W 8 Montrose rd Harrow
87 S 10 Montserrat rd SW15
142 H 10 Monument st EC3
75 P 1 Monza st E1
75 R 7 Moodkee st SE16
75 R 7 Moody st E1
4 H 12 Moon la Barnt
133 V 4 Moon st N1

94 F 11 Moons ct SE12
134 E 20 Moor la EC2
142 D 1 Moor la EC2
142 F 2 Moor pl EC2
140 G 7 Moor st W1
107 Z 6 Moorcroft rd SW16
22 A 16 Moorcroft way Pinn
95 Y 1 Moordown SE18
78 L 20 Moordown SE18
156 E 18 Moore clo Wallgtn
135 X 19 Moore Pk rd SW6
145 W 20 Moore Pk rd SW6
108 K 14 Moore st SE19
147 O 5 Moore st SW3
31 Q 9 Moorefield rd SW16
112 D 19 Moorland rd Brom
65 O 3 Moorey clo E15
65 O 4 Moorey clo E15
60 H 11 Moorfield av W5
142 E 2 Moorfields EC2
142 F 2 Moorgate EC2
137 T 5 Moorhouse rd W2
24 H 10 Moorhouse rd Harrow
38 H 3 Moorland clo Rom
152 B 11 Moormead rd Epsom
83 Z 16 Moormead rd Twick
90 B 2 Moorside rd Brom
25 O 17 Moot ct NW9
45 N 11 Mora rd NW2
44 M 11 Mora rd NW2
134 C 13 Mora st EC1
64 B 19 Morant st E14
90 E 1 Morat st SW9
46 G 16 Moravian pl SW3
63 P 8 Moravian st E2
39 O 3 Moray clo Rom
48 D 6 Moray ms N4
48 E 5 Moray rd N4
39 O 3 Moray way Rom
103 T 17 Morcoombe clo Kingst
92 Z 4 Mordaunt rd NW10
90 C 4 Mordaunt st SW9
93 U 3 Morden clo SE13
119 Z 9 Morden ct Mrdn
41 X 15 Morden gdns Grnfd
120 G 9 Morden gdns Mrdn
120 C 7 Morden hall Mrdn
120 D 6 Morden Hall park Mrdn
120 B 7 Morden Hall rd Mrdn
93 U 4 Morden hill SE13
119 U 13 Morden park Mrdn
94 F 5 Morden rd SE3
94 E 4 Morden rd SE3
106 A 20 Morden rd SW19
36 K 20 Morden rd Ilf
120 A 3 Morden rd Mitch
37 Z 20 Morden rd Rom
38 A 20 Morden rd Rom
94 E 5 Morden Rd ms SE3
93 S 5 Morden st SE13
119 X 18 Morden way Sutton
76 M 9 Morden Wharf rd SE10
65 P 17 Morden clo E16
57 Z 16 Morecambe clo E1
11 V 14 Morecambe gdns Stanm
150 C 8 Morecambe st SE17
18 A 13 Morecombe terr N18
18 J 15 Moree way N18
94 H 8 Morehead way SE3
133 Y 12 Moreland st EC1
20 E 10 Moreland way E4
88 L 18 Morella rd SW12
110 H 9 Moremead rd SE6
110 N 10 Moremead rd SE6
93 R 18 Morena st SE6
117 T 17 Moresby av Surb
49 Z 5 Moresby rd E5
50 A 4 Moresby rd E5
83 S 1 Moreton av Islwth
50 B 5 Moreton clo E5
13 Z 20 Moreton clo NW7
31 O 18 Moreton clo N15
148 C 9 Moreton pl SW1
31 P 18 Moreton rd N15
157 P 11 Moreton rd S Croy
152 H 3 Moreton rd Worc Pk
148 E 8 Moreton st SW1
148 C 9 Moreton ter SW1
33 Y 13 Morgan av E17
48 F 16 Morgan rd N7
112 E 19 Morgan rd Brom
65 P 14 Morgan st E16
63 W 9 Morgan st E3
142 J 14 Morgans la SE1
146 J 19 Morgans wlk SW11
88 A 12 Morie st SW18

50 L 4 Morieux rd E10
107 P 10 Moring rd SW17
123 S 19 Morland av Croy
99 Z 14 Morland av Drtfrd
46 B 4 Morland clo NW11
70 L 3 Morland gdns S'hall
32 G 17 Morland rd E17
110 F 16 Morland rd SE20
123 T 18 Morland rd Croy
69 T 2 Morland rd Dgnhm
24 J 14 Morland rd Harrow
53 Y 6 Morland rd Ilf
154 E 12 Morland rd Sutton
33 W 2 Morley av E4
18 K 14 Morley av N18
30 J 6 Morley av N22
12 G 9 Morley cres Edg
24 E 9 Morley cres Stanm
24 F 9 Morley Cres east Stanm
24 E 10 Morley Cres west Stanm
8 B 4 Morley hill Enf
51 U 15 Morley rd E10
65 P 6 Morley rd E15
93 U 11 Morley rd SE13
67 S 4 Morley rd Bark
37 Y 17 Morley rd Rom
119 V 20 Morley rd Sutton
84 F 16 Morley rd Twick
141 U 19 Morley st SE1
13 Z 20 Morlton clo NW7
91 N 3 Morna rd SE5
50 B 17 Morning la E9
152 L 3 Morningside rd Worc Pk
135 N 8 Mornington av W14
126 M 7 Mornington av Brom
35 V 20 Mornington av Ilf
21 S 13 Mornington clo Wdfd Grn
132 A 8 Mornington cres NW1
64 A 9 Mornington gro E3
132 A 9 Mornington pl NW1
131 Z 8 Mornington pl NW1
52 B 2 Mornington rd E11
20 J 2 Mornington rd E4
75 Z 20 Mornington rd SE8
58 K 12 Mornington rd Grnfd
21 S 13 Mornington rd Wdfd Grn
131 Y 8 Mornington st NW1
132 A 9 Mornington ter NW1
131 Y 7 Mornington ter NW1
102 E 9 Mornington wlk Rich
142 J 19 Morocco st SE7
63 S 4 Morpeth gro E9
63 S 9 Morpeth rd E9
63 S 9 Morpeth st E2
148 B 3 Morpeth ter SW1
54 K 9 Morrab gdns Ilf
53 T 15 Morris av E12
87 X 17 Morris gdns SW18
84 D 15 Morris rd E14
51 Y 12 Morris rd E15
56 C 7 Morris rd Dgnhm
83 V 7 Morris rd Islwth
39 Z 1 Morris rd Rom
63 N 18 Morris st E1
90 A 19 Morrish rd SW2
31 S 10 Morrison av N17
66 K 6 Morrison rd Bark
89 O 6 Morrison st SW11
129 W 14 Morshead rd W9
113 T 10 Morston gro SE9
89 X 16 Morten clo SW4
31 O 4 Morteyne rd N17
64 L 4 Mortham st E15
107 X 3 Mortimer clo SW16
129 Y 6 Mortimer cres NW6
132 D 18 Mortimer mkt WC1
129 X 6 Mortimer pl NW6
66 F 9 Mortimer rd E6
128 D 12 Mortimer rd NW10
134 K 2 Mortimer rd N1
49 S 20 Mortimer rd N1
60 C 17 Mortimer rd W13
81 Z 17 Mortimer rd Erith
120 L 5 Mortimer rd Mitch
138 H 11 Mortimer sq W11
140 I 33 Mortimer st W1
139 Z 4 Mortimer st W1
47 R 12 Mortimer ter NW5
85 Y 6 Mortlake High st SW14
65 W 16 Mortlake rd E16
54 D 13 Mortlake rd Ilf
85 S 4 Mortlake rd Rich
73 P 19 Mortlake rd Rich
91 Z 2 Mortlock gdns SE15
16 J 13 Morton rd N14

Ref	Entry
135 X 6	Morton ms SW5
149 S 2	Morton pl SE1
65 O 2	Morton rd E15
134 D 2	Morton rd N1
80 L 9	Morton rd Blvdr
120 F 12	Morton rd Mrdn
16 H 12	Morton way N14
90 F 14	Morval rd SW2
100 L 6	Morven rd SW17
64 A 6	Morville st E3
140 F 2	Morwell st WC1
137 X 8	Moscow pl W2
137 W 4	Moscow rd W2
91 P 1	Mosedale st SE5
30 H 6	Moselle av N22
30 B 12	Moselle clo N8
31 V 2	Moselle pl N17
22 D 8	Moss clo Pinn
15 O 19	Moss Hall cres N12
15 N 19	Moss Hall gro N12
22 C 8	Moss la Pinn
39 V 18	Moss la Rom
56 F 20	Moss rd Dgnhm
36 A 9	Moss ter Ilf
88 K 9	Mossbury rd SW11
81 T 12	Mossdown clo Blvdr
35 Z 8	Mossford ct Ilf
36 B 10	Mossford grn Ilf
36 B 5	Mossford la Ilf
63 X 12	Mossford st E3
151 Z 6	Mossington rd SE16
57 P 11	Mossington rd SE16
110 C 16	Mosslea rd SE20
127 C 12	Mosslea rd Brom
146 M 6	Mossop st SW3
119 V 7	Mossville gdns Mrdn
43 N 14	Mostyn av Wemb
42 L 14	Mostyn av Wemb
128 F 11	Mostyn gdns NW10
63 Z 7	Mostyn gro E3
119 W 1	Mostyn rd SW19
90 F 3	Mostyn rd SW9
26 A 3	Mostyn rd Edg
25 Z 2	Mostyn rd Edg
127 R 15	Mosul way Brom
139 S 20	Motcombe st SW1
13 R 7	Mote end NW7
89 U 4	Motley av EC2
13 N 17	Motorway m1 NW7
118 G 13	Motspur pk New Mald
113 O 2	Mottingham gdns SE9
112 K 2	Mottingham hall SE9
112 L 1	Mottingham la SE9
113 N 2	Mottingham la SE9
94 K 19	Mottingham la SE9
19 S 1	Mottingham rd N9
113 U 8	Mottingham rd SE9
80 A 10	Mottisfont rd SE2
79 Z 9	Mottisfont rd SE2
63 R 2	Moulins rd E9
62 D 4	Moulton av Hounsl
113 V 8	Mound the SE9
31 X 19	Moundfield rd N16
91 X 19	Mount Adon pk SE22
86 E 19	Mount Angelus rd SW15
84 K 13	Mount Ararat rd Rich
109 Z 7	Mount Ash rd SE26
110 A 6	Mount Ash rd SE26
20 C 11	Mount av E4
60 G 14	Mount av W5
58 G 18	Mount av S'hall
60 E 15	Mount clo W5
6 B 15	Mount clo Barnt
113 P 20	Mount clo Chisl
155 H 19	Mount clo Wallgtn
159 Z 2	Mount ct W Wkhm
115 X 15	Mount Culver av Sidcp
97 Y 13	Mount dri Bxly Hth
22 E 15	Mount dri Harrow
43 V 7	Mount dri Wemb
108 C 6	Mount Earl gdns SW16
20 D 6	Mount Echo av E4
20 E 4	Mount Echo dri E4
107 K 5	Mount Ephraim rd SW16
109 Z 6	Mount gdns SE26
12 K 12	Mount gro Edg
48 K 9	Mount Grove rd N5
49 L 7	Mount house Barnt
133 Y 15	Mount mills EC1
108 C 6	Mount Nod rd SW16
155 P 18	Mount pk Wallgtn
41 S 7	Mount Pk av Harrow
156 J 20	Mount Pk av S Croy
60 G 17	Mount Pk cres W5
60 G 15	Mount Pk rd W5
41 R 9	Mount Pk rd Harrow
133 R 17	Mount pleasant WC1
133 R 18	Mount pleasant WC1
5 Y 14	Mount pleasant Barnt
6 A 14	Mount pleasant Barnt
60 K 2	Mount pleasant Wemb
61 N 2	Mount pleasant Wemb
48 C 2	Mount Pleasant cres N4
50 B 6	Mount Pleasant hill E5
50 A 4	Mount Pleasant la E5
32 H 7	Mount Pleasant la E17
128 C 2	Mount Pleasant rd NW10
31 R 7	Mount Pleasant rd N17
93 T 15	Mount Pleasant rd SE13
60 E 13	Mount Pleasant rd W5
117 X 5	Mount Pleasant rd New Mald
48 C 1	Mount Pleasant vlls N4
98 K 14	Mount Pleasant wlk Bxly
44 L 9	Mount rd NW4
26 G 20	Mount rd NW4
105 Z 4	Mount rd SW19
5 W 16	Mount rd Barnt
97 X 13	Mount rd Bxly Hth
56 C 3	Mount rd Dgnhm
99 U 15	Mount rd Drtfrd
120 G 2	Mount rd Mitch
117 X 6	Mount rd New Mald
139 W 9	Mount row W1
139 W 10	Mount st W1
24 F 20	Mount Stewart av Harrow
143 V 2	Mount ter E1
46 D 10	Mount the NW10
118 E 7	Mount the New Mald
43 U 7	Mount the Wemb
152 K 9	Mount the Worc Pk
46 C 12	Mount vernon NW3
12 L 11	Mount vernon NW7
20 J 3	Mount View E4
25 X 14	Mount View rd N4
30 F 19	Mount View rd N4
48 B 1	Mount View rd N4
108 J 7	Mount vills SE27
155 P 20	Mount way Wallgtn
23 Y 6	Mountbell st Stanm
118 E 7	Mountcombe clo Surb
66 H 8	Mountfield rd E6
27 X 9	Mountfield rd N3
60 H 18	Mountfield rd W5
93 W 15	Mountfields ct SE13
49 W 15	Mountford rd E8
133 R 1	Mountfort ter N1
126 C 18	Mounthurst rd Brom
80 D 5	Mountjoy clo SE2
93 W 4	Mounts Pond rd SE3
23 X 4	Mountside Stanm
67 T 4	Movers la Bark
45 T 19	Mowbray rd NW6
109 V 19	Mowbray rd SE19
12 D 13	Mowbray rd Edg
102 D 7	Mowbray rd Rich
38 K 6	Mowbrays clo Rom
38 K 7	Mowbrays rd Rom
63 O 5	Mowlem st E2
135 Y 7	Mowlem st E2
149 S 20	Mowll st SW9
139 V 2	Moxon st W1
4 H 13	Moxon st Barnt
135 T 7	Moye st E2
51 U 2	Moyers rd E10
144 M 15	Moylan rd W6
61 N 7	Moyne pl NW10
107 U 14	Moyser rd SW16
129 N 14	Mozart st W10
19 E 17	Mt Ephraim la SW16
120 E 14	Muchelney rd Mrdn
56 G 12	Muggeridge rd Dgnhm
78 F 3	Muir st E16
85 X 10	Muirdown av SW14
62 C 18	Muirfield W3
71 T 9	Muirkirk rd SE6
20 C 8	Mulberry clo E4
58 A 6	Mulberry clo Grnfd
72 C 19	Mulberry cres Brentf
54 K 19	Mulberry ct Bark
157 V 1	Mulberry la W Wkhm
74 E 14	Mulberry pl W6
143 S 3	Mulberry st E1
81 Y 5	Mulberry way Blvdr
140 G 13	Mulberry wlk SW3
44 E 13	Mulgrave rd NW10
135 O 14	Mulgrave rd SW6
60 H 10	Mulgrave rd W5
157 O 7	Mulgrave rd Croy
153 V 16	Mulgrave rd Sutton
154 A 14	Mulgrave rd Sutton
41 X 8	Mulgrave rd Wemb
47 Y 4	Mulkern rd N19
89 Y 17	Muller rd SW4
85 Y 7	Mullins path SW14
22 J 3	Mullion st Har
130 J 19	Mulready st NW8
88 G 20	Multon rd SW18
142 C 5	Mumford ct EC2
90 H 14	Mumford rd SE24
89 N 12	Muncaster rd SW11
135 P 11	Mund st W14
92 B 15	Mundania rd SE22
65 S 19	Munday rd E16
144 K 6	Munden st W14
50 C 6	Mumford rd E5
54 E 4	Mundon gdns Ilf
10 A 8	Mungo Pk clo Bushey Watf
57 W 17	Mungo Pk rd Rainhm
83 P 14	Munnings gdns Islwth
28 M 20	Munro ms W10
85 T 13	Munro dri SW14
82 C 12	Munster av Hounsl
17 X 13	Munster gdns N13
87 U 2	Munster rd SW6
144 K 18	Munster rd W6
102 C 16	Munster rd Tedd
131 Z 14	Munster sq NW1
150 D 5	Munton rd SE17
97 Y 20	Murchison av Bxly
51 U 5	Murchison rd W9
63 W 10	Murdock cottages E3
133 P 7	Muriel st N1
93 Y 11	Murillo rd SE13
141 S 19	Murphy st SE1
126 J 3	Murray av Brom
82 K 14	Murray av Hounsl
134 E 19	Murray gro N1
47 X 19	Murray ms NW1
14 C 20	Murray rd NW7
105 P 15	Murray rd W5
72 D 12	Murray rd W5
102 C 4	Murray rd Rich
65 U 19	Murray sq E16
47 W 19	Murray st NW1
144 L 14	Muscal rd W6
91 V 8	Muschamp rd SE15
154 J 3	Muschamp rd Carsh
142 L 9	Muscovy st EC3
140 J 2	Museum st WC1
5 R 6	Musgrave clo Barnt
87 Z 1	Musgrave cres SW6
147 V 20	Musgrave cres SW6
83 V 1	Musgrave rd Islwth
92 G 3	Musgrove rd SE14
88 H 6	Musjid rd SW11
49 Z 6	Muston rd E5
29 R 6	Muswell av N10
29 T 11	Muswell hill N10
29 R 12	Muswell Hill bdwy N10
29 T 12	Muswell Hill pl N10
29 R 16	Muswell Hill rd N10
29 S 9	Muswell ms N10
29 T 9	Muswell rd N10
129 V 3	Mutrix rd NW6
117 V 4	Muybridge rd New Mald
149 X 20	Myatt rd SW9
90 J 1	Myatt rd SW9
77 S 18	Mycenae rd SE3
17 X 2	Mycenae gdns N21
133 T 12	Myddelton gdns N21
15 V 8	Myddelton pk N20
30 C 1	Myddelton pk N22
30 B 11	Myddelton rd N8
133 T 11	Myddelton sq EC1
133 U 14	Myddelton st EC1
8 F 4	Myddleton av Enf
8 G 5	Myddleton clo Enf
30 B 12	Myddleton rd N8
110 A 9	Mylis clo SE26
133 T 11	Mylne st EC1
80 A 11	Myra st SE2
143 V 4	Myrdle st E1
51 S 5	Myron pl SE13
16 A 5	Myrtle clo Barnt
99 S 1	Myrtle clo Erith
99 R 1	Myrtle clo Erith
71 T 2	Myrtle gdns W7
110 G 10	Myrtle gro SE26
8 C 4	Myrtle gro Enf
117 W 4	Myrtle gro New Mald
32 J 19	Myrtle rd E17
66 E 4	Myrtle rd E6
17 Z 11	Myrtle rd N13
73 W 2	Myrtle rd W3
159 P 5	Myrtle rd Croy
100 M 16	Myrtle rd Hampt
62 G 1	Myrtle rd Hounsl
53 Z 7	Myrtle rd Ilf
154 D 10	Myrtle rd Sutton
134 J 11	Myrtle st N1
49 V 19	Myrtleberry st E8
80 A 13	Myrtledene rd SE2
88 M 9	Mysore rd SW11
89 N 9	Mysore rd SW11
109 N 7	Myton rd SE21
72 B 14	M4 motorway Brentf
70 G 15	M4 motorway Hounsl

N

Ref	Entry
32 G 18	N Access rd E17
32 L 4	N Countess rd E17
77 Y 15	Nadine st SE7
97 P 7	Nags Head la Welling
48 B 20	Nailour st N7
51 S 5	Nairn st E14
91 P 12	Nairne gro SE24
122 C 8	Namton dri Thntn Hth
150 H 9	Namur ter SE17
13 S 8	Nan Clarks la NW7
64 B 19	Nankin st E14
64 B 19	Nansen rd E15
89 P 9	Nansen rd SW11
45 V 6	Nant rd NW2
87 V 7	Napier av SW6
134 C 9	Napier gro N1
145 O 2	Napier pl W14
51 Z 11	Napier rd E11
52 A 9	Napier rd E11
65 N 6	Napier rd E15
66 H 4	Napier rd E6
62 K 8	Napier rd NW10
31 S 10	Napier rd N17
123 Z 10	Napier rd SE25
145 N 2	Napier rd W14
81 P 12	Napier rd Blvdr
126 J 8	Napier rd Brom
157 O 16	Napier rd Croy
9 U 17	Napier rd Enf
83 Y 11	Napier rd Islwth
42 H 17	Napier rd Wemb
75 Y 18	Napier st SE8
133 V 3	Napier ter N1
84 B 18	Napoleon rd Twick
89 U 14	Narbonne av SW4
87 Z 6	Narborough st SW6
45 X 16	Narcissus rd NW6
11 R 18	Naresby fold Stanm
49 X 8	Narford rd E5
63 U 20	Narrow st E14
127 R 14	Narrow way Brom
62 M 17	Nascot st W12
136 B 5	Nascot st W12
46 E 19	Naseby clo NW6
83 U 2	Naseby clo Islwth
109 O 15	Naseby rd SE19
56 E 10	Naseby rd Dgnhm
35 T 5	Naseby rd Ilf
112 F 17	Nash grn Brom
19 P 8	Nash rd N9
92 G 12	Nash rd SE4
74 J 8	Nasmyth st W6
86 D 3	Nassau rd SW13
82 D 2	Nassau st W1
46 L 12	Nassington rd NW3
16 M 17	Natal rd N11
107 Y 13	Natal rd SW16
53 Y 13	Natal rd Ilf
123 N 6	Natal rd Thntn Hth
79 V 19	Nathan way SE18
42 E 6	Nathans rd Wemb
20 G 4	Nation way E4
141 P 13	National Film theatre SE1
140 H 11	National gallery WC2
140 H 11	National Portrait gallery WC2
146 F 3	Natural History museum SW7
64 H 20	Naval row E14

49 Y 17 Navarino gro E8
49 Y 16 Navarino rd E8
66 E 5 Navarre rd E6
34 M 15 Navarre st E2
34 L 4 Navestock cres Wdfd Grn
89 X 7 Navy st SW4
15 P 8 Naylor rd N20
151 W 18 Naylor rd SE15
58 F 10 Neal av S'hall
140 J 6 Neal st WC2
140 J 6 Neal yd WC2
90 B 7 Nealden st SW9
28 D 12 Neale clo N2
98 J 1 Neals yd Erith
44 B 14 Neasden clo NW10
44 B 11 Neasden la NW10
43 Y 9 Neasden la NW10
44 C 17 Neasden la NW10
55 P 16 Neasham rd Dgnhm
151 O 14 Neate st SE5
150 K 14 Neate st SE5
120 C 15 Neath gdns Mrdn
142 D 19 Nebraska st SE1
151 O 1 Neckinger SE1
93 S 4 Nectavine way SE13
137 T 6 Needham rd W11
45 P 10 Needham ter NW2
26 J 16 Neeld cres NW4
43 P 16 Neeld cres Wemb
93 P 19 Nelgarde rd SE6
144 F 14 Nella rd W6
151 Z 6 Nelldale rd SE16
75 O 11 Nelldale rd SE16
38 G 6 Nelson clo Rom
82 G 15 Nelson gdns Hounsl
106 C 20 Nelson Gro rd SW19
133 X 10 Nelson pl N1
73 T 2 Nelson pl W3
115 N 10 Nelson pl Sidcp
34 G 13 Nelson rd E11
20 C 20 Nelson rd E4
31 S 12 Nelson rd N15
30 C 18 Nelson rd N8
19 N 9 Nelson rd N9
76 H 17 Nelson rd SE10
106 B 18 Nelson rd SW19
81 P 12 Nelson rd Blvdr
126 M 9 Nelson rd Brom
9 T 19 Nelson rd Enf
41 S 3 Nelson rd Harrow
118 A 11 Nelson rd New Mald
117 Z 12 Nelson rd New Mald
115 N 10 Nelson rd Sidcp
11 R 18 Nelson rd Stanm
82 G 16 Nelson rd Twick
83 N 17 Nelson rd Twick
141 X 16 Nelson sq SE1
63 N 16 Nelson st E1
143 W 4 Nelson st E1
65 P 19 Nelson st E16
66 K 4 Nelson st E6
133 X 10 Nelson ter N1
89 X 10 Nelsons row SW4
61 V 20 Nemoure rd W3
88 J 6 Nepaul rd SW11
86 G 17 Nepean st SW15
75 P 7 Neptune st SE16
95 O 9 Nesbit rd SE9
151 S 2 Nest st SE16
21 O 18 Nesta rd Wdfd Grn
75 R 4 Neston st SE16
7 W 19 Nestor av N21
27 Y 1 Nether clo N3
14 L 18 Nether Court av N3
14 L 18 Nether Court Golf course N3
15 P 17 Nether st N12
27 X 3 Nether st N3
14 L 20 Nether st N3
74 D 15 Netheravon rd SW4
74 D 12 Netheravon rd W4
71 V 2 Netheravon rd W7
72 F 9 Netherbury rd W5
6 M 14 Netherby gdns Enf
92 C 18 Netherby rd SE23
14 L 19 Nethercourt N3
54 E 19 Netherfield gdns Bark
15 O 16 Netherfield rd N12
107 O 7 Netherfield rd SW17
89 V 6 Netherford rd SW4
46 E 15 Netherhall gdns NW3
46 D 16 Netherhall way NW3
15 V 2 Netherland rd N20
5 T 19 Netherlands rd Barnt
39 S 7 Netherpark dri Rom
146 C 15 Netherton gro SW10
83 Z 13 Netherton rd Twick
84 A 14 Netherton rd Twick
136 F 20 Netherwood rd W14
45 V 19 Netherwood st NW6
128 F 20 Nethwood rd W10
159 V 16 Netley clo Croy
153 P 11 Netley clo Sutton
120 C 16 Netley gdns Mrdn
36 E 16 Netley rd Ilf
120 C 16 Netley rd Mrdn
132 A 14 Netley st NW1
43 P 17 Nettleden av Wemb
108 J 8 Nettleford clo SE27
92 G 1 Nettleton rd SE14
107 Y 19 Nettlewood rd SW16
110 K 4 Neuchatel rd SE6
76 H 18 Nevada st SE10
135 V 6 Nevern pl SW5
135 T 7 Nevern rd SW5
135 T 7 Nevern sq SW5
49 S 9 Nevill rd N16
103 Z 20 Neville av Kingst
114 M 9 Neville clo Sidcp
28 D 19 Neville dri N2
55 U 8 Neville gdns Dgnhm
65 T 2 Neville rd E7
129 S 9 Neville rd NW6
60 P 10 Neville rd W5
123 P 17 Neville rd Croy
55 V 8 Neville rd Dgnhm
36 C 4 Neville rd Ilf
117 R 3 Neville rd Kingst
102 C 5 Neville rd Rich
146 F 9 Neville st SW7
146 F 9 Neville ter SW7
120 J 18 Neville wlk Carsh
20 F 6 Nevin dri E4
39 R 1 Nevis clo Rom
107 N 3 Nevis rd SW17
65 U 12 New Barn st E13
121 X 10 New Barns av Mitch
139 Y 7 New Bond st W1
81 Y 10 New br Erith
141 W 7 New Br st EC4
26 M 15 New Brent st NW4
27 N 14 New Brent st NW4
142 H 3 New Broad st EC2
60 F 20 New broadway W5
140 A 9 New Burlington ms W1
140 A 8 New Burlington pl W1
140 A 9 New Burlington st W1
142 A 6 New change EC4
150 D 18 New Church rd SE5
65 Y 8 New City rd E13
120 D 4 New clo SW19
100 B 12 New clo Felt
140 H 5 New Compton st WC2
140 G 10 New Coventry st W1
92 H 1 New Cross rd SE14
75 P 19 New Cross rd SE14
141 P 5 New ct WC2
141 R 8 New ct WC2
46 E 11 New end NW3
46 F 11 New End sq NW3
126 E 8 New Farm av Brom
141 U 3 New Fetter la EC4
142 H 10 New Fresh wharf EC3
143 N 4 New Goulston st E1
70 F 18 New Heston rd Hounsl
144 C 17 New House wlk Mrdn
134 L 15 New Inn sq EC2
134 K 15 New Inn st EC2
134 K 16 New Inn yd EC2
150 D 4 New Kent rd SE1
76 A 16 New King st SE8
87 W 4 New Kings rd SW6
143 R 10 New Martan st E1
64 K 2 New Mount st E15
134 J 17 New North pl EC2
36 D 1 New North rd Ilf
132 M 20 New North st WC1
28 F 8 New Oak rd N2
140 V 4 New Oxford st WC1
140 K 19 New Palace yd SW1
17 Z 12 New Park av N13
18 A 12 New Park av N13
89 Z 20 New Pk rd SW2
107 Y 1 New Pk rd SW2
65 O 4 New Plaistow rd E15
51 U 15 New Providence st E15
139 R 6 New Quebec st W1
143 V 4 New rd E1
20 F 13 New rd E4
13 S 2 New rd NW7
27 R 1 New rd NW7
31 U 3 New rd N17
30 L 5 New rd N22
29 Z 16 New rd N8
18 L 10 New rd N9
80 J 13 New rd SE2
72 H 15 New rd Brentf
69 U 6 New rd Dgnhm
100 B 11 New rd Felt
82 K 11 New rd Hounsl
54 H 6 New rd Ilf
103 P 17 New rd Kingst
121 O 19 New rd Mitch
102 E 8 New rd Rich
97 P 6 New rd Welling
41 V 12 New rd Wemb
17 V 12 New River cres N13
48 L 18 New River wlk N1
140 J 9 New row WC2
141 R 5 New sq WC2
142 L 3 New st E1
141 U 4 New St sq EC4
141 U 5 New Street hill EC4
112 J 13 New Street hill Brom
28 F 9 New Trinity rd N2
34 E 17 New wanstead E11
26 C 14 New Way rd NW9
132 M 8 New Wharf rd N1
61 Y 9 Newark cres NW10
157 O 14 Newark rd S Croy
143 W 2 Newark st E1
63 N 16 Newark st E1
26 H 11 Newark way NW4
99 T 1 Newberry rd Erith
92 B 2 Newbold rd SE15
153 O 10 Newbolt av Sutton
10 H 18 Newbolt rd Stanm
117 Y 9 Newborough grn New Mald
73 V 2 Newburgh rd W3
140 B 7 Newburgh st W1
149 P 9 Newburn st SE11
9 X 2 Newbury av Enf
40 D 17 Newbury clo Grnfd
152 D 8 Newbury gdns Epsom
20 H 20 Newbury rd E4
126 E 7 Newbury rd Brom
36 G 19 Newbury rd Ilf
40 C 17 Newbury way Grnfd
8 F 9 Newby clo Enf
64 F 19 Newby pl E14
89 T 6 Newby st SW8
133 U 16 Newcastle row EC1
141 W 4 Newcastle st EC4
139 X 1 Newcavendish st W1
108 B 8 Newcombe gdns SW16
13 O 16 Newcombe pk NW7
61 N 2 Newcombe pk Wemb
137 U 13 Newcombe st W8
52 B 9 Newcomen rd E11
88 F 7 Newcomen rd SW11
142 E 16 Newcomen st SE1
130 K 10 Newcourt st NW8
63 Y 19 Newell st E14
100 G 20 Newfield clo Hamp
100 H 19 Newfield clo Hampt
100 G 20 Newfield clo Hampt
24 M 4 Newgale gdns Edgw
122 M 19 Newgate Croy
100 C 6 Newgate clo Felt
141 X 4 Newgate st EC1
20 M 12 Newgate st E4
142 L 20 Newhams row SE1
95 N 9 Newhaven gdns SE9
123 P 11 Newhaven rd SE25
149 S 1 Newhaven ter SE1
37 W 10 Newhome ave Rom
37 W 10 Newhouse av Rom
118 B 18 Newhouse clo New Mald
98 G 15 Newick clo Bxly
50 B 10 Newick rd E5
149 Y 6 Newington butts SE11
149 Z 2 Newington causeway SE1
149 Y 8 Newington cres SE17
49 O 14 Newington grn N16
49 O 16 Newington Grn rd N1
43 P 7 Newland ct Wemb
71 Y 6 Newland gdns W13
30 A 10 Newland rd N8
78 E 3 Newland st E16
11 X 10 Newlands clo Edg
70 B 13 Newlands clo S'hall
42 E 17 Newlands clo Wemb
110 D 13 Newlands pk SE26
4 B 16 Newlands pl Barnt
122 B 3 Newlands rd SW16
21 R 9 Newlands rd Wdfd Grn
158 K 19 Newlands wood Croy
40 C 2 Newlyn gdns Harrow
31 U 6 Newlyn rd N17
4 G 15 Newlyn rd Barnt
96 K 5 Newlyn rd Welling
140 D 3 Newman pas W1
65 U 10 Newman rd E13
126 G 2 Newman rd Brom
140 C 2 Newman st W1
141 R 20 Newman ter SE1
142 G 6 Newmans ct EC2
141 P 3 Newmans row WC2
5 S 7 Newmans way Barnt
40 K 16 Newmarket av Grnfd
95 P 18 Newmarket grn SE9
120 D 15 Newminster rd Mrdn
40 M 16 Newnham clo Grnfd
40 M 16 Newnham gdns Grnfd
30 E 4 Newnham rd N22
143 P 7 Newnham st E1
24 L 14 Newnham way Harrow
127 V 6 Newnhams clo Brom
134 E 8 Newnorth rd N1
49 O 1 Newnton clo N4
140 G 8 Newport ct WC2
140 G 8 Newport pl WC2
51 V 6 Newport rd E10
32 J 14 Newport rd E17
86 H 1 Newport rd SW13
149 O 6 Newport st SE11
40 C 7 Newquay cres Harrow
111 S 4 Newquay rd SE6
83 Z 12 Newry rd Twick
31 O 15 Newsam av N15
94 C 17 Newstead rd SE12
105 R 8 Newstead way SW19
120 D 17 Newstead wlk Carsh
29 R 3 Newton av N10
73 V 6 Newton av W3
134 H 7 Newton gro N1
74 A 10 Newton gro W4
40 H 7 Newton park Harrow U C
51 Y 14 Newton rd E15
44 M 11 Newton rd NW2
31 W 14 Newton rd N15
105 U 18 Newton rd SW19
137 W 5 Newton rd W2
23 T 6 Newton rd Harrow
83 V 4 Newton rd Islwth
96 M 8 Newton rd Welling
60 M 1 Newton rd Wemb
140 M 4 Newton st WC2
17 Z 16 Newton way N18
87 Z 14 Newtons yd SW18
72 C 10 Niagra av W5
23 T 15 Nibthwaite rd Harrow
112 G 17 Nichol la Brom
72 F 4 Nicholas gdns W5
107 N 13 Nicholas glebe SW17
142 G 8 Nicholas la EC3
63 R 12 Nicholas rd E1
156 B 8 Nicholas rd Croy
56 B 8 Nicholas rd Dgnhm
47 Y 5 Nicholay rd N19
82 G 11 Nicholes rd Hounsl
135 S 7 Nicholl st E2
60 J 14 Nichols grn W5
123 V 20 Nicholson rd Croy
141 X 14 Nicholson st SE1
23 R 7 Nicola clo Harrow
156 L 14 Nicola clo S Croy
26 K 26 Nicoll pl NW4
62 B 4 Nicolle rd NW10
10 A 7 Nicolson dri Bushey Watford
88 H 18 Nicosia rd SW18
110 G 8 Niederwald rd SE26
74 J 12 Nigel Playfair av W6
52 M 15 Nigel rd E7
91 Y 7 Nigel rd SE15
77 Z 19 Nigeria rd SE7
20 L 15 Nightingale av E4
20 L 13 Nightingale clo E4
73 V 18 Nightingale clo W4
155 N 3 Nightingale clo Carsh
93 X 13 Nightingale gro SE13
34 G 15 Nightingale la E11
29 Z 13 Nightingale la N8
88 L 19 Nightingale la SW12
89 O 17 Nightingale la SW12
126 L 4 Nightingale la Brom
127 N 5 Nightingale la Brom
84 K 18 Nightingale la Rich

78 K 16 Nightingale pl SE18
49 Y 10 Nightingale rd E5
62 E 7 Nightingale rd NW10
30 C 3 Nightingale rd N22
19 S 7 Nightingale rd N9
71 V 2 Nightingale rd W7
155 N 4 Nightingale rd Carsh
100 H 15 Nightingale rd Hampt
89 O 18 Nightingale sq SW12
78 K 16 Nightingale vale SE18
89 R 15 Nightingale wlk SW4
65 X 7 Nile rd E13
134 D 12 Nile st N1
151 O 12 Nile ter SE15
91 S 12 Nimegen way SE22
10 D 4 Nimmo dri Bushey Watford
107 T 12 Nimrod rd SW16
138 C 17 Nine Elms la SW8
79 N 18 Nithdale rd SE18
78 M 18 Nithdale rd SE18
4 B 19 Niton clo Barnt
85 P 8 Niton rd Rich
144 G 17 Niton st SW6
19 S 17 Nobel rd N18
142 B 4 Noble st EC2
30 F 9 Noel Park rd N22
66 C 12 Noel rd E6
133 X 8 Noel rd N1
6 P 17 Noel rd W3
51 T 1 Noel sq Dgnhm
140 C 6 Noel st W1
152 L 15 Nonsuch park Epsom Sutton
153 N 13 Nonsuch park Epsom Sutton
153 P 20 Nonsuch wlk Sutton
153 O 19 Nonsuch wlk Sutton
27 P 13 Nora gdns NW4
41 T 3 Nora ter Harrow
135 U 13 Norah st E2
117 R 3 Norbiton av Kingst
117 U 6 Norbiton Comm rd Kingst
63 X 17 Norbiton rd E14
62 D 19 Norbroke st W12
136 J 2 Norburn st W10
108 C 20 Norbury av SW16
122 E 1 Norbury av SW16
83 P 11 Norbury av Hounsl
108 H 19 Norbury clo SW16
122 C 1 Norbury cres SW16
121 Z 5 Norbury cross SW16
122 C 4 Norbury Ct SW16
121 Z 4 Norbury Ct SW16
37 V 16 Norbury gdns Rom
13 O 10 Norbury gro NW7
108 J 17 Norbury hill SW16
20 A 15 Norbury rd E4
122 M 4 Norbury rd Thntn Hth
123 N 4 Norbury rd Thntn Hth
121 Z 5 Norbury ri SW16
122 A 5 Norbury ri SW16
24 D 17 Norcombe gdns Harrow
49 W 8 Norcott rd N16
91 W 17 Norcroft gdns SE22
101 T 1 Norcutt rd Twick
17 X 20 Norfolk av N13
31 Y 18 Norfolk av N15
17 X 19 Norfolk clo N13
28 H 10 Norfolk clo N2
6 B 14 Norfolk clo Barnt
84 B 15 Norfolk clo Twick
138 L 5 Norfolk cres W2
96 H 18 Norfolk cres Sidcp
98 B 1 Norfolk gdns Bxly Hth
82 E 13 Norfolk gdns Hounsl
107 Z 6 Norfolk Ho rd SW16
138 H 5 Norfolk pl W2
96 M 4 Norfolk pl Welling
32 G 7 Norfolk pl E17
66 H 3 Norfolk rd E6
62 B 1 Norfolk rd NW10
43 W 18 Norfolk rd NW10
130 J 5 Norfolk rd NW8
106 J 16 Norfolk rd SW19
67 U 2 Norfolk rd Bark
4 M 12 Norfolk rd Barnt
56 H 15 Norfolk rd Dgnhm
9 O 18 Norfolk rd Enf
22 L 16 Norfolk rd Harrow
54 H 1 Norfolk rd Ilf
38 L 18 Norfolk rd Rom
122 M 6 Norfolk rd Thntn Hth

149 O 4 Norfolk row SE11
138 G 5 Norfolk sq W2
138 H 6 Norfolk Sq ms W2
52 F 14 Norfolk st E7
141 P 8 Norfolk st WC2
89 P 20 Norgrove rd SW12
123 U 5 Norhyrst av SE25
136 G 14 Norland gdns W11
136 L 14 Norland pl W11
136 H 15 Norland rd W11
136 L 14 Norland sq W11
104 H 1 Norley vale SW15
51 V 4 Norlington rd E10
30 K 4 Norman av N22
100 C 4 Norman av Felt
58 C 19 Norman av S'hall
84 C 18 Norman av Twick
134 B 15 Norman bldgs EC1
38 J 6 Norman clo Rom
63 X 7 Norman gro E3
126 J 14 Norman park Brom
51 X 8 Norman rd E11
66 H 11 Norman rd E6
31 V 15 Norman rd N15
76 E 17 Norman rd SE10
106 D 17 Norman rd SW19
81 U 4 Norman rd Blvdr
57 X 1 Norman rd Horch
54 A 16 Norman rd Ilf
53 Z 16 Norman rd Ilf
153 X 11 Norman rd Sutton
153 W 10 Norman rd Sutton
122 J 11 Norman rd Thntn Hth
134 B 15 Norman st EC1
17 N 9 Norman way N14
16 L 9 Norman way N14
61 T 16 Norman way W3
44 E 13 Normanby rd NW10
144 M 13 Normand ms W14
145 N 13 Normand rd W14
4 H 14 Normandy av Barnt
90 F 2 Normandy rd SW9
99 P 2 Normandy way Erith
97 W 3 Normanhurst av Bxly Hth
83 Z 13 Normanhurst dri Twick
84 D 15 Normanhurst dri Twick
108 D 3 Normanhurst rd SW2
43 X 18 Normans clo NW10
43 X 18 Normans mead NW10
102 E 18 Normansfield av Tedd
20 C 14 Normanshire dri E4
105 X 5 Normanton av SW19
20 M 10 Normanton pk E4
21 N 9 Normanton pk E4
157 R 13 Normanton rd S Croy
110 G 5 Normanton st SE23
108 F 11 Normington clo SW16
28 F 17 Norrice lea N2
140 E 11 Norris st SW1
87 R 11 Norroy rd SW15
5 Z 15 Norrys clo Barnt
5 Y 15 Norrys rd Barnt
104 F 4 Norstead pl SW15
32 G 18 North Access rd E17
61 Y 8 North Acton rd NW10
19 T 8 North Audley st W1
18 L 13 North av N18
60 B 15 North av W13
155 N 16 North av Carsh
24 L 18 North av Harrow
85 O 3 North av Rich
58 F 20 North av S'hall
51 X 10 North Birbeck rd E11
53 R 16 North Circular rd E12
33 X 5 North Circular rd E17
19 W 17 North Circular rd E4
66 F 10 North Circular rd E6
61 R 2 North Circular rd NW10
43 W 18 North Circular rd NW10
08 C 16 North Circular rd NW2
45 N 1 North Circular rd NW2
17 V 16 North Circular rd N13
18 F 15 North Circular rd N18
28 C 8 North Circular rd N2

27 X 11 North Circular rd N3
60 L 8 North Circular rd Wemb
97 W 10 North clo Bxly Hth
69 S 4 North clo Dgnhm
119 S 8 North clo Mrdn
60 L 20 North Common rd W5
32 L 6 North Countess rd E17
115 Y 15 North Cray rd Sidcp
27 V 9 North cres N3
132 E 20 North cres WC1
91 V 12 North Cross rd SE22
91 A 14 North Cross rd Ilf
132 C 20 North ct W1
12 L 10 North dene NW7
82 J 3 North dene Hounsl
159 T 20 North Downs cres Croy
159 S 20 North Downs cres Croy
107 U 9 North dri SW16
83 O 6 North dri Hounsl
46 C 5 North end NW3
21 Y 3 North end Buck Hl
156 L 3 North end Croy
46 D 6 North End av NW3
145 N 7 North End cres W14
45 Z 4 North End rd NW11
46 A 4 North End rd NW3
144 L 5 North End rd W14
145 R 13 North End rd W14
43 R 10 North End rd Wemb
46 C 7 North End way NW3
74 E 13 North Eydt gdns W6
106 C 17 North gdns SW19
98 B 20 North glade Bexley
31 O 16 North gro N15
47 O 2 North gro N6
29 N 9 North hill N6
29 N 17 North Hill av N6
70 A 13 North Hyde la Shall
78 G 11 North Kent gro SE18
101 V 14 North la Tedd
87 P 14 North Lodge clo SW15
133 P 18 North ms WC1
87 Y 12 North pas SW18
95 U 17 North pk SE9
135 S 18 North pl E1
106 L 17 North pl Mitch
101 V 15 North pl Tedd
136 B 3 North Pole rd W10
47 N 7 North Pole rd W10
47 Z 17 North rd N1
47 P 1 North rd N6
48 B 16 North rd N7
18 M 4 North rd N9
79 W 9 North rd SE18
106 D 15 North rd SW19
72 G 9 North rd W5
81 U 6 North rd Blvdr
112 H 20 North rd Brom
99 U 17 North rd Drtfrd
25 T 3 North rd Edg
54 G 7 North rd Ilf
85 O 8 North rd Rich
37 X 16 North rd Rom
58 F 20 North rd S'hall
70 G 1 North rd Shall
116 G 14 North rd W Wkhm
125 S 20 North rd W Wkhm
139 T 7 North row W1
93 Y 4 North several SE3
27 Z 17 North sq NW11
66 T 6 North st E13
27 N 15 North st NW4
89 U 6 North st SW4
54 A 20 North st Bark
67 N 1 North st Bark
126 E 2 North st Brom
98 E 9 North st Bxly Hth
154 M 8 North st Carsh
155 N 9 North st Carsh
83 N 6 North st Islwth
39 O 14 North st Rom
143 P 6 North Tenter st E1
146 J 4 North ter SW3
104 L 12 North view SW19
60 D 11 North view W5
35 N 7 North View dri Wdfd Grn
29 Y 11 North View rd N8
47 Y 18 North vlls NW1
25 S 10 North way NW9
19 S 8 North way N9
138 F 3 North Wharf rd W2
159 U 13 North wlk Croy
77 X 3 North Woolwich rd E16

85 Z 7 North Worple way SW14
84 A 7 North Worple way SW14
98 J 6 Northall rd Bxly Htl
133 U 16 Northampton bldgs EC1
49 N 16 Northampton gro N1
49 N 16 Northampton rd EC1
133 T 16 Northampton rd N1
157 X 2 Northampton rd Croy
133 X 13 Northampton sq EC1
48 L 20 Northampton st N1
107 Z 16 Northanger rd SW16
130 J 14 Northbank NW8
33 T 7 Northbank rd E17
121 Y 5 Northborough rd SW16
122 C 4 Northborough rd SW16
126 F 16 Northbourne Brom
89 Y 12 Northbourne rd SW
93 Y 12 Northbrook rd SE1
4 F 20 Northbrook rd Barn
123 N 11 Northbrook rd Croy
53 V 7 Northbrook rd Ilf
30 B 1 Northbrooke rd N2
133 X 17 Northburgh st EC1
49 O 20 Northchurch rd N1
43 O 18 Northchurch rd Wemb
134 J 1 Northchurch ter N1
14 H 5 Northcliffe dr N20
60 J 20 Northcote av W5
58 C 19 Northcote av S'hall
70 D 1 Northcote av S'hall
17 S 16 Northcote av Surb
83 Y 12 Northcote av Twick
32 J 14 Northcote rd E17
62 K 1 Northcote rd NW10
88 K 12 Northcote rd SW11
123 O 14 Northcote rd Croy
117 X 7 Northcote rd New Mald
114 H 10 Northcote rd Sidcp
84 A 12 Northcote rd Twick
83 Z 12 Northcote rd Twick
30 A 4 Northcott av N22
72 B 7 Northcroft rd W13
152 A 17 Northcroft rd Epsom
31 U 19 Northdene gdns N1
36 G 15 Northdown gdns Ilf
57 Y 2 Northdown rd Hornch
97 R 5 Northdown rd Welling
132 M 10 Northdown st N1
99 S 2 Northend rd Erith
18 F 9 Northern av N9
142 J 8 Northern Langbourn champs EC3
65 W 5 Northern ri E13
9 X 15 Northern rd Enf
119 T 10 Northernhay wlk Mrdn
63 W 20 Northey st E14
72 B 3 Northfield av W13
153 S 9 Northfield cres Sutton
56 B 12 Northfield gdns Dgnhm
53 V 20 Northfield rd E6
49 T 1 Northfield rd N16
72 A 5 Northfield rd W13
5 W 12 Northfield rd Barnt
56 B 12 Northfield rd Dgnhr
9 P 19 Northfield rd Enf
87 X 11 Northfields SW18
61 U 14 Northfields rd W3
14 M 12 Northiam N12
63 O 4 Northiam st E8
135 Y 6 Northiam st E8
133 O 19 Northington st WC1
90 L 6 Northlands st SE5
12 K 14 Northolm Edg
25 P 4 Northolme gdns Edg
48 K 11 Northolme rd N5
40 K 12 Northolt gdns Grnfd
40 K 12 Northolt rd Harrow
41 O 7 Northolt rd Harrow
112 C 7 Northover Brom
134 H 7 Northport st N1
14 K 12 Northram N12
108 G 4 Northstead rd SW2
142 M 7 Northumberland all EC3
52 L 4 Northumberland av E12
9 N 5 Northumberland av Enf

83 V 1 Northumberland av Islwth
96 G 9 Northumberland av Welling
140 K 13 Northumberland ave WC2
18 H 10 Northumberland gdns N9
121 Y 11 Northumberland gdns Mitch
31 Z 2 Northumberland gro N17
31 Y 1 Northumberland pk N17
81 X 19 Northumberland pk Erith
137 U 5 Northumberland pl W2
51 N 1 Northumberland rd Barnt
15 P 1 Northumberland rd Barnt
22 H 16 Northumberland rd Harrow
140 J 12 Northumberland st WC2
99 N 2 Northumberland way Erith
64 B 17 Northumbria st E14
44 C 13 Northview cres NW10
28 B 15 Northway NW11
27 A 15 Northway NW11
119 T 8 Northway Mrdn
119 S 8 Northway Mrdn
155 V 8 Northway Wllgtn
12 L 12 Northway cir NW7
12 M 13 Northway cres NW7
90 L 8 Northway SE5
123 U 16 Northway rd Croy
23 Z 19 Northwick av Harrow
24 A 20 Northwick av Harrow
24 D 18 Northwick cir Harrow
130 F 17 Northwick clo NW8
42 B 2 Northwick park Harrow
23 X 18 Northwick Pk rd Harrow
60 H 4 Northwick rd Wemb
130 E 17 Northwick ter NW8
41 W 1 Northwick wlk Harrow
49 Y 2 Northwold rd E5
57 X 12 Northwood av Hornch
15 T 16 Northwood gdns N12
41 W 15 Northwood gdns Grnfd
35 W 12 Northwood gdns Ilf
47 T 1 Northwood rd N6
110 K 2 Northwood rd SE23
155 O 14 Northwood rd Carsh
122 L 3 Northwood rd Thnt Hth
117 T 16 Norton av Surb
20 B 15 Norton clo E4
8 M 9 Norton clo Enf
122 A 3 Norton gdns SW16
50 M 3 Norton rd E10
57 N 18 Norton rd Dgnhm
42 G 18 Norton rd Wemb
42 C 5 Norval rd Wemb
63 X 18 Norway pl E14
76 E 16 Norway st SE10
52 E 16 Norwich rd E7
135 U 5 Norwich rd E8
- 69 S 7 Norwich rd Dgnhm
58 L 3 Norwich rd Grnfd
122 M 7 Norwich rd Thntn Hth
141 T 3 Norwich st EC4
25 W 2 Norwich wlk Edg
57 P 3 Norwood av Rom
60 M 5 Norwood av Wemb
70 F 12 Norwood clo S'hall
70 F 12 Norwood clo Shall
22 G 18 Norwood dri Harrow
70 D 10 Norwood gdns S'hall
70 H 12 Norwood Grn rd S'hall
108 K 8 Norwood High st SE27
108 M 12 Norwood Pk rd SE27
109 N 12 Norwood Pk rd SE27
108 J 5 Norwood rd SE27
70 E 10 Norwood rd S'hall
32 L 15 Notley rd E17
56 E 18 Notley st SE5
123 Z 10 Notson rd SE25

137 T 12 Notting Hill ga W11
65 Y 16 Nottingham av E16
140 K 6 Nottingham ct WC2
131 T 19 Nottingham pl W1
33 U 18 Nottingham rd E10
106 L 2 Nottingham rd SW17
83 V 4 Nottingham rd Islwth
156 L 10 Nottingham rd S Croy
131 U 20 Nottingham st W1
122 K 18 Nova rd Croy
114 B 2 Novar rd SE9
87 X 2 Novello st SW6
74 G 17 Nowell rd SW13
22 E 12 Nower hill Pinn
106 M 6 Noyna rd SW17
93 P 8 Nuding clo SE13
67 P 4 Nugent rd N4
123 T 6 Nugent rd SE25
130 C 11 Nugent ter NW8
22 C 4 Nugents pk Pinn
142 E 3 Nun ct EC2
68 K 1 Nuneaton rd Dgnhm
91 Y 8 Nunhead cres SE15
92 A 7 Nunhead grn SE15
92 B 8 Nunhead gro SE15
92 A 8 Nunhead la SE15
7 Z 8 Nunns rd Enf
4 A 19 Nupton dri Barnt
28 C 7 Nursery av N2
98 C 7 Nursery av Bxly Hth
158 E 3 Nursery av Croy
158 K 4 Nursery clo Croy
9 T 6 Nursery clo Enf
37 W 19 Nursery clo Wdfd Grn
21 U 16 Nursery clo Wdfd Grn
31 U 3 Nursery ct N17
9 T 6 Nursery gdns Enf
52 G 17 Nursery la E7
16 H 3 Nursery rd N14
105 R 19 Nursery rd SW19
90 D 9 Nursery rd SW9
120 J 7 Nursery rd Mitch
120 A 1 Nursery rd Mrdn
154 D 9 Nursery rd Sutton
12 L 3 Nursery rd Thntn Hth
150 D 8 Nursery row SE17
31 U 3 Nursery st N17
26 L 10 Nursery walk NW4
39 N 20 Nursery wlk Rom
81 T 20 Nurstead rd Erith
128 K 12 Nutbourne st W10
91 W 8 Nutbrook st SE15
69 P 3 Nutbrowne rd Dgnhm
151 V 18 Nutcroft rd SE16
54 L 7 Nutfield gdns Ilf
51 V 12 Nutfield rd E15
44 F 9 Nutfield rd NW2
91 V 11 Nutfield rd SE22
122 H 9 Nutfield rd Thntn Hth
139 N 4 Nutford pl W1
108 D 3 Nuthurst av SW2
46 E 17 Nutley ter NW3
11 U 8 Nutt gro Edg
151 P 18 Nutt st SE15
134 L 7 Nuttall st N1
34 K 16 Nutter la E11
81 R 14 Nuxley rd Blvdr
79 T 18 Nyanza st SE18
85 P 4 Nylands av Rich
75 V 18 Nynehead st SE14
110 K 5 Nyon gro SE6

O

29 S 2 Oak av N10
31 P 1 Oak av N17
29 Z 14 Oak av N8
159 P 1 Oak av Croy
7 P 3 Oak av Enf
100 D 14 Oak av Hampt
70 A 20 Oak av Hounsl
159 V 13 Oak bank Croy
25 D 3 Oak clo N14
154 D 4 Oak clo Sutton
62 C 17 Oak comm W3
112 A 2 Oak Cottage clo SE6
71 S 6 Oak cotts W7
60 A 14 Oak dene W13
39 Y 19 Oak Dene clo Rom
159 O 1 Oak gdns Croy
25 U 2 Oak gdns Edg
45 R 12 Oak gro NW2
159 V 1 Oak gro W Wkhm
34 H 19 Oak Hall rd E11

116 K 16 Oak hill Surb
34 A 2 Oak hill Wdfd Grn
33 Z 1 Oak hill Wdfd Grn
33 X 1 Oak hill Wdfd Grn
34 B 3 Oak hill Wdfd Grn
33 X 2 Oak hill clo Wdfd Grn
33 Y 1 Oak Hill cres Wdfd Grn
34 A 3 Oak Hill gdns Wdfd Grn
46 C 12 Oak Hill pk NW3
46 B 11 Oak Hill way NW3
63 X 19 Oak la E14
16 L 19 Oak la N11
28 F 7 Oak la N2
83 Z 19 Oak la Twick
83 U 9 Oak la Twick
21 R 13 Oak la Wdfd Grn
103 O 3 Oak lodge Rich
125 S 18 Oak Lodge dri W Wkhm
44 A 20 Oak rd NW10
81 X 20 Oak rd Erith
99 X 3 Oak rd Erith
117 X 3 Oak rd New Mald
72 H 1 Oak st W5
3 J 14 Oak st Rom
60 E 18 Oak Tree clo W13
24 C 3 Oak Tree clo Stanm
25 X 16 Oak Tree dell NW9
15 O 6 Oak Tree dri N20
112 J 11 Oak Tree gdns Brom
130 J 14 Oak Tree rd NW8
124 K 19 Oak View grn Croy
47 O 13 Oak village NW5
16 D 2 Oak way N14
119 N 9 Oak way SW20
74 A 2 Oak way W3
124 G 13 Oak way Croy
90 L 10 Oakbank gro SE24
88 A 5 Oakbury rd SW6
93 W 5 Oakcroft rd SE13
16 G 4 Oakdale N14
24 K 15 Oakdale av Harrow
51 W 7 Oakdale rd E11
34 J 8 Oakdale rd E18
52 J 20 Oakdale rd E7
30 M 18 Oakdale rd N4
31 N 18 Oakdale rd N4
108 B 12 Oakdale rd SW16
149 U 6 Oakden st SE11
113 V 11 Oakdene av Chisl
81 X 17 Oakdene av Erith
117 V 19 Oakdene dri Surb
27 W 1 Oakdene pk N3
116 K 17 Oakenshaw clo Surb
47 P 6 Oakeshott av N6
24 B 11 Oakfield av Harrow
118 D 12 Oakfield clo New Mald
8 C 14 Oakfield gdns N18
59 P 10 Oakfield gdns SE19
109 T 12 Oakfield gdns SE19
125 P 13 Oakfield gdns Bcknhm
120 K 20 Oakfield gdns Carsh
59 P 10 Oakfield gdns Grnfd
32 J 7 Oakfield rd E17
66 C 4 Oakfield rd E6
17 N 9 Oakfield rd N14
28 A 5 Oakfield rd N3
48 F 1 Oakfield rd N4
30 F 20 Oakfield rd N4
108 B 17 Oakfield rd SE20
105 R 6 Oakfield rd SW19
122 L 20 Oakfield rd Croy
54 A 9 Oakfield rd Ilf
146 A 13 Oakfield rd SW10
27 V 17 Oakfields rd NW11
47 V 12 Oakfield rd NW5
124 C 2 Oakgrove rd SE20
34 J 18 Oakhall ct E11
126 D 10 Oakham dri Brom
27 P 3 Oakhampton rd NW7
46 A 12 Oakhill av NW3
22 A 7 Oakhill av Pinn
116 K 16 Oakhill cres Surb
116 L 17 Oakhill dri Surb
116 J 15 Oakhill gro Surb
16 B 1 Oakhill gro Surb
15 Z 1 Oakhill park Barnt
116 J 15 Oakhill path Surb
87 X 12 Oakhill pl SW15
87 X 12 Oakhill rd SW15
122 B 2 Oakhill rd SW16
125 T 4 Oakhill rd Bcknhm
116 K 16 Oakhill rd Surb
154 B 6 Oakhill rd Sutton
98 E 12 Oakhouse rd Bxly Hth
15 V 1 Oakhurst av Barnt
80 L 20 Oakhurst av Bxly Hth

33 Z 12 Oakhurst clo E17
21 P 5 Oakhurst clo E4
33 Z 13 Oakhurst gdns E17
21 P 5 Oakhurst gdns E4
91 X 10 Oakhurst gro SE22
40 G 2 Oakington av Harrow
42 M 9 Oakington av Wemb
43 O 9 Oakington av Wemb
43 P 15 Oakington Mnr dri Wemb
129 U 17 Oakington rd W9
30 A 20 Oakington way N8
152 A 13 Oakland way Epsom
21 P 8 Oaklands N21
19 N 1 Oaklands av N9
9 N 20 Oaklands av Enf
71 W 16 Oaklands av Islwth
39 S 12 Oaklands av Rom
96 K 18 Oaklands av Sidcp
122 F 8 Oaklands av Thntn Hth
159 T 5 Oaklands av W Wkhm
98 C 13 Oaklands clo Bxly Hth
42 F 16 Oaklands ct Wemb
74 H 3 Oaklands gro W12
54 C 7 Oaklands Park av Ilf
45 O 13 Oaklands rd NW2
14 G 2 Oaklands rd N20
85 X 8 Oaklands rd SW14
71 W 5 oaklands rd W7
112 B 17 Oaklands rd Brom
98 B 12 Oaklands rd Bxly Hth
116 H 16 Oaklea pas Kingst
35 Y 10 Oakleafe gdns Ilf
15 V 7 Oakleigh av N20
25 T 5 Oakleigh av Edg
16 A 10 Oakleigh cl N11
15 X 10 Oakleigh cres N20
25 V 8 Oakleigh ct Edg
15 S 5 Oakleigh gdns N20
12 A 15 Oakleigh gdns Edg
15 V 2 Oakleigh park Barnt
127 X 2 Oakleigh Park av Chisl
15 V 2 Oakleigh pk Barnt
15 U 5 Oakleigh Pk north N20
15 V 4 Oakleigh Pk south N20
15 U 7 Oakleigh Rd north N20
16 A 11 Oakleigh Rd north N20
16 C 13 Oakleigh Rd south N11
121 S 1 Oakleigh way Mitch
61 P 19 Oakley av W5
54 L 20 Oakley av Bark
156 B 8 Oakley av Croy
133 X 10 Oakley cres N1
59 S 19 Oakley cres W7
151 N 11 Oakley pl SE1
49 O 20 Oakley rd N1
123 Z 11 Oakley rd SE25
124 A 11 Oakley rd SE25
127 P 20 Oakley rd Brom
23 S 17 Oakley rd Harrow
132 C 8 Oakley sq NW1
146 K 14 Oakley st SW3
146 K 14 Oakley st SW3
12 K 13 Oakmead av Brom
107 R 2 Oakmead rd SW12
121 X 20 Oakmead rd Mitch
80 A 16 Oakmere rd SE2
109 P 11 Oakridge rd SE19
100 A 4 Oaks av Felt
38 L 8 Oaks av Rom
152 L 8 Oaks av Worc Pk
20 M 8 Oaks ct E4
36 G 14 Oaks la Ilf
157 Z 10 Oaks rd Croy
158 C 8 Oaks rd Croy
79 O 15 Oaks the SE18
154 M 17 Oaks way Carsh
155 N 17 Oaks way Carsh
109 Z 8 Oaksford av SE26
111 Y 9 Oakshade rd Brom
17 S 15 Oakthorpe rd N13
17 U 10 Oaktree av N13
111 R 12 Oakview rd SE6
118 M 9 Oakway SW20
125 W 4 Oakway Brom
97 Z 16 Oakway clo Bxly

95 Y 15 Oakways SE9
155 T 19 Oakwood Wallgtn
125 U 3 Oakwood av Bcknhm
120 G 3 Oakwood av Mitch
58 H 20 Oakwood av S'hall
70 H 1 Oakwood av S'hall
6 J 20 Oakwood clo N14
113 V 16 Oakwood clo Chisl
7 O 18 Oakwood cres N21
42 A 18 Oakwood cres Grnfd
42 Z 17 Oakwood cres Grnfd
137 O 20 Oakwood ct W14
145 O 1 Oakwood ct W14
98 L 9 Oakwood dri Bxly Hth
12 G 18 Oakwood dri Edg
54 K 7 Oakwood gdns Ilf
17 N 1 Oakwood Pk nth N14
16 M 2 Oakwood Pk nth N14
122 F 15 Oakwood pl Croy
27 Z 14 Oakwood rd NW11
28 A 15 Oakwood rd NW11
104 H 20 Oakwood rd SW20
122 F 15 Oakwood rd Croy
16 L 1 Oakwood view N14
136 E 1 Oakworth rd W10
142 B 3 Oat la EC2
65 Z 10 Oatlands ri Enf
65 Z 10 Oban ct E13
123 P 7 Oban rd SE25
57 S 6 Oban rd Bark
64 K 16 Oban st E14
88 G 10 Oberstein rd SW11
90 K 14 Oborne pl SE24
137 U 17 Observatory gdns W8
85 V 11 Observatory rd SW14
95 Z 1 Occupation la SE18
72 G 11 Occupation la W5
150 A 9 Occupation rd SE17
72 B 4 Occupation rd W13
72 A 10 Occupation rd W13
80 L 8 Occupation rd Blvdr
63 U 14 Ocean st E1
49 O 19 Ockendon rd N1
115 O 18 Ockendon rd Orp
107 Z 8 Ockley rd SW16
122 C 17 Ockley rd Croy
83 V 6 Octavia la Islwth
88 J 3 Octavia st SW11
76 A 19 Octavius st SE8
150 M 11 Odell st SE5
52 E 14 Odessa rd E7
42 H 7 Odessa rd NW10
75 X 7 Odessa rd SE16
88 M 5 Odger st SW11
113 U 9 Offenham rd SE9
89 V 8 Offerton rd SW4
4 H 16 Offham slope N12
149 S 18 Offley rd SW9
48 D 20 Offord rd N1
78 F 12 Ogilby st SE18
91 V 8 Oglander rd SE15
140 A 1 Ogle st W1
56 D 9 Oglethorpe rd Dgnhm
65 P 13 Ohio rd E13
107 O 11 Okeburn rd SW17
15 T 15 Okehampton clo N12
80 D 20 Okehampton cres SE18
80 H 20 Okehampton cres Welling
97 S 1 Okehampton cres Welling
128 E 6 Okehampton rd NW10
141 X 5 Old bailey EC4
153 S 16 Old Barn clo Sutton
98 L 9 Old Barn way Bxly Hth
139 T 18 Old Barrack yd SW1
135 U 12 Old Bethnal Green rd E2
141 R 4 Old bldgs WC2
140 A 11 Old Bond st W1
116 F 2 Old Bridge st Kingst
142 H 3 Old Broad st EC2
111 X 12 Old Bromley rd Brom
146 B 9 Old Brompton rd SW5
140 A 10 Old Burlington st W1
143 O 4 Old Castle st E1
139 X 5 Old Cavendish st W1
142 A 7 Old Change ct EC4
43 X 7 Old Church la NW9
11 T 20 Old Church la Stanm
24 E 1 Old Church la Stanm
11 R 20 Old Church la Stanm
11 T 20 Old Church la Stanm
63 T 17 Old Church rd E1
20 B 11 Old Church rd E4
146 J 15 Old Church st SW3
140 F 7 Old Compton st W1
70 G 17 Old Cote dri Hounsl
137 X 17 Old Ct pl W8
84 F 7 Old Deer park Rich
84 K 8 Old Deer Pk gdns Rich
89 S 20 Old Devonshire rd SW12
77 U 19 Old Dover rd SE3
16 H 2 Old Farm av N14
114 E 2 Old Farm av Sidcp
82 E 9 Old Farm clo Hounsl
100 G 15 Old Farm Rd Hampt
114 M 3 Old Farm Rd east Sidcp
114 L 3 Old Farm Rd west Sidcp
4 G 7 Old Fold clo Barnt
4 G 7 Old Fold la Barnt
4 A 12 Old Fold view Barnt
135 Z 11 Old Ford rd E2
63 U 5 Old Ford rd E3
64 C 7 Old Ford rd E3
10 M 14 Old forge Stanm
10 M 13 Old Forge cl Stanm
8 G 4 Old Forge rd Enf
132 L 20 Old Gloucester st WC1
22 C 5 Old Hall clo Pinn
22 B 5 Old Hall dri Pinn
113 Y 20 Old hill Chisl
105 S 12 Old Ho clo SW19
126 L 8 Old Holmsdale rd Brom
91 Z 8 Old James st SE15
142 D 6 Old jewry EC2
150 K 7 Old Kent rd SE1
75 O 18 Old Kent rd SE14
151 X 16 Old Kent rd SE14
25 T 16 Old Kenton la NW9
10 L 16 Old Lodge way Stanm
83 O 15 Old Manor dri Islwth
98 M 7 Old Manor way Bxly Hth
145 W 8 Old Manor yd SW5
34 K 9 Old Mill ct E18
79 S 16 Old Mill rd SE18
141 T 6 Old Mitre ct EC4
143 R 2 Old Montague st E1
135 U 20 Old montaguest E1
135 N 15 Old Nichol st E2
134 M 15 Old Nichol st E2
141 N 1 Old North st WC1
62 B 12 Old Oak Comm la NW10
62 C 18 Old Oak Comm la W3
62 C 9 Old Oak la NW10
74 E 3 Old Oak rd W3
84 E 12 Old Palace la Rich
156 K 4 Old Palace rd Croy
84 F 12 Old Palace yd Rich
149 O 5 Old Paradise st SE11
89 P 16 Old Park av SW12
7 Z 12 Old Park av Enf
7 Y 15 Old Park gro Enf
139 W 16 Old Park la W1
17 R 12 Old Park rd N13
80 A 14 Old Park rd SE2
7 W 12 Old Park rd Enf
7 V 14 Old Park rd South Enf
7 X 18 Old Park ridings N21
7 U 11 Old Park view Enf
114 G 17 Old Perry st Chisl
148 F 1 Old Pye st SW1
139 R 7 Old Quebec st W1
142 G 19 Old Queen st SW1
93 Z 11 Old rd SE13
94 A 11 Old rd SE13
98 M 12 Old rd Drtfrd
9 P 6 Old rd Enf
12 C 18 Old Rectory gdns Edg
10 C 14 Old redding Harrow
152 D 19 Old Schools la Epsom
141 W 5 Old Seacoal la EC4
148 L 18 Old South Lambeth rd SW8
141 R 4 Old sq WC2
134 J 14 Old st EC1
65 W 7 Old st E13
127 W 1 Old Station hill Chisl
89 U 8 Old town SW4
156 K 4 Old town Croy
76 K 15 Old Woolwich rd SE10
12 M 19 Oldberry rd Edg
42 D 9 Oldborough rd Wemb
131 T 19 Oldbury pl W1
8 L 9 Oldbury rd Enf
57 P 1 Oldchurch park Rom
39 P 19 Oldchurch rd Rom
39 P 20 Oldchurch rise Rom
48 D 18 Oldershaw rd N7
127 V 9 Oldfield clo Brom
41 T 17 Oldfield clo Brom
10 L 15 Oldfield clo Stanm
59 P 4 Oldfield Farm gdns Grnfd
75 T 11 Oldfield gro SE16
41 S 18 Oldfield la Grnfd
59 P 5 Oldfield la Grnfd
41 S 17 Oldfield la Grnfd
44 C 20 Oldfield rd NW10
49 S 9 Oldfield rd N16
105 S 14 Oldfield rd SW19
74 D 5 Oldfield rd W12
127 U 8 Oldfield rd Brom
97 Z 5 Oldfield rd Bxly Hth
98 A 5 Oldfield rd Bxly Hth
41 O 17 Oldfields cir Grnfd
153 X 3 Oldfields rd Sutton
73 V 4 Oldham ter W3
49 W 3 Oldhill pl N16
49 X 3 Oldhill st N16
89 R 18 Oldridge rd SW12
111 X 10 Oldstead rd Brom
63 S 15 Olds pl E1
63 W 7 Olga st E3
76 H 9 Oliffe st E14
31 V 19 Olinda rd N16
128 K 11 Oliphant st W10
65 Z 9 Olive rd E13
45 N 13 Olive rd NW2
44 L 12 Olive rd NW2
106 D 18 Olive rd SW19
72 G 8 Olive rd W5
39 N 15 Olive st Rom
123 U 7 Oliver av SE25
51 P 7 Oliver clo E10
123 V 6 Oliver gro SE25
51 P 7 Oliver rd E10
33 V 14 Oliver rd E17
117 W 3 Oliver rd New Mald
154 F 9 Oliver rd Sutton
79 O 11 Oliver st SE18
87 P 9 Olivette st SW15
16 K 17 Ollerton rd N11
151 R 13 Olmar st SE1
149 Z 14 Olney rd SE17
150 C 12 Olney rd SE17
97 X 14 Olron cres Bxly Hth
79 P 18 Olven rd SE18
97 O 3 Olveston wlk Carsh
144 L 4 Olyffe av Welling
137 Z 9 Olympia W14
91 W 3 Olympia way W2
43 P 10 Olympic way Wemb
44 K 13 Oman av NW2
93 T 13 Omborough way SE13
142 C 15 Omeara st SE1
132 M 10 Omega pl N1
92 G 3 Ommaney rd SE14
91 U 9 Ondine rd SE15
92 C 17 One Tree clo SE23
33 O 20 Onga clo Rom
84 K 14 Onslow av Rich
20 H 9 Onslow clo E4
115 V 5 Onslow dri Sidcp
34 J 10 Onslow gdns E18
29 S 15 Onslow gdns N10
7 U 17 Onslow gdns N21
146 F 8 Onslow gdns SW7
155 U 16 Onslow gdns Wllgtn
146 E 8 Onslow ms SW7
122 F 19 Onslow rd Croy
118 F 8 Onslow rd New Mald
84 K 14 Onslow rd Rich
146 G 6 Onslow sq SW7
133 U 19 Onslow st EC1
149 Y 2 Ontario st SE1
53 Z 8 Opal mews Ilf
149 V 8 Opal st SE11
80 C 11 Openshaw rd SE2
106 E 2 Openview SW18
91 W 3 Ophir ter SE15
131 O 1 Oppidans ms NW3
131 O 1 Oppidans rd NW3
75 P 6 Oran pl SE16
25 V 1 Orange Hill rd Edg
75 P 9 Orange pl SE16
140 F 11 Orange st WC2
140 G 6 Orange yd W1
150 E 8 Orb st SE17
144 M 19 Orbain rd SW6
88 H 3 Orbel st SW11
16 H 1 Orchard av N14
15 U 8 Orchard av N20
27 X 10 Orchard av N14
81 N 16 Orchard av Blvdr
80 M 16 Orchard av Blvdr
124 J 18 Orchard av Croy
124 J 20 Orchard av Croy
99 Y 20 Orchard av Drtfrd
70 C 20 Orchard av Hounsl
121 O 19 Orchard av Mitch
118 C 5 Orchard av New Mald
70 Z 2 Orchard av S'hall
118 L 8 Orchard clo SW20
10 C 5 Orchard clo Bushey Watf
97 Y 2 Orchard clo Bxly Hth
11 Y 18 Orchard clo Edg
41 N 17 Orchard clo Grnfd
116 B 19 Orchard clo Wemb
60 K 2 Orchard clo Wemb
12 H 17 Orchard cres Edg
8 G 6 Orchard cres Enf
101 O 3 Orchard ct Twick
152 E 1 Orchard ct Worc Pk
93 X 4 Orchard dri SE3
11 Z 15 Orchard dri Edg
42 B 17 Orchard ga Grnfd
153 X 10 Orchard gdns Sutton
124 J 17 Orchard gro Croy
25 R 5 Orchard gro Edg
25 N 15 Orchard gro Harrow
93 S 3 Orchard hill SE13
155 N 10 Orchard hill Carsh
99 O 12 Orchard hill Drtfrd
104 X 20 Orchard la SW20
21 X 13 Orchard la Wdfd Grn
109 X 20 Orchard lodge SE20
64 M 18 Orchard pl E14
31 U 3 Orchard pl N17
29 T 20 Orchard pl N6
4 G 14 Orchard rd Barnt
81 R 12 Orchard rd Blvdr
72 E 16 Orchard rd Brentf
112 M 20 Orchard rd Brom
69 T 3 Orchard rd Dgnhm
70 F 17 Orchard rd Enf
100 F 17 Orchard rd Hampt
82 F 12 Orchard rd Hounsl
116 J 5 Orchard rd Kingst
121 O 19 Orchard rd Mitch
85 P 9 Orchard rd Rich
38 G 6 Orchard rd Rom
114 J 9 Orchard rd Sidcp
153 Y 10 Orchard rd Sutton
83 Z 14 Orchard rd Twick
84 A 14 Orchard rd Twick
97 R 6 Orchard rd Welling
124 K 19 Orchard ri Croy
103 V 20 Orchard ri Kingst
85 S 11 Orchard ri Rich
96 J 13 Orchard Ri east Sidcp
96 G 13 Orchard Ri west Sidcp
32 H 12 Orchard st E17
139 T 6 Orchard st W1
27 X 16 Orchard the NW11
93 X 4 Orchard the SE3
73 Z 10 Orchard the W4
8 A 19 Orchard the Enf
124 J 16 Orchard way Croy
8 D 11 Orchard way Enf
154 G 8 Orchard way Sutton
9 O 9 Orchardleigh av Enf
8 B 19 Orchardmede Enf
130 F 18 Orchardson st NW8
16 G 3 Orchid rd N14
62 G 20 Orchid st W12
133 N 19 Orde Hall st WC1
63 Z 7 Ordell rd E3
76 M 5 Ordnance cres SE10
130 G 6 Ordnance hill NW8
78 J 18 Ordnance rd E16
65 S 14 Ordnance rd E16
75 V 16 Oreborough st SE8
53 S 11 Oregon av E12
101 V 5 Orford gdns Twick
34 G 10 Orford rd E17
33 R 15 Orford rd E17
20 G 9 Organ la E4
121 X 7 Oriel clo Mitch
35 T 11 Oriel gdns Ilf
46 E 13 Oriel pl NW3
40 K 20 Oriel way Grnfd
149 W 4 Orient st SE11
78 A 3 Oriental rd E16
64 B 19 Oriental st E14

50 G 17 Oriol rd E9
79 U 13 Orissa rd SE18
89 U 9 Orlando rd SW4
109 P 17 Orleans rd SE19
84 C 19 Orleans rd Twick
48 G 18 Orleston ms N7
48 G 18 Orleston rd N7
41 S 11 Orley Farm rd Harrow
76 L 14 Orlop st SE10
109 Y 11 Ormanton rd SE26
137 Y 10 Orme ct W2
137 Y 10 Orme Ct ms W2
137 Y 10 Orme la W2
117 T 3 Orme rd Kingst
137 X 10 Orme sq W2
102 J 7 Ormeley lodge Rich
89 S 20 Ormeley rd SW12
121 P 2 Ormerod gdns Mitch
59 N 7 Ormesby gdns Grnfd
24 M 17 Ormesby way Harrow
74 H 3 Ormiston gro W12
77 S 14 Ormiston rd SE10
100 K 20 Ormond av Hampt
132 M 19 Ormond clo WC1
100 L 19 Ormond cres Hampt
100 L 18 Ormond dri Hampt
132 M 18 Ormond ms WC1
48 A 4 Ormond rd N4
67 A 2 Ormond rd Rich
140 C 12 Ormond yd SW1
67 U 11 Ormonde ga SW3
85 U 1 Ormonde pl SW1
21 Y 5 Ormonde rd Buck Hl
131 O 6 Ormonde ter NW8
49 T 10 Ormsby pl N16
135 N 8 Ormsby st E2
75 O 16 Ormside st SE15
151 Z 14 Ormside st SE15
46 H 15 Ornan rd NW3
49 S 11 Orpen rd N16
91 N 3 Orpheus st SE5
48 C 9 Orpingley rd N7
18 D 12 Orpington gdns N18
17 V 6 Orpington rd N21
144 B 6 Orris ms W6
138 A 4 Orsett ms W2
137 Z 4 Orsett ms W2
149 P 9 Orsett st SE11
137 Z 4 Orsett ter W2
138 A 4 Orsett ter W2
34 K 3 Orsett ter Wdfd Grn
134 L 5 Orsman rd N1
143 T 14 Orton st E1
88 G 4 Orville rd SW11
65 X 5 Orwell rd E13
49 W 5 Osbaldeston rd N16
148 E 7 Osbert st SW1
54 C 12 Osberton rd SE12
143 P 3 Osborn st E1
94 C 11 Osborn ter SE3
124 J 9 Osborne clo Becknhm
39 Z 19 Osborne clo Hornch
27 O 2 Osborne gdns NW7
122 L 3 Osborne gdns Thntn Hth
51 S 8 Osborne rd E10
52 H 15 Osborne rd E7
50 M 17 Osborne rd E9
44 J 17 Osborne rd NW2
17 U 11 Osborne rd N13
48 E 4 Osborne rd N4
75 X 3 Osborne rd W3
81 O 15 Osborne rd Blvdr
21 V 6 Osborne rd Buck Hl
56 C 14 Osborne rd Dgnhm
9 V 9 Osborne rd Enf
39 Y 18 Osborne rd Hornch
82 E 9 Osborne rd Hounsl
102 K 17 Osborne rd Kingst
58 M 17 Osborne rd S'hall
122 L 3 Osborne rd Thntn Hth
56 B 13 Osborne sq Dgnhm
150 G 7 Osborne st SE17
93 N 3 Oscar st SE8
47 W 16 Oseney cres NW5
63 Y 3 Oshea gro E3
16 F 3 Osidge la N14
63 R 12 Osier st E1
87 Y 11 Osiers rd SW18
111 S 12 Oslac rd SE6
31 P 18 Osman clo N15
18 K 12 Osman rd N9
41 O 7 Osmond clo Harrow
155 V 10 Osmond gdns Wllgtn
62 E 16 Osmund st W12
131 Z 17 Osnaburgh ter NW1
128 G 14 Osney wlk Wallgtn
47 U 13 Ospringe rd NW5

48 D 1 Ossian rd N4
139 T 1 Ossington bldgs W1
137 W 10 Ossington clo W2
137 W 11 Ossington st W2
151 R 12 Ossory rd SE1
132 F 10 Ossulton st NW1
28 D 11 Ossulton way N2
90 D 18 Ostade rd SW2
145 Z 3 Osten ms SW5
71 P 19 Osterley la Islwth
83 U 1 Osterley cres Islwth
122 L 2 Osterley gdns Thntn Hth
70 K 13 Osterley la S'hall
70 M 10 Osterley park Islwth
71 O 15 Osterley Park house Islwth
70 D 7 Osterley Pk rd S'hall
71 U 6 Osterley Pk View rd W7
15 S 20 Osterley rd N16
71 S 20 Osterley rd Islwth
83 S 1 Osterley rd Islwth
70 C 2 Oswald rd S'hall
50 G 11 Oswald st E5
158 M 20 Osward Croy
106 M 3 Osward rd SW17
149 X 4 Oswin st SE11
91 S 4 Oswyth rd SE5
63 X 6 Otford clo Brom
98 G 16 Otford clo Bxly
92 K 16 Otford cres SE4
64 F 9 Otis st E3
35 Z 18 Otley appr Ilf
35 Y 17 Otley dri Ilf
36 A 17 Otley dri Ilf
65 X 16 Otley rd E16
50 E 8 Otley ter E5
69 Z 1 Ottawa gdns Dgnhm
59 N 13 Otter rd Grnfd
20 K 11 Otterbourne rd E4
71 Y 19 Otterburn gdns Islwth
107 N 15 Otterburn st SW17
111 N 9 Otterden st SE6
149 W 14 Otto st SE17
49 X 10 Ottoway st E5
54 K 16 Oulton cres Bark
31 P 15 Oulton rd N15
10 B 1 Oundle av Bushey Watf
106 M 1 Ouseley rd SW1
131 W 10 Outer circle NW1/NW8
130 M 11 Outer circle NW1/NW8
44 D 20 Outgate rd NW10
66 C 3 Outram rd E6
29 X 4 Outram rd N22
157 W 2 Outram rd Croy
132 L 4 Outram st N1
142 K 4 Outwhich st EC3
149 P 15 Oval Cricket ground SE11
131 X 5 Oval rd NW1
157 W 2 Oval rd Croy
69 V 4 Oval Rd north Dgnhm
69 U 6 Oval Rd south Dgnhm
135 W 8 Oval the E2
97 N 18 Oval the Sidcp
149 P 12 Oval way SE11
124 K 17 Ovenstone gdns Croy
111 O 13 Overbrae Becknhm
125 U 4 Overbury av Becknhm
125 T 5 Overbury av Becknhm
31 O 19 Overbury rd N15
50 G 11 Overbury st E5
93 P 8 Overcliff rd SE13
97 S 14 Overcourt clo Sidcp
117 X 3 Overdale av New Mald
72 D 8 Overdale rd W5
69 P 9 Overdown rd SE6
91 X 19 Overhill rd SE22
125 V 12 Overhill way Becknhm
49 X 2 Overlea rd E5
96 E 16 Overmead Sidcp
74 L 10 Overstone rd W6
144 B 5 Overstone rd W6
83 U 3 Overton clo Islwth
52 G 2 Overton dri E11
37 O 20 Overton dri Rom
50 J 3 Overton rd E10
6 M 18 Overton rd N14
7 N 17 Overton rd N14
80 H 8 Overton rd SE2
90 G 6 Overton rd SW9

153 Y 17 Overton rd Sutton
156 L 4 Overtons yd Croy
40 D 5 Ovesdon av Harrow
146 L 2 Ovington gdns SW3
146 M 2 Ovington ms SW3
146 M 2 Ovington sq SW3
146 M 4 Ovington st SW3
147 N 5 Ovington st SW3
17 Y 15 Owen rd N13
133 V 1 Owen st EC1
35 V 4 Owen Waters ho Ilf
80 D 11 Owenite st SE2
133 V 11 Owens ct EC1
133 V 1 Owens row EC1
152 G 20 Ox la Epson
87 S 3 Oxberry av SW6
140 F 10 Oxendon st SW1
91 U 8 Oxenford st SE15
42 L 2 Oxenpark av Wemb
75 W 13 Oxestalls rd SE8
119 S 2 Oxford av SW20
70 F 15 Oxford av Hounsl
140 A 5 Oxford cir W1
140 A 6 Oxford Cir av W1
18 M 7 Oxford clo N9
12 U 7 Oxford clo Mitch
117 V 14 Oxford cres New Mald
142 E 8 Oxford ct EC4
15 S 6 Oxford gdns N20
73 A 19 Oxford gdns W10
136 J 4 Oxford gdns W10
73 R 15 Oxford gdns W4
51 Y 18 Oxford rd E15
129 W 7 Oxford rd NW6
15 U 4 Oxford rd N20
48 F 4 Oxford rd N4
19 N 8 Oxford rd N9
109 O 15 Oxford rd SE19
87 S 12 Oxford rd SW15
72 H 1 Oxford rd W5
60 H 20 Oxford rd W5
154 J 11 Oxford rd Carsh
9 N 18 Oxford rd Enf
23 V 11 Oxford rd Harrow
23 O 18 Oxford rd Harrow
54 C 14 Oxford rd Ilf
15 R 13 Oxford rd Mitch
101 R 12 Oxford rd Tedd
55 U 12 Oxford rd Wallgtn
21 Z 16 Oxford Rd north W4
73 T 13 Oxford Rd north W4
73 S 14 Oxford Rd south W4
138 L 6 Oxford sq W2
140 E 4 Oxford st W1
139 T 6 Oxford st W1
44 L 7 Oxgate gdns NW2
44 J 6 Oxgate la NW2
127 X 13 Oxhawth cres Brom
96 E 6 Oxleas clo Welling
40 F 4 Oxley av Harrow
118 A 11 Oxleigh clo New Mald
56 D 12 Oxlow la Dgnhm
120 F 6 Oxted clo Mitch
121 X 2 Oxtoby way SW16

P

143 Y 7 Pace pl E1
65 T 17 Pacific rd E16
133 P 15 Packenham st WC1
73 T 7 Packington rd W3
133 Y 4 Packington st N1
134 A 6 Packington st N1
96 P 14 Packmores rd SE9
135 P 14 Padbury ct E2
74 H 8 Paddenswick rd W6
138 G 1 Paddington grn W2
139 S 1 Paddington st W1
131 T 20 Paddington st W1
138 F 5 Paddington station W2
110 E 9 Paddock rd SE26
40 K 12 Paddock clo Harrow
44 G 8 Paddock rd NW2
97 Z 11 Paddock rd Bxly Hth
40 A 9 Paddock rd Ruis
114 F 19 Paddock way Chisl
43 T 7 Paddocks the Wemb
90 K 7 Padfield rd SE5
37 V 10 Padnall rd Rom
7 W 7 Padstow rd Enf
110 C 20 Page av SE20
24 M 20 Page clo Harrow
156 H 10 Page cres Croy
31 W 15 Page Green N15
31 U 16 Page Green ter N15
127 R 5 Page Heath la Brom

13 V 20 Page st NW7
26 G 3 Page st NW7
148 G 5 Page st SW1
123 Y 17 Pagehurst rd Croy
29 R 7 Pages hill N10
29 R 8 Pages la N10
150 L 3 Pages wlk SE1
154 G 6 Paget av Sutton
101 O 10 Paget clo Hampt
66 E 14 Paget gdns E6
49 P 4 Paget rd N16
53 Y 13 Paget rd Ilf
78 K 18 Paget rd SE18
133 W 12 Paget st EC1
78 K 18 Paget ter SE18
75 X 20 Pagnell st SE14
84 M 8 Pagoda av Rich
93 X 6 Pagoda gdns SE3
31 S 19 Paignton rd N15
49 S 8 Paine rd N16
22 C 10 Paines clo Pinn
22 B 10 Paines la Pinn
36 L 9 Painters rd Ilf
37 O 9 Painters rd Ilf
30 J 4 Paisley rd N22
120 F 19 Paisley rd Carsh
48 C 10 Pakeman rd N7
137 Z 17 Palace av W8
137 W 10 Palace av W8
24 J 18 Palace ct Harrow
25 U 9 Palace Ct gdns N10
138 B 19 Palace ga W8
29 Z 6 Palace Gates rd N22
8 A 13 Palace gdns Enf
137 W 12 Palace Gdns ms W8
137 W 14 Palace Gdns ter W8
158 M 17 Palace grn Croy
109 U 18 Palace gro SE19
126 G 1 Palace gro Brom
147 U 7 Palace ms SW1
8 B 13 Palace ms Enf
29 Z 2 Palace rd N11
29 Y 15 Palace rd N8
109 V 17 Palace rd SE19
108 D 2 Palace rd SW2
126 G 1 Palace rd Brom
116 G 10 Palace rd Kingst
40 A 11 Palace rd Pinn
109 U 17 Palace sq SE19
148 B 2 Palace st SW1
126 J 2 Palace view Brom
158 L 7 Palace view Croy
20 E 16 Palace View rd E4
51 N 3 Palamos rd E10
49 T 12 Palatine av N16
49 T 12 Palatine rd N16
62 H 7 Palermo rd NW10
120 F 1 Palestine gro SW18
85 Z 12 Palewell Comm dri SW14
85 Y 10 Palewell pk SW14
58 G 20 Palgrave av S'hall
74 D 8 Palgrave rd W12
138 N 14 Palissy st E2
140 E 13 Pall mall SW1
140 G 12 Pall mall east SW1
140 C 11 Pall Mall pl SW1
95 P 1 Pallett way SE18
144 K 10 Palliser rd W14
115 W 15 Palm av Sidcp
72 J 7 Palm gro W5
38 L 16 Palm rd Rom
63 U 8 Palm st E2
98 D 6 Palmar cres Bxly Hth
97 W 7 Palmar rd Bxly Hth
153 N 10 Palmer av Sutton
152 M 9 Palmer av Sutton
82 F 2 Palmer clo Hounsl
116 J 5 Palmer cres Kingst
48 F 16 Palmer pl N7
65 W 13 Palmer rd E13
140 D 20 Palmer st SW1
148 E 1 Palmer st SW1
16 T 8 Palmers la Enf
68 T 8 Palmers rd E2
6 G 16 Palmers rd N11
85 W 8 Palmers rd SW14
122 C 3 Palmers rd SW16
17 P 17 Palmerston cres N13
79 P 17 Palmerston cres SE18
105 Y 18 Palmerston gro SW19
32 K 14 Palmerston rd E17
52 H 17 Palmerston rd E7
45 W 20 Palmerston rd NW6
17 P 18 Palmerston rd N22
30 C 1 Palmerston rd N22
45 V 11 Palmerston rd SW14
105 Y 19 Palmerston rd SW19
73 U 7 Palmerston rd W3

Ref	Name
155 N 7	Palmerston rd Carsh
23 V 11	Palmerston rd Harrow
154 E 10	Palmerston rd Sutton
83 U 16	Palmerston rd Twick
123 N 11	Palmerston rd Thntn Hth
135 Z 6	Palmiter pl E9
135 Y 9	Palmiter st E2
136 F 6	Pamber st W10
156 K 17	Pampisford rd S Croy
142 D 7	Pancras la EC4
132 F 7	Pancras rd NW1
45 X 16	Pandora rd NW6
80 B 6	Pangbourne av W10
136 D 1	Pangbourne av W10
11 X 15	Pangbourne dri Stanm
58 L 19	Panhard pl Shall
5 S 18	Pank av Barnt
104 K 20	Panmuir rd SW20
110 A 7	Panmure rd SE26
127 R 6	Pantiles the Brom
10 D 4	Pantiles the Bushey Watf
81 O 20	Pantiles the Bxly Hth
140 G 10	Panton st WC2
141 T 8	Paper bldng EC4
108 H 3	Parade ms SW2
147 S 16	Parade the SW11
90 A 4	Paradise rd SW4
143 Y 19	Paradise st SE16
147 P 13	Paradise wlk SW3
116 M 14	Paragon gro Surb
94 C 4	Paragon pl SE3
50 B 18	Paragon rd E9
150 D 6	Paragon row SE17
94 D 4	Paragon the SE3
92 H 16	Parbury rd SE23
122 K 4	Parchmore rd Thntn Hth
122 K 3	Parchmore way Thntn Hth
73 T 5	Pard Rd north W3
133 Y 16	Pardon st EC1
143 U 4	Parfett st E1
151 Y 8	Parfitt rd SE16
75 N 12	Parfitt rd SE16
144 E 13	Parfrey st W6
35 Y 17	Parham dri Ilf
29 U 8	Parham way N10
141 V 13	Paris gdn SE1
110 E 17	Parish la SE20
P9 P 9	Park appr Welling
51 Z 18	Park av E15
66 S 4	Park av E6
61 N 8	Park av NW10
46 A 4	Park av NW11
44 L 18	Park av NW2
17 U 12	Park av N13
18 J 14	Park av N18
30 C 5	Park av N22
28 C 4	Park av N3
85 Z 11	Park av SW14
54 D 18	Park av Bark
112 F 16	Park av Brom
155 O 13	Park av Carsh
8 E 20	Park av Enf
82 K 15	Park av Hounsl
53 X 5	Park av Ilf
107 S 18	Park av Mitch
70 E 4	Park av S'hall
159 U 3	Park av W Wkhm
21 U 16	Park av Wdfd Grn
60 L 7	Park av Wemb
152 H 15	Park Av east Epsom
44 K 15	Park Av north NW10
29 X 13	Park Av north N8
29 W 14	Park Av south N8
152 F 15	Park Av west Epsom
32 A 2	Park Avenue rd N17
39 T 6	Park blvd Rom
42 M 12	Park chase Wemb
43 N 11	Park chase Wemb
61 N 7	Park clo NW10
44 H 10	Park clo NW2
155 N 13	Park clo Carsh
23 T 3	Park clo Harrow
83 N 13	Park clo Hounsl
28 C 3	Park cres N3
131 X 18	Park cres W1
8 B 16	Park cres Enf
81 Y 17	Park cres Hornch
23 T 4	Park cres Harrow
39 V 20	Park cres Hornch
131 Y 18	Park Cres Ms east W1
131 W 19	Park Cres Ms west NW1
25 W 4	Park croft Edg
25 W 4	Park croft Edgw
31 Y 1	Park ct N15

117 Z 9	Park ct New Mald
42 L 14	Park ct Wemb
45 Z 4	Park dri NW11
17 Y 1	Park dri N21
7 Y 20	Park dri N21
78 D 15	Park dri SE7
85 Z 11	Park dri SW14
73 P 8	Park dri W3
56 L 10	Park dri Dgnhm
10 D 20	Park dri Harrow
22 F 20	Park dri Harrow
39 P 12	Park dri Rom
78 D 15	Park Dri clo SE7
46 K 12	Park end NW3
112 C 20	Park end Brom
39 R 13	Park End rd Rom
127 O 1	Park Farm clo N2
102 L 17	Park Farm rd Kingst
28 H 10	Park ga N2
17 O 3	Park ga N21
60 F 13	Park ga W5
103 T 14	Park Ga clo Kingst
25 U 11	Park gdns NW9
81 Y 11	Park gdns Erith
103 O 14	Park gdns Kingst
65 S 3	Park gro E15
29 Y 2	Park gro N11
126 H 1	Park gro Brom
98 J 11	Park gro Bxly Hth
12 A 16	Park gro Edg
51 Z 7	Park Gro rd E11
28 K 12	Park hall rd N2
109 N 6	Park Hall rd SE21
110 B 3	Park hill SE23
89 Y 12	Park hill SW4
60 H 15	Park hill W5
127 T 9	Park hill Brom
154 L 13	Park hill Carsh
84 M 16	Park hill Rich
125 Y 3	Park Hill rd Brom
157 R 8	Park Hill rd Croy
114 G 6	Park Hill rd Sidcp
155 S 16	Park Hill rd Wallgtn
157 T 4	Park Hill ri Croy
17 O 2	Park ho N21
64 D 14	Park Ho gdns Twick
64 H 2	Park la E15
32 A 3	Park la N17
31 W 3	Park la N17
18 H 12	Park la N9
139 T 11	Park la W1
165 P 9	Park la Carsh
157 N 4	Park la Croy
40 J 9	Park la Harrow
57 Y 17	Park la Hornch
84 G 11	Park la Rich
37 V 19	Park la Rom
153 R 14	Park la Sutton
101 W 15	Park la Tedd
42 L 14	Park la Wemb
57 V 2	Park lane Hornch
40 K 10	Park mead Harrow
97 S 15	Park mead Sidcp
62 E 5	Park pde NW10
140 B 14	Park pl SW1
73 R 9	Park pl W3
72 H 3	Park pl W5
100 M 15	Park pl Hampt
43 N 13	Park pl Wemb
42 M 13	Park pl Wemb
130 D 20	Park Pl vlls W2
51 O 4	Park rd E10
52 J 5	Park rd E12
65 R 3	Park rd E15
32 L 16	Park rd E17
65 Y 3	Park rd E6
131 O 17	Park rd NW1
62 A 3	Park rd NW10
73 U 4	Park rd NW3
26 K 20	Park rd NW4
130 L 13	Park rd NW8
43 Y 1	Park rd NW9
29 Z 2	Park rd N11
16 K 4	Park rd N14
30 J 14	Park rd N15
18 J 13	Park rd N18
28 H 11	Park rd N2
18 H 9	Park rd N8
29 W 15	Park rd N8
123 T 9	Park rd SE25
106 H 15	Park rd SW19
90 B 18	Park rd SW2
73 Y 16	Park rd W4
59 X 19	Park rd W7
4 H 13	Park rd Barnt
5 X 15	Park rd Barnt
111 O 19	Park rd Becknhm
110 M 17	Park rd Becknhm
126 G 2	Park rd Brom
114 A 14	Park rd Chisl
100 L 11	Park rd Hampt

82 L 13	Park rd Hounsl
83 N 13	Park rd Hounsl
54 D 9	Park rd Ilf
84 A 4	Park rd Islwth
103 O 14	Park rd Kingst
116 D 1	Park rd Kingst
117 Z 9	Park rd N Mald
84 M 15	Park rd Rich
117 N 12	Park rd Surb
153 S 14	Park rd Sutton
153 S 14	Park rd Sutton
101 W 15	Park rd Tedd
84 E 14	Park rd Twick
155 R 3	Park rd Wallgtn
155 S 10	Park rd Wallgtn
42 K 18	Park rd Wemb
103 N 14	Park Rd east Kingst
73 Y 15	Park Rd north W4
103 N 12	Park Rd west Kingst
23 T 5	Park ri Harrow
110 J 1	Park Ri sE23
30 E 10	Park ridings N8
76 J 15	Park row SE10
61 S 8	Park royal NW10
61 W 12	Park Royal rd NW10
105 N 9	Park side SW19
131 X 17	Park Sq east NW1
131 W 17	Park Sq ms NW1
131 W 17	Park Sq west NW1
142 B 12	Park st SE1
139 S 7	Park st W1
156 M 4	Park st Croy
101 U 14	Park st Tedd
9 V 4	Park ter Wemb
152 F 1	Park ter Worc Pk
46 A 4	Park the NW11
29 P 20	Park the N6
109 T 18	Park the SE19
110 B 3	Park the SE23
72 G 4	Park the W5
155 N 12	Park the Carsh
114 M 11	Park the Sidcp
17 P 2	Park view N21
61 N 14	Park view W3
118 F 6	Park view New Mald
22 F 3	Park view Pinn
43 U 14	Park view Wemb
16 E 14	Park View cres N11
27 O 17	Park View gdns NW4
30 G 4	Park View gdns N22
67 O 4	Park View gdns Bark
35 T 13	Park View gdns Ilf
44 E 12	Park View rd NW10
31 X 10	Park View rd N17
28 B 4	Park View rd N3
113 Y 3	Park View rd SE9
60 K 14	Park View rd W5
70 G 1	Park View rd Shall
97 U 8	Park View rd Welling
131 Y 9	Park Village east NW1
131 X 8	Park Village west NW1
76 L 16	Park vista SE10
37 W 19	Park vils Rom
27 T 16	Park way NW11
16 M 7	Park way N14
15 Y 14	Park way N20
119 O 9	Park way SW20
25 T 6	Park way Edg
7 S 10	Park way Enf
39 U 19	Park way Hornch
39 T 7	Park way Rom
21 Z 16	Park way Wdfd Grn
29 P 20	Park wlk N6
146 D 13	Park wlk SW10
128 L 17	Park yd W10
94 B 18	Parkcroft rd SE12
79 U 14	Parkdale rd SE18
86 F 1	Parke rd SW13
74 E 20	Parke rd SW13
156 M 8	Parker rd Croy
78 C 3	Parker st E16
140 M 4	Parker st WC2
143 R 19	Parkers row SE1
86 A 10	Parkfield av SW14
58 A 6	Parkfield av Grnfd
22 M 7	Parkfield av Harrow
58 A 7	Parkfield av Harrow
58 C 5	Parkfield clo Grnfd
22 M 8	Parkfield cres Harrow
40 B 8	Parkfield cres Ruis
58 A 7	Parkfield dri Grnfd
22 L 10	Parkfield gdns Harrow
44 H 20	Parkfield rd NW10
58 A 6	Parkfield rd SE14
58 B 5	Parkfield rd Grnfd
41 N 9	Parkfield rd Harrow
133 U 8	Parkfield st N1

127 V 13	Parkfield way Brom
86 M 11	Parkfields SW15
124 L 19	Parkfields Croy
43 Z 3	Parkfields av NW9
44 A 3	Parkfields av NW9
118 J 1	Parkfields av SW20
103 N 13	Parkfields rd Kingst
94 D 9	Parkgate SE3
5 P 5	Parkgate av Barnt
85 X 14	Parkgate cres Barnt
102 M 7	Parkgate gdns SW14
146 L 19	Parkgate house Rich
155 S 11	Parkgate rd Wallgtn
108 M 6	Parkhall st SE27
88 H 2	Parkham st SW11
154 K 12	Parkhill clo Carsh
20 H 4	Parkhill rd E4
46 M 17	Parkhill rd NW3
98 B 19	Parkhill rd Bxly
98 C 19	Parkhill rd Bxly
49 W 18	Parkholme rd E8
150 G 17	Parkhouse st SE5
98 D 19	Parkhurst gdns Bxly
53 W 14	Parkhurst rd E12
16 C 15	Parkhurst rd N11
31 W 7	Parkhurst rd N11
32 J 14	Parkhurst rd N17
30 D 1	Parkhurst rd N22
17 R 20	Parkhurst rd N22
48 A 12	Parkhurst rd N7
98 E 18	Parkhurst rd Bxly
154 F 7	Parkhurst rd Sutton
39 S 9	Parkland av Rom
34 G 2	Parkland av Wdfd Grn
116 M 13	Parklands Surb
27 S 11	Parklands dri N3
107 T 12	Parklands rd SW16
120 A 2	Parkleigh rd SW19
102 H 10	Parkleys Rich
86 J 16	Parkmead SW15
8 A 2	Parknook gdns Enf
84 H 10	Parkshot Rich
44 H 11	Parkside NW2
13 T 19	Parkside NW7
26 E 1	Parkside NW7
28 A 3	Parkside N3
101 O 13	Parkside Hampt
115 R 6	Parkside Sidcp
153 S 14	Parkside Sutton
105 O 1	Parkside av SW19
127 R 9	Parkside av Brom
99 S 6	Parkside av Bxly Hth
39 N 10	Parkside av Rom
99 O 5	Parkside cres Bxly Hth
117 V 15	Parkside cres Surb
12 B 12	Parkside dri Edg
105 O 10	Parkside gdns SW19
16 A 4	Parkside gdns Barnt
6 G 2	Parkside house Barnt
81 W 10	Parkside rd Blvdr
82 J 12	Parkside rd Hounsl
89 N 2	Parkside rd SW11
18 A 13	Parkside ter N13
22 M 13	Parkside way Harrow
23 N 12	Parkside way Harrow
86 H 13	Parkstead rd SW15
18 F 18	Parkstone av N18
33 U 10	Parkstone rd E17
91 Y 5	Parkstone rd SE15
22 K 19	Parkthorne clo Harrow
22 J 19	Parkthorne dri Harrow
80 X 19	Parkthorne rd SW12
123 Y 19	Parkview rd Croy
145 O 19	Parkville rd SW6
131 X 5	Parkway NW1
111 O 19	Parkway Becknhm
159 T 20	Parkway Croy
54 K 10	Parkway Ilf
105 W 13	Parkwood rd SW19
98 C 20	Parkwood rd Bxly
83 W 1	Parkwood rd Islwth
46 L 11	Parliament hill NW3
140 J 19	Parliament sq SW1
140 J 18	Parliament st SW1
88 L 10	Parma cres SW11
63 O 6	Parmiter st E2
12 G 12	Parnell clo Edg
63 Y 2	Parnell rd E3
63 W 17	Parnham st E14
47 W 4	Parolles rd N19
81 R 9	Paroma rd Blvdr
66 A 4	Parr clo E6
24 J 4	Parr rd Stanm
134 D 7	Parr st N1

66 G 19 Parry av E6
152 H 15 Parry clo Epsom
79 N 10 Parry pl SE18
123 R 7 Parry rd SE25
148 K 14 Parry st SW8
45 Y 13 Parsifal rd NW6
56 B 16 Parsloes av Dgnhm
55 X 14 Parsloes av Dgnhm
55 X 17 Parsloes park Dgnhm
87 X 3 Parson grn SW6
27 O 9 Parson st NW4
26 M 12 Parson st NW4
8 A 10 Parsonage gdns Enf
8 B 9 Parsonage la Enf
81 T 17 Parsonage Mnr way Blvdr
76 G 12 Parsonage st E14
12 B 10 Parsons cres Edg
87 W 1 Parsons Grn la SW6
12 C 10 Parsons gro Edg
78 H 9 Parsons hill SE18
156 K 1 Parsons mead Croy
122 J 20 Parsons mead Croy
63 X 7 Parsons rd E13
87 Y 2 Parthenia rd SW6
14 C 16 Partingdale la NW7
113 V 6 Partridge grn SE9
114 G 8 Partridge rd Sidcp
148 H 18 Pascal st SW8
93 X 13 Pascoe rd SE13
149 Z 11 Pasley rd SE17
32 J 10 Pasquier rd E19
95 U 15 Passey pl SE9
64 E 14 Passfield dri E14
16 K 20 Passmore gdns N11
147 T 8 Passmore st SW1
17 X 17 Pasteur gdns N18
18 A 17 Pasteur gdns N18
94 J 19 Paston cres SE12
149 Y 4 Pastor st SE11
42 B 10 Pasture clo Wemb
112 B 1 Pasture rd SE6
56 A 14 Pasture rd Dgnhm
42 A 8 Pasture rd Wemb
14 H 5 Pastures the N20
89 S 1 Patcham ter SW8
145 T 2 Pater st W8
142 A 5 Paternoster row EC4
141 Y 5 Paternoster sq EC4
106 A 20 Path the SW19
107 Y 15 Pathfield rd SW16
88 J 6 Patience ct SW11
89 X 15 Patio clo SW4
89 V 1 Patmore st SW8
149 W 20 Patmos rd SW9
90 H 1 Patmos rd SW9
64 B 8 Paton clo E3
134 A 14 Paton st EC1
65 Z 9 Patrick rd E13
63 O 7 Patriot sq E2
135 Y 10 Patriot sq E2
93 R 17 Patrol pl SE6
47 V 18 Patshull pl NW5
47 U 18 Patshull rd NW5
84 H 14 Patten all Rich
18 J 19 Patten rd SW18
110 M 2 Pattenden rd SE6
109 U 17 Patterson ct SE19
109 U 16 Patterson rd SE19
45 X 10 Pattison rd NW2
79 P 12 Pattison rd SE18
157 U 4 Paul gdns Croy
134 H 18 Paul st EC2
64 L 2 Paul st E15
90 K 4 Paulet rd SE5
24 G 12 Paulhan rd Harrow
17 T 2 Paulin dri N21
100 M 1 Pauline cres Twick
83 N 20 Pauline cres Twick
126 D 3 Pauls sq Brom
146 H 14 Paultons sq SW3
146 H 15 Paultons st SW3
47 V 5 Pauntley st N19
89 V 10 Pavement the SW4
56 G 18 Pavet clo Dgnhm
147 P 4 Pavilion rd SW1
139 P 20 Pavilion rd SW1
53 U 1 Pavilion rd Ilf
147 P 3 Pavilion st SW1
110 C 19 Pawleyne rd SE20
122 L 13 Pawsons rd Croy
42 A 7 Paxford rd Wemb
85 N 4 Paxton clo Rich
109 P 10 Paxton pl SE27
74 A 17 Paxton rd N17
64 C 7 Payne rd E3
75 Z 18 Payne st SE8
85 Y 9 Paynesfield av SW14
10 G 3 Paynesfield rd Bushey Watf
147 X 11 Peabody av SW1

31 R 5 Peabody cotts N17
90 K 19 Peabody est SE24
153 S 17 Peaches clo Sutton
77 P 9 Peachum rd SE3
142 J 13 Peacock all SE1
149 Y 7 Peacock st SE17
149 Z 8 Peacock yd SE17
142 H 4 Peahen ct EC2
110 C 10 Peak hill SE26
110 C 10 Peak Hill av SE26
110 C 10 Peak Hill gdns SE26
110 C 8 Peak the SE26
35 O 14 Peaketon av Ilf
59 Y 10 Peal gdns W13
122 C 14 Peall rd Croy
25 Y 14 Pear clo NW9
141 T 17 Pear pl SE1
75 O 2 Pear st E17
133 U 17 Pear Tree clo EC1
99 N 2 Pear Tree clo Erith
55 P 13 Pear Tree gdns Dgnhm
133 Z 15 Pear Tree st EC1
134 A 15 Pear Tree st EC1
110 C 2 Pearcefield av SE23
51 W 7 Pearcroft rd E11
89 T 5 Peardon st SW8
24 H 6 Pearswood gdns Stanm
110 G 6 Pearfield rd SE23
33 N 10 Pearl rd E17
143 Z 12 Pearl st E1
141 T 18 Pearman st SE1
83 O 7 Pears rd Hounsl
88 A 3 Pearscroft ct SW6
88 B 3 Pearscroft rd SW6
134 M 1 Pearson st E2
135 N 8 Pearson st E2
120 K 4 Peartree clo Mitch
38 G 7 Peartree gdns Rom
8 E 12 Peartree rd Enf
41 Y 6 Pebworth rd Harrow
109 X 6 Peckarmans wood SE26
90 F 6 Peckford pl SW9
90 F 6 Peckford yd SW9
150 K 18 Peckham gro SE15
91 W 2 Peckham High st SE15
91 X 1 Peckham Hill st SE15
151 R 19 Peckham Hill st SE15
151 U 14 Peckham Pk rd SE15
91 S 2 Peckham rd SE5
91 Y 9 Peckham rye SE15
92 B 11 Peckham Rye east SE15
92 A 13 Peckham Rye park SE22
47 V 16 Peckwater st NW5
48 A 18 Pedlars way N7
135 R 18 Pedley st E1
50 G 11 Pedro st E5
75 P 11 Pedworth gdns SE16
151 Z 7 Pedworth rd SE16
105 P 12 Peek cres SW19
26 F 11 Peel dri NW9
35 R 8 Peel gro Ilf
63 O 7 Peel gro E2
123 Z 10 Peel gro E2
34 A 6 Peel rd E18
129 S 11 Peel rd NW6
23 U 10 Peel rd Harrow
42 F 9 Peel rd Wemb
137 V 14 Peel st W8
134 E 14 Peerless st EC1
19 P 13 Pegamoid rd N18
149 S 13 Pegasus pl SE11
156 F 15 Pegasus rd Croy
112 G 3 Pegley gdns SE12
79 U 18 Pegwell st SE18
64 B 18 Pekin st E14
85 N 12 Peldon av Rich
84 M 12 Peldon pas Rich
67 W 4 Pelham av Bark
91 S 7 Pelham clo SE5
146 J 7 Pelham cres SW7
146 J 6 Pelham pl SW7
34 G 10 Pelham rd E18
31 U 13 Pelham rd N15
30 F 8 Pelham rd N22
105 Y 18 Pelham rd SW19
106 A 17 Pelham rd SW19
124 D 3 Pelham rd Becknhm
98 F 8 Pelham rd Bxly Hth
54 F 8 Pelham rd Ilf
146 J 6 Pelham st SW7
150 B 13 Pelier st SE17
111 Y 5 Pelinore rd SE6
110 D 17 Pell st E1
144 M 16 Pellant rd SW6
30 E 5 Pellatt gro N22

91 V 14 Pellatt rd SE22
49 S 14 Pellerin rd N16
64 A 17 Pelling st E14
17 S 11 Pellipar clo N13
78 F 12 Pellipar rd SE18
65 T 4 Pelly rd E13
76 U 3 Pelton rd SE10
32 G 11 Pembar av E17
128 F 13 Pember rd NW10
39 Z 10 Pemberton av Rom
47 X 8 Pemberton gdns N19
37 Y 16 Pemberton gdns Rom.
30 H 17 Pemberton rd N4
141 U 5 Pemberton row EC4
47 V 9 Pemberton ter N19
100 D 1 Pembridge av Twick
137 S 9 Pembridge cres W11
137 U 11 Pembridge gdns W2
137 S 9 Pembridge ms W11
137 U 8 Pembridge pl W2
137 T 10 Pembridge rd W11
137 S 9 Pembridge sq W2
137 T 8 Pembridge vlls W11
9 N 7 Pembroke av Enf
23 Z 9 Pembroke av Harrow
24 A 9 Pembroke av Harrow
117 T 11 Pembroke av Surb
139 U 18 Pembroke clo SW1
121 O 4 Pembroke clo Mitch
145 S 5 Pembroke gdns W8
56 G 10 Pembroke gdns Dgnhm
145 S 4 Pembroke Gdns clo W8
102 M 3 Pembroke lodge Rich
145 T 3 Pembroke ms W8
145 T 3 Pembroke pl W8
25 P 3 Pembroke pl Edg
33 R 15 Pembroke rd E17
29 P 3 Pembroke rd N10
17 Z 12 Pembroke rd N13
18 A 12 Pembroke rd N15
31 V 15 Pembroke rd N15
30 A 12 Pembroke rd N18
123 R 9 Pembroke rd SE25
145 R 6 Pembroke rd W14
126 M 4 Pembroke rd Brom
127 N 4 Pembroke rd Brom
81 Y 12 Pembroke rd Erith
58 L 10 Pembroke rd Grnfd
54 K 2 Pembroke rd Ilf
42 G 10 Pembroke rd Wemb
145 T 4 Pembroke sq W8
132 M 3 Pembroke st N1
145 R 3 Pembroke studios W8
145 T 4 Pembroke vlls W8
84 F 11 Pembroke vlls Rich
145 T 4 Pembroke wk W8
118 G 18 Pembury av Worc Pk
126 D 17 Pembury clo Brom
115 Y 5 Pembury gro Sidcp
49 Z 14 Pembury rd E5
31 U 5 Pembury rd N17
123 Y 9 Pembury rd SE25
80 M 18 Pembury rd Bxly Hth
81 N 17 Pembury rd Bxly Hth
122 H 17 Pemdevon rd Croy
63 R 11 Pemell clo E1
75 O 2 Penang st E1
32 L 7 Penant ter E17
31 N 4 Penarth st SE15
70 D 12 Penberth rd SE6
50 H 12 Penda rd E5
81 W 18 Penda rd Erith
104 L 20 Pendarves rd SW20
118 M 1 Pendarves rd SW20
31 O 10 Pendennis rd N17
108 B 8 Pendennis rd SW16
76 C 18 Pender st SE8
82 H 12 Penderell rd Hounsl
111 V 4 Penderry ri SE6
107 T 13 Pendle rd SW16
33 P 17 Pendlestone rd E17
112 D 7 Pendragon rd Brom
92 G 6 Pendrell rd SE4
79 T 17 Pendrell st SE18
111 S 1 Penerley rd SE6
115 W 2 Penfold la Bxly
19 S 5 Penfold rd N9
95 N 8 Penfold rd SE9
130 J 20 Penfold pl NW1
90 J 4 Penford st SE5
97 W 14 Pengarth rd Bxly
110 D 17 Penge la SE20
65 X 3 Penge rd E13
123 X 6 Penge rd SE25

77 Z 10 Penhall rd SE7
97 U 18 Penhill rd Bxly
108 A 17 Penistone rd SW16
41 P 9 Penkeith dri Harrow
80 B 8 Penmont rd SE2
58 M 7 Penn clo Grnfd
24 C 19 Penn clo Harrow
38 E 1 Penn gdns Rom
33 O 6 Penn rd E17
44 A 14 Penn rd N7
134 G 5 Penn st N1
151 P 15 Pennack rd SE15
145 X 4 Pennant ms W8
74 M 5 Pennard rd W12
136 C 16 Pennard rd W12
151 V 20 Pennethorne rd SE15
45 S 5 Pennine dri NW2
99 P 3 Pennine way Bxly Hth
143 V 11 Pennington st E1
64 A 20 Pennyfields E14
50 A 17 Penpoll rd E8
97 R 9 Penpool la Welling
33 O 4 Penrhyn av E17
32 M 6 Penrhyn av E17
33 P 4 Penrhyn cres E17
85 W 10 Penrhyn cres SW14
33 N 5 Penrhyn gro E17
116 H 8 Penrhyn rd Kingst
57 X 16 Penrith clo Hornch
108 H 4 Penrith pl SE27
31 O 15 Penrith rd N15
117 Z 8 Penrith rd New Mald
122 M 2 Penrith rd Thntn Hth
107 U 14 Penrith st SW16
150 A 11 Penrose gro SE17
150 L 8 Penrose st SE17
150 L 8 Penry st SE1
25 R 3 Penrylan pl Edg
132 E 8 Penryn st NW1
89 V 4 Pensbury pl SW8
89 V 3 Pensbury st SW8
85 R 4 Pensford av Rich
97 O 15 Penshurst av Sidcp
126 E 19 Penshurst gdns Edg
128 C 12 Penshurst grn Brom
63 T 2 Penshurst rd E9
31 U 2 Penshurst rd N17
98 B 1 Penshurst rd Bxly Hth
36 A 2 Penshurst rd Ilf
122 H 11 Penshurst rd Thntn Hth
20 G 12 Pensmead ter E4
33 W 5 Pentire rd E17
45 S 8 Pentland clo NW11
88 C 16 Pentland st SW18
121 R 6 Pentlands clo Mitch
86 M 6 Pentlow st SW15
19 O 9 Pentney rd E4
107 U 1 Pentney rd SW12
105 R 19 Pentney rd SW19
133 S 9 Penton gro N1
149 X 9 Penton ms SE17
149 X 8 Penton pl SE17
150 A 10 Penton pl SE17
133 P 11 Penton rise WC1
133 S 9 Penton st N1
133 R 10 Pentonville rd N1
8 K 4 Pentrich av Enf
150 M 19 Pentridge st SE15
18 B 16 Pentyre av N18
71 N 20 Penwerris av Islwth
105 Z 3 Penwith rd SW18
106 A 3 Penwith rd SW18
107 T 14 Penwortham rd SW16
145 V 9 Penywern rd SW5
136 L 12 Penzance pl W11
136 L 13 Penzance st W11
151 O 12 Pepler rd SE15
128 H 9 Peploe rd NW6
142 A 16 Pepper st SE1
4 B 17 Pepys cres Barnt
92 F 2 Pepys rd SE14
104 L 19 Pepys rd SW20
118 M 1 Pepys rd SW20
142 G 12 Pepys st EC3
46 H 15 Perceval av NW3
49 V 13 Perch st E8
31 V 1 Percival ct N17
37 U 18 Percival gdns Rom
85 V 11 Percival rd SW14
8 H 14 Percival rd Enf
133 W 15 Percival st EC1
80 G 10 Percival st EC1
133 P 12 Percy cir WC1
17 T 17 Percy gdns Enf
117 Z 19 Percy gdns Worc Pk
140 E 3 Percy ms W1
33 Z 20 Percy rd E11
65 N 14 Percy rd E16

129 U 10 Percy rd NW6
15 R 16 Percy rd N12
17 Z 3 Percy rd N21
124 E 1 Percy rd SE20
123W 11 Percy rd SE25
74 G 6 Percy rd W12
97 Z 6 Percy rd Bxly Hth
98 A 6 Percy rd Bxly Hth
100 G 17 Percy rd Hampt
37 N 20 Percy rd Ilf
83 Z 9 Percy rd Islwth
121 O 17 Percy rd Mitch
38 J 9 Percy rd Rom
82 H 20 Percy rd Twick
100 K 3 Percy rd Twick
140 E 2 Percy st W1
100 M 1 Percy way Twick
135 N 11 Perham rd W14
144 M 12 Perham rd W14
109 N 1 Perifield SE21
60 E 5 Perimeade rd Grnfd
102 B 8 Peripheral rd Rich
95 N 11 Periton rd SE9
60 A 11 Perivale gdns W13
59 Z 8 Perivale la Grnfd
59 T 10 Perivale la Greenford
42 A 14 Perkin clo Wemb
36 E 16 Perkins rd Ilf
148 F 2 Perkins rents SW1
96 F 17 Perpins rd SE9
108 H 2 Perran rd SW2
47 S 18 Perren st NW5
74 J 8 Perrers rd W6
42 A 14 Perrin rd Wemb
46 E 13 Perrins la NW3
46 D 13 Perrins wlk NW3
79 P 10 Perrott st SE18
2 J 20 Perrott villas E4
61 Z 17 Perry av W3
69 Z 6 Perry clo Rainhm
31 R 18 Perry ct N15
18 C 10 Perry gdns N9
110 L 5 Perry hill SE6
118 C 19 Perry how Worc Pk
7W 7 Perry mead Enf
110 J 8 Perry rd E14
114 K 15 Perry st Chisl
114 H 16 Perry St gdns Chisl
110 D 4 Perry vale SE23
26 E 20 Perryfield way NW9
102 B 6 Perryfield way Rich
36 D 17 Perrymans Farm rd Ilf
87 Z 4 Perrymead st SW6
73 Y 1 Perryn rd W3
61 Z 19 Perryn rd W3
140 E 5 Perrys pl W1
111 Z 5 Persant rd SE6
120 G 14 Pershore gro Carsh
43 Z 2 Perth av NW9
118 F 3 Perth clo SW20
50 K 4 Perth rd E10
65 V 8 Perth rd E13
30 H 5 Perth rd N22
48 F 4 Perth rd N4
67 S 5 Perth rd Bark
125 U 3 Perth rd Becknhm
35 X 18 Perth rd Ilf
54 B 1 Perth rd Ilf
36 A 20 Perth rd Ilf
63 R 16 Perth st E1
54 C 2 Perth ter Ilf
40 E 5 Perwell av Harrow
44 J 20 Peter av NW10
62 J 1 Peter av NW10
140 E 7 Peter st W1
87 X 4 Peterborough ms SW6
33W 18 Peterborough rd E10
87 X 4 Peterborough rd SW6
120 H 13 Peterborough rd Carsh
41 V 2 Peterborough rd Harrow
41 U 2 Peterborough rd Harrow
88 A 2 Peterborough vlls SW6
88 D 10 Petergate SW11
11 U 18 Peters clo Stanm
141 Z 7 Peters hill EC4
133 X 20 Peters la EC1
17 Y 16 Petersfield clo N18
73W 5 Petersfield rd W3
86 J 20 Petersfield ri SW15
102 H 3 Petersham clo Rich
153W 12 Petersham clo Sutton
146 B 2 Petersham la SW7

146 B 2 Petersham ms SW7
102 L 2 Petersham park Rich
146 C 1 Petersham pl SW7
102 J 1 Petersham rd Rich
84 J 17 Petersham rd Rich
80 D 7 Peterstone rd SE2
49 N 13 Petherton rd N5
144 E 16 Petley rd W6
131 Y 17 Peto pl NW1
65 O 19 Peto st E16
78 D 10 Pett st SE18
39 R 6 Pettits blvd Rom
39 P 7 Pettits clo Rom
39 P 7 Pettits la Rom
39 N 4 Pettits La north Rom
56 D 16 Pettits pl Dgnhm
56 D 15 Pettits rd Dgnhm
39 N 16 Pettley gdns Rom
42 E 14 Petts Grove av Wemb
40 K 14 Petts hill Grnfd
140 D 20 Petty france SW1
42 E 20 Petworth clo SW1
15 X 17 Petworth rd N12
98 D 14 Petworth rd Bxly Hth
88 K 2 Petworth st SW11
146 J 15 Petyt pl SW3
146 M 7 Petyward SW3
16 K 17 Pevensey av N11
8 C 8 Pevensey av Enf
52 D 12 Pevensey rd E7
106 G 10 Pevensey rd SW17
100 B 2 Pevensey rd Felt
101 R 12 Peveril dri Tedd
146 L 20 Peveril st SW11
19 Z 17 Pewsy cl E4
76 G 19 Peyton pl SE10
150 E 13 Phelp st SE17
146 L 14 Phene st SW3
145 T 9 Philbeach gdns SW5
143 T 7 Philchurch st E1
57 N 4 Philip av Rom
158 K 2 Philip clo Croy
31 U 11 Philip la N15
91 Y 7 Philip pl SE15
65 R 12 Philip st E13
95 U 16 Philipot path SE9
95 N 12 Phillimore gdns SE9
62 L 3 Phillimore gdns NW10
128 B 4 Phillimore gdns NW10
137 S 19 Phillimore gdns W8
137 T 19 Phillimore pl W8
137 U 20 Phillimore wlk W8
134 L 6 Phillipp st N1
142 H 9 Philpot la EC3
143 X 4 Philpot st E1
95 R 7 Phineas Pett rd SE9
134 J 17 Phipp st EC2
106 G 20 Phipps Br rd SW19
120 E 4 Phipps Br rd SW19
7 Z 2 Phipps Hatch la Enf
8 A 3 Phipps Hatch la Enf
147 X 4 Phipps ms SW1
120 F 1 Phipps ter SW19
63 Z 20 Phoebe st E14
93 O 13 Phoebeth rd SE4
133 R 16 Phoenix pl WC1
132 G 10 Phoenix rd NW1
110 C 16 Phoenix st WC2
140 H 6 Phoenix st WC2
118 K 10 Phyllis av New Mald
81 U 7 Picardy Mnr way Blvdr
81 S 3 Picardy rd Blvdr
81 S 9 Picardy rd Blvdr
139 Y 14 Piccadilly W1
140 B 3 Piccadilly W1
140 C 12 Piccadilly arcade SW1
140 E 10 Piccadilly cir W1
140 C 11 Piccadilly pl W1
133 Y 12 Pickard st EC1
66 K 7 Pickering av E6
137 Y 5 Pickering ms W2
133 Z 3 Pickering st N1
10 D 5 Pickets clo Bushey Watf
89 R 18 Pickets st SW12
24 F 5 Pickett croft Stanm
19 U 8 Picketts Lock la N9
97 Y 5 Pickford clo Bxly Hth
97 Z 2 Pickford la Bxly Hth
97 Y 9 Pickford rd Bxly Hth
126 B 19 Pickhurst grn Brom
126 A 13 Pickhurst la W Wkhm
125 Z 12 Pickhurst la W Wkhm
126 B 17 Pickhurst mead Brom
126 B 13 Pickhurst pk Brom

126 A 18 Pickhurst ri W Wckhm
125 V 19 Pickhurst ri W Wkhm
142 L 14 Pickle Herring st SE1
91 R 17 Pickwick st SE21
142 B 18 Pickwick st SE1
148 K 19 Pickworth st SW8
139 U 5 Picton pl W1
150 F 19 Picton st SE5
79 T 14 Piedmont rd SE18
78 J 4 Pier parade E16
78 J 4 Pier rd E16
76 H 10 Pier st E14
88 B 10 Pier ter SW18
91 Z 13 Piermont grn SE22
91 Z 13 Piermont rd SE22
61 T 19 Pierrepoint rd W3
133W 7 Pierrepont row N1
63 Z 18 Piggot st E14
64 A 17 Piggot st E14
108 L 8 Pilgrim hill SE27
17 E 14 Pilgrim st EC4
142 F 19 Pilgrimage st SE1
46 G 13 Pilgrims la NW3
5 X 17 Pilgrims ri Barnt
157 V 12 Pilgrims way S Croy
43 S 4 Pilgrims way Wemb
147 P 14 Pilke st SW3
115 S 17 Pilkington rd SE15
113 N 16 Pilmans clo Sidcp
147 U 8 Pimlico rd SW1
20 K 8 Pimp Hall park E4
143 T 8 Pinchin st E1
106 B 20 Pincott rd SW19
98 E 11 Pincott rd Bxly Hth
134 K 20 Pindar st EC2
129 Z 18 Pindock ms W9
125 R 19 Pine av W Wkhm
16 H 3 Pine clo N14
158 F 9 Pine coombe Croy
117 R 14 Pine gdns Surb
14 K 5 Pine gro N20
48 B 7 Pine gro N4
45 N 12 Pine rd NW2
16 A 8 Pine rd N11
155 O 19 Pine ridge Carsh
133 T 16 Pine st EC1
117 R 13 Pine wlk Surb
64 D 18 Pinefield clo E14
127 R 3 Pines rd Brom
6 H 15 Pines The N14
21 R 10 Pines the Wdfd Grn
114 J 2 Pinewood av Sidcp
158 H 6 Pinewood clo Croy
60 E 17 Pinewood gro W13
80 H 16 Pinewood rd SE2
72 H 18 Pinewood rd Brom
108 A 9 Pinfold rd SW16
16 F 19 Pinkham way N11
98 H 11 Pinnacle hill Bxly Hth
95 O 12 Pinnell rd SE9
22 J 14 Pinner ct Pinn
23 O 19 Pinner gro Pinn
23 N 17 Pinner park Pinn
94 G 10 Pinner Pk av Harrow
48 C 17 Pinner Pk av Harrow
117 O 5 Pinner Pk gdns Harrow
25W 17 Pinner rd Harrow
11 Y 12 Pinner rd Harrow
120 H 14 Pinner view Harrow
124 C 4 Pinto way SE3
159 V 14 Piper clo N7
87 X 20 Piper rd Kingst
77 V 3 Pipers grn NW9
106 M 17 Pipers Grn la Edg
89 S 6 Pipewell rd Carsh
64 L 2 Piquet rd SE20
43 N 1 Pirbright cres Croy
43 N 18 Pirbright rd SW18
94 E 17 Pirie st E16
94 E 17 Pitcairn rd Mitch
156 J 2 Pitcairn st SW8
63 T 18 Pitchford st E15
63 T 18 Pitfield st N1
60 D 12 Pitfield way NW10
60 B 9 Pitfold clo SE12
105 Z 9 Pitfold rd SE12
106 A 10 Pitlake Croy
122 M 11 Pitsea pl E1
137 V 17 Pitsea st E1
142 K 14 Pitshanger la W5
Pitshanger park Grnfd
Pitt cres SW19
Pitt cres SW19
Pitt rd Thntn Hth
Pitt st W8
Pitts ct SE1

139 V 14 Pitts Head ms SW1
126 E 18 Pittsmead av Brom
123 X 5 Pitville gdns SE25
63 Y 17 Pixley st E14
158 H 20 Pixton way Croy
142 F 18 Plaintain pl SE1
65 O 4 Plaistow gro E15
112 G 18 Plaistow gro Brom
112 G 18 Plaistow la Brom
126 M 2 Plaistow la Brom
65 U 5 Plaistow Pk rd E13
65 R 6 Plaistow rd E15
109 Z 8 Plane st SE26
55W 2 Plantagenet gdns Rom
55 X 2 Plantagenet pl Rom
5 P 14 Plantagenet rd Barnt
99 V 1 Plantation rd Erith
94 F 5 Plantation the SE3
65 Y 2 Plashet gro E6
66 A 1 Plashet gro E6
53 O 20 Plashet gro E7
93 S 19 Plassy rd SE6
134 G 17 Platina pl EC2
90 A 11 Plato rd SW2
132 F 9 Platt st NW1
87 R 8 Platt the SW15
45 Y 11 Platts la NW3
9 R 7 Platts rd Enf
110 G 20 Plawsfield rd Becknhm
126 L 2 Plaxtol clo Brom
77 T 14 Plaxtol pl SE10
81 T 18 Plaxtol rd Erith
121 N 13 Player rd Mitch
144 E 12 Playfair st W6
38 J 4 Playfield av Rom
91 T 13 Playfield cres SE22
25W 6 Playfield rd Edg
48 E 7 Playford rd N4
48 E 6 Playford rd N4
48 E 8 Playford rd N4
5 11 Playgreen way SE6
141 X 7 Playhouse yd EC4
86 J 12 Pleasance rd SW15
86 J 11 Pleasance the SW15
158 L 5 Pleasant gro Croy
133 Y 1 Pleasant pl N1
131 Z 5 Pleasant row NW1
60 F 5 Pleasant way Wemb
20 B 8 Pleasaunce E4
132 B 6 Plender st NW1
47W 13 Pleshey rd N7
31 S 1 Plevna clo N15
31 S 1 Plevna cres N15
18 L 10 Plevna rd N9
76 F 7 Plevna st E14
66 K 18 Plevna st E6
109 V 17 Pleydell av SE19
74 E 10 Pleydell av W6
141 U 6 Pleydell st EC4
64 D 18 Plimsoll st E14
142 G 8 Plough ct EC3
91W 17 Plough la SE22
106 C 11 Plough la SW19
155 A 12 Plough la Wallgtn
155 Z 8 Plough la Wallgtn
155 Z 10 Plough La clo Wallgtn
141 T 4 Plough pl EC4
88 G 10 Plough ter SW11
88 G 10 Plough ter SW11
75W 20 Plough way SE16
134 K 18 Plough yd EC2
72 F 19 Plough yd Brentf
70 B 9 Pluckington pl Shall
79 O 18 Plum garth Brentf
78 A 18 Plum la SE18
93 U 2 Plumb st SE10
133 U 15 Plumbers st EC1
143 S 3 Plumbers row E1
120 L 2 Plummer la Mitch
89 X 18 Plummer rd SW4
40 L 7 Plumpton clo Grnfd
78 L 15 Plumstead Comm rd SE18
79 P 16 Plumstead Comm rd SE18
79W 1 Plumstead High st SE18
79 O 10 Plumstead rd SE18
141 V 3 Plumtree ct EC4
65 S 16 Plymouth rd E16
112 J 20 Plymouth rd Brom
129 N 2 Plympton av NW6
130 K 18 Plympton pl NW8
129 O 1 Plympton rd NW6
130 K 18 Plympton st NW8
80 F 20 Plymstock rd Welling
141 X 17 Pocock st SE1
88 C 11 Podmore rd SW18

49 N 14	Poets rd N5
87 X 11	Point pleasant SW6
28 D 6	Pointalls clo N3
40 C 5	Poland st W1
72 B 8	Pole Hill rd E4
94 L 6	Polebrook rd SE3
10 L 4	Polescroft la SE6
55 X 20	Polesworth rd Dgnhm
68 K 1	Polesworth rd Dgnbm
65 S 19	Pollard clo E16
20 G 12	Pollard rd N20
35 U 13	Pollard rd Mrdn
35 U 13	Pollard row E2
35 U 13	Pollard st E2
22 B 6	Pollards cres SW16
22 C 5	Pollards Hill east SW16
22 C 5	Pollards Hill north SW16
22 C 7	Pollards Hill south SW16
22 B 6	Pollards Hill west SW16
22 A 5	Pollards Wood rd SW16
39 Z 7	Pollen st W1
50 C 5	Pollock rd SE17
92 M 19	Polstead rd SE6
79 R 10	Polthorne gro SE18
08 A 13	Polworth rd SW16
32 D 11	Polygon rd NW1
89 U 9	Polygon the SW4
75 K 11	Polytechnic st SE18
75 P 26	Pomeroy sq SE14
75 R 20	Pomeroy st SE14
75 R 20	Pomeroy st SE14
90 K 7	Pomfret st SE5
94 E 5	Pond clo SE3
146 J 7	Pond pl SW3
79 R 10	Pond rd E15
94 D 5	Pond rd SE3
47 P 3	Pond sq N6
46 H 14	Pond st NW3
102 D 16	Pond way Tedd
142 A 12	Pond yd SE1
48 C 20	Ponder st N7
126 A 20	Pondfield rd Brom
56 G 14	Pondfield rd Dgnhm
153 R 12	Pondhill gdns Sutton
143 V 7	Ponler st E1
50 D 16	Ponsard rd NW10
50 D 16	Ponsford st E9
148 H 9	Ponsonby pl SW1
88 J 19	Ponsonby rd SW15
148 H 9	Ponsonby ter SW1
147 R 2	Pont st SW1
147 O 2	Pont St ms SW3
112 D 12	Pontefract rd Brom
148 F 15	Ponton rd SW8
112 D 12	Pontypool pl SE1
82 B 4	Poole Ct rd Hounsl
50 E 19	Poole rd E9
134 E 6	Poole st NJ
123 R 17	Pooles bldgs WC1
68 M 5	Pooles la Dgnhm
48 E 7	Pooles pk N4
48 E 7	Pooles pk N4
26 B 13	Poolsford rd NW9
N 12	Pope rd Brom
142 M 19	Pope st SE1
51 S 3	Popes av Twick
158 L 4	Popes gro Croy
51 S 3	Popes gro Twick
142 F 7	Popes Head all EC3
72 G 9	Popes la W5
90 F 9	Popes rd SW9
134 A 3	Popham rd N1
134 A 3	Popham st N1
134 A 3	Popham st N1
120 M 1	Poplar av Mitch
70 K 8	Poplar av S'hall
64 E 19	Poplar Bath st E14
105 Y 11	Poplar ct SW19
117 Z 4	Poplar gdns New Mald
136 D 20	Poplar gro W6
117 Z 6	Poplar gro New Mald
43 W 9	Poplar gro Wemb
64 D 20	Poplar High st E14
81 V 10	Poplar mt Blvdr
137 Y 9	Poplar pl W2
119 Y 6	Poplar rd SW19
119 U 20	Poplar rd Sutton
38 M 5	Poplar st Rom
156 M 1	Poplar wik Croy
90 L 9	Poplar Wik rd SE24
44 M 19	Poplars av NW2
33 R 18	Poplars rd E17
6 F 16	Poplars the N14
141 V 5	Poppins ct EC4
34 A 20	Poppleton rd E11
15 Y 11	Porch way N20
137 Z 7	Porchester gdns ms W2
138 L 6	Porchester pl W2
137 Y 5	Porchester rd W2
117 T 4	Porchester rd Kingst
137 Y 4	Porchester sq W2
137 Z 5	Porchester Sq ms W2
138 K 4	Porchester st W2
138 D 10	Porchester ter W2
137 Z 3	Porchester Ter north W2
137 Z 7	Porchester terr W2
113 S 4	Porcupine clo SE9
90 D 11	Porden rd SW2
41 N 3	Porlock av Harrow
18 F 3	Porlock rd Enf
142 F 18	Porlock rd SE1
108 G 6	Portal clo SE27
8 B 11	Portcullis Lodge rd Enf
63 S 10	Portelet rd E1
144 J 2	Porten rd W14
138 E 1	Porters av W2
131 S 20	Porter st W1
55 U 15	Porters av Dgnhm
50 F 5	Portersfield E10
110 J 10	Porthcawe rd SE26
97 N 9	Porthkerry av Welling
63 Y 13	Portia rd E3
87 U 14	Portinscale rd SW15
49 U 2	Portland av N16
18 E 16	Portland av New Mald
97 O 17	Portland av Sidcp
113 P 4	Portland cres SE9
58 L 13	Portland cres Grnfd
24 J 8	Portland Cres east Stanm
24 G 8	Portland Cres west Stanm
30 K 19	Portland gdns N4
37 X 15	Portland gdns Rom
90 B 1	Portland gro SW8
139 Y 2	Portland ms W1
140 C 7	Portland ms W1
139 Y 1	Portland pl W1
131 Y 19	Portland pl W1
31 T 13	Portland rd N15
123 Y 10	Portland rd SE25
113 R 4	Portland rd SE9
136 M 12	Portland rd W11
112 L 11	Portland rd Brom
116 K 7	Portland rd Kingst
120 J 3	Portland rd Mitch
70 D 7	Portland rd S'hall
48 K 4	Portland ri N4
48 K 4	Portland Ri est N4
150 E 11	Portland st SE17
84 G 11	Portland ter Rich
85 Y 9	Portman av SW14
139 S 4	Portman clo W1
35 N 7	Portman dri Wdfd Grn
25 X 9	Portman gdns NW9
139 S 6	Portman ms W1
63 R 9	Portman pl E2
117 N 4	Portman pl Kingst
139 S 5	Portman sq W1
139 R 6	Portman st W1
129 O 11	Portnall rd W9
137 T 10	Portobello ms W11
137 T 10	Portobello mws W11
136 M 2	Portobello rd W10
137 S 10	Portobello rd W11
128 K 19	Portobello rd W11
133 S 20	Portpool la EC1
64 K 16	Portree st E14
27 T 19	Portsdown av NW11
9 X 1	Portsdown ms NW11
138 M 6	Portsea ms W2
138 M 6	Portsea pl W2
89 V 4	Portslade rd SW8
104 J 1	Portsmouth av SW15
86 L 19	Portsmouth rd SW15
86 L 20	Portsmouth rd SW15
116 F 12	Portsmouth rd Surb & Kingst
141 O 5	Portsmouth st WC2
143 O 8	Portswood pl SW15
86 D 17	Portugal gdns Twick
141 P 5	Portugal st WC2
152 G 20	Portway E15
152 G 20	Portway Epsom
142 F 7	Post Office ct EC3
150 G 2	Potier st SE1
63 N 10	Pott st E2
135 X 14	Pott st E2
87 P 19	Potterne clo SW19
142 L 15	Potters fields SE1
117 W 9	Potters gro New Mald
107 X 14	Potters la SW16
-4 L 15	Potters la Barnt
5 O 13	Potters la Barnt
143 V 18	Pottery la SE16
136 L 12	Pottery la W11
101 X 2	Poulet gdns Twick
62 J 5	Poulett rd E6
120 J 13	Poulter park Carsh
154 H 5	Poulton av Sutton
142 D 6	Poultry EC2
109 O 19	Pound clo Surb
44 F 19	Pound la NW10
78 B 12	Pound Pk rd SE7
95 V 15	Pound pl SE9
154 L 11	Pound st Carsh
89 O 7	Pountney rd SW11
82 E 20	Powder Mill la Twick
100 G 1	Powder Mill la Twick
11 Z 18	Powell clo Edg
155 Z 16	Powell clo Wallgtn
56 D 12	Powell gdns Dgnhm
50 A 11	Powell rd E5
21 Z 3	Powell rd Buck HI
74 B 17	Powells wlk W4
73 R 12	Power rd W4
50 D 11	Powerscroft rd E5
115 T 17	Powerscroft rd Sidcp
29 X 14	Powis gdns NW11
137 P 5	Powis gdns W11
137 R 5	Powis ms W11
132 L 19	Powis pl WC1
50 D 9	Powis rd E3
137 R 6	Powis sq W11
64 L 9	Powis st E15
137 R 3	Powis st SE18
137 R 5	Powis ter W11
47 R 19	Powlett pl NW1
82 L 10	Pownall gdns Hounsl
135 R 4	Pownall rd E8
82 L 10	Pownall rd Hounsl
52 E 9	Powster rd Brom
80 K 18	Powys clo Bxly Hth
17 N 14	Powys la N13
16 M 14	Powys la N13
16 M 13	Powys la N14
89 V 18	Poynders gdns SW4
89 W 18	Poynders rd SW4
47 U 9	Poynings rd N19
14 K 17	Poynings way N12
114 F 20	Poyntell cres Chisl
8 J 18	Poynter rd Enf
31 Z 6	Poynton rd N17
88 M 6	Poyntz rd SW11
83 N 7	Poyser st E2
135 X 11	Poyser st E2
138 G 5	Praed ms W2
138 F 6	Praed st W2
65 X 8	Pragel st E13
112 X 3	Pragnell rd SE12
48 G 8	Prah rd N4
89 R 4	Prairie st SW8
85 T 20	Pratt ms NW1
52 B 3	Pratt st NW1
149 O 4	Pratt wlk SE11
45 P 3	Prayle gro NW2
74 D 11	Prebend gdns W4
134 B 5	Prebend st N1
94 A 7	Prendergast rd SE3
74 A 11	Prentis rd SW16
78 A 11	Prentiss ct SE7
118 B 10	Presburg rd New Mald
25 N 5	Prescelly pl Edg
143 O 8	Prescot st E1
127 Y 15	Prescott av Brom
89 X 9	Prescott pl SW4
134 A 13	President st EC1
43 Z 9	Press rd NW10
129 O 19	Pressland st W10
64 H 20	Prestage st E14
52 L 20	Prestbury rd E7
113 T 9	Prestbury sq SE9
88 J 9	Prested rd SW11
20 J 20	Preston av E4
101 S 5	Preston clo Twick
34 K 16	Preston dri E11
97 W 2	Preston dri Bxly Hth
52 C 13	Preston dri Epsom
44 C 18	Preston gdns NW10
29 X 1	Preston gdns Enf
35 S 19	Preston gdns Ilf
44 H 18	Preston hill Harrow
42 K 1	Preston hill Harrow
42 H 1	Preston pl NW2
61 N 18	Preston pl Rich
84 L 13	Preston pl Rich
34 A 20	Preston rd E11
64 G 20	Preston rd E14
64 G 3	Preston rd E15
108 J 15	Preston rd SE19
104 E 18	Preston rd SW20
42 K 2	Preston rd Harrow
42 J 3	Preston waye Harrow
76 G 3	Prestons rd E14
70 B 14	Prestwick clo S'hall
24 B 13	Prestwood av Harrow
24 C 13	Prestwood clo
32 G 12	Pretoria av E17
31 U 1	Pretoria clo N17
20 H 6	Pretoria cres E4
51 X 4	Pretoria rd E11
65 O 11	Pretoria rd E16
20 H 5	Pretoria rd E4
31 U 1	Pretoria rd N17
107 T 13	Pretoria rd SW16
53 Y 14	Pretoria rd Ilf
38 J 14	Pretoria rd Rom
18 G 18	Pretoria Rd north N18
16 B 7	Prevost rd N11
108 L 8	Price clo SW17
156 J 10	Price rd Croy
141 Y 14	Prices st SE1
133 O 4	Prices yd N1
5 O 19	Pricklers hill Barnt
133 R 12	Prideaux pl WC1
90 A 7	Prideaux rd SW9
123 N 10	Pridham Rd east Thntn Hth
110 J 7	Priestfield rd SE23
114 L 7	Priestlands Pk rd Sidcp
37 P 19	Priestley gdns Rom
31 V 20	Priestly clo N16
121 P 2	Priestly rd Mitch
50 E 15	Priestly st E9
39 N 8	Priests av Rom
86 B 9	Priests br SW15
142 A 5	Priests ct EC2
149 T 17	Prima rd SW9
8 C 5	Primrose av Enf
37 P 20	Primrose av Rom
55 R 1	Primrose av Rom
34 H 7	Primrose clo E18
40 D 11	Primrose clo Harrow
46 K 17	Primrose gdns NW3
141 V 7	Primrose hill EC4
46 L 19	Primrose Hill rd NW3
131 N 1	Primrose Hill rd NW3
131 S 3	Primrose Hill stds NW1
51 R 4	Primrose rd E10
34 G 7	Primrose rd E18
134 X 20	Primrose st EC2
60 F 6	Primrose way Wemb
62 F 18	Primula st W12
131 P 6	Prince Albert rd NW1
130 K 11	Prince Albert rd NW1
46 E 13	Prince Arthur ms NW3
46 E 14	Prince Arthur rd NW3
94 B 3	Prince Charles rd SE3
138 E 20	Prince Consort rd SW7
66 A 17	Prince Edward cres E16
50 M 17	Prince Edward rd E9
6 H 15	Prince George av N14
7 N 18	Prince George av N14
49 S 12	Prince George rd N16
119 N 3	Prince Georges av SW20
106 H 20	Prince Georges rd SW19
78 B 19	Prince Henry rd SE7
78 H 20	Prince Imperial rd SE18
95 R 13	Prince John rd SE9
47 R 19	Prince Of Wales cres NW1
88 L 2	Prince Of Wales dri SW11
147 Y 20	Prince Of Wales dri SW11
89 O 1	Prince Of Wales dri SW8

65 Y 18 Prince Of Wales rd E16
26 L 12 Prince Of Wales rd NW4
47 T 18 Prince Of Wales rd NW5
94 C 3 Prince Of Wales rd SE3
154 G 3 Prince Of Wales rd Sutton
74 A 13 Prince Of Wales ter W4
137 Z 19 Prince Of Wales ter W4
123 R 10 Prince rd SE25
65 X 12 Prince Regent la E13
82 L 7 Prince Regent rd Hounsl
95 T 8 Prince Rupert rd SE9
75 Z 16 Prince st SE8
76 A 16 Prince st SE8
135 P 20 Princedale rd W11
140 C 12 Princelet st E1
25 P 13 Princes av NW9
29 R 11 Princes av N10
17 V 17 Princes av N13
29 Y 4 Princes av N22
27 Z 4 Princes av W3
73 R 7 Princes av W3
154 K 18 Princes av Carsh
58 L 16 Princes av Grnfd
21 X 14 Princes av Wdfd Grn
25 P 13 Princes clo NW9
12 B 16 Princes clo Edg
115 V 7 Princes clo Sidcp
101 P 10 Princes clo Tedd
42 K 14 Princes ct Wemb
23 T 11 Princes dri Harrow
138 G 19 Princes ga SW7
146 H 2 Princes Ga ms SW7
138 G 19 Princes gate SW7
146 H 1 Princes gdns SW7
138 H 20 Princes gdns SW7
61 R 14 Princes gdns W3
60 D 13 Princes gdns W5
29 R 11 Princes la N10
137 W 9 Princes ms W2
27 T 17 Princes Pk av NW11
140 C 13 Princes pl EC4
136 L 13 Princes pl W11
127 T 19 Princes plain Brom
19 P 13 Princes rd N18
110 F 16 Princes rd SE20
85 Z 8 Princes rd SW14
105 X 15 Princes rd SW19
72 C 2 Princes rd W13
21 Y 8 Princes rd Buck Hl
36 D 13 Princes rd Ilf
103 P 19 Princes rd Kingst
84 M 12 Princes rd Rich
85 N 1 Princes rd Rich
39 V 18 Princes rd Rom
101 P 11 Princes rd Tedd
99 X 17 Princes Rd north Drtfrd
93 U 5 Princes ri SE13
137 W 8 Princes sq W2
142 E 5 Princes st EC2
18 E 20 Princes st N17
140 H 19 Princes st SW1
139 Z 6 Princes st W1
98 A 9 Princes st Bxly Hth
84 J 11 Princes st Rich
154 F 8 Princes st Sutton
65 W 4 Princes ter E13
87 P 19 Princes way SW19
105 S 2 Princes way SW19
21 Y 8 Princes way Buck Hl
123 N 12 Princes way Croy
40 B 12 Princes way Ruis
136 L 14 Princes yd W1
42 L 6 Princess av Wemb
48 K 6 Princess cres N4
49 S 13 Princess May rd N16
131 U 3 Princess rd NW1
129 U 9 Princess rd NW6
122 M 14 Princess rd Croy
123 N 12 Princess rd Croy
110 E 10 Princethorpe rd SE26
141 N 1 Princeton sq WC1
107 U 10 Pringle gdns SW16
141 X 8 Printing Hse sq EC4
77 X 14 Priolo rd SE7
154 H 15 Prior av Sutton
48 K 19 Prior Bolton st N1
76 G 20 Prior st SE10
32 J 8 Priors croft E17
93 U 1 Priors Point hill SE10
33 O 15 Priory av E17
19 Z 11 Priory av E4

20 B 11 Priory av E4
29 Y 13 Priory av N8
74 B 9 Priory av W4
153 P 8 Priory av Sutton
41 X 12 Priory av Wemb
34 E 4 Priory clo E18
19 Z 11 Priory clo E4
6 F 17 Priory clo N14
14 G 3 Priory clo N20
124 J 7 Priory clo Becknhm
127 U 2 Priory clo Chisl
100 F 19 Priory clo Hampt
10 J 10 Priory clo Stanm
41 W 12 Priory clo Wemb
109 N 18 Priory cres SE19
153 P 8 Priory cres Sutton
41 Y 10 Priory cres Wemb
32 K 8 Priory ct E17
89 Z 1 Priory ct SW8
80 J 14 Priory dri SE2
10 H 10 Priory dri Stanm
29 S 18 Priory gdns N16
86 C 8 Priory gdns SW14
89 Z 1 Priory gdns SW8
89 Z 2 Priory gdns SW8
74 A 10 Priory gdns W4
60 K 8 Priory gdns W5
100 E 19 Priory gdns Hampt
41 X 11 Priory gdns Wemb
89 Z 3 Priory gro SW8
41 Y 11 Priory hill Wemb
86 D 10 Priory la SW15
89 Y 2 Priory ms W8
94 C 9 Priory pk SE3
129 S 3 Priory Pk rd NW6
41 X 12 Priory Pk rd Wemb
81 P 6 Priory rd E6
46 A 19 Priory rd NW6
129 X 1 Priory rd NW6
29 X 13 Priory rd N8
106 F 18 Priory rd SW19
73 X 9 Priory rd W4
54 E 20 Priory rd Bark
122 F 17 Priory rd Croy
100 E 19 Priory rd Hampt
83 O 13 Priory rd Hounsl
73 P 18 Priory rd Rich
153 P 9 Priory rd Sutton
64 E 8 Priory st E3
37 S 4 Priory ter NW6
10 E 3 Priory view Bushey Watf
22 K 12 Priory way Harrow
146 C 11 Priory wlk SW10
64 B 9 Priscilla rd E3
135 V 8 Pritchards rd E2
151 T 2 Priter rd SE16
151 T 3 Priter way SE16
18 C 17 Private rd Enf
90 C 12 Probert rd SW2
108 H 4 Probyn rd SW2
141 N 2 Procter st WC1
30 F 4 Progress way N22
156 D 3 Progress way Croy
8 L 19 Progress way Enf
74 A 20 Promenade Appr rd W4
86 C 2 Promenade the W4
93 U 2 Prospect clo SE10
81 S 12 Prospect clo Blvdr
82 F 3 Prospect clo Hounsl
87 X 11 Prospect cottages SW18
83 N 16 Prospect cres Twick
33 S 12 Prospect hill E17
31 S 4 Prospect pl N17
28 H 12 Prospect pl N2
126 H 7 Prospect pl Brom
38 K 8 Prospect pl Rom
116 D 15 Prospect pl Surb
312 L 20 Prospect rd E17
45 W 9 Prospect rd NW2
109 Z 9 Prospect rd SE26
8 M 14 Prospect rd Barnt
5 N 14 Prospect rd Barnt
21 Z 17 Prospect rd Wdfd Grn
28 H 11 Prospect ring N2
133 N 15 Prospect ter WC1
132 M 15 Prospect ter WC1
78 D 11 Prospect vale SE18
63 T 8 Prospect wk E2
97 K 14 Prospero rd N19
26 K 15 Prothero gdns NW4
145 N 17 Prothero rd SW6
44 C 13 Prout gro NW10
64 A 9 Prout rd E5
134 A 8 Provence st N1
139 U 3 Providence ct W1
133 V 5 Providence pl N1
38 B 5 Providence place Rom
46 M 19 Provost rd NW3

134 E 13 Provost st N1
10 A 8 Prowse av Bushey Watf
47 U 20 Prowse pl NW1
16 J 9 Pruden clo N14
142 D 5 Prudent pass EC2
75 O 2 Prusom st E1
143 Z 12 Prusom st E1
142 H 10 Pudding la EC3
64 E 5 Pudding Mill la E15
141 X 9 Puddle dock EC4
87 V 19 Pulborough rd SW18
31 P 18 Pulford rd N15
148 E 10 Pulford st SW1
28 E 12 Pulham av N2
4 E 10 Puller rd Barnt
66 E 8 Pulleyns av E6
86 M 15 Pullman gdns SW15
90 C 9 Pulross rd SW9
34 G 10 Pulteney gdns E18
133 R 5 Pulteney st N1
133 R 5 Pulteney ter N1
145 T 19 Pulton pl SW6
72 H 18 Pump all Brentf
141 S 7 Pump ct EC4
156 L 7 Pump pail Croy
74 B 18 Pumping Station la W4
74 B 18 Pumping Station rd W4
63 N 8 Pundersons gdns E2
135 X 12 Pundersons gdns E2
118 D 15 Purbeck av New Mald
118 E 15 Purbeck av New Mald
45 R 6 Purbeck dri NW2
57 X 2 Purbeck rd Hornch
142 M 20 Purbrook st SE1
144 J 17 Purcell cres SW6
58 K 13 Purcell rd Grnfd
134 J 9 Purcell st N1
12 B 15 Purcells av Edg
132 G 9 Purchese st NW1
64 C 11 Purdy st E3
56 B 4 Purland clo Dgnhm
79 Z 6 Purland rd SE18
45 S 8 Purley av NW2
35 X 8 Purley clo Ilf
48 H 20 Purley pl N1
18 C 11 Purley rd N9
157 N 18 Purley rd S Croy
122 D 19 Purley way Croy
156 E 4 Purley way Croy
95 N 10 Purneys rd SE9
94 M 9 Purneys rd SE9
79 X 13 Purrett rd SE18
87 W 2 Purses Cross rd SW6
26 K 1 Pursley rd NW7
128 C 10 Purves rd NW10
62 M 7 Purves rd NW10
87 S 8 Putney bridge SW6
87 S 7 Putney Bridge app SW6
87 U 10 Putney Bridge rd SW15
86 L 7 Putney comm SW15
86 L 17 Putney heath SW15
87 O 16 Putney heath SW15
104 M 3 Putney heath SW19
87 P 17 Putney Heath la SW15
87 R 11 Putney High st SW15
87 P 14 Putney hill SW15
86 H 10 Putney Pk av SW15
86 J 10 Putney Pk la SW15
14 H 14 Pyecombe corner N12
100 L 1 Pyecroft av Twick
153 Z 6 Pylbrook rd Sutton
5 U 17 Pym clo Barnt
109 N 1 Pymers mead SE21
17 O 17 Pymms la N13
18 H 12 Pymmes Gdns north N9
18 H 12 Pymmes Gdns south N9
16 F 12 Pymmes Green rd N11
18 G 13 Pymmes park N18
17 O 18 Pymmes rd N13
80 B 9 Pynham clo SE2
11 O 16 Pynnacles clo Stanm
49 N 15 Pyrland rd N5
85 N 16 Pyrland rd Rich
108 H 7 Pyrmont gro SE27
73 P 16 Pyrmont rd W4
54 B 8 Pyrmont rd Ilf
108 M 16 Pytchley cres SE19
91 T 8 Pytchley rd SE22

Q

47 N 16 Quadrant gro NW5
84 H 11 Quadrant rd Rich
122 J 8 Quadrant rd Thntn Hth
75 S 20 Quadrant the SW20
80 K 20 Quadrant the Bxly Hth
84 J 11 Quadrant the Rich
94 F 10 Quaggy wlk SE12
43 V 19 Quainton st NW10
83 Z 1 Quaker la Islwth
71 X 19 Quaker la Islwth
135 N 18 Quaker st E1
8 A 19 Quakers wlk Enf
141 S 3 Quality st WC2
45 O 7 Quantock gdns NW2
99 R 3 Quantock rd Bxly Hth
120 G 14 Quarr rd Carsh
87 Y 4 Quarrendon st SW6
153 U 13 Quarry Pk rd Sutton
88 E 15 Quarry rd SW18
153 U 13 Quarry ri Sutton
51 P 12 Quartermile la E10
139 P 6 Quebec ms W1
36 B 19 Quebec rd Ilf
54 A 1 Quebec rd Ilf
110 D 17 Queen Adelaide rd SE20
120 K 6 Queen Ann gdns Mitch
50 F 19 Queen Ann rd E9
126 D 7 Queen Anne av Brom
139 Y 3 Queen Anne ms W1
139 X 3 Queen Anne st W1
31 T 15 Queen Annes av N15
101 R 7 Queen Annes clo Twick
140 F 19 Queen Annes ga SW1
74 A 8 Queen Annes gdns W4
72 J 6 Queen Annes gdns W5
8 E 20 Queen Annes gdns Enf
74 A 9 Queen Annes gro W4
72 K 5 Queen Annes gro W5
18 C 2 Queen Annes gro Enf
8 F 19 Queen Annes pl Enf
74 L 14 Queen Caroline st W6
144 C 10 Queen Caroline st W6
17 N 3 Queen Elizabeth dri N14
159 W 20 Queen Elizabeth dri Croy
141 P 13 Queen Elizabeth hall SE1
32 H 10 Queen Elizabeth rd Kingst
116 L 3 Queen Elizabeth rd Kingst
143 O 17 Queen Elizabeth st SE1
49 N 6 Queen Elizabeths clo N16
17 N 4 Queen Elizabeths dri N14
16 M 6 Queen Elizabeths dri N14
49 N 4 Queen Elizabeths wlk N16
155 Y 8 Queen Elizabeths wlk Wallgtn
49 R 16 Queen Margarets gro N1
119 O 12 Queen Mary av Mrdn
108 K 14 Queen Mary rd SE19
154 L 17 Queen Marys av Carsh
131 S 15 Queen Marys gardens NW1
132 K 19 Queen sq WC1
142 C 9 Queen st EC4
139 X 13 Queen st W1
98 A 9 Queen st Bxly Hth
54 J 16 Queen st Croy
39 O 17 Queen st Rom
142 C 10 Queen St pl EC4

42 B 8 Queen Victoria st EC4
41 Y 8 Queen Victoria st EC4
35 X 12 Queenborough gdns Ilf
58 A 20 Queenhill rd S Croy
42 B 10 Queenhithe EC4
53 R 16 Queens acre Sutton
29 R 10 Queens av N10
15 U 9 Queens av N20
17 X 6 Queens av N21
28 D 4 Queens av N3
98 M 16 Queens av Grnfd
24 D 9 Queens av Stanm
21 W 16 Queens av Wdfd Grn
59 N 16 Queens ave Grnfd
47 X 20 Queens cir SW11
12 C 17 Queens clo Edg
55 S 10 Queens clo Wallgtn
45 N 13 Queens Club gdns W14
44 M 13 Queens Club gdns W14
84 F 6 Queens cottage Rich
47 O 18 Queens cres NW5
51 N 13 Queens cres Rich
10 B 3 Queens ct SE23
48 J 6 Queens dri N4
61 O 17 Queens dri N4
60 M 18 Queens dri W3
17 R 15 Queens dri W5
46 G 11 Queens dri Surb
46 D 3 Queens Elm sq SW3
46 B 3 Queens Ga SW7
Queens Ga gdns SW7
46 C 1 Queens Ga ms SW7
46 D 3 Queens Ga pl SW7
46 D 4 Queens Ga Pl ms SW7
46 C 1 Queens Ga ter SW7
39 Z 19 Queens gallery SW1
38 C 20 Queens gate SW7
27 N 16 Queens gdns NW4
38 C 8 Queens gdns W2
60 E 13 Queens gdns W5
82 B 2 Queens gdns Hounsl
69 Z 7 Queens gdns Rainham
30 F 7 Queens gro NW8
20 K 5 Queens Grove rd E4
33 Y 5 Queens Head st N1
62 E 15 Queens Head yd SE1
76 L 17 Queens house SE10
29 S 10 Queens la N10
26 B 4 Queens Mead rd Brom
137 Y 8 Queens ms W2
15 Z 18 Queens Parade clo N11
28 K 7 Queens park NW6
15 Y 18 Queens pde N11
51 Y 1 Queens rd E11
61 Z 6 Queens rd E13
32 L 19 Queens rd E17
33 N 17 Queens rd E17
26 M 17 Queens rd NW4
27 N 16 Queens rd NW4
16 M 20 Queens rd N11
28 D 5 Queens rd N3
18 M 9 Queens rd N9
92 E 2 Queens rd SE14
147 U 17 Queens rd SW11
85 Z 14 Queens rd SW14
105 Z 14 Queens rd SW19
106 B 13 Queens rd SW19
60 J 16 Queens rd W5
54 A 20 Queens rd Bark
24 C 13 Queens rd Barnt
24 J 3 Queens rd Becknhm
26 F 3 Queens rd Brom
21 W 7 Queens rd Buck HI
14 A 15 Queens rd Chisl
122 K 14 Queens rd Croy
8 E 13 Queens rd Enf
100 K 10 Queens rd Hampt
82 J 7 Queens rd Hounsl .
54 B 8 Queens rd Kingst
103 R 19 Queens rd Kingst
119 Z 8 Queens rd Mrdn
Queens rd New Mald
84 L 17 Queens rd Rich
85 N 12 Queens rd Rich
85 N 14 Queens rd Rich
70 A 7 Queens rd S'hall
101 W 16 Queens rd Tedd
83 X 20 Queens rd Twick
101 Y 1 Queens rd Twick
55 S 10 Queens rd Wallgtn
97 P 3 Queens rd Welling

65 U 5 Queens Rd west E13
84 M 15 Queens ri Rich
86 G 9 Queens ride SW13
150 D 13 Queens rowe SE17
83 Z 8 Queens sq Islwth
18 E 20 Queens st N17
65 W 4 Queens ter E13
130 F 7 Queens ter NW8
83 Z 9 Queens ter Islwth
27 N 15 Queens way NW4
156 E 12 Queens way Croy
20 J 4 Queens wlk E4
43 W 6 Queens wlk NW9
60 D 14 Queens wlk W5
23 S 12 Queens wlk Harrow
29 T 17 Queens Wood rd N10
146 E 5 Queensberry ms SW7
146 E 5 Queensberry pl SW7
146 F 5 Queensberry way SW7
138 A 8 Queensborough pas W2
138 A 9 Queensborough pas W2
137 Z 8 Queensborough ter W2
138 A 10 Queensborough ter W2
83 T 14 Queensbridge pk Islwth
49 V 18 Queensbridge rd E8
135 P 3 Queensbridge rd E8
24 M 12 Queensbury park Harrow
43 X 2 Queensbury rd NW9
61 O 5 Queensbury rd Wemb
60 M 6 Queensbury rd Wemb
134 C 2 Queensbury st N1
25 N 10 Queensbury Stn pde Edg
42 K 12 Queenscourt Wemb
95 P 15 Queenscroft rd SE9
136 J 14 Queensdale pl W11
136 H 15 Queensdale rd W11
136 K 14 Queensdale wlk W11
49 Z 12 Queensdown rd E5
17 Z 18 Queensland av N18
106 A 20 Queensland av SW19
48 G 13 Queensland rd N7
48 F 13 Queensland rd N7
130 G 4 Queensmead NW8
153 N 20 Queensmead Sutton
105 O 5 Queensmere clo SW19
105 O 5 Queensmere rd SW19
144 G 19 Queensmill rd SW6
110 E 10 Queensthorpe rd SE26
147 W 17 Queenstown rd SW8
89 R 6 Queenstown rd SW8
89 X 19 Queensville rd SW12
137 Y 6 Queensway W2
9 P 16 Queensway Enf
15 W 12 Queenswell av N20
33 U 6 Queenswood av E17
100 K 15 Queenswood av Hampt
82 E 4 Queenswood av Hounsl
122 G 12 Queenswood av Thntn Hth
155 X 9 Queenswood av Wallgtn
110 G 8 Queenswood rd SE23
96 K 15 Queenswood rd Sidcp
48 C 14 Quemerford rd N7
94 A 8 Quentin rd SE13
30 F 19 Quernmore rd N4
112 E 15 Quernmore rd Brom
88 C 5 Querrin st SW6
129 U 4 Quex ms NW6
129 V 3 Quex rd NW6
74 A 14 Quick rd W4
133 X 9 Quick st N1
64 A 10 Quickett st E3
106 C 17 Quicks rd SW19
46 K 20 Quickswood NW3
130 M 1 Quickswood NW3
87 P 10 Quill la SW15
142 B 17 Quilp st SE1
135 R 12 Quilter st E2
63 P 7 Quinn sq E2
4 A 18 Quinta dri Barnt

119 U 1 Quintin av SW20
125 V 6 Quinton clo Becknhm
155 R 8 Quinton clo Wallgtn
106 C 5 Quinton st SW18
64 J 20 Quixley st E14
91 T 9 Quorn rd SE22

R

146 D 17 Raasay st SW10
137 V 12 Rabbit row W8
53 R 11 Rabbits rd E12
117 Z 8 Raby rd New Mald
63 V 17 Raby st E14
157 U 5 Racewood gdns Croy
141 V 5 Racquet ct EC4
145 S 15 Racton rd SW6
72 E 10 Radbourne av W5
89 W 19 Radbourne rd SW12
107 W 1 Radbourne rd SW12
62 F 5 Radcliffe av NW10
8 A 5 Radcliffe av Enf
154 J 18 Radcliffe gdns Carsh
17 W 4 Radcliffe rd N21
157 V 3 Radcliffe rd Croy
23 Y 8 Radcliffe rd Harrow
87 P 15 Radcliffe sq SW15
149 U 11 Radcot st SE11
137 N 1 Raddington rd W10
96 F 18 Radfield way Sidcp
93 V 15 Radford rd SE13
87 V 1 Radipole rd SW6
65 R 18 Radland rd E16
110 B 5 Radlet av SE26
130 K 5 Radlett pl NW8
54 L 13 Radley av Ilf
34 E 8 Radley la E18
145 W 4 Radley ms W8
31 T 7 Radley rd N17
56 G 18 Radleys mead Dgnhm
51 N 4 Radlix rd E10
23 V 3 Radnor av Harrow
97 R 13 Radnor av Welling
35 T 17 Radnor cres Ilf
8 E 5 radnor gdns Enf
101 V 3 Radnor gdns Twick
138 H 6 Radnor ms W2
138 J 6 Radnor pl W2
128 L 5 Radnor rd NW6
151 S 17 Radnor rd SE15
151 S 18 Radnor rd SE15
23 T 16 Radnor rd Harrow
101 W 2 Radnor rd Twick
134 C 14 Radnor st EC1
148 X 17 Radnor ter W8
147 N 12 Radnor wlk SW3
146 M 11 Radnor wlk SW3
23 Z 11 Radstock av Harrow
24 A 11 Radstock av Harrow
146 K 18 Radstock st SW11
99 Z 14 Raeburn av Drtfrd
117 S 19 Raeburn av Surb
96 J 16 Raeburn clo NW11
25 O 6 Raeburn rd Edg
96 J 16 Raeburn rd Sidcp
90 B 11 Raeburn st SW2
126 G 4 Rafford way Brom
113 X 20 Ragglesworth Chisl
156 K 10 Raglan ct S Croy
71 S 15 Raglan rd E17
81 O 12 Raglan rd Blvdr
126 M 9 Raglan rd Brom
18 F 2 Raglan rd Enf
47 T 17 Raglan st NW5
41 N 18 Raglan way Grnfd
38 F 5 Raider clo Rom
47 U 14 Railey ms NW5
84 A 10 Railshead rd Twick
90 G 12 Railton rd SE24
29 G 19 Railway appr N8
142 F 14 Railway appr SE1
23 V 13 Railway appr Harrow
83 Y 20 Railway appr Twick
155 S 12 Railway appr Wllgtn
75 P 5 Railway av SE16
68 G 17 Railway cuttings Twick
75 X 19 Railway gro SE14
101 X 15 Railway pas Tedd
142 L 8 Railway pl EC3
105 V 16 Railway pl SW19
81 T 8 Railway pl Blvdr
80 H 9 Railway rd Tedd
101 V 11 Railway rd Tedd
86 B 7 Railway side SW13
132 L 9 Railway st N1

55 T 2 Railway st Rom
33 V 5 Railway ter E17
93 R 13 Railway ter SE13
150 J 17 Rainbow st SE5
75 N 2 Raine st E1
96 F 15 Rainham clo SE9
128 D 13 Rainham rd NW10
56 H 9 Rainham rd North Dgnhm
57 T 18 Rainham rd Rainhm
56 K 19 Rainham rd South Dgnhm
64 C 9 Rainhill way E3
75 V 12 Rainsborough av SE8
61 S 7 Rainsford rd NW10
138 J 4 Rainsford st W2
57 U 4 Rainsford way Hornch
77 U 13 Rainton rd SE7
144 E 16 Rainville rd W6
16 K 12 Raith av N14
76 H 2 Raleana rd E14
101 U 16 Raleigh av Tedd
155 X 8 Raleigh av Wllgtn
26 L 15 Raleigh clo NW4
15 X 10 Raleigh dri N20
117 V 20 Raleigh dri Surb
30 G 13 Raleigh rd N8
85 N 8 Raleigh rd Rich
70 B 12 Raleigh rd S'hall
133 Z 6 Raleigh st N1
15 T 15 Raleigh st Wallgtn
155 S 14 Raleigh st Wallgtn
16 L 4 Raleigh st N14
150 C 1 Ralph st SE1
147 O 11 Ralston st SW3
50 C 17 Ram pl E9
41 T 7 Rama ct Harrow
11 O 1 Ramillies pl W1
13 O 9 Ramillies rd NW7
73 Y 9 Ramillies rd W4
97 P 16 Ramillies rd Sidcp
140 B 5 Ramillies st W1
75 O 11 Ramouth rd SE16
143 W 6 Rampart st E1
148 F 9 Rampayne st SW1
20 A 10 Rampton clo E4
37 Z 12 Rams gro Rom
52 C 11 Ramsay rd E7
73 V 7 Ramsay rd W3
18 C 4 Ramscroft clo N9
107 R 13 Ramsdale rd SW17
38 F 3 Ramsden dri Rom
15 Z 16 Ramsden rd N11
89 P 20 Ramsden rd SW12
81 Z 20 Ramsden rd Erith
122 E 13 Ramsey rd Croy
135 T 16 Ramsey st E2
16 H 4 Ramsey way N14
49 V 17 Ramsgate st E8
36 K 14 Ramsgill appr Ilf
36 K 14 Ramsgill dri Ilf
95 P 9 Ramsgill gdns Ilf
66 F 7 Rancliffe rd E6
44 C 8 Randall av NW2
76 F 18 Randall pl SE10
149 N 8 Randall rd SE11
39 T 18 Randall rd Rom
149 N 8 Randall row SE11
64 L 13 Randall's st E16
132 L 3 Randell's rd N1
102 K 9 Randle rd Rich
111 R 7 Randlesdown rd SE6
33 S 15 Randolf rd S'hall
129 Z 12 Randolph av W9
130 C 17 Randolph av W9
130 B 17 Randolph cres W9
129 X 10 Randolph gdns NW6
130 C 18 Randolph ms W9
65 Y 18 Randolph rd S'hall
70 D 5 Randolph rd S'hall
132 B 1 Randolph st NW1
22 K 7 Randon clo Harrow
86 G 5 Ranelagh av SW13
87 U 7 Ranelagh av SW6
12 B 13 Ranelagh clo Edg
12 B 13 Ranelagh dri Edg
84 C 12 Ranelagh dri Twick
34 K 15 Ranelagh gdns E11
87 U 8 Ranelagh gdns SW6
73 U 18 Ranelagh gdns W4
53 U 3 Ranelagh gdns Ilf
147 V 9 Ranelagh gro SW1
51 Z 11 Ranelagh rd E11
65 O 6 Ranelagh rd E15
66 J 4 Ranelagh rd E6
62 D 7 Ranelagh rd NW10

31 T 10 Ranelagh rd N17
30 C 6 Ranelagh rd N22
148 C 11 Ranelagh rd SW1
72 G 5 Ranelagh rd W5
70 A 1 Ranelagh rd S'hall
42 H 17 Ranelagh rd Wemb
153 Z 2 Ranfurly rd Sutton
111 Z 11 Rangefield rd Brom
112 C 13 Rangefield rd Brom
31 V 15 Rangemoor rd N15
21 R 2 Rangers rd E4
93 W 1 Rangers sq SE10
142 M 7 Rangoon st EC3
81 P 19 Ranleigh gdns Bxly Hth
89 T 20 Ranmere st SW12
23 R 14 Ranmoor rd Harrow
23 S 13 Ranmoor gdns Harrow
157 V 7 Ranmore av Croy
153 O 20 Ranmore rd Sutton
144 E 16 Rannoch rd W6
44 A 1 Rannock av NW9
44 A 2 Rannock av NW9
77 Y 12 Ransom rd SE7
130 K 20 Ranston st NW1
45 V 11 Ranulf rd NW2
63 X 4 Ranwell clo E3
63 X 4 Ranwell st E3
99 S 4 Ranwell clo Erith
19 O 10 Ranworth rd N9
39 S 9 Raphael av Rom
39 T 8 Raphael park Rom
139 N 19 Raphael st SW3
89 T 6 Rashleigh st SW8
15 S 9 Rasper rd N20
107 X 3 Rastell av SW2
52 K 16 Ratcliff rd E7
63 U 18 Ratcliffe clo E14
63 T 18 Ratcliffe cross E1
63 T 19 Ratcliffe orchard E1
63 N 20 Ratcliffe st E1
140 E 3 Rathbone pl W1
65 O 16 Rathbone st E16
140 D 2 Rathbone st W1
30 D 15 Rathcoole av N8
30 D 15 Rathcoole gdns N8
110 M 2 Rathfern rd SE6
92 V 6 Rathgar av W13
27 V 16 Rathgar clo N3
90 J 7 Rathgar rd SW9
89 X 16 Rathmell dri SW4
77 V 13 Rathmore rd SE7
90 F 11 Rattray rd SW2
90 F 12 Rattray rd SW2
91 X 3 Raul rd SE15
47 U 13 Raveley st NW5
34 K 6 Raven rd E18
143 X 1 Raven row E1
63 N 14 Raven row E1
106 M 8 Ravenfield rd SW17
65 Y 6 Ravenhill rd E13
87 P 12 Ravenna rd SW15
58 M 9 Ravenor park Grnfd
59 N 9 Ravenor Pk rd Grnfd
58 L 8 Ravenor Pk rd Grnfd
126 C 5 Ravens clo Brom
8 D 9 Ravens clo Enf
94 E 12 Ravens way SE12
125 Y 1 Ravensbourne av Brom
111 X 19 Ravensbourne av Brom
60 A 15 Ravensbourne gdns W13
36 A 5 Ravensbourne gdns Ilf
35 X 4 Ravensbourne gdns Ilf
93 N 18 Ravensbourne pk SE6
92 M 18 Ravensbourne Pk cres SE6
92 K 20 Ravensbourne rd SE6
126 E 6 Ravensbourne rd Brom
99 V 7 Ravensbourne rd Dartford
84 D 14 Ravensbourne rd Twick
120 D 11 Ravensbury av Mordn
121 N 4 Ravensbury clo Mitch
120 F 9 Ravensbury gro Mitch
120 F 9 Ravensbury la Mitch
120 F 8 Ravensbury path Mitch
105 Z 3 Ravensbury rd SW18

111 Z 10 Ravenscar rd Brom
74 G 11 Ravenscourt av W6
74 F 10 Ravenscourt gdns W6
74 G 11 Ravenscourt pk W6
74 H 11 Ravenscourt pl W6
73 W 11 Ravenscourt rd W4
74 H 11 Ravenscourt rd W6
16 G 14 Ravenscraig rd N11
27 W 20 Ravenscroft av NW11
42 L 3 Ravenscroft av Wemb
45 V 1 Ravenscroft ave NW11
65 S 14 Ravenscroft clo E16
4 D 13 Ravenscroft pk Barnt
4 D 12 Ravenscroft Pk rd Barnt
65 T 14 Ravenscroft rd E16
124 F 1 Ravenscroft rd Becknhm
135 P 10 Ravenscroft st E2
15 S 14 Ravensdale av N12
31 V 20 Ravensdale rd N16
82 B 7 Ravensdale rd Hounsl
149 U 11 Ravensdon st SE11
55 X 12 Ravensfield clo Dgnhm
152 B 10 Ravensfield gdns Epsom
45 W 17 Ravenshaw st NW6
127 Y 2 Ravenshill Chisl
26 L 12 Ravenshurst av NW4
88 M 19 Ravenslea rd SW12
111 X 18 Ravensmead rd Brom
26 E 19 Ravenstone rd NW9
30 E 11 Ravenstone rd N8
107 R 2 Ravenstone st SW12
115 Z 1 Ravenswood Bxly
125 T 20 Ravenswood av W Wkhm
156 J 6 Ravenswood clo Croy
40 D 7 Ravenswood cres Harrow
125 T 19 Ravenswood cres W Wkhm
103 U 16 Ravenswood ct Kingst
83 T 1 Ravenswood gdns Islwth
33 T 14 Ravenswood rd E17
89 S 19 Ravenswood rd SW12
156 J 6 Ravenswood rd Croy
62 K 8 Ravensworth rd NW10
113 T 8 Ravensworth rd SE9
134 J 16 Ravey st EC2
79 U 17 Ravine gro SE18
87 V 20 Rawcaster clo SW18
147 N 6 Rawlings st SW3
158 K 16 Rawlins clo S Croy
133 W 2 Rawstone pl EC1
133 W 2 Rawstorne st EC1
68 A 6 Ray gdns Bark
11 P 16 Ray gdns Stanm
21 Z 18 Ray Lodge rd Wdfd Grn
133 U 18 Ray st EC1
4 M 18 Raydean rd Barnt
47 S 7 Raydon st N19
55 Z 14 Raydons gdns Dgnhm
55 Y 15 Raydons rd Dgnhm
56 A 14 Raydons rd Dgnhm
127 P 14 Rayfield clo Brom
94 C 19 Rayford av SE12
18 A 10 Rayleigh clo Kingst
117 O 3 Rayleigh rd N13
17 Z 10 Rayleigh rd N13
105 U 20 Rayleigh rd SW19
34 L 1 Rayleigh rd Wdfd Grn
21 X 20 Rayleigh ri S Croy
157 S 14 Rayleigh ri S Croy
27 N 11 Raymead NW4
122 G 11 Raymead av Thntn Hth
79 T 19 Raymere gdns SE18
34 B 9 Raymond av E18
71 Z 8 Raymond av W13
110 C 11 Raymond clo SE26
65 X 2 Raymond rd E13
105 T 15 Raymond rd SW19

54 D 2 Raymond rd Ilf
151 Y 6 Raymouth rd SE16
34 C 12 Rayne ct E18
40 F 4 Rayners la Harrow
22 F 20 Rayners la Pinn
31 Y 13 Rayners rd SW15
52 L 1 Raynes av E11
18 A 5 Raynham av N18
18 K 16 Raynham rd N18
18 K 17 Raynham terr N18
70 D 3 Raynor clo S'hall
40 B 3 Raynton rd Harrow
19 P 15 Rays av N18
19 P 15 Rays rd N18
89 T 1 Raywood st SW8
50 A 18 Reading la E8
50 A 18 Reading la E8
40 L 14 Reading rd Grnfd
154 D 12 Reading rd Sutton
143 X 15 Reardon path E1
75 N 2 Reardon st E1
143 X 13 Reardon st E1
79 R 19 Reaston st SE14
75 P 9 Rebecca ter SE16
73 Z 14 Reckitt rd W4
75 O 15 Record st SE15
106 J 12 Recovery st SW17
38 L 17 Recreation la Rom
110 E 9 Recreation rd SE26
126 B 3 Recreation rd Brom
70 A 10 Recreation rd S'hall
121 Y 8 Recreation way Mitch
134 A 5 Rector st N1
27 W 6 Rectory clo E4
27 W 6 Rectory clo N3
99 R 11 Rectory clo Drtfrd
11 O 17 Rectory clo Stanm
116 C 20 Rectory clo Surb
143 X 18 Rectory cres E11
77 X 18 Rectory Field cres SE7
30 A 12 Rectory gdns N8
58 F 2 Rectory gdns Grnfd
124 M 1 Rectory grn Becknhm
89 V 7 Rectory gro SW4
156 J 4 Rectory gro Croy
100 F 4 Rectory gro Hampt
107 P 13 Rectory la SW17
12 C 17 Rectory la Edg
115 R 11 Rectory la Sidcp
115 U 11 Rectory la Sidcp
11 O 17 Rectory la Stanm
116 C 20 Rectory la Surb
155 V 7 Rectory la Wallgtn
58 D 7 Rectory park Grnfd
78 B 7 Rectory Pk av Grnfd
73 P 11 Rectory pl SE18
53 U 16 Rectory rd E12
33 R 12 Rectory rd E17
49 V 9 Rectory rd N16
30 A 14 Rectory rd N8
86 G 4 Rectory rd SW13
73 U 2 Rectory rd W3
111 O 20 Rectory rd Becknhm
124 M 2 Rectory rd Becknhm
56 F 20 Rectory rd Dgnhm
70 E 9 Rectory rd S'hall
153 Z 7 Rectory rd Sutton
75 S 13 Rectory sq E1
142 E 10 Reculver rd SE16
113 Y 13 Red Bull yd EC4
121 X 13 Red Ho chl Chisl
97 Y 11 Red Ho of Croy Hth
81 R 17 Red Leaf clo Blvdr
141 U 5 Red Lion ct EC4
28 F 8 Red Lion hill N2
78 J 20 Red Lion la SE18
95 W 1 Red Lion la SE18
95 W 2 Red Lion pl SE18
117 O 20 Red Lion rd Surb
150 D 14 Red Lion row SE17
141 N 2 Red Lion sq WC1
141 O 2 Red Lion st WC1
84 H 13 Red Lion st Rich
125 V 17 Red Lodge rd W Wkhm
139 T 8 Red pl W1
137 Y 8 Redan pl W2
144 G 1 Redan st W14
90 K 5 Redan ter SE5
146 H 15 Redanchor clo SW3
110 C 6 Redberry gro SE26
27 Z 4 Redbourne av N3
34 L 18 Redbridge La west E11
35 N 14 Redbridge lane S11

147 N 12 Redburn st SW3
40 K 16 Redcar clo Grnfd
150 A 19 Redcar st SE5
63 P 20 Redcastle clo E1
135 N 16 Redchurch st E2
145 W 10 Redcliffe clo SW5
145 Y 10 Redcliffe gdns SW10
146 B 14 Redcliffe gdns SW10
53 V 3 Redcliffe gdns Ilf
145 Z 12 Redcliffe ms SW10
146 B 15 Redcliffe pl SW10
146 C 13 Redcliffe rd SW10
145 Z 11 Redcliffe sq SW10
119 X 12 Redclose av Mrdn
65 Y 4 Redclyffe rd E6
58 M 18 Redcroft rd S'hall
142 C 15 Redcross way SE1
13 S 12 Reddings clo NW7
13 S 11 Reddings the NW7
151 R 16 Reddins rd SE15
110 G 18 Reddons rd Becknhm
71 X 19 Redesdale gdns Islwth
146 M 12 Redesdale st SW3
82 G 19 Redfern av Hounsl
62 B 1 Redfern rd NW10
93 U 18 Redfern rd SE6
145 W 6 Redfield la SW5
122 D 9 Redford av Thntn Hth
155 Z 14 Redford av Wallgtn
87 P 9 Redgrave rd SW15
25 U 8 Redhill dri Edg
131 Y 11 Redhill st NW1
157 R 20 Redington clo S Croy
46 B 11 Redington gdns NW3
46 A 10 Redington rd NW3
9 N 4 Redlands rd Enf
90 B 19 Redlands way SW2
83 W 9 Redlees park Islwth
83 Y 11 Redlees clo Islwth
68 P 14 Redman's rd E1
143 U 13 Redmead la E1
74 J 10 Redmore rd W6
91 N 11 Redpost hill SE24
75 U 8 Redriff rd SE16
38 J 7 Redriff rd Rom
65 R 5 Redriffe rd E13
63 S 3 Redruth rd E9
29 W 12 Redston rd N8
30 F 7 Redvers rd N22
50 G 13 Redwald rd E5
83 O 19 Redway dri Twick
104 F 1 Redwoods SW15
146 E 6 Reece ms SW7
65 S 16 Reed clo E16
94 F 13 Reed clo SE12
47 U 19 Reed pl NW1
39 U 7 Reed Pond wlk Rom
31 W 9 Reed rd N17
56 G 16 Reede gdns Dgnhm
56 D 17 Reede rd Dgnhm
56 G 17 Reede way Dgnhm
91 W 6 Reedham st SE15
49 P 12 Reedholm vlls N16
11 U 13 Reenglass rd Stanr
123 U 14 Rees gdns Croy
134 D 5 Rees st N1
26 B 18 Reets Farm clo NW9
43 X 1 Reeves ms W1
139 U 10 Reeves ms W1
64 D 10 Reeves rd E3
31 V 7 Reform row N17
88 M 5 Reform st SW11
24 N 19 Regal ct N18
131 V 5 Regal la NW1
24 K 19 Regal way Harrow
134 J 9 Regan way N1
39 R 18 Regarth av Rom
100 E 11 Regency clo Hamp
83 T 14 Regency ms Islwth
148 F 8 Regency st SW1
124 L 15 Regency wlk Croy
15 R 17 Regent clo N12
24 J 19 Regent clo Harrow
140 C 9 Regent pl W1
90 J 4 Regent rd SE24
117 O 12 Regent rd Surb
132 L 14 Regent sq WC1
81 U 11 Regent sq Blvdr
128 G 14 Regent st SW1
139 Z 4 Regent st W1
140 B 10 Regent st W1
73 P 15 Regent st W4

Ref	Name
131 U 4	Regent's Park rd NW1
131 W 4	Regent's Park ter NW1
17 S 17	Regents av N13
157 S 13	Regents clo S Croy
11 X 14	Regents ct Edg
131 T 13	Regents Park rd NW1
27 V 11	Regents Park rd N3
131 T 8	Regents Park Zoological gdns NW1
135 R 5	Regents row E8
48 D 4	Regina rd N4
123 Y 6	Regina rd SE25
21 Z 3	Regina rd W13
70 B 10	Regina rd S'hall
72 A 3	Regina ter W13
52 D 19	Reginald rd E7
76 B 20	Reginald rd SE8
76 B 20	Reginald sq SE8
132 C 15	Regnart bldgs NW1
133 R 5	Reid st N1
79 U 10	Reidhaven rd SE18
80 B 19	Reigate av Sutton
112 D 6	Reigate rd Brom
54 J 8	Reigate rd Ilf
156 B 10	Reigate way Wallgtn
49 Y 8	Reighton rd E5
91 X 7	Relf rd SE15
146 L 1	Relton ms SW7
93 Y 11	Rembrandt clo E14
25 P 6	Rembrandt rd Edg
31 P 18	Remington rd N15
133 Y 10	Remington st W2
74 F 18	Remnant st WC2
134 F 8	Rempstone mews N1
64 A 1	Remus rd E3
128 L 19	Rendle st W10
49 Y 10	Rendlesham rd E5
7 X 4	Rendlesham rd Enf
75 R 7	Renforth st SE16
82 A 5	Renfrew clo Hounsl
149 M 6	Renfrew rd SE11
82 A 4	Renfrew rd Hounsl
103 U 17	Renfrew rd Kingst
106 M 15	Renmuir st SW17
93 U 8	Rennell st SE13
32 J 11	Renness rd E17
96 F 13	Rennets clo SE9
96 E 14	Rennets Wood rd SE9
141 V 12	Rennie st SE1
38 F 4	Renown clo Rom
32 F 17	Rensburg rd E17
27 O 19	Renters av NW4
26 M 19	Renters av NW4
68 E 10	Renwick rd Bark
150 H 2	Rephidim st SE1
105 W 1	Replingham rd SW18
144 M 20	Reporton rd SW6
78 G 15	Repository rd SE18
39 W 11	Repton av Rom
42 D 13	Repton av Wemb
154 H 12	Repton clo Carsh
111 R 20	Repton ct Becknhm
35 U 4	Repton ct Ilf
39 W 12	Repton dri Rom
39 W 11	Repton gdns Rom
35 U 4	Repton gro Ilf
25 N 14	Repton rd Harrow
63 V 16	Repton st E14
38 F 4	Repulse clo Rom
6 G 16	Reservoir rd N14
92 H 5	Reservoir rd SE4
77 N 16	Restell clo SE10
138 B 20	Reston pl SW7
96 G 16	Restons cres SE9
47 T 6	Retcar st N19
20 D 9	Retingham way E4
24 F 16	Retreat clo Harrow
50 D 18	Retreat pl E9
84 G 13	Retreat rd Rich
25 X 15	Retreat the NW9
86 B 8	Retreat the SW13
40 J 2	Retreat the Harrow
117 N 15	Retreat the Surb
81 N 8	Retreat the Thntn Hth
152 K 4	Retreat the Worc Pk
117 U 2	Revell rd Kingst
153 U 13	Revell rd Sutton
79 X 17	Revell ri SE18
92 H 9	Revelon rd SE4
105 X 4	Revelstoke rd SW18
114 B 2	Reventlow rd SE9
151 R 6	Reverdy rd SE1
116 H 15	Revesby rd Carsh
44 E 6	Review rd NW2
69 T 4	Review rd Dgnhm
146 A 20	Rewel st SW6
146 A 20	Rewell st SW6
120 F 15	Rewley rd Carsh
38 H 3	Rex clo Rom
139 U 11	Rex pl W1
34 K 17	Reydon av E11
127 W 5	Reynard clo Brom
109 T 18	Reynard dri SE19
30 M 2	Reynardson rd N17
31 N 2	Reynardson rd N17
17 W 19	Reynold's pl SE3
53 Y 15	Reynolds av E12
37 U 19	Reynolds av Rom
55 T 1	Reynolds av Rom
46 A 2	Reynolds clo NW11
155 N 1	Reynolds clo Carsh
121 N 20	Reynolds clo Carsh
25 N 9	Reynolds dri Edg
92 D 12	Reynolds rd SE15
73 W 7	Reynolds rd W4
117 Z 17	Reynolds rd New Mald
157 S 8	Reynolds way Croy
78 F 3	Rhea st E16
133 Z 7	Rheidol ter N1
31 V 6	Rheola clo N17
135 O 15	Rhoda st E2
29 T 5	Rhodes av N22
48 C 17	Rhodes st N7
51 X 6	Rhodesia rd E11
90 A 5	Rhodesia rd SW9
119 Y 14	Rhodesmoor Ho ct Mrdn
63 X 6	Rhodeswell pl E3
63 X 17	Rhodeswell rd E14
63 X 15	Rhodeswell rd E14
63 X 9	Rhondda gro E3
59 X 6	Rhyl rd Grnfd
47 P 17	Rhyl st NW5
93 U 8	Rhyme rd SE13
29 Y 1	Rhys av N11
121 P 2	Rialto rd Mitch
40 L 18	Ribblesdale av Grnfd
30 C 14	Ribblesdale rd N8
107 S 14	Ribblesdale rd SW16
59 W 8	Ribchester av Grnfd
64 C 18	Ricardo st E14
105 W 12	Ricards rd SW19
120 M 14	Rice la Mitch
121 N 14	Rice la Mitch
63 Z 19	Rich st E14
73 U 3	Richard cotts W3
65 S 15	Richard st E16
38 L 17	Richards av Rom
33 O 11	Richards pl E17
64 M 6	Richardson rd E15
132 A 19	Richardson's ms W1
133 N 20	Richbell pl WC1
149 P 18	Richborne ter SW8
45 R 13	Richborough rd NW2
10 B 4	Richfield rd Bushey Watf
10 B 3	Richfield rd Bushey Watf
65 P 3	Richford rd E15
74 L 8	Richford st W6
136 B 19	Richford st W6
144 B 1	Richford st W6
74 L 7	Richford st W6
152 H 9	Richlands av Epsom
20 J 16	Richmond av E4
44 L 19	Richmond av NW10
119 U 2	Richmond av N1
119 U 2	Richmond av SW20
140 E 6	Richmond bldgs W1
84 G 14	Richmond dri Rich
20 K 16	Richmond cres E4
133 K 3	Richmond cres N1
18 K 5	Richmond cres N9
26 H 15	Richmond gdns NW4
23 V 1	Richmond gdns Harrow
10 H 20	Richmond gdns Harrow
156 B 6	Richmond grn Croy
133 X 1	Richmond gro N1
116 L 15	Richmond gro Surb
84 K 17	Richmond Hill Rich
84 J 15	Richmond Hill ct Rich
140 E 7	Richmond ms W1
85 T 17	Richmond park Rich
85 X 10	Richmond Pk rd SW14
102 K 19	Richmond Pk rd Kingst
79 O 11	Richmond pl SE18
51 V 6	Richmond rd E11
32 M 19	Richmond rd E17
20 K 5	Richmond rd E4
52 J 15	Richmond rd E7
49 U 20	Richmond rd E8
50 A 19	Richmond rd E8
17 N 20	Richmond rd N11
31 R 19	Richmond rd N15
28 D 8	Richmond rd N2
86 L 7	Richmond rd SW15
113 J 1	Richmond rd SW20
72 J 4	Richmond rd W5
5 P 17	Richmond rd Barnt
156 B 5	Richmond rd Croy
5 R 17	Richmond rd East Barnt
54 B 9	Richmond rd Ilf
83 Z 8	Richmond rd Islwth
102 J 19	Richmond rd Kingst
39 T 18	Richmond rd Rom
122 J 7	Richmond rd Thntn Hth
156 B 5	Richmond rd Thntn Hth
84 D 19	Richmond rd Twick
65 U 7	Richmond st E13
140 K 16	Richmond ter SW1
140 K 17	Richmond Ter ms SW1
52 E 6	Richmond way E11
136 G 19	Richmond way W14
94 F 9	Richmount gdns SE3
12 J 14	Richmount gdns Edg
145 U 13	Rickett st SW6
48 A 7	Rickthorne rd N4
41 V 14	Ridding la Grnfd
112 L 7	Riddons rd SE12
72 C 13	Ride the Brentf
9 R 13	Ride the Enf
78 F 12	Rideout st SE18
64 C 7	Ridgdale st E3
17 Y 2	Ridge av N21
18 A 2	Ridge av N21
99 T 16	Ridge av Drtfrd
27 P 8	Ridge clo NW4
25 Z 13	Ridge clo NW9
45 T 3	Ridge crest Enf
45 W 9	Ridge hill NW11
45 W 9	Ridge rd NW2
18 A 4	Ridge rd N21
30 E 19	Ridge rd N8
107 S 17	Ridge rd Mitch
119 V 20	Ridge rd Sutton
153 U 1	Ridge rd Sutton
98 B 18	Ridge the Bxly
117 O 12	Ridge the Surb
83 P 18	Ridge the Twick
99 T 16	Ridge way Drtfrd
100 A 7	Ridge way Felt
21 Z 15	Ridge way Wdfd Grn
94 L 9	Ridgebrook rd SE3
12 J 14	Ridgemount gdns Edg
158 G 1	Ridgemount av Croy
109 Z 17	Ridgemount clo SE20
132 E 19	Ridgemount gdns WC1
7 U 10	Ridgemount gdns Enf
4 C 20	Ridgeview clo Barnt
15 P 10	Ridgeview rd N20
96 J 13	Ridgeway East Sidcp
7 T 6	Ridgeway Enf
40 K 2	Ridgeway Harrow
96 H 12	Ridgeway West Sidcp
5 Y 20	Ridgeway av Barnt
112 H 10	Ridgeway dri Brom
35 R 14	Ridgeway park E4
20 P 8	Ridgeway park E4
83 U 1	Ridgeway rd Islwth
71 T 20	Ridgeway rd Islwth
71 T 18	Ridgeway rd North Islwth
20 G 5	Ridgeway the E4
45 V 3	Ridgeway the NW11
18 B 16	Ridgeway the NW7
13 U 15	Ridgeway the NW7
13 V 13	Ridgeway the NW7
25 Z 14	Ridgeway the NW9
15 Y 14	Ridgeway the N11
17 N 8	Ridgeway the N3
28 A 3	Ridgeway the N3
73 P 7	Ridgeway the W3
156 C 7	Ridgeway the Croy
22 J 19	Ridgeway the Harrow
24 O 20	Ridgeway the Harrow
39 V 13	Ridgeway the Rom
11 R 19	Ridgeway the Stanm
69 V 2	Ridgeway clo Dgnhm
88 B 14	Ridgmount rd SW18
132 F 20	Ridgmount st WC1
105 P 16	Ridgway SW19
105 O 17	Ridgway gdns SW19
105 S 16	Ridgway pl SW19
90 J 8	Ridgway rd SW9
154 G 14	Ridgway the Sutton
65 Z 14	Ridgwell rd E16
140 A 2	Riding house W1
139 Z 2	Riding House st W1
45 V 2	Riding the NW11
7 X 15	Ridings av N21
60 M 11	Ridings the W5
61 N 12	Ridings the W5
45 V 2	Ridings the NW11
117 R 11	Ridings the Surb
8 F 4	Ridler rd Enf
72 B 8	Ridley av W13
39 Z 4	Ridley clo Rom
52 K 11	Ridley rd E7
49 U 16	Ridley rd E8
62 H 5	Ridley rd NW10
106 A 17	Ridley rd SW19
126 D 6	Ridley rd Brom
97 O 2	Ridley rd Welling
97 P 2	Ridley rd Welling
50 C 5	Ridley sq E5
96 D 14	Riefield rd SE9
44 L 15	Riffel rd NW2
136 H 12	Riffle pl W11
64 D 15	Rifle st E14
87 J 5	Rigault rd SW6
156 F 4	Rigby clo Croy
64 C 18	Rigden st E14
62 H 8	Rigeley rd NW10
50 G 4	Rigg app E13
107 V 11	Riggindale rd SW16
91 R 4	Rigold rd SE5
142 M 19	Riley rd SE1
9 R 4	Riley rd Enf
146 F 16	Riley st SW10
48 F 16	Ringcroft st N7
126 F 6	Ringer's rd Brom
87 X 15	Ringford rd SW18
87 T 3	Ringmer av SW6
8 B 18	Ringmer pl Enf
92 B 19	Ringmore ri SE23
30 D 7	Ringslade rd N22
93 S 18	Ringstead rd SE6
154 G 10	Ringstead rd Sutton
70 B 14	Ringway S'hall
28 M 9	Ringwood av N2
122 B 16	Ringwood av Croy
104 G 3	Ringwood gdns SW15
32 K 18	Ringwood rd E17
17 V 4	Ringwood way N21
100 H 10	Ringwood way Hampt
85 Z 7	Ripley gdns SW14
154 C 8	Ripley gdns Sutton
65 Y 17	Ripley rd E16
81 P 10	Ripley rd Blvdr
7 Y 4	Ripley rd Dgnhm
100 C 18	Ripley rd Hampt
54 J 8	Ripley rd Ilf
25 P 20	Ripon gdns Ilf
31 O 12	Ripon rd N17
19 N 4	Ripon rd N9
78 L 17	Ripon rd SE18
97 N 3	Rippersley rd Welling
67 P 2	Ripple rd Bark
68 C 4	Ripple rd Bark
69 N 5	Ripple rd Dgnhm
133 P 2	Ripple Vale gro N1
79 X 13	Rippolson rd SE18
40 J 16	Rippon clo Dgnhm
51 N 20	Rippoth rd E3
64 A 1	Rippoth rd E3
118 H 17	Risborough dri Worc Pk
141 Z 16	Risborough st SE1
75 P 7	Risdon st SE16
39 U 2	Rise park Rom
39 S 5	Rise Park blvd Rom
39 P 7	Rise Park pl Rom
34 D 15	Rise the E11
43 Z 11	Rise the NW10
13 S 20	Rise the NW7
17 V 15	Rise the N13
99 U 11	Rise the Drtfrd
12 E 15	Rise the Edg
41 Y 15	Rise the Grnfd
158 C 20	Rise the S Croy
97 T 19	Rise the Sidcp
13 J 6	Risebridge rd Rom
38 J 6	Risedale rd Bxly Hth
50 K 18	Riseholme st E9
92 H 17	Riseldine rd SE23
141 Y 1	Rising Sun ct EC1
133 R 8	Risinghill st N1

23 T 6	Risingholme rd Harrow	
33 X 13	Risings the E17	
30 M 5	Risley av N17	
31 O 5	Risley av N17	
148 M 16	Rita rd SW8	
149 N 17	Rita rd SW8	
30 L 16	Ritches rd N15	
124 A 15	Ritchie rd Croy	
133 T 7	Ritchie st N1	
32 H 12	Ritchings av E17	
107 P 4	Ritherdon rd SW17	
49 W 17	Ritson rd E8	
50 C 18	Rivaz pl E9	
34 B 13	Rivenhall gdns E18	
17 V 9	River av N13	
17 Y 3	River bank N21	
34 L 18	River clo E11	
8 C 12	River front Enf	
155 O 5	River gdns Carsh	
124 M 1	River Gro pk Becknhm	
102 H 1	River la Rich	
84 H 20	River la Twick	
100 J 6	River Meads av Felt	
30 D 7	River Park rd N22	
111 X 17	River Pk gdns Brom	
67 Y 14	River rd Bark	
68 B 14	River rd Bark	
102 E 14	River reach Tedd	
133 T 12	River st EC1	
74 L 14	River ter W6	
144 B 11	River ter W6	
101 W 5	River View gdns Twick	
77 O 7	River way SE10	
152 A 11	River way Epsom	
100 J 5	River way Twick	
74 H 12	Rivercourt rd W6	
84 E 14	Riverdale gdns Twick	
79 W 14	Riverdale rd SE18	
79 W 13	Riverdale rd SE18	
97 Z 17	Riverdale rd Bxly	
98 A 17	Riverdale rd Bxly	
81 W 14	Riverdale rd Erith	
100 C 9	Riverdale rd Twick	
84 E 15	Riverdale rd Twick	
12 J 12	Riverdene Edg	
152 A 19	Riverholme dri Epsom	
48 K 10	Riversdale rd N5	
38 F 2	Riversdale rd Rom	
8 E 11	Riversfield rd Enf	
44 J 1	Riverside NW4	
77 V 8	Riverside-SE7	
102 A 1	Riverside Twick	
59 U 12	Riverside clo W7	
116 Q 8	Riverside clo Kingst	
155 R 6	Riverside clo Wallgtn	
86 B 1	Riverside dri W4	
120 J 11	Riverside dri Mitch	
102 C 4	Riverside dri Rich	
74 J 12	Riverside gdns W6	
8 A 10	Riverside gdns Enf	
60 K 6	Riverside gdns Wemb	
64 H 7	Riverside rd E15	
31 Y 18	Riverside rd N15	
106 D 8	Riverside rd SW17	
115 Z 5	Riverside rd Sidcp	
97 W 19	Riverside walk Bxly Hth	
14 K 13	Riverside wlk N12	
83 U 7	Riverside wlk Islwth	
144 A 14	Riverview gdns SW13	
74 K 16	Riverview gdns SW13	
73 T 18	Riverview gro W4	
111 N 3	Riverview pk SE6	
73 T 18	Riverview rd W4	
17 U 14	Riverway N13	
35 N 6	Rivington av Wdfd Grn	
134 K 14	Rivington pl EC2	
134 L 14	Rivington st EC2	
31 N 2	Rivulet rd N17	
30 K 2	Rivulet rd N17	
39 S 5	Rix Park rd Rom	
53 R 15	Rixsen rd E12	
64 B 1	Roach rd E3	
51 O 20	Roach rd E3	
48 B 6	Roads pl N4	
76 F 18	Roan st SE10	
10 M 19	Robb rd Stanm	
125 V 2	Robbins ct Becknhm	
139 T 4	Robert Adam st W1	
130 D 18	Robert clo W9	
78 K 4	Robert st E16	
132 A 13	Robert st NW1	
131 Y 13	Robert st NW1	
79 R 11	Robert st SE18	
140 L 11	Robert st WC2	
72 G 7	Robert's all W5	
133 U 16	Robert's pl EC1	
135 T 13	Roberta st E2	
126 L 1	Roberton dri Brom	
39 Z 4	Roberts clo Rom	
147 T 2	Roberts ms SW1	
33 R 4	Roberts rd E17	
81 T 14	Roberts rd Blvdr	
120 E 18	Robertsbridge rd Carsh	
64 H 3	Robertson rd E15	
89 S 6	Robertson st SW8	
38 M 1	Robin clo Rom	
38 M 2	Robin clo Rom	
142 C 5	Robin ct EC2	
47 O 6	Robin gro N6	
79 D 17	Robin gro Brentf	
25 O 19	Robin gro Harrow	
121 V 7	Robin Hood clo Mitch	
23 V 3	Robin Hood dri Harrow	
64 G 19	Robin Hood la E14	
104 A 11	Robin Hood la SW15	
97 Z 12	Robin Hood la Bxly Hth	
121 W 7	Robin Hood la Mitch	
153 Y 11	Robin Hood la Sutton	
154 A 11	Robin Hood la Sutton	
104 C 11	Robin Hood rd SW15/SW19	
104 A 8	Robin Hood way SW15	
41 X 17	Robin Hood way Grnfd	
141 U 2	Robin Hood yd EC1	
97 X 10	Robina clo Bxly Hth	
112 K 7	Robins ct SE12	
63 P 6	Robinson rd E2	
108 K 16	Robinson rd SW17	
56 D 11	Robinson rd Dgnhm	
147 N 13	Robinson st SW3	
90 E 4	Robsart st SW9	
62 H 1	Robson av NW10	
7 V 9	Robson clo Enf	
108 K 7	Robson rd SE27	
25 N 6	Roch av Edg	
51 N 1	Rochdale rd E17	
80 B 13	Rochdale rd SE2	
122 B 1	Roche rd SW16	
120 F 15	Roche wlk Carsh	
135 N 14	Rochelle st E2	
65 X 4	Rochester av E13	
126 J 4	Rochester av Brom	
94 K 7	Rochester clo SE3	
8 F 7	Rochester clo Enf	
97 P 15	Rochester clo Sidcp	
157 T 5	Rochester gdns Croy	
53 T 2	Rochester gdns Ilf	
47 V 19	Rochester ms NW1	
47 U 19	Rochester pl NW1	
47 U 19	Rochester rd NW1	
155 N 8	Rochester rd Carsh	
148 C 5	Rochester row SW1	
47 W 20	Rochester sq NW1	
148 E 4	Rochester st SW1	
47 U 19	Rochester ter NW1	
94 H 1	Rochester way SE3	
94 K 6	Rochester way SE3	
96 C 9	Rochester way SE9	
95 V 8	Rochester way SE9	
99 O 19	Rochester way Bxly	
37 T 14	Rochford av Rom	
121 Z 15	Rochford way Croy	
85 Z 8	Rock av SW14	
56 G 15	Rock gdns Dgnhm	
151 U 4	Rock gro SE16	
109 U 10	Rock hill SE26	
25 X 2	Rock st N4	
110 E 2	Rockburn rd SE23	
92 A 17	Rockell's pl SE22	
45 O 13	Rockhall rd NW2	
108 F 10	Rockhampton clo SE27	
108 F 9	Rockhampton rd SE27	
157 R 14	Rockhampton rd S Croy	
39 Z 20	Rockingham av Hornch	
150 B 2	Rockingham st SE1	
24 C 8	Rocklands dri Stanm	
136 F 18	Rockley rd W14	
63 U 3	Rockmead rd E9	
79 V 13	Rockmount rd SE18	
86 G 8	Rocks la SW13	
59 S 2	Rockware av Grnfd	
56 G 15	Rockwell rd Dgnhm	
136 C 17	Rockwood pl W12	
133 Y 9	Rocliffe st W2	
45 W 4	Rodborough rd NW11	
123 R 15	Roden gdns SE25	
48 C 11	Roden rd N7	
53 Y 9	Roden st Ilf	
53 X 9	Roden way Ilf	
89 Y 14	Rodenhurst rd SW4	
46 M 13	Roderick rd NW3	
66 M 1	Roding av Bark	
34 M 13	Roding la Ilf	
35 O 8	Roding la North Wdfd Grn	
35 N 14	Roding la South Ilf	
35 N 12	Roding lane South Ilf	
50 G 13	Roding rd E5	
21 Y 19	Rodings the Wdfd Grn	
139 R 2	Rodmarton ms W1	
14 H 15	Rodmell slope N12	
77 O 14	Rodmere st SE10	
90 A 20	Rodmill la SW2	
32 J 7	Rodney pl E17	
150 C 5	Rodney pl SE17	
106 C 20	Rodney pl SW19	
34 G 13	Rodney rd E11	
150 F 7	Rodney rd SE17	
120 H 5	Rodney rd Mitch	
118 A 10	Rodney rd New Mald	
133 P 8	Rodney st N1	
38 F 6	Rodney way Rom	
86 G 18	Rodway rd SW15	
112 H 19	Rodway rd Brom	
91 V 14	Rodwell rd SE22	
25 V 12	Roe end NW9	
25 V 12	Roe la NW9	
158 B 14	Roe wy Croy	
78 J 4	Roebourne way E16	
86 K 5	Roebuck la Buck Hl	
21 Y 4	Roebuck clo N17	
9 O 4	Roedean av Enf	
9 O 4	Roedean clo Enf	
86 A 14	Roedean cres SW15	
86 G 11	Roehampton clo SW15	
86 B 15	Roehampton ga SW15	
86 H 18	Roehampton High st SW15	
86 F 11	Roehampton la SW15	
104 K 1	Roehampton la SW15	
104 C 6	Roehampton vale SW15	
76 F 6	Roffey st E14	
133 O 18	Roger st WC1	
56 B 18	Rogers gdns Dgnhm	
65 R 17	Rogers rd E16	
106 H 9	Rogers rd SW17	
56 F 17	Rogers rd Dgnhm	
110 E 1	Rojack rd SE23	
34 F 4	Rokeby gdns Wdfd Grn	
92 L 3	Rokeby rd SE4	
64 L 3	Rokeby st E15	
96 F 4	Rokesby clo Welling	
30 A 15	Rokesly av N8	
146 C 9	Roland gdns SW7	
33 W 14	Roland rd E17	
146 C 9	Roland way SW7	
37 X 12	Roles gro Rom	
5 X 15	Rolfe clo Barnt	
78 D 11	Rolfe rd SE7	
35 W 18	Roll gdns Ilf	
127 Z 15	Rolleston av Brom	
127 Z 16	Rolleston clo Orp	
157 O 17	Rolleston rd S Croy	
75 R 16	Rollins st SE15	
48 E 14	Rollit st N7	
82 H 13	Rollit cres Hounsl	
141 S 5	Rolls bldgs EC4	
20 C 18	Rolls Park av E4	
20 D 17	Rolls Park rd E4	
141 S 4	Rolls pas EC4	
151 R 9	Rolls rd SE1	
90 L 13	Rollscourt av SE24	
75 X 15	Rolt st SE8	
57 S 2	Rom cres Rom	
32 J 10	Roma rd E17	
53 U 7	Roman rd E3	
66 E 12	Roman rd E6	
29 R 2	Roman rd N10	
74 C 10	Roman rd W4	
54 A 17	Roman rd Ilf	
53 Z 17	Roman rd Ilf	
109 P 14	Roman ri SE19	
48 C 19	Roman way N7	
126 A 10	Romanhurst av Brom	
125 Z 9	Romanhurst av Brom	
119 X 18	Romany gdns Sutto	
107 O 7	Romany rd SW17	
93 T 13	Romborough gdns SE13	
93 U 9	Romer av SE13	
108 O 7	Romeyn rd SW16	
53 U 11	Romford rd E12	
51 Z 19	Romford rd E15	
52 K 16	Romford rd E7	
37 Z 1	Romford rd Rom	
143 U 3	Romford st E1	
140 G 7	Romilly rd N4	
109 N 8	Romilly st W1	
140 G 7	Rommany rd SE27	
26 A 4	Romney clo NW11	
31 Z 4	Romney clo N17	
40 J 1	Romney clo Harrow	
40 J 1	Romney clo Harrow	
22 H 20	Romney dri Harrow	
98 C 1	Romney dri Harrow	
76 J 17	Romney gdns Bxly Hth	
68 J 3	Romney rd SE10	
117 Y 15	Romney rd Dgnhm	
143 H 9	Romney rd New Mald	
108 H 1	Romney st SW1	
68 J 2	Romola rd SE21	
47 N 13	Romsey gdns Dgnhm	
63 H 18	Rona rd NW3	
48 G 15	Ronald av E15	
112 F 20	Ronald clo Becknh	
96 J 15	Ronald st E1	
	Ronalds rd N5	
	Ronalds rd Brom	
	Ronaldstone rd Sidcp	
45 S 14	Rondu rd NW2	
57 S 3	Roneo corner Hornch	
94 D 20	Ronver rd SE12	
142 J 9	Rood la EC3	
142 J 9	Rookery clo NW9	
69 V 1	Rookery cres Dgnh	
127 M 14	Rookery la Brom	
89 U 11	Rookery rd SW4	
26 C 16	Rookery way NW9	
29 U 12	Rookfield av N10	
106 L 13	Rookstone rd SW1	
11 F 18	Rookwood av New Mald	
155 X 8	Rookwood av Wallgtn	
21 O 7	Rookwood gdns E4	
37 O 1	Rookwood gdns Ilf	
31 W 20	Rookwood rd N16	
57 O 18	Roosevelt way Dgnhm	
78 L 8	Rope Yd rails SE18	
142 F 1	Ropemaker st EC2	
63 X 20	Ropemakers fields E14	
95 V 14	Roper st SE9	
121 P 2	Roper way Mitch	
20 G 17	Ropers av E4	
63 Y 12	Ropery st E3	
98 F 12	Rosalind cres Bxly Hth	
144 L 19	Rosaline rd SW6	
159 Z 8	Rosamund st SE18	
82 B 5	Rosary clo Hounsl	
145 O 19	Rosary gdns SW7	
145 O 19	Rosaville rd SW6	
134 C 18	Roscoe st EC1	
142 N 12	Rose all SE1	
142 A 5	Rose And Crown ct EC2	
83 Y 2	Rose And Crown pa Islwth	
140 C 13	Rose And Crown yd SW1	
34 J 7	Rose av E18	
120 M 1	Rose av Mitch	
106 M 20	Rose av Mitch	
30 A 11	Rose av Mordn	
32 L 11	Rose Bank gro E17	
109 Z 17	Rose Bank st SE20	
72 H 8	Rose gdns W5	
58 H 11	Rose gdns Shall	
25 X 12	Rose glen NW9	
57 P 4	Rose glen Rom	
37 W 10	Rose Hatch av Rom	
154 B 2	Rose hill Sutton	
144 B 20	Rose hill Sutton	
37 Z 12	Rose la Rom	
10 A 6	Rose lawn Bushey Wat	
140 J 8	Rose st WC2	
117 T 10	Rose wlk Surb	
159 W 2	Rose wlk W Wkhm	
60 A 13	Roseacre rd W.13	
97 S 9	Roseacre rd Welling	
41 V 13	Rosebank av Wemb	
33 P 19	Rosebank rd E17	

X 6 Rosebank rd E3
U 6 Rosebank rd W7
O 14 Rosebank vlls E17
X 16 Rosebank way W3
T 14 Roseberry av EC1
R 18 Roseberry av E12
C 5 Roseberry av New Mald
H 18 Roseberry gdns Sidcp
J 18 Roseberry gdns N4
U 7 Roseberry rd N10
U 8 Roseberry rd N10
K 10 Roseberry rd N9
W 7 Roseberry rd SE16
A 16 Roseberry rd SW2
Z 16 Roseberry rd SW2
O 13 Roseberry rd Hounsl
S 4 Roseberry rd Kingst
Y 7 Roseberry st SE16
Z 7 Rosebery av N17
C 11 Rosebery av Harrow
C 5 Rosebery av New Mald
M 3 Rosebery av Thntn Hth
O 15 Rosebery clo Mrdn
A 16 Rosebery gdns N8
Z 19 Rosebery gdns W13
B 8 Rosebery gdns Sutton
U 19 Rosebery pl E8
J 10 Rosebery rd N10
V 14 Rosebery rd Sutton
R 19 Rosebine av Twick
B 6 Rosebury rd SW6
C 15 Rosecourt rd Croy
Z 10 Rosecroft av NW3
G 10 Rosecroft gdns NW2
R 20 Rosecroft gdns Twick
H 12 Rosecroft rd S'hall
C 8 Rosedale clo SE2
V 6 Rosedale clo W7
O 20 Rosedale clo Stanm
C 1 Rosedale gdns Dgnhm
L 16 Rosedale rd E7
C 1 Rosedale rd Daghm
U 5 Rosedale rd Epsom
J 9 Rosedale rd Rich
L 10 Rosedale rd Rom
D 7 Rosedene av SW16
B 17 Rosedene av SW16
H 8 Rosedene av Grnfd
Y 12 Rosedene av Mrdn
X 12 Rosedene gdns Ilf
R 7 Rosedene ter E10
F 14 Rosedew rd W14
F 14 Rosedew rd W6
A 19 Rosefield gdns E14
Y 18 Rosegarden clo Edg
E 12 Roseheath rd Hounsl
W 15 Rosehill gdns Grnfd
C 1 Rosehill gdns Sutton
A 1 Rosehill park Sutton
C 1 Rosehill pk W Sutton
C 15 Rosehill rd SW18
C 19 Rosehillav Sutton
J 13 Roseleigh av N5
F 17 Roselieu clo Twick
B 8 Rosemary av N3
M 6 Rosemary av N9
N 7 Rosemary av N9
D 5 Rosemary av Enf
A 6 Rosemary av Hounsl
T 10 Rosemary av Rom
O 16 Rosemary dri Ilf
B 4 Rosemary gdns Dgnhm
W 7 Rosemary la SW14
O 18 Rosemary rd SE15
M 19 Rosemary rd SE15
L 2 Rosemary rd Welling
F 4 Rosemary st N1
V 4 Rosemead av Mitch
L 16 Rosemead av Wemb
R 19 Rosemont av N12
C 17 Rosemont rd NW3
T 1 Rosemont rd W3
V 6 Rosemont rd New Mald
L 16 Rosemoor rd Rich
N 6 Rosemoor st SW3
U 8 Rosemount dri Brom
Z 16 Rosemount rd W13
F 11 Rosen's wlk Edg
K 1 Rosenau rd SW11
K 19 Rosendale rd SE21
M 1 Rosendale rd SE21
V 5 Roseneath av N10
O 15 Roseneath rd SW11
C 14 Roseneath wlk Enf

93 S 17 Rosenthal rd SE6
92 E 13 Rosenthorpe rd SE15
76 G 6 Roserton st E14
124 E 14 Rosery the Croy
148 K 18 Rosetta st SW8
112 L 9 Roseveare rd SE12
82 G 13 Roseville av Hounsl
118 M 1 Rosevine rd SW20
91 P 17 Roseway SE21
91 X 2 Rosewell av SE15
41 Y 17 Rosewood av Grnfd
57 X 15 Rosewood av Hornch
93 T 4 Rosewood gdns SE13
155 U 13 Rosewood gdns Wallgtn
154 E 2 Rosewood gro Sutton
50 E 16 Rosina st E9
87 O 7 Roskell rd SW15
112 F 14 Roslin way Brom
120 F 3 Roslyn clo Mitch
39 S 7 Roslyn gdns Rom
31 P 15 Roslyn rd N15
88 K 2 Rosnau cres EC1
133 T 16 Rosoman pl EC1
133 U 15 Rosoman st EC1
56 A 5 Ross av Dgnhm
23 N 1 Ross clo Harrow
155 T 12 Ross pde Wallgtn
64 H 5 Ross rd E15
123 X 4 Ross rd SE25
99 V 17 Ross rd Drtfrd
100 L 2 Ross rd Twick
155 V 12 Ross rd Wallgtn
95 R 7 Ross way SE9
39 W 19 Rossall clo Hornch
60 M 9 Rossall cres Wemb
154 K 9 Rossdale Sutton
19 O 2 Rossdale dri N9
43 U 4 Rossdale dri NW9
9 O 20 Rossdale dri Enf
87 N 9 Rossdale rd SW15
94 G 1 Rosse ms SE3
82 H 12 Rossindel rd Hounsl
49 Y 6 Rossington st E5
107 T 1 Rossiter rd SW12
21 O 8 Rosslyn av E4
63 C 8 Rosslyn av SW13
15 W 1 Rosslyn av Barnt
56 D 2 Rosslyn av Dgnhm
23 W 14 Rosslyn cres Harrow
42 Y 12 Rosslyn cres Wemb
46 H 14 Rosslyn hill NW3
33 U 14 Rosslyn rd E17
67 S 1 Rosslyn rd Bark
54 F 20 Rosslyn rd Bark
84 D 16 Rosslyn rd Twick
130 L 17 Rossmore rd NW1
131 N 16 Rossmore rd NW1
106 G 10 Rostella rd SW17
31 N 19 Rostrevor av N15
70 C 14 Rostrevor gdns S'hall
105 X 13 Rostrevor rd SW19
87 U 2 Rostrevor rd SW6
141 X 20 Rotary st SE1
71 Z 20 Rothbury gdns Islwth
50 M 20 Rothbury rd E9
155 P 10 Rotherfield rd Carsh
9 T 1 Rotherfield st N1
134 B 1 Rotherfield st N1
97 Y 16 Rotherhill av SW16
75 R 11 Rotherhithe New rd SE16
151 V 11 Rotherhithe New rd SE16
75 S 10 Rotherhithe Old rd SE16
75 T 2 Rotherhithe st SE16
143 X 18 Rotherhithe st SE16
75 S 1 Rotherhithe tunnel E1
156 E 12 Rothermere rd Croy
61 O 13 Rotherwick hill W5
45 X 2 Rotherwick rd NW11
87 O 7 Rotherwood rd SW15
133 X 4 Rothery st N1
123 P 9 Rothesay av SE25
119 T 9 Rothesay av SW20
40 O 18 Rothesay av Grnfd
85 S 9 Rothesay av Rich
51 L 19 Rothsay rd E7
150 H 2 Rothsay st SE1
73 V 9 Rothschild rd W4
108 K 10 Rothschild st SE27
68 G 2 Rothwell gdns Dgnhm
68 G 3 Rothwell rd Dgnhm

131 R 3 Rothwell st NW1
89 N 1 Rotten row SW11
78 E 14 Rotunda clo SE18
151 S 5 Rouel rd SE16
19 X 15 Rougemont av Mrdn
124 G 17 Round gro Croy
110 B 6 Round hill SE26
105 P 3 Roundacre SW19
89 U 5 Roundell st SW8
110 E 5 Roundhay clo SE23
7 P 15 Roundhill dri Enf
112 D 6 Roundtable ct Brom
31 P 4 Roundway N17
30 L 7 Roundway N17
35 T 6 Roundway rd Ilf
62 F 2 Roundwood park NW10
62 G 3 Roundwood Pk av NW10
44 C 19 Roundwood rd NW10
64 B 11 Rounton rd E3
90 E 20 Roupell rd SW2
108 D 1 Roupell rd SW2
141 U 15 Roupell st SE1
133 B 1 Rousden st NW1
109 R 9 Rouse gdns SE21
88 J 19 Routh rd SW18
144 K 19 Rowallan rd SW6
19 Z 19 Rowan av E4
121 V 1 Rowan clo SW16
121 V 1 Rowan cres SW16
121 V 2 Rowan rd SW16
144 F 6 Rowan rd W6
72 B 20 Rowan rd Brentf
97 Z 8 Rowan rd Bxly Hth
98 A 8 Rowan rd Bxly Hth
144 F 6 Rowan ter W6
37 U 11 Rowan way Rom
28 E 17 Rowan wlk N2
17 X 11 Rowans the N13
18 B 4 Rowantree clo N21
7 W 9 Rowantree rd N20
18 B 4 Rowantree rd N21
18 N 5 Rowben clo N20
151 O 9 Rowcross st SE1
58 H 2 Rowdell rd Grnfd
20 C 20 Rowden rd E4
110 K 20 Rowden rd Becknhm
89 N 4 Rowditch la SW11
44 K 20 Rowdon av NW10
159 Z 20 Rowdon cres Croy
69 O 1 Rowdown rd Dgnhm
67 Z 7 Rowe gdns Bark
40 G 9 Rowe wlk Harrow
88 J 5 Rowena cres SW11
107 O 2 Rowfant rd SW17
50 H 12 Rowhill rd E5
129 X 19 Rowington clo W2
24 E 11 Rowland av Harrow
110 A 8 Rowland gro SE26
46 J 14 Rowland Hill st NW3
18 A 20 Rowland hillav N17
135 T 20 Rowland st E1
56 B 8 Rowlands rd Dgnhm
22 J 1 Rowlands rd Pinn
97 P 19 Rowley av Sidcp
43 N 20 Rowley clo Wemb
61 N 1 Rowley clo Wemb
48 K 1 Rowley gdns N4
30 L 16 Rowley rd N15
117 O 5 Rowlls rd Kingst
55 S 18 Rowney gdns Dgnhm
55 R 18 Rowney rd Dgnhm
101 S 1 Rowney rd Twick
26 L 9 Rowsley av NW4
47 Z 16 Rowstock gdns N7
79 P 18 Rowton rd SE18
41 S 1 Roxborough la Harrow
71 W 19 Roxborough av Islwth
41 T 2 Roxborough pk Harrow
23 S 20 Roxborough pk Harrow
40 A 4 Roxbourne park Rom
108 H 11 Roxburgh rd SE27
145 V 19 Roxby pl SW6
40 L 7 Roxeth Green av Harrow
40 L 12 Roxeth grn Harrow
41 R 6 Roxeth hill Harrow
93 S 16 Roxley rd SE13
159 N 12 Roxton gdns Croy
74 G 5 Roxwell rd W12
68 B 7 Roxwell rd Bark
34 M 1 Roxwell way Wdfd Grn
37 S 20 Roxy av Rom
36 J 14 Roy gdns Ilf
100 K 14 Roy gro Hampt

140 B 11 Royal academy W1
138 E 20 Royal Albert hall SW7
81 U 12 Royal Alfred home Blvdr
140 A 11 Royal arcade W1
147 O 10 Royal av SW3
152 B 3 Royal av Worc Pk
84 K 5 Royal Botanic gardens Rich
108 H 7 Royal cir SE27
132 C 3 Royal College st NW1
47 U 20 Royal College st NW1
136 J 15 Royal cres W11
40 A 11 Royal cres Ruis
136 H 15 Royal Cres ms W11
142 G 6 Royal Exch bldgs EC2
142 G 6 Royal Exchange bldgs EC2
141 O 14 Royal Festival hall SE1
76 G 19 Royal hill SE10
147 P 12 Royal Hospital rd SW3
78 F 14 Royal Military repository SE18
143 P 9 Royal mint EC3
143 P 9 Royal Mint st E1
76 H 16 Royal Naval college SE10
49 Y 18 Royal Oak rd E8
98 C 12 Royal Oak rd Bxly Hth
76 K 19 Royal observatory SE10
140 F 13 Royal Opera arcade SW4
94 B 5 Royal pde SE3
60 K 10 Royal pde W5
114 C 19 Royal pde Chisl
76 G 20 Royal pde SE10
66 A 19 Royal rd E16
65 Z 18 Royal rd E16
149 W 14 Royal rd SE17
115 W 6 Royal rd Sidcp
101 R 11 Royal rd Tedd
141 R 20 Royal st SE1
63 T 6 Royal Victor pl E3
67 X 7 Roycraft av Bark
67 X 6 Roycraft clo Bark
67 Y 6 Roycraft gdns Bark
34 H 5 Roycroft clo E18
79 U 14 Roydene rd SE18
59 Y 12 Royle cres W13
20 C 17 Royston av E4
54 G 5 Royston av Sutton
155 Y 8 Royston av Wallgtn
35 N 19 Royston gdns Ilf
154 F 5 Royston park Sutton
124 F 1 Royston rd SE20
110 F 20 Royston rd Becknhm
99 S 16 Royston rd Drtfrd
84 L 14 Royston rd Rich
63 P 7 Royston st E2
117 S 11 Roystons the Surb
89 U 6 Rozel rd SW4
110 M 5 Rubens st SE6
9 Y 11 Ruberoid rd Enf
33 O 10 Ruby rd E17
151 W 15 Ruby st SE15
51 S 10 Ruckholt clo E10
51 P 12 Ruckholt rd E10
62 E 6 Rucklidge av NW10
46 F 12 Rudall cres NW3
79 N 1 Rudd st SE18
75 W 19 Ruddigore rd SE14
98 H 8 Rudland rd Bxly Hth
89 U 17 Rudloe rd SW12
129 W 10 Rudolf rd NW6
65 R 7 Rudolph rd E13
12 H 18 Rudyard gro NW7
157 Z 15 Ruffetts clo S Croy
132 L 2 Ruffetts the S Croy
132 L 2 Rufford st N1
40 A 10 Rufus dri Ruis
40 A 10 Rufus clo Ruis
18 G 5 Rugby av N9
41 S 17 Rugby av Grnfd
42 C 14 Rugby av Wemb
23 S 14 Rugby clo Harrow
55 S 19 Rugby gdns Dgnhm
153 P 20 Rugby la Sutton
25 S 12 Rugby rd NW9
73 Z 6 Rugby rd W4
55 P 19 Rugby rd Dgnhm
83 U 15 Rugby rd Twick
133 N 19 Rugby st WC1
58 K 11 Ruislip clo Grnfd
59 P 11 Ruislip rd East Grnfd
58 L 11 Ruislip rd Grnfd

106 M 9	Ruislip st SW17
145 Y 19	Ruislip rd SW6
90 E 7	Rumsey rd SW9
136 K 9	Runcorn pl W11
26 J 17	Rundell cres NW4
150 E 9	Runham st SE17
41 T 10	Runnelfield Harrow
141 W 14	Running Horse yd SE1
106 F 20	Runnymede SW19
82 L 17	Runnymede clo Twick
107 Z 20	Runnymede cres SW16
59 T 6	Runnymede gdns Grnfd
82 K 17	Runnymede gdns Twick
47 Y 5	Runton st E13
75 P 6	Rupack st SE16
42 K 16	Rupert av Wemb
140 F 9	Rupert ct W1
90 J 6	Rupert gdns SW9
129 R 10	Rupert rd NW6
47 Y 8	Rupert rd N19
74 B 9	Rupert rd W4
140 E 8	Rupert st W1
92 D 3	Rural pl SE14
107 T 17	Rural way SW14
65 P 17	Ruscoe rd E16
156 L 3	Rush Green gdns Rom
156 K 4	Rush Gro st SE18
78 H 12	Rush Gro st SE18
89 P 8	Rush Hill rd SW11
88 M 17	Rusham rd SW12
89 N 17	Rusham rd SW12
32 M 6	Rushbrook cres E17
114 A 5	Rushbrook rd SE9
33 P 1	Rushcroft dri E4
33 R 1	Rushcroft rd E4
90 F 11	Rushcroft rd SW2
35 X 10	Rushden gdns NW7
15 X 3	Rushdene av Barnt
120 G 19	Rushen wlk Carsh
116 A 19	Rushett clo Surb
116 A 18	Rushett rd Surb
93 S 18	Rushey grn SE6
7 P 15	Rushey hill Enf
92 M 16	Rushford rd SE4
26 D 13	Rushgrove av NW9
102 B 8	Rushmead Rich
157 U 8	Rushmead clo Croy
127 R 7	Rushmore clo Brom
50 E 2	Rushmore cres E5
50 C 12	Rushmore rd E5
58 E 9	Rusholme av Dgnhm
57 R 17	Rusholme rd SW15
24 A 19	Rushout av Harrow
134 G 8	Rushton st N1
26 G 11	Rushworth av NW4
141 Y 18	Rushworth st SE1
53 T 17	Ruskin av E12
73 R 20	Ruskin av Rich
97 N 6	Ruskin av Welling
28 A 18	Ruskin clo NW11
97 N 6	Ruskin dri Welling
152 L 2	Ruskin dri Worc Pk
60 F 11	Ruskin gdns W5
25 N 13	Ruskin gdns Harrow
39 Y 4	Ruskin gdns Rom
97 N 6	Ruskin gro Welling
31 U 4	Ruskin rd N17
81 R 11	Ruskin rd Blvdr
155 O 11	Ruskin rd Carsh
83 V 8	Ruskin rd Islwth
58 A 20	Ruskin rd S'hall
89 T 5	Ruskin st SW8
18 J 8	Ruskin wlk N9
90 L 14	Ruskin wlk SE24
127 T 13	Ruskin wlk Brom
23 T 14	Rusland Pk rd Harrow
30 L 9	Rusper rd N22
55 U 18	Rusper rd Dgnhm
26 E 19	Rusper rd NW9
30 H 8	Russell av N22
61 V 1	Russell clo NW10
125 S 5	Russell clo Becknhm
98 D 10	Russell clo Bxly Hth
69 V 3	Russell clo Drtfrd
99 W 9	Russell clo Drtfrd
140 B 15	Russell ct SW1
27 T 19	Russell gdns NW11
15 X 8	Russell gdns N20
144 L 1	Russell gdns SW14
102 C 4	Russell gdns Rich
136 K 20	Russell Gdns ms W14
13 N 14	Russell gro NW7
149 U 20	Russell gro SW9
15 X 8	Russell la N20
16 A 6	Russell la N20
33 R 20	Russell rd E10
65 U 17	Russell rd E16
32 K 11	Russell rd E17
19 X 14	Russell rd E4
26 E 19	Russell rd NW9
17 O 18	Russell rd N13
31 R 16	Russell rd N15
15 X 7	Russell rd N20
105 X 17	Russell rd SW19
144 M 2	Russell rd W14
21 X 6	Russell rd Buck Hl
123 P 16	Russell rd Croy
8 G 3	Russell rd Enf
41 N 13	Russell rd Grnfd
120 K 6	Russell rd Mitch
83 V 17	Russell rd Twick
132 J 19	Russell sq WC1
65 U 6	Russell st E13
140 M 8	Russell st WC2
108 C 12	Russells footpath SW16
93 T 4	Russett way SE13
142 C 5	Russia ct EC2
63 O 6	Russia la E2
135 Z 8	Russia pl E2
142 C 5	Russia row EC2
150 D 17	Rust sq SE5
107 T 17	Rusthall av W4
107 T 17	Rustic av SW16
119 V 16	Rustington wlk Mrdn
117 S 17	Ruston av Surb
136 J 6	Ruston clo W11
136 K 5	Ruston ms W11
63 Z 3	Ruston st E3
108 A 12	Rutford rd SW16
47 F 13	Rutherglen clo Sutton
148 F 4	Rutherford st SW1
10 D 5	Rutherford way Bushey Watf
79 Z 15	Ruthergien rd SE2
152 G 14	Rutherwyke clo Epsom
77 T 16	Ruthin clo SE3
97 N 18	Rutland av Sidcp
85 U 7	Rutland clo SW14
106 H 16	Rutland clo SW19
126 C 9	Rutland clo Brom
115 W 3	Rutland clo Bxly
119 W 15	Rutland dri Mrdn
138 K 19	Rutland ga SW7
126 D 9	Rutland ga Brom
138 K 20	Rutland Ga ms SW7
81 U 14	Rutland gate Blvdr
30 J 18	Rutland gdns N4
138 L 19	Rutland gdns SW7
59 Y 15	Rutland gdns W13
157 T 9	Rutland gdns Croy
55 S 14	Rutland gdns Dgnhm
138 L 19	Rutland gdns ms SW7
74 K 14	Rutland gro W6
144 A 10	Rutland gro W6
146 K 1	Rutland Ms south SW7
110 H 16	Rutland pk SE6
45 N 18	Rutland Pk gdns NW2
34 J 14	Rutland rd E11
53 N 20	Rutland rd E12
33 O 18	Rutland rd E17
63 S 3	Rutland rd E9
104 M 18	Rutland rd SW19
9 N 18	Rutland rd Enf
23 N 18	Rutland rd Harrow
54 A 11	Rutland rd ilf
53 Z 11	Rutland rd ilf
58 G 14	Rutland rd S'hall
101 P 4	Rutland rd Twick
110 M 4	Rutland wlk SE6
105 Y 20	Rutlish rd SW19
120 E 9	Rutter gdns Mitch
92 E 4	Rutts ter SE14
10 D 5	Rutts the Bushey Watf
87 P 7	Ruvigny gdns SW15
115 X 15	Ruxley clo Sidcp
91 W 18	Ryecot path SE22
94 C 4	Ryculff sq SE3
27 R 5	Rydal clo NW4
60 C 7	Rydal cres Grnfd
98 H 3	Rydal dri Bxly Hth
26 B 15	Rydal gdns NW9
104 A 12	Rydal gdns SW15
82 K 16	Rydal gdns Hounsl
42 E 3	Rydal gdns Wemb
107 X 11	Rydal rd SW16
9 R 19	Rydal way Enf
140 B 13	Ryder ct SW1
66 K 17	Ryder gdns E6
57 U 18	Ryder gdns Rainhm
140 C 13	Ryder st SW1
140 C 12	Ryder yd SW1
130 A 8	Ryders ter NW8
107 T 3	Rydevale rd SW12
95 P 7	Rydons clo SE9
98 G 15	Rye clo Bxly
92 B 11	Rye Hill pk SE15
91 X 3	Rye la SE15
92 E 12	Rye rd SE15
16 J 2	Rye the N14
12 A 19	Rye way Edg
109 S 1	Ryecotes mead SE21
35 Z 7	Ryecroft av ilf
82 L 20	Ryecroft av Twick
100 L 2	Ryecroft av Twick
93 V 13	Ryecroft rd SE13
108 G 15	Ryecroft rd SW16
87 Z 3	Ryecroft st SW6
91 Z 16	Ryedale SE22
108 M 15	Ryefield rd SE19
105 X 6	Ryfold rd SW19
16 F 13	Ryhope rd N11
47 S 17	Ryland rd NW5
44 G 9	Rylandes rd NW2
80 B 8	Rylands clo SE2
94 J 16	Rylands cres SE12
74 D 7	Rylett cres W12
74 F 8	Rylett rd W12
135 O 16	Rylston rd E1
18 A 11	Rylston rd N13
145 O 16	Rylston rd SW6
88 B 12	Rymer rd SW18
123 T 17	Rymer rd Croy
90 J 15	Rymer st SE24
139 O 20	Rysbrack st SW3

S

139 W 7	S Moulton pass W1
65 O 18	Sabbarton st E16
88 M 7	Sabine rd SW11
89 N 7	Sabine rd SW8
118 A 10	Sable ct New Mald
48 J 20	Sable st N1
50 A 6	Sach rd E5
126 E 19	Sackville av Brom
41 P 10	Sackville clo Harrow
53 X 17	Sackville gdns ilf
153 X 17	Sackville rd Sutton
140 B 11	Sackville st W1
14 K 16	Saddlescombe way N12
112 H 4	Sadstone rd SE12
27 V 17	Saffron clo NW11
133 U 19	Saffron hill EC1
141 U 1	Saffron hill EC1
38 L 7	Saffron rd Rom
133 U 19	Saffron st EC1
149 P 4	Sail st SW11
107 P 4	Sainfoin rd SW17
109 R 12	Sainsbury rd SE19
97 O 3	St Abb's st Welling
120 L 19	St Agatha's grn Carsh
149 V 15	St Agnes pl SE11
63 P 3	St Agnes ter E9
72 C 6	St Aidan's rd W13
91 Z 14	St Aidans rd SE22
101 Z 12	St aiban's Gdns Tedd
66 J 9	St Alban's av E6
135 Z 9	St Alban's gro E9.
146 A 1	St Alban's gro W8
133 V 5	St Alban's pl N1
62 A 3	St Alban's rd NW10
47 P 9	St Alban's rd NW5
54 K 2	St Alban's rd N5
144 K 12	St Alban's ter W6
73 Y 10	St Albans av W4
30 F 6	St Albans cres N22
32 E 3	St Albans cres Wdfd Grn
120 K 18	St Albans gro Carsh
16 L 10	St Albans la NW11
4 C 4	St Albans rd Barnt
102 K 16	St Albans rd Kingst
153 U 9	St Albans rd Sutton
34 D 3	St Albans rd Wdfd Grn
140 F 12	St Albans rd SW1
37 W 15	St Aldrew's av Hornch
76 G 17	St Alfege pas SE10
78 B 15	St Alfege rd SE7
142 C 2	St Alphage gdn EC2
19 O 3	St Alphage rd N9
89 W 11	St Alphonsus rd SW4
8 C 12	St Andrew st Enf
141 V 3	St Andrew st EC4
41 Y 12	St Andrew's av Wemb
44 J 10	St Andrew's clo NW2
15 P 13	St Andrew's clo N1
24 E 7	St Andrew's clo Stanm
41 Y 11	St Andrew's clo Wemb
49 O 4	St Andrew's gro N
141 Y 7	St Andrew's hill EC
49 R 3	St Andrew's ms N1
131 X 16	St Andrew's pl NW
32 G 9	St Andrew's rd E17
44 J 19	St Andrew's rd NW10
27 W 19	St Andrew's rd NW11
43 X 5	St Andrew's rd NW
19 P 4	St Andrew's rd N9
62 B 18	St Andrew's rd W3
154 K 4	St Andrew's rd Carsh
156 L 8	St Andrew's rd ilf
53 U 1	St Andrew's rd ilf
116 G 14	St Andrew's rd Surb
116 F 14	St Andrew's sq Sur
106 C 3	St Andrews ct SW18
24 E 5	St Andrews dri Stanm
33 Z 19	St Andrews rd E11
144 M 12	St Andrews rd W7
71 S 5	St Andrews rd W7
39 O 18	St Andrews rd Rom
115 X 7	St Andrews rd Side
88 C 15	St Ann's cres SW1
47 O 18	St Ann's gdns NW
88 C 17	St Ann's hill SW18
88 C 17	St Ann's Pk rd SW18
30 J 16	St Ann's rd N15
31 T 18	St Ann's rd N15
18 G 7	St Ann's rd N9
86 D 3	St Ann's rd SW13
67 P 4	St Ann's rd Bark
23 U 18	St Ann's rd Harrow
63 Z 18	St Ann st E18
63 Z 18	St Anne's pl E14
51 V 5	St Anne's rd E11
42 H 15	St Anne's rd Wemb
156 K 15	St Anne's way Cro
156 K 15	St Anne's way Cro
140 E 6	St Annes ct W1
60 L 8	St Annes gdns Wemb
63 Y 19	St Annes pass E14
148 G 2	St Anns la SW1
86 C 7	St Anns pas SW13
80 B 13	St Anns rd N8
148 G 1	St Anns st SW1
130 G 8	St Anns ter NW8
138 J 14	St Anns vlls W11
139 V 7	St Anselm's pl W1
134 K 1	St Anthony's av Wdfd Grn
52 G 20	St Antony's rd E7
92 F 7	St Asaph rd SE4
105 U 12	St Aubyn's av SW1
109 T 16	St Aubyn's rd SE1
82 G 14	St Aubyns av Hounsl
98 F 4	St Audry av Bxly Hth
60 L 7	St Augustine's av W5
127 R 12	St Augustine's av Brom
156 L 15	St Augustine's av Croy
42 K 9	St Augustine's av Wemb
47 Y 19	St Augustine's rd NW1
81 P 9	St Augustine's rd Blvdr
24 M 8	St Austell clo Edg
93 V 4	St Austell rd SE13
67 S 2	St Awdry's rd Bark
33 N 18	St Barnabas rd E1
107 P 18	St Barnabas rd Mitch
154 F 10	St Barnabas rd Sutton
34 J 2	St Barnabas rd Wdfd Grn
154 F 10	St Barnabas ter E9
147 U 9	St Barnabus st SW
90 A 1	St Barnabus vill SW8

20 C 18	St Benet's gro Carsh
42 H 8	St Benets pl EC3
36 B 4	St Bernards rd E6
26 G 3	St Blaise av Brom
43 N 5	St Botolph st EC3
41 V 5	St Bride st EC4
41 V 5	St Bride's av Edg
41 W 7	St Bride's pas EC4
9 F 5	St Catherines dri SE14
20 B 9	St Catherines rd E4
42 M 11	St Chad's pl WC1
37 X 20	St Chad's rd Rom
32 L 12	St Chad's st WC1
55 Y 1	St Chads gdns Rom
57 V 18	St Chads park Rom
36 K 2	St Charles pl W10
36 H 2	St Charles sq W10
32 J 7	St Clair dri Worc Pk
35 V 8	St Clair rd E13
35 T 7	St Claire clo Ilf
43 N 7	St Clare st EC3
38 E 19	St Clement st N7
41 P 6	St Clement's la WC2
52 G 8	St Clements ct EC3
09 N 9	St Cloud rd SE27
58 F 16	St Crispin's clo S'hall
33 U 20	St Cross st EC1
45 U 17	St Cuthbert's rd NW2
22 F 1	St Cuthberts gdns Pinn
06 L 10	St Cyprians's st SW17
25 S 18	St David's clo W Wkhm
43 V 10	St David's clo Wemb
24 M 4	St David's dri Edg
24 J 20	St David's pl NW8
09 N 9	St Denis rd SE27
87 W 3	St Dionis rd SW6
92 K 3	St Donatts rd SE14
61 Y 19	St Dunstan's gdns W3
53 T 11	St Dunstan's hill Sutton
42 J 10	St Dunstan's la EC3
52 K 16	St Dunstan's rd E7
23 V 8	St Dunstan's rd SE25
44 F 12	St Dunstan's rd W6
71 T 6	St Dunstans rd W7
61 Y 18	St Dunstans av W3
41 U 6	St Dunstans clo W3
42 J 10	St Dunstans hill EC3
18 J 3	St Edmund's rd N9
31 N 5	St Edmund's ter NW8
30 M 7	St Edmund's ter NW8
31 N 6	St Edmunds clo NW8
24 A 4	St Edmunds dri Stanm
23 Z 4	St Edmunds dri Stanm
82 K 19	St Edmunds la Twick
35 V 19	St Edmunds rd Ilf
27 X 19	St Edwards clo NW11
74 E 5	St Elmo rd W12
67 R 2	St Erkenwald rd Bark
68 E 20	St Ermins hill SW1
08 J 2	St Faith's rd SE21
93 V 20	St Fillans rd SE6
49 Y 5	St Gabriel st SE11
5 P 15	St Gabriel's rd NW2
39 Z 8	St George st W1
25 W 12	St George's av N7
47 X 11	St George's av N7
70 E 1	St George's av S'hall
52 J 20	St George's ave E7
27 U 19	St George's cir EC1
27 U 19	St George's clo NW11
48 B 9	St George's dri SW1
47 Y 7	St George's dri SW1
42 H 9	St George's la E3
49 Y 1	St George's mkt SE1
31 P 2	St George's ms NW1
51 U 8	St George's rd E10
52 H 19	St George's rd E7
27 V 18	St George's rd NW11
18 L 10	St George's rd N9
19 X 3	St George's rd SE1
05 U 16	St George's rd SW19
73 Z 6	St George's rd W4
71 W 3	St George's rd W7
125 P 1	St George's rd Becknhm
127 T 6	St George's rd Brom
100 A 10	St George's rd Felt
53 T 1	St George's rd Ilf
103 O 19	St George's rd Kingst
121 S 6	St George's rd Mitch
115 X 14	St George's rd Sidcp
84 B 13	St George's rd Twick
155 R 11	St George's rd Wallgtn
127 S 2	St George's rd West Brom
52 J 20	St George's sq E7
148 D 9	St George's sq SW1
148 E 11	St George's Sq ms SW1
75 X 10	St George's stairs SE16
151 O 15	St George's way SE15
150 K 15	St George's way SE15
148 E 11	St George's wlk Croy
72 F 5	St Georges av W5
41 Z 10	St Georges clo Wemb
17 P 9	St Georges rd N13
56 A 12	St Georges rd Dgnhm
55 Y 14	St Georges rd Dgnhm
8 G 3	St Georges rd Enf
85 N 9	St Georges rd Enf
118 C 6	St Georges sq New Mald
131 P 2	St Georges ter NW8
94 E 2	St German's pl SE3
92 J 20	St Germans rd SE23
56 H 19	St Giles av Dgnhm
56 H 19	St Giles clo Dgnhm
140 H 5	St Giles High st WC2
140 H 6	St Giles pas WC2
91 R 1	St Giles rd SE5
150 H 20	St Giles rd SE5
109 N 10	St Gothard rd SE27
122 O 1	St Helen's cres SW16
136 G 4	St Helen's gdns W10
142 J 5	St Helen's pl EC3
122 D 2	St Helen's rd Ilf
53 S 13	St Helena st WC1
75 R 12	St Helens rd SE16
72 C 2	St Helens rd W13
35 L 19	St Helens rd Ilf
120 C 13	St Helier av Mrdn
82 G 14	St Heliers av Hounsl
33 T 19	St Heliers rd E10
74 H 16	St Hildas rd SW13
109 Z 19	St Hugh's rd SE20
39 V 12	St Ivians dri Rom
133 V 17	St James's row EC1
71 Y 3	St James av W13
90 G 7	St James cres SW9
142 K 5	St James ct EC3
136 J 13	St James gdns W11
140 E 11	St James mkt SW1
140 F 18	St James park SW1
18 M 9	St James rd N9
151 U 11	St James rd SE1
107 P 19	St James rd Mitch
92 J 2	St james' SE14
124 J 6	St James' av Becknhm
15 W 12	St James' clo N20
116 G 13	St James' rd Surb
63 R 6	St James's av E2
15 N 11	St James's av N20
100 M 13	St James's av Hampt
153 X 10	St James's av Sutton
118 C 12	St James's clo New Mald
84 J 17	St James's ct Rich
106 L 2	St James's dri SW17
60 J 1	St James's gdns Wemb
29 S 12	St James's la N10
140 B 15	St James's palace SW1
122 L 17	St James's pk Croy
140 B 14	St James's pl SW1
9 U 18	St James's pl Enf
52 C 15	St James's rd E7
151 T 1	St James's rd SE16
154 K 5	St James's rd SE1
123 O 19	St James's rd Croy
9 O 7	St James's rd Enf
100 L 12	St James's rd Hampt
116 H 4	St James's rd Kingst
153 Y 13	St James's rd Sutton
140 D 13	St James's sq SW1
143 B 13	St James's st SW1
74 M 14	St James's st W6
144 C 11	St James's st W6
131 N 7	St James's ter NW1
131 N 6	St James's Ter ms NW8
79 N 13	St James's vlls SE18
133 W 16	St James's wlk EC1
18 H 7	St Joans rd EC1
133 W 15	St John st EC1
62 D 3	St John's av N10
15 Z 18	St John's av N11
50 S 5	St John's Church rd E9
42 K 15	St John's clo Wemb
90 F 7	St John's cres SW9
83 V 5	St John's ct Islwth
110 C 18	St John's cts SE20
137 N 11	St John's gdns W11
136 M 11	St John's gdns W11
47 W 8	St John's gro N19
84 J 9	St John's gro Rich
88 H 11	St John's hill SW11
88 F 11	St John's Hill gro SW11
133 X 19	St John's la EC1
133 W 19	St John's pl EC1
33 T 9	St John's rd E17
66 E 4	St John's rd E6
31 R 19	St John's rd N15
110 C 16	St John's rd SE20
88 K 10	St John's rd SW11
105 R 16	St John's rd SW19
71 Z 1	St John's rd W13
67 U 5	St John's rd Bark
154 K 5	St John's rd Carsh
156 J 5	St John's rd Croy
100 C 10	St John's rd Felt
23 V 18	St John's rd Harrow
36 H 20	St John's rd Ilf
54 G 1	St John's rd Ilf
83 W 5	St John's rd Islwth
116 E 2	St John's rd Kingst
117 V 7	St John's rd New Mald
84 K 10	St John's rd Rich
115 P 10	St John's rd Sidcp
153 Z 3	St John's rd Sutton
97 P 8	St John's rd Welling
42 H 13	St John's rd Wemb
133 W 19	St John's st SE1
79 R 15	St John's ter SE18
128 H 15	St John's ter W10
8 B 1	St John's ter Enf
93 O 4	St John's vale SE4
47 X 6	St John's vlls N19
47 X 4	St John's way N19
130 G 7	St John's Wood barrack NW8
130 K 11	St John's Wood High st NW8
130 J 8	St John's Wood ter NW8
87 P 13	St Johns av SW15
21 X 5	St Johns ct Buck Hl
133 X 19	St Johns pass EC1
77 S 20	St Johns pk SE3
65 S 17	St Johns rd E16
20 E 13	St Johns rd E4
27 W 19	St Johns rd NW11
70 B 8	St Johns rd S'hall
52 J 17	St Johns ter E7
130 G 14	St Johns Wood rd NW8
70 D 3	St Joseph's dri S'hall
19 O 5	St Joseph's rd N9
89 S 1	St Joseph's st SW8
30 B 13	St Josephs rd N8
49 S 16	St Jude st N16
63 N 7	St Jude's rd E2
135 X 11	St Judes rd E2
108 F 11	St Julian's clo SW16
108 H 9	St Julian's Farm rd SE27
129 S 3	St Julians rd NW6
131 W 8	St Katherine's precinct NW1
142 L 7	St Katherine's row EC3
143 O 12	St Katherine's way E1
113 S 10	St Keverne rd SE9
71 Z 4	St Kilda rd W13
49 O 4	St Kilda's rd N16
23 S 18	St Kilda's rd Harrow
24 M 1	St Lawrence clo Edgw
76 H 1	St Lawrence st E14
136 L 2	St Lawrence ter W10
64 E 17	St Leonard's av E14
97 O 8	St Leonard's clo Welling
64 G 18	St Leonard's rd E14
61 Z 11	St Leonard's rd NW1/
60 C 19	St Leonard's rd W13
116 F 12	St Leonard's rd Surb
147 P 10	St Leonard's ter SW3
20 L 18	St Leonards av E4
24 C 15	St Leonards av Harrow
82 A 1	St Leonards gdns Hounsl
54 B 16	St Leonards gdns Ilf
85 U 8	St Leonards rd SW14
156 H 6	St Leonards rd Croy
47 P 18	St Leonards sq NW5
64 F 10	St Leonards st E3
147 O 11	St Leonards ter SW3
146 M 14	St Loo av SW3
109 N 10	St Louis rd SE27
31 T 9	St Loys rd N17
89 X 10	St Luke's av SW4
8 B 3	St Luke's av Ilf
53 Z 15	St Luke's av Ilf
137 P 4	St Luke's ms W11
102 L 20	St Luke's pas Kingst
65 P 17	St Luke's sq E16
146 K 9	St Luke's st SW3
129 O 11	St Luke's yd W9
137 P 4	St Lukes ms W11
137 P 3	St Lukes rd W11
1 O 9	St Malo av N9
30 J 13	St Margaret's av N15
15 R 6	St Margaret's av N20
40 M 8	St Margaret's av Harrow
114 E 6	St Margaret's av Sidcp
153 S 5	St Margaret's av Sutton
86 K 13	St Margaret's cres SW15
84 B 12	St Margaret's dri Twick
79 O 15	St Margaret's gro SE18
83 Z 5	St Margaret's gro Twick
84 A 15	St Margaret's gro Twick
93 Z 9	St Margaret's pas SE13
52 L 7	St Margaret's rd E12
128 A 11	St Margaret's rd NW10
62 L 8	St Margaret's rd NW10
31 S 9	St Margaret's rd N17
67 R 3	St Margaret's rd Bark
124 F 9	St Margaret's rd Becknhm
12 E 17	St Margaret's rd Edg
84 A 13	St Margaret's rd Twick
92 L 11	St Margaret's sq SE4
140 K 19	St Margaret's st SW1
79 P 14	St Margaret's ter SE18
143 P 7	St Mark st E1
5 N 13	St Mark's clo Barnt
131 U 4	St Mark's clo NW1
63 Y 1	St Mark's ga E9
135 Z 16	St Mark's gro SW10
116 K 13	St Mark's hill Surb
138 M 6	St Mark's pl W11
123 Y 9	St Mark's rd SE25
136 G 2	St Mark's rd W11
128 F 20	St Mark's rd W11
71 T 5	St Mark's rd W7
8 H 19	St Mark's rd Enf
121 N 4	St Mark's rd Mitch
144 M 4	St Mark's rd Mitch
102 B 17	St Mark's rd Tedd
49 V 15	St Mark's ri E8
131 T 5	St Mark's sq NW1
105 V 15	St Marks pl SW19
126 G 7	St Marks rd Brom
66 A 7	St Martin's av E6
132 A 4	St Martin's clo NW1
8 M 5	St Martin's clo Enf

140 H 9 St Martin's ct WC2
140 J 9 St Martin's la WC2
140 H 11 St Martin's pl WC2
18 M 8 St Martin's rd N9
90 C 4 St Martin's rd SW9
140 G 11 St Martin's rd E17
142 A 4 St Martins Le grand EC1
135 P 3 St Mary Abbot's pl E8
145 P 2 St Mary Abbots ter W14
142 J 10 St Mary At hill EC3
155 R 6 St Mary av Wallgtn
142 K 4 St Mary axe EC3
143 Z 18 St Mary Ch st SE16
33 P 14 St Mary rd E17
78 H 10 St Mary st SE18
53 T 15 St Mary's appr E12
27 U 7 St Mary's av N3
126 Z 6 St Mary's av Brom
126 A 7 St Mary's av Brom
70 K 11 St Mary's av S'hall
101 W 15 St Mary's av Tedd
152 E 17 St Mary's clo Epsom
71 R 19 St Mary's cres Islwth
48 K 19 St Mary's gro N1
86 J 8 St Mary's gro SW13
73 T 17 St Mary's gro W4
85 N 11 St Mary's gro Rich
133 X 4 St Mary's path N1
51 U 8 St Mary's rd E10
65 U 6 St Mary's rd E13
62 C 2 St Mary's rd N8
27 S 20 St Mary's rd NW11
30 B 14 St Mary's rd N8
19 O 5 St Mary's rd N9
92 C 3 St Mary's rd SE15
123 R 7 St Mary's rd SE25
105 U 13 St Mary's rd SW19
72 G 5 St Mary's rd W5
67 P 3 St Mary's rd Bark
15 Y 3 St Mary's rd Barnt
54 D 8 St Mary's rd Ilf
116 E 18 St Mary's rd Surb
152 C 3 St Mary's rd Worc Pk
75 P 5 St Marychurch st SE16
34 H 20 St Marys av E11
31 W 6 St Marys clo N17
26 J 11 St Marys cres NW4
72 F 5 St Marys ct W5
149 U 5 St Marys gdns SE11
138 E 1 St Marys ter W2
149 U 5 St Marys wlk SE11
148 F 2 St Matthew SW1
116 K 19 St Matthew's av Surb
127 U 6 St Matthew's dri Brom
90 E 12 St Matthew's rd SW2
135 S 15 St Matthew's row E2
72 K 3 St Matthews rd W5
87 V 2 St Maur rd SW6
79 S 18 St Merryn clo SE18
15 V 16 St Michael clo N12
19 P 4 St Michael's av N9
43 R 17 St Michael's av Wemb
93 Z 9 St Michael's clo SE13
127 P 6 St Michael's clo Brom
22 C 18 St Michael's cres Pinn
126 K 1 St Michael's gdns W10
44 L 12 St Michael's rd NW2
90 C 4 St Michael's rd SW9
122 M 20 St Michael's rd Croy
156 M 1 St Michael's rd Croy
155 V 12 St Michael's rd Wallgtn
97 P 8 St Michael's rd Welling
39 B 6 St Michaels ter N22
138 J 3 St Michaels st W2
142 E 6 St Mildred's ct EC2
94 C 19 St Mildred's rd SE12
57 X 11 St Nicholas av Hornch
127 S 1 St Nicholas la Chisl
79 Y 12 St Nicholas rd SE18
154 B 11 St Nicholas rd Sutton
92 M 3 St Nicholas st SE14
92 J 8 St Norbert grn SE4
92 H 10 St Norbert gro SE4
92 G 12 St Norbert rd SE4
135 N 19 St Olaf's rd E1
144 M 20 St Olaf's rd SW6

142 D 5 St Olave's ct EC2
66 J 3 St Olave's rd E6
121 W 3 St Olave's wlk SW16
149 O 11 St Oswald's pl SE11
108 H 20 St Oswald's rd SW16
148 H 7 St Oswulf st SW1
132 J 11 St Pancras station NW1
47 V 20 St Pancras way NW1
132 E 6 St Pancras way NW1
134 C 4 St Paul st N1
44 M 17 St Paul's av NW2
75 U 2 St Paul's av SE16
24 M 15 St Paul's av Harrow
141 Z 6 St Paul's cathedral EC4
141 Y 6 St Paul's Church yd EC4
49 N 17 St Paul's pl N1
48 L 17 St Paul's rd N1
49 N 18 St Paul's rd N1
67 P 3 St Paul's rd Bark
72 G 17 St Paul's rd Brentf
81 W 19 St Paul's rd Erith
84 M 8 St Paul's rd Rich
122 M 6 St Paul's rd Thntn Hth
49 N 17 St Paul's shrubbery N1
64 A 14 St Paul's way E14
28 A 3 St Paul's way N3
114 E 20 St Pauls Cray rd Chisl
47 Y 19 St Pauls cres NW1
51 X 16 St Pauls dri E15
31 Y 3 St Pauls rd N17
149 Y 13 St Pauls ter SE17
63 Z 15 St Pauls way E3
142 H 7 St peter's EC3
33 Y 17 St Peter's av E17
18 L 14 St Peter's av N18
135 U 11 St Peter's clo E2
36 J 13 St Peter's clo Ilf
27 N 15 St Peter's ct NW4
74 F 12 St Peter's gro W6
88 E 10 St Peter's pl SW11
19 O 6 St Peter's rd N9
74 G 13 St Peter's rd W6
157 O 9 St Peter's rd Croy
117 O 4 St Peter's rd Kingst
58 H 15 St Peter's rd S'hall
84 C 12 St Peter's rd Twick
74 F 12 St Peter's sq W6
133 X 5 St Peter's st N1
157 O 12 St Peter's st S Croy
60 H 14 St Peters way W5
94 D 12 St Peters clo SE3
145 N 20 St Peters ter SW6
74 F 12 St Peters villas W6
137 X 10 St Petersburgh ms W2
137 X 9 St Petersburgh pl W2
89 S 6 St Philip St SW8
49 W 19 St Philip's rd E8
116 G 14 St Philip's rd Surb
138 F 1 St Philips pl W2
152 J 2 St Phillip's av Worc Pk
96 L 7 St Quentin rd Welling
136 D 2 St Quintin av W10
65 X 8 St Quintin rd E13
43 X 16 St Raphaels way NW10
5 U 4 St Ronans clo Barnt
34 E 2 St Ronans cres Wdfd Grn
89 U 5 St Rule st SW8
122 L 16 St Saviour's rd Croy
90 C 14 St Saviours rd SW2
87 N 14 St Simons av SW15
60 A 16 St Stephen's av W13
58 F 16 St Stephen's clo S'hall
137 V 4 St Stephen's cres W2
84 D 17 St Stephen's gdns Twick
137 U 3 St Stephen's ms W2
84 E 17 St Stephen's pl Twick
3 S 16 St Stephen's rd E17
63 X 4 St Stephen's rd E3
60 C 16 St Stephen's rd W13

9 S 1 St Stephen's rd Enf
82 H 14 St Stephen's rd Hounsl
33 T 17 St Stephens av E17
74 K 4 St Stephens av W12
33 S 16 St Stephens clo E17
130 L 6* St Stephens clo NW8
122 E 6 St Stephens cres Thntn Hth
137 S 4 St Stephens gdns W2
93 U 7 St Stephens gro SE13
65 Z 1 St Stephens rd E6
142 E 7 St Stephens row EC4
149 N 20 St Stephens ter SW8
142 F 8 St Swithins la EC4
93 W 14 St Swithun's rd SE13
98 D 19 St Thomas ct Bxly
22 C 5 St Thomas dri Pinn
54 B 17 St Thomas gdns Ilf
65 S 17 St Thomas rd E16
16 L 3 St Thomas rd N14
142 F 14 St Thomas st SE1
73 U 18 St Thomas' rd W4
81 W 5 St Thomas' rd Blvdr
47 O 17 St Thomas's gdns NW5
50 B 20 St Thomas's pl E9
48 G 9 St Thomas's rd N4
50 B 20 St Thomas's sq E9
135 P 17 St Thomas's way E1
22 A 17 St Ursula gro Pinn
58 H 16 St Ursula rd S'hall
82 M 17 St Vincent of Twick
139 U 2 St Vincent st W1
5 V 17 St Wilfreds clo Barnt
5 V 16 St Wilfrid's clo Barnt
102 C 14 St Winifred's rd Tedd
53 U 15 St Winifride's av
149 N 7 Salamanca pl SE1
148 M 7 Salamanca st SE1&SE11
149 N 7 Salamanca st SE1&SE11
119 P 19 Salcombe dri Mrdn
38 C 20 Salcombe dri Rom
13 Z 20 Salcombe gdns NW7
50 M 1 Salcombe rd E17
49 T 14 Salcombe rd N16
88 L 13 Salcott rd SW11
156 B 7 Salcott rd Croy
138 J 3 Sale pl W2
24 K 16 Salehurst clo Harrow
92 L 16 Salehurst rd SE4
156 K 6 Salem pl Croy
137 Y 8 Salem rd W2
107 X 2 Salford rd SW2
27 U 9 Salisbury av N3
67 S 1 Salisbury av Bark
13 U 5 Salisbury av Sutton
141 V 6 Salisbury ct EC4
105 T 18 Salisbury gdns SW19
47 V 6 Salisbury ms N19
145 O 18 Salisbury ms SW6
131 P 20 Salisbury pl W1
51 V 7 Salisbury rd E10
53 O 14 Salisbury rd E12
33 T 16 Salisbury rd E17
20 C 11 Salisbury rd E4
52 E 18 Salisbury rd E7
30 G 6 Salisbury rd N22
30 K 17 Salisbury rd N4
18 J 10 Salisbury rd N9
123 X 16 Salisbury rd SE25
105 S 18 Salisbury rd SW19
72 B 6 Salisbury rd W13
13 V 13 Salisbury rd Barnt
127 P 12 Salisbury rd Brom
98 E 20 Salisbury rd Bxly
154 M 13 Salisbury rd Carsh
56 H 19 Salisbury rd Dgnhm
9 Z 1 Salisbury rd Enf
23 R 16 Salisbury rd Harrow
54 H 6 Salisbury rd Ilf
117 Y 5 Salisbury rd New Mald
84 K 10 Salisbury rd Rich
39 Z 16 Salisbury rd Rom
70 D 11 Salisbury rd S'hall
152 C 5 Salisbury rd Worc Pk
150 E 6 Salisbury row SE17
141 V 6 Salisbury sq EC4
130 H 18 Salisbury st NW8
73 W 4 Salisbury st W3
63 U 17 Salmon la E1

63 X 17 Salmon la E14
65 R 7 Salmon rd E14
81 T 14 Salmon rd Blvdr
63 Y 11 Salmon st E3
33 X 13 Salmon st E17
43 U 3 Salmon st NW9
18 K 5 Salmons rd N9
65 X 14 Salomons rd E13
32 F 18 Salop rd E17
74 A 6 Salt Coats rd W4
153 U 9 Saltash clo Sutton
107 P 14 Saltash rd SW17
36 D 1 Saltash rd Ilf
97 U 2 Saltash rd Welling
63 Z 20 Salter st E14
142 E 8 Salter's Hall ct EC4
109 N 13 Salter's hill SE19
33 X 13 Salter's rd E17
48 B 10 Salterton rd N7
90 F 11 Saltoun rd SW2
129 R 12 Saltram cres W9
85 W 11 Saltwell st E14
128 M 4 Salusbury rd NW6
129 N 3 Salusbury rd NW6
106 K 11 Salvador pl SW17
59 Z 4 Salvia gdns Grnfd
34 D 2 Salway clo Wdfd Grn
34 D 5 Salway hill E18
51 Y 19 Salway pl E15
51 X 19 Salway rd E15
150 L 20 Salwood st SE15
74 G 14 Samels clo W6
91 N 8 Samford st NW8
77 O 19 Samos clo SE3
124 A 3 Samos rd SE20
143 U 14 Sampson st E1
65 X 7 Samson st E13
76 G 7 Samuda st E14
78 E 10 Samuel st SE18
23 X 9 Sancroft rd Harrow
149 P 8 Sancroft st SE11
142 B 18 Sanctuary st SE1
97 V 17 Sanctuary the Bxly
57 Y 9 Sand hills Wallgtn
78 C 10 Sand st SE18
88 B 1 Sand's End la SW6
18 K 18 Sandal rd N18
17 Z 10 Sandal rd New Mal
118 A 10 Sandal rd New Mal
64 L 3 Sandal st E15
60 K 11 Sandall clo W5
47 W 18 Sandall rd NW5
60 J 11 Sandall rd W5
24 S 19 Sandbourne av SW19
92 H 4 Sandbourne rd SE4
60 N 8 Sandbrook rd N16
95 R 8 Sandby grn SE9
811 Z 12 Sandcliff rd Erith
141 T 14 Sandell st SE1
27 N 1 Sanders la NW7
27 O 1 Sanders la NW7
26 M 1 Sanders la NW7
45 S 8 Sanderstead av NW2
89 V 18 Sanderstead clo SW12
50 J 3 Sanderstead rd E10
157 O 18 Sanderstead rd S Croy
122 K 6 Sandfield gdns Thntn Hth
122 K 6 Sandfield rd Thntn Hth
30 L 3 Sandford av N22
66 F 11 Sandford clo E6
66 F 9 Sandford rd E6
66 F 9 Sandford rd E6
26 G 9 Sandford rd Brom
97 Z 9 Sandford rd Bxly Hth
150 F 9 Sandford row SE17
80 F 18 Sandgate rd Wellin
151 V 13 Sandgate st SE15
22 L 19 Sandhurst av Harro
57 X 7 Sandhurst av Surb
25 O 10 Sandhurst clo NW9
157 T 18 Sandhurst clo S Croy
54 L 13 Sandhurst dri Ilf
25 P 11 Sandhurst rd NW9
19 S 1 Sandhurst rd N9
111 X 1 Sandhurst rd SE6
9 R 11 Sandhurst rd Bxly
9 R 20 Sandhurst rd Enf
114 M 7 Sandhurst rd Sidcp
157 T 18 Sandhurst way S Croy
153 U 3 Sandiford rd Sutton
157 X 3 Sandilands Croy
28 A 3 Sandilands rd SW6
91 W 6 Sandison st SE15
141 O 2 Sandland st WC1

43 V7 Sandling ri SE9
90 A10 Sandmere rd SW4
49 Z9 Sandmere rd SW4
50 L12 Sandover rd SE5
46 J18 Sandown av Dgnhm
24 A11 Sandown rd SE25
23 Z11 Sandown rd SE25
40 C17 Sandown way Grnfd
1 Y13 Sandpit rd Brom
8 P7 Sandpits rd Croy
22 H3 Sandpits rd Rich
9 T2 Sandringham av SW20
8 E8 Sandringham clo Enf
46 C10 Sandringham clo Ilf
40 H8 Sandringham cres Harrow
6 H4 Sandringham dri Welling
15 T19 Sandringham gdns N12
40 B19 Sandringham gdns N8
46 C10 Sandringham gdns Ilf
43 X19 Sandringham rd E10
42 K16 Sandringham rd E7
49 W15 Sandringham rd E8
45 S2 Sandringham rd NW11
44 J17 Sandringham rd NW2
40 L9 Sandringham rd N22
4 L16 Sandringham rd Bark
12 F13 Sandringham rd Brom
22 M12 Sandringham rd Croy
40 H20 Sandringham rd Grnfd
52 H5 Sandringham rd Worc Pk
58 F8 Sandrock pl Croy
93 P7 Sandrock rd SE13
47 Y17 Sandtoft rd SE7
45 Y17 Sandwell cres NW6
32 J14 Sandwich st WC1
18 L15 Sandy Hill rd SE18
18 L13 Sandy Hill rd SE18
55 V19 Sandy Hill rd Wallgtn
21 P1 Sandy la Mitch
55 Z11 Sandy la North Wallgtn
45 X18 Sandy la Orp
02 E5 Sandy la Rich
55 X13 Sandy la South Wallgtn
53 T18 Sandy la Sutton
02 A15 Sandy la Tedd
01 Y17 Sandy la Tedd
46 B6 Sandy rd NW3
13 V15 Sandy ridge Chisl
42 L1 Sandy row E1
58 K5 Sandy way Croy
55 O8 Sandycombe rd Rich
34 C17 Sandycombe rd Twick
79 Z16 Sandycroft SE2
53 Y13 Sandyhill rd Ilf
11 T17 Sandymount av Stanm
49 U8 Sanford la N16
75 U16 Sanford st SE14
49 V8 Sanford ter N16
23 T8 Sangley rd SE25
13 R20 Sangley rd SE6
48 C11 Sangora rd SW11
13 V16 Sans wlk EC1
2 B8 Sansom rd E11
1 P1 Sansom st SE5
8 B10 Santley st SW4
43 X13 Santos rd SW18
0 E17 Santway the Stanm
2 M7 Saracen st E14
2 M7 Saracen's Head yd EC3
34 K12 Sarah st N1
02 A12 Saratoga rd E5
01 O5 Sardinia st WC2
15 V14 Sarnesfield rd Enf
5 V14 Sarre rd NW2
2 A9 Sarsen av Hounsl
16 M2 Sarsfeld rd SW1
7 N2 Sarsfeld rd SW1
0 C5 Sarsfeld rd Grnfd
43 Y13 Sarum rd E3
16 E15 Sator rd SE15
00 M13 Saunders clo Hampt
00 L13 Saunders clo Hampt
00 L12 Saunders clo Hampt

76 J12 Saunders Ness rd E14
79 X13 Saunders rd SE18
149 R5 Saunders st SE11
57 V7 Saunton rd Hornch
142 M9 Savage gdns EC3
66 H18 Savage gdns E4
47 N12 Savernake rd NW3
18 K1 Savernake rd N9
118 B12 Savile clo New Mald
21 R18 Savill row Wdfd Grn
78 D3 Saville rd E16
73 Y8 Saville rd W4
38 B20 Saville rd Rom
101 V2 Saville rd Twick
140 A19 Saville row W1
9 S10 Saville row Enf
105 R17 Savona clo SW19
148 A19 Savona st SW8
12 B16 Savoy clo Edg
141 N10 Savoy hill WC2
140 M11 Savoy pl WC2
141 N10 Savoy row WC2
141 N10 Savoy st WC2
140 M11 Savoy way WC2
74 F2 Sawley rd W12
120 H17 Sawtry clo Carsh
141 Z9 Sawyer st SE1
142 A16 Sawyer st SE1
90 A17 Saxby rd SW2
90 A17 Saxby st SW2
67 V5 Saxham rd Bark
20 L11 Saxlingham rd E4
100 G6 Saxon av Felt
93 X9 Saxon clo SE13
61 T15 Saxon dri W3
62 X7 Saxon rd E3
66 F12 Saxon rd E6
30 J4 Saxon rd N22
123 O12 Saxon rd SE25
112 D18 Saxon rd Brom
53 Z17 Saxon rd Ilf
54 A17 Saxon rd Ilf
70 C1 Saxon rd Shall
6 J19 Saxon way N14
116 E20 Saxonbury gdns Surb
58 C20 Saxton gdns S'hall
150 A4 Sayer st SE17
72 C5 Sayes Ct st SE8
114 L16 Scadbury pk Chisl
140 D1 Scala st W1
31 W10 Scales rd N17
143 W14 Scandrett st E1
51 W4 Scarborough rd E11
48 G3 Scarborough rd N4
19 P2 Scarborough rd N9
143 P7 Scarborough st E1
156 L5 Scarbrook rd Croy
42 H18 Scarle rd Wemb
111 Y6 Scarlet rd SE6
95 O7 Scarsbrook rd SE3
135 W1 Scarsdale pl E8
150 J14 Scarsdale rd SE5
41 M14 Scarsdale rd Harrow
135 U3 Scarsdale vlls W8
86 F7 Scarth rd SW13
135 P9 Scawen rd SE8
135 P9 Scawfell st E2
12 K9 Scaynes link N12
63 P9 Sceptre rd E2
14 K4 Scaynes link N12
77 U19 Schofield rd SE3
20 J6 Scholar's rd E4
107 U2 Scholar's rd SW12
47 Y5 Scholefield rd N19
63 S20 School House la E1
116 D1 School la Kingst
22 B12 School la Pinn
70 G1 School pass Shall
63 N12 School pl E1
53 T13 School rd E12
61 Z12 School rd NW10
114 C19 School rd Chisl
69 T3 School rd Dgnhm
100 M14 School rd Hampt
83 N8 School rd Hounsl
116 E1 School rd Kingst
100 M14 School Rd av Hampt
15 U19 School way N12
102 C19 Schoolhouse la Shall
76 G13 Schooner st E14
87 V13 Schubert rd SW15
146 G2 Science museum SW7
151 O18 Scipio st SE15
135 O17 Sclater st E1
49 V12 Scobie pl N16
141 X15 Scoresby st SE1
92 A6 Scorton av Grnfd
22 A2 Scot gro Pinn
125 Y3 Scot's av Brom
125 X3 Scot's la Brom

59 Z13 Scotch comm W13
60 A13 Scotch comm W13
91 T17 Scotland Green rd Enf
9 U15 Scotland Green rd N Enf
31 W6 Scotland grn N17
140 K14 Scotland gdns E4
21 Y6 Scotland rd Buck Hl
15 Z15 Scotsdale clo Sutton
94 J15 Scotsdale rd SE12
133 V16 Scotswood st EC1
99 T2 Scott cres Erith
40 J5 Scott cres Harrow
130 E14 Scott Ellis gdns NW8
143 T20 Scott Lidgett cres SE16
51 T4 Scott's rd E10
136 A18 Scott's rd W12
74 K6 Scott's rd W12
55 W3 Scottes la Dgnhm
112 E19 Scotts rd Brom
65 R17 Scoulding rd E16
64 H20 Scouler st E14
89 U8 Scout la SW4
12 M13 Scout way NW7
142 A19 Scovell rd SE1
53 Z9 Scrafton rd Ilf
68 J5 Scrattons ter Bark
135 P3 Scriven st E8
93 R17 Scrooby st SE6
62 H10 Scrubbs la NW10
89 X19 Scrutton clo SW12
134 J17 Scrutton st EC2
125 U12 Scudamore la NW9
92 C14 Scutari rd SE22
91 Y7 Scylla rd SE15
92 A7 Scylla rd SE15
159 Z3 Seabrook dri W Wkhm
56 E2 Seabrook gdns Rom
55 V9 Seabrook rd Dgnhm
141 X5 Seacoal la EC4
16 K15 Seafield rd N11
33 R11 Seaford rd E17
31 P14 Seaford rd N15
72 A3 Seaford rd W13
8 F14 Seaford rd Enf
132 M14 Seaford rd Mald
118 K9 Seaforth av New Mald
39 R1 Seaforth clo Rom
17 S4 Seaforth gdns N21
152 D9 Seaforth gdns Epsom
21 Y17 Seaforth gdns Wdfd Grn
63 Y14 Seager pl E3
135 U13 Seagrave rd SW6
34 G20 Seagry rd E11
49 V13 Seal st E8
150 F4 Searles rd SE1
150 E18 Sears st SE5
54 J14 Seaton av Ilf
83 P16 Seaton clo E13
83 P16 Seaton clo Twick
132 B16 Seaton pl NW1
99 W19 Seaton rd Drtfrd
120 J4 Seaton rd Mitch
83 O16 Seaton rd Twick
70 B20 Seaton rd Welling
60 J5 Seaton rd Wemb
18 K1 Seaton st N18
133 X14 Sebastian st EC1
82 N9 Sebastopol rd N9
133 X1 Sebbon st N1
52 L13 Sebert rd E7
135 U9 Sebright pas E2
4 D10 Sebright rd Barnt
22 M6 Secker cres Harrow
141 S15 Secker st SE1
53 S14 Second av E12
65 T9 Second av E13
33 P15 Second av E17
27 O12 Second av NW4
19 P14 Second av N18
82 A7 Second av SW14
129 N15 Second av W10
74 D3 Second av W3
69 V5 Second av Dgnhm
8 G17 Second av Enf
37 T15 Second av Rom
42 G6 Second av Wemb
101 S3 Second Cross rd Twick
43 T13 Second way Wemb
150 L13 Secretan rd SE5
150 K12 Sedan st SE17
9 S16 Sedcote rd Enf
147 S6 Sedding st SW1
120 G12 Seddon rd Mrdn
95 P6 Sedgebrook rd SE3

24 E16 Sedgecombe av Harrow
74 E2 Sedgeford rd W12
111 R12 Sedgehill rd SE6
28 D10 Sedgemere av N2
56 E11 Sedgemoor dri Dgnhm
112 B2 Sedgeway SE6
91 S1 Sedgmoor pl SE5
51 T7 Sedgwick st E9
50 F16 Sedgwick st E9
87 W15 Sedleigh rd SW18
145 S14 Sedlescombe rd SW6
139 X7 Sedley pl W1
109 T9 Seeley dri SE21
44 F2 Seelig av NW9
107 S16 Seely rd SW17
142 L9 Seething la EC3
116 E15 Seething Wells la Surb
12 K18 Sefton av NW7
25 R5 Sefton av Harrow
157 Z1 Sefton rd Croy
123 Y20 Sefton rd Croy
86 M6 Sefton rd SW15
133 W16 Sekforde st EC1
44 D15 Selbie av NW10
32 M15 Selborne av E17
115 Y1 Selborne av Bxly
26 G13 Selborne gdns NW4
59 Y5 Selborne gdns Grnfd
33 O14 Selborne rd E17
17 O10 Selborne rd N14
16 M10 Selborne rd N14
30 C6 Selborne rd N22
30 C5 Selborne rd Ilf
91 N3 Selborne rd SE5
157 T7 Selborne rd Croy
53 W8 Selborne rd Ilf
118 A3 Selborne rd New Mald
115 R10 Selborne rd Sidcp
53 W11 Selbourne av E12
58 H12 Selby gdns S'hall
120 K16 Selby grn Carsh
51 Z10 Selby rd E11
65 V14 Selby rd E13
31 R1 Selby rd N17
18 D20 Selby rd N17
123 Y3 Selby rd SE20
60 C12 Selby rd W5
120 J16 Selby rd Carsh
135 T18 Selby st E1
92 D5 Selden st E1
123 X14 Selhurst New rd SE25
123 R15 Selhurst pl SE25
18 C11 Selhurst rd N9
123 T17 Selhurst rd SE25
56 A2 Selinas la Dgnhm
106 K10 Selkirk rd SW17
100 M3 Selkirk rd Twick
101 N2 Selkirk rd Twick
27 X2 Sellers Hall clo N3
106 K13 Sellincourt rd SW17
135 R20 Sellindge clo Beckhm
149 O6 Sellon ms SE11
62 E4 Sellons av NW10
132 C5 Selous st NW1
38 J4 Selsdon clo Rom
157 O14 Selsdon la S Croy
158 S19 Selsdon Pk rd S Croy
34 E20 Selsdon rd E11
65 Y6 Selsdon rd E13
44 F8 Selsdon rd NW2
108 H8 Selsdon rd SE27
157 O12 Selsdon rd S Croy
97 V2 Selsey cres Welling
49 T14 Selsey rd N16
64 A15 Selsey st E14
12 K14 Selvage la NW7
146 E9 Selwood pl SW7
124 A20 Selwood rd Croy
157 Z1 Selwood rd Croy
119 V19 Selwood rd Sutton
146 F10 Selwood terr SW7
110 L7 Selworthy rd SE6
20 H19 Selwyn av E4
36 J18 Selwyn av Ilf
84 L8 Selwyn av Rich
82 B9 Selwyn clo Hounsl
97 O9 Selwyn cres Welling
25 R3 Selwyn ct Edg
65 U4 Selwyn rd E13
63 X7 Selwyn rd E3
31 W11 Selwyn rd N17
117 Y1 Selwyn rd New Mald
147 W7 Semley pl SW1
122 C2 Semley rd SW16
90 A10 Seneca rd SW4

122 L9 Seneca rd Thntn Hth
121 P20 Senga rd Wallgtn
153 N6 Senhouse rd Sutton
129 X20 Senior st W2
112 H2 Senlac rd SE12
18 F2 Sennen rd Enf
63 S16 Senrab st E1
10 G3 Sequoia clo Bushey Watf
141 P5 Serle st WC2
141 Z7 Sermon la EC4
151 N5 Setchell rd SE1
75 R6 Seth st SE16
68 G1 Seton gdns Dgnhm
65 S6 Settle rd E13
143 U4 Settles st E1
87 Z6 Settrington rd SW6
36 L19 Seven Kings park Ilf
54 J6 Seven Kings rd Ilf
31 P18 Seven Sisters rd N15
48 J5 Seven Sisters rd N4
48 B10 Seven Sisters rd N7
63 N20 Seven Star all E1
98 H11 Sevenoaks clo Bxly Hth
92 K15 Sevenoaks rd SE4
115 S19 Sevenoaks way Sidcp
53 H12 Seventh av E12
8 J16 Seventh av Enf
39 Z9 Severn av Rom
8 L2 Severn dri Enf
44 C15 Severn way NW10
88 J10 Severus rd SW11
139 R19 Seville st SW1
26 H19 Sevington rd NW4
120 W18 Sevington st W9
71 Y5 Seward rd W7
124 F3 Seward rd Becknhm
133 Y15 Seward st EC1
134 A14 Seward st EC1
63 R5 Sewardstone rd E2
20 C1 Sewardstone rd E4
50 E11 Sewdley st E5
80 B6 Sewell rd SE2
65 T9 Sewell st E13
39 O10 Seymer rd Rom
31 X7 Seymour av N17
152 K20 Seymour av Epsom
119 P17 Seymour av Mrdn
139 N1 Seymour bldgs W1
21 P8 Seymour ct E4
44 H7 Seymour ct NW2
53 T4 Seymour gdns Ilf
117 O12 Seymour gdns Surb
84 A19 Seymour gdns Twick
139 N3 Seymour hall W1
139 T5 Seymour ms W1
123 Z9 Seymour pl SE25
139 N4 Seymour pl W1
50 L4 Seymour rd E10
20 D4 Seymour rd E4
66 A5 Seymour rd E6
28 B2 Seymour rd N3
30 H16 Seymour rd N8
19 N8 Seymour rd N9
87 W17 Seymour rd SW18
105 P6 Seymour rd SW19
73 W9 Seymour rd W4
155 O11 Seymour rd SW19
101 N11 Seymour rd Hampt
116 F1 Seymour rd Kingst
122 F20 Seymour rd Kingst
121 O18 Seymour rd Mitch
139 R6 Seymour st W1
123 Z1 Seymour ter SE20
123 Z1 Seymour vlls SE20
146 O13 Seymour wlk SW10
76 H11 Seyssel st E14
73 Z1 Shaa rd W3
101 U10 Shacklegate la Tedd
110 B4 Shackleton clo SE23
58 F20 Shackleton rd S'hall
70 F1 Shackleton rd Shall
49 V13 Shacklewell grn E8
49 V13 Shacklewell la E8
49 U12 Shacklewell rd N16
49 U13 Shacklewell row E8
135 P15 Shacklewell st E2
143 P18 Shad thames SE1
152 D3 Shadbolt clo Worc Pk
58 E7 Shadwell dri Grnfd
63 O19 Shadwell pl E1
10 A2 Shadybush clo Bushey Watf
101 Z17 Shaef way Tedd
56 J17 Shafter rd Dgnhm
140 F9 Shaftesbury av W1
5 P13 Shaftesbury av Barnt
9 S5 Shaftesbury av Enf

40 M3 Shaftesbury av Harrow
42 J1 Shaftesbury av Harrow
24 H19 Shaftesbury av Harrow
70 H9 Shaftesbury av S'hall
145 U4 Shaftesbury ms W8
142 B2 Shaftesbury pl EC1
51 O5 Shaftesbury rd E10
33 R17 Shaftesbury rd E17
20 K5 Shaftesbury rd E4
65 X1 Shaftesbury rd E7
52 M20 Shaftesbury rd E7
18 F19 Shaftesbury rd N18
48 A3 Shaftesbury rd N4
124 M4 Shaftesbury rd Becknhm
120 H16 Shaftesbury rd Carsh
84 J9 Shaftesbury rd Rich
39 U17 Shaftesbury rd Rom
134 D9 Shaftesbury st N1
67 O5 Shaftesburys the Bark
147 P3 Shafto ms SW1
63 T3 Shafton rd E9
61 Y3 Shakespeare av NW10
16 H16 Shakespeare av N8
53 T19 Shakespeare cres E12
25 N20 Shakespeare dri Harrow
28 M13 Shakespeare gdns N2
32 G8 Shakespeare rd E17
13 T14 Shakespeare rd NW7
27 Y3 Shakespeare rd N3
90 J10 Shakespeare rd SE24
73 W1 Shakespeare rd W3
59 W19 Shakespeare rd W7
97 Y2 Shakespeare rd Bxly Hth
39 U18 Shakespeare rd Rom
49 R12 Shakespeare wlk N16
146 D15 Shalcomb st SW10
119 S11 Shaldon dri Mrdn
18 E14 Shaldon rd N18
24 M7 Shaldon rd Edg
61 U19 Shaleimar rd W3
85 T7 Shalestone rd SW10
136 E32 Shalfleet Dri est W10
61 U19 Shallimar gdns W3
113 Y9 Shallons rd SE9
116 L15 Shalston vlls Surb
122 C14 Shamrock rd Croy
89 W7 Shamrock st SW4
16 E5 Shamrock way N14
16 K5 Shand st SE1
89 V15 Shandon rd SW4
63 T13 Shandy st E1
31 X13 Shanklin rd N15
29 Y17 Shanklin rd N8
90 D10 Shannon gro SW9
130 L8 Shannon pl NW8
120 L19 Shap cres Carsh
135 N8 Shap st E2
151 U14 Shard's sq SE15
90 K13 Shardcroft av SE24
92 K3 Shardeloes rd SE14
114 M10 Sharman clo Sidcp
64 C15 Sharman st E14
116 E19 Sharon clo Surb
63 P2 Sharon gdns E9
73 Y13 Sharon rd W4
9 V8 Sharon rd Enf
131 R2 Sharpleshall st NW1
75 R17 Sharratt st SE15
149 N11 Sharsted st SE17
140 F10 Shaver's pl SW1
68 L6 Shaw av Bark
68 L6 Shaw gdns Bark
112 B8 Shaw rd Brom
9 S6 Shaw rd Enf
32 J5 Shaw st E17
125 Z15 Shaw way Wallgtn
94 M12 Shawbrooke rd SE9
95 N11 Shawbrooke rd SE9
91 V12 Shawbury rd SE22
127 O2 Shawfield pk Brom
146 M11 Shawfield st SW3
86 H19 Shawford ct SW15
159 V20 Shaxton cres Croy
48 A17 Shearling way N7
94 B9 Shearman rd SE3
26 B13 Sheaveshill av NW9
85 R12 Sheen Comm dri Rich
85 R10 Sheen Ct rd Rich

85 V10 Sheen Ga gdns SW14
133 R4 Sheen gro N1
85 W7 Sheen la SW14
84 L11 Sheen pk Rich
84 L11 Sheen rd Rich
85 P12 Sheen rd Rich
84 C10 Sheen way Wallgtn
85 V13 Sheen wood SW14
84 M9 Sheendale rd Rich
110 A11 Sheenewood SE26
135 W5 Sheep la E8
89 N5 Sheepcote la SW11
88 M5 Sheepcote la SW11
23 W19 Sheepcote rd Harrow
37 X13 Sheepcotes rd Rom
117 Z18 Sheephouse way New Mald
118 A18 Sheephouse way New Mald
141 O6 Sheffield st WC2
137 U15 Sheffield ter W8
38 G1 Sheila clo Rom
38 G1 Sheila rd Rom
22 D11 Shelbourne clo Pinn
31 Z6 Shelbourne rd N17
48 D12 Shelburne rd N7
115 N9 Shelbury clo Sidcp
92 B14 Shelbury rd SE22
46 K1 Sheldon av N6
28 M17 Sheldon av N6
35 Y7 Sheldon av Ilf
45 P13 Sheldon rd NW2
98 B3 Sheldon rd Bxly Hth
55 Y20 Sheldon rd Dgnhm
156 L6 Sheldon st Croy
137 S17 Sheldrake pl W8
49 O10 Shelford pl N16
4 A20 Shelford rd Barnt
109 T19 Shelford ri SE19
127 S15 Shelgate rd SW11
127 S15 Shell clo Brom
93 P7 Shell rd SE13
93 P7 Shell rd SE13
53 P18 Shelley av E12
59 P8 Shelley av Grnfd
57 U6 Shelley av Hornch
12 B15 Shelley clo Edg
12 C15 Shelley clo Edg
59 P9 Shelley clo Grnfd
58 F18 Shelley cres S'hall
42 D8 Shelley gdns Wemb
61 Y4 Shelley rd NW10
49 S15 Shellgrove rd N16
88 M6 Shellwood rd SW11
105 Y19 Shelton rd SW19
140 L5 Shelton st WC2
134 D15 Shene st EC1
34 G1 Shenfield clo Wdfd Grn
34 G2 Shenfield rd Wdfd Grn
134 K10 Shenfield st N1
91 S7 Shenley rd SE5
82 B2 Shenley rd Hounsl
49 O9 Shenley wlk N16
98 L11 Shenstone clo Bxly Hth
9 N5 Shepard clo Enf
37 V15 Shepherd clo Rom
39 X13 Shepherd mkt W1
29 T19 Shepherd's clo N6
99 Z19 Shepherd's la Drtfrd
46 F14 Shepherd's wlk NW3
134 D12 Shepherdess pl N1
134 B8 Shepherdess wlk N1
136 D17 Shepherds Bush common W12
136 F17 Shepherds Bush grn W12
C16 Shepherds Bush mkt W12
74 M5 Shepherds Bush mkt W12
136 G16 Shepherds Bush pl W12
136 G19 Shepherds Bush rd W6
144 D5 Shepherds Bush rd W6
136 G18 Shepherds Bush Shopping centre W12
116 E18 Shepherds grn Chisl
29 S19 Shepherds hill N6
50 E16 Shepherds la E9
139 T8 Shepherds pl W1
158 E17 Shepherds way S Croy
155 O4 Shepley clo Carsh
65 P12 Sheppard st E1L

134 C3 Shepperton rd N1
55 U20 Sheppey gdns Dgnhm
55 P20 Sheppey rd Dgnhm
66 K19 Shepstone st E6
52 K17 Sherard rd E7
95 S12 Sherard rd SE9
140 D6 Sheraton st W1
70 G10 Sherborne av S'ha
25 P10 Sherborne gdns NW9
60 B15 Sherborne gdns W13
142 F8 Sherborne la EC4
153 X1 Sherborne rd Sutt
134 E3 Sherborne st N1
31 T18 Sherboro rd N15
9 O8 Sherborne av Enf
120 H7 Sherbourne cres Carsh
60 B15 Sherbourne gdns W13
17 W3 Sherbrook gdns N
66 H16 Sherbrooke gdns S
144 L19 Sherbrooke rd SW
75 X16 Shere rd SE8
35 Y16 Shere rd Ilf
20 L17 Shereward clo SE
86 C16 Sherfield gdns SW15
24 F19 Sheridan gdns Harrow
53 T16 Sheridan rd E12
52 D10 Sheridan rd E7
119 W1 Sheridan rd Blvdr
81 R9 Sheridan rd Rich
97 Z7 Sheridan rd Bxly H
102 D8 Sheridan rd Rich
154 L12 Sheridan wlk Cars
53 U12 Sheringham av E1
6 K18 Sheringham av N1
38 L19 Sheringham av Ro
100 F2 Sheringham av Twick
54 L16 Sheringham dri Ba
48 E17 Sheringham rd N7
124 B5 Sheringham rd SE
22 H1 Sherington av Pinr
77 V17 Sherington rd SE7
83 X20 Sherland rd Twick
101 X1 Sherland rd Twick
126 G1 Sherman rd Brom
64 F8 Sherman st E3
33 T13 Sherrhall st E17
53 O16 Sherrard rd E12
4 M19 Sherrards way Ba
J15 Sherrick Green rd
45 Y19 Sherriff rd NW6
31 X7 Sherringham av N
26 H12 Sherrock gdns NW
92 F4 Sherwin rd SE14
34 H11 Sherwood av E18
108 A20 Sherwood av SW
107 Y19 Sherwood av SW1
41 U16 Sherwood av Grnfd
86 K8 Sherwood clo SW
54 E20 Sherwood gdns Ba
97 S16 Sherwood Pk av Sidcp
121 V8 Sherwood Pk rd Mitch
153 Y12 Sherwood Pk rd Sutton
27 N9 Sherwood rd NW4
26 M10 Sherwood rd NW4
105 V19 Sherwood rd SW1
123 Z18 Sherwood rd Croy
100 M11 Sherwood rd Ham
41 N8 Sherwood rd Harro
40 M8 Sherwood rd Harro
36 D14 Sherwood rd Ilf
96 G6 Sherwood rd Welling
15 S10 Sherwood st N20
140 D9 Sherwood st W1
15 T10 Sherwood ter N20
159 T2 Sherwood way W Wkhm
63 Y6 Shetland rd E13
80 E15 Shieldhall st SE2
138 M1 Shillibeer pl W1
133 X2 Shillingford st N1
88 K6 Shillington st SW1
17 X16 Shilltoe rd N13
136 R5 Shinfield st W12
62 M17 Shinfield st W12
110 G6 Shinford path SE2
81 R18 Shinglewell rd Erit
78 M8 Ship & Half Moon pas SE18
143 T9 Ship all E1

93 N 2 Ship st SE4	87 X 1 Shottendane rd SW6	93 T 5 Silk Mills path SE13	52 G 19 Skelton rd E7
42 H 7 Ship Tavern pas EC3	86 A 10 Shottfield av SW13	26 C 15 Silkfield rd NW9	51 S 1 Skelton's la E10
42 K 14 Ship yd SE1	63 X 20 Shoulder Of Mutton all E14	25 X 6 Silkstream rd Edgw	144 D 15 Skelwith rd W6
07 S 1 Shipka rd SW12	139 N 3 Shouldham st W1	30 D 10 Silsoe rd N8	75 S 13 Sketchley gdns SE16
65 X 18 Shipman rd E16	95 T 8 Shrapnel rd SE9	20 A 19 Silver Birch av E4	8 H 12 Sketty rd Enf
10 G 4 Shipman rd SE23	85 X 11 Shrewsbury av SW4	19 Y 19 Silver Birch av E4	63 V 12 Skidmore st E1
55 V 9 Shipton clo Dgnhm	24 K 14 Shrewsbury av Harrow	23 P 2 Silver clo Harrow	64 M 4 Skiers st E15
35 R 11 Shipton st E2	95 Z 3 Shrewsbury la SE18	73 T 12 Silver cres W4	142 A 12 Skin Mkt pl SE1
42 H 14 Shipwright yd SE1	137 T 3 Shrewsbury ms W2	40 L 18 Silver Join St clo Grnfd	147 T 7 Skinner pl SW1
92 D 20 Shirburn clo SE23	79 R 20 Shrewsbury park SE18	159 X 2 Silver la W Wkhm	133 V 15 Skinner st EC1
24 C 19 Shirbutt st E14	53 N 16 Shrewsbury rd E7	140 C 8 Silver pl W1	142 C 9 Skinners la EC4
95 O 6 Shirebrook rd SE3	53 N 20 Shrewsbury rd E7	18 B 15 Silver st N18	93 P 2 Skinners row SE10
27 P 18 Shirehall clo NW4	61 Y 3 Shrewsbury rd NW10	8 C 12 Silver st Enf	66 H 10 Skipsey av E6
27 N 16 Shirehall gdns NW4	16 J 18 Shrewsbury rd N11	75 X 3 Silver wlk SE16	149 Y 2 Skipton st SE1
27 P 17 Shirehall la NW4	137 T 5 Shrewsbury rd W2	5W 15 Silvercliffe gdns Barnt	63 R 3 Skipworth rd E9
27 P 19 Shirehall pk NW4	124 J 6 Shrewsbury rd Becknhm	110 D 10 Silverdale SE26	33W 3 Sky Peals rd Wdfd Grn
02 J 10 Shires the Rich	120 K 18 Shrewsbury rd Carsh	7 O 15 Silverdale Enf	99 U 1 Slade gdns Erith
29 N 5 Shirland ms W9	106 M 16 Shrewton rd SW17	36 J 17 Silverdale av Ilf	99 T 1 Slade Green rd Erith
29 P 14 Shirland rd W9	111 Z 9 Shroffold rd Brom	153 U 8 Silverdale clo Sutton	79 U 16 Slade the SE18
32 O 2 Shirley av Bxly	112 B 8 Shroffold rd Brom	20 K 19 Silverdale dri Hornch	95 O 7 Sladebrook rd SE3
58 C 1 Shirley av Croy	132 D 19 Shropshire pl W1	98 G 6 Silverdale rd Bxly Hth	72 V 4 Sladedale rd SE18
53 U 20 Shirley av Sutton	30 C 1 Shropshire rd N22	156 J 4 Silverdale rd Croy	50 B 12 Sladen pl E5
54 H 8 Shirley av Sutton	130 L 19 Shroton st NW1	83 Y 6 Silverhall st Islwth	7 T 11 Slades clo Enf
58 F 5 Shirley Ch rd Croy	34 F 7 Shrubberies the E18	78 G 3 Silverland st E16	114 B 9 Slades dri Chisl
82 M 14 Shirley clo Hounsl	17W3 Shrubbery gdns N21	121 E 11 Silverleigh rd Thntn Hth	7 S 10 Slades gdns Enf
24 G 10 Shirley cres Becknhm	18 J 12 Shrubbery rd N9	57 S 12 Silverlock st SE16	7 U 11 Slades hill Enf
82 H 19 Shirley dri Hounsl	108 A 10 Shrubbery rd SW16	93 P 17 Silvermere rd SE6	7 T 11 Slades dri Enf
71 X 2 Shirley gdns W7	70 F 1 Shrubbery rd S'hall	11 S 19 Silverston clo Stanm	93 P 12 Slagrove pl SE13
54 G 17 Shirley gdns Bark	152 L 6 Shrubland gro Worc Pk	11 S 19 Silverston way Stanm	146 C 16 Slaidburn st SW10
19 S 3 Shirley gro N9	33 P 20 Shrubland rd E10	20 C 7 Silverthorn gdns E4	93 U 11 Slaithwaite rd SE13
89 P 7 Shirley gro SW11	33 N 16 Shrubland rd E17	89 T 5 Silverthorne rd SW8	48 E 14 Slaney pl N7
58 E 8 Shirley Hills rd Croy	135 R 2 Shrubland rd E8	144 F 16 Silverton rd W6	148 B 18 Sleaford st SW8
77 Y 18 Shirley Ho dri SE7	159 O 7 Shrublands av Croy	78 B 3 Silvertown By-pass E16	140 J 8 Slingsby pl WC2
24 B 19 Shirley Pk rd Croy	15 U 7 Shrublands clo N20	52 O 3 Silvertown way E16	84 V 3 Sloane av SW3
52 A 20 Shirley rd E15	96 K 19 Shuttle clo Sidcp	65 O 18 Silvertown way E16	147 R 9 Sloane Ct east SW3
72 Z 7 Shirley rd W4	99 V 8 Shuttle rd Drtfrd	91 V 14 Silvester rd SE22	147 R 10 Sloane Ct west SW3
58 B 1 Shirley rd Croy	135 S 18 Shuttle st E1	142 D 18 Silvester st SE1	147 S 7 Sloane gdns SW1
7 Y 12 Shirley rd Enf	98 B 18 Shuttlemead Bxly	75 R 12 Silwood st SE16	147 R 7 Sloane sq SW1
14 H 7 Shirley rd Sidcp	88 H 4 Shuttleworth rd SW11	94 B 10 Sim's wlk SE3	139 P 19 Sloane st SW1
55 U 19 Shirley rd Wallgtn	89 X 6 Sibells rd SW4	15 X 7 Simmons clo N20	147 R 4 Sloane st SW1
33 P 4 Shirley st N1	53 R 20 Sibley gro E12	20 K 9 Simmons la E4	147 R 1 Sloane st SW1
58 L 4 Shirley way Croy	120 L 3 Sibthorp rd Mitch	78 L 13 Simmons rd SE18	124 K 14 Sloane ter SW1
59 N 3 Shirley way Croy	94 J 18 Sibthorpe rd SE12	15W7 Simmons way N20	100 K 17 Sloane wlk Croy
47 N 13 Shirlock rd NW3	120 J 17 Sibton rd Carsh	154 J 3 Simms clo Carsh	25 V 17 Slotts dri Hampt
46 M 12 Shirlock rd NW3	140 M 1 Sicilian av WC1	94 H 18 Simnel rd SE12	25 V 17 Slough la NW9
31 O 5 Shobden rd N17	140 L 2 Sicilian av WC1	137 S 9 Simon clo W11	143W6 Sly st E1
12 V 5 Shoe la EC4	87 S 1 Sidbury st SW6	51 O 6 Simonds rd E10	83W4 Smallberry av Islwth
53 U 20 Shoebury rd E6	114 J 12 Sidcup By Pass rd Sidcp	51 X 16 Simons wlk E15	138 E 7 Smallbrook ms W2
45 T 17 Shoot Up hill NW2	115 U 17 Sidcup By Pass rd Sidcp	82 E 17 Simpson rd Hounsl	99 V 9 Smalley rd N16
24 E 12 Shooters av Harrow	114 M 9 Sidcup High st Sidcp	57 U 19 Simpson rd Rainhm	106 F 19 Smallwood rd SW17
54 C 4 Shooters hill SE18	115 S 13 Sidcup hill Sidcp	107 C 9 Simpson rd Rich	88 C 12 Smardale rd SW18
95 N 1 Shooters Hill rd SE18	115 T 14 Sidcup Hill gdns Sidcp	85 N 18 Simpson st SW11	81 R 12 Smarden clo Blvdr
77 Y 20 Shooters Hill rd SE3	94 J 14 Sidcup rd SE9	64 E 20 Simpsons rd E14	113 T 8 Smarden gro SE9
94 A 2 Shooters Hill rd SE3	113 X 4 Sidcup rd SE9	87 Y 14 Simrose ct SW18	39 Z 4 Smart clo Rom
57 V 5 Shooters rd Enf	114 C 6 Sidcup rd SE9	39 T 14 Sims clo Rom	63 T 8 Smart st E2
100 F 4 Shore gro Felt	131 P 18 Siddons la NW1	8 H 7 Sinclair clo Enf	140 L 4 Smarts pl WC2
63 P 1 Shore pl E9	31 X 5 Siddons rd N17	136 H 19 Sinclair gdns W14	87 X 19 Smeaton rd SW18
63 P 1 Shore rd E9	110 G 5 Siddons rd SE23	27 R 18 Sinclair gro NW11	89 Y 4 Smedley st SW8&SW4
120 E 1 Shore st SW19	156 G 4 Siddons rd Croy	10 A 1 Sinclair rd E4	64 A 1 Smeed rd E3
134 L 15 Shoreditch High st EC2	32 K 16 Side of E17	19 X 18 Sinclair rd E4	72 K 17 Smith hill Brentf
115W2 Shoreham clo Bxly	114 E 1 Sidewood rd SE9	136 J 19 Sinclair rd W14	148 J 3 Smith sq SW1
88 A 13 Shoreham st SW8	149 R 2 Sidford pl SE1	144 K 1 Sinclair rd W14	65 O 19 Smith st E16
126 D 15 Shoreham way Brom	83 T 4 Sidmouth av Islwth	71 Z 1 Singapore rd W13	147 N 10 Smith st SW3
57 N 10 Shorncliffe rd SE1	51 T 7 Sidmouth rd E10	134 G 15 Singer st EC2	116 L 15 Smith st Surb
93 U 20 Shorndean st SE6	62 M 1 Sidmouth rd NW10	63W 12 Single st E3	147 N 10 Smith st SW3
97 R 15 Shorne clo Sidcp	128 C 1 Sidmouth rd NW10	14 L 15 Singleton rd Dgnhm	140 O 9 Smith's ct W1
127W5 Shornefield clo Brom	45 N 19 Sidmouth rd NW2	12 N 12 Singleton scarp N12	63 P 15 Smithey st E1
86 E 12 Shornells way SE2	80 F 20 Sidmouth rd Welling	32 F 4 Sinnott rd E17	141 X 2 Smithfield st EC1
33 R 18 Shorrold's rd SW6	132 M 15 Sidmouth st WC1	84 A 20 Sion rd Twick	80 C 11 Smithies rd SE2
14 J 12 Short ga N12	17 R 18 Sidney av N13	74 D 2 Sir Alexander rd W3	31 O 4 Smithson rd N17
82 R 18 Short hedges Hounsl	72 F 16 Sidney gdns Brentf	30 K 8 Sirdar rd N22	105 R 3 Smithwood clo SW19
51 Y 6 Short rd E11	133W11 Sidney gro EC1	136 J 11 Sirdar rd W11	150 L 9 Smyrk's rd SE17
42 J 12 Short rd E15	52 E 10 Sidney rd E7	107 N 16 Sirdar rd Mitch	129 U 2 Smyrna rd NW6
74 A 16 Short rd W4	123W11 Sidney rd SE25	67 X 3 Sisley rd Bark	64 E 19 Smythe st E14
51 Y 10 Short st E11	90 D 5 Sidney rd SW9	87 V 15 Sisparb gdns SW18	6 G 11 Snakes la Barnt
141 V 16 Short st SE1	23 O 11 Sidney rd Harrow	123 Y 17 Sissinghurst rd Croy	21 S 17 Snakes la Wdfd Grn
67 P 3 Short st Bark	84 K 11 Sidney rd Twick	89 N 8 Sisters av SW11	21 T 18 Snakes la Wdfd Grn
15 X 19 Short way N12	83 Z 16 Sidney rd Twick	107 T 1 Sistova rd SW12	21 X 20 Snakes la west Wdfd Grn
95 P 8 Short way SE9	63 O 16 Sidney sq E1	8 C 20 Sittingbourne av Enf	11 V 14 Snaresbrook dri Stanm
83 N 19 Short way Twick	143 Z 3 Sidney sq E1	18 B 1 Sittingbourne av Enf	34 E 11 Snaresbrook hall E18
83 Z 7 Short wlk Islwth	135 Z 2 Sidney st E1	10 H 17 Sitwell gro Stanm	33 Z 14 Snaresbrook rd E11
152 E 16 Shortcroft rd Epsom	63 O 17 Sidney st E1	56 H 20 Siviter way Dgnhm	34 C 14 Snaresbrook rd E11
56 B 17 Shortcrofts rd Dgnhm	143 Z 1 Sidney st E1	31 O 5 Siward rd N17	136 C 3 Snarsgate st W10
143 N 9 Shorter st EC3	63 O 16 Sidney St east E1	106 C 7 Siward rd SW17	62 M 16 Snarsgate st W10
142 F 5 Shorters ct EC2	63 N 1 Sidworth st E8	126 J 7 Siward rd Brom	75 X 19 Snead st SE16
144 G 8 Shortlands W6	135 X 2 Sidworth st E8	53 U 14 Sixth av E12	27 U 20 Sneath av NW11
12 C 12 Shortlands clo N18	77 T 17 Siebert rd SE3	128 J 15 Sixth av W10	18 H 18 Snells pk N18
126 A 2 Shortlands gdns Brom	59 S 8 Siemens rd SE18	8 J 16 Sixth av Enf	44 M 13 Sneyd rd NW2
125 X 5 Shortlands gro Brom	49 Y 15 Sigdon rd E8	100 M 6 Sixth Cross rd Twick	141W3 Snow hill EC1
144 F 7 Shortlands ms W6	76 M 8 Sigismund st W10	100 M 8 Sixth Cross rd Twick	88 B 5 Snowbury rd SW6
51 P 1 Shortlands rd E10	136 H 7 Silchester rd W10	45 S 14 Skardu rd NW2	134 J 19 Snowden st EC2
125 Y 5 Shortlands rd Brom	150 L 12 Silcote rd SE5	87 T 19 Skeena hill SW18	142 G 17 Snowsfields SE1
103 O 18 Shortlands rd Kingst	98 F 3 Silecroft rd Bxly Hth	66 F 3 Skeffington rd E6	91 U 8 Soames st SE15
102 M 19 Shortlands rd Kingst		106 C 4 Skelbrook st SW18	118 A 1 Soames wlk New Mald
55 U 13 Shorts croft NW9		87 V 11 Skelgill rd SW15	141 O 3 Soan museum WC2
140 K 5 Shorts gdns WC2			126 G 15 Socket la Brom
154 K 10 Shorts rd Carsh			
155 S 14 Shotfield Wallgtn			

140 F5 Soho sq W1	69 S5 South clo Dgnhm	143 P7 South Tenter st E1	110 L9 Southend la SE6&SE26
140 E5 Soho st W1	119 X14 South clo Mrdn	146 J5 South ter SW7	34 H6 Southend rd E18
63 V12 Solebay pl E1	40 E2 South clo Pinn	116 K13 South ter Surb	53 T19 Southend rd E6
63 X11 Solebay st E3	100 H6 South clo Twick	109 R16 South vale SE19	111 P17 Southend rd Becknhm
45 X16 Solent rd NW6	32 K10 South Countess rd E17	41 U12 South vale Harrow	35 N8 Southend rd Wdfd Grn
8 L14 Solna av SW15	140 F1 South cres WC1	126 J3 South view Brom	32 G9 Southerland rd E17
18 A3 Solon rd N21	36 A15 South Cross rd Ilf	99 O13 South view Drtfd	147 W10 Southerland row SW1
92 A9 Solomon's pas SE15	109 O6 South Croxted rd SE21	98 B17 South View clo Bxly	77 T16 Southern appr SE1
90 A10 Solon New rd SW4	12 L12 South dene NW7	35 Y18 South View cres Ilf	123 V6 Southern av SE25
90 A11 Solon rd N4	153 S20 South dri Sutton	34 J11 South View dri E18	63 Y10 Southern gro E3
82 C7 Solway clo Hounsl	72 G9 South Ealing rd W5	29 Z11 South View dri N8	29 Southern Langbourn champs EC3
30 H4 Solway rd N22	18 G11 South Eastern av N9	47 Y18 South View rd N8	65 X6 Southern rd E13
91 X10 Solway rd SE22	147 V6 South Eaton pl SW1	14 M7 South way N12	38 L13 Southern rd N2
5 U19 Somaford gro Barnt	125 R16 South Eden Pk rd Becknhm	19 R9 South way N9	128 K18 Southern row W10
45 U14 Somali rd NW2	135 X3 South Edward's sq E8	119 O9 South way SW20	133 N9 Southern st N1
54 D20 Somerby rd Bark		158 K5 South way Croy	38 F19 Southern way Rom
48 J7 Somerfield rd N4	135 X1 South end W8	22 H14 South way Harrow	144 B5 Southerton rd W6
49 U13 Somerford gro N16	156 M8 South end Croy	43 P14 South way Wemb	74 B15 Southerton rd W6
31 Y2 Somerford gro N17	46 K13 South End clo NW3	83 Z15 South Western rd Twick	90 B5 Southesk st SW9
135 X17 Somerford st E1	46 K14 South End grn NW3	84 A16 South Western rd Twick	31 S15 Southey rd N15
97 U18 Somerhill av Sidcp	46 J11 South End rd NW3	138 G4 South Wharf rd W2	105 Z18 Southey rd SW19
97 R4 Somerhill rd Welling	57 Z14 South End rd Hornch	159 Z5 South wlk W Wkhm	90 E1 Southey rd SW9
90 G10 Somerleyton rd SW9	135 Y1 South End row W8	86 A8 South Worple av SW13	110 E18 Southey st SE20
138 J6 Somers cres W2	52 K19 South Esk rd E7		4 B20 Southfield Barnt
90 C17 Somers pl SW2	106 B18 South gdns SW19	86 A8 South Worple way SW14	71 V5 Southfield cotts W7
32 L14 Somers rd E17	32 K16 South gro E17		101 V8 Southfield gdns Twick
90 C17 Somers rd SW2	31 P16 South gro N15	85 Y8 South Worple way SW14	22 J13 Southfield pk Harrow
35 T15 Somersby gdns Ilf	47 P4 South gro N6		31 T9 Southfield rd N17
118 J3 Somerset av N17	113 S16 South hill Chisl	142 E19 Southall pl SE1	73 X6 Southfield rd W4
96 L11 Somerset av Welling	41 O10 South hill av Harrow	128 M19 Southam st W10	74 H7 Southfield rd W4
118 B13 Somerset clo New Mald	41 T12 South Hill gro Harrow	129 O20 Southam st W10	9 P19 Southfield rd Enf
93 P5 Somerset gdns SE13	46 K13 South Hill pk NW3	141 R3 Southampton bldgs WC2	26 H9 Southfields N4
122 D6 Somerset gdns SW16	46 K11 South Hill Pk gdns NW3	121 Z8 Southampton gdns Mitch	87 X16 Southfields rd SW18
101 T12 Somerset gdns Tedd	126 A9 South Hill rd Brom	140 L2 Southampton pl WC1	134 G1 Southgate gro N1
141 O9 Somerset house WC2	125 Z8 South Hill rd Brom	46 M14 Southampton rd NW5	134 G3 Southgate rd N1
33 O17 Somerset rd E17	113 T17 South Hill rd Chisl	132 K19 Southampton row WC1	49 P18 Southgate rd N1
26 L13 Somerset rd NW4	149 S19 South Island pl SW9	140 L9 Southampton st WC2	64 E17 Southill st E14
31 V11 Somerset rd N17	116 G6 South la Kingst	91 T1 Southampton way SE5	79 Z18 Southland rd SE18
18 F16 Somerset rd N18	117 Z15 South la New Mald	150 G18 Southampton way SE5	83 P13 Southland way Hounsl
105 R9 Somerset rd SW19	118 A15 South la New Mald	116 A17 Southbank Surb	127 R7 Southlands gro Brom
72 C3 Somerset rd W13	117 X9 South La w New Mald	25 X8 Southborne av NW9	126 M10 Southlands rd Brom
73 X7 Somerset rd W4	149 O19 South Lambeth est SW8	116 V10 Southborough clo Surb	127 N8 Southlands rd Brom
5 O16 Somerset rd Barnt	148 L17 South Lambeth rd SW8	127 U12 Southborough la Brom	152 C16 Southmead Epsom
72 F17 Somerset rd Brentf	121 Z8 South Lodge av Mitch	63 S2 Southborough rd E9	87 S20 Southmead rd SW19
99 Z17 Somerset rd Drtfd	122 A8 South Lodge av Mitch	127 S10 Southborough rd Brom	42 L15 Southmeadows Wemb
8 B16 Somerset rd East Barnt	6 K13 South Lodge cres Enf	116 J20 Southborough rd Surb	113 V8 Southold ri SE9
22 M16 Somerset rd Harrow	6 J14 South Lodge dr N14	126 F18 Southbourne Brom	14 L13 Southover N12
117 N4 Somerset rd Kingst	7 N17 South Lodge dr N14	22 B20 Southbourne clo Pinn	14 L14 Southover N12
58 H15 Somerset rd S'hall	139 W7 South Molton la W1	27 S13 Southbourne cres NW4	54 F9 Southover rd Brom
101 U12 Somerset rd Tedd	65 T16 South Molton rd E16	94 H12 Southbourne gdns SE12	79 S11 Southport rd SE18
70 A18 Somerset waye Hounsl	139 W7 South Molton st W1	54 B16 Southbourne gdns Ilf	122 H20 Southsea rd Croy
97 Z5 Somersham rd Bxly Hth	123 T10 South Norwood hill SE25	156 K7 Southbridge pl Croy	38 J8 Southsea rd Kingst
85 S8 Somerton av Rich	112 B1 South Park cres SE6	156 M8 Southbridge rd Croy	74 D9 Southside W6
85 S9 Somerton rd NW2	94 A20 South Park cres SE6	94 C15 Southbrook rd SE12	105 O14 Southside comm SW19
92 A10 Somerton rd SE15	54 F9 South Park dri Ilf	122 A1 Southbrook rd SW16	96 F18 Southspring Sidcp
112 H5 Somertrees av SE12	54 G9 South Park dri Ilf	74 K6 Southbrook st W12	94 A5 Southvale rd SE3
24 M14 Somervell rd Harrow	157 R10 South Park Hill rd S Croy	8 K14 Southbury av Enf	44 D14 Southview av NW10
92 E3 Somerville rd SE14	106 B15 South Park rd SW19	8 G13 Southbury rd Enf	155 V17 Southview gdns Wallgtn
110 F17 Somerville rd SE20	105 X16 South Park rd SW19	66 G7 Southchurch rd E6	111 X9 Southview rd Brom
37 U15 Somerville rd Rom	54 F9 South Park rd Ilf	146 L6 Southcombe st W14	142 C11 Southwark Br SE1
48 E8 Sonderburg rd N7	54 F11 South Park ter Ilf	117 S18 Southcote av Surb	142 B16 Southwark Br rd SE1
150 F13 Sondes st SE17	146 G10 South pde SW3	32 F15 Southcote rd E17	
23 V20 Sonia ct Harrow	73 Y10 South pde W4	47 V12 Southcote rd N19	142 A14 Southwark gro SE1
44 D12 Sonia gdns NW10	54 F9 South Pk cres Ilf	124 B13 Southcote rd SE25	151 Y1 Southwark park SE16
15 P14 Sonia gdns N12	117 V10 South Pk gro New Mald	159 U3 Southcroft av W Wkhm	
70 G20 Sonia gdns Hounsl	142 G1 South pl EC2	96 H7 Southcroft av Welling	151 T5 Southwark Pk rd SE16
123 X15 Sonning rd SE25	116 L16 South pl Surb	107 N14 Southcroft rd SW17	
48 D18 Sonning st N7	148 F1 South Place mews EC2	105 U3 Southdean gdns SW19	143 X20 Southwark Pk rd SE16
51 P2 Sophia rd E10	16 F17 South rd N11	71 X9 Southdown av W7	
65 V16 Sophia rd E16	18 L5 South rd N9	40 L5 Southdown cres Harrow	151 X2 Southwark Pk rd SE16
64 C20 Sophia st E14	110 E4 South rd SE23	36 G15 Southdown cres Ilf	142 C14 Southwark st SE1
153 Z6 Sorrento rd Sutton	106 D16 South rd SW19	105 O19 Southdown dri SW20	63 Y17 Southwater clo E14
154 A6 Sorrento rd Sutton	72 G10 South rd W5	105 R20 Southdown rd SW20	28 B17 Southway NW11
48 K11 Sotheby rd N5	25 U4 South rd Edg	143 P1 Southdown rd SW20	14 L9 Southway N20
88 M3 Soudan rd SW11	100 A14 South rd Felt	155 O19 Southdown rd Carsh	119 N10 Southway SW20
144 H4 Souldern rd W14	100 D16 South rd Hampt	57 X2 Southdown rd Hornch	126 E18 Southway Brom
32 H19 South Access rd E17	37 X18 South rd Rom	95 Y16 Southend clo SE9	155 V9 Southway Wallgtn
136 A10 South Africa rd W12	70 E3 South rd S'hall	95 Y15 Southend cres SE9	74 L6 Southway clo W12
62 L20 South Africa rd W12	101 R8 South rd Twick		42 L10 Southwell av Grnfd
74 J1 South Africa rd W12	154 K19 South ri Carsh		146 B4 Southwell gdns SW7
139 V12 South Audley st W1	24 C4 South row SE3		90 L7 Southwell rd SE5
20 E1 South av E4	27 Z18 South sq NW11		122 F14 Southwell rd Croy
155 N17 South av Carsh	141 R1 South sq WC1		24 H18 Southwell rd Harrow
85 O3 South av Rich	139 T12 South st W1		51 X3 Southwest rd E11
58 D20 South av S'hall	126 F2 South st Brom		138 J5 Southwick ms W2
58 D20 South Av gdns S'hall	9 S17 South st Enf		138 J7 Southwick pl W2
116 K14 South bank Surb	69 Y7 South st Rainhm		55 N15 Southwold dri Bark
116 K15 South Bank ter Surb	39 R16 South st Rom		
51 X10 South Birkbeck rd E11			
74 F14 South Black Lion la E			
146 A10 South Bolton gdns			
29 R17 South clo N6			
4 H12 South clo Barnt			
97 W11 South clo Bxly Hth			

50 A 7 Southwold rd E5
29 R 20 Southwood av N6
03W 20 Southwood av Kingst
47 X 18 Southwood dri Surb
35 Z 14 Southwood gdns Ilf
47 P 2 Southwood la N6
29 P 20 Southwood la N6
47 S 1 Southwood Lawn rd N6
29 S 20 Southwood Lawn rd N6
47 S 1 Southwood Lawn rd N6
47 R 1 Southwood pk N6
43 Y 4 Southwood rd SE9
4 A 3 Southwood rd SE9
95 T 14 Sowerby clo SE9
57 U 17 Sowrey av Rainhm
23 N 1 Spa hill SE19
29 O 19 Spa hill SE19
51 S 2 Spa rd SE16
51 O 2 Spa rd SE16
51 S 2 Spa rd SE16
33 T 15 Spafield st EC1
07 S 13 Spalding rd SW17
64 B 12 Spanby rd E3
46 E 3 Spaniards clo NW11
46 F 4 Spaniards end NW3
46 E 6 Spaniards rd NW3
39 U 3 Spanish pl W1
88 E 12 Spanish rd SW18
23 R 2 Spar clo SE25
23 T 13 Sparkbridge rd Harrow
52 J 9 Sparrow Farm rd Epsom
56 G 8 Sparrow grn Dgnhm
14 C 1 Sparrows la SE9
96 B 20 Sparrows la SE9
10 A 4 Sparrows way Bushey Watf
48 B 3 Sparsholt rd N4
47 V 4 Sparsholt rd Bark
93 T 3 Sparta st SE10
45 V 7 Spear ms W8
78 J 17 Spearman st SE18
14 L 14 Spearpoint ter Ilf
97 N 3 Spears rd N4
70 B 20 Speart la Hounsl
76 A 20 Speedwell st SE8
32 K 14 Speedy pl WC1
88 H 8 Speke rd SW11
23 N 3 Speke rd Thntn Hth
13 U 8 Spekehill SE9
23 D 3 Speldhurst clo Brom
63 S 2 Speldhurst rd E9
73 Z 7 Speldhurst rd W4
35 R 2 Spelman st E1
43 R 1 Spelman st E1
17 R 19 Spencer av N13
61 N 7 Spencer clo NW10
23 P 17 Spencer clo Croy
21 Y 17 Spencer clo Wdfd Grn
28 D 19 Spencer dri N2
95 T 13 Spencer gdns SE9
85 V 12 Spencer gdns SW14
05 S 17 Spencer hill SW19
05 T 17 Spencer Hill rd SW14
88 F 13 Spencer pk SW18
32 D 2 Spencer pl SW1
33 U 6 Spencer rd E17
66 B 3 Spencer rd E6
16 D 14 Spencer rd N11
31 X 5 Spencer rd N17
90 G 14 Spencer rd SE24
88 G 12 Spencer rd SW18
18 K 1 Spencer rd SW20
73 V 2 Spencer rd W3
73 V 20 Spencer rd W4
12 B 18 Spencer rd Brom
23 U 8 Spencer rd Harrow
54 L 4 Spencer rd Ilf
83 O 3 Spencer rd Islwth
21 N 18 Spencer rd Mitch
23 S 11 Spencer rd S Croy
01 T 5 Spencer rd Twick
42 C 6 Spencer rd Wemb
47 T 11 Spencer ri NW5
33 X 13 Spencer st EC1
87 O 10 Spencer wlk SW15
49 R 13 Spenser gro N16
45 C 1 Spenser st SW1
79 X 13 Speranza st SE18
31 T 9 Sperling rd N17
63 V 20 Spert st E14
6 G 20 Spey side N14
39 P 2 Spey way Rom
62 G 16 Spezia rd NW10
18 E 13 Spiers clo New Mald
31 N 5 Spigurnell rd N17

58 C 18 Spikes Br rd S'hall
79 Y 14 Spindel clo S18
79 V 14 Spindel st SE18
40 D 14 Spinnells rd Harrow
56 A 14 Spinney gdns Dgnhm
127 S 3 Spinney oak-Brom
17 S 2 Spinney the N21
107 E 7 Spinney the SW16
5 O 10 Spinney the Barnt
115 Y 12 Spinney the Sidcp
11 X 14 Spinney the Stanm
152 M 9 Spinney the Sutton
41 X 10 Spinney the Wemb
127 T 3 Spinneys the Brom
134 L 20 Spital sq E1
135 R 19 Spital st E1
134 M 20 Spitalfields market E1
31 W 13 Spondon rd N15
93 U 20 Sportsbank st SE6
30 L 3 Spottons gro N17
159 O 11 Spout hill Croy
34 F 18 Spratt Hall rd E11
83 R 14 Spray la Islwth
79 N 10 Spray st SE18
78 M 10 Spray st SE18
147 N 8 Sprimont pl SW3
7 P 20 Spring bank N21
60 G 19 Spring Br rd W5
153 S 12 Spring Clo la Sutton
7 S 3 Spring Ct rd Enf
140 H 13 Spring gdns SW1
57 Y 13 Spring gdns Hornch
38 J 17 Spring gdns Rom
155 U 11 Spring gdns Wallgtn
34 J 1 Spring gdns Wdfd Grn
148 L 10 Spring Gdns wlk SE1
73 O 15 Spring gro W4
82 M 2 Spring Grove cres Hounsl
82 L 3 Spring Grove rd Hounsl
83 N 3 Spring Grove rd Hounsl
85 N 12 Spring Grove rd Rich
84 M 12 Spring Grove rd Rich
49 X 2 Spring hill E5
23 Z 14 Spring la SE25
124 A 15 Spring la SE25
11 N 13 Spring lake Stanm
139 R 1 Spring ms W1
159 T 7 Spring park Croy W Wickhm
106 E 7 Spring pk av Croy
28 E 4 Spring Pk av Croy
46 F 9 Spring Pk rd Croy
15 P 13 Spring pl NW5
152 E 2 Spring Pond rd Dgnhm
138 F 7 Spring st W2
152 O 20 Spring st Epsom
98 H 10 Spring vale Bxly Hth
25 P 1 Spring Vale rd Edg
144 G 2 Spring Vale ter W14
151 X 19 Springall st SE15
75 N 20 Springalls st SE15
17 P 1 Springbank N14
93 Z 17 Springbank rd SE13
111 U 20 Springbourne ct Becknhm
28 L 12 Springcroft av N2
72 H 13 Springdale av Brentf
49 N 12 Springdale rd N16
50 A 3 Springfield E5
49 Y 4 Springfield E5
10 C 4 Springfield Bushey Watf
29 V 11 Springfield av N22
19 U 5 Springfield av SW20
10 L 11 Springfield clo Stanm
36 B 17 Springfield dri Ilf
50 A 4 Springfield gdns E5
25 Z 16 Springfield gdns NW9
127 U 9 Springfield gdns Brom
159 T 2 Springfield gdns W Wkhm
34 L 2 Springfield gdns Wdfd Grn
77 Y 17 Springfield gro SE7
129 N 6 Springfield la NW6
126 A 15 Springfield mt NW9
49 Z 2 Springfield park E5
65 N 8 Springfield rd E15
32 K 19 Springfield rd E17
20 L 4 Springfield rd E4
53 U 19 Springfield rd E6
130 A 5 Springfield rd NW8
16 G 17 Springfield rd N11

31 X 12 Springfield rd N15
110 B 14 Springfield rd SE26
105W 13 Springfield rd SW19
71 T 2 Springfield rd W7
127 U 9 Springfield rd Brom
98 G 10 Springfield rd Bxly Hth
23 T 18 Springfield rd Harrow
116 K 7 Springfield rd Kingst
101 Y 13 Springfield rd Tedd
108 L 20 Springfield rd Thntn Hth
122 L 1 Springfield rd Thntn Hth
82 H 20 Springfield rd Twick
155 S 11 Springfield rd Wallgtn
97 P 7 Springfield rd Welling
109 Z 8 Springfield ri SE26
129W 5 Springfield wlk NW6
48 M 3 Springpark dri N4
125 V 5 Springpark dri Becknhm
93W 16 Springrice rd SE13
62 E 4 Springwell av NW10
108 D 10 Springwell clo SW16
108 E 11 Springwell clo SW16
70 A 20 Springwell clo Hounsl
12 G 7 Springwood cres Edg
12 F 7 Springwood cres Edg
52 F 16 Sprowston ms E7
52 F 16 Sprowstone rd E7
33 T 9 Spruce Hills rd E17
92 H 6 Sprules rd SE4
31 O 13 Spur rd N15
67 O 9 Spur rd Bark
11 Y 12 Spur rd Edg
71 Z 20 Spur rd Islwth
109 O 19 Spurgeon av SE19
109 O 19 Spurgeon rd SE19
150 E 1 Spurgeon st SE1
91 V 10 Spurling rd SE22
56 C 17 Spurling rd Dgnhm
49 Z 16 Spurstowe rd E8
49 Y 16 Spurstowe ter E8
155 N 10 Square the Carsh
53W 1 Square the Ilf
21 R 17 Square the Wdfd Grn
106 E 7 Squarey st SW17
28 E 4 Squire's la N3
46 F 9 Squires mt NW3
15 P 13 Squirrel clo N12
152 E 2 Squirrels grn Worc Pk
39 Y 11 Squirrels Heath av Rom
22 L 11 Squirrels the Pinn
135 T 13 Squirries st E2
132 E 5 Stable yd NW1
140 B 16 Stable yd SW1
140 B 16 Stable Yd rd SW1
19 P 15 Stacey av N18
33W 17 Stacey clo E10
140 H 6 Stacey st WC2
139 P 20 Stackhouse st SW3
78 E 18 Stadium rd SE18
95 R 1 Stadium rd SE18
146 O 19 Stadium st SW10
43 P 13 Stadium way Wemb
50 G 3 Staffa rd E10
6 H 17 Stafford clo N14
153 T 13 Stafford clo Sutton
156 O 10 Stafford gdns Croy
129 T 12 Stafford ms NW6
84 L 18 Stafford ms Rich
140 A 20 Stafford pl SW1
63 Y 7 Stafford rd E3
52 M 19 Stafford rd E7
129 S 11 Stafford rd NW6
156 D 11 Stafford rd Croy & Wallgtn
23 N 3 Stafford rd Harrow
117 V 6 Stafford rd New Mald
114 H 9 Stafford rd Sidcp
84 B 19 Stafford rd Twick
155 U 14 Stafford rd Wallgtn
156 B 12 Stafford rd Wallgtn
140 A 12 Stafford st W1
137 U 20 Stafford ter W8
91 Y 1 Staffordshire st SE15
24 E 20 Stag clo Edg
25 V 10 Stag la NW9
104 E 5 Stag la SW15
21 V 7 Stag la Buck Hl
148 A 1 Stag pl SW1

121 S 5 Stainbank rd Mitch
31 V 12 Stainby rd N15
142 H 15 Stainer st SE1
153 P 3 Staines av Sutton
80 E 10 Staines rd Hounsl
54 D 14 Staines rd Ilf
100 H 7 Staines rd Twick
101 O 4 Staines rd Twick
33 P 13 Stainforth rd E17
88 K 6 Stainforth rd SW11
36 F 20 Stainforth rd Ilf
142 B 4 Staining la EC2
114 E 20 Stanmore clo Chisl
63 R 7 Stainsbury st E2
64 A 18 Stainsby rd E14
93W 18 Stainton rd SE6
9 R 5 Stainton rd Enf
130 L 20 Stalbridge st NW1
151 Y 3 Stalham st SE16
109 S 19 Stambourne way SE19
159 V 4 Stambourne way W Wkhm
142 G 15 Stamer st SE1
74 E 10 Stamford Brook av W6
74 E 9 Stamford Brook rd W6
31 X 14 Stamford clo N15
23 T 1 Stamford clo Harrow
70 H 1 Stamford clo S'hall
126 D 10 Stamford dri Brom
68 F 2 Stamford gdns Dgnhm
68 G 2 Stamford gdns Dgnhm
49W 3 Stamford Grn east N16
49W 4 Stamford Grn west N16
49 U 4 Stamford hill N16
66 C 3 Stamford rd E6
31W 14 Stamford rd N15
68 D 2 Stamford rd Dgnhm
141 T 13 Stamford st SE1
54 F 1 Stamford rd Ilf
135 O 11 Stamp pl E2
87 N 7 Stanbridge rd SW15
80 C 6 Stanbrook rd SE2
92 B 4 Stanbury st SE15
26 A 15 Stancroft NW9
61 X 10 Standard rd NW10
81 R 14 Standard rd Blvdr
98 A 11 Standard rd Bxly Hth
9W 1 Standard rd Enf
82 C 7 Standard rd Hounsl
87 X 20 Standen rd SW18
74 G 12 Standish rd W6
65 V 10 Standrew's rd E13
56 F 17 Stanfield gdns Dgnhm
63 X 7 Stanfield rd E3
65 F 15 Stanfield rd Dgnhm
38 G 18 Stanford clo Rom
150 J 7 Stanford pl SE17
16 A 16 Stanford rd N11
45 Y 2 Stanford rd W8
55 U 20 Stanford rd Dgnhm
148 E 6 Stanford st SW1
121 X 3 Stanford way SW16
11 O 14 Stangate gdns Stanm
123 X 10 Stanger rd SE25
27W 10 Stanhope av N3
126 E 20 Stanhope av Brom
23 P 5 Stanhope av Harrow
142 C 16 Stanhope bldgs SE1
139 U 13 Stanhope ga W1
13 R 17 Stanhope gdns NW7
30 K 18 Stanhope gdns N4
22 U 19 Stanhope gdns N6
146 D 6 Stanhope gdns SW7
56 A 8 Stanhope gdns Dgnhm
53 T 3 Stanhope gdns Ilf
124 L 10 Stanhope gro Becknhm
146 D 5 Stanhope Ms east SW7
146 C 6 Stanhope Ms south SW7
146 C 5 Stanhope Ms west SW7
59 N 10 Stanhope Pk rd Grnfd
139 N 7 Stanhope pl W2
39 R 16 Stanhope rd E17
16 D 15 Stanhope rd N11
15 S 16 Stanhope rd N12
47 V 1 Stanhope rd N6
29 V 20 Stanhope rd N6
4 B 19 Stanhope rd Barnt

97 Z4 Stanhope rd Bxly Hth
155 O17 Stanhope rd Carsh
157 R7 Stanhope rd Croy
56 A8 Stanhope rd Dgnhm
59 N13 Stanhope rd Grnfd
114 M8 Stanhope rd Sidcp
139 W15 Stanhope row W1
132 A12 Stanhope st NW1
138 G8 Stanhope ter W2
136 B15 Stanlake ms W12
74 L3 Stanlake ms W12
136 A14 Stanlake rd W12
74 K2 Stanlake rd W12
136 A15 Stanlake vlls W12
74 L3 Stanlake vlls W12
67 X8 Stanley av Bark
125 U5 Stanley av Becknhm
56 C3 Stanley av Dgnhm
58 M3 Stanley av Grnfd
59 N3 Stanley av Grnfd
118 F11 Stanley av New Mald
39 W14 Stanley av Rom
60 K1 Stanley av Wemb
149 N16 Stanley clo SW8
39 X12 Stanley clo Rom
60 K1 Stanley clo Wemb
137 O9 Stanley cres W11
45 N16 Stanley gdns NW2
107 N16 Stanley gdns SW17
137 P9 Stanley gdns W11
74 A5 Stanley gdns W3
155 U15 Stanley gdns Wallgtn
101 N11 Stanley Gdns rd Tedd
89 R5 Stanley gro SW8
122 F15 Stanley gro Croy
132 J9 Stanley pas NW1
60 M2 Stanley Pk dri Wemb
154 M16 Stanley Pk rd Carsh
155 S14 Stanley Pk rd Wallgtn
33 R19 Stanley rd E10
53 R16 Stanley rd E12
64 J4 Stanley rd E15
34 C6 Stanley rd E18
20 K4 Stanley rd E4
29 R2 Stanley rd N10
16 L17 Stanley rd N11
30 X13 Stanley rd N15
28 G12 Stanley rd N2
18 F7 Stanley rd N9
85 T10 Stanley rd SW14
105 Y16 Stanley rd SW19
73 U8 Stanley rd W3
126 K8 Stanley rd Brom
155 O18 Stanley rd Carsh
122 G15 Stanley rd Croy
8 F13 Stanley rd Enf
41 N8 Stanley rd Harrow
140 M7 Stanley rd Harrow
82 M9 Stanley rd Hounsl
83 N9 Stanley rd Hounsl
54 D8 Stanley rd Ilf
119 Y8 Stanley rd Mitch
58 A20 Stanley rd S'hall
115 O8 Stanley rd Sidcp
154 A16 Stanley rd Sutton
153 Z16 Stanley rd Sutton
101 U13 Stanley rd Tedd
43 N17 Stanley rd Wemb
155 N19 Stanley sq Carsh
66 L19 Stanley st E6
75 Y19 Stanley st SE8
48 A8 Stanley ter N4
83 R3 Stanleycroft clo Islwth
88 K4 Stanmer st SW11
85 N8 Stanmore gdns Rich
154 D6 Stanmore gdns Sutton
11 O14 Stanmore hill Stanm
10 L11 Stanmore hill Stanm
131 Y4 Stanmore rd NW1
52 C4 Stanmore rd E11
30 K12 Stanmore rd N15
81 Y10 Stanmore rd Blvdr
84 M7 Stanmore rd Rich
133 N4 Stanmore st N1
125 P2 Stanmore ter Becknhm
66 K17 Stannard cres E6
49 W17 Stannard rd E8
149 T12 Stannary pl SE11
149 U12 Stannary st SE11
90 D7 Stansfield rd SW9
56 E9 Stansgate rd Dgnhm
126 C13 Stanstead clo Brom

34 H15 Stanstead rd E11
110 J1 Stanstead rd SE23
115 W2 Stansted cres Bxly
107 Z11 Stanthorpe clo SW16
107 A11 Stanthorpe rd SW16
107 Z11 Stanthorpe rd SW16
101 T14 Stanton av Tedd
153 P1 Stanton clo Worc Pk
110 K9 Stanton rd SE26
86 D4 Stanton rd SW13
119 O1 Stanton rd SW20
122 L18 Stanton rd Croy
91 W1 Stanton st SE15
73 P1 Stanway gdns W3
12 G17 Stanway gdns Edg
34 K9 Stanway st N1
145 O7 Stanwick rd W14
42 A9 Stapenhill rd Wemb
141 S3 Staple inn WC1
141 S3 Staple Inn bldgs WC1
142 G19 Staple st SE1
36 H17 Stapleford clo SW19
87 R20 Stapleford clo SW19
108 A1 Stapleford clo Kingst
117 P5 Stapleford clo Kingst
42 G20 Stapleford rd Wemb
68 D8 Stapleford way Bark
93 Y14 Staplehurst rd SE13
154 J17 Staplehurst rd Carsh
57 W19 Stapleton cres Rain
156 F10 Stapleton gdns Croy
30 F20 Stapleton Hall rd N4
48 D3 Stapleton Hall rd N4
107 N7 Stapleton rd SW17
81 R14 Staple rd Blvdr
4 F12 Stapylton rd Barnt
63 N20 Star & Garter rd E1
84 L20 Star And Garter hill Rich
99 O12 Star hill Drtfrd
64 M12 Star la E16
65 N13 Star la E16
145 N12 Star rd W14
83 P5 Star rd Islwth
138 J4 Star st W2
141 S5 Star yd WC2
76 C8 Starboard way E14
36 E7 Starch Ho la Ilf
132 C14 Starcross st NW1
74 G6 Starfield rd W12
21 U6 Starling clo Buck Hl
101 W1 Staten gdns Twick
49 N11 Statham gro N16
18 D15 Statham gro N16
16 D16 Station app N11
107 Y12 Station appr SW16
87 U7 Station appr SW6
98 F20 Station appr Bxly
127 W2 Station appr Chisl
152 F11 Station appr Epsom
100 H20 Station appr Hampt
23 U20 Station appr Harrow
117 R2 Station appr Kingst
22 B12 Station appr Pinn
85 D2 Station appr Rich
153 T16 Station appr Sutton
97 O5 Station appr Welling
42 C17 Station appr Wemb
73 V20 Station Appr rd W4
90 K7 Station av SW9
152 C19 Station av Epsom
85 O3 Station av Rich
27 Z6 Station clo N3
100 K20 Station clo Hampt
31 N14 Station cres SE3
77 S15 Station cres SE3
73 W19 Station cres Wemb
42 J17 Station gdns W4
49 K9 Station pde NW2
44 N17 Station pde NW2
57 Y13 Station pde Hornch
85 O2 Station pde Rich
48 G7 Station pl N4
51 V10 Station rd E10
53 O13 Station rd E12
51 M18 Station rd E15
32 J17 Station rd E17
20 K3 Station rd E4
52 F13 Station rd E7
26 G18 Station rd NW4
13 P18 Station rd NW7
16 E17 Station rd N11
31 Y11 Station rd N17
18 G16 Station rd N18
47 V10 Station rd N19
17 W5 Station rd N21
30 A1 Station rd N22
27 Y5 Station rd N3
28 A7 Station rd N3
110 C15 Station rd SE20

123 V9 Station rd SE25
86 E4 Station rd SW13
106 F20 Station rd SW19
61 N17 Station rd W5
71 T2 Station rd W7
81 T9 Station rd Blvdr
126 A3 Station rd Brom
98 A6 Station rd Bxly Hth
97 Z6 Station rd Bxly Hth
155 N7 Station rd Carsh
114 A17 Station rd Chisl
113 Z19 Station rd Chisl
122 L20 Station rd Croy
157 P3 Station rd Croy
99 T15 Station rd Drtfrd
12 D18 Station rd Edg
100 H20 Station rd Hampt
22 K15 Station rd Harrow
23 V19 Station rd Harrow
82 K12 Station rd Hounsl
36 F11 Station rd Ilf
53 Z8 Station rd Ilf
117 P1 Station rd Kingst
112 L19 Station rd New Mald
81 U8 Station rd North Blvdr
55 W1 Station rd Rom
101 X14 Station rd Tedd
83 W20 Station rd Twick
125 U20 Station rd W Wkhm
159 U1 Station rd W Wkhm
108 J3 Station rise SE27
64 J1 Station st E15
51 W20 Station st E15
78 L4 Station st E16
90 M2 Station ter SE5
59 P2 Station view Grnfd
153 S15 Station way Sutton
23 V19 Station yd Twick
141 X6 Stationers ct EC4
102 L17 Staunton ct Kingst
75 Y17 Staunton st SE8
85 Z1 Staveley gdns W4
92 B1 Staveley rd SE15
73 X18 Staveley rd W4
44 M19 Staverton rd NW2
48 G13 Stavordale rd N5
120 C18 Stavordale rd Carsh
63 S12 Stayners rd E1
153 X4 Stayton rd Sutton
150 D7 Stead st SE17
134 C15 Steadman st EC1
88 B6 Stebbing way Bark
76 H10 Stebondale st E14
140 J3 Stedham pl WC1
149 Z7 Steedman st SE17
28 M6 Steeds rd N10
83 Y11 Steel rd Islwth
46 M18 Steel's ms NW3
46 M18 Steel's rd NW3
51 Z12 Steele rd E11
64 M5 Steele rd E15
61 W7 Steele rd NW10
31 T9 Steele rd N17
73 X8 Steele rd W4
63 P18 Steels la E1
91 S12 Steen way SE22
107 Y8 Steep hill SW16
105 T11 Steeple clo SW6
87 T6 Steeple clo SW6
17 Y17 Steeplestone clo N18
106 C5 Steerforth st SW18
106 L20 Steers mead Mitch
120 K1 Steers mead Mitch
107 N14 Stella rd SW17
124 A4 Stembridge rd SE20
123 Z4 Stembridge rd SE20
57 V17 Stephen av Rain
140 E3 Stephen ms W1
64 M5 Stephen rd Bxly Hth
140 E3 Stephen st W1
64 M5 Stephen's rd E15
88 B6 Stephendale rd SW6
65 O4 Stephens rd E15
59 W16 Stephenson rd W7
64 M15 Stephenson st E16
62 C8 Stephenson st NW10
132 C15 Stephensons way NW1
63 T19 Stepney causeway E1
63 R13 Stepney grn E1
63 U16 Stepney High st E1
63 R13 Stepney way E1
143 W2 Stepney way E1
12 A13 Sterling av Edg
11 Z13 Sterling av Edg
32 G9 Sterling gd E17
8 A7 Sterling rd Enf
138 L20 Sterling st SW7
144 E2 Sterndale rd W14

136 F16 Sterne st W12
91 Y6 Sternhall la SE15
108 A4 Sternhold av SW2
107 Y3 Sternhold av SW2
56 D14 Sterry cres Dgnhm
152 A8 Sterry dri Epsom
56 E17 Sterry gdns Dgnhm
67 X4 Sterry rd Bark
56 D12 Sterry rd Dgnhm
137 O1 Stervans rd W10
97 U5 Stevedale rd Wellir
53 V18 Stevenage rd E6
144 E20 Stevenage rd SW6
87 O3 Stevenage rd SW6
50 D17 Stevens av E9
10 B6 Stevens grn Bushey Hth
55 R9 Stevens rd Dgnhm
74 E1 Steventon rd W12
142 B9 Stew lane EC4
134 M20 Steward st E1
142 L1 Steward st E1
25 W19 Stewart clo NW9
51 V13 Stewart rd E15
76 H6 Stewart st E14
146 J9 Stewart's gro SW3
89 T1 Stewart's la SW8
147 Z10 Stewart's la SW8
148 A20 Stewart's rd SW8
89 W3 Stewart's rd SW8
17 X17 Stewartsby clo N18
73 T2 Steyne rd W3
113 T10 Steyning gro SE9
14 K17 Steynings way N12
115 X3 Steynton av Bxly
81 S10 Stickland rd Blvdr
58 K10 Stickleton clo Grnfc
73 P14 Stile Hall gdns W4
42 B11 Stilecroft gdns Wemb
127 U13 Stiles clo Brom
74 G18 Stillingfleet rd SW13
14 C4 Stillington st SW1
92 K17 Stillness rd SE23
65 V7 Stirling rd E13
31 X5 Stirling rd N17
30 H14 Stirling rd N22
90 A6 Stirling rd SW9
73 T8 Stirling rd W3
23 V9 Stirling rd Harrow
82 H20 Stirling rd Twick
117 T14 Stirling wlk Surb
40 E10 Stiven cres Harrow
48 C14 Stock Orchard cres N7
48 C15 Stock Orchard st N7
65 T8 Stock st E13
56 B6 Stockdale rd Dgnhm
59 X9 Stockdove way Grnfd
108 D6 Stockfield rd SW16
9 X10 Stockingswater la Enf
38 M19 Stockland rd Rom
121 X1 Stockport rd SW16
107 X20 Stockport rd SW16
33 X11 Stocksfield E17
13 N10 Stockton gdns NW7
13 M10 Stockton gdns NW7
30 L3 Stockton gdns N17
30 L3 Stockton rd N17
18 L18 Stockton rd N18
90 D8 Stockwell av SW9
50 C3 Stockwell grn SW9
90 C6 Stockwell grn SW9
90 C6 Stockwell gro SW9
90 C5 Stockwell la SW9
90 D4 Stockwell Pk cres SW9
90 D4 Stockwell Pk rd SW9
90 E7 Stockwell Pk wlk SW9
90 C5 Stockwell rd SW9
76 H18 Stockwell st SE10
90 B2 Stockwell ter SW8
88 F9 Stockwood st E17
110 B20 Stodart rd SE20
124 B1 Stodart rd SE20
87 S20 Stoford clo SW19
49 O9 Stoke Newington Ch st N16
49 V8 Stoke Newington comm N16
49 U9 Stoke Newington High st N16
49 T13 Stoke Newington rd N16
62 D9 Stoke pl NW10
103 V18 Stoke rd Kingst

66 D 12 Stokes rd E6
24 G 15 Stokes rd Croy
62 E 17 Stokesley st W12
17 U 9 Stonard rd N13
55 R 13 Stonard rd Dgnhm
20 H 16 Stondon pk SE23
41 R 3 Stone bldgs WC2
11 Z 15 Stone gro Edg
17 S 2 Stone Hall rd N21
42 K 3 Stone House ct EC2
25 P 8 Stone Pk av Becknhm
52 C 2 Stone rd Worc Pk
26 D 10 Stone rd Brom
52 E 10 Stone st Croy
61 Y 1 Stonebridge pk NW10
31 U 16 Stonebridge rd N15
43 T 16 Stonebridge way Wemb
19 S 20 Stonecot clo Sutton
21 X 20 Stonecroft rd Erith
22 A 16 Stonecroft way Croy
41 V 4 Stonecutter st EC4
98 E 8 Stonefield clo Bxly
40 A 14 Stonefield clo Ruislip
33 T 4 Stonefield st N1
78 B 19 Stonefield way SE7
40 B 14 Stonefield way Ruislip
11 Y 13 Stonegrove est Edg
11 Y 14 Stonegrove est Edg
11 Y 16 Stonegrove gdns Edg
35 R 19 Stonehall av Ilf
49 Y 7 Stoneham rd E5
16 J 18 Stoneham rd N11
85 Y 13 Stonehill clo SW14
85 X 13 Stonehill rd SW14
73 R 14 Stonehill rd W4
109 T 6 Stonehills ct SE21
9 N 5 Stoneleigh av Enf
152 G 7 Stoneleigh av Worc Pk
52 E 10 Stoneleigh cres Epsom
124 G 13 Stoneleigh pk Croy
152 F 10 Stoneleigh Pk rd Epsom
136 H 10 Stoneleigh pl W13
31 V 9 Stoneleigh rd N17
120 H 16 Stoneleigh rd Carsh
35 S 11 Stoneleigh rd Ilf
38 M 15 Stonells rd SW11
48 D 5 Stonenest st N4
142 A 19 Stones End st SE1
95 Y 4 Stoney all SE18
142 N 14 Stoney la E1
109 T 17 Stoney la SE19
142 D 13 Stoney st SE1
12 J 14 Stoneyfields gdns Edg
12 J 13 Stoneyfields la Edg
89 W 9 Stonhouse st SW4
145 P 7 Stonor rd W14
65 T 3 Stopford rd E13
149 Z 11 Stopford rd SE17
78 H 5 Store E16
51 Y 16 Store st E15
140 F 1 Store st WC1
32 L 14 Storey rd E17
29 N 18 Storey rd N6
78 K 4 Storey st E16
140 H 18 Storeys gate SW1
91 R 7 Stories rd SE5
52 D 19 Stork rd E7
151 U 1 Stork's rd SE16
26 A 2 Storksmead rd Edg
46 L 1 Stormont rd N6
12 B 20 Stormont rd N6
89 O 10 Stormont rd SW11
19 O 14 Storrington rd Croy
133 N 2 Story st N1
63 P 12 Stothard st E1
153 S 10 Stoughton av Sutton
70 H 9 Stour av S'hall
64 A 2 Stour rd E3
56 B 20 Stour rd Dgnhm
99 V 8 Stour rd Drtfrd
139 N 5 Stourcliffe st W1
87 R 19 Stourhead clo SW19
100 D 9 Stourton av Felt
18 H 6 Stowe gdns N9
31 S 11 Stowe pl N15
74 J 6 Stowe rd W12
23 P 5 Stoxmead Harrow
61 Y 3 Stracey rd NW10
35 S 9 Stradbroke gro Ilf
48 L 13 Stradbroke rd N5
90 L 16 Stradella rd SE24

35 X 7 Strafford av Ilf
73 U 6 Strafford rd W3
4 E 11 Strafford rd Barnt
82 F 8 Strafford rd Hounsl
83 Z 18 Strafford rd Twick
63 W 8 Straham rd E3
70 B 6 Straight the S'hall
76 G 18 Straightsmouth
91 Z 11 Straker's rd SE15
92 A 11 Straker's rd SE15
141 P 7 Strand WC2
140 L 10 Strand WC2
73 S 17 Strand-On-The-green W4
145 O 1 Strangways ter W14
67 Z 2 Stratford clo Bark
56 J 20 Stratford clo Dgnhm
117 Y 8 Stratford ct New Mald
87 R 10 Stratford gro SW15
139 V 6 Stratford pl W1
65 S 5 Stratford rd E13
27 O 13 Stratford rd NW4
145 V 4 Stratford rd W8
70 A 11 Stratford rd S'hall
122 G 7 Stratford rd Thntn Hth
145 W 3 Stratford studios W8
47 W 20 Stratford vlls NW1
88 H 11 Strath ter SW11
87 U 16 Stratham clo SW18
94 H 15 Strathaven rd SE12
88 H 12 Strathblaine rd SW11
108 C 17 Strathbrook rd SW16
42 F 7 Strathcona rd Wemb
108 D 12 Strathdale SW16
106 F 8 Strathdon dri SW17
100 L 1 Strathearn av Twick
82 M 20 Strathearn av Twick
138 J 8 Strathearn pl W2
105 Y 11 Strathearn rd SW19
153 V 10 Strathearn rd Sutton
77 S 20 Stratheden rd SE3
94 E 1 Stratheden rd SE3
54 F 18 Strathfield gdns Bark
90 A 12 Strathleven rd SW2
28 A 16 Strathmore gdns N3
137 V 13 Strathmore gdns W8
25 S 7 Strathmore gdns Edg
57 U 5 Strathmore gdns Hornch
105 Y 6 Strathmore rd SW19
123 N 17 Strathmore rd Croy
101 S 9 Strathmore rd Tedd
151 T 7 Strathnairn st SE1
46 H 19 Strathray gdns NW3
105 Z 2 Strathville rd SW18
106 A 2 Strathville rd SW18
122 E 6 Strathyre av SW16
8 C 2 Stratton av Enf
155 X 20 Stratton av Wallgtn
119 W 3 Stratton clo SW19
97 Z 7 Stratton clo Bxly Hth
82 F 4 Stratton clo Hounsl
54 J 16 Stratton dri Bark
58 F 17 Stratton gdns Shall
119 X 3 Stratton rd SW19
98 A 8 Stratton rd Bxly Hth
97 Z 8 Stratton rd Bxly Hth
139 Z 13 Stratton st W1
76 F 8 Strattondale st E14
73 Y 7 Strauss rd W4
101 V 6 Strawberry hill Twick
101 V 7 Strawberry Hill clo Twick
101 X 6 Strawberry Hill rd Twick
155 N 5 Strawberry la Carsh
28 F 5 Strawberry vale N2
101 X 6 Strawberry vale Twick
81 R 16 Stream way Blvdr
80 B 17 Streamdale SE2
66 F 4 Streatfield av E6
24 G 10 Streatfield rd Harrow
108 C 14 Streatham Comm north SW16
108 B 15 Streatham Comm south SW16
108 A 6 Streatham ct SE16
108 A 17 Streatham High rd SW16
107 Z 12 Streatham High rd SW16
108 B 3 Streatham hill SW2
90 A 20 Streatham pl SW2
107 P 19 Streatham rd Mitch
140 J 3 Streatham st WC1

107 W 18 Streatham vale SW16
101 O 5 Streathbourne rd SW17
46 L 12 Streatley pl NW3
120 P 1 Streatley rd NW6
64 H 6 Streimer rd E15
62 A 19 Strelley way W3
123 S 17 Stretton rd Croy
102 C 5 Strettoh rd Rich
88 F 19 Strickland rd SW18
93 O 3 Strickland st SE4
52 F 12 Strode rd E7
44 H 19 Strode rd NW10
31 S 9 Strode rd N17
14 K 17 Strode rd SW6
53 O 17 Strone rd E12
52 K 19 Strone rd E7
95 T 13 Strongbow cres SE9
95 U 13 Strongbow rd SE9
74 D 5 Stronsa rd W12
56 M 4 Strood av Rom
104 F 6 Stroud cres SW15
40 K 13 Stroud ga Harrow
48 D 3 Stroud Green rd N4
124 B 15 Stroud Green way Croy
124 B 16 Stroud Grn way Croy
123 Y 15 Stroud rd SE25
105 X 6 Stroud rd SW19
118 C 18 Stroudes clo Worc Pk
148 E 3 Strutton ground SW1
142 M 2 Strype st E1
44 G 2 Stuart av NW9
73 N 1 Stuart av W5
52 E 19 Stuart av Brom
40 D 10 Stuart av Harrow
30 E 5 Stuart cres N22
158 L 6 Stuart cres Croy
97 T 7 Stuart Evans clo Welling
101 U 12 Stuart gro Tedd
106 L 20 Stuart pl Mitch
129 U 13 Stuart rd NW6
92 D 11 Stuart rd SE15
105 X 5 Stuart rd SW19
73 V 1 Stuart rd W3
67 X 2 Stuart rd Bark
15 X 3 Stuart rd Barnt
23 W 10 Stuart rd Harrow
102 C 5 Stuart rd Rich
122 M 8 Stuart rd Thntn Hth
97 R 1 Stuart rd Welling
70 M 20 Stucley rd Hounsl
33 N 1 Stucley st NW1
133 W 4 Studd st N1
87 Y 5 Studholme st SW6
75 N 19 Studholme st SE15
151 X 18 Studholme st SE15
18 R 18 Studio pl SW1
114 L 7 Studland clo Sidcp
116 E 14 Studland rd SE26
59 S 16 Studland rd W7
102 K 16 Studland rd Kingst
74 J 11 Studland rd W6
52 J 20 Studley av E4
33 W 1 Studley av E4
35 O 18 Studley dr Ilf
52 S 12 Studley clo Sidcp
111 O 16 Studley Grange rd W7
52 H 18 Studley rd E7
40 A 3 Studley rd SW4
68 K 2 Studley rd Dgnhm
65 V 1 Stukeley st WC2
140 L 4 Stukeley st WC2
52 H 20 Stukely rd E7
111 O 16 Stumps Hill la Becknhm
92 A 6 Sturdy rd SE15
33 T 8 Sturge av E17
141 Z 17 Sturge st SE1
142 A 17 Sturge st SE1
149 Z 11 Sturgeon rd SE17
52 L 15 Sturges field Chisl
44 M 1 Sturgess av NW4
26 K 20 Sturgess av NW4
64 D 18 Sturry st E14
143 U 7 Stutfield st E1
90 J 7 Styles gdns SW9
125 U 10 Styles way Becknhm
102 H 7 Sudbourne rd SW2
102 J 6 Sudbrook gdns Rich
102 J 6 Sudbrook la Rich
102 J 6 Sudbrook park Rich
87 O 17 Sudbrooke rd SW12
42 F 11 Sudbury av Wemb
112 E 13 Sudbury cres Brom
42 B 15 Sudbury cres Wemb
41 X 11 Sudbury croft Wemb

41 X 9 Sudbury Ct dri Harrow
41 X 10 Sudbury Ct rd Harrow
157 T 7 Sudbury gdns Croy
157 T 8 Sudbury gdns Croy
42 A 16 Sudbury Heights av Grnfd
41 Z 15 Sudbury Heights av Grnfd
41 U 10 Sudbury hill Harrow
41 X 10 Sudbury Hill clo Wemb
54 K 15 Sudbury rd Bark
133 X 9 Sudeley st N1
87 V 12 Sudlow rd SW18
142 A 18 Sudrey st SE1
59 W 6 Suez av Grnfd
9 W 15 Suez rd Enf
20 E 13 Suffield rd E4
31 T 15 Suffield rd N15
142 B 5 Suffield rd SE20
142 E 9 Suffolk la EC4
32 J 13 Suffolk pk E17
142 F 12 Suffolk pl SW1
65 R 10 Suffolk rd E13
62 B 1 Suffolk rd NW10
44 B 20 Suffolk rd NW10
31 O 17 Suffolk rd N15
133 V 7 Suffolk rd SE25
74 F 20 Suffolk rd SW13
67 U 2 Suffolk rd Bark
56 J 15 Suffolk rd Dgnhm
22 F 17 Suffolk rd Harrow
36 H 18 Suffolk rd Ilf
115 T 15 Suffolk rd Sidcp
152 E 3 Suffolk rd Worc Pk
52 E 14 Suffolk st E7
140 F 12 Suffolk st SW1
64 G 6 Sugar House la E15
142 B 9 Sugar Loaf ct EC4
63 P 8 Sugar Loaf wk E2
89 O 10 Sugden rd SW11
116 A 20 Sugden rd Surb
150 E 16 Sugden st SE5
67 Y 6 Sugden way Bark
136 D 19 Sulgrave rd W6
144 C 1 Sulgrave rd W6
74 M 8 Sulgrave rd W6
90 A 19 Sulina rd SW2
66 A 15 Sullivan av E16
87 Y 6 Sullivan ct SW6
87 Y 8 Sullivan rd SW6
11 S 1 Sullivan way Boreham Wd
34 G 14 Sultan rd E11
150 A 18 Sultan st SE5
124 G 3 Sultan st Becknhm
45 X 17 Sumatra rd NW6
113 Z 20 Summer hill Chisl
127 X 2 Summer hill Chisl
128 M 8 Summerfield av NW6
129 N 8 Summerfield av NW6
60 B 12 Summerfield rd W5
94 D 20 Summerfield st SE12
18 D 1 Summerhill gro Enf
31 P 13 Summerhill rd N15
82 B 1 Summerhouse av Hounsl
49 T 7 Summerhouse rd N16
29 S 11 Summerland gdns N10
73 V 1 Summerlands av W3
12 L 12 Summerlee av N12
28 L 13 Summerlee gdns N12
106 C 4 Summerley st SW18
15 X 19 Summers la N12
28 F 1 Summers la N12
15 X 19 Summers row N12
133 T 18 Summers st EC1
29 R 17 Summersby rd N6
106 D 8 Summerstown SW17
153 U 14 Summerville gdns Sutton
83 W 14 Summerwood rd Islwth
25 Y 15 Summit av NW9
25 Y 14 Summit clo NW9
16 G 8 Summit clo N14
25 P 2 Summit clo Edgw
35 O 6 Summit dri Wdfd Grn
33 T 13 Summit rd E17
58 H 1 Summit rd Grnfd
16 F 8 Summit way N14
109 T 19 Summit way SE19
146 F 7 Sumner pl SW7
91 V 1 Sumner rd SE15
151 O 15 Sumner rd SE15

122 H 19 Sumner rd Croy
41 N 1 Sumner rd Harrow
122 G 20 Sumner rd South Croy
141 Z 12 Sumner st SE1
142 A 13 Sumner st SE1
142 H 6 Sun ct EC2
77 V 20 Sun la SE10
134 H 20 Sun st EC2
142 J 1 Sun St pas EC2
61 X 12 Sunbeam rd NW10
89 P 15 Sunburgh rd SW12
12 L 15 Sunbury av NW7
85 Z 11 Sunbury av SW14
12 L 15 Sunbury av NW7
153 R 5 Sunbury rd Sutton
78 H 9 Sunbury st SE18
99 U 4 Suncourt Erith
110 B 7 Suncroft pl SE26
110 F 2 Sunderland rd SE23
72 G 8 Sunderland rd W5
137 W 5 Sunderland ter W2
62 G 19 Sundew av W12
74 F 1 Sundew av W12
123 V 5 Sundial av SE25
77 X 14 Sundorne rd SE7
127 N 1 Sundridge av Brom
113 O 19 Sundridge av Chisl
96 F 6 Sundridge av Welling
113 O 15 Sundridge park Chisl
113 N 17 Sundridge Park mansion Chisl
123 W 19 Sundridge rd Croy
77 V 19 Sunfields pl SE3
97 Z 11 Sunland av Bxly Hth
60 K 3 Sunleigh rd Wemb
59 Y 4 Sunley gdns Grnfd
62 B 19 Sunningdale av W3
67 R 2 Sunningdale av Bark
100 B 4 Sunningdale av Felt
10 M 20 Sunningdale clo Stanm
25 U 17 Sunningdale gdns NW9
127 R 10 Sunningdale rd Brom
153 V 8 Sunningdale rd Sutton
26 L 9 Sunningfields cres NW4
26 L 11 Sunningfields rd NW4
93 R 6 Sunninghill rd SE13
123 Y 7 Sunny bank SE25
61 V 1 Sunny cres NW10
26 L 9 Sunny gdns NW4
26 J 10 Sunny hill NW4
26 J 8 Sunny Hill park NW4
157 O 13 Sunny Nook gdns S Croy
9 U 7 Sunny Rd the Enf
20 G 3 Sunny Side dri E4
25 Y 14 Sunny view NW9
28 J 1 Sunny way N12
123 V 7 Sunnycroft rd SE25
82 K 5 Sunnycroft rd Hounsl
58 H 13 Sunnycroft rd S'hall
12 M 18 Sunnydale gdns NW7
94 H 12 Sunnydale rd SE12
20 L 16 Sunnydene av E4
42 E 20 Sunnydene gdns Wemb
110 G 10 Sunnydene st SE26
13 R 12 Sunnyfield NW7
108 A 9 Sunnyhill rd SW16
153 Y 5 Sunnyhurst clo Sutton
121 W 5 Sunnymead av Mitch
25 Y 20 Sunnymead rd NW9
86 J 14 Sunnymead rd SW15
152 A 18 Sunnymede av Epsom
35 Z 13 Sunnymede dri Ilf
105 S 15 Sunnyside SW19
51 N 3 Sunnyside rd E10
45 W 9 Sunnyside rd NW2
47 Y 1 Sunnyside rd N19
72 F 4 Sunnyside rd W5
54 C 9 Sunnyside rd Ilf
101 R 10 Sunnyside rd Tedd
18 J 12 Sunnyside Rd east N9
18 J 11 Sunnyside Rd north N9
18 J 12 Sunnyside Rd south N9
21 R 10 Sunnyvale Wdfd Grn
91 O 10 Sunray av SE24

127 T 13 Sunray av Brom
100 E 7 Sunrise clo Felt
20 E 4 Sunset av E4
91 O 15 Sunset av Wdfd Grn
123 T 3 Sunset gdns SE19
90 M 10 Sunset rd SE5
91 N 10 Sunset rd SE5
4 F 9 Sunset view Barnt
120 M 2 Sunshine way Mitch
92 A 3 Sunwell st SE15
116 F 19 Surbiton cres Kingst
116 F 14 Surbiton ct Surb
116 J 10 Surbiton Hall clo Kingst
116 M 12 Surbiton hill Surb
116 M 14 Surbiton Hill pk Surb
117 P 11 Surbiton Hill pk Surb
116 J 10 Surbiton Hill rd Kingst
116 H 8 Surbiton rd Kingst
78 K 8 Surgeon st SE18
48 A 16 Surr st N7
129 V 18 Surrendale pl W9
154 G 4 Surrey gro Sutton
88 J 2 Surrey la SW11
110 A 1 Surrey mount SE23
92 E 12 Surrey rd SE15
67 U 2 Surrey rd Bark
56 J 14 Surrey rd Dgnhm
22 M 16 Surrey rd Harrow
125 S 20 Surrey rd W Wrhm
141 X 17 Surrey row SE1
150 K 8 Surrey sq SE17
65 X 10 Surrey st E13
141 P 8 Surrey st WC2
156 L 4 Surrey st Croy
150 K 8 Surrey ter SE17
109 O 16 Surridge gdns SE19
38 J 11 Susan clo Rom
94 J 5 Susan d SE3
127 Y 1 Susan wood Chisl
113 X 20 Susan wood Chisl
64 F 18 Susannah st E14
83 S 8 Sussex av Islwhm
84 B 15 Sussex clo Twick
40 G 18 Sussex cres Grnfd
30 K 17 Sussex gdns N4
138 H 6 Sussex gdns W2
90 H 11 Sussex gro SW9
31 N 15 Sussex ms NW1
138 H 8 Sussex Ms east W2
138 G 9 Sussex Ms west W2
131 O 16 Sussex pl NW1
138 H 8 Sussex pl W2
144 C 9 Sussex pl W6
74 L 13 Sussex pl W6
81 V 19 Sussex pl Erith
118 B 8 Sussex pl New Mald
66 J 5 Sussex rd E6
90 H 10 Sussex rd SW9
154 M 15 Sussex rd Carsh
81 V 19 Sussex rd Erith
22 M 16 Sussex rd Harrow
23 N 17 Sussex rd Harrow
122 A 10 Sussex rd Mitch
118 B 8 Sussex rd New Mald
157 P 13 Sussex rd S Croy
70 A 8 Sussex rd S'hall
15 R 13 Sussex rd Sidcp
125 S 20 Sussex rd W Wrhm
14 L 16 Sussex ring N12
138 H 8 Sussex sq W2
65W 10 Sussex st E13
147 Z 10 Sussex st SW1
47 Z 5 Sussex way N19
48 A 7 Sussex way N4
6 D 16 Sussex way Barnt
28 B 16 Sutcliffe clo NW11
94 J 13 Sutcliffe park SE9
97 U 4 Sutcliffe rd SE18
97 U 4 Sutcliffe rd Welling
129 V 19 Sutherland av W13
130 B 15 Sutherland av W9
96 L 12 Sutherland av Welling
25 S 14 Sutherland ct NW9
86 B 9 Sutherland gdns SW13
118 J 19 Sutherland gdns Worc Pk
105 U 1 Sutherland gro SW18
87 U 20 Sutherland gro SW18
101 U 12 Sutherland gro Tedd
137 T 5 Sutherland pl W2
32 G 9 Sutherland rd E17
63 Y 6 Sutherland rd E3
31 X 3 Sutherland rd N17
18 L 5 Sutherland rd N9
59 Z 18 Sutherland rd W13
74 A 16 Sutherland rd W4

81 S 7 Sutherland rd Blvdr
122 F 18 Sutherland rd Croy
9 S 19 Sutherland rd Enf
58 E 17 Sutherland rd S'hall
150 A 12 Sutherland sq SE17
147 Z 11 Sutherland st SW1
150 B 12 Sutherland wlk SE17
77 Y 20 Sutlej rd SE7
48 B 19 Sutterton st N7
154 B 11 Sutton arc Sutton
154 A 3 Sutton Comm rd Sutton
153 Y 2 Sutton Comm rd Sutton
119 U 18 Sutton Comm rd Sutton
4 D 16 Sutton cres Barnt
73 V 17 Sutton ct W4
73V 16 Sutton Ct rd W4
154 C 13 Sutton Ct rd Sutton
82 J 3 Sutton dene Hounsl
123 V 12 Sutton gdns SE25
67 V 5 Sutton gdns Bark
154 G 10 Sutton gro Sutton
70 G 20 Sutton Hall rd Hounsl
73 W 13 Sutton la W4
82 E 6 Sutton la Hounsl
73 U 16 Sutton La south W4
154 A 13 Sutton Pk rd Sutton
50 C 15 Sutton pl E9
65 R 12 Sutton rd E13
32 F 6 Sutton rd E17
29 P 5 Sutton rd N10
67 W 4 Sutton rd Bark
67 U 5 Sutton rd Bark
82 J 1 Sutton rd Hounsl
140 G 5 Sutton row W1
82 F 2 Sutton sq Hounsl
63 O 18 Sutton st E1
128 B 19 Sutton way W10
62 M 13 Sutton way W10
82 F 1 Sutton way Hounsl
106 D 3 Swaby rd SW18
88 C 18 Swaffield rd SW18
122 M 10 Swain rd Thntn Hth
47 R 4 Swain's la N6
106 L 16 Swain's rd SW17
74 C 4 Swainson rd W3
99 T 13 Swaisland dri Drtfd
99 Z 15 Swaisland rd Drtfd
99 V 9 Swale rd Drtfd
81 U 14 Swalecliffe rd Blvdr
111 P 9 Swallands rd SE6
139 Z 6 Swallow pl W1
140 C 11 Swallow st W1
77 W 14 Swallowfield rd SE7
100 B 10 Swan clo Felt
15 R 9 Swan ct N20
15 R 9 Swan ct N29
142 F 10 Swan la E4
15 R 9 Swan la N20
150 J 3 Swan mead SE1
75 R 5 Swan rd SE16
100 B 11 Swan rd Felt
58 K 17 Swan rd S'hall
142 C 19 Swan st SE1
84 A 7 Swan st Islwth
9 S 8 Swan way Enf
142 F 10 Swan wharf EC4
10 O 14 Swan wlk SW3
48 H 19 Swan yd N1
33 U 2 Swanage rd E4
88 D 16 Swanage rd SW18
98 F 3 Swanbridge rd Bxly Hth
135 O 15 Swanfield st E2
97 U 3 Swanley rd Welling
136 H 14 Swanscombe rd W11
74 B 13 Swanscombe rd W4
9 O 14 Swansea rd Enf
105 R 1 Swanton gdns SW19
81 T 19 Swanton rd Erith
86 D 18 Swanwick clo SW15
64 C 11 Swanwick rd E3
81 S 17 Swaylands clo Blvdr
143 U 9 Swedenborg sq E1
143 U 9 Swedenborg st E1
143 O 19 Sweeney cres SE1
68 G 12 Sweet Briar grn N9
18 F 11 Sweet Briar gro N9
18 F 14 Sweet Briar wk N18
65 T 8 Swete st E13
94 G 5 Sweyn pl SE3
40 K 7 Swift clo Harrow
87 U 2 Swift st SW6
112 U 20 Swiftsden way Brom
137 N 1 Swinbrook rd W10
124 C 16 Swinburn cres Croy
86 H 12 Swinburne rd SW15

42 H 18 Swinderby rd Wemb
114 A 14 Swindon st W12
74 K 2 Swindon st W12
90 H 7 Swinfield gdns SW9
79 W 17 Swingate la SE18
50 J 16 Swinnerton st E9
43 T 5 Swinton clo Wemb
133 N 13 Swinton pl WC1
133 O 13 Swinton st WC1
113 V 9 Swinton gdns SE9
72 C 12 Swyncombe av W5
50 L 2 Sybourn st E17
72 G 8 Sycamore av W5
96 L 15 Sycamore av Sidcp
74 L 7 Sycamore gdns W12
136 A 20 Sycamore gdns W6
43 W 1 Sycamore gro NW9
117 Z 5 Sycamore gro New Mald
118 A 4 Sycamore gro New Mald
104 M 15 Sycamore rd SW19
134 A 17 Sycamore st EC1
122 E 10 Sycamore way Thntr Hth
110 A 12 Sydenham av SE26
109 Y 7 Sydenham hill SE26
110 B 8 Sydenham pk SE26
110 C 7 Sydenham Pk rd SE26
110 G 11 Sydenham rd SE26
157 N 1 Sydenham rd Croy
123 P 15 Sydenham ri SE23
110 A 3 Sydenham ri SE23
109 Z 3 Sydenham ri SE23
110 A 2 Sydenham rise SE23
49 V 11 Sydner N16
146 G 8 Sydney clo SW3
26 L 16 Sydney gro NW4
146 H 8 Sydney ms SW3
146 H 7 Sydney pl SW7
29 R 5 Sydney rd N10
30 F 12 Sydney rd N8
80 H 8 Sydney rd SE2
119 P 3 Sydney rd SW20
71 Z 3 Sydney rd W13
72 A 5 Sydney rd W13
124 J 2 Sydney rd Becknhm
97 X 10 Sydney rd Bxly Hth
8 B 14 Sydney rd Enf
153 X 9 Sydney rd Ilf
114 J 9 Sydney rd Sidcp
153 X 9 Sydney rd Sutton
101 V 13 Sydney rd Tedd
84 A 16 Sydney rd Twick
21 S 15 Sydney rd Wdfd Grn
146 J 8 Sydney st SW3
13 P 18 Sylvan av NW7
30 E 1 Sylvan av N22
27 Z 7 Sylvan av N3
38 C 18 Sylvan av Rom
116 F 19 Sylvan gdns Surb
75 N 17 Sylvan gro SE15
151 Y 16 Sylvan gro SE15
109 S 19 Sylvan hill SE19
34 E 15 Sylvan rd E11
33 N 15 Sylvan rd E17
52 C 17 Sylvan rd E7
123 V 1 Sylvan rd E17
109 U 20 Sylvan rd SE19
54 A 7 Sylvan rd Ilf
109 V 20 Sylvan Rd est SE19
55 P 11 Sylvan way Dgnhm
159 Z 8 Sylvan way Wkhm
113 T 16 Sylvester av Chisl
50 A 18 Sylvester path E8
50 A 17 Sylvester rd E8
28 F 7 Sylvester rd N2
42 E 14 Sylvester rd Wemb
43 S 20 Sylvia gdns Wemb
84 D 3 Symons st SW3
72 A 20 Syon la Brentf
71 V 16 Syon la Islwth
84 D 2 Syon park Islwth
71 V 18 Syon Pk gdns Islwth

T

142 D 18 Tabard st SE1
150 F 1 Tabard st SE1
65 T 12 Tabernacle av E13
134 G 18 Tabernacle st EC2
89 W 12 Tableer av SW4
47 Z 11 Tabley rd N7
153 T 15 Tabor gdns Sutton
105 U 17 Tabor gro SW19
74 K 9 Tabor rd W6
148 B 6 Tachbrook ms SW1

48 E 9 Tachbrook st SW1
46 C 18 Tadema rd SW10
36 E 15 Tadmor st W12
18 D 10 Tadworth av New Mald
57 Y 13 Tadworth pde Hornch
44 G 7 Tadworth rd NW2
20 K 5 Taffeys how Mitch
64 F 8 Taft st E3
23 R 16 Tailworth st E1
27 B 12 Talacre st NW5
28 F 11 Talbot av N2
3 U 13 Talbot clo N15
26 G 16 Talbot cres NW4
54 M 7 Talbot gdns Ilf
36 L 6 Talbot gro W11
36 K 7 Talbot ms W11
93 Z 3 Talbot pl SE13
94 A 3 Talbot pl SE13
54 B 3 Talbot place SE3
66 H 4 Talbot rd E6
52 E 12 Talbot rd E7
44 B 18 Talbot rd NW10
31 V 13 Talbot rd N15
29 W 6 Talbot rd N22
29 O 19 Talbot rd N6
37 P 6 Talbot rd W13
71 Y 2 Talbot rd W2
37 U 4 Talbot rd W2
26 H 7 Talbot rd Brom
55 O 10 Talbot rd Carsh
58 B 19 Talbot rd Dgnhm
23 X 9 Talbot rd Harrow
83 Z 10 Talbot rd Islwth
70 C 10 Talbot rd S'hall
23 O 9 Talbot rd Thntn Hth
83 U 20 Talbot rd Twick
101 U 1 Talbot rd Twick
42 G 17 Talbot rd Wemb
138 G 6 Talbot sq W2
42 F 15 Talbot yd SE1
91 V 2 Talfourd pl SE15
11 T 2 Talfourd rd SE15
94 V 14 Talgarth rd W14
109 W 9 Talisman sq SE26
42 L 9 Talisman way Wdfd Grn
23 U 3 Tallack clo Harrow
50 M 4 Tallack rd E10
77 W 16 Tallis gro SE7
15 U 8 Tallis st EC4
15 R 17 Tallyho' corner N12
83 T 17 Talma gdns Twick
90 G 12 Talma rd SW2
92 D 20 Talmage clo SE23
142 H 8 Talnot ct EC3
64 E 10 Talwin st E3
78 B 10 Tamar st SE7
62 E 20 Tamarisk sq W12
129 S 16 Tampin ms W9
21 N 18 Tamworth av Wdfd Grn
121 R 4 Tamworth la Mitch
121 S 7 Tamworth pk Mitch
145 T 14 Tamworth rd SW6
121 T 8 Tamworth vlls Mitch
30 J 20 Tancred rd N4
44 C 19 Tanfield av NW2
156 L 8 Tanfield rd Croy
58 T 9 Tangier rd Rich
10 F 10 Tanglewood clo Stanm
86 E 17 Tangley gro SW15
57 Z 19 Tangmere cres Hornch
132 L 13 Tankerton st WC1
107 Y 17 Tankerville rd SW16
44 K 7 Tankridge rd NW2
148 K 18 Tanner st SE1
143 O 18 Tanner st SE1
54 B 18 Tanner st Bark
92 M 3 Tanners hill SE4
93 N 1 Tanners hill SE4
36 C 10 Tanners la Ilf
111 Z 20 Tannery clo Dgnhm
110 E 12 Tannsfeld rd SE26
141 T 18 Tanswell st SE1
65 P 16 Tant av E16
89 N 20 Tantallon rd SW12
37 X 11 Tantony gro Rom
156 K 3 Tanworth pl Croy
156 K 3 Tanworth rd Croy
46 L 11 Tanza rd NW3
64 F 17 Tapley st E14
135 X 17 Tapp st E1
92 B 7 Tappersfield rd SE15
4 G 13 Tapster st Barnt
91 T 12 Tarbert rd SE22
12 E 20 Tariff rd N17
110 A 3 Tarleton gdns SE23
65 R 19 Tarling rd E16

143 Y 6 Tarling st E1
63 O 18 Tarling st E1
7 O 15 Tarn bank Enf
95 U 20 Tarnwood pk SE9
107 X 8 Tarrington clo SW16
149 Y 10 Tarver st SE17
76 E 18 Tarves way SE10
46 M 16 Tasker rd NW3
90 A 8 Tasman rd SW2
17 Z 19 Tasmania ter N18
144 K 14 Tasso rd W6
43 X 19 Tatam rd NW10
148 J 7 Tate gallery SW1
78 E 3 Tate st E16
153 X 12 Tate of Sutton
92 H 16 Tatnell rd SE23
95 R 12 Tattersall clo SE9
49 U 1 Tatton cres N16
150 G 7 Tatum st SE17
118 K 3 Taunton av SW20
82 M 4 Taunton av Hounsl
83 N 3 Taunton av Hounsl
24 K 9 Taunton av Stanm
99 O 6 Taunton clo Bxly Hth
119 X 20 Taunton clo Sutton
7 T 11 Taunton dri Enf
131 O 18 Taunton ms NW1
131 N 17 Taunton rd SE12
54 C 13 Taunton rd SE12
58 K 2 Taunton rd Grnfd
24 K 8 Taunton way Stanm
32 G 11 Tavestock av E17
60 A 6 Tavistock av Grnfd
59 Z 7 Tavistock av Grnfd
16 E 2 Tavistock cres N14
137 O 2 Tavistock cres W10
112 A 9 Tavistock cres Mitch
121 Z 9 Tavistock cres Mitch
54 H 13 Tavistock gro Croy
123 N 18 Tavistock gro Croy
137 N 5 Tavistock ms W11
132 H 16 Tavistock pl WC1
52 B 19 Tavistock rd E15
34 E 11 Tavistock rd E7
52 B 11 Tavistock rd E7
62 D 5 Tavistock rd NW10
31 N 19 Tavistock rd N4
137 O 3 Tavistock rd W11
120 G 20 Tavistock rd Carsh
123 N 19 Tavistock rd Croy
25 O 5 Tavistock rd Edg
97 T 2 Tavistock rd Welling
132 G 16 Tavistock sq WC1
140 M 9 Tavistock st WC2
141 N 7 Tavistock st WC2
47 Z 9 Tavistock ter N19
132 F 16 Taviton st WC1
75 T 10 Tawny way SE16
39 S 4 Tay way Rom
83 U 16 Tayben av Twick
89 P 10 Taybridge rd SW8
85 S 4 Taylor av Rich
101 N 12 Taylor clo Hampt
38 E 1 Taylor clo Rom
106 K 18 Taylor rd Mitch
155 R 11 Taylor rd Wallgtn
78 M 11 Taylor st SE18
44 A 20 Taylor's la NW10
62 B 16 Taylors grn W3
109 Y 10 Taylors la SE26
4 G 6 Taylors la Barnt
110 B 3 Taymount ri SE23
58 E 9 Taywood av Grnfd
135 U 8 Teale st E2
31 T 3 Tebworth rd N17
66 D 13 Tedder gdns E6
158 E 18 Tedder rd South Croy
101 X 11 Teddington lodge Tedd
101 W 11 Teddington pk Tedd
101 W 10 Teddington Pk rd Tedd
147 N 11 Tedworth gdns SW3
147 N 12 Tedworth sq SW3
59 V 6 Tees av Grnfd
83 Z 2 Teesdale av Islwth
83 Z 2 Teesdale gdns Islwth
34 B 20 Teesdale rd E11
135 V 11 Teesdale st E2
135 V 10 Teesdale yd E2
123 X 17 Teevan clo Croy
123 X 18 Teevan rd Croy
25 N 8 Teignmouth clo SE9
89 X 11 Teignmouth clo SW4
45 O 16 Teignmouth rd NW2
107 O 17 Teignmouth rd Mitch
97 T 3 Teignmouth rd Welling
45 Z 10 Telegraph hill NW3
86 K 17 Telegraph rd SW15

142 F 4 Telegraph st EC2
107 W 1 Telferscot rd SW12
108 A 2 Telford av SW2
107 Y 2 Telford av SW2
26 E 20 Telford rd NW9
16 H 18 Telford rd N11
114 D 5 Telford rd SE9
128 K 20 Telford rd W10
58 K 18 Telford st S'hall
62 A 15 Telford way W3
66 J 7 Telham rd E6
91 U 11 Tell gro SE22
95 P 1 Telison av SE18
89 P 18 Temperley rd SW12
57 W 18 Tempest way Rainhm
45 U 17 Templar ho NW2
100 H 17 Templar pl Hampt
50 D 14 Templar rd E9
32 J 3 Templar st SE5
27 W 19 Templars av NW11
27 X 8 Templars cres N3
141 U 8 Temple av EC4
15 T 3 Temple av N20
158 L 4 Temple av Croy
56 D 3 Temple av Dgnhm
27 V 8 Temple clo N3
27 Y 16 Temple Fortune hill NW11
27 X 17 Temple Fortune la NW11
27 W 18 Temple gdns NW11
55 V 9 Temple gdns Dgnhm
27 X 19 Temple gro NW11
27 Y 10 Temple gro Enf
141 U 7 Temple av EC4
51 V 14 Temple Mills la E15
51 P 13 Temple Mills rd E15
141 P 9 Temple pl WC2
66 C 3 Temple rd E6
45 N 10 Temple rd NW2
44 M 11 Temple rd NW2
30 C 13 Temple rd N8
73 V 9 Temple rd W4
72 F 9 Temple rd W5
157 O 9 Temple rd Croy
82 L 9 Temple rd Hounsl
85 N 6 Temple rd Rich
85 U 12 Temple sheen SW14
85 T 13 Temple Sheen rd SW14
51 Y 10 Temple st E11
135 V 9 Temple st E2
154 G 6 Temple way Sutton
135 Z 3 Templecombe rd E9
63 O 3 Templecombe rd E9
119 R 11 Templecombe way Mrdn
59 W 15 Templeman rd W7
20 C 12 Templeton av E4
18 C 13 Templeton clo N15
123 P 1 Templeton clo SE19
145 U 6 Templeton pl SW5
31 O 18 Templeton rd N15
60 B 14 Templewood W13
46 B 10 Templewood av NW3
46 B 10 Templewood gdns NW3
46 B 10 Temsford clo Har
24 B 8 Tenby av Harrow
89 Z 20 Tenby clo Rom
37 Y 19 Tenby clo Rom
32 G 15 Tenby rd E17
25 N 6 Tenby rd SE3
9 P 13 Tenby rd Enf
37 Y 19 Tenby rd Rom
97 V 1 Tenby rd Welling
143 W 13 Tench st E1
53 R 4 Tenda rd SE16
37 T 15 Tendring way Rom
107 X 2 Tenham av SW2
36 C 11 Tenison st W1
24 L 4 Tenison way SE1
138 A 8 Tenniel clo W2
37 Z 8 Tenniel pl W2
142 E 17 Tennis st SE1
123 T 10 Tennison rd SE25
8 E 7 Tenniswood rd Enf
52 F 1 Tennyson av E11
53 P 20 Tennyson av E12
25 V 11 Tennyson av NW9
118 K 12 Tennyson av New Mald
101 W 2 Tennyson av Twick
51 Z 19 Tennyson rd E15
32 L 18 Tennyson rd NW1
111 S 9 Tennyson rd NW6
129 P 5 Tennyson rd NW6
110 F 17 Tennyson rd SE20
106 C 14 Tennyson rd SW19
59 V 20 Tennyson rd W7

82 M 3 Tennyson rd Hounsl
89 S 5 Tennyson st SW8
57 U 6 Tennyson way Hornch
70 G 8 Tensing rd S'hall
135 V 17 Tent st E1
70 H 12 Tentelow la S'hall
143 N 2 Tenter ground E1
142 E 1 Tenter st EC2
56 B 5 Tenterden av Dgnhm
20 C 10 Tenterden clo NW4
42 J 2 Tenterden clo Harrow
27 R 11 Tenterden dri NW4
27 P 11 Tenterden gdns NW4
27 O 11 Tenterden gro NW4
31 T 2 Tenterden rd N17
139 Y 6 Tenterden st W1
123 Y 16 Tenterten rd Croy
123 Y 16 Tenterton gdns Croy
91 R 13 Terbach way SE22
56 D 5 Terling rd Dgnhm
24 L 4 Terminus pl SW1
86 C 5 Terrace gdns SW13
84 K 17 Terrace la Rich
65 U 4 Terrace rd E13
50 D 20 Terrace rd E9
129 S 3 Terrace the NW6
21 S 18 Terrace the Wdfd Grn
147 P 16 Terrace wlk SW11
56 A 16 Terrace wlk Dgnhm
23 Z 16 Terrace wlk Dgnhm
107 S 5 Terrapin rd SW17
30 A 6 Terrick rd N22
62 K 18 Terrick st W12
22 E 10 Terrilands Pinn
30 L 14 Terront rd N15
75 V 11 Terry La gdns SE8
133 V 6 Tetbury pl N1
146 B 19 Tetcott rd SW10
29 P 10 Tetherdown N10
126 E 4 Tetty way Brom
97 R 1 Teviot rd Welling
64 F 13 Teviot st E14
92 A 20 Tewkesbury av SE23
22 C 17 Tewkesbury av Pinn
31 O 19 Tewkesbury clo N15
25 U 10 Tewkesbury gdns SE9
31 O 19 Tewkesbury rd N15
120 F 19 Tewkesbury rd Carsh
16 H 18 Tewkesbury ter N11
79 V 13 Tewson rd SE18
8 B 20 Teynham av Enf
30 M 5 Teynton ter N17
31 X 8 Thackeray av N17
40 J 4 Thackeray dri Harrow
55 O 2 Thackeray dri Rom
66 B 6 Thackeray rd E6
89 S 5 Thackeray rd SW8
137 Y 20 Thackeray rd W4
129 Z 11 Thakeham clo SE26
62 A 20 Thames av Grnfd
59 V 6 Thames av Grnfd
85 W 5 Thames bank SW14
75 Z 1 Thames pl E1
78 A 4 Thames rd E16
73 R 17 Thames rd W4
68 A 8 Thames rd Bark
67 W 9 Thames rd Bark
99 W 8 Thames rd Drtfrd
102 G 17 Thames side Kingst
116 G 2 Thames side Kingst
76 F 16 Thames St SE10
38 L 8 Thameshill av Rom
48 D 9 Thame vlls N7
157 T 6 Thanescroft gdns Croy
156 M 3 Thanet pl Croy
157 N 7 Thanet pl Croy
98 E 19 Thanet rd Bxly
132 J 14 Thanet st WC1
155 X 11 Tharp rd Wallgtn
15 R 3 Thatcham gdns N20
37 Y 12 Thatches gro Rom
141 U 3 Thavies inn EC4
114 B 5 Thaxsted rd SE9
139 U 4 Thayer st W1
124 J 1 Thayers Farm rd Becknhm
27 O 15 The approach NW4
9 N 8 The approach Enf
16 P 15 The avenue N11
154 K 16 The Beeches av Carsh
146 B 10 The boltons SW10
41 X 13 The bottons Wemb
41 X 12 The bottoms Wemb
20 G 7 The bracken E4

18 C 2 The brackens Enf
20 L 14 The bramblings E4
60 H 19 The broadway W5
60 G 20 The broadway W5
22 D 13 The chase Pinn
72 E 16 The dell Brentf
14 L 20 The drive N1
118 F 12 The grange New Mald
105 O 13 The green SW19
119 R 9 The green Mrdn
159 T 6 The grove W Wkhm
96 M 20 The hollies Sidcup
13 S 9 The lincolns NW7
40 D 16 The link Grnfd
32 H 13 The links E17
99 N 11 The marlowes Drtfd
63 Y 19 The mitre E14
118 A 1 The moat New Mald
6 H 15 The pines N14
94 D 10 The priory SE3
25 X 15 The retreat NW9
62 A 17 The tee W3
61 X 20 The tiltwood W3
72 K 3 The vine W5
28 G 9 The walks N2
88 M 8 Theatre st SW11
133 V 4 Theberton st N1
141 T 14 Theed st SE1
95 P 2 Thelma gdns SE3
101 X 14 Thelma gro Tedd
22 L 5 Theobald cres Harrow
156 J 2 Theobald rd Croy
150 E 3 Theobald st E1
133 O 20 Theobald's rd WC1
15 P 14 Theobalds av N12
93 V 15 Theodore rd SE13
122 A 15 Therapia la Croy
121 X 17 Therapia la Croy
92 C 15 Therapia rd SE22
74 G 12 Theresa rd W6
74 G 12 Theresa st W6
76 E 11 Thermopylae ga E14
110 F 17 Thesiger rd SE20
89 X 3 Thessaly rd SW8
148 A 19 Thessaly rd SW8
68 K 2 Thetford gdns Dgnhm
68 K 2 Thetford rd Dgnhm
117 Z 13 Thetford rd New Mald
118 A 12 Thetford rd New Maiden
73 O 17 Thetis ter Rich
21 X 19 Theydon gro Wdfd Grn
50 C 5 Theydon rd E5
50 L 9 Theydon st E19
154 E 8 Thicket cres Sutton
109 X 17 Thicket gro SE20
55 U 17 Thicket gro Dgnhm
109 Y 18 Thicket rd SE20
110 A 16 Thicket rd SE20
154 E 7 Thicket rd Sutton
53 S 13 Third av E12
65 T 9 Third av E13
33 F 15 Third av E17
128 M 15 Third av W10
74 C 3 Third av W3
69 V 5 Third av Dgnhm
8 G 17 Third av Enf
37 T 17 Third av Rom
42 G 6 Third av Wemb
101 S 4 Third Cross rd Twick
43 U 13 Third way Wemb
25 X 4 Thirleby rd SE18
148 C 3 Thirleby rd SW1
60 C 8 Thirlmere av Grnfd
42 E 4 Thirlmere gdns Wemb
29 T 6 Thirlmere rd N10
107 X 10 Thirlmere rd SW16
98 K 3 Thirlmere rd Bxly Hth
40 J 17 Thirsk clo Grnfd
123 P 8 Thirsk rd SE25
89 N 8 Thirsk rd SW11
107 P 17 Thirsk rd Mitch
63 R 19 Thirza st E1
40 C 10 Thisledene av Harrow
146 C 9 Thistle gro SW5
24 G 6 Thistlecroft gdns Stanm
50 B 10 Thistlewaite rd E5
71 P 18 Thistleworth clo Islwth
41 W 11 Thomas A beckett clo W11
88 H 9 Thomas Baines rd SW11

93 P 19 Thomas la SE6
143 S 11 Thomas More st SE1
63 Z 16 Thomas rd E14
64 A 16 Thomas rd E14
78 K 10 Thomas st SE18
85 S 6 Thompson av Rich
91 V 16 Thompson rd SE22
56 C 10 Thompson rd Dgnhm
150 A 17 Thompsons av SE5
156 F 1 Thomson cres Croy
122 F 19 Thomson cres Croy
23 U 19 Thomson rd Harrow
151 S 7 Thorburn sq SE1
134 B 11 Thoresby st N1
116 A 17 Thorkhill rd Surb
10 A 6 Thorn av Bushey Watf
12 D 20 Thorn bank Edg
127 X 14 Thorn clo Brom
58 E 8 Thorn clo Grnfd
18 L 18 Thornaby gdns N18
71 P 20 Thornbury av Islwth
89 Z 16 Thornbury rd SW2
90 A 17 Thornbury rd SW2
83 R 4 Thornbury rd Islwth
71 R 19 Thornbury rd Islwth
50 L 10 Thornby rd E5
89 Z 17 Thorncliffe rd SW4
70 E 12 Thorncliffe rd S'hall
91 T 12 Thorncombe rd SE22
39 Y 18 Thorncroft Hornch
154 A 9 Thorncroft rd Sutton
153 Z 10 Thorncroft rd Sutton
137 W 18 Thorncroft st SW8
106 C 5 Thorndean st SW18
72 H 20 Thorndene av N11
148 E 8 Thorndike st SW1
152 C 9 Thorndon gdns Epsom
65 N 17 Thorne clo E16
117 V 8 Thorne clo New Mald
86 B 6 Thorne pas SW13
148 L 20 Thorne rd SW8
117 V 8 Thorne rd New Mald
65 R 17 Thorne st E16
86 B 6 Thorne st SW13
156 H 12 Thorneloe gdns Croy
125 T 6 Thornes clo Beckham
125 T 6 Thornes clo Becknhm
127 X 7 Thornet Wood rd Brom
73 T 12 Thorney Hedge rd W4
148 J 6 Thorney st SW1
27 S 3 Thornfield av NW7
74 K 5 Thornfield rd W12
136 A 17 Thornfield rd W12
93 U 14 Thornford rd SE13
65 W 3 Thorngrove rd E13
51 W 16 Thornham gro E15
76 E 18 Thornham st SE10
132 G 18 Thornhaugh ms WC1
132 H 19 Thornhaugh st WC1
79 V 19 Thornhill av SE18
133 O 7 Thornhill bridge N1
133 O 1 Thornhill cres N1
51 S 7 Thornhill gdns E10
54 H 20 Thornhill gdns Bark
116 A 19 Thornhill gdns Surb
133 R 2 Thornhill gro N1
51 R 7 Thornhill rd E10
51 P 2 Thornhill rd N1
133 S 2 Thornhill rd N1
122 M 17 Thornhill rd Croy
133 O 2 Thornhill sq N1
108 J 9 Thornlaw rd SE27
40 L 7 Thornley dri Harrow
76 L 13 Thornley pl SE10
111 U 3 Thornsbeach rd SE6
123 Z 4 Thornsett rd SE20
124 A 5 Thornsett rd SE20
106 B 3 Thornsett rd SW18
107 Y 2 Thornton av SW2
74 B 11 Thornton av W4
122 C 15 Thornton av Croy
125 O 3 Thornton dene Becknhm
107 X 1 Thornton gdns SW12
105 R 18 Thornton hill SW19
51 X 6 Thornton rd E11
89 W 19 Thornton rd SW12
85 X 9 Thornton rd SW14
4 E 13 Thornton rd Barnt
81 T 9 Thornton rd Blvdr
112 F 12 Thornton rd Brom
120 J 18 Thornton rd Carsh
53 Y 13 Thornton rd Ilf

122 E 13 Thornton rd Thntn Hth
105 P 17 Thornton Rd east SW19
90 E 5 Thornton st SW9
28 B 17 Thornton way NW11
56 M 5 Thorntons Farm av Rom
78 B 14 Thorntree rd SE7
93 N 3 Thornville st SE4
94 A 13 Thornwood rd SE13
93 Z 13 Thornwood rd SE13
52 A 16 Thorogood gdns E15
30 B 2 Thorold rd N22
53 Z 7 Thorold rd Ilf
54 C 4 Thorold rd Ilf
148 G 20 Thorparch rd SW8
89 Y 1 Thorpatch rd SW8
32 L 6 Thorpe cres E17
33 V 6 Thorpe Hall rd E17
33 T 7 Thorpe rd E7
66 F 4 Thorpe rd E6
52 C 11 Thorpe rd E7
31 T 19 Thorpe rd N15
54 D 20 Thorpe rd Bark
102 K 18 Thorpe rd Kingst
74 G 3 Thorpebank rd W12
35 Y 12 Thorpedale gdns Ilf
48 B 5 Thorpedale rd N4
110 B 5 Thorpewood av SE26
109 R 11 Thorsden way SE19
45 R 10 Thorverton rd NW2
63 V 7 Thoydon rd E3
107 U 13 Thrale rd SW16
142 C 14 Thrale st SE1
143 P 2 Thrawl st E1
142 G 6 Threadneedle st EC2
63 Y 19 Three Colt st E14
135 Y 16 Three Colts la E2
63 N 11 Three Colts la E2
98 J 6 Three corners Bxly Hth
121 N 6 Three Kings rd Mitch
139 W 8 Three Kings' yd W1
64 F 9 Three Mill la E3
63 X 13 Three Oak la SE1
142 E 16 Three Tuns ct SE1
136 J 9 Threshers pl W1
110 D 8 Thriftwood SE23
65 W 18 Throckmorten rd E16
142 G 4 Throgmorton av EC2
142 G 5 Throgmorton st EC2
80 E 8 Throwley clo SE2
154 C 11 Throwley rd Sutton
149 Z 9 Thrush st SE17
111 R 12 Thurbarn rd SE6
108 G 9 Thurlby rd SE27
89 P 16 Thurleigh av SW12
88 L 17 Thurleigh rd SW12
89 O 16 Thurleigh rd SW12
119 R 11 Thurleston av Mrdn
15 Y 19 Thurlestone av N12
54 K 14 Thurlestone av Ilf
108 H 9 Thurlestone rd SE27
146 J 5 Thurloe clo SW7
39 S 19 Thurloe gdns Rom
146 H 4 Thurloe pl SW7
146 G 5 Thurloe Pl ms SW7
146 H 5 Thurloe sq SW7
146 G 5 Thurloe st SW7
42 H 16 Thurlow gdns Wemb
108 K 2 Thurlow hill SE21
108 K 3 Thurlow Pk rd SE21
46 G 14 Thurlow rd NW3
71 Y 6 Thurlow rd W7
150 H 10 Thurlow st SE17
47 N 17 Thurlow ter NW5
115 Y 14 Thursland rd Sidcp
159 W 16 Thursley cres Croy
105 P 5 Thursley gdns SW19
113 S 8 Thursley rd SE9
52 S 17 Thurso st SW17
93 S 6 Thurston rd SE13
104 J 17 Thurston rd SW20
58 F 18 Thurston rd S'hall
135 O 7 Thurtle rd E2
81 W 16 Thwaite clo Erith
29 P 12 Thyra gro N12
151 S 1 Thyrland rd SE16
42 H 19 Thyrll p Wemb
64 D 11 Tibbatt's rd E3
87 O 17 Tibbets gdns SW15
105 O 2 Tibbett's clo SW19
110 J 5 Ticehurst rd SE23
131 N 7 Tichfield rd NW8
80 E 5 Tickford clo SE2
65 R 20 Tidal Basin rd E16
87 N 12 Tideswell rd SW15
158 M 5 Tideswell rd Croy
64 B 13 Tidey st E3
96 K 4 Tidford rd Welling

64 A 11 Tidworth rd E3
89 Z 20 Tierney rd SW2
90 A 20 Tierney rd SW2
108 A 1 Tierney rd SW2
75 R 8 Tiger bay SE16
126 H 8 Tiger la Brom
94 M 8 Tilbrook rd SE3
51 T 2 Tilbury rd E10
66 G 7 Tilbury rd E6
86 L 15 Tildesley rd SW15
17 Y 16 Tile Kiln la N13
106 G 2 Tilehurst rd SW18
153 R 13 Tilehurst rd Sutton
47 U 3 Tilekiln la N6
47 Z 20 Tileyard rd N1
159 U 18 Tilford av Croy
105 P 2 Tilford gdns SW19
50 A 13 Tilia rd E5
76 B 8 Tiller rd E14
27 W 11 Tillingbourne gdns N3
27 W 12 Tillingbourne way N3
14 M 13 Tillingham way N12
63 N 18 Tillman st E1
43 X 1 Tillman st E1
133 N 2 Tilloch st N1
57 P 8 Tillotson rd N9
22 K 3 Tillotson rd Harrow
53 W 1 Tillotson rd Ilf
63 S 15 Tillotson st E1
109 U 12 Tilney av SE19
21 U 8 Tilney dri Buch Hl
56 B 19 Tilney rd Dgnhm
139 U 13 Tilney st W1
89 Z 18 Tilson gdns SW2
31 X 5 Tilson rd N17
150 M 17 Tilson rd SE15
144 M 15 Tilton st SW6
95 T 16 Tiltyard appr SE9
127 W 2 Timber clo Chisl
134 X 17 Timber st EC1
152 A 8 Timbercroft Epsom
79 U 18 Timbercroft la SE18
27 R 7 Timberdene NW4
31 Y 19 Timberwharf rd N16
63 X 14 Timothy rd E3
86 G 20 Timsbury wlk SW15
149 X 20 Tindal st SW9
90 J 1 Tindal st SW9
85 Z 7 Tinderbox all SW14
63 R 14 Tinsley rd E1
91 U 10 Tintagel cres SE22
53 U 19 Tintagel dri Stanm
25 T 10 Tintern av NW9
92 N 2 Tintern gdns N14
30 L 5 Tintern rd N22
120 F 20 Tintern rd Carsh
90 B 10 Tintern st SW4
40 K 4 Tintern way Harrow
65 T 13 Tinto rd E13
65 T 13 Tinto rd E16
148 M 8 Tinworth st SE11
149 N 9 Tinworth st SE11
7 Z 7 Tippetts clo Enf
89 O 7 Tipthorpe rd SW11
89 O 7 Tipthorpe rd SW11
157 S 8 Tiptown dri Croy
156 L 15 Tirlemont rd S Croy
122 L 15 Tirrell rd Croy
140 E 8 Tisbury ct W1
121 Z 3 Tisbury rd SW16
136 G 8 Tisdall pl SE17
138 K 6 Titchbourne row W2
117 N 7 Titchfield rd NW1
130 M 7 Titchfield rd NW8
120 F 19 Titchfield rd Carsh
9 U 1 Titchfield rd Enf
120 G 18 Titchfield wlk Carsh
120 G 18 Titchwell rd SW18
147 F 13 Tite st SW3
26 F 4 Tithe clo NW7
40 G 9 Tithe Farm av Harrow
40 G 9 Tithe Farm clo Harrow
26 G 3 Tithe wlk NW7
10 E 3 Titian av Bushey Watf
20 B 16 Titley clo E4
35 W 9 Tiverton av Ilf
80 B 20 Tiverton dri SE9
114 B 1 Tiverton rd SE9
128 H 6 Tiverton rd NW10
31 N 5 Tiverton rd N15
18 D 18 Tiverton rd N18
24 M 9 Tiverton rd Edg
82 M 4 Tiverton rd Hounsl
122 F 11 Tiverton rd Thntn Hth
60 K 5 Tiverton st SE1
150 A 20 Tiverton st SE1
29 X 16 Tivoli rd N8

108 L 13 Tivoli rd SE27
82 B 11 Tivoli rd Hounsl
35 W 9 Tivoton rd lit
76 A 5 Tobago st E14
46 K 19 Tobin clo NW3
20 A 14 Tofton rd E4
142 F 5 Tokenhouse yd EC2
43 P 18 Tokyngton av Wemb
86 G 14 Toland sq SW15
42 K 2 Toley av Wemb
36 D 9 Tollesbury gdns Ilf
63 S 11 Tollet st E1
109 T 5 Tollgate dri SE21
47 V 6 Tollhouse way N19
48 D 5 Tollington pk N4
48 C 5 Tollington pl N4
48 C 12 Tollington rd N7
48 A 9 Tollington way N7
132 C 15 Tolmers sq NW1
83 Y 8 Tolson rd Islwth
118 M 1 Tolverne rd SW20
37 X 15 Tolworth gdns Rom
117 V 17 Tolworth ri Surb
67 V 4 Tom Mann clo Bark
64 B 9 Tomlin's gro E3
101 Y 1 Tomlins all Twick
83 X 17 Tomlins ter E14
133 X 14 Tompion st E1
36 C 5 Tomswood ct Ilf
36 A 2 Tomswood hill Ilf
36 C 5 Tomswood rd Ilf
24 K 12 Tonbridge cres
     Harrow
132 J 12 Tonbridge st WC1
119 V 19 Tonfield rd Sutton
88 B 13 Tonsley hill SW18
88 B 13 Tonsley pl SW18
88 B 13 Tonsley rd SW18
88 B 12 Tonsley st SW18
121 O 3 Tonstall rd Mitch
141 S 4 Took's ct EC4
22 A 4 Tooke clo Pinn
83 Z 3 Toolands rd Islwth
22 C 10 Toole st SE17
143 N 18 Tooley st SE1
142 K 15 Tooley st SE1
23 O 7 Toorack rd Har
23 P 7 Toorack rd Harrow
107 T 7 Tooting Bec
     common SW16
107 X 9 Tooting Bec gdns
     SW16
107 P 8 Tooting Bec rd
     SW17
106 G 11 Tooting gro SW17
106 J 12 Tooting gro SW17
106 J 12 Tooting High st
     SW17
125 Z 16 Tootswood rd Brom
126 A 10 Tootswood rd Brom
125 Y 11 Top pk Becknhm
149 R 5 Topaz st SE11
30 M 4 Topham sq E1
133 S 17 Topham st EC1
20 H 3 Tophouse rise E4
84 M 8 Topiary sq Rich
94 M 9 Topley st SE9
29 Z 15 Topsfield rd N8
107 N 8 Topsham rd SW17
137 U 16 Tor gdns W8
97 T 1 Tor rd Welling
129 O 2 Torbay rd NW6
40 C 5 Torbay rd Harrow
47 T 20 Torbay st NW1
24 L 2 Torbridge clo Edg
110 C 4 Torcross dri SE23
79 U 15 Tormount rd SE18
53 T 11 Toronto av E12
51 X 12 Toronto rd E11
54 A 3 Toronto rd Ilf
35 P 13 Torquay gdns Ilf
110 F 18 Torr rd SE20
120 H 19 Torre wlk Carsh
52 B 18 Torrens rd E15
90 C 13 Torrens rd SW2
52 B 15 Torrens rd E15
133 V 9 Torrens st N1
47 X 17 Torriano av NW5
47 W 16 Torriano cotts NW5
92 B 10 Torridge gdns SE15
122 J 11 Torridge rd Thntn
     Hth
111 Y 3 Torridon rd SE6
93 Y 13 Torridon rd SE6
15 U 16 Torrington av N12
40 L 11 Torrington dri
     Harrow
16 H 20 Torrington gdns N11
60 C 20 Torrington gdns
     Grnfd
15 W 16 Torrington gro N12
15 S 15 Torrington pk N12
132 D 19 Torrington pl WC1

34 F 10 Torrington rd E18
56 C 3 Torrington rd Dgnhm
60 D 3 Torrington rd Grnfd
119 Y 16 Torrington way
     Mrdn
86 H 14 Torwood rd SW15
140 G 20 Tothill st SW1
80 E 20 Totnes rd Welling
28 G 14 Totnes wlk N2
17 V 18 Tottenhall rd N13
132 C 18 Tottenham Court rd
     W1
140 F 2 Tottenham Court rd
     W1
31 U 13 Tottenham Grn east
     N15
31 V 12 Tottenham Grn
     South side N17
30 C 15 Tottenham la N8
140 C 1 Tottenham ms W1
49 P 18 Tottenham rd N1
140 C 1 Tottenham st W1
106 M 11 Totterdown st SW17
13 W 9 Totteridge common
     N20
15 N 7 Totteridge la N20
24 E 16 Totternhoe clo
     Harrow
122 G 6 Totton rd Thntn Hth
63 U 7 Totty st E3
142 A 18 Toulmin st SE1
150 A 18 Toulon st SE5
145 R 17 Tournay rd SW6
47 R 17 Tovey pl NW5
143 N 14 Tower br E1
143 O 11 Tower Br appr E1
150 J 3 Tower Br rd SE1
142 M 18 Tower Br rd SE1
109 Z 17 Tower clo SE20
30 M 6 Tower gdns N17
31 O 6 Tower Gdns rd N17
33 O 11 Tower Hamlets rd
     E17
52 D 14 Tower Hamlets rd E7
143 N 10 Tower hill EC3
142 L 10 Tower hill EC3
33 O 14 Tower ms E17
142 M 11 Tower Of london
     EC3
142 L 10 Tower pl EC3
44 G 20 Tower rd NW10
81 X 12 Tower rd Blvdr
98 F 10 Tower rd Bxly Hth
101 W 6 Tower rd Twick
142 D 7 Tower royal EC4
140 H 7 Tower st WC2
30 C 8 Tower ter N22
124 H 19 Tower view Croy
22 A 4 Towers rd Pinn
58 H 10 Towers rd S'hall
100 D 4 Towfield rd Felt
31 U 12 Town Hall Appr rd
     N15
73 X 13 Town Hall av W4
88 M 8 Town Hall rd SW11
72 H 18 Town mead Brentfd
67 N 4 Town quay Bark
18 M 8 Town rd N9
19 D 11 Town rd N9
48 M 3 Towncourt path N4
58 E 7 Towney mead Grnfd
52 C 19 Townley clo E15
91 S 13 Townley rd SE22
98 D 11 Townley rd Bxly Hth
98 B 14 Townley rd Bxly Hth
150 D 8 Townley st SE17
88 D 4 Townmead rd SW6
85 T 4 Townmead rd Rich
16 L 13 Townsend av N14
43 Z 2 Townsend la NW9
25 Y 18 Townsend la NW9
31 U 16 Townsend rd N15
70 B 2 Townsend rd S'hall
150 H 6 Townsend st SE17
84 J 12 Townshend pl Rich
130 L 8 Townshend rd NW8
113 Z 13 Townshend rd Chisl
84 M 11 Townshend rd Rich
85 O 10 Townshend ter Rich
108 L 5 Towton rd SE27
105 S 20 Toynbee rd SW20
143 N 3 Toynbee st E1
44 L 14 Tracey av NW2
149 S 7 Tracey st SE11
24 D 2 Tracy ct Stanm
84 D 20 Tradescant rd SW8
18 D 20 Trafalgar av N17
101 U 1 Trafalgar av SE15
119 P 20 Trafalgar av Worc
     Pk
63 T 13 Trafalgar gdns E1
76 K 16 Trafalgar gro SE10

76 L 15 Trafalgar rd SE10
106 C 17 Trafalgar rd SW19
101 R 4 Trafalgar rd Twick
140 H 12 Trafalgar sq SW1
140 F 10 Trafalgar sq WC2
150 F 10 Trafalgar st SE17
122 D 11 Trafford rd Thntn
     Hth
51 Y 20 Tramway av E9
19 O 4 Tramway av N9
121 N 12 Tramway path Mitch
18 G 4 Tranmere rd N9
106 D 4 Tranmere rd SW18
82 L 19 Tranmere rd Twick
94 A 5 Tranquil vale SE3
138 K 2 Transept st NW1
72 B 16 Transport av Brentfd
151 V 1 Tranton rd SE16
103 Z 19 Traps la Kingst
118 A 1 Traps la New Mald
48 E 9 Travers rd N7
10 B 7 Treacy clo Bushey
     Watf
136 H 9 Treadgold st W11
135 W 9 Treadway st E2
82 K 9 Treaty rd Hounsl
132 M 6 Treaty st N1
139 X 14 Trebeck st W1
145 U 9 Trebovir rd SW5
63 Y 12 Treby st E3
63 Y 8 Tredegar rd E3
63 Y 9 Tredegar rd E3
63 Y 9 Tredegar sq E3
63 X 8 Tredegar ter E3
135 U 3 Trederwen rd E8
110 D 13 Tredown rd SE26
127 P 9 Tredwell clo Brom
65 Y 17 Tree rd E16
147 R 16 Tree wlk SW11
86 C 8 Treen av SW13
112 H 10 Treewall gdns Brom
56 E 7 Trefgarne rd Dgnhm
88 E 14 Trefoil rd SW18
30 A 20 Tregaron av N8
89 P 10 Tregarvon rd SW11
40 G 11 Tregenna av Harrow
6 H 16 Tregenna ct N14
50 M 20 Trego rd E9
90 A 7 Tregothnan rd
     SW19
135 Z 3 Tregunter rd E2
146 A 12 Tregunter rd SW10
36 E 1 Treharn rd Ilf
85 Z 8 Treharn rd SW14
107 P 8 Treherne rd SW17
90 G 1 Treherne rd SW9
50 H 14 Trehurst st E5
51 U 10 Trelawn rd E10
90 F 13 Trelawn rd SW2
36 E 1 Trelawny rd Ilf
63 Y 8 Trellis st E3
109 O 16 Treloar gdns SE19
89 Y 9 Tremadoc rd SW4
93 O 6 Tremaine clo SE4
124 A 4 Tremaine rd SE20
47 U 18 Tremlett gro N19
54 L 9 Trenance gdns Ilf
119 Y 14 Trenchard ct Mrdn
148 K 16 Trenchold st SW8
109 Z 18 Trenholme clo SE20
109 Z 18 Trenholme ter SE20
62 K 9 Trenmar gdns NW10
72 E 8 Trent av W5
6 E 20 Trent gdns N14
16 F 1 Trent gdns N14
16 F 6 Trent park Barnt
90 C 14 Trent rd SW2
21 V 6 Trent rd Buch Hl
105 X 2 Trentham st SW18
7 O 10 Trentwood side Enf
88 B 18 Treport st SW18
111 Z 16 Tresco clo Brom
92 B 9 Tresco rd SE15
40 C 2 Trescoe gdns
     Harrow
54 L 8 Trescoe gdns Ilf
50 C 14 Tresham av E9
67 X 1 Tresham rd Bark
93 O 8 Tressillian cres SE4
92 M 9 Tressillian rd SE4
93 O 6 Tressillian rd SE4
68 M 3 Treswell rd Dgnhm
69 N 3 Treswell rd Dgnhm
13 P 12 Tretawn gdns NW7
13 O 12 Tretawn pk NW7
144 M 8 Trevarion rd W14
41 O 2 Treve av Harrow
53 U 14 Trevelyan av E12
42 J 1 Trevelyan cres
     Harrow

62 M 4 Trevelyan gdns
     NW10
128 C 5 Trevelyan gdns
     NW10
52 B 13 Trevelyan rd E15
106 J 14 Trevelyan rd SW17
141 X 14 Treveris st SE1
128 J 19 Treverton st W10
86 J 18 Treviso rd SW15
110 G 3 Treviso rd SE23
86 B 15 Trevithick st SE8
22 C 18 Trevone gdns Pinn
5 U 18 Trevor clo Barnt
126 D 18 Trevor clo Brom
23 W 1 Trevor clo Harrow
83 V 12 Trevor clo Islwth
25 Y 4 Trevor gdns Edg
138 M 20 Trevor pl SW7
105 T 19 Trevor rd SW19
25 Y 4 Trevor rd Edg
34 G 1 Trevor rd Wdfd Grn
139 N 19 Trevor sq SW7
138 M 20 Trevor sq SW7
138 M 19 Trevor st SW7
39 W 4 Trevose rd E17
118 M 1 Trewince rd SW20
106 B 4 Trewint st SW18
110 F 12 Trewsbury rd SE26
66 A 14 Triangle ct E16
89 X 10 Triangle pl SW4
135 W 3 Triangle rd E8
117 U 4 Triangle the New
     Mald
75 V 10 Trident st SE16
75 U 10 Trident st SE16
142 A 9 Trig la EC4
149 P 17 Trigon gro SW8
149 P 16 Trigon rd SW8
110 G 3 Trilby rd SE23
75 Y 18 Trim st SE14
48 B 3 Trinder rd N4
4 A 17 Trinder rd Barnt
73 N 3 Tring av W5
58 E 16 Tring av S'hall
43 P 18 Tring av Wemb
69 Z 1 Trinidad gdns
     Dgnhm
63 Z 20 Trinidad st E14
28 F 11 Trinity av N2
8 J 20 Trinity av Enf
141 T 5 Trinity Church pas
     EC4
74 K 17 Trinity Church rd
     SW13
142 C 20 Trinity Church sq
     SE1
82 B 9 Trinity clo Hounsl
157 T 19 Trinity clo S Croy
107 N 5 Trinity cres SW17
106 M 5 Trinity cres SW17
65 P 13 Trinity gdns E16
93 T 2 Trinity gdns SE10
90 C 10 Trinity gdns SW9
98 B 10 Trinity pl Bxly Hth
28 F 9 Trinity rd N2
30 C 4 Trinity rd N22
110 C 15 Trinity rd SE20
105 N 3 Trinity rd SW19
107 N 6 Trinity rd SW17
88 G 17 Trinity rd SW18
105 Z 16 Trinity rd SW19
36 A 9 Trinity rd Ilf
85 N 9 Trinity rd Rich
70 A 2 Trinity rd S'hall
90 A 20 Trinity rd SW2
142 M 9 Trinity sq EC3
51 Y 9 Trinity st E11
142 C 20 Trinity st SE1
7 Y 8 Trinity st Enf
62 D 20 Trinity way NW3
142 C 20 Trio pl SE1
94 A 8 Tristan sq SE3
112 D 9 Tristram rd Brom
156 A 7 Tritton av Croydon
109 O 7 Tritton rd SE21
88 F 9 Tritton rd SW11
156 D 4 Trojan way Croy
89 T 4 Trollope st SW8
63 U 16 Troon st E1
81 R 17 Trosley rd Blvdr
22 M 17 Trossachs rd SE22
151 T 6 Trothy rd SE1
88 H 3 Trott st SW11
77 W 13 Troughton rd SE7
92 G 2 Troutbeck rd SE14
89 U 16 Trouville rd SW4
24 L 2 Towbridge rd Edg
102 E 15 Trowlock av Tedd
109 P 15 Troy rd SE19
78 M 11 Troy st SE18
91 X 7 Trpy town SE15
31 X 2 Trulock rd N17
49 S 14 Truman's rd N16

146 K 10	Trumble gdns Thntn Hth	
142 C 6	Trump st EC2	
71 V 7	Trumpers way W7	
52 B 11	Trumpington rd E7	
10 E 5	Trundlers way Bushey Watf	
75 U 14	Trundley's rd SE8	
53 R 2	Truro gdns Ilf	
32 L 14	Truro rd E17	
30 A 3	Truro rd N22	
47 O 19	Truro rd W2	
108 H 12	Truslove rd SE27	
144 B 2	Trussley rd W6	
74 L 8	Trussley rd W6	
57 W 2	Truston's gdns Hornch	
147 N 9	Tryon st SW3	
79 R 17	Tuam rd SE18	
62 E 7	Tubbs rd NW10	
57 W 18	Tuck rd Rainhm	
86 E 18	Tuckton wlk SW15	
100 H 17	Tudor av Hampt	
39 W 11	Tudor av Rom	
152 L 9	Tudor av Worc Pk	
46 J 16	Tudor clo NW3	
13 V 20	Tudor clo NW7	
43 W 6	Tudor clo NW9	
127 V 1	Tudor clo Chisl	
113 V 20	Tudor clo Chisl	
99 Y 16	Tudor clo Drtfrd	
153 P 12	Tudor clo Sutton	
155 W 17	Tudor clo Wallgtn	
21 V 16	Tudor clo Wdfd Grn	
7 X 4	Tudor cres Enf	
32 K 20	Tudor ct E17	
43 R 16	Tudor Ct north Wembl	
43 R 17	Tudor Ct south Wembl	
103 N 14	Tudor dri Kingst	
102 H 11	Tudor dri Kingst	
143 T 17	Tudor dri Mrdn	
39 V 12	Tudor dri Rom	
43 W 7	Tudor gdns NW9	
86 C 8	Tudor gdns SW13	
61 R 15	Tudor gdns W3	
39 W 12	Tudor gdns Rom	
159 T 6	Tudor gdns W Wkhm	
135 Z 2	Tudor gro E9	
63 O 1	Tudor gro E9	
140 F 3	Tudor pl W1	
106 K 19	Tudor pl Mitch	
20 E 19	Tudor rd E4	
65 Z 4	Tudor rd E6	
135 Y 3	Tudor rd E9	
63 O 2	Tudor rd E9	
19 O 4	Tudor rd N9	
109 U 18	Tudor rd SE19	
124 B 13	Tudor rd SE25	
67 X 3	Tudor rd Bark	
5 M 11	Tudor rd Barnt	
4 M 11	Tudor rd Barnt	
125 S 6	Tudor rd Becknhm	
100 H 18	Tudor rd Hampt	
23 P 8	Tudor rd Harrow	
83 P 10	Tudor rd Hounsl	
103 P 18	Tudor rd Kingst	
58 B 20	Tudor rd S'hall	
141 U 8	Tudor st EC4	
16 K 5	Tudor way N14	
73 O 6	Tudor way W3	
48 A 11	Tufnell Park rd N7	
47 V 11	Tufnell Pk rd N19	
20 A 14	Tufton rd E4	
148 H 2	Tufton st SW1	
123 O 14	Tugela rd Croy	
10 M 4	Tugela st SE6	
135 S 9	Tuilerie st E2	
125 U 6	Tulse clo Becknhm	
108 G 1	Tulse hill SW2	
90 F 18	Tulse hill SW2	
108 M 4	Tulsemere rd SE27	
109 X 7	Tunbridge ct SE26	
18 D 12	Tuncombe rd N18	
74 L 3	Tunis rd W12	
136 A 14	Tunis rd W12	
62 B 2	Tunley rd NW10	
107 N 3	Tunley rd SW17	
65 X 10	Tunmarsh la E13	
63 T 19	Tunnel appr E1	
64 C 17	Tunnel appr E14	
76 L 6	Tunnel appr SE10	
77 P 12	Tunnel av SE10	
76 L 6	Tunnel av SE10	
75 P 6	Tunnel entrance SE16	
29 V 2	Tunnel gdns N11	
90 D 10	Tunstall rd SW9	
157 N 1	Tunstall rd Croy	
123 T 20	Tunstall rd Croy	
57 V 19	Tunworth cres NW9	

86 C 17	Tunworth cres SW15	
100 L 20	Turdinghall la Felt	
19 P 4	Turin rd N9	
135 S 14	Turin st E2	
133 W 19	Turks Head yd EC1	
147 R 9	Turks row SW3	
48 C 5	Turle rd N4	
121 Z 2	Turle rd SW16	
65 N 4	Turley clo E15	
141 W 14	Turnagain rd EC4	
55 Y 5	Turnage rd Dgnhm	
31 R 14	Turner av N15	
106 L 20	Turner av Mitch	
101 O 6	Turner av Twick	
28 A 19	Turner clo NW11	
28 A 19	Turner dri NW11	
33 U 11	Turner rd E17	
24 L 8	Turner rd Edg	
117 Z 16	Turner rd New Mald	
143 W 4	Turner st E1	
65 P 17	Turner st E1	
42 G 3	Turners all EC3	
63 Y 15	Turners rd E3	
134 K 9	Turners st N1	
46 D 2	Turners wood NW11	
35 O 13	Turneville rd E2	
145 O 13	Turneville rd W14	
90 M 19	Turney rd SE21	
91 O 18	Turney rd SE21	
74 A 11	Turnham Green ter W4	
92 H 12	Turnham rd SE4	
133 V 19	Turnmill st EC1	
30 F 12	Turnpike la N8	
157 S 4	Turnpike link Croy	
147 X 11	Turpentine la SW1	
38 E 1	Turpin av Rom	
127 T 16	Turpington clo Brom	
127 R 15	Turpington la Brom	
150 C 8	Turquand st SE17	
89 U 6	Turret gro SW4	
106 C 7	Turtle rd SW17	
42 J 16	Turton rd Wemb	
79 T 14	Tuscan rd SE18	
76 M 15	Tuskar st SE10	
75 O 18	Tustin st SE15	
151 Z 16	Tustin st SE15	
21 U 8	Tuttlebee la Buck Hl	
39 O 2	Tweed way Rom	
39 O 3	Tweed way Rom	
120 F 19	Tweeddale rd Carsh	
126 F 2	Tweedmouth rd E13	
126 F 2	Tweedy rd Brom	
141 R 8	Tweezer's all WC2	
84 D 13	Twickenham ter Twick	
41 X 15	Twickenham gdns Grnfd	
23 T 2	Twickenham gdns Harrow	
51 V 6	Twickenham rd E11	
100 C 9	Twickenham rd Felt	
84 A 1	Twickenham rd Islwth	
83 X 10	Twickenham rd Islwth	
84 A 1	Twickenham rd Iswth	
84 F 11	Twickenham rd Rich	
101 Y 9	Twickenham rd Tedd	
88 A 18	Twilley st SW18	
14 M 13	Twineham green N12	
101 O 6	Twining av Twick	
47 S 11	Twisden rd NW5	
61 W 1	Twybridge way NW10	
60 M 9	Twyford Abbey rd Wemb	
29 N 10	Twyford av N2	
28 L 11	Twyford av N2	
61 P 19	Twyford av W3	
73 P 1	Twyford av W3	
73 R 2	Twyford cres W3	
141 N 4	Twyford pl WC2	
120 F 19	Twyford rd Carsh	
40 J 2	Twyford rd Harrow	
54 B 14	Twyford rd Ilf	
78 B 4	Twyford st E16	
133 N 4	Twyford st N1	
65 O 13	Tyas rd E16	
119 X 5	Tybenham rd SW19	
9 O 10	Tyberry rd Enf	
41 U 1	Tyburn la Harrow	
63 X 17	Tye st E14	
142 U 18	Tyers gate SE1	
148 O 8	Tyers st SE11	
149 O 10	Tyers ter SE11	
81 O 14	Tyeshurst clo SE2	
121 Z 3	Tylecroft rd SW16	
122 C 3	Tylecroft rd SW16	
54 B 14	Tylehurst gdns Ilf	

111 R 20	Tyler rd Becknhm	
77 N 14	Tyler st SE10	
24 L 19	Tylers ga Harrow	
52 K 11	Tylney rd E7	
127 N 3	Tylney rd Brom	
48 J 20	Tyndale ter N1	
51 T 7	Tyndall rd E10	
96 L 8	Tyndall rd Welling	
54 A 7	Tyne rd Ilf	
143 O 4	Tyne st E1	
89 O 6	Tyneham rd SW11	
8 L 3	Tynemouth dri Enf	
31 W 13	Tynemouth rd N15	
107 O 17	Tynemouth rd Mitch	
88 C 4	Tynemouth st SW6	
126 D 11	Tynham grn Brom	
87 Z 1	Tyrawley rd SW6	
154 M 8	Tyrell ct Carsh	
114 J 11	Tyron way Sidcp	
66 H 7	Tyrone rd E6	
97 P 13	Tyrrell av Welling	
91 X 11	Tyrrell rd SE22	
93 O 6	Tyrwhitt rd SE4	
133 T 15	Tysoe st EC1	
92 D 19	Tyson rd SE23	
49 U 17	Tyssen pas E8	
49 V 17	Tyssen st E8	
47 X 10	Tytherton rd N19	

U

64 E 14	Uamvar st E14	
107 P 19	Uckfield gro Mitch	
9 U 1	Uckfield rd Enf	
148 D 6	Udall st SW1	
101 Z 13	Udney Pk rd Tedd	
62 H 3	Uffington rd NW10	
108 G 9	Uffington rd SE27	
22 L 2	Ufford clo Harrow	
22 L 2	Ufford dri Harrow	
141 V 17	Ufford st SE1	
49 R 20	Ufton gro N1	
134 H 2	Ufton rd N1	
107 V 10	Ullathorne rd SW16	
17 P 11	Ulleswater rd N13	
14 F 15	Ullin st E14	
103 Y 10	Ullswater clo SW15	
103 Y 9	Ullswater cres SW15	
104 A 10	Ullswater cres SW15	
108 J 5	Ullswater rd SE27	
74 G 20	Ullswater rd SW13	
57 W 14	Ullswater rd Hornch	
17 X 13	Ulster gdns N13	
48 C 12	Ulster ms N7	
131 W 18	Ulster ter W1	
77 N 16	Ulundi rd SE3	
87 P 12	Ulva rd SW15	
91 W 13	Ulverscroft rd SE22	
33 X 7	Ulverston rd E17	
102 J 5	Ulverstone rd SE27	
45 W 14	Ulysses rd NW6	
86 G 17	Umbria st SW15	
30 H 19	Umfreville rd N4	
9 W 10	Under Bridge way Enf	
93 P 6	Undercliff rd SE13	
4 K 16	Underhill Barnt	
131 Z 5	Underhill pas NW1	
131 Z 17	Underhill rd SE22	
131 Z 5	Underhill st NW1	
16 F 9	Underne av N14	
77 V 20	Underpass SE3	
112 B 8	Undershaw rd Brom	
159 U 12	Underwood Croy	
136 S 19	Underwood rd E1	
20 E 15	Underwood rd E4	
57 Y 5	Underwood rd W5	
113 V 5	Underwood the SE9	
106 L 12	Undine st SW17	
59 R 3	Uneeda dri Grnfd	
142 L 15	Unicorn pas SE1	
32 L 19	Union rd E17	
16 L 18	Union rd N11	
89 X 4	Union rd SW8	
127 O 11	Union rd Brom	
106 C 10	Union rd Croy	
122 M 16	Union rd Croy	
42 J 18	Union rd Wemb	
18 H 20	Union row N17	
36 L 8	Union sq N1	
64 H 4	Union st E15	
142 A 15	Union st SE1	
141 X 16	Union st SE1	
4 F 13	Union st Barnt	

116 H 3	Union st Kingst	
134 M 11	Union wlk E2	
132 E 17	University college WC1	
132 H 20	University Of london WC1	
106 G 15	University rd SW19	
132 C 18	University st WC1	
151 R 16	Unwin rd SE15	
83 U 7	Unwin rd Islwth	
81 R 10	Up Abbey rd Blvdr	
136 J 17	Up Addison gdns W14	
109 R 20	Up Beaulah hill SE19	
147 V 2	Up Belgrave st SW1	
139 P 5	Up Berkeley st W1	
92 L 4	Up Brockley rd SE4	
139 S 9	Up Brook st W1	
146 K 14	Up Cheyne row SW3	
50 A 8	Up Clapton rd E5	
49 Y 4	Up Clapton rd E5	
124 J 10	Up Elmers end Becknhm	
125 P 13	Up Elmers End rd Becknhm	
139 T 10	Up Grosvenor st W1	
101 V 4	Up Grotto rd Twick	
141 V 12	Up ground SE1	
141 V 12	Up ground SE1	
123 T 9	Up grove SE25	
81 O 16	Up Grove rd Blvdr	
102 G 8	Up Ham rd Rich	
131 V 17	Up Harley st NW1	
81 V 13	Up Holly Hill rd Blvdr	
140 C 8	Up James st W1	
140 D 9	Up John st W1	
74 H 14	Up mall W6	
141 P 20	Up marsh SE1	
139 O 1	Up Montagu st W1	
153 T 16	Up Mulgrave rd Sutton	
64 B 15	Up North st E14	
46 L 17	Up Park rd NW3	
16 G 17	Up Park rd N11	
81 U 12	Up Park rd Blvdr	
112 K 20	Up Park rd Brom	
103 O 16	Up Park rd Kingst	
137 T 19	Up Phillimore gdns W8	
57 T 11	Up Rainham rd Hornch	
85 T 10	Up Richmond Rd w Hornch	
157 T 17	Up Selsdon rd S Croy	
81 R 10	Up Sheridan rd Blvdr	
158 D 4	Up Shirley rd Croy	
82 G 2	Up Sutton la Hounsl	
102 D 19	Up Teddington rd Kingst	
142 B 9	Up Thames st EC4	
141 Z 8	Up Thames st EC4	
48 F 4	Up Tollington pk N4	
107 N 4	Up Tooting pk SW17	
106 M 4	Up Tooting pk SW17	
106 L 9	Up Tooting rd SW17	
107 N 6	Up Tooting rd SW17	
58 J 12	Up Town rd Grnfd	
90 C 18	Up Tulse hill SW2	
154 F 10	Up Vernon rd Sutton	
133 W 11	Up Walthamstow rd E17	
97 P 4	Up Wickham la Welling	
131 V 20	Up Wimpole st W1	
139 V 2	Up Wimpole st W1	
138 D 7	Upbrook ms W2	
146 B 19	Upcerne rd SW10	
75 R 17	Upcot st SE15	
12 H 14	Upcroft av Edg	
158 A 3	Upfield Croy	
157 Z 5	Upfield Croy	
59 V 13	Upfield rd W7	
53 X 11	Uphall av Ilf	
53 X 10	Uphall rd Ilf	
53 Y 12	Uphall rd Ilf	
74 B 11	Upham Pk rd W4	
13 O 15	Uphill dri NW7	
25 W 16	Uphill dri NW9	
13 P 13	Uphill gro NW7	
13 P 14	Uphill rd NW7	
65 R 12	Upland rd E13	
91 X 12	Upland rd SE22	
91 X 18	Upland rd SE22	
98 B 8	Upland rd Bxly Hth	
157 O 12	Upland rd S Croy	
154 G 14	Upland rd Sutton	
125 N 4	Uplands Becknhm	

32 F 9	Uplands av E17
85 T 13	Uplands clo SW14
35 P 2	Uplands end Wdfd Grn
7 U 9	Uplands Pk rd Enf
30 E 17	Uplands rd N8
16 B 6	Uplands rd Barnt
37 U 11	Uplands rd Rom
35 P 2	Uplands rd Wdfd Grn
7 T 16	Uplands way N21
54 L 20	Upney la Bark
67 Y 1	Upney la Bark
36 C 18	Uppark dri Ilf
16 G 16	Upper Brighton rd Surb
72 F 17	Upper butts Brentf
27 X 9	Upper Cavendish av N3
18 J 17	Upper Fore st N18
20 L 4	Upper green Mitch
65 R 9	Upper rd E13
55 Z 11	Upper rd Wallgtn
86 K 10	Upper Richmond rd SW15
87 N 11	Upper Richmond rd SW15
83 Z 7	Upper sq Islwth
48 H 20	Upper st N1
33 V 8	Upper st N1
33 W 2	Upper street N1
46 D 10	Upper ter NW3
32 G 15	Upper Woburn pl WC1
14 M 12	Upperton rd Sidcp
65 X 9	Upperton Rd west E13
65 Y 8	Upperton Rd west E13
24 E 9	Uppingham av Stanm
17 S 19	Upsdell av N13
90 L 3	Upstall st SE5
52 G 20	Upton av E7
98 B 15	Upton clo Bxly
53 Z 16	Upton dene Sutton
24 C 17	Upton gdns Harrow
65 T 1	Upton la E7
65 T 1	Upton la E7
65 V 1	Upton Park rd E7
52 H 20	Upton Pk rd E7
18 L 16	Upton rd N18
79 P 18	Upton rd SE18
A 14	Upton rd Bxly Hth
97 Y 10	Upton rd Bxly Hth
82 H 9	Upton rd Hounsl
23 N 2	Upton rd Thntn Hth
15 V 20	Upway N12
94 D 16	Upwood rd SE12
22 A 1	Upwood rd SW16
50 E 16	Urlwin st SE5
05 T 1	Urmston dri SW19
88 J 3	Ursula st SW11
68 K 1	Urswick gdns Dgnhm
50 C 15	Urswick rd E5
63 Z 4	Usher rd E3
81 F 11	Usk rd SW11
65 P 20	Usk st E16
53 S 8	Usk st E2
56 E 9	Uvedale rd Dgnhm
8 B 17	Uvedale rd Enf
46 B 18	Uverdale rd SW10
74 G 3	Uxbridge rd W12
36 B 16	Uxbridge rd W12
73 O 3	Uxbridge rd W13
73 O 2	Uxbridge rd W5
60 K 20	Uxbridge rd W5
00 L 13	Uxbridge rd Hampt
22 L 1	Uxbridge rd Harrow
23 O 1	Uxbridge rd Harrow
16 G 10	Uxbridge rd Kingst
70 L 2	Uxbridge rd S Hall
10 K 18	Uxbridge rd Stanm
1 O 17	Uxbridge rd Stanm
37 S 13	Uxbridge st W8
44 N 2	Uxendon cres Wemb
43 N 2	Uxendon hill Wemb
42 M 3	Uxendon hill Wemb

V

21 O 6	Valance av E4
30 B 13	Vale clo W9
04 B 8	Vale cres SW15
22 A 15	Vale croft Pinn
16 K 6	Vale dri Barnt
30 L 20	Vale gro N4
73 Y 4	Vale gro W3
61 P 15	Vale lane W3
52 H 17	Vale rd E7
30 M 20	Vale rd N4
31 N 19	Vale rd N4
127 V 2	Vale rd Brom
152 E 8	Vale rd Epsom
121 W 8	Vale rd Mitch
153 Z 8	Vale rd Sutton
152 F 5	Vale rd Worc Pk
45 V 4	Vale ri NW11
48 J 10	Vale row N5
132 J 1	Vale royal N1
30 L 20	Vale ter N4
45 T 6	Vale the NW11
29 O 4	Vale the N10
17 N 1	Vale the N14
16 L 3	Vale the N20
74 C 3	Vale the N3
146 G 14	Vale the SW3
158 G 3	Vale the Croy
70 B 17	Vale the Hounsl
34 F 3	Vale the Wdfd Grn
55 W 3	Valence av Dgnhm
55 X 10	Valence cir Dgnhm
55 Y 8	Valence park Dgnhm
55 X 10	Valence wood Dgnhm
56 A 9	Valence Wood rd Dgnhm
11 S 14	Valence st Stanm
115 Y 2	Valentine av Bxly
110 E 5	Valentine ct SE23
141 V 18	Valentine pl SE1
52 E 19	Valentine rd E9
40 L 10	Valentine rd Harrow
141 W 18	Valentine row SE1
53 Y 4	Valentine's clo N3
57 P 8	Valentine's way Rom
53 Y 2	Valentines park Ilf
112 B 13	Valeswood rd Brom
65 R 5	Valetta gro E13
74 C 4	Valetta rd W3
50 B 18	Valette st E8
38 F 7	Valiant clo Rom
143 U 1	Vallance rd E1
135 U 14	Vallance rd E2
29 V 6	Vallance rd N22
33 U 12	Vallentin rd E17
52 H 4	Valley av N12
99 U 15	Valley clo Drtfd
25 R 18	Valley dri NW9
106 G 17	Valley gdns SW19
42 L 20	Valley gdns Wemb
77 Y 13	Valley gro SE7
101 X 3	Valley ms Twick
108 D 10	Valley rd SW16
81 X 11	Valley rd Blvdr
126 A 4	Valley rd Brom
99 U 15	Valley rd Dartfd
115 R 20	Valley rd Orp
20 B 5	Valley side E4
4 F 19	Valley view Barnt
158 C 2	Valley wlk Croy
108 D 11	Valleyfield rd SW16
7 T 9	Valleyfields cres Enf
20 A 7	Valleyside parade E4
62 H 8	Valliere rd NW10
114 G 2	Valliers Wood rd Sidcp
59 Y 13	Vallis way W13
90 M 3	Valmar rd SE5
91 N 2	Valmar rd SE5
106 M 12	Valnay st SW17
32 H 4	Valognes av E17
87 V 15	Valonia gdns SW18
79 O 16	Vamberry rd SE18
117 Z 17	Van Dyck av New Mald
94 C 1	Vanborough ter SE3
77 O 18	Vanbrough fields SE3
77 O 17	Vanbrugh hill SE3
77 P 19	Vanbrugh pk SE3
77 P 20	Vanbrugh Pk rd SE3
77 O 18	Vanbrugh Pk Rd west SE3
73 Z 8	Vanbrugh rd W4
94 C 1	Vanbrugh ter SE3
75 W 19	Vance st SE14
110 L 3	Vancouver rd SE23
25 T 5	Vancouver rd Edg
88 C 20	Vanderbilt rd SW18
140 D 20	Vandon pas SW1
87 P 17	Vandyke clo SW19
95 P 14	Vandyke cross SE9
24 M 19	Vane clo Harrow
148 D 5	Vane st SW1
81 S 13	Vanessa clo Blvdr
38 E 8	Vanguard clo Rom
93 O 2	Vanguard st SE4
156 A 16	Vanguard way Wallgtn
112 E 8	Vanoc gdns Brom
52 D 12	Vansittart rd E7
145 U 10	Vanston pl SW6
135 P 17	Vanstone pl E1
145 U 18	Vanstone pl SW6
107 N 13	Vant rd SW17
106 M 13	Vant rd SW17
75 O 15	Varcoe rd SE16
151 Z 12	Varcoe rd SE16
143 W 3	Varden st E1
88 G 12	Vardens rd SW11
65 W 16	Varley rd E16
135 N 19	Varna rd SW6
132 A 12	Varndell st NW1
31 P 19	Vartry rd N15
149 V 20	Vassall rd SW9
151 P 3	Vauban st SE16
63 O 13	Vaudrey clo E1
26 G 16	Vaughan av NW4
74 E 10	Vaughan av W6
53 T 1	Vaughan gdns Ilf
151 X 13	Vaughan pl SE15
52 C 19	Vaughan rd E15
90 L 6	Vaughan rd SE5
22 M 19	Vaughan rd Harrow
23 R 20	Vaughan rd Harrow
116 A 17	Vaughan rd Surb
96 L 5	Vaughan rd Welling
148 J 10	Vauxhall br SW1&SE11
148 E 11	Vauxhall Br rd SW1
156 M 15	Vauxhall gdns S Croy
148 M 13	Vauxhall gro SW8
149 N 13	Vauxhall gro SW8
149 P 8	Vauxhall st SE11
148 M 10	Vauxhall wlk SE11
93 P 11	Veda rd SE13
16 N 16	Vectis gdns SW17
93 P 11	Veda rd SE13
10 A 3	Vega rd Bushey Watf
91 S 12	Velde way SE22
130 H 19	Venables st NW8
74 G 12	Vencourt pl W6
30 J 20	Venetia rd N4
72 F 7	Venetia rd W5
90 M 5	Venetian rd SE5
89 W 9	Venn st SW4
74 E 18	Venner rd SE26
99 P 4	Vennere gdns Bxly Hth
63 W 11	Venour rd E3
24 C 6	Ventnor av Stanm
15 N 9	Ventnor dri N20
54 C 19	Ventnor gdns Bark
75 T 19	Ventnor rd SE14
154 B 17	Ventnor rd Sutton
97 Y 18	Venture clo Bxly
7 U 18	Vera av N21
87 T 2	Vera rd SW6
74 F 14	Verbena gdns W6
80 A 18	Verdun rd SE2
79 T 19	Verdun rd SW13
139 X 6	Vere st W1
145 N 12	Vereker rd W14
109 P 16	Vermont rd SE19
88 B 16	Vermont rd SW18
154 A 4	Vermont rd Sutton
55 Y 19	Verney gdns Dgnhm
75 O 14	Verney rd SE16
151 V 12	Verney rd SE16
55 Y 12	Verney rd Dgnhm
43 Y 10	Verney st NW10
151 V 11	Verney way SE16
79 O 16	Vernham rd SE18
53 T 13	Vernon av E12
119 O 3	Vernon av SW20
34 G 1	Vernon av Wdfd Grn
6 B 18	Vernon cres Barnt
24 A 4	Vernon ct Stanm
23 Z 4	Vernon dri Stanm
144 L 6	Vernon ms W14
140 L 2	Vernon pl WC1
51 Z 4	Vernon rd E11
52 A 5	Vernon rd E11
51 Z 19	Vernon rd E15
52 L 14	Vernon rd E17
63 Z 6	Vernon rd E3
30 G 11	Vernon rd N8
85 Y 8	Vernon rd SW14
54 K 5	Vernon rd Ilf
154 E 10	Vernon rd Sutton
41 P 16	Vernon rd Grnfd
133 P 12	Vernon rise WC1
133 O 11	Vernon sq WC1
144 L 6	Vernon st W14
97 Y 5	Veroan rd Bxly Hth
74 E 6	Verona rd E7
57 S 5	Veronica rd SW17
36 A 15	Veronique gdns Ilf
89 R 19	Verran rd SW12
109 X 19	Versailles rd SE20
32 K 20	Verulam av E17
58 J 11	Verulam pl Grnfd
133 S 20	Verulam st EC1
22 M 8	Verwood rd Harrow
74 F 4	Vespan rd W12
92 J 5	Vesta rd SE4
110 G 4	Vestris rd SE23
33 R 14	Vestry rd E17
91 S 2	Vestry rd SE5
134 F 12	Vestry st N1
110 K 5	Vevey st SE6
56 D 9	Veysey gdns Dgnhm
141 V 2	Viaduct bldgs EC1
135 W 14	Viaduct pl E2
135 W 14	Viaduct st E2
34 G 8	Viaduct the E18
93 S 18	Vian st SE13
90 D 20	Vibart gdns SW2
47 O 14	Vicar's rd NW5
77 T 20	Vicarage av SE3
88 G 3	Vicarage cres SW11
85 X 12	Vicarage dri SW14
67 R 2	Vicarage dri Bark
82 C 3	Vicarage Farm rd Hounsl
70 C 20	Vicarage Farm rd Hounsl
137 W 16	Vicarage ga W8
79 P 14	Vicarage gdns SE18
137 W 15	Vicarage gdns W8
120 J 7	Vicarage gdns Mitch
91 P 1	Vicarage gro SE5
52 B 19	Vicarage la E15
65 O 2	Vicarage la E15
66 K 8	Vicarage la E6
152 G 19	Vicarage la Epsom
54 D 5	Vicarage la Ilf
47 Z 1	Vicarage path N19
79 P 14	Vicarage pk SE18
51 O 1	Vicarage rd E10
52 B 20	Vicarage rd E15
44 B 17	Vicarage rd NW10
26 G 20	Vicarage rd NW4
31 X 3	Vicarage rd N17
85 Y 12	Vicarage rd SW14
156 G 4	Vicarage rd Croy
56 D 20	Vicarage rd Dgnhm
57 X 4	Vicarage rd Hornch
116 G 2	Vicarage rd Kingst
153 Z 7	Vicarage rd Sutton
101 X 12	Vicarage rd Tedd
101 T 4	Vicarage rd Twick
35 S 2	Vicarage rd Wdfd Grn
43 Z 10	Vicarage way NW10
40 G 1	Vicarage way Harrow
65 S 3	Vicars clo E15
8 F 10	Vicars clo Enf
93 P 9	Vicars hill SE13
17 U 3	Vicars Moor la N21
146 D 18	Vicat st W10
90 A 1	Viceroy rd SW8
42 L 20	Victor gro Wemb
62 K 7	Victor rd NW10
48 D 7	Victor rd N7
110 F 17	Victor rd SE20
23 O 11	Victor rd Harrow
101 T 11	Victor rd Tedd
18 C 10	Victor villas N9
146 H 3	Victoria And Albert museum SW7
142 K 2	Victoria av EC2
66 A 3	Victoria av N3
27 W 5	Victoria av N3
5 U 15	Victoria av Barnt
82 G 12	Victoria av Hounsl
116 F 16	Victoria av Surb
155 P 5	Victoria av Wllgtn
5 V 15	Victoria clo Barnt
85 O 3	Victoria cotts Rich
31 R 16	Victoria cres N15
109 R 14	Victoria cres SE19
105 W 17	Victoria cres SW19
43 P 17	Victoria ct Wemb
65 T 19	Victoria Dock rd E16
65 N 17	Victoria Dock rd E16
105 R 3	Victoria dri SW19
105 S 4	Victoria dri SW19
141 S 9	Victoria emb EC4/WC2/SW1
140 L 16	Victoria emb EC4/WC2/SW1
137 S 12	Victoria gdns W11
82 A 1	Victoria gdns Hounsl
15 T 15	Victoria gro N12
146 A 1	Victoria gro W8
137 V 10	Victoria Gro ms W2
129 S 4	Victoria ms NW6
63 W 2	Victoria park E9
135 Y 5	Victoria Pk rd E9
63 P 3	Victoria Pk rd E9
135 Z 11	Victoria Pk sq E2

63 O 8 Victoria Pk sq E2
84 H 13 Victoria pl Rich
51 Y 12 Victoria rd E11
65 S 7 Victoria rd E13
33 T 7 Victoria rd E17
34 H 8 Victoria rd E18
21 N 4 Victoria rd E4
20 M 5 Victoria rd E4
62 A 12 Victoria rd NW10
27 N 13 Victoria rd NW4
129 T 4 Victoria rd NW6
13 R 15 Victoria rd NW7
31 W 14 Victoria rd N15
29 W 5 Victoria rd N22
48 E 3 Victoria rd N4
18 J 9 Victoria rd N9
85 X 7 Victoria rd SW14
61 Y 13 Victoria rd W3
60 C 14 Victoria rd W5
138 A 19 Victoria rd W8
54 A 18 Victoria rd Bark
53 Z 18 Victoria rd Bark
5 U 15 Victoria rd Barnt
127 P 12 Victoria rd Brom
98 D 12 Victoria rd Bxly Hth
113 X 12 Victoria rd Chisl
56 J 14 Victoria rd Dgnhm
36 A 15 Victoria rd Ilf
35 Z 15 Victoria rd Ilf
117 N 3 Victoria rd Kingst
106 K 19 Victoria rd Mitch
39 S 18 Victoria rd Rom
40 A 13 Victoria rd Ruis
'70 D 9 Victoria rd S'hall
114 M 8 Victoria rd Sidcp
116 G 15 Victoria rd Surb
154 F 12 Victoria rd Sutton
101 X 15 Victoria rd Tedd
84 A 18 Victoria rd Twick
89 S 10 Victoria ri SW4
129 T 4 Victoria sq NW6
147 Y 2 Victoria sq SW1
147 Y 1 Victoria sq SW1
51 Y 20 Victoria st E15
140 G 20 Victoria st SW1
148 D 2 Victoria st SW1
81 P 14 Victoria st Blvdr
147 Y 5 Victoria station SW1
48 E 4 Victoria ter N4
41 S 4 Victoria ter Harrow
129 T 5 Victoria vlls NW6
85 N 10 Victoria vlls Rich
77 W 15 Victoria way SE7
49 T 10 Victorian gro N16
49 T 11 Victorian rd N16
120 D 11 Victory av Mrdn
150 D 5 Victory pl SE17
109 T 16 Victory pl SE19
106 B 18 Victory rd SW19
150 G 17 Victory sq SE5
38 F 7 Victory way Rom
23 P 12 View clo Harrow
29 N 19 View rd N6
28 M 20 View rd N6
31 U 18 View the SE2
87 V 16 Viewfield rd SW18
97 T 20 Viewfield rd Sidcp
79 W 14 Viewland rd SE18
7 U 19 Viga rd N21
109 X 9 Vigilant clo SE26
140 B 10 Viking st S'hall
58 C 19 Viking rd S'hall
90 F 7 Viking rd SW9
150 G 12 Villa st SE17
80 A 18 Villacourt rd SE18
20 H 16 Village clo E4
99 U 11 Village Green rd Drtfrd
27 S 7 Village rd N3
8 D 19 Village rd Enf
77 Z 16 Village the SE7
78 A 16 Village the SE7
43 Z 12 Village way NW10
44 A 12 Village way NW10
91 O 15 Village way SE21
125 N 3 Village way Becknhm
40 F 1 Village way E Harrow
40 D 1 Village way Pinn
79 P 12 Villas rd SE18
116 L 11 Villiers av Surb
100 F 2 Villiers av Twick
51 O 6 Villiers clo E10
117 N 9 Villiers clo Rich
116 L 11 Villiers path Surb
44 G 17 Villiers rd NW10
124 F 4 Villiers rd Becknhm
83 S 4 Villiers rd Islwth
116 M 6 Villiers rd Kingst
140 K 12 Villiers rd WC2
70 F 4 Villiers st S'hall
82 H 18 Vincam clo Twick

134 G 14 Vince st EC1
126 J 9 Vincent clo Brom
44 E 10 Vincent gdns NW2
20 K 20 Vincent rd E4
30 L 13 Vincent rd N15
30 F 7 Vincent rd N22
79 N 11 Vincent rd SE18
73 U 8 Vincent rd SE18
123 S 18 Vincent rd Croy
68 L 2 Vincent rd Dgnhm
83 P 3 Vincent rd Islwth
117 P 5 Vincent rd Kingst
100 M 14 Vincent row Hampt
148 E 5 Vincent sq SW1
65 P 16 Vincent st E16
148 F 6 Vincent st SW1
133 X 9 Vincent ter N1
24 K 17 Vine ct Harrow
54 B 15 Vine gdns Ilf
133 S 18 Vine hill EC1
142 L 15 Vine la SE1
82 J 10 Vine pl Hounsl
86 D 9 Vine rd E15
143 N 7 Vine st EC3
38 L 14 Vine st Rom
133 U 18 Vine St br EC1
142 B 18 Vine st SE1
33 T 13 Vinegar all E17
6 H 18 Vineries the N14
8 E 11 Vineries the Enf
130 K 14 Vinery vlls NW8
28 A 5 Vines av N3
93 S 8 Viney rd SE13
27 S 2 Vineyard av NW7
105 X 9 Vineyard Hill rd SW19
84 J 13 Vineyard pas Rich
85 X 7 Vineyard path SW14
84 X 14 Vineyard the Rich
133 T 16 Vineyard wlk EC1
90 F 10 Vining st SW9
142 C 9 Vintners pl EC4
80 C 12 Viola av SE2
62 E 20 Viola sq W12
8 B 3 Violet av Enf
156 J 12 Violet gdns Croy
130 B 10 Violet hill NW8
156 J 9 Violet la Croy
33 P 19 Violet rd E17
34 H 7 Violet rd E18
64 C 12 Violet rd E3
139 N 1 Virgil pl W1
149 R 1 Virgil st SE1
36 D 8 Virginia gdns Ilf
134 M 14 Virginia rd E2
108 J 20 Virginia rd Mitch
143 T 10 Virginia st E1
134 B 19 Viscount st EC1
9 T 9 Vista av Enf
35 O 16 Vista dri Ilf
95 P 19 Vista the SE9
24 J 17 Vista way Harrow
26 J 17 Vivian av NW4
43 S 17 Vivian av Wemb
43 O 15 Vivian gdns Wemb
91 Z 7 Vivian gro SE15
63 V 6 Vivian rd E3.
32 S 15 Vivian way N2
84 F 17 Vivienne clo Twick
79 T 20 Voce rd SE18
118 D 14 Voewood clo New Mald
89 X 8 Voltaire rd SW4
34 E 18 Voluntary pl E11
47 V 7 Vorley rd N19
108 B 16 Voss ct SW16
135 U 14 Voss st E2
150 A 6 Vowler st SE17
156 C 15 Vulcan clo Croy
92 K 5 Vulcan rd SE4
14 L 4 Vulcan ter Se4
98 H 8 Vyne the Bxly Hth
61 Z 20 Vyner rd W3
63 N 4 Vyner st E2

W

97 Z 20 W woodside Bxly
65 Y 19 Wada rd E16
150 D 7 Wadding st SE17
51 X 16 Waddington rd E15
51 X 17 Waddington st E15
108 M 19 Waddington way SE19
109 N 20 Waddington way SE19
156 G 4 Waddon clo Croydon
156 E 6 Waddon Ct rd Croy

156 K 2 Waddon New rd Croy
156 F 7 Waddon Pk av Croydon
156 H 5 Waddon rd Croydon
156 F 14 Waddon way Croydon
64 C 19 Wade st E14
64 C 19 Wade's pl E14
17 T 3 Wades gro N21
17 U 3 Wades hill N21
7 T 19 Wades hill N21
135 Y 7 Wadeson st E2
63 O 5 Wadeson st E2
38 A 20 Wadeville av Rom
33 S 3 Wadham av E17
130 J 2 Wadham gdns NW3
41 P 17 Wadham gdns Grnfd
33 T 3 Wadham rd E17
87 T 11 Wadham rd SW15
73 Y 9 Wadhurst rd W4
33 Z 20 Wadley rd E11
00 C 6 Wadsworth rd Grnfd
65 T 15 Waford rd E16
63 Y 13 Wager st E3
5 P 3 Waggon rd Barnt
65 X 4 Waghorn rd E13
24 H 11 Waghorn rd Harrow
91 X 7 Waghorn st SE15
75 P 18 Wagner st SE15
18 J 20 Wagon la N17
38 K 8 Wainfleet av Rom
87 P 20 Wainford cl SW19
94 C 19 Waite Davies rd SE12
151 O 13 Wake st SE11
149 P 6 Wake st SE11
109 S 18 Wakefield gdns SE19
35 P 20 Wakefield gdns Ilf
16 L 17 Wakefield rd N11
31 U 15 Wakefield rd N15
84 H 13 Wakefield rd Rich
66 E 3 Wakefield st E6
18 K 17 Wakefield st N18
132 L 15 Wakefield st WC1
49 O 18 Wakeham st N1
22 E 11 Wakehams hill Pinn
88 L 13 Wakehurst rd SW11
89 N 12 Wakehurst rd SW11
64 M 6 Wakelin rd E15
59 W 15 Wakeling rd W7
93 U 18 Wakeling st E14
128 D 13 Wakeman rd NW10
25 Y 14 Wakemans Hill av SE9
54 B 19 Wakering rd Bark
133 X 11 Wakley st EC1
148 M 19 Walberswick st SW8
142 E 7 Walbrook EC4
150 C 8 Walcorde av SE17
149 U 4 Walcot sq SE11
148 D 5 Walcott st SW1
108 H 7 Waldeck gro SE27
30 J 12 Waldeck rd N15
85 W 7 Waldeck rd SW14
60 C 18 Waldeck rd W13
73 P 15 Waldeck rd W4
101 V 5 Waldegrave gdns Twick
101 W 9 Waldegrave pk Twick
30 G 10 Waldegrave rd N8
109 V 18 Waldegrave rd SE19
60 M 18 Waldegrave rd W5
127 S 10 Waldegrave rd Brom
55 T 6 Waldegrave rd Dgnhm
101 V 8 Waldegrave rd Twick
157 U 7 Waldegrove Croy
87 T 3 Waldemar av SW6
72 D 4 Waldemar av W13
105 X 11 Waldemar rd SW19
17 Z 13 Walden av N13
113 V 10 Walden av Chisl
69 Z 7 Walden av Rnham
81 O 13 Walden clo Blvdr
122 D 7 Walden gdns Thntn Hth
113 U 14 Walden rd Chisl
143 W 3 Walden st E1
63 N 16 Walden st E1
36 H 1 Walden way Ilf
110 C 2 Waldenshaw rd SE23
106 K 19 Waldo pl Mitch
62 J 9 Waldo rd NW10
126 M 7 Waldo rd Brom
110 D 2 Waldram cres SE23
110 E 2 Waldram Pk rd SE23
110 D 2 Waldram pl SE23

125 W 6 Waldron gdns Brom
106 D 5 Waldron rd SW18
41 S 4 Waldron rd Harrow
41 P 7 Waldron's yd Harrow
156 K 9 Waldronhyrst Croy
156 K 8 Waldrons the Croy
93 V 6 Walerand rd SE13
145 K 12 Wales av Carsh
61 Y 15 Wales Farm rd W3
63 U 14 Waley st E1
15 O 1 Walfield av N20
49 T 12 Walford rd N16
93 Y 12 Walfram rd SE13
145 A 20 Walfrey gdns Dgnhm
145 W 6 Walham gro SW6
145 T 16 Walham rd SW6
113 X 11 Walkden rd Chisl
140 E 8 Walker's ct W1
109 N 2 Walkerscroft mead SE21
108 M 1 Walkerscroft mead SE21
99 Y 14 Walkley rd Drtfrd
28 G 9 Walks the N2
66 H 2 Wall End rd E6
64 J 20 Wall rd E14
49 P 19 Wall st N1
137 T 4 Wallace collection W2
154 L 11 Wallace cres Carsh
65 N 9 Wallace rd E15
64 M 9 Wallace rd E15
48 M 17 Wallace rd N1
92 H 6 Wallbutton rd SE4
45 P 3 Wallcote av NW2
39 Z 11 Wallenger av Rom
92 E 3 Waller rd SE14
74 E 1 Wallflower st W12
145 W 6 Wallgrave rd SW5
145 V 15 Wallgrave ter SW5
136 E 4 Wallingford av W10
36 L 20 Wallington rd Ilf
51 N 18 Wallis rd E9
50 M 19 Wallis rd E9
58 K 17 Wallis rd S'hall
85 S 2 Wallorton gdns SW14
51 X 2 Wallwood rd E11
63 Z 15 Wallwood st E14
71 Z 7 Walmer gdns W13
139 N 1 Walmer pl W1
136 J 7 Walmer rd W11
139 N 1 Walmer st W1
79 R 11 Walmer ter SE18
60 B 4 Walmgate rd Grnfd
14 K 18 Walmington fold N12
154 K 11 Walnut clo Carsh
8 B 18 Walnut gro Enf
114 D 20 Walnut Tree clo Chisl
77 O 15 Walnut Tree rd SE10
72 K 17 Walnut Tree rd Brentf
55 X 7 Walnut Tree rd Dgnhm
70 F 17 Walnut Tree rd Hounsl
149 S 4 Walnut Tree wlk SE11
84 M 5 Walpole av Rich
85 N 5 Walpole av Rich
72 D 4 Walpole av W13
101 V 13 Walpole cres Tedd
73 V 13 Walpole gdns W4
101 U 6 Walpole gdns Twick
101 V 13 Walpole pl Tedd
32 J 12 Walpole rd E17
34 B 6 Walpole rd E18
65 Y 2 Walpole rd E6
30 M 7 Walpole rd N17
106 G 15 Walpole rd SW19
127 N 11 Walpole rd Brom
157 N 2 Walpole rd Surb
116 N 16 Walpole rd Surb
101 V 13 Walpole rd Tedd
101 T 4 Walpole rd Twick
75 X 20 Walpole st SE14
147 O 9 Walpole st SW3
42 L 19 Walrond av Wemb
92 E 4 Walsham rd SE14
152 C 10 Walsingham gdns Epsom
49 V 10 Walsingham rd E5
8 B 16 Walsingham rd Enf
120 M 19 Walsingham rd Mitch
63 T 9 Walter st E2
116 J 1 Walter st Kingst

63 T 16 Walter ter E1
12 J 20 Walter wlk Edg
123 S 10 Walters rd SE25
9 R 16 Walters rd Enf
126 E 2 Walters yd Brom
129 R 17 Walterton rd W9
25 R 18 Waltham av NW9
99 V 15 Waltham clo Drtfrd
25 P 9 Waltham dri Edg
120 B 8 Waltham rd Carsh
70 B 8 Waltham rd S'hall
19 Z 12 Waltham way E4
20 B 5 Waltham way E4
33 N 2 Walthamstow av E4
33 X 11 Walthamstow rd E17
31 N 5 Waltheof av N17
31 N 4 Waltheof gdns N17
40 E 12 Walton av Harrow
118 D 10 Walton av New Mald
153 U 5 Walton av Sutton
44 K 7 Walton clo NW2
23 R 12 Walton clo Harrow
40 E 12 Walton cres Harrow
23 R 13 Walton dri Harrow
61 T 15 Walton gdns W3
42 J 7 Walton gdns Wemb
159 U 17 Walton grn Croy
147 O 2 Walton dri SW3
53W 12 Walton rd E12
53W 13 Walton rd E12
65 X 6 Walton rd E13
31 V 14 Walton rd N15
23 R 12 Walton rd Harrow
38 C 2 Walton rd Rom
115 S 8 Walton rd Sidcp
147 N 3 Walton st SW3
146 L 5 Walton st SW3
8 A 6 Walton st Enf
148 K 17 Walton ter SW8
61 T 15 Walton way W3
121 U 9 Walton way Mitch
150 C 10 Walworth pl SE17
150 B 9 Walworth rd SE17
127 N 7 Walwyn av Brom
104 J 1 Wanborough dri SW15
86 J 20 Wanborough dri SW15
106 E 18 Wandle bank SW19
155 Z 6 Wandle bank Wallgtn
155 Z 6 Wandle ct Wallgtn
106 K 3 Wandle rd SW17
106 E 18 Wandle rd SW19
156 L 6 Wandle rd Croy
156 A 5 Wandle rd Croy
120 E 10 Wandle rd Mrdn
155 R 3 Wandle rd Wallgtn
156 E 6 Wandle side Croy
155 R 5 Wandle side Wallgtn
120 L 11 Wandle way Mitch
135 Z 18 Wandon rd E1
145 Z 18 Wandon rd SW6
88 A 5 Wandsworth Br rd SW6
88 G 13 Wandsworth Comm North side SW18
88 E 15 Wandsworth Comm West side SW18
88 G 15 Wandsworth common SW18
87 Y 14 Wandsworth High st SW18
87 Y 13 Wandsworth hill SW18
87 V 10 Wandsworth park SW15
87 Z 13 Wandsworth plain SW18
148 H 18 Wandsworth rd SW8
89 T 6 Wandsworth rd SW8
87 Z 15 Wandsworth stadium SW18
55 V 1 Wangey rd Rom
91 P 9 Wanley rd SE5
90 L 8 Wanless rd SE24
65W 11 Wanlip rd E13
68 Z 1 Wansbeck rd E9
50 M 20 Wansbeck rd E9
45W 18 Wansdown pl SW6
150 A 7 Wansey st SE17
34 K 4 Wansford rd Wdfd Grn
126 L 3 Wanstead clo Brom
35 N 18 Wanstead gdns Ilf
52 K 2 Wanstead house E11
35 S 19 Wanstead la Ilf
52 M 5 Wanstead Pk av E12

53 S 3 Wanstead Pk rd Ilf
35 O 20 Wanstead Pk rd Ilf
34 F 17 Wanstead pl E11
126 K 3 Wanstead rd Brom
98 L 20 Wansunt rd Bxly
94 B 13 Wantage rd SE12
56 G 15 Wantz rd Dgnhm
143 Z 14 Wapping Dock st E1
143 Y 14 Wapping Dock st E1
75 O 3 Wapping High st E1
143 T 14 Wapping High st E1
143 X 10 Wapping la E1
75 N 1 Wapping la E1
75 P 2 Wapping wall E1
74 K 4 Warbeck rd W12
30 D 6 Warberry rd N22
103 T 15 Warboys appro Kingst
20 H 17 Warboys cres E4
103 T 14 Warboys rd Kingst
10 B 19 Warburton rd Harrow
135 X 3 Warburton rd E8
100 J 1 Warburton rd Twick
33 S 8 Warburton ter E17
63 N 2 Warbutt rd E8
81 Z 17 Ward clo Erith
64 H 2 Ward rd E15
47 V 11 Ward rd N19
75 O 9 Wardale clo SE16
40 E 4 Warden av Harrow
47 R 19 Warden rd NW5
142 A 15 Wardens gro SE1
50 F 15 Wardle st E9
63 S 9 Wardley st E18
88 A 19 Wardley st SW18
87 R 2 Wardo av SW6
75 R 12 Wardon st SE16
140 D 6 Wardour ms W1
140 E 7 Wardour st W1
141 Y 7 Wardrobe pl EC4
141 Y 7 Wardrobe ter EC4
54 F 1 Wards rd Ilf
82 J 10 Wareham clo Hounsl
35 Y 15 Waremead rd Ilf
132 G 5 Warf rd NW1
9 V 19 Warf rd Enf
128 F 14 Warfield rd NW10
100 L 20 Warfield rd Hampt
141 V 18 Warfield yd SW1
31 V 18 Wargrave av N15
40 M 10 Wargrave rd Harrow
30 H 16 Warham rd N4
23W 8 Warham rd Harrow
156 M 10 Warham rd S Croy
149 X 18 Warham st SW9
115 R 7 Waring park Sidcp
108 L 9 Waring st SE27
71 Y 19 Warkworth gdns Islwth
31 P 3 Warkworth rd N17
79 T 20 Warland rd SE18
56 C 2 Warley av Dgnhm
19 P 8 Warley rd N9
35 X 4 Warley rd Ilf
34 H 2 Warley rd Wdfd Grn
122 J 8 Warlingham rd Thntn Hth
129 R 16 Warlock rd W9
48 B 12 Warlters clo N7
48 B 12 Warlters ms N7
48 B 12 Warlters rd N7
48 A 2 Warltersville rd N4
90 M 15 Warmington rd SE24
123W 4 Warminster gdns SE25
123W 6 Warminster rd SE25
123 X 3 Warminster rd SE25
121 T 2 Warminster way Mitch
24 H 11 Warneford rd Harrow
135 Y 4 Warneford st E9
153 S 2 Warner av Sutton
52 A 16 Warner clo E7
21 S 16 Warner clo Wdfd Grn
135 T 10 Warner pl E2
32 J 13 Warner rd E17
29 X 13 Warner rd N8
90 M 2 Warner rd SE5
112 C 18 Warner rd Brom
133 R 17 Warner st WC1
133 S 18 Warner yd EC1
154 M 16 Warnham Ct rd Carsh
15 V 17 Warnham rd N12
88 A 11 Warple rd SW18
74 A 4 Warple way W3
51 V 9 Warren av E11
51 X 15 Warren av E15
111 Z 17 Warren av Brom

158 E 17 Warren av S Croy
85 T 9 Warren ave Rich
19 S 5 Warren clo N9
98 E 12 Warren clo Bxly Hth
18 H 3 Warren cres N9
133 S 8 Warren ct N1
111 N 19 Warren ct Becknhm
103 X 17 Warren cutting Kingst
58 L 11 Warren dri Grnfd
57 X 10 Warren dri Hornch
117 T 20 Warren dri Surb
52 K 1 Warren Dri the E11
103W 15 Warren house Kingst
11 N 10 Warren house Stanm
78 M 9 Warren la SE18
10 K 9 Warren la Stanm
103 X 16 Warren pk Kingst
154 H 12 Warren Pk rd Sutton
21 P 3 Warren Pond rd E4
51 V 9 Warren rd E10
34 K 19 Warren rd E11
52 L 1 Warren rd E11
20 G 8 Warren rd E4
44 E 8 Warren rd NW2
106 J 16 Warren rd SW19
10 B 5 Warren rd B Watf
98 D 12 Warren rd Bxly Ht
123 T 19 Warren rd Croy
36 D 15 Warren rd Ilf
103 V 15 Warren rd Kingst
115 T 8 Warren rd Sidcp
83 O 17 Warren rd Twick
109 Y 20 Warren ri Kingst
132 B 17 Warren st W1
131 Z 18 Warren st W1
37 X 14 Warren ter Rom
53 R 12 Warren the E12
154 H 20 Warren the Carsh
70 D 20 Warren the Hounsl
7 Y 16 Warren wlk SE7
47 V 11 Warrender rd N19
89 N 2 Warriner gdns SW11
130 A 19 Warrington cres W9
130 A 19 Warrington gdns W9
156 H 6 Warrington rd Croy
55 X 7 Warrington rd Dgnhm
23 T 16 Warrington rd Harrow
55 X 7 Warrington sq Dgnhm
65 S 12 Warrington st E13
53 V 12 Warrior sq E12
78 C 8 Warspite rd SE18
64 G 3 Warton rd E15
129 Y 9 Warwick av W9
12 G 11 Warwick av Edg
40 D 13 Warwick av Harrow
5 V 16 Warwick clo Barnt
10 F 3 Warwick clo Bushey Watf
100 M 18 Warwick clo Hampt
138 B 1 Warwick cres W2
141 R 2 Warwick ct WC1
72 K 3 Warwick dene W5
86 J 9 Warwick dri SW15
135 P 3 Warwick gdns E8
30 L 17 Warwick gdns N4
145 P 3 Warwick gdns W14
54 A 5 Warwick gdns Ilf
49 Z 5 Warwick gro E5
50 A 5 Warwick gro E5
116 L 16 Warwick gro Surb
141 Y 5 Warwick la EC4
129 Z 18 Warwick ms W9
148 A 9 Warwick pl SW1
72 G 4 Warwick pl W5
130 A 20 Warwick pl W9
34 J 15 Warwick rd E11
53 R 16 Warwick rd E12
52 D 18 Warwick rd E15
32 K 6 Warwick rd E17
20 A 19 Warwick rd E4
135 P 5 Warwick rd E8
16 L 19 Warwick rd N11
18 F 15 Warwick rd N18
124 B 6 Warwick rd SE20
72 G 4 Warwick rd W5
5 N 15 Warwick rd Barnt
9 Z 1 Warwick rd Enf
117 U 5 Warwick rd New Mald
70 E 8 Warwick rd S'hall
115 R 13 Warwick rd Sidcp
154 C 10 Warwick rd Sutton
122 E 7 Warwick rd Thntn Hth
101 U 1 Warwick rd Twick
97 T 7 Warwick rd Welling

145 P 5 Warwick road W14
147 Z 2 Warwick row SW1
148 A 8 Warwick sq SW1
141 Y 5 Warwick sq EC4
148 A 8 Warwick Sq ms SW1
140 C 9 Warwick st W1
79 T 16 Warwick ter SE18
148 B 6 Warwick way SW1
147 X 9 Warwick way SW1
134 C 18 Warwick yd EC1
49 T 11 Warwickshire rd N16
75 Z 18 Warwickshire st SE8
53 S 11 Washington av E12
34 C 7 Washington rd E18
65 Y 2 Washington rd E6
74 G 19 Washington rd SW13
117 O 4 Washington rd Kingst
152 J 1 Washington rd Worc Pk
64 E 9 Washington st E3
110 G 1 Wastdale rd SE23
93W 3 Wat Tyler rd SE10
73 P 17 Watcombe cotts Rich
123 Z 11 Watcombe rd SE25
124 A 10 Watcombe rd SE25
142 K 10 Water la EC3
52 A 18 Water la E15
54 J 10 Water la Ilf
116 G 2 Water la Twick
84 G 13 Water la Rich
101 Z 1 Water la Twick
100 G 5 Water Mill way Felt
61 N 4 Water rd Wemb
155 Y 14 Water ri Wallgtn
141 R 8 Water st WC2
157 R 9 Water Tower hill Croy
156 L 5 Water Works yd Croy
111 T 18 Waterbank rd SE6
55 T 18 Waterbeach rd Dgnhm
80 A 17 Waterdale rd SE2
51 P 18 Waterden rd E15
16 G 10 Waterfall clo N14
106 H 15 Waterfall cotts SW19
16 F 14 Waterfall rd N11
145W 19 Waterford rd SW6
88 A 1 Waterford rd SW6
141 W 8 Watergate EC4
76 A 15 Watergate st SE8
140 L 12 Watergate wlk EC4
20 L 13 Waterhall av E4
141 O 11 Waterloo br WC2
39 O 18 Waterloo ct Rom
63 P 6 Waterloo gdns E2
129 R 1 Waterloo pas NW6
140 F 13 Waterloo pl SW1
84 J 12 Waterloo pl Rich
51 N 2 Waterloo rd E10
65 Y 2 Waterloo rd E6
52 D 14 Waterloo rd E7
44 G 5 Waterloo rd NW2
141 U 18 Waterloo rd SE1
36 B 7 Waterloo rd Ilf
39 O 17 Waterloo rd Rom
154 F 10 Waterloo rd Sutton
134 B 14 Waterloo st EC1
141 R 16 Waterloo station SE1
133W 2 Waterloo ter N1
47 U 4 Waterlow rd N19
87 R 9 Waterman st SW15
102 H 18 Watermans clo Kingst
120 M 15 Watermead la Carsh
111 T 9 Watermead rd SE6
102 C 8 Watermill clo Rich
115 S 17 Waters gdns Dgnhm
112 B 6 Waters rd SE6
111 Y 7 Waters rd SE6
117 S 5 Waters rd Kingst
24 H 2 Watersfield way Edg
124 M 1 Waterside Becknhm
99 S 12 Waterside Drtfrd
131 U 3 Waterside pl NW1
134 L 12 Waterson st N1
30 M 5 Waterville rd N17
50 E 8 Waterworks la E5
90 B 15 Waterworks rd SW2
119 V 2 Watery la SW20
115 S 17 Watery la Sidcp
120 L 14 Wates way Mitch
10 M 1 Watford By pass Borhm Wd

88 K 1 Watford clo SW11
41 Y 4 Watford rd Harrow
42 B 13 Watford rd Wemb
13 O 14 Watford way NW7
26 E 4 Watford way NW7
43 S 11 Watkin rd Wemb
25 U 6 Watling av SE9
26 A 1 Watling av Edg
142 B 7 Watling ct EC4
45 T 17 Watling gdns NW2
142 B 7 Watling st Bxly Hth
98 J 11 Watling st Bxly Hth
99 X 15 Watling st Drtfrd
110 H 12 Watlington gro SE26
63 N 18 Watney mkt E1
143 R 18 Watney pas SE1
85 V 6 Watney rd SW14
63 N 18 Watney st E1
63 N 17 Watney st E1
121 W 12 Watneys rd Mitch
53 W 20 Watson av E6
153 S 2 Watson av Sutton
106 K 16 Watson clo SW19
65 U 5 Watson st E13
49 P 14 Watson st N16
138 M 3 Watson's ms W1
75 Z 20 Watson's st SE8
30 D 6 Watsons rd N22
101 Y 12 Watt's la Tedd
50 C 9 Wattisfield rd E5
64 C 13 Watts gro E3
114 A 20 Watts la Chisl
113 Z 20 Watts la Chisl
75 N 3 Watts st E1
143 X 13 Watts st E1
17 V 15 Wauthier clo N13
129 W 2 Wavel ms NW6
96 J 15 Wavell dri Sidcp
73 Y 14 Wavendon av W4
92 A 10 Waveney av SE15
19 X 15 Waverley av E4
117 U 14 Waverley av Surb
154 C 4 Waverley av Sutton
100 G 1 Waverley av Twick
82 E 20 Waverley av Twick
43 N 16 Waverley av Wemb
34 K 6 Waverley clo E18
127 N 12 Waverley clo Brom
79 R 15 Waverley cres SE18
67 U 7 Waverley gdns Bark
36 D 8 Waverley gdns Ilf
27 S 10 Waverley gro N3
130 F 8 Waverley pl NW8
33 V 10 Waverley rd E17
34 K 6 Waverley rd E18
31 Y 2 Waverley rd N17
29 Z 20 Waverley rd N8
79 R 14 Waverley rd SE18
124 A 8 Waverley rd SE25
123 Z 8 Waverley rd SE25
7 X 12 Waverley rd Enf
152 J 11 Waverley rd Epsom
40 C 4 Waverley rd Harrow
58 H 19 Waverley rd S'hall
154 K 14 Waverley way Carsh
31 V 8 Waverly vlls N17
139 W 12 Waverton st W1
34 F 7 Wavertree rd E18
108 B 2 Wavertree rd SW2
58 G 17 Waxlow cres S'hall
61 X 6 Waxlow rd NW10
22 A 8 Waxwell clo Pinn
22 A 9 Waxwell la Pinn
58 A 9 Wayfarer rd Grnfd
136 G 9 Wayflete st W10
88 K 6 Wayford st SW11
49 X 16 Wayland av E8
88 F 9 Wayland rd SW11
108 J 6 Waylett pl SE27
136 G 8 Waynfere St est W10
156 J 7 Waynflete av Croy
106 D 4 Waynflete st SW18
45 T 4 Wayside NW11
85 W 12 Wayside rd SW18
159 S 14 Wayside Croy
10 C 1 Wayside av Bushey Watf
6 J 19 Wayside clo N14
39 S 10 Wayside clo Rom
56 D 14 Wayside gdns Dgnhm
113 T 10 Wayside gro SE9
23 S 5 Weald la Harrow
23 V 3 Weald ri Harrow
49 Y 6 Weald sq E5
113 U 15 Weald the Chisl
38 G 19 Weald way Rom
153 V 3 Wealdstone st NW9
20 K 10 Weale rd E4
99 Z 20 Weardale av Drtfrd

8 C 6 Weardale gdns Enf
93 X 11 Weardale rd SE13
135 S 18 Weaver st E1
108 K 10 Weaver wlk SE27
142 L 15 Weavers la SE1
50 J 3 Webb st SE1
141 U 19 Webber row SE1
141 X 18 Webber st SE1
88 L 12 Webbs rd SW11
72 G 3 Webster gdns W5
67 E 11 Webster rd E11
151 U 2 Webster rd SE16
46 G 15 Wedderburn rd NW3
67 T 4 Wedderburn rd Bark
128 M 17 Wedlake st W10
35 W 4 Wedmore av Ilf
47 X 8 Wedmore gdns N19
59 R 10 Wedmore rd Grnfd
47 Y 9 Wedmore st N19
22 U 3 Weech rd NW6
47 P 15 Weedington rd NW5
76 L 8 Weetman st SE10
94 F 12 Weigall rd SE12
139 V 7 Weighhouse st W1
123 Z 3 Weighton rd SE20
23 R 4 Weighton rd Harrow
154 G 11 Weihurst gdns Sutton
87 R 9 Weimar st SW15
18 B 19 Weir Hall av N18
18 A 15 Weir Hall gdns N15
31 P 1 Weir Hall rd N17
18 C 17 Weir Hall rd N18
83 V 19 Weir rd Bxly
98 U 19 Weir rd Bxly
132 G 13 Weir's pas NW1
15 Z 8 Weirdale av N20
15 Z 7 Weirdale ave N11
87 P 8 Weiss rd SW15
112 G 10 Welbeck clo Brom
115 N 2 Welbeck clo Sidcp
15 T 15 Welbeck clo N12
152 F 17 Welbeck clo Epsom
118 C 11 Welbeck clo New Mald
66 A 8 Welbeck rd E6
5 V 19 Welbeck rd Barnt
120 H 20 Welbeck rd Carsh
40 K 3 Welbeck rd Harrow
154 C 6 Welbeck rd Sutton
139 W 5 Welbeck st W1
139 W 4 Welbeck way W1
311 V 1 Welbourne rd N17
49 U 20 Welbury st E8
90 K 3 Welby st SE5
107 R 13 Welham rd SW17
154 H 1 Welhouse rd Carsh
4 A 16 Well appr Barnt
40 B 10 Well clo Ruis
142 C 7 Well ct EC4
95 S 10 Well Hall rd SE9
85 V 12 Well la SW14
46 G 10 Well pl NW3
46 G 10 Well rd NW3
4 A 17 Well rd Barnt
51 Y 17 Well st E15
63 P 1 Well st E9
135 Z 1 Well st E9
50 D 20 Well st E9
76 G 17 Well st SE10
24 C 18 Wellacre rd Harrow
59 V 7 Welland gdns Grnfd
143 T 8 Wellclose sq E1
143 T 10 Wellclose st E1
23 T 17 Welldon cres Harrow
142 A 17 Weller st SE1
132 J 10 Wellers ct NW1
74 H 8 Wellesley av W6
101 S 5 Wellesley cres Twick
157 N 3 Wellesley Ct rd Croy
119 T 19 Wellesley fount Sutton
157 O 3 Wellesley gro Croy
47 O 15 Wellesley pl NW5
34 F 16 Wellesley rd E11
33 O 18 Wellesley rd E17
47 O 15 Wellesley rd NW5
30 F 7 Wellesley rd N22
73 P 14 Wellesley rd W4
122 M 20 Wellesley rd Croy
156 M 2 Wellesley rd Croy
157 N 3 Wellesley rd Croy
23 T 17 Wellesley rd Harrow
53 Y 6 Wellesley rd Ilf
54 B 4 Wellesley rd Ilf
154 D 13 Wellesley rd Sutton
101 S 6 Wellesley rd Twick
134 C 11 Wellesley ter N1
29 S 9 Wellfield av N10
108 B 10 Wellfield rd SW16
108 D 11 Wellfield wlk SW16

42 A 18 Wellgarth Grnfd
46 A 4 Wellgarth rd NW11
4 B 14 Wellhouse la Barnt
125 N 9 Wellhouse rd Becknhm
97 R 8 Welling High st Welling
96 D 7 Welling way SE9
20 C 9 Wellington av E4
31 W 18 Wellington av N15
19 N 10 Wellington av N9
82 G 13 Wellington av Hounsl
22 E 4 Wellington av Pinn
97 N 15 Wellington av Sidcp
152 M 6 Wellington av Worc Pk
137 S 6 Wellington clo W11
69 X 1 Wellington clo Dgnhm
117 W 7 Wellington cres New Mald
69 Y 1 Wellington dri Dgnhm
77 X 14 Wellington gdns SE7
101 P 9 Wellington gdns Hampt
130 H 12 Wellington pl NW8
50 M 3 Wellington rd E10
34 G 14 Wellington rd E11
32 J 12 Wellington rd E17
66 G 5 Wellington rd E6
52 D 14 Wellington rd E7
18 E 12 Wellington rd NW10
15 U 2 Wellington rd NW8
105 Z 5 Wellington rd SW19
72 D 9 Wellington rd W5
81 P 12 Wellington rd Bxly
126 L 9 Wellington rd Brom
97 V 14 Wellington rd Bxly
122 J 17 Wellington rd Croy
18 E 4 Wellington rd Enf
8 E 18 Wellington rd Enf
101 P 10 Wellington rd Hampt
23 T 9 Wellington rd Harrow
82 E 10 Wellington rd North Hounsl
22 D 4 Wellington rd Pinn
85 N 15 Wellington rd Rick
82 G 14 Wellington rd South Hounsl
135 R 12 Wellington row E2
147 N 10 Wellington sq SW3
64 L 14 Wellington st E10
78 K 11 Wellington st SE18
140 M 8 Wellington st WC2
141 N 8 Wellington st WC2
67 O 2 Wellington st Bark
41 R 4 Wellington ter Harrow
64 A 11 Wellington way E3
93 Z 18 Wellmeadow rd SE13
111 Z 3 Wellmeadow rd SE6
71 Y 10 Wellmeadow rd W7
120 G 20 Wellow wlk Carsh
140 B 2 Wells bldgs W1
150 K 20 Wells cres SE5
43 X 5 Wells dri NW9
56 G 16 Wells gdns Dgnhm
53 R 1 Wells gdns Ilf
57 U 18 Wells gdns Rainhm
62 B 13 Wells House rd NW10
70 J 1 Wells la S'hall
140 B 3 Wells ms W1
110 A 8 Wells Park gro SE26
109 X 8 Wells Park rd SE26
74 M 7 Wells rd W12
136 C 19 Wells rd W12
127 U 3 Wells rd Brom
131 O 6 Wells st W1
140 B 3 Wells st W1
48 F 6 Wells ter N4
16 L 4 Wells the N14
150 H 16 Wells way SE5
150 G 15 Wells Way bridge SE5
48 E 15 Wells yd N7
4 A 15 Wellside clo Brentf
85 V 12 Wellside gdns SW14
127 W 5 Wellsmoor gdns Harrow
19 R 4 Wellstead av N9
66 J 7 Wellstead rd E6
55 N 2 Wellwood rd Ilf
88 D 13 Wellwood rd SW18
135 U 4 Welshpool st E8
74 G 13 Weltje rd W6

79 U 20 Welton rd SE18
42 L 10 Wembley Hill rd Wemb
43 N 13 Wembley Hill rd. Wemb
43 O 10 Wembley Pk dri Wemb
42 M 12 Wembley Pk dri Wemb
100 G 19 Wembley rd Hampt
43 U 17 Wembley way Wemb
47 U 1 Wembury rd N6
94 C 5 Wemyss rd SE3
41 S 8 Wendela ct Harrow
74 C 7 Wendell rd W12
154 F 1 Wendling rd Sutton
63 Z 3 Wendon st E3
118 E 14 Wendover dri New Mald
62 D 6 Wendover rd NW10
95 O 7 Wendover rd SE9
126 H 7 Wendover rd Brom
97 O 11 Wendover way Welling
8 G 19 Wendy clo Enf
60 K 4 Wendy way Wemb
134 B 10 Wenlock rd N1
12 G 20 Wenlock rd Edg
134 D 10 Wenlock st N1
63 T 6 Wennington rd E3
34 D 1 Wensley av Wdfd Grn
18 M 19 Wensley rd N18
35 S 5 Wensleydale av Ilf
100 K 18 Wensleydale gdns Hampt
100 J 17 Wensleydale rd Hampt
111 Y 4 Wentland clo SE6
111 Y 5 Wentland rd SE6
27 Z 1 Wentworth av N3
14 M 20 Wentworth av N3
119 W 17 Wentworth clo Mrdn
99 X 17 Wentworth dri Drtfrd
17 V 12 Wentworth gdns N13
42 M 3 Wentworth hill Wemb
43 N 3 Wentworth hill Wemb
27 Z 2 Wentworth pk N3
53 N 14 Wentworth rd E12
27 V 19 Wentworth rd NW11
4 D 11 Wentworth rd Brentf
122 F 18 Wentworth rd Croy
143 P 3 Wentworth st E1
22 A 13 Wentworth way Pinn
98 F 4 Wenvoe av Bxly Hth
63 X 11 Wenwith pl E3
144 M 17 Werley av SW6
24 E 3 Wernborough st Stanm
79 P 15 Wernbrook st SE18
123 X 10 Werndee rd SE25
35 V 10 Werneth Hall rd Ilf
132 D 10 Werrington st NW1
87 R 11 Werter rd SW15
61 X 8 Wesley av NW10
82 D 4 Wesley av Hounsl
41 N 6 Wesley clo Harrow
51 U 2 Wesley rd E10
61 X 3 Wesley rd NW10
139 V 1 Wesley st W1
47 R 12 Wesleyan pl NW5
119 Z 5 Wessex av SW19
99 S 3 Wessex dri Erith
45 S 3 Wessex gdns NW11
83 P 10 Wessex st E2
45 S 2 Wessex way NW11
63 R 17 West Arbour st E1
33 R 15 West av E17
27 O 15 West av NW4
14 L 19 West av N3
22 D 19 West av Pinn
58 D 19 West av S'hall
56 B 12 West av Wallgtn
33 P 14 West Avenue rd E17
49 S 2 West bank N16
66 M 3 West bank Bark
118 L 9 West Barnes la New Mald
30 G 9 West Beech rd N22
140 K 4 West Central st WC1
22 J 4 West chantry Harrow
18 H 11 West clo N9
6 B 14 West clo Barnt
59 N 6 West clo Grnfd
43 N 4 West clo Wemb
45 Y 15 West cotts NW6

14 L20	West ct N3
42 D8	West ct Wemb
42 M4	West ct Wemb
107 U9	West drive SW16
10 C19	West drive Harrow
153 P19	West drive Sutton
10 C20	West Drive gdns Harrow
147 S4	West Eaton pl SW1
62 A1	West Ella rd NW10
33 W16	West End av E10
22 A13	West End av Pinn
45 Z20	West End la NW6
129 V4	West End la NW6
45 Z20	West End la NW6
4 C14	West End la Barnt
22 A15	West End la Pinn
70 B2	West End rd S'hall
76 D12	West Ferry rd E14
43 Z10	West gdns E1
68 N20	West gdns E1
106 J19	West gdns SW17
31 P14	West Green rd N15
30 K13	West Green rd N15
21 Z17	West gro Wdfd Grn
147 S1	West Halkin st SW1
85 S3	West Hall rd Rich
113 P1	West hallowes SE9
64 M2	West Ham la E15
65 R1	West Ham park E15
45 Z19	West Hampstead ms NW6
141 T5	West Harding st EC4
45 Y5	West Heath av NW11
45 Y9	West Heath clo NW3
99 U16	West Heath clo Drtfrd
45 Y4	West Heath dri NW11
45 Y8	West Heath gdns NW3
45 Y7	West Heath rd NW3
45 B9	West Heath rd NW3
80 H17	West Heath rd SE2
99 U16	West Heath rd Drtfrd
44 H3	West Hendon bdwy NW9/NW2
87 P18	West hill SW15
41 S6	West hill Harrow
157 S19	West hill S Croy
45 O4	West hill Wemb
42 M4	West hill Wemb
87 W16	West Hill rd SW18
19 N6	West Hill way N20
98 L1	West holme Erith
45 A20	West India Dock rd E14
143 W19	West la SE16
73 P3	West Lodge av W3
137 V12	West mall W8
152 B14	West mead Epsom
111 U18	West Moat clo Beckhm
147 Z8	West ms SW1
11 W20	West oak Beckhm
113 R2	West park SE9
85 R2	West Park av Rich
37 X16	West Park clo Rom
85 R1	West Park gdns Rich
85 P3	West Park rd Rich
104 L2	West pl SW19
141 W2	West Poultry av EC1
65 R3	West rd E15
31 Z1	West rd N17
18 M20	West rd N17
85 W6	West rd SW14
147 R12	West rd SW3
89 Z12	West rd SW4
60 J14	West rd W5
16 B5	West rd Barnt
103 W20	West rd Kingst
37 X17	West rd Rom
56 M3	West rd Rom
58 M6	West Ridge gdns Grnfd
128 J17	West row W10
84 L10	West Sheen vale Rich
105 N15	West Side comm SW10
104 M13	West Side comm SW19
141 X2	West smithfield EC1
149 W1	West sq SE11
51 Z8	West st E11
33 R16	West st E17
140 H7	West st WC2
72 D18	West st Brentf
126 E2	West st Brom
98 A20	West st Bxly Hth
154 L9	West st Carsh
156 M7	West st Croy
41 S4	West st Harrow
154 A11	West st Sutton
154 M8	West St la Carsh
85 T12	West Temple sheen SW14
143 O7	West Tenter st E1
26 M15	West view N4
18 D3	West View cres N9
147 Z8	West Warwick dri SW1
43 Z10	West way NW10
62 G19	West way W12
12 G19	West way Edg
82 D1	West way Hounsl
125 Y15	West way W Wkhm
158 G2	West Way gdns Croy
60 J15	West wlk W5
16 B4	West wlk Barnt
100 M15	Westbank rd Hampt
11 U15	Westbere dri Stanm
45 T14	Westbere rd NW2
61 X18	Westbourne av W3
153 S1	Westbourne av Sutton
138 E8	Westbourne cres W2
110 E3	Westbourne dri SE23
137 X4	Westbourne gdns W2
137 W6	Westbourne gro W2
98 G11	Westbourne gro Bxly Hth
137 T7	Westbourne Gro ms W11
137 X5	Westbourne Gro ter W2
137 X5	Westbourne Pk ms W2
137 R4	Westbourne Pk rd W11
137 X4	Westbourne Pk rd W2
137 W3	Westbourne Pk vlls W2
19 N11	Westbourne pl N9
48 D17	Westbourne rd N7
61 E14	Westbourne rd SE26
80 K19	Westbourne rd Bxly Hth
123 V15	Westbourne rd Croy
138 G9	Westbourne st W2
138 A3	Westbourne ter W2
138 A1	Westbourne ter W2
138 C5	Westbourne Ter ms W2
88 H2	Westbridge rd SW11
146 J20	Westbridge rd SW11
100 E17	Westbrook av Hampt
5 U11	Westbrook clo Barnt
5 T12	Westbrook cres Barnt
94 H2	Westbrook rd SE3
70 E19	Westbrook rd Hounsl
123 O2	Westbrook rd Thntn Hth
5 T11	Westbrook sq Barnt
97 T6	Westbrooke cres Welling
114 F5	Westbrooke rd Sidcp
97 T7	Westbrooke rd Welling
32 M12	Westbury E17
30 L6	Westbury av N22
30 H10	Westbury av N22
58 G12	Westbury av S'hall
42 K20	Westbury av Wemb
14 L18	Westbury gro N3
21 Y7	Westbury la Buck Hl
72 G15	Westbury pl Brentf
33 N13	Westbury rd E17
52 J16	Westbury rd E7
44 A20	Westbury rd NW10
17 N19	Westbury rd N11
14 M17	Westbury rd N12
124 E1	Westbury rd SE20
60 J18	Westbury rd W5
67 S3	Westbury rd Bark
124 J6	Westbury rd Beacknhm
127 O1	Westbury rd Brom
21 Y6	Westbury rd Buck Hl
113 O20	Westbury rd Chisl
123 O15	Westbury rd Croy
100 A2	Westbury rd Felt
53 V7	Westbury rd Ilf
42 K20	Westbury rd Wemb
89 V4	Westbury st SW8
52 J17	Westbury ter E7
27 O10	Westchester dri NW4
118 E1	Westcombe av SW20
122 B16	Westcombe av Croy
4 L17	Westcombe dri Barnt
77 T8	Westcombe hill SE3
77 T14	Westcombe hill SE7
77 R15	Westcombe Pk rd SE10
77 R18	Westcombe Pk rd SE3
107 V13	Westcote rd SW16
159 T19	Westcott clo Croy
59 U16	Westcott cres W7
149 X12	Westcott rd SE17
45 S12	Westcroft clo NW2
119 U8	Westcroft gdns Mrdn
155 P8	Westcroft rd Carsh
74 F13	Westcroft sq W6
45 S12	Westcroft way NW2
78 M17	Westdale pas SE18
78 M16	Westdale rd SE18
112 K2	Westdean av SE12
112 L12	Westdown rd E15
93 N19	Westdown rd SE6
77 S14	Westerdale rd SE10
31 T15	Westerfield rd N15
18 D11	Westerham av N9
97 S15	Westerham dri Sidcp
33 S20	Westerham rd E10
110 L11	Westerly cres SE26
27 N11	Western av NW11
62 B19	Western av W3
61 U13	Western av W3
65 X5	Western av W5
56 L17	Western av Dgnhm
57 N17	Western av Dgnhm
58 F3	Western av Grnfd
59 S7	Western av Grnfd
60 F8	Western av Grnfd
70 D1	Western av Shall
137 V2	Western Av extension W2
14 M20	Western ct N3
61 O19	Western gdns W5
129 R19	Western ms W9
65 X5	Western rd E13
33 U16	Western rd E17
28 L12	Western rd N2
27 L12	Western rd N2
30 C9	Western rd N22
90 G8	Western rd SW9
72 H1	Western rd W5
60 K20	Western rd W5
120 J2	Western rd Mitch
39 S15	Western rd Rom
70 B8	Western rd S'hall
153 X12	Western rd Sutton
51 W19	Western st E15
74 L19	Western ter W6
14 M1	Western way N20
36 B20	Westernville gdns Ilf
12 M11	Westfield clo Enf
153 U8	Westfield clo Sutton
24 H14	Westfield dri Harrow
24 G13	Westfield gdns Harrow
64 G13	Westfield la Harrow
22 E1	Westfield pk Pinn
12 M11	Westfield rd NW7
30 B14	Westfield rd N8
71 Z3	Westfield rd W13
72 A4	Westfield rd W13
124 L3	Westfield rd Beacknhm
98 L87	Westfield rd Bxly Hth
156 J3	Westfield rd Croy
56 M15	Westfield rd Dgnhm
129 K4	Westfield rd Mitch
116 F13	Westfield rd Surb
153 U8	Westfield rd Sutton
98 B9	Westfield rd SE18
86 D7	Westfields SW3
86 C7	Westfields av SW13
61 U15	Westfields rd W3
128 J17	Westgate ms SW1
80 L15	Westgate rd SE2
123 Z9	Westgate rd SE25
124 A9	Westgate rd SE25
111 T19	Westgate rd Beacknhm
125 S2	Westgate rd Beacknhm
135 X3	Westgate st E8
145 Y12	Westgate ter SW10
93 V2	Westgrove la SE10
149 Z19	Westhall rd SE5
85 U12	Westhay gdns SW14
28 A14	Westholm NW11
94 G17	Westhorne av SE12
95 P12	Westhorne av SE9
87 N8	Westhorpe rd SW15
105 S1	Westhouse clo SW19
114 A12	Westhurst dri Chisl
17 T11	Westlake clo N13
75 R12	Westlake rd SE16
134 D12	Westland pl N1
89 U17	Westlands ter SW12
71 X8	Westlea rd W7
86 L14	Westleigh av SW15
86 O15	Westleigh av SW15
127 R2	Westleigh dri Brom
25 P6	Westleigh gdns Edg
86 J17	Westmead SW15
154 H9	Westmead rd Sutton
12 K10	Westmere dri NW7
140 J20	Westminster abbey SW1
122 H2	Westminster av Thntn Hth
140 L18	Westminster br SW1
141 P19	Westminster Br rd SE1
148 B3	Westminster cathedral SW1
36 E8	Westminster clo Ilf
101 X12	Westminster clo Tedd
17 N17	Westminster rd N13
67 U7	Westminster gdns Bark
36 D8	Westminster gdns Ilf
19 N6	Westminster rd N9
71 U4	Westminster rd W7
154 E1	Westminster rd Sutton
9 T8	Westmoor gdns Enf
9 S9	Westmoor rd Enf
78 A10	Westmoor st SE7
96 H9	Westmoreland av Welling
84 B15	Westmoreland clo Twick
137 S4	Westmoreland ms SW1
147 Y11	Westmoreland pl SW1
33 O19	Westmoreland rd E17
25 N11	Westmoreland rd NW9
150 D13	Westmoreland rd SE17
86 F2	Westmoreland rd SW13
126 B10	Westmoreland rd Brom
139 W1	Westmoreland st W1
147 X12	Westmoreland ter SW1
22 L16	Westmorland rd Harrow
121 Z10	Westmorland way Mitch
95 W10	Westmount rd SE9
19 N10	Westoe rd N9
55 N15	Weston dri Bark
24 C5	Weston dri Stanm
83 R3	Weston gdns Islwrth
56 A11	Weston grn Dgnhm
112 D19	Weston gro Brom
89 O18	Weston la SW2
30 C17	Weston pk N8
73 U9	Weston rd W4
112 D19	Weston rd Brom
55 Z11	Weston rd Dgnhm
8 C8	Weston rd Enf
133 O11	Weston rise WC1
150 G3	Weston st SE1
142 H17	Weston st SE1
142 H15	Weston st SE1
135 Z1	Weston wlk E9
88 E17	Westover rd SW18
109 T15	Westow hill SE19
109 T17	Westow st SE19
6 F15	Westpole av Barnt
63 T17	Westport rd E1
65 V13	Westport rd E1
63 T17	Westport rd E1
65 V13	Westport rd E13
54 M14	Westrow dri Bark
54 K19	Westrow dri Bark
54 L19	Westrow gdns Ilf
28 H6	Westside NW4
44 C14	Westview clo NW10

Ref	Name
74 G 6	Westville rd W12
20 A 18	Westward rd E4
19 Y 18	Westward rd E4
24 K 19	Westward way Harrow
118 K 7	Westway SW20
136 B 7	Westway W12
118 K 6	Westway clo SW20
152 E 8	Westways Epsom
107 Z 15	Westwell rd SW16
136 E 19	Westwick gdns W14
109 N 19	Westwood av SE19
40 L 12	Westwood av Harrow
86 D 8	Westwood gdns SW13
110 B 10	Westwood hill SE26
96 L 10	Westwood la Welling
97 N 13	Westwood la Welling
110 B 1	Westwood pk SE23
92 A 19	Westwood pk SE23
77 V 3	Westwood rd E16
86 D 8	Westwood rd SW13
54 L 4	Westwood rd Ilf
24 D 6	Wetheral dri Stanm
40 J 17	Wetherby clo Grnfd
146 A 8	Wetherby gdns SW5
145 Y 9	Wetherby ms SW5
146 B 7	Wetherby rd SW7
7 Z 14	Wetherby rd Enf
50 L 1	Wetherden st E17
63 T 3	Wetherell rd E9
29 P 4	Wetherill rd N10
88 L 19	Wexford rd SW12
106 C 6	Weybourne st SW18
122 G 10	Weybridge rd Thntn Hth
105 S 2	Weydown clo SW19
56 B 10	Weylond rd Dgnhm
94 M 2	Weyman rd SE3
13 O 15	Weyman av NW7
72 E 8	Weymouth av W5
153 Z 16	Weymouth ct Sutton
139 X 1	Weymouth ms W1
135 O 8	Weymouth pl E2
139 W 1	Weymouth st W1
131 X 20	Weymouth st W1
135 O 9	Weymouth ter E2
10 L 20	Weymouth wlk Stanm
48 F 7	Whadcoat st N4
38 A 18	Whalebone av Rom
142 F 4	Whalebone ct EC2
38 A 18	Whalebone gro Rom
64 M 1	Whalebone la E15
37 Y 3	Whalebone la N Rom
38 A 7	Whalebone la N Rom
56 B 3	Whalebone la S Dgnhm
38 A 17	Whalebone la S Rom
101 Y 2	Wharf la Twick
135 U 7	Wharf pl E2
64 J 3	Wharf rd E15
134 A 9	Wharf rd N1
134 B 11	Wharf rd N1
19 V 1	Wharf rd N9
9 W 18	Wharf rd Enf
64 L 15	Wharf st E16
132 L 8	Wharfdale rd N1
122 D 7	Wharfedale gdns Thntn Hth
145 X 11	Wharfedale st SW10
71 P 2	Wharncliffe dri S'hall
123 R 4	Wharncliffe gdns SE25
123 R 4	Wharncliffe rd SE25
63 R 8	Wharncliffe st E2
126 H 1	Wharton rd Brom
133 P 13	Wharton st WC1
110 F 17	Whateley rd SE20
91 U 13	Whateley rd SE22
119 R 5	Whatley av SW20
92 G 19	Whatman rd SE23
9 U 7	Wheatfields Enf
9 U 8	Wheatfields Enf
123 Z 5	Wheathill rd SE20
124 A 6	Wheathill rd SE20
70 H 17	Wheatlands Hounsl
107 O 7	Wheatlands rd SW17
18 C 9	Wheatley gdns N9
83 V 7	Wheatley rd Islwth
139 V 1	Wheatley st W1
148 K 17	Wheatsheaf la SW8
39 T 18	Wheatsheaf rd Rom
39 T 19	Wheatsheaf rd Rom
145 R 20	Wheatsheaf ter SW6
128 L 20	Wheatstone rd W10
56 K 9	Wheel Farm dri Dgnhm
48 C 20	Wheelwright st N7
135 N 18	Wheler st E1
74 A 7	Whellock rd W4
15 S 8	Whetstone clo N20
135 O 3	Whetstone pk WC2
94 L 4	Whetstone st SE3
48 A 7	Whewell rd N4
132 K 13	Whidborne st WC1
107 X 11	Whinfell clo SW16
95 R 8	Whinyates rd SE9
33 W 15	Whipps cross E17
34 B 18	Whipps Cross rd E11
33 X 16	Whipps Cross rd E11
133 U 14	Whiskin st EC1
25 N 7	Whistler gdns Edg
43 M 18	Whistler st N5
135 S 6	Whiston rd E2
134 M 7	Whiston rd N1
92 K 1	Whitbread rd SE4
45 T 13	Whitburn rd SE13
61 S 8	Whitby av NW10
25 R 10	Whitby gdns NW9
154 F 1	Whitby gdns Sutton
40 M 10	Whitby rd Harrow
41 N 10	Whitby rd Harrow
134 F 2	Whitby rd Sutton
135 N 16	Whitby st E1
47 V 19	Whitcher pl NW1
24 M 2	Whitchurch av Edg
11 Z 19	Whitchurch clo Edg
11 Z 20	Whitchurch gdns Edg
24 K 2	Whitchurch la Edg
12 B 20	Whitchurch la Edg
140 G 11	Whitcomb st WC2
103 P 5	White Ash lodge Rich
133 T 19	White Bear yd EC1
143 S 4	White Ch la E1
62 L 19	White City rd W12
136 A 9	White City rd W12
136 B 9	White City stadium W10
133 T 20	White Conduit st N1
23 V 2	White gdns Harrow
56 D 17	White gdns Dgnhm
142 J 3	White Hart ct EC2
31 S 1	White Hart la N17
30 J 2	White Hart la N22
86 B 6	White Hart la SW14
38 E 4	White Hart la Rom
79 V 11	White Hart rd SE18
142 F 15	White Hart yd SE1
11 S 14	White Ho dri Stanm
7 Z 5	White Ho la Enf
113 V 10	White Horse hill Chisl
63 T 13	White Horse la E1
63 U 17	White Horse rd E1
66 G 8	White Horse rd E6
139 Y 14	White Horse st W1
142 D 3	White Horse yd EC2
142 M 4	White Kennett st E1
142 H 6	White Lion ct EC2
133 S 9	White Lion st N1
139 Y 8	White Lion yd W1
108 K 17	White lodge SE19
103 V 1	White lodge Rich
28 H 19	White Lodge clo N2
125 V 3	White Oak dri Becknhm
50 M 19	White Post la E9
51 N 19	White Post la E9
75 P 19	White Post la SE15
52 A 20	White rd E15
143 N 2	White's row E1
89 Y 10	White's sq SW4
69 S 3	Whitebarn la Dgnhm
37 U 14	Whitebeam av Brom
143 R 3	Whitechapel High st E1
135 X 20	Whitechapel rd E1
143 U 2	Whitechapel rd E1
58 L 18	Whitecote rd S'hall
125 W 8	Whitecroft clo Becknhm
125 V 9	Whitecroft way Becknhm
134 H 20	Whitecross pl EC2
112 A 7	Whitefield av NW2
112 A 7	Whitefoot la Brom
23 S 8	Whitefoot ter Brom
23 S 7	Whitefriars av Harrow
23 S 7	Whitefriars dri Harrow
141 U 6	Whitefriars st EC4
140 J 15	Whitehall SW1
140 K 14	Whitehall ct SW1
20 L 6	Whitehall gdns E4
140 K 15	Whitehall gdns SW1
73 R 3	Whitehall gdns W3
73 T 16	Whitehall gdns W4
21 U 8	Whitehall la Buck Hl
99 Y 3	Whitehall la Erith
47 V 3	Whitehall pk N19
73 T 16	Whitehall Pk rd W4
140 K 13	Whitehall pl SW1
155 R 9	Whitehall rd Wallgtn
71 Y 7	Whitehall rd W7
127 O 10	Whitehall rd Brom
23 S 20	Whitehall rd Harrow
122 F 13	Whitehall rd Thntn Hth
21 O 7	Whitehall rd Wdfd Grn
31 U 2	Whitehall st N17
126 F 3	Whitehart slip Brom
130 J 19	Whitehaven st NW8
146 M 8	Whitehead's gro SW3
99 W 14	Whitehill rd Drtfd
123 P 8	Whitehorse la SE25
122 M 17	Whitehorse rd Croy
123 N 13	Whitehorse rd Croy
16 E 10	Whitehouse way N14
60 D 17	Whiteledges W13
109 P 12	Whiteley rd SE19
100 H 7	Whiteley's way Felt
51 X 17	Whiter wlk E15
36 G 17	Whites av Ilf
142 L 17	Whites grounds SE1
89 V 10	Whites sq SW4
72 E 13	Whitestile rd Brentf
46 E 9	Whitestone la NW3
158 A 1	Whitethorn gdns Croy
8 A 16	Whitethorn gdns Enf
64 B 13	Whitethorn st E3
65 Z 2	Whitfield rd E6
93 X 3	Whitfield rd SE3
81 N 18	Whitfield rd Bxly Hth
132 B 18	Whitfield st W1
140 D 1	Whitfield st W1
120 L 6	Whitford gdns Mitch
156 L 11	Whitgift's Croy
156 M 2	Whitgift sq Croy
149 N 6	Whitgift st SE11
156 L 5	Whitgift st Croy
67 N 1	Whiting av Bark
4 A 18	Whitings rd Barnt
154 G 1	Whitland rd Carsh
31 T 7	Whitley rd N17
47 W 7	Whitley rd N19
87 T 20	Whitlock dri SW19
63 V 10	Whitman rd E3
62 M 6	Whitmore gdns NW10
128 C 8	Whitmore gdns NW10
134 J 8	Whitmore rd N1
124 L 6	Whitmore rd Becknhm
40 M 3	Whitmore rd Harrow
41 O 2	Whitmore rd Harrow
87 O 14	Whitnell way SW15
35 N 12	Whitney av Ilf
51 P 1	Whitney rd E10
53 O 12	Whitta rd E12
34 G 14	Whittaker av Rich
65 Z 2	Whittaker rd E6
153 V 5	Whittaker rd Sutton
147 S 7	Whittaker st SW1
110 C 8	Whittall gdns SE26
40 L 15	Whitten av Grnfd
87 V 2	Whittingstall rd SW6
142 J 7	Whittington av EC3
17 O 20	Whittington rd N22
30 A 1	Whittington rd N22
92 B 1	Whittington rd SE15
22 C 16	Whittington way Pinn
58 K 17	Whittle clo S'hall
155 N 17	Whittlebury clo Carsh
22 M 3	Whittlesea clo Harrow
22 M 4	Whittlesea path Harrow
22 M 3	Whittlesea rd Har
23 N 4	Whittlesea rd Harrow
23 N 3	Whittlesea rd Harrow
141 T 15	Whittlesey st SE1
41 W 16	Whitton av East Grnfd
42 B 19	Whitton clo Grnfd
82 M 14	Whitton dene Hounsl
83 T 13	Whitton dene Islwth
41 Z 17	Whitton dri Grnfd
83 O 14	Whitton Manor rd Islwth
82 L 12	Whitton rd Hounsl
83 T 16	Whitton rd Twick
82 H 16	Whitton waye Hounsl
65 S 10	Whitwell rd E13
79 N 11	Whitworth pl SE18
78 K 18	Whitworth rd SE18
123 U 8	Whitworth rd SE25
77 N 13	Whitworth st SE10
91 Y 8	Whorlton rd SE15
30 G 10	Whymark av N22
52 H 18	Whyteville rd E7
50 E 18	Wick rd E9
102 C 19	Wick rd Tedd
143 V 7	Wicker st E1
159 O 11	Wickersley rd SW1
63 O 11	Wickford st E1
159 O 11	Wickford st E1
153 O 11	Wickham av Croy
152 M 10	Wickham av Sutton
125 X 18	Wickham chase W Wkhm
126 A 16	Wickham chase W Wkhm
9 O 11	Wickham clo Enf
159 Y 9	Wickham court W Wkhm
159 V 2	Wickham cres W Wkhm
159 V 2	Wickham Ct rd W Wkhm
92 L 8	Wickham gdns SE4
88 B 18	Wickham la SE2
79 Z 15	Wickham la SE2
33 U 1	Wickham rd E4
92 M 6	Wickham rd SE4
93 N 4	Wickham rd SE4
125 S 5	Wickham rd Becknhm
158 F 3	Wickham rd Croy
159 N 1	Wickham rd Croy
23 R 8	Wickham rd Harrow
149 O 9	Wickham st SE11
96 M 3	Wickham st Welling
97 P 1	Wickham st Welling
125 T 9	Wickham way Becknhm
79 S 3	Wickliffe av N3
43 R 6	Wickliffe gdns Wemb
132 M 12	Wicklow st WC1
133 N 12	Wicklow st WC1
90 K 6	Wickwood st SE5
40 B 7	Widdecombe av
48 C 13	Widdenham rd N9
64 L 1	Widdin st E15
121 X 6	Wide way Mitch
113 S 7	Widecombe gdns Ilf
72 F 15	Widecombe way N2
142 L 2	Widegate st E1
129 V 15	Widley rd W9
127 O 4	Widmore Lodge rd Brom
127 O 3	Widmore rd Brom
126 K 2	Widmore rd Brom
43 R 19	Wiggington av Wemb
30 G 17	Wightman rd N4
100 A 2	Wigley rd Felt
139 X 4	Wigmore pl W1
154 H 1	Wigmore rd Carsh
139 X 4	Wigmore st W1
154 G 2	Wigmore wlk Carsh
65 W 11	Wigston rd E13
24 J 5	Wigton gdns Stanm
149 T 11	Wigton pl SE11
32 L 5	Wigton rd E17
28 F 19	Wilberforce rd NW9
48 H 6	Wilberforce rd N4
105 O 15	Wilberforce way SW19
147 R 5	Wilbraham pl SW1
18 B 17	Wilbury way N18
137 P 12	Wilby ms W11
148 J 18	Wilcox rd SW1
153 Z 9	Wilcox rd Sutton
154 A 8	Wilcox rd Sutton
101 R 9	Wilcox rd Tedd
140 M 5	Wild ct WC1
27 Z 20	Wild hatch NW11
140 M 6	Wild st WC2

150 H 1 Wild's rents SE1
11 U 20 Wildcroft gdns Edg
87 O 17 Wildcroft rd SW15
86 M 20 Wildcroft rd SW15
113 Z 18 Wilderness rd Chisl
100 K 10 Wilderness the Hampt
49 T 2 Wilderton rd N16
93 R 18 Wildfell rd SE6
142 H 20 Wilds rents SE1
46 C 5 Wildwood gro NW3
46 C 2 Wildwood rd NW11
28 C 19 Wildwood rd NW11
46 E 3 Wildwood ri NW11
122 M 15 Wilford rd Croy
148 B 1 Wilfred st SW1
61 V 13 Wilfrid gdns W3
135 O 19 Wilkes st E1
77 R 17 Wilkin st NW5
106 E 9 Wilkinson rd SW17
149 N 20 Wilkinson st SW8
134 K 9 Wilks pl N1
95 N 10 Will Crooks gdns SE9
94 M 10 Will Crooks gdns SE9
31 P 8 Willan rd N17
89 S 7 Willard st SW8
73 R 3 Willcott rd W3
5 P 20 Willenhall av Barnt
78 L 15 Willenhall rd SE18
96 L 19 Willersley av Sidcp
114 K 2 Willersley av Sidcp
114 K 1 Willersley clo Sidcp
45 O 19 Willesden la NW6
128 M 1 Willesden la NW6&NW2
129 R 2 Willesden la NW6&NW2
122 F 11 Willett pl Thntn Hth
122 F 11 Willett rd Thntn Hth
47 S 17 Willey's rd NW5
113 X 5 William Barefoot dri SE9
38 L 6 William clo Rom
140 J 11 William IV st WC2
132 K 10 William Morris clo E17
139 R 18 William ms SW1
132 A 15 William rd NW1
105 T 18 William rd SW19
154 E 10 William rd Sutton
33 T 19 William st E10
51 W 19 William st E15
15 R 15 William st N12
31 U 1 William st N17
139 R 18 William st SW1
54 A 20 William st Bark
154 L 5 William st Carsh
150 H 9 William's gro SE17
71 Z 1 William's rd W13
32 K 5 Williams av E17
85 V 8 Williams gro N22
85 V 8 Williams la SW14
120 D 12 Williams la Mrdn
70 B 12 Williams rd S'hall
156 F 13 Williams ter Croy
48 A 13 Williamson st N7
27 Y 17 Willifield way NW11
21 Z 20 Willingale clo Wdfd Grn
30 J 8 Willingdon rd N22
47 W 15 Willingham clo NW5
47 V 15 Willingham Ter nw5 NW5
90 A 8 Willington rd SW9
117 P 4 Willinsam way Kingst
154 H 14 Willis av Sutton
65 P 5 Willis rd E15
122 M 16 Willis rd Croy
81 V 10 Willis rd Erith
64 E 17 Willis st E14
156 C 8 Willoughby av Croy
32 A 2 Willoughby la N17
19 N 20 Willoughby la N4
31 Z 1 Willoughby Pk rd N17
46 F 12 Willoughby rd NW3
30 G 12 Willoughby rd N8
103 N 20 Willoughby rd Kingst
84 F 14 Willoughby rd Twick
140 H 2 Willoughby st WC1
86 E 6 Willow av Sidcp
97 N 15 Willow av Sidcp
87 T 7 Willow bank SW6
102 B 6 Willow bank Rich
16 L 19 Willow Bridge rd N1
72 E 17 Willow clo Brentf
17 U 13 Willow clo Brom
98 B 17 Willow clo Bxly Hth

57 Y 10 Willow clo Hornch
122 H 14 Willow clo Thntn Hth
49 U 6 Willow cotts N16
73 O 17 Willow cotts Rich
11 Y 13 Willow ct Edg
117 S 6 Willow ct Kingst
4 F 15 Willow dri Barnt
14 K 8 Willow end N20
116 J 19 Willow end Surb
82 G 3 Willow gdns Hounsl
65 S 5 Willow gro E13
113 Z 15 Willow gro Chisl
152 M 7 Willow Hayne gdns Worc Pk
120 M 12 Willow la Mitch
157 T 7 Willow mt Croy
148 C 5 Willow pl SW1
46 G 11 Willow rd NW3
72 K 6 Willow rd W5
154 M 1 Willow rd Carsh
8 E 9 Willow rd Enf
99 X 3 Willow rd Erith
117 V 8 Willow rd New Mald
37 Y 18 Willow rd Rom
134 H 15 Willow st E3
20 K 4 Willow st E4
38 L 14 Willow st Rom
74 G 3 Willow vale W12
113 Y 15 Willow vale Chisl
120 F 1 Willow view SW19
28 A 3 Willow way N3
110 B 7 Willow way SE26
100 K 5 Willow way Twick
32 L 15 Willow wlk E17
30 J 12 Willow wlk N15
28 G 8 Willow wlk N2
7 P 20 Willow wlk N21
150 L 5 Willow wlk SE1
151 N 6 Willow wlk SE1
153 V 4 Willow wlk Sutton
21 R 14 Willow Wood cres SE25
151 P 17 Willowbrook rd SE15
24 B 16 Willowcourt av Harrow
10 D 4 Willowdene Bushey Watf
82 M 18 Willowdene clo Twick
60 F 13 Willowmead clo W5
120 A 12 Willows av Mrdn
58 B 11 Willowtree la Grnfd
80 E 12 Willrose cres SE2
82 J 17 Wills cres Hounsl
13 V 16 Wills gro NW7
49 Y 20 Wilman gro E8
125 R 20 Wilmar gdns W Wkhm
103 O 13 Wilmer cres Kingst
134 K 6 Wilmer gdns N1
64 H 1 Wilmer Lea clo E15
73 X 20 Wilmington av W4
54 G 20 Wilmington gdns Bark
54 E 19 Wilmington gdns Bark
133 S 15 Wilmington sq WC1
133 S 14 Wilmington st WC1
71 U 4 Wilmot pl NW1
71 U 4 Wilmot pl W7
87 T 1 Wilmot rd E10
31 O 10 Wilmot rd N17
99 Y 14 Wilmot rd Drtfrd
135 X 14 Wilmot st E2
78 M 11 Wilmount st SE18
88 B 20 Wilna rd SW18
136 J 12 Wilsham st W11
93 N 1 Wilshaw st SE14
40 C 16 Wilsmere dri Grnfd
24 B 17 Wilsmere dri Harrow
106 X 20 Wilson av Mitch
22 M 20 Wilson gdns Harrow
143 V 19 Wilson gro SE16
65 Z 8 Wilson rd E6
66 A 8 Wilson rd E6
91 P 3 Wilson rd SE5
22 M 20 Wilson rd Harrow
53 U 1 Wilson rd Ilf
43 G 19 Wilson st EC2
142 G 1 Wilson st EC2
65 R 5 Wilson st E13
33 T 15 Wilson st E17
17 U 3 Wilson st N21
144 H 9 Wilson's rd W14
56 H 20 Wilthorne gdns Dgnhm
74 B 14 Wilton av W4
139 S 19 Wilton cres SW1
105 V 20 Wilton cres SW19
38 L 2 Wilton dri Rom

105 V 20 Wilton gro SW19
118 D 13 Wilton gro New Mald
147 V 1 Wilton ms SW1
139 S 18 Wilton pl SW1
29 P 6 Wilton rd N10
148 A 6 Wilton rd SE2
147 Z 4 Wilton rd SW1
106 J 16 Wilton rd SW19
5 Y 13 Wilton rd Barnt
53 Y 11 Wilton rd Ilf
53 Y 11 Wilton row SW1
134 E 4 Wilton sq N1
147 W 1 Wilton st SW1
139 T 20 Wilton ter SW1
134 D 4 Wilton villas N1
49 Y 18 Wilton way E8
50 A 18 Wilton way E8
101 O 1 Wiltshire gdns N4
90 G 7 Wiltshire rd SW9
122 G 7 Wiltshire rd Thntn Hth
118 B 15 Wilverley cres New Mald
90 C 18 Wimbart rd SW2
104 E 13 Wimbledon common SW19
105 U 14 Wimbledon Hill rd SW19
87 X 17 Wimbledon Pk rd SW18
105 U 3 Wimbledon Pk rd SW18
105 O 3 Wimbledon Pk side SW19
106 E 9 Wimbolt rd SW17
135 S 11 Wimbolt st E2
70 G 11 Wimborne av S'hall
21 X 8 Wimborne av Buck Hl
25 P 10 Wimborne dri NW9
22 A 20 Wimborne dri Pinn
60 B 15 Wimborne gdns W13
18 H 8 Wimborne rd N9
124 A 8 Wimborne way Becknhm
31 S 7 Wimbourne rd E17
134 E 8 Wimbourne st N1
139 W 4 Wimpole st W1
40 J 15 Wincanton cres Grnfd
35 Z 9 Wincanton gdns Ilf
87 V 18 Winchat rd SE18
95 P 8 Winchcomb gdns SE9
120 G 18 Winchcombe rd Carsh
154 J 1 Winchcombe rd Carsh
81 O 20 Winchelsea av Bxly Hth
87 O 14 Winchelsea clo SW15
52 D 11 Winchelsea rd E7
61 Z 3 Winchelsea rd NW10
31 U 10 Winchelsea rd N17
157 U 14 Winchelsey ri S Croy
87 V 1 Winchendon rd SW6
101 R 10 Winchendon rd Teddt
128 M 2 Winchester av NW6
25 P 12 Winchester av NW9
70 F 16 Winchester av Hounsl
126 B 7 Winchester clo Brom
8 E 18 Winchester clo Enf
103 T 17 Winchester clo Kingst
46 G 20 Winchester ms NW3
126 B 7 Winchester pk Brom
49 U 16 Winchester pl E8
47 T 3 Winchester pl N6
73 U 6 Winchester pl W3
33 V 2 Winchester rd E4
20 H 20 Winchester rd E4
130 H 1 Winchester rd NW3
47 T 2 Winchester rd N6
18 H 5 Winchester rd N9
126 B 7 Winchester rd Brom
97 W 4 Winchester rd Bxly Hth
100 D 6 Winchester rd Felt
24 L 12 Winchester rd Harrow
54 D 10 Winchester rd Ilf
84 A 16 Winchester rd Twick
142 E 12 Winchester sq SE1
78 B 4 Winchester st E16
147 X 9 Winchester st SW1
148 A 10 Winchester st SW1

73 W 4 Winchester st W3
142 E 13 Winchester wlk SE1
24 E 17 Winchfield clo Harrow
110 J 11 Winchfield rd SE26
16 L 5 Winchmore Hill rd N14
17 P 2 Winchmore Hill rd N21
25 N 15 Winckley clo SE9
149 T 6 Wincott st SE11
96 E 10 Wincrofts dri SE9
155 O 17 Windborough rd Carsh
159 Z 2 Windemere rd W Wkhm
128 M 6 Windermere av NW6
27 Y 9 Windermere av N3
119 Z 6 Windermere av SW19
57 W 14 Windermere av Hornch
42 E 3 Windermere av Wemb
35 S 17 Windermere gdns Ilf
42 E 4 Windermere gro Wemb
29 S 6 Windermere rd N10
47 W 7 Windermere rd N19
104 A 11 Windermere rd SW15
121 W 2 Windermere rd SW16
72 D 7 Windermere rd W5
98 J 4 Windermere rd Bxly Hth
123 U 19 Windermere rd Croy
58 F 13 Windermere rd S'hall
88 H 4 Winders rd SW11
159 X 20 Windham av Croy
85 N 7 Windham rd Rich
55 U 9 Winding way Dgnhm
75 X 12 Windlass pl SE8
105 P 1 Windlesham gro SW19
110 C 4 Windley clo SE23
116 C 19 Windmill clo Surb
89 S 13 Windmill dri SW4
7 S 10 Windmill gdns Enf
122 L 16 Windmill gro Croy
46 C 10 Windmill hill NW3
7 X 11 Windmill hill Enf
51 X 17 Windmill la E15
10 E 5 Windmill la Bushey Watf
59 N 12 Windmill la Grnfd
116 B 17 Windmill la Surb
18 C 12 Windmill rd N18
88 F 15 Windmill rd SW18
104 K 11 Windmill rd SW19
74 A 11 Windmill rd W4
72 D 10 Windmill rd W5
72 D 13 Windmill rd W5
122 L 17 Windmill rd Croy
100 L 13 Windmill rd Hampt
121 U 11 Windmill rd Mitch
149 S 11 Windmill row SE11
140 E 2 Windmill st W1
10 F 4 Windmill st Bushey Watf
141 U 16 Windmill wlk SE1
92 W 20 Windover av NW9
110 F 6 Windrush la SE23
32 J 7 Windsor av E17
120 D 1 Windsor av SW19
12 E 12 Windsor av Edg
117 W 13 Windsor av New Mald
153 T 6 Windsor av Sutton
27 T 8 Windsor clo N3
40 H 11 Windsor clo Harrow
40 G 11 Windsor cres Harrow
43 R 9 Windsor cres Wemb
16 G 3 Windsor ct N14
5 Y 19 Windsor dri Barnt
99 X 15 Windsor dri Drtfrd
108 L 19 Windsor gro SE27
148 C 4 Windsor pl SW1
51 R 7 Windsor rd E10
52 F 6 Windsor rd E11
20 D 13 Windsor rd E4
52 H 15 Windsor rd E7
44 J 17 Windsor rd NW2
17 U 12 Windsor rd N3
31 X 7 Windsor rd N17
27 T 8 Windsor rd N13
48 A 10 Windsor rd N7
60 H 20 Windsor rd W5
72 J 1 Windsor rd W5
4 D 19 Windsor rd Barnt
97 Y 11 Windsor rd Bxly Hth

21 V 10 Woodland clo Wdfd Grn
76 L 15 Woodland cres SE10
29 S 14 Woodland gdns N10
33 T 7 Woodland gdns Islwth
09 T 14 Woodland hill SE19
20 H 5 Woodland rd E4
16 E 16 Woodland rd N11
09 T 14 Woodland rd SE19
22 G 10 Woodland rd Thntn Hth
29 S 14 Woodland ri N10
41 Z 18 Woodland ri Grnfd
49 V 19 Woodland st E8
78 C 12 Woodland ter SE7
13 P 18 Woodland way NW7
17 T 6 Woodland way N21
80 H 12 Woodland way SE2
24 H 20 Woodland way Croy
07 P 18 Woodland way Mitch
19 V 9 Woodland way Mrdn
59 U 4 Woodland way W Wkhm
21 V 10 Woodland way Wdfd Grn
76 M 14 Woodland wlk SE10
28 C 4 Woodland's av N3
33 V 10 Woodland's rd E17
25 S 17 Woodlands NW11
19 N 9 Woodlands SW20
22 F 14 Woodlands Harrow
55 R 19 Woodlands Wallgtn
52 G 4 Woodlands av E11
73 T 3 Woodlands av W3
17 X 2 Woodlands av New Mald
37 Y 20 Woodlands av Rom
14 H 1 Woodlands av Sidcp
96 H 20 Woodlands av Sidcup
152 E 2 Woodlands av Worc Pk
27 S 16 Woodlands clo NW11
127 U 4 Woodlands clo Brom
10 H 19 Woodlands dri Stanm
83 U 5 Woodlands gro Islwth
30 L 14 Woodlands Park rd N15
76 M 15 Woodlands Park rd SE10
51 Z 6 Woodlands rd E11
19 P 6 Woodlands rd N9
86 D 8 Woodlands rd SW13
127 S 4 Woodlands rd Brom
97 Z 7 Woodlands rd Bxly Hth
98 A 7 Woodlands rd Bxly Hth
8 A 5 Woodlands rd Enf
23 W 15 Woodlands rd Harrow
54 A 9 Woodlands rd Ilf
83 T 7 Woodlands rd Islwth
39 T 11 Woodlands rd Rom
70 A 2 Woodlands rd S'hall
116 Q 18 Woodlands rd Surb
93 X 17 Woodlands st SE13
16 E 6 Woodlands the N14
93 X 18 Woodlands the SE13
108 M 18 Woodlands the SE19
11 O 15 Woodlands the Stanm
87 U 12 Woodlands way SW15
100 J 3 Woodlawn av Twick
100 A 4 Woodlawn dri Felt
87 O 1 Woodlawn rd SW6
87 P 2 Woodlawn rd SW6
144 F 19 Woodlawn rd SW6
124 A 12 Woodlea dri Brom
49 R 9 Woodlea rd N16
13 X 5 Woodleigh av N12
108 A 7 Woodleigh gdns SE19
78 J 4 Woodman st E16
155 U 20 Woodmansterne la Wallgtn
107 X 20 Woodmansterne rd SW16
154 K 18 Woodmansterne rd Carsh
95 T 20 Woodmere SE9
124 D 18 Woodmere av Croy

124 G 17 Woodmere clo Croy
124 E 18 Woodmere gdns Croy
125 W 11 Woodmere way Becknhm
87 Z 7 Woodneigh st SW6
107 T 11 Woodnook rd SW16
8 M 20 Woodpecker clo Enf
158 J 19 Woodpecker mt Croy
75 V 17 Woodpecker rd SE14
90 K 13 Woodquest av SE24
22 E 4 Woodridings av Pinn
22 C 2 Woodridings clo Pinn
51 Y 1 Woodriffe rd E11
78 F 12 Woodrow SE18
69 B 2 Woodrow clo Grnfd
139 S 9 Woods ms W1
92 A 3 Woods rd SE15
135 R 20 Woodseer st E1
56 H 10 Woodshire rd Dgnhm
27 Y 14 Woodside NW11
105 V 14 Woodside SW19
21 X 8 Woodside Buck Hl
29 P 13 Woodside av N10
15 O 14 Woodside av N12
28 M 15 Woodside av N6
123 Z 13 Woodside av SE25
114 B 14 Woodside av Chisl
60 K 3 Woodside av Wemb
99 O 9 Woodside av Bxly Hth
11 N 16 Woodside clo Stanm
117 U 18 Woodside clo Surb
60 L 3 Woodside clo Wemb
114 H 7 Woodside cres Sidcp
123 Y 18 Woodside end Croy
60 L 4 Woodside end Wemb
20 E 18 Woodside gdns E4
31 T 8 Woodside gdns N17
15 O 13 Woodside Grange rd N12
123 Y 14 Woodside grn SE25
15 P 12 Woodside gro N12
15 P 11 Woodside la N11
97 X 15 Woodside la Bxly
15 P 14 Woodside Park rd N12
123 Y 13 Woodside pk SE25
33 X 14 Woodside Pk av E17
60 L 4 Woodside pl Wemb
65 X 12 Woodside rd E13
30 E 2 Woodside rd N22
123 Z 15 Woodside rd SE25
127 R 11 Woodside rd Brom
99 N 10 Woodside rd Bxly Hth
102 J 18 Woodside rd Kingst
117 Z 3 Woodside rd New Mald
118 A 4 Woodside rd New Mald
114 H 7 Woodside rd Sidcp
154 C 6 Woodside rd Sutton
21 S 12 Woodside rd Wdfd Grn
123 Z 14 Woodside view SE25
124 B 14 Woodside way Croy
121 T 1 Woodside way Mitch
47 S 10 Woodsome rd NW5
105 T 3 Woodspring rd SW19
11 Y 20 Woodstead gro Edg
45 T 1 Woodstock av NW11
71 Z 7 Woodstock av W13
83 Y 12 Woodstock av Islwth
58 F 9 Woodstock av S'hall
119 V 17 Woodstock av Sutton
98 B 20 Woodstock clo Bxly
24 L 9 Woodstock clo Stanm
8 M 19 Woodstock cres Enf
94 D 17 Woodstock ct SE12
54 M 6 Woodstock gdns Ilf
136 H 18 Woodstock gro W12
33 W 7 Woodstock ms W1
33 W 7 Woodstock rd E17
52 K 20 Woodstock rd E7
45 W 3 Woodstock rd NW11
48 G 5 Woodstock rd N4
74 A 9 Woodstock rd W4
10 G 2 Woodstock rd Bushey Watf
155 P 12 Woodstock rd Carsh

157 O 7 Woodstock rd Croy
60 M 1 Woodstock rd Wemb
119 U 18 Woodstock ri Sutton
65 N 17 Woodstock st E16
139 X 7 Woodstock st W1
64 D 19 Woodstock ter E14
121 T 2 Woodstock way Mitch
152 H 11 Woodstone av Epsom
109 V 9 Woodsyre SE26
86 K 11 Woodthorpe rd SW15
123 U 5 Woodvale av SE25
20 G 13 Woodview av E4
101 X 10 Woodville clo Tedd
45 P 1 Woodville gdns NW11
60 L 17 Woodville gdns W5
35 Z 12 Woodville gdns Ilf
52 C 3 Woodville rd E11
32 J 14 Woodville rd E17
34 H 8 Woodville rd E18
45 R 1 Woodville rd NW11
129 R 8 Woodville rd NW6
49 P 15 Woodville rd N16
60 H 18 Woodville rd W5
5 N 14 Woodville rd Barnt
19 X 8 Woodville rd Mrdn
102 C 6 Woodville rd Rich
122 M 8 Woodville rd Thntn Hth
123 N 7 Woodville rd Thntn Hth
78 E 12 Woodville st SE18
26 G 17 Woodward av NW4
55 S 20 Woodward gdns Dgnhm
68 C 1 Woodward rd Dgnhm
55 U 20 Woodward rd Dgnhm
91 T 16 Woodwarde rd SE22
83 O 16 Woodwards Foot path Twick
23 Z 17 Woodway cres Harrow
88 D 13 Woodwell st SW18
94 D 16 Woodyates rd SE12
104 K 16 Wool rd SW20
94 J 4 Woolacombe rd SE3
58 F 19 Wooler st SE17
30 H 19 Woollaston rd N4
44 F 2 Woolmead av NW9
18 L 18 Woolmer gdns N18
18 L 17 Woolmer rd N18
68 G 19 Woolmore st E14
68 A 7 Woolneigh st SW6
124 G 4 Woolstone rd SE23
78 G 9 Woolwich Ch st SE18
78 H 18 Woolwich comm SE18
78 L 4 Woolwich manorway SE18
78 K 13 Woolwich New rd SE18
77 O 13 Woolwich rd SE10
80 K 15 Woolwich rd SE2
81 P 13 Woolwich rd SE2
77 Y 12 Woolwich rd SE7
78 B 10 Woolwich rd SE7
98 D 10 Woolwich rd Bxly Hth
64 J 17 Wooster gdns E14
27 Y 6 Wootton gro N3
141 U 15 Wootton st SE1
144 B 10 Worbeck rd SE20
31 W 1 Worcester av N17
158 M 3 Worcester clo Croy
159 N 3 Worcester clo Croy
121 R 5 Worcester clo Mitch
13 O 10 Worcester cres NW7
21 X 14 Worcester cres Wdfd Grn
41 O 18 Worcester gdns Grnfd
35 R 20 Worcester gdns Ilf
154 B 15 Worcester gdns Sutton
152 C 5 Worcester gdns Worc Pk
42 B 10 Worcester pl EC4
53 T 11 Worcester rd E12
32 F 6 Worcester rd E17
105 V 13 Worcester rd SW19
153 Z 15 Worcester rd Sutton
154 A 15 Worcester rd Sutton
8 A 6 Worcesters av Enf
53 P 19 Wordsworth av E12
34 C 9 Wordsworth av E18

153 N 9 Wordsworth dri Sutton
30 H 13 Wordsworth pde N15
49 S 13 Wordsworth rd N16
110 E 18 Wordsworth rd SE20
155 W 15 Wordsworth rd Wallgtn
27 X 14 Wordsworth wlk NW11
146 M 19 Worfield st SW11
149 N 9 Worgan st SE11
52 A 20 Worland rd E15
7 S 13 World's End la Enf
146 E 17 Worlds End pas SW10
144 C 10 Worlidge st W6
74 L 13 Worlidge st W6
91 V 10 Worlingham rd SE22
74 G 3 Wormholt rd W12
142 H 13 Wormwood st EC2
128 M 19 Wornington rd W10
137 N 1 Wornington rd W10
128 K 19 Wornington rd W10
130 H 5 Woronzow rd NW8
105 P 19 Worple av SW19
83 Y 13 Worple av Islwth
40 E 3 Worple clo Harrow
105 T 18 Worple rd SW19
119 O 1 Worple rd SW20
118 M 2 Worple rd SW20
83 Z 8 Worple rd Islwth
105 U 16 Worple Rd mews SW19
85 Y 7 Worple st SW14
40 E 4 Worple way Harrow
84 L 12 Worple way Rich
134 G 19 Worship st EC2
106 F 11 Worslade rd SW17
110 M 11 Worsley Br rd SE26
111 N 13 Worsley Br rd SE26
51 Z 11 Worsley rd E11
52 A 11 Worsley rd E11
89 V 12 Worsopp dri SW4
64 M 4 Worthing clo E15
70 D 17 Worthing st Hounsl
116 M 20 Worthington rd Surb
117 N 19 Worthington rd Surb
66 A 1 Wortley rd E6
122 E 16 Wortley rd Croy
83 P 4 Worton gdns Islwth
83 R 9 Worton rd Islwth
83 P 5 Worton way Islwth
44 M 11 Wotton rd NW2
75 Y 17 Wotton rd SE8
65 O 17 Wouldham rd E16
52 A 10 Wragbey rd E11
35 W 10 Wray av Ilf
64 A 3 Wray cres N4
153 U 19 Wray rd Sutton
153 P 7 Wrayfield rd Sutton
79 P 18 Wrekin rd SE18
44 M 13 Wren av NW2
70 F 10 Wren av S'hall
55 W 14 Wren gdns Dgnhm
57 S 5 Wren gdns Hornch
91 N 2 Wren rd SE5
55 W 14 Wren rd Dgnhm
115 U 7 Wren rd Sidcp
133 O 16 Wren st WC1
128 F 7 Wrentham av NW10
111 Z 10 Wrenthorpe rd Brom
142 K 4 Wrestlers ct EC3
64 B 7 Wrexham rd E3
94 J 3 Wricklemarsh rd SE3
95 P 2 Wricklemarsh rd SE3
75 S 19 Wrigglesworth st SE14
49 S 17 Wright rd N1
150 L 3 Wright's bldgs SE1
137 M 20 Wright's la W8
105 N 16 Wrights all SW19
145 W 1 Wrights la W8
63 X 5 Wrights rd E3
123 S 6 Wrights rd SE25
155 R 9 Wrights row Wallgtn
85 X 7 Wrights way SW14
132 C 1 Wrotham rd NW1
26 C 2 Wrotham rd W13
4 E 9 Wrotham rd Barnt
97 U 3 Wrotham rd Welling
62 H 6 Wrottesley rd NW10
79 N 16 Wrottesley rd SE18
89 N 15 Wroughton rd SW11
26 K 12 Wroughton ter NW4
55 U 17 Wroxall rd Dgnhm
29 W 2 Wroxham gdns N11
92 B 5 Wroxton st SE15
154 L 5 Wrythe grn Carsh
154 M 5 Wrythe Grn rd Carsh

120 C 19 Wrythe la Carsh
154 G 1 Wrythe la Carsh
62 D 16 Wulfstan st W12
16 L 15 Wunningdale N14
60 K 2 Wyatt ct Wemb
108 B 3 Wyatt Pk rd SW2
52 F 18 Wyatt rd E7
48 K 9 Wyatt rd N5
33 U 11 Wyatt's la E17
43 V 20 Wybourne way NW10
4 H 11 Wyburn av Barnt
102 M 19 Wych Elm pas Kingst
157 N 18 Wyche gro S Croy
5 N 19 Wycherley cres Barnt
11 U 19 Wychwood av Edg
122 K 6 Wychwood av Thntn Hth
11 U 19 Wychwood clo Edg
35 V 13 Wychwood gdns Ilf
11 T 19 Wychwood wlk Edg
133 W 14 Wyclif st EC1
96 K 3 Wycliffe clo Welling
89 P 7 Wycliffe rd SW11
106 B 16 Wycliffe rd SW19
45 X 6 Wycombe gdns NW11
31 Y 5 Wycombe rd N17
35 U 16 Wycombe rd Ilf
61 R 2 Wycombe rd Wemb
123 Z 17 Wydehurst rd Croy
119 N 15 Wydell clo Mrdn
112 H 9 Wydeville Mnr rd SE12
88 G 6 Wye st SW11
36 A 5 Wyfields Ilf
35 Z 5 Wyfields Ilf
87 S 1 Wyfold rd SW6
144 L 20 Wyfold rd SW6
71 X 9 Wyke gdns W7
64 A 1 Wyke rd E3
119 N 2 Wyke rd SW20
55 U 17 Wykeham av Dgnhm
55 T 17 Wykeham grn Dgnhm
42 M 3 Wykeham hill Wemb
43 N 3 Wykeham hill Wemb
26 L 16 Wykeham rd NW4
24 A 12 Wykeham rd Harrow
14 F 5 Wykeham rise N20
43 T 17 Wyld way Wemb
46 C 4 Wyldes clo NW11
92 H 17 Wyleu st SE23
70 H 8 Wylie rd S'hall
63 O 12 Wyllen clo E1
135 Z 18 Wyllen clo E1
129 V 14 Wymering rd W9
87 N 7 Wymond st SW15
114 J 1 Wyncham av Sidcp
96 J 20 Wyncham av Sidcup
16 L 5 Wynchgate N14
11 N 4 Wynchgate N14
23 U 2 Wynchgate Harrow
158 E 20 Wyncote way S Croy
25 R 17 Wyndale av NW9
34 H 4 Wyndale rd E18
77 V 15 Wyndcliff rd SE7
7 V 12 Wyndcroft clo Enf
47 U 10 Wyndham cres N19
82 F 15 Wyndham cres Hounsl
139 O 2 Wyndham pl W1
65 Z 1 Wyndham rd E6
150 B 19 Wyndham rd SE5
149 Z 19 Wyndham rd SE5
77 A 7 Wyndham rd W13
15 Z 6 Wyndham rd Barnt
103 O 17 Wyndham rd Kingst
139 O 1 Wyndham st W1
91 O 13 Wyneham rd SE24
110 G 6 Wynell rd SE23
133 R 8 Wynford rd N1
113 U 6 Wynford way SE9
145 U 1 Wynnstay gdns W8
88 E 9 Wynter st SW11
123 T 10 Wynton gdns SE25
61 T 16 Wynton pl W3
133 W 12 Wynyatt st EC1
12 F 11 Wyre gro Edg
59 W 8 Wyresdale cres Grnfd
139 O 5 Wythburn pl W1
95 Y 15 Wythens wlk SE9
56 F 10 Wythenshawe rd Dgnhm
127 T 3 Wythes clo Brom
78 C 3 Wythes rd E16
57 T 15 Wythfield rd SE9
95 S 16 Wythfield rd SE9

148 J 17 Wyvil est SW8
148 K 16 Wyvil rd SW8
64 E 14 Wyvis st E14

Y

76 H 2 Yabsley st E14
81 R 5 Yainton way Blvdr
151 R 5 Yalding rd SE16
120 E 1 Yarborough rd SW19
143 W 3 Yarden st E1
143 W 4 Yarden st E1
133 S 14 Yardley st WC1
139 X 14 Yarmouth ms W1
40 B 5 Yeading av Harrow
22 G 16 Yeading wlk Har
29 N 19 Yeatman rd N6
144 E 10 Yeldham rd W6
88 G 5 Yelverton rd SW11
64 C 14 Yeo st E3
75 V 11 Yeoman st SE8
83 S 14 Yeomans ms Islwth
143 P 8 Yeomans yd E1
146 L 3 Yeomans' row SW3
47 Y 9 Yerbury rd N19
113 S 19 Yester dri Chisl
113 U 16 Yester pk Chisl
113 U 17 Yester rd Chisl
45 R 13 Yew gro NW2
17 T 4 Yew Tree clo N21
97 N 3 Yew Tree clo Welling
118 B 19 Yew Tree clo Worc Pk
37 Z 15 Yew Tree gdns Rom
62 F 20 Yew Tree rd W12
158 K 20 Yew Tree way Croy
82 E 13 Yew Tree wlk Hounsl
41 S 3 Yew wlk Harrow
112 A 16 Yewdale clo Brom
44 D 19 Yewfield rd NW10
124 K 5 Yewtree rd Becknhm
49 P 6 Yoakley rd N16
95 R 13 Yolande gdns SE9
48 F 8 Yong pk N4
85 W 12 York av SW14
71 U 2 York av W7
114 J 4 York av Sidcp
24 B 6 York av Stanm
140 L 11 York bldgs WC2
71 U 2 York clo W7
119 Z 9 York clo Mrdn
131 U 18 York ga NW1
16 M 2 York gate N14
92 C 2 York gro SE15
108 J 5 York Hill se27 SE27
137 X 17 York Ho pl W8
47 T 15 York ms NW5
88 E 7 York pl SW11
140 K 11 York pl WC2
71 T 2 York pl W7
51 T 9 York rd E10
32 F 17 York rd E17
72 J 18 York rd E4
52 E 19 York rd E7
26 E 20 York rd NW9
16 L 19 York rd N11
16 M 2 York rd N14
18 M 17 York rd N18
18 B 3 York rd N21
141 P 16 York rd SE1
88 E 8 York rd SW11
106 B 15 York rd SW19
61 X 16 York rd W3
72 E 9 York rd W5
5 S 16 York rd Barnt
72 G 15 York rd Brentf
122 F 16 York rd Croy
82 K 8 York rd Hounsl
53 X 8 York rd Ilf
103 N 19 York rd Kingst
84 M 13 York rd Rich
53 X 16 York rd Sutton
101 T 10 York rd Tedd
33 U 10 York ri NW5
134 M 8 York row E2
63 V 18 York sq E14
139 R 1 York st W1
67 N 4 York st Bark
121 O 18 York st Mitch
101 Y 1 York st Twick
131 T 18 York ter Enf
7 Z 3 York ter Enf
98 J 1 York ter Erith
131 J 17 York Ter east NW1
131 T 17 York Ter west NW1
132 K 4 York way N1
15 Y 10 York way N20

47 Z 19 York way N7
100 D 7 York way Felt
96 J 8 Yorkland av Welling
18 M 17 Yorkshire gdns N18
49 T 10 Yorkshire rd E14
63 V 17 Yorkshire gro N16
112 A 9 Yorkshire rd Mitch
122 A 9 Yorkshire rd Mitch
121 Z 10 Yorkshire rd Mitch
135 R 9 Yorkton st E2
137 Y 19 Young st W8
7 Z 6 Youngmans clo Enf
36 D 17 Youngs rd Ilf
36 B 18 Yoxley appr Ilf
36 B 18 Yoxley dri Ilf
89 S 18 Yukon rd SW12
44 A 19 Yuletide rd NW10

Z

75 P 14 Zampa rd SE16
95 P 2 Zangwill rd SE3
63 V 6 Zealand rd E3
89 T 20 Zennor rd SW12
91 U 10 Zenoria st SE22
122 L 10 Zermatt rd Thntn Hth
64 F 14 Zetland st E14
123 O 10 Zion pl Thntn Hth
123 O 10 Zion rd Thntn Hth

Cinemas and Theatres

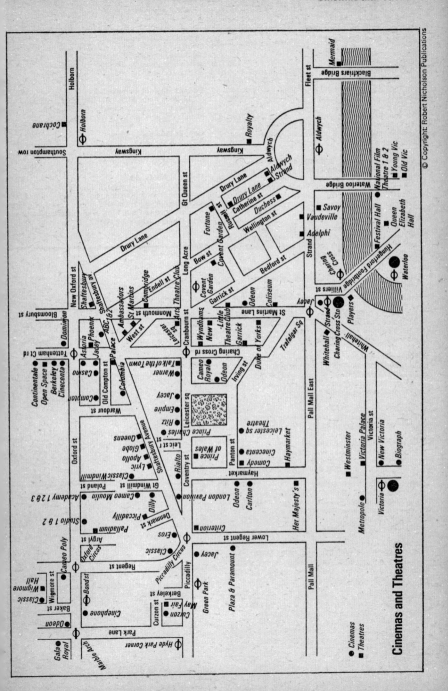

© Copyright: Robert Nicholson Publications

Cinemas and Theatres

● Cinemas
■ Theatres

London directory

Shops and services

Babyminders   139 U 5
126 Wigmore Street, W1. 935 3515. Started the whole concept of trustworthy babysitting. 25,000 children on their books. Excellent for trained short-notice sitters.

Canning School of English   146 A 1
13 Canning Place, W8. 589 4468. Small classes, 4 week intensive audio visual courses for continental businessmen.

Car Ferry Enquiries 12 Western rd. Oxford.
Oxford 48765. The only central agency for all car ferry bookings. No extra charge. Buy their 17½p 'The Lazy way to book your car ferry' which gives complete details of virtually all ferries with free brochure and booking service.

Dodo   137 S 7
185 Westbourne Grove, London W11. Pub signs, mirrors, decorations, and turn of the century advertisements brought together for their humour and atmosphere, also scientific instruments.

Ear Piercing   147 X 12
Ring 828 4167, ask for Mrs. Medway O'Mahony, she will pierce your ears painlessly under ideal aseptic conditions. Clients own or small gold stud earings.

Eros Escort & Guide Service   140 D 11
213 Piccadilly, W1. 734 0167. Attractive male and female partners for an evening in London. Am/Ex welcome. Open 2 p.m. - 8 p.m.

Fishers Hairdressers   141 Z 5
28 Cathedral Place, St. Paul's Churchyard, EC4. (01) 236 1767. Modern and pleasant, gives a 'West End' cut to city executives. Secretarial service. Refreshments and a sauna bath. 97½p.

Claude Gill Books   139 T 7
481 Oxford Street, W1. 'A department store of books.' Open Mon-Sat 09.00 to 17.30. Late Thurs to 19.00.

Government Bookshop (HMSO)   141 R 2
49 High Holborn, WC1. Chancery Lane or Holborn underground. Open 8.30 a.m. - 5.15 p.m. Monday to Friday. More than 2,000 titles always in stock.

Hachette, Librairie Francaise   140 C 9
4 Regent Place, W1R 6BH. 734 5259. London's oldest and largest shop for French books, publications, newspapers subscriptions. New art section with prints, lithographs and art books. 9.30 a.m. - 6.00 p.m. Sats till 1.00.

Lino Taboas   139 T 3
46 George Street, W1. (01) 935 0225. Modern London style haircuts. Shampoos by female staff. Drinks served. Comfortable surroundings. Extras include facial, scalp treatments. Appointment

Problem Ltd   141 T 6
178 Fleet St, EC4. (01) 828 8181. Night and day service for all sorts of office and household emergencies. The range is almost limitless. Members only. Subscription £5.50 annually (bankers order).

Rene   139 V 12
66 South Audley Street, W1. 499 3227/8

Speedwriting International   139 W 6
Avon House, 360 Oxford Street, W1. 493 3401. Intensive secretarial courses. Day or evening classes start every Monday. Shorthand 100 w.p.m. in 8/12 weeks. Typing.

Edward Stanford map specialists   140 J 8
12-14 Long Acre, WC2. (01) 836 1321. London's only shop exclusively devoted to maps, guides, atlases, globes and other geographical products.

Geo. F. Trumper   139 Y 13
9 Curzon Street, W1. (01) 499 1850. A very famous establishment. Superb shopfront and interior. The highest quality haircut for 55p.

Universal Aunts Ltd.   147 O
36 Walpole Street, Chelsea, SW3. 730 9834. All accommodation in London and country. Individual tours and guides. Travel and theatre tickets. Children met, escorted and cared for. Experienced baby sitters. Secretarial and domestic staff.

Pubs

The Antelope   147 U 7
22 Eaton Terrace, SW1. 730 7781. Good hearty male beer swilling. Old fashioned English food served upstairs in alcoved dining room.

Black Lion   74 F 14
2 South Black Lion Lane, W6. 748 7056. Riverside local with beer garden. Famous for our sandwiches. Restaurant for lunches and dinner.

The Brockley Jack   92 J 15
410 Brockley Road, SE4. (01) 699 3966. Licensee E. V. Burfield D.C.M. Originally 13th century highwaymans tavern. Music Don Parr Quintet. Buffet always available. Starring Shirley Weston of BBC and ITV Thursday to Sunday.

The Dove Inn   74 H 14
19 Upper Mall, Hammersmith, W6. 748 5405. First left past Hammersmith flyover leaving London. 17th century. Famous people. Historical. Riverside terrace. Hot-cold snacks. London hours.

Galleries

W. & F. C. Bonham & Sons Ltd.   138 M 20
Montpelier Galleries, Montpelier Street, SW7. Auctioneers and valuers. Dealers in pictures, furniture, silver, porcelain, glass, ethnography, carpets, rugs, export and home.

Ganymed Gallery   141 P 3
11 Great Turnstile, WC1. (01) 405 9836. Rare old Prints, always an interesting selection, also publishers of modern etchings and lithographs.

London Arts Gallery   139 Z 10
22 New Bond Street, W1. (01) 493 0646. Largest stock of original prints in London. Old masters, 19th & 20th century Miro Vasarely paintings, sculpture, Ernst, Arp.

Lumley Cazalet   139 X 8
24 Davies Street, W1. Specialists in 20th century original prints by Matisse, Picasso, Braque, Chagall, etc., and many lesser known and young artists.

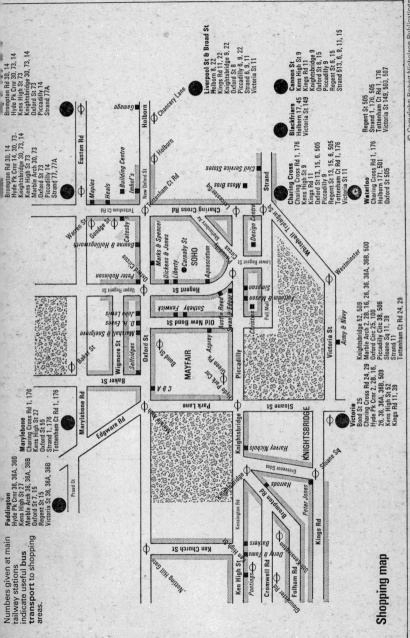

Shopping map

Numbers given at main railway stations indicate useful **bus transport** to shopping areas.

Paddington
Hyde Pk Cnr 36, 36A, 36B
Kens High St 27
Marble Arch 36, 36A, 36B
Oxford St 15
Regent St 15
Victoria St 36, 36A, 36B

Marylebone
Charing Cross Rd 1, 176
Kens High St 27
Oxford St 55
Strand 1, 176
Tottenham Ct Rd 1, 176

Brompton Rd 30, 14
Hyde Pk Cnr 14, 30, 73,
Knightsbridge 30, 73, 14
Oxford St 73
Marble Arch 30, 73
Piccadilly 14
Strand 77, 77A

Brompton Rd 30, 14
Hyde Pk Cnr 30, 73, 14
Kens High St 73
Knightsbridge 30, 73, 14
Oxford St 73
Strand 77A

Liverpool St & Broad St.
Holborn 8, 22
Kings Rd 11, 22
Knightsbridge 9, 22
Oxford St 8
Piccadilly 6, 9, 22
Strand 6, 9, 11
Victoria St 11

Cannon St.
Kens High St 9
Kings Rd 11
Knightsbridge 9
Oxford St 6, 15
Piccadilly 9
Regent St 6, 15
Strand 513, 6, 9, 11, 15

Blackfriars
Holborn 17, 45
Victoria St 149

Charing Cross
Charing Cross Rd 1, 176
Kens High St 9
Kings Rd 11
Oxford St 13, 15, 6, 505
Piccadilly 9
Regent St 13, 15, 6, 505
Tottenham Ct Rd 1, 176
Victoria St 11

Regent St 505
Strand 1, 176, 505
Tottenham Ct Rd 1, 176
Victoria St 149, 503, 507

Waterloo
Charing Cross Rd 1, 176
Holborn 171, 501
Oxford St 505

Victoria
Bond St 25
Charing Cross Rd 24, 29
Hyde Pk Cnr 2, 2B, 16,
26, 36, 36A, 36B, 509
Kens High St 52
Kings Rd 11, 39

Knightsbridge 52, 509
Marble Arch 2, 2B, 16, 26, 36, 36A, 36B, 500
Piccadilly Circ 38, 506
Sloane Sq 11, 39
Strand 11
Tottenham Ct Rd 24, 29

Underground

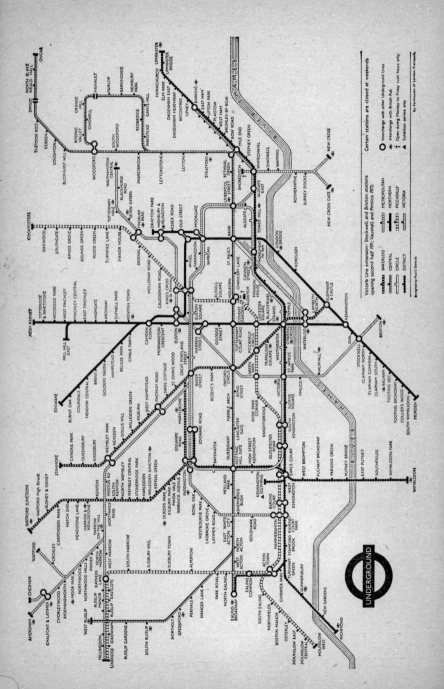